TIBET HANDBOOK

with Bhutan

Gyurme Dorje

Maps by **Sebastian Ballard, Michael Farmer
and Kevin Feeney**

These snow mountains are the navel of the world, a
  place where snow lions dance.
Their crystal-like pagodas are abodes of Supreme Bliss.
The verdant hills encircling them are fragrant sources of
  life-restoring nectar,
Where spiritual accomplishments are won and
  uncorrupted meditation thrives.
Nothing is more wondrous! Nothing more amazing!

After **Milarepa** (1040-1123), *'Encounter with Rechungma'*

2

TRADE & TRAVEL
Handbooks

Trade & Travel Publications Ltd
6 Riverside Court, Lower Bristol Road, Bath BA2 3DZ, England
Telephone 01225 469141   Fax 01225 469461
Email 100660.1250@compuserve.com

©Trade & Travel Publications Ltd., January 1996

ISBN 0 900751 69 X

CIP DATA: A catalogue record for this book is available from the British Library

In North America, published and distributed by

PASSPORT BOOKS
a division of *NTC Publishing Group*

4255 West Touhy Avenue, Lincolnwood (Chicago), Illinois 60646-1975, USA
Telephone 708-679-5500   Fax 708-679-2494   Email NTCPUB2@AOL.COM

ISBN 0-8442-4901-7

Library of Congress Catalog Card Number 95-71558

Passport Books and colophon are registered trademarks of NTC Publishing Group

**MAPS – Publisher's note: the maps in this book are not intended to have
any political significance or purport to show authenticated international
boundaries.**

**IMPORTANT: While every endeavour is made to ensure that the facts
printed in this book are correct at the time of going to press, travellers
are cautioned to obtain authoritative advice from consulates, airlines,
etc, concerning current travel and visa requirements and conditions
before embarking. The publishers cannot accept legal responsibility for
errors, however caused, that are printed in this book.**

Cover illustration by Suzanne Evans

Printed and bound in Great Britain by Clays Ltd., Bungay, Suffolk

THE DALAI LAMA
FOREWORD

For too long Tibet has been a far off country shrouded in mystery. Sheer geographical inaccessibility meant that few foreigners reached Tibet and those who did often told tales that were not easily believed. The resulting romantic reputation surrounding our country has not served us Tibetans well. At a time when we desperately needed support, there was insufficient understanding of the realities of the Land of Snow.

Tibet's high altitude clearly distinguishes it from its neighbours. However, as the source of many of Asia's great rivers and having a measurable effect on the regional climate, it cannot easily be ignored. The Tibetan people have a distinct identity. Our language, diet, dress and way of life are unique. Our rich and ancient culture, strongly influenced by Buddhism, has much of value to contribute to the welfare of the world. For example, living experience of meditation has given practitioners a profound understanding of the working and nature of the mind. Similarly, Tibetan physicians have valuable insights into the ways of maintaining the balance of physical health.

In an increasingly interdependent world, a world in which information has such power, it is important that we extend our appreciation of all the peoples and environments with whom we share the planet. The *Tibet Handbook* gives a thorough treatment to the whole of Tibet. It includes maps, detailed descriptions of specific locations, a general introduction and practical information for visitors. I am confident it will fulfil a longstanding need. It will be welcomed both by those who venture into Tibet and those armchair travellers who, for the time being, prefer to stay at home. My congratulations to all who have contributed to this effort to make more readily available clear and reliable information about Tibet.

GYURME DORJE

Gyurme Dorje was born in 1950 in Edinburgh, where he received a classical education at George Watson's College and later obtained a Masters degree in Sanskrit and Oriental Studies from Edinburgh University. He then studied for 10 years in India and Nepal, initially at the Sanskrit University in Varanasi and subsequently in Darjeeling, Himachal Pradesh and Kathmandu, where he immersed himself in the Tibetan language and cultural traditions and was commissioned to translate Buddhist texts. Returning to the West in 1980 he continued his major translation projects, with the support of Tibetan communities in Dordogne and New York; and then moved to London in 1983 where, based at the School of Oriental and African Studies (SOAS), he completed a Ph.D in Tibetan literature (1987). From 1985 onwards he has made some 29 journeys to Tibet – on family visits, academic research projects and also in the capacity of a travel guide or tour director. In 1989 he founded Trans Himalaya, the first tour operator to focus on cultural expeditions and adventure travel in relation to the Tibetan plateau as a whole, offering specialist routes through the remote regions of Kham and Amdo. The author and translator of several important works on Tibetan Buddhism, Tibetan medicine and pilgrimage routes, he is currently a research fellow based at SOAS, working on the translation and compilation of *The Greater Tibetan English Dictionary*.

AUTHOR'S ACKNOWLEDGEMENTS

Thanks are due to the following who have contributed directly to the present work: Brian Beresford prepared the preliminary text for the chapter on Far-west Tibet (Ngari). Likewise, Bradley Rowe contributed much data for the Amdo section of the chapter entitled Far-east Tibet. Some of the Author's field work on East Tibet (Kham) was generously funded by the British Academy's Stein Arnold Exploration Award; and the remainder, along with the gathering of research data on Lhasa, Gyarong, Southern, Western, and Central Tibet, was carried out under the auspices of Trans-Himalaya of London and Abercrombie and Kent of Hong Kong over the course of 29 visits to the Tibetan plateau between 1985-95. The chapters on the Kathmandu valley and Bhutan have been revised and expanded by the author on the basis of Robert Bradnock's original text. Recent travel information on Bhutan was supplied by Françoise Pommeret.

Michael Farmer prepared the regional maps, with which each section of the Tibet guide is introduced. Sebastian Ballard provided the maps of Bhutan and the Kathmandu Valley. Kevin Feeney was responsible for the town and county maps whilst Joanne Morgan and Ann Griffiths typeset the Handbook. Iconographic line drawings are reproduced from Chandra, Lokesh (1988) *Buddhist Iconography*, Aditya Prakashan: New Delhi. Tibetan script has been added by Christopher Fynn; and Chinese script by Kelzang Drukdra. Thanks are also due to the following: GT Sonam, Tsewang Sidhar, Tendzin Phuntsok Atisha, Dolma Dorje, Weisi Pelyang, Hua Qing, Michael Aris, Michael Kawaleski, Topgyel and Orgyan Dorje.

CONTENTS

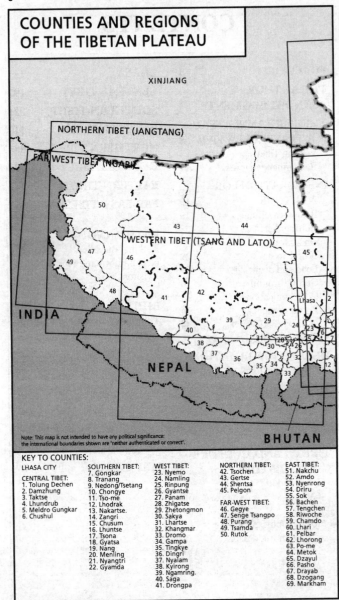

COUNTIES AND REGIONS OF THE TIBETAN PLATEAU

XINJIANG

NORTHERN TIBET (JANGTANG)

FAR WEST TIBET (NGARI)

WESTERN TIBET (TSANG AND LATO)

INDIA

Lhasa

NEPAL

BHUTAN

Note: This map is not intended to have any political significance: the international boundaries shown are 'neither authenticated or correct'.

KEY TO COUNTIES:

LHASA CITY

CENTRAL TIBET:
1. Tolung Dechen
2. Damzhung
3. Taktse
4. Lhundrub
5. Meldro Gungkar
6. Chushul

SOUTHERN TIBET:
7. Gongkar
8. Tranang
9. Nedong/Tsetang
10. Chongye
11. Tso-me
12. Lhodrak
13. Nakartse
14. Zangri
15. Chusum
16. Lhuntse
17. Tsona
18. Gyatsa
19. Nang
20. Menling
21. Nyangtri
22. Gyamda

WEST TIBET:
23. Nyemo
24. Namling
25. Rinpung
26. Gyantse
27. Panam
28. Zhigatse
29. Zhetongmon
30. Sakya
31. Lhartse
32. Khangmar
33. Dromo
34. Gampa
35. Tingkye
36. Dingri
37. Nyalam
38. Kyirong
39. Ngamring.
40. Saga
41. Drongpa

NORTHERN TIBET:
42. Tsochen
43. Gertse
44. Shentsa
45. Pelgon

FAR-WEST TIBET:
46. Gegye
47. Senge Tsangpo
48. Purang
49. Tsamda
50. Rutok

EAST TIBET:
51. Nakchu
52. Amdo
53. Nyenrong
54. Driru
55. Sok
56. Bachen
57. Tengchen
58. Riwoche
59. Chamdo
60. Lhari
61. Pelbar
62. Lhorong
63. Po-me
64. Metok
65. Dzayul
66. Pasho
67. Drayab
68. Dzogang
69. Markham

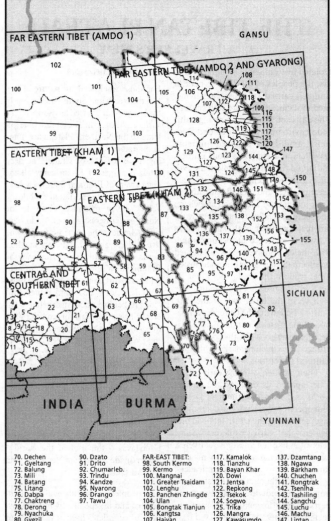

70. Dechen	90. Dzato	**FAR-EAST TIBET:**	117. Kamalok	137. Dzamtang
71. Gyeltang	91. Drito	98. South Kermo	118. Tianzhu	138. Ngawa
72. Balung	92. Chumarleb.	99. Kermo	119. Bayan Khar	139. Barkham
73. Mili	93. Trindu	100. Mangnai	120. Dowi	140. Chuchen
74. Batang	94. Kandze	101. Greater Tsaidam	121. Jentsa	141. Tsenlha
75. Litang	95. Nyarong	102. Lenghu	122. Repkong	142. Tsenlha
76. Dabpa	96. Drango	103. Panchen Zhingde	123. Tsekok	143. Tashiling
77. Chaktreng	97. Tawu	104. Ulan	124. Sogwo	144. Sangchu
78. Derong		105. Bongtak Tianjun	125. Trika	145. Luchu
79. Nyachuka		106. Kangtsa	126. Mangra	146. Machu
80. Gyezil		107. Haiyan	127. Kawasumdo	147. Lintan
81. Dardo		108. Tongkor	128. Chabcha	148. Cho-ne
82. Chakzamka		109. Ziling City	129. Tsigortang	149. Tewo
83. Jomda		110. Rushar	130. Mato	150. Drukchu
84. Gonjo		111. Gonlung	131. Machen	151. Dzoge
85. Pelyul		112. Serkhok	132. Gabde	152. Mewa
86. Derge		113. Mongyon	133. Darlag	153. Zungchu
87. Sershul		114. Chilen	134. Jigdril	154. Nampel
88. Jyekundo		115. Tsongkha Khar	135. Padma	155. Maowen
89. Nangchen		116. Drotsang	136. Serthal	156. Trochu
				157. Lungu

THE TIBETAN PLATEAU:
A TRAVELLER'S VIEW

Isolated by formidable mountain barriers, the peoples of the Tibetan plateau uniquely carried a sophisticated, living, medieval culture into the 20th century. The allure of Tibet's pristine high-altitude environment and profound Buddhist traditions attracted intrepid travellers and explorers from Europe, India, and America throughout the 19th and early 20th centuries. Many faced great physical and mental hardships in their journeys to Lhasa and elsewhere; and some tragically lost their lives, without reaching their goal. The Tibetans actively discouraged such contacts and, with the exception of a few far-sighted intellectuals and lamas, no-one inside Tibet realized the implications that Tibet's self-imposed isolation would come to have in the latter half of the 20th century. Following the Chinese occupation of the plateau and the abortive Tibetan uprising of 1959, the country was plunged into the long dark night of the Cultural Revolution.

Then, suddenly, in the early 1980s, Tibet opened its doors to the outside world as a tourist destination. Deluxe tour operators were quick to take advantage, rekindling the allure that had motivated the early explorers. Some celebrities like Tenzin Norgye of Everest who had become a legend in his own time, were even engaged as tour leaders!

Although there are still restrictions imposed on individual travel in many parts of Tibet for political reasons, ensuring that only the well-endowed traveller can afford to undertake full-scale guaranteed itineraries, bureaucracy has not deterred the adventurous hardy backpacker who can often be seen trudging through remote parts of the country, following in the footsteps of his or her illustrious predecessors.

For those fascinated by **nature**, Tibet, like the North and South Poles, is one of the last great uncharted territories on the surface of the earth. The vibrant blue salt lakes of the Northern Plateau are home to migratory birds from Siberia, including the Black-necked Crane. The deep forested gorges of Kham carry all the great rivers of East and Southeast Asia: Salween, Mekong and Yangtze; while the Yellow River meanders through the North-eastern grasslands of Amdo – ancestral home of the nomadic *drokpa*, who live in black yak wool tents, tending their herds of yak and dri. Further W, the Brahmaputra flows along the continental suture through a landscape of high-altitude desert. Vast sand dunes shift along its banks, concealing sheltered lateral valleys, where farming communities (*rongpa*) subsist on highland barley. In the Far-west are the deserted cave cities of the Sutlej valley, and the gorge of the upper Indus.

Throughout the plateau, the spectacular snow mountains have always been focal points of pilgrimage. Such are the sacred peaks of Mt Kailash in the Far-west, Amnye Machen in the NE, Kawa Karpo in the SE, and the awesome Himalayas – the roof of the world – which divide Tibet from Nepal, Bhutan and Northern India.

The **peoples** of the plateau are stout-hearted and independently minded, living in complete harmony with this environment. The upper grasslands and watersheds are the preserve of the nomads who now live their lives largely untainted by the Chinese occupation. By contrast, in the low-lying towns and cities, the palpable tension between the indigenous Tibetans and Chinese immigrant community reflects, on the one hand, the robust and courageous resolve of those who are determined to conserve their cultural heritage and, on the other, the pragmatism of those who reluctantly accommodate themselves to the ways of their colonists.

For visitors interested in the Buddhist **culture** of Tibet, only a few of the great monasteries and palaces have survived the ravages of the recent past relatively unscathed. In Lhasa, there are outstanding works of art to be seen in the Potala and Norbulingka palaces of the Dalai Lamas, in the city temples of Jokhang, Ramoche, and Lukhang; and in the surrounding monasteries of Drepung and Sera. Other monasteries in far-flung parts of the country, such as Tashilhunpo (the seat of the Panchen Lamas) and Labrang (the seat of the Jamyang Zhepas) still proudly display some of their original treasured artefacts. However, throughout the length and breadth of the country, you cannot fail to be impressed by the efforts made by local communities to restore their particular monasteries or temples, no matter which school of Tibetan Buddhism or Bon they espouse.

When visiting monasteries, you will not usually have to remove shoes, as in India, but do remember to be modestly dressed, to remove your hat, to abstain from smoking, and to proceed around or through sacred shrines in a clockwise manner. Never sit down pointing your feet towards the images of a temple or its inner sanctum! You may feel privileged to bear witness to the revival of this ancient culture, even if distressed by the obvious signs of wanton destruction, mostly dating from the 1960s, and by the apparent lack of activity in some monasteries. This can be balanced at the end of your trip by a visit to neighbouring Kathmandu or Bhutan, where many of Tibet's greatest lamas have actively resurrected their communities in exile. Independent Bhutan also preserves the ancient spiritual heritage of Tibet intact, having avoided the depradations of the Chinese Cultural Revolution. Nonetheless, in many remote monasteries of East and Far-east Tibet you will be heartened by the genuine non-sectarian approach and commitment to the meditative and scholarly life shown by elderly and young monks or nuns alike, with scant material resources.

The convergence of Tibet's spiritual and secular life can best be seen during the **autumnal festival season**, when, throughout the length and breadth of the country, finely dressed crowds assemble to spectate or participate in the diverse equestrian events, folk singing and dancing performances, contests of marksmanship and trials of strength, interspersed with the colourful pageantry of religious dance (*cham*). Tented commercial travellers vigorously ply their wares, as traditional handicrafts change hands, along with modern goods, weaponry, and religious artefacts.

VISITING TIBET

Tibet is not an easy part of the world to visit. Its physical size and height above sea level combined with red tape and bureaucracy make for adventurous travelling. Therefore if you decide to visit Tibet, whether out of a spirit of adventure, to commune with nature, or to explore the Buddhist and secular heritage, you must be prepared to endure physical hardships in the course of your journey. Read the Information for visitors section (page 19) carefully and equip yourself properly before setting out.

Tibet's climate dictates that it is only really possible to visit during the spring, summer and autumn (late Mar-Nov). Out of this period it is extremely cold and many routes are impassable as passes are closed by snow. Lhasa, the capital, is however accessible throughout the winter months by flight from Chengdu.

Decide which parts of Tibet you wish to visit

Since the plateau as a whole is as large as Western Europe, it is obviously impossible to go everywhere in the course of a single trip! There are four main gateway cities offering access to the plateau: Kathmandu (in Nepal), Chengdu (in Sichuan), Kunming (in Yunnan), and Lanzhou (in Gansu); or five with the addition of Kashgar (in Xinjiang, very difficult to enter through but easier as an exit point).

Tibet itself is conveniently divided into seven geographical regions: Lhasa (the capital); Central Tibet (Kyichu Valley); Southern Tibet and Western Tibet (the lower and upper reaches of the Brahmaputra River and its lateral valleys); Northern Tibet (Jangtang Plateau); Far-west Tibet (Ngari); Eastern Tibet (Kham); and Far-east Tibet (Amdo and Gyarong). Each region has a map showing the 5,000m line with the major rivers and their lateral valleys clearly shown.

The counties forming each of these regions have many interesting places of interest close to the motorable roads. Lesser jeep tracks and trekking routes are also described within each of the counties, usually following the contours of its river valleys and mountain passes. Each county begins with a tinted panel showing both Tibetan and Chinese names in English and script as well as population and area statistics. In most cases, a distance chart has been included, showing the accessibility of the main places of interest and towns.

NB Good, accurate maps on Tibet are extremely rare, particularly those with topographic information. This *Handbook* has drawn on extensive field visits to compile these schematic county plans. The regional maps, showing topographic features, roads, towns, and all the places of interest referred to in the text, are all drawn with the most up-to-date informa-tion available. Refer to the Introduction for the key map providing an overall view of the Tibetan plateau and the adjacent countries S of the Himalayan range – Bhutan, Nepal, and peripheral parts of N India.

Organized and FIT Travel

Having decided upon an itinerary, the next step is to determine whether you wish to go out as an individual traveller or make your travel arrangements through a tour operator. The latter option, though more expensive, is the only one which will reliably enable you to visit the so-called 'closed' areas of Eastern and Far-west Tibet. All arrangements including international flight connections to any of the five gateway cities, Chinese visas, and Tibet travel permits will be made by your tour operator. This does not imply having to take a 'package' tour as operators are quite used to organizing tours for very small groups or even single travellers.

On the other hand, if you have a low budget, time to spare, great physical endurance, and are able to accept the risk of being unceremoniously ejected from the country (or one part of it), the former option is perfectly feasible. Only certain parts of Amdo in NE Tibet are officially designated as 'open' areas, properly accessible to the individual traveller. In between, there is the grey area of Lhasa and its environs, said to be 'open', but often highly restricted. Individual travellers, after obtaining a standard Chinese visa, should first consult the information on the gateway cities given in this guide – Kathmandu (page 657, Chengdu (page 508, Kunming (page 492, Lanzhou (page 584, and Kashgar (page 440). Of these, access from Lanzhou currently offers the best prospects for the FIT travel.

Hotels and restaurants

A wide choice is only available in Lhasa, Ziling and the gateway cities. Kathmandu, Chengdu and Kunming offer the full range of luxury to budget accommodation. On the plateau itself, 3-star hotels, such as *Lhasa Holiday Inn* and the *Qinghai Hotel* in Ziling, are at the top of the range. Outside of the main towns, be prepared to sleep in government guesthouses and truck stops which are highly variable and often decidedly unclean, sometimes lacking even basic facilities. Camping is often much preferable.

Hotel categories are determined by the price of the average double room, exclusive of local taxes.

Getting around

There are only a few paved roads in Tibet. Most roads are therefore subject to clouds of dust and delays occur in summer due to landslides. Public transport is almost exclusively reserved for Tibetans but some truck drivers may be prepared to give lifts to independent travellers (hitchhiking is illegal). Make sure that you obtain adequate transport for your chosen destination. This will often be 4WD landcruisers with support trucks. For this reason alone, truly independent travel over long distances is not easy.

Tibetan and Chinese place names

It is an inescapable fact that the Tibetan Plateau is largely under Chinese control. For this reason there is a bewildering use of names and no two sources seem to agree on whether Tibetan or Chinese names are used. Do not be surprised to find a complete mixture of both – this does not present too much of a difficulty as Tibetans will be pleased to help. The *Handbook* has adopted a totally Tibetan approach and Chinese equivalents are only given for the main places. The names of the counties within each region and the names of important monasteries or places of interest within them have also been given in Tibetan and Chinese script. This information is provided, not for the specialist, but on behalf of the independent traveller who may have no means of communication with local people.

Pronunciation and spelling

The spelling adopted for the representation of both Tibetan and Sanskrit names in this work is designed with the general reader in mind, rather than the specialist. Exact transliterations have therefore been avoided.

● Tibetan

Tibetan spellings have been chosen which broadly reflect a modern Central Tibetan pronunciation (not necessarily that of Lhasa). Please note that a final e is never silent, but pronounced in the manner of the French *é*. *Ph* is never pronounced like an English *f*, but like a *p* with strong aspiration. Among the important regional variants, the general reader should be aware that in some parts of the country, *ky* or *khy* may be pronounced as *ch*, *gy* as *j*, *b* as *w*, *dr* as *b*, and *ny* as *hmy*. Also suffixes may be elided, and the basic vowel sounds may change, such that *u* becomes *i*, and so forth.

● Sanskrit

In the absence of diacritics to represent Sanskrit letters, the following simplified conventions have been observed throughout: *palatal c* is rendered as *c* (but to be pronounced as in *Italian ch*); *palatal s* is rendered *sh*, and *retroflex s* as a simple *s*. The names of all deities are given, wherever possible, in their Sanskrit rather than Tibetan forms. For a correspondence between the Sanskrit and Tibetan names see the glossary and the iconographic guide, pages 129 and 76.

RECOMMENDED TOURS

The following tours, representative of the diverse region, will assist you make your choice of destination; but they are by no means exclusive. A number of them overlap and it is obviously possible to swop between them. In each of the regional sections, the recommended route is highlighted at the beginning of each section. The right hand column cross-references their stages to specific pages of the guide, and you will be able to read around these in more detail before planning your route.

NB All except the third entail long overland journeys exceeding 1,000 km.

1. Cultural Tour of Central, Southern, and Western Tibet

Length: 15 days. *Best time to visit*: April-June, late Sept-Nov.

This itinerary is usually the one preferred by first-time visitors to Tibet, in that it combines the main historic palaces and monasteries of Tibet's heartland, with a close Himalayan encounter, and relatively comfortable travel and accommodation en route. Starting from the gateway city of Kathmandu in Nepal, you fly to Lhasa and then to the former capitals of Tsetang and Zhigatse, before cutting through the highland region, overland to Nepal. Travel by 4WD or minibus (if you do not visit Everest Base Camp).

Alternatively, you can extend the trip by organizing an extension from the Chongye Tombs to Lhodrak and reach Nakartse on the road to Gyantse from the S (see pages 129-330).

Day 1	Kathmandu	657
	Gongkar Airport	222
	Overnight: Lhasa	129
Day 2-6	Lhasa	129
Day 7	Lhasa	
	Samye Monastery	235
	Overnight: Tsetang	245
Day 8	Chongye Tombs	265
	Tradruk Temple	255
	Yumbu Lagang Palace	258
	Overnight: Tsetang	
Day 9	Mindroling	231
	Overnight: Gyantse	322
Day 10	Zhalu Monastery	341
	Overnight: Zhigatse	331
Day 11	Zhigatse	
Day 12	Sakya Monastery	348
	Overnight: Shelkar	365
Day 13	Everest Base Camp	368
	Overnight: Shelkar	
Day 14	Dingri	365
	Overnight: Dram	375
Day 15	Return to Kathmandu	

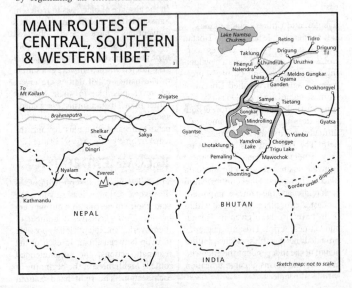

MAIN ROUTES OF CENTRAL, SOUTHERN & WESTERN TIBET

Sketch map: not to scale

2. Mount Kailash and Guge Kingdom

Length: 25 days. *Best time to visit*: May-July, Sept-Oct.

This is an itinerary for the hardy adventurer or gritty pilgrim, combining the regions of Western, Northern, and Far-west Tibet, and culminating in the circuit of the sacred Mt Kailash and the cave cities of Toling and Tsaparang. Travel by 4WD.

Day 1	Kathmandu	657
	Overnight: Dram	375
Day 2	Dingri	365
	Overnight: Shelkar	365
Day 3	Dzarongpu Monastery	368
	Overnight: Everest Base Camp	368
Day 4	*Overnight*: Shelkar	
Day 5	Lhartse	355
	Overnight: Tingkye	363
Day 6	Tsochen	388
Day 7	Gertse	390
Day 8	Gegye	400
Day 9	Senge Tsangpo	402
Day 10	Tsamda	423
Day 11	Tsaparang	429
Day 12	Toling	425
Day 13	Tirthapuri	404
Day 14	Darchen	406
Day 15-18	Mt Kailash trek	406
	Manasarovar Lake	416
Day 19-20	Manasarovar Lake	
	Chiu Monastery	418
	Overnight: Purang	405
Day 21	Mayum La Pass	385
Day 22	Baryang	385
Day 23	Saga	382
Day 24	Nyalam	374
Day 25	Dram	
	Return to Kathmandu	

3. Kyi-chu Valley

Length: 15 days. *Best time to visit*: April-Oct.

Around Lhasa, it is possible to explore the Kyi-chu valley of Central Tibet, with relatively short travel stages. For those disinclined to undertake a long expedition, this itinerary highlights rural life and the historic monasteries of the Upper Kyi-chu, in close proximity to the capital. Enjoy bathing in the hot springs at Zhoto Tidro. Travel by 4WD.

Day 1	Kathmandu	657
	Gongkar Airport	222
	Overnight: Lhasa	129
Day 2-5	Lhasa	
Day 6	Yerpa Caves	202
Day 7	Taklung Monastery	207
Day 8	Reting Monastery	208
Day 9	Zhoto Tidro Hermitage	215
Day 10	Zhoto Tidro Hermitage	
Day 11	Drigung Monastery	212
Day 12	Uruzhva Temple	
	Katsel	210
	Overnight: Gyama	210
Day 13	Ganden Monastery	203
Day 14	Lhasa	
Day 15	Return to Kathmandu	

4. Brahmaputra Gorges and the Salween-Mekong Traverse

Length: 19 days. *Best time to visit*: April-June, late Sept-Oct.

This combines a tour of the beautifully forested Kongpo region of Southern Tibet with the Northern and Southern overland routes to and from Chamdo in Kham. **NB** The route is easily reversed. The stretch from Nyangtri to Pasho is often impassable in the rainy season or when the road is cut up by glacial snowmelt. Travel by 4WD.

Day 1	Kathmandu	657
	Gongkar Airport	222
	Overnight: Lhasa	129
Day 2-3	Lhasa	
Day 4	Draksum Lake	307
Day 5	Buchu Temple	299
Day 6	Timpei Caves	296
Day 7	Nyangtri	298
Day 8	Po-me	475
Day 9	Pasho	480
Day 10	Chamdo	466
Day 11	Chamdo	
Day 12	Riwoche	460
Day 13	Riwoche Temple	461

5. Lhasa to Chengdu Overland

Length: 21 days. *Best time to visit*: April-June, late Sept-Oct.

This increasingly popular itinerary enables visitors to travel through the 'closed' areas of E Tibet from Lhasa via Chamdo and Derge to Chengdu in Sichuan. There are a number of important monasteries en route, such as those at Chamdo, Derge, Kandze, and Lhagang. **NB** The journey can be rugged and facilities are poor en route. It is easily reversed; and the northern route from Lhasa to Chamdo (pages 129 and 76) can be substituted for the southern one shown here. Also, the southern route from Chamdo via Batang and Litang to Dardo (pages 465-506) can be followed instead of that via Derge which is included here. Travel by 4WD.

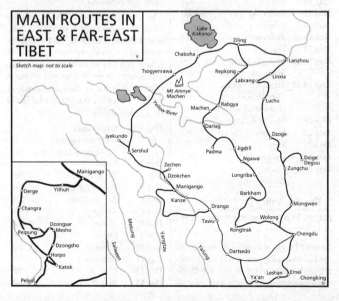

MAIN ROUTES IN EAST & FAR-EAST TIBET

Sketch map: not to scale

6. Lhasa to Lanzhou Overland

Length: 16 days. *Best time to visit*: May-Oct.

This route traverses the desolate W Kokonor plateau of the Far-east Tibet region, to reach the fabled Kokonor – one of Inner Asia's largest lakes, before travelling through Kumbum, Repkong and Labrang, which are at the cultural heart of Amdo. The Repkong style of painting is particularly renowned. **NB** This itinerary is reversible. Travel by 4WD or minibus (but take care on the stretch from Repkong to Labrang.

Day 1	Kathmandu	657
	Gongkar Airport	222
	Overnight: Lhasa	129
Day 2-4	Lhasa	
Day 5	Nakchu	451
Day 6	Amdo	452
Day 7	Toma	560
Day 8	Kermo	562
Day 9	Lake Kokonor	570
Day 10	Lake Kokonor	
Day 11	Ziling	573
Day 12	Kumbum Monastery	577
	Overnight: Ziling	
Day 13	Repkong	592
Day 14	Labrang	638
Day 15	Labrang	
Day 16	Lanzhou	584

7. Lhasa to Kunming Overland

Length: 18 days. *Best time to visit*: April-June, late Sept-Nov.

This truly memorable journey combines the route from Lhasa to Chamdo in Kham with a descent of the Mekong River, bypassing the plunging glaciers of the sacred Mt Kawa Karpo into the rich flowering landscapes of Dechen county and Yunnan. **NB** This itinerary is reversible; and the northern route from Lhasa to Chamdo (pages 129 and 330) could be substituted for the southern one shown here. Also it is possible to go from Markham across the Yangtze to Batang and thence southwards into Yunnan via Chaktreng (pages 498-498).

Day 1	Kathmandu	657
	Gongkar Airport	222
	Overnight: Lhasa	129
Day 2-4	Lhasa	
Day 5	Draksum Lake	307
Day 6	Nyangtri	298
Day 7	Po-me	475
Day 8	Pasho	480
Day 9	Chamdo	466
Day 10	Chamdo	
Day 11	Dzogang	485
Day 12	Markham	486
Day 13	Tsakhalo	486
Day 14	Dechen	487
Day 15	Gyeltang	489
Day 16	Lijiang	491
Day 17	Dali	492
Day 18	Kunming	492

8. Kham and Amdo Overland

Length: 22 days. *Best time to visit*: May-Oct.

Starting in the gateway city of Chengdu and ending in Lanzhou, this is a detailed itinerary combining the grasslands of Kham and Amdo with the Amdo cultural heartland around Kumbum, Repkong, and Labrang. There are many monasteries en route such as those at Lhagang, Kandze, Dzogchen, Zhechen, Jyekundo, Zhiwu, and so on. **NB** This itinerary is reversible. Travel by 4WD or minibus (but take care on the stretch from Repkong to Labrang.

Day 1	Hong Kong/Beijing	
	Overnight: Chengdu	508
Day 2	Chengdu	
Day 3	Wolong Panda Reserve	507
Day 4	Dartsedo	503
Day 5	Lhagang Monastery	501
Day 6	Tawu	550
Day 7	Kandze	544
Day 8	Dzogchen Monastery	524
Day 9	Dzogchen Monastery	
Day 10	Zhechen Monastery	525
	Overnight: Sershul	528
Day 11	Zhiwu	530
Day 12	Jyekundo	532

Day 13	Jyekundo	
Day 14	Mato	607
Day 15	Mt Amnye Machen	556
	Overnight: Wenchuan	605
Day 16	Chabcha	602
	Overnight: Lake Kokonor	570
Day 17	Ziling	573
Day 18	Kumbum Monastery	577
	Overnight: Ziling	
Day 19	Repkong	592
Day 20	Labrang	638
Day 21	Labrang	
Day 22	*Overnight*: Lanzhou	584

9. Golok and Gyarong Overland

Length: 21 days. *Best time to visit*: April-June, Sept-Oct.

This exciting itinerary combines the Labrang, Repkong and Kumbum heartland of Amdo with the nomadic region of Golok and the Jonangpa and Nyingmapa monasteries of the upper Gyarong in Far-east Tibet. **NB** It can easily be reversed. Travel by 4WD.

Day 1	Hong Kong/Beijing	
	Overnight: Lanzhou	584
Day 2	Labrang Monastery	638
Day 3	Repkong	592
Day 4	Ziling	573

Day 5	Kumbum Monastery	577
	Overnight: Chabcha	602
Day 6	Darlag	613
Day 7	Tarthang Monastery	615
Day 8	Jigdril	615
Day 9	Ngawa	623
Day 10	Ngawa	
Day 11	Barkham	628
Day 12	Dzamtang	621
Day 13	Dzamtang	
Day 14	Sertal	619
Day 15	Sertal	
Day 16	Drango	548
Day 17	Lhagang Monastery	501
Day 18	Dartsedo	503
Day 19	Tsenlha	633
Day 20	Wolong Panda Reserve	507
Day 21	Chengdu	508

10. Eastern Kham Overland

Length: 26 days. *Best time to visit*: May-June, late Sept-Oct.

This focuses on the gorges and grasslands of eastern Kham (currently in Sichuan). It combines the Chinese Buddhist pilgrimage site of Mt Emei Shan with a number of renowned Nyingmapa, Sakyapa and Gelukpa monasteries. **NB** This can be reversed. Travel by 4WD.

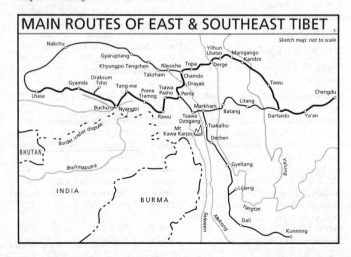

MAIN ROUTES OF EAST & SOUTHEAST TIBET

Sketch map: not to scale

Day 1	Hong Kong/Beijing	
	Overnight: Chengdu	508
Day 2	Chengdu	
Day 3	Emei Shan	507
Day 4	Emei Shan	
Day 5	Haiyan	571
Day 6	Dartsedo	503
Day 7	Nyachuka	499
Day 8	Litang	496
Day 9	Batang	495
Day 10	Litang	
	Overnight: Nyachuka	
Day 11	Nyarong	547
Day 12	Pelyul Monastery	515
Day 13	Pelyul Monastery	
Day 14	Katok Monastery	513
Day 15	Katok Monastery	
Day 16	Dzongsar Monastery	518
Day 17	Derge	520
Day 18	Derge	
Day 19	Dzogchen Monastery	524
Day 20	Dzokchen Monastery	
Day 21	Kandze	544
Day 22	Kandze	
Day 23	Lhagang Monastery	501
Day 24	Dartsedo	
Day 25	Wolong Panda Reserve	507
Day 26	Chengdu	

11. Nature Parks of Amdo

Length: 23 days. *Best time to visit*: April-Oct.

The last of these recommended itineraries runs from Chengdu to Lanzhou, passing through the beautiful nature parks of the Minjiang valley and those of the Amnye Machen range, Drakar Tredzong, and Lake Kokonor. The scenery is spectacular and rewarding. **NB** This itinerary can be reversed. Travel by 4WD or minibus; and by horse around the N side of Mt Amnye Machen.

Day 1	Hong Kong/Beijing	
	Overnight: Chengdu	508
Day 2	Chengdu	
Day 3	Zungchu	650
Day 4	Sertso Park	650
Day 5	Dzitsa Degu Park	652
Day 6	Dzitsa Degu Park	
Day 7	Dzoge	646
Day 8	Labrang Monastery	638
Day 9	Repkong	592
Day 10	Machen	609
Day 11	Xueshan	611
Day 12-14	Amnye Machen	610
Day 15	Machen	
Day 16	Tsogyenrawa	608
Day 17	Drakar Tredzong	604
Day 18	Drakar Tredzong	
Day 19	Chabcha	602
Day 20	Lake Kokonor	570
Day 21	Ziling	573
Day 22	Kumbum Monastery	577
	Ziling	
Day 23	Lanzhou	584

INFORMATION FOR VISITORS

Abbreviations

Abbreviations used in the book include:
a/c = air-conditioned; T = telephone; F
= fax; nr = near; under Hotels rm =
room/ rooms, bath = WC, shower or
bath; rec = recommended; hr =
hour/hours; N = north; S = south; E =
east; W = west.

NB For specific information on Bhutan
and Nepal, please see pages 741 and 657.

Before travelling

Entry requirements

● **Visas and permits**

A valid passport including a standard
Chinese **entry visa** is essential. Such
visas are generally obtainable from most
Chinese embassies and consulates,
sometimes on sight of flight tickets and
TCs. In the high season (Aug/Sept) confirmation of booking through a domestic
Chinese travel agency is required, and
this is all that one needs to travel to those
parts of the Tibetan plateau which are
officially designated as 'open' to individual travellers. The cost of a standard
Chinese tourist visa varies from US$12-
120 according to the nationality of the
applicant and the type of visa required.
Individual visas may be issued for single
or double entry, with a validity of 1, 2, or
3 months. Group visas may be issued for
parties of six and over, for the specific
duration of a fixed itinerary (single or
double entry). Multiple entry visas are
normally issued for business or educational purposes only, ranging in validity
from 6-12 months, and are more expensive (US$120-250). Normally three
working days is required to process an
application from the date of its submis-
sion, but express services are also available at a premium.

**Aliens' Travel Permit and Military Per-
mit** In April 1996, there are very few
parts of Tibet which are completely open
to the individual traveller who has sim-
ply obtained a standard Chinese visa.
Such areas are confined to the extreme
NE fringe of Amdo (ie certain parts of
Gansu, Qinghai and Sichuan provinces).
To visit other parts of Tibet, including
Lhasa, and the central, western, south-

INTERNAL TRAVEL: THE NEED FOR PERMITS

In order to understand these restrictions on internal travel, it is important to keep in mind the political situation in China and Tibet. It took a backward turn in 1989 with martial law being declared in Lhasa for over a year. Although martial law ostensibly has been lifted, tourists are still closely watched. It is important to be aware that Tibet is an occupied country, so one must take care not to jeopardize the position of anyone who may help while you are there. The current attitude of the Chinese authorities to foreign tourists in Tibet is ambivalent. They want their money yet know that many tourists sympathize with the Tibetans and their wish for self-determination.

For this reason and because it is more financially lucrative they have forbidden the 'backpacking lone traveller' and insist on supervised group tours at fixed rates. This they justify by saying that you are travelling on the "roof of the world" and thus, the more remote your journey the more you should pay for the privilege, despite little or no facilities! This means that your enjoyment of a journey through remote areas of Tibet will, to a large extent, depend upon your own ability not to be disturbed by repeated requests for fees, permits and even for photography, as well as some exorbitant rates for hotel accommodation.

ern, and far-western regions, as well as Kham and Golok, a standard Chinese visa is not sufficient. Individual travel is not permitted within these areas (although there are inevitably individuals who can reach Lhasa from Kermo or Chengdu overland with great ingenuity and some degree of risk). In order to visit these so-called 'closed areas', a special **Aliens' Travel Permit** (ATP) must be issued by the police in either Lhasa, Chengdu, Kunming, Lanzhou, or Ziling (sometimes reinforced by a **military permit** also).

To obtain such permits, it is necessary to make your travel arrangements through a bona fide agency, providing details of age, sex, nationality, passport number, occupation, and address, preferably 2 months before departure. The visa authorization will then be faxed or telexed to the Chinese embassy of your choice, and on that basis a standard Chinese visa will be issued. Alternatively, those who enter China with a standard Chinese tourist visa can also make ad hoc arrangements with a local agency in any of the above cities to obtain an ATP and (if required) a military

permit before entering the closed areas of the Tibetan plateau. To be safe it is better to make prior arrangements through a tour operator or travel agent before leaving home.

The permits themselves specify every destination and town that you wish to visit and cannot be changed once you have arrived in the closed area of your choice. Therefore be certain to detail all possible destinations in your request as well as the route(s) you wish to follow.

● **Embassies and consulates**
Australia: 15 Coronation Dr, Yarralumla, ACT 2600, T (062) 273 4780, 273 4781; Consulate: 77 Irving Rd, Toorak, Melbourne, Victoria, T (03) 8220604; **Austria:** Meternichgasse 4, 1030 Vienna, T (06) 753149/7136706; **Belgium:** 443-5, Avenue de Tervureen, 1150 Brussels, T (02) 7713309/7712681; **Canada:** 515 St Patrick's St, Ottawa, Ontario KIN 5H3, T (0613) 2342706/2342682; **France:** 11 Ave George V, 75008, Paris, T (1) 47.23.36.77/43.36.77.90; **Germany:** Karfurtsenallee 12, Bonn 2 (Bad Godesberg), T (0228) 361095/362350; **Hong Kong:** Visa Office, Ministry of Foreign

Affairs of the PRC, 5/F Low Block, China Resources Building, 26 Harbour Rd, Wanchai, T 5851794/5851700; **Italy:** 56 via Bruxelles, 56-00198 Rome, T (06) 841 3458/841 3467; **Japan:** 3-4-33, Moto-Azabu, Minato-ku, Tokyo, T (03) 34033380/34033065; **Nepal:** Baluwatar, Kathmandu, T 412332/415383; **Netherlands:** Adriaan Goekooplaan 7, 2517 JX The Hague, T (070) 355 1515/9209; **New Zealand:** 2-6 Glenmore St, Wellington, T (064) 4721383/4721384; **Spain:** C/Arturo Soria 113, 28043 Madrid, T (01) 519 4242/3651; **Sweden:** Lodovagen 8 115 25, Stockholm, T (08) 783 6739/783 0179; **Switzerland:** Kalecheggweg 10, 3006 Bern, T (031) 447333/434593; **UK:** 49-51 Portland Pl, London W1N 3AH, T (0171) 6311430; **USA:** 2300 Connecticut Ave NW, Washington DC 20008, T 3282500/3282517, F (202) 3282582; Consulates: 3417 Montrose Blvd, Houston, Texas 77006; 104 South Michigan Ave, Suite 1200, Chicago, Illinois 60603; 1450 Laguna St, San Francisco, CA 94115; 520 12th Ave, New York, NY 10036. The only foreign embassy on the Tibetan plateau is the Royal Nepalese Consulate: Gyatso To Lam, Lhasa, T (0891) 6322881. In Chengdu there is a US Consulate General, *Jinjiang Hotel* (West Wing), T (028) 5583520.

● **Tourist information**
The various provinces into which the Tibetan plateau is divided have their own respective tourist authorities. Tourism within the Tibetan Autonomous Region is administered by the Tibet Tourism Bureau (TTB), Yuanlin Rd, T 34315, F (0891) 6334632. For information on travel to E Tibet, contact the Sichuan Provincial Tourism Bureau, 180 Renmin Nan Rd, T (028) 5527478; the Yunnan Provincial Tourism Bureau, Huancheng Nanlou St, Kunming, T (0871) 3132895, the Qinghai Provincial Tourism Bureau, 21 Huanghe Rd, T 6143711, F (0086-971) 8238721; and the Gansu Provincial Tourism Bureau,

209 Tianshui Ave, Lanzhou, T (0931) 8426847.

● **Domestic tour companies and travel agents**
The main domestic travel agencies have already been listed under their respective cities, especially Lhasa, Kunming, Chengdu, Ziling, and Lanzhou. Among these the best are: **in Lhasa:** *China Workers' Travel Service* (CWTS): Tibet Branch, *Holiday Inn Lhasa*, Room 1104, T 6324250, 6332221 ext 1104, F (0086-891) 6334472, Tx 69025 WTBL CN; – Tibet Tourist Corporation (TTC) – also known as China International Travel Service, Lhasa Branch (CITS), W Dekyi lam, T 6336626/6335046, F (00-86-891) 6336315/6335277; *Tibet International Sports Travel* (TIST), *Himalaya Hotel*, 6 E Lingkor lam, T 6334082, F (0086-891) 6334855; and *Tibet Plateau Iron Horse Travel Service* (IHTS), W Dekyi lam, T 6336793, 6332432, F (0086-891) 6336793, Tx 68012 TTB CN. **In Chengdu:** *Golden Bridge Travel Service* (CGBTS), 18 Jinhe St, T 6630370, F (0086-28)-6642528; and *Guagda Everbright Travel Service*, Room 115, *Chengdu Hotel*, Chengdu, T 4448888 ext 115, F (0086-28) 4433632. **In Kunming:** *Yunnan Overseas Travel Corporation*, 154 E Dongfeng Rd, Kunming, T 3188905, F (0086-871) 3132508. **In Lanzhou:** CITS, Lanzhou Branch, 361 Tianshui Ave, Lanzhou, T 8826181, F (0086-931) 8418556. **In Ziling:** CITS, Ziling Branch, T 38701 ext 1307, F (0086-971) 8238721.

● **International tour companies and travel agents**
Tours in the Tibetan area vary greatly in price, depending upon the number of days, the number of persons in a group, the remoteness and distance covered by the itinerary, and the package arrangement (ie full board or half-board). Prices are slightly lower than comparable tours of Bhutan, ranging from US$100/day to

over US$200/day.

Nepal: *Summit Trekking*, Kopundol Height, Lalitpur, PO Box 1406, Kathmandu, T (977-1) 521894, F (977-1) 523737; *Arniko Travel*, PO Box 4695, Naxal, Nagpokhari, Kathmandu, T (977-1) 412667, F (977-1) 521880; *Himalayan Journeys*, PO Box 969, Kantipat, Kathmandu, T (977-1) 226138, F (977-1) 227068; *Kailash Himalaya Trek*, PO Box 4781, Bagbazar, Kathmandu, T (977-1) 229249, F (977-1) 223171; *Adventure Travel Nepal Ltd*, PO Box 272, Lazimpath, Kathmandu, T (977-1) 415995/ 223328, F (977-1) 414075/419126; *Tibet Travels and Tours Pvt Ltd*, PO Box 1397, Thamel, Kathmandu, T (977-1) 410303, F (977-1) 415126; *China Tibet Qomolangma Travelways Ltd*, PO Box 1147, Lal Durbar Marg, Kathmandu, T (977-1) 410411, F (977-1) 419778.

Hong Kong: *China Tibet Qomolangma Travelways Ltd*, 37/F Times Tower, 393 Jaffe Rd, T (852) 2838 3391, F (852) 2834 1535; *Abercrombie & Kent*, 27/F Tai Sang Commercial Building, 24-34 Hennessy Rd, Wanchai, T (852) 28657818, F (852) 28660556; *Mera Travel*, Room 1308 Argyll Centre Phase I, 688 Nathan Rd, T (852) 23916892, F (852) 27891649; *China Travel Service, Kowloon Branch*, 1/F Alpha House, 27-33 Nathan Rd, T (852) 7214481, F 7216251.

UK: *Trans Himalaya*, 30 Hanover Rd, London NW10 3DS, T (44) 181-459-7944, F (44) 181-459-8017, have the most specialized itineraries in E Tibet and Central Tibet, as well as short budget tours; *Bales Tours*, Bales House, Barrington Rd, Dorking RH4 3EJ, T (44) 1306 885991; *Encounter Overland*, 267 Old Brompton Rd, London SW5 9JA, T (44) 171 373 1433, F (44) 171 370 6951; *Himalayan Kingdoms*, 20 The Mall, Clifton, Bristol, BS8 4DR, T (44) 117 9237163; *Kailash Travel*, 116 Haverstock Hill, London NW3 2BB, T (44-71) 586 7372.

USA: *Inner Asia Expeditions*, 2627 Lombard St, San Francisco, CA 94123, T (415) 922 0448, F (415) 3465535; *Wilderness Travel*, 801 Allston Way, Berkeley, Ca 94710, T (415) 548 0420; *Mountain Travel*, 6420 Fairmount Ave, El Cerrito, CA 94530, T 415 527 8100; *Distant Horizons*, 619 Tremont St, Boston, MA 02118, T (617) 267-5343, F (617) 267 0323.

● **Tibetan Cultural Organizations**

For a comprehensive listing of such organizations, see *A Handbook of Tibetan Culture*, edited by Graham Coleman and published by Rider (1992). In the **UK**, such organizations include *Tibet House*, 1 Culworth St, London NW8 7AF (T 0171-722-5378); *Tibet Foundation*, 43 New Oxford St, London WC1 1BH (T 0171-379-0634); *Tibet Information Network*, 7 Beck Rd, London E8 4RE (T 0181-533-5458), and *The Orient Foundation*, Queene Anne House, 11 Charlotte St, Bath, Avon BA1 2NE (T 01225-336-010).

In the **United States**, contact *Tibet House*, 3/F 241 E 32nd St, New York, NY 10016 (T 0212-213-5392), *Tibetan Cultural Centre*, 3655 South Snoddy Rd, Bloomington, Indiana 47401 (T 0812-855-8222), the *Monasteries in Tibet Fund*, 256 S Robertson Blvd, Suite 9379, Beverley Hills, CA 98211; and *The Orient Foundation*, 261 Madison Ave, South Suite 103, Bainbridge Island, Washington 98110 (T 0206-842-1114).

In **India**, the most important offices are the *Library of Tibetan Works and Archives*, Gangchen Kyishong, Dharamsala, HP 176215 (T 01892-2467); the *Information Office of the Tibetan Government in Exile*, Gangchen Kyishong, Dharamsala, HP, 176215 (T 01892-2457/2598); and *Tibet House*, 1 Institutional Area, Lodhi Rd, New Delhi 110003 (T 611-515).

In **Nepal**, contact the *Office of Tibet*, PO Box 310 Lazimpat, Kathmandu (T 11660); in **Japan**, the *Tibetan Cultural Centre of Japan*, 2-31-22, Nerima, Nerima-ku, Tokyo (T 03-3991-5411); in

Canada, the *Canada-Tibet Friendship Society*, PO Box 6588, Postal Section A, Toronto, Ontario, M5W 1X4 (T 0416-531-3810); in **Australia**, *Tibet Information Service*, PO Box 87, Ivanhoe, Victoria, 3079 (T 03-663-4484); and in **France**, the *Gedun Chompel Asssociation for the Protection and Development of Tibetan Cultural Heritage*, 127 rue de Sevres, Paris 75006 (T 331-45679503).

When to go

April-June and Sept-Nov are generally the best and most popular months. The rainy season, though mild in comparison with that of India and Southeast Asia, can bring flash floods and high rivers, which break up the poor road surfaces. Be prepared to trek across landslides in the rainy season. However, the Tibetan plateau, and particularly the S is not as cold as one tends to imagine. With the exception of high passes the snow, even in winter, rarely stays on the ground for more than a few hours. The days are generally warm and it is only at night that the temperature can really drop. Rather than the cold it is the extreme dryness of the air which characterizes Tibetan weather. Nearly all of the rain falls in July and Aug, and there is practically no snow below 5,000m.

The winters are tough, especially in the N. There can be icy winds, and passes are often blocked with snow. Nevertheless, the sun shines continuously and the light is superb. Long distance travel in this period is much more rigorous. However, in the sheltered valleys of Lhasa, Tsetang, Zhigatse and Southern Kham the winter days are mild and beautiful. From Dec to Mar the streets are full of weird and wonderful peoples from the four corners of Tibet. In many respects, this is one of the best times of the year to visit not only Tibet, but also Hong Kong and Nepal. West Tibet tends to be drier, while the E is more subject to the weather patterns of Southeast Asia. During Aug, especially, Tibet can be very wet, but this is also a very good time of year to visit festival sites.

Health

No vaccinations are required for China, although anti-malaria medication is recommended for low-lying sub-tropical areas of SE Tibet during the rainy season. Immunization against polio, tetanus, rabies (fairly commonplace), hepatitis, meningitis, and typhoid should also be considered. Avoid unboiled water and ice-cubes, as well as uncooked vegetables and unpeeled fruit since dysentery is commonplace. It is strongly recommended that everyone has a check-up by their doctor before embarking on a prolonged overland journey in remote parts of Tibet, and that you prepare by undertaking some physical exercise each day (walking, swimming or jogging).

Generally, the dry and sunny atmosphere in Tibet means that bacteria are not as plentiful and as virulent as at lower altitudes in Nepal, India, and China. Thus, one remains fairly healthy while travelling in Tibet. Altitude sickness is the commonest ailment and you are advised to take plenty of fluids throughout your stay. You should have a daily intake of 4 litres at high altitude, and keep your water-bottle handy and filled up, or be sure to drink sufficient soft drinks, mineral water, or soup in the course of the day. Otherwise the effects of the high altitude are much more likely to cause you to feel headaches, lightheadedness, nausea, or sleeplessness. Always remember to replenish your water-bottle when stopping near a stream, spring or lake in the course of a long overland journey (see box on page 41 for hints on sterilization). It is important to pace yourself well when walking in Tibet. Move slowly and in a relaxed manner to minimize discomfort. Apart from paracetamol, aspirin and mild sleeping tablets which can help, the following remedies have sometimes been recommended by experienced travellers and mountaineers: Coca 30 and Phosphorum 30 (homeopathic); and acetazolomide (eg the diuretic Diamox). In view of the demanding nature of travel on the plateau, most agencies require a medical certificate signed by your doctor if you are over the age of 65.

Apart from altitude sickness, the major irritant to health in Tibet is the dryness of the atmosphere which often causes respiratory problems or cracking of the lips. You are advised to carry throat lozenges and an expectorant for dry coughs such as Actifed, as well as an effective lip-salve such as Blistease or Carmex.

In addition, you should bring: water-purifying tablets; vitamin supplements; Floradix iron supplement (to be taken 2 weeks prior to departure since it increases the red blood cells which absorb oxygen); pain killers (paracetamol, tylenol, etc); antihistamine cream and insect repellent; antiseptic cream for cuts and burns; immodium and 'Arsenicum Album 6' (a homeopathic medication for diarrhoea); streptomagma tablets, tetracycline or metronidazole (available on prescription for dysentery, infections and bronchitis); rehydration salts ('Dioralite' brand); tetranizadol and some laxatives for stomach disorders; disinfectants for wounds and latrines, and suntan cream or lotion (factor 15), in addition to a standard first-aid kit. Don't forget to consult your doctor before departure and ensure that you bring adequate supplies of any necessary prescribed drug (to be carried in hand luggage). Oxygen pillows or bottles are sometimes available on standard Central Tibetan routes, and on certain trekking routes, the first-aid kit will be carried by an 'ambulance' horse. For further details, see **Health Information**, pages 37-45.

Money

● **Currency**
The national currency is the Yuan (¥) or Renminbi (RMB), popularly called 'kwai'. 10 Jiao (pronounced 'mao') = 1 Yuan and 10 Fen = 1 Jiao. The exchange rate is approximately US$1 = ¥8. In China TCs are accepted and major currency denominations are easily changed in the larger cities. However, with the exception of *Holiday Inn* and the *Bank of China*, Lhasa Branch, credit cards are not yet used in Tibet. In general, it is more efficient to exchange money in the hotels than in the banks – particularly in Chengdu, Kunming, Ziling, and Lanzhou.

China has at long last abandoned its cumbersome dual currency system, which formerly obliged the banks and hotels to convert foreign currency into Foreign Exchange Certificates (FEC) for use in the hotels or tourist shops. The 'people's currency' (Renmimbi) is now fully convertible, leaving only the US dollar with a higher street value than the official rate of exchange.

● **Exchange**
The Bank of China has branches in Lhasa, Dram (Zhangmu), Ziling (Xining), Lanzhou, Kermo (Golmud), Chengdu, and Kunming, which will change TCs and hard currency. Unofficial money changers prefer US$ cash. Remember to carry a sufficient amount of RMB for long overland drives or treks. Even if your tour is pre-arranged, when travelling in remote areas, it is always wise to carry extra cash to cover unforeseen contingencies (such as payment of entrance and photographic fees).

What to take

It is always best to keep luggage to a minimum. A sturdy rucksack or a hybrid backpack/suitcase, rather than a rigid suitcase, covers most eventualities and survives bus boot, roof rack and plane/ship hold with ease. Serious trekkers will need a framed backpack. A complete checklist of items required for long treks or overland journeys is given below under **Trekking**, pages 31-32.

● **Checklist:**

Air cushions for hard seating
Bumbag
Contact lens cleaning equipment – not readily available in the region
Earplugs
Eye mask
Insect repellent (and/or mosquito net, electric mosquito mats, coils)
Neck pillow
International driving licence
Photocopies of essential documents
Short wave radio
Spare passport photographs
Sun hat
Sun protection cream – factor 10 plus
Sunglasses
Swiss Army knife
Tissues/toilet paper
Torch and spare batteries
Umbrella (excellent protection from sun, rain and unfriendly dogs)
Wipes (*Damp Ones* or equivalent)
Zip-lock bags

Those intending to stay in budget accommodation might also include:

Cotton sheet sleeping bag
Money belt
Padlock with chain (for hotel room and pack)
Plastic sheet to protect against bed bugs on mattresses
Soap
Student card
Towel
Toilet paper
Universal bath plug

● **Health kit:**

Antacid tablets (for Nepal and Bhutan)
Anti-diarrhoea tablets
Anti-malaria tablets (for Nepal and Bhutan)
Anti-infective ointment
Condoms/Contraceptives
Dusting powder for feet
First aid kit and disposable needles
Flea powder
Sachets of rehydration salts
Tampons
Travel sickness pills
Water sterilizing tablets

Getting there

Air

The only civilian airport currently open to foreign travellers on the Tibetan plateau is at Gongkar, although Chamdo Airport should shortly follow suit.

Transport to Lhasa from Gongkar Airport 1¾ hrs drive by bus or land coaster.

Flights to Lhasa China South-west Airlines have connections to Lhasa from Chengdu (2 hrs) daily at US$200; Kathmandu (55 mins) on Tues and Sat at US$200, and Beijing (4 hrs) on Sun at US$385. Tickets to Lhasa can be obtained from CAAC or China South-west offices in Kathmandu (T 411302), Hong Kong (T 8610322), Chengdu (T 6239991), or Beijing (T 4014441/ 6013336), but it is easiest to liaise with your travel agent.

There are also scheduled flights to Chengdu, Lanzhou, Kunming, and Lijiang: all important starting points for overland journeys through E Tibet. Specifically for Chengdu, there are daily flights from Beijing and frequent flights from Hong Kong (China South-west on Wed/Sat; Dragon Air on Tues/Sun). For Lanzhou, there are daily flights from Beijing, Guangzhou (all except Mon and Fri), and Hong Kong. For Ziling, there are flights from Beijing, and Xi'an. For Kunming (and Lijiang) there are connections from Hong Kong, Beijing, Bangkok and Rangoon. In all cases, please recheck your flight time prior to departure.

For ticketing services out of Lhasa, contact China South-west Airlines, E 14 Kharngadong Rd, Lhasa, T (0891) 6333331, F (0891) 633330.

Train

The only railway within the Tibetan plateau is that running from Ziling to Kermo in Amdo. There are daily express and local services. Plans to extend the railway from Kermo to Lhasa have so far floundered on account of the difficulty of laying tracks on a permafrost surface and boring ice tunnels through the Kunluns.

Road

The main motorable roads into Tibet commence at Kalpa in the Kinnaur region of India (presently closed), Kathmandu in Nepal, Gangtok in Sikkim (presently closed), Kunming via Lijiang in Yunnan, Chengdu via Ya'an, Han Yuan, Wolong, or Guan Xian in Sichuan, and Lanzhou via Ziling or Labrang. On some of these overland routes public transport is available but you may not be permitted to use it.

Hitchhiking is officially prohibited in the Tibetan area, but some drivers will take risks to offer a ride to foreign visitors in order to make a little money. It is useful for potential hitchhikers to know the districts to which Tibetan number plates refer: 01: Lhasa; 02: Nyangtri; 03: Chamdo; 04: Lhokha; 05: Zhigatse; 06: Ngari; 07: Nakchu; and 08: Kermo (Golmud).

All those points of land access feature long itineraries exceeding 2,000 km, and traverse the toughest watersheds in the world – those of the Indus, Sutlej, Brahmaputra, Salween, Mekong, Yangtze, Yalung, Gyarong, Yellow River, or Minjiang. It is therefore important that the correct choice of vehicle is made. Organized groups will normally travel in Japanese air-conditioned buses where the roads are good, or 4WD Toyota land-cruisers on the tougher routes, with a Dong Feng support truck to carry the baggage and camping equipment. In the case of those itineraries which emphasize trekking, horse-riding or mountaineering, baggage will be transported by yak caravans or pack-animals.

Customs

Until 1993 it was essential for all foreign visitors to complete a customs declaration form on arrival and countersign its duplicate on exiting the country, thereby keeping a close monitor on the import of luxury electronic goods in particular. Such controls have recently been relaxed for travellers arriving by air, and it is also permissable to import four bottles of liquor, two cartons of cigarettes, and 72 rolls of still film or 1,000m of video film. **NB** No 16 mm cameras are permitted, except when special licenses have been arranged for filming.

Foreigners are generally not subject to more than perfunctory baggage checks on entering and leaving Tibet, but in periods of political tension (which are commonplace) controls may be tightened. Certain items such as Dalai Lama pictures, critical literature and Tibetan national flags are sensitive; and the export of antique objects, including religious statues and jewellery, which were made before 1959 is officially prohibited. Old carpets and household items are more easily taken out, and it is best if some receipt or proof of purchase can be shown. There are shopkeepers in Lhasa who can arrange such receipts for a variety of purchases, regardless of their source!

On arrival

● **Airport information**

At Gongkar airport, transportation to Lhasa or Tsetang is normally provided by the local travel services. Infrequent public buses are also available. Airport taxes are payable at departure time: ¥30 for domestic flights to Chengdu and ¥65 for the international flights to Kathmandu.

● **Baggage**

An experienced traveller carries as little luggage as possible. Remember that you are allowed no more than the normal weight and that you may be liable to pay for excess baggage. You should also carry essentials, medication, reading material, cameras, flashlights, and other necessities (eg toilet paper) at all times in your flight bag or, as many prefer, in a lightweight backpack. If you are trekking or undertaking a long overland drive, you may have to supply your own tent and sleeping bag. Bring your own water-bottle, a screw-top cup or jar (for thirst-quenching jasmine tea), and a pocket-knife with bottle opener/corkscrew attachments, as well as a can opener, scissors, sewing kit, and pocket-size screwdriver. A complete checklist of items required for long treks or overland journeys is given below under **Trekking**, pages 31-32.

● **Clothing**

The air temperature in Tibet can change very quickly with a passing cloud and the coming of the night. A flexible system of 'layered' clothing is recommended: thermal underwear, cotton shirts, a warm pullover and windproof jacket, and some light rain-gear, as well as a sun-hat and a scarf or face-mask to ward off the dust. For overland travel or trekking, strong but lightweight walking boots are useful, and gloves, woollen hats and thick socks all have their place. For the hot springs, people may want to bring swimwear. A rucksack is indispensable for trekking and many people will find their own down jacket and sleeping bag a great asset.

Apart from the larger tourist hotels, no laundry or dry-cleaning service is available. If you wish to avoid the do-it-yourself option, it is sometimes possible to come to a private arrangement for laundry services with local guesthouse attendants.

● **Conduct**

The challenge in Tibet is to remain polite and curteous in social relationships regardless of the difficulties which arise! Remember that loss of self-control is less likely to bring about your desired response. When visiting a monastery or temple, **do not** smoke, wear a hat, or interrupt prayers and on-going ceremonies. External photography is generally allowed, whereas internal photography of the images and murals within a temple may be prohibited, or acceptable for a fee (normally imposed by the authorities). Always ask before photographing. Bribes are officially frowned upon, but often accepted when discretley offered. Small gifts, however, are widely appreciated. Photographs of important lamas from the various Buddhist or Bon traditions are revered throughout the monasteries, villages, and towns of Tibet, but photographs of the Dalai Lama, which cannot presently be sold in public, should be avoided unless they can be given discreetly in confidence. At the time of arrival or departure, it is customary to exchange gifts. See also the sections on **Trekking**, page 31, and **Communications**, page 33.

● **Hours of business**

Government buildings, banks and offices are open from Mon-Fri (0930-1230, 1530-1800). Saturday (only recently) and Sun are public holidays, as are the main festivals of the Chinese calendar: New Year's Day (1 Jan), Tibetan New Year, Chinese New Year (Spring Festival), International Working Women's Day (8 Mar), International Labour Day (1 May), Youth Day (4 May), Children's Day (1 June), Founding of the Chinese Communist Party (1 July), Army Day (1 Aug), and National Day (1 Oct).

● **Official time**

Tibetan time is absurdly the same as time in Beijing since a single time zone prevails throughout the regions controlled by China, ie GMT + 8 hrs. This accounts for the long daylight evenings and dark early mornings. Consequently, the border crossings between Tibet and Nepal or between Xinjiang and Pakistan may be the only places on the ground where travellers experience a sense of jet-lag! Daylight Savings Time does operate in summer, during which period the time difference is reduced to GMT + 7 hrs.

● **Photography**

Simple print film is commonly available in the larger towns and cities in Tibet, but slide film is hard to obtain even in the tourist shops of the *Holiday Inn* at Lhasa. You are therefore advised to stock up before leaving home. Outside photography is free of charge, but be careful not to film sensitive and strategic industrial or military installations. Internal photography in temples and monasteries may be permitted for a fee. Always ask first! Recommended films: for colour prints, Fuji HR100 or equivalent, and Fuji HR1600 for interiors; for colour slides, Kodak chrome 3 ASA 25 and 64, and Kodak Tungsten ASA 160 for interiors; for black and white, Kodak T-max ASA 100, and Kodak Tri-X for interiors. A UV filter or polarizer can help reduce the exposure problem caused by high altitude solar glare in Central and W Tibet. Mornings and late afternoons usually offer the best conditions for filming, and at other times try under-exposure by half a stop. There is some spectacular scenery, but if you go during the wet season make sure to protect film against humidity, and at all times try to protect your equipment from dust. Use a lens hood.

● **Police**

The various branches of the police force, known as the Public Security Bureau (*Tib* Chide Lekhung, *Ch* Gonganju), monitor traffic, crime, political dissent, and visa extensions. Offices are found in all cities, towns, and lesser townships, but visa extensions are only possible in Lhasa, Zhigatse, Tsetang, Kermo, and Ziling. These offices are also responsible for issuing Alien Travel Permits (ATP) for the 'closed' areas of the Tibetan plateau.

● **Safety**

In urban areas pickpockets are commonplace, and venues of entertainment, such as karaoke bars and discotheques, can sometimes erupt into flashpoints of violence, reminiscent of the Wild West. Foreign visitors should be aware of the risks facing the indigenous population who engage in acts of political dissent; and seek not to leave friends or acquaintances in a compromised position. Do not distribute photographs of the Dalai Lama in public places or even upon random request! In general it is best if unwitting visitors make little contact with Tibetans in urban areas, but, as always, what one can or cannot do will depend upon who one knows. Some secret policemen are themselves among the most affable and gracious hosts when introduced socially by those with the right connections! In general the crime rate in Tibet is low, and you will be received curteously throughout the length and breadth of the country. Some remote village communities may be suspicious of passing strangers, but you are more at risk from the dangerous road conditions than from the country's inhabitants. Overland travel in Tibet remains a pastime for the adventurous!

● **Shopping**

The Tibetans invariably bargain for their purchases and expect foreign visitors to do the same. In the markets, feel free to talk with your hands and pocket calculator! Avoid buying artefacts which have in fact been imported from Nepal! Among the most interesting objects available nowadays are traditional jewellery, metalwork, carpets, woodwork, and textiles. According to government regulations you are not to export antiques unless you have obtained a receipt or red seal.

● **Tipping**

Tipping is officially frowned upon, but widespread in hotels and travel agencies. Remember to tip your driver in Tibet as well as your guide. In view of the road conditions, the driver will often receive more than the guide.

● **Voltage**

220 volts, 50 cycles AC. The current is variable and the hours of operation unpredictable. Carry a range of plug conversion adapters. Rely on battery-operated equipment. A strong flashlight is also essential.

● **Weights and measures**

Metric – the same as in China. Traditional measurements are also in use. 1 kg equals 2 gyama (*Ch* jin), 1 ha equals 15 mu, 1 km equals 2 li, 1m equals 3 chi.

Where to stay

The **hotels** in Tibet range from 3-star downwards. Throughout the plateau there are no 4-star or 5-star hotels (although departure points in Kathmandu, Chengdu, Lanzhou, Kunming and Lijiang do have better facilities). Within Lhasa, the better hotels, such as *Holiday Inn*, *Tibet Hotel*, *Himalaya Hotel*, and *Sunlight Hotel*, vary in price from US$88 to 25, and provide a full meal plan in the range US$51 to 20. Outside Lhasa, there are large modern hotels in Ziling, Tsetang, Zhigatse, Gyantse, Bayi, Shelkar, Dram (*Ch* Zhangmu), Senge Tsangpo (*Ch* Shiquanhe), Purang, Nakchu, Chamdo, Barkham, Dartsedo, Jyekundo, and Machen. Although these establishments like to present themselves as being luxury hotels, they are in fact rather bland and basic. About half of them do at least provide hot running water and attached bathrooms, and their prices range from US$40 to 20, with full meal plan at US$30 to 15.

Some of the older, more traditional hotels offer a very good service. The *Lapulen Hotel* at Labrang (a converted summer palace) is an outstanding example, but there are also some reasonably clean and friendly **guesthouses** in places like Manigango, Drango, Ngawa, Kandze, Derge, Zhiwu, and Tawu. The traveller should be aware that such guesthouses have shared toilet and bathroom facilities. Bring your own disinfectant and toilet paper!

In smaller places, you can stay in simple **transport stations** or head out of town to set up a **camp** (in which case you will also need a stove and cooking utensils). All rooms are on a twin-share basis, although single supplements are generally available. For further details of the hotels in each city or town, see the relevant **local information** sections.

Food and drink

● **Food**

Organized tours in Tibet may include a full package with three meals daily, or a half package with breakfast and dinner only. In Lhasa a minimum package (hotel only) is also available. International cuisine (Western, Nepalese) is only available in Lhasa, at *Holiday Inn* and a small number of outside restaurants. A few specialist restaurants will offer Tibetan dishes or Peking dishes. Otherwise the standard cuisine offered in restaurants throughout the Tibetan plateau is Sichuan or Muslim style.

Tibetan cuisine, for the most part, is pretty basic, the staple consisting of large amounts of **tsampa** (roasted barley flour) and endless bowls of **butter tea**. Naturally you will have a chance to taste this delicacy during your stay, but it is highly unlikely that you will want to repeat the experience every day! On the other hand, there are some very good dishes to be had. The famous **momo**: a steamed meat dumpling which resembles the Chinese *jiaoze*, or Tibetan country-style **noodles** (*then-thuk*), and whilst you are in Lhasa you can arrange to have traditional Tibetan banquet (18 dishes), including *lasha* (lamb with radish), *gyuma* (black pudding), *thu* (cheesecake), and *dresi* (sweet rice), topped up with copious cups of 'chang', the local wine.

In nomadic areas, the staple diet consists of yak meat and mutton (fresh or dried), supplemented by delicious yoghurt. Cheese also comes in many varieties: hardened cubes which must be carefully sucked to avoid damaging the teeth, moderately soft whisps which are easy to digest, and, in E Tibet, an assortment of cheeses similar to cottage cheese and to cheddar (*Tib* Jo-she). Desserts are not generally served but delicious apples, apricots, peaches, and walnuts are available in season.

During day trips and long overland journeys, it is sometimes necessary to take a picnic lunch – either supplied by the hotels or the local travel agency. Organized tours, which entail camping, will have a cook who can prepare a full campsite meal, or take over the kitchen of a roadside restaurant. In drier regions of W and Far-west Tibet, you must carry more tinned provisions, while in the more fertile eastern regions, fresh vegetables are plentiful. To supplement this diet, you may wish to carry instant soups, cheeses, pâtés, biscuits, chocolates, coffee, and so forth, which can be very welcome if the weather suddenly turns nasty, or if you have stomach trouble.

● **Drink**

Beer and soft drinks are generally served with all meals in Tibet, but imported alcohol is available only in the larger tourist hotels. Bottled mineral water can be bought easily in the towns. Tea and thermos bottles of hot water are provided in hotel and guesthouse rooms, and this is probably the most refreshing remedy for the dry and dusty atmos-phere prevalent on the Tibetan plateau. Boiled water is essential for drinking and indeed for brushing the teeth. Some restaurants will also provide Indian style sweet milk tea or Nescafé. However, butter tea (*soja/poja*) or salted black tea (*ja-dang*) are generally drunk at home. The national alcoholic drinks are *chang* (chang), a fortified barley ale, and *arak* (arak), a type of distilled liquor. Dried fermented millet (*tomba*) is brewed in areas bordering Sikkim and Bhutan, while 'Lhasa Beer' (*Lhasa Pijiu*) and other brands of beer, as well as Chinese spirits, can be purchased throughout the plateau.

Getting around

Air and train

Once inside Tibet, there are no internal air connections for foreign travellers, although this may soon change when the new Chamdo Airport is opened up to visitors from the outside world. (Presently there are 2 flights a week from Chengdu for local traffic only.) The only rail link runs from Lanzhou through the Tsongkha valley to Ziling and on past Lake Kokonor to Kermo.

Road

In the absence of other forms of domestic transportation, people are totally dependent on the roads. The road network is extensive but extremely precarious. The only paved roads on the Tibetan plateau are those from Lanzhou to Ziling via Tsongkha, Ziling to Repkong and adjacent counties, Ziling to Lhasa via Kermo, Ziling to Wenchuan, Domda to Jyekundo, Lhasa to Tsetang via Gongkar Airport, and Dartsedo to Tawu via Lhagang. The others are all unpaved dirt roads, plagued by palls of dust and landslides in the rainy season. Roads crossing high passes are periodically snowbound from late Oct through to Mar. The principal means of road transport for local people is by public bus, and for visitors, 4WD drive land-cruisers or Japanese buses. Vehicles are always hired along with their driver. Owing to the rugged nature of the terrain, many routes in Tibet are for the adventure traveller only, but this does not preclude children. No special facilities are provided for children, but many youngsters adapt easily to the magnificent outdoor environment. Tour operators will normally offer a reduced price for children under 16 years of age.

● **Trekking**
The sheer vastness of the Tibetan plateau offers great scope for trekking. Some remote areas are even now only accessible on foot or horseback. Trekking conditions are very different from those in Bhutan and Nepal, where the travel agencies have had many years' experience at organizing treks. The best months are April-June and Sept-Nov, although even in the rainy season trekking is not always problematic.

On organized treks, tour operators will provide cooking equipment, food, and sometimes tents. In general on such expeditions you will want to travel with the bare minimum of equipment. You don't want to carry anything more than what is essential. Nonetheless, away from Lhasa the travelling is hard, so self-sufficiency is important, and there are a number of required items.

Dietary supplements for trekking First, although organized tours will have a cook

---

HIMALAYAN ENVIRONMENT TRUST CODE OF PRACTICE

Campsite Leave it cleaner than you found it.

Deforestation Make no open fires and discourage others making one for you. Limit use of water heated by firewood (use of dead wood is permitted – available in Sikkim but scarce elsewhere). Choose accommodation where kerosene or fuel-efficient wood burning stoves are used.

Litter Remove it. Burn or bury paper and carry away non-degradable litter. If you find other people's litter, remove their's too! Pack food in biodegradable containers. Carry away all batteries/cells.

Water Keep local water clean. Do not use detergents and pollutants in streams and springs. Where there are no toilets be sure you are at least 30m away from water source and bury or cover waste. Do not allow cooks or porters to throw rubbish in nearby streams and rivers.

Plants Do not take cuttings, seeds and roots – it is illegal in all parts of the Himalayas.

Giving to children encourages begging. **Donations** to a project, health centre or school is more constructive.

Respect **local traditions and cultures**.

Respect **privacy** and ask permission before taking photographs.

Respect **holy places**. Never touch or remove religious objects. Remove shoes before entering temples.

Respect local **etiquette**. Dress modestly, particularly when visiting temples and shrines and while walking through villages; loose, lightweight clothes are preferable to shorts, skimpy tops and tight-fitting outfits. Avoid holding hands and kissing in public.

to prepare main meals, the dishes will often be basic, especially if you are trekking in W or Far-west Tibet, where fresh vegetables are non-existent. Therefore it is strongly recommended that you bring a small camping stove of your own with a fuel bottle, as well as some freeze dried meals for the sake of variation in diet. You can also prepare your own hot drinks (coffee, cocoa, etc) whenever you want to. You may also like to bring some high protein fruit and nut, or muesli bars as well as chocolate, beef jerky, cheese, pâté, and so forth.

Clothing for trekking Second, because the temperatures on the Tibetan plateau are subject to extreme fluctuations you need to think in terms of 'layered clothes' that you can peel off and put on with ease. The weather will be warm to hot during the day and can be cool to freezing at night, and is often wet and windy depending on the location and season. At high altitude, the dry atmosphere stops perspiration so you won't become as dirty as usual and need not wash completely nor change clothes every couple of days. So you do not need to bring more than two or three items of any clothing. Also, if you intend to take an address book, do leave a duplicate at home in case of loss or water damage.

The following items of clothing are recommended for long treks: good comfortable walking shoes or boots (be sure to wear them in first); Band-Aid/elastoplast for blisters; thick wool socks (at least three pairs); light sandals or canvas shoes; long underwear (silk is good as winds can be icy); sufficient changes of underwear and T-shirts; cotton or woollen shirts (with pockets); wool sweaters (at least two, one to be worn over the other); trousers or jeans (possibly one heavy, one light-weight); a rain coat; a down-filled jacket; a sun hat, dark glasses, scarf or cravat (essential); and gloves. In general, Gortex is recommended for both walking boots and trekking clothes.

Trekking equipment Third, some of the following items will be supplied by the tour agency responsible for organizing your trek, but you should ensure that you obtain the others prior to your departure from Lhasa or wherever. Various camping items can be purchased or hired cheaply in Kathmandu. Carry your luggage in a backpack or heavy duty travel bag (with strong straps/handles), and keep your immediate necessities in a small knapsack, or shoulder bag (camera bag).

You should bring your own sleeping bag (suitable for all-weather outdoor conditions), an insulation mat, an umbrella, a flashlight (headlamp recommended) and extra alkaline batteries, a water flask and/or thermos bottle, a small stove (multifuel if possible) and fuel bottle, cooking and eating utensils, a Swiss-type army knife (with bottle and can openers etc), matches (waterproof preferable), a waterproof pouch or belt for money and passport, a medical kit (as outlined above under **Health**), suntan lotion, and (if possible) your own lightweight tent.

Some remote trekking trails are not well-defined, so it is easy to lose the way; and high-altitude rescue is non-existent. It is therefore essential to trek with a reliable local guide. Pack animals can be hired locally for certain treks, as in the Everest region, the Kailash region, the Kongpo region, and the upper Kyichu region.

NB When trekking in Tibet, please observe the Himalayan Code of Practice (see box), and be serious about the conservation of the ecology and the environment, even if locals or guides set a bad example. They only do so because of the general apathy or depression experienced by dispossessed persons the world over!

● **Cycling**
Some travel agencies will offer cycling trips on the plateau, especially between

Lhasa and Kathmandu. Contact Tibet International Sports Travel in Lhasa.

● **Mountaineering**
For details of climbing fees and organization in the Himalayas and in the Tibetan Autonomous Region as a whole, refer to an international tour operator, or directly to the *Tibet Mountaineering Association* (F 0891-6336366), or to *Tibet International Sports Travel* (F 0891-6334855), both in Lhasa. For the Minyak Gangkar, Kawalungring, and Minshan ranges, refer to the *Sichuan Mountaineering Association* based in Chengdu. For the Amnye Machen range refer to the *Qinghai Mountaineering Association*, and for the Kawa Karpo range, refer to the *Yunnan Mountaineering Association*. The local travel agencies listed in this guide can also provide relevant information, as can the head office of the *China Mountaineering Association* in Beijing.

● **Suggested routes on the Tibetan Plateau**
For a listing of the most popular routes on the Tibetan plateau, see above, pages 12-17. Special interest itineraries can also be arranged for Buddhist groups, botanists, mountaineers, or trekkers.

Communications

● **Language**
English is spoken by very few people in Tibet, and French or German by even fewer! The best language for communication is Tibetan, and for a brief outline of the dialects of the Tibetan language (To-ke, Tsang-ke, U-ke, Kham-ke, Amdo-ke etc), see the **Introduction**, page 59. In recent decades Chinese has become something of a lingua franca, preferred even by Tibetans from different parts of the plateau when communicating with one another. There have been conscious attempts to reverse this trend by moving towards a universally standard form of Tibetan, but the obstacles are formidable. One should not forget the minority languages spoken within Tibet: the Qiangic dialects of E Tibet, the Monpa and Lhopa dialects of S Tibet, the Mongol, Tu, and Salar languages of the NE, and so forth.

Some simple Tibetan phrases The basic word order of the Tibetan language is Subject- Object- Verb. For a list of useful works on the Tibetan language see the bibliography below. Some basic phrases include: **greetings** (Central Tibet: *tashidelek* or *chapenang*; Kham: *ka-a-te*; Amdo: *ke-demo*); **thank you** (Central Tibet: *tu-je-che* or *tu-je-nang'*; Kham and Amdo: *katro*); and **goodbye** (Central Tibet: *kalepeb* (if staying) or *kaleshuk* (if leaving); Kham: *yakpo songa* or *yamo*; Amdo: *demo che-a*).

● **Postal services**
Postage stamps for letters and postcards are available in most towns and large hotels on the plateau, but you are advised to stock up in Chengdu, Lhasa, Lanzhou, or Kunming at the beginning of your trip. Larger packages should be mailed from Chengdu, Ziling, Lanzhou, Kunming, or Lhasa. Postcards cost ¥1.60 (airmail), and aerogrammes ¥1.90. Parcels sent by surface mail begin at ¥52 to UK and ¥30.60 to USA for a 1 kg parcel; and ¥82 to UK or ¥77 to USA for a 1 kg airmail parcel. When sending mail it is best to have the country of destination written in Chinese. For collecting mail, there is a post restante facility in the Lhasa GPO, but it is better to use such facilities at the larger hotels: *Holiday Inn, Himalaya*, and so forth.

● **Telephone services**
The major hotels in Lhasa, Tsetang and Ziling have international IDD telephone connections, and in these cities, as well as the departure points (Kathmandu, Chengdu, Kunming or Lanzhou) you can send and receive telefax messages. In smaller towns, calls can be

made locally, or to the provincial capital, but be prepared for long delays. Such remote places may be contactable by telegram.

Tibet international dialling code is, of course, the same as that of China 86. Area codes: Lhasa and Tsetang 891; Ziling 971; Lanzhou 931; Kunming 871, and Chengdu 28.

Entertainment

Newspapers and books are available throughout the country. In Lhasa, try the *Xinhua Bookstore* near the Jokhang Temple, or the bookshop next to the *Tibet Hotel*. Other towns and cities have similar outlets. Few publications are in English, but there is prolific publishing in Tibetan of both classical and modern texts. The newspapers are of limited value, even for those who read Tibetan (*Mimang Tsakpar*) or Chinese (*Renmin Ribao*). The only English newspaper is the *China Daily*. There are local television and radio broadcasting services in each of the provinces or prefectures into which Tibet is now divided. Lhasa, Qinghai, and Kandze television services are all active in programme making. Some productions are voiced over or subtitled in Tibetan.

Private entertainment includes both traditional festivals (on which see the next section), sporting contests, gambling (especially Mahjong), and the new wave of cinemas, video parlours, pool tables, discotheques, clubs, bars and karaoke establishments which thrive in all urban areas.

Holidays and festivals

● **National holidays**
The dates of traditional festivals vary according to the lunar calendar, whereas most modern Chinese holidays are tied to the solar calendar.

Public Holidays: 1996
1 Jan	New Year's Day
19 Feb	Tibetan New Year
	Chinese New Year/ Spring Festival
8 Mar	International Working Women's Day
1 May	International Labour Day
4 May	Youth Day
1 June	Children's Day
1 July	Founding of the Chinese Communist Party
1 Aug	National Army Day
1 Oct	National Day

● **Festivals**
The Tibetan lunar calendar is calculated each year by astrologers from the *Mentsikhang* in Lhasa and Dharamsala. It is based on a cycle of 60 years, each of which is named after one of 12 animals and one of five elements in combination. For example, 1996 is called the fire mouse year. A calendrical year normally contains 12 months, but the addition of an extra intercalary month for astrological reasons is not uncommon. In general, the Tibetan lunar month is about 2 months behind the western calendar. Many festivals are traditionally held throughout the Tibetan calendar – some are nationwide and others applicable to a certain area only. They may also be religious or secular in character. The main horse festival season falls between the 5th and the 7th months of the year (usually July-Sept), and some are now fixed in relation to the solar calendar, eg **Jyekundo Horse Festival**, which begins on 25 July, and the **Litang Horse Festival**, commencing on 1 August.

The following is a general guide to the major events in the Tibetan calendar. In order to work out how they correspond to dates in the western calendar, it is necessary to wait until late autumn or winter, when the following year's calendar is prepared. In addition, the **10th day** of every month is dedicated to Padmasambhava who introduced the highest Buddhist teachings from India in the 8th century. The **25th day** of each month is a Dakini Day, associated with the fe-

FESTIVAL DATES, 1996

Lunar Date	Western Date	Event
1st of 1st Month	19 Feb	Losar, Tibetan New Year
8th of 1st Month	26 Feb	Monlam, the Great Prayer Festival
15th of 1st Month	5 Mar	Day of Offerings
15th of 4th Month	1 June	Enlightenment of Buddha
18th of 4th Month	4 June	Gyantse Horse Festival
15th of 5th Month	1 July	Local Deities' Day
15th of 5th Month	1 July	Tashilhunpo Festival
4th of 6th Month	19 July	Dharmacakra Day
10th of 6th Month	25 July	Birth of Padmasambhava
29th of 6th Month	13 Aug	Drepung Zhoton (Yoghurt Festival)
1st of 7th Month	15 Aug	Zhoton (Yoghurt Festival)
27th of 7th Month	9 Sept	Bathing Festival
30th of 7th Month	12 Sept	End of Rain Retreat
30th of 7th Month	12 Sept	Damzhung Horse Festival
1st of 8th Month	13 Sept	Ongkor (Harvest Festival)
22nd of 9th Month	2 Nov	Descent from the God Realms
15th of 10th Month	24 Nov	Palden Lhamo Procession in Barkhor
25th of 10th Month	5 Dec	Anniversary of Tsongkhapa
6th of 11th Month	16 Dec	Nine Bad Omens

male deities who are the agents of Buddha-activity. The **29th day** of each month is dedicated to the wrathful doctrinal protector deities, while the **15th** and **30th** are associated with the Buddha, and the **8th** with the Medicine Buddha.

Further reading

● Guidebooks

The present guidebook is the only comprehensive treatment of the Tibetan plateau, which includes Kham and Amdo, in addition to Nepal and Bhutan. For information on the Buddhist sites of Central and W Tibet, you might also refer to Stephen Batchelor's *The Tibet Guide* (Wisdom, 1987), and to Keith Dowman's *The Power Places of Central Tibet* (RKP, 1988). For trekking, the best sources are Victor Chen's *Tibet Handbook* (Moon Publications, 1994), and Gary McCue's *Trekking in Tibet* (Cordee, 1991).

● History

For a broad appraisal of Tibetan culture, refer to the classic works, RA Stein's *Tibetan Civilization* (Faber, 1972), Tsepon Shakabpa's *Tibet: A Political History* (Potala, 1984), Cristopher Beckwith's *The Tibetan Empire in Central Asia* (Princeton, 1987), and Snellgrove & Richardson's *Cultural History of Tibet* (Weidenfeld and Nicholson, 1968). For recent history and the current Tibetan situation, see the present Dalai Lama's two biographies, *My Land and My People*, and *Freedom In Exile*; also Hugh Richardson's *Tibet and its History* (Shambhala, 1984), Melvyn Goldstein's *History of Modern Tibet 1939-1959* (University of California Press, 1989), John Avedon's *In Exile from the Land of Snows* (Wisdom 1986), and Mary Craig's *Tears of Blood* (Harper Collins 1992).

● Central, Western and Far-western Tibet

In addition to the aforementioned guidebooks, the following works provide useful background reading: G Tucci's *To Lhasa and Beyond* (Instituto Poligrafico dello Stato, 1956), Charles Bell's *Portrait of The Dalai Lama* (Collins, 1946), Heinrich Harrer's *Seven Years in Tibet* (Rupert Hart-Davis, 1953), Goldstein & Bell's *Nomads of Western Tibet*, and John Snelling's *The Sacred Mountain*.

● **Eastern and Far-eastern Tibet**

There are fewer useful sources on E and Far-east Tibet. The best are Eric Teichman's *Travels of a Consular Official in Eastern Tibet* (Cambridge University Press, 1922), Andre Migot's *Tibetan Marches* (Penguin, 1957), Chogyam Trungpa's *Born in Tibet* (Unwin, 1979), Gallen Rowell's *Mountains of the Middle Kingdom*, Joseph Rock's *The Amnye Machen and Adjacent Regions* (SOR, 1956), Frank Kingdon Ward's *Mystery Rivers of Tibet* (Cadogan, 1986), Jacques Bacot's *Le Tibet Revolte* (Hachette, 1912), and for light relief Marie de Poncheville's *Sept Femmes au Tibet* (Albin Michel, 1990).

● **Religion**

For a general understanding of Mahayana Buddhism and its Tibetan context, see Tucci's *The Religions of Tibet* (Berkeley, 1980), Paul Williams' *Mahayana Buddhism* (RKP, 1989), Tulku Thondup's *Buddhist Civilization in Tibet* (RKP, 1987), Paltrul Rinpoche's (transl.) *The Words of My Perfect Teacher* (Harper Collins, 1994), and David Snellgrove's *Indo-Tibetan Buddhism* (Serindia, 1987). For detailed information on the different schools of Tibetan Buddhism, see Dudjom Rinpoche (Trans Dorje and Kapstein), *The Nyingma School of Tibetan Buddhism*, and M Ricard (trans), *The Life of Shabkar* (Suny, 1994). On the Kagyupa tradition, see Lobzang Lhalungpa's translation of *The Life of Milarepa* (Dutton, 1977), Karma Thinley's *The Sixteen Karmapas* (Shambhala, 1978), and Douglas and White's *Karmapa: the Black Hat Lama of Tibet* (Luzac, 1976); and on the Sakyapa school, *The History of the Sakya School* (Ganesha, 1983). For a detailed study of the Gelukpa school, see J Willis, *Enlightened Beings: Life Stories from the Ganden Tradition* (Wisdom, 1995), and Pabongka Rinpoche (transl), *Liberation in the Palm of Your Hand* (Wisdom, 1991). Lastly, on the pre-Buddhist Bon tradition, see Samten Karmay's *The*

Treasury of Good Sayings: a Tibetan History of Bon (OUP, 1972), and Per Kvaerne's *The Bon Religion of Tibet* (Serindia, 1995).

● **Tibetan language and medicine**

For the modern Tibetan language, the best primers are Kalzang Gyurme's *Le Clair Mirroir* (translated into French from Tibetan by Nicholas Tournade and Heather Stoddard), and on the medical tradition, see Parfianivitch, Dorje and Mayer (eds), *Tibetan Medical Paintings* (Serindia, 1993).

● **Maps**

The best maps available in Tibet are the *China Tibet Tour Map*, published by the Mapping Bureau of the TAR in 1993, and the *Map of Mountain Peaks on the Qinghai-Xizang Plateau*, published by the China Cartographic Publishing House in 1989. The *Tibetan Language Map of the Ngawa Autonomous Prefecture*, published in Sichuan, is detailed, but accessible only to Tibetan readers as is the large series of Tibetan language maps of TAR. Some Chinese maps are also useful, especially the detailed *China Road Atlas*, which provides distances between points on all motorable roads.

Among maps of Tibet published in the West, those prepared by Michael Farmer, and published in *The Nyingma School of Tibetan Buddhism* (Wisdom, 1991) have extremely accurate topographical features, and clearly contrast the river systems with a subtle use of contour shading. The maps published in Switzerland by Peter Kessler are important for their contribution to traditional Tibetan toponymics. Other maps published in the United States include the *Operational Navigational Charts* (ONC) and the *Joint Operations Graphic Series* (JOG), the latter being reproduced in Victor Chen's *Tibet Handbook*. These and others are available at Stanford's Map Centre, 12-14 Long Acre, London WC2E 9LP (T 0171-836-1321).

HEALTH INFORMATION

CONTENTS

The following information has been compiled for us by Dr David Snashall, Senior Lecturer in Occupational Health, United Medical Schools of Guy's and St Thomas' Hospitals and Chief Medical Adviser, Foreign and Commonwealth Office, London.

The traveller to the Tibetan Plateau is inevitably exposed to health risks not encountered in North America or Western Europe. Despite the fact that most of the area lies geographically within the Temperate Zone, the climate is occasionally tropical in, for example, the Himalayan foothills. In general tropical diseases are not a major problem for visitors. Because much of the area is economically underdeveloped, infectious diseases still predominate in a way in which they used to predominate in the West some decades ago. There is an obvious difference in health risks between the business traveller who tends to stay in international class hotels in large cities, and the backpacker trekking through the rural areas. There are no hard and fast rules to follow; you will often have to make your own judgements on the healthiness or otherwise of your surroundings.

There are some well qualified doctors in the area, hardly any of whom speak English but the quality and range of medical care diminishes very rapidly as you move away from big cities. There are systems and traditions of medicine wholly different from the western model and you may be confronted with unusual modes of treatment such as herbal medicine and acupuncture. At least you can be sure that local practitioners have a lot of experience with the particular diseases of their region. If you are in one of the five gateway cities, it may be worthwhile calling on your Embassy to provide a list of recommended doctors.

If you are a long way away from medical help, a certain amount of self medication may be necessary and you will find many of the drugs available have familiar names. However, always check the date stamping and buy from reputable pharmacies because the shelf life of some items, especially vaccines and antibiotics, is markedly reduced in hot conditions. Unfortunately in the sub-Himalayan areas of Nepal and Bhutan, many locally produced drugs are not subjected to quality control procedures and so can be unreliable. There have, in addition, been cases of substitution of inert materials for active drugs.

With the following precautions and advice, you should keep as healthy as usual. Make local enquiries about health risks if you are apprehensive and take the general advice of European and North American families who have lived or are living in the area.

Before travelling

Take out medical insurance. You should have a dental check up, obtain a spare glasses prescription and, if you suffer from a long-standing condition such as diabetes, high blood pressure, heart/lung disease or a nervous disorder, arrange for a check up with your doctor who can at the same time provide you with a letter explaining details of your disability. Check the current practice for malaria prophylaxis (prevention) for the countries you intend to visit.

Vaccination & immunization

The following vaccinations are recommended:

Typhoid (monovalent): one dose followed by a booster in 1 month's time. Immunity from this course lasts 2-3 years. An oral preparation is currently being marketed in some countries and a one dose injectable vaccine is also available but more expensive than monovalent: Typhin-Vi (Mevieux).

Poliomyelitis: this is a live vaccine generally given orally and a full course consists of three doses with a booster in tropical regions every 3-5 years.

Tetanus: one dose should be given with a booster at 6 weeks and another at 6 months and 10 yearly boosters thereafter are recommended. Children should, in addition, be properly protected against diphtheria, whooping cough, mumps, measles and HIB. Teenage girls, if they have not had the disease, should be given rubella (German measles) vaccination. Consult your doctor for advice on BCG innoculation against tuberculosis; the disease is still common in the region.

Meningococcal Meningitis and Japanese B Encephalitis (JBE): immunization (effective in 10 days) gives protection for around 3 years. There is an extremely small risk, though it varies seasonally and from region to region. Consult a Travel Clinic.

Hepatitis A: Havrix, Havrix Monodose and Junior Havrix vaccine give protection for 10 years after two injections (10 days to be effective). Alternatively, 1 gamma globulin injection to cover up to 6 months' travel is effective immediately and much cheaper. Regular travellers should have a blood test first to check whether they are already immune.

Rabies: pre-exposure vaccination gives anyone bitten by a suspect animal time to get treatment (so particularly helpful to those visiting remote areas) and also prepares the body to produce antibodies quickly; cost of vaccine can be shared by three receiving vaccination together.

Malaria: prophylactic tablets are strongly advised for visitors to affected countries such as Nepal and Bhutan but since a particular course of treatment is recommended to a specific part of the world (which can change in time) seek up-to-date advice from the Malaria Reference Laboratory, T 0891 600 350 (recorded message, premium rate) or the Liverpool School of Tropical Medicine, T 051 708 9393. In the USA, try Centre for Disease Control, Atlanta, T 404 332 4555.

Smallpox, cholera and yellow fever: vaccinations are not required. You may be asked for a certificate if you have been in a country affected by yellow fever immediately before travelling to the region.

Infectious Hepatitis (jaundice)

This is common throughout the region. It seems to be frequently caught by travellers. The main symptoms are stomach pains, lack of appetite, nausea, lassitude and yellowness of the eyes and skin. Medically speaking, there are two types: the less serious but more common is hepatitis A for which the best protection is careful preparation of food, the avoidance of contaminated drinking water and scrupulous attention to toilet hygiene. Human normal immunoglobulin (gamma globulin) confers considerable protection against the disease and is particularly useful in epidemics. It should be obtained from a reputable source and is certainly recommended for travellers who intend to live rough. The injection should be given as close as possible to your departure and, as the dose depends on the likely time you are to spend in potentially infected areas, the manufacturer's instructions should be followed.

The other, more serious, version is hepatitis B, which is acquired as a sexually transmitted disease, from a blood transfusion or an injection with an unclean needle or possibly by insect bites. The symptoms are the same as hepatitis A but the incubation period is much longer.

You may have had jaundice before or you may have had hepatitis of either type before without becoming jaundiced, in which case it is possible that you could be immune to either hepatitis A or B. This immunity can be tested for before you travel. If you are not immune to hepatitis B already, a vaccine is available (three shots over 6 months) and if you are not immune to hepatitis A already, then you should consider having gamma globulin.

AIDS

AIDS is not the huge problem that it is in India where it is increasing in its prevalence probably faster than in most countries with a pattern typical of developing societies. Thus, it is not wholly confined to the well known high risk sections of the population, ie homosexual men, intravenous drug abusers, prostitutes and the children of infected mothers. Heterosexual transmission is now the dominant mode and so the main risk to travellers is from casual sex. The same precautions should be taken as when encountering any sexually transmitted disease. The AIDS virus (HIV) can be passed via unsterile needles which have been previously used to inject a HIV positive patient but the risk of this is very small indeed. It would, however, be sensible to check that needles have been properly sterilized or disposable needles used. The chance of picking up hepatitis B in this way is much more of a danger. Be wary of carrying disposable needles yourself; Customs officials may find them suspicious. The risk of receiving a blood transfusion with blood infected with the HIV virus is greater than from dirty needles because of the amount of fluid exchanged.

Supplies of blood for transfusion are now largely screened for HIV in all reputable hospitals, so the risk must be very small indeed. Catching the AIDS virus does not necessarily produce an illness in itself; the only way to be sure if you feel you have been put at risk is to have a blood test for HIV antibodies on your return to a place where there are reliable laboratory facilities. The test does not become positive for many weeks.

Common problems

Altitude

Acute mountain sickness can strike from about 3,000m upwards. It is more likely to affect those who ascend rapidly (eg by plane) and those who over-exert themselves. Teenagers seem to be particularly prone. Past experience is not always a good guide: the Author, having spent years in Peru travelling constantly between sea level and very high altitude never suffered the slightest symptoms, then was severely affected climbing Kilimanjaro in Tanzania.

On reaching heights above 3,000m, heart pounding and shortness of breath, especially on exertion are almost universal and a normal response to the lack of oxygen in the air. Acute mountain sickness takes a few hours or days to come on and presents with headache, lassitude, dizziness, loss of appetite, nausea and vomiting. Insomnia is common and often associated with a suffocating feeling when lying down in bed. Keen observers may note that their breathing tends to wax and wane at night and their face tends to be puffy in the mornings – this is all part of the syndrome. If the symptoms are mild, the treatment is rest, painkillers (preferably not Aspirin based) for the headache and anti-sickness pills for vomiting. Oxygen may help at very high altitudes but is unlikely to be available unless on an organized tour in Tibet.

The best way of preventing acute

CHILDREN AND BABIES

Younger travellers seem to be more prone to illness abroad, but that should not put you off taking them. More preparation is necessary than for an adult and perhaps a little more care should be taken when travelling to remote areas where health services are primitive. This is because children can become more rapidly ill than adults, although they often recover more quickly.

Diarrhoea and vomiting are the most common problems so take the usual precautions, but more intensively. Make sure all basic childhood **vaccinations** are up to date, as well as the more exotic ones. Children should be properly protected against diphtheria, mumps and measles. Consult your doctor for advice on BCG innoculation against tuberculosis. Protection against mosquitoes and drug prophylaxis against malaria are essential. Many children take to 'foreign' food quite happily. Milk in Nepal and Tibet is generally unpasteurized and should be well boiled. Powdered milk may be the answer, although you should be certain that the water source is safe. Breast feeding where appropriate is the best option.

The treatment of **diarrhoea** is the same as for adults except that it should be started earlier and be continued with more persistence. Children get dehydrated very quickly in the tropics and can become drowsy and uncooperative unless cajoled to drink water or juice plus salts. Oral rehydration has been a lifesaving technique in children.

Upper respiratory infections such as colds, catarrh and middle ear infection are common – antibiotics should be carried against the possibility. **Outer ear infections** after swimming are also common – antibiotic ear drops will help.

Protect children against the sun with a hat and high factor sun lotion. Severe sunburn at this age may well lead to serious skin cancer in the future.

mountain sickness is a relatively slow ascent and, when trekking through the Himalayas to high altitude, some time spent in the foothills getting fit and adapting to moderate altitude is beneficial. On arrival at places over 3,000m, a few hours rest in a chair and the avoidance of alcohol, cigarettes and heavy food will go a long way towards preventing acute mountain sickness. Should the symptoms be severe and prolonged, it is best to descend to a lower altitude and to reascend slowly or in stages. The symptoms disappear very quickly with even a few 100m of descent. If a slow staged attempt is impossible because of shortage of time, then the drug Acetazolamide (Diamox) can be used as a preventative and continued during the ascent. There is good evidence of the value of this drug in the prevention of acute mountain sickness but some people do experience funny side effects. The usual dose is 500 mgs of the slow release preparation each night, starting the night before ascending above 3,000m.

Other problems experienced at high altitude are sunburn, excessively dry air causing skin cracking, sore eyes (it may be wise to leave your contact lenses out) and stuffy noses. It is unwise to ascend to high altitude if you are pregnant, especially in the first 3 months, or if you have any history of heart, lung or blood disease, including sickle cell.

There is a further, albeit rare, hazard due to rapid ascent to high altitude – a kind of complicated mountain sickness presenting as acute pulmonary oedema or acute cerebral oedema. Both conditions are more common the higher you go. Pulmonary oedema comes on quite rapidly with breathlessness, noisy breathing, cough, blueness of the lips and frothing at the mouth. Cerebral oedema usually presents with confusion, going on to unconsciousness. Anybody developing these serious conditions must be brought down to low altitude as soon as possible and taken to hospital.

Rapid descent from high places will aggrevate sinus and middle ear infections and make bad teeth ache. The same problems are sometimes experienced during descent at the end of an aeroplane flight. Do not ascend to high altitude in the 24 hrs following scubadiving. Remember that the Himalayas and other mountain ranges are very high, very cold, very remote and potentially very dangerous. Do not travel in them alone, when you are ill or if you are poorly equipped. As telephone communication can be non-existent, mountain rescue is extremely difficult and medical services may not be up to much.

Despite these various hazards (mostly preventable) of high altitude travel, many people find the environment healthier and more invigorating than at sea level.

Heat and cold

Remember that, especially in the mountains, there can be a large and sudden drop in temperature between sun and shade and between night and day, so dress accordingly. Loose fitting cotton clothes are still the best for hot weather. Warm jackets and woollens are essential after dark at high altitude.

WATER PURIFICATION

There are a number of methods for purifying water in order to make it safe to drink. Dirty water should first be strained through a filter bag, and then boiled or treated. Bringing water to a rolling **boil** at sea level is sufficient to make water safe for drinking, but at higher altitudes you have to boil the water for longer to ensure that all the microbes are killed.

Various sterilizing methods can be used, and there are propriety preparations containing **chlorine** (eg *'Puritabs'*) or **iodine** (eg *'Pota Aqua'*) compounds. Chlorine compounds generally do not kill protozoa (eg giardia). Prolonged usage of iodine compounds may lead to thyroid problems, although this is rare if used for less than a year.

There are a number of **water filters** now on the market, available both in personal and expedition size. There are broadly two types of water filter, **mechanical** and **chemical**. Mechanical filters are usually a combination of carbon, ceramic and paper, although they can be difficult to use. Ceramic filters tend to last longer in terms of volume of water purified. The best brand is possibly the Swiss-made *Katadyn*. Although cheaper, the disadvantage of mechanical filters is that they do not always kill viruses or protozoa. Thus, if you are in an area where the presence of these is suspected, the water will have to be treated with iodine before being passed through the filter. When new, the filter will remove the taste, although this may not continue for long. However, ceramic filters will remove bacteria, and their manufacturers claim that since most viruses live on bacteria, the chances are that the viruses will be removed as well. This claim should be treated with scepticism.

Chemical filters usually use a combination of an iodine resin filter and a mechanical filter. The advantage of this system is that, according to the manufacturers' claims, everything in the water will be killed. The disadvantage is that the filters need replacing, adding a third to the price. Probably the best chemical filter is manufactured by *Pur*.

Insects

These can be a great nuisance although more so in the sub-tropical areas of Nepal and Bhutan than in the high altitude plateau of Tibet. Some of course are carriers of serious diseases such as malaria, dengue fever or filariasis and various worm infections. The best way of keeping mosquitoes away at night is to sleep off the ground with a mosquito net and to burn mosquito coils containing Pyrethrum. Aerosol sprays or a 'flit' gun may be effective as are insecticidal tablets which are heated on a mat which is plugged into the wall socket (if taking your own, check the voltage of the area you are visiting so that you can take an appliance that will work. Similarly, check that your electrical adaptor is suitable for the repellent plug.)

Or you can use personal insect repellent of which the best contain a high concentration of Diethyltoluamide. Liquid is best for arms and face (take care around eyes and make sure you do not dissolve the plastic of your spectacles). Aerosol spray on clothes and ankles deter mites and ticks. Liquid DET suspended in water can be used to impregnate cotton clothes and mosquito nets. If you are bitten, itching may be relieved by cool baths and antihistamine tablets (care with alcohol or driving), corticosteroid creams (great care – never use if any hint of sepsis) or by judicious scratching. Calamine lotion and cream have limited effectiveness and antihistamine creams have a tendency to cause skin allergies and are, therefore, not generally recommended. Bites which become infected (commonly in the tropics) should be treated with a local antiseptic or antibiotic cream such as Cetrimide as should infected scratches. Skin infestations with body lice, crabs and scabies are unfortunately easy to pick up. Use Gamma benzene hexachloride for lice and Benzyl benzoate for scabies. Crotamiton cream alleviates itching and also kills a number of skin parasites. Malathion lotion 5% is good for lice but avoid the highly toxic full strength Malathion used as an agricultural insecticide.

Intestinal upsets

Generally, the dry and sunny atmosphere means that bacteria are not as plentiful and as virulent as at lower altitudes in Nepal, India and China. However, practically nobody escapes this one, so be prepared for it. Most of the time, intestinal upsets are due to the insanitary preparation of **food**. Do not eat uncooked fish or vegetables or meat (especially pork), fruit with the skin on (always peel your fruit yourself) or food that is exposed to flies (especially salads). Tap **water** may be unsafe, especially after heavy rain and the same goes for stream water or well water. Filtered or bottled water is usually available and safe. Ice for drinks should be made from boiled water but rarely is, so stand your glass on the ice cubes, instead of putting them in the drink. Dirty water should first be strained through a filter bag (available from camping shops) and then boiled or treated. Bringing the water to a rolling boil at sea level is sufficient but at high altitude you have to boil the water for longer to ensure that all the microbes are killed. Various sterilizing methods can be used and there are proprietary preparations containing chlorine or iodine compounds. Unpasteurized milk products, including cheese, are sources of tuberculosis, brucellosis, listeria and food poisoning germs. You can render fresh milk safe by heating it to 62°C for 30 mins, followed by rapid cooling or by boiling it. Matured or processed cheeses are safer than fresh varieties.

Diarrhoea is usually the result of food poisoning, occasionally from contaminated water. There are various causes – viruses, bacteria, protozoa (like amoeba), salmonella and cholera organisms. It may take one of several forms, coming on suddenly, or rather slowly. It may be accompanied by vomiting or by severe abdominal pain and the passage of blood or mucus when it is called dysentery. How do you know which type you have and how do you treat them? All kinds of diarrhoea, whether or not accompanied by vomiting respond favourably to the replacement of water and salts taken as frequent small sips of some kind of rehydration solution. There are proprietary preparations, consisting of sachets of powder which you dissolve in water, or you can make your own by adding half a teaspoonful of salt (3.5 grams) and 4 tablespoonfuls of sugar (40 grams) to a litre of boiled water.

● If you can time the onset of diarrhoea to the minute, then it is probably viral or bacterial and/or the onset of dysentery. The treatment, in addition to rehydration, is Ciprofloxacin 500 mgs every 12 hrs. The drug is now widely available.

● If the diarrhoea has come on slowly or intermittently, then it is more likely to be protozoal, ie caused by amoeba or giardia and antibiotics will have no effect. These cases are best treated by a doctor as should any diarrhoea continuing for more than 3 days. If there are severe stomach cramps, the following drugs may help: Loperamide (Imodium, Arret) and Diphenoxylate with Atropine (Lomotil).

Thus, the lynch pins of treatment for diarrhoea are rest, fluid and salt replacement, antibiotics such as Ciprofloxacin for the bacterial types and special diagnostic tests and medical treatment for amoeba and giardia infections. Salmonella infections and cholera can be devastating diseases and it would be wise to get to a hospital as soon as possible if these were suspected. Fasting, peculiar diets and the consumption of large quantities of yogurt have not been found useful in calming travellers' diarrhoea or in rehabilitating inflamed bowels. Oral rehydration has, especially in children, been a lifesaving technique and as there is some evidence that alcohol and milk might prolong diarrhoea, they should probably be avoided during and immediately after an attack. There are ways of preventing travellers' diarrhoea for short periods of time when visiting these countries by taking antibiotics but these are ineffective against viruses and, to some extent, against protozoa, so this technique should not be used, other than in exceptional circumstances. Some preventives such as Entero-vioform can have serious side effects if taken for long periods.

Malaria

Malaria is not prevalent in Tibet. Take advice from a Travel Clinic if you are likely to travel through India, Nepal, Pakistan or China where you may be subject to some risk. It remains a serious disease and you are advised to protect yourself against mosquito bites as above and to take prophylactic (preventive) drugs. Start taking the tablets a few days before exposure and continue to take them 6 weeks after leaving the malarial zone. Remember to give the drugs to babies and children and pregnant women also. The subject of malaria prevention is becoming more complex as the malaria parasite becomes immune to some of the older drugs. In particular, there has been an increase in the proportion of cases of falciparum malaria which is particularly dangerous. Some of the preventive drugs can cause side effects, especially if taken for long periods of time, so before you travel you must check with a reputable agency the likelihood and type of malaria in the countries which you intend to visit and take their advice on prophylaxis and be prepared to receive conflicting advice. Because of the rapidly changing situation in the area I have not included the names and dosage of the drugs. You can catch malaria even when taking prophylactic drugs, although it is unlikely. If you do develop symptoms (high fever, shivering, severe headache, sometimes diarrhoea) seek medical advice immediately. The risk of the disease is obviously greater the further you move from the cities into rural areas with primitive facilities and standing water.

Snake bite

If you are unlucky enough to be bitten by a venomous snake, spider, scorpion, or centipede attempt (within limits) to catch the animal for identification. The reactions to be expected are fright, swelling, pain and bruising around the bite, soreness of the regional lymph glands, nausea, vomiting and fever. If, in addition, any of the following symptoms supervene get the victim to a doctor without delay: numbness, tingling of the face, muscular spasm, convulsions, shortness of breath or haemorrhage. Commercial snake bite or scorpion sting kits may be available but are only useful for the specific type of snake or scorpion for which they are designed. The serum has to be given intravenously, so is not much good unless you have had some practice in making injections into veins. If the bite is on a limb, immobilize the limb and apply a tight bandage between the bite and the body, releasing it for 90 secs every 15 mins. Reassurance of the bitten person is very important because death from snake bite is, in fact, very rare. Do not slash the bite area and try to suck out the poison because this sort of heroism does more harm than good. Hospitals usually hold stocks of snake bite serum. Best precaution: do not walk in snake territory with bare feet, sandals or shorts.

Sunburn and heat stroke

The burning power of the sun is phenomenal, especially at high altitude. Always wear a wide brimmed hat and use some form of sun cream or lotion on untanned skin. Normal temperate zone suntan lotions (protection factor up to 7) are not much good. You need to use the types designed specifically for the tropics or for mountaineers or skiers with a protection factor between 7 and 15. Glare from the sun can cause conjunctivitis so wear sunglasses, especially near the snowline.

There are several varieties of 'heat stroke'. The most common cause is severe dehydration. Avoid dehydration by drinking lots of non-alcoholic fluid.

Other afflictions

Rabies is present in Tibet though less endemic than in other countries in the region such as India. If you are bitten by a domestic or wild animal, don't leave things to chance. Scrub the wound with soap and water/or disinfectant, try to have the animal captured (within limits) or at least determine its ownership where possible and seek medical assistance at once. The course of treatment depends on whether you have already been vaccinated against rabies. If you have (and this is worthwhile if you are spending lengths of time in developing countries) then some further doses of vaccine are all that is required. Human diploid cell vaccine is the best, but expensive: other, older kinds of vaccine such as that derived from duck embryos may be the only types available. These are effective, much cheaper and interchangeable generally with the human derived types. If not already vaccinated then anti-rabies serum (immunoglobulin) may be required in addition. It is wise to finish the course of treatment whether the animal survives or not.

Athlete's foot and other fungal infections are best treated by sunshine and a proprietary preparation such as Tolnaftate.

Influenza and **respiratory diseases** are common, perhaps made worse by polluted cities and rapid temperature, climatic changes and its proximity to

FIRST AID KITS

Although pre-packaged first aid kits for travellers are available from many camping and outdoor pursuit shops, it is unlikely that you will ever need to use at least half of their contents. If you are visiting very remote areas, for example if you are trekking, it becomes more important to ensure that you have all the necessary items. You may want to bring with you a supply of sticky plasters and corn plasters (Band Aid etc), intestinal treatments such as Imodium, and antihistamine tablets. *Flagyl* can be bought across the chemist's counter in Nepal, whereas in UK at least, a doctor's prescription is required. Paracetamol is readily available. Tibet's larger hospitals and medical centres do not seem to have any shortage of sterile, single-use needles, but to be safe you should bring your own supply, the standard 'green' size are the most versatile. If you have any specialized requirements, it is recommended that you bring them with you.

China.

Itchy rashes A very common itchy rash is avoided by frequent washing and by wearing loose clothing. It is helped by the use of talcum powder to allow the skin to dry thoroughly after washing. It may be caused by bed bugs, lice etc which are commonly found in the bedding in truck stops.

Returning home

Remember to take your anti-malaria tablets for 6 weeks if you have been travelling in endemic areas such as Nepal or S Bhutan. If you have had attacks of diarrhoea, it is worth having a stool specimen tested in case you have picked up amoebic dysentery. If you have been living rough, a blood test may be worthwhile to detect worms and other parasites.

Further information

The following organizations give information regarding well trained English speaking Physicians throughout the world: International Association for Medical Assistance to Travellers, 745 5th Ave, New York, 10022; Intermedic 777, Third Ave, New York, 10017.

Information regarding country by country malaria risk can be obtained from the World Health Organization (WHO) or the Ross Institute, The London School of Hygiene and Tropical Medicine, Kepple St, London WC1E 7HT, which publishes a strongly recommended book entitled: *The Preservation of Personal Health in Warm Climates*.

The organization MASTA (Medical Advisory Service for Travellers Abroad) also based at the London School of Hygiene and Tropical Medicine, Telephone 0171 631-4408 – Telex 895 3474) will provide country by country information on up-to-date health risks.

Further information on medical problems overseas can be obtained from the new edition of *Travellers' Health: How to Stay Healthy Abroad*, edited by Richard Dawood (Oxford University Press, 1992). We strongly recommend this revised and updated edition, especially to the travellers who go to the more out-of-the-way places.

TIBET: LAND, CULTURE AND HISTORY

LAND AND LIFE

CONTENTS

Basics

OFFICIAL NAME *Bod*

CAPITAL Lhasa

NATIONAL FLAG **Tibetan**: white snow mountain extending from lower corners to centre, with two snow-lions supporting a gemstone (symbolic of Buddhism) and *gakhyil* (symbolic of prosperity), and a yellow sun which rises behind the summit, emanating alternate red and blue rays of light representing 12 traditional regions of Tibet which reach the upper borders; bound on three edges with a yellow border symbolic of Buddhism binding the cultural life of Tibet while remaining open to other religions with one edge of the flag open. **Chinese**: the red flag of the People's Republic of China with one large yellow star representing the industrial workers, and four minor stars representing the peasants, merchants, intellectuals and military.

OFFICIAL LANGUAGES Tibetan, Chinese

MEDIUM OF INSTRUCTION IN SCHOOLS Chinese, Tibetan

KEY STATISTICS 1995 *Population*: 7,106,613 (excluding Ziling and Jang Sadam districts), of which approximately 65% are Tibetan, 28% Han and Hui, and 7% minority nationalities (including Monpa, Lhopa, Qiang, Jang, Mongol, Salar, Tu, Khazak, and Sarik). *Area*: 2,088,670 sq km (excluding Ziling and Jang Sadam districts). *Population density*: 3.403/sq km. *Birth rate*: 30:1,000. *Death rate*: 14:1,000. *Life expectancy*: 62. *Literacy*: 40%. *Land use* (TAR only): forested 1.4

billion cu m, nomadic pasture 167 million acres, agriculture 0.55 million acres. *GNP per capita*: US$200. *Religion*: Buddhist 66%, Bon 3%, Muslim 6%, Atheist 25%.

Geology and landscape

Location

The area covered by the Tibetan plateau and the adjacent Sino-Tibetan border ranges (latitude: 39-27°C N; longitude: 78-104°C E), which are sometimes poetically referred to as the 'roof of the world' or the 'third pole', forms an enormous land-locked region in Central Asia, 2,300,000 sq km in area. It encompasses Tibet (including the eastern provinces of Kham and Amdo) which is the cultural heartland of Inner Asia, and the countries to its S, Bhutan and the Kathmandu Valley of Nepal, where cultures of the Tibetan world and the Indian subcontinent converge. The Tibetan plateau is an immense region (as large as Western Europe); and has considerable importance within the biosphere as the highest region on the planet and the source of virtually all the important waterways of South and East Asia.

The indigenous name given to this region is **Bod** or **Bod-Kham**; the English equivalent (Tibet) being derived from the Mongolian *Thubet*, the Chinese *Tu-fan*, and the Arabic *Tubbat*.

Yet, the plateau includes, in addition to Tibet, the peripheral mountain areas to the S, which are defined by the Karakorum and Himalayan ranges: Gilgit and Baltistan (now in Pakistan); Ladakh, Lahoul, Spiti, Kinnaur, Tehri-Garwal, Kumaon, Sikkim, and Arunachal (now in India); Manang, Dolpo, Mustang,

Langtang, Helambu, and Khumbhu (now in Nepal); and the mountainous areas of Bhutan. The formidable terrain and its communication difficulties have ensured that the plateau has rarely been politically united in the course of its history. The defining characteristics of the region are made, rather, on the basis of topography, ethnicity, language, and religion, which together form the distinct Tibetan cultural millieu.

Provinces and terrain

Traditionally, Tibet has been divided into three provinces (*Tib* cholkha sum), namely: **Utsang** (extending from Ngari Korsum in Far-western Tibet as far as Sokla Kyawo in the upper reaches of the Salween); **Kham** (extending eastwards from Sokla Kyawo to the watershed of the Yellow and Yangtze basins); and **Amdo** (extending eastwards and north-eastwards from the source of the Yellow River and the Sertal region to Chorten Karpo on the Sang-chu tributary of the Yellow River).

Currently, the plateau is administratively divided between the **Tibetan Autonomous Region** (1,106,780 sq km) of China, and four other Chinese provinces – Qinghai, Gansu, Sichuan, and Yunnan. Of these latter provinces, the plateau incorporates virtually the entire land-mass of **Qinghai** (676,851 sq km, excluding Ziling district), the **Ganlho Autonomous Prefecture** and **Tianzhu Autonomous County** (44,323 sq km) of Gansu province, the **Kandze** and **Ngawa Autonomous Prefectures** of W Sichuan (240,154 sq km), and the **Dechen Autonomous Prefecture** of NE Yunnan (20, 562 sq km). The region is

---

GEOLOGICAL HISTORY OF THE TIBETAN PLATEAU

Precambrian

4,000-2,500 mya (million years ago): oldest stable continental rock.
660 mya: oldest Tibetan rock

Palaeozoic

500 mya: Gondwanaland included India and S Tibet.
Earliest South Tibetan fossils (1979) suggest latitude of modern Australia.
400/300 mya: Pangaea (4th) supercontinent forms; and Old Thethys Sea contracts.
300 mya: formation of Kunlun, Pamir, and Altyn Tagh ranges.

Mezozoic

200 mya: fusion of Jangtang plain and Indochina with Asia, along two connection zones of the Salween and Yangtze respectively. Consequent rising of plateau from seabed.
140 mya: India separates from Africa.
100 mya: tectonic pressure raises Kangtise and Nyenchen Thangla ranges.

Cenozoic

45 mya: Himalayas begin to form as India fully collides with Asia, subducting the Neo-Tethys sea.
20 mya: older Himalayan rock thrust upward through younger strata over 2,000 km central fault.
15-10 mya: Himalayas at 3,000m; plateau at 1,000m.
2 mya: rapid uplift of plateau and Himalayas along main boundary fault.

Pleistocene Epoch

1 mya: Himalayas at 4,500m; Plateau at 3,000m.
10,000 ya: Himalayas at 6,000m; Plateau at 4,700m.

bordered on the W by India, on the N and NW by Xinjiang (Chinese Turkestan), on the NE, E and SE by mainland China, and on the S by India, Nepal, Bhutan and Burma.

NB Many of the bordering regions of these neighbouring countries, ie Baltistan, Gilgit, Ladak, Zangskar, Lahoul, Spiti, Kinnaur, northern Nepal, Sikkim, Bhutan and Arunachal Pradesh, have at one time or another been considered Tibetan territory and their cultures, languages, and ethnic composition are still predominantly Tibetan. Taken as a whole, Tibet occupies about one fourth of China's territory.

Terrain

The Tibetan plateau covers an area as large as Western Europe, or seven times the size of France, with an elevation ranging from the low-lying southern gorges at 1,700m to the massive 8,000m Himalayan peaks. The country can conveniently be divided into four distinct geographical regions – the Northern lakeland plateau (**Jangtang**) which is sparsely populated by nomadic herdsmen, the dry far-western highlands (**Ngari**) which are the source of the Indus, Sutlej and Brahmaputra rivers, the urbanized central valleys of Lhasa and Shigatse (**Utsang**) which form the Brahmaputra River system, and the most fertile and populated eastern region (**Kham and Amdo**), which is characterized by the deep river gorges of the Salween, Mekong, Yangtze, Yalong, and Gyarong and by the high rolling pastures around the upper reaches of these rivers, as well as around the upper reaches of the Yellow River, Minjiang and Jialing.

The origins of Tibet's landscape

Most of the Tibetan plateau is considered to have formed the bed of the **Neotethys Ocean**, which was destroyed some 210-50 million years ago as the Indian sub-continental plate moved to throw up the mountains of the Himalayan region. This however is a comparatively recent geological event, and it is predated in the peripheral N and E areas of the plateau, where the oldest rocks are Precambrian granite, known to be about 1 billion years old. Unfortunately, the geological correlations of these earlier strata have been complicated by subsequent neotectonic development.

During the **Palaeozoic** era (570-245 million years ago) the **Kunlun ranges** of Tibet's northern frontier, which are largely composed of Cambrian and Triassic granites, granodiorites, and andesites, began accumulating along the southern margin of the Tarim Basin. This developing mountain range continued westwards into the Pamirs and the Hindu Kush. Then, during the **Mesozoic** era (245-66.4 million years ago), the **Jangtang** plain of N Tibet became separated from the S Tibet block by an ocean; evidence of this can be found in the Dangla mountains of N Tibet. Further movement involving the breakup of the southern supercontinent 'Pangaea' produced the granite **Gangtise**, **Nyenchen Tanglha**, and **Karakorum ranges** (180-100 million years ago).

The process continued until, during the **Cenozoic** period (66.4 million years ago – onwards), the Tibetan plateau was finally formed. The all-important collision of the drifting Indian subcontinent with Eurasia is considered to have taken place some 2,012 km S of the Indus-Brahmaputra watershed on the northern side of the Inner Himalayan range. Since then some 805 km of this horizontal movement of the continental crust northwards have been contracted to form the Himalayas – the world's highest mountain range and the largest concentration of continental crust on earth (69 km thick in places). Further S, the collision created the Gangetic basin. The massive plateau, subject to widespread volcanicity, continues to extend upwards and outwards under its own weight, as the Indian sub-continental plate moves ever northwards at a speed of about 6.1 cm/year.

Earthquake and geothermal activity

The entire region is subject to intense geological activity. Satellite photos reveal widespread thrust fault zones throughout the plateau; deep fault zones in the Himalayas, the Jangtang lakeland plain, and the river gorges of E Tibet; as well as strike-slip fault zones in the Kunlun and Altyn Tagh ranges, and in the Yalong, Yangtze, and Yellow River valleys. From 1870-1996 over 50 major earthquakes (measuring over 6 on the Richter scale) have occurred along these fault lines.

Over the plateau as a whole, there are more than 600 geothermal areas including hot springs, geysers and hydrothermal explosions. The majority of these are found in the region between the southern Himalayan watershed and the northern Gangtise/Nyenchen Tanglha watersheds.

Mountain ranges

Two principal mountain belts extend eastwards in a pincer-like manner from the **Pamir knot**. To the N, the ranges stretch through the **Kunluns** to the **Altyn Tagh** and **Chole Namgyel** mountains. In the S, they extend through the **Karakorums** and **Himalayas**, and thence SE to the **Arakan** mountains of Burma. These frontier mountain ranges

are imposingly high, with individual peaks rising above 7,000-8,000m. They have gentle interior slopes and rugged precipitous exterior slopes. This has ensured the geographic isolation of the region and its unique landscape complexes. The **plateau** extending between these two formidable mountain barriers is located between 3,990-5,000m above sea level; and its surface is a complex combination of ranges and plains, generally tilting from NW to SE. The permanent snow-line averages 4,510-5,000m; and may reach 6,400m in Central Tibet.

Karakorum mountains

The Karakorum mountains (*Ch* Kala Kunlun Shan) extend SE from the borders of **Afghanistan** for 800 km as far as the **Pang-gong** Tibet range and **Chang Chenmo Ladakh** ranges. Approximately 240 km wide, and characterized by craggy peaks with steep slopes and ravine-like transverse valleys, the Karakorums form a watershed between the **Indus River** to the S and the **Tarim basin** in the N. The average elevation is 6,100m, and there are four peaks which rise above 7,925m, the highest being **K2 (Dapsang)** at 8,611m.

The Karakoram glaciers, along with those of the Himalayas, are renowned for their immensity.

Himalayan mountains

The world's highest mountain range, which comprises 110 peaks above

---

HIMALAYA: HIGHEST PEAKS IN THE WORLD

The main Himalayan range, known as the **Inner** or **Great Himalayas**, is parallelled to the S by two minor latitudinal ranges, the southernmost being the sub-Himalayan or Outer Himalayan range of the **Shiwaliks** (274-760m); followed by the **Lesser Himalayas** (4,572m, valleys at 914m) of Kashmir and Central Nepal. The Great Himalayas comprise nine of the 14 highest peaks in the world, all above 7,925m. The most prominent peaks are (from W to E): Gangotri (6,726m), Kamet (7,756m), Nanda Devi (7,817m), Ganglung (6,324m), Kanjiroba (6,492m), Dhaulagiri (8,172m), Annapurna (8,078m), Shishipangma (8,012m), Everest (8,848m), Kangchendzonga (8,598m), Jomolhari (7,313m), Kulha Kangri (7,554m), Phulahari (7,410m), and Namchak Barwa (7,756m).

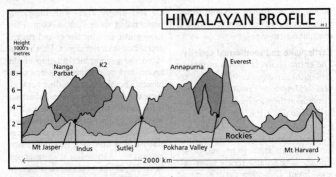

HIMALAYAN PROFILE IH 2

Height 1000's metres

Nanga Parbat — K2 — Annapurna — Everest

Rockies

Mt Jasper — Indus — Sutlej — Pokhara Valley — Mt Harvard

← 2000 km →

7,300m, and more than 30 above 8,000m, the highest being **Mt Everest** (8,848m; 29,029 ft), extends 24,500 km from **Mt Nanga Parbat** (8,108m) in the extreme W to **Mt Namchak Barwa** (7,756m) in the extreme E. From S to N the range covers an area of 200-400 km; and the total area is 594,400 sq km.

The range is a drainage area for 19 major rivers, the greatest of which – the **Indus**, **Sutlej**, **Karnali**, and **Brahmaputra**, rise N of the Himalayan range and are fed by some of the world's highest glaciers (eg the 32 km long Gangotri glacier and the Kumbhu glacier of Nepal). They flow through deep gorges between 1,524-4,877m deep and 10-48 km wide.

Kunlun mountains

The **Kunlun** mountains forming Tibet's northern frontier extend 2,000 km from the **Pamirs** in the W to the **Bayankala** and **Amnye Machen** mountains in the E. The range rarely exceeds 200 km in its width. The southern slopes, which rise only 1,500m above the plateau, are contrasted with the steep northern slopes, which form a massive rampart as they are approached from the Tarim basin and its low-lying oases of **Khotan**, **Keriya** and **Qarqan**, only 900-1,500m above sea level.

The highest peaks are located in the W Kunluns, eg **Mt Muztagh** (7,723m); **Mt Keriya** (7,120m), **Mt Kongur**

(7,719m), and **Mt Muztagh Ata** (7,546m). The Central and East Kunluns are lower, including the parallel ranges of the Kukushili (some peaks above 6,300m) and the Bayankala, characterized by their flat dome-shaped peaks and gently broken slopes. The region has long been subject to erosion, causing large sand dunes, and producing steppe and desert soils with low organic content. The high degree of evaporation has produced frequent saline depressions and largely undeveloped river systems.

Main features of the plateau

Hemmed in by those formidable mountain barriers, in the western part of the plateau, high plains predominate; while in the eastern part, there is a predominance of ranges and deep gorges.

In the W lie the **Northern Plateau (Jangtang)** and the **Tsaidam basin**. Both are hemmed in by mountain ranges with individual peaks which rise above 6,000m but, in general, their soft and smooth outlines tend not to dominate the surrounding landscape.

By contrast, the eastern sandstone ranges are deeply eroded, so that they have come to dominate the surrounding landscape. Such are: the eastern extermity of the **Nyenchen Tanglha** range dividing the Brahmaputra from the Salween River; the **Gaoligong Mountains** on the Burmese border, dividing the Irrawady from the Salween; the **Tshawagang** uplands and **Kawa Karpo** range (*Ch* Taniantaweng, Hengduan and Nushan), dividing the Salween from the Mekong River; the **Markhamgang** uplands (*Ch* Ningjing and Yunling), dividing the Mekong from the Yangtze; the **Drida Zelmogang** and **Puburgang** uplands including the Tro La (*Ch* Cholashan) and **Kawalungring** (*Ch* Shaluli) ranges, which divide the Yangtze from the Yalong River; the **Menyak Rabgang** uplands (*Ch* Daxue) dividing the Yalong from the Gyarong; the **Mardzagang** uplands along with the **Bayankala** and **Amnye Machen** ranges, dividing the Yangtze, Yalong, and Gyarong from the Yellow River and the **Minshan** range at the eastern extremity of the plateau, which divides the Yellow River from the upper Yangtze tributaries – the Minjiang and Jialing.

Soil

The far-western and northern highland regions are largely covered with detrital desert; while the deeply cut mountain ranges of the frontiers and E are subject in places to extensive glaciation, or dissected by severe erosion. The **high-altitude plateau** in the Far-west and N, sustains soils which are either weakly developed embryonic soils of detritus and stony fragments, varying from light brown to grey in colour according to the humus content; or sandy soil subject to aeolian wind-relief, thus forming a thin surface layer above gravel or shingle. Here, the vegetation is extremely sparse, and the amount of humus reduced, increasing the content of unbleached mineral salts, and intensifying the upward flow of salt solutions to the surface.

In the S, the upper reaches of the **Indus** and **Brahmaputra** River valleys lie in a deep marginal depression running parallel to the frontier Himalayan range. This is a region of immature subsidence in which thick accumulations of

earlier marine sediments and later continental deposits washed down from the mountains have been transformed into sandy deserts flanked by lateral valleys of alluvial deposits, enabling specialized agriculture to flourish in sheltered lower elevations.

South of this river system, the **Himalayas** have the most complex veriety of vegetation and soil types. On a vertical axis, low-lying forested areas or desert steppe (ie mountain chestnut soils and mountain chernozems) give way to alpine meadow or mountain tundra, and thence to detritus, snow and glaciation. Soil tends to be thicker on the N-facing slopes, which support dense forests at lower altitudes and grasslands at higher altitudes. Predominant is the alluvial soil associated with mountain tundra, which has been deposited by the gorge rivers onto the **Gangetic** plain of India.

Further E and NE the erosion processes have exposed the sandstone rocks, producing the alluvial soils of the **Mekong** and **Yangtze** gorges, the bleached podzolic grey-brown soils of the mountain slopes, the dark-coloured chernozem soils of the **Amdo** grasslands with their deep rich humus, and the thick loess deposits of the ranges around the upper reaches of the **Yellow** River. Among these the alluvial soils and chernozems, like those of the **Gangetic** plain, are more fertile than the deficient lithosols of the W and N. Generally, the major threat to agriculture in the region is the increasing salinization of the soil and the increasing erosion of the Indo-Tibetan and Sino-Tibetan rivers, as the plateau continues to be pushed upwards by tectonic movement.

Minerals

Geological surveys suggest that the Tibetan plateau is extremely rich in its accumulation of ores within the folded zone – from the **Karakorums** in the Far-west through the **Himalayas** to the **Kawa Karpo** ranges – due to intrusions of granites and igneous rock. Such deposits include ores of copper, iron, lead and zinc, as well as antimony, arsenic, molybdenum, borax, sulphur, coal, bauxite, mica, gypsum, and sapphire. Throughout the plateau, many alluvial and vein deposits of gold are to be found.

Around **Lhasa** there is hard coal and alabaster; while magnetite is common in the eastern **Brahmaputra** valley.

Further N, in the **Dangla** range, iron ore, hard coal, graphite, asbestos, and soapstone have been discovered.

The **Northern Plateau/Jangtang** lakelands have an unlimited reserve of salts: borax, gypsum, common salt, quartz, and soda.

The **Chole Namgyel** mountains on the extreme NE frontier of the plateau contain iron, chromium, copper, lead, zinc, gold, and coal from the Carboniferous and Jurassic ages.

The **Tsaidam** depression is known for its Jurassic coal and oil, which are deposited within Lower Tertiary sandstone.

Rivers

The land-locked Tibetan plateau is the primary source of the water supply for most of Central, East and South Asia. **Internal drainage** is rare, being almost invariably confined to the short rivers and saline lakes of the Northern Plateau (Jangtang) and the Lake Kokonor region of the NE.

Those rivers originating in Tibet which drain into the **Pacific Ocean** include the **Yellow** River (*Tib* Machu; *Ch* Huang Ho), the **Yangtze** (*Tib* Drichu; *Ch* Jinsha), and the **Mekong** (*Tib* Dachu; *Ch* Lancang); along with important tributaries of the **Yangtze**, namely the **Yalong** (*Tib* Dzachu/Nyachu), **Gyarong** (*Ch* Dadu), **Min**, and **Jialing**.

Those rivers which drain into the **Indian Ocean** are the **Salween** (*Tib* Gyelmo Ngulchu; *Ch* Nujiang), **Irrawaddy** (*Burmese* Nmai Hka), **Brahmaputra** (*Tib* Tsangpo; *Ch* Zangbo), **Sutlej** (*Tib* Langchen Tsangpo), **Indus** (*Tib* Senge Tsangpo), and certain **Gangetic feeder rivers** including the **Karnali** (*Tib* Mabcha Tsangpo), **Trishuli** (*Tib* Kyirong Tsangpo), **Sunkosi** (*Tib* Matsang Tsangpo), and **Arun** (*Tib* Bum-chu).

Other tributaries of the Ganges and Brahmaputra have their sources further S in Nepal and Bhutan. Among these, important **Gangetic tributaries** include the Chamlia, Seti, Bheti, and Kali-Gandaki, while those of the **Brahmaputra** include the Wang-chu, the Puna Tsangchu, the Mangde-chu and the Bumtang-chu.

Lakes

Many inland lakes have been formed on the plateau by the filling of geological basins, from volcanic debris, silting, and glacial retreat. Dehydration however suggests that the lakes of the Northern Plateau (Jangtang) S of the Kunlun range were once part of the Yangtze, and the lakes from Pang-gong Lake eastwards once part of the Salween. Some smaller lakes were once connected to larger lakes (eg Rakshas to Manasarovar, and Zigetang to Serling). The process of salination is more prominent in the northern lakes; the deep blue colour being due to paucity of silt and the intense sunlight. In general, the lakes of the plateau are important sources of minerals: mirabilite, gypsum, borax, magnesium, potassium, lithium, strontium, uranium and so forth. Among the largest are: **Kokonor** (97 km across), **Ngoring** and **Kyaring** (40 km across), **Namtso** and **Serling** (81 km across), **Dangra** (64 km long), **Yamdrok** (64 km across), **Manasarovar** (24 km across and 73m deep), **Rakshas** (24 km long), and **Panggong** (48 km by 113 km).

Climate

The climate of the plateau, conditioned by the terrain, is generally severe, dry, and continental, with strong winds, low humidity, a rarified atmosphere, and a great fluctuation in the annual and summer daytime temperatures. The region is exposed to an unimpeded access of arctic air from the N; while the southern tropical and equatorial air masses barely penetrate the Himalayan barrier into Central Asia. The contrast between the strong heating of the land in summer months and the chilling in winter produces sharp seasonal variations in atmospheric circulation and enhances the role of local centres of atmospheric activity.

In winter, the polar continental air mass originating in Siberia dominates East and Central Asia, forming a persistent high-pressure anticyclone over Tibet. Cold dry air therefore moves eastward and southward out of the continent during the winter; and the plateau experiences cold but calm weather, with little snowfall. This pattern is occasionally interspersed by cyclonic storms moving eastwards from the Mediterranean, which give rise to short periods of low-pressure, bringing snow to the higher ranges. By contrast, **in summertime**, the heating caused by the dry and dusty continental wind creates a low-pressure area, which contributes to the onset of the monsoon rains in South Asia. Nearly all the plateau's precipitation (average 460 mm) falls in summer and in specific areas.

The higher western and northern regions are less exposed to this monsoon weather pattern than the lower regions to the E and S. Thus, the former characteristically endure frost weathering for all but 45 days/annum, along with severe salt accumulation and wind activity.

In the **Kunlun** mountains to the N, where strong winds, dry dusty heat, and frost weathering predominate, the annual precipitation averages only 50-100 mm; and the temperature fluctuates between extremes: 25-28°C (foothills, in mid-summer) and -9°C (foothills, in mid-winter); 10°C (higher slopes, mid-summer) and -35°C (higher slopes, in mid-winter).

Further W, in the **Karakorum** Mountains, the climate is characterized by rarified air, intense solar radiation, and strong winds. Precipitation (100 mm/annum) is largely confined to high-altitude snow-fields above 4,877m, and to immense glaciers, which plunge on the southern slopes from 4,694-2,896m, and on northern slopes from 5,913-3,536m.

In the **Jangtang** plateau, rainfall is less than 100 mm. July temperatures fluctuate from 30°C in daytime to -15°C at night. Winter temperatures may drop to -35°C. Snow evaporates due to dryness, and wind speed exceeds 20m/second, causing severe dust storms.

Further S, in the **Himalayas**, a series of dramatic well-defined vertical climatic zones presents considerable variation in temperature and environment. The formidable mountain barrier obstructs the passage of cold continental air southwards and equally impedes the passage of warm monsoon air northwards, so that, on the southern side, precipitation varies from 1,530 mm in W Nepal to 3,060 mm in parts of Bhutan; whereas on the NW slopes (around Ladakh) the figure drops to 765 -153 mm, and in Tibet proper to even less. Winter precipitation is heavier in the W Himalayas, which are more exposed to weather patterns from West Asia, than in the E Himalayas; but this is reversed in summer when the E is directly exposed to SW monsoon currents.

Different altitudinal climatic zones are clearly defined on the southern slopes of the Himalayas, varying from the sub-equatorial and tropical climates of the foothills at the lowest level to the snowy climate of the peaks. The degree of exposure is also significant – the sunny southern slopes differing from the shady northern ones, and windward slopes exposed to moist ocean winds differing from leeward slopes. The barrier effect is most pronounced in areas where rain-bearing monsoon winds have a constant direction. Temperatures vary accordingly, so that the average pre-monsoon temperature is 11°C at 1,945m, -8°C at 5,029m, and -22°C at 5,944m.

The **gorges of Eastern Tibet** are much more accessible to South and Southeast Asian weather patterns. Here there is marked contrast between perennially snow-capped peaks, the temperate zone (1,829-3,353m), and the mild weather prevailing in the valleys below, some of which in the southernmost part of **Kham** are subject to a sultry heat and high level of humidity. Annual precipitation approximates 51 cm; and there is heavy snowfall in the mountain uplands during winter.

In **Nepal and Bhutan**, the contrast between those vertical climatic zones is seen at its greatest extent: the sub-tropical **Terai** has minimum 5°C (mid-winter) and maximum 45°C (mid-summer); the temperate **mid-mountain belt**, eg Kathmandu has minimum -3°C (mid-winter) and maximum 37°C (mid-summer); and the **alpine Himalayan belt**, eg Khumbhu has minimum -15°C (mid-winter) and maximum 35°C (mid-summer).

Vegetation, land and wildlife

Pre-historic flora and fauna

The ancient environment of the plateau can be known from the fossils discovered in recent decades. These suggest a very different landscape from the one we have today. Marine fossils, including trilobites and brachiopods, characteristic of those found on ocean beds have been dated to 500 million years ago (mya). Marine plant fossils (dated 400-300 mya) suggest there was once warm water over northern Tibet and cold water over southern Tibet. In the **Chamdo** area, fossils of tropical plants, giant horsetail plants, and the *changdusaurus* (2.7m high and 6.1m long) have been dated to 200-150 mya, as has the *ichthyosaur* fossil (9.1m long), discovered at **Nyalam** in the Himalayas. Later fossils (dated 100 mya) suggest that swampland was gradually replaced by tropical plants and broadleaf forests, which still covered much of the **Tsaidam,** the **Kunluns**, and **Jangtang** as late as 25 mya.

Gradually (10-5 mya), those forests became drier grasslands as the temperature dropped, leaving only the subtropical eastern gorges and moister Himalayas forested. The plateau was frequented by gazelles, giraffes, deer, rhino, wild cats, hyenas, 3-toed horses, and rodents. African mammal fossil remains (hippo, giraffe) have also been discovered in the **Shiwalik Hills** of southern Nepal.

During the **Ice Age** (3 mya-14,000 ya), the dry cold steppe increased and the forests decreased, causing Central Asian animals, such as cattle, sheep, goats; marmots, kiang and wild yak to reach the Tibetan plateau, and other animals such as the badger, hyena, tiger, horse, porcupine, elephant, panda, and leopard to migrate S to warmer climates. Glaciation reached its maximum during this period, with some glaciers being 130 km long in **Kham**, 20-30 km long on **Kailash**, and 40 km long in the **Himalayas**! After a subsequent period of interglacial warming (14,000 ya – 1,000 BC) during which forests again increased, the **New Ice Age** (1,000 BC) brought a harsher climate, drier lakes and fewer forests. Unfortunately, there are no surviving vegetation relics from previous geological eras due to the relative youth of the plateau and the subsequent glaciation of the Quaternary Age, which destroyed the pre-glacial vegetation.

Vegetation

The present species of flora found of the plateau appeared in the wake of the retreating glaciers and are related through migration to the adjacent desert flora of Central Asia and the mesophyte flora of East Asia. The vegetation of the region, like its climate, reflects the diversity of the topography.

The very high altitude, dryness and complex land forms create a local climatic zone on the Tibetan plateau which runs counter to the worldwide pattern. Thus, the S is more heavily forested than the N, which is mostly rocky desert; the SE is more densely forested than the Central parts, and the NE is grassland. Mountain ranges also exhibit their own vegetation and vertical climatic zones, ie from tropical forest through deciduous forest, grassland, pine forest, alpine scrub and barren rock. However this pattern is broken in the SE where mountain zones divide forest and meadowland; and on the plateau where steppe and desert prevail.

In the N and W, where there is a predominance of cold alpine desert, the soil cover is shallow and only perennial hard-frost resistant plants with roots reaching the parent rock survive. The arid climate of the **Jangtang** plateau, devoid of trees and larger plant forms, supports only grasses and a scattered vegetation of salt-tolerant bushes and Artemisia plants. The environment of the **Kunluns** is one of stark and barren

YAK, DRI, DRONG, DZO: THE HIGHLAND CATTLE OF TIBET

No creature exemplifies the uniqueness of the Tibetan plateau like the yak. From whichever of the gateway cities you approach Tibet: Kathmandu, Chengdu, Kunming, Lanzhou, or Kashgar, the initial appearance of the yak at altitudes of 8,000-9,000 ft indicates that you have arrived within the ethnic Tibetan area. For the Tibetan people and the yak are inseparable. Hardy, stubborn, frisky, and apparently clumsy though deceptively agile on precipitous rugged terrain, this 'grunting ox' (*Bos grunniens*) comes in many shapes and sizes: the male of the species is known as the yak, and the female as the dri. These animals have been domesticated and tended by Tibetan nomads for thousands of years, giving rise also to the hybrid dzo (a cross between a bull and a dri), which has become an ideal ploughing animal in Tibetan farming villages. By contrast, the wild yak (drong), like the American bison, once roamed the grasslands of Northern and Eastern Tibet, in large herds, but their numbers have been severely depleted within the last few decades, falling prey to Chinese hunters and modern weaponry.

Since antiquity, the yak has been used as a pack animal and is rarely ridden in the manner of a horse. Prior to the construction of motorable roads, yak caravans were the principal means for the transportation of freight, and they still are in many remote parts of the country. Though slow, they are untiringly capable of carrying loads of over 50 kg across 5,000m passes, and they withstand temperatures of -30°C. For the nomads who rear the yak, this creature is the source of their wealth and livelihood. The flesh provides meat (*tsak-sha*), which may be cooked or freeze dried; the milk of the dri provides butter (*mar*) and cheese (*chura*). Some Amdo towns now have meat and dairy processing factories supplied by the local nomadic communities. The hide is used for high-calved Tibetan boots, clothing, and traditional coracle construction. The soft inner hair (*ku-lu*) is now used for the production of high quality sweaters, particularly in the Repkong area of Amdo, and these are exported worldwide. The coarse outer hair (*tsid-pa*) is spun by the nomads themselves and used for making their black yak wool tent dwellings, known in Tibetan as 'ba' (*bra*).

desert rock, and stagnant pools. More variation is found in the **Karakorums**, where the lower river valleys (below 3,048m) abound in willow, poplar, and oleander; the lower slopes in artemisia, and the upper slopes in juniper.

Himalayan flora (as found in Tibet, Nepal, and Bhutan) are differentiated according to four complex vertical zones: the **tropical foothills** of the East and Central Himalayas (180-730m), which are covered in evergreens such as mesua ferrea, oak, chestnut, alder, and pandanus furcatus; the **subtropical zone** (910-1,370m) in which are found deciduous sal trees, steppe forest, and thorn steppe; the **temperate zone** (1,370-3,350m) in which grow pine, cedar, spruce, oak, and birch; and the **alpine zone** (3,200-4,450m) where juniper, rhododendron, flowering plants, moss and lichen grow.

A richer plant life is found in the river valleys and low-lying gorges of **S** and **SE Tibet**, where the humidity level is higher. Here, there are willows, poplars, conifers, teak, rhododendron, oak, birch, elm, bamboo, sugar cane, tea, tamarisk, and so forth.

On the mountain slopes dominating the **gorges** of **E Tibet** are rich virgin forests, abounding in spruce, fir, larch, juniper, pine, and medicinal herbs. The floral **grasslands** of **Amdo** and the **uplands of Kham** support grasses such as cobresia and sedge, which provide fodder and pasture for livestock.

Regional variations occur within the vertical climatic zones of **Kham**. For example, in the **Yangtze**, **Yalong** and **Gyarong gorges** of E Kham, below 610m there grow cypress, palm, bamboo, citrous fruits; from 610-1,520m there grow evergreens and oaks; from 1,520-2,430m grow mixed conifers; from 2,590-3,500m grow sub-alpine coniferous forests; and from 3,500-4,880m grow alpine shrub and meadow. Further S of Kham, in the **lower Salween** and **Mekong gorges** of **Dechen** county, the verti-

cal zones have a more pronounced subtropical vegetation: below 1,830m there is conifer forest, from 1,830-3,350m there is an abundance of azaleas, rhododendrons, camelias, roses, and primroses and from 3,350-4,570m grow fir, bamboo, dwarf juniper, and flowering herbs.

In general, therefore, a transition is clearly observable from the grassy-shrub landscapes of the uplands, through the sub-alpine coniferous forests, to the forest landscapes of the warmly temperate and subtropical belts.

Wildlife

Over 530 species of birds, 190 species of mammals, more than 40 species of reptiles, and 30 species of amphibians, and 2,300 species of insects are found in the region as a whole.

In general it is said that **E Himalayan** fauna have an affinity with those of the Chinese and Indo-Chinese region, whereas **W Himalayan** fauna are more closely related to Turkmenian and Mediterranean fauna. In the **western** and **northern Tibet plains**, there are many animal specimens, predominantly hoofed mammals (ungulates), who thrive in this open habitat, and rodents. Within the **Kunlun** ranges, these include gazelle, wild ass, wild goat, wild yak, blue sheep, urial, ibex, brown bear, and wolf.

The **saline lakes** of the Jangtang Plateau are home to varieties of waterfowl in seasonal migration. In the **Karakorums**, the urial, wild yak, ibex, and wild ass are found; while birds of prey such as the lammergeier, griffon, and golden eagle are commonplace.

In the **Himalayan** region, **above the tree-line**, are found a number of endemic species adapted to cold, such as the snow leopard, brown bear, red panda, and yak. The **lower forests** are home to the black bear, clouded leopard, and terai langur; and the **southern foothills** are frequented by the rhino, musk deer, stag, and elephant. There are distinctive varieties of fish, such as the glyptothorax, and reptiles, such as the japalura lizard, the blind snake (*typhlops*), and unusual species of insects, such as the troides butterfly. Over 800 species of birds have been identified in **Nepal** alone – including the magpie, titmouse, chough, thrush, redstart, lammergeier, kite, vulture, and snow partridge.

The deep valleys of **SE Tibet**, which are exposed to the moist humidity of the monsoon, support dense forests with a plethora of animals and birds. Here there are found the leopard, bear, wild boar, wild goat, langur, lynx, jackal, wild dog, and spotted cat. Distinctive species such as the lesser panda and ling yang antelope are found in the **Gyarong** region. In the high **grasslands of Amdo** and the **Kham uplands** are brown bears,

wild and bighorn sheep, mountain antelope, musk deer, wild ass, wild yak, snake, scorpion, and mountain lizard. Waterfowl is abundant in the lakes of **E and NE Tibet**, as are fish, frog, crab, otter, and turtle. Birds include the hoopoe, hawk, mynah, gull, crane, sheldrake, teal, owl, and magpie.

Wildlife reserves

These are extremely well developed in both **Nepal** and **Bhutan**, where ecological and environmental considerations have been given more of a priority. Among the current administrative divisions of Tibet, **Qinghai** province in the NE has advanced furthest in the establishing of wildlife reserves. The world's second largest reserve was established in the **Jangtang** region in 1993. Details on these reserves will be found below, in their relevant chapters.

CULTURE

CONTENTS

People of the region

The racial origins of the Tibetans are little known and still remain a matter of scientific speculation. A systematic research into their origins has been limited on account of the isolation and inaccessibility of the country, an instinctive in-built resistance to anthropometric examination, and the comparative lack of skeletal remains due to the paucity of archaeological excavations and perhaps to the funeral custom of dismemberment and 'sky burial'.

Ethnologists, whose opinions vary and disagree, have distinguished **two main racial types** among the **Tibetans** – one tall with long limbs and heads, and often distinct aqualine features; and another of shorter stature, with high cheekbones and round heads. The former type, found mainly among the northern and eastern nomads of Kham and Amdo, like the modern Turkic and Mongolian peoples, is considered to be descended from a tall dolicocephalous race of great antiquity. The latter, inhabiting mostly the central and western parts of the country, as well as the Himalayan valleys of Northern Nepal and Bhutan, is regarded as a descendent of the Proto-Chinese of the Paroean group from which the modern Han Chinese, Thais and Burmese are also descended.

However, this hypothesis appears oversimplified. There is evidence of great ethnic and linguistic diversity within the tribal confederations of Eastern Tibet, probably as a result of the process of intermingling with the neighbouring peoples and minority nationalities. The Tibetans themselves, according to legend, trace their ancestry to the union of an intelligent monkey and a demonic ogress, and for their part, the Chinese have always considered the Tibetans to be racially distinct.

Despite the demographic movements of the 20th century which have resulted in the widespread population transfer of ethnic Han Chinese into the Tibetan plateau, and of the Indo-Aryan Nepalese into the Himalayan valleys of Northern Nepal, Sikkim and Bhutan, the region as a whole is even now largely inhabited by a population of Tibetan origin. When the three countries are taken individually however, there are considerable variations.

The following statistics are based on 1995 projections made by the Global Demography Project, at the University of California in Santa Barbara.

Tibet

Tibet (*Area* 2,108,700 sq km) is one of the mostly sparsely populated regions on earth with an estimated population of only 7 million (1995 estimate, excluding Ziling and Jang Sadam areas). Modern census figures are complicated, owing to the current partition of Tibet into five diverse Chinese provinces, but even conservative Chinese publications have given the overall ethnic Tibetan population at 4.5 million, suggesting that they comprise 65% of the plateau's population. Tibetans in exile and a number of Tibetologists, who hold these figures to be underestimated, both on account of the non-registration of many nomadic peoples and the large number of refugees now in neighbouring countries, such as India, have given the total Tibetan ethnic population between 5-6 million. Of the remainder (max 35%), the majority (approximately 28%) are accounted for by the recent rapid influx of Han Chinese from Sichuan and other provinces of mainland China into urban areas of Tibet and the more gradual demographic movement of Hui Muslims from the Ziling region. **NB** These figures do not take into account the transient Chinese population in Tibet (including the army), who are mostly registered in other provinces of mainland China.

Among the two larger groups, the Tibetans include within their numbers the **Topa** of the highland region (Far-west Tibet); the **Tsangpa** of W Tibet, the **Upa** of Central Tibet, the **Horpa** of N Tibet, the **Khampa** of E Tibet, the **Amdowa** of NE Tibet, and the **Gyarongwa** of Far-east Tibet. In all these areas of Tibet there are both sedentary communities (*rongpa*) and nomadic groups (*drokpa*).

The situation differs in the remote border areas where smaller nationalities have lived for centuries. These minorities, comprising approximately 7% of the total population, include peoples closely related to the Tibetans, such as the Monpas (6,200m) and Lhopas (2,100m) – about 0.15% who inhabit Metok and the adjacent counties of the extreme S; the Qiangs (102,000, 1.6%) of Maowen and adjacent counties in the extreme E; and the Jang (Naxi; 245,000) and Li of Jang Sadam (Lijiang) who also inhabit the adjacent Tibetan counties of Markham, Dechen, Gyeltang, Balung, and Mili in the extreme SE. Other nationalities (totalling about 5%) found in the extreme NE are of Mongol or Turkic

origin: some 2.5% (23,750) of China's estimated Kazakhs (ie 0.35%) inhabit W Kokonor. Some 90% of the 69,100 (1%) Salar population inhabits Dowi (Xunhua Salar AC); and the 159,400 Tu (2.4%) are mostly found in Huzhu Tu AC and in the upper reaches of the Tsong-chu and Datong valleys. Mongolian populations are confined to certain parts of W Kokonor and Sogwo AC.

● **Nepal**

By contrast, **Nepal**, a mere 149,098 sq km in area, has a burgeoning population of 19.9 million, of which the majority 80% are of Indo-Aryan origin, and only 20% are of Tibetan stock. The latter include not only the Tibetan and Bhotia inhabitants of N Nepal (such as the Sharpas, the Dolpowas, and the Lowo Lhopas of Mustang) but also the related Mongoloid inhabitants of the central belt: Newars, Tamangs, Rais, Limbus, Sunwars, Magars, and Gurung peoples.

● **Bhutan**

Bhutan (*area* 42,195 sq km) has a relatively small population, currently estimated at 600,000, of which approximately 70% are Drukpas and Monpas of Tibetan origin. The minority 30% figure represents the Lhotsampa population of Nepalese origin, many of whom have in recent years been returned to Nepal in a dramatic reversal of the eastward historic migrations of the Nepalese peoples.

Apart from the industrial belts of the S Nepalese Terai and the S Bhutanese *duars*, and the comparatively small numbers employed in Tibet's recent but threadbare urban development, the vast majority of the region's population is engaged in subsistance farming or animal husbandry.

Languages

The Tibetan language is classified as one of the 23 Tibeto-Burman languages spoken within the borders of present day

China, the others including Yi, Bai, Hani, Liau, Lahu, Jang (Naxi), and Qiang. There are great variations in dialect from Ladakh in the Far-west to the Golok, Gyarong and Gyeltang dialects of the E. With remarkable differences in pronunciation and vocabulary, these dialects have sometimes been mistaken for distinct languages in their own right.

Broadly speaking, the Tibetan language comprises the Utsang, Kham and Amdo groups of dialects. The first of these includes the **U-ke** spoken in Lhasa and Lhokha, the **Tsang-ke** spoken around Zhigatse and Gyantse, the **To-ke** spoken in the highland areas and Ngari (Far-west), and the **Sharpa-ke** spoken by the peoples of the NE Nepal border. **Kham dialects** include those of Nangchen and Jyekundo in the N, Nakchu in the W, Dechen and Muli in the S, and Chamdo, Drayab, Batang, Derge, and so forth in the E. **Amdo dialects** include **drokpa-ke**, spoken by the nomads of Golok, and the adjacent areas of Sertal, Dzamtang, and Ngawa; **rongpa-ke**, spoken by the settled farming communities of Tsongka, Bayan Khar (Hualong) and Dowi (Xunhua); and the **semi-nomadic semi-sedentary** dialects spoken in Repkong, Labrang, and Luchu areas.

In general, the Tibetan language has constructed its specialized Buddhist vocabulary under Indian influence, while freely borrowing from Chinese commonplace words of everyday usage – food, drink, clothing. Tibetan writing has never made use of ideograms. The standard block-lettered script derives from the 7th century Ranjana script of N India, and the more cursive handwriting script, it has been suggested, may have an even older origin in the NW Indian Vartula script.

National language

The great disparity in pronunciation and vocabulary between the various Tibetan dialects creates many problems of communication, even for native Tibetan speakers. Nowadays, Tibetans from Amdo and Lhasa often find it easier to converse in Chinese rather than Tibetan, so that the former has become something of a lingua franca for Tibetans inside Tibet. The Tibetan Government-in-exile has for many years now been promoting the ideal of a standard form of Tibetan in its schools; and even within Tibet the need for a national Tibetan language is well understood, even if it seems a remote goal. By contrast, the written language has remained remarkably constant since the orthographic revisions of the 9th century.

Tibetan language is an important medium of instruction in primary schools and, to a lesser extent, in middle schools. Higher education almost invariably is imparted in Chinese, and there are very few scientific textbooks published in Tibetan. The situation is slightly better among the exiled community, where efforts have been made to establish a wide-ranging technical terminology for modern scientific subjects.

Chinese speakers include those of the E and SE who speak Sichuan dialect and those of the NE who speak Putonghua (standard Mandarin) or Ziling dialect. Very few Chinese living or working in Tibet have attempted to master the Tibetan language, most assuming that the indigenous peoples will have to accommodate themselves to communicate with the newcomers, who control the urban economy. This is undoubtedly the prevailing trend among the young in particular, and in parts of E Tibet it has become commonplace to see educated Tibetans adopt Chinese names in order to secure their own advancement. The greatest fear confronting the Tibetan people is not the prospect of another persecution or cultural revolution, so much as being outnumbered by an influx of Chinese immigrants in their own land. After all, there are obvious precedents in Manchuria and Inner Mongolia!

Daily life

Social customs and life Tibetan daily life and social customs have for centuries been highly influenced by Buddhism. Whenever child-naming rituals, wedding ceremonies or funerals and so forth are held, it is important that an auspicious day is chosen.

The **Tibetan calendar** is based on the 60-year cycle of the *Kalacakra Tantra* (rather than the century of the western system). Each of the years within a 60-year cycle has its own distinctive name according to the *Kalacakra Tantra*, and a derivative name formed by combining the 12 animals and five elements of Chinese geomancy. Each cycle thus begins with the fire hare year and ends with the fire tiger year. Presently we are in the 17th cycle counting from the year 1027 when this system was introduced to Tibet. Auspicious days within the lunar calendar may fall on the 15th or 30th days of any month, which are associated with Shakyamuni Buddha, or on the 8th (Medicine Buddha Day), the 10th (Padmasambhava Day), or 25th (Dakini Day). Specific events, such as the Buddha's first promulgation of the Buddhist teachings, are commemorated on set days of the year (ie the 4th day of the 6th month). In addition to such general auspicious days, there are also those which may be specific to a given individual, determined on the basis of the time of birth.

During all the important ceremonies of daily life, the offering of auspicious white scarfs along with tea or barley ale and tsampa (roasted barley flour), is a prerequisite.

Naming ceremonies following the birth of a child follow the Buddhist naming system rather than the western patronymic system. Surnames are rarely found, with the exception of aristocratic families who add their clan name as a prefix to their given Buddhist names. Weddings are generally arranged by the parents of the bride and groom, taking into account important issues such as compatability of birth-sign, social class, and absence of consanguinity. Gifts are mutually exchanged – the 'milk price' being paid by the groom's family and the 'dowry' by the bride's family.

CEREMONIAL SCARFS

During the 13th century, Drogon Chogyel Phakpa, advisor to Emperor Qubilai Qan, introduced the custom of offering ceremonial scarfs (*katak*) on special occasions. This practice subsequently became the principal means of expressing courtesy, greetings, or respect in Tibet. Often the scarfs are presented to spiritual masters or sacred images, to the victors of sporting contests or divas of theatrical performances, or to dignitaries when being granted an audience, making a petition, or receiving tidings. Commonly, kataks are also offered to those about to embark on a long journey, and to new-born babies, newly weds, or deceased persons.

Simple ceremonial scarfs are made of loosely woven cotton, and superior scarfs of silk. The shorter ones may be 1-1½m long, and the longer up to 7m in length! Most are white in colour, indicative of purity, but blue, yellow, red, and green scarfs are not unknown. Generally 5-coloured scarfs are offered only to Buddha-images, or else wrapped around a ceremonial arrow (*dadar*), used in longevity empowerments (*tsewang*) and marriage ceremonies. Most are plain, but some may be inscribed with the words 'good auspices' (*tashidelek*), or designed with the 'eight auspicious symbols' (*tashi da-gye*), the motif of the Great Wall of China, and so forth.

Funeral ceremonies assume varied forms: sky burial being the most common and compassionate form of corpse disposal in Central Tibet and W Tibet, and cremation an equally popular method in E Tibet where wood is more plentiful. The former entails the dismembering of the body and its distribution to celestial vultures. Important lamas may be cremated or embalmed within stupa reliquaries. Lesser persons may be given water burial (particularly in the fast-flowing gorges of the SE), or earth burial. The latter, which carried high prestige during the Bonpo period when the early Chongye tombs were constructed, gradually came to have inferior associations from the Buddhist perspective.

Diet The traditional staple diet of the Tibetans is somewhat bland, consisting of butter tea, tsampa (roasted barley flour), dried meat, barley ale (*chang*), and dairy products – milk, curd, and cheese. Many nomadic families still survive on this diet alone today; whereas urban communities also have rice, noodles, millet and a wide range of fresh vegetables and pulses.

Animal husbandry is still the main occupation of rural and nomadic communities, while subsistence farming is possible only in the low-lying valleys. Although Tibetans have traditionally displayed a compassionate Buddhist attitude to all forms of wildlife, the eating of meat is widespread (both out of choice and necessity) in view of the fact that, until very recently, the country was not known for its abundance of vegetables.

National dress

The inhabitants of different parts of the Tibetan plateau may be recognized by their distinctive dress, notwithstanding the ubiquitous Chinese clothing which is all too prevalent nowadays. Both men and women wear the **chuba**, a long-sleeved gown, tied at the waist with a sash. Farmers often wear sleeveless chubas and nomads sheepskin chubas. Local designs are distinctive: the black smock design of Kongpo, the otter-skin bordered chuba of Amdo, the shorter length but longer sleeved chuba of Kham, the brocade-bordered black tunic of Tsang and To, and so forth.

Head-wear is also distinctive: the coiffure of both men and women indicating the part of the country to which they belong. For example, Khampa men with black hair braids generally come from Chamdo and those with red braids from Derge. Brocade hats lined with fur are popular in Central Tibet while stetsons or Bolivian-style bowlers are widely used in E Tibet. In general Tibetans wear subdued colours, but there are areas of E Tibet in particular where maroons and shocking pinks are preferred, on festival days in particular.

Jewellery Both men and women wear jewellery, the most highly prized stone being the uniquely Tibetan **zi** (banded agate or chalcedony). Ornaments of gold, silver, coral, turquoise, amber, beryl, and ivory are also worn, but none compare in value to the zi stone.

Tibetan houses

These vary in their design and material from one part of the country to the next. In Central Tibet and W Tibet, village houses are flat-roofed and made of adobe, in Kongpo and adjacent areas, they are made with wooden shingles and decorative features, reminiscent of Bhutanese architecture, in Kham horizontal timbers painted red with intricate window sills are typical, and in Minyak or Gyarong the sturdy stone houses of Qiangic construction are commonplace. Perhaps the most beautiful village and small town architecture is to be seen in the Tawu area of E Tibet, where the building technique combines the horizontal red timber construction with pristine whitewashed adobe, and finely carved windows. In general, village

BA AND *GUR:* TIBETAN TENTS

There are basically two types of Tibetan tent: the black yak wool tent (*ba*) used as a dwelling by the nomadic populace, and the white tent with blue appliqué (*gur*) used by villagers and townspeople for picnics and recreation. The former are dotted around the high grasslands and pastures where the nomads tend their herds of yak and flocks of sheep. They are made of a coarse yak wool tweed, which is capable of withstanding the elements: wind, rain, and snow; and the design has changed little in centuries. There is a central tent pole, from which the four corners are pegged out in a rectangle and a low inner wall of earth and clumps of grass constructed on three sides. The door flap may be kept open or closed. The stove is in the centre of the tent, with a ventilation opening immediately above – the size of the opening being controlled by pulley ropes. The nomads occupy the high ground in the spring and summer seasons; and by mid-autumn, they begin their age-old transhumance, exchanging the snow-bound pastures for the comparatively well sheltered dwellings of the lower valleys. During the 1960s efforts were made to settle the nomads permanently in camps, but they have now reverted to their original lifestyle. A few of the permanent camps are still used as a winter residence for the elderly and the young. Alongside the black tents, there are sometimes small white tepee style tents to be seen. These are occasionally used for storage, but often for the daughter of a nomadic family while entertaining suitors.

The picnic tents of the townspeople are used during the festival season. Some are very large and ornate, with decorative blue appliqué designs, depicting the eight auspicious symbols (*tashi da-gye*) and so forth. The horse festivals of Gyantse and Damzhung, and those of Kham (eg at Jyekundo and Nakchu) provide an ideal opportunity for visitors to see the large variety of Tibetan picnic tents in use. Also, in Lhasa, there is a tent factory producing decorative tents and awnings to order.

houses have a lower floor for animals; and an upper floor for human habitation. Shuttered windows with a trefoil arch shape are colourfully painted. Electricity is now commonplace in towns and cities, but in the countryside oil lamps are still in use. The nomadic communities throughout Tibet live in large sturdy tents (*ba*) made of black yak wool.

Minority groups

Among the smaller minority groups within Tibet, the **Monpa** inhabit the counties of Metok, Nyangtri, and Tsona. Their customs, religion and culture are fully integrated with those of the Tibetans through long-standing political, economic and marital links. Many speak Tibetan in addition to own dialects. Both

men and women wear robes with aprons, black yak hair caps, and soft-soled leather boots with red and black stripes. Women wear white aprons, earrings, rings and bracelets. In subtropical Metok women and men both wear jackets – the women with long striped skirts. The slash and burn method of agriculture is practised here, and the staple diet consists of rice, maize, millet, buckwheat, and chilli pepper, in addition to tsampa and tea. Hunting is still important in these areas where the virgin forest is dense, and species of wild boar, bears, foxes, and langurs are to be found. Monpa houses are made of wood with bamboo/thatched roofs.

The **Lhopa** of Menling, Metok, Lhuntse, and Nang counties are largely forest

Tibet: culture

dwelling hunter gatherers and fishermen. Few of them speak Tibetan; and intermarriage is rare. The standard dress is a sleeveless buttonless knee-length smock of black sheep wool with a helmet-like hat made of bearskin or bamboo/rattan laced with bearskin, and no shoes. Men wear bamboo earrings and necklaces, and bows and arrows, while the women wear silver or brass earrings, bracelets, necklaces, and ornate waist belts. The staple diet is a dumpling made of maize or millet, as well as rice and buckwheat, in addition to tsampa, potatoes, buttered tea and chilli peppers.

In Far-east Tibet, the **Qiang** and related groups occupy fertile land and good mountain pastures. The adjacent forests are home to the giant panda, langur, and flying fox. Men and women wear long blue gowns over trousers with sheepskin jackets. The women have laced collars and sharp-pointed embroidered shoes, embroidered waistbands, and earrings. The staples are millet, barley, potatoes, wheat, buckwheat; and they have finely constructed stone blockhouses, 2/3 storeys high.

In SE Tibet the **Jang** or **Naxi** inhabit the Lijiang area and adjacent counties in Dechen, Markham and Mili. Here, the women wear wide-sleeved gowns with jackets and long trousers with an ornate waistband. The men tend to wear standard Chinese clothing. Naxi society is mostly patriarchal, but a few matriarchal elements survive in Yongining (Yunnan) and Yanyuan (Sichuan) counties. There, the children live with the mother and women comprise the main labour force.

In the extreme NW of Amdo, there are **Kazakhs** inhabiting the W Kokonor prefecture. These Turkic speaking peoples have a distinctive vocabulary assimilated from Chinese, Uighur, and Mongol. The written language is based on Arabic. Most Kazakhs are engaged in nomadic animal husbandry, dwelling in yurts (*yu*) during the spring, summer and autumn seasons. The men wear loose long-sleeved furs and skin garments, with sheepskin shawls or camel-hair stuffed overcoats in winter, and sheepskin trousers. The women wear red dresses with cotton padded coats in winter, and white-shawls embroidered with red and yellow designs. Dairy products such as milk dough, milk skin, cheese, and butter are plentiful. The diet also includes butter tea, mutton stewed in water without salt, smoked meat, horse sausage, fermented mare's milk, and sweets made of rice or wheat. Kazakh society is Muslim and patriarchal, while both monogamous and polygamous types of marriage are found.

In Dowi (Xunhua) county of Amdo, the **Salar** people of Turkic origin have lived since their arrival from Samarkhand during the Mongol period (1271-1368). Theirs is a strict Muslim society and the women are rarely permitted to appear in public. Predominantly a farming community, the Salar grow barley, wheat, buckwheat and potatoes, with secondary stock-breeding, lumbering, wool-weaving and salt production.

The **Tu** peoples of Huzhu and Tianzhu counties in the NE extremities of Amdo are said to be Chahan Mongols descended from the army of the Mongol general Gerilite, who intermarried with indigenous Turkic nomads (Horpa) during the time of Genghiz Qan. Later, they again intermingled with other Mongol groups who settled in those areas during the Ming period. Their language belongs to Mongolian branch of Altaic family and the script devised for the Mongol language by Drogon Chogyel Phakpa is still in use among them for certain literary functions. Both men and women wear shirts with finely embroidered collars and bright colours. Traditionally livestock breeders, the Tu adapted to farming from the 13th century onwards, and became converts to the Gelukpa school of Tibetan Buddhism.

The **Hui Muslim** community inhabit much of Amdo and the NE. They are predominantly Chinese-speaking urban dwellers, but maintain their distinctive religion, names, and (sometimes) dress. In Central Tibet they are often known as Zilingpa; and have a reputation for unscrupulous trading.

Mongols inhabit the W Kokonor and Sogwo areas of Amdo. They wear fur coats in winter and loose chubas in summer, generally red, yellow or dark blue in colour, with a green or red waistband, knee-length boots, and conical hats (in winter) or silk/cloth turbans (in summer). The girls have hair parted in the middle, with agate, coral and turquoise ornaments. Mongol peoples are renowned for their excellent horsemanship and archery. Their staple diet consists of beef, mutton, dairy products, and tea; and they live in felt yurts. Both traditional shamanism and Buddhism are practised.

Literature

The Tibetan language is the source of one of the world's greatest and most prolific literary heritages, rivalling those of China, India, Greece or Rome. Although most works are of a Buddhist nature, the secular tradition of poetics and drama continues to flourish. The epic poems of **Ling Gesar** are more voluminous than the great *Mahabharata* of ancient India – some 72 volumes having already been redacted and published in Tibet by the provincial publishing houses and the Chinese Academy of Social Sciences. Three million copies of these texts have been distributed throughout the Tibetan world! The development of secular Tibetan literature has also been given a new impetus by the **Amnye Machen Institute**, recently established at Dharamsala in NW India to promote the work of contemporary Tibetan writers.

The classical literature, which remains highly popular at the present day, includes the canonical texts of Buddhism and their indigenous Tibetan commentaries – amounting to hundreds of thousands of volumes; as well as the great works on the traditional sciences – grammar, medicine, logic, art, astrology, poetics, prosody, synonymics, and drama. Religious histories, biographies and hagiographies provide an important frame of reference for the adherents of the various Buddhist schools and the Bon tradition. The works are too numerous to detail here, but mention should be made of the great canonical compilations.

The Buddhist tantras translated into Tibetan during the early diffusion of Buddhism are contained in the *Nyingma Gyudbum*, the best known edition of which is preserved in woodblock form at the Derge Parkhang in Kham. The later translations of the tantras, as well as some earlier translations of both sutras and tantras, are contained in the 104 volume *Kangyur*, compiled in the 14th century by Buton Rinchendrub (1290-1364). Most extant commentaries of Indian origin are contained in a companion anthology, the 185 volume *Tangyur*, which he also compiled. There are several extant manuscript versions of these canonical texts – most of them housed in the great monasteries around Lhasa, but seven woodblock editions of the *Kangyur* survive, along with four of the *Tangyur*. At present these are being collated and republished in a new master edition by the Kangyur-Tangyur Collation Project in Chengdu.

Art

Tibetan painting and sculpture date from the 7th century onwards, coinciding with the unification of Tibet by King Songtsen Gampo and the gradual absorption of Buddhism from the neighbouring cultures of India, Nepal, China, and Central Asia. There is little evidence of Tibetan art prior to the 7th century and the earliest surviving examples so fully absorbed the impact of the surrounding artistic traditions that it is difficult to discern pre-Buddhist elements, should an earlier, purely indigenous tradition have existed.

Tibetan painting found three principal expressions: manuscript illumination (*peri*), mural painting (*debri*), and cloth-painted scrolls (*tangka*), each in-

exorably linked to the goals and practices of Buddhism. Appliqué tangkas and sand-painted mandalas also evolved as by-products. Sculpted images of deities and historical figures were mostly produced in metal, clay or stucco, and to a lesser extent in wood, stone, or even butter. In theory, Tibetan works of art served primarily as icon, intermediary between man and divinity, a function underscored by the indigenous term

WOODBLOCK PRINTING

The technique of woodblock or xylographic printing *(shingpar)* which was developed in Tang China predates the invention of movable type in Western Europe. A copy of the world's earliest extant printed book, the Chinese translation of the *Diamond Cutter Sutra (Vajracchedikasutra)*, dated 868, is preserved in the British Museum in London. This technique was slow to reach Tibet, where from the introduction of the written script by Tonmi Sambhota in the 7th century until the intervention of the Manchu emperors in Tibetan affairs during the 18th, the vast Buddhist literature – both translated and indigenous, was recorded in manuscript form only. Some precious manuscript versions of the Buddhist Canon inscribed in gold ink *(sertri)* or silver ink *(ngultri)* on black paper have survived; and the general custom of utilizing red ink for canonical works and black ink for non-canonical commentaries persists even now. The oldest woodblock edition of the Tibetan canon, prepared in China by the Ming Emperor Wan Li no longer exists (although one printed copy has been preserved in Sera Monastery).

During the 18th century, woodblock versions of the *Kangyur* and *Tangyur* – the compilations forming the Buddhist Canon, were commissioned at Nartang near Zhigatse, at Zhol Parkhang in Lhasa, at Derge in Kham, at Cho-ne in Amdo, and at Beijing. The letters are carved in reverse in oblong blocks of wood, and the paper, cut to size, is printed by impressing it with a roller against the inked surface of the woodblock. There are several teams, each of two persons, often monks, who work together, rhythmically printing multiple copies of a single page. The pages of the book *(pe-cha)* are then collated and the edges dyed red or yellow, in accordance with tradition. The pages are not bound but kept loose leaf, and wrapped in a cloth book cover *(pe-re)*. This printing technique came to permeate most of the Tibetan plateau; and many small monasteries had their own distinctive woodblock collections, often reflecting their own traditions. At the present day, the largest woodblock collections are housed at Derge, Cho-ne, Lhasa, Labrang Tashikyil, and Kumbum. Copies of the Buddhist Canon and related works once again are being actively distributed throughout the plateau in this time-honoured method.

The storage of woodblocks of course requires a large amount of space. By contrast, the techniques of modern printing, including movable type, photo-offset, and computer typesetting are now in vogue, and the various nationalities' publishing houses of the TAR, Sichuan, Qinghai, and Gansu are particularly active in the printing and distribution of conveniently bound copies of classical and modern works of Tibetan literature at affordable prices.

'tongdrol' (liberation by seeing the deity). In conjunction with ritual, a painting or a sculpted image housed a deity consecrated for purposes of worship, offering, and spiritual communication.

Among the various stylistic influences which have been observed in the art of Tibet, the oldest strand seems to be that of **Newar Nepal** (and Guptan India) as seen in the oldest door frames and pillars of the Jokhang temple in Lhasa. Early Central Asian or Khotanese influence has been discerned in the extant images of Kachu Lhakhang, Yemar, and Dratang – the last of these also containing murals indicative of the Pala style of Bengal (8th-12th century). **Kashmiri art styles** are noticeable at Tsaparang in the Gu-ge Kingdom of Far-west Tibet, although the earlier murals of nearby Toling did not survive the Cultural Revolution. Better examples can be found at Tabo and Alchi in the adjacent Indian areas of Spiti and Ladakh. During the period of Mongol influence, the monasteries of Sakya and Zhalu were lavishly decorated by Newar artists from Nepal. Subsequent indigenous developments included: the 15th century **Lato** style (eg the murals of Chung Riwoche stupa), the **Gyantse** style (of Kumbum and Pelkor Chode), the **Uri** style of Lhasa, which became the prevalent style from the 17th century onwards, the exquisite **Repkong** style of Amdo, and the **Karma Gadri** style of Kham which encorporated landscape elements and perspective from Chinese art, and later exerted considerable influence on the mainstream Central Tibetan style.

Music and dance

Song and dance have always been an important vehicle for social contact in Tibet. Apart from the epics of **Ling Gesar**, which have already been mentioned, there are free-form mountain and nomadic ballads; lyric poems such as the *Hundred Thousand Songs of Milarepa*; and regional folk-songs from To, Batang, Kham and so forth. The folk songs have a thematic character: there are wedding songs, labour songs, round dance songs, archery songs, drinking songs, love songs (such as those composed by Dalai Lama VI), and songs in the form of repartee or playful rejoinders. These songs are expressed in simple language which evokes an immediate mood or imagery, and employs both metaphor and hidden analogy. Modern songs are continually being written and performed in this traditional style, utilizing the sophisticated technology of the recording studio. Tibetan pop singers, such as Datron, Kalzang Chodron, and Tseten Dolma, are well known both inside and outside Tibet. Currently the vitality of the Tibetan folk song is under threat from the phenomenal development of Chinese karaoke throughout Tibet over the last 5 years.

Songs are frequently accompanied by folk dances. Among the most popular are the round dances known as *gor-zhe* in Lhasa, Tsang and Lhokha, and as *gor-dong* in Chamdo area. Men and women form two concentric circles around a bonfire, singing alternate choruses, while the stamping of the feet keeps the rhythm. There are other distinctive dances, such as the drum dance of Lhokha, the bell-and-drum dance of Chamdo and Kongpo, the tap dance of the highland region (*to-zhe*), and the synchronized labour songs (*le-zhe*). For a description of the religious dances (*cham*), which are distinct from these, see the section on Bhutan (see below, page 698).

The first **opera** troupe in Tibet was founded in the 15th century by Tangtong Gyelpo, the celebrated bridge-builder who may be regarded as the Leonardo da Vinci of Tibet. By the 17th century opera (*dogar*) had become an art form in its own right. A stylistic distinction developed between the traditional **White Masked Sect** and the innovatory **Blue Masked Sect**. The former, which included troupes such as the Bingdungpa from Chongye, the Nangzipa from Tolung, and the Tashi Zholpa from Nedong, were gradually supplanted by the more sophisticated exponents of the latter style, such as those of Gyelkar based at Rinpung, Shangpa and Jungpa, both based at Namling, and Kyormo-lung based at Lhasa. Nowadays there are numerous troupes throughout the country, and the best time to see their performances is during the Zhoton festival in Norbulingka at Lhasa during the month of August.

Crafts

Traditional handicrafts are made largely for the indigenous market rather than the tourist trade. Among the most widely available items are: the wooden churns (*dongmo*) used for making butter tea; birchwood bowls (sometimes inlaid with silver or pewter); jade bowls from Rinpung area; knifes and daggers with ornately carved scabbards; gold and silverware engraved with motifs such as the Eight Auspicious Symbols; engraved amulet boxes; carpets from Gyantse and other towns, the weaving of which has become the principal cottage industry in Tibet and the Tibetan communities of N India and Nepal: blankets which may be finely woven, striped or shaggy; stuffed mattresses with decorative covers; wooden household furniture including shrines, cabinets, and tables – all with decorative panelling; striped aprons from Chidezhol; bamboo artefacts from the southern counties of Nyangtri, Menling, Metok, and Dzayul; and pastoral artefacts, such as the yak hair sling and the sheepskin bellows.

RELIGION

CONTENTS

Tibetan religious traditions may conveniently be considered in three categories – animism, Bon and Buddhism. The first concerns the control of animistic forces by bards and story-tellers, and the second emphasizes the purity of space, funerary rituals, and certain meditative practices, which may have originated in either Zoroastrianism or Kashmiri Buddhism; and the third is the means of liberation from the sufferings of cyclic existence as propounded in ancient India by Shakyamuni Buddha.

Animism and the 'Religion of Humans'

The earliest form of Tibetan religion, which RA Stein has termed the 'nameless religion', is a type of animism based upon the worship of the elements and mountain deities. Incense offerings would be made to appease local mountain spirits, and 'wind-horse' (*lungta*) prayer flags or cairns affixed on prominent passes to ensure good auspices. Solemn declarations of truth (*dentsik*) and oaths would be made in the presence of local deities, to invoke good fortune (*gyang-khug*); and talismanic objects or places (*la-ne*) were revered as life-supporting forces. Enemies or hostile forces could then be overpowered by drawing in their life-supporting talisman in a ceremony known as *la-guk*.

The so-called 'religion of humans' (*mi-cho*) which evolved out of this early animism relied upon storytellers (*drung*) and singers of riddles (*de'u*) or epic poems to provide an ethical framework for social behaviour. According to a late 14th century chronicle, the religion of humans had nine aspects, represented in the body of a lion – the right foot symbolizes tales of the world's origin; the left foot symbolizes tales of the appearance of living beings; the hindquarters symbolize tales of the divisions of the earth; the right hand symbolizes tales of the geneology of rulers; the left hand those of subjects; the middle finger those concerning the origin of Buddhism; the neck those of the tribes holding allegiance to each ruler, the head those concerning patrilinear and matrilinear lines of descent, and the tail symbolizing paeans of joy.

Bon

The religion of Tazik (Persia) which was introduced into the Zhangzhung Kingdom of Far-west Tibet and thence into Central Tibet during the period of the early kings is considered to have evolved in three distinct phases, known as 'revealed Bon' (*dol-bon*), 'deviant Bon' (*khyar-bon*) and 'translated Bon' (*gyur-bon*). The original importance which Bon held for the Tibetan kings probably lay in its elaborate funerary rites and veneration of space. The earliest kings of Tibet are said to have been immortals who would descend from and ascend into the heavens on a sky-cord (*mu*); but following the death of Drigum Tsenpo, the mortal kings increasingly focussed upon funerary rites and rituals for the averting of death through 'ransom' (*lud*).

The '**revealed Bon**' refers to those rituals which were prevalent in Tibet from the time of Drigum Tsenpo until the time of King Lhatotori Nyentsen. The '**deviant Bon**' included a new wave of rituals and practices derived from Zhangzhung and Brusha in Far-west Tibet; and the '**translated Bon**' refers to the synthesis which developed following the introduction of Buddhism to Tibet and its establishment as the state religion. The Bon orders which have survived until the present are thoroughly imbued with Buddhist imagery and symbolism; and they have evolved their own parallel literature to counter-balance that of the Buddhists, ranging from exoteric teachings on ethics to highly esoteric teachings on the Great Perfection (Dzogchen).

Since the late 19th century there have been two camps: the traditionalists who claim to reject all contacts with other Buddhist schools (as at **Menri** in Tsang and **Narshi** in Ngawa), and the modernists who accept the ecumenical approach followed in Kham towards the turn of the century by Jamgon Kongtrul, Zharza Tashi Gyeltsen, and others. Certain parts of Tibet remain strongholds of this tradition, notably the **Menri** area around the Shang valley in W Tibet, the **Bonri** area of Kongpo, the **Jangtang** lakelands, the **Tengchen** area of Kham, the **Ngawa** and **Zungchu** areas of Amdo, and **Gyarong**.

In exile the principal Bon community is based at **Solon** in Himachal Pradesh, India.

Buddhism

Brief introduction

Buddhism evolved from the teachings of Siddhartha Gautama of the Shakya clan (known as the Buddha, the 'Awakened One'), who lived in northern India in the 6th or 5th century BC. The Buddha's teachings are rooted in a compelling existential observation: despite all persons' efforts to find happiness and avoid pain, their lives are filled with suffering and dissatisfaction. However, the Buddha did not stop there. He recognized the causes of suffering to be the dissonant mental states – delusion, attachment, aversion, pride, and envy, and realized that it is possible to free oneself permanently from such sufferings through a rigorous and well-structured training in ethics, meditation, and insight, which leads to a profound understanding of the way things really are, that is, enlightenment.

The Buddha was born a prince and had known great opulence but had also experienced great deprivations when he renounced his life of luxury to seek salvation through ascetic practice. He concluded that both sensual indulgence and physical deprivations are hinderances to spiritual evolution. He taught the Middle Way, a salvific path which was initially interpreted to mean isolation from the normal distractions of daily life, by living in communities devoted to the pursuit of spiritual liberation, which were disciplined but did not involve extreme deprivation. These communities, consisting of both monks and nuns, preserved and put into practice the Buddhist teachings. Initially, the teachings were preserved through an oral transmission, but by the 1st century BC were increasingly committed to written form. Unlike other of the world's leading religious traditions, Buddhism does not rely on a single literary source (eg the Bible, Koran, or Talmut), but on a vast, rich, sophisticated literary corpus. The preservation of Buddhism brought literacy to hundreds of millions in Asia.

Buddhism's path to salvation depended largely on the individual's own efforts. Its emphasis on self-reliance and non-violence appealed to the merchant class in India, and thus it spread along trade routes – N through Central Asia, into China and then into the Far-east,

Korea and Japan. It also spread S to Sri Lanka and Southeast Asia: Burma, Thailand, Indo-China, and Indonesia. Later, Nepal and Tibet embraced Buddhism at the zenith of its development in India, and it was this tradition which eventually came to permeate Mongolia, Manchuria and Kalmukya. In recent years Buddhism has also found adherents in the West.

A Buddhist is one who takes refuge in the **Three Precious Jewels** (Triratna): Buddha, Dharma (his teachings), and Sangha (the monastic community). Beyond this, Buddhism has evolved remarkably different practices to bring about liberation, its teachings having been interpreted and reinterpreted by commentators in each new generation and in each cultural milieu. Buddhism's brilliance lies in its universality – its compelling existential appeal and, crucially, its efficacy. Historically it has appealed to peasants and to kings, to philosophers and to the illiterate, to prostitutes and murderers, and to those already close to sainthood. And though it was not its intention, Buddhism has transformed the cultures in its path – imbuing them with its ideals of universal compassion and profound insight.

Buddhist teachings

The Buddhist teachings are broadly said to have developed in three distinct phases: (1) the sutra, vinaya and abhidharma texts (ie Tripitaka) of the **Lesser Vehicle** (Hinayana), which were maintained by the four great monastic orders founded in diverse parts of India by Katayayana, Rahula, Upali, and Kashyapa; (2) the sutra teachings of the **Greater Vehicle** (Mahayana), which were maintained by the followers of Nagarjuna and Asanga; and (3) the tantras or esoteric teachings of the **Indestructible Vehicle** (Vajrayana), which were transmitted by accomplished masters such as Man-jushrimitra, Indrabhuti, and Padmasambhava. These different vehicles have their distinctive points of emphasis: the **Lesser Vehicle** holding that obscurations and defilements are eliminated by renunciation; the **Greater Vehicle** holding that enlightenment can be cultivated through compassion and insight which comprehends the emptiness underlying all phenomena, including those obscurations; and the **Indestructible Vehicle** holding that all obscurations are originally pure and transmutable into their pristine nature.

A primary distinction is made between the **sutra** texts which emphasize the gradual or causal approach to enlightenment; and the **tantras** with their emphasis on the immediate or resultant approach.

Tibetan Buddhism

Among all the Buddhist countries of Asia, the highest developments of Indian Buddhism were preserved in Tibet. This was due partly to geographical proximity, partly to temporal considerations, and partly to the aptitude which the Tibetans themselves displayed for the diversity of Indian Buddhist traditions. The sparse population, the slow measured pace of daily life and an almost anarchical disdain for political involvement have encouraged the spiritual cultivation of Buddhism to such an extent that it came to permeate the entire culture.

All schools of Buddhism in Tibet maintain the monastic discipline of the **vinaya**, the graduated spiritual practices and philosophical systems based on the **sutras** and their commentaries, the shastras, and the esoteric meditative practices associated with the **tantras**. Different schools developed in different periods of Tibetan history, each derived from distinctive lineages or transmissions of Indian Buddhism.

The oldest, the Nyingmapa, are associated with the early dissemination of Buddhism during the period of the Yarlung Dynasty. The Sakyapa and the Kagyupa, along with the Kadampa, appeared in the 11th century on the basis of later developments in Indian Buddhism. The Gelukpa originated in Tibet during the 14th century, but can claim descent from the others, particularly the Kadampa and the Sakyapa. Each of these schools has had its great teachers and personalities over the centuries. Each has held political power at one time or another and each continues to exert influence in different parts of the country. Witness, for example, the strength of the Sakyapa in **Derge** and **Jyekundo**, the Kagyupa in **Tolung** and **Nangchen**, the Gelukpa in **Lhasa**, **Zhigatse**, **Chamdo** and **Tsongka**, or the Nyingmapa in **Lhokha**, **Derge**, and **Golok-Sertal**.

NB The Mongol and Chinese custom of referring to the major schools of Tibetan Buddhism by the colours of the ceremonial hats worn by their monks has been avoided in this book because it is an absurd oversimplification, containing a number of anomalies, as the great scholar Tseten Zhabdrung clearly pointed out in an article in *China Tibetology*.

Nyingmapa

The Nyingmapa school maintains the teachings introduced into Tibet by Shantaraksita, Padmasambhava, Vimalamitra and their contemporaries during the 8th century. The entire range of the Buddhist teachings are graded by the Nyingmapa according to nine hierarchical vehicles, starting from the exoteric sutras of the Lesser Vehicle and the Greater Vehicle and continuing through the classes of Outer Tantras to those of the Inner Tantras. It is the Inner Tantras known as Mahayoga, Anuyoga and Atiyoga (or Dzogchen) which are the teachings of the Nyingmapa par excellence.

Following the establishment of Buddhism in Tibet by King Trisong Detsen,

the Nyingma literature was systematically translated into Tibetan at **Samye** Monastery. The tradition survived the persecution of Langdarma thanks to the activities of yogins such as Lhalung Pelgyi Dorje, Nyak Jnanakumara and Nubchen Sangye Yeshe; and the monks who preserved the Vinaya lineage in Amdo. When Buddhism was restored in Central Tibet, the unbroken aural tradition of the Nyingmapa flourished at **Ukpalung** in Tsang under the guidance of the Zur family, and the terma traditions (comprising teachings concealed in the past by Padmasambhava and his followers to be revealed for the benefit of future generations) developed their own local allegiances throughout the country. The most outstanding scholar and promulgator of this tradition was Longchen Rabjampa (1308-63). The six main monasteries of the Nyingma school, each of which has hundreds of branches throughout the land, are: **Katok**, founded in 1159 by Katokpa Dampa Deshek (1122-92); **Dorje Drak**, founded in 1632 by Rigdzin III Ngagi Wangpo (1580-1639); **Mindroling** founded in 1670 by Rigdzin Terdak Lingpa (1646-1714); **Pelyul**, founded in 1665 by Rigdzin Kunzang Sherab (1636-98); **Dzokchen**, founded in 1685 by Dzogchen Pema Rigdzin (1625-97); and **Zhechen**, founded in 1735 by Zhechen Rabjam II Gyurme Kunzang Namgyel.

Kagyupa

The Kagyupa school maintains the lineages of the Indian masters Tilopa, Naropa, and Maitripa, which emphasize the perfection stage of meditation (*sampannakrama*) and the practice of the Great Seal (*Mahamudra*). These were introduced to Tibet by Marpa Lo-tsawa (1012-96) and Zhang Tselpa (1122-93). Marpa, who lived in the **Lhodrak** area bordering Bhutan, had four main disciples including the renowned yogin Milarepa (1040-1123), who passed many years in retreat in the mountain caves of

Labchi, and adjacent Himalayan valleys. Milarepa is one of a select group of Tibetan masters revered for their attainment of enlightenment or buddhahood within a single lifetime. His biography and songs are classic texts, available in English translation, but it was his principal student, Gampopa (1079-1153), who founded the first monastery of that school at **Daklha Gampo** in the early 12th century. Gampopa's principal students Phakmodrupa Dorje Gyelpo (1110-70) and Karmapa I Dusum Khyenpa (1110-93) respectively founded the influential monasteries of **Densatil** and **Tsurphu**. The former was the source of the eight minor Kagyu schools, including those of **Drigung** (founded by Drigung Kyopa, 1143-1217), **Taklung** (founded by Taklung Tangpa Tashipel, 1142-1210), and **Druk** (founded by Lingje Repa, 1128-88). Later, in 1717 the great monastery of **Pelpung** was founded in E Tibet by Situ Chokyi Jungne.

Kadampa

When the Bengali master Atisha (982-1054) reintroduced the teachings of the gradual path to enlightenment into Tibet in 1042, he transmitted the doctrines of his teacher Dharmakirti of **Sumatra**, which focussed on the cultivation of compassion and the propitiation of the deities Tara, Avalokiteshvara, Acala and Shakyamuni Buddha. His disciples included Ngok Lotsawa (1059-1109) and Dromton Gyelwei Jungne (1004-64) who respectively founded the important monasteries of **Sangphu Neutok** and **Reting**. During the early 15th century this tradition was absorbed within the indigenous Gelukpa school.

Sakyapa

The Sakyapa tradition represents a unique synthesis of early 8th century Buddhism and the later diffusion of the 11th century. The members of the Khon family had been adherents of Buddhism since the time of Khon Luiwangpo

Sungwa, a student of Padmasambhava. Then, in 1073, his descendent Khon Konchok Gyelpo, who had received teachings of the new tradition from Drokmi Lotsawa, founded the **Gorum** temple at **Sakya**. His tradition therefore came to emphasize the ancient teachings on Vajrakila, as well as the new teachings on Hevajra, Cakrasamvara, and the esoteric instruction known as the Path and its Fruit. The monastery was initially developed and expanded by the so-called five founders of Sakya: Sachen Kunga Nyingpo (1092-1158), Jetsun Sonam Tsemo (1142-82), Drakpa Gyeltsen (1147-1216), Sakya Pandita (1182-1251), and Drogon Chogyel Phakpa (1235-80). During the latter's lifetime, the **Lhakhang Chenmo** was built (1268) and, with the patronage of the Mongol Empire secured, a network of monasteries and temples was established throughout Central and East Tibet, comprising **Gongkar Chode**, **Jyekundo**, **Zhiwu**, **Dzongsar**, and **Lhagang**, to name but a few. After the death of the Sakya hierarch Danyi Zangpo Pal (r 1305-22), the ruling house of Sakya split into two main branches — the Phuntsok Palace and the Dolma Palace, which have until the present shared their authority on a rotational basis.

Other important sub-schools of Sakya also developed. Among them, **Ngor** was founded in 1429 by Ngorchen Kunga Zangpo, **Nalendra** in 1435 by Rongton Sheja Kunzik, **Derge Lhundrupteng** in 1448 by Tangtong Gyelpo; **Tanak Tubten Namgyeling** monastery in 1478 by Gorampa Sonam Senge; and **Dra Drangmochen** during the early 16th century by Tsarchen Losel Gyatso, who was a student of the great Doringpa.

Gelukpa

The Gelukpa school maintains the teachings and lineage of Je Tsongkhapa (1357-1419), who established a uniquely indigenous tradition on the basis of his Sakyapa and Kadampa background.

Born in the **Tsongka** valley of Amdo, he moved to Central Tibet and founded the monastery of **Ganden** in 1409. He instituted the Great Prayer Festival at Lhasa, and propagated his important treatises on the sutra and tantra traditions in and around the Tibetan capital. Two of his foremost students, Jamyang Choje Tashi Palden and Jamchen Choje Shakya Yeshe, respectively founded **Drepung** (1416) and **Sera** (1419); while others such as Gyeltsab Je and Khedrup Je, became the prime teachers of the new Gelukpa order. The latter was retrospectively recognized as Panchen Lama I. Another of Tsongkhapa's students was Dalai Lama I Gendun Drupa, who founded **Tashilhunpo** at Zhigatse in 1447.

The successive emanations of the Dalai and Panchen Lamas enhanced the prestige of the Gelukpa school, which swiftly gained allegiances among the Mongol forces of the NE. Following the civil wars of the 17th century, many Kagyu monasteries were converted to the Gelukpa tradition, and the regent Sangye Gyatso compiled his *Yellow Beryl (Vaidurya Serpo)* history of the Gelukpa tradition.

The six greatest monasteries of the Gelukpa school are those of **Ganden**, **Drepung**, and **Sera**, in addition to **Tashilhunpo**, **Kumbum Jampaling**, and **Labrang Tashikhyil** in Amdo. Along with **Chamdo**, **Dargye**, **Kandze** and many other important centres, these became important institutions for the study of dialectics and the serious practice of the sutras and tantras.

Others

The lineages of certain minor Buddhist traditions have also survived intact – among them the **Zhiche** ('pacification') and **Chodyul** ('object of cutting') which were expounded by the S Indian yogin Padampa Sangye and his female Tibetan disciple Machik Labdron (1031-1126). The rituals of the latter are particularly popular among adherents of the Nyingma and Kagyu traditions.

The **Jonangpa** tradition was founded at Jonang in Tsang by Kunpang Tü-je Tsondru (b 1243), and widely propagated through the writings of its great exponents: Dolpopa Sherab Gyeltsen (1292-1361), Jestun Kunga Drolchok (1507-66), and Taranatha (1575-1634). Its teachings combined an in-depth knowledge of the *Kalacakra Tantra* and other tantra-texts of the new translation period, with a distinctive view concerning the nature of the emptiness *(shunyata)* which, according to Buddhism, underlies all phenomena. The Jonangpa differentiated between mundane phenomena which are regarded as being 'inherently empty' and the attributes of the Buddha which are regarded as being 'extraneously empty' of mundane impurities. The school was persecuted – ostensibly for holding this view, during the 17th century and its adherents have only survived in remote parts of **Dzamtang** and **Ngawa** in the Amdo area, where there are many Jonangpa monasteries.

The **Zhalupa** tradition is that associated with **Zhalu** monastery in Tsang and particularly with Buton Rinchendrub (1290-1364) who was one of Tibet's most prolific authors and the compiler of the modern Tibetan canon – known as the *Kangyur* and *Tangyur*. The **Bodong** tradition was founded, also in Tsang, by Bodong Cho-le Namgyel, who authored 132 volumes of texts on all the subjects of classical science including Buddhism. Lastly, the **Shangpa Kagyu** lineage was based on the tantric teachings which the yogin Khyungpo Neljor (b 978) received from the Indian yogini Niguma, and the masters Maitripa and Sukhasiddhi.

Buddhism today

The Buddhist traditions permeated the social life of Tibet until the destruction of the country's 6,000 monasteries during the suppression of the recent Tibetan uprising and the Cultural Revolution. Only a few temples and shrines of historic importance survived intact, along with a small number of temples which were used as granaries. Since the demise of the Gang of Four heroic efforts have been made by the people to restore the buildings which represent their Buddhist heritage, with or without the support of the government. More difficult is the reintroduction of systematic Buddhist learning and meditation practice. Many of the great Tibetan masters who reside in exile have returned home for visits to encourage a Buddhist renaissance; but some authorities often continue to react with suspicion and misunderstanding.

Islam

The Muslim community of Tibet includes the descendents of medieval converts and merchants from **Ladakh**; as well as more recent migrants from the **Ziling** area. In Lhasa, there are mosques, such as **Gyel Lhakhang**, and Muslim cemeteries. In NE Amdo there are counties such as Bayan Khar (Hualong) and Dowi (Xunhua), where the Hui and Salar Muslim communities are predominant.

Religious and secular festivals

Religious festivals are important events throughout the Tibetan Buddhist world – commemorating the deeds of the Buddha, or those of the great masters of the past associated with one tradition or another. For a more detailed account, see the section on the religious festivals and religious dances of Bhutan in the present book (page 708), most of which also applies to Tibet.

Secular festivals include the traditional new year (*losar*) festival, the summer horse-festivals held throughout the country between the 5th and 7th months of the lunar calendar, and the more recent national festivals adopted from the Chinese calendar.

The following are the main festivals observed according to the traditional calendar:

	M	D
Losar, Tibetan New Year	1	1
Monlam, the Great Prayer Festival	1	1
Day of Offerings	1	15
Enlightenment of Buddha	4	15
Local Deities' Day	5	15
Dharmacakra Day	6	4
Birth of Padmasambhava	6	10
Yoghurt Festival	6	29
Rain Retreating Festival	7	1
Bathing Festival	7	27
Damzhung Horse Festival	7	30
Ongkor Festival	8	1
Descent from the God Realms	9	22
Anniversary of Tsongkhapa	10	25
M = Month; D = Day		

AN ICONOGRAPHIC GUIDE OF TIBETAN BUDDHISM

It is impossible to visit Tibet without being almost overwhelmed by religious imagery. The sheer scale is breathtaking – the Potala Palace in Lhasa has 1,000 rooms, housing approximately 200,000 images! Even the smallest monastery has many icons. It will help both your understanding and enjoyment if you can recognize some of these images.

This guide contains the names of the deities or images most frequently depicted in the Buddhist temples and monasteries of Tibet. Illustrations of some of these are also appended. It is important to remember that, with the probable exception of images representing the ancient historic kings of Tibet, the others are not regarded as concrete or inherently existing being in the Judeo-Christian or even in the Hindu sense. Rather, the deities are revered as pure expressions of buddha-mind, who are to be visualized in the course of meditation in their pure light forms: a coalescence of pure appearance and emptiness. Through such meditations, blessings are obtained from the mentors of the past; spiritual accomplishments are matured through the meditational deities, enlightened activities are engaged in through the agency of the dakinis, and spiritual development is safeguarded by the protector deities. These therefore are the four main classes of image to be observed in Tibetan shrines. Among them, the images representing the spiritual teachers of the past are exemplified by Buddha Shakyamuni, Padmasambhava and Tsongkhapa; those representing the meditational deities by Vajrakumara, Cakrasamvara and Kalacakra; those representing dakinis or female agents of enlightened activity by Vajravarahi; and the protector deities by Mahakala, Shridevi, and so forth.

Temples: what to expect

Most temples have an entrance portico replete with murals depicting the Four Guardian Kings of the four directions and the Wheel of Rebirth (*bhavacakra*) on the outer wall. Within the main gate, there are often images of the gatekeepers Vajrapani (E) and Hayagriva (W), watching over the portals, while the murals of the inner wall nearest the gate depict the protector deities. The central hall, which is of variable size (depending on the number of columns), contains the rows of seats which are occupied by the monastic body during ritual ceremonies, with the thrones or elevated seats of the main lamas furthest from the gate. Proceeding clockwise around the hall, the side-walls may well depict scenes from the life of Buddha Shakyamuni, or other historical figures. Eventually you will reach the innermost wall (facing the gate and beyond the thrones), against which the rows of clay or guilded copper images, sacred scriptures, and reliquary stupas are positioned. These will vary according to the tradition which the temple or monastery represents, although images of the Buddhas of the Three Times are commonly depicted here. There may additionally be an inner sanctum containing the most precious images housed within the temple, with its own circumambulatory pathway. In front of the images, offerings will be arrayed, including water offering bowls, butter lamps and torma-offering cakes, while donations will be left by the faithful as a meritorious action.

The guide

Acala (*Tib* Miyowa) one of the 10 wrathful kings (*dashakrodha*), forming a peripheral group of meditational deities in certain mandalas.

Akashagarbha (*Tib* Namkei Nyingpo) one of the eight major bodhisattvas, yellow in colour, symbolizing the buddha's sense of smell and holding a sword which cuts through dissonant emotions. See **Icon 36**.

Aksobhya (*Tib* Mikyopa) one of the five peaceful meditational buddhas forming the buddha-body of perfect resource (*sambhogakaya*), collectively known as the Buddhas of the Five Families. Aksobhya is blue in colour, symbolizing the purity of form and the mirror-like clarity of buddha-mind. He holds a vajra to symbolize that emptiness and compassion are without duality. See **Icon 4**.

Amitabha (*Tib* Opame) one of the five peaceful meditational buddhas forming the buddha-body of perfect resource (*sambhogakaya*), collectively known as the Buddhas of the Five Families. Amitabha is red in colour, symbolizing the purity of perception and the discerning aspect of buddha-mind. He holds a lotus to symbolize the purification of attachment and the altruistic intention. See **Icon 6**.

Amitayus (*Tib* Tsepame) a meditational deity with nine aspects, who is included among the Three Deities of Longevity, red in colour, and holding a vase full of the nectar of immortality. See **Icon 45**.

Amoghasiddhi (*Tib* Donyo Drupa) one of the five peaceful meditational buddhas forming the buddha-body of perfect resource (*sambhogakaya*), collectively known as the Buddhas of the Five Families. Amoghasiddhi is green in colour, symbolizing the purity of habitual tendencies and the activity aspect of buddha-mind. He holds a sword to symbolize the cutting of dissonant emotions through buddha-activity. See **Icon 7**.

Amritakundalin (*Tib* Dutsi Kyilwa) one of the gatekeepers of the mandalas of meditational deities, dark-green in colour, symbolizing the inherent purity of sensory contact, and holding a crossed-vajra which subdues egotism.

Apchi a doctrinal protectress of the Drigung Kagyu school, who assumes both peaceful and wrathful forms.

Atisha (*Tib* Jowoje) a saintly Buddhist master from Bengal (982-1054), who introduced the Kadampa teachings into Tibet. See **Icon 93**.

Avalokiteshvara (*Tib* Chenrezik) one of the eight major bodhisattvas and the patron deity of Tibet, white in colour, symbolizing the buddha's compassion and sense of taste, and holding a lotus untainted by flaws. There are various forms of this most popular bodhisattva: the 11-faced 1,000-armed form known as Mahakarunika (Tu-je Chenpo, Zhal Chu-chikpa, **Icon 42**), the four-armed form (Chenrezik Chak Zhipa, **Icon 39**), a two-armed form known as Kharsapani (**Icon 44**), the lion-riding form called Simhanada (**Icon 43**), the soothing form called Mind at Rest (Semnyi Ngalso), or Jowo Lokeshvara, and the standing form called Padmapani, the last of which is usually red in colour (**Icon 33**).

Begtse a sword-wielding form of the protector deity **Mahakala**.

Bhairava (*Tib* Jikje) a wrathful bull-headed meditational deity (in Buddhism), or a wrathful counterpart of Shiva (in Hinduism).

Bhaisajyaguru (*Tib* Sangye Menla) the central buddha of medicine, otherwise called Vaiduryaprabharaja, who is blue in colour, holding a bowl containing the panacea myrobalan. See **Icon 12**.

Bodongpa Chokle Namgyel (1375-1451) one of Tibet's most prolific writers, the author of approximately 100 treatises, a product of the Bodong E college, who established his own distinctive school of Buddhism in Tibet.

Brahma (*Tib* Tsangpa) a four-faced protector deity associated with the world system of form (in Buddhism), the creator divinity (in Hinduism).

Buddha Shakyamuni (*Tib* Shakya Tupa) the historical Buddha (6th-5th centuries BC), known prior to his attainment of buddhahood as Siddhartha or Gautama, who is also revered as the fourth of the thousand buddhas of this aeon. He is depicted in diverse forms, seated, standing, or reclining (at the point of his decease), and with diverse hand-gestures (symbolizing past merits, generosity, meditation, teaching, fearlessness and so forth). The Jowo form depicts him as a bodhisattva prior to his attainment of buddhahood, and the form Munindra depicts him as he appears among the devas. See **Icon 9**.

Buddhas of the Five Families (Skt *Pancajina*/*Tib* Gyelwa Riknga) the five buddhas of the buddha-body of perfect resource (*sambhogakaya*; **Icons 3-7**). See listed separately **Aksobhya**, **Amitabha**, **Amoghasiddhi**, **Ratnasambhava**, and **Vairocana**.

Buddhas of the Three Times (*Tib* Dusum Sangye) see listed separately the Buddha of the past **Dipamkara** (**Icon 8**), the Buddha of the present **Shakyamuni** (**Icon 9**), and the Buddha of the future **Maitreya** (**Icon 10**).

Buton Rinchendrub (1290-1364) compiler of the Buddhist canon, and major scholar within the Zhalupa tradition of Tibetan Buddhism. See **Icon 109**.

Cakrasamvara (*Tib* Khorlo Demchok) a four-faced 12-armed wrathful meditational deity, blue in colour, in union with his consort Vajravarahi, trampling upon Bhairava and Kali, and thus representing the Buddhist transmutation of the mundane Hindu divinity Shiva and his consort. See **Icon 54**.

Chenrezi Semnyi Ngalso see under **Avalokiteshvara**.

Cimara (*Tib* Tsimara) wrathful protector deity of Samye Monastery, and fore-

most of the *tsen* class of doctrinal protectors, greenish red in colour.

Cintamani(cakra) Tara see under **Tara**.

Dalai Lama (*Tib* Gyelwa Rinpoche) revered as the human embodiment of Avalokiteshvara, the patron deity of Tibet who symbolizes compassion, the successive Dalai Lamas (see page 123) have, since the mid 17th century, assumed both spiritual and temporal authority in Tibet. Among them, the most significant have probably been Dalai Lama III Sonam Gyatso (1543-88; **Icon 116**), Dalai Lama V Ngawang Lobzang Gyatso (1617-82; **Icon 118**), Dalai Lama VI Tsangyang Gyatso (1683-1706; **Icon 120**), Dalai Lama VII Kalzang Gyatso (1708-57), Dalai Lama XIII Tupten Gyatso (1876-1933; **Icon 121**), and the present Dalai Lama XIV (b 1935; **Icon 122**).

Damsi a group of nine sibling demons who have violated their commitments and are said to endanger infant children.

Dashakrodha kings (*Tib* Trowo Chu) a group of 10 peripheral meditational deities known as the 10 wrathful kings, comprising Usnisacakravartin, Prajnantaka, Yamantaka, Vighnantaka, Padmantaka, Mahabala, Takkiraja, Shumbharaja, Acala, and Niladanda.

Desi Sangye Gyatso (1677-1705) an important regent of Tibet and author of seminal commentaries on medicine, astrology, religious history, and other subjects. See **Icon 119**.

Dharmaraja (*Tib* Chogyel) see **Yama Dharmaraja**.

Dharmatala one of two peripheral figures, sometimes classed alongside the group of **sixteen elders**. He is described as a layman (*upasaka*) who looked after the 16 elders during their visit to China.

Dipamkara Buddha (*Tib* Sangye Marmedze) the third buddha of this aeon, also known as Kashyapa Buddha, who was the one immediately preceding

Shakyamuni. See **Icon 8**.

Dolpopa Sherab Gyeltsen (1292-1361) the most influential scholar of the Jonangpa school, who was a pre-eminent master of the tantras and an exponent of the *zhentong* philosophy. See **Icon 110**.

Dorje Drakden a doctrinal protector in the retinue of Pehar, who possesses the medium of Nechung, the state oracle of Tibet.

Dorje Drolo a wrathful tiger-riding form of Padmasambhava (**Icon 91**). See under **Eight Manifestations of Padmasambhava**.

Dorje Lekpa a goat-riding doctrinal protector of the Dzogchen teachings, wearing a wide-brimmed hat, who was bound under an oath of allegiance to Buddhism by Padmasambhava in the Oyuk district of W Tibet.

Dorje Yudronma a doctrinal protectress of the Menmo class, with whom the great Nyingmapa master Longchen Rabjampa is said to have had a particular affinity. See **Icon 62**.

Drigungpa Jikten Gonpo (1143-1217) one of the foremost students of Phakmodrupa and founder of the Drigung Kagyu school, based at Drigung Til Monastery. See **Icon 101**.

Dromtonpa Gyelwei Jungne (1004-64) the foremost Tibetan student of Atisha and founder of Reting Monastery. See **Icon 94**.

Drubpa Kabgye the eight wrathful meditational deities of the Nyingma school, viz: Yamantaka, Hayagriva, Shriheruka, Vajramrita, Vajrakila, Matarah, Lokastotrapuja, and Vajramanrabhiru.

Drukchen the title of the successive heads of the Drukpa Kagyu school, for an enumeration of whom, see page 322.

Dzogchen Pema Rigdzin (1625-97) the founder of Dzogchen Monastery in Kham.

Eight Awareness-holders (Skt *asta-vidyadhara*/Tib rigdzin gye) the eight Indian lineage-holders of the eight transmitted precepts of Mahayoga, who are said to have been contemporaries of Padmasambhava, namely: Manjushrimitra, Nagarjuna, Humkara, Vimalamitra, Prabhahasti, Dhanasamskrita, Rambuguhya-Devacandra, and Shantigarbha.

Eight Bodhisattvas (*Tib* nyese gye) the eight major bodhisattvas, standing figures who are often depicted flanking images of Shakyamuni Buddha. See listed separately: **Manjushri** (**Icon 31**), **Vajrapani** (**Icon 32**), **Avalokiteshvara** (**Icon 33**), **Ksitigarbha** (**Icon 34**), **Nivaranaviskambhin** (**Icon 35**), **Akashagarbha** (**Icon 36**), **Maitreya** (**Icon 37**), and **Samantabhadra** (**Icon 38**).

Eight Classes of Spirits (*lhade gye*) a series of lesser spirits or demons, who are to be appeased or coerced by means of ritual offerings.

Eight Deities of the Transmitted Precepts see **Drubpa Kabgye**.

Eight Manifestations of Padmasambhava (*Tib* guru tsen gye) the eight principal forms assumed by Padmakara at different phases of his career, namely: **Saroruhavajra** (birth; **Icon 84**), **Padma Gyelpo** (kingship; **Icon 85**), **Shakya Senge** (ordination; **Icon 86**), **Loden Chokse** (mastery of the teachings; **Icon 87**), **Padmasambhava** (establishment of Buddhism in Tibet; Icon 88), **Nyima Ozer** (subjugation of demons; Icon 89), **Senge Dradrok** (subjugation of non-Buddhists; **Icon 90**), and **Dorje Drolo** (concealment of terma; **Icon 91**).

Eight Medicine Buddhas (*Tib* menla deshek gye) the successive buddhas revered as the precursors of Buddhist medicine, viz: Sunamaparikirtana, Svaraghosaraja, Suvarnabhadravimala, Ashokottama, Dharmakirtisagaraghosa, Abhijnanaraja, Shakyaketu, and Bhaisajyaguru. For an illustration of the last of these, who is also the central medicine buddha, see **Icon 12**.

Eight Taras who Protect from Fear (*Tib* Dolma Jikpa Gye Kyobma) a group of female divinities, who offer protection from eight specific types of fear, viz: Manasimhabhayatrana (pride and lions), Mohahastibhayatrana (delusion and elephants), Dvesagniprashamani (hatred and fire), Irsyasarpavisapaharani (envy and poisonous snakes), Kudristicoropadravanivarani (wrong view and thieves), Ghoramatsaryashrinkhalamocani (avarice and fetters), Ragaughavegavartashosani (attachment and rivers), and Samshayapishacabhayatrana (doubt and carnivorous demons). See also under **Tara**.

Eighty-four Mahasiddhas (*Tib* Drubtob Gyachu Gyezhi) a group of 84 tantric masters of ancient India, for the life-stories of which, see J Robinson, *Buddhas Lions*.

Ekajati (*Tib* Ralchikma) an important protectress of the Dzogchen teachings, characteristically depicted with a single hair-knot, a single eye and a single breast.

Five Founders of Sakya (*Tib* Gongma Nga) the successors of Khon Konchok Gyelpo who founded Sakya in 1073, viz: Sachen Kunga Nyingpo (1092-1158; **Icon 104**), Sonam Tsemo (1142-82; **Icon 105**), Drakpa Gyeltsen (1147-1216; **Icon 106**), Sakya Pandita Kunga Gyeltsen (1182-1251; **Icon 107**), and Drogon Chogyel Phakpa (1235-80; **Icon 108**).

Four Guardian Kings (*Skt* Caturmaharajaika/*Tib* Gyelchen Zhi) the guardian kings of the four directions, whose martial forms are frequently depicted on the walls of a temple portico, viz: Dhritarastra (E), Virudhaka (S), Virupaksa (W), and Vaishravana (N). **Icons 123-126**.

Gampopa (1079-1153) the student of Milarepa and source of the four major and eight minor Kagyu schools. See **Icon 98**.

Ganesh (*Skt* Ganapati or Vinayaka/*Tib* Tsokdak) the elephant-headed offspring of Shiva (in Hinduism), an obstacle-causing or obstacle-removing protector deity (in Buddhism).

Genyen a group of 21 aboriginal divinities, most of whom are identified with snow peaks.

Gonpo Maning (*Skt* Mahapandaka Mahakala) a spear-wielding two-armed form of the protector deity Mahakala. See **Icon 58**.

Guhyasamaja (*Tib* Sangwa Dupa) a six-armed seated meditational deity, two forms of which are recognized: Aksobhyavajra (according to the Arya tradition) and Manjuvajra (according to the Buddhajnanapada tradition). The former is light-blue in colour, embraced by the consort Sparshavajra, and has three faces, symbolizing the transmutation of the three poisons: delusion, attachment, and hatred. See **Icon 51**.

Guru Chowang (1212-70) a great treasure-finder of the Nyingma school.

Gyelpo Ku-nga the five aspects of the important protector deity Pehar, known respectively as the kings of body, speech, mind, attributes, and activities. See **Icons 63-67**.

Hanuman the monkey god of Hinduism.

Hayagriva (*Tib* Tamdrin) a wrathful horse-headed meditational deity of the Nyingma school who is generally red in colour, symbolic of buddha-speech, and included among the **Drubpa Kabgye**. He also appears as a gatekeeper in certain mandalas, and, as the renowned tamer of the egotistical demon Rudra, is frequently positioned (along with Vajrapani) at the entrance of a temple.

Hevajra (*Tib* Kyedorje) a wrathful counterpart of the meditational deity Aksobhya, deep-blue in colour, who is depicted in a dancing posture, with 2, 4, 6, or 16 arms, and in union with the consort

Nairatmya. See **Icon 56**.

Huashang one of two peripheral figures, sometimes classed alongside the group of **sixteen elders**. He is described as a monk (*Ch* hoshang) who looked after the 16 elders during their visit to China.

Hundred Peaceful and Wrathful Deities (*Tib* Zhitro Lhatsok, Dampa Rikgya) the assembly of the 42 peaceful deities and 58 wrathful deities, according to the *Guhyagarbha Tantra*, the basis for the visionary account of the *Tibetan Book of the Dead*.

Jambhala (*Tib* Dzambhala) a protector deity of wealth, yellow in colour, frequently depicted holding a gemstone.

Jamchen Choje Shakya Yeshe a student of Tsongkhapa, who founded Sera Monastery in 1419.

Jampa see **Maitreya**.

Jamyang Choje Tashi Palden a student of Tsongkhapa, who founded Drepung Monastery in 1416.

Jangkya Qutuqtu III Rolpei Dorje (1717-86) a holder of high office in Manchu China, who was responsible for escorting Dalai Lama VII to Lhasa, and for the prolonged military campaigns against the Bonpo in Gyarong.

Je Yabsesum the collective name given to Tsongkhapa (1357-1419) and his two foremost students, Gyeltsabje Darma Rinchen (1364-1431) and Khedrubje Gelek Pelzang (1385-1438), who were the first throne-holders of Ganden Monastery and thus the founders of the Gelukpa school. The last of these was also retrospectively recognized as Panchen Lama I. See **Icons 113-115**.

Jikme Lingpa (1730-98) an important Nyingmapa yogin who revealed the highly influential teaching-cycle known as the *Innermost Spirituality of Longchenpa* (*Longchen Nyingtig*).

Jowo see **Jowo Shakyamuni**.

Jowo Lokeshvara see under **Avalokiteshvara**.

Jowo Shakyamuni a form of Buddha Shakyamuni, as a bodhisattva, prior to his attainment of buddhahood.

Kalachakra (*Tib* Dukhor, Dukyi Khorlo) a wrathful meditational deity, blue in colour, with four faces and 12 upper arms and 24 lower arms, embraced by the consort Vishvamata, symbolizing the transmutation of the wheel of time. See **Icon 53**.

Kali in Hinduism, the female consort of Mahadeva, an aspect of Shiva.

Karmapa the oldest succession of incarnating lamas recognized in Tibet, embodying Avalokiteshvara's compassion and presiding over the Karma Kagyu school. For a listing of the 17 Karmapas from Karmapa I Dusum Khyenpa onwards. See also **Icon 99**.

Katokpa the title assumed by the first 13 hierarchs of Katok Monastery in E Tibet, founded by Katokpa I Dampa Deshek in 1159.

Kharsapani see under **Avalokiteshvara**.

Krishna (*Tib* nagpo) one of the incarnations of Visnu (in Hinduism).

Ksitigarbha (*Tib* Sayi Nyingpo) one of the eight major bodhisattvas, white in colour, symbolizing the buddha's eyes, and holding a sprouting gemstone of pristine cognition. See **Icon 34**.

Kubera (*Tib* Tadak Kubera) a protectory deity of wealth, known as the 'lord of horses', black in colour, brandishing a sword and holding a jewel-spitting mongoose.

Kurukulla (*Tib* Rikchema) a red coloured female meditational deity in dancing posture, holding a flowery bow and arrow, symbolizing her charisma to fascinate and overpower even hostile forces.

Lokeshvara (*Tib* Jikten Wangchuk) an abbreviation of **Avalokiteshvara**.

Longchen Rabjampa (1308-63) preeminent scholar, treasure-finder, and systematizer of the Nyingma tradition. See **Icon 111**.

Longdol Lama Ngawang Lobzang (1719-95) an erudite encyclopaedist, who was a student of Dalai Lama VII and teacher of Jamyang Zhepa II Konchok Jikme Wangpo.

Lords of the Three Enlightened Families (*Tib* Riksu Gonpo) the three main bodhisattvas associated with the early Mahayana transmissions, namely Manjughosa symbolizing discriminative awareness; Avalokiteshvara symbolizing compassion; and Vajrapani symbolizing power. See **Icons 39-41**.

Machen Pomra protector deity embodied in the snow peaks of the Amnye Machen range; one of the **Twelve Subterranean Goddesses**.

Mahakala (*Tib* Nagpo Chenpo) a class of supramundane protector deities, 75 aspects of which are recognized. Among these, the most widespread are Four-armed Mahakala (*Caturbhujamahakala*; **Icon 57**); Six-armed Mahakala (*Sadbhujamahakala*), Gonpo Maning (Skt *Mahapandaka Mahakala*; **Icon 58**), Tiger-riding Mahakala (*Tib* Gonpo Takzhon), Begtse, and Panjaranatha (*Tib* Gonpo Gur; **Icon 59**), the last of which is preferred among the Sakyapa.

Mahakarunika (*Tib* Tu-je Chenpo) see under **Avalokiteshvara**.

Mahottara Heruka (*Tib* Chemchok Heruka) the wrathful counterpart of the primordial buddha Samantabhadra, is dark-brown, with three faces symbolizing the three approaches to liberation, six arms symbolizing the six perfections, and four legs symbolizing the four supports for miraculous ability, trampling upon Mahedeva and Umadevi.

Maitreya (*Tib* Jampa) one of the eight major bodhisattvas (**Icon 37**) and the future buddha (**Icon 10**), whitish-yellow in colour, symbolizing the buddha's loving kindness and sight, and holding an orange bush which dispels the fever of dissonant emotions.

Manjughosa (*Tib* Jampeyang, Jamyang) one of the eight major bodhisattvas (**Icon 31**) who is depicted upright, whitish-green in colour and holding a lily, which symbolizes the renunciation of dissonant emotions. In a more familiar seated posture, he is one of the lords of the three enlightened families (**Icon 40**), orange in colour, symbolizing the buddha's discriminative awareness and tongue, and holding a sword which cuts through obscurations and a book of discriminative awareness. Other important forms include Manjushri Vadisimha, Manjushri Kumarabhuta, White Manjushri, and the five aspects which appeared in the visions of Tsongkhapa.

Manjushri (*Tib* Jampel) see **Manjughosa**.

Manjuvajra (*Tib* Jampei Dorje) a form of the meditational deity Guhyasamaja, according to the tradition of Buddhajnanapada.

Marici (*Tib* Ozerchenma) the red goddess of the dawn, who is propitiated for the removal of obstacles.

Marpa (1012-96) Marpa Chokyi Wangchuk, the student of Naropa and first Tibetan exponent of the Karma Kagyu lineage, whose disciples included Milarepa. See **Icon 96**.

Matsyendranath an aspect of Avalokiteshvara ('lord of fish') which is revered in Nepal, the white form known as Jamali being enshrined in Asan, and the red form, Bukham, in Patan.

Maudgalyayana (*Tib* Maudgal bu) one of the two foremost students of Shakyamuni, who passed away before the Buddha's parinirvana. See **Icon 14**.

Milarepa (1040-1123/1052-1135) the great yogin and ascetic poet of the Kagyu lineage, who was the student of Marpa and teacher of Gampopa. See **Icon 97**.

Nairatmya (*Tib* Dakmema) female

consort of the meditational deity Hevajra, symbolizing selflessness or emptiness.

Narayana (*Tib* Jukse) one of the incarnations of the Hindu deity Visnu.

Ngok Lotsawa Lekpei Sherab founder of the Kadampa monastery of Sangpu Neutok and a major student of the 11th century Bengali master Atisha.

Ngorchen Kunga Zangpo (b 1382) who founded the monastery of Ngor Evam Chode in 1429, giving rise to the influential Ngorpa branch of the Sakya school.

Nivaranaviskambhin (*Tib* Dripa Namsel) one of the eight major bodhisattvas, reddish-yellow in colour, symbolizing the buddha's ears, and holding a wheel of gems because he teaches the Buddhist doctrine. See **Icon 35**.

Nyangrel Nyima Ozer (1136-1204) a major treasure-finder (*terton*) of the Nyingma school.

Nyatri Tsenpo the first king of the Yarlung Dynasty. See **Icon 77**.

Nyenchen Tanglha the protector deity embodying the mountain range of the same name, which forms a watershed between the Brahmaputra River and the Jangtang lakes. The main peak looms over Lake Namtso Chukmo.

Padmakara (*Tib* Pema Jungne) the form assumed by Padmasambhava at the time when he and his consort Mandarava were burnt at the stake in Zahor, but miraculously transformed their pyre into a lake. See **Icon 81**.

Padmapani see under **Avalokiteshvara**.

Padmasambhava the form assumed by Padmasambhava (ie Guru Rinpoche) while establishing Buddhism in Tibet. See **Icon 88**.

Panchen Lama the emanations of the Buddha Amitabha, ranking among Tibet's foremost incarnate successions.

Among them, Panchen Lama IV Chokyi Gyeltsen (1567-1662; **Icon 117**) was an important teacher of Dalai Lama V.

Panjaranatha (*Tib* Gonpo Gur) see under **Mahakala**.

Paramadya (*Tib* Palchok Dangpo) a major meditational deity of the Yogatantra and Mahyoga class.

Parvati consort of the Hindu deity Shiva.

Pehar an important protector deity within the Nyingma and Geluk traditions. See also **Gyelpo Ku-nga**.

Pelpung Situ the incarnations of Tai Situpa, including Situ VIII Chokyi Jungne who, in 1727, founded the largest Karma Kagyu monastery at Pelpung within the kingdom of Derge. For a full enumeration of the Tai Situpas, see page 520.

Pema Totrengtsal the form assumed by Padmasambhava while manifesting as the meditational deity Vajrakumara to subdue the demons of the Kathmandu valley at Yanglesho (Pharping).

Phadampa Sangye the 11th-12th century S Indian yogin who propagated the Chodyul and Zhiche teachings in the highland region of Western Tibet.

Phakmodrupa Dorje Gyelpo (1110-70) student of Gampopa and progenitor of the eight lesser branches of the Kagyu school, including the Drigungpa, Taklungpa and Drukpa branches. See **Icon 100**.

Phakpalha the title of the principal incarnate lama of Chamdo Jampaling Monastery in Kham, which was founded between 1436-44 by Jangsem Sherab Zangpo.

Prajnaparamita (*Tib* Yum Chenmo) the female meditational deity embodying the perfection of discriminative awareness, golden yellow in colour, and holding emblems such as the book, sword, lotus, vajra and rosary, which are indicative of supreme insight. See **Icon 48**.

Rahula (*Tib* Za) an important protector deity within the Nyingma school, depicted as a dark brown or black multi-headed semi-human semi-serpentine figure. See **Icon 61**.

Ratnasambhava (*Tib* Rinchen Jungne) one of the five peaceful meditational buddhas forming the buddha-body of perfect resource (*sambhogakaya*), collectively known as the Buddhas of the Five Families. Ratnasambhava is yellow in colour, symbolizing the purity of sensations or feelings and the equanimity or sameness of buddha-mind. He holds a gemstone to symbolize that his enlightened attributes are spontaneously present and that he fulfils the hopes of all beings. See **Icon 5**.

Ravana (*Tib* Dradrok-kyi bu) the 10-headed ogre of Lanka, slain by Rama in the course of the Hindu epic *Ramayana*.

Rechungpa (1084-1161) a yogin who, like Gampopa, was one of Milarepa's foremost students.

Remati (*Tib* Magzorma) an aspect of the protectress Shridevi, who rides a mule and holds a sickle or a sandalwood club and a blood-filled skull. She is propitiated in order to overwhelm internal passions and outer disruptions due to warfare.

Remdawa Zhonu Lodro (1349-1412) a great exponent of the Madhyamaka philosophy within the Sakya tradition, who became one of Tsongkhapa's most significant teachers.

Rigdzin Ngagi Wangpo (1580-1639) the third successive emanation of Rikdzin Godemchen, founder of the Northern Treasures (Jangter) tradition of the Nyingma school. In 1632 he established the monastery of Dorje Drak in S Tibet.

Rinchen Zangpo (958-1055) the great translator and contemporary of Atisha whose centre of activity was in Far-west Tibet and the adjacent areas of Spiti and Ladakh.

Sakya Pandita see under **Five Founders of Sakya**.

Samantabhadra (*Tib* Kuntu Zangpo) the male or subjective aspect of the primordial buddha-body of actual reality (*dharmakaya*), blue in colour, symbolizing the ground of buddha-mind or luminosity. See **Icon 1**.

Samantabhadra (bodhisattva) (*Tib* Jangsem Kuntu Zangpo) one of the eight major bodhisattvas, reddish-green in colour, symbolizing the buddha's nose, and holding a corn-ear of gemstones because he fulfils the hopes of beings. See **Icon 38**.

Samantabhadri (*Tib* Kuntu Zangmo) the female or objective aspect of the primordial buddha-body of actual reality (*dharmakaya*), blue in colour, symbolizing the ground of phenomenal appearances or emptiness. See **Icon 1**.

Samayatara (*Tib* Damtsik Dolma) a wrathful female meditational deity, consort of the Buddha Amoghasiddhi.

Sarvavid Vairocana (*Tib* Kunrik Nampar Nangze) see under **Vairocana**.

Seven Generations of Past Buddhas (*Tib* Sangye Rabdun) the seven buddhas of the immediate past, in sequence: Vipashyin (**Icon 11**), Shikhin, Vishvabhuk, Krakucchanda, Kanakamuni, Kashyapa, and Shakyamuni.

Shakyamuni see **Buddha Shakyamuni**.

Shakyamuni Aksobhyavajra (*Shakya Tupa Mikyo Dorsem*) the aspect of Shakyamuni Buddha depicted in the Ramoche Jowo image, which was originally brought to Tibet from Nepal by Princess Bhrikuti in the 7th century.

Shakyashri (1127-1225) the great Kashmiri scholar who visited Tibet in his later years, influencing all traditions.

Shantaraksita (*Tib* Zhiwei Tso/Khenpo Bodhisattva) a monastic preceptor of Zahor, who officiated at Nalanda Monastery prior to his arrival in Tibet at the invitation of King Trisong Detsen. He ordained the first seven trial monks in Tibet and was responsible for the construction of Samye Monastery, which he modelled on Odantapuri Monastery in Magadha. See **Icon 82**.

Shariputra (*Tib* Shari-bu) one of the two foremost students of Shakyamuni, who passed away before the Buddha's parinirvana. See **Icon 13**.

Shiva (*Tib* Lha Wangchuk) the Hindu divinity of destruction; a mundane protector deity in Buddhism.

Shridevi (*Tib* Palden Lhamo) a major protectress and female counterpart of Mahakala, who has both peaceful and wrathful forms, the latter being a ferocious three-eyed form, dark-blue in colour, and riding a mule. Remati (see above) is included among her aspects. See **Icon 60**.

Simhanada (*Tib* Senge Ngaro) see under **Avalokiteshvara**.

Simhavaktra (*Tib* Senge Dongma) a lion-headed meditational deity, who is the female aspect of Padmasambhava, dark blue in colour and holding a vajra-chopper and skull cup, which symbolize that she dispels obstacles to enlightened activity.

Sitatapatra (*Tib* Dukar) a female umbrella-wielding meditational deity, depicted with a thousand arms, who is propitiated in order to remove obstacles.

Six Ornaments (*Tib* Gyen Druk) the six great Buddhist commentators of ancient India, viz: Nagarjuna and Aryadeva who developed the Madhyamaka philosophy; the brothers Asanga and Vasubandhu who developed the Yogacara, Cittamatra, and Vaibhasika philosophies; and Dignaga and Dharmakirti who developed a systematic Buddhist logic. See **Icons 69-74**.

Six Sages of the Six Realms (*Tib* Tupa Druk) six buddha aspects said to appear respectively in the six realms of

existence in order to teach the way to liberation from sufferings, respectively: Munindra (among the gods), Vemacitra (among the antigods), Shakyamuni (among humans), Simha (among animals), Jvalamukha (among tormented spirits), and Yama Dharmaraja (among the hells).

Six-armed Mahakala (*Tib* Gonpo Chak Drukpa) see under **Mahakala**.

Sixteen Elders (*Tib* Neten Chudruk) a group of elders (*sthavira*) and contemporaries of Shakyamuni Buddha, who were traditionally assigned to promote the Buddhist teachings in the world throughout time, and who have been particularly venerated in Chinese Buddhism, where they are known as arhats (*Ch* lohan). See **Icons 15-30**.

Songtsen Gampo the 7th century unifying king of Tibet who made Lhasa the capital of his newly emergent nation and espoused the Buddhist teachings, revered thereafter as an emanation of the compassionate bodhisattva Avalokiteshvara. See **Icon 79**.

Taklung Tangpa Tashipel (1142-1210) a foremost student of Phakmodrupa Dorje Gyelpo, who founded the Taklung Kagyu sub-school and the monastery of the same name in 1178. See **Icon 102**.

Tangtong Gyelpo (1385-1464) the Leonardo of Tibet, renowned as a mystic, revealer of treasure-doctrines, engineer, master bridge-builder, and the inventor of Tibetan opera. See **Icon 112**.

Tara (*Tib* Dolma) a female meditational deity, who is identified with compassion and enlightened activity. There are aspects of Tara which specifically offer protection from worldly tragedies and fear of the elements (see above, **Eight Taras who Protect from Fear**), and an enumeration of 21 aspects of Tara is well-documented. Among these the most popular are Green Tara (*Tib* Doljang; **Icon 49**), who is mainly associated with protection, and White Tara (*Tib* Dolkar;

Icon 46), who is associated with longevity. In addition, the form known as Cintamani (cakra) Tara is a meditational deity of the Unsurpassed Yogatantra class.

Terdak Lingpa (1646-1714) a great treasure-finder who revitalized the Nyingmapa tradition and founded Mindroling Monastery in 1670.

Thirty-five Confession Buddhas (*Tib* ltung-bshags-kyi lha so-lnga) a group of 35 buddhas associated with the specific practice of purifying non-virtuous habits, in which the names of each are invoked in turn (usually in conjunction with physical prostrations).

Thousand Buddhas of the Aeon (*Tib* Sangye Tongtsa) the thousand buddhas of the present aeon, whose names are enumerated in the *Bhadrakalpikasutra*. Among these Shakyamuni Buddha was the fourth, and the next to appear in the world will be Maitreya.

Three Ancestral Religious Kings (*Tib* Chogyel Mepo Namsum) the three foremost Buddhist kings of ancient Tibet, namely Songtsen Gampo who unified the country and espoused Buddhism in the 7th century (**Icon 79**), Trisong Detsen who established the spiritual practices and monastic ordinations of Buddhism in the 8th century (**Icon 83**), and Tri Ralpachen who sought to end Tibetan militarism and lavishly sponsored Buddhist activity in the 9th century (**Icon 92**).

Three Deities of Longevity (*Tib* Tselha Namsum) see respectively **Amitayus** (**Icon 45**), **White Tara** (**Icon 46**), and **Vijaya** (**Icon 47**).

Thubpa Gangchentso see under **Vairocana**.

Thubwang (*Skt Munindra*) see **Buddha Shakyamuni**.

Tiger-riding Mahakala (*Tib* Gonpo Takzhon) see under **Mahakala**.

Tonmi Sambhota the 7th century inventor of the Tibetan capital letter script (*uchen*). See **Icon 80**.

Trailokyavijaya (*Tib* Khamsum Namgyel) a peripheral deity, sometimes assuming a peaceful guise alongside the eight standing bodhisattvas, and sometimes in a wrathful form alongside the Dashakrodha kings.

Tri Ralpachen see under **Three Ancestral Religious Kings**.

Trisong Detsen see under **Three Ancestral Religious Kings**.

Tsangpa Gya-re Yeshe Dorje (1161-1211) the first Drukchen (head of the Drukpa Kagyu school). See **Icon 103**. For a full enumeration of the Drukchen emanations, see above, page 322.

Tsering Che-nga five female protector deities associated with the snow peaks of the Everest Range, viz: Miyowa Zangma, Tingi Zhelzangma, Tashi Tseringma, Drozangma, and Drinzangma.

Tseringma see under **Tsering Che-nga**.

Tsongkhapa (and his foremost students) see **Je Yabsesum**.

Tuken Lobzang Chokyi Nyima (1737-1802) the third incarnation of Changkya Qutuqtu Rolpei Dorje of Gonlung Jampaling Monastery in Amdo. In 1801 he wrote the *Crystal Mirror of Philosophical Systems*.

Twelve Subterranean Goddesses (*Tib* Tenma Chunyi) a group of 12 protector goddesses of the earth, who are associated with specific mountain localities, such as Kongtsun Demo, the protectress of Kongpo; and Machen Pomra, the protectress of the Amnye Machen range.

Twelve Tenma see **Twelve Subterranean Goddesses**.

Twenty-five Tibetan Disciples (*Tib* Jewang Nyernga) the Tibetan disciples of Padmasambhava, including King Trisong Detsen, Yeshe Tsogyel, Vairotsana, Nubchen Sangye Yeshe, Nyak

Jnanakumara, and so forth.

Twenty-one Taras (*Tib* Dolma Nyishu Tsachik) see under **Tara**.

Two Gatekeepers (*Tib* gokyong nyi) in most temples the gates are guarded on the inner side by large images of Hayagriva (W) and Vajrapani or Acala (E).

Two Supreme Ones (*Tib* Chok Nyi) the ancient Indian Vinaya masters, Gunaprabha and Shakyaprabha, who are sometimes classed alongside the **Six Ornaments**. See **Icons 75-76**. Note that some traditions identify Nagarjuna and Asanga as the Two Supreme Ones and, instead, place the Vinaya masters among the Six Ornaments.

Ucchusmakrodha (*Tib* Trowo Metsek) a wrathful aspect of the meditational deity Hayagriva, in which form the spirit of rampant egotism (Rudra) is tamed.

Usnisavijaya (*Tib* Tsuktor Namgyel) a three-headed multi-armed wrathful deity, who is the first and foremost of the **Dashakrodha kings**.

Vairocana (*Tib* Nampar Nangze) one of the five peaceful meditational buddhas forming the buddha-body of perfect resource (*sambhogakaya*), collectively known as the Buddhas of the Five Families. Vairocana is white in colour, symbolizing the purity of consciousness and the emptiness of buddha-mind. He holds a wheel to symbolize that his teachings cut through the net of dissonant emotions. See **Icon 3**. Among other aspects of Vairocana are the four-faced form Sarvavid Vairocana (*Tib* Kunrik Nampar Nangze; **Icon 50**) in which all the peripheral buddhas are embodied, and Muni Himamahasagara (*Tib* Thubpa Gangchentso), in and around whose body all world systems are said to evolve.

Vairotsana one of the 25 disciples of Padmasambhava, revered as a major translator of Sanskrit texts and a lineage holder of the Dzogchen tradition.

Vaishravana (*Tib* Nam-mang To-se)

the guardian king of the northern direction, who, like Jambhala and Manibhadra, is associated with wealth, and wields a banner and a jewel-spitting mongoose in his hands.

Vajradhara (*Tib* Dorje Chang) an aspect of the buddha-body of actual reality (*dharmakaya*), appearing in a luminous form complete with the insignia of the buddha-body of perfect resource (*sambhogakaya*). He is dark blue in colour, seated, holding a vajra and bell in his crossed hands. See **Icon 2**.

Vajrakila (*Tib* Dorje Phurba) a wrathful meditational deity of the Nyingma and Sakya schools in particular, and one of the **Drubpa Kabgye**. He is depicted dark-blue in colour, with three faces, and six arms, and wielding a ritual dagger (*kila/phurba*) which cuts through obstacles to enlightened activity.

Vajrakumara (*Tib* Dorje Zhonu) an aspect of the meditational deity Vajrakila. See **Icon 52**.

Vajrapani (*Tib* Chakna Dorje) one of the eight major bodhisattvas and one of the lords of the three enlightened families, blue in colour, symbolizing the buddha's power and sense of hearing, and holding a vajra because he has subjugated sufferings. There are various forms of this bodhisattva, among which the standing peaceful form (**Icon 32**), and the two-armed wrathful form, raising a vajra in the right hand and a noose in the left (**Icon 41**) are most frequently depicted.

Vajrasattva (*Tib* Dorje Sempa) an aspect of **Aksobhya** (**Icon 4**) who may appear in a blue form or a white form, holding a vajra in his right hand and a bell in the left, symbolizing purification and the indestructible reality of skilful means and emptiness.

Vajrasattva Yab-yum (*Tib* Dorsem Yabyum) the meditational deity **Vajrasattva** in union with his female consort.

Vajravarahi (*Tib* Dorje Phagmo) a female meditational deity who is the consort of Cakrasamvara, generally red in colour and with the emblem of the sow's head above her own. See **Icon 55**.

Vajravidarana (*Tib* Dorje Namjom) a peaceful meditational deity, seated and holding a crossed-vajra to the heart with the right hand and a bell in the left.

Vajrayogini (*Tib* Dorje Neljorma) a female meditational deity, red in colour and with a semi-wrathful facial expression. There are several aspects, including the one known as Kecari, the practices of which are associated mainly with the Kagyu school.

Vijaya (*Tib* Namgyelma) an eight-armed three-headed meditational deity, who is one of the **Three Deities of Longevity**, white in colour and holding a small buddha-image in her upper right hand. Statues of Vijaya are often inserted within Victory Stupas. See **Icon 47**.

Vimalamitra (*Tib* Drime Drakpa) a Kashmiri master and contemporary of Padmasambhava who introduced his own transmission of Dzogchen in Tibet, and was responsible for disseminating the *Guhyagarbha Tantra*.

Virupa one of the Eighty-four Mahasiddhas of ancient India who was a progenitor of the profound instructions set down in the *Path and Fruit* teachings of the Sakya school.

Visnu (*Tib* Khyabjuk) the Hindu divinity of preservation; a mundane protector in Buddhism.

Yama Dharmaraja (*Tib* Shinje Chogyel) a proctector deity favoured by the Geluk school, dark blue in colour and bull-headed, and brandishing a club and a snare. He is identified with Yama, the 'lord of death'. See **Icon 68**.

Yamantaka (*Tib* Zhinje-zhed) a wrathful meditational deity, with red, black and bull-headed aspects who functions as the opponent of the forces of death. Practices associated with Yamantaka are important in the Nyingma and Geluk schools.

Yamari (*Tib* Zhinje) see **Yamantaka**.

Yangdak Heruka (Skt *Shriheruka*) a wrathful meditational deity associated with buddha-mind, from the Nyingma cycle known as the **Drubpa Kabgye**.

Yeshe Tsogyel one of the foremost disciples and female consorts of Padmasambhava, formerly the wife of King Trisong Detsen.

Yutok Yonten Gonpo (1127-1203) renowned exponent of Tibetan medicine.

Zhamarpa the title given to the successive emanations of Zhamarpa Tokden Drakpa Senge (1283-1349), a student of Karmapa III. The monastery of Yangpachen in Damzhung county later became their principal seat.

1 **Samantabdhara** with **Samantabhadri** (Tib.*Kunzang Yabyum*)

2 **Vajradhara** (Tib. *Dorje Chang*)

3 Buddhas of the Five Families: **Vairocana** (Tib. *Nampar Nangze*)

4 Buddhas of the Five Families: **Aksobhya-Vajrasattva** (Tib. *Mikyopa Dorje Sempa*)

5 Buddhas of the Five Families: **Ratnasambhava** (Tib. *Rinchen Jungne*)

6 Buddhas of the Five Families: **Amitabha** (Tib. *Opame*)

7 Buddhas of the Five Families:
Amoghasiddhi (Tib. *Donyo Drupa*)

8 Buddhas of the Three Times:
Dipamkara (Tib. *Marmedze*)

9 Buddhas of the Three Times:
Shakyamuni (Tib. *Shakya Tupa*)

10 Buddhas of the Three Times:
Maitreya (Tib. *Jampa*)

11 Vipashyin (Tib. *Namzik*), first of
the Seven Generations of Past
Buddhas (*Sangye Rabdun*)

12 Bhaisajyaguru (Tib. *Sangye Menla*),
foremost of the Eight Medicine
Buddhas (*Menla Deshek Gye*)

ༀ ། ཤ་རིའི་བུ་མཆོག་རྟོགས་ཆེ། །

13 Shariputra (Tib. *Shari-bu*)

ༀ ། རྒྱུ་འཕྲུལ་ཆེན་པོ་མོའུ་དགལ་གྱི་བུ། །

14 Maudgalyayana (Tib. *Maudgal-bu*)

ༀ ། གནས་བརྟན་ཡན་ལག་འབྱུང་ལ་ཕྱག་འཚལ་ལོ། །

15 Sixteen Elders: **Angaja** (Tib. *Yanlak Jung*)

ༀ ། བཀོལ་གྱུ་འདོད་འཇོ་འཆལ་གནས་པ་བ་ཀུ་ལ། །

16 Sixteen Elders: **Bakula** (Tib. *Bakula*)

ༀ ། ཆེ་མཆོག་བརྟེན་འབྱུང་འཕགས་པ་མ་ཕམ་པ། །

17 Sixteen Elders: **Ajita** (Tib. *Mapampa*)

ༀ ། སྒྲ་གཅན་འཛིན་སྐད་ཅིག་གནས་པ་སྒྲ་གཅན་འཛིན། །

18 Sixteen Elders: **Rahula** (Tib. *Drachendzin*)

ཀྱི་ཕྱིང་བཞིན་འཁོན་ལོགས་འཕ་ལྱལ་བ་མ་མགན་བཟླགས།

19 Sixteen Elders: **Vanavasin** (Tib. *Naknane*)

ཀྱི་འཕྲིན་ལས་གནས་མ་རབ་བཟང་ལས་ལྱན་མཇ།

20 Sixteen Elders: **Cudapanthaka** (Tib. *Lamtrenten*)

ཀྱི་ལུལ་སྤྲུལ་པ་ན་དུན་འ་གྱུར་གནས་མ་དར་གྱུར་བལ།

21 Sixteen Elders: **Kalika** (Tib. *Duden*)

ཀྱི་དུ་སྤྱུར་མེས་ར་རྱ་རྡུ་རྡི་ཝ་ལ་བཟལ།

22 Sixteen Elders: **Bharadvaja** (Tib. *Bharadvadza*)

ཀྱི། ཝ་ནཏི་དུར་ར་ཆྱེ་རྡི་རྡི་མོ་མི་སྲུ།

23 Sixteen Elders: **Vajriputra** (Tib. *Dorje Moyibu*)

ཀྱི་ག་སྤྱུར་པྱོ་ལས་རྡོ་རྒྱལ་ལས་མཁས་རྒྱུ་ལས་འདུན་ཁ།

24 Sixteen Elders: **Panthaka** (Tib. *Lamten*)

ཀ།སུ་འབྲུག་འརྟེ་བ་བདེ་ལམགནལམ་བ་ཟང་པོ་མཆོད།

25 Sixteen Elders: **Bhadra** (Tib. *Zangpo*)

ཤ།འདོ་དྷུ་རྟེ་འདོས་གྱུ་ལས་འལུ་སྐྱེ་གྱི་ཤ།

26 Sixteen Elders: **Nagasena** (Tib. *Luyide*)

ཤ།མི་འགྱོང་སྐྱོ་གྱོ་གཏེར་སྟུན་ག་མེར་འདུ།

27 Sixteen Elders: **Kanakavatsa** (Tib. *Serbe'u*)

ཤ།ཚོན་གུ་ཁམ་ཚར་རྣམ་འཇེན་སྡོན་རྗེད་ནམམཚོ།

28 Sixteen Elders: **Gopaka** (Tib. *Beche*)

ཤ།འཛོག་ནས་མེ་འནི་འབ་གྱུག་སྐྱུན་རྣ་ར་ཚ་འབྲུག་ནམ།

29 Sixteen Elders: **Kanaka Bharadvaja** (Tib. *Serchen*)

ཤ།ལམ་དྲ་འཇིགས་གུ་ལ་འབ་གས་མ་མི་འདུན།

30 Sixteen Elders: **Abheda** (Tib. *Michedpa*)

31 Eight Bodhisattvas: **Manjushri** (Tib. *Jampal*)

32 Eight Bodhisattvas: **Vajrapani** (Tib. *Chakna Dorje*)

33 Eight Bodhisattvas: **Avalokiteshvara** (Tib. *Chenrezik*)

34 Eight Bodhisattvas: **Ksitigarbha** (Tib. *Sayi Nyingpo*)

35 Eight Bodhisattvas: **Nivaranaviskambhin** (Tib. *Dripa Namsel*)

36 Eight Bodhisattvas: **Akashagarbha** (Tib. *Namkei Nyingpo*)

37 Eight Bodhisattvas: **Maitreya** (Tib. *Jampa*)

38 Eight Bodhisattvas: **Samantabhadra** (Tib. *Kuntu Zangpo*)

39 Lords of the Three Enlightened Families: **Four-armed Avalokiteshvara** (Tib. *Chenrezik Chakzhipa*)

40 Lords of the Three Enlightened Families: **Manjughosa** (Tib. *Jampeyang*)

41 Lords of the Three Enlightened Families: **Vajrapani** (Tib. *Chakna Dorje*)

42 Aspects of Avalokiteshvara: **Eleven-faced/ Thousand-armed Mahakarunika** (*Zhal Chuchikpa*)

43 Aspects of Avalokiteshvara: **Simhanada** (Tib. *Senge Ngaro*)

44 Aspects of Avalokiteshvara: **Kharsapani** (Tib. *Kharsapani*)

45 Three Deities of Longevity: **Amitayus** (Tib. *Tsepame*)

46 Three Deities of Longevity: **White Tara** (Tib. *Dolkar*)

47 Three Deities of Longevity: **Vijaya** (Tib. *Namgyelma*)

48 Meditational Deities: **Prajnaparamita** (Tib. *Yum Chenmo*)

49 Meditational Deities: **Green Tara**
(*Droljang*)

50 Meditational Deities: **Sarvavid
Vairocana** (Tib. *Kunrik Nampar
Nangze*)

51 Meditational Deities: **Guhyasamaja**
(Tib. *Sangwa Dupa*)

52 Meditational Deities: **Vajrakumara**
(Tib. *Dorje Zhonu*)

53 Meditational Deities: **Kalacakra** (Tib.
Dungkor)

54 Meditational Deities: **Cakrasamvara**
(Tib. *Khorlo Dompa*)

55 Meditational Deities: **Vajravarahi** (Tib. *Dorje Pamo*)

56 Meditational Deities: **Hevajra** (Tib. *Kye Dorje*)

57 Protector Deities: **Four-armed Mahakala** (Tib. *Gonpo Chak Zhipa*)

58 Protector Deities: **Mahapandaka Mahakala** (Tib. *Gonpo Maning*)

59 Protector Deities: **Panjaranatha** (Tib. *Gonpo Gur*)

60 Protector Deities: **Shridevi** (Tib. *Palden Lhamo*)

ཨོཾ། ཁྱབ་འཇུག་ཆེན་གཟའ་ལ་ཕྱག་འཚལ་ལོ། །

ཨོཾ། རྡོ་རྗེ་གཡུ་སྒྲོན་མ།

61 Protector Deities: **Rahula** (Tib. *Za*)

62 Protector Deities: **Dorje Yudronma**

63 Five Aspects of Pehar: **Kuyi Gyelpo**

64 Five Aspects of Pehar: **Sung-gi Gyelpo**

65 Five Aspects of Pehar: **Tukyi Gyelpo**

66 Five Aspects of Pehar: **Yonten-gyi Gyelpo**

67 Five Aspects of Pehar: **Trinle Gyelpo**

68 Dharmaraja (Tib. *Damchen Chogyel*)

69 Six Ornaments and Two Supreme Ones: **Nagarjuna** (Tib. *Phakpa Ludrub*)

70 Six Ornaments and Two Supreme Ones: **Aryadeva** (Tib. *Phakpa Lha*)

71 Six Ornaments and Two Supreme Ones: **Asanga** (Tib. *Thok-me*)

72 Six Ornaments and Two Supreme Ones: **Vasubandhu** (Tib. *Yiknyen*)

73 Six Ornaments and Two Supreme Ones: **Dignaga** (Tib. *Choklang*)

74 Six Ornaments and Two Supreme Ones: **Dharmakirti** (*Chodrak*)

75 Six Ornaments and Two Supreme Ones: **Gunaprabha** (*Yonten-o*)

76 Six Ornaments and Two Supreme Ones: **Shakyapraha** (*Shakya-o*)

77 Three Early Tibetan Kings: **Nyatri Tsenpo**

78 Three Early Tibetan Kings: **Lhatotori Nyentsen**

79 Three Early Tibetan Kings: **Songtsen Gampo**

80 Tonmi Sambhota

81 Founders of the Nyingma School: **Padmakara** (Tib. *Pema Jungne*)

82 Founders of the Nyingma School: **Shantaraksita** (Tib. *Khenpo Bodhisattva/ Zhiwatso*)

83 Founders of the Nyingma School: **King Trisong Detsen**

84 Eight Manifestations of Padmasambhava: **Saroruhavajra** (*Tsokye Dorje Chang*)

ༀ། །པདྨ་རྒྱལ་པོ་བྱིན་རླབས་བརྒྱུད་པ་རྒྱལ། །

85 Eight Manifestations of Padmasambhava: **Pema Gyelpo**

ༀ། །ཤཱཀྱ་ཐུབ་པ་བདུད་བཞི་འདུལ་བ་མཛད་སྐུ་ལ་ཤེ། །

86 Eight Manifestations of Padmasambhava: **Shakya Senge**

ༀ། །བློ་ལྡན་མཆོག་སྲེད་མཁས་གྲུབ་དགེ་སྦྱོང་གོང་དང་། །

87 Eight Manifestations of Padmasambhava: **Loden Chokse**

ༀ། །པདྨ་འབྱུང་གནས་རིག་འཛིན་འདུས་པ་སྒྱུ། །

88 Eight Manifestations of Padmasambhava: **Padmasambhava**

ༀ། །ཉི་མ་འོད་ཟེར་གྲུབ་ཐོབ་ལུས་མེད་བདེ་ཆེན། །

89 Eight Manifestations of Padmasambhava: **Nyima Ozer**

ༀ། །སེང་གེ་སྒྲ་སྒྲོག་ཡེ་ཤེས་འཁོར་ལོ་འདྲེན་ཞིང་སྒྲོགས། །

90 Eight Manifestations of Padmasambhava: **Senge Dradrok**

འ། ཕྱི་ནུབ་ཉི་རནུ་ག་གོ་གནལ་ཚ་ན་རྡོ་རྗེ་སྒྲོལ་ལོ། །

91 Eight Manifestations of Padmasambhava: **Dorje Drolo**

འ། །ཁབ་མཆོད་རྒྱུ་ལྱིན་ཁ་ཤུ་ར་འཕགས་པ་ཉི་ལ་ལ། །

92 King Ralpachen

93 Founders of Kadampa School: **Atisha** (Tib. *Jowoje*)

འ། །སྨད་ག་ཉི་སྨྱ་པ་འབྲོམ་སྟོན་མཆོ། །

94 Founders of Kadampa School: **Dromtonpa**

འ།། ངུན་གྱི་བྱོང་དེནམ་རྡོ་རྗེ་ཚོན་པ་ལགས་སུ་ལེན་བ་ལགས། །

95 Founders of Kadampa School: **Ngok Lekpei Sherab**

འ། །སྒྲུལ་ཆེན་མི་བྱིད་མ་རྒུན་སྒྲུ་ས་མར་པ་འི་ལགས། །

96 Founders of Kagyu School: **Marpa**

ༀ་ཧཱུྃ་ཀཾ་ཀྱུ་དུ་ཛ་ཀྱེ་ངྒེ་སོཤ་ཚི་ཧེ། །

97 Founders of Kagyu School: **Milarepa**

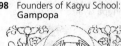

ༀ་ཀྱུ་ལ་མགུ་ས་བྱེ་རཚ་ཀྱ་མེ་ཚུ་ཧཾ་མོ་པ། །

98 Founders of Kagyu School: **Gampopa**

ༀ་ཧཱུྃ་བདུ་ཟོར་ནུ་གསུམ་ཀྱུ་ཚུ་ཙ་ཀཾ་པ། །

99 Founders of Kagyu School: **Karmapa I, Dusum Khyenpa**

ༀ་ཧཱུྃ་བདེ་ག་སུ་ས་གྱུ་བ་ཟེ་རྩུ་ས་ཀྱུ་ཙ་ཚ་ཀཾ་མོ། །

100 Founders of Kagyu School: **Phakmodrupa Dorje Gyelpo**

ༀ་ཧཱུྃ་འདི་ག་ཧཱུ་ན་གསུ་མ་མཁོ་ཨེ་རྒྱུ་བ་ཀྱེ་ཧཾ་ཟར་པ། །

101 Founders of Kagyu School: **Drigungpa Jikten Gonpo**

102 Founders of Kagyu School: **Taklung Tangpa Tashipel**

ཨ༔གཙང་པ་རྒྱ་རས་ཡེ་ཤེས་རྡོ་རྗེ་ལ་ན་མོ༔

103 Founders of Kagyu School: **Tsangpa Gya-re Yeshe Dorje**

༄༅༔རྗེ་རིན་པ་དང་བ་གཡེན་ལ༔ན་མོ༔

104 Five Founders of Sakya: **Kunga Nyingpo**

ཨ༔རྗེ་རི་སློབ་དཔོན་བསོད་ནམས་རྩེ་མོ་ལ༔

105 Five Founders of Sakya: **Sonam Tsemo**

༄༔རྗེ་རྒྱལ་ད་པ་གྲགས་པ༔རྒྱལ་མཚན་ལ་ན་མོ༔

106 Five Founders of Sakya: **Drakpa Gyeltsen**

ཨ༔རྗེ་བ་ས་ཕུ་ན་ཆེ་ན་ཆོ་ལ་ན་མ༔

107 Five Founders of Sakya: **Sakya Pandita**

༄༔རྗེ་འགྲོ་མགོན་ཆོས་རྒྱལ་འཕགས་པ་ལ་ན་མོ་ན་མཆོ་དན་༔

108 Five Founders of Sakya: **Drogon Chogyel Phakpa**

ཨ ། ཐམས་ཅད་མཁྱེན་པ་བུ་སྟོན་རིན་ཆེན་གྲུབ་པ། །

109 Buton Rinchen Drub

ཨ༑གྲུབ་ཆེན་ཤེས་རབ་པ་ཤར་པ་རྩ་ཕྱགས་མཚན་ཉིན་པ་ཕྲ།

110 Dolpopa Sherab Gyeltsen

ཨ ། ཀློང་ཆེན་རབ་འབྱམས་ཟུག་པ་དྲི་མེད་འོད་ཟེར་པ། །

111 Longchen Rabjampa

ཨ། །ཨ་ཆེ་མེ་འགྲུབ་པ་འབི་དངས་ཕྱུག་གཏན་རྒྱོ་གོ་པ།།

112 Tangtong Gyelpo

ཨ། ། དཔལ་ལྡན་བླ་མ་བཙུན་པ་རྗེ་ཙོང་ཁ་པ་འཛིན་དུ་གྱུ། །

113 Founders of Gelukpa School:
Tsongkhapa

ཨཱུ།།འཇམ་དམགས་ཀུན་དགའ་རྒྱལ་མཚན་དང་དར་མ་རིན་ཆེན་ཞལ་དཀས།།

114 Founders of Gelukpa School:
Gyeltsab Darma Rinchen

ཿ།ཨོཾ་མཁས་གྲུབ་རྗེ་དཔལ་བཟང་དགེ་ལེགས་དཔལ་བཟང་པོ།།

115 Founders of Gelukpa School: **Khedrubje Gelekpel**

ཿ།།བསྭ་སྒྲོལ་བྱོན་པ་བསོད་ནམས་རྒྱ་མཚོ་ཞེས་ཨལ་ཚའི།།

116 Masters of the Gelukpa Tradition: **Dalai Lama III Sonam Gyatso**

ཿ།བློ་བཟང་ཆོས་ཀྱི་རྒྱལ་མཚན་དཔལ་བཟང་པོར་འདུད་ལ་བཞད།།

117 Panchen Lama IV, **Lobzang Chogyen**

ཿ།།ངག་དབང་བློ་བཟང་རྒྱ་མཚོའི་སྐུ།།

118 Dalai Lama V, **Ngawang Lobzang Gyatso**

ཿ།སྡེ་སྲིད་སངས་རྒྱས་རྒྱ་མཚོའི་སྐུ་རིའི།།

119 Desi Sangye Gyatso

ཿ།།རིག་འཛིན་ཚངས་དབྱངས་རྒྱ་མཚོ་ཡུང་དྲུང་རྒྱལ་མོ་ཚོ།།

120 Dalai Lama VI, **Rigdzin Tsangyang Gyatso**

ཨོཾ་སྭ་སྟི། སྦྱིན་པ་རྒྱ་མཚོ་བློ་བཟང་།

121 Dalai Lama XIII, Tubten Gyatso

ཨོཾ་སྭ་སྟི། བསྟན་འཛིན་རྒྱ་མཚོ་ཞེས་བྱ།

122 Dalai Lama XIV, Tendzin Gyatso

123 Dhritarastra, Guardian King of the East

124 Virudhaka, Guardian King of the South

125 Virupaksa, Guardian King of the West

126 Vaishravana, Guardian King of the North

HISTORY

CONTENTS

Legend

The Tibetan Buddhist historical work known as the *Mani Kabum* mentions both the dehydration of the Tibetan lakelands and the legendary ape-like origins of the Tibetan race. The first Tibetans are said to have been the offspring of a monkey emanation of Avalokiteshvara (the patron deity of Tibet) – representing compassion and sensitivity – who mated with an ogress of the rocks – symbolizing the harshness of the Tibetan environment – at Zodang Gongpori Cave above Tsetang in S Tibet. They gave birth to six children, indicative of six types of sentient being, which later multiplied to 400, divided into four large tribes and two smaller groups. Gradually the monkeys evolved into humans, displaying both their paternal compassion and maternal aggression.

Other Bonpo (pre-Buddhist) legends, found in the *Lang Poti Seru*, trace the origin of the early tribes not to the monkey descendants of Avalokiteshvara, but to sub-human or primitive groups. Here, O-de Gung-gyel intermarries with various types of spirit – a *lhamo*, a *nyenmo*, a *mumo*, and a *lumo*, thereby giving birth to the Tibetan kings, demons, and human beings.

Meanwhile, there are other legends referring to the 10 groups of primeval non-human beings who held sway over Tibet prior to the dominion of the Tibetan monkey-tribes. Appearing in succession these were: Nojin Nagpo of Zangyul Gyen-me (who used bows and arrows), Dud of Dudyul Kharak Rong-gu (using battle axes), Sin of Sinpo Nagpo Guyul (using animal bone slings and catapults), Lha of Lhayul Gungtang (using sharp swords), Mu-gyel (using lassoes with hooks and black magic rituals), canyon-dwelling Dre (using bolos with rocks attached), the Masang brothers of Bod (using armour and shields), the Lu of Bo-kham Ling-gu (using metamorphosis), the Gyelpo of Dempotse, and the 18 classes of bewitcher demons or Gongpo (using guile but squandering good fortune). Subsequently, the monkey descendents of Zodang Gongpori emerged, perhaps indicating a shift from the primitive human culture of the Old Stone Age to a more advanced neolithic culture.

Archaeology

There has been no systematic archaeological survey of the Tibetan plateau, but the evidence that does emerge from the disparate excavated sites suggests that Tibet was inhabited during the Old Stone Age (2 mya-10,000 ya). Crude pebble choppers have been unearthed at Kukushili, flake tools at Dingri, and stone scrapers, knives, drills, and axes at

Lake Xiaochaili in the Tsaidam – the last dated to 33,000 BC. There are also primitive cave and 'nest' dwellings in Kongpo, Powo, Lhartse, Yamdrok, and the Jangtang Plateau.

A number of finely chipped blades from the Middle Stone Age (10,000 ya) have been excavated at Serling Lake, Nyalam, Chamdo and Nakchu, indicating the prevalence of a hunting culture. Nonetheless, there are also indications of early farming communities in eastern areas: at the neolithic settlement of **Go-ru** N of Chamdo, dated 3,500 BC, where the remains of 2-storey dwellings partitioned, as now, into human habitation upstairs and animal barns downstairs, have been discovered, along with stone artefacts, pottery and bone needles. Similar sites containing stone artefacts and pottery shards have been located in Nyangtri (disc 1958/1975), and above all in Amdo, where the authorities of Qinghai and Gansu have supported a number of archaeological digs. Among them are the farming villages of Ma-chia-yao and Pan-shan in Cho-ne, respectively dated 3,000 BC and 2,500 BC; the village of Ma-ch'ang to the E of Lake Kokonor dated 2,000 BC; and the sites in the Sang-chu and Lu-chu valleys dated 1,850 BC. Evidence suggests that the yak became a domesticated animal around 2,500 BC and that there was an early interdependence of the hunting, no-madic and farming lifestyles.

Megalithic sites

Megaliths, generally dated 3,000-1,000 BC, have been discovered at Reting, Sakya, Shab Geding, Zhide Khar, Chi'u near Lake Manasarovar, and Dangra Lake in the Jangtang. Sometimes these stones have an obvious formation: at Pang-gong Lake in Far-west Tibet there are 18 parallel rows of standing stones with circles at end of each row; while at Saga is a large grey stone slab sur-rounded by pillars of white quartz. Un-usually shaped and coloured stones are found also in Kongpo, Powo, and Tsari.

The early Tibetan Clans

Tibetan historians refer to either four or six distinct Tibetan clans, which claimed descent from the legendary monkey and ogress. The former comprise the Se clan, the Mu clan, the Dong clan, and the Tong clan (collectively known as the Ruchen Zhi). Sometimes, the Ba and Da clans are added to these. As the power of the 'non-human' rulers declined, the indigenous tribes took control of the land, eventually forming 12 kingdoms and 40 principalities. The 12 kingdoms were: Chimyul Drushul, Zhangzhung, Nyangdo Chongkar, Nubyul Lingu, Nyangro Shambo, Gyiri Jongdon, Ngamsho Tranar, Olphu Pangkhar, Simrong Lamogong, Kongyul Drena, Nyangyul Namsum, and Dakyul Druzhi. Only three of the 40 principalities are now known: Drokmo Namsum, Gyemo Yuldruk, and Semo Druzhi. These kingdoms and principalities are reckoned to have existed from the period before the first king of the Yarlung Dynasty (3rd/4th BC), and some, notably Zhangzhung in Far-west Tibet, maintained their inde-pendence from around 3,000 BC (according to Bonpo sources) until their absorption by Songtsen Gampo in the 7th century.

Some sources associate the four original clans with four important Tibetan cultures of antiquity: the Dong with that of Minyak (Far-east Tibet and Ningxia), the Tong with Sumpa (Jangtang), the Mu with Zhangzhung (Far-west Tibet), and the Se with Azha (Lake Kokonor). Among the aristocratic family names of Tibet, those of Lang, Gar, Khyungpo, and Khon are said to have been descend-ents of the Se clan. Illustrious descend-ents of this clan therefore include Amnye Jangchub Drekhol, who was the teacher of the epic warrior Ling Gesar, the ruling houses of Sakya and Phakmo-dru, Gar Tongtsen (the minister of Songtsen Gampo) and the Derge royal family, the great yogin Milarepa and Khungpo Neljor. By contrast, the Ba family, which assumed important military and civil positions during the period of the Yarlung Dynasty, claims descent from the Dong clan. Its members include Marpa, Phakmodrupa and Drigungpa who were all seminal figures in the development of the Kagyu school of Buddhism. The Kyura and Nyura families of Driigung and Mindroling respectively claim descent from the Tong clan, as do the Achakdru of Golok. Lastly, the ruling house of Zhangzhung in Far-west Tibet claimed descent from the Mu clan, as attested in important Bonpo historical works.

Qiang Tribes

Chinese annals suggest that the Qiang or Ti tribes inhabiting the western periphery of the Chinese Empire were of Tibetan extraction. These tribes were established by 1,500 BC W of the Shang settlements near Chang-an (modern Xi'an), from where they would raid the farming communities. By 500 BC the Qiang were organizing themselves into agricultural and cattle-rearing societies, gradually developing into 150 sub-tribes, along the easternmost borderlands of the Tibetan plateau. They are said to have constituted a significant percentage of the region's population during the Zhou and Qin dynasties. Around the 5th century (CE) the Qiang tribe known as the Tang-hsiang (identified with the Dong clan) appear to have subdivided into western and northern groups, which Chinese sources identify respectively with the Tibetan (Ch T'u-fan) tribes (dominant from the 7th century) and the Tanguts (dominant in Xixia during the 11th century). Remnants of the Qiang tribes are found today around Maowen, and in those parts of E

Tibet where the so-called Qiangic languages are spoken. Some sources suggest that it was an intermingling of Qiang tribes with the Yueh-chih and Hsiung-nu in the NE (c 175-115 BC) which gave rise to the tall aqualine Tibetans of the NE, who are distinct from the short Mongoloid type of western and southern origin.

The Yarlung Dynasty

The chronology of early Tibet is not easily determined with any degree of certainty. There are sources suggesting that by 781 BC the aforementioned primitive groups had been supplanted by the descendents of the four clans, and that until 247 BC the 12 kingdoms and 40 principalities formed by those clans held sway alone.

Seven Heavenly Kings called Tri

The first king of the Yarlung Dnasty, Nyatri Tsenpo (1) is said to have had divine origin and to have been immortal – ascending to the heavens on a sky-cord (*mu*) at the appointed time for his passing. Other sources suggest an Indian origin for the royal family – the lord Rupati who fled N India during the Pandava wars, and who is said to derive from the mountain-dwelling Shakya clan, or the Licchavi clan of Nepal – connecting him with the family line of Shakyamuni Buddha. Descending on **Mt Lhari Yangto** in Kongpo, he proceeded to **Mt Lhari Rolpa** in Yarlung around 247 BC (the time of Ashoka) and thence to **Tsen-tang Gozhi** where he encountered the local Tibetan tribes who made him their king. Carried shoulder-high, he was bourne to the site of the **Yumbu Lagang** palace, which he himself had constructed. Utilizing magical weaponry and powers, Nyatri Tsenpo defeated the shaman Oyong Gyelwa of Sumpa and the ruler of Nub.

The first seven kings of this Yarlung Dynasty, circa 247-100 BC, including

Nyatri Tsenpo himself, are known as the 'seven heavenly kings called Tri', in that they all passed away in the celestial manner, without the need for tombs. Nyatri's successors were: Mutri (2), Dingtri (3), Sotri (4), Mertri (5), Daktri (6), and Sibtri (7). Towards the end of this period, the Silk Rd was opened to the N of Tibet.

Two Celestial Kings called Teng

Sibtri's son, Drigum Tsenpo (8), is said to have fallen under the influence of the Iranian shaman Azha of Gurnavatra; who persuaded the king to adopt the fatalist line suggested by his own name 'sword-slain'. Deceived by his royal horse keeper Longam, the king accidentally cuts his own sky-cord in a contest of swordsmanship. Bereft of his divine powers the king is then killed by Longam's arrow, and thus has the dubious distinction of becoming the first mortal king of the Yarlung Dynasty. The king's three sons, Chatri, Nyatri and Shatri fled to the Powo area of SE Tibet, while the king's body was sent downstream to Kongpo in a copper casket, and Longam usurped the throne. Chatri later regained the throne in battle with Longam and adopted the name Pude Gungyel (9), after which he built the **Chingwa Taktse Castle** in Chongye.

Pude Gyungyel's ministers, including his own nephew Rulakye who had helped him regain the throne, are accredited with the introduction of charcoal, smelting, metalwork, bridge-building, and agriculture. The rituals of the Bonpo shamans of Zhangzhung also gained prominence during this period on account of their elaborate funerary rites. Henceforth, the mortal kings of Tibet would be buried in locations such as the **Chongye tombs**. Drigum Tsenpo and his son Pude Gungyel, collectively known as the 'two celestial kings called Teng', reigned approximately from 100 BC-50 BC, making them contemporaries of Han Wu Ti (140-85 BC).

Six Earthly Kings called Lek

The six 'earthly kings called Lek' like their predecessors mortal or otherwise, continued to marry into 'non-human' or rarified aristocratic lines only. Pude Gungyel's son Esho Lek (10) was the first in this line, followed by his son, Desho Lek (11), the latter's son Tisho Lek (12); and so on through Gongru Lek (13), Drongzher Lek (14), and Isho Lek (15). Their castles were all located in and around Chongye Taktse; and their tombs were located on adjacent rocky peaks or foothills. During this period (c 50 BC-100 CE) farm animals were domesticated, and irrigation and taxation developed.

Eight Middle Kings called De

The eight 'middle kings called De' (c 100-300 AD) are little known, apart from their burial sites at river banks. They were: Za Namzin De (16), De Trulnam Zhungtsen (17), Senolnam De (18), Senolpo De (19), De Nolnam (20), De Nolpo (21), De Gyelpo (22), and De Tringtsen (23). Towards the end of this period, Tibetan trade prospered with the neighbouring Shu Han Dynasty (221-263 AD), which had its capital at Chengdu. Large trade marts were established in the Kokonor region, and Tibetan horses were highly valued.

Five Linking Kings called Tsen

The 'five linking kings called Tsen' are significant in that it was during their reigns (c 300-493 AD) that the kings of Tibet first married among their Tibetan subjects. The ancient title lha-se ('divine prince') was now replaced with the title tsenpo ('king'/'potentate'). The first in this line was Tore Longtsen (24); followed by Trhitsun Nam (25), Trhidra Pungtsen (26), Trhi Tokje Toktsen (27), and Lhatotori Nyentsen (28). The important ministers during this period hailed from the Tonmi, Nub and Gar clans, and the rich heritage of Tibetan

TAMING THE OGRESS: THE GEOMANTIC TEMPLES OF TIBET

When the Tang princess Wengcheng arrived in Tibet, she introduced Chinese divination texts including the so-called Portang scrolls. According to the ancient Chinese model of government, spheres of influence were based on six concentric zones, namely: an imperial centre, a royal domain zone, a princes' domain, a pacification zone, a zone of allied barbarians, and a zone of cultureless savagery. The Tibetan geomantic temples were laid out according to four such zones, corresponding to the imperial centre, the royal domain zone, the pacification zone, and that of the allied barbarians. Just as China was conceived of as a supine turtle, so the Tibetan terrain was seen as a supine ogress or demoness, and geomantic temples were to be constructed at focal points on her body: the **Jokhang** temple at the heart, the four 'district controlling' temples (**runon**) on her shoulders and hips, the four 'border taming' temples (**tadul**) on her elbows and knees, and the four 'further taming' temples (**yangdul**) on her hands and feet.

According to literary sources such as the *Mani Kabum*, Buton, Longdol Lama, and Drukpa Pekar, the four 'district controlling' temples are: **Tradruk** (left shoulder), **Katsel** (right shoulder), **Yeru Tsangdram** (right hip), and **Rulak Drompagyang** (left hip). These same authors list the four 'border taming' temples as: **Khomting** (left elbow), **Buchu** (right elbow), **Jang Traduntse** (near Saga, right knee); and **Mon Bumtang** (left knee); while the four further taming temples are listed as: **Jang Tsangpa Lungnon** (left hand), **Den Langtang Dronma** (right hand), **Mangyul Jamtrin** (right foot), and **Paro Kyerchu** (left foot).

Other authors such as Sakya Sonam Gyeltsen, Pawo Tsuklag and Dalai Lama V list the 'district controlling' temples as: **Langtang Dronma, Kyerchu, Tselrik Sherab Dronma**, and **Jang Tsangpa Lungnon**; the four 'border taming' temples as: **Uru Katsel, Lhodrak Khomthing, Den Langtang Dronma**, and **Yeru Tsangtram**; and the four 'further taming' temples as: **Lhodrak Khomting, Kongpo Buchu, Mangyul Jamtrin**, and **Jang Traduntse**. These are the central temples among the 108 reputedly built in this period throughout Tibet.

folklore was established through the activities of the Bonpo priests known as Shen, the bards who narrated epic tales (*drung*), and singers of enigmatic riddles (*de'u*).

During the reign of the last of these kings, Lhatotori Nyentsen (374-493), Buddhism was introduced to Tibet. According to legend, in 433 certain Buddhist sutras including the *Karandavyuha* (dedicated to Tibet's patron deity Avalokiteshvara) landed on the palace roof at Yumbu Lagang, along with a mould engraving of the six-syllabled mantra of Avalokiteshvara and other sacred objects, but these were given the name '**awesome secret**' because no-one could understand their meaning. Lhatotori was rejuvenated and lived to the ripe old age of 120. His tomb is said to be at Dartang near the Chongye River, though others say he vanished into space.

More sober historians, such as Nelpa Pandita, assert that these texts were brought to Tibet by Buddharaksita and Tilise of Khotan. It appears from this and other sources, such as Fa-hien's records of Buddhism in Central Asia (dated 400 AD), that Lhatotori's discovery of Buddhism was predated by Buddhist contacts in E Tibet, where the Tibetan P'u (Fu) family formed the ruling house during the Earlier Chin Dy-

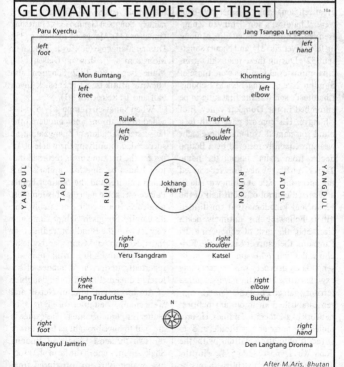

POSITION OF GEOMANTIC TEMPLES [10]

Sketch map: not to scale

TIBET

NEPAL

BHUTAN

N

* Jokhang (Lhasa)
Runon
1. Tradruk
2. Katsel
3. Yeru Tsangdram
4. Rulak

Tadul
5. Buchu
6. Khomting
7. Mon Bumtang
8. Jang Traduntse

Yangdul
9. Den Langtang Dronma
10. Jang Tsangpa Lungnon
11. Mangyul Jamtrin
12. Paru Kyerchu

GEOMANTIC TEMPLES OF TIBET [10a]

Paru Kyerchu

left foot

Jang Tsangpa Lungnon

left hand

Mon Bumtang

left knee

Khomting

left elbow

Rulak

left hip

Tradruk

left shoulder

Jokhang
heart

YANGDUL

TADUL

RUNON

RUNON

TADUL

YANGDUL

right hip

right shoulder

Yeru Tsangdram

Katsel

right knee

right elbow

Jang Traduntse

Buchu

N

right foot

right hand

Mangyul Jamtrin

Den Langtang Dronma

After M. Aris, Bhutan

nasty (351-394). Later, the seccasionist Later Chin Dynasty (384-417), also Tibetan, offered patronage to the renowned Buddhist scholar Kumarajiva, and its rulers were well acquainted with Buddhism.

Meantime, an administrator of the P'u family named Lu Kuang was sent to Xinjiang where he ruled over a mixed Tibetan and Turkic population (T'u yu-hun), and founded the Later Liang Dynasty (386-403) on the trade routes to the W.

The kings of this period were contemporaries of the Toba Wei emperors in China and the Gupta Empire in India.

Four Ancestors of the Religious Kings

The four immediate ancestors of the great religious kings of Tibet (493-630) were: Lhatotori's son Trhinyen Zungtsen (29), Drong Nyendeu (30), Mulong or Takri Nyenzik (31), and Namri Songtsen (32). During these reigns the principal ministerial families were those of Shudpu, Nyen, Nyang, Be, and Tsepong. Lhatotori's son was the first king to be entombed in the **Dongkar** valley, E of Chongye. His consort gave birth to a blind son named Mulong, whose sight was subsequently restored by a Bonpo doctor from Azha. Taking the name Takri Nyenzik, the new king reoccupied the ancestral castle at Chingwa Taktse, and seized control of about half of the 12 ancient kingdoms that constituted Tibet. Following his untimely death circa 560, the task of conquering Tri Pangsum, the usurper king of the **Kyichu** valley, fell to his son Namri Songtsen. The usurper was successfully expelled to the N and the newly acquired territory named **Phenyul**. Namri Songtsen established an important political network of aristocratic families. He promoted the horse and salt trade; and secured diplomatic relations with the Toba Wei Dynasty (386-534), with the Turkish Khanates established by the

sons of Bumin Khagan in Mongolia and Dzungaria, and finally with the Sui Dynasty which reunified China in 589. Following the Sui Emperor's annihilation of the T'u yu-un (c 600), the Tibetans of the Yarlung Dynasty (known in Chinese as T'u-fan) expanded into N Tibet to fill the vacuum. In 630, the king was poisoned by discontented nobles.

The Tibetan Empire and the Nine Religious Kings

It is not surprising that the unification of Tibet and its imperial expansion should have coincided with the adoption of Buddhism as the dominant civilizing influence in Tibetan life. This is the age of the nine great religious kings (630-836), who have been the most powerful political figures in the whole course of Tibetan history, namely: Songtsen Gampo (33), Gungsong Gungtsen (34), Mangsong Mangtsen (35), Dusong Mangpoje (36), Tride Tsukten or Me'agtsom (37), Trisong Detsen (38), Mune Tsepo (39); Tride Songtsen, also known as Mutik Tsenpo or Senalek Jinyon (40), and Tri Relpachen (41).

When Songtsen Gampo (617-650) acceded to the throne and conquered the far-western kingdom of Zhangzhung, he succeeeded in unifying the whole of Tibet for the fist time in its recorded history. **Lhasa** became the capital of this grand empire, and the original **Potala Palace** was constructed as his foremost residence. In the course of establishing his empire, Songtsen Gampo came into contact with the Buddhist traditions of India, Khotan, and China, and quickly immersed himself in spiritual pursuits, reportedly under the influence of his foreign queens Bhrikuti, the daughter of Amshuvarman, king of Nepal; and Wengcheng, daughter of Tang Taitsung, Emperor of China. These queens are said to have brought as their dowry the two foremost images of Buddha Shakyamuni – one in the form of Aksobhya, which Bhrikuti introduced from

Nepal and one in the bodhisattva form known as Jowo Rinpoche, which was introduced from China.

The king constructed a series of geomantic temples at important power-places across the length and breadth of the land, and these are revered as the earliest Buddhist temples of Tibet. He sent his able minister Tonmi Sambhota to India where the Uchen (capital letter) script was developed from an Indian prototype to represent the Tibetan language. In later years, the king abdicated in favour first of his son and later in favour of his grandson; passing his final years in spiritual retreat. His tomb is the celebrated **Banso Marpo** in the Chongye valley (although other traditions claim him to have been interred in the Jokhang).

The years immediately following Songtsen Gampo's unification of Tibet saw engagement in wide-ranging military campaigns. From 665-692 the Yarlung kings controlled the Central Asian oases and cities, and this Tibetan influence is reflected in the manuscripts and paintings preserved in the **Dunhuang** caves, which have been dated 650-747. Conflict with Tang China began in 670 and by 680 the Tibetan army had advanced as far SE as the **Nan-chao** Kingdom (modern Dali in Yunnan province). King Tride Tsukten (b 704) constructed a number of Buddhist shrines, including the temple of **Kachu**, and extended his imperial influence westwards into **Brusha** (the Burushaski region of Gilgit) by 737.

In 730, Tride Tsukten's Chinese consort Jincheng gave birth to a son – Trisong Detsen, perhaps the greatest of all the Tibetan kings, in whose reign Buddhism was formally established as the state religion. In the early years of his reign Trisong Detsen sent his armies against Tang China, eventually occupying the imperial capital **Xi'an** in 763. The **Zhol pillar** was erected at Lhasa to commemorate this event. Increasingly,

the king sought to promote Buddhism, and he invited the Indian preceptor Shantaraksita to found the country's first monastery at **Samye**. Owing to obstacles instigated by hostile non-Buddhist forces, the king accepted Shantaraksita's advice and invited Padmasambhava, the foremost exponent of the tantras and the Dzogchen meditative tradition in India to participate in the establishing of Buddhism. Padmasambhava bound the hostile demons of Tibet under an oath of allegiance to Buddhism, enabling the monastery's construction to be completed and the first monks to be ordained.

The king then instituted a methodical translation programme for the rendering of Sanskrit and Chinese Buddhist texts in Tibet. Intelligent children were sent to India to be trained as translators, and their prolific work ranks among the greatest literary endeavours of all time. Meanwhile Padmasambhava, Vimalamitra, and other accomplished masters of the Indian tantra traditions imparted their meditative instructions and lineages to the custodianship of their Tibetan disciples in remote but spectacularly located mountain caves, **Chimpu, Sheldrak, Kharchu, Drak Yangdzong, Monka Senge Dzong**, and so forth. In this way their Tibetan followers were brought to spiritual maturity and attained the highest realizations concerning the nature of mind and the nature of reality. Chinese Buddhist influence receded to some extent in the aftermath of the great debate held at Samye in 792 between Kamalasila of the Indian tradition and Hoshang Mo-ho-yen of the Chinese tradition.

The establishment of Buddhism as the state religion of Tibet, commemorated by an inscribed pillar at the entrance to Samye Monastery, was a threshold of enormous significance, in that the demilitarization of Tibet can be be traced back to that event. The great empire forged by the religious kings gradually began to recede. In 781, Dunhuang was lost, and following the king's death, conflict with China resumed.

His successors all acted as lavish patrons of Buddhism, sometimes at the expense of the older Bon tradition and the status of Tibet's ancient aristocratic families. This trend reached its zenith during the reign of Tri Relpachen (r 816-836), who had each monk supported by seven households of his subjects. Among Tri Relpachen's many achievements, the most important one politically is the peace treaty agreed with China in 823; which clearly defined the Sino-Tibetan border at **Chorten Karpo** in the Sang-chu valley of Amdo. Obelisks were erected there and in Lhasa to commemorate this momentous event, the one in Lhasa surviving intact until today. The strong Buddhist sympathies of the king attracted an inevitable backlash on the past of disgruntled Bonpo and aristocratic groups. This resulted in his assassination at the hands of his elder brother, the apostate Langdarma Udumtsen; and with this act, the period of the great religious kings came to an abrupt end.

Persecution of Buddhism and disintegration of Empire

When Langdarma (42) came to power following the assassination of his brother, the Bonpo suddenly found themselves once more in the ascendancy. Old scores against the Buddhists were settled and a widespread persecution ensued. The monasteries and temples were desecrated or closed down and Buddhist practice was driven underground. Only practitioners of the tantras survived in Central Tibet, whether in their remote mountain retreats or by living their lives incognito in small village communities. The monastic tradition could only survive in the remote NE of Amdo, where at **Dentik** and **Achung Namdzong**, three far-sighted monks

transmitted the Vinaya lineage to Lachen Gongpa Rabsel, ensuring that the lineage of monastic ordination would continue unbroken for the benefit of posterity.

Langdarma's severe persecution of Buddhism was itself brought to an abrupt end in 841/2, when he was assassinated by the Buddhist master Lhalung Pelgyi Dorje, a black-hatted and black-clothed figure, who shot the apostate king with an arrow and fled in disguise, reversing his clothes to reveal their white lining! This act is commemorated in the famous black hat dance (*shanak*). Lhalung Pelgyi Dorje eventually reached the safety of **Achung Namdzong** in Amdo where he remained in penance for the rest of his life.

The succession to the throne was then disputed by Langdarma's two sons, Tride Yumten, the son of his senior consort, and Namde Osung, the son of his junior consort. Osung gained control of Lhasa while Yumten moved to Yarlung, and this event marked the beginning of the disintegration of the royal dynasty and the corresponding disintegration of Tibet's political unity (869). The line of 42 kings which began with Nyatri Tsenpo had come to an end, and Tibet left without central authority for over 300 years.

The later diffusion of Buddhism

While anarchy prevailed in much of Central Tibet, the kingdoms of **Tsongkha** (c 900-1100) and **Xixia** (990-1227) maintained the Buddhist heritage in the remote NE parts of Amdo and the adjacent province of Ningxia. Around 953 or 978 Lu-me and his fellow monks from Utsang brought the monastic ordination back from Amdo to Central Tibet, having received it from Lachen Gongpa Rabsel. They embarked upon an extensive temple building programme in the Kyi-chu and

Brahmaputra valleys, which laid the basis for the later diffusion of Buddhism.

Further W, descendents of the royal family had effectively maintained the traditional royal sponsorship of Buddhism. The kingdom of **Gu-ge** had been established on trade routes with N and NW India along the canyons of the upper Sutlej River. One of the most important kings Lha Lama Yeshe-o and his nephew Lha Lama Jangchub-o were the patrons of both Rinchen Zangpo (958-1055), the great translator of the later diffusion, and Atisha (982-1054), the renowned Bengali Buddhist master. He reinforced the ethical discipline of the gradual path to enlightenment and its compassionate ideals, rather than the practices of the tantras, which apparently had been dangerously misapplied by some corrupt practitioners.

During this period, Tibetan translators once again began travelling to India to study Sanskrit and receive teachings in the various aspects of the Indian Buddhist tradition. The texts which they brought back to Tibet were naturally those in vogue in 11th century India, in contrast to those previously introduced during the 8th century by Padmasambhava and his followers. Consequently a distinction was recognized between the 'old translations' of the early period and the 'new translations' of the later period. Among this new wave of translators were Rinchen Zangpo and Ngok Lotsawa who represented the **Kadampa** tradition (associated with Atisha), Drokmi Lotsawa (992-1074) who represented the **Sakyapa** tradition (of Gayadhara and Virupa), and Marpa Lotsawa (1012-97) who represented the **Kagyupa** tradition (of Tilopa and Naropa). By contrast the practitioners of the earlier teachings became known as the **Nyingmapa**, and among them, during this period was the outstanding translator Rongzom Pandita (11th century).

The foundation of large temples and monasteries soon followed: **Zhalu** in 1040, **Reting** in 1054; **Sakya** in 1073,

Ukpalung in the 11th century, **Katok** in 1159, and the Kagyu monasteries of **Daklha Gampo, Kampo Nenang, Karma Gon, Tsurphu, Densatil, Drigung, Taklung,** and **Ralung** – all in the 12th century.

The Sakyapa Administration (1235-1349)

A new sense of militancy was introduced into Tibetan life during the 13th century when, in common with most peoples of Asia, the Tibetans had to come to terms with the phenomenal rise to power of the Mongols who, unified by Genghiz Qan (r 1189-1227) swept across Asia, combining great horsemanship and mobility with astute strategy. In 1206 the Mongols reached Tibet, and suzerainty was offered to **Sakya**. In order to avoid the fate of Xixia, the Tangut Kingdom, which was annihilated in 1227, the Tibetans decided to accommodate themselves to Mongol aspirations by filling a unique role – that of spiritual advisors seeking imperial patronage. Consequently, after the Mongol general Dorta Nakpo had sacked **Reting** and other northern monasteries in 1240, Sakya Pandita (1182-1251) proceeded to **Lake Kokonor** in 1244 to meet Guyug and Godan, the son and grandson of Genghiz Qan, accompanied by his nephew, Drogon Chogyel Phakpa (1235-80). A 'patron-priest relationship' was established and Goden transferred the hegemony of Utsang to Sakya Pandita in 1249.

Later, in 1253, Prince Qubilai once again offered this hegemony to his new advisor, Drogon Chogyel Phakpa. Central Tibet (Utsang) was divided into four horns (*ru*) and 13 myriarchies (*trikhor*). Among these, the horn of **Uru** was centred at **Ramoche** in Lhasa with Olka Shukpa Pundun to the E, Mala Lagyu to the S, Zhu Nyemo to the W, and Drakyi Langma Gurpub to the N, including the myriarchies of Gyama, Drigung, and Shalpa. The horn of **Yoru** was centred at

Tradruk, with Kongpo Drena in the E, Shawuk Tago in the S, Kharak Gangtse in the W, and Mala gyu in the N, including the myriarchies of Tangpoche, Pangpoche, Phakdru, and Yabzang. The horn of **Yeru** in Tsang was centred on **Namling** in Shang, with Drakyi Langma Gurpub in the E, Nyangang Yagpo'i Na in the S, Jemalagu in the W, and Smriti Chunak in the N, including the myriarchies of Chumik, Shang, and Zhalu. Lastly, the horn of **Rulak** was centred in **Drekyi Durwana**, with Jamnatra in the E, Belpo Langna in the S, Kem Yagmik in the W, and Jema Langon in the N, including the myriarchies of S Lhato, N Lhato, and Gurmo. Although the Mongols sought to govern Tibet and actually held a census there in 1268 and 1287, power remained effectively in the hands of the Sakyapas.

Drogon Chogyel Phakpa thus became the most powerful Tibetan ruler since the assassination of Tri Relpachen in 836. Although the tribal confederations and kingdoms of E Tibet maintained a degree of independence, the power of Sakya even extended deeply into Kham and Amdo. When Qubilai Qan subsequently invaded China and established the Yuan Dynasty (1260-1368), Phakpa was given the rank of Tishri, imperial preceptor, and remained in **Dadu**, the imperial capital of Qubilai Qan (Beijing), where he devised a script for the Mongolian language, based on the Tibetan script. Executive decisions on the ground were made by the Ponchen, or administrator, who was appointed to head the 13 myriarchies. Ponchen Shakya Zangpo (r 1265-68) and Ponchen Kunga Zangpo (r 1268-80) held this office during the lifetime of Phakpa; and following the latter's death in 1280, Dharmapala (r 1280-87) was appointed as imperial preceptor and Shang Tsun as Ponchen. Later, following the lifetime of the imperial preceptor Danyi Zangpo Pal (r 1305-22), the ruling house of Sakya split into four branches,

two of which – the Phuntsok Palace and the Dolma Palace, took turns at holding supreme authority in Tibet. Actual power was however exercised by the successive Ponchen.

Nonetheless, some of the other Buddhist non-Sakya traditions inside Tibet did not accept this situation with ease: Emperor Mongke had been the patron of Karma Pakshi until his death in 1260; while the Drigungpa were backed by Hulegu of the Ilkhan Dynasty (1258-1335) – a brother of Qubilai Qan, who launched an abortive attack on Sakya in 1285. This resulted in the burning of **Drigung** and its sacred artefacts in 1290. Later, in 1350, during the reign of Sonam Gyeltsen and his Ponchen, Gawa Zangpo, power was usurped by one of the myriarchs, Tai Situ Jangchub Gyeltsen of Phakmodru. The power of the Sakyapa rulers rose and fell in proportion to the rise and fall in the power of the Mongol qans in China.

The Phakmodrupa Administration (1350-1435)

The Tibetan nationalist movement which wrested power from the Mongol-backed Sakyapas in 1350 was headed by Jangchub Gyeltsen (r 1350-71), the myriarch of Phakmodru, and based at **Nedong** in S Tibet. On acquiring supreme power in Tibet, he and his successors assumed the title gongma ('king'). His power was belatedly recognized by the Mongol emperors, who additionally conferred the title Tai Situ upon him. Jangchub Gyeltsen reorganized the myriarchy system into a system of dzong or county fortresses, which persisted down to the present century. Local dzongpon officials, such as Rabten Kunzang Phak at Gyantse, came to hold considerable autonomy under this administration. During this period the rulers of Tibet firmly backed the Kagyupa school of Tibetan Buddhism, but it also coincided with the rise of the

Gelukpa tradition. Jangchub Gyeltsen's successors were Sakya Gyeltsen (1372-84), Drakpa Jangchub (1385-90), Sonam Drakpa (1391-1408), Drakpa Gyeltsen (1409-34), Sangye Gyeltsen (1435-39), Drakpa Jungne (1440-68), Kunga Lekpa (1469-73), Rinchen Dorje (1474-1513), Chenga Ngagi Wangpo (1514-64), Ngawang Tashi Drakpa (1565-78), and Drowei Gonpo (1579-1617). The power of the later gongma was gradually eclipsed by the house of Ringpung in Tsang, until by 1478 the position had little more than nominal or titular significance.

The Ringpung Administration (1478-1565)

The Rinpung princes first came to prominence during the reign of the Phakmodrupa king Drakpa Gyeltsen (r 1409-34), who appointed Namka Gyeltsen as lord of the **Rinpung** estates and governor of Sakya and Chumik. In 1435, his relation Rinpung Norbu Zangpo seized power from Phakmodru in W Tibet, gradually bringing to an end the influence of Nedong in that region. His son Donyo Dorje in 1478 finally inflicted a decisive defeat on the kings of Phakmodru; and he became the most powerful ruler in Tibet. He was a principal patron of the Zhamarpa branch of the Karma Kagyu school. The family's power was eventually eclipsed in 1565 by Zhingzhakpa Tseten Dorje of the Samdrubtse fiefdom at Zhigatse.

The Tsangpa Administration (1565-1642)

The princes of **Samdrubtse** (modern Zhigatse) became powerful patrons of the Karma Kagyu school, particularly following the foundation of the Zhamarpa's residence at Yangpachen. In 1565, the power of the Rinpungpas was usurped by Karma Tseten (Zhingshakpa Tseten Dorje) of the Nyak family. He made **Zhigatse** the capital of Tibet.

In religious affairs, he adopted a sectarian posture, which favoured the Karma Kagyu school at the expense of others. When he persecuted the Northern Treasures (Jangter) community of the Nyingmapa school, he is said to have been ritually slain in 1599 by Jangdak Tashi Topgyel; but the son who succeeded him, Karma Tensung Wangpo, maintained the same policy. He forged an alliance with the Chogthu Mongols and captured Lhasa and Phenyul in 1605. On his death (1611), he was succeeded by his son, Karma Phuntsok Namgyel, who, in 1613, established a new 15-point legal system for Tibet. His imposing castle at Zhigatse is said to have been a prototype for the Potala Palace at Lhasa.

In 1616 he forced Zhabdrung Ngawang Namgyel to flee **Ralung** Monastery for Bhutan, and following the latter's establishment there of a theocratic Drukpa state, the kings of Tsang engaged in a series of unsuccessful military campaigns against Bhutan. In 1618 he also established a Karma Kagyu Monastery, known as **Tashi Zilnon**, on the hill above Tashilhunpo, and once again sent Mongol armies against Lhasa.

Following his death in 1621, he was succeeded by his son, Karma Tenkyong Wangpo (1604-42). From 1635-42 much of Tibet was plunged into civil war, the power of the Tsangpa kings of Zhigatse and their Chogthu allies being challenged by the Gelukpas of Lhasa, who were backed by the powerful Mongol armies of Gushri Qan. Mongol forces sacked Zhigatse in 1635, and eventually occupied the city in 1642, slaying Karma Tenkyong. From this point on until the present Lhasa has functioned as the capital of Tibet.

The Depa Zhung (1642-1959)

As we have seen, from the 13th century onwards, the hierarchies of a number of Buddhist schools – the Sakyapas, the

Drigungpas, the Kagyupas and later, the Gelukpas vied for political control of the country, relying upon the military power of Mongol princes, with whom they established a 'patron-priest relationship'. The most famous of these princes were Godan, Qubilai Qan, Altan Qan, Arsalang, and Gushri Qan. While these schools managed to gain control of the country in succeeding centuries and established their capitals at Sakya, Nedong, Zhigatse and Lhasa, none of them exercised temporal authority over the whole of the Tibetan plateau in the manner of the early kings. The remote kingdoms and tribal confederations of E Tibet, whether nomadic or settled, fiercely maintained their independence and permitted a high degree of eclecticism in religious expression. The willingness of Tibetan potentates to involve Mongol princes in Tibetan political life had serious consequences for the nation's integrity.

In 1639-41, during the prolonged civil war between Zhigatse and Lhasa with their partisan religious affiliations, the Qosot Mongols decisively intervened on the side of Lhasa, enabling Dalai Lama V to establish political power for the Gelukpa school.

Reconstruction of the **Potala Palace**, symbol of Songtsen Gampo's 7th century imperial power, was undertaken by Dalai Lama V and the regent Desi Sangye Gyatso; and this building once again became the outstanding symbol of the Tibetan national identity. The new Lhasa administration gradually extended its influence over many parts of E Tibet through the agency of Gushri Qan's Mongol armies, imposing a religious and political order which was often at variance with the local traditions. Kagyu monasteries suffered in particular, and many were converted to the Gelukpa school. Nonetheless, this was the first period since the early kings in which a strong national identity and political

cohesion could develop. The Dalai Lama soon became an all-embracing national figurehead, representing not only the Gelukpa school but the aspirations of all the other traditions. As the embodiment of Avalokiteshvara, the patron bodhisattva of Tibet, his compassion permeated the land and provided a compassionate stabilizing influence in times of strife.

The predecessors of Dalai Lama V had been important figures for the early development of the Gelukpa school. Dalai Lama I (1391-1474) had been a close disciple of Tsongkhapa, founder of the Gelukpa school, and he himself had established **Tashilhunpo** monastery in Zhigatse in 1447. His mortal remains are interred in a stupa within that monastery. His successors were based at **Drepung** to the NW of Lhasa, and the Ganden Palace of Drepung remained their private residence and political power base until the construction of the Potala. The stupas containing the embalmed remains of Dalai Lamas II, III and IV are housed at Drepung. Among them, Dalai Lama III Sonam Gyatso (1543-88) travelled to Mongolia where he became spiritual advisor to Altan Qan, king of the Mongols, and received the Mongol title Dalai Lama, 'ocean of wisdom'. Subsequently he was reborn as the grandson of Altan Qan. Dalai Lama IV Yonten Gyatso is therefore the only Dalai Lama to have been born a Mongol rather than a Tibetan. From that time onwards, the backing of the Mongol armies was secured, and victory over Zhigatse in the civil war guaranteed.

The regents of the Dalai Lamas and external intrigues

The succession of Dalai Lamas who ruled Tibet from the Potala Palace were assisted by powerful regents. During the time of Dalai Lama V, there were four regents: Sonam Rabten (1642-58), Trinle Gyatso (1660-68), Lobzang Tutob (1669-

74), and Sangye Gyatso (1679-1705) – the last of whom was a prolific scholar in the fields of Tibetan medicine, astrology and history. He concealed the death of Dalai Lama V in 1682 in the interests of national stability, but was himself tragically killed by the Mongol prince Lhazang Qan who interfered to depose the libertine poet Dalai Lama VI in 1706. Lhazang was later slain by the invading Dzungarwa armies of the Mongol prince Sonam Rabten in 1717; and it was the turmoil caused by this invasion that prompted Kangxi, the Manchu emperor of China to become embroiled in Tibetan politics. Ostensibly supporting the Mongol faction of Lhazang Qan, which had abducted Dalai Lama VI and murdered the regent in Lhasa, and opposing that of the Dzungarwa, which had invaded Lhasa in response to that abduction, the Manchu armies effectively put an end to Mongol influence on Tibetan affairs.

In 1720, during the regency of Taktsewa (1717-20), the Manchus instated Dalai Lama VII, who was in their custody. **Amdo** and **Nangchen** were annexed by the new **Kokonor territory** in 1724, and in 1727 the Manchus claimed much of Kham, E of the Yangtze as their own protectorate.

The next 150 years saw periodic intervention by the Manchus in the affairs of the Lhasa government, assisting it in its wars with Nepal and intriguing against it by ensuring that few Dalai Lamas ever reached the age of majority! This was the age when powerful regents and Manchu ambassadors (*amban*) held sway during the infancy and childhood of the Dalai Lamas. Some such as Miwang Sonam Topgyel (1728-47) were highly regarded for their political acumen and secular stance; while others connived against the young Dalai Lamas within their charge.

During the lifetime of Dalai Lama VII alone there were four important regents: Taktsewa (1717-20), Khangyel (1720-27), Miwang Sonam Topgyel (1728-47), and Gyurme Namgyel (1747-50). During the lifetime of Dalai Lama VIII, there were three main regents, Delek Gyatso (1757-77), Ngawang Tsultrim (1777-91) and Tenpei Gonpo (1791-1810). The next four Dalai Lamas all passed away prematurely before reaching the age of majority. During this period the following regents held sway: Jigme Gyatso (1811-19), Jampal Tsultrim (1819-44), Panchen Lama VII Tenpei Nyima (1844-45), Ngawang Yeshe Tsultrim (1845-62), Wangchuk Gyelpo (1862-64), and Khyenrab Wangchuk

THE DALAI LAMAS OF TIBET	
Dalai Lama I Gendun Drupa	(1391-1474)
Dalai Lama II Gendun Gyatso	(1475-1542)
Dalai Lama III Sonam Gyatso	(1543-1588)
Dalai Lama IV Yonten Gyatso	(1589-1616)
Dalai Lama V Ngawang Lobzang Gyatso	(1617-1682)
Dalai Lama VI Tsangyang Gyatso	(1683- ?)
Dalai Lama VII Kalzang Gyatso	(1708-1757)
Dalai Lama VIII Jampal Gyatso	(1758-1804)
Dalai Lama IX Lungtok Gyatso	(1805-1815)
Dalai Lama X Tsultrim Gyatso	(1816-1837)
Dalai Lama XI Khedrub Gyatso	(1838-1855)
Dalai Lama XII Trinle Gyatso	(1856-1875)
Dalai Lama XIII Tubten Gyatso	(1876-1933)
Dalai Lama XIV Tendzin Gyatso	(b 1934)

(1864-73). Despite those unilateral machinations of the Manchus which were designed to divide Tibet and weaken the rule of the Dalai Lamas, it is important to note that the Tibetans still controlled their own affairs and that apart from a diplomatic legation in Lhasa there was virtually no Chinese presence on the Tibetan plateau, even in those supposedly partitioned eastern regions.

This 19th century pattern of regency power continued for a while during the childhood of Dalai Lama XIII, when Tatshak Jedrung Ngawang Palden (1875-86) and Trinle Rabgye (1886-95) held power, but the Dalai Lama himself soon took control and gained respect, not only for his spiritual status, but as the first Dalai Lama since the Great Fifth to hold genuine political power. Later regents during his lifetime, such as Lobzang Gyeltsen (1906-09) and Tsemonling (1910-34) acted more as the instruments of his policy. However, from the late 19th century onwards, Sichuan warlords began to intervene and establish military garrisons in E Tibet, wary of the declining power of the Manchu Dynasty and of the enhanced power of Lhasa in the region.

Global political concerns had a dramatic impact upon Tibet during the reign of Dalai Lama XIII. The Younghusband expedition from British India in 1904 forced the Dalai Lama to flee to Mongolia; and precipitated a new Chinese 'forward policy' in Tibet. The warlords Chao Erh-feng and Liu Wen-hui in their aggressive campaigns of 1909-18 and 1928-33 respectively attacked E Tibet, seeking to carve out a new Chinese province which they would call Xikang (W Kham). The Dalai Lama again fled into exile this time to Calcutta (1910) and the ill-equipped Tibetan forces bitterly resisted the invaders. In 1912-13 all

---

EARLY WESTERN CONTACTS WITH TIBET

1603	Portuguese merchant d'Almeida in Ladakh
1624-32	Jesuit missionaries d'Andrade, Cabral and Cacella in Gu-ge and Tsang
1661	missionaries Grueber and d'Orville visit Lhasa from China
1707-45	Capuchins in Lhasa; d'Ascoli and de Toursdella Penna and da Fano compile Tibetan dictionary
1715-17	Jesuit cartographers survey Tibet
1716-33	Jesuit Desideri in Lhasa
1774-75	George Bogel of British East India Co visits Zhikatse
1783-92	Samuel Turner's trade mission from British India
1811	Thomas Manning visits Lhasa
1823	Csoma de Koros in Zangskar
1846	Lazarist fathers Huc and Gabet visit Lhasa from Amdo
1879-80	Przevalski visits Amdo, Kham, and Tsaidam
1885-86	Carey from British India visits Tsaidam and Dunhuang
1889-90	Bonvalot visits Amdo and Kham via Lop Nor
1890	De Rhins and Grenard travel to Namtso
1895	Sven Hedin in Jangtang
1896	Wellby and Malcolm travel to Kokonor and Kunluns and thence to Kashmir
1900-1906	Hedin in West Tibet
1900	Koslov in Kokonor, Tsaidam and South Amdo
1904	Francis Younghusband leads a British military force to Lhasa
1906-7	Stein and Pelliot in Dunhuang
1906-48	British Trade Mission in Gyantse and Lhasa

Chinese were expelled from Lhasa and the Dalai Lama XIII began a period of internal reform and external independence from China. However, he was unable to change the deeply ingrained conservatism and xenophobia of the monastic and aristocratic hierarchy. Despite his warnings of what might befall the Tibetan nation if they did not heed his prophesies and change accordingly Tibet continued in blind isolation from the world forces swirling about it. The 13th Dalai Lama died in 1933.

During the infancy and childhood of HH Dalai Lama XIV (b 1934), political events were in the hands of the regents Reting (1934-40), Takdra (1941-51), and Lukhangwa Tsewang Rabten (1951/2).

Chinese Administration (1951-)

The conflict between the Tibetan forces and the Chinese Communists under Mao Zedong and the warlords in E Tibet resumed after WW2, resulting in the invasion of Tibet by the communist forces from 1951, and culminating in the forceful seizure of the country by the People's Liberation Army. The Tibetan government in Lhasa was obliged to sign a 17-point agreement in 1951, outlining the policies for the 'peaceful integration of Tibet' into the 'motherland'. In 1959 an apparent attempt to kidnap the Dalai Lama by Communist generals in Lhasa resulted in a spontaneous revolt by the Tibetan people against the Chinese invaders. The Chinese People's Liberation Army ruthlessly suppressed the Lhasa uprising, resulting in the exodus of over 100,000 refugees to India, Nepal and Bhutan.

In 1965, those parts of the country under direct control of Lhasa were proclaimed an Autonomous Region of China, known as the Tibetan Autonomous Region (TAR), while E Tibet had already been divided between four other provinces – Qinghai, Gansu, Sichuan, and Yunnan. During the dark years of suppression and the insanity of the Cultural Revolution and its aftermath (1966-77) which followed the communist invasion systematic attempts were made to obliterate Tibetan culture. Thousands of monasteries were destroyed, along with their precious artefacts and vast libraries of great literary works. Some sources suggest that as many as 1 million Tibetans died in consequence of these events, whether directly through war and persecution, or indirectly through famine and material hardships. Accusations of genocide against the People's Republic of China were upheld by the International Commission of Jurists at The Hague.

Yet Tibetans, both inside and outside Tibet, never lost their strong sense of national identity, and at every opportunity they have striven to preserve and restore their precious culture. Under the guidance of the Dalai Lama in India a Tibetan Government-in-exile has been established, and developed upon democratic principles. Moreover the main centres of Buddhist learning have been re-established in refugee settlements in Nepal and India and many of the great Buddhist masters of Tibet who followed the Dalai Lama into exile have established world-wide communities of Buddhist practitioners, holding allegiance to one or another of the schools of Tibetan Buddhism.

The influence of HH Dalai Lama XIV as an international statesman and Nobel Peace Prize holder of the Gandhian persuasion is widely acclaimed. Meanwhile, until a genuine political solution to the problems engendered by occupation can be found and the rulers of China are willing to engage in a dialogue with the Dalai Lama or his representatives, the signs of internal dissension and discontent within the country known to the world at large as 'Tibet' will remain as great as ever.

MODERN TIBET

CONTENTS

Government

Following the Chinese Communist occupation of E Tibet and Central Tibet, the country was divided between five Chinese provinces, administered, on the Soviet model, as autonomous regions, prefectures and counties. In this context it should be known that the word 'autonomous' is something of a euphemism. The Kandze area was initially an autonomous region in its own right (1950), but by 1955 it had been encorporated into Sichuan province as an autonomous prefecture. The Nagwa area was established as an autonomous prefecture of Sichuan province in 1953, and in the same year the Ganlho area of Amdo was encorporated as an autonomous prefecture of Gansu province, and the Dechen area of Kham into Yunnan province.

After the seizure of Utsang and W Kham by the PLA in 1951, and the signing of the 17-Point Agreement (see above, page 125), a preparatory committee was established to oversee the integration of Tibet into the 'motherland' in 1956. The abortive uprising against Chinese rule and policy in 1959 lead to the enforced exile of HH the Dalai Lama and many of his people, including Tibet's greatest lamas and spiritual masters. In 1965, the Tibetan Autonomous Region was inaugurated, and since then the areas of Utsang and W Kham have been so known.

Supreme authority lies in the hands of the Communist Party and the Army rather than in the civilian administration, many members of which appear to act as a rubber-stamp for decisions made elsewhere. There are numerous working committees and consultative bodies beneath the Communist Party right down to local village level. Since Oct 1992, the chairman of the party in the TAR has been Chen Kaiyuan, a technocrat who encourages economic reforms while repressing pro-independence sympathizers.

Tibetan Government in exile

In the aftermath of the suppression of the Lhasa Uprising in 1959, HH the Dalai Lama XIV fled into exile, followed by some 80,000 Tibetan refugees, who sought sanctuary in India, Nepal, Bhutan and Sikkim. By 1970 there were some 100,000 Tibetan refugees dispersed throughout 45 settlements – extending from N India through Madhya Pradesh and Orissa, to Karnataka in the S. The Dalai Lama first settled in Mussoorie, but soon moved to Dharamsala, where the Government-in-exile was established.

In exile the Tibetan Government was reorganized according to modern democratic principles. Elections were called in 1960 for the establishment of a new body known as the Commission of People's Deputies; and in 1963 a draft Constitution of Tibet was promulgated, combining the aspirations of Buddhism with the needs of modern government. This constitution was eventually published in Tibetan in 1991; and awaits the final approval of the Tibetan people.

The Government-in-exile administers all matters pertaining to Tibetans in exile, including the re-establishment, preservation and development of Tibetan culture and education, and, internationally, it leads the struggle for the restoration of Tibet's freedom. The Tibetan community in exile functions in accordance with the Charter for Tibetans in exile and is administered by the Kashag (Council of Ministers), which is accountable to the Assembly of Tibetan People's Deputies (a democratically elected parliament). The Tibetan Supreme Justice Commission is an independent judiciary body.

The Central Tibetan Administration (CTA) is comprised of three autonomous commissions – Election, Public Service and Audit, seven departments – Religion & Culture, Home Affairs, Education, Information and International Relations, Security, Health, and one council for planning.

The CTA mainly through the assistance of the Government of India and various international voluntary organizations, has successfully rehabilitated Tibetan refugees in 14 major and eight minor agricultural centres, 21 agro-industrial settlements and 10 handicraft centres throughout India and Nepal. There are also 83 Tibetan schools in India, Nepal, and Bhutan, with an approximate 23,000 children currently enrolled.

More than 117 monasteries have been re-established in exile; also a number of institutions including the Tibetan Medical and Astrological Institute; the Library of Tibetan Works and Archives, the Tibetan Institute of Performing Arts, the Centre for Tibetan Arts and Crafts – all based in Dharamsala, the Central Institute for Higher Tibetan Studies in Sarnath, and Tibet House in New Delhi. These institutions help to preserve and promote the ancient Tibetan heritage and culture, whilst enhancing the cultural life of the exiled community.

The CTA also maintains Offices of Tibet in New Delhi, New York, Zurich, Tokyo, London, Kathmandu, Geneva, Moscow, Budapest, Paris, Canberra and Washington DC. These Offices of Tibet are the official agencies representing the HH Dalai Lama and the Tibetan Government-in-exile.

Economy

The economy of Tibet has undergone considerable reform in the last few years, though not to the same extent as mainland China. The infrastructure of the country is still dependent on inferior road surfaces which are often washed away in the rainy season. Nonetheless some modest effort has been made to extend the paved road from Gongkar Airport to Tsetang, and the recent opening of Chamdo Airport is likely to have a great impact on economic and social life in E Tibet – for better or worse.

The **Tibet Development Fund** is encouraged to promote foreign investment in the economy, in education, and in health. However, such changes tend to have their impact in urban areas alone, and often to benefit the educated Chinese immigrants and shopkeepers rather than the economically dispossessed Tibetan population. Tibetans employed in cement production and mining seem to have benefited more than most, their per capita income doubling within 3 short years. **NB** Inflation and overheating account for some of this dramatic rise. Mobile phones abound in government offices and trading circles, and IDD connections can be made from Lhasa, Ziling and Tsetang.

Rural economy The rural economy has changed little. There are greenhouses in the suburbs supplying vegetables to the urban communities, but most farmers are engaged in subsistence agriculture. Highland barley is the crop; supplemented in certain areas by wheat, peas, buckwheat, and broad beans, in more sheltered valleys by rape seed, potato, turnip, apple, and walnut. Rice and cotton grow in the warmer parts of S Tibet. Nomadic groups are often better off, in that their livestock sustains the dairy and meat processing industry, as well as wool and leather production. Traditional imports from China, including tea, porcelain, and metals, are now supplemented by oil, textiles, and plastics.

Importance to China Despite the often-proclaimed expense of Chinese investment in Tibet, the advantages to China of Tibet's occupation are indeed great – providing space for China's burgeoning population and enormous exploitable resources – particularly in water, timber, livestock, herbal medications, and minerals. As the source of East and South Asia's greatest rivers, the Tibetan plateau has an enormous hydro-electric and geothermal potential which even now has hardly been exploited. There are large reserves of natural gas, and the landlocked lakes abound in borax, salt, mirabilite, and soda. The mining of gold, copper, iron, coal, mica, and sulphur has become widespread; and unregistered economic migrants from China have created serious law and order problems in the remote mining areas of E and NE Tibet. Oilfields have been opened in the Tsaidam basin of Northern Tibet.

Even prior to 1911, Sichuan had begun to export Chakla timber to China. However, since 1950 lumbering has become a systematic and incessant occupation throughout Kham. Anyone entering Kham from the E will encounter constant truck convoys from Darstedo, Batang and elsewhere carrying timber into China. Tawu has become an important centre for the lumber industry and the hillsides from Drango to Riwoche and Kongpo are scarred and devastated with little sign of reforestation, causing considerable ecological damage.

The wildlife of E Tibet which once flourished is all but extinct, while only a few nature reserves administered within Qinghai appear to have taken the idea of conservation on board seriously. The lure of valuable medications such as bear bile, musk, and caterpillar fungus often proves to be irresistible to the illegal hunter.

Economic life and minority nationalities The national minorities within Tibet have their own traditional economy: the **Monpa** grow rice, maize, buckwheat, barley, wheat, soya, and sesame. The **Lhopa** largely follow their traditional barter based economy, in which animal products and hides are traded for salt, wool, tools, clothing and tea. The **Qiang** of Far-east Tibet produce herbal medications such as caterpillar fungus, while their lands are rich in oil, coal, crystal, mica, and plaster. The **Jang** (Naxi) of SE Tibet live in a region of plentiful rainfall (average 2,700 mm), which sustains cash crops of rice, maize, wheat, potatoes, beans, hemp, and cotton; and minerals such as gold, silver, copper, aluminium, and manganese. The **Salars** of Dowi in NE Amdo grow barley, wheat, buckwheat and potatoes, with secondary occupations in stock-breeding, lumbering, wool-weaving and salt production. There is also a well-developed fruit-growing sector, including pears, apricots, grapes, jujube, apples, walnuts, and red peppers.

Tourism

This sector of the economy has been developed since the mid-1980s and reached its highpoint in 1987 prior to the recent political movement in Lhasa. Since then the movement of individual travellers has been restricted in most parts of Tibet and their activities closely monitored. However, organized cultural and trekking tours are available throughout the Tibetan plateau – mostly at premium rates but some with the budget traveller in mind. See the Information for visitors, page 19 for details.

LHASA

ལྷ་ས

CONTENTS

BASICS *Area* 664 sq km; *Alt* 3,590m; *STD code* (86)-891; *Main languages* Tibetan and Chinese; *Distance from Gongkar Airport* 96 km; *Temperature* Jan: max 10°, min -8°, July: max 25°, min 10°; *Oxygen* 68%; *Annual precipitation* 1,462 mm, of which 90% falls in summer and early autumn (July/Sept). Kyi-chu run-off approximately 16-19 litres/second/sq km.

SOCIAL INDICATORS *Population* 160,000; Han immigrant population 29% (excludes mobile unregistered Han population of approximately 80,000). *Literacy* 66%. *Birth rate* 18:1,000. *Infant mortality rate* 129:1,000. *Death rate* 14:1,000. *Religion* (Buddhist 73%, Muslim 2%, Atheist 25%).

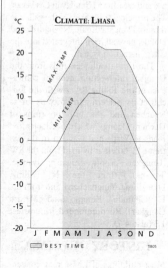

CLIMATE: LHASA

°C
MAX TEMP
MIN TEMP

BEST TIME

TIB05

The holy city of Lhasa (*Ch* Lasa Shiqu) is the historic capital of Tibet, situated on the N bank of the **Kyi-chu** River, where the valley opens out to its fullest extent. To the N of the city lies an impenetrable 5,200m range, extending from Mt Gephel Utse (above Drepung in the W) to Mt Dukri Tse (above Pawangka) and Mt Sera Utse (above Sera in the E). To the S, on the far bank of the river, is the Chakyak Karpo range. Smaller hills are located within the valley: the most prominant being Marpori ('Red Mountain') on which the Potala Palace is constructed, Chakpori (where Tibet's medical college and temples once stood, now dominated by a radio mast), and Bonpori (surmounted by a Chinese temple dedicated to Ling Gesar). The Kyi-chu River at Lhasa meanders past several island sandbanks, among which Kumalingka ('Thieves' Island'), the best known and an adjacent island are now partly owned by a Hong Kong business consortium, intent on constructing casinos and creating a Himalayan Las Vegas! The principal tributaries of the valley, ie those of Dongkar, Lhalu, Nyangdren and Dokde, have all been integrated into the Chera irrigation system.

The Lhasa valley extends from the Dongkar intersection, near the confluence of the Tolung River with the Kyi-chu at its western extremity, as far as Ngachen and the hill top ruins of Dechen Dzong, which overlooks the roads to Yerpa and Ganden in the extreme E. Access is by road from the SW (Gongkar Airport, Zhigatse, Gyantse, Tsetang), from the N (Ziling, Damzhung, Yangpachen), and from the E (Chamdo, Kongpo and Meldro Gangkar). **Recommended itineraries: 1,3 (also 4-7)**.

HISTORY OF LHASA

Most buildings of Lhasa may conveniently be assigned to one of three distinct phases of construction (although older sites have undergone extensive renovations in subsequent centuries). The earliest phase coincides with the construction of the Jokhang and Ramoche temples along with the first Potala Palace during the 7th century; the middle phase with the building of the great Gelukpa monasteries, the new Potala Palace and Norbulingka Palace during the 15th-18th centuries; and the third phase with the recent expansion of the city under Chinese rule.

Neolithic potsherds and implements of bone and stone which were excavated at Chogong near Sera in 1984 suggest that the Lhasa valley was a place of human habitation thousands of years before Songtsen Gampo unified Tibet and established his capital there. However, it was in the 6th century that Songtsen Gampo's grandfather, Takri Nyenzik, gained control over most of the 12 petty kingdoms into which Tibet had been divided. He did so by overthrowing his own brother-in-law, Tri Pangsum of Phenyul, who had usurped power from Takyawo of Nyenkar (Meldro) and tyrannized the clans of the Upper Kyi-chu valley (those of Wa, Nyang, Non and Tsepong). Takri's son, Namri Songtsen, later succeeded to the throne and gained complete control over the Kyi-chu valley, thereby establishing the framework of the Tibetan Empire; and it was the latter's son, Songtsen Gampo, who became the first king of unified Tibet. He subjugated the ancient kingdom of Zhangzhung in the W, and then moved his capital from Chingwa Taktse in Chongye to Rasa, founding the first **Potala Palace** on Mt Marpori in 637, and the Rasa Trulnang (ie Jokhang) temple in 641. Following the construction of the Jokhang temple, the original name of the city, Rasa, was altered to Lhasa or Lhaden (see below, page 139).

King Songtsen Gampo's building activities were influenced by his Buddhist consorts: in his early years, the Newar queen Bhrkuti had the **Jokhang** temple constructed at the centre of a geomantically important network of temples around the country (see below, page 139). In his later years, the Chinese queen Wengcheng constructed the **Ramoche** temple; and his Tibetan queen Monza Tricham founded the temple at **Dra Yerpa**, N of the city. Other significant constructions from that period included the 9-storey **Pawangka tower/hermitage**; and the temples of **Meru Nyingba**, **Tsamkhung**, and **Drak**

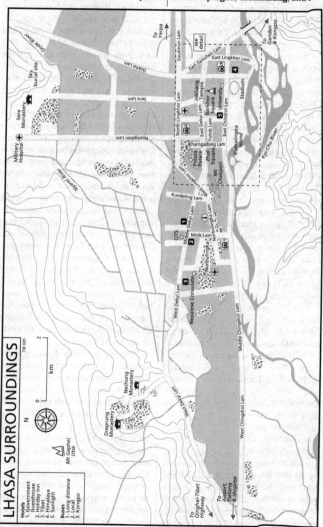

LHASA SURROUNDINGS

TIB 020

N

0   1   2
|————————|————————|
km

Mt Gephel Utse

Hotels
1. Government
   Guesthouse
2. Holiday Inn
3. Tibet
4. Himalaya
5. Sunlight

Buses
1. Long distance
2. Local
3. Kongpo

Lhaluphuk. Lhasa flourished as the capital of the Tibetan Empire until the assassination of King Relpachen by Langdarma in the 9th century resulted in the fragmentation of the country, and the desecration of the sacred sites.

The next major period of development began in 1409 when Tsongkhapa instituted the Great Prayer Festival at the Jokhang temple, and the three great monasteries of the Lhasa region were founded: **Ganden** in 1409, **Drepung** in 1416, and **Sera** in 1419. The Jokhang temple was also renovated and augmented during this period through the patronage of the kings of the Phakmodru Dynasty. Eventually, in 1642, Lhasa was restored as the capital of Tibet, following the defeat of the armies of the king of Tsang by the Mongol forces of Gushi Qan. With the latter's assistance, Dalai Lama V established a theocratic form of government (*chosi nyiden*) which endured until the occupation of Tibet by Communist forces in 1951. The four regency temples of Lhasa developed during this period; but above all, to symbolize the enhanced status of Lhasa, Dalai Lama V rebuilt the 13-storey **Potala Palace**. Later, in the 18th century Dalai Lama VII began the construction of the summer palace complex at **Norbulingka**.

Until recent decades, there were only three principal routes around Lhasa, followed by pilgrims and traders alike: the **Nangkhor** (inner circuit) around the Jokhang temple, the **Barkhor** (intermediate circuit) with its prolific market stalls, and the **Lingkhor** (outer circuit) which skirted the entire city including the Potala Palace. Pilgrims and traders alike would move around the holy city on these circuits, invariably in a clockwise direction. The great religious sites of the city were thus the focal points of attraction: Jokhang temple surrounded by its Barkhor shrines, Ramoche and Chakpori, the Potala and Norbulingka palaces, and the outlying monasteries of Drepung, Nechung, Sera and Pawangka. Residential parts of the city and its suburbs also had their distinct names: Rabsel, Hawaling and Telpung-gang to the S and SW of the Barkhor; Tromzigang, Kyire and Banak Zhol to the N of the Barkhor; Zhol village, nestling below the Potala, Denpak to the NW of the city, Lhalu, Pelding, and Nyangdreng to the N, Dokde and Tsangrel to the NE, Nachen and Changdrong to the E, and so forth. A number of the modern roads have been named after these places, which by-and-large survive, although the village of Zhol has now been relocated in apartment blocks behind the Potala at Lhalu.

The third and most recent phase of construction in Lhasa has been carried out under the Chinese occupation, during which the city has been subjected to grotesque expansion and transformation, its noble buildings obscured by the nondescript concrete tower blocks characteristic of many present day Chinese cities. Lhasa currently functions as the capital not of the whole of Tibet, but of the Tibetan Autonomous Region (*Ch* Xizang Zizhiqu). As such it is responsible for the administration of 7 districts: Lhasa, which has 7 counties under its jurisdiction; Lhokha, which has 12 counties; Nyangtri, which has 7 counties; Zhigatse, which has 18 counties; Ngari, which has 7 counties; Nakchu, which has 9 counties; and Chamdo, which has 11 counties.

Most of the new buildings constructed in Lhasa reflect a cumbersome 2-tier or 3-tier bureaucracy, in that government departments of the TAR, Lhasa District, and Lhasa Municipality have their separate offices dispersed throughout the city. However unwelcome this development may be, it cannot be ignored, and, indeed, it is with reference to the plan of contemporary Lhasa, rather than the traditional pilgrimage circuits, that the visitor will make his or her way to the ancient and medieval sites of historic importance, described in the following pages.

ORIENTATION

Most visitors will approach Lhasa from the SW or N, whether driving the short distance from Gongkar Airport, or the longer overland routes from Nepal via Zhigatse and from Ziling via Kermo and Nakchu. These approach roads converge to the W of the city at Dongkar. Just to the W of Dongkar, the valley begins to open out into a wide plain and the Potala Palace is visible from afar. A large military HQ has recently been constructed near the intersection, where an important petrol station complex and the *Dongkar Restaurant* are also located. From Dongkar two roads lead into town: the main paved route, Chingdrol lam (*Ch* Jiefang lu; also known as Tsang-gyu lam) follows the river bank upstream all the way to the E end of the city, and a dirt road extension of Dekyi lam (*Ch* Beijing lu) skirts the Lhasa Cement Factory (*Ch* Sunyitrang) to enter the city through the defile between Chakpori and Marpori hills, which formerly marked the true gateway to the city.

Chingdrol lam

Chingdrol lam, which also functions as a ring road, passes through one of the most rapidly developing parts of the city, favoured by the influx of Chinese immigrants who have established their small businesses (shops, restaurants, and karaoke bars) to service the army, which occupies much of the land in this sector of the city. The road is divided into West Chingdrol lam (Chingdrol Nub lam), Middle Chingdrol lam (Chingdrol Bar lam), and East Chingdrol lam (Chingdrol Shar lam).

Starting from **Dongkar**, you pass to the N side of **West Chingdrol lam**, an engineering and machinery institute, and a large military complex including within it warehouses, carpentry workshops, small farms, the Chinese Martyrs' Cemetery, Middle School Number Nine, the College of Agriculture and Animal Husbandry, and the Military Publications Office. Looking further N you will see the palls of smoke rising above the yellow buildings of the Lhasa Cement Factory, and behind them, like a cluster of brilliant white grains of rice on the hillside of Gephel Utse, the buildings of **Drepung Monastery**. On the S side of West Chingdrol lam, towards the river, you will pass in succession the local police station, the post office warehouse, the freight depot, the Gang-gyen Development Company, and the Hospital for Skin Diseases.

Continuing on to **Middle Chingdrol lam**, you pass on the N side the TAR Agricultural Machinery Company, the TAR schools of banking, hygene, and finance, and the Long Distance Bus Station. A memorial dedicated to the workers who died in the construction of the Ziling-Lhasa highway stands opposite the junction with Mirik lam (*Ch* Minzu lu), on which the Norbulingka Palace and *Lhasa Holiday Inn* are located (see below, page 169). Ahead at this point you will observe the radio and television mast on the summit of Mt Chakpori, where Lhasa's medical colleges and temples once stood. Continuing eastwards on Middle Chingdrol lam, you will pass to the N the Armed Police HQ and the TAR Government Offices, while the colourful prayer-flag strewn bridge to **Kumalingka** ('Thieves' Island') lies to the S.

After the intersection with Kharngadong lam, which leads towards the Potala Palace and has a number of fashionable restaurants and nightclubs, you continue on to **East Chingdrol lam**, passing in succession to the S: a large military complex, the Bank of China Lhasa Branch, the *Minorities Hotel*, the Sports Stadium, and Middle School Number One. To the N you pass the Tibetan Medical School and Middle School Number Eight; and (after the Do Senge lam turn-off leading to the Hospital of Traditional Medicine and the Jokhang temple), you pass the Peoples'

Art Museum, the *Kadak Hotel*, and the Boot Factory. At this point East Lingkhor lam bisects the road. If, at this crossroads, you continue on East Chingdrol lam, you will pass on the N side the Lhasa Municipality Government Buildings, the *Sunlight Hotel*, and the Kongpo Bus Station, and on the S the Tibet University campus. From this point the road forms a T-junction with East Zamchen lam, leading NW into town or SE across the **Lhasa Zamchen Bridge** towards the Upper Kyi-chu valley and Kongpo.

Dekyi lam

Taking the unpaved road into Lhasa from Dongkar, you follow a more traditional route, along Dekyi lam (*Ch* Beijing lu) which also stretches the entire length of the city and is divided into W, Middle and E sections. On **West Dekyi lam** (*Tib* Dekyi nub lam), you pass to the S the factories and residential compounds of the Lhasa Cement Factory (*Ch* Sunyitrang), and the Mineral Research Laboratory. Thereafter, passing through Denpak village, you will observe, on the hillside immediately above, **Drepung Monastery** and **Nechung Monastery** (see below, page 180). Then, to the N of the road you will pass the Lhasa City Engineering and Construction Unit and the TAR Rd Transport Maintenance Head Office; while to the S is the TAR Customs Office, a green painted building with a clock-tower, marking the place where Dekyi lam is intersected by lanes leading N (to Pari Zimkhang, the TAR Communist Party School and the erstwhile *TAR Tourism Bureau and guesthouse*) and S (to the Import-Export Control Bureau, the Animal and Plant Inspection Department, and Chingdrol lam).

Continuing E on **Middle Dekyi lam** (Dekyi Bar lam) you pass to the N: the TAR Hygene Head Office, the TAR Opera Troupe, the TAR Finance Head Office, the Muslim Cemetery Kache Lingka, the China Building Bank, the School of Performing Arts, the TAR Civil Administration Buildings, the TAR Scientific Association, the Tibet Tourism Corporation Offices, the Iron Horse Travel Company Office, the TAR Rd Planning Office, and the TAR Petroleum Company. To the S you will pass: the TAR Statistics Department, the TAR Insurance Offices, the *Tibet Hotel*, the Perik Bookshop, the Workers' Convalescent Home, the Lhokha District Office, and *Lhasa Holiday Inn*. In this section of the road, there are also many small Tibetan and Chinese restaurants geared to the tourist market (in contrast to those on Chingdrol lam which largely service the army).

Turning right on to **Mirik lam** (*Ch* Minzu lu) which connects Dekyi lam with Chingdrol lam, you will pass on the E the TAR Peoples' Conference Hall and Theatre, the Golden Bridge Travel Office, and the TAR Motor Parts Fitting Company; while to the W is the main entrance to *Holiday Inn*, a side road leading to the Royal Nepalese Consulate and the Yarlung Travel Service, the entrance to **Norbulingka Palace**, the TAR Cultural Relics Association, the TAR Workers' No. 2 Hospital, and the Long Distance Bus Station.

A road known as **Norbulingka lam** or **West Lingkhor lam** leads from the entrance of Norbulingka Palace towards Chakpori Hill and intersects with Middle Dekyi lam at a large roundabout dominated by two grotesquely sculpted golden yaks, before continuing into Lhalu and N Lhasa. On the N side of this road, you will pass **Kundeling Monastery**, and the *Transport Office Guesthouse*, while to the S you pass the old Television and Radio Broadcasting Offices, the Ling Gesar temple on Bonpori Hill, and the **Trak Lhaluphuk** temple complex on Chakpori Hill. The extension of West Lingkhor lam into Lhalu and N Lhasa is described below (see page 137).

Continuing E on **Middle Dekyi lam** from the Mirik lam intersection, you pass on the N side the *TAR Government Guesthouse (Xizang Zeng Fu Zhao dai suo)*, the local Dekyi lam police station, the Electrical Studies Centre, and the Foreign Trade Company, adjacent to the Golden Yak Roundabout. On the S side, you will pass the TAR High Court, the TAR Mapping and Survey Department, and the Lhasa Petrol Station.

After the roundabout, **East Dekyi lam** (Dekyi Shar lam) begins, passing through the defile between Chakpori and Marpori Hills, where a stupa gateway once more dominates the approach to the city. The road here opens out on to the vast and newly constructed **Zhol Square**. On the N side of the square you will see in succession the newly constructed TAR Television and Radio Station, the lingkhor circuit around the Potala Palace, and the renowned **Potala Palace** itself, with the 15th century Zhamarpa Palace in the foreground. To the S, is the enclosed **Zhol Doring** (see below, page 153), and the open expanse of Zhol Square (formerly the Cultural Palace Park).

At this point, crossing **Kharngadong lam** (which leads northwards to the CAAC Airline Office and the vegetable market), you pass on the N side, the Lhasa Post Office, and (after the Nyangdren lam T-junction) the local bus station, the TAR Seismology Head Office, a children's play centre, the Taxi Company, the *Yak Hotel*, the Ramoche lam turn-off leading to **Ramoche Temple** (see below, page 153), and the Peoples' Court. On the S side, you will pass the *Ying Hotel*, the Men-tsikhang lam turn-off leading to the *Snowlands Hotel* and the Hospital of Traditional Medicine (Mentsikhang), the Tromzikhang Market, the *Kyire Hotel*, and the *Banak Zhol Hotel*. After the East Lingkhor lam intersection, which leads S to the Public Security Bureau and East Chingdrol lam, the road then forms a T-junction with East Zamchen lam, heading NW into town or SE towards the bridge.

Lingkhor lam

Named after the traditional pilgrimage circuit around the city of Lhasa, this motor route is still frequented by devotees who come from all parts of Tibet to circumambulate the holy city. There are three sections: West Lingkhor lam, extending NE from the Golden Yak Roundabout towards Lhalu; North Lingkhor lam, extending due E behind the Potala Palace and Lukhang Temple, as far as the Mongolian Horseman Roundabout and the *Plateau Hotel* intersection; and East Lingkhor lam, extending due S from the latter to the riverside. On **West Lingkhor**, after passing the Foreign Trade Office on the left, you pass the main Lhasa branch of the Bank of China, the Lhalu Middle School and the District Car Rental Company; and on the right, overshadowed by the Potala Palace, the side entrance to the TAR Television and Broadcasting Head Office.

Turning onto **North Lingkhor lam** (also known as Dzuktrun lam), you then pass on the left side of the road, the TAR Political Affairs Head Office, the TAR United Front Work Division, the Peoples' Publishing House Bookstore, the TAR Geology and Mineral Head Office, the Office of Foreign Affairs, Lhasa City Police Head Office, the Gang-gyen Store, and the *Plateau Hotel* (Gao Yuan). On the S side, you will pass the N face of the Potala Palace, the **Lukhang Temple** and its surrounding park, the Peoples' Hospital (Mimang Menkhang), the newspaper publishers, Ramoche lam turn-off which leads to Ramoche Temple (see below, page 153), and the Telecommunications Building.

Lastly, **East Langkhor lam** passes the Peoples' Court, the Peoples' City Hospital, the *Banak Zhol Hotel*, the Public Security Bureau, the mosque Gyel Lhakhang, the Boot Factory, Middle School Number One, the Carpet Factory, the TAR Mountaineering Institute, the *Himalaya Hotel* and the *Xue Lian Hotel*.

Yutok lam and the Barkhor radial roads of Central Lhasa

From the entrance to the Cultural Palace and the TAR Government Buildings, **Yutok lam** (also called Mimang lam) leads eastwards to the gates of the Jokhang, Tibet's holiest shrine and the true centre of Lhasa. On the S side of this approach road, are the Xinhua Bookstore, the public baths, Middle School Number Eight, a Tibetan medical school, the Friendship Store, and the Yutok bridge. After the Do Senge lam intersection, the Lhasa City Cinema is located on the S side and the **Hospital of Traditional Medicine** (Mentsikhang) on the N side. It is from this point onwards, as the Jokhang is approached from the W, that the radial road network of ancient Lhasa begins. Although the replacement of traditional buildings has greatly diminished the appeal and warmth of the narrow lanes and gulleys around which Lhasa citizens lived their lives for centuries, the structure of the road network remains unchanged, except on the W side where the Jokhang plaza was constructed in the 1960-70 period. Four large prayer-flags are situated within the Barkhor ('intermediate circuit') market which surrounds the Jokhang, known respectively as **Ganden Darchen** in the NE, **Juyag Darchen** in the W, **Kelzang Darchen** in the SW, and **Sharkyaring Darchen** in the SE. Working clockwise from the W side, there is a northern lane, called **Mentsikhang lam**, due E of the Hospital of Traditional Medicine, which leads to East Dekyi lam and is known for its restaurants and tea houses. The regency temple **Tengye Ling** is approached via an alley behind the hospital. A second road runs NE from the plaza towards the **Tromzikhang** market

---

PRAYER FLAGS

In Tibet, any prominant place exposed to the wind may be adorned with multicoloured prayer flags (*darchok*), permitting the natural power of the wind to distribute the blessings of their inscribed prayers as they flap to and fro, for which reason they are known also as 'horses of the wind' (*lungta*). Domestic rooftops and monastery compounds often have large poles to which these flags are attached, and renewed annually on the 3rd day after the Tibetan New Year. Similarly, most mountain passes (*la-tse*) are marked by cairns of stones (some inscribed with mantras), to which sets of prayer-flags are attached. Wherever public buses or private jeeps cross over a major pass, the passengers will invariably disembark to add a stone to the cairn, or tie a newly prepared set of prayer flags and burn incense as an offering to the spirit of the mountain, who would have been tamed and appointed protector of Buddhism by Padmasambhava back in the 8th century. Some will cast paper prayer-flags into the air from the bus window, rejoicing loudly in the ancient paean: "Kyi-kyi so-so! May the gods be victorious!" (*lha-gyel-lo*).

A single set of cotton prayer-flags is ordered in the sequence: blue, white, red, green and yellow, respectively symbolizing the five elements: space, water, fire, air and earth. In each corner of the flag there may be a protective animal: garuda (top-left), dragon (top-right), tiger (bottom-left), and lion (bottom-right), while the mantra-syllables forming the main part of the inscription may vary according to the preferred meditational deity of the devotee. Those of the three bodhisattvas: Avalokiteshvara, Manjughosa, and Vajrapani are commonplace, as are the mantras of the female bodhisattva Tara, who protects travellers from the diverse dangers of the road.

via the butter and meat markets, also giving access to East Dekyi lam. Having entered upon the Barkhor circuit, the third road extends SE from the NE corner. The fourth road, known as **Waling lam** (or Dunsisung lam), leads SE from the SE corner towards the nunnery of **Ani Tsamkhung**, the mosque of Gyel Lhakhang and East Chingdrol lam. The fifth, known as **Rabsel lam**, leads SW from the SE corner, and the last **Gyedu lam**, leads SW from the SW (Barkhor Café) corner.

North Lhasa

As already indicated, there are a number of N-S roads intersecting with Chingdrol lam and Dekyi lam, the two main E-W arteries of the city. Among these, the most important are: Lhalu lam, extending due N from West Lingkhor lam via Lhalu to Pelding commune; Nyangdren lam, extending due N from the Post Office on Dekyi lam to Pawangka and Sera Monastery (see below, page 181); and Dokde lam, extending NE from the *Plateau Hotel* intersection out of town.

On **Lhalu lam**, you pass on the W side of the road, the New Zhol village, Lhalu village, and Pelding, where there is a quarry and an oxygen production plant. On the E side you pass the TAR Women's Affairs Office, the TAR Procurator's Office, and the Chamdo District Office.

On **Nyangdren lam**, you pass on the W side the TAR Government Personnel Department, Lukhang Park, the TAR Religious Affairs Office, Lhasa City Maintenance Department, the TAR Transport Company, the local police station, the Compounding Factory of the Hospital of Traditional Medicine, the TAR Gymnastics Association, the Gymnasium, the Zhigatse District Office, the Ngari District Office, Middle School Number Six, Lhasa Teacher Training College and the School of Hygene. On the E side, you will pass the Post Office, the Fine Art Company, the Nakchu District Office, the Inpatients Hospital of Traditional Medicine, the University of Traditional Medicine (Sorik Lobdra Chenmo), Ngari Branch of the Lhasa City Bank, the Race Course, Xinhua Press, and a number of workers' schools. Thereafter, the road leads due N to the Military Hospital and Pawangka, while a detour leads due E to **Sera Monastery** and the nearby Sky Burial Site.

On **Dokde lam**, you pass on the W side the Lhasa Television and Broadcasting Head Office, the Power Station Construction Company, the Epidemic Prevention Department, the North Fire Station, an armed police unit, and various electrical or engineering companies. On the E side, you pass the *Plateau Hotel*, the Ganlho Amdo Office, the armed police reserve units and TAR security offices, Middle School Number Four, the Commercial School, pharmaceutical companies, motor repair units and agricultural machine suppliers.

The Academy of Social Sciences is located in a street between Nyangdren lam and Dokde lam, alongside a satellite station, an armed police hospital, a fertilizer factory, and a hydro-electric power plant.

East Lhasa

Among the outlying easterly parts of the city, **Ngachen lam**, the extension of North Lingkhor lam, leads out of town towards a power station of the same name and the hilltop ruins of **Dechen Dzong**. En route, you pass by the International Satellite Station, a series of armed and unarmed police units, Middle School Number Three, and a flour mill.

South Lhasa

The S bank of the Kyi-chu River is relatively undeveloped. Most buildings belong to the military, but there are a number of outlying farming villages: Dekyi Khangsar, Zhapa, Nupa, Gepho and so forth. At Drib, the regency temple of **Tsekchokling** has been rebuilt.

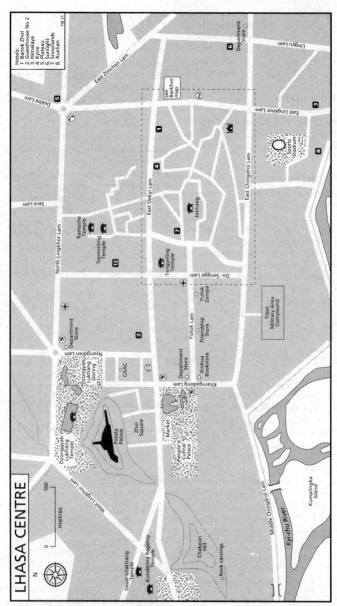

LHASA CENTRE

N

metres
0   500

Hotels:
1. Banok Zhol
2. Guesthouse No 2
3. Himalaya
4. Kyire
5. Plateau
6. Sunlight
7. Snowlands
8. Xuelian

East Zimchen Lam

Dokhe Lam

Lingyu Lam

Department Store

East Lingkhor Lam

Sports Stadium

East Chingdrol Lam

Sera Lam

North Lingkhor Lam

East Delyi Lam

Ramoche Temple

Tsemonling Temple

Tengyeling Temple

Jokhang

Do-Sengge Lam

see Barkhor map

Tibet Military Area Compound

Nyangdren Lam

Department Store

CAAC

Dzongyab Lukhang Doring

Yutok Zampa

Yutok Lam

Friendship Store

Xinhua Bookstore

Department Store

Khangpodrong Lam

West Lingkhor Lam

Dzonggyab Lukhang Temple

Potala Palace

Zhol Square

Market

Peoples Cultral Palace

Gesar Lhakhang Temple

Kundeling Regency Temple

Chakpori Hill

Rock carvings

Middle Chingdrol Lam

Kyi-chu River

Kumalingka Island

PLACES OF INTEREST
IN CENTRAL LHASA

Jokhang Temple
ཇོ་ཁང

During the reign of Songtsen Gampo's father, the king of the Kathmandu valley was one Amshuvarman, who instated his own era in 576 (he was preceded by Shivadeva and followed by the latter's son Udayadeva in 621, and thereafter by the usurper Jisnugupta/Visnugupta in 624). Udayadeva's son Narendradeva fled to Lhasa when his father was overthrown, and remained there until his return from exile, probably with Tibetan assistance, and enthronement in 641, after which he introduced the Matsyendranath cult. He is said to have vanished into the foot of Kathmandu's celebrated Matsyendranath image at the time of his death.

It was during Narendradeva's sojourn in Lhasa that Songtsen Gampo married the Nepalese princess Bhrikuti, who arrived in Lhasa in 632 or 634 and began construction of the Potala. Later, he married the Chinese princess Wengcheng who arrived in Lhasa in 641 and remained there until her death in 680/681. In consequence of this latter marriage, the Tang emperor Kao Tsung bestowed upon Songtsen Gampo the title Baowang, 'jewel king'.

Geomantic importance of the Jokhang

The Jokhang is Tibet's most sacred shrine, the focal point of pilgrims from the entire Tibetan plateau. Situated at the heart of the old town of Lhasa, it was founded by Queen Bhrikuti on a site deemed by Queen Wengcheng to be the principal geomantic power-place in Tibet, identified with the heart of the supine ogress. To facilitate the construction of the Jokhang, in 638 the Othang Lake had been filled in with earth, transported by goats. The original name of the town Rasa ('place of the goat') was subsequently altered to Lhasa ('place of the deity') following the temple's consecration.

However, further obstacles had to be eliminated by the construction of 12 outlying geomantic temples before the building of this central temple could be completed. In this way, the Jokhang came to form the centre of a grand geomantic scheme whereby temples were erected in three successive rings of four on the body of the 'supine ogress' which is Tibet (ie on her shoulders and hips, elbows and knees, and hands and feet). On the Jokhang's eventual completion (647), the temple was known as **Rasa Trulnang** ('magical apparition of Rasa'); and also as **Gazhi Trulnang** ('magical apparition endowed with four joys') because its construction was said to have brought happiness to the four classes of the populace.

The main gate of the Jokhang temple faces W towards Nepal in recognition of Queen Bhrikuti who bore the expense of the Jokhang's construction. The original design appears to have had a Newar model, and only later was it said to have been modelled on Vikramashila Monastery in NW India. The earliest phase of building, traces of which indicate distinctive Newar influence, are to be seen in the original door-frames of the four ground-floor inner chapels dedicated to Mahakarunika, Amitabha, Shakyamuni, and Maitreya; and those of the second storey at the centre of the destroyed N wing, and the Zhalre Lhakhang of the E wing, as well as the Songtsen Chapel of the W wing. The fact that the Newar queen wished to make the third storey but never did may indicate her premature death. Later, when the third storey was added, the temple was said to represent the three buddhabodies (Trikaya) or three world-systems (Tridhatu).

Bhrikuti installed the primary images in a pentoid arrangement (5 main

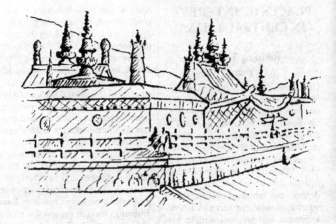

Jokhang rooftops in Lhasa

chapels flanked by vihara-like cells) within a square hall: the deity Aksobhya in the centre flanked by Amitabha and Maitreya; with Mahakarunika and Shakyamuni Acalavajra on the N and S wings respectively. There were four gates: one in each of the four walls, and 37 columns represented the 37 sections of the Vinaya.

Songtsen Gampo erected the protector shrines, with images of naga kings, Ravana and Kubera to safeguard the temple from the elements. He also concealed his treasures (*terma*) in important pillars of the Jokhang; a custom perhaps linked to the age-old Tibetan tradition of concealing wealth at the foundation of buildings or pillars.

Renovations

The Jokhang has undergone continuous renovation since its original establishment. The main phases of renovation may be attributed to the following:

a) Queen Jincheng refurbished the temple, King Senalek Jinyon cleared the outer courtyard, and King Relpachen built the Meru and Karu temples to the rear; while adding certain minor images.

b) Atisha discovered Songtsen Gampo's testament, the *Kachem Khakolma*, in the Jokhang; while Zangkar Lotsawa Phakpa Sherab enlarged the central chapel and altered the Zhelre Lhakhang.

c) Dakpo Gompa Tsultrim Nyingpo (1116-69) renovated the other chapels, including the Zhalre Lhakhang murals of the second storey and built the inner circuit (*nangkhor*).

d) Gade Zangpo and Monlam Dorje of Tsel Gungtang (14th century) renovated the first 2 storeys of the present great hall (area 25,084 sq m).

e) Phakdru Drakpa Gyeltsen built the front extension or Outer Jokhang in 1409.

f) Desi Sangye Gyatso and Dalai Lama VI added further halls, replacing the old tiled roof with a golden roof.

g) The Mongol Ta Lama of Sera added the rooftop emblem of the dharma-wheel flanked by two deer in 1927.

h) Following the damage of the Cultural Revolution, ⅓ of the complex was restored between 1972 and 1975. Presently the site is 2,600 sq m in area with

121 statues. The temple was reopened in 1979 with nine monks.

i) The most recent and extensive renovations were carried out between 1992 and 1994.

Layout

The Inner Jokhang in 3 storeys forms a square (82.5 sq m), enclosing the inner hall known as Kyilkhor Thil. This structure is surrounded by the inner circumambulation pathway (*nangkhor*), beyond which is the 2-storeyed Outer Jokhang or western extension, containing secondary chapels, storerooms, kitchens, toilets and residential quarters. The Meru Nyingba temple adjoins the Jokhang on the E side, while the S and W sides are adjoined by other buildings. This whole structure is surrounded by the intermediate circumambulation pathway (*barkhor*); which in turn is surrounded by the old city of Lhasa, with the Potala beyond. The outer walkway (*lingkhor*) on which pilgrims even now circumambulate the entire holy city of Lhasa forms an outer ring-road, and much of it has been encorporated into the modern road infrastructure of the city.

Outer Jokhang

In the square in front of the entrance, the Jokhang plaza, formerly known after its flagpole, the Juya Darchen, there is the stump of a willow reputedly planted by Princess Wengcheng. It is flanked by two more recent willows and enclosed within a new stone wall. In front of the stump is the pock-marked obelisk of 1794 admonishing against smallpox, and another inscriptionless stele. In an adjacent enclosure to the N is the 6m obelisk with an inscription commemorating the Sino-Tibetan peace treaty of 821/822.

The **entrance portico** (Khyamra Gochor) with six fluted columns is fronted by a courtyard (*dochal*) where pilgrims prostrate and have worn the flagstones smooth. Side-murals depict the Four Guardian Kings and the Four Harmonious Brethren. The structure is surmounted by a balcony hidden by a yak-hair curtain, from which dignitaries would observe ceremonies conducted below. The upper N wing of the Outer Jokhang contains the **Labrangteng**; from which successive Dalai Lamas would observe important ceremonies. It has a grand reception hall; while below are storerooms, and the **Sitar Courtyard**, where living animals would be ransomed from the slaughterhouse as an act of merit. The S wing of the Outer Jokhang contains the offices of the Panchen Lamas (formerly those of the Tibetan cabinet).

Gyalchen Zhi Lhakhang (Zimgo Chinang Nyiwar)

Entering from the left and after passing two large prayer wheels, the pilgrim first sees statues of the Four Guardian Kings backed by 17th and 19th century frescoes of gandharvas and nagas, and flanked by those of Samantabhadra's paradise. This ante-chamber leads through the inner door.

Kyamra Chenmo (Main Courtyard)

Within the main assembly hall, the 19th century murals on the W wall depict Gushri Qan, Dalai Lama V and Pancen Lama IV; and the Thousand Buddhas of the Aeon. The murals of the S wall depict the founding of the three large monasteries around Lhasa, and the life of the Buddha. The W murals above the entrance depict the nine aspects of Amitayus, and the meditational deities Guhyasamaja, Cakrasamvara, and Bhairava, as well as Kalacakra.

The hall (32m by 39m) was constructed by Tsongkhapa for the Great Prayer Festival in 1409. It is in the form of an open atrium, with large murals along its cloistered walls (dating from 1648). On the N side is the 2-storeyed residence of the Dalai Lama, with its gilded roof and window overlooking the courtyard. The rooftop view from this outer hall overlooks the elaborate western façade.

Along the N wall are, in succession:

1) The **Namthar Gosum Lhakhang**, with images of the Buddhas of the Three Times, the Eight Bodhisattvas, and the two gatekeepers. A staircase leads down from the Dalai Lama's private quarters;

2) **Shugtri Chenmo**, the Dalai Lama's stone throne, backed by paintings of Shakyamuni, Avalokiteshvara and Manjushri, with the Thousand Buddhas;

3) **Dolma Lhakhang**, containing an image of Cintamani Tara flanked by White and Green Tara, and backed on the left and right respectively by images of Nyaknyon Sewa Rinchen (who sculpted the original Cintamani image) and Atisha. Its rear (W) wall has images of the Twenty-one Taras in two tiers, originally commissioned by Dalai Lama VII, with Shantaraksita, Padmasambhava and Trisong Detsen forming a trio on the N side, along with Tsongkhapa and his foremost students. A long stone altar stands in front of the inner gateway. Outside the door is a stone bearing a handprint of Longdol Lama.

4) Embedded within the NW column at the entrance to the inner circumambulation pathway are two stones, said to have been thrown there by Tsangnyon Heruka Sangye Gyeltsen and Unyon Kunga Zangpo.

5) The **Inner Circumambulation** (*nangkhor*) is lined with prayer-wheels and murals outlined in gold on red background, which depict the Thousand Buddhas and scenes from the *Avadanakalpalata*, interspersed with stupas and relief-images. On the N side are four successive chapels entered from the westernmost one, namely: **Tamdrin Sangdrubling** (with images of Hayagriva and Kurukulla), **Mahakarunika**, **Sarvavidvairocana**, and the innermost dedicated to the **Eight Medicine Buddhas**. On the E side are: **Neten Chudruk Lhakhang**, which contains images commissioned by Desi Sangye Gyatso; the **Gurubum Lhakhang** (containing 100,000 images of Padmasambhava surrounding three central images), and the **Sera Dago**, which is a gate connecting the Jokhang with Meru Nyingba temple and the **Dago Rungkhang** kitchen (used during the Great Prayer Festival by the monks of Sera). On the S side, outside the wall, is the **Sung Chora** debating courtyard, renovated in 1986, and containing a yellow stone platform where thrones (*shugtri*) for Tsongkhapa, the Dalai Lama, and the Ganden Tripa were set up during the Great Prayer Festival, and where the annual Geshe examinations were held. Also, outside the wall on this S side are the temples dedicated to the Eight Medicine Buddhas, the Sixteen Elders, the Graduated Path (*lamrim*), and the Eight Sugatas; and a 3-storey Ngakhang, or tantric college, offering an excellent rooftop view of the Jokhang.

During the Great Prayer Festival, the monks of the three main monasteries would be seated in the assembly hall – those from Sera in the N, Drepung in the centre, and Ganden in the S. The Dalai Lama would be flanked by Shartse Choje and Jangtse Choje, the hierarchs of the two colleges of Ganden monastery, and the entire ceremony would be supervised by the Ganden Tripon (head of the Gelukpa school), and the Tsokchen Umdze from Drepung.

Inner Jokhang

Ground Floor

Main Gate (Zhung-go): embedded in the flagstones in front of the gate is a fossil known as Amolongkha, and a footprint of Dalai Lama XIII. The gate is ornamented with Derge crafted metalwork and surrounded by murals depicting Maitreya (left), Je Yabsesum (above), and Dipamkara (right).

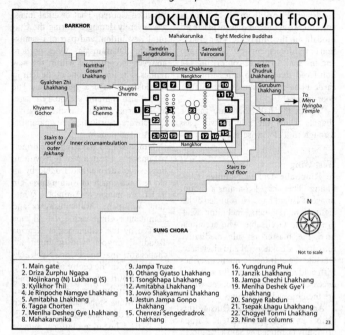

JOKHANG (Ground floor)

1. Main gate
2. Driza Zurphu Ngapa Nojinkang (N) Lukhang (S)
3. Kyilkhor Thil
4. Je Rinpoche Namgye Lhakhang
5. Amitabha Lhakhang
6. Tagpa Chorten
7. Menlha Deshek Gye Lhakhang
8. Mahakarunika
9. Jampa Truze
10. Othang Gyatso Lhakhang
11. Tsongkhapa Lhakhang
12. Amitabha Lhakhang
13. Jowo Shakyamuni Lhakhang
14. Jestun Jampa Gonpo Lhakhang
15. Chenrezi Sengedradrok Lhakhang
16. Yungdrung Phuk
17. Janzik Lhakhang
18. Jampa Chezhi Lhakhang
19. Menlha Deshek Gye'i Lhakhang
20. Sangye Rabdun
21. Tsepak Lhagu Lhakhang
22. Chogyel Tonmi Lhakhang
23. Nine tall columns

Entrance Hall

The outermost rooms of the portico including the Driza Zurphu Ngapa are empty, while the innermost chambers depict the wrathful pretector deities: yaksas (**Nojinkhang**), Shridevi and Mahakala on the N side; and benign naga kings (**Lukhang**) as well as the Othang Lake seal on the S side. These protectors are said to have appeared to Songtsen Gampo in a vision during the original construction of the Jokhang, and were charged with its protection.

Kyilkhor Thil (Inner Hall)

The 2-storey inner hall is divided into three sections – two with short columns (*kawa thungthung*) and one with long columns (*kawa ringbo*). Immediately beyond the entrance, there are two rows of short columns running N-S, the southernmost ones bearing tangkas of the Sixteen Elders. Then, in the centre of the hall, are six large statues: a 6m west-facing image of Padmasambhava (erected by Khyentse Rinpoche and consecrated by Minling Chung Rinpoche), a 4m N-facing image of Barzhi Jampa (commissioned by the Barzhi family), a 10m west-facing image of Thuwang Zangthama, a 8m N-facing image of Miwang Jampa (cast in 1736, its auras and jewels have been replaced), and at their centre a 4m Mahakarunika with a small Padmasambhava to its rear. The tallest columns (9 in 4 groups) which support the skylight are painted and date from the period of Gade Zangpo's restoration.

An inner row of 12 short columns (*kawa thung-thung*) with six to each side of the Jowo Lhakhang, running S-N in front of the inner sanctum, probably dates from the 7th century. These are characterized by short bases and round shafts, suggesting an authentic Nepalese design. Five of them (three at the N end and two at the S end) were plastered probably in the 14th century for protection or reinforcement – by Gade Zangpo and his son. A cornice comprising 144 lion-faced figures also dates from the earliest phase, as do some of the interior door-frames.

Within the hall, there are various chapels which the pilgrim will pass through in a clockwise manner, as follows:

West Wing

Je Rinpoche Dakpa Namgye Lhakhang This chapel contains a central image of Tsongkhapa, surrounded by his eight pure retainers, including Khedrubje and Gyeltsabje, who accompanied the master on his meditative retreats at Chokhorgyel and elsewhere. Outside the entrance, a monk inscribes with gold ink on red paper the names of deceased persons or petitioners, which are then burned as offerings.

Amitabha Lhakhang Outside this chapel is the Tagpa Chorten, a stupa originally fashioned by Sakya Pandita in the 13th century, and containing certain relics of King Songtsen Gampo.

North Wing

Menlha Desheg Gye Lhakhang: this chapel is dedicated to the Eight Medicine Buddhas. Outside is an earthen platform with an image of Milarepa.

Mahakarunika Lhakhang Within the chain metal curtain of this chapel, the door of which appears to have an original frame, there is a restored image of the deity Mahakarunika. The original image, known as Thuje Chenpo Rangjung Ngaden, is said to have been imbued with the life-force of five beings (*ngaden*), namely: King Songtsen Gampo, his two foreign queens, and the gatekeeping deities Amritakundalin and Hayagriva. It also contained buddha relics from Bodh Gaya in India which had been brought to Tibet by Lodro Jungne an emanation of King Songtsen Gampo. That original image was severely damaged during the Cultural Revolution, and part of it smuggled to Dharamsala. One portion, however, is contained within the new replica. The image is one of the four in the Jokhang with a gilded roof. The chapel also contains secondary images of: Khasarpani, Tara, Marici, Hayagriva, Lokeshvara, Bhrikuti, Prajnaparamita, and Amritakundalin.

Jampa Truze Lhakhang The principal image is a seated Maitreya with an impressive aureole, and fronted by an old restored image of Manjughosa. On its left are images of Amitabha, White Tara, Vajrapani, Avalokiteshvara and Manjughosa. On its right is Tsongkhapa flanked by the reliquaries of Ngaripa Tsondu Nyingpo (who sculpted the chapel's original images) and Ngok Lekpei Sherab. In the centre of the chapel is a stone butter bowl, made by Tsongkhapa. Over the door is a replica of an original Mani Stone engraving (which was one of the Jokhang's most precious artefacts). The stone platform outside the door was once used by King Songtsen Gampo and his queens while bathing, and it is said that the actual clay of the Maitreya image within was mixed with bath water prior to its construction.

Othang Gyatso Lhakhang This chapel contains a stone slab, which is said to give access to a subterranean lake below the Jokhang's foundation. Annual offerings were formerly made in this chapel by the Tibetan Government. Now it is mostly blocked-off by the Tsongkhapa Lhakhang.

Tsongkhapa Lhakhang A covered elevated platform supports a small image of Tsongkhapa called Nangyen Ngadrama, which is flanked on the left by Sakya Choje Kunga Tashi and Buton Rinchendrub, and on the right by Asanga, Sonam Gyeltsen, Dorje Gyeltsen, and Karmapa III. The original central image is said to have been made in Tsongkhapa's lifetime, but there are other traditions attributing its miraculous construction to the protector deity Dharmaraja, or alternatively to a later Mongol emperor.

East Wing

Amitabha Lhakhang (Room where final obstacles are dispelled) The entrance to this chapel is guarded by Vajrapani and Ucchusmakrodha – the former could not be budged by Langdarma's henchmen, and the latter reputedly repelled a Chinese invasion following the death of Songtsen. Note the original sloping Newar door-frame with its unpainted patina. Inside is an image of Amitabha flanked on the left by Vajrapani and on the right by Hayagriva, while the Eight Bodhisattvas are on the side-walls. Outside the chamber to the S is a stone platform with images of Songtsen Gampo, his two foreign queens, and Guru Saroruhavajra (commissioned by Dalai Lama XIII). The platform originally supported images of the Four Guardian Kings, as sculpted by Tripa Monalm Dorje, using clay from Samye. The fourth 'light-emanating' image of the Jokhang, Dolma Darlenma, was also once positioned in this chapel. The statue had received its name after reputedly requesting Sakya Pandita for an offering scarf.

Jowo Lhakhang Foyer The highly polished wooden floor of the foyer is flanked by two pairs of guardian kings (with wrathful demeanour on the S side and smiling demeanour on the N side). The original guardians, now destroyed, were attributed either to Princess Wengcheng or Princess Jincheng. The elaborately decorated high ceilings display a marked Newar influence. An image of Padmasambhava, sculpted in the 18th century by Orgyan Drodul Lingpa, admonishes the naga spirits to stay away.

Jowo Shakyamuni Lhakhang The inner sanctum, which is the largest and loftiest chapel of the Jokhang and one of four with a gilded roof, contains Tibet's most revered image – the 1.5m image of **Jowo Rinpoche**, representing the Buddha at the age of 12. This image was reputedly made of an alloy of precious metals mixed with jewels by Visvakarman in Kapalavastu, and in later times presented to China by the king of Magadha to commemorate the defeat of the Yavanas. Subsequently it was brought to Tibet by Princess Wengcheng. One tradition recorded by Tucci states that the original was partially destroyed in 1717 by the Dzungars, the present image being stylistically later. Originally housed in the Ramoche temple, it was later brought to the Jokhang by Wengcheng on the death of Songtsen Gampo and interred in a chamber on the S side behind a painting of Manjughosa. Queen Jincheng subsequently recovered it and installed it as the central image of the Jokhang. Later it was buried in sand after Trisong's disloyal Bon ministers chose to return it to China and 300 men could not move it. During that period, the temple was converted to a slaughterhouse. Subsequently the image was once again buried in sand by Langdarma who had the gates of the Jokhang plastered with the picture of a monk drinking wine. The head-dress and ear-ornaments (*na-gyen*) originally date from time of Tsongkhapa (but have been replaced in recent times), and the pearl-studded robe from that of the Da Ming emperor. The image was conserved without damage during the Cultural Revolution, during which period the temple was utilized as a military barracks and its outer courtyard as a slaughterhouse.

Entering the inner sanctum, the pilgrim finds the main image seated upon a three-tiered stone platform; flanked by smaller images of Maitreya and Manjughosa. There are ornate silver-plated pillars with dragon motifs supporting an overhead canopy; and a silver sphere above the crown, which was donated by a Mongol Qan. Side-steps at the S and

N sides grant access to the pilgrim, who can then make offerings directly to the image. Behind the Jowo Rinpoche image, there is a copper plaque with an inscription commemorating Anige's 13th century restoration of the throneback and the aureole. In front of the plaque is an E-facing image of Dipamkara Buddha called Acala, which stands back-to-back with Jowo Rinpoche, and is claimed to have once been the central image. Facing the latter, at the back of the chapel is a 6m image of Thubpa Gangchentso, flanked by the Twelve Bodhisattvas, along with the gatekeepers Vajrapani and Hayagriva – all of which were sculpted by Zangkar Lotsawa. Other statues of the inner sanctum depict Dalai Lama VII, Dalai Lama XIII and Tsongkhapa.

Outside the chapel to the S is a raised platform with images of Atisha flanked by Dromtonpa and Ngok Lekpei Sherab. Behind Dromtonpa is a mural depicting a 'speaking' form of Tara (Dolma Sungjonma).

Jestun Jampa Gonpo Lhakhang This chapel, which has an original 7th century Newar door-frame, contains as its main image Jampa Chokhor. This image is held to have been an emanation of King Krikin, which was brought to Tibet from Nepal as part of Princess Bhrikuti's dowry. The present statue is a replica but the finely carved aureole may be original. Flanking the main image are the Eight Taras Who Protect from Fear; with Avalokiteshvara in the form Chenrezi Semnyi Ngalso in front, and a replica of Princess Wengcheng's stove in the NW corner. The original Maitreya image formerly was the centrepiece of the second storey.

Outside on a platform are images of Amitayus, Dolpopa Sherab Gyeltsen, and Four-armed Avalokiteshvara.

Chenrezi Sengedradrok Lhakhang The main image here is of Amitabha, flanked by six emanations of Avalokiteshvara, of which the first left

gives the chapel its name. Outside is a 1.5m stone column with a hole at the top, to which pilgrims press their ears in order to hear the sound of the mythical anga bird at the bottom of Othang Lake.

South Wing

Yungdrung Phuk In the SE corner beyond the stairs are two images of Padmasambhava and one of King Trisong Detsen, along with a painting of the Medicine Buddha, which is said to have been fashioned out of light rays emanating from Avalokiteshvara's heart.

Janzik Lhakhang (closed) Outside are new murals depicting Songtsen Gampo and his two foreign queens with the ministers Gar and Tonmi. The original paintings had been commisssioned by Monlam Dorje of Tsel Gungtang.

Jampa Chezhi Lhakhang This chapel, which is one of the four with a gilded roof, contains an image of Maitreya, which was brought from Drepung to replace the (now destroyed) silver Maitreya, which was traditionally escorted around the Barkhor on the 25th day of the first lunar month during the Jampa Dendren ceremony. Other statues contained within this chapel include: Manjughosa, Khasarpani, Mahakarunika, Vajrasattva, and Jambhala, as well as Lharje Gewabum, who is said to have built one of the Kyichu dykes. Behind the image of the protector Gek Tarje at the NE corner of the chape, and alongside a Padmasambhava image, is a 0.5m gilded goat's head, replacing a reputedly self-arising original. This depicts the legendary Queen of Goats (Dungtse Ra'i Gyelmo) who presided over the filling-in of the Othang Lake.

Menlha Deshek Gye'i Lhakhang (Jowo Besai Lhakhang) This is the chapel in which the Jowo Rinpoche image was hidden by Princess Wengcheng within a cavity behind the buddha-image of the E wall. The main images depict Amitabha and the Eight Medicine Buddhas. The image of Manjughosa, known as Jampeyang Koyolma, which is depicted on the outer wall, is said to have spoken to Princess Jincheng, agreeing to move aside so that the statue could be extracted. West of the entrance are images of the Five Founders (Gongma Nga) of Sakya.

Sangye Rabdun Lhakhang This chapel depicts the Seven Generations of Past Buddhas, one of which supposedly flew there from India.

Tsepak Lhagu Lhakhang This chapel depicts the Nine Aspects of Amitayus, deity of longevity. Outside on the SW wall is a mural depicting Prajnaparamita, with a reputedly self-arising eye, which appeared when an old lady miraculously had her sight restored on praying to the image. Other murals in this alcove depict the Three Deities of Longevity (Tselha Namsum).

West Wing

Chogyel Tonmi Lhakhang In this royal chapel, King Songtsen Gampo is flanked (on the left) by: Gar, Bhrikuti, Nyatri Tsenpo, and Trisong Detsen; and (on the right) by: Relpachen, Lhatotori, Wengcheng, and Tonmi Sambhota. Formerly it also contained images of Mongza Tricham, Gungru Gungtsen, and Zhang Lonnyi. The room has original offering bowls and lamps. Outside are important murals depicting the foundation of the Jokhang and the events of Songtsen Gampo's reign, including the construction of the first Potala Palace.

Second Floor (access from S-E corner)

Zhalre Lhakhang The chapel immediately above the Jowo Rinpoche Lhakhang was remodelled by Zangkar Lotsawa when the lower chamber was enlarged. Only the westernmost part of the original chamber remains, offering a view of the chapel below, and this is approached by a recently constructed catwalk – the original approach being

walled-off to prevent pilgrims walking above the Jowo Lhakhang. The remaining E inner wall contains original frescoes. Unfortunately, the 7th century frescoes of the N wall were removed in the 1980s. The southern frescoes and the well-preserved three-panelled mural of the E wall suggest a synthesis of Tibetan and Pala styles, predating the integrated Tibeto-Newar style of the 15th century.

Guru Lhakhang (Barkhang Lopon) A 7th century tapering door-frame with metal lattices leads into this chapel, where the central image depicts Padmasambhava in the awesome form known as Nangsi Zilnon, flanked by his two foreign consorts and eight manifestations. The original Pala-style paintings of the outside walls (probably by Zangkar Lotsawa) were restored in 1991.

Demchok Lhakhang Here the principal image depicts the meditational deity Cakrasamvara in union with the female consort Vajravarahi.

Thuwang Tsokhor Bypassing three empty chapels, the pilgrim arrives at this shrine, which has images of Shakyamuni surrounded by the Eight Bodhisattvas; and also Jowo Shakyamuni, flanked by Shariputra and Maudgalyayana.

Ku-nga Gonkhang (Gonkhangphuk) This chapel contains nine 1.5m images of the protector deities, including the five forms of Pehar known as Gyelpo Ku-nga, as well as Hayagriva, Shridevi, and Nechung, and the gatekeepers Du-tsen and Lu-tsen.

Chogyel Songtsen Lhakhang The main shrine of the W wing, surmounted by a gilded roof, is dedicated to King Songtsen Gampo. Note the 7th century door-frames. The king's ale pot, known as Chogyel Trungben, or Chang-no Tamgochen, which may perhaps be of Scythian or Kushan origin, is kept in a cabinet on a wooden stand between the two gates. The central image of the king, flanked by his two foreign wives, is said

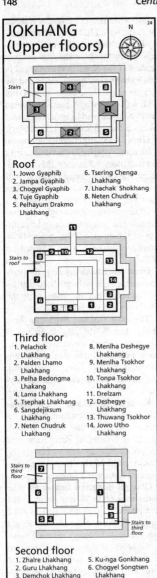

JOKHANG
(Upper floors)

N

Roof

1. Jowo Gyaphib
2. Jampa Gyaphib
3. Chogyel Gyaphib
4. Tuje Gyaphib
5. Pelhayum Drakmo Lhakhang
6. Tsering Chenga Lhakhang
7. Lhachak Shokhang
8. Neten Chudruk Lhakhang

Third floor

1. Pelachok Lhakhang
2. Palden Lhamo Lhakhang
3. Pelha Bedongma Lhakang
4. Lama Lhakhang
5. Tsephak Lhakhang
6. Sangdejiksum Lhakhang
7. Neten Chudruk Lhakhang
8. Menlha Deshegye Lhakhang
9. Menlha Tsokhor Lhakhang
10. Tonpa Tsokhor Lhakhang
11. Drelzam
12. Deshegye Lhakhang
13. Thuwang Tsokhor Lhakhang
14. Jowo Utho Lhakhang

Second floor

1. Zhalre Lhakhang
2. Guru Lhakhang
3. Demchok Lhakhang
4. Thuwang Tsokhor
5. Ku-nga Gonkhang
6. Chogyel Songtsen Lhakhang
7. Thupa Rigdruk Lhakhang

to have been originally commissioned by Bhrikuti (the middle finger of the main image is said to be that of Songtsen himself and the image an exact likeness). Behind are images of the Seven Generations of Past Buddhas and wall-painted mandalas. The S wall has further images of Songtsen Gampo with Wengcheng and his Tibetan consort.

Thupa Rigdruk Lhakhang The chapel of the NW corner is dedicated to Four-armed Avalokiteshvara, flanked by the Six Sages of the Six Realms. Note the multiplicity of murals depicting Amitayus in red on a cream background.

The chapels of the N wing and those beyond the Zhalre Lhakhang on the E-wing have been destroyed and are presently unrestored.

Third Floor (access from the SE and NW corners)

The frescoes of the third floor depict the protectors, especially Shridevi. Many murals however have four or five layers of paint, of which the lower layers have yet to be inspected. Only three chapels are open:

Pelhachok Dukhang (Meru Tshokhang) This chapel is dedicated to the protectress Shridevi, and it is cared for by the monks of Meru Sarpa Tratsang. There are new murals in white, red and gold on black background, which depict Shridevi, Mahakala, and Bhairava. The murals outside this chapel depict Six-armed Mahakala, Dalai Lama V, the regent Desi Sangye Gyatso, and Gushri Qan, with Magzorma, Shridevi, and the Twelve Tenma.

Palden Lhamo Lhakhang This chapel contains a peaceful image of Shridevi.

Pelha Bedongma Lhakhang Here, the wrathful image of frog-faced Shridevi is separated from the previous chapel by a partition wall. On the 13th day of the 10th lunar month, this image would be displayed for 3 days, and on the full-moon day it would be carried around the Barkhor during the festival known as Pelhe Rida.

Closed chapels on this floor include: (W) Lama Lhakhang, Tsephak Lhakhang, Sangdejiksum Lhakhang, Neten Chudruk Lhakhang; (N) Menlha Deshegye Lhakhang, Menlha Tsokhor Lhakhang, Tonpa Tsokhor Lhakhang, Drelzam, Deshegye Lhakhang, Thuwang Tsokhor; and (E) Jowo Utho Lhakhang.

The Roof

There are four gilded roofs (*gyaphib*) and four corner chapels on the roof of the Jokhang. The former comprise: the **Jowo Gyaphib** in the Centre-East, the largest gilded roof, which was donated by Tew Mul, the ruler of Yartse Kingdom of W Tibet in the 14th century; the **Jampa Gyaphib** in the Centre-South; the **Chogyel Gyaphib** in the Centre-West, which was commissioned by Dalai Lama V; and the **Tuje Gyaphib** in the Centre-North, which was donated by the kings Punimul and Pratimul of Yartse in the late 14th century.

As to the four corner chapels: the **Pelhayum Drakmo Lhakhang** in the SE (now closed) is dedicated to Magzorma; the **Tsering Chenga Lhakhang** in the SW (now closed) is cared for by the monks of Tsurphu; the **Neten Chudruk Lhakhang** in the NE (now closed) was formerly utilized by the Tibetan Government during the Great Prayer Festival; and the **Lhachak Shokhang** in the NW (now closed) once functioned as a government stationery supplier. Also on the Jokhang roof are the **Lhabum Lubum** charm vases; and the **Tamnyen Darchen** flag, which was erected by Desi Sonam Chopel following the defeat of Beri Kingdom during the 17th century. The bright sunlit roofs present a great contrast to the dark smoke-filled chapels of the Jokhang's interior.

Barkhor Buildings and Temples

Nangtseshak Jail

This 720 sq m 2-storey prison adjoining the N wall of the Jokhang was of great notoriety in the past, but is now disused. In front there is a square, which nowadays functions as a carpet bazaar. The lane entrance to Meru Nyingba temple is located here.

Meru Nyingba Temple

This temple is situated on the NE side of the Jokhang, and approached from the N arc of the Barkhor. It was one of six temples built by King Relpachen – this one on the site of an earlier temple where Tonmi Sambhota had finalized the Tibetan alphabet. It was destroyed by Langdarma and subsequently rebuilt by Atisha to become Gelukpa under Dalai Lama III Sonam Gyatso (1543-89). The oldest existing structure is the **Jambhala Lhakhang**, the main building being of recent 20th century construction. The temple is dedicated to doctrinal protectors, especially the diverse forms of Pehar.

Gongkar Chode Branch Temple

This Sakya protector shrine is located

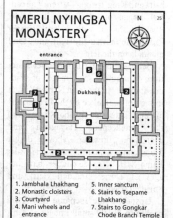

MERU NYINGBA MONASTERY

N 25

entrance

Dukhang

1. Jambhala Lhakhang
2. Monastic cloisters
3. Courtyard
4. Mani wheels and entrance
5. Inner sanctum
6. Stairs to Tsepame Lhakhang
7. Stairs to Gongkar Chode Branch Temple

up a staircase on the right of the lane entrance to Meru Nyingba temple. The central image is of the protector Gonpo Pelgon Dramtso, and was formerly flanked by images of Panjara, Shridevi, and Six-armed Mahakala.

Jambhala Lhakhang

This ancient temple lies below the Gongkar Chode branch temple. Originally it was part of King Relpachen's construction. It is only 7.5m by 7.2m with low ceiling, and is said to be where Tonmi Sambhota devised the Tibetan alphabet. Later it became affiliated to Nechung Gonpa.

The Dukhang (Assembly Hall)

This S-facing 3-storey complex is approached through a courtyard flanked by a monastic cloister. The main building, constructed by Nechung Khenpo Sakya Ngape in the 19th century, is an extremely active temple. It was renovated in 1986. Mani prayer wheels flank either side of the entrance; the left frescoes depict the protector deity Dorje Drakden; skylight frescoes depict Tsongkhapa and his foremost students; Atisha with his foremost students, and Padmasambhava flanked by Shantaraksita and King Trisong Detsen. The central image on the altar is a new Avalokiteshvara; with a large copper Padmasambhava to the right, and a sand mandala on the left.

Behind this altar is the **inner sanctum**, containing an image of Padmasambhava in the form Nangsi Zilnon in the centre flanked by the five aspects of Pehar known as Gyelpo Ku-nga; and the gatekeepers Hayagriva and Thoktsen. Frescoes above depict Tsongkhapa, Samantabhadra, and Dalai Lama XIII. The side chapels have images of Dorje Drakden (left) and Shridevi (right).

Upstairs is the **Tsepame Lhakhang** containing 1,000 small images of Amitayus.

The Pawangka Labrang

This 3-storey residence of the **Pawangka Rinpoche**, a powerful Gelukpa master who rose to prominence in the early 20th century, is located on the E side of the Barkhor.

Karmashar Lhakhang

This temple is located on the E side of the Barkhor. One of Lhasa's three oracles was based here, the others being at Nechung and Gadong in the Tolung valley. The Karmashar Choje oracle would make one annual prophecy concerning affairs of state on the 30th day of the 6th lunar month after travelling in procession from **Karmashar** to **Sera** monastery acompanied by Cham dancers drawn from the corpse-cutter (*ragyabpa*) and police (*korchagpa*) professions. The prophecy would then be written down and pinned on the door of Karmashar for public inspection.

Ani Tshamkhung Nunnery

This is one of Lhasa's three nunneries, the others being Drubtob Lhakhang on Chakpori and Chubzang Gonpa at Pawangka. It is located on the left side of Waling St, which leads SE from the Barkhor to the Mosque (Gyel Lhakhang). Passing through the perimeter wall, to which the kitchen and living quarters are attached, the yellow 2-storey building is located at the rear of the courtyard. The **Tshamkhung** (meditation hollow) of Songtsen Gampo located downstairs and approached from a small passage on the right side of the building, contains the chamber where the king meditated in order to prevent flooding of the Kyi-chu River. Inside is the meditation hollow – a 1.5 sq m whitewashed earthen well 1.5m deep and below floor level, which is approached by four steps and surmounted by a glass-framed shrine.

A reconstructed black-stone Ngadrama image of Songtsen Gampo overlooks the opening and the king's stone seat is positioned in front. During the first Great Prayer Festival (Monlam Chenmo) in 1419 the site was occupied by Drubtob Chenpo Kuchora and his successor Ngari Drubtob Chenpo. The first temple was erected by Tsong Khapa's student Tongten (1389-1445); and the second storey added by Pawangka Rinpoche in the early 20th century.

The nuns of Tshamkhung held regular fasting or *nyun-ne* ceremonies and were responsible for lighting butter lamps in the Jokhang. Restored between 1982-84, there are now more than 80 nuns at Tshamkhung. The present **assembly hall**, on the second floor, has a Thousand-armed Avalokiteshvara as its

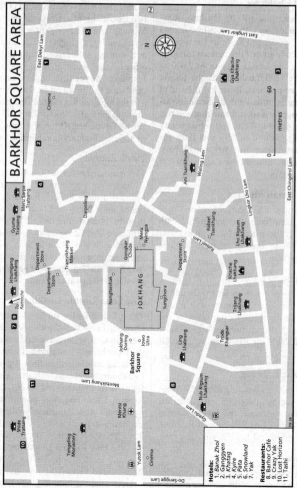

BARKHOR SQUARE AREA

N

East Dekyi Lam

Cinema

East Lingkor Lam

Gya Khache Dbakhang

Ani Tsamkhung

Wating Lam

Lingkor Lho Lam

East Chingdrol Lam

metres
0   60

Gyume Tratsang

Meru Sarpa Tratsang

To Jebumgang Lhakhang

Darpoling

Tramzikhang Market

Department Store

Department Store

Meru Nyingba

Gonpkar Circle

Rabsel Tsenkhang

Lho Rigsum Lhakhang

Nangtsesha

JOKHANG

Department Store

Khache Lhakhang

Trijang Lhakhang

To Ramoche

Sungchöra

Jokhang Doring

Jowo Utra

Ling Lhabrang

Trode Khangsar

Barkhor Square

Nub Rigsum Lhakhang

Mentsikhang Lam

Gyebti Lam

Menti Khang

Shide Tratsang

Tengteling Monastery

Yutok Lam

Cinema

Do-Senge Lam

Hotels:
1. Banak Zhol
2. Ganggyen
3. Kharag
4. Kyire
5. Pata
6. Snowland
7. Yak

Restaurants:
8. Barkhor Café
9. Crazy Yak
10. Lost Horizon
11. Tashi

main image – with (right side) Tsongk-hapa and his students, Vajrayogini, Aksobhya, Shakyamuni and White Tara; and (left side) Amoghasiddhi, Cakrasamvara, Ling Rinpoche, Pawangka Rinpoche and Green Tara. A large centrally suspended tangka depicts Tsongkhapa with his foremost students.

Gyel Lhakhang

Lhasa has some 2,000 Muslims, some descendents of 17th century immigrants from Ladakh and Kashmir, the remainder newly arrived immigrants from the Ziling and Linxia regions. At 2,600 sq m, the Gyel Lhakhang is the largest mosque in Lhasa, located at the end of Waling St, running from the Sharkyaring flagpole via Ani Tshamkhung. It was constructed in 1716, and subsequently rebuilt twice – in 1793 and 1960. Fri prayers attract over 600 worshippers. The adjacent streets have many Muslim restaurants.

The Small Mosque

Situated due S of the Jokhang and W of Gyel Lhakhang, this mosque of 20th century construction has a ground floor bath-house and an upstairs Koranic schoolroom.

Lingtsang Labrang

A 2-storey building on the S side of Barkhor Sq, with Chinese-style murals and an excellent rooftop view of the Jokhang, this was previously a residence of the late Ling Rinpoche, senior tutor to HH Dalai Lama XIV.

Trijang Labrang

This 3-storey building directly S of the Jokhang was once the seat of the late Trijang Rinpoche, the Junior Tutor of HH Dalai Lama XIV. It is now the headquarters of the Lhasa Cinema Company.

Tonpa

This now dilapidated 3-storey building on the S stretch of the Barkhor is said to have once been a residence of Tonmi Sambhota, inventor of the Tibetan script. At present, the building functions as the headquarters of the Barkhor Residents' Committee.

The Mentsikhang (Institute of Tibetan Medicine and Astrology)

The original 2-storey Mentsikhang, founded by Dr Khyenrab Norbu in 1916, is opposite the new Lhasa cinema on Mimang lam. The present multi-storeyed building slightly to its E functions as the outpatients department and the offices of the Tibetan Medical Research Institute. The penultimate floor has an exhibition of Tibetan medical artefacts; and the top floor has a shrine dedicated to Yutok Yonten Gonpo, flanked by Desi Sangye Gyatso and Khyenrab Norbu; as well as a medical tangka exhibition hall.

Yutok Zampa

This is an ancient bridge 300m W of the Jokhang, now contained within the Lhasa Customs Office. Formerly it linked the old city of Lhasa with the suburbs. Named after its 18th century turquoise-tiled Chinese roof, the bridge is 6.8m wide and 28.3m in span; with thick 2m stone walls which probably date from the 7th century. The bridge has five openings at each end.

The Four Rigsum Lhakhang

These four temples surround the Jokhang in the cardinal directions, each of them containing images of the Lords of the Three Enlightened Families. Among them, the eastern temple, **Shar Rigsum Lhakhang**, was formerly located across from the Mosque, the southern one, **Lho Rigsum Lhakhang**, was originally a royal residence and the first building of the Barkhor. Its single-storey chapel is now a private residence. The northern one, the **Jang Rigsum Lhakhang**, was formerly located opposite the Banak Zhol behind Meru Tratsang, and the western one, the **Nub Rigsum Lhak-**

LHASA OBELISKS

The obelisk or stele is a significant historical monument, constructed to symbolize royal dominion or important political and spiritual events, and often surrounded in its four directions by stupas. The obelisks of Lhasa include those in front of the **Jokhang**, namely the legible 3.5m stele constructed in 823 by King Relpachen to commemorate the peace treaty signed with Tang China, the illegible smallpox stele of 1794, and the inscriptionless stele of the Ming period with animal carvings on its plinth.

In front of the **Potala**, there are four other obelisks: the 3.5m quadrilingual Kangxi stele of 1721 commemorating the defeat of the Dzungars, and the 4m quadrilingual Qianlong stele of 1791 commemorating the two defeats of the Gorkhas in 1788 and 1791 respectively, have recently been repositioned in the foreground of the building. Considerably older than these, however, are the **Outer Zhol Obelisk** (Zhol Chima) and the **Inner Zhol Obelisk** (Zhol Nangma). The former is an 8m stele constructed by Trisong Detsen in 763 to commemorate the exploits of his General Takdra Lugong whose forces occupied the Chinese capital at Xi'an; and the latter is located below the Potala stairway.

---

hang, was located on a site W of the present Mentsikhang and N of the Yutok Zampa. Of these, only the southern temple survives intact.

Ramoche Temple and Adjacent Tratsangs

ར་མོ་ཆེ

Ramoche Temple

Founded by Princess Wengcheng at the same time as the Jokhang, Ramoche is reputed to be the princess' burial site, divined by her to be connected directly with the hells or with the subterranean crystal palace of the nagas. It originally was built to contain Tibet's holiest image – **Jowo Rinpoche**, which had been transported to Lhasa via Lhagang in a wooden cart. The construction of the temple was completed around the same time as the Jokhang. Later, when Tang China threatened to invade Tibet during the reign of Mangsong Mangtsen (649-76), the Jowo Rinpoche image was hidden by Wengcheng in a secret chamber within the Jokhang; later to be unearthed by Princess Jincheng (post 710) who then placed it within the central chapel of the Jokhang.

As a substitute the image of **Jowo Mikyo Dorje**, representing the Buddha as an 8-year-old, which had been made by Vishvakarman and brought to Tibet by the Nepali queen Bhrikuti, was taken from the S chamber of the Jokhang to Ramoche, and installed there as the main image.

Originally, Ramoche was built in Chinese-style but, after being destroyed by fires, the present 3-storeyed building was constructed in Tibetan style. In 1474 it was placed under the authority of Kunga Dondrub, a second generation student of Tsongkhapa. It then became the assembly hall of the **Gyuto Tratsang**, the Upper Tantric College of Lhasa, located further E, and housed 500 monks. During the period 1959-66, Ramoche housed a communist labour training committee. The temple has, however, been restored since 1985, and the central Jowo Mikyo Dorje image, which had been severed in two parts during the Cultural Revolution, was repaired when its torso was returned to Tibet, having been found in Beijing by the late Panchen Lama X, that same year. According to some, this image may not be the original, in that Ramoche was also damaged by Mongol incursions in

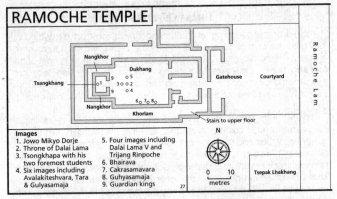

RAMOCHE TEMPLE

Images
1. Jowo Mikyo Dorje
2. Throne of Dalai Lama
3. Tsongkhapa with his two foremost students
4. Six images including Avalakiteshvara, Tara & Gulyasamaja
5. Four images including Dalai Lama V and Trijang Rinpoche
6. Bhairava
7. Cakrasamavara
8. Guhyasamaja
9. Guardian kings

0   10
metres

earlier centuries. Presently, the temple is once again occupied by the Upper Tantric College monks and undergoing repairs.

Entrance

Ramoche is located on Ramoche lam, a lane near East Dekyi lam, closeby the Tromzikhang market. The temple is entered via a large courtyard, leading up to an E-facing 3-storey gatehouse, bedecked by 10 large fluted columns and two rows of eight mani wheels. The upper chambers of the gatehouse comprise later chapels and cells for monks.

Khorlam

The circumambulatory path around the temple has new rows of mani wheels on the S, W, and N sides. Outer murals depict the Three Deities of Longevity (Tselha Namsum).

Dukhang (Assembly Hall)

The assembly hall is approached with the hermitage (*drubkhang*) on the left. The corridor has archaic bas-relief images and beams painted with the Six Syllabled Mantra, while the right wall has a painting of Dorje Yudronma, protectress of the Upper Tantric College. By the entrance at the end of the right wall is an image of Vajrapani.

The **assembly hall** has 27 lion sculptures below the skylight. The central

images flank and back the throne of Dalai Lama. Behind in a glass cabinet are Tsongkhapa with his foremost students; to the left are Gyuto Khenpo I Kunga Dondrub, Jowo Shakyamuni, Avalokiteshvara, Tara, and then, further left, Guhyasamaja. To the right of the throne are: Tsongkhapa, Trijang Rinpoche Dalai Lama V, and Shakyamuni. Against the left wall are images of the three meditational deities Guhyasamaja, Cakrasamvara, and Bhairava.

Tsangkhang (Inner Sanctum)

Surrounded by an inner circumambulation path (*nangkhor*), the **inner sanctum** is 5.4 by 4.4m. Here, **Jowo Mikyo Dorje** is seated on a large stone platform, facing W. The entrance is flanked by the Four Guardian Kings. Above the central image are the Seven Generations of Past Buddhas, with the Eight Bodhisattvas to the right and left. The rear wall has images of Tsongkhapa and Maitreya; while the gatekeepers Vajrapani and Hayagriva flank the entrance.

Upper Floors

The second floor of Ramoche is largely residential; but there is one main chapel containing images of Buddha as King of the Nagas, surrounded by the Sixteen Elders. An inner sanctum contains images of the Eight Medicine Buddhas and a copy of the *Kangyur*. On the 3rd floor, the front chambers are the Dalai Lama's private apartments, and the rear chamber a private chapel, with a gyaphib-style roof, enclosed by a wooden balustrade.

Tsepak Lhakhang

This temple is located S of Ramoche. It contains new large images of Amitayus, flanked by Shakyamuni and Maitreya. The inner walls have murals depicting the Thirty-five Confession Buddhas and lineage-holders from all the four major schools of Tibetan Buddhism. In the outer circumambulation (*korlam*), there are 1,127 wall-painted images of Amitayus, in gold outlined on a red background.

Jebumgang Lhakhang

This temple, located at the junction of Ramoche lam and East Dekyi lam, behind the public toilets, is dedicated to Tsongkhapa and it contains 100,000 small images of this master. The building was used as a granary during the Cultural Revolution.

Gyume Tratsang

Gyume Tratsang, the Lower Tantric College of Lhasa, is located on East Dekyi lam across the street from the Tibet-Gansu trade centre and the *Kirey Hotel*. A number of tantric colleges were established by Tsongkhapa's student Je Sherab Senge (1382-1445), including Se Gyupa (in Tsang), Chumelung (W of Lhasa), and Gyume Tsatsang, and those affiliated directly with Tsel Gungtang, Sera, Dechen and Meldro. Among these, the present Gyume complex dates from its reconstruction by Kalon Techen Phagto in the 18th century.

The **ground floor**, approached from the debating courtyard, houses the press for the Lhasa *Kangyur*, and a large assembly hall with an **inner sanctum** (*tsangkhang*) containing new 6m images of Tsongkhapa and his students. An ad-

jacent protector shrine contains murals of the meditational deities Guhya-samaja, Cakrasamvara and Bhairava, along with the protectors Mahakala, Shridevi, Dharmaraja and Vaishravana.

On the **second floor** of the main temple is the **Dolma Lhakhang**, the images of which include (left to right): Manju-ghosa, Vajrapani, Tara, Amitayus, Shakyamuni, Tsongkhapa with students, Maitreya in the form Jampa Cho-khorma, Cakrasamvara (with a 'speaking' Tara to the rear), Guhyasamaja, Dalai Lama XIII, Tsongk-hapa, Je Sherab Senge (the founder of Gyume), and Maitreya. New murals on the W wall depict the Eight Aspects of Tara and Vijaya. A balcony attached to the Dolma Lhakhang overlooks the aforementioned N inner chapel of the ground floor.

On the third floor is the **Kangyur Lhakhang** with an old bronze Shakyamuni as its centrepiece, flanked by a set of the *Kangyur* volumes. Its W wall has images of Tsongkhapa and his foremost students. An adjacent **Zhalre Lhakhang** overlooks the aforementioned 6m images.

The fourth level contains the private apartments (*zimchung*) of the Dalai Lamas. The Gelukpa tantric study programme at such colleges was known for its austere strictness, and, at Gyume, was accessible only to superior monks from Ganden, Sera and Drepung. Currently there are 40 monks.

Shide Tratsang

Shide Tratsang is located on the N side of East Dekyi lam, W of its intersection with the Mentsikhang lam, and down a side lane. It is said to have been founded by King Relpachen and is included among the six lhakhang surrounding the Jokhang. Fom the 14th century onwards, it has been a dependency of Reting Monastery. The extant building is entered from roof level near the **Reting Labrang** – an attractive garden-enclosed building towards Tsomonling, which is still active as the residence of the present Reting Rinpoche.

Meru Sarpa Tratsang

Meru Sarpa Tratsang is located opposite the *Kirey Hotel* on East Dekyi lam, but is now occupied by the TAR Theatre Troupe. There is an assembly hall with three small chapels. Formerly affiliated with Shide Tratsang, this college separated after 1684 and its preceptor later (post 1912) became a candidate for the regency. Its monks became affiliated with **Gyume Tratsang**. The present buildings date from the 19th century and were constructed by Sakya Nga-pe, the abbot of Nechung.

The Potala Palace
རྩེ་པོ་ཏ་ལའི་ཕོ་བྲང་

Aptly named after Mt Potalaka, the sacred mountain abode of the bodhisattva of compassion, Avalokiteshvara, the Potala Palace has been identified in different ages as the residence of Tibet's two illustrious and kingly emanations of Avalokiteshvara – Songtsen Gampo during the 7th century and Dalai Lama V during the 17th century. The building which towers above the city of Lhasa rises from the slopes of Mt Marpori, for which reason it is known locally as **Tse Podrang** ('Summit Palace'). The outer section, known as the **White Palace** has functioned as the traditional seat of government and the winter residence of the Dalai Lamas, while the inner section known as the **Red Palace** contains outstanding temples and the reliquary tombs of eight past Dalai Lamas. In terms of global perception, it is this relic of Tibet's past, present, and future national aspirations, more than any other, which uniquely symbolizes the country, like the Great Wall in China or the Vatican in Italy. This 13-storeyed edifice was among the world's tallest buildings prior to the advent of the 20th century skyscraper, and undoubtedly the grandest building in Tibet. It has many external vantage points – from the outer circumambulatory path (*lingkhor*), from Ku-

malingka Island, from the adjacent Chakpori Hill, from the Jokhang roofs, and so forth. Wherever one goes in downtown Lhasa, the resplendent golden roofs of the Potala are visible on the skyline.

Access

While tourists normally approach from the rear drive-in entrance on the N side of Mt Marpori to avoid the steep climb, the main entrance is from the Eastern Gatehouse above Zhol Square on West Dekyi lam. The outer walls of the Potala form a quadrangle, with fortified gates to the S, E and W, and Mt Marpori to the N. There are watch-towers on the SE and SW corners. The auxiliary buildings in the foreground include the Zhamarpa Palace, the Printing Press (Parkhang), the Kashag offices, and the prison.

The two printing presses are particularly significant: the **Ganden Phuntsoling Parkhang** (SE corner) is a 2-storey 600 sq m structure, contemporaneous with the White Palace. Its woodblocks which dated from 17th-18th century have been destroyed except for a few which were transferred to the Mentsikhang. The **Gang-gyen Potidengtsunkhang** was constructed during the reign of Dalai Lama XIII and funded by Genden Tripa XCI, whose reliquary is within its grounds. It is a vast 6-storey building at the western perimeter wall, containing the Zhol edition of the *Kangyur* and *Tangyur* (2nd floor). The actual printing room is on the third floor in the **Jampa Lhakhang**, where precious images of Maitreya flanked by Atisha and Tsongkhapa, Amitayus, King Trisong Detsen, Padmasambhava, and White Tara have all been destroyed. The **protector chapel** (*gonkhang*) on the third floor was built only in 1949 but its enormous Bhairava image has been destroyed. In addition to the aforementioned woodblocks, the building now houses the archives of the Tibetan Autonomous Region.

History Of The Potala Palace

Little remains of the original 11-storeyed Potala Palace which King Songtsen Gampo built on Mt Marpori in 637. An illustration of this earlier structure, which was destroyed by lightning in the reign of King Trisong Detsen, is found on the outer wall of the Lamrim Lhakhang within the Red Palace. It appears however that the foundations of the present palace do date from the earlier period, as do two of the chapels contained within the Red Palace, namely the **Songtsen Nyipuk** and the **Phakpa Lhakhang** (see below, page 162).

When Lhasa was reinstated as the capital of Tibet in the 17th century, after an interim period of 900 years, during which time the seat of government had been located successively at Sakya, Tsetang, Rinpung, and Zhigatse, one of the first acts to be carried out by Dalai Lama V was the reconstruction of this national symbol. Prior to its completion, he himself lived at the Ganden Palace in Drepung Monastery, and the largest building below Mt Marpori had been the palace of the Zhamarpas, who had dominated the political life of Lhasa until the defeat of their powerful patrons at Zhigatse in 1641. Nonetheless, the fortress (*dzong*) of the Kings of Zhigatse is said to have been taken as the prototype or model for the construction of the new Potala Palace.

Dalai Lama V preserved the original foundations of the 7th century edifice and had the **White Palace** built between 1645 and 1653. 7,000 workers and 1,500 artisans were employed on this construction, along with Manchu and Newar artists. The murals of the E Wing and the **Kangyur Lhakhang** were completed in 1648, and the following year he moved from Drepung. The **Inner Zhol Obelisk** (Doring Nangma) was constructed to commemorate this event.

The central upper part, known as the **Red Palace**, is mostly attributed to the regent Desi Sangye Gyatso (r 1679-1703) and dated 1690-93. Its interior was finished in 1697. However Dalai Lama V died in 1682 and his death was concealed by the regent until 1694, enabling him to complete the task without the distraction of political upheavals. There is also an extant Jesuit drawing, dated 1661, which interestingly suggests that 2 storeys of the Red Palace were actually constructed before his demise. Work on the funerary chapel was carried out between 1692-4, costing 2.1 million taels of silver.

Renovations

Enlargement was carried out through the 18th century. Then, in 1922, the renovation of the chapels and halls adjacent to the Phakpa Lhakhang was undertaken, along with that of the E Wing of the White Palace; and the Zhol printing press was enlarged. In 1959 the S façade was shelled during the suppression of the Lhasa Uprising, but the damaged porch of the Red Palace and the Potala School (Tse Lobdra) were subsequently restored by the late Panchen Lama X. The most recent renovations have taken place since 1991, during which period the inner walls have been strengthened, the electrical supply stabilized, and the extraneous buildings in the foreground of the palace removed to create a large square.

Altogether, the interior area of the 13-storeyed Potala Palace is 130,000 sq m. The building is 118m high, 366m from E to W, and 335m from N to S. There are 1,000 rooms, housing approximately 200,000 images.

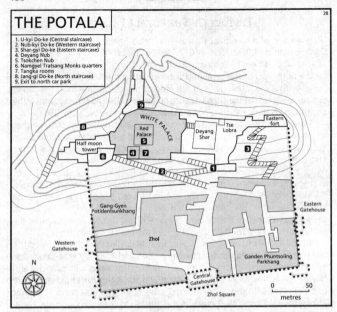

THE POTALA

1. U-kyi Do-ke (Central staircase)
2. Nub-kyi Do-ke (Western staircase)
3. Shar-gyi Do-ke (Eastern staircase)
4. Deyang Nub
5. Tsokchen Nub
6. Namgyel Tratsang Monks quarters
7. Tangka rooms
8. Jang-gi Do-ke (North staircase)
9. Exit to north car park

Traditionally the chapels of the Potala were only open to the public on set days such as the 4th day of the 6th lunar month, and in the 4th lunar month. Now, in the absence of the Dalai Lama, it has the air of a museum, and is accessible 6 days a week. Opening hours: 0900-1600 except Sun, with longer queues on Wed and Sat when pilgrims may enter throughout the day. Some rooms are closed from 1230-1430. Tourist admission fee: ¥45.

Entrance

The Potala Palace has four approaches: the **Eastern Staircase** (Shar-gyi Do-ke) which leads to the Sharchen Chok jail tower; the **Western Staircase** (Nub-kyi Do-ke) which leads into the Western Courtyard (Deyang Nub) and the Namgyel Monastery; the **Northern Staircase** (Jang-gi Do-ke) or drive-in entrance at a higher level which was formerly used only by the Dalai Lamas; and the **Central Staircase** (U-kyi Do-

ke) which bifurcates – one branch leading to the Western Gatehouse and the other to the Eastern Gatehouse. The latter is the principal entrance into the Potala, passing the Taktsang Gormo tower and the Tse Lobdra (senior seminary), before reaching the spacious Eastern Courtyard (Deyang Shar).

The White Palace

Deyang Shar (Eastern Courtyard)

This 1,500 sq m courtyard has the Tse Lobdra (senior seminary) on its NE corner and a 2-storey residential and office complex on the N and S wings. The **Tse Lobdra** was an eclectic school, founded by Dalai Lama VII (1708-57), which drew teachers from Mindroling and elsewhere.

The 4-storeyed eastern façade of the White Palace overlooks this courtyard, the Dalai Lama's private apartments being in the uppermost gallery. A triple wooden ladder (Sum-ke Go) leads from the courtyard to the entrance foyer and the main gate. The S wall of the foyer depicts the gold handprints (*chak-je*) of Dalai Lama XIII and an edict of Dalai Lama V, proclaiming Desi Sangye Gyatso as his regent. The murals here depict the Four Guardian Kings, the construction of the Mentsikhang on Mt Chakpori, the arrival of Princess Wengcheng, and the Jokhang construction.

Ascend the four flights of stairs to the roof of the White Palace, where the private apartments of the Dalai Lamas are located.

Eastern Private Apartments (Nyiwo Shar Ganden Nangsel)

The gate leading into the living quarters of Dalai Lama XIV is marked by tiger-skin maces. The **outer reception room** has an elaborately decorated throne, flanked by portraits of Dalai Lama XIII and Dalai Lama XIV. On the NW wall adjacent to the entrance there is a fine mural depicting the legendary land of Shambhala; and on the SE wall there is a cracked mural depicting the Mahabodhi Temple at Vajrasana in India. A balcony overlooks the Eastern Courtyard, and there are antechambers on the SE and SW corners, which lead into the Dalai Lama's private quarters. These rooms include an **audience chamber** for informal receptions, foreign visitors, and the sealing of official documents. Its altars contain images depicting Simhavaktra, the Three Deities of Longevity (Tselha Namsum), and so forth, and there is an interesting mural illustrating Dhanyakataka, the sacred abode in S India where the *Kalacakra Tantra* was first revealed. A small **Protector Chapel (Gonkhang)** has statues of Six-armed Mahakala, Shridevi, Dorje Drakden, and a table replete with the Dalai Lama's personal ritual implements. The **bedroom/dining room** with its images of the Three Deities of Longevity and Tsongkhapa mural is preserved as it was at the time of the Dalai Lama's depar-ture in 1959. An inner door leads to the bathroom.

Western Private Apartments (Nyiwo Nub Sonam Lekhyil)

The living quarters of the previous Dalai Lamas comprise: an ornate **reception hall** where audience would be given to the Tibetan cabinet and Manchu ambans; a **bedroom** with murals hand-painted by Dalai Lama XIII; and an **audience chamber** where government council meetings would be held. This last room contains images of Thubwang Tazurma, Je Tashi Dokarma, Padmasambhava and Dalai Lama V.

East Main Hall (Tsomchen Shar)

Within the White Palace, the East Main Hall is the largest chamber (25.8m by 27.8m), with 64 pillars, extending 3 storeys in height. It was in this hall that each successive Dalai Lama was enthroned, the New Year commemorated, and credentials received from Manchu envoys. The murals depict events from early Tibetan history and the background of the different Dalai Lamas. An inscription in Chinese above the throne reads "May the emancipating service of the Dharma be spread throughout the Universe". The **Golden Urn** from which the names of certain Dalai Lamas were latterly drawn is now kept in the Norbulingka Summer Palace (see below, page 169).

Tangka Rooms

Between the White Palace and the Red Palace, there is a yellow building in which the two extant giant applique tangkas (*go-ku*) are kept. These were traditionally unfurled from the walls of the Potala at the beginning of the Yoghurt Festival; but in recent years have only been displayed on one occasion (1994). The third tangka was offered to **Batang Monastery** in the early decades of the present century.

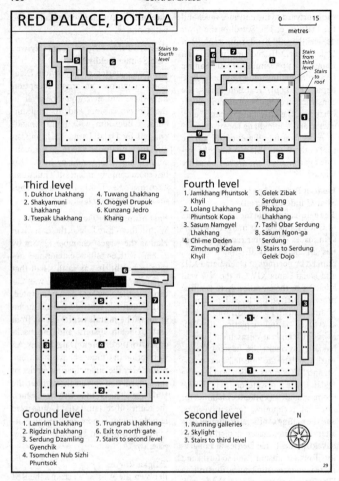

RED PALACE, POTALA

0 _____ 15
metres

Third level
1. Dukhor Lhakhang
2. Shakyamuni Lhakhang
3. Tsepak Lhakhang
4. Tuwang Lhakhang
5. Chogyel Drupuk
6. Kunzang Jedro Khang

Fourth level
1. Jamkhang Phuntsok Khyil
2. Lolang Lhakhang Phuntsok Kopa
3. Sasum Namgyel Lhakhang
4. Chi-me Deden Zimchung Kadam Khyil
5. Gelek Zibak Serdung
6. Phakpa Lhakhang
7. Tashi Obar Serdung
8. Sasum Ngon-ga Serdung
9. Stairs to Serdung Gelek Dojo

Ground level
1. Lamrim Lhakhang
2. Rigdzin Lhakhang
3. Serdung Dzamling Gyenchik
4. Tsomchen Nub Sizhi Phuntsok
5. Trungrab Lhakhang
6. Exit to north gate
7. Stairs to second level

Second level
1. Running galleries
2. Skylight
3. Stairs to third level

N

29

Namgyel Monastery and Western Courtyard

The Western Courtyard (Deyang Nub) serves as a focal point for the **Namgyel Monastery**, which was originally founded at Drepung by Dalai Lama III. At the southern perimeter of the courtyard are the monk's cells from which the aforementioned giant applique tangkas were unfurled. The walls of the Namgyel Monastery depict the protector deities and lamas of all the four major lineages.

The Red Palace

Unlike the White Palace which was used for administrative purposes and as a residence, the Red Palace which looms from the centre of the White Palace has a spiritual function. Its many temples are interspersed with the eight golden reliquary stupas (*serdung*) containing the embalmed remains of Dalai Lama V and Dalai Lamas VII-XIII. Four floors extend below the S façade of the Red Palace, but this space is demarcated only for aesthetic reasons. The N façade is constructed on solid rock. The functional part of the Red Palace has four floors, which are aligned with all but the highest of the storeys of the White Palace.

The **West Main Hall** (Tsokchen Nub) is the central structure of the Red Palace. It is flanked on all four sides by chapels 2 storeys high, entered from the ground level of the atrium; while the upper three floors have running galleries, reached in succession by a series of ladders and trap-doors. The galleries of the upper 2 storeys outwardly adjoin a further series of chapels, and inwardly they connect via footbridges with a central pavilion, the construction of which leaves sufficient space for light to filter into the West Main Hall below.

Access to the Red Palace is from the roof of the Potala via an entrance to the fourth floor facing the West Private Apartments (Nyiwo Nub Sonam Lekhyil).

Fourth Floor

Jamkhang Phuntsok Khyils (E)

This chapel contains a large gilded-copper Maitreya image, which was commissioned by Dalai Lama VIII in honour of his relative – the deceased mother of Panchen VI Palden Yeshe. Facing the image is the throne of Dalai Lama VIII. The library is positioned on the far wall – containing the *Kangyur, Tangyur*, and the *Collected Works of Dalai Lama V*. Images adjacent to Maitreya include Dalai Lama V (containing clippings from his own hair), the Three Deities of Longevity (Tselha Namsum), the Lords of the Three Enlightened Families (Riksum Gonpo), Acala, Samayatara, Padmasambhava, and Kalacakra. A wooden three-dimensional palace (*vimana*) of

the meditational deity Kalacakra is kept in the corner. Many old tangkas were destroyed in this chapel by an electrical fire in 1984.

Lolang Lhakhang Phuntsok Kopa (SE)

Originally constructed by Desi Sangye Gyatso, this chapel contains the celebrated three-dimensional mandalas of the meditational deities Guhyasamaja, Cakrasamvara, and Bhairava, which were commissioned by Dalai Lama VII in 1749. An image of that Dalai Lama is adjacent to the throne; and the murals depict his own life, as well as the ordination of Tibet's first seven trial monks in the 8th century. There are also many small images representative of all four major schools of Tibetan Buddhism.

Sasum Namgyel Lhakhang (S)

This former residential chamber was converted into a chapel by Dalai Lama VII whose throne it contains. The W wall has a large silver image of Eleven-faced Avalokiteshvara (285 kg) which was commissioned by Dalai Lama XIII. A portrait of Emperor Qianlong on the N wall was an enthronement gift to Dalai Lama VIII, dated 1762. Beneath it is the quadrilingual inscription "May Emperor Kangxi live for many thousands of years!", which was commissioned in 1722, and presented as a gift to the young Dalai Lama VII. In a glass cabinet are images of Tsongkhapa and his foremost students, Atisha, Dalai Lama VII, Panchen Lama IV, Panchen Lama VI, and so forth; and on the wall to the left is a 120 volume edition of the Manchu *Kangyur*, with trilingual covers, some samples of which have been placed in a glass cabinet in front.

Chi-me Deden Zimchung Kadam Khyil (SW)

This, the largest room on the fourth floor, functioned as a residence of Dalai Lama VI from 1697-1706. It was converted into a chapel by Dalai Lama VIII in 1797. The central image depicts Ami-

The Potala Palace in Lhasa

tayus, with a thousand small images of the same deity in surrounding niches. Other images include: a standing Avalokiteshvara, the masters of the graduated (*lam-rim*) lineage, the Sixteen Elders, the Four Guardian Kings, Tsongkhapa (from China) and the Nyingmapa protectress Ekajati. The murals depict the early Kadampa lineage-holders and Indian kings.

Serdung Gelek Dojo (W)

A gateway leads via an enclosed passageway to a staircase, through which one descends 4 storeys to enter the well-lit **reliquary chamber of Dalai Lama XIII**. A viewing gallery is constructed on the fourth floor. The ornate reliquary stupa, built between 1934-36, is 13m in height, weighing over 10,000 taels, with a central image of Eleven-faced Avalokiteshvara. In front is a newer image of Dalai Lama XIII; and on the altar is an offering mandala made of over 200,000 pearls. Murals depict events in the life of Dalai Lama XIII, including his 1910 pilgrimage to India. Ornate brocade ceiling hangings are suspended from the galleries above.

Gelek Zibar Serdung (NW)

This chamber contains the **reliquary stupa of Dalai Lama VIII**, which was constructed in 1805. The stupa has an inset image of Eleven-faced Avalokiteshvara. Other images include: Dalai Lama VIII, Buddha in the form Tuwang Dudul (commissioned by Dalai Lama IX), and an applique tangka depicting Tibet's first king, Nyatri Tsenpo.

Phakpa Lhakhang (NW)

This is the most revered chapel within the Potala Palace, dating from the original 7th century construction. It houses a **'self-arising' gilt sandalwood image of Avalokiteshvara** which was one of four discovered in Nepal by Akaramatishila in the 7th century, when a sandalwood trunk split open. The triple staircase entrance is surmounted above the door with an trilingual insciption: "Wondrous Fruit of the Field of Merit", which was presented by the Manchu Emperor Tongzhi in the 19th century. The central image is flanked by two other standing images representing Tara and Avalokiteshvara. To the left are Dalai Lama X and Tsongkhapa, while to the right are Dalai Lamas VIII and IX. Other statues include: Khasarpani from Tanak, red sandalwood images of the Eight Bodhisattvas (commissioned by Dalai Lama V), silver images of the Lords of the Three Enlightened Families, Eleven-faced Avalokiteshvara, and Shakyamuni with the Sixteen Elders.

Inside the cabinet on the left are: stone footprints of Padmasambhava (from Gungtang Pass), Tsongkhapa, and Nagarjuna; an image of Jetsun Drakpa Gyeltsen called Dzetoma, an image of Panchen Shakyashri (in Tibet from 1204-14), a jade image of Drogon Chogyel Phakpa Lodro Gyeltsen, and an image of Tangtong Gyelpo. To the right of the door, adjacent to a large Vajrapani image, is an old image of Atisha.

Outside, note the bell and the image of the late regent Reting Rinpoche overlooking the approach to this chapel.

Tashi Obar Serdung (N)

The **reliquary chapel of Dalai Lama VII** has a multi-doored entrance. The stupa itself is 9m in height, with 100,000 precious stones, and surrounded by four large images. In front is a three-dimensional depiction of the Tushita Buddhafield, and on the S wall an image of Maitreya.

Sasum Ngon-ga Serdung (NE)

This chapel contains the golden **reliquary stupa of Dalai Lama IX**, along with a silver image of this Dalai Lama; and 114 volumes of the *Kangyur* inscribed in gold, a silver image of Tsongkhapa, and further images of the Sixteen Elders, which were commissioned by Dalai Lama VIII. The chapel is flanked on the W by the **Protector Chapel** (Gonkhang) and on the E by the narrow **Neten Lhakhang**.

Third Floor

Dukhor Lhakhang (E)

The gilded copper three-dimensional palace of the meditational deity Kalacakra, contained in this chapel, was con-

structed by Desi Sangye Gyatso, 6.2m in diameter. There is also a life-size image of Kalacakra, surrounded by the 172 Kalacakra lineage-holders. On the right are seven religious kings of Tibet and the 25 kings (*khalki*) of Shambhala; as well as a gilt Enlightenment Stupa (Jangchub Chorten), eight silver stupas symbolizing the major events of the Buddha's life, and images of Manjughosha, Shridevi, Padmasambhava, and 38 deities in the retinue of Kalacakra. The murals depict Shambhala and the Kalacakra lineages.

Shakyamuni Lhakhang (SE)

This chapel contains the throne of Dalai Lama VII, and images depicting Shakyamuni, flanked by the eight standing bodhisattvas, and a manuscript edition of the *Kangyur*.

Tsepak Lhakhang (S)

This chapel contains images of the nine aspects of Amitayus; flanked by White Tara and Green Tara. The murals depict the Potala Palace during the late 18th century, as well as the charismatic master Tangtong Gyelpo and the iron bridge constructed by him across the Brahmaputra at Chuwori Chakzam.

Tuwang Lhakhang (W)

Here the central image is Shakyamuni Buddha, flanked by the Eight Bodhisattvas. There is also a throne of Dalai Lama VII, a manuscript *Kangyur*, and decorations commissioned by Dalai Lama VIII.

Chogyel Drupuk (NW)

This, along with the aforementioned Phakpa Lhakhang, is the oldest chamber of the Potala Palace, approached by a ramp which leads into a recessed cavern, supported by one large column which penetrates to the floor above and seven smaller columns. There are 28 images in the room. In a niche in the S face of the tall column is an image of Dalai Lama V, and at its base the stove of King Songtsen Gampo. Of the 28 images, the main deities depicted are Maitreya (1.5m), Avalokiteshvara (twice), Shaykamuni, Vaishravana, and White Tara. Most depict historical personages, such as the following: the youthful clean-shaven Dalai Lama V along with archaic images of Songtsen Gampo, his two foreign queens and Minister Gar Tongtsen (N); King Gungri Gungtsen and Minister Tonmi Sambhota (W); Tsongkhapa, Songtsen Gampo with Queen Mongza Tricham and other members of the royal family (E); and, lastly, Songtsen Gampo with Gungtang Lama Zhang (S).

Kunzang Jedro Khang (NE)

Here there are outer and inner chambers containing small images in Chinese bronze, as well as larger images of Tsongkhapa, Amitayus, Six-armed Mahakala, and Shridevi.

Second Floor

The chapels are closed on the second floor. However, there are **extraordinary murals** depicting the construction of the Potala Palace and various renowned monasteries, the Great Prayer Festival of Lhasa, and the funeral procession of Dalai Lama V. The gates overlooking the reliquary stupa of Dalai Lama V are particularly revered by pilgrims.

First Floor

West Main Hall (Tsomchen Nub Sizhi Phuntsok)

At 725 sq m, the West Main Hall is the largest room in the Potala Palace. It has eight tall and 36 short pillars, wrapped in raw silk material. The central throne of Dalai Lama VI is surmounted by a plaque, presented by Emperor Qianlong, which carries the legend: 'originally pure lotus place'. The 280 sq m murals, dating from the 17th century, depict Dalai Lama V, the Buddha-field of Mt Potalaka, and the Tibetan kings. There are two large embroidered tapestries depicting the Three Ancestral Religious Kings and the Dalai Lamas, which were presented by Emperor Kangxi. Applique tangkas depict Amitabha and the Seven Generations of Past Buddhas, surrounded by the Thirty-five Confession Buddhas (N); the four main Kadampa deities flanked by the Eight Bodhisattvas and Tara who Protects from the Eight Fears (E); the Buddhas of the Three Times surrounded by the Sixteen Elders (S); and the Medicine Buddhas, the Lords of the Three Enlightened Families, and the Seven Generations of Past Buddhas (W). The four side-chapels were originally constructed by Desi Sangye Gyatso:

Lamrim Lhakhang (E)

This chapel is dedicated to the ancient Indian and Tibetan masters of the 'extensive lineage of conduct' and the 'profound lineage of view', as represented by the Kadampa and Gelukpa schools. In the centre is a gilded silver image of Tsongkhapa, with Asanga (progenitor of the former lineage) to the right, and Nagarjuna (progenitor of the latter lineage) to the left. Near the right wall are two Enlightenment Stupas.

Rigdzin Lhakhang (S)

This chapel, dedicated to the ancient Indian lineage-holders of the Nyingma school, has 20 columns. The central image depicts Padmakara (40 kg), flanked by the consorts Mandarava and Yeshe Tshogyel. To the left are gilded silver images of the Eight Awareness-Holders (Vidyadhara), who were the teachers of Padmasambhava; and to the right are similar images representing the Eight Manifestations of Padmasambhava. Behind on the E, W, and S walls are the volumes of a *Kangyur* manuscript, written in gold and black ink.

Serdung Dzamling Gyenchik (W)

This chapel contains three reliquary stupas, the largest being that of Dalai Lama V, named **Unique Ornament of the World (Dzamling Gyenchik)**. It extends over 14m in height, almost to the roof terrace of the fourth storey. Its gold embellishments weigh approximately 3,700 kg, and its jewels are 10 times more valuable. It has in its lattice window a gold image of Eleven-faced Avalokiteshvara. At the western end of the chapel are the reliquaries of Dalai Lama X (**Khamsum Serdung Gyenchok**) and Dalai Lama XII (**Serdung Serjin Obar**), who both died as minors. Behind these lesser reliquaries is a gold manuscript version of the *Kangyur* and *Tangyur* and the *Collected Works* of Tsongkhapa and his students. The central stupa is flanked by eight stupas symbolizing the eight major events in the life of the Buddha; and on the E wall there are murals depicting Dalai Lama V.

Trungrab Lhakhang (N)

The images of this chapel depict the illustrious past emanations of India and Tibet. At the centre is a solid gold Shakyamuni and a solid silver Dalai Lama V. To the right are King Songtsen Gampo, Dromtonpa, and Tsharchen Losel Gyatso. To the left are the first four Dalai Lamas. In front are the Eight Medicine Buddhas, the Buddhas of the Three Times, the Lords of the Three Enlightened Families and the aspects of Padmasambhava portrayed in the teaching-cycle known as *Spontaneously Present Wishes (Sampa Lhundrub)*. Behind is a *Tangyur* manuscript presented to Dalai Lama VII by the Manchus, and a *Kangyur* offered by Desi Sangye Gyatso. On the far-left is the **reliquary stupa of Dalai Lama XI (Serdung Pende Obar)** with a silver image of King Songtsen Gampo in its lattice window.

From here, the pilgrim exits via the rear (N) gate of the Potala.

Karngadong Lhakhang

Southeast of the Potala Palace on Karngadong Rd is the Karngadong Lhakhang, which contains ancient carved stone tablets, said to have been removed from the Jokhang.

Dzong-gyab Lukhang Temple

The excavation of mortar for the construction of the Potala Palace in the 17th century left behind a crater which became Lake Lukhang (270m by 112m). The small island (40m wide) on this lake was once frequented as a retreat by Dalai Lama V, and a 3-storeyed temple dedicated to the naga spirits (Lukhang) was constructed by Desi Sangye Gyatso and Dalai Lama VI in the Zangdok Pelri style. There, annual offerings were traditionally made by the Tibetan Cabinet (Kashag) to appease the nagas. Renovations were carried out subsequently by Dalai Lama VIII in 1791, by Dalai Lama XIII in the early decades of this century, and in 1984. In recent years the temple has housed a small Tibetan language primary school.

Ground Floor

The chapel of the ground floor, known as **Meldro Sechen Lhakhang**, has a raised platform supporting images of Nagaraja, riding an elephant and with five snakes above the head, and White Tara. The murals of the vestibule depict the buddha-fields of Zangdok Pelri and Abhirati.

Second Floor

Here the principal image depicts Shakyamuni Buddha in the form Nagendraraja, with nine snakes above the head, symbolizing the nine naga kings. Eleven-faced Avalokiteshvara is to the left and the Twenty-one Taras to the right. A 'self-arising' stone image of Padmasambhava sits in front. The murals of the S and E walls depict the life of Pema Obar – one of the immortal themes of Tibetan opera; while those of the W and N depict the legend of the Indian king Gyelpo Lek-kye.

Third Floor

The murals of this floor are outstanding, those of the E wall depicting the Eighty-four Mahasiddhas of ancient India, Padmasambhava's Twenty-five Tibetan disciples (Jewang Nyer-nga) and a number of sacred sites, such as Mindroling Monastery, Samye Monastery, Gangri Tokar hermitage, Sakya Monastery, and Mt Kailash. On the S side is the private apartment of the Dalai Lamas, who would traditionally visit the temple during the 4th month of the lunar calendar. The W wall uniquely depicts the yogic postures of the Anuyoga and Atiyoga meditations – each vignette captioned with the appropriate instructions. Lastly, the N wall depicts the Hundred Peaceful and Wrathful Deities and after-death scenes.

Drak Lhalupuk and other Chakpori Shrines

བྲག་ལྷ་ཀླུ་ཕུག

Chakpori

Opposite the Potala to the SE is the 3,725m Chakpori, an S-shaped hill, considered sacred to Vajrapani. The slopes of Chakpori contain more than 5,000 rock-carvings, some of which were reputedly carved by Newar sculptors so as to correspond to the visions of King Songtsen Gampo, who saw images emerge from the hillside during his retreat on the adjacent Mt Marpori.

The E ridge of Chakpori is separated from Mt Marpori by the newly constructed stupas on West Dekyi lam. Traditionally, this marked the entrance to the city of Lhasa (**Dago Kani**). Beneath the cliffs on the E side are the caves and temple complex of **Drak Lhalupuk**. On the summit a nunnery was constructed in the 15th century by Tangtong Gyelpo, but this was relocated further downhill in 1695 by Desi Sangye Gyatso and Nyingto Yonten Gonpo, who built in its place the **Medical College** (Menpa Tratsang). A celebrated hilltop temple affiliated with the Medical College, which contained an outstanding coral image of Amitayus made by Tangtong Gyelpo, a pearl image of Mahakarunika and a tur-

quoise image of Tara, was destroyed in 1959, and subsequently replaced by a radio mast. Lhasa Television and Lhasa Radio have their offices below the W slopes of the hill; while the TAR Television and Radio stations are now relocated on the N side of West Dekyi lam, next to the Potala.

Drak Lhalupuk

Follow a dirt road hugging the base of Mt Chakpori's SE ridge to the **Drak Lhalupuk Cave**, also called Chogyel Zimpuk. Beyond the gateway to the site is the monastic residential building and the **Karzhung Cave**, containing new religious posters. A flight of stone steps then leads up to the 2-storey grotto chapel. On the first floor is the **Tungshak Lhakhang**, containing images of Shakyamuni Buddha, Manjughosa, Tangtong Gyelpo, and the Three Deities of Longevity. The murals here depict the Thirty-five Confession Buddhas.

On the second floor is the **Zhalye Lhakhang**, containing the throne of the Dalai Lamas, and the actual **grotto entrance** on its right wall. An inscribed history of the site and images of Padmasambhava and Amitayus, along with large stone butter lamps, mark the entrance to the grotto. This original habitation was founded circa 645 by Songtsen Gampo's Tibetan queen Ruyong Gyelmo Tsun, reputedly at a site where the subterranean nagas had been detained during the draining of the marsh for the Jokhang's construction. The grotto later came to be associated with Padmasambhava, Nyang Tingzin Zangpo and Phakpa Chegom.

The **oblong cave** measures 27 sq m, its width varying between 4.5m and 5.5m. A central column of rock supports the ceiling, which forms a narrow circumambulatory passage with the walls. There are 71 sculptures within the grotto, the earliest of which were sculpted by Newars. Of these, 69 are carved directly into the granite, 47 of them dating from the earliest period, 19 from the 12th/13th century, and three from the 14th/15th century.

Fourteen of those sculptures are on the surfaces of the central column. Its E face has sculpted images of Shakyamuni (1.3m), with Shariputra and Maudgalyayana, flanked by Maitreya and Avalokiteshvara. The S face depicts Aksobhya Buddha flanked by the bodhisattvas Samantabhadra and Akashagarbha. The W face depicts three medicine buddhas; and the N face Shakyamuni with his two students.

The **S wall of the grotto** has 32 statues in three rows (17, 1, 14). Of these the **top row** has an image of Drubtob Nyima Ze – the yogin who opened and decorated the grotto; along with Yeshe Tsogyel, Dipamkara Buddha and Manjughosa; followed by Longchenpa; Avalokiteshvara with Vajrapani and Amitabha; Ksitigarbha; Shakyamuni with Samantabhadra and Nivaranaviskambhi; Maitreya with Namkei Nyingpo and Yeshe Tsogyel; and Shaykamuni with Yeshe Tsogyel and Tara. The **middle row** has a small Shaykamuni image; and the **lower row** has fine Newar style images of Ksitigarbha, Avalokiteshvara, Maitreya, Samantabhadra, crouching Maitreya, Akashagarbha, Ksitigarbha, Acala, Nivaranaviskambhi, peaceful Vajrapani, Tara, Dolma Rechikma, and Tara. Next to the Ksitigarbha image of the lower row is a **clacking stone**, said to have been used by King Songtsen Gampo when communicating with his Chinese consort Wengcheng, who was in retreat in the adjacent cave.

The **W wall of the grotto** has six images: Khasarpani, the Buddhas of the Three Times, Mahakala, and Padmasambhava. The NW corner has a freestanding Shridevi, flanked by Padmasambhava and Vajrapani.

Lastly, the **N wall** has 17 images in two rows, including Amitabha and Shakyamuni (**top row**), and Maitreya (thrice), Avalokiteshvara (thrice), Ni-

varanaviskambhi, Tonmi Sambhota, King Songtsen Gampo with his two foreign queens, Minister Gar Tongtsen, and Shakyamuni Buddha with his two students (**lower row**).

Neten Lhakhang

Adjacent to the grotto is the Neten Lhakhang, a new 3-storey yellow building, constructed in 1987 by adolescents and consequently nicknamed the Youth Monastery. The ground floor has monastic quarters. The **main chapel on the second floor** has an entrance passage with (on the left) Tsongkhapa and his two foremost students, and (on the right) 11 statues, including two arhats, Shakyamuni, Khedrupje, and Shakyamuni on the upper row; and Huashang, Dharmatala, and the Four Guardian Kings on the lower row.

The central shrine has a new image of Shakyamuni Buddha with his two main disciples (donated by Dharamsala) and the Sixteen Elders in two rows on either side. There is also a private apartment set aside for the Dalai Lama. The balcony overlooks the Potala Palace and the city. This second floor chapel also has a landing which opens onto the **Gyaza Drubpuk** – the meditation cave of Princess Wengcheng. The latter contains a bas-relief 1m image of Avalokiteshvara, and on the right wall Wengcheng's clacking stone cavity. On the left of the landing is another rock face, with a 'self-arising' relief image of Vajrapani.

Drubtob Lhakhang

The nunnery of Drubtob Lhakhang, named after Tangtong Gyelpo (1385-1464), stands above and to the right of the Drak Lhalupuk Cave. It is considered a branch of Shugseb Nunnery (see below, page 219). The original site was consecrated by the meditations of Tangtong Gyelpo, and earlier by those of Nyang Tingzin Zangpo. The central image is Tangtong Gyelpo, while the right wall has an image of Yutok Yonten Gonpo and the reliquary stupa of Dr Khyenrab Norbu, founder of the Lhasa Mentsikhang. The back wall has paintings of the Three Ancestral Religious Kings and the Medicine Buddha in gold line on a red background.

Regency Temples of Tengyeling and Tsomonling

བསྟན་རྒྱས་གླིང་དང་ཚོ་སྨོན་གླིང

The regency temples of Kundeling, Tengyeling, Tsomonling and Tsechokling were constructed during the 17th century after Dalai Lama V had assumed both spiritual and temporal power. Among these, Tengyeling and Tsomonling are located within Inner Lhasa; Kundeling lies to the S of Parmari, in the western area of the city, and Tsechokling lies S of the Kyi-chu River.

Tengyeling

Tengyeling is located behind the Mentsikhang and on a lane, the entrance of which directly faces the *Snowland Hotel*. The main assembly hall once contained three eastern chapels, approached by a triple entrance, and an interior western hall; but the compound of the monastery is presently occupied by Tibetan homes and the Lhasa No. 1 Middle School. Only the **Protector Chapel (Gonkhang)**, at roof level, is now active. Affiliated with Samye Monastery. it contains reconstructed images of Cimara flanked on the left by Pehar and Padmasambhava, and on the right by Hayagriva and Vajrakumara. Formerly the most important of the regency temples, Tengyeling was the seat of the successive Demo Qutuqtus, who provided three regents of Tibet – the first during the period of Dalai Lama VIII from 1757-77, the second during the period of Dalai Lamas IX and X from 1810 to 1819, and the third during the period of Dalai Lama XIII from 1886-95 when the incumbent

qutuqtu was deposed by the Dalai Lama XIII on his assumption of temporal power. When Chao Erh-feng invaded Lhasa in 1910, Tengyeling offered support – for which reason the monastery was later damaged by the Tibetans in 1912, and converted temporarily into a post office. In its place, Meru Sarpa (opposite the *Kirey Hotel*) was classed as a regency temple.

The residence of the Demo Qutuqtu (**Demo Labrang**) to the N is entered from either Tengyeling or directly from East Dekyi lam. Slightly W of this building is a new Government Reception Centre, built to receive Tibetans returning from abroad.

Tsomonling

Tsomonling (properly pronounced Tsemonling) is located S of Ramoche. The large courtyard is surrounded on three sides by 2-storey monastic cells, which are now occupied by the laity. The building on the N side of the courtyard has two wings: the **Karpo Podrang** in the E and the **Marpo Podrang** in the W. The former is a 3-storey building, dating from 1777, which contains: the assembly hall, the reliquary chamber of Numun Qan I and II, and six chapels (ground level), the protector chapel (2nd level), and the residence of the monastic preceptors (3rd level). The latter, dating from the 19th century, contains: the assembly hall with reliquaries of Nomun Qan III and IV, two protector chapels, and a chapel dedicated to the Eight Medicine Buddhas. Tsomonling is the residence of the successive Nomun Qan Qutuqtus, two of whom served as regents: during the period of Dalai Lama VIII from 1777-84, and during the period of Dalai Lamas X and XI from 1819 until 1844, when the incumbent was exiled to China.

PLACES OF INTEREST IN WEST LHASA

Bonpori Gesar Lhakhang

South of Mt Chakpori, on the summit of Parmari, a mountain sacred to the bodhisattva Manjughosa, is the **Gesar Lhakhang**, a temple in Chinese style, which was built in 1792 by the Manchu ambans on behalf of the Qianlong emperor to commemorate the defeat of the Gorkhas. The temple was dedicated to the Chinese god of war and justice Guan Di, who for political reasons was identified with Gesar. A Chinese inscribed obelisk on the western side is dated 1793.

The temple, under the jurisdiction of Kundeling which lies at its base, comprises a lower **southern courtyard** containing the obelisk and leading to the main temple, and a higher northern chapel known as the **Jamyang Lhakhang**. The **main temple** has a new image of Gesar, backed by a thousand images of Tara, while the side walls have a thousand images of Padmasambhava.

Kundeling Regency Temple

Kundeling, one of the four regency temples, is located to the W of the Potala Palace and S of Parmari, at the end of a side-road which branches off West Dekyi lam at the petrol station. The original complex was large and several chapels stood within a pleasant wooded garden. Kundeling's main 4-storey temple housed an assembly hall with a ceiling nearly the height of the building. The **main chapel**, dedicated to Tsongkhapa, once contained the reliquary stupas of the successive Tasak Qutuqtus, two of whom served as regents of Tibet – one during the period of Dalai Lama VIII and Dalai Lama IX between 1791 and 1819, and the other during the period of Dalai Lama XIII from 1875 to 1886. Presently, there is a small rebuilt chapel on the site.

Norbulingka Palace

ནོར་བུ་གླིང་ཁ

This 40 ha park is entered from a main gate on Mirik lam, S of the *Holiday Inn* and the Nepalese Consulate. The site was developed as the Summer Palace of the Dalai Lamas, from the mid-18th century, when Dalai Lama VII selected it on account of a medicinal spring where he would bathe owing to his frail disposition. Thus the initial **Uyab Podrang** was built, and its site subsequently augmented in 1755 by the construction of the **Kelzang Podrang**. Later, the complex became known as the Summer Palace because the Tibetan government would move here from the Potala on the 18th day of the 3rd lunar month. Dalai Lama VIII (1758-1804) expanded the complex, building the debating courtyard *(chos-rva)*, the **Tsokyil Podrang** (marking the location of the original medicinal spring), the **Lukhang Lho Pavilion**, the **Druzing Podrang**, and the adjacent SE perimeter wall. Dalai Lama XIII (1876-1933) later upgraded the gardens of the Kelzang and Chensel palaces, developed the Tsokyil Podrang area, and finally in 1930 oversaw the construction of the **Chensel Lingka** in the NW area of the park. This new complex itself contains three palaces: **Chensel Podrang**, **Kelzang Dekyil Podrang**, and **Chime Tsokyil Podrang**. Finally, Dalai Lama XIV constructed the new palace or **Takten Migyur Podrang** between 1954-56.

Norbulingka is divided into three areas: the palaces, the opera grounds, and the government buildings, among which the opera grounds comprise the open air stage and gardens to the E of the complex, adjacent to the entrance, where operatic performances are held during the Yoghurt Festival. Further N and to the W of the Takten Migyur Podrang are the government offices and Lonyenkhang, now occupied by the park attendants and the Cultural Office

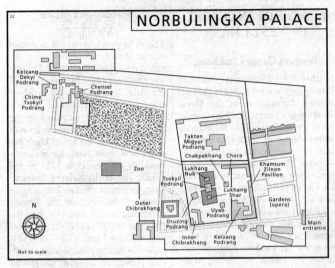

NORBULINGKA PALACE

of Tibet.

The actual palace section comprises four integral complexes which are visited by the pilgrim in the following sequence: Kelzang Podrang (SE), Takten Migyur Podrang (N), Tsokyil Podrang (C), and Chensel Podrang (NW).

Kelzang Podrang Complex

This 3-storey palace is named after Dalai Lama VII, Kelzang Gyatso, who commissioned its construction in 1755. The central feature of the complex is the N-facing reception hall known as **Tshomchen Nyiwo**, entered via a S-facing cloister, which permits bright sunlight to enter the chamber through its large skylight. The centrepiece is the Dalai Lama's throne, backed by images of Shakyamuni, the Eight Medicine Buddhas, and the Sixteen Elders. Murals depict the Lords of the Three Enlightened Families, the Three Ancestral Religious Kings, and there are also 100 applique tangkas depicting the Three Deities of Longevity.

On the second floor (approached by stairs at the SW of the portico) are the following chapels: **Nechu Lhakhang** (N) has images of the Buddha and the Sixteen Elders, the complete works of Tsongkhapa, and murals depicting the Yarlung kings; **Tashi Namrol Lhakhang** (E) is a protector chapel containing images of Six-armed Mahakala, Shridevi, Dharmaraja, Yamantaka, and the meditational deities Guhyasamaja, Cakrasamvara and Bhairava. There are two libraries (NW and NE); and the private apartments of the Dalai Lamas. The latter include: the study room known as **Tosam Gokyil** (SE), which has murals depicting Shakyamuni, Tsongkhapa's five visions, and Manjushri riding a snowlion; the **Reception Hall** with its life-size images of Buddha and Kalacakra, and murals depicting the life of Dalai Lama XIII and his retinue; and the **Cultural Hall** (Rik-ne Khang), which functions as a library and has murals depicting Avalokiteshvara, Tsongkhapa's five visions, and the symbol of elemental power and buddha attributes (*namchu wangden*).

The single-storey east-facing **Uyab**

Lhakhang is the oldest building in Norbulingka. It is located W of the Kelzang Podrang and was used as a meditation chamber by the Dalai Lamas. Note the simpler construction. The central room contains a golden throne and image of Shakyamuni Buddha, with murals depicting the Three Ancestral Religious Kings, the Sixteen Elders, the Potala Palace, the Jokhang Temple, Reting Monastery, and Norbulingka Palace. There is also a small study library (**Chakpe Khang**) and a meditation room (**Nyendzok Khang**).

The 2-storey **Khamsum Zilnon** Pavilion is located 70m NE of the Kelzang Podrang, and built into the grounds of the palace. It was formerly used as an observation point for the Dalai Lamas and their entourage during the Yoghurt Festival. Originally constructed by Dalai Lama XIII, it was replaced with a more elaborate structure by the Reting regent during the present century. The chambers of the Dalai Lamas, their tutors and officials are on the second floor.

The S-facing **Chakpekhang**, located N of the Uyab Phodrang, houses metaphysical texts and its murals depict Shakyamuni Buddha, the great Buddhist commentators of ancient India known as the 'six ornaments and two supreme ones', Kalacakra, the Sixteen Elders, the Eight Medicine Buddhas, and so forth. The S-facing **Debating Courtyard** (Chora), located N of the Chakpekhang, was once reserved for metaphysical discussions between the Dalai Lamas and their tutors.

Takten Migyur Podrang Complex

Also known as the New Palace (Podrang Sarpa) on account of its recent construction (1954-56), the Takten Migyur Podrang is an elaborate 2-storey building, located N of the Tsokyil Podrang. The roof is surmounted by the wheel and deer emblem, and the S-facing façade has large glass windows.

Ground Floor

Tiger-skin maces symbolizing royal dominion flank the entrance. The **Tshomchen Nelenkhang** in the SE is a European-style reception room distinguished by a gold image of Manjushri flanked by gilded copper images of the Eight Medicine Buddhas.

Second Floor

The **South Assembly Hall** (Tshomchen Lhoma Sizhi Dogukyil) has two entrances on the W side, while the S wall is composed of floor-to-ceiling windows. The N wall has images of Shakyamuni Buddha flanked by Manjushri and Maitreya, surmounted by a wall-length embroidered frieze depicting the great Indian Buddhist commentators. On the E wall there is an applique tangka of Yamantaka, suspended above the splendid throne of the Dalai Lama. The **celebrated murals** of the W, N, and E walls depict 301 scenes from Tibetan civilization – commencing with its legendary origins and continuing down to the period of Dalai Lama XIV.

The **Zimchung Drodren Semchokkhang** is the name given to the Dalai Lama's private quarters, comprising an **anteroom** and an inner chamber. The former has an embroidered sofa, above which is an ornate silk applique depicting Atisha, Ngok Lekpei Sherab and Dromtonpa, surmounted by the Kadampa protector deities. There is an altar on the N wall with silver images of the Lords of the Three Enlightened Families, and an old Philips gramophone, complete with 78 rpm records. The **inner chamber** to the E is the bedroom, bedecked with an Indian-style silver altarpiece dedicated to images of Avalokiteshvara, the Three Deities of Longevity, and Green Tara. A tangka depicts Tsongkhapa and various Gelukpa masters. Other items of interest include an art-deco bed, British plumbing and a Russian radio.

North of the anteroom is another

west-facing chamber with a sofa of Indian sandalwood and a shrine containing an image of Shakyamuni Buddha flanked by a silver Vajrayogini and a gilded copper Tsongkhapa. The **Library** (Zimchung Chakpekhang), located in the NW corner, has a principal image of Manjushri, a throne of the Dalai Lamas, and the murals of its W wall depict the great pilgrimage sites of Indian Buddhism. The **Zimchung Evam Gakyil**, located within this library, is the meditation room of the Dalai Lama, surmounted by paintings of the three meditational deities Guhyasamaja, Cakrasamvara and Bhairava; as well as Padmasambhava flanked by Shantaraksita and King Trisong Detsen. A silver shrine contains images of Guhyasamaja, Mahakala, and Manjushri; while a low table supports the three-dimensional celestial palace (*vimana*) of Mahakarunika.

The **North Assembly Hall** (Ogmin Goden Choling) is the principal reception room of the New Palace, dominated by its elevated gold throne, backed by gilded copper images of Maitreya flanked by Atisha and Tsongkhapa. The outer murals of the W and E walls depict the 56 episodes of the Buddha's life (above) and the 202 deeds of Tsongkhapa (below). The inner murals of the W wall depict the court of the present Dalai Lama, including the foreign envoys present in Lhasa during the 1940s; while those of the inner E wall depict the entire series of Dalai Lamas. Notice that the first four lack the wheel emblem, indicating that they lacked the unique fusion of spiritual and temporal power held by their successors. The murals of the S wall depict the legendary abode of Shambhala, the Sixteen Elders, and the Four Guardian Kings.

The **Zimchung Dogu Phuntsok**, entered from the E wall of the North Assembly Hall, functioned as an office and the daytime quarters of the Dalai Lama's mother. It has a white sandalwood shrine replete with sandalwood images of Shakyamuni, the Six Ornaments and Two Supreme Ones of ancient India, Milarepa, and Atisha. On the N wall are gold images of Atisha with Ngok Lekpei Sherab and Dromtonpa; while its murals depict Tsongkhapa and his eight main students, with the founders of the major Gelukpa monasteries.

The **Zimchung Jeltrekhang** (SE corner) where the Dalai Lama would relax with his family members has French furniture, and its white sandalwood shrine, holding images of Shakyamuni Buddha and the Sixteen Elders, was presented in 1956 by the Mahabodhi Society of India.

Outside this room on a landing, there are murals depicting the omni-directional wheel-shaped geometric poems (*kunzang khorlo*), which cleverly illustrate the names of the Tibetan Kings and the Dalai Lamas. Other murals depict Padmasambhava, flanked by Shantaraksita and King Trisong Detsen, the symbol of elemental power and buddha attributes (*namchu wangden*), the Four Harmonious Brethren (*tunpa punzhi*), the Twenty-five Kulika Kings of Shambhala and the Three Deities of Longevity. Lastly, there is an enigmatic drawing known as Domtson Dampa, which was used to refer obliquely to the great masters of the early phase of Buddhist propagation in Tibet during the persecution of Langdarma. It encorporates a lotus motif, symbolizing Padmasambhava, a book symbolizing Shantaraksita, a sword symbolizing King Trisong Detsen (who are also identified respectively with the Lords of the Three Enlightened Families), a two-headed duck indicative of Shantaraksita and Kamalashila, and a two-headed parrot representing the translators Kawa Peltsek and Chogrolui Gyeltsen.

Tsokyil Podrang Complex

The 18th century recreational complex of Tsokyil Podrang comprises three islands on an artificial lake. Among these, the central island accommodates the **Lhundrub Gyatsel Tsokyil Podrang**, the site of the original medicinal spring used by Dalai Lama VII. The palace was built in Chinese style with a pagoda roof in 1784 by the regent Demo Qutuqtu Delek Gyatso. A boating lake was subsequently added in 1887 by the young Dalai Lama XIII, and, at the same time, animals were first introduced to Norbulingka Zoo.

The **Lukhang Nub** pavilion was constructed on the N island, also in 1784. Its pagoda roof is supported by several Tibetan-style architectural features including an architrave of *pema* twigs. The shrine is dedicated to Nagaraja, its murals depicting Ling Gesar and the legendary competition of magical prowess held between Milarepa and the Bonpos at Mt Kailash. The **Lukhang Shar** pavilion, E of the lake, houses ritual implements.

West of the lake is the 2-storey **Druzing Podrang**, also known as Dekyi Kunga Kyilwei Podrang, which was built by Dalai Lama XIII as a library and retreat. Pebbles deposited as a cairn by him are still visible outside the entrance. The building was renovated in 1982.

On the ground floor, the **assembly hall** (Tsomchen Chime Gatsel) contains a wooden image of Avalokiteshvara, which replaces an original Thousand-armed Mahakarunika image now in the White Palace of the Potala. Flanking it are images of Amitayus and a Shakyamuni (in stone from Bodh Gaya), along with the Eight Bodhisattvas. There are also 1,000 small images of Amitayus, and a library with a good collection of medical, historical, and Buddhist works, some in Chinese and Mongolian. On the **second floor**, the bedroom (NW) has murals depicting Yamantaka, the Eight Manifestations of Padmasambhava, and the Eight Taras who Protect from the Eight Fears.

An **inner meditation cell** used by Dalai Lama XIII for Yamantaka meditation has images of Shakyamuni and Tsongkhapa. Further E is an **official chapel** containing images of Padmasambhava, Tsongkhapa with his foremost students, Avalokiteshvara, Manjushri, Amitayus and Shakyamuni, along with a throne surmounted by murals depicting the Five Buddhas of the Enlightened Families.

Chibrakhang

The stables (Chibrakhang) occupy two buildings to the rear of the Tsokyil Podrang and Kelzang Podrang complexes. Of these, the **Inner Chibrakhang** has murals depicting the rearing of horses. It contains a 2-storey building, the upper one being where the Dalai Lamas prepared for outings. The **Outer Chibrakhang** with its stables contains three rusting motor cars – a 1931 Dodge and two 1927 Austins; and to its E is an outdoor stage platform, utilized during the Yoghurt Festival.

Chensel Podrang Complex

A pathway leads through the zoo behind the three aforementioned palace complexes, to the **Chensel Podrang**, at the NW extremity of Norbulingka. The main 3-storeyed building was commissioned by the minister Chensel during the early years of Dalai Lama XIII, and rebuilt by the latter in 1926-28. A second floor balcony overlooks the courtyard where monks from Drepung would once perform religious dances.

Ground Floor

The **Main Audience Hall** (Tsomchen Nyiwo) is where monastic ceremonies and *geshe* examinations were once held. The throne is on a raised platform at the N side, with an image of Dalai Lama XIII to its rear and a cabinet containing a silver image of Dalai Lama I in front. The side cabinets contain 36 silver statues of the Three Deities of Longevity. Murals depict the 108 deeds of Shakyamuni Buddha and the 80 aspects of Tsongkhapa's career.

Second Floor

The study room, known as **Rabsel Paksam Dokyil**, is entered from the W side, its walls decorated by black and white photos taken in 1910 during the Dalai Lama's flight to Calcutta. Also on this floor are the rooms of the Dalai Lama's attendants; and the **Dingjakhang** – a well-lit S-sided balcony.

Third Floor

On the third storey is the **Sizhi Pelbar Assembly Hall**, where the Dalai Lama would give empowerments and private teachings. It contains images of Thousand-armed Mahakarunika (lifesize) and Thousand-armed Sitatapatra, along with the protector Dorje Drakden. The murals depict the successive Dalai Lamas, from I to XIII, and the main Gelukpa monasteries. There is also an inner meditation chamber called **Tsungdrel Teksum Juggo**.

There are also two smaller palaces within the complex. Some l60m W of the main Chensel Podrang is the 2-storey **Kelzang Dekyi Podrang**, which was constructed between 1926-28, as an audience hall and later as a residence. On its ground floor, the **Zimchung Tashi Onang** contains the personal treasury of Dalai Lama XIII, while on the second floor (entered from the E staircase) there is a **Reception Room** with smaller partitioned chambers to the W. Images include Shakyamuni, Avalokiteshvara, and Khedrupje; while the murals include the sacred abodes of Mt Potalaka, Vajrasana, Wutaishan, Tushita and Dhanyakataka.

Further W of this building is the simply constructed **Chime Tsokyil Podrang**, in which Dalai Lama XIII passed away in 1933, and S of that is the **Usilkhang**, a dilapidated pavilion where the Dalai Lamas would wash their head.

Khache Lingka

The original Muslim quarter of Lhasa is the Khache Lingka, 3 km W of the Potala

Palace towards Drepung. It contains two mosques and a cemetery.

Drepung Monastery
འབྲས་སྤུངས་དགོན་པ

Drepung Monastery is located 8 km NW of Lhasa on the Gephel Utse ridge above West Dekyi lam. It was founded in 1416 by Jamyang Choje Tashi Palden (1397-1449), and named after the sacred abode of Shridhanyakataka in S India. Jamyang Choje was one of Tsongkhapa's foremost disciples, and it is known that Tsongkhapa himself taught at the site of the new monastery. The complex developed rapidly with the assistance of the Phakmodru kings, especially Nedong Namka Zangpo, so that there were 2,000 monks in its second year of existence. In the early years of the 16th century, Dalai Lama II took possession of the **Ganden Podrang** at Drepung, which was later to become an important centre of political power in Tibet. At the time when Dalai Lama V assumed spiritual and temporal power in 1641, Drepung had over 10,000 monks, who hailed from 321 different branch monasteries and lived according to nationality in 50-60 different houses, making it the largest monastery in the world. Drepung's influence within the Gelukpa world extended far to the E and NE through Amdo and Mongolia. The abbot-preceptor of Drepung, known as the **Tripa Khenpo**, was formerly an influential figure within the Tibetan government.

Much of the 20,000 sq m complex at Drepung has survived unscathed, despite repeated plunder inflicted upon it – by King Tsangpa Desi of Zhigatse during the civil war in 1618, by the Mongols in 1635, by Lhazang Qan in 1706, and by the Chinese during the recent Cultural Revolution. Many of the surviving buildings date from the 17th-18th century. The monastery reopened in 1980, with a population of approximately 500,

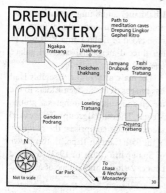

DREPUNG MONASTERY

Path to meditation caves Drepung Lingkor Gephel Ritro

Ngakpa Tratsang

Jamyang Lhakhang

Tsokchen Lhakhang

Jamyang Drubpuk

Tashi Gomang Tratsang

Loseling Tratsang

Ganden Podrang

Deyang Tratsang

N

Not to scale

Car Park

To Lhasa & Nechung Monastery

30

most of them young novices.

The complex comprises the **Central Assembly Hall** (Tsokchen Lhakhang), the **Ganden Palace** (Ganden Podrang), and a series of seven colleges (Tratsang), each originally under the control of one or other of Jamyang Choje's students, and each containing its own residential units (Khangtsang). Four of these colleges survive to the present, namely: **Ngakpa**, **Loseling**, **Deyang**, and **Tashi Gomang**. The other three, Dulwa, Shakhor, and Tosamling, unfortunately declined during the 18th century. The pilgrim's circumambulatory route around Drepung follows the sequence described here, viz: Ganden Podrang, Assembly Hall, Ngakpa Tratsang, Jamyang Lhakhang, Loseling Tratsang, Tashi Gomang Tratsang, and Deyang Tra-tsang.

Ganden Podrang

In 1518 the magnificent residence of **Dokhang Ngonmo** in the SW corner of Drepung was offered by Miwang Tashi Drakpa of Phakmodru to Dalai Lama II, and its name was thereafter changed to **Ganden Podrang**. It continued to function as the residence of the successive Dalai Lamas until Dalai Lama V moved into the newly reconstructed Potala Palace in the late 17th century. Nonetheless, the government established by him continued to refer to itself by the name Ganden Podrang until 1959.

Left of the entrance gateway is the **Sangak Podrang**, which serves as a protector shrine. The outer chamber contains an image of Dalai Lama V, the throne of the Dalai Lamas, backed by glass-cased images of the meditational deities Guhyasamaja, Cakrasamvara, and Bhairava; as well as Tsongkhapa and his foremost students. Attached to the side walls are elevated bookcases containing manuscript volumes of the *Kangyur* and *Tangyur*. The **inner sanctum** with its distinctive gold on black murals contains images of Dharmaraja, Bhairava, Six-armed Mahakala, and Shridevi.

At the northern perimeter of the terrace, is a steep flight of stairs leading to the **main courtyard**, where religious dances were once performed and where the Drepung Yoghurt Festival even now begins in summertime. This courtyard is flanked by 2-storey residential quarters, which were once occupied by the monks of Namgyel Monastery (before their move to the Potala Palace).

Beyond the courtyard, the lower storey of the palace contains an **Assembly Hall**, which houses Atisha's personal image of 'speaking' Tara (Dolma Sungjonma), and other images of Mahakarunika, and the protector deities. The **upper storey** contains the Private Apartments of the Dalai Lamas, which have images of Tsongkhapa with his main students, and an elaborate throne.

Central Assembly Hall (Tsokchen Lhakhang)

The 4,500 sq m 3-storey central assembly hall is the largest and grandest building in Drepung, rebuilt by Miwang Sonam Topgyel in 1735. Its wide terrace, approached by a flight of 17 steps, overlooks the city of Lhasa and the Kyi-chu valley. The entrance actually in use is a gateway on the left side of the building.

Ground Floor

The main hall on the ground floor (50m by 36m) has 183 columns and the 2-storeyed central atrium is well lit from above. On the left side of the hall are the **Lubum Lhakhang**, containing two sunken stupas blessed by the nagas, and the silver-plated **reliquary stupas of Dalai Lama III and Dalai Lama IV**, which are accessible to the public only on the 8th day of the 7th lunar month during the Yoghurt Festival. Beyond the Lubum Lhakhang is the **Lhamo Lhakhang**, containing a painting of the protectress Shridevi, made from the nose-blood of Dalai Lama V, as well as her three-dimensional celestial palace (*vimana*).

The **main altar** of the Assembly Hall has images of the Sixteen Elders to the far left and right in symmetrical groups of eight. The central group of images and sacred objects comprises: the reliquary of the 95th Ganden Tripa, a silver image of Sitatapatra (built in 1951), a gilded copper 2-storey high image of Manjug-

---

STUPAS

The stupa (*Tib* chorten) is a receptacle of offerings, symbolizing the buddha-mind, and the 'actual reality' (*dharmata*) or 'emptiness' (*shunyata*) behind the phenomenal appearance of the buddha-body in the world. When Shakyamuni Buddha passed away, poignantly offering his disciples a final instruction on the impermanence of conditioned phenomena, the funerary relics were interred in eight stupas, symbolic of that underlying reality, and distributed among the princes of the eight kingdoms which were his devotees: Kushinagara, Magadha, Vaishali, Kapilavastu, Calakalpa, Ramagrama, Visnudvipa, and Papa. Later, the practice of errecting such stupas as repository of offerings at crossroads and geomantic sites became popular in ancient India, particularly among some of the Mahasanghika schools. Emperor Ashoka then is credited with the multiplication of the original buddha-relics, which he reputedly inserted within 84,000 stupas constructed throughout the far-flung reaches of his Mauryan Empire and adjacent kingdoms. Some of these are said to survive at the present day, at Patan in Nepal and elsewhere.

The original stupas appear to have had a central axis, with an outer dome shape, forming a bulbous container where the relics would be interred. Books and sacred artefacts would also be inserted. As a ubiquitous Buddhism monument, the stupa has taken on a diversity of forms throughout the Buddhist world, in SE Asia, China, Japan, and so forth. The later stupas of Tibetan and Nepalese design came to have five characteristic parts: a squarish plinth or base, a rounded dome, an oblong harmika, a tiered triangular spire, and a bindu-shaped finial, respectively symbolizing the five elements: earth, water, fire, air, and space. Tibetan stupas also adopted eight distinct motifs, which together form a set, indicative of the eight principal deeds of Shakyamuni Buddha: his birth, victory over cyclic existence, enlightenment, teaching, descent from Tusita, resolution of schism, performance of miracles, and final nirvana. Such sets can be seen throughout the Tibetan plateau: for example, at Kumbum in Amdo, Zhiwu and Takzham in Kham, and at Chorten Rang-go N of Damzhung in Central Tibet. The original functionality of the stupa was never forgotten, and in Tibet the custom of cremating important lamas in a temporary funerary stupa (*purdung*), or of interring their embalmed bodies within a reliquary stupa (*dungten*) or 'golden reliquary stupa' (*serdung*) is still widely practised. The golden reliquaries of the Potala Palace, in which past Dalai Lamas are interred, are particularly renowned.

hosa in the form Chokhorma Sungjonma, and other statues of Shakyamuni Buddha, Tsongkhapa Khamsum Zilnon (donated by Longchen Shatra), Thuba Tsultrima, Dalai Lama XIII, Jamyang Choje Tashi Palden, and Dalai Lamas VII, III, IV, V, IX, and VIII. The 18th century murals depict scenes from the *Avandanakalpalata*.

Behind this wall is the **western inner sanctum** known as the **Temple of the Buddhas of the Three Times** (Dusum Sangye Lhakhang), which retains original 15th century features. Its W wall has images of Hayagriva, the gatekeeper, and four standing bodhisattvas, the N wall has silver-plated images of the Buddhas of the Three Times, with smaller gilded copper images of Shakyamuni and his two foremost disciples in front, and the Nine Stupas of Dhanyakataka to the rear. The E wall has images of Tsongkhapa, four standing bodhisattvas, and the gatekeeper Vajrapani. Small images of King Songtsen Gampo, his queens and entourage are additionally attached to the columns. Formerly, a Kalacakra ceremony was held in this temple on the 15th day of the 3rd lunar month. East of this chapel is the second or **eastern inner sanctum**, known as the **Miwang Lhakhang**, which contains an 18th century 2-storey high image of Miwang Jampa.

Second Floor

The NW corner of the second storey contains the most venerated chapel in Drepung, known as the **Jampa Tongdrol Lhakhang**. The central 15m image depicting Maitreya Buddha at the age of eight was constructed by the Phakmodru kings according to the instructions of Tsongkhapa, and it contains a hair from the head of the master himself. The entrance to this chapel is closed, and access is only gained from the floor above. The Chinese plaque above the chapel entrance was donated by one of the Manchu ambans in 1846.

Also on the second floor is the **Kangyur Lhakhang** which contains three of the 17 *Kangyur* manuscripts and blockprints kept in Drepung, viz: the Litang edition donated by Muji, the king of Jang; the Qing edition donated by the Kangxi Emperor; and a gold inscribed edition donated by Depa Lobzang Todol as a birthday gift to Dalai Lama V.

Third Floor

The **Zhelre Lhakhang**, which permits a view of the head and torso of the Maitreya image below, has a portico where pilgrims prostrate. The chapel also contains over 400 original bronze images, and, until 1994, the image was also graced by the presence of a celebrated white conch with a counter-clockwise spiral, which is said to have been buried by Shakyamuni Buddha, rediscovered by Tsongkhapa, and then presented to Jamyang Choje following the construction of Drepung. This has sadly been stolen by art thieves. Two reliquaries contain the remains of Dalai Lama II and Jamyang Zhepa, while the smaller images in front of Maitreya are (left to right): Tog-me Zangpo, Tsongkhapa, Seu Rinchen, Tsongkhapa (again) and Jamyang Choje. Eleven other images, including various Dalai and Panchen Lamas, grace the side-walls.

The **Dolma Lhakhang** contains three 'self-arising' and 'speaking' 17th century images of Tara, namely: the Nedong Chime Dolma who protects the water source at Drepung; the Yamdrok Dolma who protects the monastery's wealth; and the Gyantse Tsechen Dolma who confers authority on Drepung. The chapel also contains the edition of the Dzamling Yashak *Kangyur*, its 114 volumes inscribed in gold ink with ornately carved sandalwood covers. Other images include: Six-armed Mahakala, and Prajnaparamita whose heart contains an amulet box with a Tsongkhapa tooth relic. At the exit of this chapel is a tangka depicting the Hundred Peaceful and Wrathful Deities.

An adjacent **Printery** contains the *Collected Works of Tsongkhapa*, the *Collected Works of Dalai Lamas I & II*, various editions of the *Kangyur*, the *Biography of Atisha*, and the *History of Ganden*, as well as treatises on vinaya, grammar and a catalogue of publications.

Roof

The Assembly Hall has two golden roofs, one covering the temple dedicated to the Buddhas of the Three Times, and the other covering the Jampa Tongdrol temple. Other rooftop chapels include the **Gyelpo Lhakhang** which has images of the early kings and the Dalai Lamas flanking the central enthroned image of Dalai Lama V; the **Tsokchen Jowo Khang** which contains a silver Jowo Shakyamuni image flanked by 13 silver stupas; and the **Jampakhang** dedicated to Maitreya.

Jamyang Drubpuk

A small meditation cave at the eastern base of the Assembly Hall contains bas-relief images of Tsongkhapa and Jamyang Choje, and an old painting of Tsongkhapa. The rear cave wall backs onto the Assembly Hall.

Jamyang Lhakhang

Located behind the Assembly Hall, this shrine supported by a single pillar has a 'self-arising' image of Manjushri and murals depicting Jamyang Choje, his first disciple, and the Twelve Tenma protectresses. An iron staff substitutes for Jamyang Choje's lost walking stick which pilgrims once rubbed on their backs to cure rheumatic pains. Adjacent reliquary stupas contain the remains of Lama Umapa of Gadong and Bumdrak Dunpa.

Ngakpa Tratsang

This college dedicated to tantric studies is located W of the Central Assembly Hall. It was founded in 1419, originally to admit into tantric studies graduates of the other exoteric colleges. Adepts of the Ngakpa Tratsang would subsequently be admitted to the Upper Tantric College (Gyuto) or the Lower Tantric College (Gyume) in Lhasa. The **assembly hall** (Dukhang) which is the later of the two main buildings has images of the Indo-Tibetan *lamrim* lineage-holders, with Tsongkhapa and various Dalai Lamas at the centre. The **Jikje Lhakhang** behind the assembly hall was constructed by Tsongkhapa himself, and houses the sacred image of Bhairava known as 'Chogyel Caktakma', Dharmaraja holding an iron chain. The embalmed remains of Ra Lotsawa are contained within this image. Other statues here depict: Dorje Drakden, Mahakala, Shridevi, Dalai Lama V and Tsongkhapa.

Loseling Tratsang

The college of dialectics, known as Loseling (1,860 sq m), is located SE of the Central Assembly Hall. The abbot-preceptor of Loseling was highly influential, presiding over 23 residential units (*khangtsang*). The **assembly hall** has 102 columns, and it contains numerous volumes of scripture. From left to right the main images and sacred objects are: the reliquary stupa of Loseling Tripa I Legden Rinpoche; the reliquary stupa of the late Kangyur Rinpoche; images of Dalai Lamas V, VIII, and VII; a Bhairava mandala and image of Jamyang Choje; an image of Ganden Tripa XV Sonam Drakpa alias Dorje Shukden; images of Tsongkhapa and Dalai Lama XIII; the throne of Sonam Drakpa; the reliquary stupa of Loseling Dedrub Rinpoche; and images of Tsongkhapa with his foremost students, and Sitatapatra. The niches of the side walls hold 1,000 small images of Amitayus.

There are three inner sanctums. In succession, these are: **Neten Lhakhang** which has images of the Sixteen Elders in three tiers flanking an Enlightenment Stupa; the **Jampa Lhakhang** which has a large Maitreya with Shakyamuni Buddha (left), Tsongkhapa (right), and Dalai Lama XIII (centre), as well as Atisha flanked by Dromtonpa and Ngok Lekpei Sherab; and the **Tubpa Lhakhang** which has a small Shakyamuni image flanked by stupas. The upper level has a **Protector Chapel** accessible only to males. Here, Bhairava is flanked by the meditational deities Guhyasamaja, Cakrasamvara, and the protector Mahakala.

Tashi Gomang Tratsang

Located E of Loseling, this is the second largest college at Drepung, with 16 residential units (*khangtsang*). Traditionally it housed monks from Amdo, Mongolia and Nakchuka. The **assembly hall** has 102 columns, and images (left to right) of: Six-armed Mahakala (twice), Dalai Lama VI, Tsongkhapa (four), Dipamkara Buddha, Avalokiteshvara (twice), Dalai Lama VII, Maitreya, Amitayus, and Jamyang Choje. Distinctive murals depict the 108 episodes in the life of Shakyamuni Buddha.

There are three inner sanctums, in succession: **Tsepak Lhakhang** which has images of the Three Deities of Longevity; the **Mikyopa Lhakhang** which has three tiers of images, with Aksobhya at the centre of the top tier, flanked by Shakyamuni and a smaller Aksobhya. The middle tier has Shakyamuni, Avalokiteshvara, Maitreya, and a small Tsongkhapa in front; and on the lowest tier, there are five images of the celebrated Gomang lama Jamyang Zhepa. Lastly the **Dolma Lhakhang** has tiered images of the Twenty-one Taras and the Sixteen Elders. In its second storey is a protector shrine dedicated to Dorje Drakden. Here, the central image is Mahakala, flanked by Bhairava and various local deities.

Deyang Tratsang

This, the smallest of the four Tratsang, is dedicated to the Medicine Buddhas. The **assembly hall** has images of Tsongkhapa with his foremost students, Sitatapatra, White and Green Tara, and Dalai Lama V; while its gatekeepers are the protector deities Dorje Drakden and Shridevi. The **Jowokhang** at the rear of the assembly hall contains an image of Maitreya flanked on the left by Deyang Jangchub Palden and Dalai Lama VII, and on the right by Tsongkhapa, Shakyamuni, Dalai Lama III, Rato Tripa I Yonten Gyatso, and Deyang Tripa II. The monastic kitchen lies E of the assembly hall.

Five Meditation Caves of Jamyang Choje

Around Drepung there are five cave hermitages once associated with the monastery's founder. These are: the destroyed **Nyare Barti Chikhang** (near Ganden Podrang); the enclosed **Warti Shobokhang** (at the western perimeter where water is drawn for the monastery); the aforementioned **Jamyang Druphuk**; **Wartsokhang** (in the willow garden of Deyang Tratsang); and **Gozhima Shamma** (S of Loseling near Tewu Khangtsang).

Drepung Lingkor

There is a 1½ hr pilgrim's circumambulation of Drepung Monastery, which leads W of the perimeter wall and uphill to Gephel Ritro, before descending in the direction of Nechung. En route the following features of sacred geography are observed: four 'self-arising' golden fish at Ganden Podrang, Tashi Kangsar, Ngakpa Tratsang and Gungru Khamtsang respectively; a 'self-arising' Green Tara called Dolma Kangchakma; other paintings of Tara at Chiri Rizur, a 'self-arising' Jambhala, a stone throne associated with Dalai Lama V; and a 'self-arising' stone engraved with the Six Syllable Mantra of Avalokiteshvara.

Gephel Ritro

The hermitage known as Gephel Ritro is located 3-4 hrs' walk above Drepung Monastery on the Lingkhor. It was founded by Tsepa Drungchen Kunga Dorje in the 14th century. Here, monk herders produce excellent curd, which was formerly reserved for the Dalai Lamas. The ascent from the hermitage to the summit of Gephelri takes another 2 hrs. Juniper offerings are regularly made at the summit, especially on the full moon of the 4th month of the lunar calendar.

Nechung Monastery

གནས་ཆུང་དགོན་པ

Located 1 km SE of Drepung, Nechung Monastery is the abode of the protector deity Pehar and the seat of the State Oracle of Tibet. Pehar is said to have had legendary associations with Zahor and later, under the name Shingjachen, with the Bhatahor Kingdom of Central Asia. Following the subjugation of that kingdom by the Tibetan army under Prince Murub Tsepo, Padmasambhava converted Pehar's five forms to Buddhism, renaming them Gyelpo Ku-nga. The first Tibetan abode of Pehar was at Peharling in Samye. Later a second abode was established at Tsel Gungtang but the image of Pehar in that locale caused havoc, prompting Lama Shang to expel it in a casket into the Kyi-chu River. Retrieved from the river at Drepung, the Pehar image escaped from the casket in the form of a dove which flew into the tree at Nechung. This tree is nowadays in the rear left-side chapel, along with an image of Pehar and photo of the Nechung Oracle.

The first temple at Nechung was constructed in the 12th century; and Pehar since then is said to have periodically left the tree to fortell the future through his medium Dorje Drakden who would possess the Nechung Oracle, making pronouncements on natural disasters, political appointments and so forth. Originally a Nyingmapa establishment, Nechung later developed a close relation with nearby Drepung; and from the time of Dalai Lama V its oracles have held highly influential positions within the political life of Tibet, acting frequently as an intermediary between Pehar and the Dalai Lama.

Each Great Prayer Festival at Lhasa, the oracle would leave Nechung for Meru Monastery via the Barkhor and appear publicly on the 24th day of the 1st month of the lunar year to ward off obstacles. Above all, the oracle was required to undertake a rigorous training in tantric liturgies. When possessed by Dorje Drakden, the oracle would whisper his pronouncements, which would then be interpreted and written down by monk attendants on long blackboards dusted with limestone powder.

The oracle was also generally accessible to the nobility who paid generously for private divinations. In 1904, the medium was obliged to abdicate by Dalai Lama XIII owing to false prognostications concerning the Younghusband Expedition. In 1930 a new medium emerged to confirm the recognition of the new Dalai Lama XIV in 1937. He gave advice during the 1950s concerning the movement of the Dalai Lama and his *geshe* examinations of 1958. The following year, he fled to India with his entourage of six monks. The present incumbent, Lobzang Jikme, was not discovered as a tulku but appointed in Dharamsala where he presently resides with 20 monks. In 1976 the Drepung monks of Mungod were alarmed by his predictions concerning the well-being of the Dalai Lama.

The buildings of Nechung mostly survived the Cultural Revolution apart from its guilded roofs and embellishments. The complex, nestling within a grove of juniper and fruit trees, is approached via a lane marked by a water tower, SE of Drepung. The **residence of** the **Nechung Oracle** is located behind the main buildings, while the **School of Buddhist Dialectics** (Nangten Lobdra) is located down a lane to the left of the main entrance.

The courtyard is entered by three gates, of which the southern one is always closed, reputedly because Dorje Shugden is said to be waiting constantly outside this gate to usurp power on the departure of Pehar. Murals here depict Pehar and retinue; and there is an inscriptionless obelisk dedicated to Pehar. The 3-storeyed temple at the N end of the courtyard is approached by steps flanked by stone lions. The portico is flanked by murals depicting Pehar and Dorje Drakden.

Ground Floor
The assembly hall with its dark murals depicting the Deities of the Eight Transmitted Precepts (Kabgye) is adjoined by three chapels: among these, the **Jordungkhang** (W) contains the sacred tree stump abode of Pehar's dove emanation, flanked by two Pehar images in peaceful and wrathful guises, along with further images of Padmasambhava and Tsongkhapa; the **Tsenkhang Uma** (C) has a central image of Shakyamuni flanked by the pedestals of the now destroyed Eight Bodhisattvas. Formerly it also housed the throne of the Nechung Oracle backed by the Kutshab Rinpoche image of Padmasambhava through which Pehar was controlled. Lastly, the **Gonkhang** (E) is dedicated to Magzorma, and has images of Nyima Zhonu and (formerly) of Pehar in the form Kundu Gyelpo. **NB** This last image was regarded as the regent of Nechung in times when no oracle was recognized.

Second Floor
There are two chapels on the second floor, the larger of which is the audience room of the Dalai Lamas, containing a throne and images of Tsongkhapa, Dalai Lama V, Shakyamuni Buddha, Maitreya, and Avalokiteshvara. The smaller chapel has images of Tsongkhapa and his foremost students, Shakyamuni Buddha, Avalokiteshvara, and Tara.

Third Floor
Here there is a single chapel with an image of Padmasambhava in the charismatic form Nangsi Zilnon, which was constructed in 1981. Formerly, the temple also housed the national treasures known as the **Pehar Kordzo**.

PLACES OF INTEREST IN NORTH AND EAST LHASA

Sera Thekchenling Monastery
སེ་ར་ཐེག་ཆེན་གླིང་

Located at the base of Mt Purbuchok, which forms part of the watershed between the Kyi-chu and the Penpo-chu rivers, Sera Thekchenling was founded in 1419 by Tsongkhapa's disciple Jamchen Choje Sakya Yeshe of Tsel Gungtang (1355-1435). Prior to this foundation, Tsongkhapa and his foremost students had established hermitages in the ridge above (Sera Utse). In time, the monastic community at Sera came to number between 5,000 and 6,000 monks. The complex comprises the Great Assembly Hall (Tsokchen), three colleges (previously there were four or five, including Sera To which were gradually amalgamated), and 30 residential units (*khangtsang*). A long driveway divides the complex into eastern and western sectors – the former containing the Great Assembly Hall and the Homdong Kangtsang, and the latter containing the three colleges. The pilgrimage route follows a clockwise circuit in the sequence: Sera Me Tratsang, Ngakpa Tratsang, Sera Je Tratsang, Hamdong Khangtsang, Tsokchen Assembly Hall, and Tsongkhapa's hermitage on Mt Phurbuchok.

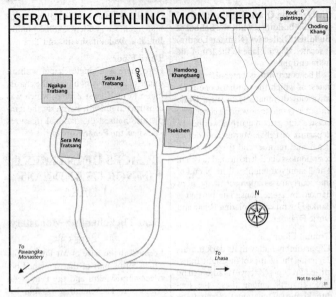

SERA THEKCHENLING MONASTERY

(Map labels: Rock paintings; Choding Khang; Ngakpa Tratsang; Sera Je Tratsang; Chora; Hamdong Khangtsang; Sera Me Tratsang; Tsokchen; N; To Pawangka Monastery; To Lhasa; Not to scale; 31)

Sera Me Tratsang

The Sera Me college, constructed in 1419, covers a large area (1,600 sq m) and has 13 residential units (*khangtsang*). It is the college promoting elementary studies at Sera. Its **assembly hall** was destroyed by lightning and rebuilt in 1761 by Kunkhyen Jangchub Penpa. It now has eight tall and 62 short columns, with main images of Shakyamuni (in copper) flanked by Maitreya, Manjushri and Amitayus, as well as by Bhaisajyaguru, Tsongkhapa and his students, Dalai Lama VII, Pawangka Rinpoche, and various former monastic preceptors of Sera Me.

There are five inner chapels attached to the assembly hall, here described from W to E (ie left to right): **Tawok Lhakhang** contains an image of Tawok, protector of the E; **Je Rinpoche Lhakhang**, contains a stupa with an inset image of Tsongkhapa flanked by images of Tsongkhapa and Shakyamuni; **Neten Lhakhang** contains images of the Buddhas of the Three Times flanked by the Sixteen Elders in their mountain grottoes, and volumes of the *Prajnaparamita*; **Jowokhang** once contained the celebrated image of Miwang Jowo Shakyamuni, which has now been replaced with a large new Buddha image, flanked by the Eight Bodhisattvas, and guarded at the gates by Hayagriva and Acala; and lastly, **Tsongkha Lhakhang** contains an image of Je Rinpoche flanked by Atisha, Dromtonpa, Dalai Lamas I-III, Dalai Lama V, Jamchen Shakya Yeshe, Gyeltsen Zangpo, who was the first preceptor of Sera, and Kunkhyen Jangchub Penpa, the founder of the college, and so forth.

The second storey contains the **Nyima Lhakhang** which has a central image of Shakyamuni Buddha in the form Tuwang Tsultrim; and the **Kangyur Lhakhang**, now containing 1,000 small images of Tara since its volumes were destroyed during the Cultural Revolution. The third storey has the Dalai Lamas' private apartments.

Ngakpa Tratsang

This 3-storeyed college building was built in 1419 by Jamchen Choje Shakya Yeshe and refurbished by Lhazang Qan in the early 18th century. It is the smallest of the current three colleges at Sera, focussing, as its name suggests, on tantric studies. The ground floor contains the assembly hall and two inner chapels.

The **assembly hall** has 42 short and four tall columns with elaborately carved capitals. The central image is an original Jamchen Choje Shakya Yeshe wearing a black hat, which was probably presented to Sera by Emperor Yongle (1360-1424) of the Ming Dynasty. Flanking this image are: Maitreya, Gyeltsen Zangpo, who was the first preceptor of Sera, Pawangka Rinpoche, Tsongkhapa with his foremost students, Dalai Lama XIII, Chokyi Gyeltsen, and Sera Je's founder Lodro Rinchen.

As for the two chapels: **Neten Lhakhang** contains images of Shakyamuni Buddha flanked by two sets of the Sixteen Elders, the upper series in Tibetan style and the lower series in Chinese lacquer, which was presented by Emperor Yongle to Jamchen Choje Shakya Yeshe. **Jigje Lhakhang** contains an original 15th century image of Bhairava, flanked by Mahakala, Dharmaraja, Shridevi, and so forth.

The second storey of the building has the **Tsepame Lhakhang** where the central image of Amitayus is flanked by the reliquary stupas of Gyeltsen Zangpo and Jetsun Chokyi Gyeltsen, as well as by images of the Eight Medicine Buddhas. The third storey has the Dalai Lamas' private apartments.

Sera Je Tratsang

Sera Je is the largest of the three colleges at Sera, covering an area of 1,700 sq m, with 17 residential units (*khangtsang*) which housed mostly immigrant monks from E Tibet and Mongolia. It was founded by Gungyel Lodro Rinchen

Senge, a student of Tsongkhapa and Jamchen Choje Shakya Yeshe. The building originally had 3 storeys, the 4th being added during a period of expansion in the 18th century when the number of columns in the assembly hall was increased to 100. The finely decorated **assembly hall** has murals depicting the deeds of the Buddha, the thrones of the Dalai Lamas and Panchen Lamas, and, on its N wall, a series of reliquary stupas, and images of Dalai Lamas VIII and XIII, Reting Tulkus II and IX, and Sera Je's founder, Lodro Rinchen.

The following chapels are visited sequentially on the W and N sides of the assembly hall: **Dusum Sangye Lhakhang** contains images of the Buddhas of the Three Times and the Eight Bodhisattvas. **Tamdrin Lhakhang** contains the most sacred image of Sera Monastery, **Hayagriva**, sculpted by Lodro Rinchen himself, and enclosed within a gilded copper embossed shrine. The upper left compartment of the shrine contains the **Sera Phur Zhal** dagger, which is traditionally placed on public view only on the 17th day of the 12th lunar month once the Dalai Lama has touched it. The dagger reportedly flew from India to Mt Phurbuchok near Sera and was hidden as a treasure (*terma*) at Yerpa before being unearthed by the treasure-finder (*terton*) Darcharuba. The chapel is also bedecked with military regalia befitting a protector shrine room. **Jampa Lhakhang** contains images of Maitreya, Eleven-faced Mahakarunika, and Tsongkhapa with his foremost students, all surrounded by an impressive library. The **Tsongkhapa Lhakhang** contains images of Tsongkhapa with his foremost students, and important lamas of Sera Je as well as Nagarjuna and the other great Buddhist commentators of ancient India, and the gatekeepers Hayagriva and Acala. **Jampeyang Lhakhang** (NE) contains two Manjushri images and one Maitreya image, the central Manjushri in the teaching gesture (*dharmacakramudra*) looking out onto the debating courtyard.

On the second floor, the **Zhelre Lhakhang** (W) permits a view of the sacred Hayagriva image on the floor below, but also contains a small image of Nine-headed Hayagriva, flanked by Padmasambhava, Dalai Lama V, and the protector deities. On the third floor, there is the **Namgyel Lhakhang**; and on the fourth, the private apartments of the Dalai Lamas and the preceptors of Sera Je.

The famous **Debating Courtyard** (Chora) contains a stone into which 13 syllables A are said to have dissolved once Tsongkhapa had completed his commentary on Madhyamaka philosophy, written in the hermitage above Sera.

Hamdong Khangtsang

This is one of the principal residential units (*khangtsang*) attached to Sera Je college. Its **assembly hall** has minor images of Tsongkhapa, Chokyi Gyeltsen, Shakyamuni Buddha, and the Three Deities of Longevity. It has two inner chapels: The **Jampakhang** contains a 'speaking' image of Tara, which is said to guard the spring water of Sera, and an image of the late lama Tubten Kunga who renovated Sera before the Cultural Revolution. The **protector chapel** (Gonkhang) contains an image of the protector deity Gyelchen Karma Trinle.

Great Assembly Hall (Tsokchen)

The 4-storeyed S-facing **Great Assembly Hall** is the largest building in Sera Monastery (2,000 sq m), with 89 tall and 36 short columns. It was constructed in 1710 by Lhazang Qan. It is entered via a 10 columned portico. Large applique tangkas are suspended from the ceiling along the side walls and there is a central skylight. The main image is that of Jamchen Choje Shakya Yeshe, the founder of Sera, flanked by Dalai Lamas V, VII, and XII, as well as by a 5m gilded Maitreya supported by two lions, Tsongkhapa and his foremost students, Chokyi Gyeltsen, Desi Sangye Gyatso, and others.

There are three inner chapels, described here in succession: **Jampa Lhakhang** contains a 6m 2-storey high image of Maitreya, which is the centrepiece of the building, flanked by the Eight Bodhisattvas and the gatekeepers Hayagriva and Acala. On the S wall is a Yongle 8th year edition of the *Kangyur* (dated 1410), originally in 108 volumes although three have been lost. This is the oldest extant *Kangyur* printed from woodblocks, and each volume has a cover carved in gold on red lacquer. The **Neten Lhakhang** contains clay images of the Sixteen Elders, each of which encloses an authentic wooden image – the original wooden series having been presented to Sera by the Ming emperor Xuan Zong. Lastly, the **Jigje Lhakhang** contains images of Bhairava and consort flanked by Shridevi and other protectors.

The second floor contains the **Zhelre Lhakhang** (C), affording a view of the large Maitreya below, with a small Tsongkhapa at its heart. The **Tu-je Chenpo Lhakhang** contains a large image of Eleven-faced Avalokiteshvara, which was originally discovered at Pawangka, and which is said to have a blessing transmitted via a staff from its heart directly to the pilgrim's head. Other images here include Tara and Six-armed Mahakala. The **Shakyamuni Lhakhang** has an image of Shakyamuni, flanked by images of various Gelukpa lamas.

The third and fourth floors contain the private apartments of the Dalai Lamas and those of the monastic preceptors of the Great Assembly Hall.

Choding Khang

The hermitage of Je Tsongkhapa, known as **Choding Khang**, is located behind the Great Assembly Hall, on the slopes of Sera Utse Hill. It is entered at roof level via a path adjacent to the painted rock carvings of Tsongkhapa, Jamchen Choje Shakya Yeshe, and the protector Dharmaraja. The building replaces the original hermitage, which was destroyed during the Cultural Revolution. Further up the slope is the meditation cave associated with the master, while the hermitages of the Upper Tantric College (Gyuto) and Lower Tantric Colleges (Gyu-me) of Lhasa are located in front.

Sera Utse

Continuing up the trail from Choding Hermitage for 1½ hrs, the pilgrim will reach the **Sera Utse**, a hermitage predating the construction of Sera itself. It comprises a 2-storeyed chapel, with monks' quarters which afford a wondrous view of the city of Lhasa, and a protector shrine dedicated to Pehar and Shridevi. An eastward trail leads around the mountain to Ragachok and Phurbuchok in the upper Dode valley; while a westward trail leads to the Tashi Choling hermitage in the Pawangka valley, 2¼ hrs distant.

Pawangka Monastery and Adjacent Sites

ཕ་འབང་ཁ

Pawangka is located some 8 km NE of Lhasa, in a defile on the lower slopes of Mt Dukri to the W of Sera Monastery, and it is approached from behind the Lhasa Military Hospital. The original temple was constructed as a tower on the 300 sq m plinth which surmounts an enormous 20m high granite rock, itself said to represent an obelisk upon a turtle. The building is said to have been modelled on Devikoti, a temple in Guwahati, Assam, which in turn had associations with Kusinagara, the sacred place where the Buddha himself passed away. (Other Tibetan sites linked to Devikota include Ragya near Lhasa, Sheldrak near Tsetang and Phurmoche

near Tashilhungpo.)

Below, at the entrance to the Pawangka defile, is a boulder, painted white with a red border along the top, where the local protector Gonpo Drashe Marpo is said to reside. Above, is a smaller whitewashed monolith – the two respectively being known as the female and male turtles (Rubal Pomo).

The original structures at Pawangka may well predate the Jokhang and Ramoche because King Songtsen Gampo and his queens seem to have gone there on the advice of Shridevi in order to suppress the supine ogress. They constructed a 9-storey palace, known as **Nyangdren Pawangka Podrang**, and there they went into retreat in order to determine the best sites for the construction of their geomantic temples. The Lords of the Three Enlightened Families affirmed their support for this endeavour by leaving 'self-arising' impressions of themselves in stone, which were later placed within the **Rigsum Gonpo Lhakhang**, which the king constructed along with 108 stupas. This temple also contains an original stone inscription of the Six-syllabled Mantra, prepared by Tonmi Sambhota who created the Tibetan alphabet here during a 3-year sojourn, following his return from India.

Above the main chapel is the **Gyaza Gonchu Podrang**, the residence of Princess Wengcheng. At the eastern extremity of the site is the **Pawang Durtro**, Lhasa's most important charnel ground, symbolizing the skull of Cakrasamvara; while there is also the **Tashi Choling** mountain hermitage, the newly reconstructed **Chubzang nunnery**, and the ridge-top **Tokden Drubpuk cave retreat** dedicated to Cakrasamvara.

Subsequently, during the 8th century, King Trisong Detsen and Padmasambhava stayed 7 days in the **Tsechu Lhakhang cave** at the base of the site. Tibet's original seven trial monks lived here for some time, but the buildings and stupas were destroyed by

Langdarma in 841, in consequence of which the protectress Shridevi advised Lhalung Peldor to kill the apostate king. A 2-storey monastery was reconstructed in the 11th century by Potowa's student Drakar, and it housed 200 monks, who gradually rebuilt the 108 stupas. Chogyel Phakpa later carried out further renovations; and the monastery was eventually completed by Khonton Peljor Lhundrub in 1619. A block of stone was brought from Devikota in Kamakhya, Assam, giving Pawangka the name Devikota. Dalai Lama V added an extra floor in the course of his renovations; so that subsequently the site was visited by all Dalai Lamas when they had obtained their *geshe* degree. The preceptors of Pawangka were later appointed directly by the Tibetan Cabinet (Kashag). In the 19th century, the hierarch of Pawangka was the teacher of the late Trijang Rinpoche, senior tutor to the present Dalai Lama.

Pawangka Circumambulation

The entire pilgrim's circuit of Pawangka takes approximately 1 day in summertime, following the sequence: Pawangka, Tashi Choling, Tokden Drubpuk, and Chubzang Nunnery.

A shorter circuit around the base of **Pawangka Rock** begins at the main steps, and runs clockwise. The **E face of the rock** contains: a cave shrine containing 1m images of the Lord of the Three Enlightened Families, Shakyamuni and Acala. The **S face** contains: rocks representing the buttocks and sexual organs of the female tortoise; and King Songtsen Gampo's cave retreat (8m by 12 m) with its original 'self-arising' bas relief image of Shridevi, and other images including the king with his two foreign queens, and Padmasambhava, flanked by Shantaraksita and King Trisong Detsen. The **W face** has a shrine dedicated to Ganden Tripa Tenpa Rabgyel who passed away here.

Nyangdren Pawangka Podrang

The present complex is a 3-storey circular building, the remains of King Songtsen Gampo's original tower, which is approached from the N by a series of steps. The other three sides are sheer rock faces. The interior floor plan is semi-circular, except for the northern section which is square. Repairs were made to this surviving structure in the 1980s; and 18 of the 108 stupas have now been rebuilt. The ground floor contains the storerooms but no chapels; while the second floor contains the assembly hall (*tsokhang*), the protector chapel (*gonkhang*), and the Four-pillared Temple (Kabzhima Lhakhang).

Among these, the **assembly hall** contains a central reliquary stupa, with an original Shakyamuni in its inner sanctum, flanked by (left side) a 'self-arising' statue of Jowo Lokeshvara, transported from Gyama, the birthplace of King Songtsen Gampo; and (right side) a 'self-arising' image called Chubzang Doku Chenrezi which was brought from Chubzang; and (below in front) another Shakyamuni image, returned recently from Beijing. On the N wall of the assembly hall (adjacent to the protector chapel entrance) are in succession images of: Shantaraksita, Dalai Lama V, King Songtsen Gampo with his foreign queens, and Dalai Lama XIII. On the W wall are Padmasambhava flanked by Shantaraksita and King Trisong Detsen, while on the E (next to the window) are old tangkas with the throne of the late Panchen Lama X below.

The **protector chapel**, entered from the E side of the assembly hall, contains the following newly constructed images: Dorje Yudronma, Vaishravana, Dharmaraja, Guhyasamaja, Cakrasamvara, Bhairava, Magzorma, Gonpo Taksha Marpo (the local protector), and Lhamo Duzorma.

The **Four-pillared Temple**, entered from the left of the assembly hall, has new images of: Tonmi Sambhota, the kings Lhatotori Nyentsen, Trisong Detsen, Songtsen Gampo and Relpachen, Minister Gar Tongtsen, Khonton Peljor Lhundrub, Reting Trichen, Tenpa Rabgyel, and Lhatsun Rinpoche. On the roof is the private apartment of the Dalai lamas, containing images of: Cakrasamvara, Tara, Atisha, Tsongkhapa with his foremost students, and Avalokiteshvara.

Rigsum Gonpo Lhakhang

The **Rigsum Gonpo Lhakhang**, located SE of the main building, was founded by King Songtsen Gampo. Beyond its entrance courtyard and within the portico to the left is the stone slab carved by Tonmi in person with the Six-syllabled Mantra of Avalokiteshvara, contained within a glass case. The left wall contains: new images of Tsongkhapa with his foremost students, Shakyamuni, and Eleven-faced Avalokiteshvara. Beyond is an **inner sanctum** containing murals of Thousand-armed Avalokiteshvara and Cakrasamvara, with the throne of the Dalai Lamas and the aforementioned highly venerated 'self-arising' images of the Lords of the Three Enlightened Families, which are of archaic design and were reputedly embellished by Newar craftsmen in the 7th century.

Adjacent to the entrance is a small shrine containing one of Cakrasamvara's three stone eyes (the others are at Tokden above and at Gari nunnery W of Pawangka). Northwest of this chapel is a newly constructed white reliquary; while N of the main building is a shrine containing 'self-arising' images of Tara (left) and Bhaisajyaguru (right). Below this shrine is a single-storey hermitage where Tsongkhapa stayed for 1 year in retreat.

Gyaza Gonchu Podrang

Uphill from Rigsum Gonpo Lhakhang is the yellow chapel of the **Gyaza Gonchu Podrang**. The ground floor contains the **Zikpa Lhakhang**, which commemorates Tsongkhapa's five visions (Zikpa Ngaden), and contains new 2m images of Tsongkhapa with his foremost students, murals of Vajrapani and Manjushri, and images of Tiger-riding Mahakala and Hayagriva. A side chamber to the left has new images of the Eight Medicine Buddhas, and some old tangkas.

Upstairs is the main chapel, dedicated to Princess Wengcheng, with images of Tara, Shakyamuni Buddha, Tsongkhapa with his students, and King Songtsen Gampo with his foreign queens.

Lhatsun Labrang

To the right (E) of the Gyaza Gonchu Podrang is the ruined Lhatsun Labrang; along with the ruined Tsongkha Lhakhang and the Karthog Lhakhang Khapa. The **Lhatsun Labrang** is entered through a S-facing courtyard, and at its rear, approached through a 1m high passage is a meditation cave of King Songtsen Gampo. To the W of the complex is a white washed rock carving of the Arapacana mantra (ie that of the bodhisattva Manjushri).

Upper White Rock

To the N of the Lhatsun Labrang is the rocky abode of the protector of Pawangka – a 15m high boulder, symbolizing the male turtle, which was formerly separated from its lower counterpart by King Songtsen Gampo's 108 stupas in order to prevent their meeting which was predicted to presage various national disasters. The rock was formerly linked to Pawangka by a heavy iron chain, which was destroyed by Langdarma along with the upper 6-storeys of the original tower. Left of the upper monolith and halfway up Mt Dukri are the **Sepuk meditation caves**, which contain 'self-arising' images of the Twenty-one Taras.

Tashi Choling Hermitage

The Tashi Choling hermitage is located on the slopes above the charnel ground, and is accessible by a pathway leading uphill from the Lhatsun Labrang. A 2-storey building stands at the N side of the courtyard and below a backdrop of ruins. On the right is a shrine containing original images of the Three Deities of Longevity, and smaller images of Shakyamuni, Bhaisajyaguru, the previous Pawangka Rinpoche, and so forth. The central pillar has a finely carved head of Hayagriva.

Tokden Drubpuk

Located 45 mins' walk above Pawangka, this hermitage comprises three caves, the main one containing one of Cakrasamvara's three eyes carved in stone, and a 'self-arising' spring, dedicated to Vajravarahi. It was a former retreat of the previous Pawangka Rinpoche, while one of the lesser caves was that of his disciple Tokden Gyaluk.

Chubzang Nunnery

Chubzang Nunnery is located at the floor of a ravine, 30 mins' walk SE of Tashi Choling. The complex comprises an enclosed debating courtyard and an assembly hall, with an entrance courtyard and kitchen. The **inner sanctum** of the assembly hall contains two sets of Tsongkhapa with his foremost students. There are over 80 Gelukpa nuns presently at Chubzang.

PLACES OF INTEREST IN SOUTH LHASA

Tsechokling Regency Temple

བཀྲ་མཆོག་གླིང་

Tsechokling, classed as one of the four regency temples, is located on the S bank of the Kyi-chu in Drib village. Constructed in 1782 by Yeshe Gyeltsen, tutor of Dalai Lama VIII, the main building (700 sq m) formerly contained a set of the Nartang *Kangyur* and a copper image of Tsongkhapa. It never actually provided a regent, but has survived the Cultural Revolution and is now under the guidance of Tsechok Rinpoche.

Ramagang

སྐུ་རྟེན་རམ་སྒང

The temple of Ramagang, in the extreme SW of the Lhasa valley, was constructed during the reign of King Relpachen, in traditional design, with a central temple and obelisk surrounded by four stupas in the cardinal directions. Nothing survives of this structure at the present day, although the stupas were photographed by Hugh Richardson in the 1940s.

LOCAL INFORMATION

● Accommodation

A *Lhasa Holiday Inn (Lhasa Fandian)*, 1 Minzu Rd, T 6322221, F (86-891) 63225796, a 3-star hotel, has 450 rm, superior category in S and C blocks with piped oxygen in rooms (US$93/room), and the inferior category in N block without piped oxygen (US$61), all rooms have attached bath, 5 restaurants (*Himalayan* for Tibetan and Nepalese dishes, *Sichuan* for Chinese dishes, *Everest* and *Gallery* for western buffet, and the *Hard Yak Café* for á la carte western meals), a full meal plan costs US$54, and breakfast US$16, also has swimming pool, *Tin Tin Bar*, coffee shop, karaoke bar, business centre, tour agency, gift shop, hairdressing and massage service, beauty salon, medical consultations (inc Tibetan traditional medicine), and in-house movies.

B *Tibet Hotel*, West Dekyi Rd, Lhasa, T 6324554, has 200 beds (US$50/double room), with attached bathrooms, restaurant (full meal plan US$32, breakfast US$8.5), travel agency, and discotheque; and *Number One Municipal Guesthouse*, Yutok Rd, has both expensive and basic accommodation, and good but plain Chinese meals.

C *Himalaya Hotel*, 9 East Lingkor Rd, Lhasa, T 6334082, F (86-891) 6334855, is located nr the river and within easy walking distance of the Barkhor, it has 116 bedrooms with attached bath (US$27/double), Chinese and Tibetan restaurants (full meal plan at US$21, breakfast US$6.5), shop, business centre facilities, and travel agency; **Sunlight Hotel**, 27 Linju Rd, Lhasa, T 6322227, F 6335675, has 133 beds (US$40/double room), some with attached bathrooms, and restaurant (full meal plan US$32, breakfast US$8.5); **Xuelian Hotel**, East Lingkor Rd, T 6323824, has 80 beds; also in this category is the **TAR Government Guesthouse (Xizang Zeng Fu Zhao dai suo)**, Middle Dekyi Rd.

D Kadak Hotel, East Chingdrol Rd, has double rooms with attached bathrooms at US$20; also **Ying Hotel**, Yutok Rd.

E Yak Hotel, 36 East Dekyi Rd, T 6323496, has 170 beds (range ¥200-90), and shared bathing facilities; **Snowlands Hotel**, Mentsikhang Rd/Tuanji lu, T 6323687, has 30 rm and Sichuan restaurant but poor washing facilities; **Kyire Hotel**, East Dekyi Rd, T 6323462, has 266 beds, big rooms (range ¥80-25), and shared showers; **Banak Zhol Hotel**, East Dekyi Rd, T 6323829, has 246 beds, thin walls, and shared shower facilities; **Plateau (Gaoyuan) Hotel**, North Lingkor Rd, T 6324916, has 180 beds, good rooms and showers; and also in this category is **Transport Office Guesthouse**, West Lingkor Rd.

● **Places to eat**
Among the major hotels, only *Holiday Inn* offers a wide range of Himalayan, Chinese, and Continental dishes. Good Chinese cuisine is available at the *Himalaya Hotel* and the *Tibet Hotel*. Lhasa city has many restaurants of varying cuisine and standard. For Tibetan food, try momo, and thukpa try the **Sonam Dokhang**, West Dekyi lam, T 6332985, where the food is excellent but expensive; **Yeti Restaurant**, West Dekyi Rd, T 6333168, which is good and reasonably priced; **Friend's Corner**, Tsomoling; **Jamdrol Restaurant**, Karma Kunzang, T 6336093, which caters exclusively to TTC tour groups; **Yak Café**, Minzu Rd, T 6334967; **Dakini Restaurant**, West Dekyi Rd; **Crazy Yak**, nr Yak Hotel, East Dekyi Rd, T 6336845, which is good and reasonably priced, with Tibetan operatic and folk dance performances in the evenings; **Yutok Restaurant**, Yutok Zampa, T 6330931; **Tibetan Corner Restaurant**, T 6325915; **Tashi Restaurant**, Tsomoling; **Tashi Restaurant Number Two**, Kyire Hotel, T 6323462; **Tibet Unute Restaurant**, Tsomoling; and **Lost Horizons Café**, Tsomoling.

For Amdo food, try the **Amdo Zakhang**, Beautiful World Entertainment Centre, Tsomoling. For Sichuan food, the **Thanduohua** is excellent and cheap. For Hotpot dishes, try **Yangyang Restaurant**, Tsomoling. For Cantonese dishes and seafood, in addition to Sichuan cuisine, try the **Crystal Palace (Ch Shuijing Gong)**, 180 Dekyi Rd, T 6333885; and for Peking duck, try the new **Gau Ya Restaurant**, on Kharngadong Rd.

For the best and most expensive Nepalese dishes (also Thai and Continental cuisine) in sophisticated surroundings with Nepalese and Indian dance performances, try the **Grand Highland Palace**, 3/F Luga Market, nr CAAC, T 6339391; **Snowland Restaurant**, Mentsikhang Rd, which is owned by Nepalese Tibetans; and **Mountain Restaurant**, Kyire, T 6338307. For Western dishes, try **Friend's Corner**, Tsomoling, where the food is good, clean and cheap; **Yak Café**, nr Holiday Inn on Mirik Lam, T 6334967, which serves clean but expensive food, and is popular with tour groups; **Tashi Restaurant**, Tsomoling, which caters mostly to individual tourists; **Snowland Restaurant**, Mentsikhang Rd, and **Lost Horizons Café**, Tsomoling.

● **Airline offices**
CAAC, Kharngadong Rd nr Potala Palace.

● **Banks & money changers**
Bank of China, West Lingkhor Rd. Limited exchange facilities are also available at *Holiday Inn*, and *Himalaya Hotel*. Larger hotels will accept credit card payments. Money changers in Barkhor will accept and change US dollars into RMB at a rate slightly above that of the banks.

● **Embassies & consulates**
Royal Nepalese Consulate, Gyatso To Rd, nr Norbulingka, T 6322881, issues 30-day tourist visas for Nepal within 24 hrs.

● **Entertainment**
Lhasa has many varied forms of entertainment. The local people devote much time to picnics, parties, and board games, especially Majong. The drinking songs of Lhasa are particularly renowned. Tibetan operas are performed at the **TAR Kyormolung Operatic Company**, the **TAR Academy of Performing Arts**, the **Lhasa City Academy of Performing Arts**, and in Norbulingka Park during the Yoghurt Festival in summer (see below, local festivals). Traditional Tibetan music may also be heard at the *Himalayan* restaurant in *Holiday Inn*, and

the *Crazy Yak Restaurant*. There are a number of nightclubs, fashion shows, discotheques, and a profusion of karaoke bars and video parlours. The **Lhasa City Cinema** is located on Yutok Rd. However, the museums such as the **Potala Museum and Exhibition Hall** on Middle Dekyi Rd, and the **Peoples' Art Museum** on the corner of East Chingdrol Rd and Do Senge Rd have little to offer in contrast to the magnificence of the city's temples, monasteries, and palaces.

● **Hospitals & medical services**
Peoples' Hospital, West Lingkhor Rd, T 6322200 (emergency department); *TAR No 2 Hospital*, Gyatso To Rd, T 6322115 (emergency department).

● **Post & telecommunications**
Fax: *Holiday Inn Business Centre*, *Himalaya Hotel Business Centre*.

General Post Office: East Dekyi Rd. Postal facilities also available in major hotels.

● **Shopping**
Books, maps, cards & newspapers: *The Perik Bookshop*, West Dekyi Rd, next to *Tibet Hotel*, has a wide range of Tibetan cultural publications. Try also the *Xinhua Bookstore*, on Yutok Rd, and the *Peoples' Publishing House Bookstore*, on North Lingkhor Rd.

Handicrafts: the traditional market of Lhasa is located around the Jokhang temple in the Barkhor and its radial road system. Tibetan handicrafts may be found here, inc textiles, carpets, jewellery, metalwork, leather goods, photographs, and religious artefacts, inc paintings, incense, and books. Antiques are available, but can only be exported with discretion. Bargaining here is the norm and, as a visitor, you should strive to reduce the proposed price by as much as 50%. Handicrafts are also available from the *Friendship Store* on Yutok Rd, and from more expensive shops in *Holiday Inn* and the *Himalaya Hotel*. For Tibetan tents and tent fabrics, contact *Tent Factory*, off East Dekyi Rd; and for new carpets, contact the *Carpet Factory*, off East Chingdrol Rd. The *Boot Factory*, on East Chingdrol Rd is also worth visiting. The Barkhor nowadays also has a number of department stores, inc a new 2-storeyed shopping complex with escalator access, opened in 1994. Chinese textiles, clothing, household utensils, and electrical goods are available here. Most shops will accept only RMB currency, and a few will be happy to receive payment in US dollars. Unofficial cur-

rency exchange facilities are instantly available; and the Bank of China is not too far distant on West Lingkhor Rd. There are interesting open air markets around Tromzikhang, N of Barkhor and on Kharngadong Rd, nr the Potala.

Photography: print film and processing are available at photographic shops on Middle and East Dekyi Rd, and on Kharngadong Rd; both slide and print film are available at *Holiday Inn*, though you are advised to carry all your film supplies from home.

Stamps: are available at GPO, on corner of East Dekyi Rd and Nyangdren Rd; and also at the reception counters or shops in the major hotels.

Textiles: *Friendship Store* on Yutok Rd, and the shops around the Barkhor offer traditional fabrics inc brocade silk, and traditional ready-to-wear Tibetan clothing.

● **Sports**
Gymnasium: on Nyangdren Rd.

Health clubs: at massage and beauty parlour in *Holiday Inn*, on Mirik Rd.

Race course: on Nyangdren Rd.

Sports Stadium: on East Lingkor Rd.

● **Tour companies & travel agents**
Tibet Tourist Corporation (TTC) also known as *China International Travel Service* – Lhasa Branch (CITS), West Dekyi Rd, T 6336626/6335046, F 6336315/6335277; *China Workers' Travel Service (CWTS)*: Tibet Branch, *Holiday Inn*, Lhasa, Rm 1104, T 6324250, 6332221 ext 1104, F 6334472, Tx 69025 WTBL CN, highly rec; *Tibet International Sports Travel (TIST)*, *Himalaya Hotel*, 6 East Lingkhor Rd, T 6334082, F 6334855; *Holiday Inn Lhasa-Tour Department*, *Holiday Inn*, 1 Mirik Rd, T 6324509, F 6334117; *Tibet Mountaineering Association (TMA)*, 8 East Lingkor Rd, T 6322981, F 6336366; Tx 68029 TMA CN; *Lhasa Travel Service*, *Sunlight Hotel*, 27 Linju Rd, T 6335196, 6333944, F 6335675, Tx 68016 TRCLS CN; *Tibet Plateau Iron Horse Travel Service (IHTS)*, West Dekyi Rd, T 6336793, 6332432, F 6336793, Tx 68012 TTB CN; *China Youth Travel Service (CYTS)*, Rm 1103, *Holiday Inn*, 1 Mirik Rd, T 6324173, F 6323329, Tx 68017 CYTS CN; *Golden Bridge Travel Service (GBT)*, Lhasa Branch, 13 Mirik Rd, T 6323828/6324063, F 6325832, Tx 68002 GBTCL CN; *China Tibet Qomolungma Travel (CTQT)*, Rm 1112, *Holiday Inn*, 1 Mirik Rd, T 6336863, F 6336861;

Asia Dragon Tour Corporation (Yarlung Travel Service), 3 Mirik Rd, T 6335181, F 6335182.

● **Tourist offices**
Tibet Tourism Bureau (TTB), Yuanlin Rd, T 6334315, F 6334632.

● **Useful addresses**
Police & public security: Foreigners' Registration Office, East Lingkhor Rd, nr *Banak Zhol Hotel*; **TAR Foreign Affairs Office**, on West Lingkhor Rd, T 6324992; **Lhasa City Police**, nr Academy of Social Sciences.

● **Transport**
Local Road Most visitors to Lhasa, whether arriving by air or land, will have their transportation organized by the travel services. Within the city, the public buses running the length of Dekyi Rd and Chingdrol Rd are inexpensive and convenient. Taxis and cycle rickshaws are also widely available, and it is always possible to hire a bicycle. For longer drives, private vehicle hire with a driver is possible. Contact any of the aforementioned agencies, or the **Taxi Company**, adjacent to the *Yak Hotel* on East Dekyi Rd; or the **District Car Rental Company**, on West Lingkhor Rd. Long distance travel by public bus is uncomfortable, irregular, and slow. There are three public bus stations: one at the West Chingdrol Rd/Mirik Rd intersection (for Zhigatse), a second off East Dekyi Rd (for Kermo), and a third on East Chingdrol Rd (for Kongpo). Hitchhiking is officially discouraged, but not impossible for the adventurous and well seasoned traveller.

Air Lhasa is connected via Gongkar Airport (96 km SE) to Chengdu (daily flights), Kathmandu (Wed/Sat), Beijing (Sun), and Guangzhou (Wed), and Shanghai (Tues/Fri).

● **Local festivals**
For the dates of traditional Tibetan festivals, inc those of Lhasa, see below, **Information for visitors**, page 34.

CENTRAL TIBET
THE KYI-CHU VALLEY

INTRODUCTION

The fertile **Kyi-chu Valley** in which the city of Lhasa is located is one of the more densely populated parts of Tibet. The valley extends from the river's glacial sources in the northern snow ranges of **Nyenchen Tanglha**, which form a watershed between the Salween and Brahmaputra, as far as its southern confluence with the **Brahmaputra** (*Tib* Yarlung Tsangpo) at **Chushul**. Upper Kyi-chu includes the districts of **Tolung**, **Phenyul**, **Lungsho**, **Dri** and **Meldro**, which lie to the NW and NE of Lhasa, while the valley downstream from Lhasa is known as **Lower Kyi-chu**. Currently, the entire Kyi-chu area is divided into six counties administered from Lhasa, namely: Tolung Dechen, Damzhung, Taktse, Lhundrub, Meldro, and Chushul. **Recommended itineraries: 3 (also 4, 6).**

TOLUNG DECHEN COUNTY

སྟོད་ལུང་བདེ་ཆེན

堆龙德庆县 Doilungdeqen

Population: 38,204   Area: 2,926 sq km

The paved Lhasa-Ziling Highway leads NW from the Dongkar intersection, W of Lhasa, and follows the E bank of the Tolung-chu upstream via Tolung Dechen to Yangpachen (77 km). Here, the northern route to Zhigatse branches off to the SW, following the Lhorong-chu tributary upstream and across Zhugu La pass into Tsang (see below, page 310), while the highway turns NE for Damzhung (85 km from Yangpachen).

The Tolung valley has for centuries been the stronghold of the Karma Kagyu school in Central Tibet owing to the presence there of three great monasteries: **Tsurphu**, **Nenang**, and **Yangpachen**. The present county capital of **Tolung Dechen** is located at **Namka Ngozhi**, a rapidly developing town 1 km beyond the Dongkar intersection.

LOWER TOLUNG

Gadong Monastery

དགའ་གདོང་དགོན་པ

Located on the slopes above Namka Ngozhi, this Kadampa monastery was founded by Zingpo Sherapa in the 11th century. It subsequently became the seat of an important oracle, and there is a meditation cave where Tsongkhapa had visions of Manjughosa. A trail leads from the monastery to the summit of Gephel Utse, above Drepung, from where there is also a trekking route into Phenyul.

Kyormolung Monastery

སྐྱོར་མོ་ལུང་དགོན་པ

If you continue on the Chushul road from Dongkar (rather than taking the Ziling highway), you will immediately cross the Dongkar Bridge. An unpaved track to the right leads up the W bank of the Tolung-chu for 7 km to Kyormo-lung. Founded by the Kadampa Vinaya master Balti Wangchuk Tsultrim (1129-1215), it was later associated with Tsongkhapa and three Gelukpa colleges were established. The fine masonry and murals of the main temple have survived the ravages of recent decades. From Kyormolung there are also trekking routes to Nam and Chushul.

Zhongwa Lhachu

ཞོང་བ་ལྷ་ཆུ

Near Kyormolung is the sacred site of Zhongwa Lhachu, where there is a natural spring, said to have been brought forth by Padmasambhava's magical prowess. The staff of Padmasambhava was formerly kept in the chapel constructed by Balti Rinpoche, and the spring itself is said to offer visions of the Eight Manifestations of Padmasambhava.

TOLUNG DECHEN TIB500

To Damzhung (85 km)

Yangpachen

To Zhugu La Pass (56 km)

50

Lungpa Zampa

LHASA

Nenang 5 14 Nakar 26

14 Namka Ngoshi 11

Dongkar 1

Tsurphu

Zhongwa Lhachu

To Nyetang (17 km)

Sketch map: not to scale

CENTRAL AND SOUTHERN TIBET (U, LHOKHA AND KONGPO)

NAKCHU

NORTHERN

PALGON

Namtso Chukmo

Lhachen La

Tashidor

Namtso

Zangzhung La

DAMZHUNG *Dam-chu*

Omatang

Gyutse La

Miri Tsangpo

Drakar

Sebrong

Reting Tsangpo

DAMCHUKA

Reting

Nyenchen Tangha

THUNDRUB

Nyingdrong

Kong-chu

Tango

Reting Tsangpo

Yangpachen Gon

Nyondrong

Pha-chu

PHODO DZONG

Drong La

Zhoto Tidro

Yangpachen

Chak La

Ngamang

Zhorong Tsangpo

Drigung Til

Shogu La

TOLUNG

Lhoroag

Dechen

DECHEN

Lhundrub *Yi-chu*

Drigung

Jomo

Gangtse

Yangra

CENTRAL

Nalanda

Phenpo-chu

Phenbo Tangkya

Urushya

Mar

Gyedal

Nenang

Pempdro La

Lamo

Katsel

MELDRO GUNGKAR

Mamzhong La

Kumalungpa

Tsurphu

NAMKA NGOZHI

Yerpa

Ganden

Gyama

Rutok Gonpa

Gangri Pelyke CHUSHUL

Nakar

Kyormolung

Nyetang

LHASA

Sangda

Lushon

DECHEN DZONG

Rutok

MELDRO GUNGKAR

Zhagong La

Sagang

Rato

Nam

TAKTSE

Onphu Taktsang

Khachu

Mabon La

Kundeling

Dzingchi

NYEMO

Angang

DARDRONG

Gangpa La

Sa-me

Shngseb Potje Drak

Drak Yangdzong

Chimpu

ZANGRI

Taktse Dzong

Kharak

Ngawari

Chedezhol

Jampaling

Drinzang

Samye

ZANGRI

Olka

Ode Gungyel

RINPUNG

Yazla

Peldi

DONGKAR

Zhung Teeshing

Mindroling

Dingpoche

ZANGRI

Yumbu

EYUL

Ngarab

Nojin

Gangzang

Dohang

GONGKAR

Namgyel

Zhol

Drong

CHONGYE

Podrang

Tsetang

Tradruk

LHAGYABRUMPA

Lhasol

NAKARTSE

Samling

Yongpado

DRATANG

Pelri

Tseringjong

Shakjang

Loklen

Khari

Gyetong

Lango

Yamdrok

Lhomo

DRANANG

Gyelmen

Yabzang

CHUSUM

Chumdo Gyang

Soksum

Jangzang

Lho Taklung

Zhandola

Chungkha

Mori

Lugu La

Yarlha Shempo

Phume Jangtang

Ling

NAKARTSE

Pagyutso

Zholchen

Droktri

Chaktse Trigu

Phudrok

Phuma

Yutso

Ve La

Tu

Chenri

Sharma

Trigu Tso

Shobotak La

TSO-ME

LHUNTSE

Yope

Zholsar

Telma

Monda La

Monda

Zhelra-chu

Shar Khaleb La

Ritang

Shopo Shar

Nyel-me

Tre La

Kangri

BOWA

DZONG

Danglhari

TAMZHOL

Takhar

Nangme-chu

Nyel-chu

KYITANG

Monda

Kuru-la

Karpo

Lu-me

Nezhi

Mish

NaraYutso

Loroto

Tritongmon

LHODRAK

Pemahal-chu

Ngamogong

Cavzhang-chu

Dokhar

Laro Karpo-chu

Khartak

Gersum

Pemaling

Dengpa

Benpa

Se-chu

Senge

Langdo

Sekhar

Gutok

Lhakhanh

Pode La

Shinbe

Lekpo

Chunak

ZHOLSHAR

TSONA

Kulha Kangri

Monla Karchung La

Namgung La

Kharcu

Me La

Shawuk Tago

Loro Narpo-chu

BHUTAN

Senge Dzong

Nyebzhang-chu

De-facto Border

Lhuntse

Jangpu

Tawang

0   100

km

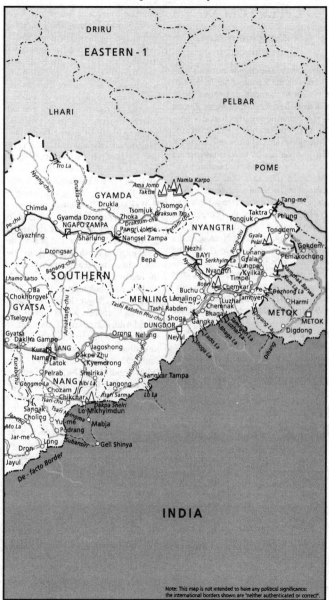

UPPER TOLUNG

Nenang Monastery

གནས་ནང་དགོན་པ

Following the Ziling highway from Tolung Dechen on the E bank of the Tolung-chu for 26 km (to kilometre road marker 3,853), you cross the river via the **Lungpa Zampa** bridge (ignoring an earlier bridge of similar iron construction), and enter the Drowolung valley where both Tsurphu (28 km) and Nenang (19 km) monasteries are located. The valley begins at Gurum township, and divides after 8 km, the southern trail leading via Nampa village and Nampa La pass to Chushul, and the western road to **Nakar** from where the Tsurphu and Nenang paths diverge. A signpost by the roadside marks the way to **Nenang**, on the far side of the ridge above Nakar. The monastery was founded by Zhamarpa I Tokden Drakpa Senge in 1333, and it later became the seat of the successive incarnations of Pawo I Chowang Lhundrub (1440-1503), the most renowned of whom was the historian Pawo II Tsuklak Trengwa (1504-66). The previous Pawo Rinpoche X (b 1912) recently passed away in France, where he had lived for a number of years. The principal temples at Nenang are the Lhakhang Chenmo and the Jampa Lhakhang.

Tsurphu Monastery: the Seat of the Karma Kargyu Tradition

སྟོད་ལུང་མཚུར་པ

Continuing along the main pathway from Nakar, which follows the Tsurphu Phu-chu upstream, after 14 km, you reach Tsurphu Monastery, the seat of the Karmapa, and one of the two main strongholds of the Karma Kagyu school in Tibet (the other being at Karma Gon in Lhato, see below, page 470). As you approach the monastery you will pass the ruins of the Karmapa's summer palace to the left.

The Site The temples, palaces, and monastic colleges of Tsurphu were severely damaged during the 1960's, following the flight of Karmapa XVI to India, but rebuilding has progressed steadily since 1983-4, largely through the efforts of Drupon Dechen Rinpoche and the good auspices of the Hawaian based Tsurphu Foundation. As you drive into the courtyard, to the left you will observe the terraced slope on which the applique scrolls of Tsurphu were once hung during religious festivals. An obelisk stands within the courtyard. Turning to face the main buildings, on the left is the Zhiwei Tratsang, in the middle is the Karmapa Labrang and Assembly Hall (Karmapa Tsokhang), and to the right is the Zuri Tratsang. The ruins of the Lhakhang Chenmo with its massive 4m thick walls are located behind the Assembly Hall, while higher up the slope stands the reconstructed palace of the regent of Tsurphu, known as Gyeltsab Podrang Chokhang or 'upper citadel of Dharma' (Chogar Gong). The regent, Gyeltsab Rinpoche, would preside over Tsurphu during the interregnum following the death of one Karmapa and the investiture of the next. The first to assume this role was Gyel-tsab I Goshi Peljor Dondrub (1427-89) who installed Karmapa VII Chodrak Gyatso (1454-1506), and from the time of Karmapa X Choying Dorje (1604-74), who offered the site to Gyeltsab VI (1659-98), the successive Gyeltsab Rinpoches have occupied this building. The present incumbent, Gyeltsab XII (b 1960), resides at Rumtek in Sikkim.

Among these buildings, the **Zhiwei Tratsang** was the first to be restored. The lower throne room with its fine murals in Chinese style depict the Sixteen Elders and its images include those of Karmapas I, II and XVI. There is also an interesting mural depicting the traditional plan of Tsurphu. Nowadays this chamber functions as a monastic assembly hall, while the upper storey contains a series of protector shrine rooms, dedi-

HISTORY OF TSURPHU

Tsurphu was founded in 1187 by Karmapa I Dusum Khyenpa (1100-93) who hailed from the Trehor region of Kham, and was one of the principal followers of Gampopa. The construction marked the site where he had received a vision of the Cakrasamvara mandala. As the founder of the Karma Kagyu school, renowned for its ascetic discipline and yogic prowess, Dusum Khyenpa is also credited with the inception of the tulku institution, which later came to dominate Tibet's spiritual and political life during the middle ages. It was he who clearly predicted the circumstances of his subsequent rebirth, and his successor, Karma Pakshi (1204-1283) became the first formal incarnation *(tulku)* to be recognized in Tibet.

Karma Pakshi constructed the main temple in 1263. It housed an image of the Buddha called Dzamling-gyen, which was said to contain original relics. Since that time altogether 17 Karmapa incarantions have occupied Tsurphu Monastery, some, such as Rangjung Dorje, renowned for their profound spiritual insights, and others such as Chodrak Gyatso and Mikyo Dorje for their vast scholarship. During the age of the Mongol Qans and Ming Emperors, the Karma Kagyu school flourished, and when Sakya's power was eclipsed, it became the most influential force in Tibetan political life under the successive dynasties of Phakmodru, Rinpung and Tsang. During this period (16th-early 17th century), when the capital of Tibet was located in Tsetang and Zhigatse, it was the Karma Kagyu school based in Tsurphu and Yangpachen which held sway throughout the Lhasa region. However, the defeat of the Tsangpa kings by the Mongol armies of Gushi Qan in 1642 at the culmination of a prolonged Civil War left the school isolated and cut off from its political power base, enabling Dalai Lama V to establish the Gelukpa theocracy at Lhasa, which persisted until the Chinese occupation of Tibet. Since 1959, when the previous Karmapa XVI established his residence at Rumtek in Sikkim, the Karma Kargyu school has developed an extensive network of Buddhist organizations and centres throughout the world.

cated to Mahakala in the form of Bernakchen, to Shridevi, and Dharmaraja, as well as to the wrathful form of Padmasambhava known as Dorje Drolo. There are some fine images of the founders of the Kagyu tradition in Tibet: Marpa, Milarepa, and Gampopa, as well as of the various Karmapas.

To the E of the Zhiwei Tratsang, is the reconstructed **Karmapa Labrang** and **Assembly Hall** (Tsokhang), which have been built on their original site. It now functions as the main temple for Tsurphu, standing in lieu of the ruined **Lhakhang Chenmo** to its rear, and upstairs is the residence of the newly recognized Karmapa XVII (b 1985). Behind, the ruins of the Lhakhang Chenmo are testament to the wanton destruction carried out against the culture of Tibet in the 1960s. This massive fortress once contained Tsurphu's most highly venerated image: an enormous 20m bronze cast statue of Shakyamuni Buddha, known as the 'Ornament of the World' (Dzamling-gyen), which had been commissioned by Karma Pakshi in the 13th century. Reconstruction of the outer walls has begun, and visitors can see a handprint left by the new incarnation in the masonry.

Further E is the partially restored **Zuri Tratsang**, an upper chamber of which contains the room used by Situ Rinpoche on his recent visit to Tsurphu from India. Here, there are documents describing the account of his recognition of the new Karmapa incarnation in 1992.

THE SEVENTEEN KARMAPAS

Karmapa I	Dusum Khyenpa (1110-1193)
Karmapa II	Karma Pakshi (1204-1283)
Karmapa III	Rangjung Dorje (1284-1339)
Karmapa IV	Rolpei Dorje (1340-1383)
Karmapa V	Dezhin Shekpa (1384-1415)
Karmapa VI	Tongwa Donden (1416-1453)
Karmapa VII	Chodrak Gyatso (1454-1506)
Karmapa VIII	Mikyo Dorje (1507-1554)
Karmapa IX	Wangchuk Dorje (1556-1603)
Karmapa X	Choying Dorje (1604-1674)
Karmapa XI	Yeshe Dorje (1677-1702)
Karmapa XII	Jangchub Dorje (1703-1732)
Karmapa XIII	Dudul Dorje (1733-1797)
Karmapa XIV	Tekchok Dorje (1798-1868)
Karmapa XV	Khakhyab Dorje (1871-1922)
Karmapa XVI	Rikpei Dorje (1921-1981)
Karmapa XVII	Orgyen Trinle Dorje (b 1985)

Further uphill and behind this entire complex are the reconstructed buildings of the independently functioning **Gyeltsab Podrang**, which includes a vast assembly hall, where the monks under the authority of Gyeltsab Rinpoche convene. The original 5-storey structure dates from 17th century.

The precipitous cliffs above Tsurphu contain the hermitage known as **Drubdra Samtenling**, and to its left is the hermitage of **Pema Khyung Dzong**, once frequented by Karma Pakshi and Karmapa III Rangjung Dorje (1284-1339). Higher up is the cave where Karma Pakshi performed a meditative retreat in darkness (*muntsam*), and a number of smaller hermitages. There is a pilgrim's circuit around Tsurphu, which takes about 3 hrs, commencing W of the perimeter wall and encompassing the Tsurphu charnel ground to the N and the aformentioned cliff-side hermitages.

Trekking

There are also three trekking routes from Tsurphu: N via the 5,300m Lhasar La pass to the Lhorong-chu valley and Yangpachen (3/4 days); S via Nampa La pass to Chushul (2/3 days); amd SW via the Tsurphu La pass to Nyemo in Tsang (2/3 days).

Tupten Yangpachen Monastery

ཐུབ་བསྟན་ཡངས་པ་ཅན་དགོན་པ

From Lungpa Zampa (see above page 196), the Ziling highway continues N, following the E bank of the Tolung-chu to Yangpachen, via the township of Mar and the old Dechen Dzong. The town of Yangpachen is the site of a geothermal power plant and hot houses which supply vegetables to the Lhasa area. There is a small hospital, a petrol station, an army compound, and a few Sichuan-style restaurants.

Yangpachen monastery is located about 14 km along the turn-off for Zhugu La pass (5,300m) and Zhigatse. It was founded in 1490 by Mu Rabjampa Thujepel on the advice of Zhamarpa IV Chokyi Drakpa (1453-1524), with funds provided by Donyo Dorje of Rinpung. Since that time it has been the main residence of Chokyi Draakpa's subsequent incarnations, the Zhamarpa hierarchs, who wear a red hat in contrast to the black hat worn by the Karmapa. The Zhamarpas held sway in Upper Tolung until 1792 when the status of Zhamarpa X (1742-92) was anulled by the Tibetan government, following his alliance with the Gorkha invasion force in an attempted restoration of Kagyu power. The woodblock edition of Golotsawa's *Blue Annals* were removed from the library at Yangpachen and transferred to Kundeling in Lhasa at that time.

The monastery has been under reconstruction since 1986, and in its **Pelkor Gonkhang**, there is an original image of the protector Six-armed Mahakala. The present incumbent, Zhamarpa XIII (b 1952), resides in India.

From Yangpachen, the northern route to Zhigatse follows the Lhorongchu upstream to Zhugu La pass for 56 km, and thence descends into the Upper Nyemo and Oyuk districts of Tsang (see below, page 310). To the S of the road, near Yangra, the Kagyu nunnery of **Dorjeling** is once again active.

DAMZHUNG COUNTY

འདམ་གཞུང་

当雄县 Damxung

Population: 21,138   Area: 8,094 sq km

The Ziling highway leading NE via Yangpachen opens out into Damzhung county, the capital of which is located at Damchuka. To the N, the road skirts the **Nyenchen Tanglha** range (7,088m), abode of the protector deity of the same name, which divides the Upper Kyi-chu region from the Jangtang Plateau and the Salween. The Dam-chu and Nyingdrong-chu rivers, which have their sources near Damzhung flow SE to converge with the Reting Tsangpo at Phodo before flowing down through Meldro and Taktse counties to Lhasa.

Damzhung town has sprung up as an important stopping point on the highway for freight trucks and buses. There are a

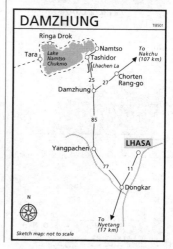

The eight stupas at Chorten Rang-go symbolizing events in the Buddha's life

number of roadside restaurants, serving Tibetan, Sichuan, and Muslim food; and in the government compound there is a large guesthouse, a public security bureau, and cinema.

After Damzhung, the highway continues NE for a further 27 km to **Chorten Rang-go** in Umatang, before cutting through the Nyenchen Tanglha range to enter the Salween River system. This point is marked by a series of eight roadside stu-

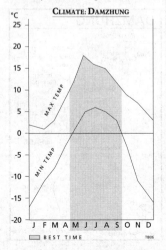

CLIMATE: DAMZHUNG

pas, symbolising the eight major events in the life of Shakyamuni Buddha. There is also a trekking route from here, which descends into the upper Reting Tsangpo valley.

Namtso Chukmo Lake

གནམ་མཚོ་ཕྱུག་མོ

An unpaved road cuts across country from a turn-off SW of Damzhung, passes via the cliff-hanging **Jangra Monastery** of the Gelukpa school, and after 25 km crosses the Lhachen La pass (5,150m). On the descent from the pass there are spectacular views of the tidal **Namtso Chukmo lake**, which is 70 km long and 30 km wide, making it the second largest saltwater lake on the Tibetan plateau (after Kokonor). The average altitude is 4,718m, and the landscape is dominated by the snow peak of Nyenchen Thanglha to the SW.

Namtso township, near the E corner of the lake has a small guesthouse and pack animals, which are hired out to those taking the pilgrimage circuit around the lake. The full circuit takes about 18 days on foot, and it is possible to drive only was far as **Tashidor**, a cave hermitage near the bird sanctuary, marked by two lofty sheer rock towers.

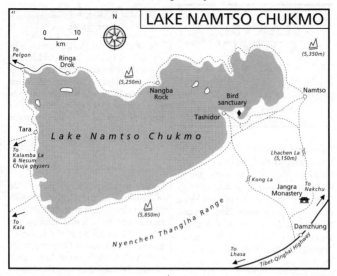

LAKE NAMTSO CHUKMO

The hermitage caves, which are said to have particular associations with Padmasambhava and his consort Yeshe Tsogyel, were frequented by many great lamas of the past, including Karmapa III Rangjung Dorje. Nowadays, they are occupied by occasional hermits of the Nyingma and Kagyu schools. The **bird sanctuary** itself teems with migratory flocks from April to Nov, and you may glimpse the rare black-necked crane.

There is a short pilgrimage circuit of the Tashidor promintory with its long *mani*-stone wall, passing near the shore; but the longer 18 day circuit of the lake requires careful preparation. Moving anteclockwise (in the Bon manner) you will reach the N promintory of **Nangba Rock** on the 8th day, **Ringa Drok** near the NW corner on the 10th day, and **Tara** on the W shore on the 12th.

ROUTES From Ringa Drok, there is a motorable road to Pelgon; and from Tara, there is another 12-day wilderness trek leading southwards via Kalamba La pass (5,240m) and the **Nesum Chuja geysers** (which freeze in winter) to Zabulung in N Shang (see below, page 318).

TAKTSE COUNTY

སྟག་རྩེ

达孜县 Dagze

Population: 21,216   Area: 1,354 sq km

Taktse county extends from the N of Lhasa Zamchen bridge as far as Lamo on the S bank of the Kyi-chu, and Logon on the N bank. As such, it includes two very important sites: the caves of Drak Yerpa and Ganden Monastery, both situated NE of Lhasa. The county capital is nowadays located at Taktse or Dechen Dzong, 21 km distant from Lhasa; and from here there are trekking routes to Samye (see below, page 235).

Tsel Gungtang

ཚལ་གུང་ཐང་

The residence of Lama Zhang, the 11th century founder of the Tselpa Kagyu school, was formerly situated 10 km E from Lhasa and S of the present Lhasa-Kongpo highway. The complex included a Kumbum stupa, two early temples, a residential building, and a later Tsuklakhang. None of these structures have yet been restored.

TAKTSE   TIB502

Sketch map: not to scale

Drak Yerpa

To Taklung (99 km)

LHASA

16   25

To Lamo (10 km)

10   11   18

Tsel Gungtang   Dechen Dzong

N

6

Ganden Namgyeling

Dechen Dzong

བདེ་ཆེན་རྫོང་

The county capital, located near the hill-top ruins of Dechen Dzong, which once guarded the approaches to Lhasa from the N, contains a Gelukpa temple, known as **Samdrubling**, which was preserved as a granary during the 1960s, and therefore has kept some of its original frescoes undamaged.

Dromto

འབྲོམ་སྟོད་

Dromto township, situated on the N side of the Taktse Zampa bridge, which spans the Kyi-chu upstream from Taktse, is surmounted by a stupa, marking the meditation hermitage of the Kadampa master Nyen Lotsawa Darmatra (11th century). Two roads diverge here on the N side of the bridge: left to Drak Yerpa and right to Phenyul and Jang (see below, page 206).

Drak Yerpa: the Caves of Mystic Realisation

བྲག་ཡེར་པ

It takes about 2 hrs to drive to the caves of Drak Yerpa, situated NE of Lhasa, either via the Taktse Zampa bridge or via Kawa and Yerpa Da villages on the more direct route from Lhasa (16 km). Following the Yerpa-chu tributary of the Kyi-chu upstream, and past a reservoir, you will arrive at this historic complex of caves and temples, some of which date from the earliest period of Buddhist activity in Tibet. The amphitheatre ridge of Yerpa and some of its larger caves are visible afar from the Lhasa-Kongpo road on the S bank of the Kyi-chu. The highest point on the ridge is the peak of **Yerpa Lhari**, abode of the local deity, at the extreme NE end of the ridge.

The Site The caves are approached via the ruined 11th century Kadampa monastery of **Yerpa Drubde**, situated

HISTORY OF DRAK YERPA

King Songtsen Gampo and his two foreign queens are said to have meditated here in the **Peu Marsergyi Lhakhang**, where they discovered 'self-arising' symbols of buddha-body, speech and mind, and in the **Chogyel Puk**. Later, Padmasambhava concealed many terma objects around Yerpa, including the celebrated ritual dagger of Sera (**Sera Phurzhal**), which was eventually rediscovered by the treasure-finder Darcharuba at Sewalung. Padmasambhava also passed some 7 months in retreat in the **Dawa Puk**, which is regarded as one of his three foremost places of attainment (*drub-ne*). In the 9th century Lhalung Pelgyi Dorje stayed at Yerpa in solitary meditation, both prior to and after his assassination of the apostate king Langdarma.

Then, following the later phase of Buddhist propagation in Tibet, Yerpa came to greater prominence under Kadampa influence: Lu-me founded 108 temples on the hillside, including a **Vairocana Lhakhang**. Marton Chokyi Jungne founded the **Jampa Lhakhang**, and Atisha himself passed 3 years here, constructing with the aid of his foremost disciples, the **Kyormo Lhakhang** and the **Chokhang**.

some 100m below the dark cavernous grottoes of the white cliffs.

Among the many caves and ruined shrines, the following (described from W to E) are most important: **Tendrel Drubpuk** associated with Atisha and his Kadampa followers; **Chakna Dorje Puk**, containing a 'self-arising' stone images of Vajrapani; **Jampa Lhakhang**, the largest cave, which once contained a celebrated 13th century image of Maitreya along with the Eight Bodhisattvas, and below which are relief images of the Lords of the Three Enlightened Families; **Drubtob Puk**, dedicated to the Eighty-four Great Accomplished Masters (*mahasiddha*) of ancient India; **Chogyel Puk**, where King Songtsen Gampo meditated in the 7th century and which once contained images of the king and the protectress Shridevi; **Dawa Puk**, containing a sculpted image of Padmasambhava, a 'self-arising' image of Ekajati and stone footprints of Padmasambhava and his student Lhalung Pelgyi Dorje; **Lhalung Puk**, where Lhalung Peldor hid for some years during the period of Langdarma's persecution; and **Neten Lhakhang**, which was constructed by Lu-me in 1011 and formerly contained images of Shakyamuni Buddha surrounded by the Sixteen Eld-

ers. Below this last shrine is the stone throne used by Atisha and a charnel ground. Atisha's hermitage, the ruins of which are even now visible had 300 monks as recently as the 19th century, when it served as the summer residence for the Upper Tantric College (ie Ramoche).

Ganden Namgyeling

དགའ་ལྡན་རྣམ་རྒྱལ་གླིང་

Situated 45 km E of Lhasa, the monastery of Ganden Namgyeling was founded in 1409 by Tsongkhapa on the Gokpori ridge of Mt Wangkur, overlooking the S bank of the river and the Phenyul valley beyond. It is approached via a turn-off at a village 39 km from Lhasa (road markers 1,529 and 4,591 km) and thence by a zigzagging motorable road for a further 6 km.

Named after the paradise of Maitreya, Ganden was the first and foremost Gelukpa monastery, constructed by Tsongkhapa himself. The site, where he himself had meditated was known to have had ancient associations with King Songtsen Gampo and his queens in that **Mt Wangkur** was named after a coronation ceremony performed at the birth of the king, and the adjacent **Mt Tsunmo Dingri** was named after the queens' favourite picnic ground. The sacred Jowo Rinpoche image of Lhasa is said to have indicated the significance of the site to Tsongkhapa, who founded the monastery in 1409 and the Chikhorkhang in 1415. The Assembly Hall (Tsokchen) was built in 1417, and the two colleges of Ganden known as Jangtse (North Point) and Shartse (East Point) were respectively founded by two of his closest disciples – respectively Namka Pelzangpo and Neten Rongyelwa. A tantric college (Gyudra) was also established by another of his students named Je Sherab Senge.

Following the death of Tsongkhapa in 1419, the succession passed first to Gyeltsabje and later to Khedrupje. In this way, the Ganden Tripa (throneholder of Ganden) came to preside over the Gelukpa school, each generally holding office for 7 years (although originally longer periods of office were observed). Formerly there were over 3,000 monks at Ganden, but following the brutal destruction of the complex during the Cultural Revolution (more severe than at any of the other five large Gelukpa es-

tablishments), the number has been reduced to about 300.

Ngachokhang

This small temple, located to the right of the trail after the bus stop, is where Tsongkhapa instructed his students. The main chamber accordingly has images of Tsongkhapa, flanked by his two foremost students, while the extremely active protector chapel to its left (out of bounds to women) has images of Shridevi, Mahakala, Dharmaraja, and Bhairava. Upstairs are the Dalai Lamas' private apartments and throne.

Serdung Lhakhang

Passing the debating courtyard and the meditation hermitage (**Gomde Khang**) on the right, the pilgrim reaches the restored **Serdung Lhakhang**, a red painted building with a large white stupa. On the ground gloor there is an interior courtyard and a Dharmaraja chapel. The main chamber or **Yangpachen Chapel** is on the second floor, containing the restored golden reliquary of Tsongkhapa (serdung), known as Tongwa Donden ('Meaningful to Behold'). Constructed in 1629, the chapel is named after a stone to the rear of the golden reliquary, which is said to have flown miraculously from Shravasti (Yangpachen) in India. The present silver stupa replaces the original, destroyed in 1959, which had been gilded by Gushi Qan's grandson and covered with a felt and sandalwood tent by Dzungarwa Tsering Dondrup in 1717. A few retrieved relics and skull fragments of Tsongkhapa have been placed within the restored stupa, and a cabinet to the left contains the master's celebrated tooth relic, within a small stupa casket, as well as his begging bowl, tea cup and vajra. The tooth relic is used in the making of barley impressions for consecrating miniture terracotta images (tsatsa), or for distribution to the faithful. Large images of Tsongkhapa and his foremost

GANDEN NAMGYELING

Vision rock
Tsongkhapa's prostration spot
Charnel ground
Guage of Negativity
Ganden Lingkhor
Nesel rock
Ozer Puk
Dreu Khangtsang
Amdo Khangtsang
Sertrikhang
Prayer flags
Serdung Lhakhang
Zimchung Tritokhang
Gomde Khang
Debating courtyard
Ngachokhang
Car park
N
Not to scale

students stand in front of the stupa. Left of the entrance is the main Assembly Hall, the side-chapels of which contain images representing the Buddhas of the Three Times, and 1,000 small images of Tsongkhapa.

Sertrikhang

Uphill and to the right of the Serdung Lhakhang is the **Sertrikhang Chapel**, containing the throne of Tsongkhapa and the succesive Ganden Tripas, which is flanked by the volumes of the *Kangyur* and backed by large images of Tsongkhapa with his two foremost students. The throne is a replica of a 15th century original made by Newar craftsmen. This chapel was originally the inner sanctum of Ganden's largest assembly hall – yet to be reconstructed.

Zimchung Tritokhang

Adjacent to the Sertrikhang and to the right is the Official Residence of the Ganden Tripa, known as **Zimchung Tritokhang**. The upper storey contains images of Tsongkhapa and his foremost students, with a full set on the *Kangyur* stacked on the wall behind. A throne used by the Ganden Tripa is located at the far end of the room. On the ground floor, there are four chapels: Among them, the **Demchok Lhakhang** contains an awesome image of Cakrasamvara, flanked by others representing Gyeltsabje, Mahakala, and Vajrayogini (closed to women). The **Dzomchen Lhakhang** contains images Tsongkhapa and students, flanked by recent lamas Pawangka Rinpoche and Trijang Rinpoche. The **Nyangde Lhakhang** is the simple chamber where Tsongkhapa passed away, and the **Gyelwa Lhakhang** is the private apartment reserved for the visiting Dalai Lamas. It contains images of Tsongkhapa, Panchen Lama X, and the Thirty-five Confession Buddhas.

Amdo and Dreu Khangtsang

Following the track uphill to the left the pilgrim passes in succession the **Amdo Khangtsang** and the **Dreu Khangtsang**. The former has brocade hangings depicting the Thirty-five Confession Buddhas and Sixteen Elders, with an image of the protectress Machen Pomra and the eye of Dharmaraja (kept in a cabinet). The latter has images of Tsongkhapa with his two foremost students.

Pilgrim's Circuit of Ganden

Thereafter, the pilgrim's circumambulatory route follows the 1 hr. Lingkhor around the hilltop, starting from a prominant group of prayer-flags. There are 'self-arising' imprints of Phadampa Sangye, the Sixteen Elders, Dharmaraja, Tsongkhapa's hat, the Lords of the Three Enlightened Families, and so forth. Passing the **Vision Rock**, which induces supernatural visions when viewed through a hole made by a fist, the pilgrim reaches the highest point on the circuit, **Tsongkhapa's prostration spot**, and then descends to the charnel ground (*durtro*) and the narrow cleft called **Gauge of Negativity** (which is said to measure the extent of the pilgrim's negativity). Thereafter, the pilgrim will pass the rock impressions of Tsongkhapa and his students, said to have been made by Tsongkhapa's own fingernails, and other impressions representing Simhavaktra, Dharmaraja's tongue, and a nectar-dripping rock.

Tsongkhapa's **Ozer Puk** hermitage contains 'self-arising' and 'speaking' images of Shridevi, Shakyamuni, Amitayus, and Tsongkhapa himself, surmounted by Atisha and Dromtonpa. Further uphill is another Dharmaraja shrine. Lastly, the pilgrim visits the black cone shaped **Nesel Rock**, on which pilgrims place their stomachs while spitting or even vomiting out disease!

LHUNDRUB COUNTY

ལྷུན་གྲུབ

林周县 Lhunzhub

Population: 65,066   Area: 6,795 sq km

The districts of Phenyul and Jang which lie to the N of Lhasa include the valley of the Lha-chu or Phenpo-chu, which rises near Yangpachen and flows SE to converge with the Kyi-chu opposite Ganden Monastery, and the 'northern region' (Jang) of the Pa-chu and Reting Tsangpo, which converge with the Kyi-chu further upstream at Phodo Dzong, the county capital, 148 km driving distance from Lhasa. These two river systems are divided by the Chak La pass (5,300m).

There are three points of access from the S: via the paved Lhasa-Kongpo road and Taktse Zampa bridge, via Drigung and Lhundrub/Phodo Dzong; or via the unpaved

road from Sera Monastery, Dokde and Yerpa. There are also trekking routes leading into Phenyul: from Lhasa via Pempogo La pass; from Tolung via Mt Gephelri ridge; and from Damzhung into Jang. Culturally, this region of Tibet has had strong associations with both the Kadampa school (especially at Reting, Nalendra, and Langtang), and with the Kagyu school (at Taklung). The Kadampa establishments were in later centuries adopted by the Gelukpa and Sakya schools.

PHENYUL

འཕན་ཡུལ

Logon

ལོ་དགོན

Located on the NW bank of the Kyi-chu, 20 km NE of the Phenyul turn-off, Logon Monastery was founded by the Kadampa master Chengawa Tsultrim Bar (1038-1103) and maintained by his illustrious student Jayulpa. Later it was adopted by the Gelukpas and became the seat of the incarnate master Lo Sempa Chenpo.

Langtang Monastery

གླང་ཐང་དགོན་པ

Located some 6 km SW of Phenpo township, on a track which crosses the Phenpo-chu (and continues over Pempogo La pass to Lhasa), the Kadampa monastery of Langtang was founded in 1093 by Langritangpa Dorje Senge (1054-1123). At its high point there were over 2,000 monks, but in later centuries its status greatly diminished and it was absorbed by the Sakya school. More recently, many of its buildings were encorporated within a local farming commune, leaving only one temple and assembly hall, with Langtangpa's revered 'speaking image' of Tara intact. Below are the ruins of the Lhakhang Chenmo and a Kadam stupa containing Langtangpa's own relics.

LHUNDRUB

TIB503

N

To Drigung Til (47 km)

47 Reting

Phodo Dzong

20

Drigung

43

Taklung (5,300m)

Logon Lamo

20

65 Phenpo

34

6

Langtang

12

25 Dechen Dzong

Nalanda

Yerpa

16 21

LHASA

Sketch map: not to scale

Nalanda Monastery

དཔལ་ནའ་ལེན་ད

Located 12 km W of Langtang near the S bank of the Phenpo-chu, Nalanda Monastery was founded in 1435 by the renowned scholar Rongton Chenpo Mawei Senge (1367-1449), and later absorbed by the Sakyapa, who recognized him as one of the 'six jewels of Tibet'. The ruins at Nalanda are extensive, but there is a renovated assembly hall, including an image of Rongtonpa himself and a stone bearing his footprint. There are also two restored residential buildings and a large Kadam stupa.

Ganden Chungkor

དགའ་ལྡན་ཆུང་འཁོར

The monastery of Ganden Chungkor is located at Phenpo township, the most fertile part of Phenyul. There are still original murals, well worth a visit.

Shara Bumpa

ཤར་འབུམ་པ

The large Kadam stupa known as Shara Bumpa is located W of Kusha village on the road to Langma and the Chak La pass. It was constructed by Sharapa Yonten Drak (1070-1141), and is revered by pilgrims who believe that by circumambulating it blindness can be cured.

JANG

བྱང

Taklung Monastery

སྟག་ལུང་དགོན་པ

Driving through the valley of the old Lhundrub Dzong, past Rinchen Tang, and the village of Langma, the road leaves the Phenyul valley and crosses Chak La pass (5,300m) before dropping sharply to Taklung (4,084m) in the upper Pha-chu valley, 120 km from Lhasa. Nomadic camps will be seen on the high pastures.

The Kagyu monastery of Taklung was founded by Taklung Tangpa Tashipel (1142-1210) in 1180 on a location previously inhabited by the Kadampa lama Potowa. Taklung Tangpa Tashipel was one of the foremost students of Phakmodrupa Dorje Gyelpo, renowned for his austere observation of monastic discipline. Through his efforts and those of his nephew Kuyalwa and the latter's successor Sangye Yarjon, the monastic population of Taklung eventually expanded to 7,000; and it survived the Mongol incursions of General Dorta Nakpo unscathed. The main temple, the Tsuklakhang, was completed in 1228. An eastern branch of Taklung was also established by the fourth preceptor, Sangye On, at Riwoche in Kham (see below, page 460), and this eventually came to eclipse the mother monastery in its importance. Mangalaguru, the fifth preceptor, continued to develop this original seat, but from the 16th century onwards, Gelukpa influence at Taklung became pronounced, as the hierarchs of Sera and Drepung sought to control the appointment of its preceptors and the instatement of its incarnate lamas.

The monastery lies along a track to the W of the Pha-chu River, below a mountain which is said to have a rock near its summit inscribed with a 'self-arising' seed-syllable A, symbolic of the emptiness underlying all phenomena. A nectar stream, descending from that seed-syllable, flows down towards the Pha-chu. At the end of the approach road, three buildings are visible across the stream, and above the ruins on the left side: **Jampa Lhakhang**, dedicated to Maitreya; the **Reliquary Lhakhang**, containing the remains of the three enormous stupas which once held the relics of Taklung's three founders, Taklung Tangpa Tashipel, Kuyalwa, and Sangye Yarjon; and the **Dargyeling Temple**, containing a large image of Aksobhya Buddha and a side-chapel which functions as a protector shrine.

The protector deities favoured here are Genyen, Nyenchen Tanglha, and Tseringma.

Looking downhill to the right of the road, the residence of Taklung Tsetrul, the incarnate lama of Taklung, has now been obscured within a cluster of village houses. Further uphill are the ruins of the great **Tsuklakhang** (the Jokhang of Taklung), the monastic kitchen, and finally, the reconstructed **Assembly Hall** (Zhelrekhang), which contains images of Taklung Tangpa Tashipel and Tangtong Gyelpo, as well as frescoes depicting the meditational deity Cakrasamvara, surrounded by the Taklung lineage-holders.

Sili Gotsang Hermitage

 སེ་ལི་གོད་ཚང་

Continuing downstream from Taklung, you drive past a sheer cliff on the left, where the Sili Gotsang Hermitage is located, adorned with prayer flags. This retreat was founded by Taklung Tangpa Tashipel in the 12th century and used also by the great Drukpa Kagyu master Gotsangpa (1189-1258). It has recently been renovated by the monks of Taklung, and contains in addition to the hermitages a protector shrine dedicated to Mahakala.

Also on the left side of the road, is a Tashi Gomang style stupa with multiple appertures, originally constructed by the Tibetan Government to mark the place where the Kyi-chu waters first flow southwards in the direction of Lhasa.

Lhundrub/Phodo Dzong

ལྷུན་གྲུབ་རྫོང་

Following the Pha-chu downstream to Lhundrub (Phodo), the county capital, you will pass on the right a strikingly conical mountain peak which forms the backdrop to the town. Three rivers converge at Lhundrub: the Pha-chu flowing from Taklung; the Rong-chu/Dam-chu flowing from the Damzhung area; and the Reting Tsangpo (or Miggi) flowing from the N of Reting. The swelling waters of the Kyi-chu, formed by this confluence, are crossed by two suspension bridges, one which leads up the Reting valley, and a second which spans the Kyi-chu to the E of town. Below the fort (*dzong*), there is also an extant iron-chain bridge dating from the age of Tangtong Gyelpo. This is the valley of **Lungsho**, which extends SE as far as Drigung, and once contained importanrt 11th century Kadampa temples, such as Tsongdu and Gyel Lhakhang.

Reting Monastery

རྭ་སྒྲེང་དགོན་པ

The road follows the Reting Tsangpo upstream for 47 km through the beautiful Miggi valley to arrive at Reting, located at 4,100m, amidst a remarkable juniper wood on the lower slopes of **Mount Gangi Rarwa**. The monastery was constructed in 1056 by Dromtonpa, the foremost Tibetan student of the great Bengali Buddhist master Atisha, 2 years after the latter had passed away at Nyetang, S of Lhasa. Here it was that Dromtonpa established the principal seat of his **Kadampa school**, and, according to legend, 20,000 juniper trees and springs emerged from the hairs of his head.

His successors Neljorpa Chenpo and Potowa expanded the monastery following Dromtonpa's death in 1064; but the Mongol armies of Dorta pillaged the site in 1240. Later, in the 14th century, Tsongkhapa visited Reting and experienced a vision of Atisha, on the basis of which he composed his celebrated *Great Treatise on the Graduated Path to Enlightenment* (*Lamrim Chenmo*). From the time of Dalai Lama VII, the abbots of Reting became eligible to serve as regent of Tibet, and they in fact did so from 1845-55, and 1933-47.

Amid the ruins of Reting, which was badly damaged in the 1960s, it is hard to grasp the former splendour of the buildings. To the extreme W of the hillside there once stood the 5-storeyed **Reting Labrang**, the palace of Reting Rinpoche, flanked by stupas. In the centre, stood the **Assembly Hall** (*du-khang*), or **Chokhang Chenmo**, containing a highly revered solid gold image of the meditational deity Guhyasamaja in the form of Manjuvajra, 45 cm in height, which was the principal meditative object of Atisha, said to have been naturally formed from the union of the primordial buddha Vajradhara and his consort. The hall also once contained a 'speaking image' of Tara and a stupa known as Tashi Pelbar. Only part of this magnificent building has been reconstructed in recent years, and the image of Manjuvarja is still the most venerated object of offering.

To the left of the building, is a consecrated spring; and to its right there was formerly the residence of Dromton and a chamber containing his teaching throne. Immediately above the Assembly Hall was the residence of Tsongkhapa, where the aforementioned *Lamrim Chenmo* was composed, and where a lifelike (Ngadrama) image of Atisha was formerly housed. The residence of Tsongkhapa's teacher Remdawa was situated higher still. On the upper E slopes of the hillside, there was a nunnery known as **Samtenling**.

Dromtonpa's meditation cave is located in a restored chapel on the hilltop Drak Senge ridge, adjacent to a shrine dedicated to the local deity **Garwa Nagpa**. Outside the cave are a sacred spring, the life-supporting tree of Dromtonpa, and a willow tree embodying Mahakala.

Other hermitages located on the ridge contain the remains of Dromtonpa's stone seat, from which Tsongkhapa later delivered his *Foundation of All Excellence*; while adjacent stone thrones have been adorned with images of Atisha, Dromtonpa and Maitreya. A red painted rock on the same ridge indicates the residence of Chingkawa, the protective divinity of Reting, which Atisha himself has brought from Nalanda in India.

Below the monastery, in the 'plain of boulders' (**Pawang Tang**), there is a large rock, known as Khandro Bumdzong, which is revered as the abode of the female deity Sangwa Yeshe.

Lamo Monastery

ལ་མོ་དགོན་པ

Located 49 km NE of Lhasa near the Taktse-Meldro road, Lamo Monastery (1109) was one of the earliest shrines constructed by Lu-me following his return to Central Tibet, when he initiated the later phase of Buddhist propagation.

MELDRO GUNGKAR COUNTY

མལ་གྲོ་གུང་དཀར

墨竹工卡县 Maizhokunggar
Population: 28,510   Area: 4,679 sq km

Meldro county, administered from the town of Meldro Gungkar, 67 km E of Lhasa, extends from the Gyamazhing Valley, due E of Lamo in the S, as far as Drigung in the N. The capital **Meldro Gungkar**, which has a small guesthouse and roadside restaurants, stands at the confluence of the Kyi-chu and Meldro Phu-chu rivers, controlling the northern approaches to Drigung and Lungsho valleys, and the eastern approaches to the forested region of Kongpo. The most important sites within the county are: Gyama, birthplace of King Songtsen Gampo; Uru Katsel, a 7th century geo-

MELDRO GUNGKAR

TIB504

Zhoto Tidro ○————○ Drigung
To Reting ◄   Til
              47
           ○ Drigung
          1.5
           ○ Uruzhva
          25   Lhakhang
Meldro Gongkar ○
              10
           ○ Ngonda
          8 ○ Gyama
           ○ Lamo

          49

○ LHASA
N   Sketch map: not to scale

mantic temple; Tangkya Lhakhang on the N bank of the Kyi-chu; Uruzhva Lhakhang, an ancient 9th century Nyingma temple; Drigung Til Monastery, and Zhoto Tidro hermitage.

Gyama

རྒྱ་མ

The turn-off for the Gyamazhing valley is located 58 km NE of Lhasa and 10 km SW of Meldro Gungkar, at the village of **Ngonda**. Within the lower reaches of this valley is the reconstructed temple of **Gyelpo Khangkar**, containing images of Songtsen Gampo and his two foreign queens, which is said to be situated near the birthplace of the king himself.

Further up the valley, you will pass in succession the former Kadampa monasteries of Dumburi, Gyamo Trikhang, and Rinchen Gang. Among these, the monastery of **Dumburi**, founded in the 12th century by Dumburipa Dawa Gyeltsen, is still in ruins. **Gyamo Trikhang**, founded by Sangye Onton, the monastic preceptor of neighbouring Rinchen Gang, has a renovated assembly hall and two chapels, upper and lower. One of its four earthen stupas (originally consecrated by Gyar Gomchenpo Tsultrim Senge in the 12th century) still stands. Lastly, **Rinchen Gang**, which was founded in 1181 by Gyar Gomchenpo Zhonu Drakpa and expanded by his nephew Sangye Onton, has a reconstructed roof-top shrine with new frescoes and relief images. The monastery had past connections with the Kashmiri Pandita Shakyashri and later came under the influence of the Sakyapa tradition.

Uru Katsel

དབུ་རུ་བཀའ་ཚལ

Situated N of the confluence of the Kyi-chu and Meldro Phu-chu rivers, Katsel was originally one of the four district-controlling geomantic temples, specifi-

Uru Katsel: a 7th century geomantic Temple

cally constructed by King Songtsen Gampo on the right shoulder of the supine ogress, who represented the rigour of the Tibetan terrain. The antiquity of the **Tukdam Tsuklakhang** at Katsel, with its unusually sloping walls, has been remarked upon by Hugh Richardson, who visited the site during the 1940s. Subsequent temples were added to the complex from the time of Padmasambhava onwards, and the monastery was later adopted by the Drigungpas.

The main building at Katsel has been reconstructed in 3 storeys, the lowest of which has three successive chapels. Of these, the **innermost chapel** contains central images of the Buddhas of the Three Times; and side images of Green Tara and Drigung Rinchen Phuntsok, as well as a stupa in which the latter's relics are preserved. The **middle chapel** contains a library, including the volumes of the *Kangyur* and *Tangyur*.

The **second storey** contains images of the Three Deities of Longevity, namely: Amitayus, White Tara and Vijaya, in the inner sanctum, and other images of Tsongkhapa, Shakyamuni, Drigungpa Jikten Gonpo, and Mahakarunika along the left wall. In the far left corner there is an applique depicting the protectress Tseringma; while adjacent to the door are the volumes of the *Collected Works of Ratna Lingpa* and the *Biography of Drigung Rinchen Phuntsok*.

The **third storey** has a large chapel with fine murals depicting the lamas of the Drigungpa lineage, flanked by tangkas of Padmasambhava, Lama Chodpa, Machik Labdron, and Shakyamuni Buddha, and surmounted by tangkas depicting Padmasambhava, Shantaraksita, and King Trisong Detsen. The inner wall has images of the Drigung protectress Apchi in her peaceful and wrathful forms, as well as Dorje Yudronma, Pehar in the form Tukyi Gyelpo, and Cimara, along with tangkas depicting Vajrasattva, Apchi and Mahakala.

Tangkya Lhakhang

ཐང་སྐྱ་ལྷ་ཁང

Located in the village of Tangkya on the N bank of the Kyi-chu, and accessible via a bridge a few kilometres N of Katsel, this geomantic temple was originally constructed in the 7th century by King Songtsen Gampo, and later restored by Lu-me during the 12th century. Further shrines were later added to the complex, including the 12th century temple built to house the remains of the Nyingma lama Zhikpo Dudtsi (1149-99). Subsequently, the temple came under the influence of other traditions: the Taklung Kagyupa, the Jonangpa, and the Gelukpa, before being absorbed by the Namgyel Monastery of the Potala Palace. The present temple appears to contain three original clay images, extracted from one of the earlier (long destroyed) structures, and some bronze Kadam-style stupas.

Uruzhva Lhakhang

Uruzhva Lhakhang (also written as Zhayi Lhakhang) is located on the S bank of the Mangra-chu, about 1.5 km upstream from Drigung township (see below, page 212). It is a small temple of considerable historic significance for two reasons. Firstly, there are original 9th century obelisks flanking the entrance gate, which have inscriptions proclaiming the royal rewards and estates granted to Nyangben Tingzin Zangpo, the childhood friend of King Trisong Detsen who helped ensure the succession of the latter's son Senalek Jinyon in 804. The obelisk on the left is in good condition, while the one on the right is fragmented. It was Nyangben who persuaded Trisong Detsen to invite Vimalamitra, the Buddhist master of the Dzogchen esoteric instructions (*mengakde*), from India, and who then became the principal recipient of these teachings in Tibet. Vimalamitra concealed the teachings at Uruzhva in the early 9th century and these were subsequently rediscovered in the 11th century by the temple caretaker Dangma Lhundrub Namgyel, from which time their transmission has continued unbroken until the present. The second reason for the importance of Uruzhva is that the temple complex was restored during the 14th century by the great Nyingmapa master Longchen Rabjampa who fully comprehended its earlier significance for the Dzogchen tradition. Later in the 18th century the site came under the influence of Sera Monastery and was reconstructed by Dalai Lama VII.

The original chapels of the temple, including the shrine dedicated to the Eight Manifestations of Padmasambhava (**Guru Tsengye Lhakhang**) were destroyed during the Cultural Revolution. The restored building is on two levels, the lower storey containing three chapels, and the upper storey a single chamber. Downstairs, the chapel to the left is still bare, the chapel to the right contains images of Padmasambhava along with the three important protectors of the Dzogchen teachings, namely: Dorje Lekpa, Ekajati, and Rahula, and a torma offering shrine. The rear chapel, in the form of an open air gallary, contains the reconstructed **Tramen Chorten**, under which Longchen Rabjampa interred the sacraments of the Damsi demons at the time of his 14th century renovations. The upper shrine, used as an assembly hall, contains a solitary image of Longchen Rabjampa.

To the left and right of the courtyard in front of the temple are the monastic residential buildings (*tratsang*), and behind the left wing there is another newly reconstructed stupa. The **Zangyak Drak** hillside to the left contains a meditation cave associated with the temple's founder Nyangben Tingzin Zangpo, and the **Karpo Drak** peak to the right has caves associated with both Padmasambhava and Dangma Lhundrub Namgyel.

Drigung Til Monastery
འབྲི་གུང་མཐིལ་དགོན་པ

The Monastery of Drigung Til is located some 72 km N of Meldro Gungkar, in the valley of the Zhorong Tsangpo, the principal NE tributary of the Kyi-chu, which

HISTORY OF DRIGUNG TIL

The Drigungpa are one of the eight schools derived from the teachings of Phakmodrupa Dorje Gyelpo (1110-1170), whose seat was established at Densatil, NE of Tsetang (see below, page 282). In 1167, a hermitage was founded at Drigung Til by Minyak Gomring, a disciple of Phakmodrupa, and in 1179, one of Phakmodrupa's most senior disciples, named Jikten Gonpo (1143-1217), inaugurated the monastery. Drigung Til acquired a high reputation for its excellence in meditation, and during the 13th century even rivalled Sakya in its political influence until its destruction by the Mongols in 1290. Following its rebuilding, the monastery once again acquired great wealth, but ceased to have a political role in the affairs of Tibet. The Drigung Kagyu tradition has several connections with that of the Nyingmapa, particularly the tradition of Longchen Rabjampa, who during the 14th century was a most influential figure in the Drigung region. The high point of its development is assigned to the 16th century, during the period of Drigung Rinchen Phuntsok, who is also considered as a Nyingmapa lineage holder. In recent centuries the Drigungpa have had two important incarnating lamas, the Chetsang and the Chungtsang; and in 1959 there were over 500 monks.

flows from its source above the nomad encampment of **Tantuk Sumdo** for over 60 km to enter the Kyi-chu opposite the ruins of the old hilltop Drigung Dzong. There are trekking routes which lead from the upper reaches of this valley into the Nyangchu district of Kongpo and the Nyiphu district of Pome (see below, page 475). The township of **Drigung qu**, which has a small guesthouse, is located near the confluence, on a promontory between the Zhorong Tsangpo and the Mangra-chu estuaries.

The road to Drigung Til Monastery runs upstream from Drigung township through the deep Zhorong Tsangpo gorge to Yangri Gonpa (now destroyed and integrated within a military compound), and thence for 30 km to the township of Menpa. The monastery is located above, on the slopes of a steep cliff overlooking the valley. The name Drigung ('back of the dri') refers to the distinctive contour of the cliff and its ridge, which resembles the back of a dri ('female of the yak').

There are more than 50 buildings scattered across the upper slopes of the ridge, but three central temples act as a focal point for the entire complex. The **Assembly Hall** (*dukhang*) contains exquisite images of Vajradhara and Shakyamuni Buddha, as well as Padmasambhava in the form of Nangsi Zilnon, Drigung Jikten Gonpo, the founder of the monastery, and Rinchen Phuntsok, who presided over its greatest development. In the centre of the hall are further images depicting Jikten Gonpo and his two immediate successors, Sherab Jungne and Drakpa Jungne, who are collectively known here as Yabsesum.

The other important temples are connected by an open air gallery. Among them, the **Serkhang** to the right of the gallery contains the reliquary stupa, stone footprint and conch of Jikten Gonpo, along with images of Manjughosa, Jikten Gonpo (twice), Ksitigarbha, the protectress Apchi in her peaceful and wrathful forms, and the thrones of the Chetsang and Chungtsang incarnations.

The **Dzamling Gyen** Temple to the left of the gallery contains the reliquaries of Drigung Rinchen Phuntsok, Dorje Rinchen, and the yogin Bachung

Sky Burial

The Tibetan custom of 'sky burial' in which corpses are dismembered and fed to vultures has attracted mixed feelings of revulsion, fear, and awe among outside observers. Yet it is important that the custom is seen properly in context. Firstly, 'sky-burial' is not the only means of disposing of the dead in Tibet; but it is the most popular.

Following the moment of death, the body of the deceased should be left untouched for 3 days, during which time an officiating lama should perform the transference of consciousness (pho-wa) which emancipates the consciousness (nam-she) of the deceased into a buddha-field or pure land; or else whisper advice into the ear of the deceased, informing him or her of the nature of the inner radiance experienced in the first of the successive intermediate states (bar-do) to be experienced after death. If the body is at all touched, it should be touched at the crown of the head, because the anterior fontanelle is the optimum point of exit for the consciousness. Touching the body elsewhere could result in the consciousness exiting from a lower unfavourable orifice. Relatives are encouraged neither to laugh and shout, nor to weep and cry during the period when the deceased's consciousness traverses the intermediate states. After 3 days, the officiating lama should continue offering advice to the deceased over the following 7 weeks, during which the consciousness may attain liberation from rebirth, or assume a subsequent rebirth. On the last day of each of the 7 weeks special prayers are recited and offerings made, culminating in the final ceremony. The purpose is to accumulate merits on behalf of the deceased, and to ensure his or her future well being, to which end a special tangka or image may be commissioned.

The disposal of the body is generally regarded as a separate, lesser matter. 'Sky-burial' in which the corpse is dismembered, the inner organs removed, the flesh cut into shreds, and the bones crushed and mixed with tsampa-flour, before being fed to the vultures is said to offer great merit. The vultures, who frequent the most popular 'sky-burial' sites and are summoned by an offering of incense, are revered as birds of purity, subsisting only on corpses and casting their droppings onto high mountain peaks. There are several well-known charnel grounds (durtro) on the plateau, including those at Sera and Drigung in Central Tibet; and Darling Monastery in Golok. Corpses may be carried long distances for dismemberment at one of the preferred sites.

Alternative forms of funeral are also current. 'Water burial' is regarded as a pure but inferior method of disposal in that fish are traditionally protected by the Buddhist community. 'Earth burial' is less frequently used, but preferred by the Chinese and Muslim communities. Traditionally earth burial was in vogue in Tibet during the period of the Yarlung dynasty, when massive tumluli were constructed in Chongye and elsewhere. However, later it came to be regarded as a lower form of burial reserved for robbers, murderers, and plague victims. Cremation is utilized in parts of Eastern Tibet where wood is more plentiful; and particularly for lamas and aristocrats. Lastly, the embalmed mortal remains of certain great lamas may be interred within a reliquary stupa, or 'golden reliquary' (serdung), as an object of offering for the sake of posterity.

Rinpoche, who passed away in 1989 after devoting many years to Drigung's reconstruction. Towards the NE of the ridge, there is a **Protector Chapel** (*gonkhang*) containing images of the protectress Apchi, and a hermitage, once frequented by Jikten Gonpo, and more recently by Bachung Rinpoche. It contains another stone footprint of Jikten Gonpo, along with a clay image of Tara, and tangkas depicting Shakyamuni and Tara.

The ruins of the residence (*labrang*) of the Drigung Chetsang and Chungtsang incarnations have not as yet been renovated, but there are active meditation hermitages (*drubkhang*) scattered across the hillside. To the NW of the ridge is the famed **Drigung Charnel Ground** (Drigung Durtro) to which the dead will be brought from far-off districts of Central Tibet, Kongpo and Nakchuka for sky burial. The circle of stones on which the corpses are dismembered, some 12m in diameter is said to represent the mandala of Cakrasamvara. Around the charnel ground are stupas and a third stone footprint of Jikten Gonpo. Two recently constructed chapels are located to the left, one containing murals of the Hundred Peaceful and Wrathful Deities (which appear to the deceased during the intermediate state after death and before rebirth), and the other containing the shaven hair of the dead. The pilgrim's circumambulation route encompasses the main temples, hermitages and charnel ground of Drigung.

Zhoto Tidro Hermitage
གནས་སྟོད་ཏི་སྒྲོ

The hermitage of Zhoto Tidro (also written as Zhoto Terdrom) is located in a side-valley which branches N off the Zhorong Tsongpo valley a few kilometres before Mepa township at the base of Drigung Til. The approach to the hermitage follows a narrow but drivable track

which ascends a precipitous cliff above the Rep-chu River and comes to a halt at a vantage point overlooking a gorge containing the hotsprings (**Chutsen Chugang**) and the nunnery. Two guesthouses have been constructed beside the hot springs, which offer relaxing bathing facilities. One is run by the nunnery and the other by TTC, Lhasa.

History In 772 when King Trisong Detsen offered his queen Yeshe Tsogyel to Padmasambhava, hostile Bonpo aristocrats forced the master and his new consort to flee the royal court for the sanctuary of the limestone caves and hot springs of Zhoto Tidro. Padmasambhava concealed a number of treasures (*terma*) in the **Kiri Yangdzong** cave above Tidro, which were discovered in later centuries by Dorje Lingpa, Drigung Rinchen Phuntsok and others. Yeshe Tsogyel herself remained in meditation at Tidro for many years, for which reason the original nunnery was constructed at this particular site. The earliest buildings appear to date from the Kadampa period, but reconstruction has taken place on a number of occasions, the most recent being after the Cultural Revolution. The nunnery, presently housing more than 80 nuns, is headed by the elderly Khandro-la, a veritable emanation of Yeshe Tsogyel, and in its temple there are splendid images of Padmasambhava, his two consorts, and eight manifestations, as well as Shakyamuni Buddha, and a Drigungpa throne.

Tidro Pilgrimage

Starting from the **hot springs**, the hardy traveller may follow the pilgrim's route to the Padmasambhava caves high in the mountains above Tidro. Immediately below the springs, there is a 15m long subterranean channel through which the river passes. Legend says that Padmsambhava himself created the tunnel in order to drain a lake inhabited by malignant water spirits by throwing his vajra at the ridge above, and the mark of the vajra can still be observed in the rocks at the tunnel entrance. He then created the hot springs for the benefit of future practitioners.

The **inner circumambulation** (*nangkor*) leads from the hot springs and the nunnery towards a W ridge which is reached by crossing a bridge over the river. The trail then ascends the Norbu La pass and plunges into another valley before rising to a charnel ground site and the ridge from which the **Kiri Yang-dzong** cave is accessible by traversing a limestone rock face with natural hand and foot holds. This 50m high cavern contains active hermitages and important meditation caves, the most significant being the **Tsogyel Sangpuk**, where Yeshe Tsogyel received the empowerments and teachings of the *Innermost Spirituality of the Dakinis* (*Khandro Nyingtig*) from Padmasambhava, and subsequently passed many years in retreat. The circuit is completed by descending the limestone face and the scree slopes below to enter a gorge containing the ruined hermitage of Drigung Rinchen Phuntsok (**Drang Monastery**). From here, the path leads back to the hot springs. There is also an **outer circumambulation** (*chikor*), which encircles the entire Tidro and Drigung region, by taking an E valley from the base of the limestone rock face.

CHUSHUL COUNTY

ཆུ་ཤུལ

曲水县 Quxu

Population: 20,642   Area: 1,482 sq km

The valley of the Lower Kyi-chu extends from Lhasa southwards, and includes important sites on both banks of the river, as far as its confluence with the Brahmaputra, which is spanned by the **Chushul Zamchen** bridge. On the S bank of the Brahmaputra opposite the Chushul confluence is the sacred Mt Chuwori (see below, page 222). Four main roads diverge at Chushul: due W to Zhigatse via Nyemo and NE to Lhasa (both on the N bank of the Brahmaputra), and SW to Gyantse via Gampa La and Lake Yamdrok, or due E to Gongkar Airport and Tsetang (both on the S bank

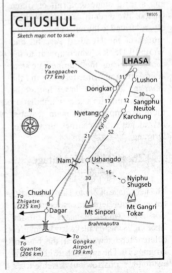

CHUSHUL   TIB505

Sketch map: not to scale

LHASA

To Yangpachen (77 km)

Dongkar   11   Lushon

30

17   12   Sangphu Neutok
Nyetang   Karchung

21   52

Nam   Ushangdo

30   16   Nyiphu Shugseb

To Zhigatse (225 km)

Chushul

8   Dagar   Mt Sinpori   Mt Gangri Tokar

Brahmaputra

To Gyantse (206 km)   To Gongkar Airport (39 km)

of the Brahmaputra). The distance from Lhasa to Chushul is 36 km on an excellent paved surface, and a further 8 km to the bridge at Dagar.

THE WEST BANK OF THE LOWER KYI-CHU

Tashigang

Following the paved Lhasa-Chushul highway SW from the Dongkar intersection for 15 km, you will reach on the left the turn-off for Tashigang, a Sakya monastery under the guidance of Bero Khyentse Rinpoche. The assembly hall (*dukhang*) has an image of Sakya Pandita, flanked by images of Shakyamuni, Avalokiteshvara, and Mahakala. Skylight murals depict the Sixteen Elders, Shakyamuni, Tara, and Atisha. Above the throne of the Dalai Lama, there is a 17th century tangka depicting Bhaisajyaguru, the Buddha of Medicine. The protector shrine is located upstairs. Currently, there are about 30 monks at Tashigang.

Nyetang Dolma Lhakhang

 སྙེ་ཐང་སྒྲོལ་མ་ལྷ་ཁང་

Located 17 km SW of Dongkar on the right side of the highway, a short distance after passing a large painted relief image of Shakyamuni on the rock face, this celebrated temple dates from the time of the great Bengali master Atisha, who passed away at Nyetang in 1054. The temple is said to have survived the Cultural Revolution virtually unscathed owing to the intervention of Chou En Lai at the expressed request of the Government of E Pakistan (now Bangladesh). An adjacent 15th century Gelukpa Monastery, known as Dewachen, was destroyed at that time. From the outside, the temple appears to be insignificant, but the sacred artefacts contained within it testify to the importance of the Kadampa tradition in 11th-13th century Tibet.

A double gateway leads via a courtyard to a covered terrace, where there are 11th century images of the Four Guardian Kings, and two sunken stupas containing the robes of Atisha and his disciple Dromtonpa. In the extreme left and right corners of the terrace there are large prayer wheels, while the murals inset between the chapel doors depict Atisha with his two foremost students, Dromtonpa and Ngok Lekpei Sherab, as well as Shakyamuni, Maitreya, and Manjughosa.

There are three interconnecting chapels, entered from the door to the left and exited by the door to the right. The first, known as the **Namgyel Lhakhang**, contains a large Victory Stupa (Namgyel Chorten), flanked on the left and right by smaller Kadam-style stupas containing relics of Naropa, among which the 3m high **Naropa Dungten** holds the precious skull of Naropa, along with Atisha's books and begging bowl. In front of the stupas are small 500 cm images of the Eight Medicine Buddhas with a clay representation of Atisha at the centre. Images on the left wall depict Tara, Avalokiteshvara, and Amitayus.

The second chapel, known as the **Dolma Lhakhang**, contains 17th century bronze images of the Twenty-One Taras, which are stacked in two tiers, occupying three walls of the chamber. The central images in the **upper tier** represent Shakyamuni (dated 1288), White Tara (a 'speaking image'), Serlingpa Dharmkirti, who was the teacher of Atisha, and Dalai Lama XIII. Other images of the Buddhas of the Five Families (*Pancajina*), dating from 11th century, are in the upper right corner. In the **lower tier**, the central objects of offering preserved inside a glass cabinet include a conch shell from Nalanda, an image of Thousand-armed Mahakarunika, a stupa containing Serlingpa's remains, a small image of Shakyamuni brought by Atisha from India, and a tangka depicting Six-armed Mahakala, which is said to have been painted with the blood from Atisha's nose. An original 'speaking image' of Tara disappeared from the cabinet during the Cultural Revolution. Other sacred objects within this chapel include a round urn containing Atisha's bone relics, a bronze 13th century image of Avalokiteshvara Karsapani from India, and an image of Maitreya known as Atsa Jampa, which was reputedly spared the wrath of the Mongols by uttering the exclamation atsa ('ouch!').

Lastly, the **Tsepak Lhakhang** contains large 12th century images of the Buddhas of the Three Times and the Eight Bodhisattvas. Among these, the central image is of the Buddha of the Present in the form of Amitayus, fashioned by Dromtonpa from the funerary ashes of Atisha. In the centre of the chapel is the backrest of Atisha's clay throne, with an attached image of Atisha himself, said to have been made in his own lifetime. The inner gates of this last chapel are guarded by large images of the gatekeepers Vajrapani (E) and Hayagriva (W).

Rato Monastery
ར་སྟོད་དགོན་པ

Located at Rato village in a side-valley, some 5 km behind Nyetang Dolma Lhakhang, Rato Monastery was founded in the 11th century by Taktsangpa; and it had later associations with the Kadampa master Ngok Loden Sherab and Tsongkhapa. Noted for the study of Buddhist logic and metaphysics, the monastery had about 400 monks at the height of its development. The principal incarnate lamas of Rato are all in exile, living in India, Germany, and the United States; and there are presently no more than 50 monks.

The **Assembly Hall** (*Dukhang*) at Rato has central images of Tsongkhapa with his foremost disciples, and an image of Tara, said to have been the personal property of Atisha. Behind these

along the rear wall are images of Shakyamuni Buddha and Atisha, flanked by the Kadampa lamas: Luchok Dorjechang, Ngok Loden Sherab, Manga Draksang, Chokla Ozer, Ngok Lekpei Sherab, and Yonten Phuntsok.

Behind, within the **inner sanctum** (*tsangkhung*) is an image of Tsongkhapa, standing in lieu of the former magnificent images of the Buddhas of the Three Times and the Eight Bodhisattvas. The extant murals of the assembly hall appear to date from the 17-18th century. These depict protector deities, such as Dharmaraja and Tsedrekpa; bodhisattvas such as Tara, Manjughosa, Avalokiteshvara, Vajrapani, and Sitapatatra; the lamas of the *lamrim* lineage, and the buddhas of confession and medicine.

Among the other reconstructed temples at Rato: the **Nyitri Lhakhang** contains a protector shrine and the Dalai Lama's private apartments in its upper storeys, the **Jamkhang** contains a large Maitreya, and the **Rinchen Ritro Hermitage** has associations with Longdol Lama. In the mountains to the N there are also meditation caves belonging to Rato Monastery.

Chushul
ཆུ་ཤུལ

The highway from Lhasa to Chushul continues SW from Nyetang Dolma Lhakhang, via the village of Nam, opposite which a new bridge has been constructed across the Kyi-chu, leading to Shugseb Nunnery (see below, page 219). Inland from Nam there was the original Drukpa Kagyu Monastery of **Druk Jangchub Choling**, founded before Ralung by Tsangpa Gyare in 1189.

The town of **Chushul** has grown considerably in recent years, owing to its position at the intersection of the four main roads of Central, Western and Southern Tibet. There is a large 2-storey guesthouse, and an overt military presence at **Dagar**, location of Chushul Zamchen bridge. Formerly, an iron suspension bridge made by Tangtong Gyelpo spanned the Brahmaputra slightly downstream from here, but it was damaged in the mid 20th century.

THE EAST BANK OF THE LOWER KYI-CHU

Karchung Ramagang

ཤར་ཆུང་ར་མ་སྒང་

From the military compound at Drib near the regency temple of Tsechokling on the S bank of the Kyi-chu opposite Lhasa, there is an unpaved road which follows the river downstream in a SW direction. Ramagang, the site of **Sangda Karchung Monastery**, is located slightly inland from Lushon village about 12 km along this track. The monastery was founded by King Senalek Jinyon (r 804-814), who erected an inscribed obelisk and stupas in each of the temple's four directions, along the design of Samye Monastery. Drepung is visible across the river from the ruins of Sangda Karchung.

Sangphu Neutok Monastery

Located about 30 km S and inland from Lushon village, on the upper slopes of a side-valley which forks to the left, Sangphu Neutok Monastery was founded in 1073 by Ngok Lekpei Sherap and developed by his nephew, Ngok Loden Sherab. These scholar translators were close disciples of Atisha. Originally there were two Kadampa colleges here, known as Lingto and Lingme. Under the guidance of Chapa Chokyi Senge (1109-69) the monastery eventually gained renown for its eclectic approach to the study of Buddhist philosophy, and it became a mixed institution with seven Sakyapa and four Gelukpa colleges. The meditation caves of Yakde Pancen and Rongton Sheja Kunzi were located in the upper ranges; while lower down by the river at Sangda,

some 16 km distant, the reliquary of Ngok Loden Sherab was formerly preserved. In recent centuries the monastery declined but it was restored by Dalai Lama XIII prior to its more recent destruction during the Cultural Revolution.

Ushangdo Peme Tashi Gephel

Following the Kyi-chu downstream from Sangda for approximately 52 km, via the villages of Sheldrong, Namgyel Gang, and Tshena Sha, a side-valley leads across the plain of Nyinda (sometimes called Shuntse) to the ruins of Ushangdo Temple. This area is also accessible from Nam on the W bank, via the new Kyi-chu suspension bridge.

The 9-storey temple of Ushangdo was the greatest construction project undertaken by the Tibetan king Relpachen (r 815-838). It is said to have been a pagoda-style building with a Chinese roof of blue turquoise. The three lower floors were used by the king and his ministers, the three middle floors by the Indian panditas and their Tibetan translators for the revision of the translation methodology; and the upper 3 storeys contained images. The building appears not to have survived Langdarma's persecution; but a small temple with a remarkable Jowo Shakyamuni image was later constructed on the site. Unfortunately, today only its ruins are visible.

Nyiphu Shugseb Nunnery

སྙི་ཕུ་ཤུག་གསེབ

Shugseb is located 16 km above Ushangdo in the uplands of Nyiphu. The site was originally consecrated by the *yogini* Machik Labron (1055-1149), who meditated in the caves of Shugseb, but the first retreat centre was actually established here by Gyargom Tsultrim Senge (1144-1204), a student of Phakmodrupa, and founder of the Shugseb Kagyu order. From the 14th century onwards, Shugseb has been an important centre for nuns of the Nyingma school, owing to the teaching activity of Longchen Rabjampa at nearby Gangri Tokar; and the female incarnation of Shugseb, the Shugseb Jetsunma, ranks as one the the highest female incarnations in the whole of Tibet.

There are presently 80 nuns living in huts around the restored temple of Shugseb. Downstairs, the temple has new images of Padmasambhava and Machik Labron, while the upper storey contains the residence of the Jetsunma. From Shugseb there are 3-4 days trekking routes E to Dorje Drak and S to Sinpori.

Gangri Tokar
གངས་རི་ཐོད་དཀར

The ridge of Mt Gangri Tokar (5,336m) is located about 1 hr hiking distance above Shugseb Nunnery. From the perspective of pure sacred vision, the site is said to represent the left knee of the female deity Vajravarahi, whose breasts and vagina are identified with the springs arising nearby. The great Nyingma master Longchen Rabjampa (1308-63) arrived here at the invitation of his protectress Dorje Yudronma. Here, in the cave hermitage of **Orgyan Dzong** and its inner sanctum, called **Dawa Chushel Puk**, he meditated, and redacted his *terma* revelations (entitled *Kandro Yangtig, Zabmo Yangtig*, and *Lama Yangtig*); and composed his great treatises including the *Seven Treasuries (Dzodun)* and the *Three Trilogies (Korsum Namsum)*.

The cave presently contains a new image of Longchen Rabjampa. The stumps of two juniper trees (the abodes of Longchen Rabjampa's protectors Rahula and Dorje Yudronma) are visible outside the entrance to the cave. A natural stone image of Rahula and rock abode of Dorje Yudronma are also to be seen. East of Orgyan Dzong are the other meditation caves, among them the **Melong Puk** hermitage of Melong Dorje, **Samten Puk**, **Dewa Puk**, and **Shar Zimpuk**, the last and most remote being especially favoured for the practice of the highest Dzogchen teachings, known as All-surpassing Realisation (*thogal*).

Riwo Tsenga
རི་བོ་རྩེ་ལྔ

Southwest of Gangri Tokar is the 5-peaked ridge known as Riwotsenga, which is named after the celebrated Buddhist range of Wutaishan in China. There are a number of meditation caves here, including the Zangyak Namka Dzong, the Guru Drupuk, and Lharing Longchen Drak.

Sinpori
སྲིན་པོ་རི

Mount Sinpori lies 30 km S of Ushangdo, on a promontory between the Kyi-chu and Brahmaputra rivers, E of the confluence. This barren desert-like terrain once contained an important 13th century Sakya temple which had been constructed by the Bengali scholar Vibhuticandra on the advice of Panchen Shakyashri. The temple was dedicated to the deity Cakrasamvara, and housed a 'speaking image' of Cakrasamvara.

Sinpori is also accessible by ferry from Chushul, by trekking from Shugseb via Leuchung, or walking from Dorje Drak on the N bank of the Brahmaputra.

SOUTHERN TIBET
THE LOWER BRAHMAPUTRA VALLEYS OF LHOKHA AND KONGPO

INTRODUCTION

Southern Tibet is the region demarcated by the lower Brahmaputra (*Tib* Yarlung Tsangpo) valley, extending E from its confluence with the Kyi-chu as far as Kongpo on the borders of Powo and Pemako, where it turns through narrow gorges and flows SW into India. As such, the region includes the lateral valleys adjoining the Brahmaputra on both its N and S banks, and the valleys of its south-flowing tributaries, which enter East Bhutan and Arunachal Pradesh to converge with this great river S of the Himalayas in West Bengal or Assam. Currently, this vast region, revered as the cradle of Tibetan civilization, is divided into 16 counties, four of which are administered from Nyangtri (ie Gyamda, Nyangtri, Nang, and Menling), and the remainder from Tsetang, the capital of the Lhokha district (ie Gongkar, Dranang, Nedong, Chongye, Tso-me, Lhodrak, Nakartse, Zangri, Chusum, Lhuntse, Tsona, and Gyatsa). The distance from Lhasa to Gongkar Airport is 96 km and to Tsetang 183 km. **Recommended itineraries: 1 and 4 (also 7).**

GONGKAR COUNTY

གོང་དཀར

贡嘎县 Gonggar

Population: 39,680   Area: 2,532 sq km

Gongkar county is located on the banks of the Brahmaputra at a point where the river valley reaches its widest extent, for which reason **Gongkar Airport** (the civilian airport serving Lhasa) was constructed there in the late 1970s. A second runway and terminal facilities were completed in 1994. The airport lies to the W of **Rawa-me**, the county capital at the entrance to the Namrab valley; 96 km from Lhasa and 87 km from Tsetang. The borders of Gongkar county extend from the sacred Mt Chuwori opposite Chushul, southwards to Gampa La pass (4,794m), which is the gateway to Lake Yamdrok and W Tibet, and eastwards as far as the Dol valley on the S bank of the Brahmaputra and Dorje Drak monastery on the N bank. Thus, it includes the southern lateral valleys of Gongkar, Namrab, and Drib; as well as the northern lateral valleys of Leuchung and Trango.

Mount Chuwori

ཆུ་བོ་རི

The sacred mountain of Chuwori which broods over the sandbanks around the confluence of the Kyi-chu and Brahmaputra rivers is considered to be one of the most auspicious places for meditation practice in Tibet. In the past, the mountain is said to have had 108 springs and 108 hermitages dating from the time of King Trisong Detsen in the 8th century. Padmasambhava had a hermitage near the summit at **Namkading**, and it is said that 108 of his yogin followers attained the body of light here at Chuwori. Later, during the 12th century, new hermitages were constructed by the Nyingmapa lama Taton Joye, Karmapa I Dusum Khyenpa, and Tsangpa Gya-re, and in the 13th century by Dorje Drak Rigzin II Lekdenje.

On the lower slopes of the mountain, the monastery of **Chakzam Chuwori** was founded by Tangtong Gyelpo, facing the celebrated iron suspension bridge which he constructed across the Brahmaputra to Yolri Gong near Chushul (damaged in the early decades of this century, and now replaced by the Chushul Zamchen bridge). At the S end of the old suspension bridge, there was also a Kumbum stupa, containing an image and relics of Tangtong Gyelpo himself.

The monastery of **Pema Wangchuk** was located on a NW spur of Mt Chuwori, and on the E side, near the Tsechu ('water of life') Spring where pilgrims flock even now, there was once an active Nyingmapa monastery called **Tsechu Kopa** or Tsechuling, founded by Menlungpa Lochok Dorje. All these sites are in ruins at the present day; but this does not deter pilgrims who make the circuit of the mountain via Phab La (4,250m) in 4 hrs.

Gampa La Pass

སྒམ་པ་ལ

The approach to Gampa La pass (4,794m), which offers spectacular views of the **Nojin Gangzang** snow ranges and the turquoise **Yamdrok Yutso Lake** is 28 km from the S end of the Chushul Zamchen bridge. The switchback road winds its way up from Samar, past deep barren gorges, which are evidence of the Brahmaputra tectonic fault line. Near the pass, which is bedecked with colourful prayer flags, there is a turn-off to the right side of the road, leading to a sensitive mining installation. For the route from Gampa La to Nakartse, see below, page 279.

Gongkar Valley

Driving E from the southern end of the Chushul Zamchen bridge for 26 km, you will observe to the left the hilltop ruins of **Gongkar Dzong**, from which the entire Gongkar region was ruled until the 1950s. This is usually the first glimpse a visitor arriving in Tibet by air will have of the wanton destruction inflicted on Tibetan culture since the Chinese occupation.

Gongkar Chode

Just beyond this hilltop promontory, at the entrance to the Gongkar valley, there is an important monastery called **Gongkar Chode** or Gongkar Dorjeden, which was founded in 1464 by Dorjedenpa Kunga Namgyel of the Sakya School. Here there are important extant murals typical of the free-flowing Khyenri school of painting, which were the original work of Jamyang Khyentse Wangchuk (b 1524). The 64 pillared **Assembly Hall** (*dukhang*) has new images of Dorjedenpa, Padmasambhava, Shakyamuni Buddha, and Sakya Pandita, and original Khyenri murals of the Five Founders of Sakya (Gongma Nga) flanking the entrance to the inner sanctum. The walls of the circumambulatory walkway around the inner sanctum have original murals depicting the Twelve Deeds of Shakyamuni and the Thousand Buddhas of the Aeon, although no trace remains of the original 3-storey high image of Shakyamuni containing the skull of the Indian master Gayadhara, which once graced the inner sanctum.

The **Gonkhang** to the left contains gold on black painted murals of Mahakala in the form Panjaranatha (Gonpo Gur), and his retinue, the preferred protectors of the Sakya tradition.

Upstairs, there are exquisite murals depicting the plan of the original monastery, and the Sakyapa meditational deities, headed by Hevajra (in the **Kyedor Lhakhang**), as well as others depicting the Sakya *Lamdre* lineage; and also a **Kangyur Lhakhang**. On the third storey the **Lama Lhakhang** is dedicated to the monastery's founder Dorjedenpa Kun-ga Namgyel. Formerly, there were other buildings at Gongkar Chode, including a distinctive 3-storeyed **Lamdre Lhakhang** and four colleges, which are all in a bad state of disrepair.

Following the road inland from Gongkar Chode for 5 km, you will reach **Dechen Chokhor**, a 13th century hermitage and monastery of the Drukpa Kagyu school, located on the slopes 150m above the road. One small chapel has been rebuilt amid the ruins. Further inland there are 1-2 day trekking routes from Gongkar valley to Lake Yamdrok via the Dra La pass (5,342m) and Chilung.

Namrab Valley

རྣམ་རབ

Continuing E on the main road below Gongkar Chode, Gongkar Airport and the entrance to the Namrab valley will be reached after a further 10 km.

- **Facilities** Accommodation is available at the *Gongkar Hotel* nr the Airport.

Rawa-me

The Sakyapa monastery of **Tubten**

Rawa-me, founded by Rawalepa (1138-1210) is situated within the town. It is in a state of disrepair, and has a prominant TV antenna on the roof. By the roadside in Rawa-me, the county town, there are a number of small Tibetan and Chinese restaurants, and a clean tea-shop selling Indian-style sweet milk tea.

Some 5 km inland from Rawa-me in the Kyishong township area is the Sakya monastery of **Dakpo Tratsang**, founded by Tashi Namgyel (1398-1459), a disciple of the illustrious Rongton Sheja Kunzik. There is a large renovated assembly hall with some original murals and new images of Sakya Pandita, Tashi Namgyel and Gorampa Sonam Senge. The adjacent protector shrine is dedicated to the deity Pangboche.

Further inland and situated 150m on a remote hillside is **Zhung Trezhing**, a hermitage frequented by Ngokton Choku Dorje (1036-1102), a close disciple of Marpa Lotsawa. After he passed away at that site, his nephew Ngok Kunga Dorje (1157-1234) founded the Trezhing monastery, where a distinct Kagyu lineage (apart from those derived from Milarepa and Gampopa) was maintained. In the past Marpa's skull was preserved here in a reliquary stupa.

Drib Valley
གྲིབ

The main road E from Gongkar Airport to Tsetang passes through the township of Chedezhol, at the entrance to the Dol or Drib valley after 17 km. Here there is an active cottage industry engaged in the production of colourful striped ladies' aprons (*pangden*). The ruins of **Chedezhol Dzong** can be seen on a ridge to the E.

Dungpu Chokhor

Some 4 km inland is the monastery of **Dungpu Chokhor**, originally founded by Drapa Ngonshe in the 11th century; and later absorbed by the Sakyapas in

the 15th century. The **Assembly Hall** has some old frescoes, depicting Mahakala in the form Panjaranatha flanked by other protectors, and the Twelve Deeds of Shakyamuni Buddha, as well as important Sakya meditational deities headed by Hevajra, the Five Founders of Sakya, and (under the skylight) the lamas of the *Lamdre* lineage. The **inner sanctum** has an original 'speaking' Tara image, adorned with coral; and there are side chambers containing a printery (left) and a Vairocana image surrounded by Taras (right). Upstairs is a chamber where HH Dalai Lama XIV stayed during his flight from Lhasa to India in 1959.

About 3 km further inland and on a side-valley E of Khyimzhi village is the monastery of **Sungrabling**, which was originally founded as a Sakya establishment by Nyakton Sonam Zangpo in the 14th century and later absorbed by the Gelukpa.

Trekking

Further up the Drib valley, via the township of Namgyel Zhol and Drib La pass, there are 3-4 day trekking routes to the N shores of Lake Yamdrok.

Dorje Drak Monastery
གྲུབ་བསྟན་རྡོ་རྗེ་བྲག

ACCESS Accessible by ferry from Chedezhol (50 mins), the monastery is located at the base of a vajra-shaped rock on the N bank of the Brahmaputra.

The celebrated Nyingma monastery of Tubten Dorje Drak maintains the *terma* tradition of the Nyingma school known as the Northern Treasures (Jangter), which derives from Rigdzin I Godemchen Ngodrub Gyel-tsen (1337-1409). In 1632, the monastery was relocated on its present secure site from Tsang, when the young Rigdzin III Ngagiwangpo and his guardian Jangdak Tashi Topgyel were forced to flee the wrath of the kings of Tsang. The site was greatly developed by Rigdzin IV Pema Trinle (1641-1717) before his untimely death at the hands of the Dzungar Mongols. Thus, the monastery was sacked by the Dzungars in 1717, and again obliterated during the 1960s. Nonetheless it has been gradually restored in recent years through the efforts of the present incarnation of Dordrak Rigdzin, who resides in Lhasa, and those of Kelzang Chojor and the local community.

Assembly Hall

The Assembly Hall (*tshokchen*) has a large image of Padmasambhava, replacing an original made by Rigdzin IV Pema Trinle, as well as painted scrolls depicting the Hundred Peaceful and Wrathful Deities, and murals depicting the Eight Manifestations of Padmasambhava. There are three thrones, the central one reserved for Dordrak Rikdzin himself, and the others for Taklung Tsetrul Rinpoche (who resides in exile in Simla and Ladakh), and Chubzang Rinpoche. In the **inner sanctum** there is a 'self-arising' stone image of Two-armed Avalokiteshvara, a collection of relics retrieved from images destroyed in the 1960s, and a library containing the *Kangyur* and the *Nyingma Gyudbum*.

The **oldest chapel** to the right (in which no women are allowed) once contained images of the 'three roots' (guru, meditational deity and dakini) of the Dorje Drak tradition; but now it contains a few old images, a copy of the Derge edition of the *Nyingma Gyudbum*, and a number of precious objects: the vajra and bell of Rigdzin IV Pema Trinle, a treasure chest (*terdrom*), part of Milarepa's staff, and a detailed plan of how the monastery once looked. Prior to the Dzungar army's destruction of Dorje Drak in 1717, this ancient chapel had been renowned for its enormous columns and skull-painted gates.

Upstairs

Upstairs there is a newly installed **printing press**; and to the left of the complex there is a **Protector Chapel**, containing images of Vajrakila and so forth. Another recently rebuilt temple contains new images of the aforementioned 'three roots'; but the ruined residences of Dordrak Rigdzin and Taklung Tsetrul have yet to be restored.

Kora

The pilgrims' circuit leads around the 'vajra rock' to the hermitage of **Dorje Drak Utse**, passing en route rock paintings and sacred footprints.

Trekking

A hermitage of the Drukpa Kagyu master Lingje Repa is nearby at **Napu Cholung**. There is also a 4-day trekking route from Dorje Drak to Lhasa, via Phushar, Trango township, and Trango La pass (4,977m) to the N.

DRANANG COUNTY
གྲ་ནང་

扎囊县 Zhanang

Population: 18,622 *Area:* 1,426 sq km

Dranang county, with its administrative capital at **Dratang**, is made up of a series of lateral valleys adjoining the Brahmaputra valley, both N and S of the river. These include the Drakyul, Zurkhar and Drakmar valleys on the N bank, and those of Dranang and Drachi on the S bank. The distance from Chedezhol to Dratang along the main Gongkar-Tsetang highway is 23 km.

DRAKYUL VALLEY
སྒྲགས་ཡུལ

The cave complexes of **Drak Yangdzong** and **Dzong Kumbum**, are a maze of interconnecting limestone passages and natural caverns, replete with bizarre rock formations, stalagmites and stalactites.

ACCESS Drakyul is most easily approached by ferry from **Yangkyar**, a

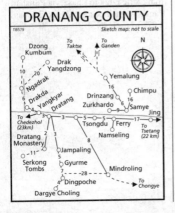

DRANANG COUNTY

Sketch map: not to scale

TIB579

Dzong Kumbum — To Taktse — To Ganden — N

Drak Yangdzong

Ngadrak — Yemalung

Drakda — Drinzang — Chimpu

Yangkyar — Zurkhardo — Samye

Dratang — Tsongdu Ferry — Jing — To Tsetang (22 km)

To Chedezhol (23km) — Namseling

Dratang Monastery — Jampaling

Serkong Tombs — Gyurme — Mindroling

Dingpoche — To Chongye

Dargye Choling

hydro-electric station 3 km W of Dranang on the Gongkar-Tsetang highway; or alternatively via the Dorje Drak ferry from Chedezhol. The pilgrimage or trek begins at **Drakda**, birthplace of Nubchen Sangye Yeshe, 4 km from the N ferry station, where the Drak-chu flows into the Brahmaputra. **NB** Alternative routes are also possible: trekking via Dorje Drak monastery and Phushur (2 days); trekking from Samye via Zurkhar (1 day); or even from Lhasa via Trango La pass (4 days) and from Taktse (4 days).

Tsogyel Latso

From the ferrry station you should first visit the Tsogyel Latso in Drakda village (4 km distant). This is an oracle lake revered as the life-supporting talisman of Yeshe Tsogyel, and is said to reveal the secrets of past and future events in its waters. Opposite, on the N shore, is **Kazhima Lhakhang**, an undestroyed branch of Samye Monastery, containing images of Padmasambhava, Vajrayogini, and Yeshe Tsogyel herself.

Ngadrak

Then, proceed to **Ngadrak**, a Karma Kagyu monastery on the W bank of the Drak-chu, some 6 km further inland. This large establishment, under the authority of Nenang, comprises an assembly hall adjoined by five chapels, and a monastic residential area, where the caretakers of the Drakyul caves can be found. 2 km further N from Ngadrak is **Pema Dzong**, a relatively intact fortress dating originally from the 14th century.

Drak Yangdzong caves

Assisted by the caretakers of Drakyul (a strong flashlight is essential), the pilgrim will approach **Drak Yangdzong** via the **Chusi Nunnery** (approximately 20 km/5¼ hrs), which is still largely in a ruinous state. The three main caves, which are all south-facing, are then reached by climbing a white limestone cliff (named Shinje Rolpei Podrang). Many carved relief images are visible

HIDDEN LANDS

The cave complexes are revered as Padmasambhava's foremost pilgrimage place of buddha-body in Central Tibet. From the perspective of the pilgrim's pure sacred vision assume the atttributes of diverse deities. These caves have been renowned since the time of Padmasambhava, when 55 of his disciples are said to have attained the body of light after meditating here. Padmasambhava himself frequented these caves, along with his consort Yeshe Tsogyel, whose birthplace, **Sewalung** in Karchen, is in the lower reaches of Drakyul. Other major disciples of Padmasambhava associated with the valley and its natural hermitages were Nubchen Sangye Yeshe and Nanam Dorje Dudjom. Subsequently in the 13th century, the Dzogchen master Melong Dorje occupied the **Ngarpuk** cave in upper Drakyul; but the caves have always been remote from mundane human habitation. It is said that even now there are 'hidden lands' (*beyul*)* at Drakyul, inaccessible to all but the fortunate.

near the cave entrances, depicting Padmasambhava, Shakyamuni Buddha, Milarepa, animal figures, and so forth.

The first cave, **Shinje Drup-ne Zho**, is a vast cavern, 100 sq m in area, with walls 15m high and 10m wide. The cave is presently occupied by hermits from Dorje Drak, but the paintings of the interior chapel depict the Mindroling lineage. The main images are of Padmasambhava in the form Nangsi Zilnon, flanked by his consorts: Mandarava and Yeshe Tsogyel.

The second cave, **Shinje Rolpei Drub-ne**, further W, is entered via a ladder and a narrow tunnel with a rope pulley, which exits into a deep cavern by way of a sandalwood ladder. Here are the **Guru Drupuk**, with its divinely shaped rocks representing Maitreya and other deities, and the **Guru Sangwa Drupuk** – the foremost goal of the Drakyul pilgrimage, where Padmasambhava passed 3 years in retreat.

The third cave, called **Jago Rangjung Drupuk** (or Nego Sarpa), 40m further W, is 8m wide, 50m deep, and in places over 10m high. The amazing limestone formations within it are held to be part of a 'hidden land' (*beyul*) replete with nectar, which was revealed for the first time in the 17th century by Rigdzin IV Pema Trinle of

Dorje Drak. The **Shiwa-tsel Charnel Ground** is located higher up the hillside to the W.

Dzong Kumbum caves

The **Dzong Kumbum** cave complex (4,800m) lies about 10 km above Ngadrak. As at Drak Yangdzong, the approach to the cave is bedecked with multiple rock carvings. The entrance is 30m high, and it is 35m deep, with five labyrinthine tunnels behind – all of them associated with Padmasambhava.

DRANANG VALLEY

གྲ་ནང

The Dranang valley is well endowed with an unusual variety of interesting sites, both prehistoric and Buddhist, for which reason it is renowned as the abode of the '13 saints or holymen of Dranang' (Dranang Kyebu Dampa Chuksum), who include illustrious figures such as Drapa Ngonshe, Tsangpa Gya-re, Orgyen Lingpa, Longchen Rabjampa, and Terdak Lingpa.

● **Accommodation** To spend some time in this district, you can stay at the small guesthouse in Dratang, the county capital, or commute from Tsetang, 47 km further E.

Dratang Monastery

A short 2 km drive inland from Dratang town on the W fork of the track leads to Dratang Monastery, an important conservation site for the artistic heritage of Tibet.

History

The temple complex was founded in 1081 by Drapa Ngonshe, a native of Dranang valley and one of the 13 saints associated with it, and completed in 1093 by his nephews.

The complex was later absorbed by the Sakyapas in the 14th-15th century, damaged by the Dzungar armies in the 18th, repaired in the 1920s and 1930s by the later Reting Rinpoche, regent of Tibet from 1922-41, and once again severely damaged by the Chinese in the 1960s. Nonetheless, despite these vicissitudes of time, the ground floor of the main building has preserved a series of frescoes which are unique in Tibet, in that they are said to represent an important synthesis of the Pala Indian style and Central Asian style (Tucci: 1949).

The Complex

Like Samye, the main temples of Dratang are surrounded by an eliptical wall (the only surviving one of three original concentric walls around the complex). No images survive at Dratang. The 20-pillared **Assembly Hall** and protector shrine to its left are empty, but for late murals from the Sakyapa period in the former.

The **inner sanctum** to the W is entered through a triple gateway, adorned with paintings of the Four Guardian Kings and various bodhisattvas. The corridor murals depict the life of Shakyamuni and the careers of major bodhisattvas, such as Amitayus and Avalokiteshvara. The 8-pillared inner sanctum itself once contained a large 3.4m image of the Buddha as Thubpa Jangchub Chenpo, flanked by the Eight Bodhisattvas, but these have all been destroyed. The murals have survived –

> ### DRAPA NGONSHE AND TIBET'S MEDICAL TRADITION
>
> Drapa Ngonshe was particularly renowned throughout Tibet as the discoverer (in 1038) of the *Four Medical Tantras (Gyud-zhi)*, said to have been redacted from Indian sources by Vairocana and concealed at Samye in the 8th century. These texts form the basis of the entire Tibetan medical tradition. However, Drapa Ngonshe is also credited with the construction of 128 Buddhist temples and shrines throughout Central and Southern Tibet, among which the Dratang Monastery was the most significant. An eclectic spiritual teacher, who had associations with the Nyingma, Zhiche, and Kadampa schools, he established Dratang as a preeminent centre for the study of tantra among the New Translation Schools (Sarmapa).

those on the S, N, and W walls dating from the 11th century, and those of the E extremities of the N and S walls (near the gates) from the later Sakyapa period. There are some 10 groups of early paintings, depicting Buddha figures surrounded by large throngs of bodhisattvas; the stylistic features of physionomy, clothing, jewellery and ornamentation all being suggestive of non-Tibetan influences – both Indian Pala, and Central Asian Khotanese. The best preserved are those of the W wall, where the stylistic line and vibrant colours can be seen to their best advantage.

Jampaling

Located on the slopes about 3 km to the E of Dratang, and reached via the E fork on the inland track, is the Gelukpa monastery of Jampaling, founded in 1472 by Tonmi Lhundrub Tashi, a descendent of Tonmi Sambhota. There were formerly nine buildings within the complex, all of which have been partially or completely destroyed in the 1960s. The 13-storey stupa of Jampaling, known as **Kumbum Tongdrol Chenmo**, was formerly the largest of its type in Tibet, exceeding the dimensions of the great stupa at Gyantse (see below, page 321), but constructed in a similar multi-chapel style. The murals were the work of Jamyang Khyentse Wangchuk, founder of the free-flowing Khyenri style of painting, extant examples of which are still seen at Gongkar Chode (see above, page 223).

Reconstruction proceeds at a slow pace here, but the **Maitreya Temple (Jampa Lhakhang)** has been rebuilt on its original site NE of the stupa. The rear wall of its assembly hall contains some old murals which survive from the earlier structure. Among the other buildings, the 18m **Tangka Wall** is in a good state of preservation, as is the **Jungden Monastery** of the Sakya school, some 200m E of the temple. The monastic college, the Jampaling Labrang, and the unusual series of shops formerly maintained on the site by Bhutanese and Nepalese traders have been erased.

Serkong Tombs

Located in a side-valley, some 11 km W of Dratang Monastery, are the 11 trapezoid and single stupa-shaped tumuli of Serkong. The largest tumulus which is in the NE is 20m high at the front and 7m high at the rear, with sides 96m long, rear 87m, and front 92m. To its left there is an excavated tomb. Four chambers were dug into the bedrock of the hill below the tumulus: an entrance passage, an entrance cavity, a tomb chamber, and an extension chamber where the deceased's personal effects would be interred. The tombs here are probably contemporaneous to those of Chongye (where the Yarlung Dynasty kings were buried) and those of Nang Dzong further E (see below, page 289). The Serkong tombs appear to have been plundered after the collapse of the Yarlung Dynasty, and later in the 18th century by the Dzungar armies.

The vast ruins of **Pema Choling Nunnery** extend for some 5,000 sq m across the hillside above Serkong. Only the lowest storey of the assembly hall survives.

Riwo Namgyel Monastery

Driving the short 15 km distance from Dratang to Dingpoche in upper Dranang valley, you will have an opportunity to visit other places of interest en route. The Gelukpa monastery of **Riwo Namgyel** is located on the E slopes of the valley (3,900m), about 6 km above the village of **Gyurme** where Tsangpa Gya-re was born. The monastery was founded ca 1470 by Gonten Gyelpo, and it developed into an extensive site (11,000 sq km) with over 60 monks. Later it was absorbed by the Namgyel Monastery of the Potala School in Lhasa. The severely damaged assembly hall has recently undergone restoration.

Gyeling Tsokpa Monastery

This eclectic establishment was founded in 1224 by students of the Kashmiri Panchen Shakyashri, and was in the 15th century adopted as a residence by Go Lotsawa Zhonupel, author of the *Blue Annals*.

The 3-storey temple is surrounded by a wall and moat, and the lowest storey functions as a basement. The **second storey** contains the assembly hall and three chapels forming an inner sanctum. Of these, the central **Jokhang** contains old murals depicting Shakyamuni Buddha, Avalokiteshvara, Amitayus, and the Four Guardian Kings. The side chapels are utilized as protector shrines, and the entrance to the assembly hall has murals depicting the progenitors of the Nyingma lineage in Tibet: Padmasambhava, Shantaraksita, King Trisong Detsen, and the Twenty-five

Disciples (Jewang Nyernga). The main relics of the monastery, including old tangkas and a small 'self-arising' statue of Shakyashri, have been removed to the **Gatsel Puk** hermitage, 4 km higher up the ridge, where there is also a new temple containing images associated with the *Longchen Nyingtig* tradition.

ACCESS About 8 km S of Dratang and beyond Gyurme village, the road passes through Gyeling township, where Gyeling Tsokpa monastery is located.

Nyingdo Monastery

This Mindroling branch monastery was originally constructed by Rinchen Lingpa in the 13th century and developed by his successor Nyingdo Tamched Khyenpa (1217-77). The most important object in this monastery (which is now being rebuilt) is a talismanic pillar from Khyungpo in the upper Salween region of East Tibet, said to offer protection from pestilences, drought and hail.

ACCESS Following a westerly trail which begins some 5 km S of Gyeling township, you will reach Peldrong township, where there are 10 plundered neolithic tombs, and from where the Nyingmapa monastery of Nyingdo is accessible.

Dingpoche Monastery

This monastery was founded in 1567 by Rinchen Pelzang, a student of Pema Karpo (1526-92) on the summit of a secluded flat spur; and yet it has not escaped destruction over the course of its history – whether at the hands of the Dzungars in the 18th century, or at the hands of the Chinese more recently. The 4-storeyed temple, said to represent the mandala of the deity Cakrasamvara, once contained large images of Shakyamuni and his two foremost disciples.

Amid the ruins, some rebuilding has taken place since 1984: there is a new assembly hall (*dukhang*), a new **Jokhang** (with images of Jowo Shakyamuni, White Tara, and Rinchen Pelzang), a new **Guru Lhakhang** (with images of Padmasambhava and his two main consorts), and a **Gonkhang** (with images of Four-armed Mahakala, Shridevi, and Dingpoche Chokyong). The **courtyard** (Chora) to the S of the complex contains a series of meditation cells (*chokhung*), dug into the ground and covered with blue and white tent canopies, which are utilized even now for solitary retreat. A rebuilt Victory Stupa (Namgyel Chorten) lies outside the perimeter wall to the SW, and a partially destroyed Enlightenment Stupa (Jangchub Chorten) within the SE corner.

At the hermitage of **Dra Yugang Drak** in the cliffs above Dingoche, there is a Padmasambhava cave, where Orgyen Lingpa subsequently (14th century) discovered a number of *terma*-texts that are no longer extant. Minling Trichen Terdak Lingpa stayed here in retreat and constructed an image of Padmasambhava; but the complex was badly damaged in the 1960s.

ACCESS The road continues S, via Rinchengang (or Raldrigang), from which there is a trekking route NE to Mindroling in the Drachi valley (28 km), as far as Kyilru township, where there is a yellow-walled temple, recently renovated. From Kyilru, there is a trail to the W, leading via Dekyiling village to the fortified Drukpa Kagyu monastery of **Dingpoche**.

Yarje Lhakhang

Southwest of Kyilru township and Dekyiling village, the jeep road continues to Yarje Lhakhang, the birthplace of the renowned treasure-finder Orgyen Lingpa, which structurally survived the persecution of the 1960s, and contains new images of Padmasambhava and Avalokiteshvara in the form Simhanada ('Lion's Roar'). There is also a wall painting which depicts Yarje Orgyen Lingpa himself.

Derong Nunnery

Continuing S from Kyilru township and SE of Dingpoche, you will reach the village of Tashiling and, on the slopes above, the nunnery of **Derong** (also written Drophu Todrong). Below the nunnery is the ruined house, reputed to be the birthplace of Longchen Rabjampa (1308-64), the most illustrious of all Nyingmapa masters in Tibet. The buildings are currently undergoing reconstruction.

Dargye Choling Monastery

The last site of interest in the upper Dranang valley is the ruined Nyingmapa monastery of Dargye Choling, some 4 km SW of Dingpoche. Founded by Natsok Rangdrol and developed by Sangdak Trinle Lhundrub during the 17th century, it was the precursor of Mindroling Monastery in the neighbouring Drachi valley. The latter's son, Minling Trichen Terdak Lingpa, was born here in 1646.

DRACHI VALLEY

གྲ་ཕྱི

There are two entrances to the Drachi valley from the main Gongkar-Tsetang highway, the first 3 km due E of Dratang, on the W bank of the Drachi-chu, and the second a further 5 km to the E on the E bank. The valley is broad but infertile, for which reason there are fewer habitations here than in neighbouring Dranang. Two sites of great importance stand out, namely: Tsongdu Tsokpa in lower Drachi, and Mindroling in upper Drachi. There are also three clusters of ancient burial sites which were recently discovered in the valley.

Tsongdu Tsokpa Monastery

Located 250m inland on the E approach road, the large Sakyapa monastery of Tsongdu Tsokpa mostly survived the ravages of the 1960s because, like other Sakya monasteries in this part of Southern Tibet, it was utilized as a granary during the Cultural Revolution. Originally a Kadampa establishment founded by Lu-me, the later Sakya foundation is attributed to the Kashmiri pandita Shakyashri during the 13th century, who set up four Buddhist groups in Tibet, known as the Tsokpa Zhi. Other teachers have also had associations with this site, notably: Khyungpo Neljor Tsultrim Gonpo of the Shangpa Kagyu school (12th century) and Go Lotsawa Zhonupel (15th century).

The main temple, formerly four storeys and now only three storeys high, is entered via a staircase, which leads to the middle storey. No trace remains of the clay image of Shakyashri and the heart of Khyungpo Neljor, which were once preserved here. Few old paintings remain and these appear to date from the 19th century. Among them the most interesting are the representations of Two-armed Avalokiteshvara at the entrance, the skylight murals depicting the Eight Medicine Buddhas and the Eight Manifestations of Padmasambhava, and the Thousand Buddhas and Eight Bodhisattvas depicted within the inner sanctum.

Orgyen Mindroling Monastery

ཨོ་རྒྱན་སྨིན་གྲོལ་གླིང་

ACCESS Mindroling is some 8 km inland on the W approach road to upper Drachi, above the village of Mondrub.

This, the largest Nyingmapa monastery in Central Tibet (100,000 sq m) was founded in 1670 by Terdak Lingpa Gyurme Dorje, on a site where, in the 11th century, Lu-me Tsultrim Sherab had built the Kadampa chapel of Tarpaling. Terdak Lingpa thus became the first Minling Trichen (throneholder of Mindroling), a position held by his familial descendents until the mid-19th century, after which the succession fell to the familial descendents of his incarnation.

THRONEHOLDERS OF ORGYEN MINDROLING	
Minling Trichen I	Terdak Lingpa Gyurme Dorje (1646-1714)
Minling Trichen II	Pema Gyurme Gyatso (1686-1717)
Minling Trichen III	Gyelse Rinchen Namgyel (1694-1760)
Minling Trichen IV	Gyurme Pema Tendzin
Minling Trichen V	Trinle Namgyel
Minling Trichen VI	Pema Wangyel
Minling Trichen VII	Gyurme Sangye Kunga
Minling Trichen VIII	Trichen Yizhin Wangyel
Minling Trichen IX	Dechen Chodrub [aka Minling Chung Khenpo]
Minling Trichen X	Kunga Tendzin [son of Terdak Lingpa's incarnation, Rangrik Dorje]
Minling Trichen XI	Dondrub Wangyel [the latter's son]
Minling Trichen XII	Kunzang Wangyel, the latter's son (b 1931)

The present throneholder, Minling Trichen XII Kunzang Wangyel, resides at the Mindroling branch monastery in Dehra Dun, India. Mindroling's extensive buildings have been severely damaged by the Dzungar armies in the 18th century, and subsequently by the Chinese. Nonetheless, reconstruction has been continuing in recent decades through the efforts of the late Minling Chung Rinpoche Ngawang Chodrak (1908-80) and Kusho Jampal, and there is much of interest to see.

The Courtyard

There are two gates leading into the courtyard of the former monastic citadel – the main gate on the NE side and the second gate on the SE, where vehicles are parked. To enter via the main gate, walk around the residential compound on the SE wing. Inside the courtyard (from left to right) are: the east-facing **Tsuklakhang** with its impressive masonry façade, the north-facing **Drubcho Sangak Podrang**, the east-facing **Namgyel Podrang**, and the south-facing **Labrang Chokhor Lhunpo Podrang**. On the E wing of the courtyard are the monastic quarters and guesthouse. Among these, the **Namgyel Podrang** (restored as recently as 1944) is in ruins, and the 13-storey stupa named **Kumbum Tongdrol Chenmo**, which had

been constructed by Terdak Lingpa himself has been completely erased. The other three buildings will be described in turn.

Tsuklakhang

Lowest Level The 3½-storey **Tsuklakhang** has an assembly hall on its lowest level, with adjoining chapels on three sides. To the S are the **Panchen Lhakhang** and the **Zhalyekhang**, the latter containing exquisite Kadam-style stupas, the silver reliquary of Minling Trichen IX Dechen Chodrub, a clay image of Terdak Lingpa, and images of the Eight Manifestations of Padmasambhava. On the N side is the protector shrine which formerly housed a central image of Mahottara Heruka (Chemchok Heruka), and now has wrathful protectors within. The large **inner sanctum** on the W has a 4m high ornate image of Shakyamuni, flanked by his two foremost disciples, and the Eight Bodhisattvas. Its gates are guarded by Vajrapani and Hayagriva.

Second Level On the second storey, the main chapel is the **Tersar Lhakhang** on the SE side. It contains 3-dimensional mandalas of the cycles entitled *Wrathful Deities of the Magical Net (Mayajala)*, and the *Gathering of the Sugatas of the Eight Transmitted Precepts (Kabgye Deshek Dupa)*, as well as deities corresponding to

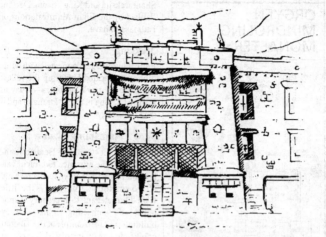

The façade of Mindroling Tsuklakhang

the new *terma* revelations of Terdak Lingpa, the silver reliquary of Minling Trichen X Kunga Tendzin, and the Nartang *Kangyur*. There is also a collection of sacred objects: a part of Guru Chowang's wrist bone with a natural buddha image growing therefrom, an image consecrated by Terdak Lingpa in person, and precious images discovered by the treasure-finders Guru Chowang, Jigme Lingpa, Dorje Lingpa and others. There is also a set of the *Nyingma Gyudbum*, published in India by the late Dilgo Khyentse Rinpoche.

To the right of this chapel is the **Jetsun Migyur Peldron Lhakhang**, containing the silver reliquary of Terdak Lingpa's daughter, and various scriptures. Beyond it are the rooms of the monastic steward and caretaker. Facing the Tersar Lhakhang is the **Neten Lhakhang** (now empty).

On the left side, in the **Pema Wangyel Lhakhang**, there are reliquaries including that of Minling Trichen VI Pema Wangyel. Adjacent to that is the **Lhakhang Onangkyil**, with reliquaries in-

cluding the silver stupa of Minling Trichen VII Gyurme Sangye Kunga. To its left are smaller chapels named **Changlochen** and **Silweitsal**.

Third level The highest chapels are those on the third storey and above. Among them, the **Lhakhang Dewachen** is the hermitage of Lochen Dharmashri, the learned brother of Terdak Lingpa, containing images of Lochen Dharmashri and a painting of Terdak Lingpa consecrated with his own handprints and footprints in gold. The **Lama Lhakhang** contains a central image of the primordial Buddha Samantabhadra in union with his consort Samantabhadri, and **outstanding murals**, which depict the entire Nyingmapa lineages, from ancient India until the 18th century.

Drubcho Sangak Podrang
On the N side of the courtyard, the **Drubcho Sangak Podrang**, which has been utilized as a granary since the 1960s, contains some original murals, although its foremost image: Four-armed Avalokiteshvara, no longer exists. Its outer walls do preserve a famous

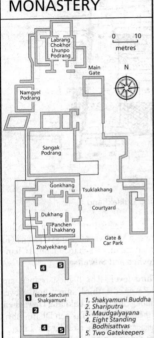

ORGYEN MINDROLING MONASTERY

0   10
metres

N

1. Shakyamuni Buddha
2. Shariputra
3. Maudgalyayana
4. Eight Standing Bodhisattvas
5. Two Gatekeepers

fresco of Padmasambhava which is said to have spoken to Terdak Lingpa, requesting him to remain in the world to help living beings and not pass away into the light body.

Labrang Chokhor Lhunpo Podrang
The lowest storey of the **Labrang Chokhor Lhunpo Podrang** has been well renovated in recent years. Its central image depicts Terdak Lingpa, and the throne is that of the Minling Trichen. The floor surface of the hall is utilized for the construction of large sand-mandalas during the 4th month of the lunar calendar. Within the inner sanctum are large 4m images of Padmasambhava,

Shantaraksita and King Trisong Detsen, flanked by the Eight Manifestations of Padmasambhava.

Trekking

Retreat hermitages connected with Mindroling are located higher up the valley; and there are trekking routes – 1 day to Dargye Choling in upper Dranang and 4 days to Chongye in the E.

Namseling Manor

Following the Gongkar-Tsetang highway E from the entrance to Drachi valley, you reach the Samye ferry crossing, after 5 km. Inland from here is the little visited but elegant 15th century manor house of Namseling. This 7-storey building is a rare example of the Tibetan noble fiefs, hardly any of which survived the Cultural Revolution.

Jing Okar Drak

On the Gongkar-Tsetang highway, 22 km E of Drachi valley entrance, there is a turn-off which leads to Okar Drak in Jing. The meditation caves here have associations with Padmasambhava and the Dzogchen master Dzeng Dharmabodhi (1052-1169). Later, *termas* were discovered here by Dorje Lingpa (1346-1405) and Terdak Lingpa of Mindroling.

ZURKHAR VALLEY

ACCESS The ferry crossing to Samye is located 13 km E of Dratang and 39 km W of Tsetang. There are no fixed departure times and the crossing takes 1-1½ hrs, zigzagging to avoid sandbanks. From the jetty on the N bank at Zurkhardo there are trucks and tractors available to transport pilgrims and tourists to the monastery, some 9 km further E. Samye can also be approached by trekking from Taktse, Ganden, and Gyama to the E of Lhasa.

Zurkhardo

From the village of Zurkhardo there is an inland route via Nekar and Kharu villages to **Dongakling**, a 15th century monastery founder by Tsongkhapa's disciple Jangsem Kunga Zangpo. The inner sanctum of the monastery contains the founder's mummified remains.

Taking the road to Samye from the ferry, after a short distance you will pass on the left side a series of five resplendent white stupas, which stand out at intervals against the sandy rocks. These are the **Stupas of Zurkhardo**, reputedly constructed by Shantaraksita to commemorate the place where King Trisong Detsen first met Padmasambhava. These stupas, which symbolize the Buddhas of the Five Families, are in an archaic style, their plinth and *bumpa* surmounted by a tall spire and *bindu*. They are visible from afar on the S bank of the Brahmaputra.

● **Accommodation** Zurkhardo has a clean and pleasant guesthouse.

SAMYE: TIBET'S FIRST MONASTERY

བསམ་ཡས་ཆོས་ར

History of Samye

Tibet's first monastery was constructed

most probably between 775 and 779, although there are other sources suggesting alternative dates, eg 763 (Tang Annals) and 787-799 (Buton). King Trisong Detsen, revered by Tibetans as an emanation of Manjushri, acceded to the throne at the age of 13, and with the assistance of Ba Trizhi he invited Shantaraksita of Zahor, who presided over Vikramashila monastery, to formally establish Buddhist monasticism in Tibet. Buddhist geomantic temples had been constructed in Tibet by King Songtsen Gampo and his queens some 130 years earlier; but owing to the hostility of Bonpo aristocratic families, the formal institutions of the Buddhist religion had not emerged. So it was that when Trisong Detsen directly confronted this arcane opposition to Buddhism, he invited Padmasambhava of Oddiyana (modern Swat) to subdue the hostile elemental forces of Tibet and make them amenable or subservient to Buddhism. Padmasambhava traversed the entire plateau, transforming negative forces into Buddhist protectors, and introducing the highest tantras and their teachings to his fortunate disciples. On the sum-

Samye Monastery

SAMYE MONASTERY

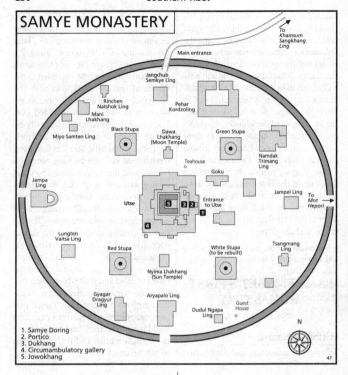

To Khamsum Sangkhang Ling

Main entrance

Jangchub Semkye Ling

Rinchen Natshok Ling

Mani Lhakhang

Pehar Kordzoling

Miyo Samten Ling

Black Stupa

Dawa Lhakhang (Moon Temple)

Green Stupa

Namdak Trimang Ling

Teahouse

Goku

Jampa Ling

Utse

Entrance to Utse

Jampel Ling

To Mnt Hepori

Lungten Vaitsa Ling

Red Stupa

White Stupa (to be rebuilt)

Tsangmang Ling

Nyima Lhakhang (Sun Temple)

Gyagar Dragyur Ling

Aryapalo Ling

Dudul Ngapa Ling

Guest House

N

1. Samye Doring
2. Portico
3. Dukhang
4. Circumambulatory gallery
5. Jowokhang

47

mit of Mt Hepori (see below, page 243), E of Samye, he crushed the local demons and consecrated the site for the construction of Tibet's first monastery.

The preceptors of Samye Monastery were held in high esteem, both socially and politically, throughout Tibet from the 8th until the late 10th century. But following the disintegration of the Yarlung Dynasty and the introduction of the second phase of Buddhist propagation, the site gradually came under the influence of other non-Nyingma traditions: the Kadampas, during the period of Ra Lotsawa; the Sakyapas during and after the period of Lama Dampa Sonam Gyeltshen (14th-16th century), and the Gelukpas under the rule of the Dalai Lamas. Samye thus became a symbol of

Tibet's national identity, in which Nyingma, Sakya and Geluk schools have all had strong interests.

Sadly, the original buildings are no longer intact, having been damaged by civil war (11th century), fires (mid 17th century, and 1826), earthquakes (1816), and the Chinese occupation (1960s). Yet, the Tibetans have always endeavoured to rebuild and enhance the complex after each round of destruction. Notable among these were the renovations carried out by Ra Lotsawa (11th century), Sonam Gyeltsen (14th century), Dalai Lama VII (1770), the Tibetan government (1849), and the late Panchen Lama X (1986 onwards). During the Chinese occupation, the village was encouraged to encroach upon the temple, and even in the late

1980s pigs and other farm animals could be seen wandering through the sacred shrines. The current policy is to redefine the area of the monastery by pushing back the village.

Khamsum Sangkhang Ling

Driving into Samye, you pass on the right the edifice of Khamsum Sangkhang Ling, which is the only extant temple among the three built outside the perimeter wall by King Trisong Detsen's three queens. This is a 4-storey building, which was reconstructed by Reting Rinpoche during the 1940s. It contains interesting murals. The high ceilinged assembly hall occupies two floors. Its inner sanctum has paintings of the Sixteen Elders and, in its circumambulatory corridor, of Shakyamuni Buddha. On the third floor, there are murals depicting the 1849 reconstruction of Samye, as well as Padmasambhava, Shakyamuni Buddha, Amitabha, and so forth. An unusually well-lit chapel on the fourth floor contains the protector shrine, with finely carved beams and columns, as well as extant murals of Shakyamuni, Amitabha, Amitayus, and the protectors.

• **Accommodation** One of the best camp sites at Samye is located in a meadow to the SW of this building.

Perimeter Wall and Stupas

The road into Samye, after by-passing the Khamsum Sangkhang Ling, skirts the reconstructed perimeter wall, distinctively crowned with a succession of 1,008 small stupas. The wall, which is now oval-shaped (the original having had a zigzag design), is over 1 km in circumference, 3-4m high, and over 1m thick. There are four gates: one in each of the intermediate sectors (NE, SE, SW and NW) of the perimeter wall, each leading to the central Utse temple via an enormous 40-50m high stupa. Three of the four stupas have been recently reconstructed: the green one to the NE, the red one to the SW and the black one to the NW. The white stupa of the SE is soon to be rebuilt. The main gate lies to the NE, and it is through this that the truck from the ferry will enter. Within the perimeter wall, there are two pilgrim's circuits, an outer route which encompasses all the secondary temples, and an inner route which encompasses the Utse temple at the centre.

Samye Utse

The east-facing Utse temple has four storeys, the second of which also has a terrace at a lower level than its entrance. Each of the three lower storeys are 5-6m high. Traditionally, the three lowest storeys and their interiors are said to have been fashioned by craftsmen from neighbouring Buddhist lands: the lowest in Indian style, the second in Chinese style, and the third in Khotanese style. Another view, perhaps based on the appearance of the Utse following its later renovation, suggests that the first is in Tibetan style, the second in Chinese style, and the third in Indian style. At the present day, these stylistic features are not self-evident, although one can observe elements of Chinese Buddhist architecture in the beams and columns of the second floor, and Central Asian features in the dress and inwardly sloping posture of the new images on the third.

To the left of the entrance is a 5m-high stone obelisk, the **Samye Doring**, dating from the original construction, which proclaims Buddhism as the state religion of Tibet. Pairs of ancient stone lions and elephants flank the entrance; and above, in the portico, there is a large 8th century bronze bell which the king's Tibetan queen Poyong Gyelmotsun offered at the time of the original construction. This is one of three once extant bells from the period of the Yarlung Dynasty – the others being in the Jokhang of Lhasa, and at Tradruk (see below, page 255).

The Utse Temple at Samye

Entering through the portico, with its inscriptions documenting the history of the monastery and murals depicting the Four Guardian Kings, there is a circumambulatory gallery complete with prayer wheels. Murals here depict the Thirty-five Confession Buddhas, the land of Shambhala, and the renovation work of 1849.

First Floor

The inner building has three main doors, one leading to the central assembly hall (*dukhang*), a second to the Avalokiteshvara chapel in the S wing and a third to the protector shrine in the N wing. Entering the large **Assembly Hall** (actually by a small door to the left of its main gate), there are E-W running rows of monks' seats. The images to the left depict in succession: Tangtong Gyelpo, Buton Rinchendrub, Shantaraksita, Kamalashila, Vimalamitra, and Yudra Nyingpo (S wall), and Vairocana, Shantaraksita, Padmasambhava, Trisong Detsen, and Songtsen Gampo (W wall). Among these, the Padmasambhava image replaces an outstanding original, which is said to have "resembled him in person" (Ngadrama). The Dalai Lama's throne in the centre

of the hall is backed by images of Longchen Rabjampa and Jigme Lingpa (twice). The images on the right depict Atisha, flanked by his Kadampa students Dromtonpa and Ngok Lekpei Sherab, and the three celebrated emanations of Manjushri: Longchen Rabjampa, Tsongkhapa, and Sakya Pandita.

The assembly hall leads into the inner sanctum or **Jowokhang** via three tall gates, symbolizing the three approaches to liberation: emptiness, signlessness, and aspirationlessness. Here, there is an inner circumambulatory corridor, with interesting murals depicting the past and final lives of Shakyamuni Buddha. The walls of the inner sanctum are more than 2m thick, and the ceiling has wonderful painted mandalas. The principal image is a 4m Shakyamuni in the form Jowo Jangchub Chenpo, flanked by 10 standing bodhisattvas (ie the standard set of eight plus Trailokyavijaya on the left and Vimalakirti on the right), and the gatekeepers Hayagriva and Acala. On the left, next to Shakyamuni, is Padmasambhava in the wrathful form Nangsi Zilnon. Many books including the *Kangyur* and *Tangyur* fill the rear wall, and in the outer right corner is a

THE ESTABLISHMENT OF BUDDHISM IN TIBET

Padmasambhava's labour in crushing the local demons on Mt Hepori paved the way for the establishment of Buddhist monasticism in Tibet. King Trisong Detsen, at Shantaraksita's suggestion, ensured that the complex was to be modelled on the plan of **Odantapuri Monastery** (modern Bihar Shariff), where the buildings themselves represented the Buddhist cosmological order (with Mt Sumeru in the centre, surrounded by four continents and eight subcontinents, sun and moon, all within a perimeter wall known as the Cakravala). This construction would therefore come to symbolize the establishment of a new Buddhist world order in Tibet. Humans were engaged in this unprecedented building project by day, and spirits by night. Hence the monastery's full name: **Glorious Inconceivable Temple of Unchanging Spontaneous Presence** (Pel Samye Migyur Lhundrub Tsuklakhang).

King Trisong Detsen then established an integrated programme for the translation of the Buddhist classics into Tibetan, bringing together teams of Indian scholars (*pandita*) and Tibetan translators (*lotsawa*). He and a celebrated group of 24 subjects received instruction on the highest tantras from Padmasambhava in particular, but also from Vimalamitra, Buddhaguhya and others, and through their meditations they attained the supreme realizations and accomplishments of Buddhist practice. In addition, Shantaraksita was requested to preside over the ordination of Tibet's first seven trial monks, namely: Ba Trizhi (Srighosa), Ba Selnang (Jnanendra), Pagor Vairocana (Vairocanaraksita), Ngenlam Gyelwa Choyang, Khonlui Wangpo Sungwa (Nagendraraksita), Ma Rinchen Chok, and Lasum Gyelwei Jangchub.

In 792 a debate was held between Kamalashila, an Indian proponent of the graduated path to buddhahood, which emphasizes the performance of virtuous deeds, and Hoshang Mo-ho-yen, a Chinese proponent of the instantaneous path to buddhahood, with its emphasis on meditation and inaction. Kamalashila emerged as the victor, but it is clear from Nubchen's treatise *Samten Migdron* that both views were integrated within the overall path to buddhahood. It was in these ways that the king established the future of Buddhism in Tibet.

Dalai Lama throne, backed by a tangka depicting Kalacakra.

The **Protector Chapel** (Gonkhang) is entered through a door on the right side of the assembly hall. It contains (from left to right) images of: Ekajati, Mahakala in the form Panjaranatha (Gonpo Gur), and Vajrakumara (W wall); Peldon Masung Gyelpo, Cimara, and Shridevi (N wall), and the retinue of Panjaranatha (E wall). A large stuffed snake and assorted weaponry are also kept in this room.

On the S wing of the Assembly Hall, entered by a separate east-facing gate, is the chapel dedicated to Thousand-armed Avalokiteshvara, known as **Chenrezi Chaktong Chentong Lhakhang**. Built in the 14th century by the Sakya Lama Dampa Sonam Gyeltsen in memory of his deceased mother, it contains an enormous Avalokiteshvara image. On the S wall are an incomplete series of relief images depicting the Eight Manifestations of Padmasambhava, as well as Milarepa, Atisha, and Green Tara. In the NE corner, there is a glass case containing some mortal remains of Jangsem Kunga Zangpo (on which see above, page 235).

Second Floor

The second floor is approached via a staircase to the left of the main entrance

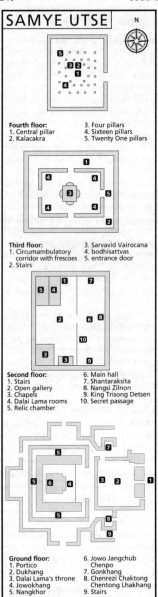

SAMYE UTSE N

Fourth floor:
1. Central pillar
2. Kalacakra
3. Four pillars
4. Sixteen pillars
5. Twenty One pillars

Third floor:
1. Circumambulatory corridor with frescoes
2. Stairs
3. Sarvavid Vairocana
4. bodhisattvas
5. entrance door

Second floor:
1. Stairs
2. Open gallery
3. Chapels
4. Dalai Lama rooms
5. Relic chamber
6. Main hall
7. Shantaraksita
8. Nangsi Zilnon
9. King Trisong Detsen
10. Secret passage

Ground floor:
1. Portico
2. Dukhang
3. Dalai Lama's throne
4. Jowokhang
5. Nangkhor
6. Jowo Jangchub Chenpo
7. Gonkhang
8. Chenrezi Chaktong Chentong Lhakhang
9. Stairs

48

and a low terrace, where the monks quarters are located. There is an open gallery with remarkable murals, 92m in length, which depict the history of Tibet, from the Yarlung period and the life of Padmasambhava, through the Sakya and Phakmodru periods, to the accession of Dalai Lama V and his successors. Notice the striking depictions of the white-bearded Terdak Lingpa and the Mongol king Gushi Qan. There are also scenes depicting athletic contests and sports.

In the NE corner there are two chapels, the one to the left is an active protector shrine, and the other dedicated to the Nine Aspects of Amitayus.

In the SE corner, a passageway leads into the **private apartments of the Dalai Lama**. Here, there are interesting murals depicting the former appearance of Samye. There is also a relic chamber, where the most precious objects of the monastery are now housed. These include: an image of Padmasambhava in the form Guru Saroruhavajra which had been discovered by Nyangrel, the skull of Shantaraksita, a turquoise buddha retrieved from the kingdom of Bhatahor, a turquoise amulet containing hairs of Padmasambhava, the left stone footprint left by Padmasambhava at Gungtang La (the right one being in the Phakpa Lhakhang of the Potala Palace), the staff of Vairocana, a meteorite vajra, and a vajra from the ancient perimeter wall.

The spacious **main hall**, which exhibits some Chinese architectural features at the roof, contains large gilded images of Shantaraksita (S), Padmasambhava in the form Nangsi Zilnon (W) and King Trisong Detsen (N). Flanking Padmasambhava are smaller images of Amitayus, Padmasambhava's tiger-riding form Dorje Drolo (offered by Semo Dechen of Lamaling), an old image of Jigme Lingpa, and Shakyamuni. To the right of the entrance there is a secret passage, where Vairocana is said to have hidden in order to escape the wrath of Queen Tsepong.

Third Floor

The newly reconstructed third floor is approached via a staircase on the left side of the second storey. There is a circumambulatory corridor with gates on each of its four sides. The outer walls of the corridor depict the Twenty-five Disciples of Padmasambhava (Jewang Nyernga), and above these there are lattices through which the outer satellite temples of Samye are visible. The inner walls of the corridor depict the Buddhas of the Five Families: Aksobhya (E), Ratnasambhava (S), Amitabha (W), and Amoghasiddhi (N).

Entering the E door, the central image is that of the 4-faced Sarvavid Vairocana (Kunrik Nampa Nangze), flanked by Vairocana and Vimalamitra on the left and Padmasambhava, and Shantaraksita on the right. Each of the four doors is guarded by two gatekeepers (Hayagriva and Acala), and in each of the corners formed by the doors there are sets of the standing bodhisattvas, distinctively robed and sloping inward, in the Central Asian manner.

Fourth Floor

The highest floor of the Utse temple is approached via a step-ladder on the W side of the third floor and a passageway which leads around to the entrance on the E. There is a central image of Kalacakra and the central pillar of juniper (formerly sandalwood) which acts as the life-axis of the building. Surrounding it are three rows of columns: the innermost with four pillars symbolizes the Four Guardian Kings, the second with 16 pillars symbolizes the Sixteen Elders, and the third with 21 pillars symbolizes the Twenty-one Taras. The splendid gilded roofs, which were fully restored in 1989, can be seen from the S bank of the Brahmaputra many miles distant.

Outer Temples

Restoration has begun on the outer temples within the complex. These include the four temples of the cardinal directions: Jampel Ling (E), Aryapalo or Tamdrin Ling (S), Jampa Ling (W), and Jangchub Semkye Ling (N); along with the eight temples of the intermediate directions: Namdak Trimang Ling (NE), and Tsangmang Ling (SE); Gyagar Dragyur Ling (SW) and Dudul Ngapa Ling (SE); Lungten Vaitsa Ling (SW) and Miyo Samten Ling (NW); and Rinchen Natshok Ling (NW) and Pehar Kordzoling (NE). The Dawa Lhakhang lies to the N of the Utse while the Nyima Lhakhang (S of Utse) has yet to be restored. According to the traditional colour symbolizm, the temples to the E were white, those to the S yellow, those to the W red, and those to the N black or dark green. In the case of the current phase of reconstruction, these distinctions are not always apparent.

The Eastern Temples

The temple of **Jampel Ling**, dedicated to Manjughosa, is currently undergoing restoration. There are murals depicting Manjughosa and the Thousand Buddhas of the aeon; and a large *mani* wheel. During the 1980s it served as a commune office.

The satellite temple to its NE, **Namdak Trimang Ling**, was formerly the residence of Shantaraksita and the Vinaya college. Within its inner sanctum were images of the Buddhas of the Three Times. To the SE of Jampel Ling, **Tsangmang Ling** formerly contained the printing press of Samye monastery.

Other buildings on the E side include the remains of the stone platform to the NE of the Utse, once used for displaying applique tangkas at festival times, a throne utilized by the late Panchen Lama X when he visited Samye in the 1980s, and on the W side a small shop and tea house.

The Southern Temples

The temple of **Aryapalo**, dedicated to Hayagriva, which originally predates the Utse, has already been restored. It is

CIMARA, THE RED PROTECTOR: JUDGEMENT NIGHT

Tseumar Chok was the abode of Cimara, the red protector of Samye who took over Pehar's role after the latter had been transferred to Nechung near Drepung (see above, page 243). In an awesome room adjacent to the protector shrine, which was opened once a year, Cimara would by night dispense the judgement of the dead upon evil-doers, chopping them to shreds on a wooden block. The monks of Samye were often, it is said, aware of the thudding sound of the chopping block and the bloody stench which filled the air during the night. This wooden block required replacement once a year.

a 2-storeyed building, entered from the S. The ground floor temple contains images of Hayagriva (E), Lokeshvara, Chenrezi Semnyi Ngalso, and Four-armed Avalokiteshvara (N), and within a W side chapel, images of the Three Ancestral Religious Kings (Chogyel Namsum), Avalokiteshvara and Manjushri.

Among its peripheral temples, **Gyagar Dragyur Ling** in the SW is located in a beautiful courtyard, with W and E cloistered galleries depicting the Indian panditas and Tibetan translators of the 8th century. This was where the Buddhist translation programme was established by King Trisong Detsen back in the 8th century. Within the chapel are images depicting Avalokiteshvara in the form of Simhanada, and the Indian yogin Padampa Sangye. In front is an applique frieze depicting the Eight Manifestations of Padmasambhava. **Upstairs** there are images of Padmasambhava flanked by the kings Songtsen Gampo and Trisong Detsen. To the left are images of the Indian panditas, including the Six Ornaments, the Two Supreme Ones, and Jinamitra; while to the right are the Tibetan translators, including Nubchen Sangye Yeshe, Vairocana, Zhang Yeshede, Kawa Paltsek, Chokrolui Gyeltsen, Khonlui Wangpo Sungwa, Jnanendraraksita, and so forth.

The temple of **Dudul Ngapa Ling** to the SE of Aryapalo temple was formerly a tantric chapel, as yet unrestored. There is a small occasional guesthouse in the village on the S side of the complex.

The Western Temples

Jampa Ling temple, dedicated to Maitreya, was where the Chinese monks resided during the 8th century; and it was the venue of the Great Debate between Kamalashila and Hoshang Moho-yen (see above, page 239). The inner sanctum is semi-circular, corresponding to the shape of the western continent in Indian cosmology; its murals depict Maitreya and Shakyamuni, and there is a new image of the latter.

Its peripheral temple to the SW, **Lungten Vaitsa Ling**, dedicated to the translator Vairocana, has some extant murals depicting Shakyamuni Buddha and the translator. **Miyo Samten Ling**, which lies to the NW, was a meditation hall utilized by Chinese monks in the 8th century.

The Northern Temples

Jangchub Semkye Ling, dedicated to Prajnaparamita, has been used for storing timber in the recent past, but is currently undergoing renovation. To its NW is the peripheral temple, **Rinchen Natshok Ling**, a small chapel with murals depicting Shakyamuni; and to the NE is the renowned temple of **Pehar Kordzoling**, where Samye's ancient Sanskrit texts were stored in the care of the protector deity Pehar. A turquoise image of this deity, also known as Shingjachen, was brought to Samye from Bhatahor in Turkestan following a successful military campaign in the early 9th century. Among the temple's treasures there was also a talismanic leather mask, called Sebak Muchung, which was believed to come alive. Nowadays, there is a **small teahouse** within the village on the N side of the complex.

Sun and Moon Temples

The clinic located S of the Utse was formerly the **Nyima Lhakhang** or Sun Temple. This shrine was dedicated to the Yaksa Cimara and is therefore sometimes called **Tseumar Chok**. The **Dawa Lhakhang**, N of the Utse, is a particularly archaic structure, with murals depicting the Thousand Buddhas.

Hepori

Mount Hepori is approached to the E of Samye Utse, beyond the government buildings of Samye township. This hill, which offers incredible bird's eye view of the Samye complex, is revered as one of the four sacred hills of Central Tibet (along with Chakpori at Lhasa, Chuwori at Chushul, and Zodang Gongpori at Tsetang). It was from here that Padmasambhava bound the local divinities of the region under an oath of allegiance to Buddhism. On the summit of Hepori is a rebuilt **Lhasangkang**, or Temple for the Smoke Offering to the Local Deities, and to its NE is a Padmasambhava meditation cave. On its slopes there were once reliquary stupas, containing the remains of Shantaraksita (E), and those of three of the greatest 8th century translators, namely: Kawa Peltsek (N), Zhang Yeshede (S ridge), and Chokrolui Gyeltsen (S end).

CHIMPHU CAVES

མཆིམས་ཕུ

ACCESS The Chimphu hermitage is located some 16 km NE of Samye in the upper reaches of the adjacent Chimyul valley. Pilgrims begin the 5-hr walk to the caves before sunrise, but it is also possible to hire a tractor at Samye village, which would take you to a clearing some 30 mins walking distance below the Chimphu Utse Temple.

Taking the right path from the N end of Samye, you will cross the local irrigation canal and the Samye River before turning left into the Chim valley. Passing the deserted villages of Chimda, you then climb steeply through a sylvain grove where aromatic herbs are in evidence to reach a stupa.

The upper valley, Chimphu, forms a natural amphitheatre, its W and E ridges divided by the waters of a sacred stream. To the SE, there is the **Chimphu Utse nunnery**, which has a large newly constructed temple containing images of Hayagriva (left); Jowo Shakyamuni, Padmasambhava, and Four-armed Avalokiteshvara (centre); and Vajrasattva Yabsum, Ekajati, Gonpo Maning, Rahula, Dorje Lekpa and a local protector (right).

Currently there are over 100 retreatants and hermits at Chimphu – the majority from E Tibet. Most of the caves are accessible from this temple to the NW, clustered around the 15m high Zangdok Pelri rock.

Caves on the ascent

At the base of the Zangdok Pelri rock, is the **Sangwa Metok Cave**, where Jigme Lingpa in the 18th century received the visions of Longchen Rabjampa, which inspired him to reveal the *Longchen Nyingtig*, and compose the *Yonten Dzo*. Outside is a rock-carved image of Manjushri, said to have been executed by Padmasambhava's own hand. Nearby is the **Lower Cave of Nyangben Tingdzin Zangpo** (**Nyangpuk Ogma**), where both Nyangben and King Trisong Detsen stayed in retreat, the **Meditation Cave of Yeshe Tsogyel** (**Tsogyel Drubpuk**), and a rock bearing an impression of Padmasambhava's hat and Yeshe Tsogyel's foot.

The trail divides into upper and lower branches at the 12m long **Guruta Rock**, where there is an enormous Padmasambhava footprint. On its lower side is the **Upper Cave of Nyangben Tingdzin Zangpo** (**Nyangpuk Gongma**), where the *Vima Nyingtig* was concealed by Nyangben in the 9th century and later mastered by Longchen Rabjampa in the 14th. Further W there is a small charnel ground, and above the rocks there are further hermitages – those of Ma Rinchen Chok, Shubu Pelzang, and the **Tamdrin Puk**, where Gyelwa Choyang propitiated Hayagriva.

Drakmar Keutsang cave

100m above the Zangdok Pelri rock is the most important of all the caves at Chimphu, the **Drakmar Keutsang**. This is revered as the primary pilgrimage place of buddha-speech in Central Tibet, where Padmasambhava first gave teachings on the eight meditational deities known as Drubpa Kabgye to his eight main disciples, including the king Trisong Detsen. A 2-storey temple has been constructed around the cave, which is at the rear on the ground level. On the altar in the temple there are new images of Padmasambhava, flanked by his two foremost consorts and eight manifestations. Formerly the most precious objects here were the Jema Atron image of Padmasambhava which had been fashioned by Vairocana and Tami Gontson, and the image of Prajnaparamita which belonged to King Trisong Detsen. The present cave does contain an image of Padmasambhava, a blue Vajravarahi, and a Jowo image, the vision of which is said to equal the vision of Padmasambhava in person.

The Drakmar Keutsang is renowned for another reason, in that it was here that Padmasambhava temporarily resuscitated the deceased Princess Pemasel and taught her the *Kandro Nyingtig* for the first time. The place where this resurrection occurred is a flagstone bearing the imprint of her body in front of the cave entrance, known as the **Pemasel Durtro**. Pilgrims are rubbed vigorously on the back and shoulders with a stone reputedly brought from the Shitavana charnel ground in India.

Above the ground level, there is a terrace offering spectacular views of the Brahmaputra valley below, and in the W side of the upper chamber there is a 4m tunnel leading to the **Meditation Cave of Vairocana (Bairo Drubpuk)**. This cave contains images of the translator Vairocana and Longchen Rabjampa.

Ridge-top caves

There are some cave hermitages at the top of the Chimphu ridge, including the **Longchen Gurkarpuk** (associated with Padmasambhava and Trisong Detsen's chief minister), the **Tsogyel Zimpuk** (associated with Yeshe Tsogyel), the cave utilized by the latter's Nepalese consort Atsara Sale, the **Longchen Puk** (associated with Longchen Rabjampa), and on the far side of the ridge, the **Chimphu Drigugu**, where Padmasambhava stayed in retreat and Vimalamitra concealed the *Vima Nyingtig* texts. High up on the NE ridge of Chimphu is **Rimochen**, a site associated with Longchen Rabjampa.

Caves on the descent

On the descent from the Drakmar Keutsang, the trail passes a hermitage containing the reliquary of Gonjo Rinpoche from Kham, and the **Reliquary of Longchen Rabjampa** (Longchen Dung-ten), who passed away at Chimphu in 1363. The site is marked by a commemorative obelisk. There is a water-of-life spring (*tshe-chu*) by the trail, and on the descent from there, a hermitage with a stupa consecrated by Karmapa III Rangjung Dorje in the 14th century and another once frequented by Nubchen Sangye Yeshe. From here the trail leads down to the Chimphu Utse nunnery and the road back to Samye or to Lo at the mouth of the Chim River.

Drakmar Drinzang

བྲག་དམར་མགྲིན་བཟང་

Following the Drakmar valley 6 km N

from Samye through Yugar and Samphu village, on the W bank of the Drakmar-chu, you will arrive at Drinzang, the birthplace of King Trisong Detsen. This was once the country residence of the latter's parents, King Tride Tsukten and Queen Jincheng. The ruins of the palace and a temple, formerly housing images of the religious kings, can be seen. The house where the king was born once had red and white sandalwood trees growing in its courtyard, but only ruins now remain.

Yemalung Hermitage
ག་ཡའ་ཛམ་ལུང་

About 16 km further inland from Drakmar Drinzang, on an E fork in the road above Ninggong village, you will reach the remote hermitage of Yemalung. The trail leads past a charnel ground and sacred spring, to the narrow rock tunnel called **Bardo Trang** where pilgrims crawl through to test their degree of preparation for the intermediate state after death! The cliff-top cave hermitage of Padmasambhava contains a new image of the master himself; and rocks marked with his handprints and mantra inscriptions. The meditation cave of his disciple Vairocana is located in the slopes above. The *terma* text entitled *Innermost Spirituality of the Awareness Holder (Rikdzin Tuktik)*, which was concealed at Yemalung by Padmasambhava was subsequently unearthed here in 1663 by Terdak Lingpa of Mindroling.

Trekking

From Nyinggong, below Yemalung, there are 3-4 day trekking routes across Gokhar La pass (5,357m) to Taktse Dzong; and across Jukar La to Ganden.

TSETANG AND NEDONG COUNTY
ཉེད་ཐང་ སྣེ་གདོང་

乃东县 Tsetang and Nedong
Population: 50,725   Area: 2,339 sq km

Tsetang is one of Tibet's largest cities, and the capital of Lhokha district of the Tibetan Autonomous Region, exercising direct control over the affairs of 13 counties: Gongkar, Tranang, Nedong, Chongye, Tso-me, Lhodrak, Nakartse, Zangri, Chusum, Lhuntse, Tsona, Gyatsa, and Nang. The county capital is located at **Nedong**, which, as the seat of the Phakmodru Dynasty, functioned as the capital of the whole of Tibet from 1349 until its eclipse by the Rinpung fiefdom in 1435.

Tsetang is considered to be the cradle of Tibetan civilization, in that the Zodang

Gongpori caves above the town are said to be the place where the Tibetan race originated. Further S in the Yarlung valley kingship and agriculture were first introduced. The first palace is at Yumbu Lagang and the first Buddhist temple at Tradruk.

ACCESS The distance from Tsetang to Lhasa is 183 km, to Gongkar Airport 87 km, and to Dranang 47 km. The county of Nedong extends on the N bank of the Brahmaputra from Do Valley in the W as far as On Valley in the E; and the entire length of the Yarlung Valley (72 km) from Jasa and Sheldrak in the NW as far as Mt Yarlha Shampo.

TSETANG

(*Pop* 40,000; *Alt* 3,100m; *STD Code* (86)-891/893; *Oxygen* 68%.)

Orientation

There are two main roads which intersect at the crossroads in downtown Tsetang. A bizarre sculpture symbolizing the play of the monkey and ogress has been erected as a landmark at this road junction. The road W from the crossroads leads to Gongkar and Lhasa,

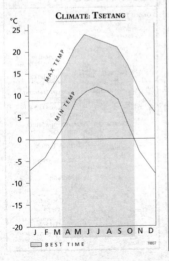

CLIMATE: TSETANG

°C

25
20
15
10
5
0
-5
-10
-15
-20

MAX TEMP
MIN TEMP

J F M A M J J A S O N D

☐ BEST TIME   TIB07

while the E road leads to Gyatsa and Menling, the N road to the Brahmaputra River bank and the On Valley ferry, and the S road to Chongye and Tsona. The Yarlung River (Yarlha Shampo-chu) flows due northwards on the W side of the intersection, and is spanned by two bridges – one on the Gongkar highway and the second (the old Namo Zampa) on the Chongye road further S.

Approaching the city from the Gongkar/Lhasa direction, the triangular peak of **Mt Zodang Gongpori** is visible long before the buildings are seen nestling below it. At the entrance to the city, on the right side of the road, there is a petrol station and a bus station. A turn-off on the right bypasses the city centre, leading to the SW and on to Sheldrak and Chongye. Continue on the main road, crossing the Yarlung bridge, with the Tsetang Hospital on the left. Both sides of the road are then occupied by truck stops and down market karaoke bars. As you approach the crossroads, there are grocery and electrical shops. Turning left at the crossroads, beside the *Himalayan Tibetan Hotel*, you will reach the vegetable, butter and meat markets, where there are small tea shops (left), and, opposite the entrance to Tsetang Commune Number Nine, a discotheque (right, upstairs).

Turning right at the crossroads into **Nedong Rd**, you will pass, on the left side, a large department store, a turn-off into the open-air market, a carpet store, a book store, a souvenir store, the Public Security Bureau, the Nedong County Government Buildings, the Post Office, and a military barracks. On the right you will pass grocery and electrical stores, some of which are run by Hui Moslems from Ziling area, the Tsetang Middle School, the Lhokha District Government Offices, the *Tsetang Guesthouse*, the *Tsetang Hotel*, and (just before the Chongye turn-off) the small *Nedong Guesthouse*.

If at the crossroads, you drive due E, onto **Gyatsa Rd** you will reach on the

TSETANG: PLAYGROUND OF THE MONKEY AND OGRESS

Tsetang means 'playground' – a reference to its importance as the place where a monkey emanation of Avalokiteshvara frolicked in the company of an ogress, thereby giving birth to the six progenitors of the original Tibet clans (see above, page 246). The monkey thus symbolizes the compassion of the bodhisattvas and the ogress the destructive or violent aspect of the Tibetan character. Legend associates **Mt Zodang Gongpori** behind Tsetang with the location of the monkey's cave.

right side a turn-off leading to the monasteries and houses of the old town: **Tsetang Monastery, Ngachopa Tratsang, Trebuling Monastery** and **Sangak Samtenling Nunnery**. On the left, you will pass the telecommunications building, the trade department and commercial buildings, before eventually reaching the Brahmaputra River, where a new bridge from Tsetang to On is currently under construction at the site of Tangtong Gyelpo's former **Nyago Chakzam** bridge.

If you take the aforementioned turn-off into the open-air market from Nedong Rd, you will find rows of stalls selling cheap Chinese household articles, clothing and shoes. A few stalls have traditional Tibetan items: tangkas, books, and religious artefacts. Behind these stalls there is a square, where the Bank of China, the cinema and dance hall are located. Turning left in front of the bank and first right, you will enter the old Tibetan quarter, where the aforementioned monasteries are located.

History

Mount Lhababri on the W side of the valley is regarded as the place where the first Tibetan king of the Yarlung Dynasty, Nyatri Tsenpo arrived from the heavens, or from India, to rule among men. He occupied the fortress of **Yumbu Lagang** to the S of Tsetang, and his descendents introduced agriculture into the valley at a place called **Zortang** (which some identify as a plot of land at Lharu below Yumbu Lagang, and others

with one to the N of town (now within Commune Number Nine).

After Songtsen Gampo unified Tibet in the 7th century and moved his capital to Lhasa, the Tsetang area gradually declined in its importance. But in 1349, **Nedong**, which is now a suburb of Tsetang, became the capital of the Phakmodrupa Dynasty which ruled Tibet until the end of the 15th century. It was during this period that the important monasteries of Tsetang were originally constructed by Tai Situ Jangchub Gyeltsen and his successors. Tsongkhapa received his ordination at **Bentsang Monastery** (Tse Tsokpa), which had been founded by Shakyashri in the early part of the 13th century.

Later, during the 18th century, Dalai Lama VII encouraged the development of the Gelukpa school in the Tsetang area, in consequence of which Tsetang Monastery was transformed into **Ganden Chokhorling**, and the **Sangak Samtenling** nunnery was established.

Places of interest

Tsetang Monastery

Located near the entrance to the old Tibetan quarter, Tsetang Monastery was originally a Kagyu site, founded in 1351 by Tai Situ Jangchub Gyeltsen of the Phakmodrupa Dynasty. As such, it held allegiance to Densatil as its mother monastery (see below, page 282). Later, in the mid-18th century, during the lifetime of Dalai Lama VII Kelzang Gyatso, the Kagyu buildings were dismantled and a Gelukpa monastery named **Ganden Chokhorling** erected to replace it. Refurbishing took place from 1900-12, but in the 1960s only the outer shell was spared. There are two main buildings, which have more recently been undergoing renovation: the assembly hall (*dukhang*) with a large skylight overlooking its Jokhang, and a residential *labrang* with attached debating courtyard.

Ngachopa Monastery

Located slightly to the E of Tsetang Monastery, this Kagyu site was also constructed by Tai Situ Jangchub Gyeltsen in the 14th century. There were fine images of Shakyamuni, Amitabha, and Maitreya. Although the complex was severely damaged during the civil war of the 16th century and the Dzungar occupation of the 17th century, it is now being actively rebuilt.

Trebuling Monastery

Trebuling Monastery is located NE of Ngachopa within the Shannan Diesel Factory compound. Its asssembly hall (*tsokchen*) and residential building still stand. However, the sacred images of Tara and Shakyamuni in the form Thupa Ngadrama which it once housed have not survived.

Sangak Samtenling Nunnery

This active nunnery, located on the slopes of Mt Zodang Gongpori above Tsetang monastery, was originally a 14th century Sakyapa establishment of the Tsarpa sub-school. It was founded on a former meditation site of Lama Dampa Sonam Gyeltsen and his student Yarlung Senge Gyeltsen. From the mid-18th century, however, it came under the influence of the Gelukpas, and a new foundation was established by Kyerong Ngawang Drakpa. Some of its sacred relics were salvaged during the 1960s. The main image within the assembly hall is a reputedly 7th century Mahakarunika, flanked by Tara, Tsongkhapa, and Tangtong Gyelpo, with the Sixteen Elders and Thirty-five Confession Buddhas behind in their individual stucco grottoes. Rear chapels contain further images of Kyenrong Ngawang Drakpa flanked by Avalokiteshvara, in the form Simhanada, and Manjughosa; and of Tsongkhapa with his foremost students, along with Atisha and Tangtong Gyelpo.

Excursions

Zodang Gongpori

Mount Zodang Gongpori is one of the four sacred hills of Central Tibet, renowned for its remote cave (4,060m), where the monkey emanation of Avalokiteshvara is said to have impregnated a demonic ogress, thereby giving birth to the six ancient Tibetan clans. The cave, which is located at 4,060m near the summit, is perched precipitously 500m above the Yarlung Valley. Within the cave is a naturally produced rock image of the monkey, and there are paintings of simian figures on the SE wall. Legend holds that a 'hidden land' (*beyul*) is contained within Mt Zodang Gongpori, its entrance (*bego*) being located on the E side of the mountain. A 2-day pilgrim's trek leads around the mountain, via the monkey cave, Gonpo La pass (4,750m), and the celebrated Tubpa Serlingpa Cave, which functioned as a retreat centre for Ngachopa Monastery.

Nyago Chakzam Bridge

Five large stone bridge supports are all that remain of the 14th century iron bridge, which provided a vital link between Tsetang and the On valley until the present century. With a span of 150-250m this was one of the celebrated engineer's greatest construction projects. The ruins on the S bank have long been regarded as a shrine to Tangtong Gyelpo's memory, but nowadays a modern bridge is under construction at Nyago.

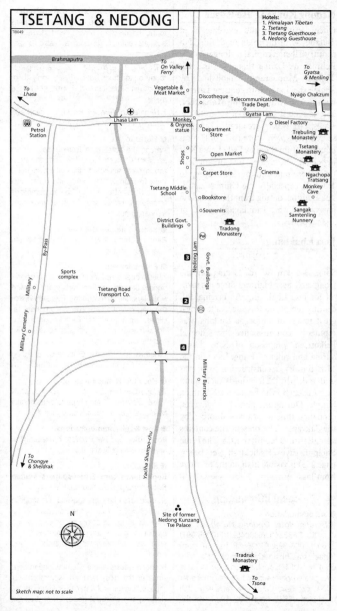

TSETANG & NEDONG

TB049

Hotels:
1. *Himalayan Tibetan*
2. *Tsetang*
3. *Tsetang Guesthouse*
4. *Nedong Guesthouse*

Brahmaputra

To On Valley Ferry

To Lhasa

To Gyatsa & Menling

Nyago Chakzum

Vegetable & Meat Market

Discotheque

Telecommunications, Trade Dept.

Lhasa Lam

Petrol Station

Monkey & Orgress statue

Gyatsa Lam

Diesel Factory

Trebuling Monastery

Department Store

Tsetang Monastery

Shops

Open Market

Carpet Store

Cinema

Ngachopa Tratsang

Monkey Cave

Tsetang Middle School

Bookstore

Souvenirs

Sangak Samtenling Nunnery

District Govt. Buildings

Tradong Monastery

By-Pass

Sports complex

Pol

Nedong Lam

Govt. Buildings

Military

Military Cemetary

Tsetang Road Transport Co.

Military Barracks

Yaciha Shampo-chu

To Chongye & Sheldrak

N

Site of former Nedong Kunzang Tse Palace

Tradruk Monastery

To Tsona

Sketch map: not to scale

Nedong Kunzang Tse Palace

Once located in the extreme S of Tsetang, W of the main road, this 15th century Tibetan capital no longer exists. Behind the Dzong there was the **Tse Tsokpa Monastery**, established by Shakyashri in the 13th century. Later, it became known as **Bentsang Monastery**, and as such it survived intact until the 1960s. This was where Orgyen Lingpa's sacred relics were stored and pills compounded from them by Dala Lama XIII in person. The greatest treasures of Bentsang were removed for safe-keeping to Tradruk, especially the Chinese applique Buddha, dating from the Ming Dynasty, and the Padmapani made of 29,000 pearls.

Jasa Lhakhang

གུ་ས་ལྷ་ཁང

Some 3-4 km W of Tsetang on the Gongkar/Lhasa highway, there is a turn-off for Jasa Lhakhang. An original 9th century temple on this site, containing a great image of Vairocana Buddha, was reputedly commissioned by Chogyel Pelkortsen, grandson of King Langdarma and ruler of Tsang. Later, in the 11th century, reconstruction work was undertaken by the local lords Yuchen and Jasa Lhachen, who founded a Kadampa temple. During the period of Sakya ascendancy, this in turn was absorbed by the Sakyapas. The present site contains a small shrine, rebuilt in 1988. The Pema Shelpuk cave of Sheldrak (see below, page 253) is visible high on the SE ridge from Jasa.

Local information

● **Accommodation**

B *Tsetang Hotel (Zedong Hotel)*, 21 Nedong Rd, T 6332603/63804520, F (0086-891) 32603/(0086-893) 63216688, has 118 comfortable rm with attached bath and television, on 4 flrs (US$45/double room), no elevator, solar heated water supply, most effective after 2000, excellent Cantonese restaurant (full meal plan US$33, breakfast U$9), under the careful management of Mr Sonam Tendzin, souvenir and gift shop, foyer bar and games room, hairdressing service, and occasional business centre, large rooms available for special functions.

C *Tsetang Guesthouse*, has clean superior rooms on top floor, but cold water only, there are 2 Chinese restaurants, 1 with set Chinese meals.

E *Himalayan Tibetan Hotel*, is cheap and centrally located at the crossroads.

● **Places to eat**

Among the hotels, the *Tsetang Hotel* offers excellent Chinese food. The *Tsetang Guesthouse* has Chinese set meals which are good value for money. There are smaller restaurants in the city centre, serving Tibetan dumplings (momo) and noodle soup (thukpa); and simple Sichuan dishes.

● **Banks & money changers**

Bank of China, Town Square, nr old Tibetan quarter of Tsetang.

● **Entertainment**

Tibetan operas and traditional music are occasionally performed at concerts in the *Tsetang Hotel* (enquire at reception). There are discotheques, karaoke bars, and video parlour facilities, up-market nr *Tsetang Hotel* and down-market, nr the truck stops on Lhasa Rd and the old Town Square.

Cinemas: the *Tsetang Cinema* is located on the Town Square, nr the **Bank of China**.

● **Hospitals & medical services**

Tsetang City Hospital, W of crossroads on N side of Lhasa Rd; *Tsetang Hospital of Traditional Medicine*, E of crossroads on Gyatsa Rd.

● **Post & telecommunications**

Post Office: opp *Tsetang Hotel* on Nedong Rd; another also on Gyatsa Rd.

● **Shopping**

Books, maps, cards & newspapers: *Xinhua Bookstore*, nr crossroads on E side.

Handicrafts: there are souvenir gift shops in the *Tsetang Hotel* and nr the crossroads on the E side. Look out for leather goods, carpets, and religious artefacts. Imported liquor and cigarettes are available at the shop in the *Tsetang Hotel*.

Modern goods: there is a new department store, nr the crossroads, and several smaller shops selling mineral water, beer, tinned foods, clothing and electrical goods. Almost all the shops will accept only RMB currency, and rarely accept payment in US dollars. It is best to change currency in Lhasa before reaching Tsetang, but the **Bank of China** can reputedly assist in emergencies. The open-air market nr the old city is well worth a visit, although unique products and antiques are hard to find.

Photography: print film and processing are available at *Tsetang Hotel* gift shop, and at photographic shops, especial Muslim owned electrical stores on the W side nr crossroads.

Stamps: are available at Post Office, SE of *Tsetang Hotel* on opp side of the road, or at the *Tsetang Hotel* reception counter.

● **Sports**

The sports ground is S of *Tsetang Hotel* on Nedong Rd.

● **Useful addresses**

Police & public security: Tsetang City Police and Public Security Bureau, S of crossroads, on E side of *Tsetang Hotel* approach road.

● **Tour companies & travel agents**

Tsetang Hotel Travel Company, and *CITS*, Shannan Branch, both based at the *Tsetang Hotel*.

● **Transport**

Air Tsetang is connected via Gongkar Airport (87 km SE) to Chengdu (daily flights), Kathmandu (Wed/Sat), Beijing (Sun), and Guangzhou (Wed), and Shanghai (Tues/Fri).

Road Most visitors to Tsetang, whether arriving by air or land, will have their transportation organized by the travel services. Long distance car and jeep transportation is more easily available from Lhasa, but also through the Tsetang Road Transport Company, located behind the *Tsetang Hotel*, on the Chongye side-road. Long distance travel by public bus is more common. The bus station for Lhasa is located to the W of Lhasa Rd, nr the Petrol Station.

DO VALLEY

From the village of Lo, where the Chim River enters the Brahmaputra, E of Samye, there is a track which follows the river bank eastwards to Kyerpa, and thence inland to Do Podrang in the Do valley. At Lowo Dongteng, there was formerly a stupa dedicated to Tashi Obar, a deity in the retinue of Cimara.

ON VALLEY

The On valley may be approached by a 7-hr trek from Kyerpa at the entrance to the Do valley, or, more easily, by boat from the **Nyago Druka ferry station**, 4 km E of Tsetang. A bridge is currently being constructed across the Brahmaputra at this point, and when completed the many interesting sites in On will become more accessible. The valley extends N from Ngari Tratsang at its entrance to the Padmasambhava cave of Onphu Taktsang in its upper reaches. In its mid-reaches, there is the hermitage of Tashi Doka, the Choding monastery, and the Khachu (Keru) Lhakhang.

Ngari Tratsang

The ruins of Ngari Tratsang stand guard over the entrance to the On valley from the S. This was a Gelukpa monastery, constructed in 1541 by Dalai Lama II Gendun Gyatso, for the training of monks from Far-west Tibet. It once contained relics which the Tibetan army had plundered from Central Asia, back in the 8th century. From here, there are jeepable roads leading inland through the On-chu valley to On township and Ahor; or via the Brahmaputra River bank to Zangri and Olka.

Tashi Doka hermitage

This site resembles an oasis, endowed with mountain willows and a sacred spring. In 1415, Tsongkhapa meditated here, in a cave hermitage (*zimpuk*) higher up the slopes, and encountered his disciple Gendun Drupa, the future Dalai Lama I, for the first time. While in retreat, Tsongkhapa is also said to have been approached by a celestial sculptor named Tashi who made seven images of the master in a single day. Hence the name Tashi Doka. Tsongkhapa reputedly shaved his head seven times in the course of a single day to provide relics for the statues. Within the cave there are some extant images of Tsongkhapa, and down below, in the assembly hall (*dukhang*), there are images of Tsongkhapa, Avalokiteshvara, the Eight Medicine Buddhas, Amitayus, Tara, and the Sixteen Elders.

ACCESS The hermitage of Tashi Doka is located some 8 km inland, above the village of Trimon, and to the E of the On-chu River.

Choding Monastery

This monastery appears to have been founded by four Nyingmapa disciples of Dampa Sedrakpa, and named by Lama Zhang Tselpa in the 12th century. Later it became the most powerful Gelukpa institution in the On valley, and its incarnate lama, Gyese Rinpoche XIV Jigme Yeshe Drakpa was appointed regent of Tibet between 1728-35.

ACCESS The ruins of Choding lie further NE in a side-valley, which is remotely visible from Kachu Lhakhang.

Khachu (Keru) Temple

Some of the earliest statues in Tibet are to be seen here – the central Buddha image reputedly dating from the period of King Tride Tsukten, father of Trisong Detsen (8th century). The buildings at Khachu (Keru) comprise: the ruined **Namla Lhakhang**, which originally may have been constructed by King Tride Song-tsen and was later rebuilt as recently as 1957; the **Jowo Lhakhang**, or inner sanctum of the assembly hall, which appears to be of early 8th century construction and contains 13 highly significant images; the **Katang Chugong**, an 11th century temple once frequented by Atisha; the **Assembly Hall** (*dukhang*) and adjacent buildings, which were developed ca 16th-17th century; and the peripheral temples and monastic residential compound, which were renovated in 1957.

Epigraphic and documentary evidence attributes the main **Jowo Lhakhang** to the reign of King Tride Tsukten; who is believed to have founded altogether five temples to house Buddhist texts bequeathed by the Indian masters Buddhaguhya and Buddhashanti. The antiquity of this temple is also suggested by the architecture of its walls, ceiling beams, and columns, and the regal motifs of its capitals. The chamber is unusually high – 6.5m in contrast to its width 8.8m and depth 7.6m; suggesting that it was first built to contain the massive 3.2m Buddha image within it; and the originality of its sculpted clay images also suggests a Khotanese influence. The well-rounded 3.2m Buddha image has a compassionate but stern visage, with a massively thick chest. The Eight Bodhisattvas (3m) are well-proportioned and elegant with fine Mongoloid features, but distinctive shoulder-drapery and bare arms and chests. By the left wall are two bodhisattva-like figures representing King Tride Tsukten and Queen Jincheng, the parents of Trisong Detsen. Lastly, the gatekeepers Hayagriva and Vajrapani are robust and muscular. The peripheral figures probably date from the second phase of building, carried out by Dro Trisumje, a chief minister of King Relpachen, in the 9th century.

ACCESS This early 8th century building is located at Gyelzang village, about 2 km N of On township (*Tib* Samkhar), on the W bank of the On-chu.

Tshezik Stupa

North of On township (Samkhar), the trail leads to Dikna township and Chabtang village, where five interconnected stupas can be seen, upon an L-shaped platform. These were constructed by Lama Zhang Tselpa during the 12th century, and are now in a state of disrepair. A branch of Lhalung Monastery (see below, page 277) was also once located on the summit of Mt Utse Teng (4,600m) nearby. Heading N from Chabtang, the On valley then divides into three branches, one of which leads SW to Do Podrang in Do valley, the second slightly NW to Onphu Taktsang, and the third N to Balo on the Meldro-Gyamda highway.

Onphu Taktsang

Among the many tiger lairs frequented by Padmasambhava in his meditations, three are pre-eminent: Onphu Taktsang in Lhokha, Paro Taktsang in Bhutan, and Rongme Karmo Taktsang in Derge. Among these, Yeshe Tsogyel twice visited Onphu Taktsang in the course of her life to flee from an unwanted suitor and to receive the Vajrakila empowerments from Padmasambhava. In addition to the Nyingmapa, the site also once had strong associations for the no longer extant Taktsangpa Kagyu school (founded 1405).

ACCESS Taking the NW trail from Chabtang, follow the power lines as far as Drigang, and then **Ahor**, beyond which point no motor vehicle can travel. The cave hermitages are 4½ hrs uphill trekking distance from Ahor, passing en route a destroyed nunnery.

YARLUNG VALLEY
ཡར་ལུང

The 72 km long Yarlung valley, which gave its name to the ancient line of Tibetan kings and is sometimes called the cradle of Tibetan civilization, is replete with interesting temples, monasteries, castles, caves, stupas and peaks. Three power places (*nesum*): Sheldrak, Tradruk and Yumbu Lagang (or Rechung Puk), and three stupa receptacles (*ten-sum*): Takchen Bumpa, Gontang Bumpa, and Tsechu Bumpa are particularly important.

The Lower Yarlung Valley

Sheldrak Caves

There are three important caves in the Pema Tsekri range, which dominates the W entrance to the Yarlung valley: The east-facing **Sheldrak Drubpuk** is the first of Padmasambhava's meditation caves in Tibet, from where the indigenous hostile forces and demons were bound under on oath of allegiance to Buddhism. The NE facing **Tsogyel Sangpuk**, or secret meditation cave of Yeshe Tsogyel, is identified by a distant prayer flag to the S of the main cave; and the west-facing **Pema Shelpuk** is the celebrated *terma*-site where Orgyen Lingpa revealed the seminal text entitled *Life and Liberation of Padmasambhava (Pema Katang)*. It is accessible from the Sheldrak Monastery or more directly by traversing a somewhat dangerous ridge above the main cave. The last of these caves is also visible from Jasa to the W of Tsetang.

ACCESS To reach Sheldrak from Tsetang, take the Chongye road and turn off on the right at a dirt track before the Tsechu Bumpa Stupa. Jeeps can negotiate this track, which follows a Yarlung tributary upstream, for 4-5 km, and tractors can reach the village of Sekhang Zhika which lies at the top of the ridge. From here, it is a tough 3-hr trek to the cave. If you walk all the way from Tsechu Bumpa Stupa, it will take 5-6 hrs.

Sheldrak Monastery

Above the village of **Sekhang Zhika** is a charnel ground, marked by a stupa consecrated to Hayagriva. The pathway then follows the ridge to the right, leading up to **Sheldrak Monastery**. This restored temple has six monks (the original was apparently dedicated to the 14th century treasure-finder Sangye Lingpa). It contains images of Padmasambhava with his two foremost consorts, the Eight Manifestations of Padmasambhava, and Karmapa III Rangjung Dorje. There are photographs depicting the *Longchen Nyingtig* assemblage of deities.

Sheldrak Drubpuk Cave

Continuing uphill to the right, the path crosses a sacred spring (*drubchu*) and climbs steeply for 100m via a rock-hewn stairway to the **Sheldrak Drubpuk Cave**

(4,550m). The cave, which is itself at the base of a rock pinnacle called **Kritkita Dzong**, offers through its window a bird's eye view of the contours of the Yarlung valley below: Tradruk, Rechung Puk, Yumbu Lagang, and Mt Yarlha Shampo are all discernible at a glance.

The Sheldrak Drubpuk cave is one of the most revered pilgrimage places on the Tibetan plateau, symbolizing Padmasambhava's buddha attributes. As such, it is classed alongside Drak Yangdzong symbolizing buddha-body, Chimphu Drakmar Keutsang symbolizing buddha-speech, Lhodrak Kharchu Chakpurchen, symbolizing buddhamind, and Monka Nering Senge Dzong in Bhutan, symbolizing buddha-activities. Thirty-five mantra adept followers of Padmasambhava were associated with Sheldrak during the 8th-9th century, and later masters such as Orgyen Lingpa and Terdak Lingpa discovered *termas* in the nearby Pema Shelpuk cave.

The original **'speaking' image of Padmasambhava**, which once graced the cave, has been relocated at Tradruk Monastery, and the altar now has newly constructed images of the Great Master flanked by his two foremost consorts. The rock surface of the W wall has natural impressions representing Avalokiteshvara, the Twenty-five Disciples of Padmasambhava, the Boudhnath Stupa in Nepal, and a crescent moon of the 3rd day of the month.

Northwest of the cave is the **sacred spring** which one of Padmasambhava's disciples, named Nyak Jananakumara, is said to have brought forth from dry rock. Below the cave entrance, there is a reconstructed 2-storey temple, with complete images of the Eight Manifestations of Padmasambhava on each level. This is where the caretaker of Sheldrak resides.

Tsechu Bumpa Stupa

Just S of the turn-off for Sheldrak on the main Tsetang-Chongye road, there is the reconstructed Tsechu Bumpa stupa – one of the three sacred stupas of Yarlung. Circumambulation of this stupa has long marked the beginning or end of the Sheldrak pilgrimage. This stupa is said to have at its core a rock-crystal Buddha image from India, which was presented to King Trisong Detsen by the translator Chokrolui Gyelsten. Others believe it to contain the armour of King Songtsen Gampo himself. On full moon days the stupa is said to exude the water of life (*tsechu*). The site is marked by a large collection of *mani* stones.

Tsentang Yui Lhakhang

East of the Tsechu Bumpa Stupa, at the village of **Khartok**, are the ruins of the Tsentang Yui Lhakhang, a temple which has been attributed to Queen Jincheng, mother of Trisong Detsen, or alternatively to one of Songtsen Gampo's queens. The temple once had distinctive blue glazed turquoise roof tiles, which would corroborate the reports of its Chinese origin. During the 15th century, this temple was an important centre for the development of dialectics within the Sakya school. Nearby, at **Tsentang Gozhi**, the first king of ancient Tibet, Nyatri Tsenpo, is said to have made contact with his Bonpo subjects after descending from the heavens at **Lhababri**. And since 1984, some 233 earth and stone mound tombs have been discovered in the vicinity of Tsentang.

Mount Lhababri

At the southern extremity of the Pema Tsekpa range, below Sheldrak, there are three hills, the highest of which is Lhababri. This so-called 'hill of divine descent' is where Tibet's first king Nyatri Tsenpo is said to have alighted from the heavens – although there are early historical accounts (eg that of Nelpa Pandita), which claim the king to have been a descendent of the Licchavi king Rupati (*Tib* Magyapa). The king was carried shoulder-high as if on a sedan chair (*nyatri*) to Yumbu Lagang, where the first palace of the Yarlung kings was constructed.

Tradruk Temple

ACCESS Located on the E side of the Yarlung valley, only 7 km S of Tsetang, Tradruk temple nowadays lies within Tradruk village to the S side of the Tsetang-Podrang road.

History

Tradruk temple is the earliest of Tibet's great geomantic temples apart from the Jokhang (some sources even claim it to predate the latter). It was reputedly constructed by King Songtsen Gampo on the left shoulder of the supine ogress, symbolizing the rigours of the Tibetan terrain (see above, page 48). The name Tradruk is said to be derived from a 'falcon' (*Tra*) emanated by the power of Songtsen Gampo's meditations, which overwhelmed a local 'dragon' (*druk*) divinity to facilitate the temple's construction. Later, the site was venerated as one of the three royal temples of Tibet by the kings Trisong Detsen and Mune Tsepo. During that period, offering ceremonies pertaining to the Vinaya and Abhidharma were performed at Tradruk. Plundered during the persecution of Langdarma, the site was renovated and expanded in 1351, and later by Dalai Lama V, who added the golden roof, and Dalai Lama VII. By the late 18th century, Tradruk had 21 temples. The assembly hall and many of the chapels were obliterated during the Cultural Revolution, but the newly reconstructed buildings were reconsecrated in 1988.

Lower Floor Chapels

As you approach the entrance, which still has its splendid original timbers intact, there is a **Mani Lhakhang** on the right, containing a large *mani* wheel. The portico no longer has its ancient bell – one of three which dated from the Yarlung period (the others are at Samye and the Jokhang – see above, pages 235 and 139). An intermediate pilgrim's circuit (*barkor*) is accessible from the courtyard beyond the portico. Continuing into the main temple, the **Tsuklakhang**, the plan of which is reminiscent of the Jokhang, you will find the assembly hall surrounded by a series of 12 chapels. From left to right, these comprise: the Ngakpa Lhakhang (W), the Gonkhang (N) and the Tuje Lhakhang (N); the Rabten Lhakhang (N), the Sangye Lhakhang (N), the Chogyel Lhakhang (E), the Dolma Lhakhang Tashi Jamnyom (E), the Tuje Lhakhang (E), the Tsepak Lhakhang (S), the Menlha Lhakhang (S), the Orgyen Lhakhang (S), and the Tongdrol Lhakhang (W).

Among these, the most important is the inner sanctum – the **Dolma Tashi Jamnyom Lhakhang**. This is the original Songtsen Gampo geomantic temple – once containing natural stone images of the Buddhas of the Five Families from Mt Zodang Gongpori, and a standing image of Tara, known as Dolma Shesema ('Tara who consumes her offerings'). New clay images of the Buddhas of the Five Families now replace the original stone statues, the fragments of which have been inserted within their respective replicas as a consecratory core. These are flanked by the Eight Bodhisattvas, and the gatekeepers.

To the left of the inner sanctum, the **Chogyel Lhakhang** contains new images depicting King Songtsen Gampo, his two foreign queens and chief ministers. To the right of the inner sanctum is the **Tuje Lhakhang**, containing an old image of Thousand-armed Mahakarunika flanked by Manjughosa and Vajrapani. In the corner is a stove reputedly used by Queen Wengcheng in person.

Among the chapels of the W wing, the **Ngapa Lhakhang** contains images of Dalai Lama V flanked by other Gelukpa and Kadampa masters, the **Tongdrol Lhakhang** depicts Tsong-khapa surrounded by his major disciples, and the **Gonkhang** has images of Mahakala and his retainers. Among the

TRADRUK TEMPLE

TIB055

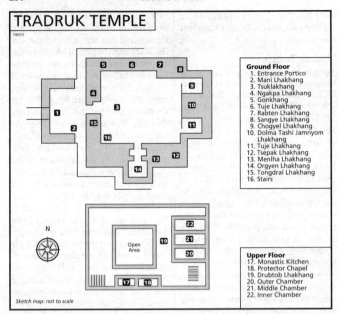

Ground Floor
1. Entrance Portico
2. Mani Lhakhang
3. Tsuklakhang
4. Ngakpa Lhakhang
5. Gonkhang
6. Tuje Lhakhang
7. Rabten Lhakhang
8. Sangye Lhakhang
9. Chogyel Lhakhang
10. Dolma Tashi Jamnyom Lhakhang
11. Tuje Lhakhang
12. Tsepak Lhakhang
13. Menlha Lhakhang
14. Orgyen Lhakhang
15. Tongdral Lhakhang
16. Stairs

Upper Floor
17. Monastic Kitchen
18. Protector Chapel
19. Drubtob Lhakhang
20. Outer Chamber
21. Middle Chamber
22. Inner Chamber

N

Open Area

Sketch map: not to scale

chapels of the N wing, both the **Tuje Lhakhang** and the **Rabten** temples contain images of the Eleven-headed Thousand-armed Mahakarunika; while the **Sangye Lhakhang** has Shakyamuni flanked by Shariputra and Maudgalyayana. Among the chapels on the S wing, the **Tsepak Lhakhang** has images of Amitayus flanked by White Tara and Vijaya; and the **Menlha Lhakhang** has images of all the Eight Medicine Buddhas, with Bhaisajyaguru at the centre. Lastly, the **Orgyen Lhakhang** has an outer chamber with images of Amitayus and Mahakala, and an inner chamber with Padmasambhava flanked by Mandarava and Yeshe Tsogyel.

Upper Floor Chapels

Ascending to the second floor, on the right side there is a monastic kitchen and a **protector chapel** with images of Mahakala and Brahma. The main chapel is the **Drubtob Lhakhang** at the

rear, which has three chambers. The outermost chamber is empty. The **middle chamber** contains the remnants of a set of the Eighty-four Mahasiddhas (from whom the chapel derives its name), the 16 volumes of the *Shatasahasrikaprajnaparamita*, and a wonderful tangka depicting Padmapani, made of 29,000 pearls, which had been originally housed at Bentsang/Tse Tsokpa monastery (now destroyed, see above, page 250).

The **innermost chamber** contains on the rear wall the wonderful original Padmasambhava image which had been salvaged from Sheldrak cave, flanked by new images of his foremost consorts, and on the right, a series of extremely rare applique tangkas, which had also been retrieved from Bentsang. These include an exquisite applique tangka of White Manjushri, others of Avalokiteshvara and Naropa, and, above all, the large applique tangka of the Buddha clad in red robes against a blue background, which may perhaps date from the Ming period, but is reputedly one of three of a kind in Tibet made by Wengcheng (the others are kept in the Reliquary Stupa of Dalai Lama V in the Potala Palace and in the Maitreya Lhakhang at Zhigatse).

Outer temples

There are four places of interest outside the temple proper: the **Neten Lhakhang** (W), dedicated to the Sixteen Elders, where there were formerly images of Songtsen Gampo and Padmasambhava; the **Sangak Podrang** (S) where monks from Mindroling have performed tantric rituals since the 17th century; the **Guru Lhakhang** (SE), and the site of the now destroyed **Namgyel Lhakhang** (N), a branch of Bentsang Monastery (see above, page 250) where Tsongkhapa received monastic ordination in the 14th century.

Rechung Puk

ACCESS The hermitage of Rechung Puk is approached via a turn-off on the right, 3 km S of Tradruk.

This famous Kagyupa hermitage sits atop the **Mila Tse** spur which overlooks the bifurcation of the Yarlung and Chongye valleys. This is the retreat of Milarepa's illustrious disciple Rechungpa Dorje Drak (1083-1161) of Loro, who, following the example of his teacher, practised asceticism and meditation here. The site thus became known as Rechung Puk. Later, in 1488, while residing at Rechung Puk, the yogin Tsangnyon Heruka, whose actual name was Sangye Gyeltsen, composed the *Life of Milarepa* and the *Hundred Thousand Songs of Milarepa*, which have since become classic texts of Tibetan Buddhism, well-known throughout the world.

Formerly there were 1,000 monks at Rechung Puk, and some rebuilding has taken place since the destruction of the 1960s. The temple contains images of Padmasambhava flanked by his fore-

most consorts, and Tsangnyon Heruka. Rechungpa's cave to its rear contains the stone seat of Rechungpa and new images of Marpa, Milarepa, and Rechungpa. Gotsangpa's highly esteemed sculpture of Tsangnyon Heruka, which once graced this cave, no longer exists; but there are rock footprints attributed to Milarepa, Rechungpa, Karmapa I, and also to Tsangnyon Heruka. A new assembly hall (*dukhang*) and retreat centre (*drubkhang*) have been constructed above the cave. At the top of the ridge is the ruined base of the **Mila Tse Watchtower**, dating from the Phakmodrupa period.

Gongtang Bumpa Stupa

At the foot of the Mila Tse spur on its W side is the 6m Gongtang Stupa, one of the three major stupas of the Yarlung valley. This stupa is said to have been built on the advice of Vairocana, the 8th century translator, who resolved a boundary dispute between the rulers of Nedong and Chongye while he was meditating in a nearby cave. The stupa therefore has come to define the entrance to the Chongye valley. A new temple to the W contains images of Hayagriva, flanked by Padmasambhava and Lhodrak Longka Geling.

Bairo Puk

Slightly S of the Gongtang Bumpa Stupa at the E side of the approach to Chongye valley, there is a meditation cave associated with the great translator Vairocana, one of the foremost disciples of Padmasambhava and Dzogchen lineage-holder. Nowadays, it contains only the copper base of its former image, but there is a more enduring rock handprint of Vairocana, and some rock-inscriptions. Heading S from here, you will enter the Chongye and Tso-me counties of Southern Tibet, see below, page 265 and 270.

Riwo Choling Monastery

East of Tsharu village, which lies to the S of Tradruk, are the vast ruins of the

Gelukpa monastery of Riwo Choling, originally founded by Tsongkhapa's student, Panchen Lama I, Khedrup Je in the 15th century. The monks of Riwo Choling have long acted as caretakers of the Yumbu Lagang Palace.

Yumbu Lagang

ཡུམ་བུ་བླ་སྒང་

History

The resplendent hilltop Yumbu Lagang is reputedly a reconstruction of Tibet's oldest building. Some sources state that when Nyatri Tsenpo emerged as the first king of Tibet in 247 or 127 BC he was escorted to Mt Tashitseri, the 'talismanic hill' (**Lagang**) of 'tamarisk' (**Ombu**), by his Bonpo followers, and there the first palace, Yumbu Lagang, was established on its summit. This is also suggested by the theme of the murals depicted inside the second storey of the building. Later, the palace appears to have been refurbished by Lhatotori Nyentsen, the 28th king (b 374 CE). In 433 or 446 CE, Buddhist texts including the *Karandavyuhasutra*, are said to have miraculously fallen upon the palace roof; heralding the first appearance of Buddhism in Tibet. In Nelpa Pandita's *History*, however, it suggests that the Indian scholar Buddharaksita arrived in Tibet with these texts, and deposited them there for the sake of posterity. Known as the 'awesome secret' (*nyenpo sangwa*), the texts were not understood but venerated until Songtsen Gampo embraced Buddhism, five reigns later. According to the *Injunctions of the King (Gyelpo Katang)*, Lhatotori Nyentsen's tomb is located within the ridge above Yumbu Lagang. Extensions to the palace were added in subsequent centuries: the two lower chapels by Songtsen Gampo, and the gold roof by Dalai Lama V. These ancient structures were obliterated during the Cultural Revolution.

The present building dates only from 1982. The 3-storey tower is 11m high, and its sides measure 4.6m and 3.5m. Its two lower storeys are entered from behind the shrines of their adjoining chapels, and the third by a ladder from the roof terrace. At its apex, the central pillar (*tsokshing*) of the tower is bedecked by kataks and sacred threads, and on each side, there is an observation window.

The site

The **ante-chamber to the lower chapel** has murals depicting the mystical visions of Tsongkhapa. Then, inside the **lower chapel** (originally constructed by King Songtsen Gampo) there is a central image of Buddha Shakyamuni in the form Jowo Norbu Sampel. This image is flanked by regal statues: Nyatri Tsenpo on the left and Songtsen Gampo on the right. Further images on the left are: Tonmi Sambhota, Trisong Detsen, and Lhatotori Nyentsen; and on the right: Relpachen, Namde Osung, and Minister Gar Tongtsen.

The **second floor chapel** is entered via an open terrace. Inside there is a gallery around which pilgrims walk to observe its fascinating murals and images, as well as those of the Buddha and the kings below. Here there is a gilded sandalwood Lokeshvara image (reminiscent of the sandalwood Lokeshvara in the Potala), as well as others depicting Amitayus, Shakyamuni, and Padmasambhava flanked by Shantaraksita and Trisong Detsen.

The murals are particularly relevant. **On the left** are depicted: Nyatri Tsenpo's descent from the heavens at Mt Lhababri and his arrival at Yumbu Lagang; the descent of the 'awesome secret' on the palace roof during the reign of Lhatotori Nyentsen; the arrival of Padmasambhava in the Sheldrak cave; and the Twenty-one Taras. **On the right** are the Eight Manifestations of Padmasambhava, and Shakyamuni with the Sixteen Elders; while beside the door are the protectors Shridevi and Yarlha

Yumbu Lagang, Palace of the Early Kings

Shampo.

ACCESS Yumbu Lagang Palace is located 6 km S of Tradruk and 3 km after the turn-off for Rechung Puk (see above, page 257).

Zortang

Below Yumbu Lagang to the NW is Zortang, the first cultivated field in Tibet. Farmers even now ensure a good harvest by sprinkling soil from this field on their own fields. The temple of **Lharu Menlha**, containing images of the Eight Medicine Buddhas, was formerly built near this field.

The Upper Yarlung Valley

Podrang Township and Takchen Bumpa Stupa

5 km S of Yumbu Lagang is **Podrang** township, described as the oldest inhabited village in Tibet. Here there is a turn-off on the left, leading NE, eventually to Eyul. Along this road in Shangyang commune, are the 119 stupas

known as **Gyatsagye**, dated to the 17th century, and on a nearby slope, the 6-7m high **Takchen Bumpa Stupa**, which is one of the three major stupas of Yarlung (see above, page 253). This stupa is named after Sadaprarudita (*Tib* Taktu Ngu), a bodhisattva figure who appears in the *Prajnaparamita* literature, and whose 'constantly weeping' left eye is said to be preserved within it. The construction dates from the Kadampa period and is attributed to one Geshe Korchen (12th century). Adjacent to the stupa, there is a small Drukpa Kagyu monastery named **Takchen Bumoche**.

Chode O and Chode Gang

ACCESS After Podrang the Yarlung valley begins to narrow. 17 km further S, there is the side-valley in which Chode O (Lower Chode) monastery is located, and after a further 6 km, the road passes through Chode Gong (Upper Chode) monastery in Yarto township.

Chode O was founded by Dalai Lama V

and expanded by Dalai Lama VII. Its assembly hall has three storeys, the middle one containing the principal images of Shakyamuni with his foremost disciples, the Sixteen Elders and Eight Medicine Buddhas.

Chode Gong is an older institution, founded by Ra Lotsawa during the 11th century and developed later by the Gelukpas. Its 4-storey temple has an assembly hall and inner sanctum dedicated to Tsongkhapa and his students, as well as Dalai Lama XIII, the Buddhas of the Three Times and the Eight Bodhisattvas.

Yabzang Monastery

At Yarto township, 1 km after Chode Gong, there is a further bifurcation – one track leading SE, and the other W for 3 km to Yabzang monastery. **Yabzang**, founded by Gyurme Long in 1206, was the seat of the small Yabzang Kagyu school, which derives from the latter's teacher Geden Yeshe Chenye, himself a disciple of Phakmodrupa. The site is largely ruinous at the present. Its approach has a ramp reminiscent of the Potala at Lhasa.

Mount Yarlha Shampo

24 km beyond Yarto township, the road crosses Yarto Drak La pass (4,970m). The main peak, abode of the protector **Yarlha Shampo** (6,636m) lies SW from here. At this watershed pass, the Yarlung valley comes to an end and the road passes via Nyel valley (Lhuntse county) into Tsari (see below, page 289) and via Droshul valley (Tsona county) to the Bhutanese and Indian borders.

LHUNTSE COUNTY
ལྷུན་རྩེ

隆子县 Lhunze
Population: 20,858   Area: 5,991 sq km

The county of Lhuntse extends from the watershed at Yarto Drak La pass, through the valleys of the Nyel-chu and Jar-chu, as far as their confluence with the Tsari-chu. Together these rivers (along with the Loro-chu in Tsona county) form the headwaters of the **Subansiri** (*Tib* Shipasha-chu), a major south-flowing tributary of the Brahmaputra, which enters the Indian state of Arunachal Pradesh (*Tib* Monyul Tsona), immediately after the confluence. The road from Tsetang to Yarto Drak La pass is 61 km and thence to **Kyitang**, the capital of Lhuntse county, a further 80 km. Kyitang lies 21 km E of the main Tsetang-Tsona frontier road.

In the E of the county, 108 km from Lhuntse by motor road, is Sangak Choling, one of the three main gateways to Tsari, the sacred mountain of Southern Tibet which attracts pilgrims from all over the country (see below, page 262).

Upper Nyel Valley (Nyelto)
གཉལ་སྟོད

Following the main road S from Tsetang across Yarto Drak La pass, there is a turn-off on the left after 10 km (at marker 194) for Chumdo Gyang and Eyul. Crossing Shopotak La pass (5,001m) after a further 23 km, you will enter the upper reaches of the **Nyel** valley. The Gelukpa monastery of **Gateng** is passed on the descent from the pass after 15 km, and then, at **Shobo Shar** village, another turn-off to the left leads to **Shopo** township in Upper Nyel. The routes from Shopo to Jarto (Upper Jaryul) and Sangak Choling will be described below, page 262.

Continuing on the main Tsetang-Tsona highway for a further 4 km (Tsona lies 90 km to the S), you will arrive at the **Kyitang turn-off**, again on the left. The road to the right leads on to Tsona, via Ritang township and monastery. Taking the left road, which follows the Nyel valley, after 21 km you will reach Kyitang.

Kyitang

The administrative capital of the county, the town is largely comprised of government buildings and military compounds; but there are some monasteries of interest in the Kyitang area, especially **Chi-le Gonpa** of the Kagyu school, near the old Lhuntse Dzong and **Trakor Monastery**, which are both located to the W of Kyitang; as well as **Tebura Monastery** to the NW, and **Shangtse (Yangtse) Monastery** near Lower Nyel (Nyel-me) to the NE.

Lower Nyel Valley (Nyel-me)
གཏལ་སྲུང་

A motorable road continues for 48 km from Kyitang down the Nyel-chu valley via **Zhingpa** township as far as **Jaryul** township, which lies E of the Nyel-chu's confluence with the Loro-chu. The Loro-chu valley is nowadays administered by Tsona county (see below, page 263).

Trekking

From Nyenrong on this road, there is a 3-day trekking route via Le La pass (5,240m), Khyimpu and Jar-me, to Sangak Choling, which is the gateway to Tsari in the NE.

An alternative more difficult trek follows the Nyel-chu downstream from this confluence with the Loro-chu, to a second confluence with the Jar-chu at **Lung**. The rapids form a deep gorge which must be crossed and recrossed by a precarious bridge and ladder! The village of **Dron** is the last Tibetan village on the Nyel/Loro-chu, and further downstream the territory is occupied by Assamese Lopas. Many of Dron's villagers are engaged in guiding pilgrims to Tsari, which is still 10 trekking days to the E from this point. At Lung, the combined headwaters of the Subansiri flow S into India.

NB There is a strong military presence at Lung. The border is disputed, and travel restrictions apply. From Lung there is a jeep road leading through Jar-me (Lower Jaryul) to Sangak Choling, 33 km to NW.

Upper Jaryul Valley (Jarto)
བྱང་སྲུང་

From **Shopo** township in Upper Nyel (1 km E of the main Tsetang-Tsona highway, see above, page 261), a jeep road crosses the Ba-re La watershed (4,630m) between the Nyel and Jarto valleys to

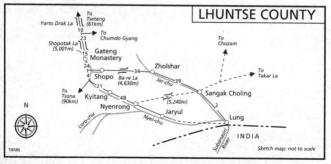

Zholsar township (34 km). En route, you should stop to visit **Dzongka Chode** monastery, which has a collection of old Buddhist texts. From Zholsar, the road follows the narrow Jarto valley downstream and SE to **Sangak Choling**, 39 km distant.

Trekking

There are two trekking routes which diverge from this road: a 1-day trek from **Shoposang** (opposite the ruins of Tengtse monastery) which leads SW via the Mo La pass (5,400m) to Lower Nyel (Nyel-me); and another 5-day trek from **Pejorling**, which leads N via the Kharpo-chu valley to **Chozam**, the northern gateway to the Tsari pilgrimage in Nang county (see below, page 288). It is also possible to make a 4-day trek from **Chumdo Gyang**, following the Eyul road, and then diverging from it to cross the Pu La watershed pass to Zholsar, via Drongzhu, Kyekye, Tengchung, and Phudrok in Jarto.

Sangak Choling

The monastery of Sangak Choling was founded by Pema Karpo of the Drukpa Kagyu school (1527-92); and expanded by his successor Drukchen V Paksam Wangpo (1593-1641). This is one of the main gateways to the Tsari pilgrimage circuit, which lies only 2-days trek to the E. The Drukpa Kagyu school had a particular affinity with Tsari, in that it was

Tsangpa Gya-re, the founder of the principal Drukpa monasteries in West and Central Tibet who first opened Tsari as a place of pilgrimage.

Sangak Choling, destroyed in the 1960s, has been under reconstruction since 1986, and now stands within a township of the same name. The main temple has a central Shakyamuni image.

Tsari Pilgrimage

To reach the pilgrim's circuit from Sangak Choling, it is necessary to trek via Cha La pass (5,060m). Begin by following the Kyu-chu gorge upstream through a glacial valley. After 12 km the road divides, the NE track leading to **Takar La** and the lesser circuit, and the N track leading to **Chozam** on the higher circuit. Traditionally, the latter, which is also known as the 'circumambulation of the ravines of Tsari' was undertaken only once every 12 years. For a description of the Tsari pilgrimage routes, see the section on Nang county below, page 288.

Lower Jaryul Valley (Jarme)

བྱར་སྨད

Below Sangak Choling, the jeep road continues for 25 km, following the Jarchu downstream to its confluence with the Nyel/Loro-chu at Lung. Arunachal Pradesh (India) lies a short distance to the S. The border is sealed and it is not possible to enter into India.

BONPO TOMB CULTURE

The funeral custom of earth-burial is rare in Central Tibet, where charnel ground dismemberment (sky burial) is the norm (for ordinary people) and cremation or embalming preferred (for important lamas). Nonetheless, during the Yarlung period, when Bonpo tomb culture was at its most influential (see above, page 112), the Tibetan kings were traditionally interred in colossal tumuli, along with their worldly wealth (and in the earliest cases with their retainers buried alive). After the collapse of the Yarlung Dynasty, the custom of burying kings in tombs came to an end. During the 1980s a number of other tomb sites have been excavated in Southern Tibet in the lateral valleys of the Brahmaputra, such as Dranang, Yarlung, and Nang, but, however large, none appear to have the grandure and historic significance of the Chongye tombs.

chronicle in Jigme Lingpa's *Collection of Tales (Tamtsok)*, an 18th century essay based on earlier sources, such as the *Gar Karchag* and *Tentsik Gyatso*, and composed by a native of Chongye, who happens to have been one of Tibet's greatest and most incisive writers of all time.

The tombs of the earliest legendary and prehistoric kings are no longer visible. The first seven kings, from Nyatri Tsenpo to Sibtri Tsenpo, are said to have ascended to the heavens at the time of their demise by means of a sky-cord (*mu*). The 8th and 9th kings (known as the 'two celestial kings of Teng') are said to have been interred at Ya and Dza; the 10th to 16th (known as the 'six earthly kings of Lek') were interred at Yapangtsam; and the 17th to 24th (known as the 'eight middle kings of De') were buried at Chuwo'i Zhung. None of these sites have been identified as yet, their tombs having 'vanished like snow falling on a lake'. Subsequent kings were buried in the plain of **Chinyul Darmotang** (at Chongye), where there are many unidentified mounds of earth, perhaps containing the tombs of the 'five linking kings of Tsen'. The last of these, the 28th king Lhatotori Nyentsen is said to be interred within Chingwa Taktse Castle.

Nowadays, there are 16 identifiable tombs – 10 in the Chingwardo valley, and six in the adjacent Dungkhar valley. Some of these are on the slopes of Mulari

hill, which divides these two valleys. Songtsen Gampo's immediate ancestors and descendents are all interred here.

Chongye/Chingwardo Tombs

Banso Marpo or **Muri Mukpo** Among the 10 tombs of the Chongye/Chingwardo valley, the largest (1) is that of Tibet's unifying 33rd king, Songtsen Gampo. This enormous tomb, is 13.4m high with its sides each measuring 129m. Literary sources describe in detail the vast treasures and entire chapels contained within it. Yet, there are other traditions claiming that Songtsen Gampo vanished into light at the time of his passing, into either the Jowo Rinpoche image or the Rangjung Ngaden image of Lhasa!

On the summit of the tomb, offering a bird's eye view of the entire Chongye valley, there is a reconstructed 13th century temple, originally attributed to the Nyingmapa lama Menlungpa Shakya-o. The temple is entered through an outer annex with a **Mani Lhakhang** on the right (murals here depict the primordial Buddha Samantabhadra in union with Samantabhadri). Beyond an inner courtyard, the **chapel** contains images of Songtsen Gampo, flanked by his two foreign queens and chief ministers. The **inner sanctum** has images (left to right) of: Amitayus, the Buddhas of the Three Times, and Padmasambhava in the form Nangsi Zilnon.

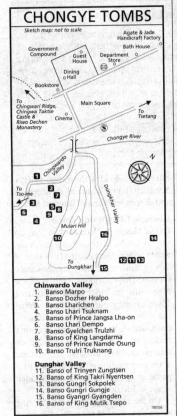

CHONGYE TOMBS
Sketch map: not to scale

Agate & Jade Handicraft Factory

Government Compound

Guest House

Department Store

Bath House

Dining Hall

Bookstore

To Chingwari Ridge, Chingwa Taktse Castle & Riwo Dechen Monastery

Main Square

Cinema

To Tsetang

Chongye River

Chingwardo Valley

To Tso-me

Dungkhar Valley

Mulari Hill

To Dungkhar

Chinwardo Valley
1. Banso Marpo
2. Banso Dozher Hralpo
3. Banso Lharichen
4. Banso Lhari Tsuknam
5. Banso of Prince Jangsa Lha-on
6. Banso Lhari Dempo
7. Banso Gyelchen Trulzhi
8. Banso of King Langdarma
9. Banso of Prince Namde Osung
10. Banso Trulri Truknang

Dunghar Valley
11. Banso of Trinyen Zungtsen
12. Banso of King Takri Nyentsen
13. Banso Gungri Sokpolek
14. Banso Gungri Gungje
15. Banso Gyangri Gyangden
16. Banso of King Mutik Tsepo

The gatekeepers are Vajrapani and Hayagriva. The murals depict the Thirty-five Buddhas of Confession (left) and the Eight Manifestations of Padmasambhava (right).

The other nine tombs on the Chongye/Chingwardo side of the valley are visible from the summit of Songtsen Gampo's tomb. As described by Jigme Lingpa, these comprise:

Banso Dozher Hralpo (2), the mausoleum of the 35th king Mangsong Mangtsen (left of Songtsen Gampo tomb).

Banso Lharichen (3), the mausoleum of the 36th king Dusong Mangpoje, aka. Trulgyi Gyelpo (right of Mangsong Mangtsen's tomb).

Banso Lhari Tsuknam (4), the mausoleum of the 37th king Tride Tsukten Me Aktsom (on the slopes of Mulari, left of Dusong Mangpoje's tomb).

Banso (5) of Prince Jangsa Lha-on (front of Tride Tsukten Me Aktsom's tomb).

Banso Lhari Dempo (6), the mausoleum of the 39th king Mune Tsepo (right of Tride Tsukten Me Aktsom's tomb).

Banso Gyelchen Trulzhi (7), the mausoleum of the 41st king Tri Relpachen (front of Dusong Mangpoje's tomb, with an inscribed obelisk outside; Jigme Lingpa adds that this tomb has also been wrongly attributed to Dengtri, the son of Senalek Jinyon).

Banso (8) of the 42nd and last king Langdarma (between those of Dusong Mangpoje and Relpachen).

Banso (9) of prince Namde Osung (behind Dusong Mangpoje's tomb).

Banso Trulri Truknang (10), the mausoleum of the 38th king Trisong Detsen (behind and to right of Tride Tsukten Me Aktsom's tomb, on the left slopes of Mulari, adjacent to Dungkhar valley. **NB** Local reports suggest this tomb is on the far side of Mulari. The ancient obelisk marking this tomb has been missing since the 18th century. Jigme Lingpa notes that it was removed by farmers.

Dungkhar Valley Tombs
In the adjacent Lower Dungkhar valley, there are six further identified tombs:

Banso (11) of the 29th king, Trinyen Zungtsen.

Banso (12) of the 31st king Takri Nyentsen (right of Trinyen Zungtsen's tomb).

Banso Gungri Sokpolek (13), mausoleum of the 32nd king Namri Songtsen (left of Trinyen Zungtsen's tomb).

Banso Gungri Gungje (14), mausoleum of the 34th king Gungri Gungtsen (left of Namri Songtsen's tomb).

Banso Gyangri Gyangdem (15), mau-

TEMPLE AT CHONGYE BANSO MARPO

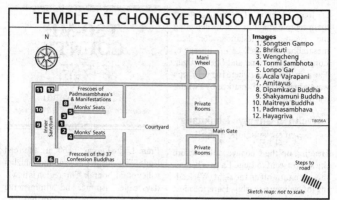

N

Mani
Wheel

Frescoes of
Padmasambhava's
& Manifestations

Monks' Seats

Private
Rooms

Inner
Sanctum

Monks' Seats

Courtyard

Main Gate

Frescoes of the 37
Confession Buddhas

Private
Rooms

Steps to
road

Images
1. Songtsen Gampo
2. Bhrikuti
3. Wengcheng
4. Tonmi Sambhota
5. Lonpo Gar
6. Acala Vajrapani
7. Amitayus
8. Dipamcaka Buddha
9. Shakyamuni Buddha
10. Maitreya Buddha
11. Padmasambhava
12. Hayagriva

TIB056A

Sketch map: not to scale

soleum of prince Murub Tsepo (W side of valley).

Banso (16) of the 40th king Mutik Tsepo, aka. Senalek Jinyon (nearby Murub Tsepo's tomb, although some say it is in front of Dusong Mangpoje's tomb).

Tseringjong Nunnery
ཚེ་རིང་ལྗོངས

The Dungkhar valley where the last six tombs are located is also the abode of Jigme Lingpa, the great Nyingmapa yogin (1729-98), who established his hermitage above Dungkhar village, 12 km from Chongye. It was from this hermitage that his *Longchen Nyingtig* tradition spread throughout Tibet. Since the 19th century, Tseringjong has been an active nunnery for practitioners of the *Longchen Nyingtig*. There are now 30 nuns at Tseringjong, which has been under reconstruction since 1985. The meditative spirit which gave rise to this powerful hermitage is still apparent at the present day.

Approaching the temple from the road, there is a Mani Wall to the right, with stones depicting the Thirty-five Buddhas of Confession, and a sacred spring to the left. Then, passing a tree and teaching throne of Jigme Lingpa's on the left, and another tree reputedly grown from the hair of Jigme Lingpa on

the right, the building is entered via a door next to the kitchen.

An antechamber then leads into the temple proper (door on right). The central images depict Padmasambhava flanked by Songtsen Gampo and Trisong Detsen. Behind these images against the rear wall are further images, depicting Longchen Rabjampa and Jigme Lingpa among others. In front of all these images is a throne, and on the left wall (next to the door) an image of the protectress Dorje Yudronma. An edition of the Lhasa *Kangyur* sits against the right wall. Within the **inner sanctum**, there is the most precious silver reliquary containing the remains of Jigme Lingpa, flanked by images of Longchen Rabjampa (left) and Jigme Lingpa (right).

Pelri Tekchenling Monastery
དཔལ་རི་ཐེག་ཆེན་གླིང

Located in a NE side-valley, and approached via a turn-off to the left a few kilometres upstream from Songtsen Gampo's tomb is the monastery of Pelri Tekchokling. The original temple was founded in the 15th century by Sonam Tobgyel, lord of Chongye. It subsequently became the residence of the Nyingmapa *terton* Sheab Ozer (1517-84), but it is most renowned as the birthplace of Jigme Lingpa. The reconstructed main temple contains murals depicting the Eight Manifestations of Padmasambhava, as well as the lineage of Longchen Rabjampa and Sherab Ozer. The ruined building where Jigme Lingpa was born is currently marked by a white-washed stone.

Gyelmen Chen-ye Lhakhang

རྒྱལ་སྨན་སྤྱན་གཡས་ལྷ་ཁང་

Heading up the Chongye valley, before the steep ascent to Lugu La pass begins, there is a turn-off on the right (W), leading to Gyelmen township. Here, the most important site is the **Chen-ye Lhakhang**, a Kadampa centre renowned for its monastic discipline, which was initially established by Geshe Drapa, and later absorbed by the Gelukpa school. The most precious relic here was the right eye of Shariputra, foremost student of Shakyamuni Buddha, after which the temple was called 'right-eye temple' (Chen-ye Lhakhang).

The main road continues uphill through **Chugo** township, near the source of the Chongye-chu River, as far as the **Lugu La** pass (4,600m), which forms the watershed between the north-flowing tributaries of the Brahmaputra, and the Lhodrak region to the S. The pass offers fantastic views of the nomadic grasslands and lakelands around Trigu Lake.

TSO-ME COUNTY

མཚོ་སྨད་

措美县 Comai

Population: 10,575   *Area:* 6,075 sq km

From Lugu La pass (4,600m), the road leads SW to Trigu Lake and the Tamzhol valley of E Lhodrak. This region is nowadays called Tso-me, and administered from its county capital at **Tamzhol**. The distance from Chongye to Tamzhol is 83 km. At the NW shore of Trigu Lake, S of the pass, **Chaktse Trigu** township lies in a vast exposed lakeland plain. Almost every building has a windmill attached. The township is an important intersection, since roads lead from here NW towards Lake Yamdrok (motorable for 34 km); SE to Ritang (76 km) near Lhuntse, and SW to Tso-me (46 km).

Trigu Lake

གྲི་གུ་མཚོ་

The bird sanctuary of Trigu Lake is located in a pristine nomadic area of

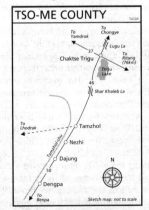

internal drainage. There are hot springs near its NW corner; and yak pastures all around. The motion and subtle colour tones of its waters are said to portend good and bad auspices; and, like neighbouring Lake Yamdrok, it is said to have a talismanic connection with the well-being of the Tibetan nation. Prosperity is considered directly proportionate to the rise in its water level.

The 46 km drive from Trigu to Tamzhol (Tso-me) town is one of the most memorable in Southern Tibet. The road cuts SW away from the lake shore, and ascends the Shar Khaleb La pass (5,129m). Beyond, there is a remarkable canyon where the bare red hillsides are severely contorted and eroded, like those around Tsaparang in Far-west Tibet (see below, page 429). To the W, you can see the peaks of Chungkha Mori (5,220m), Droktri Sharma (5,837m) and Zholchen Chenri (6,166m), which partake of this landscape and its tectonic upheavals, forming a definite watershed between the N and S flowing tributaries of the Brahmaputra. The descent to Tamzhol gives access through lateral valleys to the ruined monasteries of Rimon and Tashi Choling.

Tamzhol (Tso-me) Town

The town of **Tso-me** is dramatically set within the eroded gorge of the Tamzhol-chu (sometimes known as Lhodrak Shar-chu), which rises from the watershed at Shar Khaleb, and surges SW through the E Lhodrak region to converge with the Kuru-chu (Lhodrak Nub-chu) below Kharchu (see below, page 273).

Trekking

From Tso-me, the main road leads downstream to Benpa and Khomting Lhakhang (84 km); but it is also possible to undertake a 4-day trek to Lhodrak (Dowa Dzong), via Zholra valley, Menzang La pass, and Shera La pass.

Mawochok Monastery

 སྨ་བོ་ལྕོག་ནས

Revered as one of the supreme places for meditation in Tibet since the time of Padmasambhava, the distinctive Mawochok ridge known as **Drakmar Dorje Tsenga** ('five-fold indestructible peak of red rock') dominates the town of Tso-me from the NE. The site is said to derive its power from the three mountain abodes of the three main bodhisattvas: Avalokiteshvara, Manjushri and Vajrapani, which lie immediately to the S.

History

The monastery was the seat of Nyangrel Nyima Ozer (1136-1204), a revered incarnation of King Trisong Detsen, who, along with Guru Chowang and Rigdzin Godemchen, is regarded as one of the three supreme treasure-finders (*terton*) of Tibet. As a child, he meditated at the base of Mawochok mountain and received the name Nyima Ozer in a vision. Thereafter, he established his residence on the ridge above, from which time the monastery developed. The original buildings were destroyed in the 1960s, along with most of Mawochok's treasures, including a famous set of images depicting the three bodhisattvas (Avalokiteshvara, Manjushri, and Vajrapani), King Trisong Detsen's own master copy of the *Gathering of the Eight Transmitted Precepts* (a text rediscovered as *terma* by Nyangrel himself), and a large bronze stupa.

Main temple

Approaching the main temple from the E, there are three buildings to its left: a **protector shrine**, dedicated to Six-armed Mahakala, and two enormous stupa reliquaries, known as **Tukten Chorten** and **Tashi Obar**, which are greatly revered. They contain the relics of Nyangrel and his son Drogon Namka Pelwa. Among these, Nyangrel's own stupa is said to have been consecrated by the Kashmiri pandita Shakyashri, who was invited to Mawochok in 1204 during the funeral ceremonies.

The **main temple** is entered from the E, although the main images and inner sanctum are to the N. Inside in the NW corner, next to a wooden prostration board, there are **amazing murals** depicting the life of Nyangrel himself. On the E wall is a copy of the Derge version of the *Kangyur*. The main images are of Padmasambhava and Nyangrel. Within the **inner sanctum**, are new images of the three bodhisattvas: Manjushri, Avalokiteshvara, and Vajrapani, interspersed with other images of Amitayus, Vajrasattva, Avalokiteshvara (again), Nyangrel, and an old image of the latter's son Ngadak Drogon Namka Pelwa. There are currently 23 monks, and the reconstruction is the work of Mawochok Chozang Tendzin Gyatso Rinpoche, an aged incarnate lama who resides at Tsetang.

Pilgrimage Circuit

The pilgrim's circuit around the mountain top encompasses Nyangrel's sacred spring and meditation cave, as well as a charnel ground, and rock impressions of snowlions and Eleven-faced Avalokiteshvara. Nearby are the three scared peaks of the three bodhisattvas: Vajrapani on the left, Avalokiteshvara in the centre, and Manjushri on the right. Further to the S are the mountains of Benpa in lower Tamzhol and, beyond, the high Himalayas on the Bhutan-Tibet border.

● **Facilities** It is possible to stay within the simple guesthouse compound, which caters mostly to truckers and government employees. The town has a general store, a cinema, and a few shops, mostly owned by its expanding Chinese population.

Nezhi Zhitro Lhakhang

གནས་གཞི་ཞི་ཁྲོ་ལྷ་ཁང་

A few kilometres below Tamzhol (Tso-me) town, following the Tamzhol-chu downstream, the road passes a ruined watchtower and Phakmodrupa's earthen stupa of **Na'okyok** on the far bank of the river. After Letang village, the road crosses the river to the W bank and descends to **Nezhi** township. Here, you can visit **Nezhi Zhitro Lhakhang**, the residence of the descendents of the Nyingmapa *terton* Guru Chowang (1212-70), where the images are dedicated to the latter's particular *terma* tradition. Guru Chowang, like Nyangrel, is one of the supreme *terton* of the Nyingma school and, again like Nyangrel, hailed from the Lhodrak region of Southern Tibet. As a young man, he received the *bodhicitta* vows from Sakya Pandita here in 1229. Formerly the golden reliquary of Guru Chowang was housed here.

The temple

Within the reconstructed temple, which is entered from the E side, the central images are of Padmasambhava and his two foremost consorts. In the far NW corner there is a large image of Guru Chowang, and by the central pillars tangkas depicting the assemblies of the Hundred Peaceful and Wrathful Deities. There are **two inner sanctums**: the one to the W is dedicated to the Eight Deities of the Transmitted Precepts, who are the wrathful meditational deities of the Nyingma school, in the form revealed by Guru Chowang's own *terma* revelation, entitled *Kabgye Sangwa Yongdzok*. The second to the N was formerly dedicated to the peaceful deities but now contains images of the Buddhas of the Three Times, flanked by Atisha and the Eight Bodhisattvas. Hayagriva and Vajrapani guard its gates.

Watchtowers

The road continues SW from Nezhi, through **Dajung** and **Lu-me**, passing en route a riverside Padmasambhava cave. Below Lu-me, clusters of 15-20m high **watchtowers** are frequently to be seen. The construction of such defensive towers, especially in border areas, is well known in other parts of Tibet, including Kongpo and Gyarong. The road then winds its way downstream to **Darma Dzong** (in Dengpa township), before climbing high above the river to enter Benpa township.

LHODRAK COUNTY
ལྷོ་བྲག

洛扎县 Lhozhag

Population: 14,022 *Area:* 4,027 sq km

Traditionally the Lhodrak region of Southern Tibet included both the Kuru-chu (Lhodrak Nub-chu) and the Tamzhol-chu (Lhodrak Shar-chu) river valleys, which respectively extend SW and SE to converge below Kharchu, N of the Bhutanese border. Currently, Lhodrak is divided between Tso-me and Lhodrak counties, the latter comprising the upper reaches of the Kuru-chu, from Monda La pass as far as Kharchu; and the lower reaches of the Tamzhol-chu, from its Benpa-chu confluence as far as Kharchu.

The entire county lies to the S of the Brahmaputra watershed, and yet N of the Himalayan massives. This geographically confined but stunningly beautiful region has long been one of great historic importance, where vital traditions of both the Nyingma and Kagyu schools have flourished, acting as a cultural bridge between Tibet and E Bhutan.

The county capital is located at **Dowa Dzong** on the Zhung-chu tributary of

the Kuru-chu. The distance from Tso-me to Khomting Lhakhang is 84 km, and the distance from Dowa Dzong to Khomting Lhakhang is 67 km.

NB The rapid rivers of Lhodrak are best traversed in spring, early summer, and autumn. During the rainy season flash flooding can seriously disrupt itineraries.

Benpa Township
འབའ་ན་པ

ACCESS Benpa township is located on the west-flowing Benpa-chu tributary of the Tamzhol River. The valley formed by the Benpa-chu connects with the Khechu and Drushul valleys of Tsona county (see above, page 263) via the Ngamogong La pass.

Benpa Drukrel Lhakang once contained a large gilded copper image of Padmasambhava. Also, 1 km upstream from Benpa township, is the Kagyu monastery of **Benpa Chakdor**, named after its large image of the bodhisattva Vajrapani (*Tib* Chakdor). The assembly hall contains stone footprints of Milarepa, Karmapa I, and Gotsangpa. Within the temple to its rear are renovated images of Vajrapani, flanked by Marpa and Padmasambhava.

The main road from Benpa to Khomting Lhakhang (34 km) leads via **Drak Sinmo Barje** (also called Sengeri), where the clawmarks of the ogress of the rocks, who gave birth to the Tibetan race (see above, page 111) can be seen on the

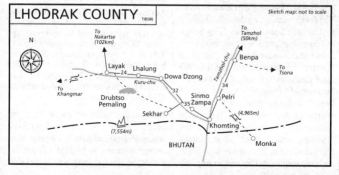

LHODRAK COUNTY　TIB586

Sketch map: not to scale

N

To Nakartse (102km)

Layak 24 — Lhalung — Dowa Dzong

Kuru-chu 32

To Khangmar

Drubtso Pemaling

Sekhar

(7,554m)

To Tamzhol (50km)

Benpa

To Tsona

Tamzhol-chu

Pelri

Sinmo 35 Zampa

34

(4,965m)

Khomting

BHUTAN

Monka

cliff face. From Pelri there is a side-valley leading to Pode La pass (4,965m) on the Bhutanese border. This leads to **Monka Nering Senge Dzong**, in Bhutan – the foremost hermitage of Padmasambhava symbolizing buddha-activities.

Khomting Lhakhang

མཁོ་མཐིང་ལྷ་ཁང་

Lhakhang Township

Lhakhang overlooks the confluence of the Kuru-chu and Tamzhol rivers. It was once an important trading post between E Bhutan, Lhasa and Tsetang.

● **Facilities** There is a pleasant guesthouse, general store and outside pool.

The Temple

This geomantic temple, which stands in the middle of Lhakhang township, is one of the border-taming (*thadul*) series of temples constructed by Songtsen Gampo during the 7th century: specifically located on the left elbow of the supine ogress, who represents the rigours of the Tibetan terrain (see above, page 48).

It is a yellow building with a shingled roof, surrounded by four large trees, which are said to have been planted by Guru Chowang in the 13th century. It once contained a renowned image of Four-faced Sarvavid Vairocana, who embodies all the Buddhas of the Five Families, flanked by the Eight Bodhisattvas. The face representing Amoghasiddhi is said to have been made by King Songtsen Gampo in person. It was within this image that Nyangrel Nyima Ozer (12th century) discovered his terma texts entitled *Gathering of the Sugatas of the Eight Transmitted Precepts (Kabgye Deshek Dupa)*. Nothing remains of these images apart from their plinths, but the painted columns and the murals above the door depicting the three bodhisattvas, Avalokiteshvara, Manjushri and Vajrapani, are exquisite. This temple urgently

requires funds for its restoration. Upstairs, in the **Tsedak Gonkhang**, there are some small extant images and black-on-gold murals of the protectors.

South to Bhutan

Below Khomting Lhakhang, a 2-hr trail to the left leads below Chakpurchen towards the **Kharchu Pelgyi Pukring** cave, where in the 15th century Ratna Lingpa discovered *terma* concealed by Namkei Nyingpo. Opposite the cave is the cliff-top **Senge Zangpo Dzong**, where a temple associated with the Dzogchen lineage-holders Melong Dorje (1243-1303) and Rigdzin Kumaradza (1266-1343) can be seen. On the W bank of the river (reached by crossing the bridge over the Kuru-chu/Lhodrak Nub-chu below Khomting Lhakhang), there is the **Tselam Pelri**, where caves of both the Nyingma and Drigung Kagyu tradition are found. This road leads S to **Ngotong Zampa** bridge on the Bhutan border.

Kharchu Monastery

མཁར་ཆུ་དགོན་པ

Situated 2³⁄₄ hrs' walking distance above Khomting Lhakhang, on a spacious hilltop alpine meadow is **Kharchu Monastery**, the seat of Namkei Nyingpo Rinpoche of the Nyingma school. The monastery lies above a semi-nomadic camp, where the dwellings have yak wool tents covering adobe and stone walls, and picturesque flower gardens.

ACCESS To reach Kharchu follow the path uphill from the *Lhakhang Guesthouse* and turn right, behind the military barracks. The trail bifurcates after 15 mins. Take the left track, and ascend to a second bifurcation after 1 hr at a rock painted image of Jambhala, god of wealth, and bear right. This will lead after a further arduous 1¹⁄₂ hrs to the summit.

Built on a promontory overlooking the deep forested gorge of Chakpurchen, where Padmasambhava's supreme hermitage symbolizing buddha mind is located, the site has long been associated with some of the greatest figures of the Nyingma and Kagyu traditions: Namkei Nyingpo, Vairocana and Yeshe Tsogyel (among Padmasambhava's 25 disciples), Shelkar Dorje Tsodron, Gotsangpa, Nyangrel Nyima Ozer, Guru Chowang, Melong Dorje, and Drukchen Pema Karpo, the last two of whom respectively founded the main temple and the monastery. From the time of Dalai Lama V, the monastery has been the seat of the reincarnations of Namkei Nyingpo.

The rebuilt 2-storeyed temple has (downstairs) an **assembly hall** containing new large images of Padmasambhava and Aksobhya Buddha, along with Marpa and Milarepa. The exquisite murals depict the lineage holders of both the Nyingma and Kagyu schools. **Upstairs**, there is a skylight offering a splendid view of the images and murals below, and the *labrang* residence containing the throne of the present Namkei Nyingpo Rinpoche, who currently resides at Bumtang in Bhutan (see below, page 737). The complex also includes a kitchen and residential area for monks, a large stupa, a sky-burial site, and a 2m high water-powered *mani* wheel. This monastery has one of the most idyllic settings in Tibet, and its lofty isolation can best be seen from a high point on the road to Senge township on the W bank of the Kuru-chu River (see below, page 273).

Chakpurchen Cave

Padmasambhava's supreme cave of buddha-mind is reached via a steep forested trail below the hermitages next to the stupa at Kharchu. En route the pilgrim's circuit takes in the **Lhamo Kharchen** hermitage of Phakmodrupa, the **Khandro Dora** platform, the **Chakpurchen Cave**, and the meditation caves of Namkei Nyingpo. The 3-storey hermitage of **Lhamo Kharchen**, containing rock footprints of Phakmodrupa, is reached along this trail, across the Kharchu River by means of an old wooden

bridge. Back on the near side of the bridge a trail then climbs uphill to the **Khandro Dora**, where there is an inscribed stone obelisk, and then plunges abruptly to **Chakpurchen Cave**.

The cave entrance is approached by means of a perilously unstable wooden bridge. Inside the cave is a multi-storey wooden hermitage of the Kagyu school, from the top of which there is a long dark passageway zigzagging toward the cave of buddha-mind, shaped like Padmasambhava's own body. (Tradition holds that he created this meditation cavern by tunnelling directly into the mountain, and remained there in dark retreat for 7 years.) The cave contains a natural rock impression of Padmasambhava's iron dagger (*chakpur*), hence the name of the cave. Lastly, the meditation caves of Namkei Nyingpo are reached to the left of Chakpurchen.

Sekhar Gutok

སྲས་མཁར་དགུ་ཐོག

This most revered site of the Kagyu school in Tibet comprises the residence of Marpa Chokyi Wangchuk (1012-96) at Drowolung and the 9-storeyed tower constructed as an ascetic penance by his foremost disciple Milarepa (1040-1123; or 1052-1135).

ACCESS These places are located in the township of **Se**, 35 km NW of Khomting Lhakhang, in the valley of the Se-chu, an east-flowing tributary of the Kuru-chu (Lhodrak Nub-chu). Access by vehicle is extremely difficult during the rainy season (July-Aug), when the road is susceptible to severe mud avalanches.

Senge

The road from Khomting Lhakhang crosses both the Tamzhol-chu and the Kuru-chu in quick succession and then climbs NE, past a hydroelectric station and large military complex, to reach **Senge** township at the top of the ridge. The views of the Kuru-chu gorge to Bhutan in the S are fantastic from this vantage point. Nearby is the **Senge Dru-puk** cave, which has associations with Padmasambhava, Yeshe Tsogyel, and Milarepa.

• **Facilities** The town has guesthouse facilities, but is there basically to service the army.

The main road then descends to recross the Kuru-chu at **Sinmo Zampa** bridge. After 8 km, it divides – the E fork leading to Lhodrak Dzong and the W to Se. Take the latter. At **Gosung Nangma** a trail on the right leads off to Drubtso Pemaling (see below, page 276). The main road leads SW to Se township, passing on the left side the **Menchu hot spring** (an important health spa).

Sekhar Gutok

The 9-storeyed tower of **Sekhar Gutok** was constructed as a great act of penance by Milarepa on behalf of Darma Dode, the son of Marpa. For adherents of the Kagyu school, and the Tibetan population as a whole, this single building and the manner of its construction encapsulate the self-sacrifice and renunciation required for success on the Buddhist spiritual path. The tower still stands, its distinctive pagoda roof now replaced with a flat roof; and three of its seven floors contain original murals. Marpa's chapel has some excellent old tangkas. The adjacent 2-storey monastery which once housed 100 monks, still contains some original images of the Karmapas, and precious relics such as the skull fragment of Dagmema (wife of Marpa).

Drowolung Monastery
གྲོ་བོ་ལུང་དགོན་པ

The residence of Marpa Chokyi Wangchuk at **Drowolung**, near Sekhar Gutok, is the original Kagyu foundation in Tibet. It was here that Marpa engaged in the translation of the texts which he had brought from India, and transmitted his teachings and realizations to the four 'great pillars' who were his foremost disciples: Ngok Choku Dorje, Tsurton Wangi Dorje, Meton Tsonpo, and Milarepa. The

ruined **Podrang Marpa** residence once contained Marpa's reliquary, and images of Marpa and his son Darma Dode. Behind this building is the retreat centre (*drubkhang*) and to its left is the stone throne of Karmapa I. A hill-side stupa marks the way to the cave hermitage, where the grottoes of Marpa, Milarepa and Gampopa are all discernible.

• **Facilities** Simple guesthouse facilities and groceries are available.

Trekking

There is also a trekking route to Sekhar Gutok from Senge township via the Khana La and Rolpa La passes.

There is another 3-4 hrs' trek from Sekhar Gutok to the remote cave of **Taknya Lungten Puk**, where Milarepa undertook his first 1 year retreat. Guides from Sekhar can show the way. Marpa's birthplace at **Zhe** lies 2-3 hrs' walking distance N of Sekhar at the foot of Mt Tashi Denga. Trekking routes also lead S to Namgung La pass and SW to Monla Karchung La pass, both on the Bhutanese border.

Drubtso Pemaling
སྒྲུབ་མཚོ་པདྨ་གླིང

This glacial lake nestling in the shadows of the Kulha Kangri Himalayan massive (7,554m) was consecrated by Padmasambhava as one of the main places for meditation in Tibet.

ACCESS There are three points of access to the lake: a relatively easy 5-6 hrs' trek from Sekhar Gutok to Drubtso Pemaling, via Gosum Nangma and Chupak; a harder 7-8 hrs' trek from Sekhar Gutok via Tuk and Rongpo La pass (5,050m); and a 9-hr trek from Lhalung via Drum La pass (5,135m). A trail SW from Tuk on the second of these treks also leads to Langdo and the main trade route to the Bumtang district of Bhutan (via Mongla Karchung La pass).

Padmasambhava's meditation cave is located on the slopes of **Mt Damchen Gara Nakpo**, overlooking the magical turquoise-coloured lake. The trail to the cave follows a precipitous track, leading firstly down to the lake-shore ruins of **Pemaling Monastery**, which was founded by Pema Lingpa (1450-1521). Here, there was once a renowned image of Vajrapani, as well as smaller images of Padmasambhava, Phakmodrupa, and Karmapa I. The cave, where Padmasambhava subdued the demon Gara Nakpo through his meditative powers, lies 1 hr above the ruins (there is one restored building where pilgrims stay), and is surrounded by glaciers on three sides. The nearby **Lhachu** waterfall is said to be the entrance to a 'hidden land' (*beyul*) within Mt Kulha Kangri. The lake is said to emit mystical or atmospheric apparitions and sounds, notably those of the so-called 'ox of the lake' (*tsolang*). The lake also forms part of the 8-9 day Kulha Kangri pilgrimage circuit, which can only be undertaken by crossing into Bhutan.

Dowa Dzong

དོ་བ་རྫོང་

The road from Sekhar Gutok to Dowa Dzong, the capital of Lhodrak county, follows the Kuru-chu upstream for 32 km (or 67 km from Khomting Lhakhang). En route it passes through **Karpo** township, where there is a small shop/restaurant next to a freight truck checkpoint. Before entering town, the valley widens and the ruined fortress of **Dowa Dzong** is visible above the road on the left. The town has an increasing number of Chinese immigrants.

● **Accommodation** There is a 3-storey guesthouse with restaurant facilities.

● **Banks & money changers** The Bank of China is located to the right of the road, adjacent to the square.

● **Entertainment & shopping** On the main street, N of the square, there are several karaoke bars and shops.

● **Government buildings** The PSB, Post Office and government compound are located to the left of the road, adjacent to the square.

Lhalung Monastery

ལྷ་ལུང་དགོན་པ

This fascinating monastery is located to the W of Dowa Dzong, on the N bank of the Kuru-chu.

History
Although it is the principal seat of the Lhodrak Sungtrul and Lhodrak Tuk-se incarnations, following in the *terma* tradition of Pema Lingpa (1450-1521), it has also had earlier associations with the Karma Kagyu school and later connections with the Gelukpa. The original foundation is attributed to Lhalung Pelgyi Dorje, the 9th century assassin of Langdarma who hailed from this part of Southern Tibet. Later, in 1154, Karmapa I Dusum Khyenpa developed the site into a monastery, and from the 17th century onwards the buildings were occupied by the Lhodrak incarnations of the Nyingma school, with the approval of Dalai Lama V and the Tibetan government.

The present buildings largely date from the period of Lhodrak Sungtrul III Tsultrim Dorje (1598-1669) and they were later expanded by Lhodrak Sungtrul VIII Kunzang Tenpei Nyima (1763-1817). Formerly the monastery had a grand appearance, its perimeter wall surrounded by 108 stupas and 108 willow trees (which have since been destroyed).

The Temple
Beyond the entrance courtyard, the assembly hall has a Zhitro Lhakhang to its right, and to the rear a Gonkhang and the *labrang* residence of Lhodrak Tuk-se. On the hills to the NE is a nunnery founded by Longchen Rabjampa.

The **ground floor** of the **Assembly Hall** once housed important 8m high clay images of the Seven Generations of Past Buddhas (Sangye Rabdun), along with other images of the first seven lineage-holders of Pema Lingpa, and the Three Deities of Longevity (Tselha Namsum). These and the tangkas painted by Lhodrak Tuk-se Gyurme

Dorje (b 1641) no longer exist. There is a new image of Padmasambhava against the N wall, and on the W, some damaged murals depicting his life. The decorated pillars have archaic features. In the centre of the hall are the thrones of the Lhodrak Sungtrul and Lhodrak Tuk-se incarnations, both of whom are currently in Bhutan.

The **second storey** has a central skylight overlooking the lower hall, surrounded by a gallery from which various chapels extend. On the S side, next to the staircase, there is an oblong room with an image of Pema Lingpa and extremely valuable **frescoes** of historic importance depicting in three successive panels the lives of Nyangrel Nyima Ozer, Pema Lingpa, and Guru Chowang – the three greatest figures of the Lhodrak region. Adjacent to the door are further murals depicting the deities of the *Barchad Lamsel*, and above the door is Hayagriva. On the W side, the **protector shrine room** has an image made personally by Tilopa, and on the N side there are two chapels: the first houses the foremost objects of the monastery in a glass case. These include a stupa containing the heart of Lhalung Pelgyi Dorje, the vajra of Jatson Nyingpo, stone footprints of Guru Chowang aged 8 and 13, and original images of Amitayus in union with consort. The second contains the reliquary of Lhodrak Sungtrul X. On the E side, there is a chapel containing the life-supporting stone (*lado*) of Guru Chowang.

In the reconstructed **Zhitro Lhakhang** to the E of the assembly hall there are new images on the N wall representing: Garab Dorje, Srisimha, Padmasambhava, Yeshe Tsogyel, and Pema Lingpa. On the W and E walls respectively there are relief images of the Hundred Peaceful and Wrathful Deities, each in their respective grottoes. Behind the assembly hall, in the **Gonkhang**, where Lhodrak Sungtrul VIII had a meditative vision of Padmasambhava, is

a 'speaking' image of Padmasambhava in the form Guru Saroruhavajra, with a teardrop trickling from its eyes. Upstairs is the residence named **Orgyen Zimpuk**.

Further E from the Gonkhang is the **Mani Ratna Labrang** or residence of the Lhodrak Tuk-se incarnations. It contains the throne and stone footprint of Lhodrak Tuk-se, aged 7, with a mat used only by the Karmapas, and a sealed meditation recess. Outside in the courtyard is a stone *udumbara* lotus.

Layak Guru Lhakhang

ལ་ཡག་གུ་རུ་ལྷ་ཁང

West of Lhalung in Monda township is the temple of **Layak Dzara Guru Lhakhang**, also called **Samdrub Dewachenpo**, which was constructed in the 13th century by Guru Chowang. Formerly this temple contained a Jowo image discovered by Guru Chowang in person, along with relics and a painting of this master. The original temple, styled after the ramparts of Nalanda monastery in India, is illustrated in the Lhalung frescoes. It is not yet possible to determine whether the 1949 reconstruction bears any resemblance to the original, since the temple is firmly locked and still used as a granary. The rear annex is now a private residence. Southwest of Layak at **Negon** there is a reconstructed branch of this monastery.

From **Monda** the road climbs NW to ascend Monda La pass (5,266m), the watershed between the lakeland plateau to the N and the south-flowing rivers of Lhodrak. The view of **Kulha Kangri** from Monda La is unrivalled. Beyond the pass is the **Monda Kangri** (6,425m). The distance from Monda township to Nakartse is 102 km, and to Lhasa, 256 km. South of the watershed, there is a trail leading W of Monda township across the Trel La pass, leading to Khangmar county of West Tibet.

NAKARTSE COUNTY

སྣ་དཀར་རྩེ

浪卡子县 Nagarze

Population: 20,003   Area: 7,660 sq km

The county of Nakartse is a vast high altitude depression containing the two largest lakes in Southern Tibet: Phuma Yutso and Yamdrok Yutso. Along with Trigu Lake (see above, page 270), these form a natural barrier between the Brahmaputra valley to the N and the watershed passes of Lhodrak to the S. The county also acts as a major road link between Central Tibet (U), to the N of Gampa La pass, and W Tibet (Tsang), to the W of Nojin Ganzang range and Khari La pass (5,045m). It has for centuries therefore been a vital trading link between Lhasa and Bhutan, Sikkim, Nepal and W Tibet. The county capital is located at Nakartse, 154 km from Lhasa, 118 km from Gyantse, and 102 km from Lhodrak.

NAKARTSE COUNTY

Sketch map: not to scale

Phuma Yutso Lake

ཕུ་མ་གཡུ་མཚོ

From Monda La pass, the sound of Lhodrak's rushing rivers is left behind, and the road to Nakartse descends into the awesome tranquillity of the lakeland plains to the N. It skirts the E shore of Phuma Yutso (5,040m), a superb turquoise-coloured lake with three small islands in a vast but sparsely populated high-altitude setting. Apart from seasonal nomadic camper groups, their herds of yak, and fierce mastiffs, there are only three lakeside villages: **Tu** in the E (on the main road), **Talma** in the S, and **Phuma Jangtang** in the W.

Beyond the Ye La pass at the NE extremity of the lake, the road enters a slightly lower tundra plain, where the rivers drain N into Lake Yamdrok Yutso. Here, large flocks of sheep and goats can be seen grazing, and large villages dot the landscape: notably **Ling** to the E and **Zhamda** on the motor road.

Trekking

Tu, Tulma and Phuma Jangtang are linked by a trekking route that encircles the lake in 8-9 days. Locals undertake this pilgrimage circuit in the springtime, culminating at the Nyingma monastery of **Sengegon** near the NE end of the lake. Strange mists and lights are often seen refracted on its surface. Perennial snow peaks grace the NW horizon, the nearest being Gyetong Soksum (6,244m) and Jangzang Lhomo (6,324m), with **Nojin Gangzang** (7,191m) in the far distance. There is a trekking route from the NW corner of the lake via Chanda La pass, to Ralung monastery in Tsang (see below, page 321).

Lho Taklung

ལྷོ་སྟག་ལུང

The township of Taklung (or Lho Taklung) lies a few kilometres N of Zhamda village, near the SE shore of Lake

Yamdrok Yutso. At 4,450m, this is the largest market town between Gyantse and Lhodrak, and the site of an important summer trade fair, attended by Bhutanese merchants from Bumtang, as well as native Tibetans from Tsang and Southern Tibet. From here, there are trekking routes along the southern shore of Yamdrok Yutso, to Docho township, and thence to Dramda township on the E shore.

Places of interest

The town has two principal monasteries and a ruined dzong. The hilltop **Taklung Monastery**, presently unrestored, is a major branch of Dorje Drak (see above, page 224), maintaining the tradition of the Northern Treasures. Its incarnate lama, Taklung Tsetrul Rinpoche now lives in Simla and Ladakh.

The Sakyapa monastery of **Tarling Chode** lies below the hill, within the township. This is the residence of Taktsang Lotsawa, a vociferous 14th century debating opponent of Tsongkhapa. There are two main buildings separated by a courtyard. The **Assembly Hall** has a large image of Padmasambhava, backing on to a protector shrine where the main image is of Panjaranatha (Gonpo Gur). Its **inner sanctum** contains the reliquary of Taktsang Lotsawa, images of the Buddhas of the Three Times, and Hevajra murals.

The second building has a **Mani Lhakhang**, and a 2-storey **Guru Lhakhang**, containing a giant image of Padmasambhava in the form Nangsi Zilnon, surrounded by his eight manifestations in their respective grottoes. On the adjacent wall is an image of Ekajati, protectress of mantra. The upper floor, entered by a staircase behind the Main Lhakhang offers a close-up view of Nangsi Zilnon's charismatic face.

● **Accommodation** Simple accommodation is available in the government guesthouse and the primary school compound.

Yamdrok Yutso Lake

ཡར་འབྲོག་གཡུ་མཚོ

The sacred lake of Yamdrok Yutso (4,408m) is revered as a talisman, supporting the life-spirit of the Tibetan nation. It is said that should its waters dry, Tibet will no longer be habitable. By far the largest lake in S Tibet (754 sq km), the pincer-shaped Yamdrok Yutso has nine islands, one of which houses a monastery and a Padmasambhava stone footprint. Within its hook-shaped western peninsula, there is another entire lake, **Dremtso** and beyond its SE extremity yet another, named **Pagyutso**. There are good motorable roads skirting the N and W shores of the lake, and trekking routes which complete the circuit. The Yamdrok region is traditionally famous for its salty dried meat, and, more recently, for its fishing.

The main highway from Lhasa to Gyantse descends to the northern lakeshore from Gampa La pass (4,794m) where the visitor from Lhasa or Tsetang will enjoy the unforgetable vista of its pincer-shaped expanse of turquoise water, with the mysterious **Mt Donang Sangwari** (5,340m) on the peninsula beyond, and the snow peaks of **Nojin Gangzang** (7,191m) in the distance. Passing a new but dysfunctional hydroelectric power station, and reaching the shore at **Tamalung**, from which there is a ferry crossing to the peninsula, the highway runs SW to **Peldi Dzong** and around the **Yarzik** inlet. At this point, there is a trekking route leading W to **Rampa** township and Ringpung valley in Tsang (see below, page 319). The highway then runs due S as far as **Nakartse**, via Dablung, where another ferry crossing leads to the peninsula. Thereafter, it cuts away from the lake to **Lango**, and ascends towards the **Khari La** pass (5,045m) – a defile between the formidable roadside glaciers of Nojin Gangzang (N) and Jangzang Lhomo, which also marks the border between S Tibet and W Tibet (Tsang). Just before Lango, the Lhodrak highway turns off the Gyantse highway on the left, and leads SE towards Lho Taklung and Zhamda (see above, page 279).

Trekking

There is a 7-day trekking circuit around the Yamdrok peninsula, commencing from and ending at **Nakartse**, via Samding Monastery, Sharwa (S of Dremtso Lake), Ngardrak township (NE of Dremtso), and Mekpa (NW of the peninsula). En route, you can visit the sacred **Mt Donang Sangwari**, where there are Padmasambhava and Yeshe Tsogyel caves; and which offers outstanding views of the snow peaks of Southern and Central Tibet from its summit.

A second 4-day trek leads eastward from the Tamalung ferry to **Dramda** on the E shore of the lake, from where there are further trekking options to Yarlung, Chongye, and Trigu Lake.

A third trekking route crosses the peninsula, via the **Tamalung** ferry on the N shore, as far as Tab, and then crosses the main body of the lake to the southern shore, via **Yongpado** island monastery. From here the townships of the nomadic pasture to the S of the lake can be reached – Ling and Docho among them.

Nakartse

 སྣ་དཀར་རྩེ

The county town of **Nakartse**, situated

on the Lhasa-Gyantse highway, has grown in recent years on the basis of the wool trade and its status as a transit point for freight trucks and passenger buses. A wool processing factory has been constructed here. The Chinese population influx is evident in the number of Chinese-owned shops and Sichuan-style eateries. On the ridge above the town is the rebuilt **Nakartse Monastery**; and the ruins of the old dzong, birthplace of the mother of Dalai Lama V.

● **Facilities** Guesthouse facilities are available. There is one excellent little Tibetan restaurant, popular with travellers, truckers, locals and even Chinese, serving noodles, momo, Tibetan butter tea, and sweet Indian-style tea.

Samding Monastery

བསམ་སྡིང་དགོན་པ

This celebrated monastery, 8 km E of Nakartse, commands the isthmus between the Yamdrok Yutso Lake pincer and Dremtso. Founded in the 12th century by Khetsun Zhonudrub, Samding has since the 14th century been a bastion of the Bodongpa school, derived from Bodongpa Chokle Namgyel (1306-86). The abbess of Samding, Samding Dorje Phagmo, has long been revered as the highest female incarnation in Tibet. In 1716 she is renowned for having transformed her nun followers into sows in order to thwart the wrath of the Dzungar armies! The present incarnation resides at Lhasa.

ZANGRI COUNTY

ཟངས་རི

桑日县 Sangri

Population: 15,043   Area: 2,469 sq km

The county of Zangri lies downstream from Tsetang on both banks of the Brahmaputra. On the S bank it extends for some 35 km as far as Rong township, including the villages situated between the Yarlung and Eyul (Si-chu) valleys. On the N bank it extends from the village of Jang below Densatil monastery (16 km E of Ngari Tratsang) as far as Mt Ode Gungyel (6,998m), including the valleys of Zangri, Olka and Dzingchi. The present district capital is located at **Zangri**.

Densatil Monastery

གདན་ས་མཐིལ་དགོན་པ

Rong

Rong township, some 35 km from Tsetang, lies on the S bank of Brahmaputra. Here

ZANGRI & CHUSUM
TI8591

To Rutok Zampa
To Chokhorgyel
Magon La
Dzingchi
Olka Taktse
Densatil
Olka Power Station
Zangri
Jang
Si-chu
Brahmaputra
Tsetang
Rong
Eyul Lhagyari
Eyul Chundo Gyang
Shakjang
To Gyatsa (27km)
Podrang La (5,030m)
To Lhuntse
Sketch map: not to scale

are the ruins of **Langkor Dzong** and **Chagar Monastery**, which was founded by Dalai Lama III.

● **Facilities** There is a fine but simple Tibetan restaurant at the crossroads in Rong, serving noodles, momo, fresh butter tea, and chang.

ACCESS To reach Densatil, take the track leading to the river bank and the **Lukhang Druka ferry** across to the N shore. At this point the river has narrowed to some 300m and the crossing is swift. After 1 km the road forks – W to Jang and E to Zangri. Take the former road, following the Brahmaputra upstream to **Jang**, which lies at the entrance to the concave valley of Densatil. From here there is a steep 3-hr climb to the monastery. A slightly longer 4-hr climb is possible from a point further upstream, approaching the monastery from the rear side of Mt Drakri Karpo, via a zigzagging track which almost reaches the summit before cutting around to enter the valley from the W side at a point higher than the monastery itself. The first route is preferable, in that it offers the shade and refreshing streams of the woodlands, whereas the latter is dry and dusty. Either of these points of access can also be reached on foot from Ngari Tratsang N of Tsetang.

History

Located amid a juniper and rhododendron woodland, within a sheltered concave ridge near the summit of **Mt Drakri Karpo**, is the Kagyu monastery of Densatil (4,750m). Founded in 1158 by Phakmodrupa Dorje Gyelpo (1110-70), this monastery became one of the most influential in Tibet, giving rise to eight diverse branches of the Kagyu school – the Drigungpa, Taklungpa, and Drukpa foremost among them. Between 1349 and 1435 or 1478, the Phakmodrupa family ruled Tibet from their castle at Nedong, near Tsetang (see above, page 121), and their ancestral monastery at Densatil acquired great wealth and precious religious artefacts. The main temple, **Tsuklakhang Marpo**, once contained 18 exquisitely engraved silver-plated reliquaries containing the relics of the past lineage-holders of

Densatil, and six gold pendants. Little evidence of this grandure remains at the present day.

The site

Approaching the monastery from the W, below the meditation hermitages, the road follows the contours of the ridge to reach what remains of the complex. Adjacent to the kitchen, there is a small temple containing a copy of the *Kangyur*, and fine old images of Vajravidarana, Cakrasamvara, and Vajravarahi. A ladder leads up to the next level, where to the left, is the chapel built on the site of Phakmodrupa's celebrated straw meditation hut (**Chilpei Khangpa**), and to the right a chapel containing an image of Vajravarahi and stone footprint of Phakmodrupa. Behind these chapels are the massive red walls of the ruined **Tsuklakhang Marpo**.

Take the pilgrim's circuit around the temple, and see the large elegantly carved **Mani Wall** on the E side. From the ridge to the W of the monastery there are stupendous views of the Brahmaputra valley – both upstream towards Tsetang and downstream towards Gyatsa.

Zangri Kharmar Temple
ཟངས་རི་མཁར་དམར་ལྷ་ཁང་

Retracing the jeep road from Jang towards the ferry, take the left fork to **Zangri**, the county capital. This is a relatively prosperous town, with its wide streets and walled orchards. The grand mansion house of the noble lords of Zangri, named **Samdrub Podrang**, still stands within the township. About 8 km E of town, on a 50m red rock promontory above the Zangri-Olka road, there is the reconstructed temple and cave hermitage of **Zangri Kharmar**. This was once the residence of Tibet's celebrated female yogini Machik Labdron. Both the temple and the cave have fine images of Machik Labdron and her Indian teacher Phadampa Samgye, as well as Karmapa Rangjung Dorje, who later (14th century) redacted

the *Chodyul* cycle of practices associated with her.

● **Facilities** Unfortunately a hardline and doctrinaire attitude towards outsiders prevails in Zangri. Camping may be preferable to the unwelcoming guesthouse facilities here.

Mount Ode Gungyel
འོད་དེ་གུང་རྒྱལ

From Zangri, the road continues NE, following the N bank of the Brahmaputra, as far as the power station of Olka Lokhang. Here, it leaves the river, which, from this point onwards, flows rapidly through a narrow gorge no more than 200m wide. Mt Palungri/Draklho Kyizhung (5,730m) slopes down to the S river bank, as does the sacred **Mount Ode Gungyel** (6,998m) on the N bank. The latter is the abode of the mountain deity of the same name, regarded as the father of Mt Nyenchen Tanglha (see above, page 83), and revered by Buddhist and Bon pilgrims alike. Tibet's second mortal king, Pude Gungyel, a culture hero who discovered base metals and agriculture, was named after this protector deity.

Olka
འོལ་ཁ

Olka Takste Dzong
འོལ་ཁ་སྟགས་རྩེ

The township of Olka, 20 km inland from the power station, lies at the bifurcation of two valleys. It is dominated by the ruins of **Olka Takste Dzong**, which the Dzungar Mongols pillaged in the 18th century. The motor road runs N following the fertile **Dzingchi** valley, but soon comes to an end.

Trekking

A 4-day trek leads on via Dzingchi township and Magon La pass to **Rutok Gonpa** (on the Meldro-Gyamda road). The other track runs NE into the more arid **Olka** valley, from which there is another 4-day trek, via the Lung La pass, to Chokhorgyel and Lhamo Latso oracle lake (see below, page 286).

Dzingchi Monastery

This ancient monastery was founded in the 10th century at the inception of the later diffusion of Buddhism in Tibet by Garmiton Yonten Yungdrung, a student of Lachen Gongpa Rabsel, who maintained the monastic ordination in Amdo during the interregnum following Langdarma's persecution. The most important image was of Maitreya. Later, in 1339, Tsongkhapa renovated the temple and refurbished its Maitreya image. His student, Gyeltsabje Darma Rinchen, who became the first throne-holder of Ganden and first head of the Gelukpa school, was firmly associated with Dzingchi, and his subsequent incarnations resided there. Taranatha's silver reliquary was kept in the Maitreya temple for almost 300 years until its destruction during the Cultural Revolution. Three temples have been recently renovated – the **Assembly Hall** (*tsokhang*), the **Maitreya Temple**, and the **Labrang** residence of the Gyeltsab Rinpoches. A large stone mansion in the W of Dzingchi is the birthplace of Dalai Lama XI.

Garpuk

This Padmasambhava meditation cave is situated in the hills E of Dzingchi, but may also be reached from Samtenling in Olka. In later centuries, Gampopa and Tsongkhapa both spent time meditating in the cave. No restoration appears to have been yet carried out.

Olka Cholung Monastery

Cholung is an important Gelukpa hermitage, founded by Tsongkhapa on the N slopes of Mt Ode Gungyel. There are many stone prints attributed to the master himself; and the reconstructed buildings have an impressive ambience. Located 1½ hrs' trekking distance from Olka Taktse, within the Olka valley, Cholung has guesthouse facilities and food is available. Further NE at **Chuzang**, there is another Tsongkhapa hermitage with two reconstructed chapels and stone imprints of the master's feet and hands.

Olka Samtenling Monastery

This ruined hermitage has been associated at different times with the Kagyupa followers of Gampopa and the Gelukpa followers of Tsongkhapa.

CHUSUM COUNTY

ཆུ་གསུམ

曲松县 Qusum

Population: 14,208   Area: 2,332 sq km

GYATSA COUNTY

རྒྱ་ཚ

加查县 Gyaca

Population: 9,733   Area: 3,727 sq km

Chusum county is the modern name for the ancient principality of **Eyul Lhagyari**, whose inhabitants have long claimed descent from King Songtsen Gampo. This broad valley is formed by the arid gorge of the Si-chu River, which rises near the Podrang La pass (5,030m) and flows NW to enter the Brahmaputra downstream from Rong. The county capital is located at **Eyul Lhagyari** (Chusum), 59 km from Tsetang, and 24 km from Rong, on a turn-off to the left side of the road. Notice the distinctive yellow markings on the traditional buildings of Eyul: its palace, monastery and farm houses. Iron ore mining is an important industry here.

The ascent from Chusum to Podrang La follows a gradual gradiant along an unusually straight road. At **Shakjang** township (8 km from Eyul Lhagyari), there is a turn-off on the right leading to Tozik, **Eyul Chumdo Gyang** (36 km) and thence to Lhuntse county (see above, page 260). Beyond Shakjang, the valley widens to 2 km and the gorge deepens to 70m. There are cave habitations on the eroded upper ridges; and it was here at **Zarmolung**, in a former Padmasambhava meditation cave called Khyungchen Dingwei Drak, that the Nyingmapa yogini Jomo Menmo (1248-83) received the visionary *terma* text entitled *Gathering of All the Secrets of the Dakinis (Khandro Sangwa Kundu)*. The distance from Shakjang to the pass is 61 km; and from there to Gyatsa, a further 27 km.

Gyatsa county lies at the heart of W Dakpo, a region of S Tibet renowned for its walnuts and apricots. On the S side of the Brahmaputra, it extends along the highway from Podrang La pass downhill through Lhasol township to the riverside at Dzam, and thence downstream via Drumpa and Lingda to Pamda (55 km). The county capital is located at **Drumpa**, alongside the Dakpo Tratsang Monastery. A trekking route leads SE from here, via Loklen (Darmar) township and Ke La pass, to Sangak Choling, the gateway to Tsari. On the N bank of the Brahmaputra, the county also includes the townships of Ngarab and Gyatsa, which are reached via a modern suspension bridge. A motorable track follows the Terpulungchu valley upstream, to Chokhorgyel monastery in Metoktang (35 km). From here, it is a 4-hr trek to Lhamo Latso, Tibet's celebrated oracle lake, on whose waters visions portending the rebirth of Dalai Lamas can be seen. From Gyatsa township, yet another route leads SE via Lung (20 km), to Daklha Gampo monastery, in the lower reaches of the Gyabpurong-chu.

WEST DAKPO

Dakpo Tratsang Monastery

Dakpo Tratsang, also known as **Dakpo Shedrubling**, was original a Karma Kargyu monastery belonging to the Zhamarpas. In 1589, Zhamarpa VI Chokyi Wangchuk (1584-1635) was enthroned here. Later in the 17th century,

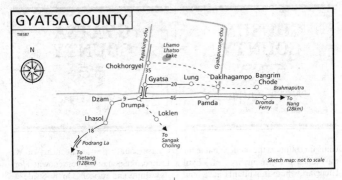

GYATSA COUNTY

TIB587

N

Terpulung-chu

Lhamo Lhatso Lake

Chokhorgyel

35

Gyatso

Gyabpucong-chu

Lung — Daklhagampo — Bangrim Chode

20

Brahmaputra

Dzam — 9 — Drumpa — 46 — Pamda — Dromda Ferry — To Nang (28km)

Lhasol — Loklen

18

To Sangak Choling

Podrang La

To Tsetang (128km)

Sketch map: not to scale

this establishment, like many other Karma Kagyu monasteries in Tibet, was converted to the Gelukpa tradition by Mongol force of arms. Many of the original buildings including the main temple have survived intact, and there is a recently restored debating courtyard. Accommodation and food are available here, or at the guesthouse in **Drumpa**, the county town, which lies alongside the monastery.

Chokhorgyel Monastery

A 35 km drive from Gyatsa township on the N bank of the Brahmaputra (across the suspension bridge E of Drumpa) passes through the valley of the Terpulung-chu. Half way up this valley, at **Tselgyu**, there is an attractive village of stone houses with thatched and shingled roofs. The marshland of its upper reaches, known as the **Plain of Flowers (Metoktang)**, abounds with a rich diversity of flora and vegetation: rhododendron, poplar, willow, walnut, apricot, and medicinal herbs, including the highly valued caterpillar fungus (*Cordiceps sinensis*; *Tib* yartsa gunbu).

At **Chokhorgyel**, the headwaters are hemmed in by three peaks, abodes of the protector deities Zhidag (N), Shridevi (S), and Begtse (E), and three valleys diverge: the NW route to Olka across Gyelung La pass and Loyul (3 days trekking distance); the NE route to Lhamo

Latso Lake (4 hrs); and the S route to Gyatsa.

The ruins of **Chokhorgyel Monastery** are extensive, including two large temples – the Lukhang and Tsuklakhang, and two colleges. The foundation dates from 1509, when Dalai Lama II Gendun Gyatso (1476-1542) had a hermitage and meditation cave here. The Dalai Lamas subsequently constructed a residence at the base of the northern peak, and would spend time here in the course of their visionary pilgrimages from Olka to Lhamo Latso Lake.

Lhamo Latso Lake

ལྷ་མོ་བླ་མཚོ

ACCESS To reach the oracle lake from Chokhorgyel, it is necessary to trek for 4 hrs. The trail passes below the ruins of **Nyingsaka Monastery**, and, crossing a stream, turns N at the base of **Mt Lhamonying** (abode of the protector Begtse). A sharp ascent leads, often through snow-covered ground, to an amphitheatre-shaped ridge (5,300m), and an ancient stone throne of the Dalai Lamas, dramatically overlooking the visionary lake, 150m below.

Lhamo Latso Lake is considered sacred to Gyelmo Makzorma, a form of the protectress Shridevi, and it is revered as the life-supporting talisman (*la-ne*) of the Dalai Lamas. Visions portending the circumstances of the rebirth of future Dalai

Lamas and Panchen Lamas are observed in its sacred waters. For example, in 1933, the regent Reting Rinpoche had a vision of the present Dalai Lama's birthplace and circumstances in Amdo. There is a pilgrim's circuit around the shores of the lake and at the eastern extremity prayer flags mark the spot where Shridevi's shrine once stood.

Trekking A 4-5 day trekking route from the N end of the lake also leads down into the Gyabpurong-chu valley, through the villages of Ba and Che, to reach Daklha Gampo monastery.

Daklha Gampo Monastery

དགས་ལྷ་སྒྱུ་སྒམ་པོ་དགོན་པ་

The Kagyu monastery of **Daklha Gampo** lies on a ridge to the NE of the eight-peaked Daklha Gampo mountain range, in the lower reaches of the Gyabpurong-chu valley. The distinctively contorted pinnacles of this range stand as an obvious landmark from the highway on the opposite bank of the Brahmaputra.

ACCESS To reach the monastery drive E from Gyatsa township for 20 km, hugging the river road as far as **Lung**. From here, there is a 6¼-hr trek to the monastery, via the villages of Rukhag Nyipa, and Ngakhang; but the trail is hard to find without the assistance of a local guide from Lung. Alternatively, there is a 2-day trek from **Bangrim Chode** monastery further E, accessible via the Dromda ferry on the Brahmaputra.

The complex was founded in 1121 by Gampopa Dakpo Lharje (1079-1153), on a site previously sanctified as a geomantic power place ('head of the ogress') by King Songtsen Gampo and transformed into a repository of *terma* by Padmasambhava. Gampopa came to meditate at the nearby **Namkading** after receiving the teachings and transmissions of the Kagyu lineage from Milarepa. He established three early chapels: **Jakhyil**, **Gomde Zimkhang** and **Chokhang Nyingma**; and gave instructions to his foremost students, who became the fountainheads of their great Kagyu lineages: Phakmodrupa Dorje Gyelpo, Karmapa I Dusum Khyenpa, and Seltong Shogom. They acquired their realizations in the many meditation caverns dotted across the range. Daklha Gampo is therefore revered as the primary Kagyu monastery for the teaching and practice of *Mahamudra* in Tibet, and it was carefully developed by the successive generations of Gampopa's familial lineage, such as Gampo Tsultrim Nyingpo, and those of his incarnation lineage, such as Gampopa Tashi Namgyel (1512-87). In 1718 the Dzungar armies sacked the monastery, but it was soon rebuilt, its national influence restored. A few chapels have been renovated following the more recent depradations of the 1960s, including original images of Avalokiteshvara and Cakrasamvara.

This region of Dakpo is also the birthplace of Karma Lingpa – one of Tibet's greatest treasure-finders (*terton*). During the 14th century he unearthed at Mt Gampodar within the Daklha Gampo range the *terma* of Padmasambhava, which has received most worldwide acclaim: *The Tibetan Book of the Dead (Bardo Thodol Chenmo)* and its cycle known as *Zhitro Gongpa Rangdrol*.

NANG COUNTY

ནང་རྫོང་

朗县 Nang Xian

Population: 5,637   Area: 6,477 sq km

Nang county is the name given to the present administrative division of E Dakpo, the principal gateway to the sacred mountain of Tsari, and the region through which the Brahmaputra River cuts its way through an unnavigable 33 km horse-shoe gorge as it flows towards Longpo and Kongpo. The county extends along the main Tsetang-Menling highway for 79 km, from Dromda Druka ferry in the W (46 km from Gyatsa), as far as Zhu in the E. Both banks of the river are characterized here by windswept sandbanks interspersed with small oases of walnut and apricot. The county capital is located at **Lang** (Nang Dzong) where the gorge begins, 28 km E of Dromda. The north-flowing Kurab-chu, Lapu-chu and Kyemtong-chu tributaries all offer trekking access to Tsari region in the S.

By contrast, on the N bank of the Brahmaputra, the only major valley is Arnaktang.

KURAB-CHU VALLEY

On the S bank of the Brahmaputra, commencing from **Dromda Druka**, there is a trekking route to Sangak Choling, the SW gateway to Tsari. The route follows the Kurab-chu tributary upstream via **Ganden Rabten** (7 km), Kurab Namgyel (5 km), and Sinmonang, before bifurcating. Take the E track, crossing the watershed passes of Gongmo La pass (5,298m) and Kharpo La (5,001m). **Ganden Rabten Monastery** is a branch of Ganden Phuntsoling near Lhasa. At **Kurab Namgyel** you can see the hilltop ruins of the dzong from which the whole Tsari was once administered.

Trungkhang

Back on the highway, at **Trungkhang Druka** (5 km E of Dromda) there is a ferry crossing to **Lhenga** on the N bank of the Brahmaputra. The birthplace of Dalai Lama XIII (1876-1933) lies 4 km E of Lhenga at **Trungkhang**. The former residence of Tibet's previous spiritual and temporal leader is sealed at present.

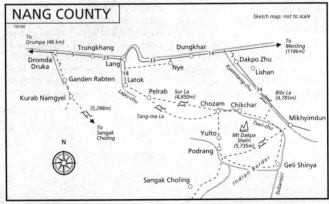

NANG COUNTY

Sketch map: not to scale

TIB588

To Drumpa (46 km)
Trungkhang   Dungkhar   To Menling (118km)
Dromda Druka   5   23   Lang   14   2   Dakpo Zhu
7   33   Nye   Lishan
Ganden Rabten   18   Latok
5   Lapu-chu   Pelrab   Sur La (4,850m)
Kurab Namgyel   Chozam   Chikchar   Mikhyimdun
(5,298m)   Tang-ma La   Tsari-chu
To Sangak Choling   Yulto   Mt Dakpa Shelri (5,735m)
N   Podrang   Geli Shinya
                                       Sangak Choling   Indian Border
Kyemtang-chu   Bibi La (4,785m)   34
Subansiri

Lang

The small county town of **Lang** (Nang Dzong) is a riverside settlement, which has grown up along the Brahmaputra's sharp bend.

● **Facilities** Guesthouse and simple restaurant facilities are available.

From here, there are three routes: the riverside highway to Nye and Dungkar (33 km), the short-cut to Nye via Kongpo Nga La pass (4,400m); and the inland route, following the Lapu-chu valley upstream to **Latok** township (18 km).

Taking the last of these routes, there is a scenic 2-day trek to **Chozam**, the main gateway to Tsari. En route, you pass through the small logging villages of Bara and Pelrab, after which the trail bifurcates: the E track leading alongside the beautiful forested alpine lake of **Tso Bunang** and across Sur La pass (4,850m) to Chozam; and the W track crossing the Tangma La pass to **Chorten Namu** and thence to Chozam.

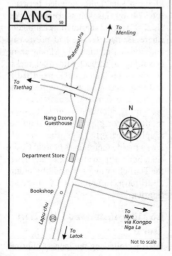

LANG

To Menling

Brahmaputra

To Tsethag

Nang Dzong Guesthouse

N

Department Store

Bookshop

Lapu-chu

To Nye via Kongpo Nga La

To Latok

Not to scale

Dungkar

Both the riverside highway and the Kongpo Nga La short-cut lead from Lang to Nye village and Dungkar township. A ferry leads across to **Dungkar monastery**, the seat of Tibet's celebrated contemporary historian, Dungkar Lobzang Trinle.

Dakpo Zhu

Some 14 km E of Dungkar, there is a turn-off, which leaves the highway at the entrance of the Kyemtong-chu valley. Following this road for a further 2 km, you will arrive at **Dakpo Zhu**, a one time haunt of the Nyingmapa yogin Dzeng Dharmabodhi (1052-1136).

KYEMTONG-CHU VALLEY

The main pilgrimage route to Tsari follows the Kyemtong-chu valley upstream, and across the Bibi La pass (4,785m) to Chozam and **Mikhyimdun**. North of Kyemdrong township on the E bank of the Kyemtong-chu, at **Lishan**, there is a large recently discovered archaeological site (815,000 sq km), including 184 tombs which have been dated to 700 CE. Above Kyemdrong township, there are trails leading up the valley through Shelrika towards Mt Dakpa Shelri. However, the road to Tsari, motorable for 34 km, cuts SW to leave the valley. It passes through a deep shrub-filled gorge to level out at an alpine riverside meadow near **Sumbatse**, and then ascends through conifer and rhododendron forest to cross the Bibi La. Lush meadows give way to stunning forests on the descent into **Mikhyimdun** (Tsari township).

TSARI

Mount Dakpa Shelri (5,735m) and its environs in Tsari form one of Tibet's most revered pilgrimage circuits – generally ranking alongside those of Mt Kailiash and Mt Amnye Machen. For the Kagyu school in particular, Tsari is classed along with Mt Kailash and Lapchi Gang as one of the three essential power places of the meditational deity Cakrasamvara. Two of Cakrasamvara's 24 power-places mentioned in the *Root Tantra of Cakrasamvara* are said to be within Tsari, Caritra and Devikota.

This holy land of Mt Dakpa Shelri is described as having four gateways, associated with the four bodhisattvas: Manjushri (E), Vajrapani (S), Tara (W) and Avalokiteshvara (N). During the earliest phase of Buddhist propagation in Tibet, Padmasambhava and Vimalamitra (8th-9th century) are said to have entered through the southern gate, and made Tsari a repository of *terma*. Kambalapada and Bhusuku (10th-11th century) entered via the eastern gate. Tsangpa Gya-re Yeshe Dorje (1161-1211) entered through the western gate at the third attempt; and lastly Sonam Gyeltsen of Ralung entered via the northern gate. There four gateways may be identified respectively with Geli Shinya (S), Mikhyimdun (E), Sangak Choling/Podrang Yutso (W), and Chikchar (N).

The main impetus for the opening of the Tsari region as a sanctuary for meditation and focal point of pilgrimage came from Phakmodrupa Dorje Gyelpo (1110-70), who on the advice of Gampopa, encouraged his students to go there. The major sites have therefore come to be associated with Tsangpa Gya-re and his Drukpa Kagyu followers, and to a lesser extent with the Drigung and Karma Kagyu schools. As explained in the *Guidebook to Tsari*, composed by Drukchen VIII Chokyi Nangwa (1768-1822), there are three distinct focal points in Tsari: **Mt Dakpa Shelri**, **Lake Tsokar**, and **Mt Tsari Sarma Tashijong**, which are likened to the parts of a symbolic vajra: the western prong, the central knob, and the eastern prong.

Among these, the first two come within the **Old Tsari (Tsari Nyingma)** pilgrimage route, and the last within the **New Tsari (Tsari Sarpa)** pilgrimage route.

Tsari Nyingma

Chikchar

Located on a beautifully forested mountain ridge above Chozam, **Chikchar** marks the beginning of all the pilgrimage circuits around Mt Dakpa Shelri. The blue and yellow mountain poppies (*Meconopsis*) which are well-known throughout the higher elevations of E Tibet are in evidence here. And it was here, in close proximity to the sacred snow peak, that in the 12th century Tsangpa Gya-re had a vision of the Cakrasamvara assemblage and consecrated the locale. In the 13th century, after the arrival of Sonam Gyeltsen of Ralung and many hermits who left the neighbouring districts of Dakpo and Kongpo to avoid an epidemic, Drukpa Kagyu monasteries were founded within the Chikchar valley at Densa Pangmo, Uripangmo, and Gopangmo. The most important building, however, was the **Dorje Phakmo Lhakhang**, founded between 1567-74 by Drukchen Pema Karpo (1527-92) at Bodo or Bokhung Zhungdo, where Tsangpa Gya-re had previously had a vision of the deity Simhavaktra becoming absorbed into the rocks. Northwest of Chikchar, at **Dotsen Tsuklakhang**, there were stones representing the sexual organs of Cakrasamvara and his consort Vajravarahi, which became a focal point of pilgrimage for childless couples. Formerly, no pilgrims were allowed to ride their horses beyond Chikchar, but a jeep road now extends down the Tsari-chu valley to **Lo Mikhyimdun** (Tsari township) on the present Indian frontier.

Lo Mikhyimdun and Lake Tsari Tsokar

Pilgrims following the longest pilgrim-

TSARI NYINGMA PILGRIMAGE

The Tsari Nyingma pilgrimage around Mt Dakpa Shelri has three distinct routes: shortest, intermediate and longest. The longest and most arduous, known as **Tsari Rongkor**, took 10-15 days. It became an official pilgrimage at the behest of the Tibetan Government, and was held once every twelve years in a monkey year to commemorate the date of Tsangpa Gya-re's original opening of Tsari. Sometimes 100,000 people would participate. The shorter routes would be followed between Apr and Sep of any year. Dalai Lama XIII undertook the Tsari pilgrimage in person. Unfortunately, the route passed through Lhopa aboriginal territory in the S, and the government was often obliged to send an armed escort, notwithstanding oaths of fealty sworn by the natives. The route follows the Tsari-chu downstream from Chozam and Chikchar, via Mikhyimdun and on to its confluence with the Subansiri (*Tib* Shipasha) at Geli Shinya. It then follows the latter river upstream to its confluence with the Yulme-chu, before cutting NW through the Yul-me valley to Yulto and Chozam. On the map the route therefore inscribes a diamond shape. At the present day it is impossible to complete the whole circuit since its southern tropical sections lie within the Indian territory of Arunachal Pradesh across a disputed frontier. The major sacred sites, which are all in the N, can still be visited, taking the lesser pilgrimage circuit via the Dolma La pass.

age in former times would trek to **Lo Mikhyimdun**, and thence continue downstream to the Subansiri confluence. Below **Chikchar**, the Tsari-chu enters a narrow gorge, and around **Poso Sumdo** the landscape abounds in rhododendrons, hemlock and juniper. (A trail from here leads across Bibi La pass to Kyemtong, see above, page 289). The border township of **Lo Mikhyimdun** is now the site of an army garrison; and the local population is more than half Lhopa. Cultivated fields of barley and potatoes are found beyond this point. From here, there is an essential 2-day trek to the sacred lake of Tsari Tsokar, further E.

Tsari Tsokar is a stunningly beautiful clear milky lake, surrounded by glaciers and forested shorelines. It was opened for meditation and pilgrimage by Karmapa III Rangjung Dorje (1284-1339) and Karmapa IV Rolpei Dorje (1340-83), and the slopes around its shores harbour meditation grottoes such as the **Khyungtsang Puk**.

The Inner Pilgrimage Circuit (Kyilkhor)

This 7-day trek, which is still followed at the present day, is best undertaken between July-Sept. In spring and autumn, the passes may be closed by snow. The route ascends the Chikchar valley to **Lapu**, location of Kambalapada's Lawapuk cave and the abode of the protectress Dorje Yudronma. Higher up there is the hermitage of Drukchen V Paksam Wangpo (1593-1641). It then crosses the **Dolma La** pass (4,910m) to the talismanic lake of Cakrasamvara, the **Demchok Latso**, and the **Miphak Gonpo** ravine. No female pilgrims were traditionally allowed to venture beyond the pass. Ascending the glacial Shakam La pass (4,910m), skirting en route a lake sacred to Avalokiteshvara, the trail then continues SW, to Droma La (4,390m) and Go La passes, before reaching **Podrang**, high above the E bank of the Yulme-chu River. Here is the most sacred of Tsari's many lakes, the **Podrang Yutso**, revered as the talismanic lake of Vajravarahi,

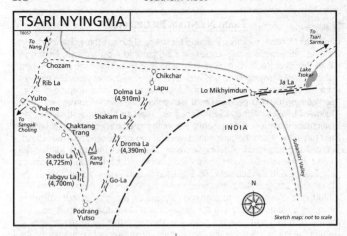

TSARI NYINGMA

To Nang — Chozam — Rib La — Yulto — Yul-me — To Sangak Choling — Chaktang Trang — Shadu La (4,725m) — Kang Pema — Tabgyu La (4,700m) — Go-La — Podrang Yutso — Droma La (4,390m) — Shakam La — Dolma La (4,910m) — Lapu — Chikchar — Lo Mikhyimdun — Ja La — Lake Tsokar — To Tsari Sarma — INDIA — Subansiri Valley — N

Sketch map: not to scale

where Tsangpa Gya-re and Gotsangpa both meditated. The latter's hermitage is above the lake, at **Namkapuk**, on the slopes of Mt Khandro Doi Lhakhang.

From Podrang the route turns sharply N, following the Yulme-chu upstream. It crosses Tabgyu La pass (4,700m) to enter the **Taktsang** ravine (4,025m), and the Shadu La pass (4,725m). Just beyond, at **Kaladungtso Lake**, there is the hermitage of the yogin Dungtso Repa.

The trail then descends into the **Domtsang** ravine, from which point women may again participate in the pilgrimage, and passing through **Chaktang Trang**, it reaches in succession **Yul-me** (3,500m) and **Yulto** (4,025m) villages. This is the stronghold of the Drigung Kagyu school at Tsari, and there is a temple dedicated to Vajravarahi.

From Yulto, there is a trek SW across the Takar La (5,090m) and the Kyu valley to Sangak Choling (see above, page 262). The main trail, however, turns NE to reach the **Chozam** plain, via either the Dorje Drak La or Rib La pass.

Chozam, a village of shingled stone houses, marks the end of the Tsari pilgrimage; and there are access points

from here to the main highway in Dakpo (Kurab Namgyel, Lang, and Zhu). The lush plains of **Senguti**, which extend for some 10 km below Chozam and alongside the meandering headwaters of the Tsari-chu, abound in silver firs, primulas, rhododendrons, honeysuckle, and so forth.

Tsari Sarma

Tsari Sarma is the name given to the sacred wildlife sanctuary around the headwaters of the Nelung Phu-chu, which flows NE to join the Brahmaputra in Menling county. There are three points of access: a 6-day trek from Kyemtong via the Lang La pass (4,815m), Nepar village, and the upper reaches of the Nelung Phu-chu; a 4-day trek from Nelung township on the highway in Menling county; or a shorter trek from Lake Tsari Tsokar (see above, page 291) via the Langtsang La pass and Langong.

The sanctuary of **Tsari Sarma** was founded by Rigdzin Kumaradza (1266-1343), a lineage-holder of the Nyingmapa school and the principal teacher of Longchen Rabjampa. Until recent times, the prohibition on hunting in this region was strictly enforced, and there was an abundance of wildlife: pheasants, deer, wild sheep, musk deer, wolves, and foxes. The 3-day pilgrimage around Tsari Sarma commences from **Tashijong** village, passing the sacred lakes of **Yutso Sarma** and **Tsonyam Sarma**, abode of secret dakinis. To the S, the Lo La pass leads across the Assamese Himalayas (Pachakshiri) into the Indian state of Arunachal Pradesh.

MENLING COUNTY
སྨན་གླིང་
米林县 Mainling

Population: 7,588   Area: 8,718 sq km

Menling county is the name currently given to the old districts of **Longpo** and **Lower Kongpo**, S of the Brahmaputra. It extends for 195 km, from a small estuary 13 km E of Dakpo Zhu, as far as Pe township in Lower Kongpo, where the Brahmaputra is channelled through a mighty gorge between Mts Namchak Barwa and Gyala Pelri at the eastern extremity of the Himalayas. At this point, the river changes its eastern course irrevocably, first to the N and then abruptly to the SW. The county capital is located at **Dungdor**, now encorporated within Nyangtri (rather than Lhokha) district. From here Tsetang lies 368 km due W, and Lhasa 550 km (via Bayi and

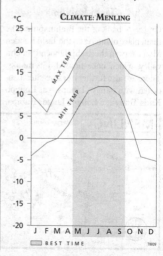

CLIMATE: MENLING

BEST TIME

Gyamda). The successive lateral valleys extending S from the Brahmaputra towards the Indian border are home to the tribal Monpa and Lhopa populations.

LONGPO

Orong and Nelung

The highway from E Dakpo enters Longpo 13 km E of Dakpo Zhu and after 42 km reaches Orong township in Orong valley. There are a number of sites in Longpo connected with the Nyingmapa *terton* Sangye Lingpa of Kongpo (1340-96), who, throughout his life, also maintained close connections with the Karma Kagyu tradition. At **Jagoshong**, he discovered *terma* concerning Mahakarunika and the *Extraction of Elixirs* (*chulen*). In the Orong area, at **Orsho Lungdrom**, he unearthed a precious gemstone called 'tiger-meat god'; and in the **Nelung** township area, 22 km further E, the site at Drongsar where he first encountered Karmapa IV Rolpei Dorje is still revered. From Nelung, there is a trekking route to Tsari Sarma (on which see above, page 292).

Tashi Rabden

On the N bank of the Brahmaputra, the main place of interest is the Tashi Rabden Monastery, in the Tashi Rabden Phu-chu valley, which once housed 130 monks. There are also further treasure-sites associated with Sangye Lingpa – at **Longpo Kada Trang** and **Longpo Jangde Bumpa**.

On the S bank, opposite the confluence of the Tashi Rabden-chu, is the Yulsum Phu-chu valley, which once marked the western extremity of Kongpo.

Dungdor (Menling Dzong)

Dungdor, the county capital, is located 41 km downstream from Nelung. The climate is warm and humid; and the countryside quite thickly forrested with conifers and junipers.

● **Facilities** Here, there is a government guesthouse, pleasantly constructed of wood, and hot water for washing is available in an outhouse. Sichuan restaurants, Chinese shops, Tibetan market stalls and karaoke bars provide some fascination for the Lhopa tribal visitors.

Inland from Dungdor, there is a military road following the Neyul Phu-chu upstream for 21 km to **Lago Zampa bridge**, and thence to the Neyul Dom La and Dungkar La passes, which lead across the border into India.

Further E, at **Shoga**, there is a stone footprint of Padmasambhava and a ruined stupa, which once rotated at the sound of the Vajra Guru mantra. From here, there is another trail following the Shoga Phu-chu upstream to Shoga La pass, and the Indian border; and at Gangka, 19 km E of Dungdor, the large **Gangka Zamchen** suspension bridge leads over to the N bank of the Brahmaputra. This last bridge is also rumoured to have a military underpass, ensuring that access to the frontier cannot be cut off.

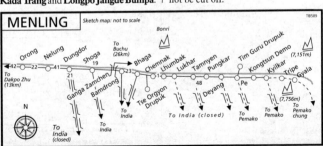

LOWER KONGPO

If you cross the Gangka Zamchen bridge to the N bank, you will reach the area of Middle Kongpo and Upper Kongpo (see below, page 307). Continuing, instead, on the S bank, where the road rapidly deteriorates, you will bypass the lateral valleys of **Bamdrong** and **Bhaga**, which respectively lead a short distance to Lado La and Bhaga La passes on the Indian border. The latter route has an important military installation, and an extremely well-lit and well-maintained military road.

Tse Orgyen Drupuk

Driving along the S bank from Gangka Zamchen bridge, notice on the opposite bank, the large estuary of the Nyang-chu, which flows into the Brahmaputra from the N, alongside the town of Nyangtri, and in the shadows of the sacred mountain, Kongpo Bonri. In the hills high above Chemnak, is the meditation cave of **Tse Orgyen Drupuk**.

At this site in the 8th century, Padmasambhava gave a longevity-empowerment to an old woman who was the only one able to reach the cave and receive the empowerment. The juniper tree next to the cave is said to have sprung from his *khatvanga*. Inside the cave is a 'self-arising' Padmasambhava image in stone and a nectar-producing rock. Older people from Chemnak claim to have seen nectar coming out of the rock. On the altar lies a new brass image of Padmasambhava.

On the ascent to the cave there are several decaying stupas and a sacred stone reputedly shaped like a dying person on all fours, prostrating before a lama with two vultures in attendance, one on either side. Once there was also a temple dedicated to Amitayus, named **Lungtok Chime Lhakhang**, where a stupa made from Padmasambhava's nasal blood (**Shangtrak Chorten**) was preserved.

ACCESS After the military installations of Bhaga and before reaching the township of Chemnak (Chabnak), there is a turn-off on the right, which leads SW and close to the Indian border.

Chemnak (Chabnak) Monastery

ACCESS Chemnak township lies 23 km E of the Gangka Zamchen bridge. It is also possible to reach Chemnak by coracle from Karma (Tsela Dzong) on the northern bank of the Brahmaputra below Drime Kunden.

The Gelukpa monastery of Chemnak, also called **Demo Chemnak**, is an imposing building with a shingled roof, situated on a wooded ridge above the road. The temple was restored in 1983. An ante-chamber has fine murals depicting the Four Guardian Kings and the protectors: Six-armed Mahakala, Bhairava, Dharmaraja, and Shukden. Within the main **assembly hall**, there are 21 tangkas and a series of murals depicting the Thirty-five Buddhas of Confession. The main images, behind the throne, are of Maitreya, flanked by a 'speaking' image also of Maitreya, and Tsongkhapa with his foremost students, flanked by two forms of Avalokiteshvara. Along the left wall are images of Padmasambhava with Shantaraksita and King Trisong Detsen; while the right wall has a very large image of Padmasambhava in the form Nangsi Zlinon. The **inner sanctum** contains 1,000 small images of Tsongkhapa. The imagery reflects the eclectic nature of the community at Chemnak, who include followers of the late Dudjom Rinpoche, head of the Nyingma school, among their numbers.

Chemnak to Pe

About 1 km E of Chemnak, there is a coracle ferry at **Lhumbak** village; and further E, at **Luzhar**, a dirt track leads down to a cable ferry across the Brahmaputra. Both of these crossings

BLACK FLAYED HIDE AND MOSQUITOES

Padmasamhava encountered Yamsha Nakpo (Black Flayed Hide) at Chaktak Bumpu. According to the Guru's biography, when the demon blocked his passage by placing one foot firmly on Mt Doshong La and the other on Mt Gyela Pelri, the Guru clapped his hands in astonishment, making the sound "Chaktak Bumbu". He promptly turned into a fish which swam upstream and then into a bird. Yamsha Nakpo turned into a bird of prey and went in swift pursuit, but the Guru evaded his grasp by vanishing into the cave-wall (hence the name of the cave). The demon could not follow. Padmasambhava remained in meditation in the cave for 3 years, 3 months and 3 days until he could manifest signs of accomplishment*. He then pierced the cave-wall with his ritual dagger*, stabbing the demon in the process. The stab-mark can still be seen above the altar.

Local informants further explain that Padmasambhava also tamed the wild beasts of Tim Gura Drupuk, including many man-biting birds, and instead permitted the relatively minor irritation of midges and mosquitoes which still thrive here!

offer access to important sites on the N bank, such as Mt Bonri, Demo Chemkar monastery, Menri, Chu Jowo, and Nyangtri, on which see below, page 298. Inland from the ferry crossing on the S bank, a trail follows the Luzhar phu-chu upstream to Luzhar La pass and the Indian border.

After Luzhar, the road passes through **Tamnyen** township, where glacial streams burst forth from Tamnyen La pass (on the Indian border) to devastate the motorable surface. At **Pungkar**, there is a small general store, and rudimentary guesthouse facilities. Then, approaching **Deyang**, where flash seasonal flooding again is a serious hazard, there is a trail leading up to Deyang La on the border. Finally, at **Pe** township, 48 km from Chemnak, there is a Chinese compound, with medical facilities, a small guesthouse and some supplies. Better to camp near the Tibetan village of Pe, where there are excellent campsites, offering wonderful majestic views of **Mt Namchak Barwa** (7,756m), until 1992 the world's highest unclimbed peak. Here, the Brahmaputra narrows to only 100m; and there are ferry boats crossing to Timpei on the N bank.

Tim Guru Drupuk

Above the village of **Timpei** in Yulsum district on the N bank of the Brahmaputra and dominated to the SE by Mt Namchak Barwa are the celebrated caves where Padmasambhava and his students practised meditation in the 8th century. Outside the main cave if one looks across the river one will see a group of prayer-flags marking the site called **Chaktak Bumbu**. This is where Padmasambhava reputedly encountered the demon Yamsha Nakpo (Black Flayed Hide).

The cave hermitage of **Tim Guru Drubpuk**, rebuilt under the guidance of Nakpo Zilnon Rinpoche of Buchu in Kongpo, is approached via a steep flight of steps. An **ante-chamber** contains a verandah and three large prayer wheels. Within the temple, which is cared for by the old Khampa ladies of Timpei village, the **chapel** has a single column supported by a Tibetan-style capital (*zhu*). The window on the right offers incredible views of Mt Nakchak Barwa. Tangkas, including two of the Peaceful and Wrathful Deities, adorn the walls, and on the left there is the entrance to the **cave** – an inner recess, containing three images of Padmasambhava, concealed images of

Mandarava and Yeshe Tsogyel, and in the centre of the floor an as yet unopened *terma* repository. The aperture in the cave wall forming the shape of a ritual dagger is above the *terma* rock.

As well as Padmasambhava, several of his most important students are said to have occupied other caves higher up the hillside. There are eight caves altogether, those of Padmasambhava, Namkei Nyingpo, Yeshe Tsogyel, Tamdrin Tulku, Chung Tulku, Vairotsana, Guru Drakpo and Senge Dongma, while the last is called Tsalung Jangsa (the place where yogic exercises were practised).

From Tim Guru Drubpuk, there is a 3-day trekking route via Sekundo and Nyima La pass to **Dongpatral** near the Kongpo to Po-me highway. The route abounds in diverse species of flowers.

Kongtsun Demo

On the S bank of the Brahmaputra, the motorable road continues beyond Pe for a few kilometres as far as **Kyilkar**, passing beyond the approach to Dozhong La pass (4,115m) and towards Mt Namchak Barwa. This is the district called **Yulsum Trenadong** ('defile where three regions of Puwo, Kongpo and Pemako converge'). It marks the beginning of the Brahmaputra rapids. Here, Padmasambhava is said to have subdued one of the 12 subterranean goddesses (*Tenma Chunyi*) of Tibet, and nearby there is a cave known as **Trekar Drupuk** where Padmasambhava stayed in meditation.

The name Kongtsun Demo has also been identified as the secret name for the deity Dorje Pokham Kyong. According to various descriptions she is either black or cherry-brown in colour with gold and turquoise head ornaments, holding a vessel of blood or a divination arrow and chest. She rides a horse with a turquoise mane, or a garuda.

The site at the present time shows few signs of repair. There is a small pilgrim's resthouse consisting of a single room, beside which a large prayer flag has been erected.

Mount Namchak Barwa

The Pepung La pass above Pungkar, the Dozhong La pass (4,115m) above Pe township, and the Nam La pass (5,225m) above Kyilkar all give access to the hidden valley of **Pemako** in Metok county (see below, page 477).

The motorable road on the S bank of the Brahmaputra comes to an end at Kyilkar, but a 3-day trekking route continues on to **Gyala**, via Tripe, which is the base camp for **Mt Namchak Barwa** (7,756m), and Lungpe. The **Nambulung** valley before Tripe also leads to Mt Namchak Barwa, and it is revered as an abode of the epic hero Ling Gesar. This mountain is the highest peak of the E Himalayas; and it has a towering snow pinnacle shaped like a ritual dagger (*phurba*), for which reason it is known as 'blazing meteorite' (*namchak barwa*) in as much as the best ritual daggers are made of meteorite. Sanctified as a repository of *terma* – some of which were discovered by Sangye Lingpa (1340-96) and others by Dudul Dorje (1615-72), the mountain remained unclimbed until a Japanese expedition of 1992 astonishingly scaled its snow pinnacle.

Gyala Shinje Badong

Gyala village is situated on a plain above the river. Its approach entails a tough climb up the Tsalung cliff-face. The white sands of the river bank below Gyala offer an attractive camp site. Here the river is navigable, and on the far bank, at **Gyala Shinje Badong**, there is the **Dampa Chokhang** temple, dedicated to Yama Dharmaraja, the 'lord of death' (*Tib* Shinje Chogyel), which contains an image of Padmasambhava. Alongside the derelict temple there are five rocks shaped like banners with water streaming down between them.

Behind the waterfalls, a rock image of Yama in either black or white form is visible during the spring and autumn when the river level is at its lowest. Here, the *terton* Sangye Lingpa discovered his Yamantaka texts, entitled *Yamantaka Lord of Life (Shinje Tsedak)*.

ACCESS The cave and its adjacent temple can be reached by dug-out log boat. From the N bank, at **Pe Nub** village, the 2-day Bonpo pilgrimage circuit of Mt Gyala Pelri (7,151m) begins.

The Brahmaputra Gorges

During the winter when the Brahmaputra is at its lowest level it is possible to undertake the extremely difficult 5-day trek to **Pemakochung**, following the course of the surging rapids through one of the world's deepest gorges, formed by the Namchak Barwa and Gyala Pelri massives, which are only 21 km apart. Within a contorted stretch of 45 km, the river plunges 3,000m to the Pemako foothills and the Indian plains beyond.

The trail passes the hot springs of Kenda-chu, the Gotsangpa Drupuk, the Nyuksang cliff, and the Senge Dzong cliff. Before Pemakochung, the trail hugs the river bank (winter access only), and passes the **Kinthup Falls**. At Pemakochung itself, there is a small Nyingmapa monastery. 2 days further trekking downstream is the **Drakpuk Kawasum Cave**, repository of the key and gateway to the 'hidden valley' of Pemako. Beyond this point, the virtually impenetrable trail follows the river's course as it is propelled N via a series of mighty cascades, including the **Rainbow Falls**. The region is sparsely inhabited by Lhopa peoples. Crossing Sordem La pass and Karma La pass (2,560m), it eventually reaches **Tongdem**, where the river converges with the Po Tsangpo in Po-me county (see below, page 475).

NYANGTRI COUNTY
林芝县 Nyingchi
Population: 25,158   Area: 9,634 sq km

Kongpo is the name given to the Nyang-chu River valley and the area of the Brahmaputra into which it flows, extending from the high Mamzhong La pass (5,000m) W of Gyamda to Menling in the SW and the massive snow peaks of Namchak Barwa and Gyala Pelri in the SE. It may for practical purposes be divided into three areas: **Lower Kongpo** includes the sites on the S bank of the Brahmaputra, from Menling to Pemakochung, which have already been described. **Middle Kongpo** includes the sites on the N bank of the Brahmaputra and the Nyang-chu River and its estuary below Bepa; and **Upper Kongpo** includes the upper reaches of the Nyang-chu from Bepa to Mamzhong La and Kongpo Bar La passes. Middle Kongpo corresponds to present day Nyangtri county, and Upper Kongpo to Gyamda county.

The capital of Nyangtri county (nowadays mispronounced and misspelt Nyingtri) was formerly located at **Nyangtri**, a small town on the E bank of

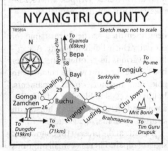

NYANGTRI COUNTY

Sketch map: not to scale

To Gyamda (69km)
Bepa
To Po-me
Bayi
Tongjuk
Serkhyim La
Lamaling
Buchu
Gomga Zamchen
Nyangtri
Chu Jowo
Luding
Mnt Bonri
Brahmaputra
To Dungdor (19km)
To Pe (71km)
To Tim Guru Drupuk

the Nyang-chu estuary, but its role has in recent years been increasingly usurped by the city of **Bayi**, 19 km to the N. As its name suggests, **Bayi** (1st Aug, ie Chinese Army Day) was originally a military base, which has undergone rapid development and is now the preferred settlement for Chinese immigrants, since it is considerably lower than Lhasa and has a pleasant climate. Bayi is now the capital of the recently formed Nyangtri District, which includes the seven counties of Menling, Nyangtri, Gyamda, Nang, Metok, Pome and Dzayul. From Dungdor (Menling Dzong) to Bayi via the Gangka Zamchen bridge the distance is 74 km.

ACCESS From Lhasa to Bayi via Gyamda the distance is 476 km; from Bayi to Nyangtri 19 km; and from Bayi to Pome 226 km.

MIDDLE KONGPO

Buchu Sergyi Lhakhang

Driving across Gangka Zamchen bridge from Dungdor (Menling),

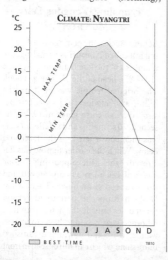

°C
CLIMATE: NYANGTRI
25
20
15
MAX TEMP
10
MIN TEMP
5
0
-5
-10
-15
-20
J F M A M J J A S O N D
☐ BEST TIME

Buchu township, on the W side of the Nyang-chu estuary, will be reached after 26 km.

The golden roof of **Buchu Sergyi Lhakhang** is visible from afar, on the E side of the 3 km wide estuary at Nyangtri, and on the S bank of the Brahmaputra, near Chemnak. This is the most ancient Buddhist shrine in Kongpo and one of four 'border taming' temples (Tadul Lhakhang) built by King Songtsen Gampo in the 7th century. It was constructed according to geomantic theory on the right elbow of the ogress who represented the Tibetan landscape. Originally therefore the temple was associated with the Nyingma tradition. By the 17th century however three schools of Buddhism had developed a strong presence in Buchu valley, namely the Drukpa Kagyu at Do Chorten, the Nyingmapa at Dechenteng, and the Gelukpa at Buchu Sergyi Lhakhang itself; for the temple was adopted by the Gelukpa in the time of the regent Demo Rinpoche (r 1886-95). Once there were only eight monks based in Buchu.

The temple has two storeys, surmounted by a golden roof. On the lower level, it formerly contained images of the Eight Manifestations of Padmasambhava and upstairs were eight images of Amitayus. These latter have not yet been restored, and of the eight manifestations, only the lower part of the large Padmasambhava survives with mantra-core (*zungjuk*) intact.

The outer structure of the building was protected in the 1960s when it was used as a granary. Around the outer walls are 50 prayer wheels. Within the gates, there is a courtyard with a small flower garden and an incense burner. An **antechamber** contains inscriptions on the left and right entrances, outlining the history of the temple, and murals depicting Shridevi and Dorje Lekpa (left), Damchen Karnak, Kongtsun Demo, and the Wheel of Rebirth (right), and the Four Guardian Kings (front). On the

The Zangdok Pelri Temple at Lamaling

right side there is also a large prayer wheel.

Beyond the antechamber, there are two main halls. The 2-pillared **outer hall** contains the volumes of the *Kangyur* and *Tangyur*, a magnificent but rarely seen image of Padmasambhava in the standing form called Pema Totrengtsal (right side), smaller images of Amitabha and White Tara (left side), the protectors Dorje Lekpa and Kongtsun Demo, and 1,000 small images of Shakyamuni Buddha. In a glass case to the left of these there is the 'life-supporting stone' (*lado*) of the oathbound protector of the temple. It has a hole, reputedly pierced in former times by Padmasambhava's ritual dagger.

The **inner hall** contains images of Padmasambhava, Shantaraksita and King Trisong Detsen, and (flanking the altar), images of Songtsen Gampo and Mahakarunika. Behind the main altar on a circumambulatory path is a 'self-arising' *terma* stone (*rangjung terdo*), dating from the era of King Songtsen Gampo. It has a hole in the middle and is now used as a butter-lamp offering. The rear wall has small images of the Thousand Buddhas; and in the right corner, adjacent to the door, is a finely decorated *torma*-offering shrine.

Lamaling (Zangdok Pelri Monastery)

Behind Buchu on the ridge of a low-lying hill called **Norburi** is Lamaling, the main seat of the late Dudjom Rinpoche (1904-87), head of the Nyingma school. The original temple was built on the hilltop in Zangdok Pelri style, but destroyed by an earthquake in 1930. The second, 20 sq metres and smaller in size, was then constructed on the tableland below. When the earlier temple was destroyed, the 'life-supporting' stone (*lado*) of Buchu reputedly moved and this was seen as an omen. Then, when Dudjom Rinpoche performed certain ceremonies outside the new building, a 3-horned goat is said to have appeared, wandered up and down, and vanished into a stone, which can still be seen in front

DRIME KUNDEN: THE COMPASSIONATE PRINCE

Prince Vasantara (Drime Kunden), as recounted in a sutra and in a later opera bearing his name, was an emanation of Avalokiteshvara sent into exile by his father for giving a precious gemstone to an enemy. In the course of his wanderings, Drime Kunden reputedly lived for 12 years in a hermitage behind the waterfall, formed of his own tears. When Drime Kunden first arrived in Kongpo a yogin emerged from the woods and asked whence he had come. He answered, saying he had been sent there by his father. The yogin recognized him and asked him to stay.

As a bodhisattva, he tamed the wild tigers and bears which previously ate stray humans and he made them respect human life. After 12 years he gave his final teaching to the beasts, saying that as long as they were to practice loving kindness and compassion his presence or absence would make no difference.

of the ruined temple. The new temple was destroyed during the 60s. In 1987, its ruined walls still bore the fingerprints of Dudjom Rinpoche's son Dorje Pasang, who was killed at that time.

The only extant original image from Lamaling is of Mahottara Heruka. It is kept along with a stone footprint of Padmasambhava. A Dorje Trolo stupa was erected to the W of the ruined temple walls in 1987; and since 1989, restoration began in earnest under the supervision of Dudjom Rinpoche's daughter Semo Dechen and her husband, Lama Chonyi Rinpoche. An exquisite **Zangdok Pelri Temple** and garden complex has been newly constructed on the hillside, and a motorable road now links Lamaling with the Buchu valley below. The new images of Lamaling represent the best metal casting tradition of the artisans from Chamdo.

Dechenteng Monastery

Southwest of Lamaling in the direction of Drime Kunden, and separated from it by a small evergreen forest is a branch monastery of Mindroling, called **Dechenteng**. The site was donated by Mindroling to the late Dudjom Rinpoche, and was used by him as the venue for an important series of empowerments (*Rinchen Terdzo*) on one occasion. As in the case of Lamaling, the original

structure was destroyed by the 1930 earthquake, and then replaced by a smaller building. At present the site is overgrown by incarvelia flowers and walnut trees.

Chokhorling Monastery

Southwest of Lamaling and below the abode of Drime Kunden are the ruins of two monasteries bearing the name of Chokhorling; one is Nyingma, the other known as **Ganden Chokhorling** is a branch of Sera. The latter, a 19th century temple founded by Nyiden Loyang, formerly had 100 monks. Huge tangkas were once hung out from the temple walls during religious dance performances. Now its ruined walls have magnificent frescoes of the Buddhas of the Three Times and a Wheel of Rebirth, which survived despite their exposure to the elements.

Drime Kunden Hermitage

Above Chokhorling is a beautiful waterfall concealing the Kongpo retreat of the legendary compassionate prince Vasantara (Drime Kunden).

On the ascent to the waterfall and hermitage, you pass many important sites. The rocks and groves are identified with major events in the life of Drime Kunden. Ascending from Chokhorling one first passes his protector shrine, a bank of rhododendron flowers, and a series of his footprints, handprints and knee-prints in stone. Higher up the hillside, there is a spring, the water of which he brought forth when Ma Khandro offered him ale to drink. The water is said to benefit the eyesight, the significance lying in the legend that Drime Kunden's own sight was restored after he had offered up his own eyes. The waterfall itself is said to benefit bathers to the extent of an empowerment ceremony received by 108 monks. Above the waterfall is the hermitage of Drime Kunden's wife, Tsampo Mendrel Tsema. It comprises a dakinis' dancing platform and a cave where pregnant women go to find omens. If the cave closes behind them, remedies have to be applied to avoid stillbirth or miscarriage and perhaps the mother's death.

In the **main hermitage** is a footprint of Drime Kunden covered by a stone. It also contains a tangka of White Tara which, when regarded purely without clinging, enables one to see the deity rather than the tangka. During each 4th month a fasting ceremony is held here. Opposite this hermitage is the residence of the protector, Chokyong Jarok Dongchen, and a 'self-arising' rock shaped like the *kalantaka* bird which

would bring messages from Drime Kunden's parents. Above the hermitage, the circumambulation of the Pabri mountain (4,350m) is said to have the same blessing as 10 million recitations of the *Vajra Guru* mantra.

In a clearing, on the descent, is a stupa below which there is a footprint and imprint of the seat where Drime Kunden would teach birds and wild beasts. The tree above the seat served as a canopy at that time. Nearby there are also the elbow-prints and handprints of his wife, who waited for him during this final teaching.

From Chokhorling and Drime Kunden, the road leads down to the village of **Karma**, near the ruins of **Tsela Dzong** (2,955m), and the main road to Dungdor (Menling). From Karma, there is also a coracle ferry to Chukhor on the E side of the Nyang-chu estuary, and to Chemnak on the S bank of the Brahmaputra.

Bayi

Following the road from Buchu along the W bank of the Nyang-chu for 29 km, you will reach Bayi. The village of **Drakchi**, which once occupied this strategic site, has been completely absorbed by the recent urban development. The current

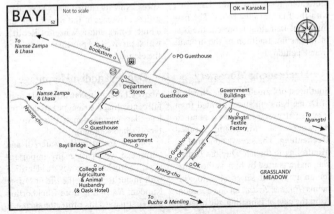

population, largely Chinese, exceeds 25,000. Here, the **Bayi Zamchen** bridge spans the Nyang-chu River.

Orientation

Approaching the town, before the bridge, you will pass the College of Agriculture and Animal Husbandry (Zhingdrok Lobdra) on the left. This complex contains the *Oasis Hotel*. A temple under the supervision of Tibet's great historian, Dungkar Lobzang Trinle, is nearby.

Crossing the long bridge, you then enter the main part of town on the E bank of the Nyang-chu. The main roads of Bayi form a grid pattern, with two N-S streets intersected by two E-W streets. The N-S street immediately across the bridge has a number of small general stores, several Sichuan restaurants, a cinema and several late-night karaoke establishments.

Two streets branch off this road, the first leading E towards an intersection with the main Lhasa-Nyangtri road. At that intersection there is the 4-storeyed *Government Guesthouse*. The second turn-off leads E into the main commercial street. Continuing along this commercial thoroughfare, you reach the town's major crossroads, where there is a large roundabout. The Government Buildings and the Bus Station are to the S, the Post Office and Xinhua Bookstore are on the E, and a high-rise modern department store with large display windows is on the E. Electrical goods are available here. From this crossroad, the main road to Lhasa (476 km) runs N, passing the *Government Guesthouse* on the left, and the main road to Nyangtri (19 km) runs S, passing the Nyangtri Textile Factory on the right.

Excursions

A short distance E of Bayi town is **Mount Pelri**, a sacred peak from whose summit Padmasambhava reputedly dried up a lake covering the valley below, to ensure the region's future habitation. Pilgrims circumambulate the mountain in 2-3 hrs, paying their respects to Padmasambhava's rock handprint, kneeprint, as well as a stupa dedicated to Phakmodrupa Dorje Gyelpo.

● **Accommodation** *Oasis Hotel*, (¥45 pp), best and most comfortable accommodation in town, hot water is available in the washrooms, and there is a student cafeteria open to hotel guests; *Government Guesthouse*, Lhasa-Nyangtri Rd, best rooms ¥65, privately owned guesthouse and *Post Office Guesthouse* just off Commercial St.

● **Places to eat** There are a number of Sichuan restaurants nr the bridge fronted by waitresses who seductively and competitively flaunt their cuisine. Restaurants and coffee shops can also be found on Commercial St.

● **Entertainment** Cinema and karaoke.

● **Transport** The bus station is located to the S of the roundabout on the Lhasa-Nyangtri road.

Nyangtri

The old county capital stands below Bonri, the sacred Bon mountain of Kongpo, at the E estuary of the Nyang-chu River, 19 km S of Bayi. The streets of Nyangtri form a T-junction: the main road to Po-me and Chamdo, turning E to ascend the Serkhyim La pass, and the S road following the riverside to Luding, and then following the Brahmaputra downstream on the N bank. Towards the

NW of town, at **Kushuk Drong**, there is a 2,000-year-old juniper tree, sacred to the Bonpo, which is protected within a walled enclosure.

• **Facilities** The bus station and guesthouse compound are beyond the intersection, on the S road out of town. Nearby are small restaurants and teashops. The government buildings, public security bureau, and larger shops are all situated further N, close to the main intersection.

Sigyel Gonchen

The Bonpo monastery of Sigyel Gon-

KARAOKE: THE END OF TIBETAN SONGS?

Walking through the streets of any town or city in Tibet during the evening, look out for the neon lights flashing above a darkened doorway, and you will have found the local karaoke parlour. Often the legend **OK** boldly pulsates above the entrance. Thopere are upmarket and downmarket sorts, but one thing is certain: the remarkable pervasiveness of this popular Asian pastime has taken hold even in the most remote places in Tibet over the last five years. The large expensive establishments often have spacious dance floors, fluorescent strobe lighting, multicoloured smoke effects, and disco or live Chinese pop and dance music interspersed with the actual karaoke. The disco formation dance known as "thirty-six" (_Ch_ sansi-liu), in which a large group of dancers pirouette in unison is always popular. The big moment comes when some budding impresario orders and pays for a requested song, and then takes the floor, microphone in hand to croon the latest number from Taipei, Hong Kong or mainland China, or perhaps a long-standing favourite. A good turn is rewarded by generous applause and the gift of a scented artificial flower. Tibetans often surpass the Chinese immigrants in their renditions of these Chinese songs, and couples take to the dance floor, accompanying the soloist. The karaoke repertoire includes a few pleasant duets; but, alas, no Tibetan music. In fact, there is a danger that traditional Tibetan singing which still has great popularity will be eclipsed by this all-powerful medium. Some speculate that the plain-clothed public security policemen intentionally run the show, and it is true that in this environment many of them become the most congenial of drinking companions. The best hope for Tibetan popular song at this juncture is that the karaoke medium can be adapted to the advantage of the Tibetans as well as for the promotion of popular Chinese culture. Sometimes in the small hours of the morning, the Tibetans will switch off the big wall screen, and take the microphone to sing impromptu Tibetan songs. Everyone will join in, including the secret policemen and their girlfriends!

The downmarket places can often be found beside truck stops or military barracks. To enter is to experience the seedy side of life in Tibet.

Drinking is an important element of this popular culture, and some groups of revellers will often carry crates of green-bottled Chinese or Tibetan beer into the karaoke bar. A bucket of cold water may be placed on the floor for refridgeration! As the evening wears on, even the most secret of policemen will loosen up and reveal all! On the other hand, drunkenness can lead to flashpoints of violence; and macho Khampa men may be quick on the draw with their long ornate knives! Brawling between rival groups has been known to close down certain establishments not long after their opening.

Apart from karaoke clubs, the small towns also have a number of exceedingly boring Chinese video parlours, and a large number of pool tables or even electronic gambling machines.

chen, approached via a turn-off on the left below Nyangtri, is a major pilgrimage attraction for the Bonpo adherents of Khyungpo Tengchen and Hor. Founded in the 14th century by Kuchok Rikpa Druk-se, it once housed 100 monks.

Taktse Yungdrungling Monastery

The motor road passes through Taktse township, above which is another Bon monastery known as Yungdrungling. Originally founded by a Bonpo from Amdo named Dongom Tenpa Lhundrub, it has recently undergone limited reconstruction, and is popular with Bonpo pilgrims from Ngawa and other parts of Amdo. There are precious relics housed here, including a tooth relic of Shenrab Miwoche, founder of the Bon religion.

Mijik Tri Durtro

This Bonpo burial ground, believed to contain the tumulus of Tibet's first mortal king, Drigum Tsenpo, lies a short distance N of Luding at the confluence of the Nyang-chu and Brahmaputra rivers. Bon literary sources refer to this tomb as **Gyangto Labub**, and there are many dire prophecies pertaining to its subsidence, as it appears over time to have moved closer to the river bank! From Luding there is a ferry crossing to the S bank of the river; and slightly further, at Drena (on the N bank), there is the place where King Drigum Tsenpo's funeral was conducted, in the shadows of **Mt Lhari Gyangto**. At Yungdrung Dzin village, there is a 9th century obelisk, with an inscription recounting the affinity which King Drigum Tsenpo's sons had with the local divinity of Mt Lhari Gyangto.

Chu Jowo Temple

Slightly E of the confluence, on the N bank of the Brahmaputra, stands the temple of Chu Jowo. This contains a relief image of Jowo Rinpoche in the guise of Four-armed Avalokiteshvara. In this form, Jowo Rinpoche, Tibet's most sacred image contained in the Lhasa Jokhang, is said to have appeared in the Brahmaputra River, honouring a pledge he had made to Kongpo Ben, a devout shoemaker from Kongpo while on a previous pilgrimage to Lhasa. Before returning to Lhasa, Jowo Rinpoche vanished into a stone, taking on the form of the relief image which is revered today. The place where the image is said to have appeared in the river is close by the present temple. The site was restored through local patronage in 1985.

Mount Bonri

Mount Bonri is the highest of the three sacred Bonpo peaks on the N bank of the Brahmaputra (Muri is further W and Mt Lhari Gyangto SW). Bonpo pilgrims from all parts of Tibet circumvent the slopes of Bonri, particularly during the winter months. Starting at Menri township (41 km from Nyangtri), where there are guesthouse facilities and shops, the 3-day trek passes to the left of the Demo valley. Here are the ruins of **Demo Chemkar** monastery, a Gelukpa monastery, which was once the residence of Tibet's regent Demo Tupten Jigme (r 1810-17). The route towards Bonri La (4,540m) passes many sites associated with Shenrab and his epic struggle against the demon Kyapa Lagring; as well as the sacred tree, **Sembon Dungshing**, which has been revered as a cemetery for babies since its consecration by Kuchok Ripa Druk-se in 1330. The summit is said to have a stone footprint of Tibet's first king Nyatri Tsenpo. The descent from the pass leads via Zhabchin Dong and Darbong to Nyangtri.

Rong chu Valley

From Nyangtri, the highway to E Tibet ascends for 32 km and then cuts across the Serkhyem La pass, to enter the north-flowing **Rong-chu valley**. This valley, which is renowned for its poppies, giant rhubarb, and other diverse species of flora, can also be reached by trekking from Tim Guru Drupuk via the Nyima La (see above, page 296). From Serkhyem La pass to Tongjuk township the distance is 46 km. En route you pass through a logging centre at **Lunang**, and **Chu Nyima**, the traditional border between Kongpo and Powo regions. For a detailed description of the route from here to Chamdo in E Tibet via Powo and Pasho, see below, page 494.

Bepa

The road N from Bayi follows the Nyang-chu upstream, passing large well-established military camps and installations on both sides of the road. The rushing waters of the Nyang-chu, flanked by beautiful conifer forests on both banks, ranks among the most memorable sights in Tibet. Pristine streams surge down to swell the river, among them the Zha-chu and Nezhi-chu, which converge at **Nezhi**. At **Bepa** township, 58 km from Bayi, you reach the border between Nyangtri and Gyamda counties, and thence enter into Upper Kongpo.

GYAMDA COUNTY

རྒྱ་མདའ

工布江达县 Gongbogyamda

Population: 12,593   Area: 14,467 sq km

This is an area of stunning natural beauty: verdant alpine forests and clear running streams abound, and there are incredible lakes, epitomized by the island lake of **Draksum Tso**. Upper Kongpo extends from the **Nangsel Zampa** bridge where the Nyang-chu River merges with its Drak-chu tributary, NW of Bepa township, as far as the **Mamzhong La pass** (5,000m), which forms the watershed between the Meldro and Nyang-chu rivers. The county capital is located at **Ngapo Zampa** (Kongpo Gyamda), 127 km N of Bayi, and 206 km NE of Lhasa. Other feeder rivers swell the river's current, notably the Banang-chu (which flows N through Drongsar township), and the Pe-chu (which flows NE through Gyazhing township).

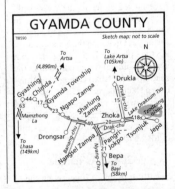

GYAMDA COUNTY

Sketch map: not to scale

TIB590

UPPER KONGPO

Pangri Jokpo Hermitage

Driving N from Bepa township, you will notice on the right the 15m high stone defense towers, which are found in many parts of Upper Kongpo. At Nangsel Zampa bridge, 21 km from Bepa, the valley of the Drak-chu abuts the Nyang-chu valley from the NE. Turn right along a dirt track before crossing the bridge, and you will shortly reach the path leading to the ridge-top Pangri Jokpo hermitage.

A steep 2 hrs' climb through barley fields, shrubbery and forested slopes brings you to a clearing below this isolated tranquil retreat, founded by the *terton* Jatson Nyingpo (1585-1656). The hermitage, which for many years has been tended by two elderly female hermits from Nangchen, comprises a **Mani Lhakhang** and the **main temple**, built against the rock walls. The temple is exceptionally well lit through its NW facing glass windows, and the views it offers of the Nyang-chu valley below are suggestive of Swiss or Austrian landscapes. The temple has both outer and inner chapels. The former contains images of Padmasambhava, Guru Drakpo, and Simhavaktra – a trio renowned as the *Union of All Rare and Precious Things (Konchok Chidu)*, described in *terma* texts revealed by Jatson Nyingpo himself. The liturgies of these texts are popular throughout both the Nyingma and Kagyu traditions. Alongside these images, to the right is a bass-relief image of Jatson Nyingpo, with a longevity-arrow (*dadar*), which is claimed to have been his personal possession. *Prajna-paramita* texts and small images of Padmasambhava are in the background. The **inner chapel** contains images of Ling Gesar (in peaceful and wrathful forms), and of Avalokiteshvara (twice), and Shakyamuni Buddha. An **inner sanctum** contains 1,000 small images of Padmasambhava.

Jatson Nyingpo passed away at Pangri Jokpo. His birthplace at **Waru Namtsul** is on the opposite side of the valley.

Lake Draksum Tso

Returning to the Nangsel Zampa bridge, cross over, and take the right turn-off (on the N bank of the Drak-chu River). The road leads to **Zhoka** township (20 km), near the ruins of the old Zhoka Dzong. En route, you will pass on the left **Len** village, noted for its 12-cornered defence towers. These ancient fortifications, which resemble those of Lhodrak (see above, page 273) and Gyarong (see below, page 626), are said to have been made by demons headed by Ling Gesar's enemy Dud Achung Gyelpo in the remote past.

At **Zhoka**, there is a hydroelectric power station and a small market. Two roads diverge here, the N route leading to **Drukla** township, following the Drukla-chu upstream, and the E route, following the Draksum-chu upstream to the lake which is its source. Take the latter, and cross the **Zhoka Zampa** bridge. The road now passes through a disused but somewhat surreal complex of telecommunication and remote tracking systems (one motorable trail leads through a fenced perimeter directly towards a hewn-out mountainside bunker!).

Continue to follow the river upstream for 18 km to **Tsomjuk**, where a bridge crosses it at the point where it exits from the lake. At **Jepa**, on the S side of the lake, the road ends at a newly constructed series of log cabins, owned by the local Tsomgo Tourist Bureau. Large applique Tibetan tents dot this idyllic campsite. Below you have a wonderful view of the jade-green lake, 16 km long by 3 km wide, girded by steep forested slopes, and with the Tsodzong Island (3,600m) positioned like a pearl at its centre. The flat-bottomed ferry boat is drawn across to the island by an overhead cable.

Tsodzong Island

The temple on Tsodzong Island is the birthplace of the *terton* Sangye Lingpa (1340-96), although there are earlier associations with Padmasambhava and King Trisong Detsen. In the early years of the 20th century, the complex was refurbished by the late Dudjom Rinpoche (1904-87); and is now undergoing further renovation, following its destruction during the 1960s. Konchok Tsering is sponsoring the project, under the guidance of Dudjom Rinpoche's daughter, Semo Dechen, and her husband Chonyi Rinpoche of Lamaling. The present caretakers, Neten and Atsang, are practitioners of the Dudjom lineage.

The main image of the temple depicts Guru Drakpo. Its head was originally brought to the island by Sangye Lingpa, riding a tigress which left its paw marks among the rocks to the W of the island. Other images depict Padmasambhava, Shakyamuni Buddha, Avalokiteshvara, and the protectress Kongtsun Demo. There is also a 'self-manifesting' stone letter A, as described in Jatson Nyingpo's own *terma*. The caretakers' house holds other treasures: a royal seal of King Songtsen Gampo, the bowls used by Sangye Lingpa and the late Dudjom Rinpoche, and a precious manuscript said to be in Jatson Nyingpo's own handwriting.

The pilgrim's circuit of the island begins with this temple, and then moves clockwise, passing the hermitage of Dudjom Rinpoche, a rock from the Shitavana charnel ground, the body imprint of Ling Gesar, the stone paw of the tigress, the stone prints of Sangye Lingpa (**all on W side**); the 'life-supporting' tree (*lashing*) of the demon Dud Achung Gyelpo which was cut down by Gesar's golden axe, a treasury belonging to the Karmapa, a tree associated with Ma Khandro, the consort of Drime Kunden (see above, page 301) which has leaves naturally inscribed with seed-syllables and animal year-signs (**all on N**

side); a stone snake which has associations with Ling Gesar, and the Tashi Obar stupa, under which is a nectar stream (**all on E side**). Finally, a white stone represents the mistress of the lake, Tsomen Gyelmo (**S side**).

Beyond the far shore of the lake, there are four prominant snow peaks: Mt Ama Jomo Taktse (5,963m) to the NW, Mt Namla Karpo (6,750m) to the N, Mt Naphu Gomri (5,663m) to the NE, and Mt Darchenri to the E. These sites also have associations with Ling Gesar.

Pilgrim's circuit

There is a 2-day pilgrims' circuit around the lake, commencing from the bridge of **Tsomjuk** and passing by the ruined Gelukpa monastery of **Pibang**, the Vajravarahi cave, the two glacial feeder rivers on the lake's E side (Ortse-chu and Nangu-chu), the ruined Kagyupa monastery of **Darchenri**, and **Tsomgo** township, at the head of the lake. Near the **Jepa** campsite on the S side, there is another glacial feeder river, known as the Penam-chu.

Returning to Zhoka, if you take the N turn-off, you will reach **Drukla** township after 15 km. Here there are more ancient defence towers and the ruins of the **Drukla Monastery**. A trekking route leads further N, for 105 km to join the old Lhasa-Chamdo caravan highway near Lake Atsa (see below, page 450).

Gyamda Town (Ngapo Zampa)

Returning to Nangsel Zampa bridge, turn right, and follow the main highway W along the course of the Nyang-chu. After 40 km, you will pass the **Sharlung Zampa** bridge at Sharlung township, where the Banang-chu tributary flows into the Nyang-chu from the S. There is a side-road from here leading S to **Drongsar**.

8 km further along the main highway, you will reach the county capital, known as **Ngapo Zampa** (Kongpo Gyamda; *alt* 3,200m). This is a small

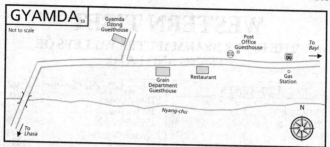

town comprising one main street reached via bridges at its W and E ends.

Above the town of Gyamda is the monastery of **Neu Dechen Gon**, associated with the late Dudjom Rinpoche's teachings on Vajrakila. In a nearby mountain-hermitage are the **Tselha Namsum** meditation caves, associated with the female yogini Machik Labdron.

• **Facilities** *Gyamda Dzong Guesthouse* (¥8/bed) and the *Post Office Guesthouse* (Yigzam Dronkhang, ¥8/bed) are both on the N side of the main street, W of the Bus Station. The *Grain Department Guesthouse* (Drurik Lekhung Dronkhang, ¥15/bed) is on the S side of the main street, W of the Petrol Station. There are a number of good and inexpensive Sichuan restaurants.

Gyamda Township and the Chamdo Caravan Trail

23 km NW of Ngapo Zampa, the road passes through Gyamda township, formerly known as **Gyamda Dzong**. From here, there is a 4-day trek following the headwaters of the Nyang-chu through **Nyangpo** district and across Tro La pass (4,890m) to **Artsa**, where a motorable dirt road leads NW to Nakchu and SE down the Yi'ong Tsangpo valley. This latter route follows the old caravan trail from Lhasa to Chamdo (see below, page 450), which commenced at Gyamda Dzong.

Nyang-chu Headwaters

Beyond Gyamda township the highway continues to **Chimda** (17 km), where Padmasambhava's student Nyak Jananakumara once fled from violent assailants, and where, later, in the 14th century Sangye Lingpa discovered *terma* pertaining to the cycles of wrathful mantras. The road continues from there to **Gyazhing** township (44 km) and eventually, after a further 63 km, to the watershed pass of **Mamzhong La** (5,000m). Near the pass, 13 km after Gyazhing, the road diverges from the main river. (A trekking trail leads upstream to Azhang Kongla pass and thence to Dakpo.) From the watershed to Lhasa via Meldro Gungkar and Taktse counties, the distance is 149 km.

WESTERN TIBET
THE UPPER BRAHMAPUTRA VALLEYS OF TSANG AND LATO

INTRODUCTION

Western Tibet is the region demarcated by the Upper Brahmaputra (*Tib* Yarlung Tsangpo) valley, extending upstream from its confluence with the Kyi-chu River, as far as the headwaters in Drongpa county (E of Mt Kailash). Separated on the S from Nepal, Sikkim and W Bhutan by the high Himalayan range, and separated on the N from the Jangtang Plateau by the Gangtise and Nyenchen Tanglha ranges, this region includes the traditional provinces of **Tsang** and **Lato**. As such, it embraces the lateral valleys adjoining the Brahmaputra on both its north and south banks, the valleys of the south-flowing Gangetic tributaries which traverse Nepal, and those of the south-flowing Brahmaputra tributaries which traverse Sikkim and W Bhutan.

The distance from Lhasa to Zhigatse is: 281 km via Nyemo and Chakdam; 348 km via Gampa La pass and Gyantse; 338 km via Yangpachen and Zhugu La pass. **Recommended Itineraries**: 1, 2.

NYEMO COUNTY

སྙེ་མོ

尼木县 Nyemo

Population: 14,462   Area: 2,077 sq km

The county of **Nyemo** extends from the upper reaches of the Lhorong-chu in the N, across the watershed formed by the snow peaks of **Jomo Gangtse** (7,048m) and **Kumalungpa Gangri** (5,858m), and through the fertile valleys of the Nyemo Ma-chu and its tributaries, the Zhu-chu and Phakpu-chu. The county capital is located at **Dardrong**, where the Nyemo Ma-chu and Zhu-chu rivers converge.

ACCESS There are two motorable routes into Dardrong: one from Markyang township (50 km) on the northern Lhasa-Zhigatse highway and another from Ton township (25 km) on the central Lhasa-Zhigatse highway.

NYEMO COUNTY

510

Zhugu La (5,454m)

Zhuguu La — To Yangpachen (56 km)

Jomo Gangtse (7,048m)

30

Markyang   Kumalungpa Gangri (5,858m)   Gyedar   To Yangpachen

7

Senshang

To Oyuk

Phakpu-chu

To Tsurphu

Zhu-chu

Zhagong La

Sagang

Jekhar

Angang   To Nakar

50   19

Brahmaputra

Nyemo Ma-chu

Dardrong   To Lhasa (57 km)

5   Ton

To Zhigatse (170 km)

20   Sa-me   Dagar

25

To Gyantse (206 km)

To Gongkar Airport (39 km)

Sketch map: not to scale

Trekking

Nyemo is a wonderful area for trekking in close proximity to Lhasa. There is a trail from **Dorjeling nunnery** near Yangpachen (see above, page 199), following the Lhorong-chu upstream via Gyedar and Yangyi, before crossing the Zhagong La pass into the Upper Zhu valley. Another trek from Tsurphu monastery links up with that trail at Gyedar; and a third leads from Nakar, S of Tsurphu, to Angang township in the Lower Zhu valley (see above).

Of all these the easiest point of access is via the central highway. Driving W from Chushul, you continue on the N bank of the Brahmaputra, passing the **Chushul Zamchen** bridgehead at **Dagar** (8 km), and the townships of Sa-me (25 km), and Ton (30 km), before reaching the turn-off for **Dardrong** at the mouth of the Nyemo Ma-chu (20 km). Dardrong is 5 km inland.

Nyemo Ma-chu valley

From **Dardrong**, a jeep track follows the Nyemo Ma-chu upstream for 50 km to **Markyang** on the northern Lhasa-Zhigatse highway. En route, you will pass through **Lhundrubgang** in Zangri township, which was once the base of an important Tibetan opera troupe. Following its amalgamation with the Jago troupe in neighbouring Zhu valley, it became renowned throughout Tibet as the **Nyemowa Opera Troupe**. Further upstream at **Jekhar** in Dragor (Pagor) township, where the Phakpu-chu converges with the Nyemo Ma-chu, there is the birthplace of **Vairotsana**, the greatest native of Nyemo, who ranks among Tibet's finest translators of the 8th century; and a foremost student of Padmasambhava. His footprint, impressed in rock at the age of eight, is said to be kept there as an object of veneration.

At Markyang on the northern highway, you can turn SW for **Oyuk** valley (see below, page 315) or NW, heading across

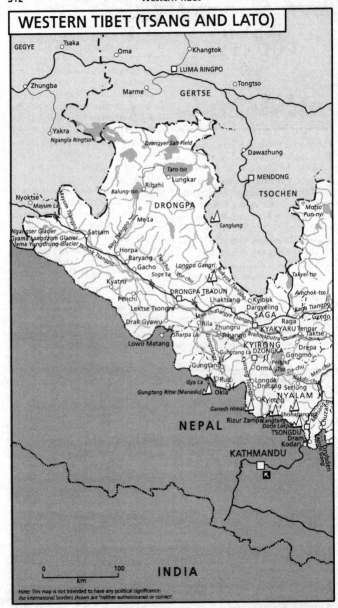

WESTERN TIBET (TSANG AND LATO)

GEGYE

Tsaka

Oma

Khangtok

Zhungba

☐ LUMA RINGPO

Marme

GERTSE

Tongtso

Yakra

Ngangla Ringtso

Drangyer Salt Field

Dawazhung

Taro-tso

☐ MENDONG

Nyoktse

Balung-tso

Ribzhi

Lungkar

TSOCHEN

Mayum Tsangpo

Mayum La

DRONGPA

Motso Pun-nyi

Me La

Sanglung

Ngangser Glacier

Gyama Langdzom Glacier

Jema Yungdrung Glacier

Satsam

Nu Tsangpo

Tachok Tsangpo

Horpa

Baryang

Longpo Gangri

Takyel-tso

Gacho

Soge La

Tsechu

Chukyot Tsangpo

Amchok-tso

Kyatru

Yur-chu

DRONGPA TRADUN

Lhaktsang

Kylbuk

Raga Tsangpo

Penchi

Dargyeling

SAGA

Gyedo

Lektse Tsongra

Men-chu

Dargye Sangpo

Rila

Raga

KYAKYARU

Tengar

Taktse

Drak Gyawu

Sharpa La

Zhungru

Trhango

Brahmaputra

Lowo Matang

Gungtang

KYIRONG

DZONGKA

Drepa

Gongmo

Gungtang La

Orma

Tso pa-chu

Nakdo-chu

Gungtang

Gya La

Rud

Kyirong Tsangpo

Longda

Drotang

Serlung

Men-chu

Gungtang Ritse (Manaslu)

Okla

NYALAM

Matsang Tsangpo

Kyirong

Ganesh Himal

Shishapangma

Dzuzang

Bhote Kosi

Rizur Zampa

Langtang

Dorje Lakpa

☐ TSONGDU

Dogubden Gung

NEPAL

Dram

Kodari

KATHMANDU

◻

◼

0   100

km

INDIA

Note: This map is not intended to have any political significance:
the international borders shown are 'neither authenticated or correct'.

THE BRAHMAPUTRA/YARLUNG TSANGPO RIVER

The **Brahmaputra** is one of Asia's major rivers, extending 2,900 km from its source in Far-west Tibet to its confluence with the Ganges in India. There are three head-streams: **Kabji**, **Angsi**, and **Tachok Khabab**, the last of which rises in the Jemayungdrung glacier 60 km SE of Lake Manasarovar. From their convergence these headwaters, known initially as the **Tachok Tsangpo** and later as the **Yarlung Tsangpo**, flow E for 1,127 km along the tectonic suture line. Then, after being forcibly channeled S through the awesome gorges between Mt Namchak Barwa and Mt Gyala Pelri, the river enters the Arunachal Pradesh province of India where it is known as the **Dihang**. In Assam it is joined by several Himalayan streams: the Lohit, Dibang, Subansiri, Kameng, Bhareli, Dhansiri, Manas, Champamati, Saralbhanga, and Sankosh. Lastly, in the Duars, it is joined by the Tista, before finally converging with the Ganges N of Goalundo Ghat.

In its upper reaches the river is navigable for 644 km from **Lhartse** eastwards, and there are coracles crossing the river at 3,962m.

The flora along the banks of the Upper Brahmaputra is confined to shrubbery, interspersed with dwarf willow and poplar trees. The true forests begin growing only in the mid-reaches, in **Dakpo** and **Kongpo**, where the climate is moister and warmer. In the SE, around **Po-me** and **Pemako**, coniferous forests cover the mountain slopes in thick areas. Conifers with an undergrowth of rhododendron grow at 3,000-4,000m; hemlock, spruce, and larch at 2,500-3,000m; pine trees at 1,500-2,500m; and tropical monsoon forest below 1,500m.

the high **Zhugu La** pass (5,454m) with its stupendous views of the Jomo Gangtse snows. Yangpachen in the Upper Tolung valley lies 56 km beyond Shogu La pass. If you take the Oyuk road, after 7 km you will pass through **Senshang** township. From here there is a long and arduous trekking route to **Lake Namtso** via the Kyangu La pass (5,769m) and Putserteng hamlet.

Nyemo Zhu valley

From Dardrong, a trail follows the Zhuchu upstream through a fertile valley to Angang township (19 km). Here are the ruins of **Zhu Kungarawa**, an 11th century Kadampa monastery founded by Ngok Lotsawa. At **Jago**, NE of Mt Gangri Pelkye (5,894m), there is the former home of Nyemo's second opera troupe, prior to its amalgamation with the troupe of Lhundrubgang (see above). From here there is a trekking route to Nakar near Tsurphu monastery (see above, page 311). Another trekking route leads from **Sagang** in the Upper Zhu valley across Zhagong La pass to Gyedar, where trails bifurcate for Yangpachen and Tsurphu.

NAMLING COUNTY

 རྣམ་གླིང་

南木林县 Namling
Population: 59,076   Area: 9,695 sq km

Namling is the current administrative name given to the valleys of **Oyuk**, **Tobgyel**, and **Shang**, which all have long and illustrious associations with both Buddhism and Bon. Through these valleys there respectively flow the Nang-gung-chu, Tobpu-chu, and Shang-chu rivers, with their various tributaries, which rise amid the southern slopes of the Nyenchen Tanglha range to the N, and flow southwards to converge with the Brahmaputra.

ACCESS The northern and central Lhasa-Zhigatse highways meet at **Trakdruka** on the S bank of the Brahmaputra, opposite Lower Oyuk. The former winds its way from Senshang across the Do-ngu La pass (4,846m) to Oyuk township and thence to Trakdruka ferry (65 km). The latter follows the N bank of the Brahmaputra upstream from Nyemo, via Dzongkar to the **Nub Khulung Zamchen** bridge in Lower Oyuk, after which it runs along the S bank to Tradruka (75 km). The Tobgyel and Shang valleys are both accessible by ferry crossings from the S bank of the river, the former at **Drakchik** ferry (19 km W of Tradruka) and the latter at **Tama** ferry (58 km W of Tradruka) or **Dongkar** ferry (at Zhigatse, 80 km W of Tradruka). The county capital is located at **Ringon** in the Shang valley.

OYUK VALLEY

Dingma Monastery

Descending from the Do-ngu La pass into Upper Oyuk, the northern Lhasa-Zhigatse highway enters the Nang-gung-chu valley. Below Rinchenling, 27 km after the pass, the Mang-chu tributary converges with the Nang-gung-chu at Domtang village. A trekking route to **Zabulung** in Upper Shang (see below, page 318) follows the **Mang-chu valley** NW via Rikdzom and Mangra township, and across the Mang La pass. Near the entrance to this valley you can see on a hill the remains of the ancient 11th century Kadampa monastery of **Dingma**, founded by Ram Dingma Deshek Jungne, a student of the Geshe

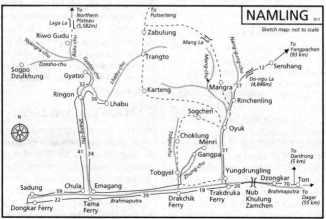

Potowa (1031-1105). At **Lukdong** in this vicinity there is also a meditation hermitage associated with Padmasambhava.

Oyuk Gongon Lhakhang

Oyuk township (Taktse) lies 7 km below the confluence of the Nang-gung-chu and Mang-chu rivers.

The principal shrine is the **Gongon Lhakhang**, which was reputedly constructed by King Songtsen Gampo as one of a series of peripheral geomantic temples. Some even classify it among the 'border-taming' temples. Later in the 8th century, the temple was frequented by Padmasambhava and his students, among them Namkei Nyingpo and King Trisong Detsen. The latter's personal weapons were once housed here.

● There are guesthouse facilities here.

Trekking
From Oyuk township, there are 3-day trekking routes, which lead SW via Sogchen township into the valley of the Tobpu-chu, or into that of its eastern tributary, where **Menri Monastery** is located (see below, page 317). A jeepable dirt road also leads NW to Karteng and the Shang Lhabu-chu valley (see below, page 317).

Oyuk Jara Gon

At **Jarasa** in Lower Oyuk, there is the abode or castle (Kukhar) of the protector deity Dorje Lekpa: guardian of the Dzogchen teachings. Here, at the hermitage called **Oyuk Chigong** or Oyuk Jara Gon, the great meditation master Chetsun Senge Wangchuk (10th-11th century) remained in retreat, and received the teachings of the *Innermost Spirituality of Vimalamitra* (*Bima Nyingthig*) in a vision from Vimalamitra. Some of these teachings he concealed and others he imparted to his foremost student, Zhangton (1097-1167). Eventually he passed into rainbow light at the age of 125! There are graphic descriptions in Tibetan literature of how Zhangton was assisted by the protector Dorje Lekpa in his efforts to rediscover the concealed teachings of the *Innermost Spirituality of Vimalamitra*. Later, in the 19th century, when Jamyang Khyentse Wangpo was on pilgrimage here from E Tibet, he recollected the teachings he had received in a past life (as Chetsun Senge Wangchuk) and redacted them into the teaching cycle now known as the *Innermost Spirituality of Chetsun* (*Chetsun Nyingthig*).

ROUTES Passing due S through the villages of Nubmalung and Tashigang, the road eventually reaches the Brahmaputra ferry crossing at Tradruka, 31 km S of Oyuk township.

Yungdrungling Monastery

Located above the E bank of the Nang-gung-chu near its confluence with the Brahmaputra, this is one of the most influential Bonpo monasteries in recent Tibetan history. Founded during the 19th century by Nangton Dawa Gyeltsen on the ridge of the holy Bonpo mountain, **Olha Gyel**. The complex had 700 monks prior to its destruction in 1959, but now there are scarcely more than 30. Amid the ruins of its assembly hall, residential buildings, hermitages and colleges, a few shrines have been reconstructed. The **Tongrol Lhakhang** contains the reconstructed reliquary of the monastery's founder; and murals depicting the Bonpo lineage-holders and ritual mandalas.

TOBGYEL VALLEY

Following the river upstream from its mouth, at **Tobgyel** township (Magada), the valley bifurcates: the W branch or Tobpu-chu leading upstream to Tshar, Choklung, the Gelukpa monastery of **Drungzhi**, and **Sogchen**. The E branch, or Zhung-chu, leads via Gangpa into a Bonpo stronghold.

Here are the celebrated Bonpo monasteries of Ensakha, Kharna, and Menri.

ACCESS The entrance to the **Tobgyel** valley may be approached by coracle from the **Drakchik** ferry (19 km W of Tradruka) on the S bank of the Brahmaputra, or by trekking – either along the N bank from Yungdrungling in Lower Oyuk, or via the Tobpu-chu headwaters from Oyuk township and Sogchen.

Ensakha and Kharna Monasteries

The Bon monastery of **Ensakha** was founded in Lower Topgyel by Druje Yungdrung Lama in 1072. Following its devastation by floods in 1386, the Bon community moved to Menri. Ensakha was eventually reconstructed and continued to function as a small monastery until recent times. Further upstream are the **Kharna-ri** caves, where Bonpo meditators and hermits have practiced for centuries; and where a new monastery was founded in 1838 by Sherab Yungdrung.

Menri Monastery

The Bonpo monastery of **Menri**, higher up the slopes of the Zhung-chu valley, was established in 1405 by Nya-me Sherab Gyeltsen, following the destruction by floods by its precursor, Ensakha monastery. This event is said to have been predicted by Shenrab Miwoche, legendary founder of the Bon religion. For centuries Menri functioned as the most important Bon teaching centre in the country, attracting monks from Tengchen, Ngawa, and Gyarong in E Tibet. Prior to its destruction in 1959 there were 350 monks at Menri; but now there are about 50. The ruins are extensive: formerly there were four colleges, a school of dialectics, and a large assembly hall. The oldest building is the **Red Meditation Hermitage** (**Drubkhang Marpo**), constructed by the monastery's founder.

SHANG VALLEY

ACCESS The Shang valley may be approached from the S bank of the Brahmaputra, either via the **Tama ferry** (58 km W of Tradruka), or the **Dongkar ferry** (80 km W of Tradruka). The former crossing alights near **Emagang** on the W bank of the Shang-chu river estuary; and the latter at **Sadung**, from where the road leads downstream to Chula on the W bank of the Shang-chu. Both roads into Shang are motorable, the W bank as far as Gyatso township (73 km) and the E bank as far as Lhabu (70 km) and Trangto. (There is also a jeep trail from Oyuk township via Karteng to Trangto; and another from Lower Tobgyel to Emagang.) A bridge for motor vehicles spans the river at **Ringon**, the county capital, and above Takna the two main branches of the Shang-chu River diverge: the valley of the Gyatso-chu extending NW and that of the Shang Lhabu-chu extending E and NE.

Emagang Shangda Palchen

In Lower Shang, the most important site is **Shangda Palchen**, the seat of the Zur family in Emagang township. Here, near the village of **Trampa**, the successive generations of the Zur family made their hermitages and securely established the transmission of the *Nyingmapa Oral Teachings* (*kama*) during the 10th century, in the aftermath of the interregnum following Langdarma's persecution. This family lineage originated with Zur Shakya Jungne (10th-11th century), his nephew Zurchungpa Sherab Drak (1014-74), and the latter's son Zur Drophukpa Shakya Senge (1074-1135), whose students carried the Nyingmapa teachings throughout Tibet. The detailed accounts of their lives are among the most lively biographical passages of Nyingmapa literature. When the Sakyapas became the dominant force in Tibetan political life during the 13th century, they maintained a close rapport with the Zurs, encouraging Zur Zangpopel to redact the Nyingmapa anthology of tantras. Later

Zurchen Choying Rangdrol (1604-69) established a close connection with Dalai Lama V.

Ringon (Namling)

Four roads intersect at **Ringon**, the county capital of Namling: the two southern routes to Dojo and Emagang and the northern routes to Gyatso and Lhabu. The cliff-hanging monastery of **Ganden Chokhorling** at Ringon has, in recent centuries, been the largest monastery in Shang: shared by both the Gelukpa and Sakyapa schools. Above the monastery are the ruins of **Ringon Taktse Dzong** fortress. Another small monastery, **Dechen Rabgye Gonpa**, is associated with the Panchen Lamas.

Gyatso-chu Valley

The motor road continues on the W bank of the river upstream from Ringon. Below Luya, the Shang Lhabu River branches to the E. Heading NW along the course of the Gyatso-chu tributary, you will reach Gyatso township after 32 km. Here the Dzesho, Nyangra, and Ridu headwaters of the Gyamtso-chu converge. Of these, the Ridu-chu leads to the **Riwo Gudu** or **Drak Gyawo** hermitage of the master Zurchung Sherab Drak; and the Dzesho-chu to the limestone cave complex of **Sogpo Dzulkhung** hermitage. In the latter, there is a Padmasambhava cave containing the impression of the master's penis in rock. From **Ridu**, the Laga La pass (5,582m) leads through the Nyenchen Tanglha range N towards the Jangtang lakes.

Zhang Zhang Dorjeden

Located 5 km E of Ringon, on the S bank of the Shang-chu, this is one of the best known of the 108 monasteries reputedly established by Khyungpo Neljor, founder of the Shangpa Kagyu school. It was here that this master passed away and was interred in a reliquary fashioned of gold and silver.

Zabulung

Padmasambhava is said to have consecrated five entire valleys for Buddhist practice in each of the four cardinal directions and at their centre. **Zabulung** valley lies at the centre of this grand design, and as such is the most revered pilgrimage place in the province of Tsang. Located NE of Ratang (Lhabu), Karteng, and Trangto, in the Shang Lhabu-chu valley, this site is renowned for its spectacular **hot springs** and the **Shang Zabulung Monastery**, where there is a meditation cave associated with Padmasambhava and his consort Yeshe Tsogyel. Throughout history, important Nyingmapa *tertons* have undergone profound spiritual experiences here: Dorje Lingpa (1346-1405) and Lhatsun Namka Jigme (b 1597) among them.

Trekking

A trekking route continues NE following the Shang Lhabu-chu upstream to the nomadic areas of **Lhabupu**, **Serka**, and eventually to **Putserteng**.

RINPUNG COUNTY

 རིན་སྤུངས

仁布县 Rinbung

Population: 19,686   Area: 1,885 sq km

Rarely visited by outsiders at the present day, **Rinpung** in Rong Valley was once the citadel of the Rinpung princes who ruled Tibet from 1435 until 1565. The county is located on the S bank of the Brahmaputra; extending from the S side of the **Nub Khulung Zamchen bridge**, 20 km E of Tradruka ferry, and downstream as far as **Samda** (W of Kharak). Most settlements are to be found in the lateral valley of the **Rong-chu**, which rises at **Yarzik** in Pelde township on the extreme NW tip of Lake Yamdrok and flows into the Brahmaputra at **Shangpa** (Rinpung township); but the county also includes the valleys of the Yakde-chu and the Bartang-chu; as well as the SW running valley of the Men-chu, the principal tributary of the Rong-chu. The county capital is located at **Jamchen Zhol** in the Rong-chu valley, 31 km SE of the Nub Khulung Zamchen bridge.

Rinpung Dzong

This fortress town is located on a ridge overlooking the W bank of the Rong-chu River. The ruined fortress or **Dzong** of **Ringpung** is further inland on a ridge to the W of the river. It overlooks a large village of some 100 houses.

The Rinpung princes first came to prominence during the reign of the Phakmodrupa king Drakpa Gyeltsen (1374-1440), who appointed **Namka Gyeltsen** as Lord of the Rinpung estates and Governor of Sakya and Chumik.

In 1435, his relation **Rinpung Norbu Zangpo** seized power from Phakmodru, gradually bringing to an end the influence of this aristocratic house of Nedong (see above, page 250). Finally in 1478 his son **Donyo Dorje** inflicted a decisive defeat on the kings of Phakmodru; and founded Yangpachen, the seat of the Zhamarpas of the Karma Kargyu school. The family's power was eventually eclipsed in 1565 by **Zhingzhakpa Tseten Dorje** of the Samdrubtse fiefdom at Zhigatse.

ACCESS Via the road from Nub Khulung Zamchen bridge, which enters the Rong-chu valley at Shangpa.

Rong Jamchen

The road continues inland, following the Rong-chu upstream, past a hydroelectric power station, to **Jamchen Zhol**, the county capital. The most important site is the 3-storeyed **Rong Jamchen Chode** – a Sakyapa monastery which later also acquired Gelukpa associations

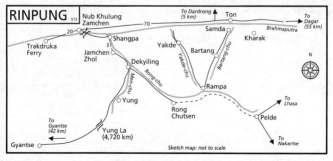

RINPUNG 512
To Dardrong (5 km) — Ton — To Dagar (55 km)
Nub Khulung Zamchen — 70 — Samda — Brahmaputra
20 — Shangpa — Yakde — Bartang — Kharak
Trakdruka Ferry — 31 — Jamchen Zhol — Dekyiling — Bartang-chu
Yakde-chu — Rong-chu — Rampa
Men-chu — Yung — To Lhasa
To Gyantse (42 km) — Rong Chutsen — Pelde
Yung La (4,720 km) — To Nakartse
Gyantse — *Sketch map: not to scale*
N

– originally founded by Zhonu Gyel-chok in 1367. The Rinpungpa prince Norbu Zangpo donated an enormous 10m high Maitreya image. In the early decades of the present century there are said to have been 1,500 Gelukpa and Sakyapa monks based here. The present reconstructed assembly hall lies below the ruins of the original complex.

• **Facilities** There is a government compound with shops and spartan guesthouse facilities, and a military barracks.

Dekyiling

The road continues to follow the river upstream as far as **Dekyiling**, where the Men-chu tributary flows into the Rong-chu from the SW. A motorable road follows the Men-chu upstream and across the Yung La pass (4,720m) to **Gyantse** (42 km). In this valley you can visit the college of **Dreyul Kyemotsel**, founded in 1449 by Rinpungpa Kunzang, who was a patron of the Sakyapa lamas Sangyepel and Gorampa Sonam Senge (1429-89).

Also, 10 km up the valley near Kyishong is **Khambulung**, where Jangdak Tashi Topgyel of the Northern Treasures (Jangter) tradition (b 1557) discovered certain *terma* revelations. The **Ngurmik Drolma Lhakhang** once contained a celebrated image of Tara, which is now housed at Tashilhunpo in Zhigatse (see below, page 333). 7 km further S is the **Gongra Lhundrubding**; also known as **Gongra Ngeden Dorje Ling**, an important Nyingmapa centre, where the *Anuyoga* texts were transmitted by Gongra Lochen Zhenpen Dorje (1594-1654).

Rong Chutsen Hot Springs and Rampa

The small hot spring known as **Dumpa Chutsen** is located at Chutsen village, just before the Rong-chu valley forms a narrow gorge. Within the gorge at **Rampa** is the hermitage of Padmasambhava's 8th century disciple, **Nanam Dorje Dujom**. The trail continues SE to **Yarzik** on the shore of Lake Yamdrok (see above, page 319).

Yakde and Bartang valleys

From Rampa, there are two side-valleys branching NE which lead to the Brahmaputra via Yakde and Bartang respectively. **Yakde** is the birthplace of Yakde Panchen Khyenrab Gyatso (1299-1378), a foremost student of Karmapa III, Rangjung Dorje, who also has associations with the Sakyapa school.

GYANTSE COUNTY

རྒྱལ་རྩེ

江孜县 Gyangze

Population: 43,810   Area: 3,595 sq km

The fertile valley of the **Nyang-chu** River, which is the principal tributary of the Brahmaputra in Tsang, rivals the Kyi-chu valley of Central Tibet in its importance as a prosperous farming region and centre of population. The valley is divided into upper and lower reaches; **Upper Nyang**, corresponding to present day Gyantse county, and **Lower Nyang** to Panam county. Upper Nyang therefore extends from the watershed of the Khari La pass as far as the town of Gyantse, and includes the peripheral valleys formed by the tributaries: Nyeru Tsangpo, Lu-chu, and Narong Dung-chu.

The county capital is located at **Gyantse**, a strategic intersection of great historic importance, 91 km E of Khari La pass (262 km from Lhasa), 67 km SE of Zhigatse, and 189 km NE of Yadong.

Ralung

ར་ལུང་དངོ་ན་ལ

Ralung Monastery, the principal seat of the **Drukpa Kagyu school** in Tibet, is located in a spectacularly dramatic setting below the snow peaks and glaciers of Nojin Gangzang (7,191m), Jangzang Lhamo (6,324m), and Gyetong Soksum (6,244m).

ACCESS The turn-off for Ralung is signposted above Ralung village, 16 km after Khari La pass (5,045m) on the left (S) side of the Lhasa-Gyantse highway (51 km from Gyantse). Access is also possible by trekking from Lake Phuma Yutso (see above, page 279) or from Yakde and Rampa (see above, page 320). From the turn-off, the trail follows the **Zhak-chu** valley for 7 km to reach the monastery.

To the right of the massive ruined ramparts of the Central Temple, the **Tsuklakhang** (which formerly contained large images of Amitayus and Lingje Repa), more modest temples have recently been reconstructed. Beyond this complex are the ruins of the **Ralung Kumbum** stupa and the cave hermitage attached to the monastery, which has always been renowned for its ascetic and meditative approach.

Founded by Tsangpa Gya-re (1126-1216) in 1180, on a site consecrated with the name Ralung by his own master Lingje Repa (1128-88), the monastery quickly supplanted **Druk Monastery** (see above, page 321) as the foremost seat of the Drukpa Kagyu school in Tibet. It was maintained originally by the so-called 'nine hierarchs named

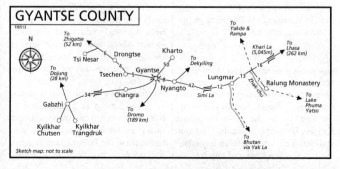

GYANTSE COUNTY

TIB513

N

To Zhigatse (52 km) · 6 Drongtse · Kharto
Tsi Nesar 4
To Dojung (28 km) · Tsechen 5 Gyantse 8 50 To Dekyiling
To Yakde & Rampa
Khari La (5,045m) · To Lhasa (262 km)
16
Lungmar 13 Zhak-chu Ralung Monastery
34 Changra Nyangto 42 12 Simi La
Gabzhi To Dromo (189 km) To Bhutan via Yak La To Lake Phuma Yatso
Kyilkhar Chutsen Kyilkhar Trangdruk

Sketch map: not to scale

HIERARCHS OF THE DRUKPA KAGYU SCHOOL	
Drukchen I	Tsangpa Gya-re (1161-1211)
Drukchen II	Cho,e Kunga Peljor (1426-76)
Drukchen III	Jamyang Chodrak (1477-1523)
Drukchen IV	Pema Karpo (1527-92)
Drukchen V	Paksam Wangpo (1593-1641)
Drukchen VI	Mipam Wangpo (1641-1717)
Drukchen VII	Trin-le Shingta (1718-1766)
Drukchen VIII	Kunzik Chokyi Nangwa (1767-1822)
Drukchen IX	Jigme Migyur Wangyel (1823-1883)
Drukchen X	Mipam Chokyi Wangpo (1884-1930)
Drukchen XI	Tendzin Khyenrab Gelek Wangpo (1931-1960)
Drukchen XII	Jigme Pema Wangchen (b 1963)

Senge', and subsequently by the successive incarnations of Tsangpa Gya-re, among whom the most renowned was the writer and historian Drukchen Pema Karpo (1527-92). The present incarnation, the 12th, resides in India. During the 17th century, Zhabdrung Ngawang Namgyel (1594-1651) fled from Ralung to establish a Drukpa theocracy in **Bhutan** (see below, page 332).

Some 21 km below the Ralung turn-off, the highway passes through **Lungmar** township at the entrance to the **Nyerulung** valley. Here there is a large hydroelectric project under construction. The valley of the Nyeru Tsangpo leads directly upstream to the Yak La pass on the frontier of the Bhutanese district of Gasa. The main road then climbs from Lungmar to cross Simi La pass after 12 km, en route for Gyantse. After Nyangto township, it is joined 8 km before reaching town by the road from Dekyiling on the E (see above, page 320).

Gyantse

Gyantse was once considered to be Tibet's third largest town – after Lhasa and Zhigatse, but nowadays its status has undoubtedly diminished, in size being surpassed by Tsetang, Chamdo, Derge, Kandze, Dartsedo, Jyekundo, Chabcha and Barkham, among others. Nonetheless Gyantse has preserved much of its

old-world atmosphere, and Tibetan rural life continues here, virtually unchanged, against a backdrop of magnificent 14th-15th century fortresses and temples. The hilltop fortress commands a strategic view of all approaching roads: from Zhigatse in the NW, Simi La pass (and Lhasa) in the SE, and Yadong on the Sikkim frontier in the SW. For centuries it has dominated the wool and timber trade routes from Nepal, Sikkim and Bhutan.

Orientation

Four routes intersect at a crossroads to the S of town: the southern highway to Lhasa leading SE (262 km), the local road to Kharto township leading NE (50 km), the Zhigatse and Yadong road (which bifurcates on the E bank of the Nyang-chu, across the Gyantse Zamchen bridge) leading SW, and the main road into town leading NW. The *Gyantse Hotel* is located to the left of this intersection; where there are also a number of small Sichuan restaurants catering to truckers and bus drivers. Taking the NW road into town, there are small guesthouses on both sides of the street. The road known as **Dzongdun** cuts NW to circumvent the castle hill, and then runs due N to approach the vast enclosure of the Pelkor Chode temple. A secondary loop known as **Chak-**

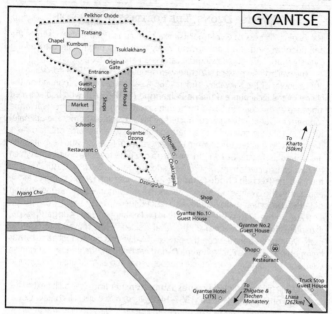

rigyab runs behind the hill to complete the castle's circumambulatory path. On the left side of Dzongdun Rd, as you approach the temple gates, you will pass small restaurants, a school, and two guesthouses. The right side comprises a number of shops selling groceries, electrical goods, and traditional wares (Gyantse was once renowned for its Tibetan carpets). To the E of this main street, an older parallel lane runs between cramped village houses towards the original gates of the precinct.

Gyantse Dzong

The hilltop offers an unrivalled view of Gyantse town, and there is a small museum, documenting the excesses of the British **Younghusband** expedition, which severely damaged the fortress in 1904. For the history of the fortress, see box, page 324.

Pelkhor Chode Temple Complex and Monasteries

དཔལ་འཁོར་ཆོས་སྡེ

History

The great monastic complex of Gyantse is known as **Pelkhor Chode** after the name of Langdarma's son Pelkhor-tsen who is said to have resided here in the 9th century. The main temple, the **Tsuklakhang** was built by **Prince Rabten Kunzang Phak** between 1418-25. Reflecting the eclectic spiritual background of his ancestors who had long been affiliated to both the Sakyapa and Zhalupa schools, the prince sought to establish an ecumenical community, and he was aided in this task by Khe-drupje Gelek Pelzangpo (1385-1438), a foremost student of Tsongkhapa, retrospectively recognized as the first Panchen Lama.

Within the high perimeter walls, other buildings were gradually estab-

GYANTSE DZONG, THE FORTRESS OF GYANTSE

The original fortress of **Gyel-khar-tse** is attributed to **Pelkhor-tsen**, son of the anti-Buddhist king Langdarma, who vainly sought to perpetuate the Yarlung Dynasty from W Tibet following the assassination of his father.

The walls of the present structure were reputedly built in 1268, following the rise to power of the Sakyapas, and in 1365 a palatial castle was founded on the hilltop by the local prince, **Phakpa Pelzangpo** (1318-1370), who had acquired influence at the court in Sakya through his reputation as a brave general in the southern military campaigns conducted by his Sakyapa overlords, and at Zhalu, where in 1350 he entered into a marriage alliance with the lords of Zhalu. As a dowry he was granted the fiefdom of Changra, W of Gyantse, and he invited the great Buddhist master **Buton Rinchendrub of Zhalu** to reside in a temple which he had constructed there. In 1365, in addition to the Gyantse Castle, he also founded the **Tsechen Chode (Shambu Tsegu)** castle and temple complex at the entrance to the Gyantse valley and adopted it as his principal seat. The incarnation of Buton, Drubchen Kunga Lodro, also resided there.

Later, in the 14th century, when Phakpa Pelzangpo's son, **Kunga Phakpa**, expanded the Gyantse complex, the royal residence was moved into Gyantse itself. During this period when the power of Sakya and its Mongol patrons was being eclipsed by the Phakmodrupa Dynasty at Nedong, the princes of Gyantse were able to maintain considerable independence and exerted great influence in both camps.

The first hilltop temple, known as **Sampel Rinchenling**, was built next to the castle by Prince Kunga Phakpa (1357-1412). Its ruined walls still contain extant 14th century murals – some executed in an authentic Newari style, and others in the Gyantse Tibetan style, which evolved therefrom.

lished: the great **Kumbum** stupa was completed in 1427; followed by an increasing number of colleges which by the end of 17th century numbered 16: representing the Sakyapa, Zhalupa and Gelukpa schools.

At the beginning of the 19th century, there were 18 colleges: the Karma Kagyu and Drukpa Kagyu schools also being represented. However, the **Pelcho Khenpo** or preceptor who presided over the whole monastery and had administrative powers in Gyantse town, was Gelukpa. Only two of these outlying college buildings are now extant; and they contain little of interest.

The NE corner of the enclosure wall comprises the **Goku Tramsa**, on which large applique tangkas would be displayed during the Gyantse festival (4th month of the lunar calendar). Commis-

sioned by the prince Rabten Kunzang Phak between 1418 and 1419, these enormous hangings depict Shakyamuni Buddha flanked by his two foremost students, as well as Maitreya, Manjushri, and so forth.

The Main Temple

The **main temple (Tsuklakhang)**, which does survive intact, contains important 15th century murals and images.

Ground Floor The Ground Floor, entered via a portico with new images of the Four Guardian Kings, has a protector shrine (**Gonkhang**) on the left, between the stairs and the main assembly hall entrance. This is a strongly atmospheric chapel, in which the images depict the main Sakya protectors: Panjaranatha (Gonpo Gur), Six-armed Mahakala, Shridevi and Ekajati. The terrifying frescoes depict charnel ground scenes in bold

The Kumbum and Pelkhor Chode at Gyantse

colours. Within the 48-pillared assembly hall, there are a few original paintings and sculptures from the 15th century, which reveal a distinctive Tibetan style.

The **inner sanctum** (N), which is surrounded by a corridor painted with scenes from the *Sutra of the Auspicious Aeon* (*Bhadrakalpikasutra*), contains enormous images of the Buddhas of the Three Times – the central Shakyamuni flanked additionally by standing images of Manjughosa and Maitreya.

To the left (W), there is the **Vajradhatu Chapel (Dorje Ying Lhakhang)** containing a central clay image of Sarvavid Vairocana, surrounded by the other four meditational buddhas and 20 peripheral figures of this mandala. There is also a gold inscribed manuscript version of the *Kangyur* dated 1431 – one volume of which is currently on display.

To the right (E) is the **Royal Chapel (Chogyel Lhakhang)**, containing exquisite clay images of the ancient kings: Songtsen Gampo, Trisong Detsen and Tri Ralpachen. The latter also contains images of Atisha, Kamalashila, Padmasambhava, Shantarakhita, Manjushri, 11-faced Avalokiteshvara, Vajrapani, and Shakyashri of Kashmir. The large Maitreya in the centre of the chapel appears to have been added subsequently when the Gelukpa tradition became the dominant school at Gyantse (no mention of it is made in the *Nyang Chojung* inventory). A recessed chamber on the S wall of this chapel contains the **Silver Reliquary of Prince Rabten Kunzang Phak**, the temple's founder, and many volumes of canonical texts. There are also small images of Amitabha, Shakyamuni, Khedrupje, Panchen Lama IV and Dalai Lama V.

Upper Floor The Upper Floor has five chapels which open out on to a central gallery. The staircase is located at the SW corner of the antechamber. To the left (W) is the **'Path and its Fruition' Temple (Lamdre Lhakhang)**, containing clay images of the lineage-holders of the Sakyapa school, from Vajradhara, Nairatmya, and Virupa onwards. In the centre of the chapel is a 3-dimensional mandala palace of the deity Cakrasamvara. Exquisite murals depict the yogic activities of the Eighty-four Mahasiddhas of ancient India. Next, the **Maitreya Chapel** contains bronze images of Indian or Newari origin, the most sacred being a small

GYANTSE KUMBUM, THE STUPA OF 100,000 DEITIES

The principal deities of the 75 chapels are outlined according to the following scheme; but for a detailed description, please consult *The Great Stupa of Gyantse* by F Ricca and E Lo Bue.

First Storey Here there are staircases in each of the four cardinal directions, leading to the temples of the second storey. The principal entrance is on the S side.

Second Storey 20 chapels (of which one constitutes the staircase). These depict the deities of the *Kriyatantras* in the following clockwise sequence:

1 (S Centre) Mahamuni with Bhaisajyaguru and Suparikirtinamasriraja; 2 (S) Marici; 3 (S) Bhutadamara Vajrapani; 4 (W) Krodha Bhurkumkuta/Ucchusmakrodha; 5 (W) Aparajita Sitapatatra; 6 (WC) Amitayus in Sukhavati; 7 (W) Parnasabari; 8 (W) Hayagriva; 9 (N) Acala; 10 (N) Mahavidya/Grahamatrika Kurukulla; 11 (NC) Dipamkara Buddha; 12 (N) Vasudhara; 13 (N) Vyaghravahana Mahakala; 14 (E) Mahabala; 15 (E) Dhvajagra; 16 (EC) Maitreya in Tusita; 17 (E) Vaishravana; 18 (E) Four Guardian Kings (staircase to third storey); 19 (S) Panjaranatha Mahakala; and 20 (S) Usnisavijaya.

Third Storey 16 chapels, depicting the deities of the *Kriyatantras* and *Caryatantras*, in the following clockwise sequence:

1 (S) Vadisimha Manjughosa; 2 (S) Avalokiteshvara Jaganatha; 3 (S) Amitayus; 4 (S) Khadiravani Tara; 5 (W) Avalokiteshvara Simhanada; 6 (W) Avalokiteshvara Amoghapasha; 7 (W) Black Hayagriva; 8 (W) Kurukulla; 9 (N) Manjughosa; 10 (N) Vajravidarana; 11 (N) Vimalosnisa; 12 (N) White Tara; 13 (E) Samantabhadra; 14 (E) Vajrapani; 15 (E) Aksobhya Buddha; 16 (E) Five Protective Dharanis (Pancaraksa murals; ascending staircase).

Fourth Storey 20 chapels, depicting the deities of the *Yogatantras*, in the following clockwise sequence:

1 (S) Vajravalanalarka; 2 (S) Vajrasattva; 3 (SC) Amitayus (with Paramadya mandalas); 4 (S) Vajrasattva; 5 (S) Jvalana; 6 (W) Prajnaparamita; 7 (W) Vairocana; 8 (WC) Ratnasambhava; 9 (W) Jnanasattva Manjushri; 10 (W) Vajrasattva; 11 (N) Vajrapani; 12 (N) Jvalanalarka; 13 (NC) Amoghasiddhi; 14 (N) Sarvavid Vairocana; 15 (N) Amitayus; 16 (E) Buddhardharmaraja; 17 (E) Buddhavishvarupa; 18 (EC) Aksobhya; 19 (E) Buddhasurya; 20 (E) ascending staircase and murals depicting the Eight Stupas.

Fifth Storey 12 chapels, depicting lineage-holders, in the following clockwise order:

1 (S) Atisha and his Kadampa followers; 2 (S) Buton Rinchendrub and his Zhalupa followers; 3 (S) Virupa and the *Lamdre* lineage of Sakya; 4 (W) Togme Zangpo and his Kadampa followers; 5 (W) Phadampa Sangye and his Chodyul and Zhiche followers; 6 (W) Tilopa and his Kagyupa followers; 7 (N) Dolpopa Sherab Gyeltsen and his Jonangpa followers; 8 (N) King Songtsen Gampo and the royal family; 9 (E) Shantarakshita, Padmasambhava and Kamalashila, with a select group of translators; 10 (E) Padmasambhava with his consorts Mandarava and Yeshe Tsogyel; 11 (E) Shakyashri and his followers; 12 (E) ascending staircase; murals of the Dashakrodha kings.

Sixth Storey (the 'Bowl' or Bum-pa) 4 chapels, depicting *Yogatantra* deities in the following clockwise order:

1 (S) Vajrasana Shakyamuni; 2 (W) Shakyasimha Buddha; 3 (N) Prajnaparamita; 4 (E) Vairocana.

Seventh Storey (Lower 'Spire' or Harmika) 1 chapel depicting the 10 mandalas of the Father Class of *Unsurpassed Yogatantras*.

Eighth Storey (Upper 'Spire' or Harmika) 1 chapel depicting the 11 mandalas of the Mother Class of *Unsurpassed Yogatantras*.

Ninth Storey (the 'Pinnacle' or Bindu) 1 chapel depicting a gilded-copper image of Vajradhara Buddha, flanked by the masters of the *Kalacakra*.

GYANTSE KUMBUM

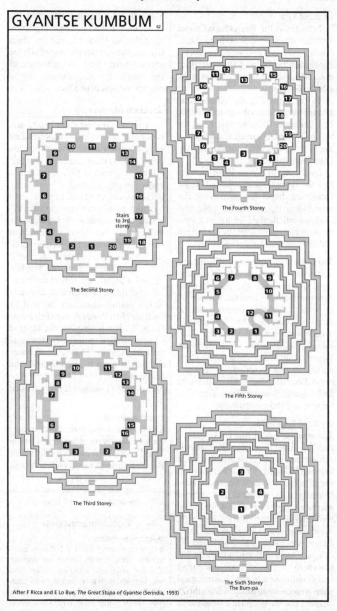

The Fourth Storey

The Second Storey

Stairs to 3rd storey

The Fifth Storey

The Third Storey

The Sixth Storey
The Bum-pa

After F Ricca and E Lo Bue, *The Great Stupa of Gyantse* (Serindia, 1993)

image of Tara.

In front (N), the **Tsongkhapa Chapel** contains images of Tsongkhapa, Dalai Lama VII, Shakyamuni, Buton Rinchendrub, Sakya Pandita, Padmasambhava, and Sakyapa lamas of the *Lamdre* lineage.

To the right (E), the **Neten Lhakhang** is dedicated to the Sixteen Elders, each image in Chinese style being set within a grotto. There are also images of the Five Aspects of Manjushri and the Four Guardian Kings.

Lastly, on the Upper Floor, just before the stairs there is a second **Neten Lhakhang** chapel dedicated to the Sixteen Elders (E) containing images of Shakyamuni flanked by his two foremost students and backed by the Sixteen Elders in their individual grottoes.

Top Floor The **Uppermost Floor** has a single chapel: the **Zhalyekhang**, containing 15 magnificent wall-painted mandalas, each 8m in diameter. They are all associated with the foremost meditational deities of the Unsurpassed Yogatantras (*Anuttaryogatantras*): Kalacakra, Guhyasamaja, Cakrasamvara, Hevajra, Yamantaka and so forth. There are also images depicting Jowo Shakyamuni, Maitreya, Manjushri, Tsongkhapa with his students, Amitayus, Tara, Sitatapatra, and Padmasambhava.

Gyantse Kumbum

The great octagonal stupa of Gyantse – one of Tibet's outstanding artistic achievements, was built and decorated between 1427-39 by Prince Rabten Kunzang Phak in the style known as Tashi Gomang or Kumbum, which combines a terraced stupa exterior with multi-layered interior chapels. Rising 35m high, the stupa is said to have 108 gates, nine storeys (including the base) and 75 chapels. One tradition identifies the 108 gates with the nine storeys (representing space) multiplied by the 12 astrological signs (representing time). Within the 75 chapels, the images form a progressive

hierarchy of 3-dimensional mandalas, as outlined in the Sakyapa compilation known as the *Drubtob Gyatsa*, ensuring that the stupa encapsulates within it the entire spiritual path and gradation of the tantras. For diagram and key to chapels see box, page 326.

Tsechen Monastery

Crossing the **Gyantse Zamchen** bridge, turn right (NW) in the direction of Zhigatse. Formerly in the 15th century the princes of Gyantse constructed a fine bridge, surmounted with a decorative stupa gateway, across the Nyang-chu, but no trace of it remains. Even the town has been rebuilt in recent decades following its devastation by floods in the 1950s. From here there are excellent views of the town and its fortress. Continuing NW, you quickly pass, after 5 km, the hilltop ruins of **Tsechen** (**Shambu Tsegu**), the seat of the incarnation of Buton Rinchendrub, known as Kunga Lodro, which was founded by Gyantse's first Prince Phakpa Pelzangpo (1318-70). It was here that the kings of Gyantse resided until the expansion of the town in the early 15th century. Later, the Sakyapa master Rendawa Zhonu Lodro Zhonu (1349-1412), who was Tsongkhapa's principal teacher, resided here.

Local festivals

The Gyantse horse-festival and archery contest is one of the oldest in this part of Tibet, having been introduced by prince Rapten Kunzang Phak in 1408. It lasts for 5 days, commencing on the 18th day of the 4th month of the lunar calendar. In 1996, this corresponds to 4 June.

Local information

● **Accommodation**
B *Gyantse Hotel*, T 357, has 200 beds, comfortable rooms in both Tibetan and Western (Chinese) style, with attached showers and television, on 4 flrs, a double room costs US$43, no elevator, solar heated water supply, most effective after 2000, good Chinese res-

taurant (full meal plan US$33, breakfast US$9), souvenir and gift shop, foyer bar and games room.

D *Gyantse No 1 Guesthouse*, on the left side of Dzongdun Rd, has 3-bed rooms, and cold running water; **D** *Gyantse No 2 Guesthouse*, has dormitory accommodation, but cold water only, nr bus station.

● **Places to eat**
Gyantse Hotel has reasonable but expensive Chinese food. For simpler fare, try the truck-stop restaurants nr the crossroads. Tibetan dumplings (*momo*) and noodles (*thukpa*) are available at the *No 2 Guesthouse* restaurant, ground flr.

● **Banks & money changers**
Not available.

● **Entertainment**
Outside the festival season, the only forms of entertainment are pool and karaoke.

● **Hospitals & medical services**
Gyantse Hospital, W of crossroads.

● **Shopping**
Handicrafts: there is a souvenir gift shop in the *Gyantse Hotel*; but try the stores on the E side of Dzongdun Rd for Tibetan textiles, carpets, handicrafts and religious artefacts.

Modern goods: there are large department stores on the E side of Dzongdun Rd, selling modern Chinese goods: clothing, tinned foods, and basic electrical supplies. **NB** Shops will accept only RMB currency. It is best to change currency in Lhasa before reaching Gyantse.

● **Tour companies & travel agents**
CITS, Gyantse Branch, based at *Gyantse Hotel*.

● **Useful addresses**
Police & public security: Gyantse City Police and Public Security Bureau, S of crossroads, nr *Gyantse Hotel*.

● **Transport**
Road Most visitors to Gyantse will have their transportation organized by the travel services. Long distance car and jeep transportation is more easily available from Lhasa or Zhigatse. Long distance travel by public bus is more common; and Gyantse is on one of the principal routes between Zhigatse and Lhasa. The bus station for Lhasa is located by the crossroads, nr the Petrol Station.

Drongtse Monastery

14 km N of Tsechen, overlooking the highway, is the renovated assembly hall of **Drongtse Monastery**, a Gelukpa institution founded in 1442 by the ascetic yogin Rinchen Gyatso, in accordance with a prophecy of Tsongkhapa. Later, Drongtse was adopted as a branch of Tashilhunpo. The ancient colleges for the study of the sutras and tantras have not been rebuilt, but the yellow **Assembly Hall** has been reconstructed in the 1980s. It contains a renovated image of Shakyamuni, and (in its upper storey) old images of Manjushri and Maitreya. Behind the monastery is a small chapel containing rock-carved images of Amitayus, Padmasambhava, Tara, and other deities.

Tsi Nesar

In a side-valley 100m to the left of the highway, 6 km N of Drongtse, are the reconstructed buildings of **Tsi Nesar**, an ancient geomantic temple (ie a peripheral temple of the 'district-controlling' or 'border-taming' class) attributed to King Songtsen Gampo. No trace remains of its precious murals and images, which reputedly dated back to the 12th century. An adjacent 8th century temple constructed by King Trisong Detsen to house an image of Prajnaparamita, which was consecrated by Padmasambhava, has also been destroyed.

Kyilkhar Caverns

The **Six Tunnels of Kyilkhar** (Kyilkhar Trangdruk) is an elaborate complex of limestone grottoes, which is associated with Padmasambhava and his consorts. It can be circumambulated by pilgrims in a single day.

A large outer cavern known as the **Assembly Hall** (Dukhang) serves as an antechamber, leading into the **Guru Lhakhang** cave (left side) where there are relief images of Padmasambhava and a stone footprint of Yeshe Tsogyel, aged eight. Adjacent to it is the **Gonkhang** cavern, where protector rituals would be performed. A long 10m tunnel extends from this ante-chamber towards an inner recess at the rear of the Dukhang. This is the **meditation cave of Yeshe Tsogyel**; and within it a tunnel leads, via a ladder and suspended rope, to the **Eighteen Tunnels of the Intermediate State** (Bardo Trangchen Chobgye) and the slippery **Elephant's Stomach Tunnel** (Langchen Tropa). Returning to the Dukhang, opposite the entrance to the cave of Yeshe Tsogyel is the **Cave of Mandarava**. Throughout the complex there are many natural rocks forming sacred images discerned by those of pure vision.

ACCESS Cross the Gyantse Zamchen bridge and turn right towards Zhigatse. After 1 km, a dirt road on the left leads to **Changra** township. From here, a 34 km drive SW crosses Namru La pass to reach **Gabzhi** in Kyilkhar township. An alternative 46 km route is also possible from Panam, via **Dojung** (see below). The valley bifurcates at Gabzhi. The SW branch, marked by the **Kyilkhar hot springs** and a stupa built by Tibet's 8th century physician Yutok Yonten Gonpo, leads to **Se** township (see below, page 348). Take the SE branch to the caverns.

PANAM COUNTY

པ་སྣུམ

白朗县 Bainang

Population: 29,373   Area: 2,410 sq km

The county of **Panam** is a prosperous farming belt, extending from Jangto township on the E bank of the Nyangchu, downstream as far as Gadong township (20 km), and from **Sharchok Zampa bridge**, following the Gyelkhar Zhung-chu tributary upstream to **Dojung** and **Wangden** townships (28 km).

The county capital is located at **Panam**, on the W bank of the Nyangchu, 37 km SE of Zhigatse and 40 km NW of Gyantse (or in local terms 16 km W of Jangto and 4 km S of Norbu Khyungtse). Jangto and the Gyelkhar Zhung-chu valley are all traditionally part of **Upper Nyang**; while **Lower Nyang** is said to begin from Norbu Khyungtse township, and extends as far as Zhigatse.

This relatively low-lying area has been targeted in recent years for Chinese settlement; and there have been protracted negotiations with the European Union Development Fund for aid to im-

plement a massive programme of agricultural development and irrigation, largely, it is feared, at the expense of the delicate eco-system and for the well-being of the immigrants rather than the locals.

Pokhang Monastery

Located above Jangto township on the E bank of the Nyang-chu, this temple was founded in 1213 by Jangchub Pelzangpo, a student of the Kashmiri pandita Shakyashri. Formerly, it contained the robe, bowl and shoes of Shakyashri.

Nyangto-kyi Phuk

Above Pokhang, is **Nyangto-kyi Phuk**, a hermitage associated with Zhalu which was responsible for training adepts in yogic practices, such as the 'inner heat' (*tummo*) and the 'control of vital energy' (*lungom*). Accomplished masters from this hermitage would sometimes participate in the **Yuldruk Barkor cross-country run**: a seemingly impossible 2-week marathon tour of Utsang and Lhokha, starting and ending in Zhalu, which was instituted on a 12-yearly basis (pig year) by Buton Rinchendrub in the 13th century and later adopted by the Tibetan government.

ZHIGATSE COUNTY
གཞིས་ཀ་རྩེ

日喀则县 Xigaze

Population: 46,625   Area: 2,678 sq km

ZHIGATSE TOWN

Zhigatse, commanding the confluence of the Nyang-chu and Brahmaputra rivers, is still Tibet's second largest city, but it may not remain so for long in view of the recent rapid development of other cities in E Tibet, such as Chamdo, Kandze, Dartsedo and Barkham. The city is slightly higher than Lhasa, at 3,900m; with an oxygen content of 67% and average annual temperatures are 16° in midsummer and -5° in mid-winter.

History

Originally known as the **Samdrubtse Estate (Zhika Samdrubtse)** it was until

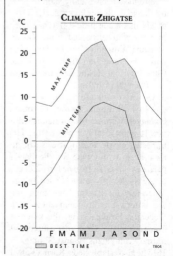

CLIMATE: ZHIGATSE

°C

MAX TEMP

MIN TEMP

J F M A M J J A S O N D

BEST TIME

the 16th century far less significant than the other great sites of the Nyang-chu valley and its environs: **Zur Sangakling**, **Zhalu**, **Nartang**, **Ngor**, and **Gyantse**. Further SW lay **Sakya**, the capital of Tibet from 1268 to 1365. During the 14th-15th century the estate became a fiefdom of the Phakmodrupa kings; and after the usurption of power by the Rinpungpa princes, it was developed as a royal residence. **Tashilhunpo Monastery** was founded under their auspices in 1447 by Dalai Lama I Gendun Drupa.

Yet, the princes of Zhigatse became powerful patrons of the Karma Kagyu school, particularly following the foundation of the Zhamarpa's residence at Yangpachen (see above, page 319).

In 1565, the power of the Rinpungpas was itself usurped by **Karma Tseten (Zhingshakpa Tseten Dorje)** of the **Nyak** family. He made Zhigatse the **capital of Tibet**. In religious affairs, he adopted a sectarian posture, which favoured the Karma Kagyu school at the expense of others. When he persecuted the Northern Treasures (*Jangter*) community of the Nyingmapa school, he is said to have been ritually slain in 1599 by Jangdak Tashi Topgyel. Unfortunately this made little difference since the son who succeeded him, **Karma Tensung Wangpo**, maintained the same policy. He forged an alliance with the Chogthu Mongols and captured Lhasa and Phenyul in 1605.

On his death (1611), he was succeeded by his son, **Karma Phuntsok Namgyel**, who, in 1613, established a new 15-point legal system for Tibet. His imposing **castle** at Zhigatse is said to have been a prototype for the Potala palace at Lhasa. In 1616 he forced Zhabdrung Ngawang Namgyel to flee Ralung Monastery for Bhutan, and following the latter's establishment there of a theocratic Drukpa state, the kings of Tsang engaged in a series of unsuccessful military campaigns against Bhutan. In 1618 he also established a Karma Kagyu

Monastery, known as **Tashi Zilnon**, on the hill above Tashilhunpo, and once again sent Mongol armies against Lhasa.

Following his death in 1621, he was succeeded by his son, **Karma Tenkyong Wangpo** (1604-42). During this period (1626) Zhigatse was visited by Jesuit missionaries. From 1635-42 much of Tibet was plunged into civil war, the power of the Tsangpa kings of Zhigatse and their Chogthu allies being challenged by the Gelukpas of Lhasa, who were backed by the powerful Mongol armies of Gushri Qan. Mongol forces sacked Zhigatse in 1635, and eventually occupied the city in 1642, slaying Karma Tenkyong. From this point on until the present Lhasa has functioned as the capital of Tibet.

Though deprived of its primary political power, Zhigatse continued to flourish as the seat of government in **Tsang** and as the residence of the **Panchen Lamas**. It became an important trading centre. Goods imported from India included ironwares, cotton, dyes, spices and sugar; from China they included porcelain, tea and figs; from Ladakh came dried fruits and turquoise, while various grains and yak products came from within Tibet. The old hilltop castle was damaged by the Dzungar armies in 1717, and finally ruined after the communist invasion of 1959.

At present, **Zhigatse** is the capital of Zhigatse district of the Tibetan Autonomous Region, responsible for the administration of 19 counties.

The distance from Zhigatse to Lhasa is 348 km via Gampa La pass and Gyantse, 281 km via Nyemo, or 338 km via Yangpachen and Shogu La pass. From Zhigatse to Dram (*Ch* Zhangmu) on the Nepalese border the distance is 475 km; and to Darchen at Mt Kailash in Farwest Tibet the distance is 1,018 km.

Orientation

There are four approaches into town: the southern route from **Gyantse**, the eastern route from **Nyemo**, the western route from **Lhartse**, and the north-western route from the outlying areas of **Dongkar**, **Tanak**, and **Phuntsoling**. Of these, the southern approach offers the most dramatic views of Tashilhunpo's red masonry and resplendent golden roofs against the stark background of **Dolmari Hill**, and in the distance, beyond the haze of the Brahmaputra, the darker higher peaks of the **Gangtise** watershed range.

A petrol station on the left side of this approach road marks the beginning of town, after which the dirt road gives way first to cobbles and then to a paved surface. This is the **Lho** (Southern) quarter of town. The *Zhigatse Hotel* is passed on the right side, and beyond on the left is the bus station and its guesthouse. A number of small restaurants and tea-shops are passed on the right. Then, a turn-off to the left called Mt Everest Rd leads W towards **Tashilhunpo Monastery**, and eventually out of town in the direction of Lhartse. Staying on the main road, you will pass large glass-fronted department stores, palatial karaoke nightclubs, the **Bank of China** (on the left) and (on the right) the **Peoples' Hospital**, followed by the **Hospital of Tibetan Medicine**. A second intersection leads W (left) from here, towards the entrance to Tashilhunpo. Continuing along the main road, you reach the commercial centre of the town and residential districts (**2nd**, **3rd** and **4th Dronglhan**). The next main turning on the right is the road to Lhasa via Nyemo and Yangpachen. Beyond, on the left, you pass into the **Jang** (Northern) quarter of town. After the People's Cinema, you reach a T-junction. Turn right for Lhasa and left for the Dongkar ferry.

Returning to the *Zhigatse Hotel*, after the Bus Station, turn left on Mt Everest Rd towards Tashilhunpo. Soon you cross a road parallel to the first. This is the main street, leading to the town centre, the **1st Dronglhan**. Here are the **Post Office**, further department stores, Muslim tea-houses, a cinema, and the **Zhigatse District Government Buildings**. A T-junction at the end of this street leads W towards the monastery (via the Public Security Bureau). Take this road, and soon, on the right, another turn-off leads into the commercial centre and open-air market, below the ruined fortress of the **Zhigatse Dzong**. The market is one of the best outside the Barkhor in Lhasa, and traditional artefacts of value can occasionally be found amongst the tourist trinkets. The privately run *Tendzin Hotel* overlooks the market. North of the market, and below the Zhigatse Dzong you pass into a residential area of town houses. A road leads NW of the Dzong towards the **Dongkar ferry**.

Returning to the bank at the intersection of main street, continue W towards **Tashilhunpo Monastery**. Walled enclosures on the left and right sides lead respectively into the compounds of the **Zhigatse Gang-gyen Carpet Factory** and the **Red Cross Medical Training Centre**. Beyond these, there is another intersection, opposite the entrance to Tashilhunpo (which leads down to the Public Security Bureau and the market). Here, on the left, you will find the *Kun-khyabling Guesthouse*. West of the intersection, a turn-off on the left leads to the **Palace of the Panchen Lamas**, while the houses of the old quarter of **Tashi Getsal** are clustered around the base of **Dolmari** on the right, beyond the monastery.

Tashilhunpo Monastery

History Tashilhunpo, the seat of the Pancen Lamas, was founded in 1447 by **Dalai Lama I**, **Gendun Drub**, on the slopes of Drolmari, W of the fortress of Zhigatse Dzong. The original building

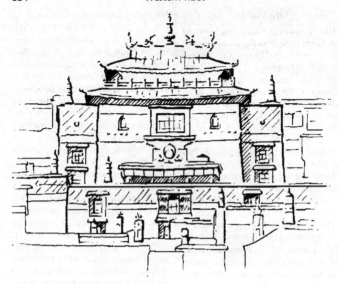

The Mausoleum of Panchen Lama IV at Tashilhunpo

(the assembly hall known as **Kelzang Lhakhang**) was built above a sacred sky-burial site, the stone slab of which is still to be seen on the floor within. An adjacent chamber, the **Tongwa Donden Lhakhang**, containing the silver reliquaries of Dalai Lama I Gendun Drub, Panchen Lama II and Panchen Lama III, dates from 1478.

In 1618 a Karma Kagyu monastery known as **Tashi Zilnon** ('suppressor of Tashilhunpo') was constructed on the higher slopes of Dolmari by Karma Phuntsok Namgyel, but no traces of it are now to be seen. The assembly hall of Tashilhunpo and its connecting chapels were refurbished and enlarged following the Civil War by Dalai Lama V and his teacher Panchen Lama IV.

A **Kudung Lhakhang**, containing the reliquary of Panchen Lama IV was built in 1662; and the splendid **Labrang Gyeltsen Tonpo** residence of the Panchen Lamas dates from the period of Panchen Lama VI (1738-80).

The **Namgyel Lhakhang** and the massive **Jamkhang Chenmo**, containing the world's largest gilded bronze image (26m high), were subsequently added to the W of the complex by Panchen Lama IX (1883-1937). Formerly, the site also contained five distinct gold-roofed mausolea enshrining the relics of Panchen Lamas V-IX, but these were erased during the 1960s.

The late Panchen Lama X (1938-89) towards the end of his life commissioned a new collossal mausoleum named **Dungten Tashi Namgyel** on the N side of the assembly hall courtyard. Within it he personally reinterred the mortal remains of his five predecessors side-by-side. The most recent construction at Tashilhunpo is the new mausoleum, the **Dungten Sisum Namgyel**, which was built to house his own relics, following his untimely death in 1989.

Around the assembly hall there were formerly four colleges: **Shartse** teaching general subjects, **Ngakpa** teaching the

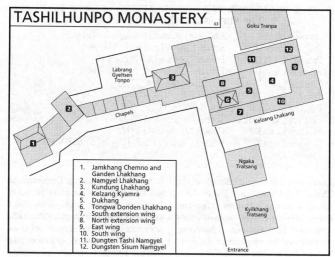

TASHILHUNPO MONASTERY

63

Goku Tranpa

Labrang Gyeltsen Tonpo

Chapels

Kelzang Lhakang

Ngaka Tratsang

Kyilkhang Tratsang

Entrance

1. Jamkhang Chemno and Ganden Lhakhang
2. Namgyel Lhakhang
3. Kundung Lhakhang
4. Kelzang Kyamra
5. Dukhang
6. Tongwa Donden Lhakhang
7. South extension wing
8. North extension wing
9. East wing
10. South wing
11. Dungten Tashi Namgyel
12. Dungsten Sisum Namgyel

tantras, **Tosamling** teaching dialectics, and **Kyilkang**. Of these **Ngakpa** has now been relocated to the front of the assembly hall; while **Kyilkhang** has assumed the functions of the other defunct colleges combined, particularly dialectics.

One of Tibet's most influential monasteries, Tashilhunpo's many branches extend from **Yong He Gong** in Beijing and **Chengde** in Manchuria to **Gyantse**, and in more recent years to **Karnataka** state in South India.

Orientation

Tashilhunpo Monastery is counted among the six largest Gelukpa monasteries in Tibet, formerly housing 4,700 monks at its peak. Like Labrang Tashikyil and Kumbum Jampaling Monastery in Amdo, it has the appearance of a monastic city. There is a 3 km pilgrimage circuit (*lingkor*) around the complex, including the Dolmari ridge to the rear, and the buildings should ideally be visited in a clockwise sequence, from W to E. Insist on following the correct route if your local tour guide tries to lead you through in reverse! The main

buildings are therefore to be visited in the following sequence:

Jamkhang Chenmo

This tall building to the W of the complex houses the world's largest gilded copper image, 26m in height. Constructed during WW1, this massive **Maitreya**, embodying loving kindness, contains 6,700 teals of gold and 150 metric tons of copper, and within it an enormous juniper tree from **Reting** monastery functions as a life-supporting axis (*sok-zhing*). The body of the image is encrusted with ornaments and precious stones, and its overwhelming visage exudes an aura of calm benevolence. The surrounding murals of the chapel depict a 1,000 Maitreyas, drawn in gold line on a red background.

Other murals near the entrance depict the three Kadampa teachers: Atisha, Dromtonpa and Ngok Lekpei Sherab; as well as the triad of meditational deities: Guhyasamaja, Cakrasamvara, and Bhairava. Fifteen other small chapels extend throughout the lower and upper floors, and among these

THE SUCCESSION OF PANCHEN LAMAS

Panchen Lama I	Khedrub Je Gelek Pelzangpo (1385-1483)
Panchen Lama II	Sonam Chokyi Langpo (1438-1504)
Panchen Lama III	Ensapa Lobzang Dobdrub (1505-1566)
Panchen Lama IV	Lobzang Chokyi Gyeltsen (1567-1662)
Panchen Lama V	Lobzang Yeshe (1663-1737)
Panchen Lama VI	Palden Yeshe (1738-1780)
Panchen Lama VII	Tenpei Nyima (1782-1854)
Panchen Lama VIII	Tenpei Wangchuk (1855-1882)
Panchen Lama IX	Chokyi Nyima (1883-1937)
Panchen Lama X	Trinle Lhundrub Chokyi Gyeltsen (1938-1989)
Panchen Lama XI	Gendun Chokyi Nyima (b 1989)

special mention should be made of the **Zhelre Lhakhang** and **Utrok Lhakhang**, from which Maitreya's face and crown are respectively seen at close quarters. The **Ganden Lhakhang**, which faces the entrance to the Jamkhang Chenmo, contains 1,000 images of Tsongkhapa.

Namgyel Lhakhang

Constructed by Panchen Lama IX (1883-1937), the Namgyel Lhakhang contains large impressive images of Tsongkhapa and his two foremost students, flanked by Maitreya and Manjushri. In recent years it has been used as a school of dialectics, and is sometimes closed to the public. The impact of this chapel is understandably dwarfed by the awesome majesty of Maitreya in the previous chapel.

Labrang Gyeltsen Tonpo

The residence of the Panchen Lamas, which was founded by Gendun Drubpa in 1447, and developed and refurbished by Panchen Lama VI Palden Yeshe (1738-80), is a 3-storeyed white building, with a series of seven interconnecting red-painted chapels along its front façade. More recent renovations were carried out between 1976-78.

From W to E (left to right) the outer chapels are as follows: **Gyanak Lhakhang** was built by Panchen Lama VI in honour of the Qianlong Emperor, who was his disciple, and it contains images of Vajradhara, Bhaisajyaguru, Tsong-khapa and Tara. **Lhendzom Zimpuk** is the chamber where the Panchen Lamas would receive official visitors including the Manchu amban. It contains two thrones and a series of 17 applique tangkas depicting the previous lives of the Panchen Lama, which were commissioned in Hangzhou by Panchen Lama IX.

Chime Peldrub Lhakhang is dedicated to Amitayus, flanked by Shakyamuni and Manjughosa. The chapel also contains a full set of the *Kangyur* and *Tangyur*. The next chamber, **Dzegya Gonkhang**, approached via a staircase, contains an image of the protectress Chamsing.

The **Puntsok Kunkyil Lhakhang** contains images of Tsongkhapa and his foremost students. **Kuntu Lhakhang** contains an assemblage of smaller images. Lastly, **Yulo Dolma Lhakhang** contains images of the 21 forms of Tara. Upstairs in the front wing of the Labrang is the chamber where the late Panchen Lama X's embalmed remains were placed within a glass shrine from 1989 until the construction of his mausoleum was completed in 1994.

Kudung Lhakhang

This red gold-roofed chapel contains the silver reliquary of Panchen IV Lobzang Chokyi Gyeltsen (1567-1662) – teacher of Dalai Lama V and the first to be recognized by the title Panchen Erdeni, embodiment of Buddha Amitabha. His predecessors were retrospectively recognized as such. The importance of this reliquary is known by the fact that among all the mausolea of Tashilhunpo, only this one was left standing during the Cultural Revolution. The 11m high reliquary stupa contains an image of Panchen Lama IV in its niche, and in front are images of the deities symbolizing longevity: Amitayus, White Tara, and Vijaya. The courtyard has a fine bell.

Kelzang Tsuklakhang

The Courtyard
The large flagstoned courtyard known as **Kelzang Khyamra** is E of the Kudung Lhakhang and approached via a high-walled lane. Notice the tall prayer-flag pole (Dukar Khorlo Darchen) which is refurbished each New Year and is said to have talismanic properties. The courtyard is where religious dances would be performed. On its W wing is the **Kelzang Tsuklakhang** and on the N are the colossal new mausolea constructed in recent years to hold the relics of past Panchen Lamas. An additional 2-storey complex of chapels flanks the E wing of the courtyard.

West Wing of the Courtyard: The Assembly Hall
Turning to the W wing, the Kelzang Tsuklakhang is a 3-storey complex. The outer walls have murals depicting the Thousand Buddhas of the Auspicious Aeon (Bhadrakalpa), each with its own verse inscription taken from the *Bhadrakalpika-sutra*.

The downstairs **Assembly Hall** (**Dukhang**) is the oldest structure at Tashilhunpo, founded in 1447 by Dalai Lama I and completed in 1459. Measuring approximately 274m by 46m, its interior is supported by 48 columns. It was constructed above a **sky-burial slab**, which is still visible on the floor between

the high rows of seats. Alongside the massive throne of the Panchen Lama, there are main images of Maitreya in the form Ajita flanked by Avalokiteshvara and Manjughosa, and a series of images attached to the pillars – depicting the deities of longevity, Amitayus, White Tara, and Vijaya, as well as peaceful and wrathful forms of Avalokiteshvara. Applique tangkas made in Hangzhou depict 17 past incarnations of the Panchen Lamas.

The dark **inner sanctum** comprises two chapels: the **Dolma Lhakhang** containing a Newari sculpted image of Cintamanicakra Tara, flanked by Green Tara (twice), Amitayus, and Je Sherab Senge; and the **Jowo Lhakhang**, containing images of Shakyamuni flanked by his foremost students, the Eight Bodhisattvas, and two additional images of Manjughosa. Attached to the pillars in the latter chapel are images of Dalai Lama I and Panchen Lama IV.

South Extension Wing of the Assembly Hall
Above the Assembly Hall, the 2-storeyed S extension wing of the Kelzang Tsuklakhang contains seven chapels, three of which are downstairs and four upstairs. In clockwise sequence (E to W), the former comprise: the **Ngonga Lhakhang**, containing a central Kadam-style stupa; the **Gyanak Lhakhang**, containing a silver image of Jowo Shakyamuni, flanked by the Sixteen Elders and Panchen Lama IX; and the **Rinchen Lhakhang**, containing a natural Chinese bronze image of Maitreya, flanked by Vajradhara, Tara, and Avalokiteshvara.

A staircase leads from here to the upper storey, where the four chapels are as follows: the **Ngurmik Lhakhang**, containing a miraculous Tara image of Indian origin which was brought to Tibet at the request of Ngurmikpa Darma Nyingpo in the 12th century; the **Pandrub Lhakhang**, containing a silver image of Panchen Lama IV flanked by Sitatapatra and 11-faced Mahakarunika; the **Gadong Lhakhang**, containing a large bronze image of Maitreya, which was commissioned by Panchen Lama IV; and the **Natsok Lhakhang**, containing images representative of the diverse Buddhist traditions, with Tsongkhapa and his foremost students at the centre. From here, a staircase leads down to the ground level and to the N wing of the Tsuklakhang complex via a passageway.

North Extension Wing of the Assembly Hall

Above the Assembly Hall, the 2-storeyed N extension wing of the Kelzang Tsuklakhang contains three chapels on its lower level and two on its higher level (each of the last two being approached via a separate staircase).

From W to E these comprise: (downstairs) the **Gonkhang**, containing images of the dharma protectors Bhairava flanked by 6-armed Mahakala, Dharmaraja, and Shridevi; (downstairs) the **Zhelre Lhakhang**, which offers a view of the head and shoulders of Maitreya in the Assembly Hall below, flanked by smaller exquisite images of Manjushri and Avalokiteshvara which were sculpted personally by Panchen Lama VI; (upstairs) the **Kunzik Dukhang**, containing images of Shakyamuni, his foremost disciples and the Sixteen Elders, as well as an active shrine dedicated to the protectress Shridevi in a recess to the right; (downstairs) an oblong-shaped **Zhelrekhang**, offering an excellent view of Shakyamuni within the inner sanctum of the Assembly Hall below, and housing a mandala of the Medicine Buddha and tangkas which depict the Six Ornaments and Two Supreme Ones of ancient India; and, lastly, (upstairs) the **Tongwa Donden Lhakhang**, containing eight stupas among which are the precious reliquaries of Dalai Lama I, Panchen Lama II and Panchen

Lama III, and a stone footprint of the celebrated Nyingma lama Guru Chowang (see above, page 338).

East and South Wings of the Courtyard

On the E and S wings of the courtyard, there is a further series of 11 chapels connected by L-shaped galleries on two levels, those on the lower floor having been constructed by Panchen Lama IV and those on the upper floor by Panchen Lama V.

Clockwise (from NE to SE and SE to SW), the former comprise: the **Jowokhang**, containing Jowo Shakyamuni surrounded by the Thousand Buddhas of the Auspicious Aeon; the **Nguldung Lhakhang**, containing an image of Vajradhara and a central silver stupa donated by Gushri Qan; the **Parkhang** (Printery), housing the extant **Nartang** woodblocks for a complete set of the *Kangyur* and a partial set of the *Tangyur*; the **Jokhang**; the **Dolma Lhakhang**; and, finally, the **Ganden Lhakhang**, the last of which contains a central image of Tsongkhapa.

The chapels of the upper floor (again clockwise) comprise: the **Tsepak Lhakhang**, dedicated to Amitayus; the **Kangyur Lhakhang**, with images of Shakyamuni and his foremost disciples, where monks congregate each morning to recite texts from the Buddhist Canon, the *Kangyur* stored herein; the **Dechen Lhakhang**, containing images of Amitabha flanked by Maitreya and Manjushri; the **Ganden Lhakhang**, containing images of Tsongkhapa flanked by Dalai Lama V, Panchen Lama VI, Panchen Lama VIII, and the Indian and Tibetan lineage-holders of their *Lamrim* tradition; and, finally, the **Tingye Dolma Lhakhang**, containing a fire-protecting image of Tara, attributed to Shakyashri, the Pandita of Kashmir (1145-1243).

North Wing of the Courtyard

On the N wing of the courtyard there are two extraordinary new mausolea, the larger of which, named **Dungten Tashi Namgyel**, was consecrated in 1988 by the late Panchen Lama X to replace the five older reliquary buildings destroyed during the Cultural Revolution. It houses an enormous reliquary stupa containing, side by side, the mortal remains of Panchen Lamas V-IX. Alongside this building is an even more recent construction: the mausoleum of the late Panchen Lama X, named **Dungsten Sisum Namgyel**, which was consecrated in 1994. The sum of US$7.75mn is said to have been spent on the construction of these mausolea. Both of these new buildings require an additional admission fee.

Ngakpa Tratsang

South of the entrance to the **Kelzang Khyamra** courtyard, a passageway leads downhill, back towards the gates of Tashilhunpo. To the right of the main path (as you exit), there is the reconstituted **Ngakpa** college. A flight of stairs leads to the assembly hall, where there are images of Tsongkhapa, flanked by his two foremost disciples and Panchen Lama IV. Next to the central throne, there is a canopied mandala of the deity Yamari. Liturgical rituals are performed here each morning.

Kyilkhang Tratsang

This college, dedicated to formal debate and the study of dialectics, has an assembly hall containing images which include Shakyamuni Buddha, Dalai Lama I, Tsongkhapa, and Panchen Lama IV. The **inner sanctum** contains images of Shakyamuni flanked by his two foremost students, the Eight Bodhisattvas and Sixteen Elders, and with a small image of Panchen Lama IX in front. Upstairs the **Gonkhang** is dedicated to the protectress Chamsing.

Goku Trampa

Northeast of Tashilhunpo Monastery is the 9-storeyed tangka wall known as **Goku Trampa**, where a 40m applique depicting the Buddhas of the Three Times is ceremonially displayed during the winter and summer prayer festivals.

Dechen Phodrang

Outside the monastery grounds, and on a branch road to the SW (see above, page 340) is the **Summer Palace of the Panchen Lamas**, which was constructed between 1956-59 to replace the former summer residence. The building is not presently open to the public.

Local festivals
For the dates of traditional Tibetan festivals, see below, **Information for visitors**, page 37. Tashilhunpo's main festival is held on the 15th day of the 5th lunar month, which in 1996 corresponds to 1 July.

Local information

● **Accommodation**
C *Zhigatse Hotel (Rikaze Hotel)*, T 22525, has 250 beds, comfortable but poorly maintained rooms with attached showers and television, on 4 flrs (US$43/double room), no elevator, solar heated water supply, sometimes effective after 2000, vastly improved Chinese restaurant (full meal plan US$32, breakfast US$9), souvenir and gift shop, foyer bar, large rooms available for special functions.

D *Kunkhyabling Garden Hotel*, well located opp Tashilhunpo Monastery, is run by Tibetans and has a Tibetan restaurant, no attached baths, but communal showers are available, rooms at US$22/double, and full meal plan at US$18 (breakfast US$5); **D** *Tendzin Hotel*, 20 rm, is cheap, friendly, Tibetan-run and centrally located, opp the open-air market, showers available; **D** *Zhigatse Guesthouse No 2*, opp Zhigatse Government Buildings and cinema, has superior accommodation and cheaper dormitory-style accommodation, good value.

E *Bus Station Guesthouse*, N of the bus station on main road into town from Gyantse, has dormitory-style accommodation, cheap restaurants located nearby.

● **Places to eat**
Among the hotels, the *Zhigatse Hotel* offers reasonable Chinese food, and the *Kunkhyabling* has

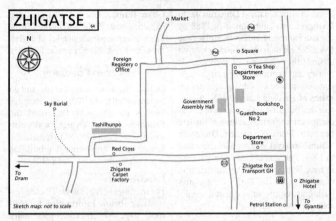

ZHIGATSE 64

Sketch map: not to scale

To Dram

To Gyantse

Market · Pol · Square · Pol · Foreign Registery Office · Tea Shop · Department Store · Government Assembly Hall · Bookshop · Guesthouse No 2 · Sky Burial · Tashilhunpo · Department Store · Red Cross · Zhigatse Carpet Factory · Zhigatse Rod Transport GH · Zhigatse Hotel · Petrol Station

simple Tibetan dishes. There are many smaller cheap road-side restaurants, serving Sichuan, Tibetan, and Muslim cuisine.

● **Banks & money changers**
Bank of China, at crossroads, opp *Hospital of Tibetan Medicine*.

● **Entertainment**
There are discotheques, upmarket karaoke cabaret and low-market karaoke bars, and video parlour facilities, mostly on the main motor road N of Bus Station. There are 2 cinemas: one adjacent to the Government Buildings and a second, the Peoples' Cinema, towards the N of town, E of the market.

● **Hospitals & medical services**
Peoples' Hospital, E of Gyantse Rd, N of *Zhigatse Hotel*; *Zhigatse Hospital of Tibetan Medicine*, at crossroads, N of *Peoples' Hospital*, opp Bank of China.

● **Post & telecommunications**
Post Office: at S end of main commercial street.

● **Shopping**
Handicrafts: there is a souvenir and gift shop in the *Zhigatse Hotel*. The Gang-gyen Carpet Factory, Mt Everest Rd, Zhigatse, T 2733, SE of Tashilhunpo entrance, has a wide selection of carpets in various designs. Credit card payment and shipping facilities are available. For metalwork, jewellery, and traditional religious or household artefacts, try the open-air market.
Modern goods: there are large glass-fronted department stores in the main commercial

street, nr Government Buildings, and on the main motor road from Gyantse, selling textiles, groceries, electrical goods. Smaller grocery and electrical stores are also to be found. The shops will generally accept only RMB currency, and rarely accept payment in US dollars. It is best to change currency in Lhasa or Dram (Ch Zhangmu) before reaching Zhigatse, and not depend upon the banks or money changers.

Photography: print film and processing are available at the department stores, and smaller electrical shops in town.

Stamps: are available at *PO*, on main commercial street, or at the *Zhigatse Hotel*, reception counter.

● **Tour companies & travel agents**
CITS, Zhigatse Branch, based at *Zhigatse Hotel*, T 2525.

● **Useful addresses**
Police & public security: Zhigatse City Police and Public Security Bureau, E of Tashilhunpo Monastery, nr market.

● **Transport**
Road Most visitors to Zhigatse, whether arriving via Lhasa, Dram (Zhangmu) or Kailash, will have their transportation organized by the travel services. Long distance car and jeep transportation is more easily available from Lhasa, but occasionally through CITS, Zhigatse branch, based in the *Zhigatse Hotel*. The public bus station is located to the SE of town on the Gyantse Rd, opp the *Zhigatse Hotel*.

Air Zhigatse Airport, located in Jangdong

township, 45 km E of town, on the central Lhasa highway, is not open to civilian traffic. The distance from Zhigatse to Gongkar Airport is 264 km due E. There are flights to Chengdu (daily), Kathmandu (Tues/Sat), Beijing (Sun), Guangzhou (Wed) and Shanghai (Tues/Fri).

SOUTHERN ZHIGATSE COUNTY

Zhalu Monastery, the Seat of Buton Rinpoche

ACCESS Some 18 km SE of Zhigatse (or 49 km from Gyantse), at Khyungram in Gyatso township, there is a turn-off on the right, which leads (4 km) to Zhalu Monastery, the seat of Buton Rinchendrub (1290-1364) who was the great codifier of the Tibetan translations of the Indian Buddhist canon.

Gyengong Lhakhang

Approaching Zhalu by this road, you will pass on the right the smaller 2-storeyed **Gyengong Lhakhang**, said to be the first temple built in Tibet at the beginning of the Later Diffusion of Buddhism in 997. Its founder was Loton Dorje Wangchuk, a disciple of Lachen Gongpa Rabsel, and teacher of Jetsun Sherab Jungne. The main image here is of Rabtenma, a form of the protectress Shridevi; and it was here that in the 13th century the Sakya Pandita received ordination as a Buddhist monk. Nowadays, pilgrims are aware of a curious mushroom growing from one of the entrance pillars, which is said to have miraculously appeared and is protected by a glass covering.

Serkhang Tramo Temple

The **Serkhang Tramo** temple of Zhalu, which stands within a walled enclosure at Zhalu village, was built originally in 1040 by Jetsun Sherab Jungne of Zhangzhung, and renovated in 1290 and 1333 by Gonpopel, Drakpa Gyeltsen, and Buton Rinchendrub with funds provided by the Mongol emperor Oljadu (1265-1307). This east-facing building has a striking Chinese-style roof, made of yellow and green glazed 'turquoise' tiles with porcelain relief carvings; and its interior murals reveal an important synthesis of Pala, Newari, Tibetan, and Chinese forms, suggesting that the art of Zhalu became the precursor for the later Gyantse style.

Entering the courtyard, there is a monastic residential compound on the N wing (upstairs), where Zhalu's 23 monks now live. Formerly, there were 3,800 monks at the highpoint of the complex's development. Most belonged to the **Zhalupa** school, a minor but highly influential Buddhist tradition, founded by Buton Rinchendrub on the basis of the Sakya and Kadam teachings.

On the S (left) of the courtyard, there is a staircase leading to the former residence of the encyclopediaist **Buton Rinchendrub**, who redacted the 227 manuscript volumes of the *Tibetan Buddhist Canon* and the 26 volumes of his own *Collected Works* here in the 14th century. An inscribed stone plaque is said to date from the temple's foundation in 1040.

The **Serkhang Tramo** itself has been entered via a NE extension area since the original E gateway was sealed by the construction of a **Protector Temple** or **Gonkhang** annex in the early 14th century.

Ground Floor

The temple has three storeys, the ground floor containing an assembly

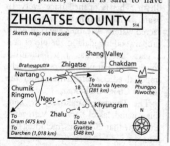

ZHIGATSE COUNTY
514

Sketch map: not to scale

Shang Valley

Brahmaputra Zhigatse Chakdam

Nartang 14 40 Mt Phungpo Riwoche

Chumik Ringmo 18 To Lhasa via Nyemo (281 km)

Ngor Khyungram

Zhalu 4

To Dram (475 km) To Lhasa via
To Darchen (1,018 km) Gyantse (348 km) N

hall (Tsokhang) with seven abutting chapels and a pilgrim's circuit (*khorlam*). An empty chapel is located immediately to the W (right) of the entrance, and the murals of the E wall are currently undergoing restoration.

To the E (left) of the entrance is the **Protector Temple**, the **Gonkhang**, a 14th century T-shaped chapel dedicated to Vaishravana, which incorporates within it sections of the original 11th century walls. The murals here interestingly juxtapose the **East-Indian Pala-syle** paintings of the original building with the work of the celebrated Newar artist **Anige** (1245-1306), who developed his distinctive 'western style' at the Yuan capital in Dadu (modern Beijing).

Continuing past the Protector Temple, you will reach the entrance to the **pilgrim's circuit**, decorated with extraordinary vivid and detailed murals of the 100 deeds of Shakyamuni Buddha, which represent the Anige school. Each band of painting has its unique inscription, taken from texts such as the *Jatakamala* and the *Ratnakuta sutras*, which describe the deeds of the Buddha. Here the influence is predominantly Newar, interspersed with a few figures suggestive of Chinese or Central Asian styles. Three small chapels are entered from the pilgrim's circuit, on the S, W and N sides; but of these, only the last has well preserved murals, depicting Avalokiteshvara, Hayagriva, and so forth.

Exiting from this passageway, the four central chapels are then approached. The **Segoma Lhakhang** (S) which once housed the renowned **Zhalu Library** contains a fragmented *Kangyur* and wall paintings of the Buddhas of the Five Families in Newari style. The **Lkakhang Lhoma** and **Lhakhang Jangma** (W) now contain only painted *tsatsa* (attributed to Atisha) and stucco halos (*torana*). Lastly, the **Gosum Lhakhang** (N) contains a number of damaged images and quite well preserved Newar-style murals.

Middle and Upper Floors

Ascending to the middle floor, there is a **chapel dedicated to Prajnaparamita**, which was renovated in the 14th century. It has a circumambulatory passageway (*khorlam*) with fascinating murals, which illustrate the synthesis of Newar and Yuan styles developed by Anige and his followers, among whom the Tibetan artist Chimpa Sonambum is identified by name. The chapel itself has been used as a storage chamber for religious dance masks and costumes.

The upper floor has four chapels, dating from the restoration work undertaken by Kunga Dondrub and Buton Rinchendrub in the 14th century.

Among these, the **Deden Lhakhang** (W) contains faded 4m mandalas of the *Yogatantras* and a number of images, including the most precious relic of Zhalu Monastery: a self-originated **black stone image of Avalokiteshvara Kharsapani**, with a natural Vajrabhairava image at its rear side. There are also many fine Indian and Kashmiri bronze images, some of which are associated with the pandita Shakyashri. The gilded copper stupas contain relics of Atisha and Buton Rinchendrub. The other images are also notable: a large austere figure of Buton Rinchendrub, the Eight Medicine Buddhas, Maitreya, Amitayus, Padmasambhava, Vajrasattva, and Vajrapani. There is a sealed ritual vase of the Indian tantric Mahasiddha Virupa, known as **Bumchu Nyongdrol**, which was brought to Tibet by Gayadhara. This is opened once every 12 years, so that pilgrims can partake of its sacred waters. A leather bag contains a sandalwood mandala in 108 pieces and a glass cabinet has a self-sounding conch-shell. Formerly, there were eight imperial edicts here dating from the time of **Chogyel Phakpa**.

The **Tsepame Lhakhang** (N) contains mandalas of Sarvavid Vairocana, and more than 20 images, including fine bronzes.

The **Tangyur Lhakhang** (E) where Buton's manuscript version of the *Tangyur* was housed before its destruction, has mandalas of Maitreya, and a circumambulatory passageway with murals depicting Avalokiteshvara and the eight stupas, which suggest a later Tibetan development of the Anige style.

Lastly, the **Neten Lhakhang** (S) contains mandalas of Paramadya, Vajradhatu, Vajrashekhara, and Trailokyavijaya; an image of Kalacakra, and images of Buton Rinchendrub and his disciple Rinchen Namgyel, along with a set of the former's 26 volume *Collected Works*. The outer walls of this chapel depict the life of Buton, an allegorical chart on the taming of mental excitement and sluggishness in the course of the meditation known as calm abiding (*satipathana*), and an astronomical chart, which reflects one of Buton's own particular interests.

Ripuk Retreat

This cave hermitage attached to Zhalu Monastery was developed by Buton, on a site sanctified for retreat by Atisha himself. **Ripuk** over the centuries acquired renown as a centre for meditative retreat, and developed into a complex with two assembly halls, housing over 300 monks. Formerly, it contained a precious image of Buton Rinchendrub and a stupa called **Tongdrol Chenmo**, which Buton himself dedicated on behalf of his deceased mother. South of Zhalu in the mountains is **Tarpaling**, the residence of Buton's teacher Tarpa Lotsawa. There is also a 2-day trek eastwards to Ngor Monastery via the Showa La and Cha La passes.

Zur Sangakling

Within Chakdam township to the E of Zhigatse, and opposite the estuary of the Shang River (see above, page 321), there is an area of great importance to the Nyingma school of Tibetan Buddhism.

This is **Zur Ukpalung**, the seat of Zurpoche Sakya Jungne, who preserved and propagated the Nyingma teachings following Langdarma's persecution and the subsequent interregnum. It is located in **Phaktangma** district and, although no longer extant, the impact of the Zur family's activities in this retreat centre over 5 centuries should not be underestimated. At the village of **Zur Sangakling**, where a temple was restored in 1421, the ritual dagger (*phurba*) of the Zur family was formerly preserved.

Upstream, closer to Zhigatse, the road passes the derelict site of **Thubten Serdokchen**, the residence of Zilungpa Sakya Chokden, which was founded in 1469 as a school of dialectics.

Phungpo Riwoche

Downstream from **Phaktangma** district, on the S bank of the Brahmaputra is **Mt Phungpo Riwoche**, one of the 'four sacred mountains of Tibet'. Padmasambhava passed time here in the **Yupuk** cave retreat, and later in the 10th-11th century it was an important site for the Dzogchen lineage since the master Nyang Jangchub Dra attained the rainbow body here. Subsequently the mountain became a favourite haunt of Yungtonpa Dorjepel (1284-1365). Also, at Yupuk, in the hermitage of Padmasambhava, the treasure-finder Dumpa Gyazhangtrom discovered Yamantaka *terma*, and Dorje Lingpa (1346-1405) discovered an image of Vajrasattva.

Nartang Monastery

Turning right at the **Zamshar** bridge, on the S side of town, the Zhigatse-Dram highway cuts SW towards the Tak La Nub pass, which forms a watershed between the Dzirak-chu and Shab-chu (Re-chu) rivers.

Nartang Monastery is located 14 km from Zhigatse on the N side of this road. This prominant Kadampa monastery was founded in 1153 by Tumton Lodro Drakpa, a disciple of Sharapa. Formerly, there was a **Kumbum (Tashi Gomang)** style stupa here, constructed during the 15th century, but it was destroyed during the Cultural Revolution. The main image was a form of Tara known as **Chumik Drolma**.

In the 17th century, Nartang came under the influence of Tashilhunpo; and it acquired particular renown for its xylograph (woodblock) compilation of the the Buddhist canon, the *Kangyur* and *Tangyur*, which was carved here between 1730-42 at the behest of Miwang Pholhane Sonam Topgyel, the then ruler of Tibet. A series of eight woodblocks depicting the Sixteen Elders were also commissioned; but only one now survives. Along with the extant fragments of the xylographs of the Nartang Canon, it is now preserved at Tashilhunpo.

The high ruined walls of Nartang are extensive, and only one small temple has been rebuilt. North of Nartang in the mountains is the **Jangchen Ritro** hermitage, where monks affiliated to Nartang would spend time in retreat.

Ngor Evam Chokden Monastery

Southwest of the Nartang turn-off, the highway passes N of **Chumik Ringmo**, where Chogyel Phakpa held a conclave concerning the Sakya hegemony of Tibet in 1277. The local monastery was destroyed by floods in the 15th century.

ACCESS Jeepable tracks lead SE from Chumik Ringmo and due S from Nartang to **Norburi** hill and **Berong** village, from which Ngor Monastery is accessible on foot.

Ngor Evam Chokden was founded in 1429 by Ngorchen Kunga Zangpo (1382-1444) of the Sakya school. The monastery became an important independent bastion of the *Lamdre* teachings, and developed its own branches throughout Tibet, as far as Jyekundo and Derge in Kham.

It was formerly renowned for its San-

TIBETAN CARPETS

Tibetan carpets are traditionally made on tall free-standing looms, on which pre-dyed woollen weft is threaded through a cotton warp and around a horizontal rod. The loops thus formed are then cut in half with a knife, which forms the pile and releases the rod. This so-called cut-loop method facilitates speedy production, in contrast to the slowly crafted Persian carpet (in which thousands of individual knots are tied). The density of the carpet is determined by the number of knots or loops per square inch, and the use of a wooden mallet to beat down each row. Most Tibetan carpets have had a fairly low density (40-80 knots or loops per square inch), and it was only in the early 1980s that the first 100 knot carpets were made by the Tibetan refugees Mr Topgyel and Mr Tseten Gyurme based in Nepal. After cutting, the carpets are trimmed, sculpted, and washed.

Traditionally Tibetan carpet making was a cottage industry, which developed in the Khampa Dzong area S of Gyantse, and the carpets produced even now in the Gyantse area are renowned. Many motifs are found, including dragons, flowers, medallions, birds, tiger-skins, and various natural scenes. There are 36 natural pigments in use; and these are now supplemented by a variety of chemical dyes. The size varies considerably; from the small square cushion-sized mats and single bed-sized rugs (ka-den), to the large floor-sized carpets (sa-den). There are production outlets for Tibetan carpets in Gyantse, Zhigatse and Lhasa; and in E Tibet, at Kandze, where there are local variations in design including the renowned rainbow border. Some of the best Tibetan carpets in both traditional and modern designs are now made, however, by Tibetan refugees living in Nepal and India.

skrit library and Newar-style murals. There were once five assembly halls, 18 colleges, and 400 monks, but presently it is restricted to only 25 monks.

The main temples are the **Lamdre Lhakhang** and the **Tartse Lhakhang**, the former (restored) containing images of Hayagriva, Mahakala, Virupa, Ngorchen Kunga Zangpo, Shakyamuni, and various hierarchs of the monastery. Below, there is a row of 60 renovated stupas, which once contained valuable mandala paintings, now preserved, documented and published in Japan.

Southwest of Berong are the **cave hermitages of Ngorchen Kunga Zangpo**, one of which contains his stone footprint. **Berong** village below Ngor may also be reached by trekking from Jamchu on the Zhigatse-Gyantse road via the Dzirak-chu or Zha-chu valleys; and another trek leads up the Dzirak-chu valley from Chumik to Chushar, and thence across Dug-nga La pass, into the Shab valley (see below, page 352).

ZHETONGMON COUNTY

བཞད་མཐོང་སྨོན

谢通门县 Xaitongmoin
Population: 15,271 Area: 8,772 sq km

The county of Zhetongmon, reached from Zhigatse via the Dongkar cable ferry to the N of town, comprises three major lateral valleys on the N bank of the Brahmaputra. These are, namely: **Tanak**, the valley of the Tanakpu-chu and its Namoche-chu tributary which supply Zhigatse with much of its electricity; **Zhe**, the valley of the Rong-chu and Zhe-chu rivers; and the upper headwaters of the **Mu Tsangpo** valley, comprising the Langna-chu and Gya-me-chu. The county capital is located at **Zhe Geding**, 138 km NW of Zhigatse.

TANAK

From **Dongkar** and **Zhudrong** villages

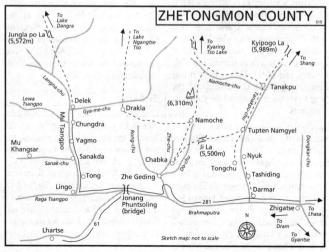

ZHETONGMON COUNTY

To Lake Dangra
Jungla po La (5,572m)
To Lake Ngangtse Tso
To Kyaring Tso Lake
Kyipogo La (5,989m)
To Shang
Namoche-chu
Tanakpu
Langna-chu
Lewa Tsangpo
Delek
Gya-me-chu
Drakla
(6,310m)
Namoche
Tupten Namgyel
Mu Tsangpo
Chungdra
Rong-chu
Zhe-chu
Dongkar-chu
Yagmo
Ji La (5,500m)
Nyuk
Mu Khangsar
Sanakda
Chabka
Tongchu
Tashiding
Sanak-chu
Tong
Zhe Geding
Darmar
Lingo
Jonang Phuntsoling (bridge)
281
Zhigatse
To Lhasa
Raga Tsangpo
Brahmaputra
N
Lhartse
61
To Dram
To Gyantse
Sketch map: not to scale

on the N bank of the Brahmaputra, take the W track which follows the river upstream. The **Upper Dongkar** valley is largely inhabited by nomads, but it does contain a productive coal mine. Continuing upstream, you will pass the villages of Chonyi, Tangpe, and Gede, before reaching the entrance to the **Tanak** valley at **Darmar**. Leave the Brahmaputra here and head into the valley.

Above Tashiding on the E bank of the Tanakpu-chu, there is a 1 hr trek to **Dolma Puk**, the cave hermitage of the Nyingmapa teacher Tanak Dolma-wa Samdrup Dorje (1295-1376). It was here that this renowned master transmitted the oral teachings of the Nyingma school, including the Mahayoga and Anuyoga texts, to his own son Sangye Rinchen (1350-1431), and student Zurham Shakya Jungne. It was here, in turn (and the nearby hermitages of **Namkading** and **Lagungo**), that Sangye Rinchen passed the teachings on to Zhangton Namka Dorje and he to his own student Rikdzin Yudruk Dorje. Samdrub Dorje's birthplace lies further upstream at **Nesar**.

At **Nyuk**, a village known for its terracotta pottery, there is the hermitage and nunnery of **Orgyen Guru**, associated with Padmasambhava. The Dzogchen master Kumaradza passed one winter season in retreat here during the 13th century, and in the 15th century it was here that Rigdzin II Lekdenje of the Jangter tradition conferred the Anuyoga teachings.

Across the Tanakpu-chu River, on the W bank is the **Tongchu Power Station**, which supplies Zhigatse town. Further upstream is **Tupten Namgyel**, an illustrious Sakya monastery founded in 1478 by Gorampa Sonam Senge. At **Tanakpu** township there is the **Bur Chutsen** hot springs, known for their medicinal properties. Trails lead from the upper reaches of the Tanak valley, via the Kyipogo La pass, to **Shang** in the NE and, via the

Namoche-chu valley and Lungzang La to **Kyaring Tso Lake** on the Jangtang plateau.

ZHE VALLEY

ACCESS The broad 100 sq km Zhe valley, in which the county capital **Zhe Geding** is located, may be reached from **Darmar** at the entrance to Tanak by following the Brahmaputra further upstream via Orgyen, Rungma and Kharu villages; or from **Tupten Namgyel Monastery** via a side-valley and the Ji La pass (5,500m). The plain is drained by the Rong-chu in the W, the Zhe-chu in the Central and the Do-chu in the E.

Heading inland from **Kharu** up the **Do-chu** valley, you will reach the Bon monastery of **Ser Darding**, where a small temple has been rebuilt. The ruined assembly hall was sacked by the Dzungar armies in the 18th century and more recently by the red guards.

Zhe Geding has guesthouse and restaurant facilities in the government compound; as well as an open air market, a post office and a tea shop. A track leads N out of town across a bridge to the renovated monastery of **Zhe Tratang Chenpo**, where there are some original murals. In the SW of the county, there is **Zhe Ngulchu Chodzong**, the residence of Gyalse Tokme Zangpo (1295-1359) who propagated the compassionate cult of Avalokiteshvara in Tibet.

Trekking

Heading inland from Chabka township, **Namoche** village is located beyond the head of the Do-chu valley, nestling below the snows of **Mt Zhe Lapu Gangri** (6,310m). A trail from here follows the Namoche River downstream to its confluence with the Tanakpu-chu; and an arduous 17-day trekking route can be undertaken via Khampalho village and Drakla township to **Lake Ngangtse Tso** in the Jangtang Northern Plateau (see below, page 390).

UPPER MU VALLEY

The **Mu valley**, extending through dramatic gorges towards the Nyenchen Tanglha range, has long been an important caravan route for traders. The lower reaches of the valley may be reached from **Zhe** by following the Brahmaputra upstream, or more easily via the motorable bridge at **Phuntsoling** (see below, page 360). The village of Lingo stands at the arid confluence of the Mu-chu and Raga Tsangpo rivers. Entering the gorge of the **Mu-chu**, there are many rock carvings and paintings to be seen. Above **Tong**, the river banks are terraced and cultivated.

At **Sanakda**, where the Sanak-chu converges with the Mu-chu, a trail leads W to **Mu Khangsar**. The ritual dagger discovered as terma by Darcharuwa was kept at **Mu-se**, before being transferred to Sera Monastery in Lhasa (see above, page 185). The main trail continues N via **Yagmo** and **Chungdra**, where the Lewa Tsangpo converges from the W, and **Delek** township where the Gyame-chu and Langna-chu headwaters come together. En route, you can detour to visit the ruins of **Lelung Monastery**, which has both Bonpo and Buddhist associations; and, in the upper reaches, the monastery of **Takmolingka**, which was founded by Muchen Konchok Gyeltsen of the Ngorpa Sakya school in 1436.

Trekking

It is possible to undertake a demanding 30-day trek through the gorges of the Mu valley, following the well travelled yak caravan route across Janglapo La pass (5,572m) to the Bon pilgrimage sites of **Lake Dangra** in the Jangtang Plateau (see below, page 396).

SAKYA COUNTY

ས་སྐྱ

萨迦县 Sakya

Population: 28,991   Area: 6,661 sq km

The county of **Sakya** comprises the lateral valleys of the **Shab-chu** and the **Trum-chu**, which flow NW to converge with the Brahmaputra respectively at **Rungma** and **Lhartse**. The main Zhigatse-Dram highway crosses the Shab-chu at **Shab Geding**, 60 km from Zhigatse; and a motorable track extends SE through the long Shab valley for 35 km as far as **Se** township. Beyond Se, there are trekking trails which lead via the remote upper reaches of this valley to **Gampa** county on the Sikkim border. The shorter **Trum-chu** valley, extending from the **Sakya Zampa** bridge as far as **Drongu La** pass, is motorable for its entire length. The route continues beyond the pass via **Mabja** to **Tingkye** county (106 km from the bridge), from where branch roads diverge: W to **Shelkar** (123 km), E to **Gampa** (129 km), and

SAKYA COUNTY   516   Sketch map: not to scale

S to **Drentang** in the **Bum-chu** (**Arun**) valley on the E Nepal border (87 km).

The administrative county capital is located at **Sakya** in the Trum-chu valley, 21 km upstream from the Sakya Zampa bridge. It was from this renowned monastery and town that the whole of Tibet was governed during the period of the Sakyapa hegemony (1268-1365), and there are buildings of historic importance to be seen, which were spared the destruction of the Cultural Revolution.

SHAB VALLEY

Tropu Jamchen Chode Monastery

Located E of **Shab Geding**, and in a gorge N of the highway, this ruined but important monastery was founded in the mid-12th century by Rinpoche Gyeltsa, a student of Phakmodrupa, and developed by his own student Jampapel, otherwise known as Tropu Lotsawa (1173-1225). He studied Sanskrit in Nepal, and was instrumental in inviting many Indian panditas to Tropu, notably Shakyashri of Kashmir, Mitrayogi, and Buddhashri. He had a large 80 cubit image of Maitreya constructed there, and a large Kumbum-style stupa was added later in the 15th century. The lineage became known as the Tropu Kagyu; its most renowned adherent being Buton Rinchendrub of Zhalu (see above, page 347).

Se Township and the Upper Shab-chu Valley

Shab Geding was formerly the residence of the preceptors of Sakya. A ruined fortress is prominent on the hillside to the N of the road. Here, the highway crosses the river via the **Shab Geding Zampa bridge**; and there are side-roads leading N towards **Rungma** on the Brahmaputra and S to **Se** township in the **Shab** valley. Taking the latter route,

you can drive through **Tsesum** and as far as Se. An alternative 2-day trekking route leads from Ngor Monastery to Se via Duk-ngal La pass (4,550m) and Rabdeling.

3 hrs trekking above Se, you can visit the fortified monastery of **Se Rinchentse**, and the nearby birthplace of Remdawa Lodro Zhonu, a celebrated master of the Sakya school who was Tsongkhapa's main teacher. Little but ruins remain, though the site does contain a sacred spring (associated with Padmasambhava) and a hilltop shrine dedicated to the local deity Pen-je.

Trekking

From Se township, there is a 4-day trek via **Lazhung** to **Sakya**; and from **Mula**, further SE in the **Shab** valley, there is another 4-day trek via the **Gye-chu** valley, **Yago** and **Gurma** to **Gampa** county (see below, page 366). Alternatively, if you continue to trek upstream along the course of the Shab-chu, at **Netsi**, the valley bifurcates: the left branch following the Tradong-chu source, and the right following the Chusum-chu, both of which lead in the direction of S **Khangmar** county (see below, page 363).

TROM-CHU VALLEY

Sakya Monastery

ས་སྐྱ་དགོན་ན་པ

The Sakya tradition is one of the four main Buddhist schools in Tibet. It was from here that the whole of Tibet was governed during the period of the **Sakyapa hegemony** (1268-1365), and even now there are buildings of historic importance to be seen, which were spared the destruction of the Cultural Revolution.

ACCESS After crossing the **Tso La pass**, which acts as a watershed between the Shab-chu and Trum-chu rivers, turn left (S) at the **Sakya Zampa** bridge to leave the highway, and follow the latter upstream to **Sakya** township (21 km). The great monastery of Sakya is located 3 km to the left

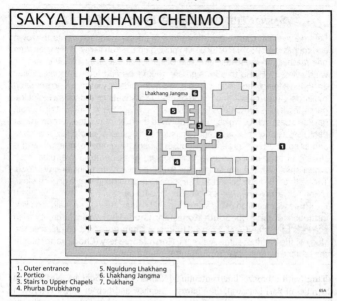

SAKYA LHAKHANG CHENMO

Lhakhang Jangma **6**

1. Outer entrance
2. Portico
3. Stairs to Upper Chapels
4. Phurba Drubkhang
5. Nguldung Lhakhang
6. Lhakhang Jangma
7. Dukhang

65A

(E) of the township on a side road.

The Five Patriarchs of Sakya

The **Khon** family had been influential in Tibet since the 8th century, when **Khon Luiwangpo Sungwa** ranked among the foremost translators of Buddhist Sanskrit texts. Subsequently, during the 11th century, **Khon Konchok Gyelpo** (1034-1102) moved from Southern to Western Tibet, where he studied with Drokmi Lotsawa – a foremost translator and mystic who had also taught Marpa. Drokmi himself had studied with many great Indian masters such as Gayadhara and Virupa, from whom he had received the lineage of the *Hevajra Tantra*. In 1073, Khon Konchok Gyelpo founded the temple of **Gorum Zimchi Karpo** on the N bank of the Trum-chu River, which eventually became the heart of the complex known as **North Sakya (Chode Jang)**. The foremost images of the Gorum Temple were a bronze Manjughosa in the form Jamy-

ang Zi-o Barwa and the leather mask known as Gorum Sebakma, which was kept in the Protector Chapel (Gonkhang). This temple is now destroyed; and the whereabouts of its precious relics are unknown.

The son of Khon Konchok Gyelpo was **Sachen Kunga Nyingpo** (1092-1158), who is revered as the first patriarch of Sakya. He studied with Zhangton Chobar, a second-generation student of Drokmi's, and was able to codify the Sakya teachings known as the *Lamdre*, the 'Path and its Fruit', as well as the *Two Recensions of the Hevajra Tantra (Tak-nyi)*. Two of Sachen Kunga Nyingpo's four sons, **Sonam Tsemo** (1142-82) and **Drakpa Gyeltsen** (1147-1216) also became renowned patriarchs of Sakya; and throughout this period the vast complex of North Sakya was developed into 108 temples. Among these, the most important extant or renovated structures are: the **Tantric College (Ngakpa Tratsang)**, the **Dolma Lha-**

SAKYA: THE 'PALE EARTH' RELIGIOUS COMPLEX

Before arriving at Lhartse a side road turns S off the main highway to the town and monastery of Sakya. After 21 km driving up the lush valley of the river Trum one reaches the monolithic structure of the Great Sakya Temple. The massive windowless walls, up to 35m high are 100m long and form a square citadel enclosing a temple and monastic complex. Its formidable presence is accentuated by its dark grey colour and its protruding rain spouts carved as mythological gargoyles. It rises above fields to the W and S, a village to the E in front of its main gate and past a slope which runs N, down to the river. Above the river on the far bank rises a jumble of houses and ruins surrounding a second complex of temples and living quarters. This array of houses is about a kilometre in length and is striking in appearance since all buildings are painted with a grey/blue wash embellished with red, white and blue stripes below the roof line and windows. The earth of the ridge behind and for some distance around is pale grey in colour, giving Sakya its name (*Tib* "sa" = earth; "kya" = pale).

These two areas on either side of the river demarcate the two main monastic institutions of Sakya. The **South Monastery (Chode Lho)** within the great walled citadel is called the Great Temple (**Lhakhang Chenmo**) and it emphasized the study of the Buddhist sutras, while the **North Monastery (Chode Jang)** taught the esoteric Buddhist practices of tantra.

khang (with a bronze Tara containing the relics of Bari Lotsawa), the **Victory Stupa** containing the relics of Khon Konchok Gyelpo, the **Demchok Lhakhang** (dedicated to Cakrasamvara), the **Mukchung Gonkhang**, the **Yutok Lhakhang**, the **Zhitok Labrang** (containing a number of reliquaries), the **Dolma Lhakhang**, the **West Protector Chapel (Gonkhang Nub)** which contained images of the Chamdrel protectors, and the **Zurkhang Tsuklakhang**, containing an image of Drakpa Gyeltsen named Dzetoma.

The fourth patriarch of Sakya was **Sakya Pandita Kunga Gyeltsen** (1182-1251), a grandson of Sachen Kunga Nyingpo, who was universally regarded as the greatest lama and most prolific scholar of his age. He was invited by Godan Qan to the Mongolian royal court in 1244, and remained there until his death in 1251, the same year in which the Qan himself passed away.

Drogon Chogyel Phakpa (1235-80), also known as Lodro Gyeltsen, was the last of the so-called 'five patriarchs of Sakya' (Sakya Gongma Nga). As the nephew and heir of Sakya Pandita, he accompanied his uncle to Mongolia, and later was appointed as the personal mentor and advisor to Godan's successor **Qubilai Qan** (1216-94). Drogon Chogyel Phakpa is credited with the invention of the first Mongolian script, known as Hor-yig, which is still utilized by the Tu peoples of NE Tibet. With Mongol support, he became the first effective ruler of Tibet since the fragmentation of the Yarlung Dynasty during the 9th century. He established a network of Sakya temples and monasteries throughout the remote parts of E Tibet, particularly around Dzongsar, Derge, Jyekundo, Kandze and Minyak, and he received the title Rinchen Chogyel, 'precious spiritual ruler'. To set the seal on his assumption of power, he oversaw the building of the Great Temple on the S bank of the Trum-chu. This imposing **Lhakhang Chenmo**, predating the building of its outer walls, was begun in 1268 at his behest, with funds provided by Qubilai Qan, who by this time

QUBILAI QAN'S MONGOL TRIBUTE

The Mongol armies conquered almost the whole of Asia and eventually extended their rule into Europe as far as Hungary. The Mongol qans ruled an empire which, at its greatest extent, was among the largest in the history of mankind. Their 'patron-priest' relationship with the throne-holders of Sakya reflects the unique rapport established by Sakya Pandita and his nephew at the Mongol court. It was they who foresaw that only by such a means could Tibet avoid the tragic fate of Xixia and other kingdoms which had pointlessly attempted to resist the advance of the Mongol armies by military means.

The model established by the Sakyapas was later adopted by the Tsangpa and Gelukpa rulers of Tibet, and it has in recent times been used by China as one of the main historical justifications for their occupation of Tibet. Qubilai Qan's relationship with Drogon Chogyel Phakpa, and the tributes which they mutually offered at that time are now cited as proof that Qubilai 'ruled over Tibet'. The implication that China has ruled Tibet ever since could, it has been suggested, by the same logic be made against Hungary or any other country conquered by the Mongols, who racially are quite distinct from the Chinese! At the present day, Outer Mongolia is an independent nation. Inner Mongolia has been occupied by China, and its Han Chinese immigrant population now outnumbers the original Mongol inhabitants, despite its 'autonomous' status.

had become the Emperor of China. The construction was eventually completed in 1276 by the regent Shakya Zangpo. Its contents will be described below (see pages 356).

In the first half of the 14th century, as a result of Chogyel Phakpa's system of dividing the large monastic structures into smaller units led by their own spiritual preceptors, the then throne-holder **Kunga Lodro Gyeltsen** divided the ruling Khon family into four houses (*labrang*), each of which would take turns to provide the throne-holder. However, by the 15th century two of these houses failed to produce heirs and the rivalries between two brothers of the Ducho Labrang eventually led to a reduction in their number. Power was consequently divided between the two houses of **Dolma Podrang** and **Phuntsok Podrang**, who over succeeding centuries provided the throne-holder in rotation. Two chapels in the upper storey of the **Lhakhang Chenmo** were built by the early throne-holders of these families and named after their illustrious houses.

By 1354, in the interim, the political power of the Sakyapas in Tibet had diminished, both as a result of internal feuding and in consequence of the collapse of the Mongolian Yuan Dynasty in China. The political vacuum was filled by the Phakmodrupa family, who were based at Tsetang and favoured the Kagyu tradition.

The unique familial succession of Sakya, nonetheless, continued down to the present day, and its throne-holders are even now revered as important spiritual and regal figures in the Tibetan world. The present throne-holder of the **Dolma Podrang** house, HH Sakya Trizin (b 1945), is the 42nd in line (or 44th if Khon Konchok Gyelpo and Bari Lotsawa are included) and he resides at Rajpur in N India. He has an outstanding command of English and lucidly communicates the philosophical perspective and tradition of the Sakya school throughout the world.

Sakya Sub-schools

In the first half of the 15th century,

Ngorchen Kunga Zangpo (1382-1457) founded the Ngor sub-school, and, later, in the first half of the 16th century, **Tsarchen Losal Gyatso** (1502-56) founded the Tsarpa sub-school. The former established a number of important branches in Jyekundo and Derge districts of Kham.

The Temples of North Sakya

The temples on the N bank of the Trum-chu were built first. Among these the Gorum Temple to the NE was the oldest, built in 1073 by Khon Konchok Gyelpo. The Utse Nyingba, Utse Sarpa, and Manjughosa temples were constructed successively by Sachen Kunga Nyingpo, Choje Drakpa Gyeltsen, and Sakya Pandita Kunga Gyeltsen around the meditation cave of Sachen. Most of these original temples were destroyed during the 1960s, but there are a number of lesser chapels and residential buildings which are well worth visiting. Some of these have been enumerated above. The **Four-Storey Palace (Zhitok Podrang)** and the **Blissful Abode of Secret Mantra (Sangak Dechenling)** are particularly memorable. Aware of the importance of the ancient complex of North Sakya, the monastic preceptors of the present day spend much of their time here.

The Temples of Sakya South

On the S bank of the Trum-chu, dominating the surrounding college buildings and palaces, is the impressive citadel known as the **Lhakhang Chenmo**. At present there are five rooms open to the public, four of which house images and reliquary stupas containing the mortal remains of Sakya's past throne-holders, including some of the original five patriarchs (Gongma Nga). The fifth contains manuscript fragments and images retrieved from the ruins of the older temples close to the patch of pale earth on the N bank.

The main entrance faces E and is

offset from the central axis of the outer gateway. The building is over two storeys high, and has an inner courtyard which gives access to the main temples.

The Upper Chapels

The upper chapels are approached via a flight of stairs accessed from the portico of the inner gateway. Among them, the **Phuntsok Podrang Lhakhang** is, as its name suggests, the chapel associated with the ruling house of Phuntsok Podrang. It contains fine murals and statues, the principal image depicting Manjughosa. There are also statues of the past lineage-holders and reliquary stupas containing the tombs of early throne-holders associated with this branch of the family line.

On the E side is the **Dolma Podrang Lhakhang**, containing five reliquary stupas of important throne-holders hailing from this branch of the family. The altar has images depicting the Three Deities of Longevity, with White Tara first and foremost.

On the NE corner, there is a locked chamber containing Sakya's precious collection of Sanskrit palm-leaf manuscripts.

The Lower Chapels

On the S (left) side of the inner courtyard is the **Phurba Drubkhang**, a large well-lit chamber in which Vajrakila rituals are performed, and which has a number of bookcases, positioned between images of Shakyamuni Buddha and Manjushri. All these contents were retrieved from the rubble of the temples of North Sakya, following the destruction of the Cultural Revolution. On the left wall is the wrathful figure of Havajra in union with the female consort Nairatmya. This is the deity described in the main tantra practiced in the Sakya tradition. It was Drokmi Lotsawa who first translated the text into Tibetan, and it thereafter became the main meditational practice of Khon Konchok Gyelpo.

On the N (right) side of the inner

courtyard, is the **Nguldung Lhakhang**, which has as its inner sanctum, the **Lhakhang Jangma**. The former houses 11 silver reliquary stupas containing the remains of past throne-holders of Sakya, with that of Ngakchang Kunga Rinchen foremost among them. The 12-pillared **Lhakhang Jangma** has six reliquary stupas containing the remains of important past abbots of Sakya who did not belong to the familial line; and in addition, a series of outstanding wall-painted mandalas, including those of Sarvavid Vairocana and Mayajala.

The Assembly Hall (Dukhang)

Facing the entrance inside the courtyard is the enormous **Assembly Hall (Dukhang)**. This is nowadays the most significant of the temples at Sakya. Its walls are 3.5m thick and up to 16m high. The roof is supported by 40 huge wooden columns made from entire tree trunks. Among these, the four central columns near the entrance are about 2m in circumference. The NW pillar, known as **Sechen Kawa**, was a gift from Qubilai Qan. It was moved by hand from Drentang. The SE pillar, known as **Takmo Kawa** ('tigress pillar'), is said to have been transported from India by a large tigress whose skin, 6m long, was tied to the column. The one to the SW, known as **Drongpo Kawa**, is said to have been brought by a wild yak who wept tears at a pass on the way, thus giving rise to a miraculous spring. Lastly, the NE pillar, known as **Nakpo Trakdzak Kawa** ('pillar bleeding black blood'), is named after a serpent spirit (*naga*) who reputedly wept black blood when it was cut down. The trunk is said to cure diseases when a nail is driven into it.

Around the three walls facing the entrance are a superb series of larger than life-size images, many of them refinely cast. Made at different times and showing a variety of different styles and influences, they mostly depict Shakyamuni Buddha, and contain the relics of the main masters of the Sakya tradition. This is not usually found in Tibetan temples.

Passing clockwise along the SE, S, W and N walls in succession from the eastern door, you will notice the following images and precious objects: **SE Wall**: a gold manuscript edition of the *Kangyur* commissioned by Chogyel Phakpa (1); **S Wall**: a gold manuscript edition of the *Kangyur* commissioned by Yumchok Tendzin Wangmo (2); a cast image of Shakyamuni Buddha (Tubwang Totsema) containing the relics of Shakya Zangpo (3); an image of Shakyamuni Buddha with a hair-ringlet made of white conch, containing the relics of Sharpa Rinchen Gyeltsen (4); images of Avalokiteshvara and Padmasambhava (5); **W Wall**: an image of Shakyamuni Buddha containing the relics of Sakya Pandita (6); the reliquary stupa of Trichen Ngawang Tutob, previous throneholder of Sakya (7); a cast 'speaking' image of Shakyamuni Buddha, named Tuwang Sungjon Tatsema, commissioned by Sachen Kunga Nyingpo (8); a cast image of Shakyamuni Buddha named Lhachen Pelbar, which contains the relics of Chogyel Phakpa (9); the renowned white conch-shell of Sakya, kept in a glass case (10); a cast image of standing Tara which was brought to Tibet by Atisha (11); a cast image of Tara containing the Jamyang Tsogyelma image on which Sakya Pandita meditated when he defeated a Hindu zealot in debate at Kyirong (12); the main image of the temple – a cast Shakyamuni Buddha named Tuchen Totsema, which was commissioned by Drogon Chogyel Phakpa (13); images of the 37 deities of the *Sarvavid Vairocanatantra* in the foreground (14); a large throne named Zhuktri Tarchikma which the first three patriarchs of Sakya once used, and a smaller throne in front used by the monastic preceptors of Sakya (15); three white-robed images depicting the first three patriarchs of Sakya (16); an image of Manjughosha named Jamyang Metubma,

THE BIGGEST BOOK IN THE WORLD?

Near the far NW corner of Sakya's Great Library is what could be the largest book in the world. It is a fully illuminated manuscript in gold lettering of the "*Sutra of the Perfection of Discrimination Awareness in One Hundred Thousand Fascicules*" (*Prajnaparamitasutra*). It lies in a special rack and its pages, in traditional single leaf format, are approximately 1.75m wide by 0.75m deep by 0.5m thick bound between two huge cover planks.

containing the relics of Tekchen Chokyi Lama (17); a cast image of Maitreya named Jamgon Totsema, containing the relics of Jetsun Pejung (18); a cast image of Vajradhara containing the relics of Dharmatala (19); a reliquary stupa named Chodong Dzamling Osel, containing the relics of Trichen Tutob Wangchuk (20); a clay image of Shakyamuni Buddha named Tuwang Totsema, containing the relics of the minister Anglen (21); a cast image of Manjughosa named Jamyang Chokhorma, containing the relics of Sharpa Dukhorwa (22); and **N Wall**: a cast image of Shakyamuni, containing the relics of Sabzang Mati Panchen (23); a cast image of Jowo Aram, containing the relics of Gangkarwa Rinchenpel (24).

Of these objects, the White Conch is revered as the most sacred object in the temple. It was given to Drogon Chogyel Phakpa by Emperor Qubilai Qan, and is regarded as the remains of the Buddha from a previous existence when born as a shellfish. It existed at the time of the present Shakyamuni Buddha, and was used by him in antiquity before being transported from India to China, and thence to Tibet. You may have to persist in order to be shown it!

The **murals** of the upper gallery depict the lamas of the *Lamdre* lineage; those of the S wall the Hundred Deeds of Shakyamuni Buddha; those of the W wall the life of Drogon Chogyel Phakpa; and those of the N wall the five original patriarchs of Sakya. On the ceiling are hundreds of mandalas representing the outer and inner tantras of the New Translation Schools.

Under these statues in a series of glass cases to the right of the central shrine are objects of art from the Emperors of Mongolia and China that no doubt represent a small part of the treasures of tribute or offerings made to the Sakya masters before the ravages of the Cultural Revolution.

The Great Library

It is well worth asking your guide to show you the library (Chotsek or 'Pendzo-khang'). To do so you may have to pay something extra (anything from ¥1.00 to ¥5.00). However once this is done you will be led behind the line of statues to a vast collection of Buddhist texts towering to the ceiling that have been gathering dust for centuries. They are stacked two storeys or eight stacks high in racks, made up of 'pigeon holes' in more than 60 sections, the length of the whole Assembly Hall. There in the gloom are thousands of texts the extent of which are only seen with a strong torch. It brings to mind what a portion of the great library of Alexandria must have been like.

Sakya town

The town and villages of Sakya are very poor, as is much of Tibet these days, and it is not unusual to be vigorously pursued by gangs of children begging you for money. Do give whatever you can manage but do not give away large amounts randomly just because one child may be more appealing. It is always good to make a donation in the main shrines by placing it on the altar

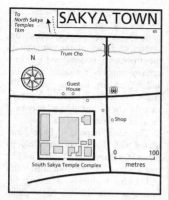

or on Offering Mandalas that usually hold some donations from prior visitors. This will benefit the whole monastery. If you give money to an individual it is normally used by that person alone.

Also the monks and guides of Sakya are obliged to collect the maximum in fees and taxes from every visitor. These are then paid to the government. If not they can be severely punished for showing any generosity to the tourists. Be warned.

● **Accommodation** There is a rest house next to the Great Temple at its NE corner. Rooms of between 5 and 10 beds are available and cooking remains one's own responsibility. Another guest house lies a few 100m E on the eastern side of the main street which runs N-S, located E of the Great Citadel. The rate for foreign tourists may be approximately ¥10 to ¥20/night.

Mabja and the Upper Bum-chu (Arun) River valley

The dirt track continues S from Sakya to leave the **Trum-chu** River valley via the **Drongu La pass**, for Mabja in the upper reaches of the **Bum-chu** (**Arun**) River valley. **Tingkye** county lies further S (see below, page 367), some 85 km from Sakya township; and there is also a 4-day trekking route to **Kharda** and the E face of **Mt Everest** (see below, page 371).

LHARTSE COUNTY

ལྷ་རྩེ

拉孜县 Lhaze

Population: 32,668 *Area:* 4,170 sq km

Lhartse county, traditionally known as **Nyingri** district, is located on the S bank of the Brahmaputra, E of the Shab-chu valley. It extends upstream from **Phuntsoling** at the confluence of the **Raga Tsangpo** (Dokzhung Tsangpo) and Brahmaputra, as far as **Chushar** (**Lhartse**), where the **Chushar**, **Mangkar**, and **Trum-chu** rivers all flow into the Brahmaputra. The county capital at **Chushar** straddles three important motor roads: E to **Zhigatse** via Chutsen and Lepu (157 km), S to **Dram** (*Ch* Zhangmu) via Shekar and Dingri (315 km), and W to **Ngamring** (60 km), the gateway to Mt Kailash in Far-western Tibet.

Bodong Monastery

བོ་དོང་དགོན་པ

16 km W of **Shab Geding**, there is a turn-off on the N side of the Zhigatse-Dram highway, leading to **Tashigang** (14

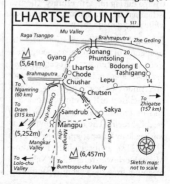

km) and **Jonang Phuntsoling** (20 km). The **Monastery of Bodong E**, located near Tashigang, was founded by Geshe Mudrapachenpo in 1049. It subsequently became the residence of Tibet's great grammarian Pang Lotsawa Lodro Tenpa (1276-1342) and of the Bodong Panchen Cho-le Namgyel (1375-1451). The latter was the prolific writer of some 100 volumes of treatises on sutra, tantra and traditional sciences including poetics and monastic discipline. The temple at Bodong, which gave rise to an independent Buddhist lineage in Tibet, once contained a revered image made from the ashes of Bodong Panchen himself. At **Nyenyo Jagoshong**, further N, there was once a peripheral 'border-taming temple', attributed to King Songtsen Gampo, containing an image of Vaishravana.

Jonang Phuntsoling

ཇོ་ནང་ཕ་ན་ཚོ་གས་གྲུ་ང

ACCESS Phuntsoling township is located at the confluence of the Brahmaputra and Raga Tsangpo (Dokzhung Tsangpo) rivers, 50 km from **Shab Geding** on a branch road to the NW of the Zhigatse-Dram highway, and 61 km from **Lhartse** county town via another dirt road which follows the Brahmaputra downstream to the confluence. A weak suspension bridge spans the river here, immediately above the defunct **Phuntsoling Chakzam**, which was constructed by Tibet's famous bridge-builder Tangtong Gyelpo during the 15th century. The area is dominated by an enormous shimmering white sand dune to the W.

Jonang Phuntsoling was formerly the stronghold of the Jonangpa school, which since the 17th century has been confined to remote areas of Dzamtang and Ngawa in S Amdo (see below, page 627), following the closure of their mother monastery and its transformation into a Gelukpa establishment. The original foundation was made by **Kunpangpa Tu-je Tsondru** (1243-1313), a lineage-holder of Yumo Mikyo Dorje who received the Kalacakra teachings from the Kashmiri pandita So-

manatha in the 11th century, and founded the school, renowned for its philosophical exposition of 'extraneous emptiness' (*zhentong*), the view that all the attributes of Buddhahood are extraneously empty of mundane impurities and defilements, but not intrinsically empty in a nihilistic sense, their experience thereby transcending all notions of existence and non-existence.

The most important figure connected with this school was **Dolpopa Sherab Gyeltsen** (1292-1361), a prolific commentator on the combined sutra and tantra traditions including the *Kalacakra Tantra*. He refined the philosophical exposition of 'extraneous emptiness' and expanded the monastery. In particular, nearby to his own hermitage, which lies below a Padmasambhava meditation cave on **Mt Jomo Nagyel** (5,744m), he built the Kumbum-style stupa named **Tongdrol Chenmo** in the side-valley of **Jonang**, a 2 hrs walk from the monastery. This 20m high stupa is almost of the same dimensions as the Kumbum at Gyantse. It is octagonal in shape and has seven storeys. The extant murals are said to reflect the provincial **Lato** style, which represents an early synthesis of Nepalese **Newar** and indigenous Tibetan elements, incorporating fewer Chinese inspired elements than the paintings of Zhalu or Gyantse.

The main monastery at Phuntsoling and the Kumbum were subsequently expanded by **Taranatha** (1575-1634), with funds provided by the kings of Tsang; and given the name **Takten Phuntsoling**. Following the civil war, the monastery was absorbed by the Gelukpa school and its name was altered to **Ganden Phuntsoling** during the lifetime of Taranatha's fifth incarnation.

The red buildings of the monastery presently stand within **Phuntsoling village**. The main 4-storey temple has an inner sanctum containing images of Aksobhya Buddha, flanked by the Eight Bodhisattvas. The library containing gold-inscribed texts on black or indigo paper is no longer extant; though some of its woodblocks have been preserved at Derge in Kham, and elsewhere. The hilltop **residence of Taranatha** is in ruins; whereas the **Tangka Wall** (**goku**) and **Mani Stone Wall** have survived. A protector shrine dedicated to Bektse, named **Drakram Gonkhang**, was founded nearby by Bodong Rinchentse.

Gyang

The district traditionally known as **Gyang** or **Drampa** lies 50 km SW of **Phuntsoling**, to the E of the Lhartse plain. Here in the 7th century, King Songtsen Gampo founded one of his primary geomantic temples, the **Drampagyang Lhakhang**, which once contained a celebrated image of Vairocana Buddha, but is now in ruins.

At neighbouring **Gyang Yonpolung**, there are the ruins of a small Nyingmapa temple below meditation caves associated with Padmasambhava, Yeshe Tsogyel, and Namkei Nyingpo. It was in this locale that, during the 14th century, the treasure-finder Zangpo Drakpa discovered the popular liturgical text known as the '*Seven Chapters*' (*le'u bdunma*). This text included an inventory, which paved the way for Rigdzin Godemchen's revelation of the **Northern Treasures** (*Jangter*) at **Zangzang Lhadrak** (see below, page 385) in 1366.

Further NW, and on the other side of the Lhartse-Phuntsoling road, is the destroyed Kumbum-style stupa of **Gyang Bumpoche**, built by the Sakyapa Sonam Tashi (1352-1417) and Thangtong Gyalpo (1385-1464), and decorated in the **Lato** style of painting.

From the 17th century onwards, this area was developed by the Panchen Lamas, who had a summer palace constructed nearby, and made lavish donations to the temple and the stupa.

Lhartse Chode and Gayadhara Lhakhang

The Gelukpa monastery of **Lhartse Chode** is located 10 km N of **Chushar**, the modern county town of Lhartse. Behind the monastery on a hill are the ruins of the old **Lhartse Dzong**, and to the E are the buildings of old Lhatse village. Formerly there were 1,000 monks in this institution, which dates originally to the 13th century. The assembly hall contains some 17th century murals, and restoration work is continuing.

Below the ruined fortress is the **Gayadhara Lhakhang**, which was built around the cave hermitage of Drokmi Lotsawa (993-1050) and his contemporary, the Kashmiri pandita Gayadhara. These figures were the teachers of Khon Konchok Gyelpo who founded the original Gorum Temple at Sakya in 1073, giving birth to the Sakyapa school.

Chushar Town

10 km S of Lhartse Chode and the old Lhartse village, is **Chushar**, the county capital of modern Lhartse. The town is an important staging post on the roads from **Zhigatse**, **Dram** (**Zhangmu**) on the Nepal border, and **Mt Kailash** in Far-west Tibet. Three river valleys extend upstream to the S: the Trum-chu, which leads via the **Zhichen Chutsen hot springs** to **Sakya** (see above, page

351 which leads to the **Mangkar** hermitages; and the Chushar, which leads across **Gyatso La** pass (5,252m) on the main highway, eventually reaching **Shelkar** at the confluence of the **Bumchu (Arun)** river and its **Lolo-chu** tributary. The distance from **Chushar** to **Shelkar** is 75 km. The road for **Ngamring** and **Mt Kailash** branches off the Gyatso La road after the **Chushar Zampa** bridge and crosses the Brahmaputra via the **Drapu ferry** or the newly-built **Lhartse Chakzam bridge**. Here **Mt Yakri** (5,641m) dominates the road on the far bank of the river.

Until recently **Chushar** was a small 'one horse' Tibetan town, with one main government shop down a side street, three guesthouses, a post office, a grocery store, a cinema and one petrol pump consisting of a rubber hose protruding from the broken window of an oil-stained mud hut. The petrol station had been a popular meeting point! It lay opposite the two small Sichuan and Muslim restaurants in town. In 1993 Chushar underwent a radical transformation. It was inundated with Han Chinese who held permits for shops on the main high street. This coincided with a modern Chinese petrol station at the E edge of town and the construction of the bridge across the Brahmaputra. The main street has now begun to take on the characteristics of thousands of other towns across China. The rows of concrete cubicle boxes for shops that stretch down either side of the main street, selling little of practical use, are all, bar one, run by Han Chinese (who, before 1992, never were seen in any numbers in Lhartse). Perhaps for the traveller it gives a sense of security in its familiarity! Here one can pick up any last minute purchases, such as 3 mins noodles or Chinese beer, for the journey across the Jangtang Northern Plateau.

Mangkar valley

The track to **Mangkar** leaves Chushar via the street running due S between the post office and the cinema. Take the E track at the next intersection, and head S to **Samdrub** and **Mangpu**, deep in the Mangkar gorge. The snow peaks of **Lhago Gangri** (6,457m) dominate its upper reaches. From **Mangpu**, a trekking trail leads to the right into the Mangkar valley, where there are said to be 13 great meditation caves. Among these, the cave hermitage of Tsarchen Losal Gyatso (1502-67), founder of the Tsarpa sub-school of the Sakyapa tradition, lies within the **Monastery of Tubten Gepel**, and his tomb is located at the nearby monastery of **Dar Drongmoche**. Ma Rinchen Chok, one of Padmasambhava's 25 disciples, was born in middle Mangkar.

In the upper reaches are the ruins of **Ganden Dargyeling**, a Gelukpa monastery, and various meditation caves associated with Drokmi Lotsawa, who transmitted the Sakyapa teachings here to Khon Konchok Gyelpo. These include: the **Osel Dawa Puk**, where Drokmi meditated; the **Dragyur Puk**, where he translated Sanskrit texts; and the **Sungak Lamdre Puk** where he received the transmission of the 'Path and its Fruit' (*Lamdre*). At nearby **Mugulung hermitage**, Drokmi gave teachings to Marpa Lotsawa of the Kagyu school and Zurpoche Shakya Jungne of the Nyingma school.

Trekking

From Mangkar, there is a 3-day trekking route to Sakya via **Drumchok**, a shorter trek SW to the Lolo-chu valley, and yet another due S to the Bumtsopu-chu valley.

KHANGMAR COUNTY

ཁང་དམར

康马县 Kangmar

Population: 13,505   Area: 5,172 sq km

Khangmar county includes the valleys of the **Drumpayu-chu** and **Nyeru-chu** rivers, which flow due N from their Himalayan watersheds to converge with the **Nyang-chu**, at **Nenying** and **Lungmar** respectively. The main highway from Gyantse to **Dromo** (*Ch* Yadong) on the Bhutan and Sikkim borders passes through the **Drumpayu** valley; and from the **Nyeru** valley, there are mountain passes leading directly into the **Gasa** district of **N Bhutan**.

The county capital is located at **Khangmar** (Nyangchu), 48 km S of Gyantse. At **Kala** township (44 km further S), there is a security checkpost which monitors all traffic heading towards the border. **Nenying** and **Yemar** temples are sites of historic importance located in Khangmar county.

KHANGMAR COUNTY

Sketch map: not to scale

Zhigatse
Changra
Gyantse
Nenying
To Lhasa
Sapugang
Lungmar
Gamrupu-chu
Khangmar
Ralung Monastery
Gamru
Yemar
Salu
Samada
Nyeru
Tradong-chu
Drumpayu-chu
Kala Tso
Mangdza
Kala
To Gampa (110 km)
To Dromo (97 km)
To Bhutan
To Bhutan
Nyeru Tsangpo

Nenying Monastery

15 km S of Gyantse, in the lower valley of the Drumpayu-chu, you can visit the monastery of **Nenying**, which was founded in the late 11th century by Jampel Sangwa of Samye. Over subsequent centuries, Nenying was developed eclectically by the Bodongpa and the Gelukpa traditions, amongst others. The renovated assembly hall contains a large new image of Tsongkhapa, and further N there is an old temple, probably surviving from the original complex, which contains faded murals of the Pala style, reminiscent of those at Gyantse Dzong. Neying is currently administered from **Sapugang** township, 11 km further S, where there are interesting coloured rock carvings.

Gamru

At Sapugang, the road crosses to the E bank of the **Drumpayu-chu**, and 1 km further S, at **Darmar**, there is a trail turning SW from the main highway. This trail follows the **Gamrupu-chu** upstream, through a wide side-valley, to **Gamru** township. Above Gamru, the trail eventually crosses the **Drulung La** pass, which forms a watershed between the **Tradong** source of the **Shab-chu** and the **Drumpayu-chu** rivers.

Khangmar

The county capital is located 18 km S of **Darmar**, in a sheltered side-valley close to the highway. The government buildings have guesthouse and dining facilities; but the PSB vigilantly inspect passers-by to ensure that those heading S towards the sensitive Sikkim and Bhutanese borders have bona fide travel permits.

Nyerulung

From **Khangmar**, a motorable side-road leads SE to cross the Nelung La pass and enter **Nyeru** township in the Nyeru Tsangpo valley. Trekking routes from here follow the valley downstream to

Lungmar and **Ralung Monastery** (see above, page 325), or NE across country to **Phuma Yutso Lake** and **Lhodrak** (see above, page 280). There are also trails into the **Gasa** district of **N Bhutan** via the **Yak La pass** (E of Lake Drumpa Yutso) and via **Wakye La pass** above the source of the Nyeru-chu.

NB These passes are only accessible to local Bhutanese traders who ply their wares in Dromo county.

Yemar

Yemar Temple, located 12 km S of **Khangmar** and just to the N of **Salu** township, on a ridge above the highway, is a deserted but extremely important temple, where life-size images survive from the 11th century. Its foundation is attributed to one Lharje Chojang, considered to be a previous emanation of the Kashmiri pandita Shakyashri, who himself visited the site in 1204. The temple has three chapels surrounded by a perimeter wall and an inner circumambulatory path. The **central chapel** (N) is dedicated to the Buddha Amoghadarshin, flanked by six forms of Maitreya; the **West chapel** (left) to Amitayus, flanked by 16 standing bodhisattvas; and the **East chapel** (right) contains a relief sculpture depicting the Buddha's **Subjugation of Mara**. The Italian Tibetologist Prof Tucci has compared the images of Yemar (Iwang) with those of **Tsi Nesar**, **Kyangpu**, and **Dratang**, which are no longer extant, and concluded that the garments and facial features suggest an early Tibetan synthesis of Indian **Pala** and **Khotanese** Central Asian styles.

Kala

The highway continues S from **Yemar**, passing through **Samada** township, where the ruined **Kyangpu** temple is located, and **Mangdza**, from where a side-trail follows the Drumpayu-chu to its source and the Yak La pass to Bhutan. At **Mangdza**, the main road leaves the valley and enters the **Kala plain**. 34 km S of Yemar at Kala township, the highway skirts the NE shore of **Lake Kalatso**. Here there is an important police checkpoint, which can only be passed by unauthorized travellers prepared to undertake a cross country trek around **Lake Kalatso** to the W, or via **Lapchi Gonpa** to the E. A motorable branch road leads W from Kala to **Gampa** county (110 km). From **Lapchi Gonpa**, a difficult trek leads to **Gasa** in Bhutan.

DROMO COUNTY

བྲོ་མོ

亚东县 Yadong

Population: 6,906   *Area:* 3,968 sq km

Dromo county is a stunningly beautiful area, comprising the valley of the **Amochu** (or Dromo Machu) River, also known in neighbouring Sikkim as the **Chumbi valley**, and the parallel valleys of its more westerly tributaries: the **Tangkarpu-chu** and **Khambuma-chu**. These three rivers all converge at **Sharsingma**, the county capital of Dromo (*Ch* Yadong), before flowing into the **Ha** (Lhade) district of W Bhutan. The terrain varies dramatically: N of the Tang La pass (4,639m), which marks the Himalayan watershed, the landscape of the Tibetan plateau is barren; but offering stupendous views of the snow peaks of **Jomolhari** on the Bhutanese border, and **Longpo Gyeldong** on the Sikkimese border. Further S, the roads plunge

through lush gorges, where alpine forest and flowers abound. **Sharsingma** (2,865m) is 160 km S of **Khangmar**, 18 km NW of **Dorin** in N Bhutan, and 16 km NE of **Dzaleb La pass** (4,386m), on the Sikkimese frontier.

Himalayan Watershed

From **Kala**, the highway skirts the W shore of **Lake Dochentso**, and continues S, passing through **Guru**, where Younghusband's British Expeditionary Force engaged the Tibetan army in 1904. At **Duna** township, 40 km S of the Kala checkpoint, there is a trekking route NW to the Butang-chu valley, a tributary of the **Khambuma-chu**. The main road gradually ascends **Tang La**, the Himalayan watershed pass (4,639m), from which the snow peaks of **Jomolhari** (7,314m) and **Longpo Gyeldong** (7,128m) are clearly visible, the former only 8 km distant. The pass is crossed 22 km S of Duna.

Phari Dzong

Below the **Tang La pass**, the highway enters the valley of the **Amo-chu** (Chumbi), and continues gently downhill to **Phari Dzong** (4,360m), 9 km distant. Phari township is a bustling market town located on an exposed 'sow-shaped' hilltop and was often given the dubious distinction of being the dirtiest town in Asia! It strategically overlooks the trading route via **Tremo La pass** to **Paro** in W Bhutan (see below, page 724), and the various westerly trails which penetrate the **Dongkya** range into inner Sikkim. From here, there are two motorable roads to **Sharsingma** (Yadong), one via the **Khambuma-chu** valley and the other via the **Dromo** valley.

Khambuma Valley

22 km drive NW from Phari, you will reach **Tengkar** in the upper Khambuma-chu valley. From here, **Khambu Monastery** and its 12 medicinal hot-springs are

in close proximity. The glacial waters of this alpine valley, hemmed in by the Dongkya Sikkim range and the Himalayas, are highly revered.

Trekking

Trekking routes lead from the Khambuma valley into NE Sikkim, ie from **Khambu-to** via the **Tso La pass**, and from **Khambu-me** via the **Chimkipu** valley. Further S, the Khambuma-chu merges with the Tangkarpu-chu, and thereafter with the Dromo Amo-chu at **Sharsingma** (Yadong).

Dromo Valley

The fertile Dromo valley, which yields an abundance of buckwheat, barley, and potatoes, is divided into three sectors: **Dromo-to** township, where the river flows through gentle alpine meadows, bypassing the Bonpo settlements of **Zhulung**, **Sharmang** and **Nubmang**; **Sharsingma** (Yadong), a relatively low-lying town (2,865m) where the three rivers converge; and **Dromo-me** where flowering plants and conifer forests abound.

Logging is the main industry; and the gorges still are relatively rich in wildlife, including pheasants, Tibetan snowcocks, and Himalayan black bears with their characteristic white V-shaped markings. The capital, **Sharsingma**, is 46 km S of **Phari Dzong**. It is a hospitable town, despite the security concerns entailed by its proximity to the border. Indian-style sweet tea and Himalayan-style fermented millet (*tongba*) are popular beverages in this part of the country.

● **Accommodation** The town has guesthouse and restaurant facilities, in addition to schools, a bank, a post office, and hydro-electric station.

Crossing the **Dromo Zamchen** bridge the highway leads SW and steeply uphill from Sharsingma through rhododendron forests to the **Natho La** and **Dzaleb La passes** on the Sikkim border.

GAMPA COUNTY
བགམ་པ

岗巴县 Gamba
Population: 6,927   *Area:* 3,979 sq km

Gampa county is the region covered by the headwaters of the **Yeru Tsangpo**, which rises N of the snow peaks of the Tibet-Sikkim Himalayas: **Mt Lonpo Gyeldong** (7,128m), **Mt Lhachen Zangdrak** (6,889m), and **Mt Tarchen Drokri** (6,830m) at the eastern extremity of the **Chorten Nyima La** (see below, page 368). The Yeru Tsangpo meanders W into Tingkye county, where it converges with the Bum-chu (Arun) before flowing S into E Nepal. Also included in Gampa county are the side-valley of its major tributary: the **Kholchu Tsangpo**, which flows S to its confluence W of Dargye village; and those of the latter's minor tributaries, the **Jemalung-chu** and **Gye-chu**, which converge at Gyelung.

GAMPA AND TINGKYE COUNTIES
TIB520

Sketch map: not to scale

The county capital is located at **Gampazhol**, 110 km W of Kala (on the Gyantse-Dromo road), and 95 km NW of Drakang (below Duna on the Gyantse-Dromo road). Access is also possible by undertaking a 4-day trek from **Badur** in the Shab valley (see above, page 352) to **Gampa Dzong** via Yakgo La pass, Gyechu valley, Gurma village, and Dargye township.

Gampa Dzong This impressive old fortress was frequently photographed by British Everest Expeditions during the early decades of this century, overlooks the new county town, where the Chinese bureacrats have something of a hardline reputation. The main focal point of pilgrimage in this county is the **Chorten Nyima** hermitage (see below, page 368) on the S border of **Gampa** and **Tingkye** counties. The hermitage can be approached by a motorable track from **Gampa Dzong**, via **Mende** (Gampa township), and **Drangling** village.

TINGKYE COUNTY
གདིང་སྐྱེས
定结县 Dinggye
Population: 8,529   Area: 4,900 sq km

Tingkye county comprises the lower valley of the **Bum-chu (Arun)** River, from the point below **Tsogo** where it flows due S to enter E Nepal via **Drentang** township, and the valleys of its major tributaries: the **Yeru Tsangpo** and **Chenlung-chu** (the latter flowing into the Yeru Tsangpo via the Bumtsopu-chu). The county capital, **Tingkye Dzong**, is located above the confluence of the **Bum-chu** and **Yeru Tsangpo**, at a strategic intersection. The distance from Tingkye Dzong to Sakya is 85 km, to Shelkar: 134 km, and to Gampa Dzong: 129 km.

Lower Bum-chu Valley

From **Jigkyob Zampa bridge**, located 31 km N of **Tingkye Dzong**, 92 km E of Shelkar, and 54 km S of Sakya, there is a 4-day trekking route to **Kharda** in the Lower Bum-chu valley. Passing S of the confluence of the Bum-chu and Yeru Tsangpo, the trail skirts on the E the snow peak of **Mt Nyarori** (6,724m) in the Ama Dribma range, which acts as a watershed between these rivers. Continuing on the E bank of the river, it then cuts through several lateral ravines, via **Kharkung**, and ascends the Chokchu La pass, offering wonderful views of **Mt Makalu** (8,470m).

Descending to the confluence of the Trakar-chu with the Bum-chu above **Chugo**, the trail subsequently crosses the Bum-chu by bridge to the W bank, and heads S through alpine forest for **Kharda**, the gateway to the **Khangzhung** E face of **Mt Everest**, and the Kharda glacier (see below, page 373).

Below **Kharda**, a difficult trail heads down the W bank of the Bum-chu to **Drentang** township, joining the main road from **Tingkye** and **Zar** (45 km). South of Drentang, the river flows into Nepal, where it is known as the **Arun**. A major dam is to be constructed in the deep **Arun** gorges of E Nepal.

Lake Tsomo Dramling

Southeast of Chenlung township, there is a sacred lake known as **Tsomo Dramling**, where pilgrims undertake a circumambulation, starting from **Tashitse** on the SW shore and passing through Dotra on the NE shore.

Zar Monastery

In the county capital, **Tingkye Dzong**, there is an important petrol station, and various amenities geared to service the army, which has a large base in town. From here, the motor road follows the Yeru Tsangpo upstream for 42 km to **Zar** bypassing Chushar across the river. At **Pukhu**, N of **Zar**, there is a small rebuilt Kagyu monastery.

Zar township, with its ruined fortress and monastery, lies on a ridge below **Mt Gang Langchen**, which is 'shaped like the head of an elephant'. The monastery, which belongs to the Gelukpa school, has two renovated buildings, including a 3-storey assembly hall. On the slopes of Mt Gang Langchen there are meditation caves and lakes associated with Padmasambhava, Yeshe Tsogyel, and Yutok Yonten Gonpo.

ACCESS Above **Zar**, the road bifurcates, the southerly track leading across **Nye La pass** to **Dekyi** and **Drentang** on the Nepal border (45 km); and the easterly road to **Tingkye** township. Below **Tashi Rabka** on the former, there are also trekking routes into Nepal via the **Rabka La pass** (4,972m) and the **Yangmagang La pass** (5,182m).

Chorten Nyima

ACCESS Driving E from Zar, after 26 km, you will reach the prosperous farming village of **Muk**. Take the left turn at the next intersection, 1 km beyond Muk (the right leads to **Gye Gonpa** and **Jewo Gonpa** in the Gen-chu valley). Then, leave the main Tingkye-Gampa road at the subsequent junction, 8 km further on, turning right to head due S. A river bed trail leads directly to the snow peaks of the **Chorten Nyima range**, nestling on the frontier between Sikkim and Nepal. The world's third highest peak **Mt Kangchendzonga** (8,585m) lies further S. The range has 13 peaks, the highest being **Mt Chorten Nyima** (6,927m) itself. Glacial streams rise within the range, heading S to converge with the **Tista** River in Sikkim.

Chorten Nyima is regarded at the gateway to the hidden land of Sikkim (Drejong), the heart of which lies within the folds of Mt Kangchendzonga. It is an extremely active pilgrimage centre, and there is a nuns' retreat hermitage to the W. The three cliff-top stupas, which are the focal point of pilgrimage, are attributed to Namkei Nyingpo and Yeshe Tsogyel, students of Padmasambhava, who himself meditated here.

The largest of the stupas, known as **Rangjung Shelgyi Chorten**, contains a crystal stupa which reputedly fell from the sky. Additionally, there are three sky burial sites, consecrated originally by Padmasambhava and Namkei Nyingpo, and medicinal springs, renowned for possessing the 'eight attributes of pure water'. These are now utilized as the source of the fabled Chorten Nyima Mineral Water, which is bottled and marketed inside Tibet! The **assembly hall** in its upper storey contains images of Hayagriva and Manjughosa, as well as a small 'self-arising' ritual dagger (*phurba*) engraved with an image of Hayagriva.

The **Tamdrin Lhakhang** contains within it the meditation cave of Padmasambhava, and relics such as the Guru's stone footprint and a bronze image of Jowo Shakyamuni. The site can also be approached from **Gampa Dzong**, via **Dranglung** (see above, page 367).

DINGRI COUNTY

དིང་རི

定日县 Tingri

Population: 24,645   Area: 14,156 sq km

The westernmost parts of Tsang province are traditionally known as **Lato**, the 'highland' region of Tibet; and this vast area is divided into N Lato and S Lato. The former comprises the upper reaches of the Brahmaputra and Raga Tsangpo, corresponding to present day Ngamring, Saga, and Drongpa counties, and the latter comprises the Bum-chu (Arun), Matsang Tsangpo (Sunkosi), and Kyirong Tsangpo (Trishuli) valleys, corresponding to present day Dingri, Nyalam, and Kyirong counties.

Among these, Dingri county occupies the upper reaches of the **Bum-chu (Arun) River**, and the lateral valleys formed by its tributaries, the foremost of which are: the Lolo-chu, Shel-chu, Rongpu-chu, Trakar-chu, Kharda-chu, Ra-chu Tsangpo, and Langkor Gya-chu. It also includes the valleys of the **Rongshar Tsangpo** and **Lapchi Gang Tsangpo** which flow SW into Nepal to join the **Sunkosi River**. The county is bordered on the S by the formidable barrier of the high Himalayan range, including **Mt Everest** (Jomolangma/Jomo Gangkar), **Makalu**, and **Cho Oyo** (Jowo Oyuk).

LOCATION The county capital is located at **Shelkar**, 75 km from **Lhartse**, 123 km from **Tingkye**, and 240 km from **Dram** (Zhangmu) on the Tibet-Nepal border.

Shelkar

The Zhigatse-Dram highway runs SW from Lhartse, across the high **Gyatso La pass** (5,252m), and then descends steeply into the barren Lato plains, following the Lolo-chu downstream. On the descent, the Everest range can be

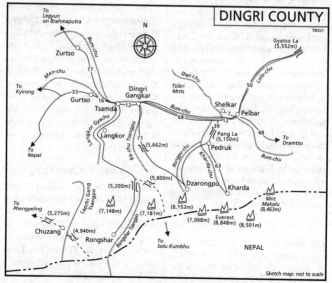

DINGRI COUNTY

TIB521

To Legyun on Brahmaputra

Zurtso — Bum-chu

Gyatso La (5,552m)

N

Men-chu — 17

Shel-chu

Lolo-chu — 50

To Kyirong — 33

Gurtso — 16

Tsamda

Dingri Gangkar — 12

Tsibri Mnts

Bum-chu — 68

Shelkar — 7 — Pelbar

Langkor Gyachu

Langkor

Ra-chu Tsangpo — 71 (5,662m)

39

Pang La (5,150m)

Rongpu-chu

Pedruk

48

To Dramtso

(5,800m)

(5,200m)

Kharda-chu — 63

Bum-chu

To Nepal

Lapchi Gang Tsangpo

Dzarongpu

Kharda

To Phengyeling

(5,275m)

(7,148m)

Rongshar Tsangpo

(7,181m)

(8,153m)

(7,068m)

Everest (8,848m)

(8,501m)

Mnt Makalu (8,463m)

Chuzang

(4,940m)

Rongshar

To Solu Kumbhu

NEPAL

Sketch map: not to scale

seen in the distance, and the **Lolo hot springs** are visible by the roadside, 38 km below the pass.

Below Pelbar, 12 km further on, a turn-off on the right leads into **Shelkar**, following the **Shel-chu** tributary upstream (7 km). The ruined fortress and monastery are prominent on the upper slopes of **Mt Shelkar Dorje Dzong**, overlooking the town. The headquarters of the **Jomolangma Nature Preserve** is located here. Since its inception in 1989 it has assumed some responsibility for the maintenance and ecology of the entire Everest region, 27,000 sq km.

● **Accommodation Pelbar** The _Everest Hotel_ is located at the small township of **Pelbar**, and most groups will stay here rather than at the old guesthouse in **Shelkar**. The rooms have attached bathrooms, generally without water! (double room US$32, breakfast US$7, full meal plain US$28).

● **Facilities Shelkar** Simple guesthouse with an excellent Chinese restaurant, a grocery store, a bookshop.

Shelkar Chode Monastery, founded originally in 1266 by the Kagyu lama Sindeu Rinchen, has been a Gelukpa monastery since the 17th century. There were formerly some 300 monks here, and an active branch of the monastery has been established in Boudha, Nepal. The restored **assembly hall** contains images of Tsongkhapa and his foremost students, alongside Padmasambhava and Vajradhara.

A motorable road leads up the **Shelchu valley** from Shelkar as far as **Gemar** township (50 km), on the N side of the **Tsibri** range. Pilgrims can sometimes be seen approaching as they circumambulate the sacred Tsibri mountain in a clockwise direction.

Tsibri

The **Tsibri** mountain range, true to its name, resembles a series of protruding ribs (_tsibma_). During the 11th century, the remote crags of Tsibri were inhabited by Padampa Sangye, the Indian master who introduced the lineages of **Chod** and **Zhije** into Tibet. Subsequently, Gotsangpa Gonpopel (1189-1258) of the Drukpa Kagyu school founded his hermitage on the SE cliff-face. His own student, Yangonpa Gyeltsenpel (1213-58) was born locally at **Lhadrong**; and his successors effectively established many Drukpa foundations around the mountain.

In the present century, a series of 11 retreat hermitages was established around the mountain by Tsibri Tripon Lama who came here from Central Tibet in 1934. Among them were **Dingpoche**, **Langtso** and **Tashi Tongmon**. Some of these sites are functioning at the present time. However, the large **Nerang Printery** which he also founded to the SW of Tsibri is no longer extant.

The nuns of **Nabtra**, the Nyingmapa monastery on the NE side of Tsibri, under the guidance of Nabtra Rinpoche, were renowned for their meditative excellence and expertise in the traditions of Mindroling and _Longchen Nyingtig_. The previous Nabtra Rinpoche was a mantrin of great status; and his present incarnation now lives in Nepal. Pilgrims often undertake the 5-day circuit of **Tsibri** mountain on foot via **Khangsar**, **Nakhok**, **Ngonga**, **Pangleb**, and **Tsakor**. Further N from Tsibri is the watershed range dividing S Lato from N Lato. **Mt Drakri** (5,871m) is the highest of these peaks.

Lake Tingmo Tso

Below Shelkar, the highway from Lhartse intersects the roads leading E to Tingkye and W to the Nepal border. Taking the Tingkye road, after some 48 km you will reach **Dramtso** township on the N shore of **Lake Tingmo Tso**. **Tsogo** township lies S of the lake and on the S bank of the Bum-chu.

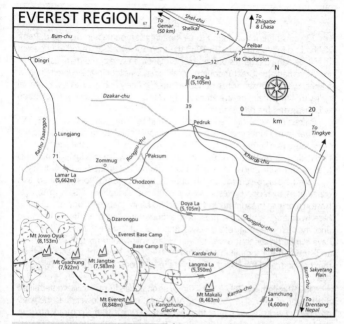

EVEREST REGION

Everest Range

Bounded on the E by the deep gorge of the **Bum-chu (Arun) River** and on the W by that of the **Matsang Tsangpo (Sunkosi)** are some of the world's highest mountains of the E Himalayan range, forming a natural barrier between Tibet and Nepal. Clustered together in close proximity, these comprise: **Makalu** (8,463m), **Lhotse** (8,501m), **Everest**, known locally as Jomolangma or Jomo Gangkar (8,848m), **Bumo Ritse** (7,068m), **Jowo Oyuk** (8,153m), **Jowo Guru** or Menlungtse (7,181m), and **Jowo Tseringma** or Gauri Shangkar (7,148m). There are stunningly beautiful treks in the environs of each of these peaks, and among them, those around **Mt Everest** are particularly well known.

On the Tibet side, **Mt Everest** may be approached from the N face at **Dzarongpu**, or the E **Kangzhung** face at **Kharda** or Karma. A motorable dirt track leaves the Shelkar-Dram highway on the left (S) 12 km after **Pelbar** and 5 km after the police checkpoint at **Tse**. Take this turn-off and drive across **Pang La pass** (5,150m) to the cultivated valley of **Pedruk** (39 km). From the pass there are wonderful views of the Everest range.

● **Pedruk facilities** At Pedruk there is a run-down hotel named *Jomolangma* (camping preferable), a noodle restaurant cum tea shop, and a well-stocked general store.

Two roads diverge at **Pedruk**, the 63 km E track leading to **Kharda** (see below, page 368) and the W track to **Dzarongpu**. Take the latter, and continue up the **Rongpu-chu** valley to **Paksum** and **Chodzom** (4,510m). Above **Chodzom** is the deserted Nyingmapa hermitage of **Chopuk**, which is built into the limestone cliffs to the W of the road. Here, a 71 km motorable track (3 days trekking) from **Dingri Gangkar**

EVEREST

For 13 years after it was found to be the highest mountain in the world, **Peak XV** had no European name. In 1865 the then Surveyor Gen of India suggested that it be named after his predecessor, Sir George Everest, the man responsible for the remarkable Great Trigonometrical Survey which ultimately determined its height. Everest himself, while honoured, was privately unhappy, as it was official policy that mountains be given their local vernacular name. However, an exception was made and the name stuck.

Everest has been climbed many times and by many routes since 1953. The route taken by Hunt's expedition is the 'Ordinary Route', disparagingly called the 'Yak' route by Sherpas. The first Chinese expeditions to reach the summit from the N side did so in 1960 and 1975. We shall never know if the British mountaineers Mallory and Irvine preceded them in 1924, when they perished on the mountain! Following his achievement on Annapurna's S Face, Chris Bonington led two expeditions to tackle Everest's SW Face and succeeded in 1975, with Dougal Haston reaching the summit. In 1970 Yuichiro Muira tried to ski down the Lhotse Face from the S Col, spent most of it airborne and out of control and ended unconscious on the edge of a crevasse! Rheinhold Messner and Alison Hargreaves have climbed it without oxygen. Peter Hillary followed in his father's footsteps and stood on the summit in 1990. In Apr 1988, two teams of Japanese met on top, having scaled the N and S Faces. There to record the event was a television crew!

On 29 September 1992 a 'GPS' survey using signals from satellites determined the height of Everest as 8846.1m. Although this is 2m lower than believed previously, Everest is still higher than K2, despite claims to the contrary made in the *New York Times* in Mar 1987. In Apr 1993 the team that first climbed Everest trekked to the Base Camp for a 40th anniversary reunion – to find 1,500 other climbers waiting their turn to go to the top of the world.

---

village via the **Rachu Tsangpo** valley and **Lamar La** pass (5,662m) connects with the route, which then continues up to **Dzarongpu Monastery** (4,980m).

Dzarongpu Monastery

Communities of nuns affiliated with the Nyingmapa monastery of Mindroling have been living in the Dzarongpu area since the late 18th century. The complex was revitalized at the beginning of the 20th century by Trulzhik I Ngawang Tendzin Norbu (d 1940) who constructed a temple named **Do-ngak Choling**. Branch monasteries were also established across the **Nangpa La** pass in the **Shar Khumbu** region of E Nepal (see below, page 375). At the high point of its development, Dzarongpu had over 500 monks and nuns.

Early British mountaineering expeditions have provided invaluable documentary evidence concerning the monastery's development and Trulzhik Rinpoche's activities. The recently renovated **assembly hall** contains an image of this master, whose present incarnation lives in Nepal, alongside an image of Terdak Lingpa, founder of Mindroling. In addition to the liturgical texts of the Mindroling cycle, the *Longchen Nyingtig* is also an important spiritual practice for the small number of monks and nuns (20) who live here.

● **Accommodation** A small guesthouse offers simple accommodation adjacent to the temple; and there is a large camping space below the stupa.

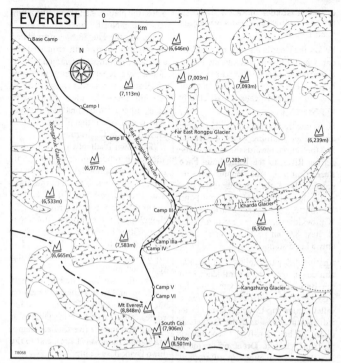

EVEREST

Base Camp
Camp I
Camp II
Camp III
Camp IIIa
Camp IV
Camp V
Camp VI
Mt Everest (8,848m)
South Col (7,906m)
Lhotse (8,501m)

Rongpu Glacier
East Rongphu Glacier
Far East Rongpu Glacier
Kharda Glacier
Kangzhung Glacier

(6,646m)
(7,003m)
(7,093m)
(7,113m)
(7,283m)
(6,239m)
(6,977m)
(6,533m)
(6,550m)
(7,583m)
(6,665m)

Rongpu Face

Above Dzarongpu Monastery, the trail continues up to the **Everest Base Camp** (5,150m), located in a sheltered spot below the morraine slopes leading up to the **Central Rongpu Glacier**. Memorial plaques, including one dedicated to Mallory, stand alongside a traditional Tibetan stupa. The views of the N face of Everest from this vantage point are particularly fine. A trail skirts the E side of the glacier and crosses a creek to reach the **Advanced Base Camp** (5,760m), from which mountaineering ascents of the N face and the NE ridge can be made. **Camp I** is located at 5,460m, **Camp II** at 6,088m, and **Camp III** at 6,368m.

NB Trekking above the Everest Base Camp should only be undertaken by those who have fully acclimatized and are properly prepared for high altitudes. Nonetheless it is possible to reach Camp III without resorting to professional mountaineering equipment.

Kangzhung Face

Taking the E track from **Pedruk** village to **Kharda** (63 km), the motor road first follows the **Trakar-chu** downstream to its confluence with the **Bum-chu (Arun)**, and then traces the latter downstream to **Kharda** township (see above, page 368).

An alternative route from Everest Base Camp entails 6 days trekking via Doya La pass and Chongpu valley, as far as Kharda. Situated deep in the Bum-chu gorge, **Kharda** is a forested, fertile, and heavily populated area.

● **Kharda facilities** There is a small guesthouse, a general store, and a government compound.

Follow the Kharda-chu upstream to **Yulbar**, where the 4-day trek to the **Kangzhung face** via Langma La pass (5,350m) begins. The view from the pass of Makalu's jagged peaks is particularly impressive.

Head into the **Karma** valley, where there are further stunning views of Makalu; and then climb towards the source of the Karma River, to the **Kangzhung Face Base Camp** in the Petang Ringmo meadow. Here, the campsite offers dramatic close-up views of Mt Everest and Mt Lhotse. A 5,950m ridge further to the W provides even closer views of all three of these 8,000m peaks – Everest being only 5 km distant.

Another 4-day trek follows the **Karma-chu** downstream to its confluence with the **Bum-chu**, crossing Samchung La pass (4,600m), and passing through a valley containing 13 glacial lakes of varied pristine hues, and the **Sakyetang plain**. The low-lying confluence (2,300m), close to **Drentang** on the E Nepal border, abounds in subtropical vegetation and flora. From here, you can follow the Bum-chu upstream towards Tingkye or Shelkar.

Dingri Gangkar

Dingri Gangkar (4,500m) lies on the slopes of a ridge, overlooking the Everest range, at the heart of the wide 80 km plain formed by the **Bum-chu (Arun) River**. Two major tributaries converge with the Bum-chu at Dingri: the **Rachu Tsangpo**, which rises near Dzarongpu below Mt Everest and the **Langkor Gyachu**, which rises above Rongshar.

For centuries the town has dominated the trade routes linking Tibet with **Shar Khumbu** in E Nepal via the Nangpa La pass (2 days trekking), and **Kodari** via the Nyalam Tong La pass (182 km). Trekking routes also lead N

across the plain to Zangzang and Chung Riwoche in **North Lato**.

During the late 18th century when the Tibetan government requested the assistance of Emperor Qianlong's Chinese army to repel the Gorkha invasions of Tibet, a fortress was constructed on the hill above the town. Along with many other fortifications from that period which cover the plain as far as **Gurtso**, it now lies in ruins.

The town itself has in recent decades been rebuilt in cramped conditions to accommodate the military camp, which lies to the S of the highway. The village houses lie to the S of the army camp in close proximity (although only the camp has functional electricity). From the rooftops there are memorable views of the entire Everest range – particularly clear during full-moon nights.

The distance from **Shelkar** to **Dingri** is 68 km, and from **Dingri** to **Dram** on the Nepal border 182 km. Trekking routes also extend from Dingri to Dzarongpu and the Everest Base Camp, via Lamar La pass (71 km), and to the Jowo Oyuk Base Camp.

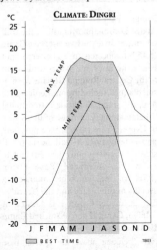

°C
CLIMATE: DINGRI

MAX TEMP

MIN TEMP

J F M A M J J A S O N D

☐ BEST TIME

TB03

• **Accommodation** On the N side, at the **Dingri bridge**, there is the *Sunshine Hotel*, owned by a local entrepreneur, who can organize pack animals for local treks. Another guesthouse is located within the army camp. Both have restaurant facilities: one traditionally Tibetan and the other essentially Sichuanese.

Dingri Langkor

Drive W from Dingri along the highway for 12 km as far as **Tsamda**, where there is a hot spring bathing facility. From here there is a motorable dirt track leading to **Langkor Monastery**. Avoid driving in the summer months when the **Langkor Gyachu River** bursts its banks. Otherwise hire a horse and cart from Dingri Gangkar. Langkor village and monastery are located inland from the highway on a south-facing ridge, in full view of **Mt Jowo Oyuk**.

This is the most important pilgrimage place of the entire Lato region, in that it was here in 1097 that the Indian yogin Phadampa Sangye founded a hermitage and disseminated the teachings of Chod and Zhije in Tibet for the first time. His foremost Tibetan student was the yogini Machik Labdron (on whom see above, page 78). Here, Phadampa Sangye delivered a memorable teaching on ethics and conduct to the people of Dingri, entitled *"Hundred Verses of Admonition to the People of Dingri"* (*Dingri Gyatsa*).

A festival is held here each year on the 14th day of the 6th month of the lunar calendar. The **temple** is located within the village of **Langkor**. The track follows the contour of the hillside, passing a medicinal spring said to have been brought forth by Padmasambhava. The temple contains images of Phadampa Sangye and Tangtong Gyelpo, and partially faded original murals depicting Padmasambhava and Milarepa. Adjacent cave hermitages are associated with Padmasambhava, Phadampa Sangye, and Machik Labdron.

Trekking

A 3-day trek from **Langkor** also leads to **Nyalam** via the **Tong La** pass. This was the traditional trading route between Dingri and Central Nepal prior to the construction of the motor road.

Rongshar

The beautiful **Rongshar** valley, SW of Dingri, is the sacred abode of the 11th century yogin Milarepa, and at the same time a botanist's paradise, nestling below the high snow peak of **Mt Jowo Tseringma** (Gauri Shangkar). To reach Rongshar, head due S from Dingri in the direction of the **Nangpa La pass** (5,800m), which eventually leads into the **Shar Khumbu** area of E Nepal.

Passing through the villages of Penak, Shator-me, and Shator-to, the trails divide at **Kyarak** (38 km). For the pass cross over to the E bank of the **Kyarakchu** and trek due S via the glaciers of **Jowo Oyuk** base camp. For **Rongshar**, remain on the W bank of the river, and head SW towards **Puhrel La** pass (5,200m), 1-day drive or 3 days trekking from Dingri. Crossing this pass, and entering into the **Rongshar** valley, the barren landscape gives way to junipers and rhododendrons (4,650m), and the road soon plunges down, following the course of the **Rongshar Tsangpo** via **Taktsang** (4,030m), where side-valleys branch off to **Salung** (NW) and **Zhung** (SE). The valley abounds in large fragrant white rose bushes.

On the descent to **Tsamgye** (Rongshar township), **Mt Jowo Tseringma** (7,148m) comes into view, dominating the valley from the S. Avoid the bureaucrats here, and continue downstream to **Chuwar Monastery** (3,300m), dramatically situated above the confluence of the **Rongshar Tsangpo** and **Menlungchu**. The gorge of the latter leads E to **Mt Menlungtse** (7,181m).

Many sites in this region have associations with Milarepa, who lived in the remote hermitages of the Rongshar valley for many years, eventually passing away at Chuwar. The Nepalese-style temple at **Chuwar Monastery** is therefore the focal point of pilgrimage in the valley. Downstream from **Drubden**, where there are cave hermitages of both Milarepa and Gampopa, the Rongshar Tsangpo enters Nepal (2,750m), where it is known as the **Sunkosi River**. Another trail climbs 400m from Drubden to **Drintang** and the **Drakmar caves**, where Milarepa taught his disciple Rechungpa. Here the cave hermitages directly face the snow peaks of Mt Jowo Tseringma.

Lapchi Gang

From **Drintang** in lower Rongshar, a trekking route leads via Trode and N across Gangchen La pass (4,940m) into the forested valley of **Lapchi Gang**. The snow peaks of this revered valley are regarded as the abodes of the meditational deities Cakrasamvara, Vajrapani, Manjughosa, and Avalokiteshvara. Here, the **Lapchi Gang Tsangpo** flows in a course parallel to that of the Rongshar Tsangpo, crossing the Tibet-Nepal border.

There are a number of 11th century hermitages associated with Milarepa in the upper and lower reaches, including the **Dudul Cave**, **Bepa Gong Cave**, and **Se Cave**, which are classed among his 'four great meditation caves'. The pagoda-roofed monastery, known as **Chura Gepheling**, is situated above the confluence of the E and W tributaries of the Lapchi Gang Tsangpo. The **assembly hall** contains a venerated image of Milarepa, reputedly made by Rechungpa from his master's nose-bleed, and a stone said to be the master's life-supporting talisman (*lado*).

Ascending the valley of the W tributary, you pass through **Chuzang**, where Milarepa subdued a hostile demon who sought to obstruct the opening of the Lapchi Gang hermitages to Buddhist practitioners. **Jamgang La pass** (5,275m) at the head of the valley leads across the watershed to **Pengyeling Monastery** on the Dingri-Nyalam stretch of the Nepal highway.

NYALAM COUNTY

གཉའ་ལམ

聶拉木县 Nyalam

Population: 4,848   Area: 5,570 sq km

Nyalam county comprises the townships of **Menpu** and **Zurtso** around the headwaters of the **Bum-chu River**, and those of **Tsangdong**, **Tsongdu**, and **Dram** in the **Matsang Tsangpo (Sunkosi)** valley. The highway from Lhasa traverses the Great Himalayan range at **Yakrushong La pass** (5,200m), also known nowadays as **Nyalam Tong La**, and then precariously follows the course of the **Matsang Tsangpo** downstream to the Tibetan customs barrier at **Dram (Zhangmu/Khasa)**, and the **Friendship Bridge** on the Nepal border. This is currently Tibet's most important land border with the outside world. The trading community of **Dram** are among the most prosperous people in all Tibet.

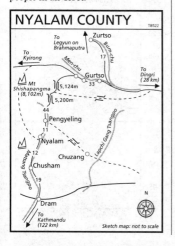

NYALAM COUNTY

The county capital is located at **Tsongdu (Nyalam)**, 30 km N of the border, and 152 km from **Dingri**. The **Arniko Highway** which runs from **Kodari** to **Kathmandu** (122 km) via **Barabise** was constructed by the Chinese in 1960s.

Bum-chu (Arun River) Headwaters

From **Dingri**, the highway cuts NW to **Gurtso** (28 km), where the **Men-chu River** joins the **Bum-chu**. The township of **Zurtso** is located 17 km further N near the source of the Bum-chu, and a jeepable track leads via Zurtso to **Legyun** and **Taktse** on the Brahmaputra in N Lato.

Gurtso has a military camp with spartan guesthouse facilities, and a vital road maintenance depot, responsible for clearing snowfall from the high Himalayan passes to the S. The highway follows the **Men-chu** upstream (SW) from Gurtso, passing Menpu township and **Menkhab-to** village, where ruined 18th century fortifications can be seen.

After 33 km (road marker 614), the road bifurcates: the W route leading to **Kyirong** and Far-west Tibet (see below, page 399). Striking views of **Mt Shishapangma** (8,012m), the highest peak entirely inside Tibetan territory, dominate the W horizon.

Mount Shishapangma

There are three approaches to the spectacular snow peaks of **Shishapangma** (Goshainathan), which at 8,012m was the last of the world's 8,000m peaks to be climbed. The northern base camp is accessible from **Serlung** on the Kyirong road, the eastern side from a turn-off 42 km S of the **Lalung La pass**, and the southern base camp from Nyalam by trekking upstream through the **Tsongdupu-chu valley**. The latter also offers fine views of the **Langtang Himalayan** peaks to the SW.

Himalayan Passes

The highway cuts through the Himalayan range via the Lalung La pass (5,124m) and the Yakrushong La pass (5,200m), which are crossed in quick succession. The latter is sometimes known as **Nyalam Tong La** ('pass from which Nyalam is visible'), although the original Tong La pass lies further E on the traditional Dingri-Nyalam trade route. Pilgrims stop at the second pass to raise prayer flags, burn incense, scatter 'wind-horse' paper inscription, and build cairns. This is the last contact with the Tibetan plateau. Below the passes, the road descends steeply into the valley of the **Matsang Tsangpo** (Sunkosi River). Trails to the E lead directly to **Langkor** and **Dingri** via the Tong-La. At **Tsangdong** township, also known as **Ne-sar**, 40 km below the second pass, the atmosphere is no longer that of the dry plateau. The warm moist air of the Indian subcontinent prevails. A trail to the E leads to **Lapchi Gang** via Tashigang.

Pengyeling Monastery

The temple of **Pengyeling**, 44 km S of the last Himalayan pass, is built around the sacred **Namkading Cave** of Milarepa, which overlooks the approach to the hidden valley of **Lapchi Gang**. The buildings are invisible from the motor road (at road marker 683), some 3 km below the highway, and above the W bank of the **Matsang Tsangpo**. An antechamber contains on its side-walls a detailed description of the pilgrimage sites associated with Milarepa in the environs of Pengyeling and Lapchi. The **Namkading Cave** contains rock impressions of Milarepa's seated meditation posture and handprint – the latter having appeared in the rock when Milarepa assisted his student Rechungpa prop up the low ceiling with a boulder. Images include Milarepa, Tsongkhapa, and the protectress Shridevi, whose mule also

reputedly left a footprint in the stone when she appeared in a vision to Milarepa.

The **main temple**, to the E of the cave entrance contains an assembly hall with a principal image of Padmasambhava. The caretaker of Pengyeling lives above and behind the temple where there are smaller caves associated with Rechungpa and the protector deities of the Gelukpa tradition. This one-time Kagyu temple complex has been affiliated to the Gelukpa monastery of Sera since the late 17th century.

Nyalam

The town of Nyalam (3,750m) traditionally known as **Tsongdu**, lies 11 km S of **Pengyeling**, deep within the gorge of the **Matsang Tsangpo** at the point where both the river and the road cut through the Himalayan range. **Mt Dorje Lakpa** rises above the town to the W. For centuries this has been the main trading post between Tibet and Nepal. The valley of the **Tsongdupu-chu** tributary runs NE towards the southern base camp of **Mt Shishipangma**. The Bod-chu tribu-

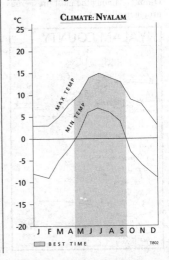

CLIMATE: NYALAM

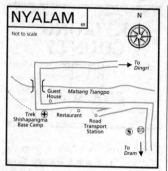

NYALAM

Not to scale

To Dingri

Guest House · Matsang Tsangpo

Trek Shishapangma Base Camp · Restaurant · Road Transport Station

To Dram

tary joins the Matsang Tsangpo from the E below the town.

● **Facilities** There are three simple guesthouses (the best being the *Nyalam Hotel* to the E of the highway). Small roadside restaurants serve Sichuan country-style cuisine. There is also an important truck stop, a petrol station, and a small hospital.

Dram (Zhangmu)

Below Nyalam, the road plunges through the **Matsang Tsangpo** gorge, hugging a precipice above the rapids. There are spectacular waterfalls on both sides of the gorge. 12 km below Nyalam, there is the 54 bed *Chusham Hotel*, which is well-located in a tranquil part of the valley near the **Chusham hot springs**, but often lacking in electricity.

The border town of **Dram** (*Ch* **Zhangmu; N Khasa**) lies 31 km below Nyalam at an average altitude of 2,300m. The sprawling town extends down the hillside for over 4 km through a series of switchback bends. In the rainy season (July-Sept) motor vehicles are sometimes unable to reach the town from Nyalam (and also from the **Friendship Bridge**) owing to landslides which are a constant hazard to the local population. Nonetheless, the people of Dram tend to be among the wealthiest in Tibet. Black market trading in assorted commodities, gold, and currency is rife.

The **Gonpa Sarpa** monastery located at the lower end, adjacent to the **China Customs Building**.

Local information
● **Accommodation**

Zhangmu Hotel, double rooms are available at US$32 (breakfast US$7; full meal plain US$28), lower end of town, adjacent to the China Customs Building. Curiously, this 5-storeyed hotel has its reception office on the top flr, which is at road level, and its restaurant on the lowest flr. Electricity supplies are erratic and the rooms are often damp.

● **Places to eat**

There are many small roadside restaurants in

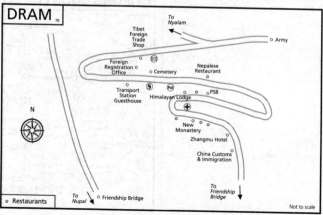

DRAM

To Nyalam

Tibet Foreign Trade Shop

Army

Foreign Registration Office · Cemetery · Nepalese Restaurant

Transport Station Guesthouse · Himalayan Lodge · PSB

N

New Monastery · Zhangmu Hotel

China Customs & Immigration

To Friendship Bridge

○ Restaurants · To Nupal · ○ Friendship Bridge

Not to scale

town, where Sichuan, Tibetan and Nepalese cuisines are available.

● **Banks & money changers**
Located in the upper end of town.

● **Post & telecommunications**
Post Office: located in the upper end of town.

● **Border facilities**
The customs and immigration posts open at 1000 Beijing time, and by the time you have gone through all formalities and driven or walked the 8 km downhill to the actual frontier on the **Friendship Bridge** (Dzadrok Zampa), the Nepalese customs will be on the point of opening at 0930 Nepal time (some 2½ hrs difference).

KYIRONG COUNTY

སྐྱིད་གྲོང

吉隆县 Gyirong
Population: 7,720   Area: 8,869 sq km

Kyirong county in **S Lato** occupies the valleys of the **Kyirong Tsangpo River** (Trishuli) and its tributaries as well as the adjacent **Gungtang-chu** headwaters and the basin of **Lake Pelkhu Tso**. To the S straddling the Tibet/Nepal border lie the mighty snow peaks of the Himalayan range: Ganesh Himal (7,406m), Langtang (7,232m), and Shishapangma (8,012m). Further N there are trails crossing the high watershed passes into N Lato, and the Brahmaputra valley. The Kyirong gorge and valley form one of Tibet's most beautiful picturesque alpine regions; and it boasts sites of historic importance, connected with King Songtsen Gampo, Padmasambhava, Milarepa, and Sakya Pandita, among others. The county capital is located at **Dzongka**,

KYIRONG COUNTY

Sketch map: not to scale

127 km E of the turn-off on the Gurtso/Nyalam road (see below, page 381), 103 km S of Saga, and 75 km N of Rizur Zampa on the Nepal border.

Lake Pelkhu Tso

On the Gurtso-Nyalam road, which connects with the Arniko Highway to Kathmandu, there is a turn-off below **Lalung La pass**, N of the Himalayan range, which cuts westwards, following the **Nakdo-chu** tributary of the **Men-chu** (itself a source of the Bum-chu) upstream to Serlung. The road passes through the desolate plain of Digur Tang, with its enormous sand dunes and the snow peaks of **Shishapangma** (8,012m) and **Langtang** (7,232m) in close proximity to the S. Leaving the Bum-chu basin, it then descends into the depression of **Pelkhu Tso** (4,600m), a stunningly beautiful lake into which the glacial streams of the Da-chu and Lha-chu drain.

Below the cliffs on the E shore is the cave hermitage of Milarepa, known as **Laphu Pemadzong**. The road skirts the S shore of the lake and then turns abruptly N, following the W shoreline. In the afternoons this terrain is exposed to strong biting winds, reminiscent of those in the Dingri plains. Reaching the base of **Jakhyung La pass** (5,180m), also known as Ma la, the road forks. Take the right turn which leads N into **Saga** county (69 km), via a small lake called **Tso Drolung**; or cross the pass (left) to reach the county capital at **Dzongka**.

Trekking

Trekking routes also skirt the N shore of the lake to reach **Gongmo**, from where the trail crosses **Shakyel La pass**, to reach Trepa and **Drakna** township on the Brahmaputra. **Drakna Druka** is an important ferry crossing on the Brahmaputra; and trails lead downstream from here to Lhartse or upstream to Tango and Saga county.

Dzongka

Dzongka, the county capital, lies 34 km below **Jakhyung La pass**, overlooking the confluence of the **Kyirong Tsangpo** and its main tributary, the **Zarong-chu**. There is a trail following the latter upstream and across Tagya La pass to Achen and the Brahmaputra.

Owing to its mild climate and location, Dzongka thrived over the centuries as an important centre for Nepalese trade. Most of the ancient perimeter walls were destroyed by the Gorkha armies of the 18th century; but a significant portion of the SW section survives even now. Within this enclosure is the Gelukpa monastery of **Ganden Palgyeling** which has some original murals and sculptures. Further N are the new buildings of Dzongka – the government compound and the commercial quarter. The once inhabited cave settlement of **Lhamog Gonpa** is located on a hill promontory above the town.

Upper Kyirong Gorge

If you take the S road from Dzongka, following the **Kyirong Tsangpo** downstream, you will reach the township of Kyirong after 68 km. At **Orma** village the river valley narrows into a spectacular 35 km gorge devoid of settlements. Side-valleys occasionally extend E or W from the gorge. At Gun, a trail leads E to **Tsalung**, the birthplace of Milarepa in Gunda district (4,300m). Further S, at Longda, a trail leads W from the gorge to the ruined **Drakar Monastery**. Above it the important cave hermitage of Milarepa, known as **Drakar Taso** (3,600m), contains wood-carved images of Padmasambhava, Milarepa, and Maitreya.

The main road continues its descent of the gorge to **Drotang** (3,320m), from where another trail leads W to Kyangpa Monastery and Milarepa's cave hermitage at **Kyangpa Namka Dzong**. Mt Riwo Pelbar is visible to the SW. The Kyirong gorge eventually opens out at **Ragma** (3,000m), where there are cultivated fields.

Lower Kyirong Valley

The **Ragma** valley, extending eastwards from the Kyirong Tsangpo, contains the **Jangchub Dzong** cave hermitage of Milarepa and **Riwo Pelbar Monastery** with its nearby Padmasambhava power place. The main Kyirong valley, forested and alpine in character, descends through Magal, Garu Monastery, and Pangzhing village, before reaching the heart of Kyirong.

Jamtrin Temple

Jamtrin Gegye Lhakhang, NE of Kyirong township, is one of the four geomantic 'further taming temples' (*yangdul lhakhang*) founded by King Songtsen Gampo during the 7th century. The 4-storey temple in an unusual pagoda design is said to be located on the right foot of the supine ogress.

Phakpa Wati Lhakhang

The most historically significant building in the township of Kyirong (2,774m) is the 4-storeyed Phakpa Wati Lhakhang. This Nepalese pagoda-style temple once contained the renowned Phakpa Wati image of standing Lokeshvara, the bodhisattva of compassion. According to legend, King Songtsen Gampo during the 7th century despatched the incarnate monk Akarmatishila to Nepal, where in a forest of the Indo-Nepalese borderland, he found a sandalwood tree-trunk, which had split open in four segments to reveal the four 'self-arising' images of Lokeshvara. Known collectively as the 'four sublime brothers' (Phakpa Chezhi) these are:

Phakpa Lokeshvara (the most sacred image in the Potala Palace; Phakpa Ukhang (in Khorzhak); Phakpa Jamali (in Nepal); and Phakpa Wati. This last image was originally brought to Lhasa with the others, but expelled to Kyirong by Bonpo ministers during the 8th century. There it remained, in the Phakpa Wati Lhakhang until 1656 when it was transported back to Lhasa for safekeeping. The temple has outer murals depicting the great monasteries of Lhasa.

Jadur Bonpo Monastery

The important Bonpo site known as Jadur, near Yangchu Tangkar village outside Kyirong township, is a focal point for Bonpo pilgrims heading in the direction of Mt Kailash. A festival is held here during the 4th month of the lunar calendar.

Samtenling Monastery

Accessible by a full day trek from Kyirong township via Neshar, Samtenling Gonpa is the largest monastery of the valley. Originally a Kagyu site, frequented by the yogin Repa Zhiwa, it was later converted to the Gelukpa school in the 17th century, following the defeat of the Tsangpa kings in the civil war; and thereafter regarded as a branch of Shelkar Chode. The large complex of ruined buildings at Samtenling testifies to the monastery's former grandure, and the snow peaks of Langtang and Ganesh Himal form a memorable backdrop. A flourishing branch of Kyirong Samtenling was established at Boudha in Kathmandu during the early 1960s.

STABBING AT SHADOWS

In the 13th century, Sakya Pandita visited Phakpa Wati Lhakhang, and it was here that he defeated the Hindu master Haranandin in debate. In order to subdue the intruder he requested help from the Nyingma yogin Darcharuwa, who had discovered a renowned ritual dagger (*kila*) at Yerpa and acquired extraordinary yogic prowess. Legend recounts that when Haranandin flew into the sky, 'flapping his hands like wings', Dracharuwa stabbed his shadow with the ritual dagger, causing him to fall to the ground, 'like a bird struck by a stone'! Subsequently no non-Buddhist masters from India sought to propagate their views inside Tibet.

Kyirong-Nepal

Two roads diverge S of Kyirong township, the westerly one following the **Kyirong Tsangpo** downstream to the Nepal border (29 km) – passing through **Khimbuk** village, **Rizur Zampa** bridge (spanning the Lende Khola-chu), and **Rashuwa Dzong**. On the Nepal side, the road passes through Syabunbesi and Dunche, before reaching Trishuli and Kathmandu. The easterly road is motorable only as far as **Langchu**, and thereafter it becomes a trekking route, passing through Dra, Kharbang, and Sale, before fording the border stream at **Chusumdo**. On the Nepalese side, it continues on to Sadang Kadu and the Langtang National Park. Without crossing the border, you can follow another trail eastwards to the Laga La glacier (W of Mt Shishapangma).

Gungtang

The **Gungtang** valleys, which form part of the **Gandaki** headwaters, are more remote than that of Kyirong, located on a jeepable side-road 187 km from Saga and 216 km from Dzongka. This road crosses the celebrated **Gungtang La pass** (also known as Jang La), from which Padmasambhava entered Tibet during the 8th century. Stone footprints of Padmasambhava from the rocks of Gungtang La are kept in the Phakpa Lhakhang of the Potala Palace and at Samye Monastery. A trekking route also leads more directly from Dzongka to Chang and thence into the heart of Gungtang.

The southern approaches from Nepal are more rugged – traversing the passes of Gya La, Lachen La, Lachung La, and Monla Drakchen. The main settlements of Gungtang are Rud, Nying, Nyam, and **Chang** – the last of which has a medicinal hot spring. **Okla Gonpa** is the principal monastery.

NGAMRING COUNTY

ངམ་རིང་

昂仁县 Ngamring

Population: 15,497   Area: 17,804 sq km

The region of N Lato comprises the counties of **Ngamring**, **Saga** and **Drongpa**, which occupy the upper reaches of the Brahmaputra, and those of its major tributaries, including the **Raga Tsangpo** and **Rikyu Tsangpo**. Among these, Ngamring county, sometimes referred to as the gateway to Mt Kailash and Far-western Tibet, is the barren area which divides the Raga Tsangpo and the Brahmaputra. The main road runs NW from Lhartse, crossing the Brahmaputra via the Lhartse Chakzam bridge or the Drapu ferry, to enter the county. It then passes through Gekha and Zangzang townships to rejoin the river at Saga. The most important historical sites are located at **Chung Riwoche** and **Zangzang Lhadrak**. The county capital of **Ngamring** is located to the NE of Gekha on a turn-off, 60 km from Lhartse, and 240 km from Saga.

Gekha and Ngamring

After crossing the Brahmaputra at

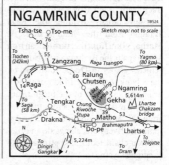

Lhartse Chakzam bridge, the recent construction of which has put an end to the adventures of the ferry crossing, the road ascends a rocky river valley, with **Mt Yakri** (Yakpo Gangri, 5,614m) to the NE and the bright blue waters of **Lake Langtso** to the S. A longer valley then leads up to **Gekha** township, 53 km from Lhartse. Gekha lies at the SE corner of **Lake Ngamring Kye-tso**, and has a road transport station, with simple accommodation and dining facilities. The county capital, **Ngamring** is located on a side-road 7 km NE of Gekha, on the NE shore of the lake. There are excellent views of the lake from the road. In town, the main site is **Ngamring Monastery**, an original 13th century Sakyapa foundation, which was partially converted to the Gelukpa school in the 17th century.

Dokzhung Tsangpo valley

From Ngamring there is a branch road which follows the **Dokzhung Tsangpo** section of the Raga Tsangpo downstream towards Lingo at its arid confluence with the Mu-chu in Zhetongmon county (see above, page 351). This jeepable trail passes through **Chowok** (Mekhang) township after 57 km, and terminates at **Yagmo** township after a further 23 km.

Chung Riwoche Kumbum

Some 500m before reaching Gekha township on the drive from Lhartse, there is a seemingly insignificant dirt track leading left (SW), which crosses the low ranges dividing the Raga Tsangpo from the Brahmaputra. At **Matho**, 39 km from that turn-off, an iron bridge spans the Brahmaputra, carrying vehicles across to **Do-pe** township on the S bank. A further 14 km drive will bring you into view of the magnificent Chung Riwoche stupa across the river on the N bank. A motorable iron bridge spans the river here, alongside an original iron-chain footbridge attributed to Tangtong Gyelpo.

The stupa of **Chung Riwoche** overlooks the Brahmaputra, from its vantage point at the base of **Mt Pal Riwoche** and the ruins of Chung Riwoche Monastery. It was constructed during the period 1449-56, and had associations with both the Sakyapa school and Tangtong Gyelpo's own Chakzampa tradition. The design and extant murals are reminiscent of similar stupas at Jonang Phuntsoling and Gyang Bumpoche (see above, page 360 and page 361). According to the biography of Tangtong Gyelpo, it is largely the work of local artists of the so-called **Lato style**, which derives from the art of **Zhalu** but exhibits a more naive brushstroke and line technique than the cosmopolitan style of the **Gyantse Kumbum** (see above, page 71).

The stupa has 8 storeys and a basement with its own interior circumambulatory walkway. The rectangular chapels on the floors from the 2nd to the 5th are contained within the terraced steps (*bangrim*) of the stupa, while the circular chapels of the 6th and 7th are in the bulbous dome (*bumpa*). The 8th floor is in the form of an open circular roof terrace, surmounted by a recently restored bell. The extant wall-painted mandalas are representative of the Sakyapa school.

Trekking

Chung Riwoche can also be approached on the N bank of the Brahmaputra, from a poor road surface from **Matho** and **Nyinkhar**, or by trekking from **Zangzang** via Choka. A more ambitious 7-day trek from S Lato follows the old trade route from **Dingri Gangkar** (see above, pages 374). It crosses the **Bum-chu (Arun) River** and Khangsar village, before traversing the watershed **Me La** pass (5,224m), which offers distant views of **Mt Drakri** (5,871m) and **Mt Bulhari** (6,040m) to the east. A second pass, **Kure La** (5,498m) is then crossed, and on the descent the trail passes W of **Yulchen** township before reaching the

S bank of the Brahmaputra at Chung Riwoche. Trails also follow the river banks upstream from Chung Riwoche to **Drakna** township in Kyirong county (see above page 381).

Ralung Chutsen

If one continues NW from Gekha on the main route, a hot spring known as **Ralung Chutsen** comes into view on the right side of the road a few kilometres past the NW shore of Ngamring Kyetso lake. Here there is a hot spring bathing house with simple guest rooms; and, if you arrive in the late afternoon, is a reasonable place to stop for the night. Apart from the guest rooms there are good grass-covered campsites. The baths themselves consist of square stone pools inside private rooms with large skylights open to the stars (if you bathe in the evening). The elderly Tibetans who manage it will flush the existing water away and replace it with fresh water if you ask politely. A small fee is charged pp whether you stay in a tent or in a room. A stop here is preferable to **Raga** which is 2 hrs or so further on. **NB** If you stay at the hot springs and intend travelling on the **northern route to Mt Kailash**, it is important to leave early the next day in order to reach **Tsochen** before nightfall.

Zangzang Lhadrak

The district of Zangzang is renowned as the birthplace of **Rigdzin Godemchen** (1337-1408), the celebrated treasure-finder (terton) of the Nyingmapa school, who discovered and revealed the **Northern Treasures** (*Jangter*). On the 60 km drive from Gekha to Zangzang township, **Mt Trazang** is passed to the SW of the road. The master's birthplace is at Toyor Nakpo, NE of this mountain, on the summit of which he unearthed the keys to his treasure-texts in April 1366. Almost 2 months later, in the nearby cave of **Zangzang Lhadrak**, he

discovered the 500 seminal works of the Northern Treasures tradition in a blue treasure-chest with five compartments. The tradition which he founded spread throughout remote areas of Ladakh and S Tibet, as far as Dartsedo in Kham; and these original sites continue even now to be revered focal points of pilgrimage for adherents of this lineage. The new town of **Zangzang** has a somewhat drab and bleak appearance. Most traffic does not stop here, but instead continues on to **Raga**, 122 km beyond Zangzang.

Jangtang routes from Zangzang

A few kilometres NW of Zangzang township on the main road, there is a turn-off which heads due N in the direction of the **Jangtang Plateau**. Following this jeepable trail, after **Kang-lhe** village, the road leaves the Raga Tsangpo basin and crosses the watershed into the Jangtang lakeland. Some 55 km from the turn-off, the trail bifurcates, one branch following the **Taklung-chu** NW for 50 km to **Tsha-tse** township, on the SE shore of **Lake Zhuru-tso**; and the other heading N for 76 km along the valley of the **Tatok Tsangpo**, to **Tso-me** township. Arduous trekking routes from these two townships skirt the E shore of the large lake **Dangra Yutso**, as far as **Ombu** on the N shore. From there, a jeep road leads 167 km to join the main Amdo-Gertse road at **Nyima** (see below).

Upper Raga Tsangpo

The main road from Zangzang to Saga runs W, following the S bank of the Raga Tsangpo upstream. After 39 km it crosses **Gye La pass**, and then, at **Gyedo** village, there is a turn-off on the right (N) for the lakes **Chudrang-tso** and **Amchok-tso**.

Raga township lies on the main road, 69 km beyond the pass and near the source of the Raga Tsangpo. It is merely a cluster of mud-walled compounds used as rest rooms for truckers. A jeepable dirt trail leads S for 26 km to **Tengkar** on the Brahmaputra, from where it is possible to trek to **Drakna** township and **Pelkhu Lake** (see above, page 381 and page 381).

Raga's importance lies in the fact that it is the closest settlement to one of W Tibet's most important road junctions. Some 14 km after Raga, the main road splits in two: the northern branch heading into the Jangtang Plateau for **Tsochen** (242 km), and thence to **Gertse**, **Gegye** and **Senge Tsangpo**; and the southern branch rejoining the Brahmaputra at **Saga** (58 km), and following it upstream to its source in Drongpa county. The former is sometimes known as the **northern route to Mt Kailash** and the latter as the **southern route to Mt Kailash**. In this text, the southern route will be described first, since it remains within the **N Lato** district of W Tibet as far as Drongpa.

SAGA COUNTY

ས་དགར

萨嘎县 Saga

Population: 11,641   Area: 13,374 sq km

Saga county in **N Lato** is the region occupied by the upper Brahmaputra and its tributaries: the **Rukyok Tsangpo** and **Kyibuk Tsangpo**. The county capital is located at **Kyakyaru**, 58 km from the Raga junction on the N Lato or Lhartse road, 105 km from Dzongka on the Zhangmu or S Lato road, and 146 km from Drongpa on the southern route to Mt Kailash.

Tengkar

A jeep track leads 26 km S from Raga to **Tengkar** township on the N bank of the Brahmaputra. Downstream from here (and still on the N bank) are the villages of Sharu, Salung and Taktse, the last of which has a hot spring. Fording the Brahmaputra at Tengkar, a trail continues from **Drakna** township on the S bank to Lake Pelkhu and Dzongka (see above, page 381 and page 381).

Kyakyaru

Saga county town (*Tib* Kyakyaru) straddles the **Dargye Tsangpo** above

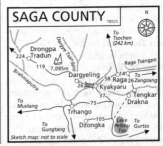

SAGA COUNTY   TIB525

Drongpa
Tradun
224   119   7,095m
Dargyeling
Brahmaputra
Raga Tsangpo
58   14   To
Raga   26   Zangzang
Kyakyaru
37   Tengkar
Drakna
To Mustang   Trhango
75
105   To
Gungtang   Dzongka   Lake   Gurtso
Pelkhu
Tso
To Tsochen (242 km)
Sketch map: not to scale

itsconfluencewiththeBrahmaputra,14 km W of old **Kyakya** village and 58 km SW of the Raga road-junction. The river is crossed here via the **Saga Chakzam** bridge. The town is strategically located at the intersection of three motor routes: the Lhartse road from the E, the Dzongka road from the S, and the Purang and Drongpa road from the W. The town of Saga (ironically meaning 'Happy Land') has grown in recent years to service an important Chinese military garrison, which functions as the headquarters of the border patrol force, monitoring the entire length of the Tibeto-Nepalese frontier as far W as the Indo-Nepalese border. Soldiers from the garrison also are likely to have target practice near the centre of town; so don't be surprised if you hear machine gun fire at any time of the day. As you leave town heading W they may give a friendly wave from the low side of the road while they shoot bullets over your head aiming at targets placed on the slope above. There is little of interest here in Saga, so rest well!

● **Facilities** On the southern route to Mt Kailash, Saga is the last town with a reasonable transport station since it has a shop and restaurant at the W end of its courtyard. The transport station is located near the SE corner of the main side street, which leaves the highway via a bridge leading directly to the town hall and cinema. It is important to reach the truck stop as early as possible since it usually fills up each night and there is little alternative accommodation. A short walk down the main road leads past local shops and the new Chinese small business ventures to a hospital and dispensary.

Dzongka and Zhungru roads

A few kilometres S of Saga, the road reaches the **Kyakya Druka** ferry, leading to the S bank of the Brahmaputra. Heading S on this jeepable road, after 37 km there is a turn-off on the right (W), which leads to **Zhungru** township. The main road continues due S for a further 32 km, after which it again bifurcates, the right (W) branch leading to **Dzongka** (34 km) in Kyirong county, and the left (E) branch leading around the southern shores of **Lake Pelkhu** to join the Dram (Zhangmu) highway. Take the latter route if you wish to reach Nepal quickly and avoid the Lhartse detour.

If you take the **Zhungru** turn-off, you will reach the township of Trhango after 75 km. Trhango lies close to the S bank of the Brahmaputra, and it is also the road-head for the renowned Gungtang La (Jang La) pass through which Padmasambhava first entered Tibet in the 8th century. A ferry crossing, **Zhungru Druka**, links Pudrak, Zhungru and other villages on the N bank with those on the S bank, including Trhango and Rila.

Dargyeling

The **southern route to Mt Kailash** and Purang leaves Saga town, following the **Dargye Tsangpo** upstream in a NW direction. After **Garshok**, it reaches the township of **Dargyeling**, 26 km from Saga. Further upstream, the road passes the confluence of the combined waters of the **Rukyok Tsangpo** and **Kyibuk Tsangpo**, before following the **Men-chu** tributary of the Brahmaputra, via Lhaktsang, into Drongpa county. The valleys are rugged with little vegetation. The distance from Dargyeling to Drongpa is 119 km.

DRONGPA COUNTY

འབྲོང་པ

仲巴县 Zhongba

Population: 25,192   Area: 28,940 sq km

Drongpa county is the region around the source of the Brahmaputra River, which in its uppermost reaches is known as the **Tachok Tsangpo**. To the S lies the Nepalese enclave of **Lowo Matang** (Mustang) and the glacial sources of the Brahmaputra. To the N are some of the great Jangtang lakes – Ngangla Ringtso, Taro-tso, and the Drangyer saltfields. The main road following the course of the Brahmaputra through Drongpa county is the **southern route to Mt Kailash**, rich in nomadic grassland pastures. The county capital is located in the environs of **Drongpa Tradun**, 145 km from Saga and 224 km from Mayum La pass, which divides W Tibet from the Ngari region of Far-west Tibet.

Drongpa Tradun

The road leading from the Men-chu valley of Saga county into Drongpa initially passes through vast sand dunes, and for

DRONGPA COUNTY

To Mnt Kailash
Lungkar
Lake
Balungtso 105
Maryum La
58 Ribzhi
Satsam
50 Horpa
20
Baryang   Gacho
14 36 4,725m
Drongpa Tradun
7,095m
Brahmaputra
119
Dargyeling
26
Kyakyaru
Sketch map: not to scale

a large part of the distance stays close to the N bank of the Brahmaputra. From the pass on the border which separates these two counties, there are fine views of **Mt Longpo Gangri** (7,095m) to the NE and the Himalayan ranges to the S. The road thereafter deteriorates considerably, making travel much slower than before.

The Drongpa river valley, formed by the combined waters of the **Tsa-chu** and **Yur-chu**, is a broad delta of sand and low-lying scrub. The waters of the river flow S into the Brahmaputra. One of King Songtsen Gampo's geomantic temples of the 'further-taming' (*yangdul*) class, named **Jang Traduntse**, is said to have been located in this valley, on the 'right knee' of the supine ogress. It was from here and from neighbouring **Zhungru** that Tibetan traders and lamas would traditionally make their way into **Lowo Matang** (Mustang), via the **Lektse Tsongra** market and the **Chu'arok** river valley.

Like Saga, **Drongpa** county town was developed originally as a military base, and it was once the main check post for illegal traffic (such as hitchhiking tourists). It had no restaurant save a public kitchen where local people could come and pick up a bowl of rice and greasy gruel. It was located on the S side of a wind-swept sand dune and was singularly uninviting. Then, abruptly, in 1993, the town was moved about 25 km W! That is, at least the military garrison and administrative buildings moved, leaving a semi-ghost town at the old site, which is inhabited mostly by local Tibetans. However, it is easy to miss the **new Drongpa** completely, in that it is concealed some distance away from the main road on the far W side of the Drongpa river valley. Look out for the turn-off some 8-10 km W of the new bridge and just before the road enters the Brahmaputra gorge. However, since there is nowhere to stay at new Drongpa, if it is not late you are advised to press on.

Baryang

From Drongpa, the main road continues to follow the Brahmaputra valley upstream, ever closer to its source. After 71 km, it crosses **Soge La pass** (4,725m), and descends 36 km to the small township of **Gacho**. Some 9 km beyond Gacho, after crossing some of the large sand dunes, there is a small hamlet of Tibetan houses, known locally as **Dutu**. Located on the eastern side of a rocky ridge on the S side of the road it is the focus for a number of families who graze their animals on the rich surrounding pastures. Nomads pitch their tents here, and there is a fine water supply nearby. From this point on, healthy, growing herds of yaks and goats are to be seen on both sides of the road. The next main settlement is **Baryang**, 14 km after Gacho; but since the township has little of interest, it is better to camp.

Horpa

Some 20 km after Baryang, the road fords the **Neu Tsangpo River** at **Horpa**. This river eventually flows into the Brahmaputra below Baryang. The crossing is dangerous and vehicles are often trapped midstream. Whether the whole **southern route to Mt Kailash** is open or not depends largely on this one crossing. If the weather is fine you should attempt to make the crossing as early as possible in the day, before the snow melt has swollen the river. If it has been raining it may be necessary to wait for assistance to arrive. It is always sensible to make this crossing together with other vehicles. Once across, the road continues through sandy grasslands.

Lungkar

From Horpa, a side-road leaves the Brahmaputra valley to follow the **Neu Tsangpo** upstream. Crossing the high **Me La** watershed, it descends into the Jangtang Plateau after 58 km. It then bypasses **Ribzhi** village on the E shore of Lake Balungtso, and after a further 105 km it comes to a halt at **Lungkar** township on the SW shore of **Lake Tarotso**. There are old trade routes heading N from here to the **Drangyer saltfield** and the vast lake **Ngangra Ringtso**.

Mayum La pass

From Horpa, the main road continues to follow the N bank of the Brahmaputra upstream to **Satsam** (50 km) and, then, after crossing to the S bank, traces the course of the **Mayum Tsangpo** feeder river towards the **Mayum La pass**, which marks the frontier between W Tibet and Far-west Tibet. The distance from Satsam to the pass is 50 km. The road across Mayum La may be impassable if it has been raining heavily. It is often practical to camp out before the pass and negotiate it in the morning while the earth may be frozen. It is a long, gradual pass that consists largely of marshy soil. Once over it, however, the road to **Barga** and **Mt Kailash** is straightforward.

On the NE side of the **Ganglungri** range, which divides Drongpa county from the **Simikot** region of NW Nepal, there are the glaciers of **Jema Yungdrung**, **Ngangser** and **Gyama Langdzom** which are included among the sources of the *Brahmaputra*.

NORTHERN TIBET
THE JANGTANG PLATEAU

INTRODUCTION

The northern plateau of Tibet, known as the **Jangtang**, is a vast lakeland wilderness, over 438,000 sq km in area. The average elevation is 4,500m, and the distance from the easternmost parts which adjoin Nakchu and Amdo counties to Lake Pang-gong in the far-west exceeds 1,300 km. The northern limits of the plateau are demarcated by the Kunlun Mts and the southern edge by the Gangtise and Nyenchen Tanglha ranges. The basin of the upper Indus lies to the W, and those of the upper Salween and Yangtze are to the E and NE. In general the western parts of the plateau are higher than the eastern parts.

The Jangtang plateau itself has no external drainage, but it is dotted with brackish salt lakes, some of which were once part of the Yangtze and Salween basins, and others remnants of the Neo-Tethys Sea. Most of these are at elevations of 4,500-5,000m; and among them the largest include **Namtso** and **Serling** (both 81 km across), **Dangra Yutso** (64 km long), **Ngangla Ringmo**, and **Lake Pang-gang** (48 km by 113 km). It is clear that these lakes are relics of once significantly larger bodies of water, the traces of which can be observed in the relief of the ancient shorelines. Certain lakes have become salt swamps, while others are connected by small streams.

The internal river network is largely undeveloped – the longest being the **Tsakya Tsangpo** which drains into Lake Serling. In winter, the rivers freeze to the bottom, thus confining drainage to the summer months. These processes and frost weathering have lead to the formation of colossal accumulations of friable material, which has levelled the relief. Due to the winnowing of fine particles, the coarser gravel-pebble material is gradually compacted and polished, forming a shiny mantle that is subject to no further deflation. In addition, the thickness of certain salt swamps is so great that they form entire beds which have acquired unique and strange shapes – pyramids, spheres and cones.

The Jangtang plateau is mostly contained within the Tibetan Autonomous Region, although the extreme NE parts currently fall within Qinghai province. Four counties form its heart: among them are **Tsochen** and **Gertse** counties in Ngari district, through which the northern route from Raga to Mt Kailash passes; and **Shentsa** and **Palgon** in Nakchu district, which link the Lhasa-Ziling highway with Far-west Tibet. **Recommended itineraries**: 2, 6.

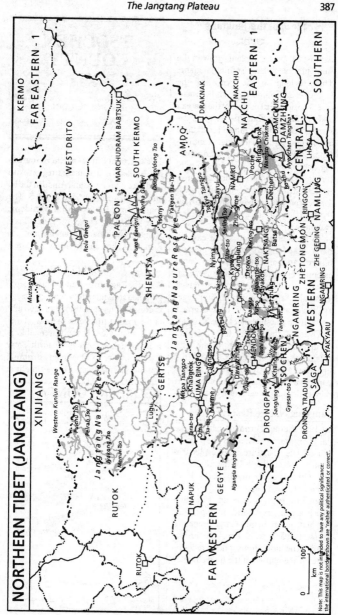

NORTHERN TIBET (JANGTANG)

Note: This map is not intended to have any political significance;
the international borders shown are neither authenticated or correct.

Flora of the Jangtang

བྱང་ཐང་

At least 53 species of plants grow in the stony tundra landscape of the Jangtang. These belong to the genus of the Gramineae, Compositae, and Cruciferae. The **northern** portion of the **plateau** and the **Eastern Kunluns** are more desertified. On the better drained areas there are creeping shrubs of teresken, acantholiumn, capsella, astragalus, thermopsis, sage, and saussurea. Along the shores of certain lakes with internal drainage grow sedges and in poorly drained swampy areas Tibetan cobresia. In ravines sheltered from the winds there are poa, sheep's fescue and reaumurea.

In the **southern** and **south-eastern** parts of the **Jangtang** where the precipitation marginally increases, the alpine èsteppes encourage the growth of poa, sheep's fescue, feather grass, and quack grass; also sandwort, delphinium, sage, astragalus and saussurea. Juniper grows sparsely on the shores of Lake Namtso.

Overall, there are few creeping shrubs capable of growing in the salty Jangtang soils: caragana, myricaria, ephedra, and tansy among them, but extensive areas of salt swamp are completely devoid of vegetation cover.

Jangtang Nature Reserve

In 1993 the northernmost parts of the Jangtang were declared as the world's second largest nature reserve (300,000 sq km), exceeded only by the ice-caps of the Greenland National Park. Here roam the much depleted herds of wild ungulates (wild yak, wild ass, blue sheep, argali, gazelle and antelope); and the plateau's remaining large predators (snow leopard, wolf, lynx and brown bear). The ubiquitous pika predominates at the bottom of the food chain.

TSOCHEN COUNTY

མཚོ་ཆེན

措勤县 Coqen

Population: 31,239   Area: 35,887 sq km

Tsochen county on the **northern route to Mt Kailash** is a nomadic region with road access to Gertse and Amdo in the N, and to Ngamring or Saga in the S. The county capital is located at **Mendong**, near the NW shore of Lake Tashi Namtso. The distance from the capital to Raga is 242 km, and to Gertse 257 km.

Places of interest

After the **Raga** turnoff and a long, deeply potholed straight road, a concrete bridge is crossed. Down the slope to the right of the road at this point there is a large geothermal area. If the water table is high enough geysers spout forth every few minutes or so. One shoots steaming water over 15m high. At one time it is

TSOCHEN COUNTY 530

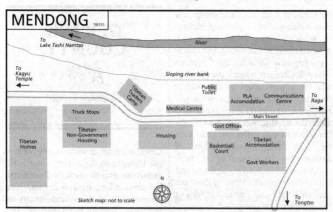

MENDONG TIB151

To
Lake Tashi Namtso

River

To
Kagyu
Temple

Sloping river bank

Tibetan
Cadres
Camp

Public
Toilet

PLA   Communications
Accomodation   Centre

To
Raga

Truck Stops

Medical Centre

Main Street

Tibetan
Non-Government
Housing

Housing

Govt Offices

Tibetan
Accomodation

Tibetan
Homes

Basketball
Court

Govt Workers

N

To
Tongtso

Sketch map: not to scale

said that there were over one hundred geysers here. Ruins of a bath house are now all that remain. The road skirts a small lake and then passes along the full length of **Lake Takyel-tso**, which is teeming with fish.

Snaking its way N up long valleys, the road crosses over small passes offering a vista of ever-changing scenery. Snow-capped peaks, among them **Mt Sanglung** (6,174m), rise far to the W through the occasional huddle of wind-whipped Chinese road gang buildings or small Tibetan hamlets nestled against the leeside of a stony ridge. The lake **Gyesar-tso** lies to the S of Mt Sanglung.

Late in the long day the road descends into the broad sandy plains of the **Yutra Tsangpo** valley – a river which drains into the small **Lake Lungkar-tso** to the SE. The drivers must be careful to follow recent tracks since they can be led into treacherous quicksands. Some 35 km before Mendong (Tsochen), there is a turn-off on the left (W) which leads 14 km to **Kyanghreng** township, on the shore of **Lake Kering-tso**. The main road continues N, crossing the **Tsochen Tsangpo**, to reach the capital around dusk.

Mendong

Mendong (Tsochen) is a barren town near the NW corner of the large Lake Tashi Namtso. It consists of one main street and little else. Existing hotel space is taken up by Chinese soldiers or officials. It can be a somewhat frustrating exercise to find the truck stop at the N end of town, and then the manager, or the caretaker who has the key to the room after a long and tiring day on the road. All this has to be done before one can think about boiling water for tea, eating dinner and falling asleep. Therefore be prepared to pitch a tent in a sheltered courtyard! Recently, there were no restaurants in Tsochen, but this may well have changed owing to the constant influx of Chinese settlers, and there may even be a new guesthouse designated for foreign travellers.

A motorable side-road from Tsochen leads 50 km to **Tseri** township, NE of **Lake Tashi Namtso**. There are a number of small hamlets in this nomadic pastureland, interspersed between smaller lakes, such as Ngangkok-tso.

Continuing on the northern route to Mt Kailash from Tsochen, the trip now changes from a rugged journey to an arduous expedition. It soon reaches the shore of the wide **Lake Dawa-tso**, around which are clusters of nomad tents. This is a traditional grazing land for herds of yaks, goats and sheep. You may notice well-made cairns of rock up to 2m high. They are actually hollow and, if undamaged, hold cooking and camping equipment for a family of nomads who will have left it there the previous year before setting out for their winter dwelling. The goods will remain untouched until they return. After driving along the NE shoreline, the road climbs through a narrow valley and comes out on the lush marshy plain of **Dawazhung**. Here there is an abundance of wildlife. Wild geese, storks and many other types of waterfowl share the area with yaks and gazelles as well as the occasional lammergeier.

The road crosses a high pass, 98 km N of Tsochen, and then sweeps down 72 km into a vast salt plain, where it spreads out into dozens of tracks. These eventually veer W for 16 km, and, near **Tongtso**, meet up with the main Jangtang lateral road which links Amdo county in the E with the region of Far-west Tibet. The raw force of the late noon sun blasts the landscape into a bleached monochrome over a featureless terrain. The town of Gertse lies 81 km W of this road junction.

GERTSE COUNTY
སྒེར་རྩེ
改则县 Gerze
Population: 340,440   Area: 97,771 sq km

Gertse is a large, desolate county bordering Drongpa in the S, Gegye in the W, and the Kunlun Mts in the N. The capital is located at Lumaringpo, 257 km from Tsochen, 836 km from Amdo county in the upper Salween basin, and 385 km from Gegye in the upper Indus valley.

Places of interest

Near Tongtso township where the roads from Tsochen and Amdo converge, you can head E in the direction of Shentsa county or W for Gegye on the northern route to Mt Kailash. Taking the latter route, you will pass **Lake Tongtso** to the N side of the road. After 81 km Lumaringpo, the county capital, suddenly appears in the distance beyond a conical, solitary hillock. It lies in the middle of nowhere; another one-street town.

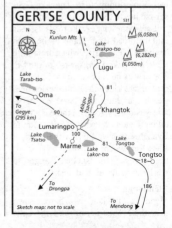

GERTSE COUNTY 531

N
To Kunlun Mts
Lake Drakpo-tso
(6,058m)
(6,282m)
(6,050m)
Lugu
81
Lake Tarab-tso
Oma
Milpu Tsangpo
Khangtok
To Gegye (295 km)
90
35
Lumaringpo
100
Lake Tsatso
Marme
81
Lake Tongtso
Lake Lakor-tso
Tongtso
18
To Drongpa
186
To Mendong

Sketch map: not to scale

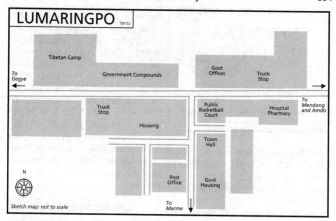

LUMARINGPO TIB152

To Gegye

Tibetan Camp

Government Compounds

Govt Offices

Truck Stop

Truck Stop

Housing

Public Basketball Court

Hospital Pharmacy

To Mendong and Amdo

Town Hall

N

Post Office

Govt Housing

Sketch map: not to scale

To Marme

Lumaringpo

Lumaringpo is larger than Mendong and it is the foremost administrative centre for the nomads of the Jangtang plateau. Its main street is bisected N-S by a second street down which, to the S, is the post office and the town hall. At the E end of the town is the hospital and dispensary (often strangely empty), the telecommunications centre and the larger government guesthouses. At the other end of town, a few hundred metres away, is the quarter occupied by Tibetan itinerants. This features the busiest and liveliest area of town: namely the pool halls, electric games parlours, 'chang' drinking houses, and gambling dens. Around here the traders from Kham, E Tibet, pitch their tents and sell all kinds of goods. The cheap truck stops are also to be found at this end of town.

There are side-roads extending from Lumaringpo into remote parts of the Jangtang plateau. One leads due S for 100 km to **Marme** township, nestling between

lakes Tsatso and Lakor-tso. From there, an old trade and trekking route runs further southwards, following the **Dobrong Tsangpo** valley into **Drongpa** county (see above, page 384). Another road leads northwards from Gertse for 35 km to **Khangtok** township in the **Mikpa Tsangpo** valley, and thence for 154 km to the remote outpost of **Lugu** by the shore of **Lake Drakpo-tso**. There are several 6,000m peaks in the region to the E of Lugu, bordering Shentsa county. Trekking routes also run from Lugu through the lakeland region bordering the Kunlun Mts, and thence out of Tibet into Xinjiang. The northern parts of Gertse county are occupied by the Jangtang Nature Reserve (see above, page 388).

The **northern route to Mt Kailash** runs NW from Gertse, passing **Oma** township after 90 km. **Lake Tarab-tso** lies beyond, on the border of Gertse and Gegye counties. The town of **Gegye** is 295 km from Oma, in the upper Indus valley.

SHENTSA COUNTY

ཤན་ཚ

申扎县 Xainza

Population: 178,630   Area: 205,202 sq km

From **Tongtso** where the Tsochen and Gertse roads intersect, you can head eastwards across the length of the Jangtang plateau towards the Lhasa-Ziling highway. On the way you will pass through Shentsa and Palgon counties. **Shentsa** is by far the largest of the Jangtang counties, extending from the present day Xinjiang and Qinghai provincial borders in the N to the Brahmaputra watershed (Mu-chu and Shang-chu tributaries) in the S. As such the county is larger than the United Kingdom! There are 67 lakes, including some of Tibet's largest: Serling, Dangra Yutso, Ngangtse-tso, Kering-tso, Taktse-tso and Uru-tso among them. In the NE of the county there are a number of 6,000m peaks including **Purok Gangri** (6,482m) and **Norlha Gangri** (6,136m), not to mention the Kunlun Mts on the Xinjiang border

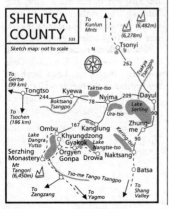

SHENTSA COUNTY 533
Sketch map: not to scale
N
To Kunlun Mts
(6,482m)
(6,278m)
Tsonyi
To Gertse (99 km)
Taktse-tso
262
Tsakya Tsangpo
Tongtso 244 Kyewa
Nyima 209 Dayul
Boktsang Tsangpo
78
To Tsochen (186 km)
Ura-tso
Lake Serling
90
Ombu 167 Kanglung
Zhungme
Lake Dangra Yutso
Khyungdzong
Gyakok
Kering-tso
Serzhing Monastery
Orgyen Gonpa
Lake Nangtse-tso
Drowa
Naktsang
Mt Tangori (6,450m)
Tso-me Tango Tsangpo
Batsa
To Zangzang
To Yagmo
To Shang Valley

further N. The entire northern region forms part of the Jangtang Nature Reserve. 10 large salt fields including those of Yibuk, Shotsa, and Deumar, testify to the importance of this region for the traditional trading commodity of the Jangtang plateau. The county capital is located at **Naktsang** (Shentsa), 805 km from Gertse, and 232 km from Palgon. However, owing to the enormity of this sparsely populated region, there is a second administrative centre at **Tsonyi** (Twin Lakes) in the N. The distance from Naktsang (Shentsa) to Tsonyi is 442 km.

Dangra Yutso Lake

ACCESS Driving eastwards from **Tongtso**, the road reaches **Kyewa** township in the valley of the **Boktsang Tsangpo** after 244 km, and then passes S of Lake Taktse-tso for 78 km to **Nyima** township. Here, there is a turn-off which leaves the main road, heading SW for 167 km via Kanglung to **Ombu** township on the northern shore of **Lake Dangra Yutso**.

The entire Dangra region is sacred to the Bonpo, and at Ombu itself there is a small Bonpo temple and hermitage complex, affiliated to Menri Gonpa. Bonpo pilgrims come from afar to circumambulate the lake, most following their preferred anti-clockwise route. The trek takes 11 days, and it is important to carry all essential supplies and camping equipment. 3 days into the trek, the trail passes through an area rich in wildlife and thence to **Serzhing Monastery**, beyond the SW corner of the lake. This is revered as one of the most important ancient Bonpo monasteries in Tibet, and, although it is largely in ruins at the present day, the site is still impressive. On the 5th day the trail passes through the **Tango Tsangpo** valley in view of the glaciers of **Mt Tangori** (6,450m), frequented largely by Bon hermits (and a few Nyingmapa). At **Tso-me** township in this valley, there is a motorable route to **Zangzang**, and a 14-day trek through the **Mu-chu** valley to **Phuntsoling**.

Continuing on the circuit of the lake, on the 10th day the trail reaches **Orgyen Gonpa** – a small rebuilt Bonpo monastery with a cave temple containing a rock hand-print of Shenrab Miwoche, founder of the Bon religion. Nearby at **Khyungdzong**, there was once an important Bonpo terma-site and hermitage, as well as a 7th century castle belonging to the kings of Zhangzhung. There is also a trail leading due E from here to **Gyakok** township, on the shore of Lake Ngangtse-tso, and eventually to **Drowa** township.

Naktsang

To reach the county capital from Ombu, you must return to the turn-off at **Nyima** township on the main Gertse-Amdo road, and continue driving eastwards, along the N shore of the enormous **Lake Serling**. You will cross the **Tsakya Tsangpo** near its confluence with the lake, and after 204 km, you will reach a major intersection, where side-roads branch off both to the N and S. The former leads to **Tsonyi** district, 262 km in the direction of the Qinghai border. Taking the latter, the road cuts SW via Zhung-me township to **Naktsang**, 180 km distant. This is the largest settlement within the county, located SE of the elongated lake Kering-tso. There are simple but spartan guesthouse facilities. An ancient trade and pilgrimage route leads from here southwards, through **Batsa** township into the **Shang** valley of Tsang (page 317).

PALGON COUNTY

དཔལ་དགོན

班戈县 Baingoin

Population: 86,277   *Area*: 99,112 sq km

Palgon county in the hinterland of **Lake Namtso Chukmo** is relatively close to the Lhasa-Ziling highway. The circuit of this amazing lake and nature reserve has already been described (see above, pages 200-201). In addition, there are 46 lesser lakes and 21 rivers, of which the **Tsakya Tsangpo**, draining into Lake Serling, is the longest.

If you approach the county capital, **Namru**, from the N, you should take the turn-off at **Dayul** which leads to Shentsa, and then after 10 km cut SE in the direction of Namru, 62 km distant. There is simple transport station accommodation here.

A jeepable trail leads directly S from Namru to Lake Namtso Chukmo, passing through the townships of **Poche** (52 km) and **Dechen** (65 km); and from Dechen due W to **Shelyer** along the

PALGON COUNTY 532

To Gertse (625 km) and Ombu (371 km)

To Ziling

Amdo 17 81

Dayul 211

10

62 Namru 226

To Naktsang 52

Nakchu

Poche 65

Lake Namtso Chukmo

Shelyer Bo-chu 52

Dechen

Damzhung

To Lhasa

Yangpachen

N

Sketch map: not to scale

Bo-chu valley (52 km). Another jeep track heads from Namru directly for 226 km to join the Lhasa-Ziling highway. Alternatively, from Dayul on the main road to Amdo county, the distance is 211 km. In the N, the Jantang Nature Reserve occupies the part of Palgon County adjacent to the Qinghai border.

FAR-WEST TIBET
MOUNT KAILASH AND GU-GE KINGDOM

CONTENTS	

MAPS	

INTRODUCTION

The vast region of Far-west Tibet, known as **Ngari**, in Tibetan (*Ch* Ali), is, like the neighbouring Jangtang plateau, one of the least populated parts of the country. Access into this region can be made from the bordering countries of Nepal, and India (the latter closed to non-Indian nationals), or from Pakistan and Kazakhstan via the Xinjiang Autonomous Region (E Turkestan). Within Tibet, the region may be approached via the northern route (Amdo or Tsochen, and Gertse), or the southern route (Saga and Drongpa). At the heart of the region is **Mt Kailash**, the focal point for most visitors, renowned for its natural beauty. Furthermore, within the canyons and valleys of the upper Sutlej River are numerous ruins of ancient cities that once comprised the kingdom of **Gu-ge**. A number of temples are still intact and contain exquisite murals and decorative motifs, some dating back more than 1,000 years. Close to the Indian border this area has only recently been opened for western travellers and is well worth including in an itinerary.

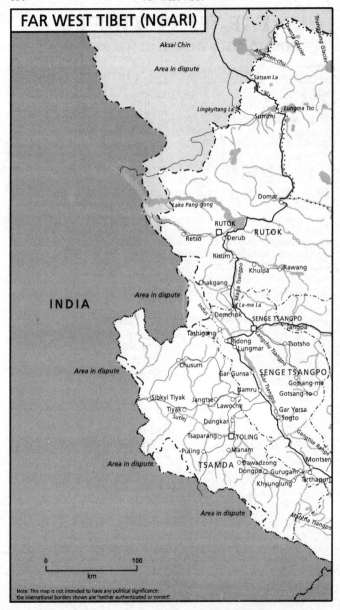

FAR WEST TIBET (NGARI)

Aksai Chin

Area in dispute

Darbuk Glacier

Trungzung Glacier

Abachen-chu

Satsam La

Lingkyitang La

Sumzhi

Lungma Tso

Domar

Lake Pang-gong

RUTOK

RUTOK

Retso

Derub

Risum

Khulpa

Rawang

Chakgang

Maga Tsangpo

INDIA

Area in dispute

La-me La

Demchok

Langchu Tsangpo

SENGE TSANGPO

Jangpa

Tsotsho

Tashigang

Ridong

Lungmar

Chusum

Area in dispute

Gar Gunsa

SENGE TSANGPO

Namru

Gotsang-me

Sibkyi Tiyak

Jangtse

Lawoche

Gotsang-to

Tiyak

Sutlej

Dungkar

Gar Yersa

Sogto

Tsaparang

TOLING

Gangtise Range

Puling

Manam

Montsen

Area in dispute

Dawadzong

TSAMDA

Dongpo

Gurugam

Tirthapuri

Khyunglung

Area in dispute

Mab-cha Tsangpo

0   100

km

Note: This map is not intended to have any political significance;
the international borders shown are 'neither authenticated or correct'.

Traditionally, the region of Ngari is said to have comprised three districts (Ngari Korsum): the district of **Rutok** and **Ladakh**; the district of **Maryul** and **Zhangzhung**; and the district of **Gu-ge** and **Purang**. However Tibetan influence in Central Asia was particularly strong during the periods of the Zhangzhung and Yarlung dynasties and some hold the three districts of Ngari to have been much larger.

Nowadays, Far-west Tibet comprises five of the seven counties in Ngari district of the Tibetan Autonomous Region: **Gegye** and **Senge Tsangpo**, which are situated in the upper Indus valley, **Rutok** county in the Aksai Chin and Northern Plateau, **Tsamda** county in the upper Sutlej valley, and **Purang** county where the Karnali and Brahmaputra rivers have their sources to the S and W of Mt Kailash. The district capital is located at **Senge Tsangpo** (*Ch* Shiquanhe).

In the description which follows, the northern route to Kailash passing through the counties of the upper Indus will be described first, followed by the southern route from Tsang, the western route through Gu-ge, and the north-western route through Xinjiang.
Recommended itinerary: 2.

Land and life

Geography
The region is demarcated by the Himalayas in the S, and the Gangtise Range (or Trans-Himalayan Range) in the N. The **Gangtise** Range (5,500-6,000m) forms a watershed between the upper Brahmaputra River and the landlocked plateau of Northern Tibet (Jangtang). The northern and southern slopes are gentle, marked by flat peaks, low elevations relative to the Tibet plateau, and intensive weathering, whereas the western slopes are broken by the deep gorges of the Indus and the heavily eroded sandstone canyons of the Sutlej.

The unique 6,658m pinnacle of **Mt Kailash**, (*Tib* Gang Ti-se/Gang Rinpoche), lies at the geographic watershed of South Asia. Before it, a few kilometres to the S, are two lakes, **Mapham Yutso** (Manasarovar) and **Lakngar** (Rakshas Tal), shaped respectively like the sun and the moon. The sources of four major rivers rise from this geomantic crown and flow in the four cardinal directions: the **Indus** (N), **Brahmaputra** (E), **Karnali** (S) and **Sutlej** (W). It is for this reason and because of the unique beauty of the region that Mt Kailash has been looked upon as a sacred realm – a goal of pilgrimage by peoples from India, Tibet and Asia for thousands of years.

Further N, the **Nganglung Gangri** range (elevation 5,700-6,300m) separates the upper Indus from the Jangtang plateau. The highest peak is **Ngari Gangri** (6,348m); and the range is less rugged than the Himalayas, with more rounded and weathered hills.

Climate
Ngari is marked by the greatest extremes of dryness and the lowest temperatures. In Senge Tsangpo (4,600m) the annual precipitation is less than 100 mm and the mean Jan temperature -12°. In recent years however the climate has become more inconsistent. During the Indian monsoon from late June to mid-Sept heavy rains often reach as far as the northern slopes of the Gangtise range, causing rivers to become impassable and increasing erosion. Deforestation of the Himalayas is thought to be the main cause.

Flora and fauna
The landscape is barren, reminiscent of the Jangtang steppes N of the Gangtise range, but there are some variations in flora. Here juniper grows, along with barberry and honeysuckle.

The region between the source of the Brahmaputra and Mt Kailash abounds with wildlife, especially after the rainy season of July and Aug. Apart from the herds of **yak** there are large herds of **wild**

KHAMPA TRADERS OF NGARI

The vast region is strikingly reminiscent of the wide open spaces of the American Wild West, especially as seen in countless Hollywood films. The inhabitants also bring to mind images of the Wild West. The nomads bear a strong physical resemblance to North American Indians, such as the Navaho. In the towns tall Khampa traders from E Tibet are like 'macho' cowboys. They swagger about, gold teeth flashing behind a wide knowing smile, long hair wound in red or black braid embellished with a large gold and turquoise earring, their feet balanced on high-heeled riding boots or showing through holes in Chinese canvas trainers, and wearing a bulky gown or 'chuba' (Tibet's national costume) tied loosely round the waist with a fat money belt from which dangles a long knife in a silver scabbard. They stand outside their tented shops on the edge of town selling everything from batteries to baseball hats, from music cassettes to motor spare parts. There is a similar sense of lawlessness to the cowboy west in this land that is free of any visible boundaries. It makes the accounts by previous travellers to Tibet of robbers raiding the caravans of traders and pilgrims all too real.

ass (*kyang*), a large and vividly marked creature which gallops away from the road when disturbed. You have to be quick to take photographs. More common throughout W Tibet are the Tibetan **gazelle** (*Tib* gowa; Procapra picticaudata) and **Hodgson's antelope** (*Tib* tso; Pantholops hodgsoni). The former is small and similar to the wild chamois of the European Alps. The latter is larger, distinguished by its long, slightly curved horns and white buttocks or hindquarters. Other animals commonly seen are the **marmot** (*chiwa*), which resembles a brown, furry football with legs, and the **abra**, a small Tibetan rodent like a gerbil that lives in large colonies of burrows in the midst of healthy grasslands.

Huge flocks of migrating birds can also be seen throughout the late summer, making their way S over the Himalayas to India for the winter. In addition there are indigenous birds such as the graceful **Brahmany geese** which have golden coloured bodies and a black head, and which maintain a life-long mating relationship. They have become the subject of numerous love songs and poems in Tibet. It is well known that if one should die or be killed, the mate will pine and grieve until it too passes away.

Transport

The journey across the great Northern Plain into Far-west Tibet passes through a land where the lifestyle remains close to what it has been for centuries. The landscapes and vistas are vast and sparsely inhabited but exhilarating, like a treeless moonscape. Lone groups of nomads dwelling in low, black tents, tend flocks of sheep and goats as well as herds of the ubiquitous yak (the 'grunting ox' according to its Latin name).

Towns are few and far apart and generally consist of one main street bisected by another, neither being more than a few hundred metres long. The main building invariably is a Chinese communist party meeting hall, and one is not always assured of finding a shop or restaurant, hotel or water, or any facilities at all for the average intrepid traveller, let alone a tourist. However, one is continually assured that, "Next year we will have made much improvement in our service!" For example, every room in the district's premier hotel, the *Ali Hotel* at Senge Tsangpo, has been tastefully laid out in a universal motel design with en-suite bathroom, toilet and shower, only lacking one element – water! Such a minor shortcoming, however, did not stop the manager (a party cadre and retired army captain) from charging the special double rate for western tourists. This situation and the lack of water has continued over the last 10 years, despite the hotel being located next to the bank of the Indus River!

Much of the journey consists often of little more than parallel tracks across the flat expanse of the plateau. The distances to be covered each day entail many hours of bumpy riding. Transport is usually arranged through the Tibetan (or Chinese) tour operator. It is likely to consist of a small convoy led by one or more 4WD Toyota landcruisers accompanied by one or two support trucks carrying food, baggage and fuel. It will be the pace of the truck that determines how quickly the distances can be covered. Although this involves long, somewhat gruelling days, the faster the grand scope of the Northern Plateau is traversed the more time that can be spent within the environs of the sacred Mt Kailash.

NB Special travel permits required for entry into Ngari and other 'closed' areas of Tibet. See also **Information for visitors** page 19.

GEGYE COUNTY

དགེ་རྒྱས

革吉县 Gegyai

Population: 47,777   Area: 54,885 sq km

Gegye county on the **northern route to Mt Kailash** extends from Lake Tarabtso, on the edge of the Jangtang plateau, as far as Dongpa and Gegye in the upper Indus valley. The capital is located at **Napuk** (Gegye) town, 383 km from Gertse town, and 112 km from Senge Tsangpo.

Driving W from **Oma** township in Gertse county, the road passes S of **Lake Tarab-tso**, and on for 94 km to **Tsaka** (*Ch* Yanba), where there are commercial salt fields. It then cuts SW for 96 km to **Zhungba** township on the Shang-chu River, passing **Lake Nyer-tso** to the W. A jeepable side-road leads S from Zhungba to **Yakra** (130 km) on the SE shore of **Lake Tsonak**, and from here there is a trekking route to the large lake **Ngangla Ringtso** on the border of Drongpa county (see above, page 384).

The main road from Zhungba cuts NW, with **Mt Tsotra** (6,046m) to the right. After 75 km, it reaches **Dongba** township, descending into the valley of the upper Indus. Trekking routes follow

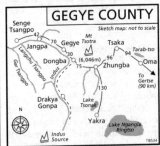

GEGYE COUNTY

Sketch map: not to scale

THE UPPER INDUS VALLEY

The Indus is 2,900 km in length, encompassing a drainage area of 1,165,500 sq km (of which 453,248 sq km are within the mountain area). The annual flow is 207 billion cu m. The actual source of the Indus is the stream known in Tibet as the Senge Khabab or Jang Senge Khabab ("northern source from the lion-shaped rock"). This source lies to the N of Mt Kailash at 5,500m in a remote valley within the Sengto district of Gegye county. In its uppermost reaches the river which emerges from this glacial source is called the Senge Tsangpo. It flows NW for about 320 km through Drakya Gonpa, Dongpa, and Napuk townships of Gegye county, and then W to Senge Tsangpo, where it converges with the Langchu Tsangpo and the Gar Tsangpo, before cutting NW through Tashigang and Demchok. Here, the river leaves Tibet, crossing into India at about 4,570m. The river volume in Tibet is mainly snow-fed, but thereafter it passes through Ladakh, Baltistan, and the alluvial plains of Pakistan, where it provides the life support for millions of people. Over 5,000 years ago its waters sustained the Indus Valley Civilization, one of the earliest settlements of mankind. Major tributaries include the Zangskar, Shyok, Shigar, Gilgit, Astor, Kabul, and the five Punjab rivers.

the river upstream to **Drakya Gonpa** and the broad **Yalung Selung** range (largest peak 6,105m), giving access to Mt Kailash. The motorable route, however, follows the Indus gorge downstream to **Napuk**, the county capital of Gegye, only 30 km distant. **Mt Dongri** (5,825m), a major landmark, lies to the E as the town is approached.

Gegye

In the past Gegye was renowned for its remote branch of the East Tibetan monastery of Dzokchen, known as **Gegye Dzokchen Gon**. The present county capital is a completely new town, poorly located at the base of a cliff where the prevailing winds create a semi-permanent sand storm. Such is the 'skill' of the latter-day Chinese geomancers who created it! This very bleak town, which was set up mainly to control the nomads, will be reached in the late afternoon if you have left Gertse early in the morning. The road now is quite straightforward and the average speed can be increased accordingly. It may be best to continue on to Senge Tsangpo, the district capital, because accommodation is difficult to find. If the transport station is full camp out against a sheltered bluff, 2 km out of town. Perfectly adequate for the few hours rest that one needs, this bluff is formed by an uninhabited complex of buildings, originally made for the Muslim construction workers who were brought down from Xinjiang province.

To reach Senge Tsangpo from Gegye, continue following the Indus downstream towards **Jangpa** (70 km) and thence for 42 km to the district capital.

SENGE TSANGPO COUNTY

 སེང་གེ་གཙང་པོ

噶尔县 Shiquanhe

Population: 10,273   Area: 11,802 sq km

Senge Tsangpo county, formerly known as Gar, straddles the confluences of the Indus River and two of its tributaries: the Langchu Tsangpo, which converges at Senge Tsangpo town, and the Gar Tsangpo, which converges S of Tashigang. The former, which is both the district and county capital, is located 112 km from Gegye, 127 km from Rutok, 255 km from Toling, and 428 km from Purang.

Senge Tsangpo

The **northern route to Mt Kailash** continues following the upper Indus valley through **Jangpa** village (70 km beyond Gegye) and on to **Senge Tsangpo** (42 km from Jangpa), which is by far the largest town in the entire region. It is a new Chinese built town, named after the **Indus River** (*Tib* Senge Tsangpo, *Ch* Shiquanhe), which has its confluence with the **Langchu Tsangpo** here. The traditional capital of the Ngari region was Gartok, a nomadic encampment in the Gar Tsangpo valley (see below, page 403).

After the long, arduous journey across the Northern Plateau this is an opportunity to spend 1 or 2 days washing clothes etc while preparing for the last, most important stage of the journey to Mt Kailash. One should also check or obtain **permits** for Tsaparang, Toling and Mt Kailash.

There are four roads which diverge at the capital: one leading NE to Gegye and Gertse (see above, page 400 and page 390), another leading due N to Rutok (see below, page 437), a third leading W to the confluence of the Indus with the Gar Tsangpo, and a fourth which leads SE to Tsotsho township.

From Senge Tsangpo you can go directly to Mt Kailash, but to reach it in 1 day it is essential to depart well before sunrise. Otherwise you should break the journey at Montser.

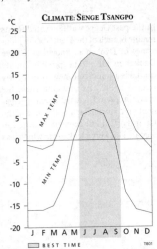

CLIMATE: SENGE TSANGPO

SENGE TSANGPO COUNTY

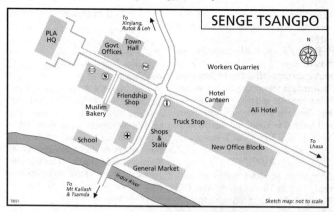

SENGE TSANGPO

To Xinjiang, Rutok & Leh

PLA HQ

Govt Offices

Town Hall

N

Workers Quarries

Hotel Canteen

Friendship Shop

Muslim Bakery

Ali Hotel

Truck Stop

School

Shops & Stalls

New Office Blocks

To Lhasa

General Market

Indus River

To Mt Kailash & Tsamda

Ti891

Sketch map: not to scale

Local information
● Accommodation
In town, the ostentatious and 'modern' *Ali Hotel* provides compulsory accommodation for foreign visitors. Since its inception, it has been generally managed by ex-public security or ex-PLA officers who know little about running a hotel. **NB** If you try to camp out at Senge Tsangpo, the police can arrest you and fine you the price of a night's stay at the hotel (US$10-33), and then charge the hotel's rate on top! Although the *Ali Hotel* has all the right fittings in its attached bathrooms, until now there has been no running water, despite promises of hot showers!

● Places to eat
The meals at the *Ali Hotel* are good (breakfast US$7; full meal plan US$28) but be sure to arrive on time otherwise you will miss out.

● Shopping
Friendship Shop at the town crossroads allow the purchase of food and other supplies.

● Hospitals & medical services
In town there is a modern hospital, which also dispenses Tibetan medicine.

Langchu Tsangpo Valley
A jeepable side-road goes SE from Senge Tsangpo town, following the **Langchu Tsangpo** upstream. After 40 km it reaches its terminus at **Tsotsho** township, and an ancient trekking route leads on into the upper reaches of this valley to **Gotsang-me** and **Gotsang-to**.

Tashigang and Demchok
Taking the westerly road from Senge Tsangpo, you will reach the confluence of the Indus with the Gar Tsangpo at **Ridong** after about 30 km. From here the main road to Mt Kailash follows the Gar Tsangpo upstream (SE), while a jeepable side-road continues NW following the course of the Indus downstream to **Tashigang** (21 km). The pot-holed surface of the latter continues on through the upper Indus gorge to reach **Demchok** and the Indian frontier (closed to tourists), where the river flows into Ladakh.

Gar Tsangpo Valley
Turning SE at **Ridong**, the confluence of the Indus with the Gar Tsangpo, the main **northern route to Mt Kailash** follows the latter upstream. It passes through **Lungmar** and then bypasses **Gar Gunsa**, the ancient winter capital of Ngari district, 111 km from Senge Tsangpo.

On old maps Gar Gunsa is referred to as Gartok. In former times it was the seat of a viceroy appointed by the central government in Lhasa to whom all foreign travellers were supposed to apply for travel permission. It lay on one of the main caravan routes. Today it is nearly impossible to see where it once was situated. All that remains are mounds of rubble.

Further S, the road passes through **Namru** after 23 km, where there is an important turn-off leading to Toling and Tsaparang in the upper Sutlej valley (see below, page 425 and page 429). Continuing along the Gar Tsangpo valley, you will reach **Gar Yersa**, the ancient summer capital of Ngari, and **Sogto** village.

Montser

After Sogto, the road crosses a watershed, leaving the source of the Gar Tsangpo behind, and following the SW side of the **Gangtise** range into a wide sandy valley which forms part of the upper Sutlej basin. This road can be quite treacherous in the rainy season because it follows a poorly cut track along the sandy floor of the river valley. Bumpy ruts cut through the sandy surface, causing vehicles to toss about. Sections of the road also ford streams and rivers which can be deceptive as far as their depth is concerned. However an experienced driver should be familiar with hazards and cover the journey safely. Eventually the road reaches the new township of **Montser**, 237 km from Senge Tsangpo.

Montser

Montser is a coal mining town with little of redeeming interest. There are no streets to speak of, nor a town centre, just housing compounds and open space. Therefore you need to enquire where the truck stops are. There are at least two truck stops in Montser, which is usually reached at dusk.

- **Accommodation** One is very basic, just beds with thin mattresses. The other is cleaner and better equipped, with beds, mattresses, and a quilted sheet, but may have no empty rooms.

- **Places to eat** One restaurant will be open, if you arrive early enough.

Tirthapuri

Before setting out from Montser on the road to Darchen, you can take a detour to visit the hot springs, picnic ground and pilgrimage site of **Tirthapuri**. It is about 6 km SW of Montser. Here is a cave associated with Padmasambhava, the Indian master who established Buddhism in Tibet in the 8th century and his Tibetan consort Yeshe Tsogyel. You may prefer just to spend a short time here and return after the circuits of Mt Kailash and Lake Manasarovar. Tirthapuri is one of the traditional pilgrimage sites visited after Mt Kailash, see below, page 404.

Gurugam Monastery

ACCESS The road to **Khyunglung**, which leaves the main road 8 km S of Montser, passes SW through a broad agricultural valley dotted with single family compounds. The Bonpo Monastery of **Gurugam** is located about 15 km from the turn-off, at the western limit of this valley. Camp here!

This is one of the most important Bonpo monasteries in Far-west Tibet. Today it has a strong connection to the main Bonpo settlement at **Dolanji** in N India where many of its monks gathered after the Chinese invasion and have successfully re-established the Bon tradition in exile. Gurugam was rebuilt in 1989-91 from walled ruins and is one of the finest examples of a Bon monastery within Ngari district. An earlier site, known as **Zhangzhung Gonpa**, is located at a square mound within a number of collapsed stupas a few hundred metres E of Gurugam. This must have been active over the same era as Khyunglung.

It was here, in one of the cave hermitages situated in the cliffs above, that the Bonpo master **Drenpei Namka** lived and meditated. He was also renowned as a great doctor – his mortar and pestle for grinding herbs and medications can still be seen to the side of the pathway leading up to his room. A steep climb leads through a series of staircases and tunnels before reaching Drenpei Namka's meditation cave, cut deep into the cliff above the temple. Inside the cave you can feel a palpable sense of sanctity amidst a remarkable wealth of religious objects.

The other major temple associated with Drenpei Namka is a box-like shrine on the top of a canyon directly to the E. Inside is a statue of the master himself, which was decapitated by the Chinese and has now been given a new head by devotees. Unfortunately the replacement is two or three times larger than normal – obviously the devotion exceeded any sense of the conventional!

Khyunglung

From Gurugam, you can also make a secondary expedition to the ruins of one of Tibet's earliest cities, known as **Khyunglung** ("Garuda Valley"). Dating back to 2,000 BC or even earlier it was established by the first kings of Zhangzhung, the original name for Far-west Tibet, and it continued to be occupied for 3,000 years. For a description of Khyunglung (which is in Tsamda county), see below, page 424.

PURANG COUNTY

སྤུ་ཧྲེང་

普兰县 Bulan
Population: 10,132   Area: 11,641 sq km

Purang county is the heart of Far-west Tibet, where the four great rivers of South Asia diverge from their glacial sources around Mt Kailash. It is the goal of the great pilgrimage routes which approach this sanctified mountain from the N (Gegye or Xinjiang), from the W (Kinnaur in India), from the S (Almora in India and Simikot in Nepal), and from the E (Drongpa). The county capital is located at **Purang**, known as Taklakot in Nepali, which lies 104 km S of Barka township, in the valley of the Karnali River (*Tib* Mabcha Tsangpo). The distance from here to Senge Tsangpo, the district capital, is 428 km, to Drongpa in Tsang 487 km, and to Toling in the upper Sutlej valley 434 km.

PURANG COUNTY   TIB535

To Senge Tsangpo (237 km)

Sketch map: not to scale

Montser

8

Tirthapuri   Drirapuk   (5,723m)

15   Mnt Kailash (6,658m)

Gurugam   60   Zutrulpuk

N   Barka   22 Darchen

28   Hor

Lake   Seralung   To Drongpa (387km)
Rakshas
Tal   Lake
Manasarovar

Chiu Gon   23

Trugo Gon

Rigong   Mnt Nemo Nanyi (7,728m)

Purang   15

18   Khorzhak
(5,090m)

To India

India   Nepal

Darchen

ACCESS The 68 km road from Montser to **Darchen**, where the circuit of Mt Kailash begins, follows the Gangtise or Trans-Himalayan Range directly down (SE) to the **Barka** Plain between Mt Kailash and the two lakes. Before leaving Montser you may decide to take a detour to visit Tirthapuri and Gurugam Monastery (in Senge Tsangpo county) and Khyunglung (in Tsamda county). Otherwise drive directly to Darchen.

Darchen was formerly an important sheep station for the nomads and their flocks. Until the late 1980s it still consisted of only two permanent buildings. One had survived the mass destruction of religious shrines during the Cultural Revolution since it was said to have belonged to the Bhutanese government through the Drukpa Kagyu tradition which still claimed jurisdiction over it. Resembling a temple, it is coloured in red ochre and serves as a shelter for Tibetan pilgrims. The second building was created in the 1980s to accommodate the first wave of pilgrims from India. It is thus known as the *IP (Indian Pilgrim) Guest House*. In 1995 a medical centre and dispensary was inaugurated. Sponsored by a Swiss Tibetan benefactor it is intended to become a centre for training doctors and for dispensing medicine and treatment for the various illnesses that afflict the local nomadic community.

● **Facilities** The large *Darchen Guesthouse* has expanded from the *IP Guesthouse* with rooms available for mainly western travellers, each room has at least 5 beds each for ¥25 each. The main compound also has a shop selling souvenirs, canned food, and the ever-present green-bottled beer.

MOUNT KAILASH

གངས་རིན་པོ་ཆེ

For most travellers to Far-west Tibet the prime focus of their journey is the sacred peak of **Mt Kailash** (6,658m). This extraordinary mountain is regarded as the 'heart of the world', the '*axis Mundi*', the centre of Asia, by Buddhists, Hindus, Jains and followers of other spiritual traditions. Of all the special destinations for the traveller to reach, Mt Kailash is surely one of the most sublime and sacred. Its geographical position as the watershed of South Asia is unique and it is this which gives it a cosmic geomantic power. From its slopes flow four great rivers in the four cardinal directions – the Indus north, the Brahmaputra east, the Karnali into the Ganges south, and the Sutlej west.

Before Mt Kailash lie the twin lakes of **Manasarovar** (4,600m) and **Rakshas Tal** (4,584m), shaped respectively like the sun and moon, and which are said to have associations respectively with the forces of light and dark. Further S, just on the edge of the Tibetan plateau and near the Himalayas is another snow-capped peak, **Mt Nemo Nanyi** (Gurlamandhata; 7,728m), which is one of the highest inside Tibet. Its three peaks and four ridges form a swastika, an ancient symbol of the universe's infinity.

Mount Kailash itself is known in the Tibetan language as **Gangkar Ti-se** and informally as **Gang Rinpoche** ("Precious Snow Mountain"), and in Chinese as **Gang Rinboqe Feng**. Though only 6,714m high, it stands quite alone like a great white sentinel guarding the main routes into Tibet from India and Nepal in the S and W.

Traditionally a pilgrim undertakes the 58 km trekking circuit or circum-ambulation (*khorlam*) around Mt Kailash commencing at **Darchen** (4,575m) and crossing the 5,723m high **Dolma La pass** on the second day of the 3-day walk. This is followed by a trek of the same duration around the beautiful turquoise **Lake Mansarovar**. The journey is then completed with a rest and camp at the hot springs and geysers of **Tirthapuri**, a few hours drive away and especially associated with Padmasambhava. All along the pilgrimage route are places of historical and spiritual interest.

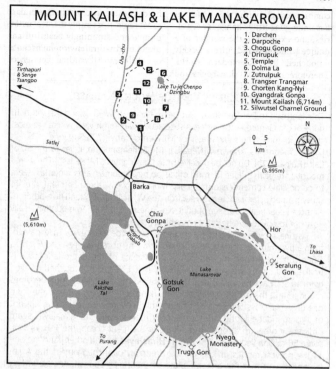

MOUNT KAILASH & LAKE MANASAROVAR

1. Darchen
2. Darpoche
3. Chogu Gonpa
4. Drirupuk
5. Temple
6. Dolma La
7. Zutrulpuk
8. Trangser Trangmar
9. Chorten Kang-Nyi
10. Gyandrak Gonpa
11. Mount Kailash (6,714m)
12. Silwutsel Charnel Ground

The Rigour of the Routes to Mt Kailash

Although Mt Kailash and its environs are of exceptional natural beauty it can only be reached via lengthy and often arduous travel along one of several routes into the region. Rivalry for the tourist business between the authorities of various Chinese provinces and districts has led to the imposition of travel restrictions by Lhasa on foreigners travelling in outlying regions. Only the most determined or wealthy travellers can therefore hope to circumvent such obstacles.

Despite the lifting of some of these bureaucratic restrictions, facilities for the foreign traveller are sparse and the way itself, from whichever direction, is rugged and often tiring. Travel in this region takes one into contact with a lifestyle that has probably suffered the least change as a result of the Chinese occupation. Local food is basic and needs to be supplemented. Thus a large degree of self-reliance and fortitude is essential. Furthermore, the sacred Mt Kailash has never easily allowed visitors into its sanctum, but with fortitude, patience and a pure, constant intention to reach and circle its snow-capped peak, one will succeed in the venture. For all these reasons, the journey to and through Farwest Tibet requires the appropriate preparation, both logistically and mentally.

The traveller who is prepared to undergo the rigours of this journey will come into contact with a way of life that has undergone little change for centuries, and experience the wonder of a unique wilderness and culture largely untouched by the modern world. Therefore, despite all drawbacks and hardships, to participate in a pilgrimage to Mt Kailash or simply to travel in this unique and stunningly beautiful and unpolluted natural environment can be one of life's most rewarding experiences.

A PILGRIM'S VIEW OF MOUNT KAILASH

The approach to Darchen from Montser, passing eastwards along the southern ridge of the Gantise range, offers a spectacular panoramic view where the most striking feature is the snow massif of **Mt Nemo Nanyi** (7,728m), one of Tibet's highest mountains, known in Nepali as Mt Gurlamandhata. It lies to the SE of **Lake Rakshas Tal**. Do not be deceived into thinking this is Mt Kailash! The sacred mountain remains hidden for most of the journey. Mountain after mountain seem to be possible contenders until, finally, it rises above all those before it; a giant snow-capped pyramid when viewed from the W; majestically standing aloof from all those lesser peaks that surround it. Now these neighbouring mountains really do seem to bow down before its magnificence!

As one moves closer, its form seems to change with every mile passed; from a pyramid, to a breast, to a dome. Now one observes clearly how it rises alone, unique among mountains. Its dominance of the entire landscape is unlike anything in the mighty Himalayas. Its 6,658m is not touched or even glanced at by any mountain near it. As Darchen comes closer its form becomes rounded and the extraordinary black markings on its faces cut into the form of a universal cross or eternal swastika through its snow capped mass. It is not of this mundane world because it now makes even the Himalayas seem ordinary. It grew up through the depths of the great ocean, the **Tethys Sea**, some 50 million years ago. The **Great Himalayas** on the other hand are one of the newest ranges on the planet, arbitrarily wrenched out of the Asian landmass as it met the tectonic plate of the Indian subcontinent, buckling skyward from the massive forces unleashed below the surface some 20 million years ago.

Mount Kailash's very whiteness and convex S face, like a mirror, is said to reflect the sun's rays out, beyond the confines of the planet. Like a giant crystal, its three faceted sides encompass a trinity that rises glittering at the nexus of the Hindu and Buddhist planetary universe. From the stark duality of its white sheen and black mystery etched into its every face – the inner and outer, splits the triad of its faces, complete and self-contained. Grudgingly through the valleys and folds of the land it then manifests into four, the great rivers of the world flowing in the four cardinal directions: the sacred rivers which are the sources of civilizations and knowledge: N the **Indus**, spawning the earliest, the Indus Valley civilization; E, the **Brahmaputra** feeding the mystics of Tibet before cutting through the eastern Himalayas and cascading down into Bengal and the source of the great philosophy and knowledge of ancient India; S via the **Karnali** into the **Ganges**, India's life-blood and the well-spring of its spiritual inspiration and ongoing timeless presence; and W, along the **Sutlej**, little known but in fact the link with the mystics of the Indian Himalayas and the sustainer of the richness of life in the NW of India. Thus the mountain would appear, just on its own to a viewer from afar.

Five Routes to Mt Kailash

There are four main approaches, each of which roughly follows one of four great river valleys, located in the four cardinal directions of the mountain. It is only recently that such diverse routes have become available for the foreign traveller. In addition, there is a fifth traditional route reserved for Indian pilgrims. Yet another, the route from Simla and Kinnaur along the Hindustan Highway into Tsamda county, is still closed for political reasons.

The Northern Plateau Route

2,021 km from Lhasa; 1,670 km from Lhartse: **1**. *Lhartse-Raga* (241 km); **2**. *Raga-Tsochen* (242 km); **3**. *Tsochen-Gertse* (260 km); **4**. *Gertse-Gegye* (370 km); **5**. *Gegye-Senge Tsangpo* (112 km); **6**. *Senge Tsangpo-Montser* (237 km); **7**. *Montser-Darchen* (68 km).

Departing from Lhartse on the Lhasa-Dram highway, the northern route traverses the Jangtang Plateau to **Senge Tsangpo**, the district capital of Far-west Tibet (Ngari) in the upper Indus valley, and then cuts S to **Mt Kailash** directly or via Tsamda, where the great sites of **Tsaparang** and **Toling** can be visited. Until the 1990s this was the only legitimate route open to foreign travellers, and of the four main routes it is still the most commonly used since it remains open throughout the year.

The Southern Brahmaputra Route

1,338 km from Lhasa; 847 km from Lhartse: **1**. *Lhartse-Saga* (293 km); **2**. *Saga-Drongpa* (145 km); **3**. *Drongpa-Barka* (387 km); and **4**. *Barka-Darchen* (22 km). *993 km from Kathmandu*: **1**. *Kathmandu-Dram* (122 km); **2**. *Dram-Dzongka* (204 km); **3**. *Dzongka-Saga* (103 km); **4**. *Saga-Drongpa* (145 km); **5**. *Drongpa-Barka* (387 km); and **6**. *Barka-Darchen* (22 km).

Departing from Kathmandu via Dram and Kyirong, or from Lhartse via Ngamring, this route follows the course of the Brahmaputra upstream through Saga and Drongpa counties. The road is generally impassable from late June until early Sept due to snow-melt, or during the monsoon when heavy rainfall swells the several rivers which need to be forded.

This southern road is the most direct route to Mt Kailash, closely following the valley of the upper **Brahmaputra** to and past its source. However until recently it was off-limits because of the Chinese military presence and border patrols. Those setting out from Lhasa will take the route via Lhartse and Ngamring. Alternatively, if you make the journey direct from Kathmandu across the Nepal border, you will meet up with the Lhasa/Lhartse approach at Saga.

The Northwestern Xinjiang Route

1,671 km from Kashgar: **1**. *Kashgar-Yarkand/Yecheng* (249 km); **2**. *Yarkand-Mazar* (249 km); **3**. *Mazar-Tserang Daban* (456 km); **4**. *Tserang Daban-Domar* (172 km); **5**. *Domar-Rutok* (123 km); **6**. *Rutok-Senge Tsangpo* (117 km); **7**. *Senge Tsangpo-Montser* (237 km); and **8**. *Montser-Darchen* (68 km).

Departing from **Hunza** in Pakistan via the Karakorum highway or from **Alma Ata** in Kazakhstan, this route effectively begins at **Kashgar** in the Xinjiang Autonomous Region, N of Tibet. Kashgar can also be reached by air from Beijing.

Leaving Kashgar, the road skirts the northern frontiers of Pakistan, Kashmir and Ladakh in NW India, cutting across the disputed territory known as the **Aksai Chin**, for which reason it has been strictly off limits for foreign travellers. The Aksai Chin is a large region claimed by India, and it can be difficult or impossible to obtain the necessary permits to leave Kashgar because there are also ongoing uprisings by the indigenous Uigur population. Although technically a 'closed' area, this can be circumvented either by guile and courage (just try your luck or hide in the back of a truck going to Senge Tsangpo), or by making prior arrangements with a tour operator who has connections with an authorized travel company either based in Ngari (Far-west Tibet) or in Kashgar. On the other hand if flying from Beijing to Kashgar it is possible to make all arrangements for permits to enter this region with a Beijing-based travel agent. If you enter China from Pakistan over the Kunjerab Pass and along the Karakoram Highway from Hunza to Kashgar it becomes a memorable and economic journey. Remember however to obtain a double entry permit to Pakistan if you wish to exit via the same way.

NB At present, this northwestern route is more commonly undertaken in reverse, to exit from Far-west Tibet into Pakistan or Kazakhstan. Nonetheless, the tourist authorities of Far-west Tibet are trying to have the approach from Kashgar officially opened.

The West Nepal Route

1. *Kathmandu-Nepalganj*; 2. *Nepalganj-Simikot-Tuling*; 3. *Tuling-Kermi*; 4. *Kermi-Yangar*; 5. *Yangar-Torea*; 6. *Torea-Sibsib*; 7. *Sibsib-Purang*; 8. *Purang-Darchen*.

Over the last 2 years it has been possible to travel on this route under the auspices of certain trekking and travel agencies in Kathmandu, but is somewhat expensive. It begins with a flight from Kathmandu via Nepalganj to **Simikot**, a small village nestling on the spur of a mountain. An intense 5 or 6 day trek following the **Karnali river** valley takes one over the **Nak La** pass (4,877m) before crossing the Tibet border and going on to **Purang**. This ancient town at the base of Mt Nemo Nanyi (Gurlamandhata) has been the focus for Nepalese traders and pilgrims from India for thousands of years. One can then travel by bus, truck, or pre-arranged land-cruiser for a half-day to Darchen at the base of Mt Kailash.

The Indian Pilgrim Route

866 km from Delhi: 1. *Delhi-Almora* (395 km); 2. *Almora-Bhirinaga* (68 km); 3. *Bhirinaga-Dardu La pass* (78 km); 4. *Dardu La*

pass-*Garyang* (157 km); 5. *Garyang-Jang La pass* (38 km); 6. *Jang La pass-Purang* (18 km); 7. *Purang-Darchen* (112 km).

This was first reopened in 1980, a remarkable act resulting from the first international agreement between India and China since the Chinese invasion of Northern India and the ensuing 1962 war. Thus it was the Hindu pilgrims who were the first to make their way to Mt Kailash since the Cultural Revolution. Until 1980 even local Tibetans had been forbidden to circumambulate or visit the sacred mountain.

Today the Indian pilgrimage is organized as a lottery by the Delhi government. Each year 5,000-10,000 Hindus apply from all parts of India. Approximately 700 are chosen and after medical examinations and fitness tests this number is reduced to 300 to 400 pilgrims, the current annual quota. (Earlier, in the 1980s, only 200 could make the journey each year.) Departing from Delhi via Almora and Bhirnag, they travel in groups of 30-40, for 10 days commencing in June/July. After 5 days trekking they cross the **Jang La** (Lipulekh) pass where they are exchanged with the outgoing group and met by Chinese tour guides, before being driven to **Purang** and the *Indian Pilgrim's Guest House*. Following a rest day, they journey to Mt Kailash where half commence the circuit of the mountain while the other half go to Lake Manasarovar. After 3 days they switch around before beginning their journey home 3 days later.

The pilgrims must bring all their supplies with them from India. Most are ill-prepared in terms of equipment and clothing however. Many arrive clad in light cotton clothes and flimsy canvas sneakers, usually topped by a woollen balaclava or plastic rainhat. Despite this, their strong and genuine devotion carries them through the experience. For Hindus, Mt Kailash is the abode of Shiva, the God of Destruction, and it has been one of the most sacred pilgrimage destinations for over 5,000 years.

The Circumambulation of Mt Kailash

Preparation

Darchen is the starting and completion point for the general circuit of the sacred mountain. It is wise to spend at least a day here in preparation.

NB It is possible to leave extra baggage at the *Darchen Guesthouse*.

Weather

Observe the weather conditions and ask those who have made the trek in the past few days the conditions you are likely to encounter. The weather will determine to a large extent the amount of baggage you need. Do not be concerned with a change of clothes for each day. Extra pairs of socks and underwear are the most that are needed. Do not forget a good raincoat, and parka all-weather jacket even if the sky is clear blue. A strong pair of walking shoes are essential.

Acclimatization

By the time you arrive in Darchen (4,880m) you should be reasonably acclimatized to the altitude (it is said that over 3,660m it takes from 10 days to 3 weeks for the blood count to adjust to less oxygen). Remember the Dolma La pass is not far under 5,790m: plan to carry as little extra weight as possible.

Porter

Arrange for a Tibetan porter or yak to carry your baggage in Darchen. The price ranges from around ¥45 for a yak, the same for a yak-herder or porter and ¥50 for a horse/day. This can be done by approaching likely looking people or by making arrangements through the guesthouse manager. If you have arranged your travel through an agency all will be handled by your tour guide.

Provisions

Water It is said that one should drink around 4 litres of liquid a day to replace the fluid lost through perspiration at high altitude. So it is important to stock up whenever you come across a spring or fresh stream. Dehydration leading to digestion problems is always possible at high altitude. Arrange to carry a good-sized water bottle with you and drink from it throughout the day. Orange or fruit flavour powders such as 'Tang' are good to mix in the water.

Food You need to plan the food to take. Each day the body burns a lot of energy so you need to start with a substantial breakfast of carbohydrates and glucose. Muesli, granola, and porridge oats are all beneficial. Do not hold back on sugar or glucose either. A large mug or two of tea, coffee or cocoa is vital. Carry at least six muesli-type bars (two a day) and when you feel your energy flagging, stop and enjoy. Glucose tabs are also helpful. In the evening you need to make up a thick soup or dehydrated stew and hot tea or chocolate.

Apparatus

This means your luggage should include a stove, fuel and cooking utensils as well as cleaning soap and scourer. Also candles, matches, torches, batteries, ground sheet, sleeping bag and tent if you want to sleep outside the pilgrim shelters.

Gyangdrak Gonpa

Gyangdrak Gonpa is an easy trek from Darchen and can be done whilst waiting for porters etc. It is a Drigung Kagyu monastery in the central approach valley of Mt Kailash and has been rebuilt in the 1980s. This is said to be the actual place where the founding master of the Bon tradition, Shenrab Miwoche, stayed when he came to Tibet several thousand years ago and imparted the prime Bon ritual practices. It is said that he was only able to teach basic rituals relating to the pacification of the spirits who control mountains and environment. The more advanced Bon teachings of Dzogchen arose much later. The ruins of the Drigung Kagyu monastery of **Selung** lie beyond Gyangdrak. Both these sites are located within the inner circuit (*nangkor*) of Mt Kailash and towards its S face. The inner circuit is usually undertaken only by those who have already made 12 circuits on the standard outer route!

Day One: Darchen to Drirapuk (22.5 km)

Leave as soon as possible after breakfast. The trail follows along the western spur of the foothills before reaching a cairn of prayer stones where it turns N into the great western valley. After about 1 km it reaches **Chorten Kang-nyi** ('Two Legged Stupa'). This was blown up in the 1960s and rebuilt in 1987, being the first Buddhist structure on the circuit to be replaced. A few hundred metres E of this is the **Darpoche** ('Great Prayer Flagpole') which is taken down and redecorated on the full moon day of the Buddha's Enlightenment Festival (around April/May each year). Hundreds of Tibetan pilgrims come for this event. It marks the beginning of the pilgrimage season since the Dolma La pass is blocked by snow until April.

Above the shallow depression of **Darpoche** is a large flat ledge of red rock. On the surface many prayers and mantras are carved. It was here that the Buddha came with 500 disciples from India. They were said to have flown there over the Himalayas by means of their supernatural powers. The view from this place looks down upon a wide flat expanse of the valley floor. Steep cliffs rise high on either side. The **Lhachu** ('Divine River') flows down from the valley ahead and pours out onto the gentle slope of the **Barka Plain**, flowing into the waters of the **Rakshas Tal** ('Demonic Lake') in the far distance. On the valley floor are ruins of 13 stupas, dynamited in the 1960s.

A footbridge now crosses the river and above it, nestling in the cliff face is the rebuilt **Chogu Gonpa**. Below this

but not discernible is the **Langchen Bepuk** ('Hidden Elephant Cave') where Padmasambhava stayed and meditated when he came to Mt Kailash.

One can climb down from the **Buddha's Platform** directly to the trail below, or return to the **Two Legged Stupa** and rejoin the circuit. If time permits a walk over the bridge to the **Chogu Gonpa** is worth including in the trek. The view of the S face of the mountain, if clear, is striking. Do not be surprised if the attendant monk here is not very cooperative. Photos are strictly forbidden of the shrines. In 1991 a gang of art thieves from Nepal and working for western art dealers broke into the shrine and stole 16 ancient statues. Two of the gang were caught and told how they were stealing to order, using photos taken by 'tourists' the previous year. This helps one to understand the cool reception one often receives in such places.

The trail now continues up the valley. The path is not steep but climbs steadily. The red escarpments of the eastern wall tower above the valley obscuring the peak from view. After some time you pass the **Three Pinnacles of Longevity** above the opposite cliff face. They represent the Three Deities of Longevity: Amitayus, White Tara and Vijaya. Above the trail the right-hand cliffs become smooth and form what seems to be a giant seat. Rising higher behind this is the rock formation regarded by Hindus as the monkey god Hanuman in prayer to the mountain. Buddhists call it the "**Torma-offering of Padmasambhava**".

After some hours more one comes upon a grassy flat populated by marmots. Rivulets of pure sweet water cross the trail. There is a rock in the middle of this spot which is associated with **Mahakala**, one of the main Buddhist protectors. From here the valley begins to turn E and, as though gazing down from the heavens, directly above is the western face of Mt Kailash, a triangular facet of rock dripping with great drops of overhanging snow. This is a face of the mountain rarely seen in photos, yet it has a power and beauty of its own.

From this turn in the valley it is another 2 hrs at least before reaching **Drirapuk**. At this point the going is not so easy and, if it is late afternoon or near sunset, each step seems a race against time. If your yaks and porters have not gone ahead (unlikely by now) you may prefer to camp along this northeastern part of the valley. It is best to proceed on and up.

NB Once Drirapuk is in sight it is important to keep to the trail. Do not be hasty. It actually passes your destination on the far side of the river. Unless you are prepared to remove shoes and socks and chance a wade through the river (which can be risky when the water is high) it is better to keep walking past Drirapuk and you will find a bridge which crosses the river over two spans. Many pilgrims drowned here before it was built in 1986. Now follow the trail down the opposite bank and traverse a second bridge of one span which crosses a tributary from the valley N. A short distance away is the *Indian Pilgrims' Rest House* at Drirapuk.

Drirapuk Temple
This is further up the hill behind the rest house. It encloses a retreat cave associated with the great yogin Gotsangpa. Drirapuk ('Cave of the Female Yak Horn') is so named because its walls bear indentations of a *dri's* horn. Gotsangpa, who stayed here from 1213 to 1217 was a disciple of one of Milarepa's disciples and is known as the author of the first history and guide book of Mt Kailash.

The north face
The location here presents one with a spectacular view of the great N face of the mountain. Unlike the S face which has a smooth slope, usually covered in snow apart from the unique vertical striations down its centre, the N face is a near-vertical sheer cliff some 1,520m high consisting of jet black rock. In only

a few places does the snow cling to it, creating extraordinary oval panels like massive eyes sited within long mask-like bands of horizontal strata, all framed by the near-circular dome of the peak which itself is flanked by two symmetrical mountains. It is as though the gods rent the mountain with a cosmic sword and then swept the rubble of the one shattered half into two tidy piles.

The 'pile' to the right is the mountain associated with the bodhisattva **Vajrapani**, the one to the left, the peak associated with **Avalokiteshvara** and beyond that a third is known as the mountain of **Manjughosa**. These three patron bodhisattvas of Tibet respectively embody enlightened power, compassion and discriminative awareness.

The view of the N face is equally spectacular at midnight (under the moonlight) as at midday.

Day Two: Drirapuk to Zutrulpuk (22.9 km)

This day is the climax of the pilgrimage. The **Dolma La pass** lies 6.4 km ahead but 762m above Drirapuk. Physically it is the most arduous day.

Breakfast early and set off as the sun's rays break over the ridges above. After the footbridge the trail rises up a rocky slope. Take this gently but steadily. It soon reaches a level walk. The peak of Mt Kailash rises to the right and can now be seen linked to a long spur which joins the eastern ridge. This is the top edge of the glacial valley from which the **Lhachu** ('Divine River') flows.

Silwutsel charnel ground
The trail continues to meander along levels and then up short staircases. At one point it passes by a broad pile of discarded clothes, utensils and personal items including hair and teeth. This is the **Silwutsel charnel ground**, the place of death. Named after a famous cremation ground near Bodh Gaya in India. Tibetan pilgrims discard something of

their possessions here. It represents the renouncing of attachment to worldly objects and to this life. Without such an understanding death remains a moment to fear.

Just above Silwutsel is a knoll over which all loose rocks have been piled up into small cairns. This is a place linked to Vajrayogini, a *dakini* who inhabits fearsome places such as charnel grounds. She is the consort of the wrathful meditational deity Cakrasamvara (Khorlo Demchok), who is said to preside over Mt Kailash.

Dolma La

All along the path now are special places connected to the history and mythology of the mountain. The air becomes more rarefied and it is essential to take short rests, breathing deeply, before continuing on. Shortly after passing a small azure pool below the trail it turns right and begins the ascent to the **Dolma La** ('Pass of Tara'). Now one's steps only cover a few metres before one must stop, gulping in air, before covering the next short distance. At last one reaches the 5,723m pass and is able to sit down and take in the meaning of that moment. At the pass is a large boulder depicting Tara, festooned with prayer flags. Here too Tibetans leave a momento of themselves such as a tooth, a lock of hair or even a personal snapshot.

Dolma La to Zutrulpuk

After perhaps 30 mins and a warm drink we descend a steep, rock-strewn path to the valley below. Just below the pass is **Lake Tu-je Chenpo Dzingbu** (Skt. Gauri Kund; Eng. 'Pool of Great Compassion'). Take great care now because it is easy to sprain your ankle or worse. You must negotiate steep staircases down to a snowfield. The only way down is to jump from boulder to boulder across a large rockfall. On the ridge above is a formation known as the **Lekyi Ta-re** ('Axe of Karma'), as though one's previous actions, if ignored, may, at any

moment ripen in an accident, suffering or death.

A final steep descending staircase brings you to the valley floor. From here it is still about 5 hrs to the day's destination with no shelter in between. It is *vitally* important to remain on the right hand side of the river, the W bank. If not, you will get trapped, unable to cross it. The walk now becomes very pleasant and relaxing (as long as the weather is clear and there is no howling gale). The path follows the gentle slope of the valley over grassy fields and clear brooks for several kilometres before it narrows and turns further S to merge with another valley before reaching **Zutrulpuk**, the 'Miracle Cave' of Milarepa.

Day Three: Zutrulpuk to Darchen (11.3 km)

Stay in the rest house and the next morning can be spent exploring the caves and visiting the temple and shrine that has been built around Milarepa's cave. A married elderly couple supervise the temple which is usually an active residence for over half a dozen Tibetan devotees, helpers, or relatives who continuously busy themselves with the tasks of maintaining the buildings. Perhaps for this reason they often seem quite impatient with visitors.

Milarepa's cave

The main temple encloses Milarepa's cave which is capped by a large slab of rock, said to be impressed on its underside with the shape of Milarepa's shoulders and upper back. This was formed when he forced the huge rock higher to make the cave more roomy. Unfortunately it now was too high and draughty. So the top of the slab (which is encased inside a mud wall) is said to hold imprints of his feet and hands where he pressed down on the rock to make it lower and just right!

You may sit within the cave. A torch is useful. It is appropriate to make an offering either by placing money on the altar or giving it to a temple attendant. They may then offer you blessed relics which look like large white pills. These are made from deposits gathered during the cleaning of the rock roof of the shrine. Do not assume that they are freely given. The residents rely upon donations and gifts from pilgrims for their sustenance. Even then the 'price' of such relics is equal to perhaps 5 pence or 15 cents or less.

Outside the temple a few metres to the S is a huge hexagonal boulder. It

MILAREPA AND MOUNT KAILASH

For Buddhists Milarepa's influence in the history of Mt Kailash is most important. Although the Buddha himself was said to have flown there with 500 saints by means of their miraculous powers the mountain had been the most sacred place for followers of the Bon religion for hundreds of years. It was to Mt Kailash that the founder of Bon, Shenrab Miwoche, first came and taught in Tibet perhaps several thousand years before Christ (his dates are imprecise). Even after Buddhism became established in Tibet by Padmasambhava and other Indian masters, Mt Kailash continued to be venerated especially by the Bonpos. This changed when Milarepa became a mendicant master and began teaching a small band of disciples. He travelled to Mt Kailash on the basis of a prophecy of the Buddha which states that "this mountain at the navel of the world ... like a crystal stupa is the abode of Cakrasamvara, a great place of accomplished yogins ... nowhere is more marvellous or wonderful ...".

When he arrived there Milarepa met a powerful Bonpo master called **Naro Bonchung** who presided over Mt Kailash and Lake Manasarovar. Each disputed the other's authority and they agreed to resolve this in a competition of their magical powers. First they tested each other at Lake Manasarovar. Naro Bonchung stood astride in one step. Milarepa spread his body over the whole surface and then balanced its waters on his finger. Not satisfied they went to the mountain and circumambulated it in their opposite directions. They met at Dolma La pass and thus began a series of feats of strength, power and magic which still left the contest unresolved.

Naro Bonchung then suggested the first to the summit after dawn on the full moon day would be the victor. Before sunrise Naro Bonchung appeared in the sky flying on his drum to the top. Despite the concern of his disciples Milarepa did not appear to be worried. Naro's ascent had ceased and he was just flying around on his drum at the same level. Then, as the rays of the sun first struck the top Milarepa joined with them and was instantly transported to the summit. Naro the shaman was shocked and fell from his drum. It dropped from the sky and tumbled down the S face of Kailash gouging out a vertical line of pits and crevices. The Bonpo conceded defeat and was given jurisdiction over a neighbouring mountain to the E.

From that contest by Milarepa until today the mountain has been influenced primarily by Buddhist adherents of Cakrasamvara, the wrathful meditational deity, who is the Buddhist tantric aspect of Great Compassion. At the same time Mt Kailash remains a major pilgrimage for Tibetan Bonpos whose custom is to circle it anticlockwise and who revere the Dalai Lama as strongly as other Tibetans. For Hindu pilgrims from India, Mt Kailash is the abode of Shiva, the Lord of Destruction and one of the triumvirate which includes Brahma and Vishnu. Jains too have traditionally made pilgrimage to Mt Kailash.

LAKES MANASAROVAR AND RAKSHAS TAL

Below the sacred Mt Kailash, there is the contrast and balance inherent in the two majestic lakes. Here the symbiosis is complete. One, **Lake Manasarovar** ("Lake Conceived from the Mind of God") is a disc of turquoise brilliance, passive, at peace, whole in its very nature and presence. Shimmering blue at 4,572m, it is one of the highest bodies of pure water on the surface of the earth. Its waters are not just fresh, they are pure beyond conventional scientific confirmation, remaining pure for at least six years. Upon its surface the great dome of Mt Kailash is reflected for much of the year. In the winter it then freezes over as great ice sheets explode like voices from the underworld. It is alive, sustaining a teeming richness of trout, carp and huge freshwater dolphins. Migrating birds from Europe, Central Asia and Siberia rest here on their journeys south to the Indian subcontinent.

A short distance down the riverbed of the **Langchen Khabab**, which is the source of the Sutlej River, leads one to the dark and stormy shores of **Lake Rakshas Tal**, some 15m lower and totally disconnected from Lake Manasarovar. Shaped like the crescent moon it embodies the forces of the night, the dark and unknown side of the psyche, yet is essential for the wholeness of life. Without the cool mystery of the night and the presence of the lunar phases sunrise could not sustain the fullness of life. Life would be consumed by the solitary brilliance of the sun.

stands upright as though placed there by hand. It once stood alone but has been half encircled by a stone wall built in the late 1980s. This wall now is beginning to collapse. It is said that Naro Bonchung hurled this boulder at Milarepa in the midst of their contest of magical powers. Milarepa caught it and placed it down gently, just above his meditation cave.

Surrounding the boulder and the temple complex are dozens of stacks of Mani Stones, rocks carved with prayers and quotations from the scriptures. Hardly a stone remains untouched. Hundreds of thousands of prayers cover the valley's slope. They continue in heaps up until reaching a vertical cliff face. Along its base is a strata into which retreat caves have been created. One imagines Milarepa's disciples meditating here, following his example by living off soup made from the abundant nettles that grow all about. Many of the caves contain meditation platforms, self-contained by dry stone walls which divide them from their cooking partitions and entrance areas. It is well worth the short climb up to these caves before beginning the final stage of the trek.

The return to Darchen

The walk back to Darchen is easy and the exit from the valley can be reached within a few hours. Just as the valley allows the river to flow out into the Barka plain, the walls become steep and the trail passes through multicoloured stratas of rock changing from red to yellow, from black to purple. This section is known as the **Trangser Trangmar** ('Gold and Red Cliffs'). The trail now turns right as it skirts the base of the foothills before finally returning to Darchen.

NB There are many more sites of lesser significance on the 3-day circuit of Mt Kailash, but those just described are all that an average pilgrim would be able to absorb in the short time available.

Circumambulation of Lake Manasarovar

After completing the circuit of Mt Kailash, the next day you can embark on the circuit of **Lake Manasarovar**. The Tibetan names for the lake are **Mapham Yutso** and **Tso Madropa**, the later being a translation of a secondary Sanskrit

BLESSED OBJECTS FROM THE LAKE

Apart from the numerous *abra* rodent colonies between Hor and Seralung, lapping the NE shoreline are strange **egg-shaped bundles of lake grass**. They occur nowhere else, which is enough to confer on them sacred status. Devotees take one or two for their blessings. Also along this stretch it is possible to find small **stones of black jet**. These are treasured for their association with the Karmapas. The shoreline sand changes continuously. Along a short stretch just S of Seralung it is made of five coloured grains: black, white, red, yellow and greenish-blue. If you find such sands, they are of special value. Moreover one often finds the dried-out bodies of fish, which are highly treasured for their medicinal properties and are said to ease the pains of childbirth if just a small piece is eaten.

name, **Anavatapta**. From Darchen drive 22 km to Barka township, at the crossroads.

Barka is a small administrative base for the people living in the environs of Mt Kailash and the lakes. It is newly made, replacing the original **Barka** hamlet, which is some 8 km to the W. Here, the roads from Senge Tsangpo, Drongpa and Purang all converge.

Day One

To reach the starting point for the circuit of Lake Manasarovar, take the Drongpa (E) road, and continue on to **Hor** township 28 km distant. Hor is a haphazard collection of mud-walled houses and assorted compounds, located slightly inland from the NE corner of the lake. It may be possible to find the only store in town open if you wish to buy any extra provisions. Otherwise drive on to **Seralung Gon**, the so-called eastern gateway to the lake. The rebuilt compound here replaces a monastery that originally was sited a few hundred metres up the valley behind. The family of a local lama and shaman live here and if possible they may have a room which you can use for the night. Don't forget to offer them a payment for the room before you leave. Otherwise it is better to camp out.

Day Two

The trek now covers some 22.5 km to reach **Trugo Gon**, a monastery at the southern gateway to the lake. Although

level, the sandy trail becomes arduous by the day's end. For the first few kilometres you should keep to the shoreline but then the trail cuts across a sandy headland, heading towards the bridge which crosses the **Trak Tsangpo** River. Wildlife abounds and herds of wild ass (*kyang*) graze on the valley floor. Soon Trugo Gon comes into view. The distance is deceptive for now, no matter how much ground one seems to cover, it never appears to be any closer. It is best not to look ahead and instead to enjoy the grassy fields abounding with flowers and mosses. Eventually, the track passes the ruins of **Nyego Monastery** at the lake's edge. It once was associated with Atisha, the Indian master who revived Buddhism in 11th century Tibet. Trugo Gon is now a simple walk away.

Day Three

Trugo Gon is the most active monastery around Lake Manasarovar. It is supervised by a young reincarnate Gelukpa monk from NE Tibet named Lama Lobzang. He is training a small number of young monks and has rebuilt the main compound as well as arranged the construction of a pilgrims' guest house nearby. He has also built a stupa outside the entrance. One can stay in the guest house if beds are available for around ¥25/night. Be careful with your possessions however since thefts have been reported. As in many similar places the Tibetans put in charge can be far from cooperative and have little idea of good public relations.

Trugo Gon is also a location where Nepalese Brahmins come to make ritual ablutions in the lake waters. They trek up from the Nepalese Terai on the Indian border and follow ancient trails right through the Himalayas. Most are very poor and only visit the lake. The main date for them is the full moon in Aug during the monsoon when the rain and wind is numbingly cold. These thin, frail men recite mantras and prayers building up the strength to walk naked into the lake and immerse themselves completely before rushing out to huddle around a small fire.

From Trugo Gon one follows the shoreline for most of the day. Before the SW corner however be prepared to encounter swarms of mosquitoes or midges. It may be necessary to cover your mouth, nose and ears with a cloth or scarf for this section. Having turned N, the western shoreline becomes a low cliff face. After a few kilometres there is evidence of caves with blackened ceilings that once were inhabited. Above them is a rebuilt monastery called **Gotsuk Gon**. An elderly lama and a few monks reside here. It is well worth the climb since there is a superb view of the lake from its roof.

Continue following the shoreline and the trail will turn left, pointing almost directly to the peak of Mt Kailash in the distance. Again the shore swings N towards the final *Indian Pilgrims' Guest House*. It is said that some of Mahatma Gandhi's ashes were brought here and cast into the lake's waters. You can stop here since the road is nearby, or continue on to Chiu Monastery, the appropriate destination for the day.

Chiu Gonpa

Chiu Gonpa ('Sparrow Monastery') at the lake's western gateway sits atop a conical outcrop of red rock. Inside is a small shrine and cave where Padmasambhava

was said to have meditated with his consort Yeshe Tsogyel before leaving this world. Various objects are to be found inside the cave, such as the granite rocks with clear imprints of Padmasambhava's hands and feet.

Here too is the **source of the Sutlej River**, known as the Ganga or Langchen Khabab, which at times links Lake Manasarovar with neighbouring Lake Raksas Tal (*Tib* Lakngar Tso). When the fortunes of Tibet are low, it is almost dry, as is the present situation. The only water that remains is the brackish cusp of hot springs behind Chiu Gonpa. The Tibetans however have created several open-air stone baths where one can wash body and clothes in the clean hot water.

Here one should meet up with one's transport and either begin the return journey (whichever way that may be) or go on to Tirthapuri, traditionally the third and final destination of the pilgrimage.

Tirthapuri: the Cave of Padmasambhava

Concluding the pilgrimage is a visit to **Tirthapuri**. Here hot springs and a geyser add to the power of the place. Inside a temple enclosure is a small cave where Padmasambhava meditated with his Tibetan consort Yeshe Tsogyel. It contains two granite stones in which indentations of their footprints are clearly present. Photography inside is forbidden.

The surrounding landscape consists mainly of red and white earth. Around the cave are dozens of unusual rock formations, almost all of which have become imbued with religious significance. Events from the lives of the buddhas and bodhisattvas are associated and recounted with each place, in accordance with the Tibetan concept of 'sacred outlook'.

The hot springs at Tirthapuri are clean to bathe in. In the past there was a geyser that erupted every few minutes

THE GRANDEST LIGHTSHOW ON EARTH

The area around the source of the **Brahmaputra** is undeniably beautiful. Parallel to the road, the Tibetan plateau rolls S to the white jagged wall of the Himalayas. At dusk, as whisps of smoke drift above the black silhouettes of the nomads' tents, the herds of yak lumber back home to camp, spurned on by hoots and whistles from the yak-herders and their sons. The folds in the hills turn a deep indigo while the snow teeth of the Himalayas, now cobalt blue in the eastward shadowlands, gleam with gold caps across the horizon as the sun sets, giving its last caress of the day to these crown jewels of Asia.

It sets, slipping away in the W and, if one turns toward the E a miraculous sign seems to hint at the sun's rise the next day – high in the sky above, vast rays of pink and red light streak across the deep blue stratosphere to converge on a now-vacant point in the distant E. It is the grandest lightshow on the planet; the shadows of peaks hundreds of miles away in the W are cast through the heavens, parallel to infinity but appearing to converge as the viewer perceives their perspective played out on a cosmic plane. This unique, awesome display may be seen just after sunset when few clouds remain, depending upon the conditions, along much of the Upper Brahmaputra, as well as at Lake Manasarovar and perhaps most vividly at Toling in the Upper Sutlej.

spraying water 6m or so into the air. The water table must be lowering because this has not happened since the late 1980s. From one of the blowholes however small white flecks or 'pills' of lime can be found. Tibetans strain the water for these and use them for medicinal purposes, since they are said to have a consecrated power to cure disease.

At Tirthapuri, the quiet waters of the Sutlej pass by grassy paddocks that are ideal for picnics or camping. The tranquility of the place is the attraction for most Tibetan pilgrims who come here to rest and relax after the intensity of their Mt Kailash and Lake Manasarovar circuits. The pilgrim now has the opportunity to confirm and assimilate the experiences of the previous days. The spaciousness and blessings here provide a means for uniting the power and majesty of Kailash with the peace and beauty of Lake Manasarovar. In this way the pilgrimage is completed.

Tachok Khabab Source

From Hor township, drive SE for 92 km to reach the village of Nyoktse on the N shore of **Lake Gung-gyu**, and then continue climbing for 40 km to reach the **Mayum La** pass. The source of the Brahmaputra, known as the **Pakshu** or **Tachok Khabab**, lies on the far side of the pass, in the glaciers of the **Ganglung-ri** range (see above, page 385).

Mabcha Tsangpo Valley

The **Mabcha Khabab**, rising near Shiri Langdor NW of **Mt Nanda Devi** (7,815m), on the Tibetan side of the Indo-Tibetan border, is a major source of the **Karnali** River. It flows SE from its source to **Rigong** township, where it becomes known as the Mabcha Tsangpo (Karnali). The motor road from Barka which cuts through the isthmus between Lake Manasarovar and Lake Raksas Tal enters the valley of the Mabcha Tsangpo at Rigong, and then continues downstream to Purang, the county capital, 104 km from Barka.

Purang

About 112 km S of Mt Kailash, past the twin lakes and Mt Nemo Nanyi, is the ancient township of **Purang** (*Ch* Bulan),

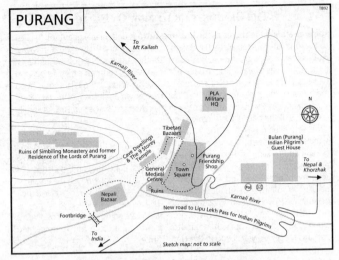

PURANG

To Mt Kailash

Karnali River

PLA Military HQ

N

Tibetan Bazaars

Bulan (Purang) Indian Pilgrim's Guest House

Ruins of Simbiling Monastery and former Residence of the Lords of Purang

Cave Dwellings & The 9 Storey Temple

Purang Friendship Shop

To Nepal & Khorzhak

General Medical Centre

Town Square

Nepali Bazaar

Ruins

Karnali River

Footbridge

New road to Lipu Lekh Pass for Indian Pilgrims

To India

Sketch map: not to scale

which the Nepalis and Indians call **Tak-lakot** (a corruption of the Tibetan **Takla Khar**). It is the administrative base for the Kailash region and traditionally it has been the focus for pilgrims from India coming via **Almora** and the **Jang La** pass (Lipulekh; 5,090m). Purang lies on the Mabcha Tsangpo, the Tibetan tributary of the Karnali, which rises in the peacock-shaped rocks of the **Mab-cha Khabab** ('Peacock Source'), S of lake **Rakshas Tal**. South of Purang, the river, now known as the **Mabcha Tsangpo** ('Peacock River') flows through the villages of **Khorzhak**, **Zher**, **Lemi** and **Omlho**, before cutting through a deep gorge into Nepal.

Purang is a fascinating trading station on the Tibetan border with India and Nepal. It was here that most of the early travellers from India would reach and make their first contact with the Tibetan authorities. It has been a capital of the early kingdoms of Far-west Tibet and has been inhabited for at least 3,000 years. It was where **Sudhana**, a previous incarnation of Buddha, reputedly lived. His exploits are recounted extensively in the *Gandhavyuhasutra*, a section of the voluminous *Avatamsakasutra*, which describes the events in a bodhisattva's life exemplifying the development of great compassion and the awakening of enlightened mind (*bodhicitta*).

● **Accommodation** To rest and recuperate from the difficulties of travel one can stay in the *Pulan Hotel* (double room US$33/night, breakfast US$7; full meal plan US$28); *Pulan Indian Pilgrim Guest House*, simple but comfortable, with individual bungalows and well-prepared Chinese meals.

The Ruins of Simbiling Monastery
Rising above the town of Purang is a high, steeply sloping ridge capped with a large complex of ruins. Before the Chinese invasion this was the residence of the regional administrator as well as the temple and monastic complex for several hundred monks. In those days it was referred to as the 'Dzong' or fortress of **Simbiling**. Such buildings on commanding positions were once common throughout Tibet. The main monastery was of the Gelukpa school but there was also one large part that held a Sakya monastery.

To walk up and explore the ruins gives

one an excellent view taking in the N slopes of the Himalayas from Nepal to India and the **Jang La** pass as well as the whole southern face of **Mt Nemo Nanyi**. It takes less than an hour at leisurely pace from the cave dwellings to reach the top. Across the Karnali River is the Chinese cantonment and the military garrison.

Cave dwellings and Tsegu Gonpa

From the road on the E bank of the Karnali River you can cross a suspension bridge to the W side where, in the cliff above the Tibetan traders' houses, there are ancient cave dwellings. Remarkably many are still inhabited. This was probably the original town of **Purang** and it may date back several thousand years to the time when cave cities were created across Asia. It is likely that it was in such cave cities man first lived in secure settlements instead of following a nomadic lifestyle.

At the western end of the caves is an ancient temple cut into the cliff. It is known as **Tsegu Gonpa** ('Nine-Storey Monastery') and includes many terraced levels going up the cliff. It can be reached by steps, ladders and platforms hanging off the wall. In the lower levels there is a residence of the family who look after the temple. Be polite as you approach and wait to be asked to enter. You will have to walk through the house, which itself is fascinating, and then be lead up to the temples above. Take shoes off before entering. The walls are covered in highly polished murals that are unique in style. They have been darkened from the smoke of lamps over hundreds of years. It is helpful to bring a torch with you.

The temple belongs now to the Drigung Kagyu or Gelukpa school, yet it may even predate the founding of these schools of Buddhism.

NB Photography here is strictly forbidden and the supervisor gets very nervous if you bring cameras out so it is best not to intimidate him.

Trading markets

At Purang one can still see how many of the Tibetan border towns were used as trading posts for the nomadic produce of the **Jangtang**, such as wool and salt which would be bartered for the rice and palm sugar of Nepal and the Indian plains. This centuries-old trade continues here today. Below the cave dwellings a trading camp forms over the summer and autumn months when large encampments of Nepalese appear. Those in front of the caves come for the salt and rice trade. Sheep and goats are loaded up with a double back-pack holding up to 30 kg of produce before they make their way over the trail on a 3-week journey to the Indo-Nepalese Terai.

Tanga Follow the path past the caves to quickly reach the busy trading camp, known as Tanga. This larger camp below the Simbiling ruins consists of streets of temporary one room residences over which the traders must sling a tarpaulin for the roof. The prohibition against permanent roofs is said to date back to a 1904 treaty between Tibet and Britain! Here there is a fascinating glimpse of a bustling bazaar that has been barely touched by time. The Nepalese bring every kind of practical item, from cooking utensils to cotton cloth and manufactured goods from India, to sell or trade for the wool and salt brought by the Northern Plateau nomads. The wool bales, resembling giant doughnuts, are carried by yaks and, once sold are undone into long skeins which are stretched down the alleyways and prepared for transport S.

The Chinese authorities today let this small trade continue (although Indians are now excluded) probably because the traders barely eke out an existence from it.

Khorzhak Temple and Village

About 15 km further down the Karnali river valley, the motorable road comes to an end at the small village of **Korzhak**

GANGES AND KARNALI RIVERS

The **Ganges**, sacred river of India, flows for 2,510 km from its sources to its confluence with the Brahmaputra in Bengal. There are five headwaters, namely: the Bhagirathi, Alaknanda, Mandakini, Dhauliganga, and Pindar, that all rise in **Uttarakand** in India, not in Tibet. Of these the two main sources, Alakanda and Bhagirathi, originate at an elevation of about 3,050m in an icy cavern below **Gangotri Glacier**. **Gaumukh**, 21 km SE of Gangotri is often cited as the Ganges' actual source.

However, in close proximity to these, a major source of the **Karnali**, one of Ganges' main tributaries, does rise in Tibet, to the S of **Lake Rakshas Tal**. It flows through **Purang** to cut SE of **Mt Nemo Nanyi** (Gurlamandhata) and enter NW Nepal. There it converges with other tributaries of the Karnali, and flows into India, where, as the **Gogra**, it eventually converges with the Ganges at **Patna**.

(*Ch* Korqag), or Kojanath as it is known in Nepal. Literally, this name indicates a sacred place where a 'retinue' or 'a venerable object and its surroundings' (*khor*) is 'placed' (*zhak*). The venerable object that was once 'placed' here was one of the four sacred images of standing Avalokiteshvara (Phakpa Chezhi) in the form Padmapani, which were brought from Nepal to Tibet by Akarmatishila during the 7th century after he extracted them intact from a split sandalwood tree-trunk. From the few existing photos of the Khorzhak image it appears to have represented the Pala style of Indian Buddhist art. All that remains today is part of its lotus flower base. The Chinese had it destroyed.

The village is situated on a beautiful bend in the Karnali River and is dominated by the large red wall of the **Khorzhak Temple** which faces the river with an enormous inscription of Avalokiteshvara's 6-syllable mantra: OM MANI PADME HUM.

Ritual masked dances

On certain special days of the month monks from the region come here to perform a day-long series of ritual masked dances. They still use many of the costumes and masks made before 1959. Local maidens who are betrothed come out on such occasions and display their family jewellery and fine clothes. This usually takes place in Sept or after the harvest in early Oct. Enquire at the *IP Guest House* to see whether any festivals are coming up.

Trekking

From Purang, you can trek out of Tibet via **Zhingpa** township and **Jang La** pass (18 km) into India, if you are an Indian pilgrim, or via Piling La, Chema La, or **Nak La** passes into Nepal, providing you have the right permits and visas. If you lack such travel documents, you will be placed under arrest inside Nepal and sent back to Tibet. The alternative is to begin the return journey through Purang and then along one of the other routes described above. If you haven't yet been to Gu-ge and have the time, it is a very worthwhile side-trip on the way back to Senge Tsangpo.

TSAMDA COUNTY

ཙ་མདའ་ར་

札达县 Zanda

Population: 24,402   Area: 28,033 sq km

Tsamda county is the current name for the region which once was known as the **Gu-ge** kingdom. It extends along the banks of the upper **Sutlej** from Khyunglung, SW of Montser, as far as the Indian border, where the river flows into Kinnaur below the Sibkyi La pass. The valley of the **Rashok Tsangpo**, which gives access to Southern Ladakh and Spiti also lies within Tsamda, as does the valley of the **Gyaza Kar-chu**, through which the Uttarakashi district of Uttar Pradesh can be reached. The county capital is located at **Toling**, 278 km from Senge Tsangpo, and 443 km from Purang. The new county name, Tsamda, is a contraction of **Tsa** (parang) and **Da** (wa-dzong), which are two of the most important sites within the upper Sutlej valley.

The Tsamda area is characterized by the striking complex of canyons cutting through the red sandstone composite of what was once an ocean floor, all descending into the upper Sutlej River. For much of the year these canyon tributaries are dry, only becoming impassable or hazardous in the monsoon. Those S of the Sutlej, such as the Manam Tsangpo, Dapa-chu, and Tophu-chu, arise in the Himalayas near the Indian border, which is heavily patrolled. The N is bounded by the Gar Tsangpo valley and southern slopes of the Gangtise Range.

It was in this region of Far-west Tibet that Tibetans appear to have first established permanently inhabited cities. At that time, in the antiquity of the pre-Christian era, the kingdom was known as **Zhangzhung**. From Bon chronicles that have recently come to light, the Far-west area was known (reputedly as

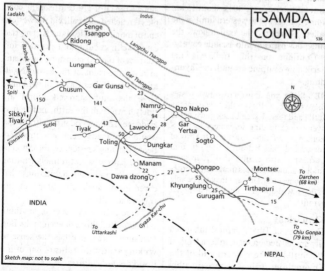

Sketch map: not to scale

far back as 2,800 BC!) as the 'heartland', in contrast to Central Tibet, which was known as the 'outlying' area, and the regions of Kham and Amdo, which were termed the 'gateway' lands. However Tibet was not a unified country at that time – the vast distances and geography being more conducive to the development of independent semi-feudal states.

Khyunglung Ngulkhar: the capital of Zhangzhung

ACCESS From **Montser** township on the main Senge Tsangpo-Darchen road, take the trail which cuts S for 8 km to the **Tirthapuri** hot springs (see above, page 418 and page 404) on the banks of the Sutlej. An alternative trekking route from **Chiu Gonpa** on the shore of Lake Manasarovar follows the Sutlej downstream from its source near Lake Raksas Tal for 79 km via Gyanyima Dzong to reach Tirthapuri.

The road cuts westward from here, at first passing through a broad agricultural valley dotted with single family compounds. Camp at the Bonpo monastery of **Gurugam** (see above, page 404), about 15 km from Montser at the western limit of the valley. Thereafter the trail follows the Sutlej downstream into Tsamda county.

Continue on this trail, via the Gerikyung camping ground, to **Khyunglung**.

NB Since you must cross two passes above the steep cliffs on the N bank of the Sutlej and then descend back down to the river before fording its waters to the S bank, it is preferable to arrange the hire of horses and yaks before setting off from Gurugam. Also ensure that your local guide is allowed to cross this county border (since some local Tibetans may not be able to do so without first obtaining a special permit).

Khyunglung

The ruins of Tibet's earliest inhabited city are located on the northern bank of the Sutlej at the western end of the Khyunglung valley, approximately

25 km SW of Tirthapuri. First noted by Prof Tucci in 1932 as a "troglydite settlement", it is a vast cave city sprawling over lesser valleys and canyons which, at its peak must have held a population of 2,000-3,000 people. In 1988, on the basis of recently discovered chronicles, Prof Namkei Norbu confirmed this as the location where the earliest kings of Zhangzhung such as Limichar had established their dynasty in antiquity.

On reaching the entrance of this valley, you will pass the small village of Khyunglung after approximately 5 km, and from there it is another 2 km to the western end of the valley, where you can camp near an outcrop of white limestone facing the broad complex of caves on the far bank of the river. A suspension bridge below the white limestone traverses the Sutlej at its narrowest point and leads left to the cave city. To the right another pathway leads towards a hot springs and a series of white and blue lime terraces.

The cave city itself extends 1 km along a red cliff. The centre of the complex is reached via a valley at the western end of the city. This leads up past myriad cave dwellings cut into the conical formations of the red sandstone aggregate, to reach the ruins of the actual **Ngulkhar**, or the 'Silver Castle' of the kings. Here the multi-storeyed rooms are finely hewn from the earth, and there is evidence of outer wooden structures that would have made them very imposing. Below the king's residence, the city consists of pathways and tunnels winding past walls and cave habitations that cover every serviceable slope of the ridges and valleys.

There is little evidence of anything related to Buddhism or even to the Bon tradition so that one has the sense of walking amidst the ruins of one of the world's oldest cultures.

Dawadzong

མ་དའབ་རྫོང་

From Khyunglung the trail continues on the S side of the Sutlej at some distance from the river, reaching the large Gelukpa monastery of **Dongpo** after 53 km (3 days). **Dawadzong** lies 27 km further W on the Dawa-chu tributary. Here there is a fabled landscape of natural pyramid formations. The ridge-top Gelukpa monastery known as **Dawa Gon**, comprises an assembly hall, a Maitreya Temple (Jamkhang) and a Labrang. For a vivid description of this area, see Lama Govinda's account in *The Way of the White Clouds*.

Manam Tsangpo Valley

The trail continues from Dawadzong in the direction of the county capital, crossing the **Manam Tsangpo** River after 22 km. Here at **Manam Gonpa**, there is an enormous complex of ruins which even now holds untold precious works of art, buried beneath the rubble. A further trek of 21 km will bring you to Toling, capital of Tsamda county, on the left bank of the Sutlej.

Toling

མཐོ་ལྡིང་

The county capital of Tsamda, known as **Toling** or Toding, may be reached by two motorable routes which turn S off the Senge Tsangpo-Darchen road to cross the watershed leading into the Sutlej valley.

ACCESS One turns off the main highway at **Namru**, 23 km SE of Gar Gunsa (see above, page 403), and the second at **Dzo Nakpo**, a few kilometres further S, where the Bauer Army Camp is also located. The latter road passes through **Dungkar** where spectacular caves have recently been discovered (see below, page 436). Taking the former, you will cross two passes, reaching the crossroads of **Lawoche** after 94 km. Here there are three possible routes: one driving NW via **Chusum** (141 km) to **Sibkyi Tiyak** on the Kinnaur frontier (150 km); a second leading W to **Jangtse** and **Tiyak**

townships (48 km); and a third heading SE for 50 km to **Toling** in the Sutlej valley.

Taking the last of these roads, you will soon see far down below in the valley floor the capital of the ancient kingdom of Gu-ge. From various vantage points on the descent into Toling, there are some of the most spectacular views in Tibet. The vast sweep of the Himalayas is discernible, as the range turns NW from Nepal and along the Indian border as far as Ladakh and Kashmir, spanning several hundred kilometres. One of the marvels of this vista is the awareness that one is apparently looking down on the Himalayas. It gives one the real sense of Tibet as the roof of the world. If you are driving from Senge Tsangpo, you must leave early because it will take a full day to reach Toling.

● **Accommodation** The *Tsamda Hotel* is about 500m down the main (only) street on the left.

The Temples of Toling

History

The temples and religious buildings of **Toling** are the most significant in Farwest Tibet. They were constructed under the guidance of the great Tibetan translator **Rinchen Zangpo** (985-1055), around 1014-25. During his lifetime he is said to have built 108 temples throughout Far-west Tibet and Ladakh, and although few still exist, those at Toling and Tsaparang are considered to be the finest repositories of the **Gu-ge style** of Buddhist art. Even though the city was subsequently replaced as a political centre of power by the citadel of Tsaparang, where the later kings of Gu-ge established their capital, slightly closer to the Indo-Tibetan trade routes, the importance of the Toling temples for the cultural heritage of Ngari remained unsurpassed.

It was primarily due to the influence of Rinchen Zangpo that Toling had become the main religious centre of the

MANDALA CHAPEL OF KING YESHE-O

The most impressive building at Toling is at the western focal point of the entire complex. The walled remains of King Yeshe-o's Mandala Chapel are unlike any seen elsewhere in Tibet. Superficially it resembles many other ruins from the Cultural Revolution and although there is an entrance from the E, the central shrine itself is given access through a gap in the SE inner wall. One enters a square hall with secondary chapels opening off from the middle of each wall. Around the mud-streaked walls of the central and secondary shrines are aureoles in relief, spaced equally about 2m apart above metre-high pedestals which once must have supported life-size images of deities. At first there appears to be no main shrine, that is until one begins to imagine the object to which all these figures face, and one's gaze moves from the vivid blue sky above the walls to the mounds of earth and mud on the ground below. There in the rubble it is just possible to make out the shape of a broad lotus with a pedestal at its heart situated in the centre of the inner shrine.

At this point, one is, in fact, standing in the midst of the central sphere of a life-sized three-dimensional mandala, which in most circumstances would only be represented in two dimensions on a mural or scroll painting. A large statue of the main tantric deity would have been on the lotus pedestal, facing E, embellished with gold, precious jewels, ornaments and robes, probably surrounded by four or eight secondary figures on the petals of the lotus. Initiates and devotees would have been led into this inner sanctum in a state of reverence and wonder, awed by the beauty, balance and harmony of this extraordinary display which would have been illuminated by soft light cascading from the windows in the bell-tower directly above the central deity. The figures on the surrounding walls would have been gilded and painted and the walls themselves no doubt embellished with

Gu-ge kingdom prior to the visit of the great Indian master **Atisha** (982-1054) in 1042. The great translator was himself the monastic preceptor of Toling at the time of Atisha's arrival. Yet, without the support of the King of Gu-ge, **Yeshe-o**, the impact of these two great masters on Tibetan Buddhism would have been far less significant. The king, a devout patron of Rinchen Zangpo's activities, sacrificed everything over several years, culminating in his own life, to invite the illustrious and peerless 11th century pandita Atisha to Tibet. After refusing several requests made by those Tibetan translators and scholars studying at Vikramashila and Odantapuri monasteries in N India, Atisha finally agreed to travel when he heard of the death of the king. Yeshe-o had been captured by invading troops from a neighbouring tribe who demanded ransom. When his nephew

Jangchub-o came to see him the king responded by saying, "I am an old man. My life now is short. Use the ransom to invite and assist Atisha to come to Tibet." Consequently, when Atisha arrived in Gu-ge he was amazed to see Buddhism flourishing.

He also must have been impressed with the architectural style of the Toling temples which were based upon the Kashmiri style and the Pala/Sena style of Bengal, his homeland in NE India. An effort had also been made to incorporate Indian elements found in Samye, Tibet's first monastery. The interiors were solidly embellished with paintings in the contemporary Indian and Nepalese styles, following formal conventions that within a few centuries were to be obliterated by the Muslim invasions of India. This artistic tradition that has come to be known as the Gu-ge style

buddhas, bodhisattvas and tantric deities along similar lines to those in the Dukhang (Red Temple) or the White Temple at Tsaparang (see below and page 431). The mandala itself was most likely that of Vajradhatu or Vairocana, the main tantra practised by Rinchen Zangpo and one which encompasses and synthesizes many of the other *Yogatantras*.

The central hall is encircled by a series of shrines and chapels (similar to those in the Jokhang in Lhasa), facing inwards and today mainly filled with dirt and rubble through which here and there protrude torsos and remnants of what once were objects of profound faith and devotion. In the centre of the W wall of this hall is a tall shrine that once held a 5m standing figure of Avalokiteshvara. There then follow a series of rooms which now contain the relief remains of two-dimensional mandalas.

Towering above each of the four corners of the temple are the only stupas of the Indian *prasada* style in existence. They are also uncommon in being made up of terracotta units since most Tibetan stupas are made from mud and stone. Within each are chambers that contain pages from Buddhist manuscripts and hundreds of thousands of small, palm pressed votive images known as **Tsa-tsa**. Despite being only around 10 cm in size, the attention to detail is remarkable, including not only a perfect figure of the deity but a depiction of the appropriate mantra or tiny stupas in the background. Such objects are added to the 'core' of any large stupa in order to enhance its sanctity and power.

These Tsa-tsa can also be found spilling out from the broken shell of many of the stupas that stand in rows of 108 outside the Toling complex on land adjacent to the cliffs above the Sutlej river. Sadly in the last few years even these have begun to be destroyed, or given an enhanced help in their collapse by local people wishing to gain more land.

provides a unique link to the Buddhist art of N India that today can only be found in a few other temples exemplary of Rinchen Zangpo's work in Ladakh (at **Alchi**) and Spiti (at **Tabo**) during the early 11th century.

The site

The Toling complex originally comprised six major buildings. The entrance was from the E where today is a run-down concrete town hall. Clockwise from here within the compound were the **Neten Temple**; the **Tongyu Lhakhang**; the **Assembly Hall (Dukhang)**, still intact and commonly known as the Red Temple due to the colour of its outside walls; the **Mandala Chapel of Yeshe-o**, which is sometimes called the Golden Temple (today only its walls remain), at the W end of the compound; the **Lhakhang Karpo** (White Temple), which is still intact although

vacant; and the **Serkhang**, the actual Golden Temple (now destroyed).

The Dukhang (Assembly Hall or Red Temple)

ACCESS It is absolutely essential to bring with you a strong flashlight in order to see the paintings clearly.

This is the largest temple at Toling and would have been used by the monastic assembly for gatherings, discourses and collective ritual practices. Distinguished by its red-washed outer walls, inside it contains the largest and earliest display of Indian and Gu-ge painting at Toling (c 13th-14th century, though some scholars cite 15th-16th century). The highly organic form of the decorative embellishments such as the flora which entwine each of the figures shows the overriding influence to be Indian/Kashmiri with a hint of Nepalese style. The artists must still have held the principles transmitted to them from the Kashmiri masters brought into Tibet by Rinchen Zangpo a century or two earlier.

Along the left-hand wall are floor-to-ceiling rows of deities entwined in wreath-like borders interweaving each into a whole organic complex across the entire space. Nearly all the deities are peaceful in form and many are in blissful union with their consorts (symbolizing the integration of skilful means and emptiness). These paintings were heavily coated with mud and dust on account of the temple's neglect, but they have now been partially cleaned.

The rear wall (W) held the main shrines and altars beneath a large statue of the Buddha (added long after the original construction). Within the inner pilgrim's walkway (*korlam*), which passes along the left, back and right sides of the altar, there is a series of paintings depicting the life of the Buddha. Nearly all are miniatures which include amusing details of rural and domestic life that reflect the individuality of the painter. The colours are still vivid and the expressions specific to each figure depicted in the paintings. Also included are stories from the early kings of Gu-ge and the development of Buddhism in Tibet.

The right (N) wall of the temple was once similar to its opposite wall but has been seriously ruined. A basic shrine now provides the focus for the temple with a few images and framed photos on it. In the early 1980s this was full of extremely precious images that had been donated during the period of 're-laxation'. It also then held over a dozen other statues and sacred images that had been released from storage by the authorities for reconsecration and worship. In the early 1990s it is alleged that a gang of art thieves based in Kathmandu stole everything, having sent photos around the world to determine the highest bidder. For this reason, the Tibetan people may object strongly to the photography of such objects today.

Lhakhang Karpo (The White Temple)

Nearly opposite the red walled Assembly Hall there is an unimpressive, squat portico leading into what appears to be a shabby windowless block. Normally closed it is necessary to rouse the caretaker in the Red Temple or at his farmhouse 100m S. This portico although painted is wooden, framed by two stout, short pillars and probably 500 years old. It opens into a long rectangular temple with a pebble stone floor and lines of thin pillars supporting a multipanelled, multidecorated ceiling culminating in a large, one-eyed Buddha statue (the other eye having been broken).

Along the left and right walls are respectively a series of the main male and female bodhisattva deities. Over 3m high, each is seated within a framework which reflects specific attributes and qualities, whether these are presented within a formal aureole, a palace, or a representation of mountains and forests in a natural landscape. Arrayed along the left (W) wall is a pantheon of the male deities, and along the opposite wall are the female deities. Unfortunately most murals of the male deities have been seriously affected by water seepage which has caused streaking, pigment destruction and complete erosion of the figures. Those that remain however, such as Avalokiteshvara, Vajradhara, Vajrasattva, Vajrapani and Manjughosa are sublime examples of the Gu-ge art form.

Of greater value still is the intact wall depicting the female deities: they begin near the door with a depiction of the life of the Buddha above a graphic presentation of life in the world and, with the surface peeled back, in the underworld, bringing to mind images from Heironymous Bosch. The line of female deities includes Vijaya, ensurer of long life, wrathful White Tara an opponent to life's inner dangers; Bhuvatrayacalanatara, 'earth mother' and protector from dangers in forest, jungles and wild lands, Sarasvati the muse of music and poetry, Red Tara the protector over earthquakes and natural disasters, Mahaprajnaparamita the 'Great Mother' of discriminative awareness, bestower of intelligence and knowledge, and Green Tara the compassionate bestower of protection out of good actions.

Created in the 16th century they depict the major pantheon of peaceful and semi-wrathful deities that are central to the renaissance of Buddhism in Tibet as expressed by the Drigung Kargyu tradition (whose founder and disciples feature at the end of the line of female deities) and the Gelukpa (whose verses of praise to "*The Foundation of Good Qualities*" (*Yon-ten Shi-gyur-ma*) by its founder Tsongkhapa is inscribed below the entire freeze). Prior to the Chinese invasion Toling had 400 Gelukpa monks, most of whom later found sanctuary in India.

The Hermitages above Toling

Along the cliff walls of the canyons above Toling one can see the caves and now crumbling walls of what once were retreat quarters for the monks. These can be reached by road by turning left of the main route to Toling and climbing into the canyons. Once on top an entire new complex opens out, for along each ridge to the S is a series of temples and caves hardly seen by foreign eyes. Once they were reached by climbing through man-made tunnels and staircases cut into the cliff face. Paths zigzagged up to the top from where one was also afforded a vast panoramic view of the upper Sutlej valley. It may still be possible to reach the peak directly above Toling provided that one carries a shovel for cutting stairs and a rope for safety.

Routes to Uttarakashi and Chamoli

In addition to the two motorable routes into Toling from the Senge Tsangpo-Darchen road, the county capital can also be approached by trekking from Tirthapuri and Dawadzong (see above, page 404 and page 425). Another jeepable road leads out of town to the W, passing through Tsaparang (26 km) and **Puling** (56 km). From Puling there are trekking routes to **Uttarakashi** in N India via Tajak La pass, and to **Chamoli** via Dronyi La pass.

Tsaparang

History

The founding of the Gu-ge kingdom in the 9th century evolved as a result of the collapse of the Yarlung Dynasty under the anti-Buddhist ruler Langdarma. After his assassination of one of his sons, Namde Osung, who had fled to Far-west Tibet, founded the Gu-ge kingdom. Before he died he assigned rule over the three provinces of Far-west Tibet, or Nga-ri, comprising **Gu-ge**, **Purang** and **Ladakh/Rutok** to his three sons in the hope of binding the realm together. Later in the 10th and early 11th century the religious king Yeshe-o sponsored the great translator Rinchen Zangpo, who had built over 100 temples throughout Far-west Tibet, to construct temples at Tsaparang and Toling. These are generally regarded as the most sublime of his work. After the Indian master Atisha came to Gu-ge, Buddhism was further revitalized and the kingdom flourished.

However, in 1624 the first European to reach Tibet, a Portuguese Jesuit based in Goa named Antonio del Andrade, arrived at Tsaparang. At this time the kingdom had less than 50 years to endure before its total collapse. It is often said that because the king favoured Andrade and allowed him to build a church jealousies arose on the part of the Buddhist lamas and officials who entered into a conspiracy with the ruler of Ladakh to bring about the kingdom's untimely end. However, according to local historical knowledge, the downfall of the kingdom of Gu-ge is far more dramatic. Why the city was never reinhabited has always remained something of a mystery.

Apparently relationships between the rulers of the three kingdoms gradually deteriorated over the centuries. This was especially true in the case of the kings of Ladakh/Rutok. Battles had been fought between these rulers from the N and their cousins in the S at both Gu-ge and Purang. Over 40 years after the Jesuit was recalled to India in 1685 a youthful king in his early twenties was forced to confront armies from the N. Deeply loved by his subjects his own forces were able to repel the aggressors repeatedly. It became clear to the king of Ladakh that he could only succeed with help from outside forces. Thus the supposedly Buddhist king of Ladakh paid for the assistance of Muslim tribal mercenaries.

With this additional strength his army soon laid seige to the city, encircling the population of several thousand in Tsaparang town around the base of the citadel. With their army decimated the people had no protection. The Ladakhi ruler then threatened to slaughter 50 people a day until the young king capitulated. From the heights of the royal citadel, impregnable and secure with its own secret water source, the King volunteered to renounce his position and depart from the realm saying that he would devote himself to the anonymity of a monastic life. He promised never to lay claim to the throne in the future on the condition that his subjects were spared their lives and that his queen and family, along with the ministers of court be guaranteed free and safe passage out of the land. To the relief of the people of Tsaparang the invaders agreed to these conditions.

The young king, his queen and their children as well as the ministers and commanders of the army descended from the heights of the citadel, bypassing a huge seige tower that was being built up the side of the 170m high cliffs. They presented themselves to the invaders and were all immediately bound and taken prisoner. The young king and his family were slaughtered immediately in full view of the population. Members of the court, ministers and generals were led down the hillside where they were all beheaded, their bodies tossed into the ravine below. The heads were then impaled upon spears and poles, forming a circle around the entire town. In this way a Muslim army repeated its ruthless techniques of war, ensuring that the 'infidels' immediately departed and never returned. A tragic testimony to this episode still exists in a secret cave where the headless torsos of the ministers were laid to rest over 300 years ago.

From the 1680s until the first half of the 20th century, Tsaparang was a ruin intact in time, virtually untouched by human forces except for the removing of the valuable timbers for new accommodation. Its major temples such as the **White**, **Red**, **Vajrabhairava** and **Demchok** temples, were intact when Prof Tucci visited in 1932 and still later when Lama Govinda and Li Gotami documented them in 1948-49. However the ravages of the Cultural Revolution swept through in the 1960s and wrecked the finely detailed surroundings of the statues, broke open their hearts and reduced the main figures to rubble. It was as though the apparent physicality of the statues presented a greater threat to the new, abstract ideology of communism for the masses than plain 2-dimensional murals. Today the ruins of Tsaparang, because they were already vacant when the Chinese invaded and thus were only lightly affected by the Cultural Revolution, are one of the finest examples of early historical ruins in Tibet, and now deemed part of the 'great artistic and historical treasures of ancient China'.

The Citadel of Tsaparang

To reach **Tsaparang**, 26 km W from Toling, it is best to leave before sunrise. Exploring this vast ruin takes all day. In the lower reaches of the city there are four main temples. One of these dates back nearly 1,000 years. The wall paintings and statues display some of the earliest examples of Tantric Buddhist art in existence. High above these temples is the citadel of the kings. One must climb up through a secret tunnel cut into the interior of the hillside to reach the top of this natural fortress, which was the residence of the later kings of Gu-ge. All that now remains intact is a small temple known as the **Demchok Mandala**. It has exquisite tantric murals inside.

The entire complex is located around a spur in the canyons S of the Sutlej. Like Khyunglung further E and upstream, Tsaparang lies on one of the main trade routes linking India and Kashmir in the W with Central Tibet in the E or the Silk Rd in the N. At its height Tsaparang was a bustling city and home to perhaps several thousand people, giving rest and support to caravans of traders, as well as a refuge and religious knowledge to members of the monastic community. The diversity of the population is vividly depicted in murals of the construction and consecration of the Red Temple.

Lhakhang Karpo (The White Temple)

After passing through the newly-built gate at the base of the city's slopes the bulk of the **Lhakhang Karpo** looms immediately to the right. To the left is the small shrine dedicated to Shakyamuni Buddha. Bypassing this, a few steps higher one will reach a porch in front of the entrance to this temple.

One enters, stepping down the dusty floor of a high ceilinged hall, diffused with a soft white light that lingers on the particles of dust, covering the room with a silvery glow. The silence is total and yet it feels as though one is being watched. One begins to explore to corners of gloom and just as one turns around one's gaze is met by a ferocious set of eyes above a snarling mouth and fangs. Over 3m high it is joined by another so that either side of the doorway is protected. These would have been forms of Hayagriva and Acala.

Now as your eyes adjust you can begin to make out the extraordinary contents of this temple. Around the walls were once larger than lifesize statues of the Buddhas of the Five Families. Each was seated upon a 1m high pedestal that is individually appropriate to each deity. All once were framed in elaborate terracotta aureoles that were easily broken in the 1960s. The finest record we have is the photographic archive of Li Gotama and Lama Govinda, dated 1948-9.

On the background walls there is a series of painted panels stretching from floor to ceiling. Each is unique in its content and proportions. Some are merit-gaining repetitive images of hundreds or thousands of buddhas; others consist of a series of vignettes depicting the lives of the tantric masters, including one or two incomplete panels that reveal the means by which they were made; yet others include detailed large images of Thousand-armed Avalokiteshvara and other deities.

The main feature of the statues (and paintings) is that they are executed in a highly distinctive style found nowhere else in Tibet. The work certainly appears to have been influenced by India, if not actually supervised by Indian master artists from Kashmir or Bengal. The torsos are elongated, the robing of the figures is loose, the ornamentation and crowns are unlike the later form of deities in Tibetan art; and perhaps most of all, the rendering of the background wall design is flexible and varied within the confines of its purpose, to an extent that is paralleled only in the temples at **Alchi**, Ladakh, in a slightly more rigid form.

Sadly all the 3-dimensional figures, in addition to the destroyed aureoles, have been broken in one way or another. Usually each had its heart ripped open, revealing little more than the sacred prayers of consecration and the life-pole which rises through the centre of the figure giving it strength and symbolic life. Most also had their arms and hands which were once displaying mudras, broken or torn off. Despite this destruction the statues retained a kind of dignity which today has been ruined by the botched attempt at restoration. Mud has been slapped into the cavities and smeared over the facial gashes without any skill such that now, with the addition of gold enamel paint, many of the figures appear to be afflicted by some disease.

The ceiling of the temple is composed of panels painted with individual decorative motifs, which are generally illustrative of Gu-ge art. At the altar end of the temple which once held a large statue of the Buddha there is a magnificent wooden skylight. Fashioned of painted beams forming a hollow square, it gradually reduces in size at 45 degree turns, making a small tower which allows a shaft of light to enter and illuminate the shrine. On its side walls the chapel has pedestals upon which still sit figures in armour. These are likely to be some of the religious kings of Gu-ge and Yarlung. Painted on the lower walls are episodes from the life of the Buddha.

NB Photography inside the temples is forbidden and you are likely to shadowed by a zealous Tibetan guide. Don't be surprised and do complain about this restriction if you wish to.

Lhakhang Marpo (The Red Temple)
Directly above the White Temple, up some steep steps is the **Lhakhang Marpo** (Red Temple). The doors are original, possibly dating from the 13th century. They were either carved in Kashmir or under the guidance of Kashmiri artisans in Tsaparang. Each has three panels containing the Sanskrit seed syllables of the mantra of great compassion OM MA-NI PAD-ME HUM. The door frame has weather-beaten figures of kings and bodhisattvas. The only other comparable doorway is found in the inner sanctum of the Jokhang in Lhasa.

The doors open onto a tall hallway filled with piles of rubble in its centre merging with a broken stupa to the right. The back wall where the central shrine once stood is vacant except for the upper decorative tendrils that held offering gods and goddesses surrounding the 3m high central figure of Amitabha. To either side of the altar the rear walls of deep blue hue have deities seated on lotus platforms. A few of the figures still remain. They comprise some of the Thirty-five Confession Buddhas. The rubble in the centre of the room once was a throne supporting an image of Shakyamuni Buddha and was probably added some time after the completion of the temple. The stupa to the right was also a later addition and appears to be in the Kadam-style associated with Atisha.

The most outstanding feature of the Red Temple is the series of murals which rise from 0.6m above the floor to the ceiling. They are comprised of two levels. The lower 0.6m consists of a frieze while the remaining upper area contains a series of images which, together with their thrones and the surrounding aureoles, are approximately 4m high. Both the frieze and the deities are rendered in the highly decorative form of the Gu-ge style, covered in a high gloss varnish that perhaps has helped preserve their deep, rich colours.

The **frieze**, commencing on the N wall to the right of the altar, depicts episodes from the life story of the Buddha. Each story is contained in a panel of flat colour. The temptation of the demons and the Buddha's enlightenment are two of the most outstanding. Copies made by Lama Govinda are supposed to exist in the Prince of Wales Museum, Bombay. On the rear wall (E) there is a set of the eight stupas symbolizing the major acts of the Buddha. These are followed by the emblems of a universal emperor as encorporated in the mandala offering of the material world. On the right side of the door is a remarkable depiction of the construction of the Red Temple, and the dignitaries attending its inaugural consecration. Animals and humans are shown carrying wood and building materials; musicians and dancers celebrate the festivities; dignitaries from both Tibet and foreign lands dressed in their respective costumes are seated in ranks; ministers, generals, relatives and close family members sit in line before the king, who is flanked by his queens, princesses and princes; all turning in devotion to the radiant central image of Amitabha to whom the temple is dedicated. Amitabha himself is flanked on the far side by rows of monks, teachers and illustrious monastic preceptors.

The magnificent paintings above the frieze on the side walls are the Buddhas of the Five Families and the Medicine Buddhas. On the rear wall are the commonly known figures of Padmasambhava, Avalokiteshvara, Green Tara and a protector flanking either side of the doorway. To the right of the door are Manjughosa, White Tara, and Vijaya. All are seated on individually elaborate thrones and literally melting into the swirling decorative elements characteristic of the Gu-ge style.

Dorje Jigje Lhakhang (Vajrabhairava Temple)

Just a few metres in front of the Red Temple's courtyard is a small protector's chapel known as the Vajrabhairava shrine. This, together with the **Neten Lhakhang** below it, was created at a later date than either the White or Red temples. Both are distinctly decorated in accord with the pantheon of the Gelukpa tradition. On the altar, now vacant, once stood a large wrathful image of Yamantaka, the bull-headed tantric emanation of Manjughosa. This is most likely the deity that Lama Govinda saw from the skylight in 1948, the photo appearing in *The Way of the White Clouds*.

On the walls of the shrine are images of deities from the *Unsurpassed Yogatantras*, such as Cakrasamvara, Hevajra, Guhyasamaja; Green Tara and the protectors near the door: Mahakala, Shridevi, Dharmaraja, and so forth. The figures on the walls to the side of the altar are of Tsongkhapa and Atisha along with their closest disciples. All are interspersed with miniature paintings of the mahasiddhas and lineage masters. The extraordinary feature of this entire room is that all the paintings are reduced to a range of colours limited to black, red and pure gold. Every figure has been covered in gold leaf and the ornaments embossed in relief. Moreover the crowns and rendition of the jewels is strikingly real in the style peculiar to Gu-ge. The overall effect is one of light and richness despite the fact that the paintings are heavily covered with centuries of candle soot and dust. This combination of gold and grime is like the radiance of a jewel penetrating the gloom of fog at dusk.

The Regent's Shrine

This, the smallest shrine, is to the left of the main entrance to Tsaparang. Built around the late 16th century it was the private chapel of the Regent of Tsaparang, attached to his winter residence. It too follows the style of the Vajrabhairava Temple with the figures gilded and the remaining colours limited to black and red. Most of the paintings are heavily coated in black soot from smoke and may even have been scorched by fire. It has no altar as such but the rear wall features a central image of the Buddha seated with his right hand in the gesture of calling the earth as a witness to his past merits (*bhumisparshamudra*). His main disciples, Sariputra and Maudgalyayana stand on the throne with him. On either side are two important masters of the *Lam-rim* teachings: Tsongkhapa, on the left and Atisha, on the right. These murals are seriously ruined and stylistically flat, lifeless and uninspiring.

The Township

The jail The lower slopes of Tsaparang are covered with pathways, staircases, tall mud walls and caves cut into the soft sandstone. Some of the caves were small shrines and still have paintings and charcoal drawings of the Buddha and other figures. Some are repositories for **tsatsa** votive images. About halfway up the lower slope is a huge cave cut into the heart of the hillside which curves down for at least 15-20m like a large well. Surprisingly it was used as a jail or detention pit for men. Another for women was also excavated.

The siege wall Near the top of the slope is a strange windowless structure of dressed granite, the only one of its kind. Between 3-5m high it is rectangular, about 15m wide and sited at the base of the cliff to the citadel. This was the base of a huge seige tower built by the invading Muslim army who destroyed the kingdom on behalf of the King of Ladakh at the beginning of the 18th century. It seems improbable that the tower would have reached a height of over 150m, but perhaps it helped convince the king safe in the citadel to give himself up to the invaders.

The Citadel of the Kings

Above the siege tower there are a number of caves and tunnels. The one on the extreme right is the entrance to a staircase that twists and turns upwards through the interior of the citadel. The way is lit every now and then by shafts of light or windows offering a view from the top of a sheer cliff down to a dry river valley. The height of the citadel is 170m from the top of the slope. The exit opens out onto a complex of collapsing walls and pathways that covers the top from edge to edge. Along the western edge runs a pathway protected by a low wall.

At the far end (S) the ridge narrows and becomes totally impassable. Here the cliff has caved in; for once there was a narrow road that allowed horses access to the top. The first structure to the S is a large open corral with attached stables. Next to it is a deep well which provided water along an aquaduct through a tunnel to the S. Walking back to the entrance one passes the high walls of what once was an assembly hall before reaching the only intact building, a square red walled temple known as the **Demchok Mandala**. Directly beneath this is a cave with dusty murals of wrathful deities. The lower torso of a statue remains. This was a shrine of the protector Mahakala.

The Demchok Mandala Shrine

Built as late as the 16th century this small shrine was probably created under the personal instructions of the king and his spiritual mentor. The walls are covered from floor to ceiling in a precise arrangement of deities, corresponding to the mandalas of the *Unsurpassed Yogatantras*. Each of the roof panels has one of the peaceful symbols of the Buddhist doctrine, such as the wheel, the lotus, the three jewels, the eternal knot, the vajra, and so on.

The temple takes its name from a miniature 3-dimensional mandala that once stood in the now vacant space in the centre of the room. It was dedicated to Cakrasamvara, considered by Buddhists to reside at Mt Kailash. It once held 32 miniature figures of the peripheral deities and was about 2.5m in diameter. All that remains now are some of the outer walls and the lotus petal floor of the mandala. It was partially intact when Govinda saw it in 1948 and it is widely believed that Prof Tucci removed most of the figurines of deities and dakinis in 1932.

The bands of figures on the walls begin at the base with a frieze depicting the charnel grounds where Indian yogins would meditate on death and confront ghosts or spirits. These places of terrifying events are vividly rendered, replete with corpses, beasts, demons, yogins, birds of prey, and atmospheric jungle. Traditionally there were eight great cemeteries in India. Above these is a frieze depicting the dakinis, the messengers of buddha-activity, embodying emptiness. Next is the broad band of tantric deities.

Each wall has five main figures, representing the central figure of the mandala and those of the four cardinal directions. On the left (S) wall are the aspects of Cakrasamvara himself, on the rear (W) wall the forms of Guhyasamaja, on the right (N) side are the aspects of Hevajra, and on the rear walls on either side of the door the protector Mahakala as well as labelled images of the king, his retainers, and contemporary masters. Above the main deities, there is a long frieze depicting the mahasiddhas and important lamas from the Tibetan lineages.

The rendering of these deities is superb in its refinement of the torsos, the power and dynamism of the wrathful figures (Cakrasamvara and Hevajra) and the sublime gentility of the peaceful figures (Guhyasamaja). The ornaments and decorative elements in the fabric are as fine as the designs of a master jeweller. The pigments of the colours are still fresh and are not overwhelmed by an excess of gilding. Overall the content of this small temple amply rewards one for undertaking the rigours of the journey.

Outside the Demchok Mandala and adjacent to it is a newly built rest room where beer and soft drinks are served!

The Winter Palace

Along the path toward the N end of the citadel is the entrance to the King's **Winter Palace**. This comprises a series of seven rooms branching off a central hallway dug from the very heart of the mountain approximately 12m below the surface. Access is down a nearly vertical tunnel with aid of an iron railing for support. The warmth of the earth sheltered the king and his retinue from the bitter cold of winter. Secret tunnels led to a water supply and could be used to make an escape in the event of danger. Windows are cut through the outside wall, providing light to the interior and a breathtaking view to the valley below.

From the northernmost ramparts one has a vertigo-inducing view down the cliff face to the complex of buildings and temples spread around the lower slopes. Stupas stand on the spurs of ridges and across the small stream to the E is another large stupa in an Indian style, as at Toling. The Sutlej valley's gorge cuts the broad vista from E to W and far in the distance under the bleached blue midday sky are the snow dusted peaks of the Gangtise Range.

Dungkar and Piyang

In 1992-93 a series of painted caves was discovered further E up the Sutlej from Toling at the small village of **Dungkar** and some 6 km away amidst the ruins of **Piyang**.

ACCESS To reach Dungkar you must drive back out of Toling, follow the canyon N until the fork in the road. Take the branch leading E to **Dzo Nakpo** on the Senge Tsangpo-Darchen road (see above, page 425). After approximately 20 km, turn off down a poorly marked side-road, heading S. After 8 km the valley opens out into green pastures alongside a small village. You will have to find the caretaker for the caves. A surly character, he will lead you 2 km down the valley and then up to caves at the base of a cliff. He will probably ask for ¥20-50 to open the doors to two of them.

Dungkar

Inside are possibly the earliest murals in Far-west Tibet, on walls carved in the form of a mandala interior. The shelves cut into the rear wall are altars which once held stucco statues of the Buddha and still have one or two images on them. Others are mingled with rubble on the floor.

The first feature that strike one is the similarity of the paintings with those of the early art at the caves of **Dunhuang** at the eastern edge of the Silk Route. In the first cave are large mandalas as well as repeated rows of Buddhas, whereas the second is almost totally covered in small Buddha figures. The figures have elongated torsos and sit on semi-spherical lotuses like those in the Dunhuang mandalas. The most distinctive feature is the manner in which the spaces surrounding the mandalas are encorporated. Instead of the precise decorative patterns of the Gu-ge style there are hosts of flying *apsara*, or offering goddesses. Their diaphonous gowns waft around them in soft breezes in a similar way to 10th century figures at Dunhuang. Even the colour of the murals is similar – a light blue overall, featuring pastel colours. Perhaps these works were created by Indian painters on their way to the cities of the Silk Route 1,000 years ago.

Other caves nearby which have not been locked up also contain paintings although seriously damaged by age and weathering.

Piyang

Down the valley at its far end is the extensive ruins of Piyang monastery. Both complexes were once Gelukpa monasteries under the control of Tashilhunpo in Zhigatse. There are also cave paintings at Piyang and perhaps more in the side valleys if one had the time to engage in a little exploration. Without doubt throughout the upper Sutlej valley there are other important sites waiting to be discovered.

Roads to Kinnaur, Spiti and Ladakh

Driving N from Toling, via the **Lawoche** intersection, you will reach **Chusum** township after 141 km, and **Sibkyi Tiyak** in the Sutlej gorge after 150 km. Here you reach the Indian border which is currently closed and across which lies the ethnic Tibetan region of **Kinnaur** (*Tib* Kunu). In Kinnaur, the Hindustan Highway leads through Kalpa to Simla in Himachal Pradesh.

The traditional trade route to Kinnaur is a caravan trail, leading directly from **Jangtse** township to **Tiyak** in the Sutlej valley and thence to Sibkyi Tiyak.

Trekking

From Chusum there is also another trekking route which leaves the Sutlej basin, crossing into the valley of the **Rushok Tsangpo**. Here there are two trails, one following the river downstream via Sumdo to **Tabo**, across the Indian border in Spiti, Himachal Pradesh; and the other following the river upstream via Khayungshing La pass into Southern **Ladakh**.

RUTOK COUNTY

༣ུ་ཐོག

日土县 Rutog

Population: 59,724   Area: 68,609 sq km

The county of Rutok in the extreme NW of Tibet borders the Xinjiang Autonomous Region and Ladakh. Geographically it forms part of the Northern Plateau (Jangtang) in the sense that its rivers drain internally into lakes, such as the long tapering **Lake Pang-gong**, which lies half inside Tibet and half inside Ladakh. None of its waterways drain into the Indus basin, which lies just a short distance to the S. The county capital is located at **Rutok**, 127 km from Senge Tsangpo and 1,239 km from Kashgar in Xinjiang.

Maga Tsangpo Valley

The road from **Senge Tsangpo**, the district capital of Far-west Tibet to Kashgar in Xinjiang province passes through Rutok county. It crosses **La-me La** pass after 31 km, leaving the Indus basin to descend into the valley of the **Maga Tsangpo**. The township of **Chakgang** is 26 km below the pass, and from there to **Risum** township it is a further 30 km. At Risum there are remarkable prehistoric rock carvings (see below, page 438). From here, a motorable side-road leads eastwards, following a tributary of the Maga Tsangpo upstream to Khulpa and **Rawang** (60 km), where there are a number of small salt lakes.

The main road from Risum continues to follow the Maga Tsangpo downstream for 30 km, as far as **Derub**, where a turn-off cuts NW for Rutok, the county capital, 10 km distant. The river itself flows immediately into Lake Pang-gong.

Rutok

In the 9th century Namde Osung, the younger Buddhist son of the apostate king Langdarma, fled Central Tibet and established Buddhism in Far-west Tibet. He divided Ngari into three regions at **Guge**, **Rutok** and **Purang**, giving authority to rule to each of his three sons and their descendants. Thus **Rutok** became the capital of the kings of northern Ngari. Over 500 years later political rivalries saw **Rutok** join with **Ladakh** to lay waste the kingdom of **Guge**, and wage war against the kingdom of **Purang**.

Today the newly built town of Rutok is basically a Chinese military garrison. Located in a slight depression its two main thoroughfares hold a few small groups of laconic soldiers in their ill-fitting green uniforms. Apart from the army, the residents of this sleepy town seem to be mainly Tibetan as well as a few Muslim traders from Xinjiang. Dust-covered Tibetan children with spikey, uncut hair and ragged clothes are sometimes the only people one sees in the single main street.

● **Accommodation** There is a truck station with overnight accommodation.

A road leads due W from Rutok for 65 km to **Retso** township, giving access to a traditional trade route via **Lake Mendong-tso** and across the Chugu La and Kharmar La passes into **Ladakh**.

RUTOK 538

To Kashgar (954 km) — 27
Tserang Daban
Pang-gong Lake — 172
Retso — 65 — Domar
To Ladakh — Rutok — 113
10
Derub
30
60 — Rawang
Risum
30
Chakgang — 26
La-me La — 31 — Senge Tsangpo
N
Sketch map: not to scale

Pang-gong Lake

The long (113 km) **Lake Pang-gong**, located N of Rutok, straddles the Indo-Tibetan border and is said to be patrolled by the highest navy in the world! This is a Chinese claim boasted by eager officials. They also say that the waters at the Tibetan end are fresh while those at the Ladakh end are saline. Be that as it may, the region surrounding the lake is renowned for its wildlife. Massive flocks of migrating birds rest here on the way from Siberia S to India. In the late summer and autumn seasons thousands of birds can be seen. Muslim fishermen from **Xinjiang** are often seen paddling out from the shore on large inner tubes to net the fish that abound in the lake. Tibetan Buddhists generally never go fishing. The surrounding area is a natural habitat for various types of wild animals, for which reason there are now plans to establish a wild game hunting

THE RUTOK PREHISTORIC ROCK CARVINGS

About 40 km S from **Rutok** at **Risum** hamlet, the road crosses a low culvert and turns left around the corner of a cliff facing flat wet lands from which fresh springs bubble forth. On the cliff to the left of the road one suddenly comes across a mass of ancient carvings chiselled into the surface of the red and black schist rocks. These remarkable images were discovered only in 1985 by the Lhasa Cultural Relics Institute and are extremely important for the insight they give into the key elements in the ancient nomadic way of life.

Included are stylized figures of deer, sheep, yak, antelope, wolf or dog, fish and men. Most are rendered in outline only and in many panels the figures are realistically portrayed rearing up or galloping. Their physicality is accented by spiral swirls and elaborate curving branches on the body, antlers or tail. Birds are also present although they are eagle-like, and yet in the midst of what seems a shower of sparks. In this way they reflect the features of the mythical Garuda, a half-man half-eagle that flies in the midst of a blazing fire eliminating all negativity. There are also abstract carvings of strange bicellular forms, evoking the cosmic egg, one of the images found in the Bon philosophy for the origin of existence.

These rock carvings are possibly the most significant prehistoric images in Tibet. Petroglyphs in the same style have recently been unearthed inside burial mounds on the steppes of Central Asia.

On the main road there are two distinct groups of petroglyphs at the location known as **Rimotang**, 1.5 km SE of **Risum**. After crossing the culvert the first is a few hundred metres on the left. The second is about a hundred metres further on. The figures are cut into a dark red coloured schist or granite. Some were defaced recently by devout Buddhists carving mantras over portions of the petroglyphs. This Buddhist graffitti is most abundant at **Rimotang**. The location is alongside a broad lush valley which may be a reason why the images are located here. It is ideal for the nomads to graze their animals while enroute. Directly beneath the rock face is a small, natural spring.

Another set is located 32 km W of **Rutok** town, on the N bank of the Chulung River and is known as **Luri Langkar**. They are similar to those of **Rimotang** and are spread over six panels less than 4m above ground.

One final group known as **Karke Sang** lies 159 km NE of Rutok and about 25 km S of **Domar township**. They are sited in a cave and along a ridge W of the **Karke Sang cave**. Downstream one can see evidence of a more intensively cultivated landscape.

park, with a sliding scale of rates according to the rarity of the animal killed, along the lines of the Balun hunting park in Qinghai province (see below, page 565).

Domar

Rejoining the highway at Derub, 10 km SE of Rutok, you can continue driving northwards to **Domar** township, 113 km distant in the Northern Plateau. At the outset, the road follows the eastern shoreline of Lake Pang-gong, and the landscape along this stretch is breathtaking in its beauty. The extreme clarity of the atmosphere gives the strange, multicoloured earth of the hills, cliffs and plains a surreal visionary quality. Have your camera ready to take some memorable landscape photos.

The drive to Domar from Rutok takes only half a day. The surrounding terrain, as the name suggests, is deep red in colour. The township is a bleak military garrison, that must be the last outpost for a soldier coming from remote mainland China. One could not get posted to a more remote location than here! It is also within the **Aksai Chin**, a disputed region claimed by India, who belatedly discovered a Chinese road traversing the middle of the territory in the 1960s.

● **Accommodation** At Domar empty rooms are usually available and, although there are 1 or 2 restaurants just outside the gates to the garrison's main courtyard, you are likely to be offered the choice of one item/dinner. They are also ready to overcharge on every item inc hot water should you ask for it.

Xinjiang Border

From Domar, the road continues crossing the Aksai Chin to leave the Northern Plateau of Tibet for Xinjiang province. The last settlements on Tibetan territory are at **Sumzhi** and **Tserang Daban** transport station, 172 km from Domar, where it is possible to stay overnight. The advantage of staying at such a place

is that you may be able to order a meal from the army camp mess. It takes half a day to reach this bleak outpost, and the actual border lies 36 km further N.

Khotan and Mazar

The road from the Tibet-Xinjiang border to Kashgar initially continues passing through the Aksai Chin. Occasionally Tibetan nomads can be seen leading their herds of yak and sometimes 2-humped camels across the plateau. Alongside the highway are many forms of flora which are unique to the region. A number of these plants have highly prized medicinal properties, considered to be especially efficacious in Tibetan pharmacopaea. The road then descends initially into the **Karakax River** valley and then into the **Yarkand River** basin, which lies between the great snow ranges of the Karakorum and the Western Kunluns.

The former cuts through the Kunlun range to **Khotan** at the southern extremity of the Taklamakhan Desert on the Silk Route. Perhaps as sparsely populated as the Arabian Desert, Khotan is a region comprised of barren wastelands and ethereal blue lakes which are among the last remnants of the Ice Age. As they melted and formed rivers flowing N through the Kunlun range they once fed the renowned Khotanese Buddhist civilization. The merchants and scholars of Khotan travelled along this route to India and China, trading in Chinese silk and other commodities, or studying and translating the Sanskrit Buddhist scriptures, several hundred years before Buddhism was established in Tibet. However, as the great rivers from Tibet's Northern Plateau dried up, the Khotanese civilization collapsed. It was buried under the desert sands until European explorers uncovered its traces at the turn of the century.

The highway running through the Yarkand valley offers wonderful panoramic views of the **Karakorums** (see above, page 49) on the Pakistan border. **K2**, the world's second highest peak, is passed in close proximity. Spend the night at **Mazar**, 456 km from Tserang Daban. Mazar is a ghost town of long concrete compounds. It is preferable to keep going and camp out somewhere near fresh water.

Yarkand and Kashgar

Yarkand (*Ch* Yecheng), is another ancient town of the southern branch of the Silk Route. However, the recent influx of Chinese settlers into this region, as in Tibet, has altered its traditional character. Generally it is not permitted for foreigners to stop over for even a day here. Yarkand is 249 km distant from Mazar. Normally one will arrive soon after lunchtime and, after a short stop for food, continue onto **Kashgar**, a further 249 km. Transport to **Khunjerab** pass leading into Pakistan is best obtained at Kashgar, rather than Yarkand. At Kashgar, accommodation is available at the former British and Russian consulate buildings, or at the *Xin Binguan Hotel* outside town. There are daily bus services between these two towns, and from Kashgar directly to **Pakistan** and **Kazakhstan**. Flights are also available to **Urumqi**, the provincial capital of Xinjiang and to **Beijing**.

EASTERN TIBET
THE RANGES AND RIVERS OF KHAM

INTRODUCTION

Eastern Tibet or Kham presents an amazing contrast to the landscape of the Brahmaputra valley and is characterized by extremely rugged mountains in parallel ranges extending from NW to SE, broken by very deep alpine gorges. The ranges are narrow and rocky with steep slopes and sharp ridges, while some peaks are covered by glaciers. Eroded narrow valleys and deep gorges have been cut by the Salween, Mekong and Yangtze rivers and their numerous tributaries, hence the name traditionally given to the region of Kham: **'four rivers and six ranges'** (*chuzhi gangdruk*).

The main topographical features are the high altitude nomadic grasslands in the far N and W, and the great rivers which flow from them in parallel SE courses, through deep forested limestone and sandstone gorges.

Nowadays this vast, fertile and most populated region of Tibet is divided for political and historical reasons between four Chinese provinces, comprising altogether 47 counties. **Tibetan Autonomous Region** includes 7 counties in Nakchu district, 11 in Chamdo district and 3 in Nyangtri district. **Yunnan province** includes the 3 counties of Dechen Tibetan Autonomous Prefecture; **Qinghai** includes the 6 counties of Yushu Tibetan Autonomous Prefecture; and **Sichuan** includes 16 counties of Kandze Tibetan Autonomous Prefecture, in addition to the Mili Tibetan Autonomous County.

The most important cities of Kham are Chamdo, Derge, Jyekundo, Dartsedo, and Gyeltang, and among these **Chamdo** is generally regarded as the main centre.

The distance from Lhasa to Chamdo is 1,066 km via Nakchu; and 1,179 km via Kongpo. The distance from Chamdo to Chengdu is 1,325 km; from Chamdo to Kunming 1,789 km; and from Chamdo to Ziling 1,542 km.

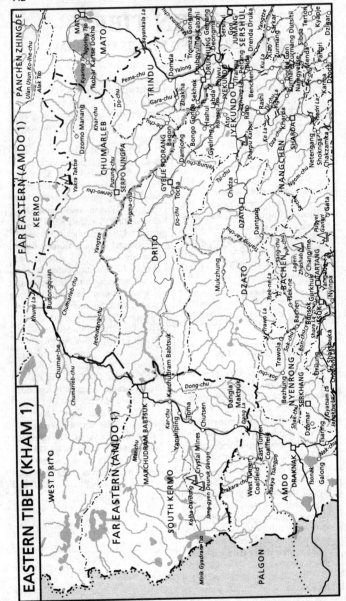

EASTERN TIBET (KHAM 1)

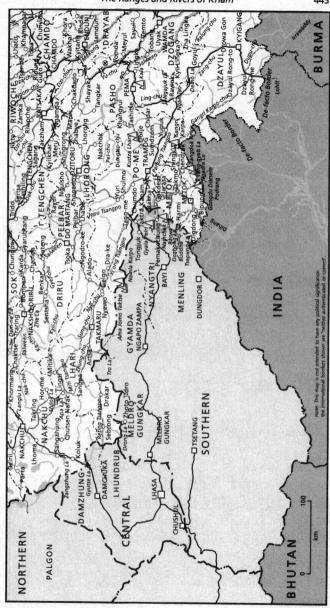

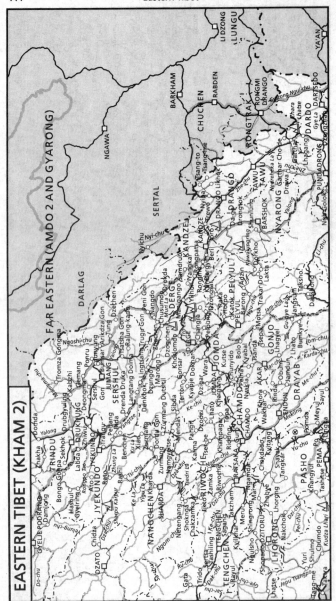

EASTERN TIBET (KHAM 2)

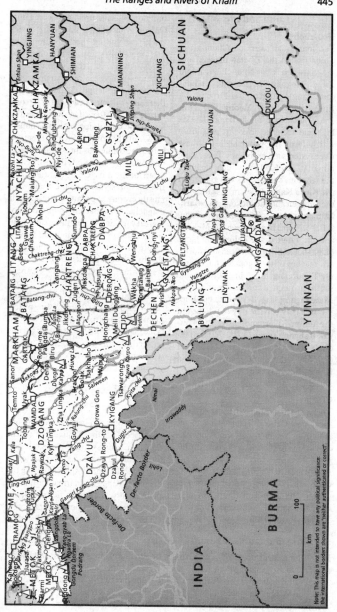

Note: This map is not intended to have any political significance; the international borders shown are neither authenticated or correct.

Land and life

Geography

The four great rivers of Kham, all of which rise on the Tibetan plateau, are: the **Salween** (*Tib* Ngul-chu, *Ch* Nu jiang), **Mekong** (*Tib* Da-chu, *Ch* Lancang jiang), **Yangtze** (*Tib* Dri-chu, *Ch* Jinsha jiang), and **Yalong** (*Tib* Dzachu/Nya-chu, *Ch* Yalong jiang). The six highland ranges (*chu-zhi gang-druk*) which form the watersheds for these river systems are as follows: **Tsawagang** range (5,100-6,700m) which includes the fabulous snow peaks and glaciers of **Mt Kawa Karpo** (6,702m) lies between the Salween and the Mekong; the **Markhamgang** range (*Ch* Ningjing Shan; 5,100-5,700m) lies between the Mekong and the Yangtze; the **Zelmogang** range (4,800-5,400m) lies between the northern reaches of the Yangtze and Yalong; the **Poborgang** range lies between the southern Yangtze and the lower Yalong; **Mardzagang** (5,100-5,700m) occupies the area between the upper Yalong and the Yellow River; and, lastly, the **Minyak Rabgang** range (4,800-7,750m) including **Mt Minyak Gangkar** (7,756m), the highest mountain in Kham, lies between the lower Yalong and the Gyarong.

Climate

The climate is milder here than in W Tibet and Central Tibet owing to the penetration of monsoon winds and precipitation from Southeast Asia, yet the great ruggedness of the terrain contributes to localized climatic diversity. Generally, there is little precipitation in winter, and abundant rainfall in summer; the annual average varying from 500 mm to 1,000 mm.

Flora and fauna of Kham

In the more **arid areas** of NW Kham adjacent to the Jangtang Plateau, alpine steppes and meadows predominate on rock soil. Cobresia grows, along with rock jasmine, arenaria, rhubarb, gentian, buffalo pen, saussurea, and astragalus. On lower mountain slopes are shrub thickets including rhododendron, willow, cinquefoil, spirea, and juniper. Towards the SE, the precipitation increases and the alpine steppes give way to forest steppe. At 3,000-3,900m there are balfour spruce, purple cone spruce and fir trees. On dry slopes the forests include juniper, oak, and pine.

Within the **gorges** of Kham there are subalpine coniferous forests growing on podzolic soils. In the NE these are characteristically mixed temperate and subtropical forests; and in the S and SW mostly evergreen or laurel forests, with magnolia, michelia, and so forth. There is great variation within these subalpine coniferous forests: ie fir in humid areas, spruce in dry areas; with numerous shrubs, grasses and mosses. In the far N gorges where winter is cold and dry there are mixed forests of oak and pine; and in the wetter SE with precipitation exceeding 2,000 mm, there are fir, spruce, hemlock, lithocarpus, birch, and poplar. As for fauna: there are fewer ungulates and rodents, but more badgers, lynxes, wild cats, monkeys, and occasionally tigers or giant pandas.

History of Kham

ཁམས

The kingdoms and tribal confederations of E Tibet, whether nomadic or sedentary, have been shaped by this vast and formidable terrain. Since the disintegration of the Tibetan Empire following the demise of King Langdarma, for most of their history, they have fiercely maintained their independence from Lhasa, China and indeed from each other. Among them the most important states in Kham were the five kingdoms ruled by hereditary kings (*gyelpo*), viz. **Chakla**, **Derge**, **Lingtsang**, **Nangchen**, and **Lhato**; the five Trehor states ruled by hereditary chieftains (*ponpo*), viz. **Drango**, **Kangsar**, **Mazur**, **Trewo** and

Beri; the diverse grassland states of the upper **Yalong** and of **Nyarong**, **Sangen**, **Gonjo**, and **Khyungpo**, which were also ruled by hereditary chieftains; the southern states of **Batang**, **Litang**, **Markham**, **Tsawarong**, **Powo** and **Kongpo** which were governed by appointed regents; and the western states of **Chamdo**, **Drayab** and **Riwoche**, which along with **Gyarong** and **Mili**, were governed by lama dignitaries.

Social history and religious impact

In Kham, religious and secular festivals have had great impact on the lives of the people since earliest times. Each region has its horse-riding festival at a fixed date in the calendar – an occasion for song, dance and various athletic competitions, at which the boisterous Khampa crowds display their local costume and traditions. Traders and spectators would often travel throughout Kham from one region to the next, planning their travels to coincide with local festivals.

Similarly, each region also has its distinctive spiritual affinities. The pre-Buddhist Bonpo have their most important strongholds in the **Khyungpo** region of the present Tibetan Autonomous Region and the **Ngawa** (Aba), **Beri** and **Gyarong** regions of Sichuan.

Pilgrimage is as important here as in Central Tibet. When Buddhism was established in the 8th century, Padmasambhava roamed throughout E Tibet in the company of his students, and he is reputed to have concealed his teachings as *terma* in many parts of the country. Twenty-five such ancient pilgrimage sites are esteemed above all others in E and NE Tibet. They are considered to have special affinity with either buddha-body, speech, mind, attributes or activities.

Buddha-body The **Kyadrak Senge Dzong** in the Upper Yalong valley is the main site. It has five aspects, viz. Chijam Nyinda Puk in the Yalong valley (body),

Lotu Karma (speech), Nyen in the Yangtze valley (mind), Khala Rongo in Nangchen (attributes) and Hekar Drak (activities).

Buddha-speech Powo Gawalung is the main site. It also has five aspects, viz. **Mt Kawa Karpo** in Tsawarong (body), **Pema Shelri** (speech), **Nabun Dzong** in Nangchen (mind), **Yegyel Namka Dzong** near Riwoche (attributes) and **Hor Tresho** or **Chakdu Khawa Lungring** near Kanze (activities).

Buddha-mind The **Dentik Shelgi Drak** in Ma-khok, Amdo, near the Huangho River is the main site. Its five aspects are: **Zhara Lhatse** in Minyak (body), **Warti Trak** (speech), **Dorje Drak** in lower Machu (mind), **Khandro Bumdzong** in lower Nangchen (attributes), and **Po-ne Drakar** near Riwoche (activities).

Buddha-attributes Rudam Gangi Rawa, is the main site, ie the mountain Trori Dorje Ziltrom above Dzogchen. Its five aspects are: **Ngulda Podrang** in front of Derge Lhundrupteng (body), **Pema Shelphuk** in lower Mesho Dzomnang (speech), **Tsandra Rinchen Drak** at Pelpung (mind), **Dzongsho Deshek Dupa** in Dzing (attributes), and **Dzomtok Puseng Namdrak** by the Yangtze (activities). All these sites are in Derge district.

Buddha-activity Katok Dorjeden is the main site. Its five aspects are: **Ngu** (body), **Tsangshi Dorje Trolo** (speech), Tashi or **Kampo Kangra** (mind), **Hyelgi Trak** (attributes), and **Drakri Dorje Pungpa** (activities). These sites are in and around Katok in southern Derge.

These power places later came to be closely associated with the Nyingma, Kagyu and Sakya traditions. Despite intertribal rivalries, the diverse states of Kham were noted for their religious tolerance until the 17th century. The Nyingma, Kagyu, Sakya and Geluk schools of Tibetan Buddhism were represented, alongside the adherents of Bon. Among areas of Kagyu influence, the strongest were **Nangchen** and **Derge**. For the Sakya school the most influential regions were **Jyekundo** and **Derge**, and for the Nyingmapa the **Zelmogang** and **Southern Derge** regions. Prior to the 17th century, the Gelukpa had their greatest centres at **Chamdo** and **Litang**.

The Mongols

A fundamental change occurred in the 17th century, however, and this is closely connected with the rise to political power of the Dalai Lama V in Lhasa. The long civil wars waged between the supporters of the Kagyu and Geluk schools in Central Tibet had some impact in the E. The zealous Mongol Gushri Qan of the Qosot tribe sought to intervene on behalf of the Gelukpa faction by sending his Mongol armies against Donyo Dorje, the king of **Beri** who adhered to the Bon religion. That kingdom was subdued between 1639-41, and the region from Beri to Drango was settled by Mongol tribesmen (Horpa), who forcibly converted and renamed some monasteries belonging to the Kagyu and other traditions. The **five Hor states** of Drango, Kandze and Beri district with their partisan affiliation thus came into being. Great monasteries were built at **Kandze** and **Dargye** near Rongpatsa. Gradually, the new administration at Lhasa was able to exert its influence on other regions to the S: **Drayab**, **Markham**, **Batang**, **Chakla** and so forth. In the 18th century, the Changkya Qutuqtu conducted a campaign against the Bonpo of the **Gyarong** region. Only the kingdoms of Derge, Nangchen and Khyungpo with their strong traditions could withstand the sectarian attacks.

Mongol intervention in Tibetan politics had even more serious repercussions in the 18th century. In 1705-06, the Manchu emperor Kangxi had supported the Qosot leader Lhabzang Qan in his abduction of Dalai Lama VI and murder of the regent Desi Sangye Gyatso. The Dzungar Mongols then intervened in 1717 to kill Lhabzang and plunder Central Tibet. Although the Tibetan forces were eventually able to gain the upper hand, the Manchu emperor who had custody of the new Dalai Lama VII, sent armies to vanquish the Dzungars and instate Kelsang Gyatso (1720). Campaigns then followed against the Qosot in Amdo leading to the annexation of Amdo and Nangchen by the new Qinghai province in 1724. Finally, in 1727 the Manchus claimed much of Kham E of the Yangtze as their own protectorate, and from 1728 they posted two representatives in Lhasa.

Manchu Warlords and occupation

While Manchu China unilaterally claimed a nominal suzerainty over much of Kham and Amdo, the reality of the situation was that the kingdoms and tribes of Eastern Tibet were de facto independent. When the forces of **Nyarong Gonpo Namgyel** overran the territories from Drango to Derge, it was the Tibetan government which came to their assistance and subdued the power of Nyarong in the campaign of 1863-65. Sichuan warlords, among them Chao Erh Feng, began to intervene from 1894, but direct interference in the affairs of E Tibet by Beijing was precipitated by Chinese reaction to the arrival of the Younghusband expedition in Lhasa (1904). In 1909, Chao Erh Feng was dispatched to adopt a 'forward policy' which sought to carve out a new and governable 33 district province called **Xikang**. The proposed territory would encompass the entire region from **Gyamda** in Kongpo to **Dartsedo**. The 1909-18 campaign, which devastated much of Kham, resulted in the eventual Chinese withdrawal from the region, despite British diplomatic efforts to maintain the artificial boundaries devised by the Manchu emperors. The conflict was later resumed with the arrival in Kham of the PLA during the 1950s. The retribution exacted on Kham for its militancy resulted in the massacre of the population and the total destruction of the region's great Buddhist artefacts. Only a few key sites, exemplified by the printery at Derge, were spared.

Further reading

There are few well-informed works on these regions of Kham available in languages other than Tibetan. Among them the most important are RA Stein, *Les tribus anciennes des marches sino-tibetaines*, Eric Teichman, *Travels of a Consular Official in Eastern Tibet*, the writings of the botanist F Kingdom Ward who travelled throughout Konpo and Southern Kham between 1913-20, and the more recent cartographic studies of Pieter Kestler in Rikon, Switzerland. Among travelogues, the most readable include A Migot, *Tibetan Marches*; C Trungpa, *Born in Tibet* and the works of the American evangelist M Duncan.

Accessibility

While individual travellers have ventured through the 'closed' areas of Eastern Tibet over the last few years with or without official sanction, the authorities of TAR, Qinghai, Yunnan, and Sichuan have for their own reasons been slow to accept the great potential for tourism in Kham. The situation is somewhat different in Amdo, where the peripheral areas of NE Tibet, around Ziling and Labrang are open to individual travel, and where tour groups frequently traverse the rail and road link from Ziling in the NE to Lhasa via Golmud, Amdo, Nakchu, Damzhung, and Yangpachen. This entails a 21-hr journey by train, followed by a 1,155 km drive across the desolate Qinghai plateau.

The disadvantages of travel on this route are that, apart from Kumbum, Labrang and so forth, the great cultural centres of Kham are bypassed.

With proper organization and travel permits, it is nonetheless possible for those able to pay the high daily rates charged by the provincial tourism bureaux to travel throughout the 'closed' areas of Kham. These routes are often impassable in winter and in the rainy season (July-Aug). The best time to make this journey is therefore between April-June or Sept-Nov. Nonetheless, owing to communication difficulties one may also face unexpected problems during these optimum periods.

There are presently two fully motorable roads leading from Lhasa to Chamdo in the heart of Kham: a **northern route**, which passes through Nakchu, Sok Dzong, Hor Bachen, Khyungpo Tengchen, and Riwoche; and a **southern route**, via Gyamda, Bayi, Powo, and Tsawa Pasho. A third and more direct motorable route will soon be fully operational, via Gyamda, Lhari, Pelbar, and Lhorong. This corresponds to the **old caravan trail**, which predates the other two roads. Until the final section is completed between Lhari and Pelbar, this trail still requires some trekking through the Nyenchen Tanghla watershed.

Of the two current motorable routes, the northern one is now in greater use, since it permits faster driving and is more reliable during the rainy season. The southern route, by contrast, is subject to recurring landslides due to the glacial snow-melt and deep river gorges around Powo. All three routes offer considerable variation in landscape and cultural programmes.

LHASA TO CHAMDO
THE NORTHERN ROUTE VIA NAKCHU

T he northern route, described in this section, comprises the counties of Nakchu, Sok Dzong, Hor Bachen, Khyungpo Tengchen, Riwoche, and Chamdo. In addition, three outlying counties of Nakchu district: Amdo, Nyenrong, and Driru, are also included. **Recommended itineraries: 4, 5 (and 7).**

NAKCHU COUNTY
ནག་ཆུ

那曲县 Nagqu
Population: 44,903   Area: 17,194 sq km

Nakchu district, traditionally known as **Jang Nakchuka**, is the name given to the high nomadic terrain of the E Jangtang Lakes and the Salween headwaters, average altitude 4,500m. This is a vast wilderness region through which the Nak-chu, Shak-chu, and Sok-chu tributaries flow to form the **Salween** (*Tib* Nak-chu): a 2,784 km river rising in the Dangla range to the N, which has its estuary at the Gulf of Martaban, S of Burma. The city of

NAKCHU, AMDO & NYENRONG

TIB539

Tumen Dosol Terka — 59 — (5,220m)
106
To Senge Tsangpo (1,333km)
Draknak
98
Serkhang
Tsaring 40 38 44
Nakchu 10 49
Takring 1
Lhoma 50
66 53
(4,727m)
Koluk
41
Artsa 38 68
To Gyamda (104km)
Omatang
Damzhung
To Lhasa

Nak-chu
Shak-chu
Khormang
Drilung
To Driru
Horme
Shakchuka
Lhari
N

Sketch map: not to scale

Nakchu, which has undergone unprecedented development within the last 2 years, is the administrative capital of nine counties within the upper Salween region, as well as having its own county-level bureaucracy. It is located on the Ziling-Lhasa highway 315 km NE of Lhasa, near the headwaters of the Nak-chu tributary, from which it derives its name. The actual sources of the Nak-chu are at **Chutsen Narak** (Jukchu), N of the Brahmaputra-Salween watershed, and at **Galong** on the southern shore of the freshwater **Lake Tsonak** to the NW. The distance from Damzhung to Nakchu is 239 km, and from Nakchu to Amdo township, 138 km along the Ziling highway.

Koluk and Lhoma

Heading NE from Lhasa via Yang-pachen and Damzhung, the paved Ziling-Lhasa highway enters Nakchu county 27 km beyond **Omatang**. Passing through **Koluk** township after 14 km, it rises slowly towards **Zangzhung La** pass (4,727m), which forms the watershed between the Brahmaputra and Salween river systems, and after crossing this

divide, it bypasses **Sangzhung** township on the W. The road now crosses the Nak-chu southern source, and runs parallel to it. Light snowfall is a normal occurrence in this exposed and sparsely populated Jangtang region, even in summertime! The township of **Lhoma** straddles the highway, 66 km NE of Koluk, and 17 km further on there is a turn-off on the right (E), which follows the Nak-chu through **Takring** and **Horme** townships in the direction of **Lhari**. This is part of the central Lhasa-Chamdo road network, on which see below, page 472.

Nakchu City

ACCESS Continue along the highway for 10 km, and soon the city of **Nakchu** comes into view, impressively large in its wilderness setting. Cross the Nakchu Zamchen bridge on the right (E), which leads off the highway into town.

The phenomenal growth of this city is due to its important location on the Lhasa-Ziling highway, and as the centre of trade for the entire nomadic region of N Tibet, which urban and farming communities refer to as **Hor**. There are strategic petrol stations, both civilian and military to the W of town, and to the S is the **Nakchu Race Course**, where an important horse festival is held each year, commencing on 10 August. More than 10,000 visitors from the Lhasa and Nakchu regions attend the events, which also provide an occasion for traditional barter, and regional folk dances. The colourful appliqué tents which surround the race track, some of them larger than houses, are particularly impressive.

Within the town the crossroads is the commercial centre. Here there are grocery, textile, and electrical stores, as well as shops selling traditional crafts. Local industry is mostly a derivative of nomadic animal husbandry: dairy products and meat processing, and cashmere wool production (also including yak and sheep wool). The Chinese population is

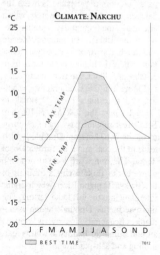

°C
CLIMATE: NAKCHU

MAX TEMP

MIN TEMP

J F M A M J J A S O N D
☐ BEST TIME

less pronounced in this high inhospitable climate (4,300m) than in other Tibetan cities. The mean temperature is 10° in mid-summer and -10° in mid-winter, and the oxygen content only 61%. Muslim shopkeepers from the Ziling area do have their own quarter.

There are two main temples in town, one Nyingma and the other Gelukpa, both of which are extremely active and well-supported by the local community. The former, **Zhabten Gonpa**, recently reconstructed and with outstanding murals, houses 80 monks of the Nyingma school.

● **Facilities Accommodation** The 3-storeyed *Nakchu Hotel* on 262 Senidong Rd, T 22424, 22739, cable 7391, has 250 beds (¥140/room). Accommodation is adequate, but the attached bathrooms lack running hot water, which has to be supplied by thermos bottles. The hotel has its own shop, karaoke bar, and two restaurants. **Places to eat** There are a number of small street restaurants: Sichuan, Muslim, and Tibetan.

From Nakchu, if you wish to continue travelling along the **Ziling** highway, retrace the route W out of town, and then turn N onto the highway. Those intending to take the **northern route to Chamdo** or visit **Driru** county should turn left (E) on exiting from the *Nakchu Hotel*, drive along the dirt track which leads out of town, and across the **Langlu La** pass (4,300m), through **Khormang** township, and via the **Jangkhu La** pass (4,700m) to **Shakchuka**. The distance from Nakchu to Khormang is 49 km, and from Khormang to Shakchuka township, another 49 km.

AMDO COUNTY
ཨ་མདོ
安多县 Amdo

Population: 9,289   Area: 22,159 sq km

The Ziling highway continues NW from Nakchu, following the valley of its source tributary upstream to **Tsaring** (40 km), and thence to **Draknak**, the capital of Amdo county, which is located to the NE of **Lake Tsonak**, the fabled source of the Nak-chu branch of the Salween River. This town is 98 km from Tsaring on a side-road, which leaves the Ziling highway after 81 km. At an altitude of 4,600m, Draknak is even more inhospitable than Nakchu. Nonetheless, it is an important crossroads town.

From here, a westerly route (see above, page 386) cuts across the exposed saltpans and lakes of the **Jangtang Plateau** to **Senge Tsangpo**, near Mt Kailash (1,333m). The main highway runs N to cross the **Dang-La pass** (5,220m), a watershed between the Salween and Yangtze headwaters, which also marks the present-day boundary between the Tibetan Autonomous Region and Qinghai province. The Dangla mountains, where the highest peaks range from 5,700m to 6,300m, are rich in minerals, including iron-ore, coal, graphite, asbestos, and soapstone. From Draknak to Dang La pass the distance is 106 km. Before reaching the pass, there is a turn-off on the W, 67 km from Draknak, which leads to the coal mines at **Tumen Dosol Terka**. The mines are located near the source of the **Trakara-chu**, a tributary of the **Tsakya Tsangpo** River, which drains internally into the salt Lake Serling. The life-style of the Draknak region is nomadic. Economic activity is centred around animal husbandry, as well as coal-mining and salt-panning.

NYENRONG COUNTY

སྣན་རོང་

聂荣县 Nyainrong

Population: 12,637   *Area:* 7,259 sq km

DRIRU COUNTY

འབྲི་རུ

比如县 Biru

Population: 29,496   *Area:* 11,295 sq km

Nyenrong county is a large sparsely populated area to the S of the Dangla Range. It comprises both the sources of the **Shak-chu** and the **Sok-chu** tributaries of the Salween. The townships of Serkhang and Dzamar are to be found near the source of the Shak-chu, and those of Bezhung and Trawola around the source of the Sok-chu.

Taking the Ziling highway from Nakchu, after 11 km there is a turn-off on the right (N), which leads to **Serkhang**, the capital of Nyenrong county, 82 km distant. The watershed between the Nak-chu and Shak-chu is crossed at **Gyatsam La** pass, 38 km along this road. **Shachuka** is the name given to the barren upper reaches of the Shak-chu valley, which extends through both Nyenrong and Driru counties, as far as the confluence with the Nak-chu.

Taking the Chamdo road from Nakchu, via the **Langlu La** and **Jangkhu La** passes (see above, page 452), you will reach the township of **Shakchuka**, 49 km E of Khormang. Here the motor road cuts across the Shak-chu valley, which extends SE from its upper reaches in Nyenrong county to its lower reaches and confluence with the Nak-chu in Driru county. The road follows a tributary of the Shak-chu upstream beyond **Drilung**, and after 22 km there is a major turn-off on the right (SE), which leads into the heart of Driru county.

Taking this branch road, you will pass through **Chaktse** township after 39 km, and then cross the **Dam-ne La** (5,013m). The barren landscapes of the upper Salween tributaries now give way to a forested valley, passing through **Traring**, where the Ka-chu River comes in from the SW to swell the combined waters of the Nak-chu and Shak-chu. **Naksho Driru**, the county capital, is located 16 km downstream in the Salween gorge. Timber is the main industry and logging trucks can frequently be seen plying the road between Driru and Nakchu. The

region is characterized by small Gelukpa monasteries interspersed with those of the Bonpo, representing two distinct phases of religious propagation.

From Driru, there are two tracks leading towards **Pelbar** county in Chamdo district, which link up with the Central Lhasa-Chamdo road (see below, page 472). Of these, the SE track crosses **Zha La** pass (5,090m) after 27 km, and descends via Sentsha (after 35 km), and Benkar (after 8 km), to join the Kyil-chu tributary of the Salween. It then heads due E to **Sateng** township in Chamdo district, 59 km distant, where the Kyil-chu converges with the Salween. The other track is a trekking route, which heads E from **Naksho Driru**, following the main Salween gorge, through **Bompen** and **Chamda**, and on downstream to Sateng. The forests of this middle Salween region are delightful but rarely visited.

SOK COUNTY
སོག་རྫོང་

索县 Sog Xian

Population: 20,331   Area: 5,839 sq km

If you continue due E on the main Chamdo road from Nakchu and Shachuka, without taking the Driru turn-off, after 35 km, the road soon crosses the **Gang La** pass (4,811m), which forms a watershed between the Shak-chu and Sok-chu. A second slightly lower pass named **Shara La** (4,744m) quickly follows, and the road then descends to join the Sok-chu valley above **Nyinpa** (72 km).

Sok Tsanden Zhol

Sok Tsanden Zhol, the county town, is located some 22 km upstream from Nyinpa within the Sok-chu valley. The terrain here is arid and barren. The lower reaches of the Sok-chu valley are administered from this town (whereas the upper reaches are within the neighbouring county of Hor Bachen).

● **Facilities** The *Yigzam Guesthouse* has clean rooms (¥14/bed) adjoining a small compound. Barking dogs are unavoidable at night. There is a good Sichuan restaurant, NE of the guesthouse, on the main road.

Sok Tsanden Gonpa

As you drive into town from Nakchu and Shakchuka, you will notice across the

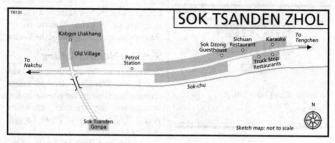

TIB130

SOK TSANDEN ZHOL

Kabgye Lhakhang

Old Village

To Nakchu

Petrol Station

Sok Dzong Guesthouse

Sichuan Restaurant

Karaoke

To Tengchen

Truck Stop Restaurants

Sok-chu

Sok Tsanden Gonpa

N

Sketch map: not to scale

river the hilltop Gelukpa monastery of **Sok Tsanden Gonpa**, which was founded by the Mongol chieftain Gushi Qan Tendzin Chogyel during the 17th century. Prior to the civil war between Lhasa and Zhigatse, the region had been a stronghold of the Bon religion. The recently renovated temple, which once housed 600 monks, is currently home to 200 monks. The main images in the assembly hall are of Shakyamuni, Tara, and Tsongkhapa with his followers. In the upper storey, there is a renowned sandalwood image of Avalokiteshvara, from which the monastery acquired its name ('tsanden' means sandalwood); and other images including Padmasambhava. The protector shrine is dedicated to Shridevi, and adjacent to it is the residence of the incumbent lama Kangyur Rinpoche. On the lowest level, there is a *mani* wheel chamber.

Kabgye Lhakhang
Southwest of Sok Tsanden Gonpa, on the W side of the Sok-chu, within the old quarter of town, is the Nyingmapa temple known as **Kabgye Lhakhang**. This shrine was founded in 1169 by the renowned treasure-finder Nyangrel Nyima Ozer (1136-1204). Following its destruction by Gushi Qan's Mongol army in the 17th century, it was restored by *terton* Nyima Drakpa. There are 30 married *mantrins* now living around the temple, where the main spiritual practices followed are all derived from the *terma* traditions, including Nyangrel's *Kabgye Deshek Dupa*, the *terma* doctrines of Nyima Drakpa, the *Lama Gongdu* of Sangye Lingpa, and the *Rigdzin Dupa* of Jigme Lingpa. The temple is in need of further funds to complete its restoration.

Further downstream below Nyinpa, a trail leads towards the confluence of the Sok-chu and Salween at **Shamchu**. The townships in the SE of the county include Chungpa and **Chamda**, where there are six cave hermitages associated with Padmasambhava. One of these, **Dorje Sherdzong**, has a cave temple complex. Rongpa township in the extreme E of the county will be described along with Hor Bachen, since it follows Hor Bachen on the motor road.

BACHEN COUNTY

སྒ་ཆེན

巴青县 Baqen

Population: 23,918   Area: 13,738 sq km

Bachen county, more properly known as **Hor Bachen**, comprises the upper reaches of the Sok-chu and its feeder rivers, the Bon-chu and Bachen-chu, all three of which converge above **Gurkhuk**. The county capital is located at **Tartang**, 37 km NE of Sok Dzong on the Chamdo road, and a short distance beyond **Patsang Monastery** (Yeta).

Tartang

This area was formerly the centre of the **Hor Jyade** camper groups, who successfully maintained their nomadic lifestyle and relative independence until the present century. A large horse-festival is held on the **Tartang** plain in summertime; and the Bon tradition survives, alongside a Gelukpa nunnery.

● **Facilities** The town has both civilian and military guesthouses, a petrol station, a few shops, and a small roadside restaurant cum tea-house.

The townships within Bachen county are located in the upper reaches of the various feeder rivers: **Bonsok** on the Bonchu, **Bachen** township (not to be confused with Bachen county town at Tartang) on the Sok-chu, **Tsek-ne** on the Bachen-chu, and **Chang-me** on the Ye-chu.

Trekking North of Tartang

Trekking routes lead up these river valleys to the **Dangla** watershed range, crossing the Salween-Yangtze watershed into present day Qinghai (see below, page 570). Among these **Trawo La** pass (4,930m) crosses directly from the Sok-chu valley, and **Tsek-ne La** (5,140m) from the Bachen-chu valley.

The main road East of Tartang

Taking the main **Chamdo highway**, 44 km E of Tartang, at **Yangada**, the road crosses yet another tributary of the Salween, which flows downstream through Chungpa to its confluence above **Chamda**. The road then cuts SE via **Chak La** pass (4,502m) into the **Rongpo Gyarubtang** region, where an important battle was fought between the Tibetan government forces and the Kuomintang in the early decades of this century.

Rongpo Gyarubtang

The township of **Rongpo Gyarubtang**, on the meandering Ri-chu tributary of the Salween, is 33 km beyond Chak La pass, at the base of the **Pugyel Gangri** snow range (6,328m). There is a small guesthouse with a congenial attendant, but lacking in electricity. SW of town at **Sertram Drak**, there is a thriving Nyingmapa monastery. The road now ascends the high **Shel La** pass (4,830m) on a spur of the Pugyel Gangri range. The forested alpine terrain of the middle Salween is visible to the SW. On reaching the pass, 44 km from Rongpo, there is a spectacular view of the **Dangla** range to the NE and the cragged **Tanlan Taweng** range to the SE.

Dangla Watershed
4,930m
Bachen-chu
5,140m
Chang-me
Tsek-ne
Bon-chu
Ye-chu
Bonsok
Yangada
44
Tartang
Sok Tsanden Zhol
4,502m
To Khyungpo Tengchen
37
33
6,328m
Rongpo Gyaruptang
4,830m

BACHEN

TIB541

N

Sketch map: not to scale

TENGCHEN COUNTY

སྟེང་ཆེན་

丁青县 Dengqen

Population: 38,911   Area: 11,175 sq km

On the descent from Shel La pass, the road enters the **Khyngpo** district of Kham, where the Bon tradition predominates. **Khyungpo Tengchen** county comprises the valleys of the south-flowing Ga-chu and Ru-chu tributaries of the Salween and those of their northwest-flowing feeder rivers, the Dak-chu and Kyilkhar-chu. The county capital is located at Khyungpo Tengchen, also known as **Gyamotang**, 269 km SE of Sok Dzong, 98 km from Shel La pass, and 143 km NW of Riwoche.

Routes from Shel La

18 km from Shel La pass, the Chamdo road cuts across the Ga-chu River at **Trido**. A trekking route leads off on the left (N) through the upper Ga-chu valley to **Gata** township, and the river's source SE of **Mt Lagen Zhushab**. Another trekking route leads due S from Trido to the river's confluence with the Salween in **Lhorong** county (see below, page 474). The **highway**, however, cuts SE from

Trido, following a tributary of the Ga-chu upstream to Sertsa (35 km), where the Ru-chu also flows in from the N and the Dak-chu from the SE.

Sertsa

This small township of Sertsa has several monasteries. Among them, the largest Bonpo monastery is **Sertsa Yongdzong**; and the largest Gelukpa monastery is **Sertsa Tashiling**. The latter is located across the **Tsuri La** pass (4,200m) from Sertsa township, and on the right (S) side of the motor road. Originally a Kagyupa monastery, Tashiling was converted to the Gelukpa school by the armies of Gushi Qan in the 17th century. It also has affinities with the Nyingma school, as evidenced by its main chapel, which contains large images of Padmasambhava flanked by Shantaraksita and King Trisong Detsen. The traditions of this renovated monastery which once housed 300 monks are being revived under the guidance of Tulku Ngawang Zangpo, who presides over a group of 80 monks.

● **Facilities** Sertsa has a government compound with guesthouse and dining facilities, a motor repair shop, and a petrol station.

Tengchen

Following the Dak-chu downstream from Sertsa, after 45 km the road reaches **Tengchen**, the capital of the Khyungpo district, situated in a wide cultivated

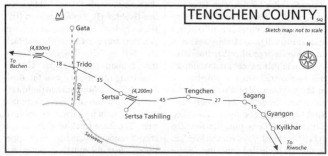

TENGCHEN COUNTY

Sketch map: not to scale

Gata

To Bachen — (4,830m) — 18 — Trido

Ga-chu

35

Sertsa — (4,200m) — 45 — Tengchen — 27 — Sagang — 15 — Gyangon

Sertsa Tashiling

Salween

Kyilkhar

To Riwoche

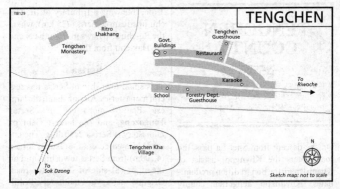

TB129 TENGCHEN

Sketch map: not to scale

valley, hemmed in by red sandstone hills. The old Tibetan village of **Tengchen Kha** and the county town of **Tengchen** face each other across the river, as if worlds apart.

The inhabitants of **Tengchen Kha** village are extremely hospitable, and display a remarkable sense of religious tolerance. At a Padmasambhava 10th day ceremony in 1988 attended by the author, Nyingmapa *mantrins*, Gelukpa monks, and Bonpo practitioners participated together with an exemplary sympathy. A branch road to the NW leads 25 km along the Zhe-chu valley to Zhezhung township.

Tengchen Monastery

The region of Khyungpo, as its name suggests, is one long connected with the Bon tradition; for **Khyunglung** ('Garuda Valley') in Far-west Tibet was an original Bon stronghold, and many later Bon communities also utilized this name. Most religious establishments in the region are Bon rather than Buddhist, and among them, there are two important monasteries situated side-by-side on the northern ridge which overlooks the town: **Tengchen Monastery** and **Ritro Lhakhang**. The former, also called Namdak Pema Long-yang, was founded in 1110 by Sherab Gyeltsen and Monlam Gyeltsen who hailed from the 'White

Lineage of the Chen family'. The third lineage-holder (ie the successor of those two) greatly expanded the community of practitioners around Tengchen and established the **Ritro Lhakhang** hermitage above the temple in 1180. The two monasteries have had long close connections with the Bon communities of **Yungdrungling** and **Menri** in W Tibet, and with those of the **Ngawa** region of Amdo.

Renovations began in 1986; and are still continuing under the guidance of Lama Sherab Gelek. Of the original vast complex of buildings, two chapels have been restored in each monastery. The **Ritro Lhakhang** comprises the **Serdung Chewa**, a chamber containing the reliquary of the second lineage-holder, Monlam Gyeltsen; and the **Serdung Chungwa**, containing the reliquaries of the six other early lineage-holders: Nyima Gyeltsen (I), Kunga Gyeltsen (III), Jinpa Gyeltsen (IV), Tsultrim Gyeltsen (V), Yungdrung Gyeltsen (VI), and Tsultrim Nyima (VII). **Tengchen Monastery** contains the **Nampar Gyelwa Lhakhang** (downstairs) and the **Residence of Lama Monlam** and the library (upstairs), which are finely decorated with frescoes of Bon divinities and *mandalas*. The **Ritro Lhakhang** also has an abbot's residential chamber, in its upper storey, where the murals depict scenes from the life of Shenrab, and a copy of the *Bon Kangyur*, recently reprinted in Chengdu, is housed. Formerly both monasteries had 300 monks each, but now the Tengchen Monastery has only 85 and the Ritro Lhakhang a mere 23.

Local information

● Facilities

In town, both the *Tengchen Guesthouse* (left of the square) and the *Forestry Guesthouse* (next to the school below the motor road) have clean but simple accommodation (¥10/bed, television inc). Hot water is provided in thermos bottles. A Sichuan-style restaurant and shop are attached to the *Tengchen Guesthouse*, and in the square outside the hotel compound gates, there are karaoke bars, pool tables, etc. The government buildings and public security bureau are located on a side-road to the left, which adjoins the square near the Guesthouse entrance.

Kyilkhar Lhakhang

Continuing along the main highway from Tengchen, the route follows the Dak-chu downstream through **Sagang** (27 km) and the valley of its feeder river, the Kyilkhar-chu, upstream through **Gyangon** (15 km). This region contains a number of large Bon monasteries perched on remote precipices, high above the motor road. At **Kyilkhar**, where the Kyilkhar-chu thrusts its way out of a long narrow red sandstone gorge, there is a large *mani* stone mound and an important branch monastery of Chamdo Jampaling. Two temples have been restored in recent years and there are now 300 monks. Inside are fine murals and images depicting Shakyamuni, Tsongkhapa flanked by his foremost students, Green Tara, White Tara, and three meditational deities: Guhyasamaja, Carasamvara, and Vajrabhairava.

Rotung Gonpa

This monastery of the Karma Kagyu school, adjacent to Kyilkhar Lhakhang, is currently undergoing renovation. Images include Mahakarunika, flanked by Padmasambhava and Vajrakila; and there are tangkas depicting the Karmapas. Presently there are 60 monks at Rongtung. Beyond Rotung, the road bypasses the grassy knoll of Kharje and plunges into the **Kyilkhar gorge**. The red sandstone walls rise sharply on both banks of the river. Only in the summer months is there evidence of vegetation. A hydro-electric power station has been constructed at **Meru** within the gorge.

RIWOCHE COUNTY

རི་བོ་ཆེ

类乌齐县 Riwoqe

Population: 24,807   Area: 5,699 sq km

Riwoche county extends from the **Dzekri La** pass (4,809m), which forms the watershed between the Salween and Mekong river systems, as far as the **Zhopel La** pass (4,688m), which divides the Dzi-chu and Ngom-chu tributaries of the Mekong. The county capital is located at Ratsaka, 143 km SE of Tengchen and 105 km E of Chamdo.

Kharmardo

After passing through the Kyilkhar gorge, the highway to Riwoche and Chamdo crosses the **Dzekri La**, 66 km from Gyangon in Tengchen county. Then, descending abruptly into the **Kharmardo** valley, the terrain is utterly transformed. High altitude barren landscape is replaced by juniper and conifer forests, and rolling alpine meadows, carpeted with blue gentian and white edelweiss. To the SE large outcrops of red sandstone and white marble are strewn across the undulating slopes. After Kharmardo, the road drops due N into

the lower Ke chu valley at **Sibta**. A motorable side-trail follows the Ke-chu upstream (NW) from Sibta, reaching **Tramoling** after 55 km. The main road follows the Ke-chu downstream from Sibta to its confluence with the Dzi-chu at **Riwoche** (35 km from Dzekri La pass).

Takzham Monastery

In the lower Ke-chu valley, some 20 km before Riwoche county town, the road passes **Takzham Monastery** on the left. This was the residence of Takzham Nuden Dorje, an 18th century treasure-finder who discovered various texts hidden by Yeshe Tsogyel including her own biography, and who held the lineages of Katok Monastery and Choje Lingpa. The main temple, constructed in Zangdok Pelri style, contains images of Padmasambhava, Amitayus, Vajrasattva, and Shakyamuni, as well as several large prayer wheels replete with the mantras of Vajrasattva, Padmasambhava and Amitabha. The central throne bears a photograph of the present Takzham Rinpoche, who resides in Switzerland. The newly painted murals depict the Takzham lineage. Outside and to the left of the temple entrance there are sets of stupas symbolizing the deeds of the Buddha, both in traditional stone design and in the distinctive Khampa wooden style. A nomadic camper group occupies the grassland behind the monastery.

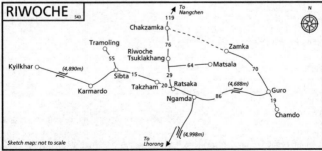

RIWOCHE 543

To Nangchen

Chakzamka — 119

Tramoling — 76 — Zamka

Kyilkhar — (4,890m) — Riwoche Tsuklakhang — 64 — Matsala — 70

Karmardo — Sibta — 15 — Takzham — 29

Ratsaka — 20 — (4,688m) — Guro

Ngamda — 86 — 19

Chamdo

Sketch map: not to scale

To Lhorong — (4,998m)

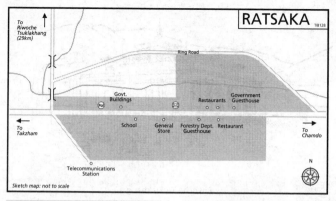

Sketch map: not to scale

Ratsaka (Riwoche town)

Entering the town of Riwoche (**Ratsaka**) from the W, you first pass the turn-off to the N which crossss the Dzi-chu bridge, heading in the direction of Riwoche Tsuklakhang. The paved main street contains all the buildings of note: the Public Security Bureau and government buildings are at the W end, while the two hotels are at the E end. The largest general store is on the S side, to the W of the hotels, and the Post Office is on the N side. Entertainment is minimal, being confined to open-air pool tables and a video parlour.

● **Facilities** *Riwoche Government Guesthouse* (Sizhung Nelen Khang) on the N side of the street, recently refurbished, best rooms upstairs, ¥8/bed and ¥20/room. The *Forestry Department Guesthouse* on the S side of the street has only 8 dormitory style rooms. There are a number of Sichuan-style restaurants and small shops on both sides of the street nr the hotels.

Riwoche Temple or Tsuklakhang

ACCESS If you wish to visit **Riwoche Tsuklakhang**, situated in the old Riwoche valley (which is the only reason for spending time in Ratsaka), you should first obtain clearance from the Public Security Bureau in town. Take the turn-off at the W end of the main street, which leads across the Dzi-chu Bridge, and then head N, following the Dzi-chu upstream on its

W bank for 29 km. En route you will pass a turn-off on the right, across the river, which leads through a defile to the **Matsala Coal Mines**, located on a prominant spur of the **Tanyi Tawun** range, 64 km distant. It is on account of these peaks that the valley received the name Riwoche. The track continues through **Nyinta**, and then opens out into a wide plain, where the resplendent Riwoche Tsuklakhang is visible in the distance.

History

The great temple, known as **Riwoche Tsuklakhang**, was founded in 1276 by Sangye On, a student of Sangye Yarjon, the third lineage-holder and abbot of the Taklung branch of the Kagyu school. Following the death of Sangye Yarjon, who was interred at Taklung in a stupa reliquary alongside his two predecessors Taklung Tangpa Tashipel and Kuyalwa, Sangye On took charge of the mother monastery for some time, but then departed abruptly for Kham, leaving Taklung in the hands of Mangalaguru, in order to fulfil a prophecy to the effect that he should found an even greater branch of the monastery at Riwoche. As such it became the main branch of Taklung in Kham, and according to Go Lotsawa, author of the *Blue Annals*, it had the greatest reputation among Khampa monasteries. From the time of its foundation, the Taklung Kagyu school was

Riwoche Tsuklakhang

considered to have upper and lower branches, the former being the original monastery at Taklung and the latter the Riwoche Tsuklakhang. The lineages associated with both are recounted in the religious history called *Chojung Ngo-tsar Gyatso*, composed in 1648 by Ngawang Damcho Zangpo.

The temple

The temple at Riwoche is physically imposing in the manner of the main temples at Samye and Sakya, with enormous tree trunk columns supporting its three storeys. It is painted in the distinctive black, white and red vertical stripes, which are a hallmark of the Taklung lineage. In the early 15th century Tsongkhapa is known to have praised the community at the Tsuklakhang for their expertise in the meditation practices of Hevajra and other deities. The surrounding community of practitioners, married or monastic, adhered to both the Taklung Kagyu and the Nyingma lineages. The Nyingmapa element in Riwoche has been especially strong since the time of Jedrung Rinpoche (Trinle Jampa Jungne), who was the teacher of both the late Dudjom Rinpoche (1904-87) and the late Kangyur Rinpoche (1888-1975).

Dwarfing the surrounding Riwoche village, which contains the government compound, the residence of Jedrung Rinpoche and other outbuildings, the temple is well-supported by those members of the local community, who are engaged in the rebuilding project and in spiritual pursuits.

The 3-storeyed temple has been undergoing restoration since 1985. The outer wall is surrounded by a pilgrim's walkway complete with rows of prayerwheels on all four sides. The temple is entered from the E side. The **ground floor** comprises the assembly hall with enormous larger-than-life size images on all four walls, separated from the hall by wooden lattices. Proceeding clockwise from the left you will pass on the E wall: Maitreya and Eight Stupas (symbolizing the deeds of the Buddha); then on the S wall: Shakyamuni, Vajrapani, Amitayus, Padmasambhava in the form Nangsi Zilnon, the Eight Manifestations of Padmasambhava, and another Shakyamuni. On the W wall, which is the **inner sanctum**, there are images of the Buddhas of the Three Times and two images of Sangye Yarjon. On the N wall are: Shakyamuni, Sangye Yarjon, Sangye On, Sarvavid Vairocana, Dipamkara Buddha, Sakyamuni, and Bhaisyaguru. Lastly, on the

E wall near the exit, you will pass Eleven-faced Avalokiteshvara and the protector deities including Magzorma.

One thousand small statues of Padmasambhava surround these principal images.

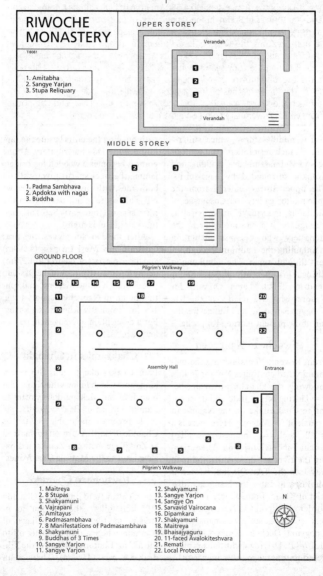

RIWOCHE MONASTERY

TIB081

1. Amitabha
2. Sangye Yarjan
3. Stupa Reliquary

UPPER STOREY

Verandah

1
2
3

Verandah

MIDDLE STOREY

1. Padma Sambhava
2. Apdokta with nagas
3. Buddha

2
3
1

GROUND FLOOR

Pilgrim's Walkway

Assembly Hall

Entrance

Pilgrim's Walkway

1. Maitreya
2. 8 Stupas
3. Shakyamuni
4. Vajrapani
5. Amitayus
6. Padmasambhava
7. 8 Manifestations of Padmasambhava
8. Shakyamuni
9. Buddhas of 3 Times
10. Sangye Yarjon
11. Sangye Yarjon
12. Shakyamuni
13. Sangye Yarjon
14. Sangye On
15. Sarvavid Vairocana
16. Dipamkara
17. Shakyamuni
18. Maitreya
19. Bhaisajyaguru
20. 11-faced Avalokiteshvara
21. Remati
22. Local Protector

N

MEKONG RIVER

The Mekong (Tib Da-chu, Ch Lancang jiang) is the world's 12th longest river, and the 7th longest in Asia, extending 4,350 km from its high altitude Ngom-chu and Dza-chu sources (4,900m) in the Tangula Mts of present-day Qinghai province, to its delta in Vietnam. The river has a total drainage area of 810,600 sq km. In its upper reaches, the Mekong flows through the deeply eroded narrow gorges of E Tibet and Yunnan for 1,955 km. Its waters have a distinctly greenish hue, except during the rainy season, when its flow is faster and turbid silt abruptly turns it reddish brown. Overall, the river has an annual sediment of 187 million tons. The lower reaches of the Mekong are wide, meandering for 2,390 km through the Khorat plateau of Thailand, Annamese Corderilla, and Cambodia, from where it eventually enters S Vietnam to form a wide delta.

The **middle storey**, which still requires much restoration, contains images of Padmasambhava, Buddha, and Ardokta surrounded by naga-spirits. The **upper storey**, entered from the open rooftop gallery, contains images of Amitabha, and Sangye Yarjon, as well as a reliquary of a late preceptor of the monastery, who was instrumental in maintaining the tradition through recent difficult times. The rebuilding at Riwoche is currently supervised by Tendzin Tulku, Lama Orgyan, Mr Ngadra, who is a relative of the late Kangyur Rinpoche, and Kunga Tre, the son of the present Jedrung Rinpoche.

Riwoche to Nangchen

From **Riwoche Tsuklakhang** the motorable road continues NW for 76 km, following the Dzi-chu upstream, before cutting NE to **Jikto** and descending to **Chakzamka** on the Ngom-chu branch of the Mekong. Here there is a small Gelukpa monastery called **Gozhi Tubden Dorjeling**. After crossing the river at Chakzamka, the road traverses the TAR-Qinghai border at **Shoknga** to enter the Nangchen district of Kham. Immediately above the border checkpoint is **Netengang**, the seat of the great Nyingmapa *terton* Chogyur Dechen Zhikpo Lingpa (1829-70). Driving conditions rapidly deteriorate as the road becomes a rocky

path hugging the cliffs beside the rapidly flowing Do-chu tributary. At one point it becomes a wooden log bridge, jammed between sharp canyon walls on both sides, with the river rushing below. **NB** This route is not passable in the rainy season (June-early Sept) or when the water level is high.

After the Do-chu gorges, the road crosses **Churi Meri La** pass (4,504m) and the triple pass of **Tsedri La** (4,277m) before fording a tributary of the Dza-chu (the E branch of the Mekong) and continuing on to **Nangchen** county town, 189 km from Riwoche Tsukla-khang. For a description of Nangchen, see below, page 535.

Chakzamka to Chamdo

From **Chakzamka**, there is also a trekking route which follows the Ngom-chu branch of the Mekong downstream to **Zamka** township. Below Zamka, the track becomes motorable as far as **Chamdo** (89 km). A turn-off on this road at **Zo** village, between Zamka and Sagang leads to the **Matsala Coal Mines**.

Riwoche to Chamdo

The highway from Ratsaka to Chamdo (105 km) follows the Dzi-chu downstream to the farming village of **Ngamda**, where a trail branches off to the SW for Lhorong county via the **Yik-druk La** pass (4,998m). There is an attractive Gelukpa monastery here, with a series of the Eight Stupas by its entrance.

At **Teda** the highway leaves the Dzi-chu valley and ascends **Zholpel La** pass (4,688m), at the southern extremity of the high **Tanlan Taweng** range. The terrain beyond the pass is a spectacular fusion of alpine conifer and deciduous forest. If you cross in the summer or early autumn, the rich diversity of the forest hues never ceases to amaze. On its descent the road plunges deeply through this forest to emerge in the Ngom-chu valley at **Guro** (sometimes written Karu), an important neolithic site, 19 km above Chamdo.

CHAMDO COUNTY

ཆབ་མདོ

昌都县 Qamdo

Population: 68,249   Area: 9,800 sq km

Chamdo (literally meaning 'river confluence') usually refers to the **city of Chamdo** (Chamdo Drongkhyer) which straddles the Mekong at the point where its Ngom-chu and Dza-chu branches converge. It may also refer to **Chamdo district** (Chamdo sa-khul), which is the administrative headquarters for 11 counties of Kham, extending from Tengchen to Jomda in the N and from Pasho to Markham in the S. In addition, it may refer specifically to **Chamdo county** (Chamdo Dzong), a triangular shaped wedge of territory, including the upper reaches of these Mekong branch rivers, as well as the Lhato and Menda areas, which lie respectively on the Ri-chu and Ke-chu tributaries of the Dza-chu. Both the county and district capitals are located in Chamdo city, one of the largest conurbations of E Tibet.

DISTANCES The distance from Chamdo to Lhasa is 1,066 km via Nakchu; and 1,179 km via Kongpo. The distance from Chamdo to Derge is 345 km; and to Kunming 1,789 km.

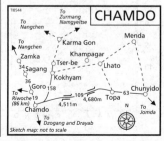

Chamdo City

Orientation

Approaching Chamdo city from Riwoche (105 km), you will reach the Ngomchu valley at **Guro** and follow the W bank of that river downstream to enter the city on **Gyelsung Lam** (Chotrika). Passing large military garrisons, the petrol station, and the Bus Station, you drive down into **Ozer Lam** (Daratang), where the *Chamdo Hotel* is located. The Public Security Bureau is to the N of the hotel, and the Chamdo District Government Compound is behind a high enclosure wall on the opposite side of the road. In this area there are a number of small Chinese restaurants and noodle bars. An L-junction at the lower end of this road leads into **Zetotang Lam**, at the top end of which is the entrance to the Chamdo District Government Compound, the Bank of China and the Post Office. Lower down on both sides of this street there are new glass-fronted department stores, schools, and electrical supply shops.

Two bridges span the Ngom-chu, the upper one being a foot-bridge (*Chaktak Zampa*) reached via an alleyway on the E side of **Zetotang Lam**. The second, the **Ngom-chu Suspension Bridge** or **West Bridge** (Nubkyi Zamchen), lies just above the river's confluence with the Dza-chu, and provides vehicular access for traffic heading to and from Derge (see below, page 518). Chamdo's main karaoke bar and discotheque is upstairs to the W of the street, opposite the approach to this lower bridge.

Crossing the Ngom-chu via the foot-bridge, you reach the peninsula of land between the two rivers, where the monastery occupies the high ground. Turn right and then sharp left into **Dekyi Lam** (Sarkyelam/Zetsongsing), which is the original commercial heart of the city. On the N (left) side of the street there is the Xinhua Bookstore, the Bank of China, the Chamdo City Government Buildings, the local police station; and a number of tea houses and coffee shops. On the S side (right) there is the Peoples' Cinema, and the open-air market (Tromzikhang), where Chamdo's stall-holders intermingle with Chinese traders. The costumes and coiffures of the people are a colourful spectacle in the market, but the diversity of traditional merchandise has diminished in recent years due to an increase in the availability of bland Chinese products. Look out for textiles, Tibetan books and the occasional trader who claims to possess antiques.

At the E end of the street, there is a T-junction, leading on to **Mimang Lam** (Gyelzam drong). Turning left and heading uphill, you now notice the Dza-chu River on the E (right). The road passes the **Chamdo Mentsixhang** on the left, and then runs due N as far as the **Dza-chu Suspension Bridge**, which leads NE out of town towards Derge. A lane on the left side of the road called Gyelkalam (Barongka) leads steeply to **Galden Jampaling Monastery** and the sky-burial ground,

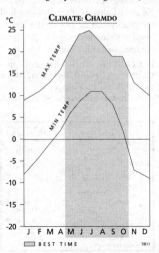

°C **CLIMATE: CHAMDO**

25

20

MAX TEMP

15

10

MIN TEMP

5

0

-5

-10

-15

-20

J F M A M J J A S O N D

☐ BEST TIME

passing the Armed Police Compound on the right. If you turn right at the aforementioned T-junction, and follow the Dza-chu downstream, the road connects with the Ngom-chu Suspension Bridge. On both sides of the street there are small restaurants, some of them Muslim owned.

Recrossing the Ngom-chu via the Suspension Bridge, you rejoin **Zetotang Lam**. Turn uphill to reach the *Chamdo Hotel*, or downhill to head out of town in the direction of Pamda, Drayab, and Markham. The **Tatsatang Zamchen** bridge leads across the combined Mekong waters to the Tatstang

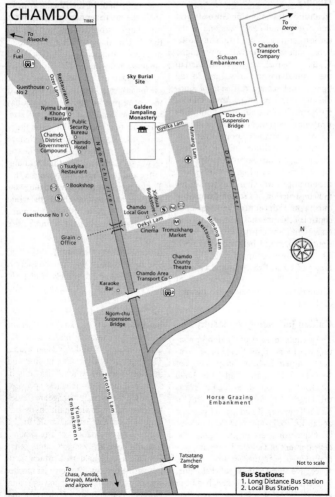

CHAMDO TIB82

To Riwoche

Fuel 🏠1

Guesthouse No 2

Ozer Lam
Restaurants

Nyima Lharag Khong Restaurant

Public Security Bureau

Chamdo District Government Compound

Chamdo Hotel

Tsudyita Restaurant

Bookshop

Guesthouse No 1

Grain Office

Karaoke Bar

Ngom-chu river

Sky Burial Site

Galden Jampaling Monastery 🏛

Gyelka Lam

Xinhua Bookstore

Chamdo Local Govt

Dekyi Lam
Cinema Tromzikhang Market Ⓜ

Chamdo County Theatre

Chamdo Area Transport Co

🏠2

To Derge

Sichuan Embankment

Chamdo Transport Company

Dza-chu Suspension Bridge

Mimang Lam

Dza-chu river

Mimang Lam
Restaurants

N

Ngom-chu Suspension Bridge

Zetotang Lam

Yunnan Embankment

Horse Grazing Embankment

Tatsatang Zamchen Bridge

To Lhasa, Pamda, Drayab, Markham and airport

Not to scale

Bus Stations:
1. Long Distance Bus Station
2. Local Bus Station

pasture. Continuing on the W bank, you will reach the Chamdo Cement Factory complex, located on the W of this road on the outskirts of town near **Chaka** township. **Chamdo Airport** is also located on this latter road, 128 km to the S, near Pamda.

History

Neolithic excavations at **Guro** suggest that the Chamdo area was one of the earliest centres of population on the Tibetan plateau. In **Drayab** county to the SE there are rock carvings attributed to the royal dynastic period; and in the light of the second diffusion of Buddhism the area became a stronghold for the Karma Kagyu tradition. The obvious strategic importance of the Mekong confluence at Chamdo combined with the relatively low altitude, and the excellent climate to generate a considerable population density. The high ground above the monastery was chosen as the site for the construction of **Galden Jampaling** during the 15th century; and ever since control of this area has been regarded as essential for the control of communications throughout Kham. Between 1909-18 Chamdo was occupied by the Chinese forces of Chao Erh Feng and General Peng, and later in 1950 the fall of Chamdo was a key even in the advance of the PLA into Tibet.

Galden Jampaling Monastery

The great monastery of **Galden Jampaling** was founded by Tsongkhapa's student Jangsem Sherab Zangpo between 1436-44. It formerly had over 1,000 monks and ranked alongside Kandze as the largest Gelukpa establishment in Kham. However, it had greater prestige and influence insofar as it was the oldest Gelukpa monastery in the region. The development of Galden Jampaling was maintained over the centuries by the successive incarnations of Pakpalha; whose father, Kuchor Tokden, had been an actual disciple of Tsongkhapa. The other important incarnate successions associated with the monastery were those of Phakpalha's own disciples Zhiwalha and Chakra Tulku.

The original monastery was destroyed in 1912-13 by Chao Erh Feng, who had captured the town in 1909. After the Chinese retreat following the seige of Chamdo by the Tibetan army in 1917, the monastery was rebuilt, but it was again destroyed during the Cultural Revolution, along with a multitude of precious artefacts – 800-year-old tangkas among them.

During recent renovations, the site of the monastery, which formerly occupied the entire plateau above the town, has been considerably reduced in size. There are four major buildings on the N and E sides of the compound which have now been restored: the **Gonkhang** (NW), the **Labrang** (N), the **Dukhang** (NE), and the **Lhakhang Nyingba** (E). The kitchen is located between the Dukhang and the Lhakhang Nyingba, while the quarters of the monks who now number 700, are mostly on the W and S sides of the compound.

Assembly Hall (Dukhang)

The largest building at the monastery is the wide 3-storey **Assembly Hall** (*dukhang*), on the right. Its red columns and silk pendants lead to the central throne of the Dalai Lama, behind which, in the **inner sanctum**, is an exquisite image of Shakyamuni flanked by his foremost students Shariputra and Maudgalyayana. The altar below this image is in silver and inscribed with the words "Shakyamuni, supreme guide and matchless speaker". To the left of this central image are statues representing the earlier traditions of Padmasambhava and Atisha, while to the right are representations of Tsongkhapa, Jangsem Sherab Zangpo and other Gelukpa lineage-holders. **Upstairs** there is a shrine dedicated to Jowo Rinpoche, containing an image of Jowo Yizhin Norbu, flanked by Maitreya and

Guhyasamaja. The body of the Jowo image is original but the head has recently been replaced. Smaller images of Pakpalha are interspersed with these. There is also an inner chamber on this level where the present Dalai Lama resided in 1954 en route for Beijing.

The ante-chamber has posters describing the daily and monthly rituals performed at Chamdo.

Old Temple (Lhakhang Nyingba)

To the right of the assembly hall and beyond the kitchen is the old temple (**Lhakhang Nyingba**), which is presently used as a college for dialectics (*tsenyi tratsang*). Inside (from left to right) are images depicting Vaishravana, Manjushri (standing), Four-armed Avalokiteshvara, Tsongkhapa flanked by his foremost students, Eleven-headed Avalokiteshvara, and Amitayus.

The Protector Temple (Gonkhang)

Situated to the left (NW side) of the compound, the **Gonkhang** contains images of Bhairava flanked by Four-armed Mahakala and Dharmaraja on the inner wall, Kongtsun Demo, Shridevi, and Guhyasamaja on the W wall, and Magzorma and the tutor of Phakpalha on the E wall. Upstairs is the library.

The Master's Residence (Labrang)

The recently restored residence of Phakpalha and the other main tulkus of Chamdo is a tall 4-storey building set further back to the N of the compound, between the Gonkhang and the Assembly Hall. This building, under reconstruction since 1988, was formerly known as the Palace of Chamdo. The present Phakpalha incarnation, Gelek Namgyel, resides in Lhasa.

Festivals

For the dates of certain traditional Tibetan festivals, see below, **Information for visitors**, see page 19.

Local information

● Accommodation

C *Chamdo Hotel (Qamdo Hotel)*, T 21231 (reception), T 21026 (manager), has 4 storeys, with comfortable rooms, attached bathrooms, and television, ¥50/bed, hot water supplied in thermos bottles, no elevator, mediocre but expensive Chinese restaurant, large rooms available for special functions.

D *Guesthouse Number 2*, adjacent to the Bus Station, no attached baths, but communal showers are available.

● Places to eat

There are many street restaurants in the upper and lower parts of town. For excellent Sichuan dishes, try *Nyima Lharag Khang*, opp the *Chamdo Hotel*; and for noodles and Chinese dumpling dishes, the *Tsudyita Restaurant*, at the top of Zetotang Lam.

● Banks & money changers

Bank of China, Dekyi Lam; subsidiary branch on Zetotang Lam.

● Entertainment

The main discotheque cum karaoke club is located on Zetotang Lam, opp the Ngom-chu Suspension Bridge. The *Peoples' Cinema* is located in Dekyi Lam (Sarkyelam/Zetsongsing), W of the open-air market.

● Hospitals & medical services

Peoples' Hospital, T 21745 (direct), T 22965 (in-patients), T 22947 (out-patients); *Military Hospital*; *Chamdo Hospital of Tibetan Medicine*.

● Post & telecommunications

Post Office: on Zetotang Lam, adjacent to Chamdo District Government Buildings.

● Shopping

Books: are available at *Xinhua Bookstore* on Dekyi Lam.

Handicrafts: for textiles, Khampa knives, metalwork, jewellery, and traditional religious or household artefacts, try the open-air market (Tromzikhang).

Modern goods: there are large glass-fronted department stores in Zetotang Lam, selling groceries, electrical goods, ready-to-wear clothes, and so forth. Official currency exchange is impossible; but a few market traders will accept payment in US dollars. It is best to change currency in Lhasa, Kunming, or Chengdu long before reaching Chamdo.

Photography: print film and processing are available at the department stores, and smaller electrical shops in town.

Stamps: are available at PO, on Zetotang Lam, nr Chamdo District Government Buildings.

● **Tour companies & travel agents**
Chamdo Travel Service, Chamdo Hotel.

● **Useful addresses**
Police & public security: Chamdo District Police and Public Security Bureau, Ozer Lam, nr *Chamdo Hotel*; **Chamdo City Police**, Dekyi Lam, opp open-air market.

● **Transport**
Road Most visitors to Chamdo, whether arriving via Lhasa, Kunming or Chengdu, will have their transportation organized by the travel services. Long distance car and jeep transportation is more easily available from Lhasa, but occasionally through the **Chamdo Transport Company**, nr Dza-chu Suspension Bridge. The public bus station is located on Ozer Lam, NW of *Chamdo Hotel*.

Air Chamdo Airport, located in Pomda township, 128 km S of town, has been recently constructed, the radar equipment having been purchased from Australia. There are twice weekly flights from Chengdu to Chamdo, but these are not available to foreign travellers at present.

Ngom-chu Valley

At the intersection above Guro, 19 km N of Chamdo, take the riverside road which follows the Ngom-chu upstream. The road passes through the townships of **Sagang** (36 km), where there is a small Gelukpa monastery, and **Zamka** (34 km), after which it forks, one trail leading to **Chakzamka** (see above, page 464) and the other clinging to the W bank of the river. Both of these trails eventually lead into the Nangchen district of Kham (in present day Qinghai), but they are only passable when the river levels are at their lowest: from late Sept until March.

Dza-chu Valley

Cross the Dzachu Suspension Bridge to the NE of Chamdo city, and take the road which follows the river upstream (rather than the highway to Derge). This

route is motorable for 158 km as far as **Tser-be**, passing through **Ridung** and **Kokhyam**, where the Ri-chu tributary flows into the Dza-chu from Lhato. Above Tser-be, a trekking trail continues following the river bank upstream to **Karma** township. En route, it passes through the important **Karma Gon**, the original Karma Kagyu monastery, which was founded in 1147 by Karmapa I Dusum Khyenpa (1110-93). Formerly, its 100-pillared Assembly Hall was one of the largest in Tibet, with 12 chapels and outstanding murals depicting the deeds of the Buddha and the history of the Karma Kagyu school. The inner sanctum contained enormous gilded brass images of the Buddhas of the Three Times. The central Shakyamuni image and the sandalwood throne were designed personally by Karmapa VIII. Little remains of these splendours.

Above Karma, the trail forks at the confluence of the Dza-chu and Ke-chu rivers, the former branch leading to **Nangchen** and the latter to **Zurmang Namgyeltse** – both in present day Qinghai (see below, page 570).

Lhato

One of the five formerly independent kingdoms of Kham, **Lhato** comprises the river valley of the Ri-chu and those of its tributaries: the Drugu-chu and the A-chu. The Ri-chu rises NE of Lhato township, in the stunning limestone crags of the **Tanyi Tawun** range (5,082m), which thrust upwards through the red sandstone landscape. It flows SE to **Lhato**, where it is joined by the Drugu-chu, and then due W to converge with the Dza-chu at **Kokhyam**. The most important monastery in the upper Ri-chu valley is **Dzodzi Gon**.

The A-chu follows a parallel SE course to enter the Drugu-chu, S of Lhato. In the nomadic grasslands of this **A-chu** valley, is the famous Drukpa Kagyu monastery of **Khampagar**, founded during the 18th century by Khamtrul IV Chokyi Nyima under the inspiration of his great predecessor Khamtrul III Ngawang Kunga Tendzin (1680-1728). Formerly there were two temples here and over 300 monks, with 200 affiliated branches throughout this part of Kham. An important college was founded at Khampagar by the late Khamtrul Dongyud Nyima.

ROUTES To reach **Lhato**, there is a trekking route from **Kokhyam**, but the easier road follows the Drugu-chu downstream from **Topa** on the main Chamdo-Derge highway. To reach Topa from Chamdo, follow the Derge highway on the E bank of the Dza-chu, and drive through Tayer township, and across the **Tama La** pass (4,511m), from where there are fine views of the city. A second pass, **Jape La** (4,680m) is then crossed, offering a clear vista of the ranges around Lhato and Nangchen (N) and around Drayab and Gonjo (S). Descending from this pass you arrive at Topa township, in the grasslands of the Drugu-chu valley. The distance from Chamdo to Topa is 109 km.

Ke-chu Valley

Menda township is located in the extreme NE of Chamdo county at the confluence of the Ke-chu and the Kyang-chu. The Ke-chu rises in SE Lhato and flows NW in an arc to Menda on the frontier of TAR and Qinghai, where its waters are swollen by the Kyang-chu, flowing S from **Zurmang Dutsitil** (see page 536). SW of Menda, the river is joined by the Tsi-chu, which flows S from **Zurmang Namgyeltse**, and the combined waters then converge with the Dza-chu branch of the Mekong above Karma. The entire region bounded by the Tsi-chu and Ke-chu rivers, including Zurmang, is sometimes known as **Tsike**. The landscape is typically nomadic, interspersed by these fast-flowing Mekong tributaries. Historically, the Karma Kagyu and the Nyingmapa have both had a strong presence in Tsike over the centuries.

Two trails lead to **Menda** from Chamdo – one via Lhato and Pangri; and the other following the Ke-chu downstream from its source near **Chunyido** and via **Sibda**. Another jeepable approach can be made from Zurmang Dutsitil in Qinghai province (see below, page 536).

472

LHASA TO CHAMDO
THE CENTRAL ROUTE VIA LHARI

CONTENTS

The central route from Lhasa to Chamdo, which is not yet fully motorable, corresponds to the old caravan trail, which was followed by pilgrims and traders alike for centuries before the construction of the northern and southern highways. The route eastwards into Kham begins at Artsa township in Lhari county, and cuts through the Nyenchen Tanglha range at ShargangLa pass (5,037m) to enter the Salween basin. Artsa is accessible 202 km driving distance from Nakchu City, following the Nak-chu valley SE to Taksar, and thence across the Salween-Brahmaputra divide to Mitika

Trekking Access

Routes also lead to Artsa from Gyamda, Drigung and Reting. The trail from **Gyamda** (104 km) in the S follows the Nyang-chu upstream to its source and across the **Tro La** pass (4,890m) and the scenic **Lake Artsa**. The latter trails follow the **Reting Tsangpo** upstream through the townships of **Sebrong**, **Drakar** and **Sangpa**.

This ancient direct trading route to Kham passes through three present day counties: **Lhari**, which is administered from Nakchu, as well as **Pelbar** and **Lhorong**, which are administered from Chamdo. The overall distance from Artsa to Chamdo is 638 km.

LHARI COUNTY
 བ་ལྷ

嘉黎县 Lhari

Population: 6,512 Area: 7,483 sq km

The county of Lhari comprises the upper reaches of the **Reting Tsangpo River** (which eventually flows into the Kyi-chu at Pondo) and the feeder rivers of the **Yi'ong Tsangpo** (which eventually joins with the Parlung Tsangpo to merge with the Brahmaputra NE of Mt Gyala Pelri).

This sparsely populated nomadic area holds strong allegiance to the Nyingmapa tradition, particularly the teachings of the treasure-finders Sangye Lingpa (14th century) and Nyima Drakpa.

ACCESS 10 km S of Nakchu on the Lhasa-Ziling highway, there is a turn-off on the E, which follows the Nak-chu River downstream and then cuts across the **Shilok La** pass (5,100m) and the **Apa La** pass (5,140m) in quick succession to enter the upper Reting Tsangpo valley. Ford the latter river at **Mitika**, via the Miti Tsangpo Zamchen bridge, and then cross the watershed to reach **Artsa**, on the banks of the Zhung-chu. The county capital is located at **Takmaru (Lhari)**, 38 km downstream from Artsa.

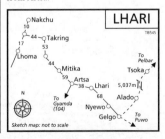

Below Takmaru the Zhung-chu merges with the Sung-chu (source above Lharigo), and thereafter is known as the **Nye-chu**. The road follows this river downstream for 68 km to **Nyewo** township. Below Nyewo, the Zha-chu tributary joins the river from the NE at **Gelgo**, and their combined waters are then known as the **Yi'ong Tsangpo**. The motor road presently does not continue beyond this point; but trekking routes follow the Yi'ong Tsangpo downstream into **Puwo** and the Zha-chu tributary upstream through **Alado** to the Brahmaputra-Salween divide.

Trekking

Taking the last mentioned trail, the Salween basin can be reached within 4 days' trek. From **Nyewo to Alado** the trail is particularly difficult and precipitous, passing through the gorge of the Zhachu rapids. Above **Alado**, the trail through the upper Zha-chu valley becomes easier, passing Ngodroke township and the monasteries of **Arig** and **Namgyel**. Eventually it crosses the watershed pass of **Shargang La** (5,037m) in the Nyenchen Tanghla range, and connects once again with a motorable track at **Tsoka** in the Salween basin. On the ascent of Shargang La, there are wonderful views of the high 6,000m peaks of this barrier range.

PELBAR COUNTY

དཔལ་འབར

边坝县 Banbar

Population: 22,565   *Area: 8,641 sq km*

Pelbar county is the thickly forested region of the middle Salween basin, extending from **Sateng** township in the NW as far as **Rayul** in the NE, and including the north-flowing tributaries of the Me-chu and the Gye-chu. To the S and W the county is bounded by the Nyenchen Tanglha watershed range. After crossing **Shargang La** pass, you rejoin the motorable road to Chamdo at **Tsoka**, below the village of **Orgyen Tamda**, where there was once an important Nyingmapa temple. The county capital is located at **Do Martang** (Pelbar) in the Me-chu valley, some 4 km N of Tsoka. Trekking routes also reach the capital from **Sateng** on the border of Driru county (see above, page 453) and from **Tengchen** county (see above, page 457).

The Chamdo road runs E from Tsoka, traversing the upper reaches of the Mechu and Gye-chu tributaries. En route it passes through **Pelbar** township (27 km), and **Lhatse** township (3 km), each of which has a Gelukpa monastery. From Lhatse a southerly trekking route also crosses the watershed and follows the Jepu Tsangpo downstream to **Puto**.

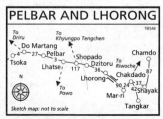

PELBAR AND LHORONG

TIB546

To Driru — Do Martang

To Khyungpo Tengchen

Tsoka — ○4—○27—○Pelbar — Shopado — Chamdo
3 — ○Dzitoru — To Riwoche
Lhatse — 117 — 36 — Chakdado — 87
Lhorong — 90 24 37 42 Shayak

N — To Powo — Mar-ri — Tangkar

Sketch map: not to scale

LHORONG COUNTY

ཀྲུའོ་རོང་

洛隆县　Lhorong

Population: 23,427　　Area: 6,728 sq km

The county of Lhorong is (in Tibetan terms) a densely populated area of the middle Salween basin through which the river completes its east-flowing course and turns S in the direction of Tsawagang. A trekking route follows the main Salween gorge downstream on the N bank from **Rayul** through Ngulsho and Shingrong townships, and thence to **Zhabye**.

The main central highway runs further S from Lhatse and crosses the Dakwang-chu tributary to reach **Shopado** and **Dzitoru** after 117 km. **Shopado** was formerly the seat of the Martsang Kagyu school in Tibet, and its main monastery was extensive, with 12 chapels and over 200 monks at its height. **Dzitoru** (nowadays known as Lhorong town) is the county capital. Here, the Gelukpa tradition predominates, its monasteries for the most part being affiliated to Chamdo.

Trekking

A 4-day trekking route follows the Dakwang-chu downstream from **Shopado** to its Salween confluence and thence via the Dak-chu valley on the N bank to **Khyungpo Tengchen** (see above, page 457). A motorable 55 km side-road from **Dzitoru** heads SE, initially following the Malatso-chu tributary, and then cutting across a watershed pass to **Nakchok**. Below Nakchok, the SE flowing tributaries: Dzi-chu, Pel-chu, and Dungtso-chu converge with the Salween, now itself plunging southwards.

Dzitoru to Chamdo

The main road from Dzitoru to Chamdo continues eastwards as far as **old Lhorong township** (36 km), and then fords the Salween at Zhabye Zampa bridge. After **Mar-ri** (90 km from old Lhorong) it crosses the Salween/Yu-chu divide, and passes into the border area of Riwoche, Pasho and Drayab counties.

The 18th century **Dolma Lhakhang**, the seat of Akong Rinpoche, who resides at Samye Ling in Scotland, is located near **Chakdong** in the upper Yu-chu valley, 24 km beyond Mar-ri. Within its vicinity there is a Padmasambhava meditation cave and a Bonpo power place at **Kulha**. A trail from here crosses the Yikdruk La pass (4,998m) to reach Riwoche; while a jeepable track leads S to **Tangkar** township in Pasho county (42 km).

The main road follows the upper Yu-chu for 37 km as far as **Shayak** township (in Pasho county), where it connects with the Chamdo-Kunming highway. From **Shayak to Chamdo via Kyitang** the distance is 87 km.

PO-ME COUNTY

 སྤོ་སྨད

泼密县 Bomi

Population: 27,981   *Area:* 16,072 sq km

The **Powo** region, nowadays known as Po-me county, includes both **Upper Powo** (Poto) and **Lower Powo** (Po-me). The former comprises the valleys of the Poto-chu and its tributary, the Yarlung-chu, which converge below **Chumdo**. The latter comprises the lower reaches of the Yi'ong Tsangpo and Parlung Tsangpo rivers which converge above **Tang-me** to join the Rong-chu and the Brahmaputra in quick succession, NE of **Mt Gyala Pelri**. The county capital is located at **Tramog**, 182 km beyond Serkhyim La pass in the lower gorge of the Parlung Tsangpo.

PO-ME (LOWER POWO)

The southern highway descends through a series of switchbacks from **Serkhyim La** into the flowering Rong-chu valley where **Tongjuk** (46 km) is located. There are spectacular views of **Mt Namchak Barwa** (7,756m) and **Mt**

The southern route from Lhasa to Chamdo is by all accounts the most scenic, and yet road conditions are often precarious, particularly in summer, when glacial melt and rainfall can cause havoc. Most drivers prefer to take the northern route via Nakchu and Riwoche. The route eastwards into Kham begins at SerkhyimLa pass (4,515m) in Nyangtri county, and traverses the present day counties of Po-meand Pasho The virgin forests and sub-tropical areas of low-lying Po-me county are unique on the Tibetan plateau. Trails also lead S from the highway into Pemako (Metok), one of Tibet's remote 'hidden lands' and largest wildlife reserves; and into Dzayul where the Lo-hit River winds its course through tribal areas to join the Brahmaputra in India. The counties of this region are administered from Nyangtri, with the exception of Pasho and Drayab which are administered from Chamdo. The distance from Lhasa to Serkhyim La is 452 km (via Kongpo Gyamda), and from Serkyim La to Chamdo 653 km. **Recommended itineraries: 4, 5 and 7.**

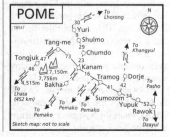

POME

TIB547

To Lhorong
Yuri
Tang-me 30
Shulmo
29
Chumdo
To Khangyul
Tongjuk 47
73 23
Kanam
46 7,150m
16
7,756m
Tramog 41 42 Dorje
To Pasho
4,515m Bakha
To Lhasa (452 km)
Sumozom 34
To Pemako
To Pemako
Yupuk 52
Rawok
To Dzayul

Sketch map: not to scale

Gyala Pelri (7,150m) to the E and NE respectively. Below Tongjuk, the road reaches its lowest point at **Taktra**, where the Rong-chu converges with the Parlung Tsangpo to flow into the Brahmaputra gorges.

Slightly further on, at **Tang-me** (47 km from Tongjuk), the Yi'ong Tsangpo and Parlung Tsangpo rivers converge. At Tang-me, a low-lying jungle settlement (1,700m), the road branches: a **trekking route** leads NW up the Yi'ong Tsangpo valley to **Dra-ke** and **Nyewo** townships. Crossing the Tang-me Zampa bridge, the **highway**, by contrast, follows the E bank of the Parlung Tsangpo upstream in a SE direction. After 73 km it reaches **Kanam** (Khartak), the traditional seat of government in Powo.

Kanam

The rulers of Kanam traditionally claimed descent from Prince Jatri Tsenpo, the younger son of Tibet's first 'mortal' king, Drigum Tsenpo, who fled here following the death of his father. Henceforth, the **Kanam Depa** was regarded as one of Tibet's princely states until the unification of the county was achieved by Songtsen Gampo in the 7th century. Special privileges were granted to the rulers of Kanam by the Yarlung Dynasty monarchs in recognition of their royal descent. The region maintained its independence from Lhasa in later centuries, despite the military intervention of 1834, which sought to quell civil unrest. Eventually, in 1928, Kanam was absorbed by the government of Dalai Lama XIII, and its ruler fled to India. In recent times, the most illustrious scion of the house of Kanam has been the late head of the Nyingmapa school Dudjom Rinpoche (1904-87).

At Kanam, the Khartak Zampa bridge crosses the Parlung Tsangpo to **Bakha**, where the Nyingmapa residence of Bakha Tulku is located.

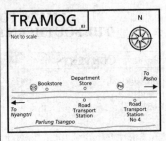

Trekking

A trekking route leads SW across the **Zholwa La** pass to the Brahmaputra gorge, and thence downstream to **Pemako** (see below, page 477).

Tramog

Continuing SE from Kanam, the highway crosses the entrance to the Poto-chu valley and reaches **Tramog** (2,743m) the county capital after 16 km, set deep within the thickly forested gorge of the Parlung Tsangpo. Timber is not surprisingly the primary source of wealth and industry. SW of town, and across the river, the **Galung La** pass leads SW into Pemako (see below, page 477).

● **Facilities** There are guesthouse and restaurant facilities in this town.

The forested valleys of Powo are intimately connected with Padmasambhava. **Gawalung** is the main pilgrimage site of buddha-speech in Kham. The great treasure-finders Sanggye Lingpa (1340-96) and Dudul Dorje (1615-72) also meditated in the region and discovered treasures at **Pukmoche** and **Takdzong** respectively. Treasure-sites (*terkha*) of Dudul Dorje are to be found, additionally, in the environs of **Mt Namchak Barwa**.

Upstream from Tramog, another trail fords the Parlung Tsangpo and leads into NE Pemako via the **Chendruk La** pass.

Side-valleys of the Parlung Tsangpo in Po-me

Continuing upstream from Tramog and

Khamog, the somewhat treacherous road reaches the entrance to the **Chodzong** valley at **Sumdzom** after 41 km. A motorable track branches off here, following the Chodzong Tsangpo upstream for 42 km to **Dorje** township. From here, a trekking route leads across **Kudza La** pass to **Khangyul** in the Salween basin.

The side-valleys of the Moglung-chu, Yupuk-chu, and Midpa-chu rivers are similarly accessible from the highway. Of these, the entrance to **Yupuk valley** is at the township of the same name, located some 34 km SE of Sumdzom. Above Yupuk, the road continues SE to the stunningly beautiful glacial lake known as **Ngan Tso** (see below, page 480).

POTO (UPPER POWO)

Upper Powo comprises the valley of the Poto-chu, and those of its main tributaries: the Dong-chu (W) and Yarlung-chu (E), which converge at **Chumdo**.

ACCESS From Kanam, leave the Parlung Tsangpo valley, and head N to Chumdo (23 km).

The **Dong-chu valley** is intimately associated with the activities of the treasure-finder Dudul Dorje. It was here that he discovered a *Guidebook to the Secret Land of Pemako*, and practices pertaining to the meditational deities Yamari and Bhairava. In the **Dechen Sangwa** cave in this same valley, he then discovered the text entitled *Gathering of the Entire Intention of the True Doctrine (Damcho Gongpa Yongdu)*. Below the cave, at **Dechen Tang** he established his main residence.

Above Chumdo, the road follows the Dong-chu as far as **Shulmo** (29 km) and **Yuri** (9 km), before cutting NE towards the **Zhartse La** pass for a further 30 km. From here, you can trek across the watershed to Lhorong county in the Salween basin. At **Yuri Gango**, there was a second temple founded by Dudul Dorje.

METOK COUNTY
མེ་དོག

墨脱县 Medog

Population: 5,906   Area: 6,787 sq km

The **Pemako** region, one-third of which currently lies within Tibet and the remainder within the **Arunachal Pradesh** province of India, is the name given to the wild jungle terrain of the Brahmaputra valley, SE of the foaming rapids formed where the river plunges 5,000m through the gorge between the E Himalayan peaks of **Mt Namchak Barwa** and **Mt Gyala Pelri**. Pemako is exposed to the full force of the Assamese monsoon (over 300 cm per annum), and its altitude is low (4,500m to 600m). The climate is hot, tropical and humid, and its virgin forests form one of the **largest wildlife preserves** on the Tibetan plateau. A haven for bears, wild cats, snakes, leeches, and countless species of insects, the region is even now extremely isolated. No proper motorable road links Pemako with the rest of the country. Most supplies are flown in by helicopter from **Nyangtri** to the county capital at **Metok**; and tractors sometimes

PEMAKO   *Sketch map: not to scale*

To Pe · 5.225m · 4.115m · 3.713m · Kanam · 16 · Tramog · Brahmaputra · Bakha · Pangzhing · Harmi · Takmo · Lake Bokun · N · Metok · Zhumo-chu · Patengtsa · Bipung · Rinchenpung · Digdong · Gongdu Dorsem Podrang · Indian Border

TIB548

negotiate the main trail from **Tramog** in Po-me, across the **Galung La** pass. The population is predominantly tribal, comprising the jungle-dwelling **Abor (Lhopa)**, who subsist as hunter-gatherers, and the **Monpa**, who also cultivate the land. Later influxes of Tibetan peoples from Kongpo and Powo have added to the population diversity, and the indigenous Abors have been pushed into peripheral border areas.

Despite the inhospitability of the terrain and its inhabitants, the Pemako region has long been regarded as one of the prime pilgrimage sites in Tibet. When Padmasambhava propagated Buddhism during the 8th century, he included Pemako at the head of a select number of 'hidden lands' (*beyul*), as an ideal environment for Buddhist practice in the future. Even now there are caves and *terma*-sites in Pemako associated with the great master and his 25 Tibetan disciples.

Later, during the 17th century, the treasure-finder Dudul Dorje discovered a pilgrim's guide to Pemako near his hermitage in Poto. Accordingly, the valley was identified as the abode of Vajravarahi, her head at **Mt Gangri Karpo** (NE), her neck at **Mt Dorjeyang**, her navel at **Mt Rinchenpung**, and her breasts as **Mt Gongdu Podrang** and **Pemasiri**. The gateway to the 'hidden land' is located at **Pemakochung** in the Brahmaputra gorge (see above, page 476). It was only during the late 18th century, that Pemako was formally opened as a place of pilgrimage by Gampopa Orgyen Drodul Lingpa (b 1757), Choling Garwang Chime Dorje (b 1763), and Rikdzin Dorje Tok-me (1746-97).

Trekking

Various trekking routes lead into Pemako. From Tramog the most important are via Galung La, Chendruk La, and Pokhung La passes, and from Kanam via Bakha and the Zhowa La pass. From Pe in Kongpo

there are most direct trekking routes from S Tibet, via the Tamnyen La, the Deyang La (3,713m), Buddha Tsepung La, Dozhong La (4,115m), and Nam La (5,225m). Of these latter passes, **Dozhong La** is the most direct, reaching Metok county town from Pe within 4 days. The best times to trek from Kongpo are in July or late Sept, but Pemako is a destination recommended only for pilgrims and explorers of great stamina and physical endurance.

Metok

Trek across **Zhowa La** pass from Kanam to reach the E bank of the Brahmaputra at **Pangzhing** township, and continue S to **Takmo**, where the Chendruk Tsangpo flows in from the E. The trekking routes from Tramog via Galung La and Chendruk La also converge here.

The main trail continues to follow the E bank of the river downstream to the county capital at Metok. A trail also follows the W bank from **Jarasa** down through **Muknak Gonpa**, to Dezhing township, and thence to **Metok**, which is at the low altitude of 760m. A trail leads W from this riverside track towards **Mt Namchak Barwa**, and Dudjom Rinpoche's sacred *terma*-site known as **Phurparong**.

Zhumo Valley

From the confluence of the Brahmaputra and Zhumo-chu at Metok, follow the latter upstream to reach **Mt Zangdok Pelri**, and **Rinchenpung Monastery**, where there is a sacred image of Hayagriva. A 3-day trek from Rinchenpung leads SE to **Gongdu Dorsem Podrang**, a wildlife sanctuary close to the de-facto Indian border, consecrated to the meditational deity Vajrasattva.

Bipung

Bipung or Drepung township lies SW of Metok on the E bank of the Brahmaputra. Within this township, at **Tirkhung**, is the birthplace of the late Dudjom Rinpoche (1904-87), head of the Nyingmapa school. Across on the W bank is the village of **Patengtsa**, from where a 3-day trek leads to **Buddha Tsepung La** pass. The valley approaching the pass is the location of the fabled talismanic lake **Chime Dutsi Latso**, otherwise known as **Lake Bokun**, which is set against the backdrop of a sheer forested mountain, its slopes harbouring temples dedicated to Vajravarahi. **Phukmoche**, a meditation cave of Padmasambhava, is also located here.

A parallel valley leads via **Harmi** and across **Dozhong La** to Kongpo. South of Bipung the trail follows the Brahmaputra downstream, passing through **Digdong** village and thence directly to the de-facto Indian border. The river from this point on is known as the **Dihang**.

DZAYUL COUNTY

ཛ་ཡུལ

察隅县 Zayu

Population: 17,142   Area: 19,693 sq km

Dzayul county comprises the upper reaches of the Dzayul-chu (**Lohit**), which is fed by two main sources: the Zang-chu (E) and the Gangri Karpo-chu (W). These tributaries converge at Lower Dzayul township before flowing S into Arunachal Pradesh.

Towards the SE of the county, is the valley of the Kyita-chu (Burmese: Nmai), a major source of the 2,170 km long **Irrawaddy** River, which rises at the Languela glacier in Dzayul and enters Burma via Yunnan province.

The county capital of Dzayul is located at **Kyigang** (formerly known as

Sangak Chodzong) in the Zang-chu valley, 258 km SE of **Sumdzom**, and 172 km SE of **Rawok**. Dzayul shares its S borders with India (which controls one third of its territory), Burma, and Gongshan county of Yunnan. The sparse population is both Tibetan and tribal Lopa.

ROUTE To reach Dzayul, leave the highway at **Rawok**, and drive SE across **Demo La** pass. The road follows the Zang-chu tributary of the **Lohit** through **Goyul** township (92 km from Rawok), and thence downstream to **Drowa Gon** (63 km) and the county capital at **Kyigang** (17 km). Here, the river changes course SW, and the motorable road follows it for 61 km as far as its confluence with the Gangri Karpo-chu at **Lower Dzayul township (Dzayul Rong-me)**.

The Gangri Karpo-chu, which rises in the snow range of the same name in NE Pemako, passes through **Upper Dzayul township (Dzayul Rongto)** and eventually merges with the Zang-chu at **Lower Dzayul township (Dzayul Rong-me)**. The only motorable stretch is between these townships (66 km), but there are also trekking routes leading NW from Upper Dzayul to **Pemako** and SE from Lower Dzayul to **Burma** and **India**.

The extreme E of the county comprises the lower Salween gorge, from the villages of **Golak** township on the Ralungchu tributary as far S as Tsawarong, on the E bank of the Salween. According to one tradition, it was to **Gyelmo Taktse** in Tsawarong that Vairocana, the great translator, was exiled during the 8th century; and where he taught the Dzogchen practices to his foremost students Sangton Yeshe Lama and Pangen Sangye Gonpo. At **Wa Senge Puk (Wapuk)** in **Tsawarong**, three successive generations of Dzogchen masters, who had received teachings from Vairocana, attained the rainbow-light body.

NB The Salween in this stretch is not motorable, but trekking routes follow the river downstream from Pasho county, through Golak to Tsawarong. Below Tsawarong, the trail continues downstream into Yunnan.

PASHO COUNTY

དཔའ་ཤོད་

八宿县 Baxoi

Population: 21,901   Area: 12,580 sq km

The highway from Po-me to Chamdo continues to follow the Parlung Tsangpo upstream through alpine forested landscape for 127 km as far as **Rawok** township, where it enters Pasho county. Rawok is located on the N shore of the blue lake **Ngan Tso**, dramatically girded by snow peaks. The ruins of the Gelukpa **Shukden Gonpa** lie to the S of the lake; and there is a turn-off for Dzayul in the SE. Keep to the highway, which then turns abruptly N on its 23 km ascent of **Ngajuk La** pass (4,468m).

Pema

Crossing this pass, which forms a watershed between the Brahmaputra and Salween river systems, the beautiful alpine forests recede; and the road follows the barren Ling-chu valley downstream for 67 km to **Pema (Pasho)**, the capital of **Tsawa Pasho** county, in the mid-Salween basin. En route it passes through **Chidar** township, **Tashitse Dzong** and

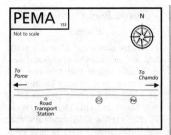

PEMA 153
Not to scale
N

To Pome ←
To Chamdo →
Road Transport Station

Rangbu Gonpa. At **Pema** there are simple guesthouse and restaurant facilities. The highway continues to follow the Ling-chu downstream from Pema to its confluence with the Salween at **Po**, bypassing a turn-off on the right (S) which leads to **Lingka** township. The ruins of **Nera Gonsar** monastery are visible here. After crossing the Salween via the **Ngulchu Zampa** bridge, the highway then rises steeply from the gorge through 180 switchbacks to scale the **Gama La** pass (4,618m).

Pomda

The descent on the far side of the pass is much more gradual, leading down to the rolling grasslands of **Pomda** in the Yu-chu valley. Here, 92 km from Pema, the southern highway from Lhasa finally connects with the Chamdo-Kunming highway. Pomda township (4,084m) lies 13 km further upstream in the wide Yu-chu valley. It is an important crossroads for traffic heading W to Lhasa, N to Chamdo, and S to Yunnan or Sichuan. A small Gelukpa monastery, named **Pomda Sangak Dechen**, was founded by Phakpalha Tongwa Donden as a branch of Chamdo. Destroyed by the Bonpo king of Beri in the 17th century, it was subsequently rebuilt by Phakpalha Gyelwa Gyatso. It had 70 monks, and was formerly the main attraction of the valley, prior to the construction of the highway.

● **Facilities** The town has Sichuan restaurant facilities and a transport station guesthouse, beloved by truck drivers. When the southern highway to Lhasa is blocked by landslides or snowmelt in summer, the trucks often remain stationary at Pomda for prolonged periods.

The gently sloping grasslands of the Yu-chu valley (the principal tributary of the Salween) lie in the highlands of **Tsawagang**, N of the Tsawarong (Salween) gorges. The new **Chamdo Airport** (4,300m) has recently been constructed here, 25 km N of Pomda and 128 km S of Chamdo, but it has not yet been officially opened to foreign travellers. Locals can fly to and from Chengdu twice weekly. From Pomda the combined highway follows the Yu-chu valley upstream to **Shayag** (59 km). A turn-off on the left (NW) connects with the old caravan trail to Lhasa via Shabye Zampa and Lhorong (see above, page 474).

The main road then cuts E across the **Lona La** pass (4,511m), which is a watershed between the Mekong and Salween river systems. **Kyitang** (Jyitang) village lies beyond the pass, above the Mekong valley, in Drayab county, and from here to Chamdo the distance is only 65 km.

DRAYAB COUNTY

བྲག་གཡབ

察雅县 Zhagyab

Population: 42,097   Area: 9,672 sq km

Drayab county extends SE from **Kyitang** on the Pomda-Chamdo highway through the valley of the Me-chu tributary of the Mekong and those of its small feeder rivers, the Leb-chu, Do-chu, and so forth. **Kyitang** township is distinguished by its sturdy houses with horizontal timbers: a typical feature of Khampa domestic architecture. Descend into the Mekong gorge, and follow the river downstream, reaching the Drayab turn-off at the Me-chu confluence after 10 km. The county capital is located at **Endun** (Drayab town), 34 km from Kyitang.

Returning to the Me-chu/Mekong confluence from Endun, take the right turn and follow the Mekong upstream on the highway. Soon you will pass the Dzi-chu (Riwoche) River confluence on the left (W) side of the road; and continue on to Chamdo. The entire 234 km drive from Pasho to Chamdo can be covered in a single day in optimum road conditions.

Sketch map: not to scale

Nyagre Rock Carvings and Images

In **Nyagre** district of Drayab county, there are ancient rock carvings and statues which suggest that this area had close connections with the Yarlung Dynasty kings of Tibet. At **Denma Drag** (now known as Rinda Dekyiling) there is a relief carving of Vairocana Buddha, said in the *Mani Kabum* to have been commissioned by Princess Wengcheng in the 7th century. An important inscription suggests that the image was actually fashioned in the time of his descendent King Tride Songtsen (9th century).

Drayab Endun (Mother Monastery)

In 1621, Drayab Kyabgon I Ngupe Trakpa Gyatso (1572-1638) founded the Gelukpa monastery of **Drayab Tashi Chodzong**, and unified the surrounding areas: three agricultural valleys including Nyag-re, and two outlying nomadic tracts. The original monastery became known as the **Magon** ('mother monastery') following the foundation of the **Bugon** ('son monastery') at Jamdun in 1640; and since that time Drayab county has comprised both the **Endun** area, under the authority of the Magon, and the **Jamdun** area under the authority of the Bugon.

Drayab Tashi Chodzong

The **Magon** monastery rapidly became one of the most influential cultural centres of E Tibet, developing under the guidance of the nine successive Drayab Kyabgon incarnations (also known as Tulku Chetsang) and the successive incarnations of Sangye Tashi, who are known as the Tulku Chungtsang. The monastery housed over 1,000 monks. It has been destroyed twice in the present century – once by Chao Erh Feng's forces and more recently by the Communists. Reconstruction is proceeding apace through the effort of the local populace and the development project initiated by Drayab Kyabgon IX who resides in Germany.

Of its former 32 temples, which symbolized the 32-deity mandala of Guhyasamaja, a 3-storeyed **Assembly Hall (Dukhang)** has been restored. On the ground level, the spacious **Jamkhang temple** contains images of Drayab Kyabgon IX Loden Sherab, Ngok Lekpe Sherab, Atisha, and the protector Ksetrapala, among others. The residence of the Kyabgon is on the 3rd floor of this building. Below the monastery the restored **Drayab Gonkhang** contains images of Dorje Drakden, Dorje Shukden, Ksetrapala (6 forms), and Dorje Yudronma, as well as fine murals depicting the 12 *Tenma* protectors.

Formerly the Magon monastery had 33 branches throughout Drayab county, including the nunneries of **Dolma Ritro** and **Evam Ritro** hermitages. Currently there are about 100 registered monks at the Magon, and approximately 900 unofficial monks.

● **Facilities** The town of **Drayab** (Endun), which lies at 3,660m, below the Magon Monastery, has simple guesthouse facilities. There are 3 small Sichuan-style restaurants on the main street, and small grocery stores. The government buildings and public security bureau are located within a compound at the end of the main street.

Jamdun

Further S at Jamdun, there is a life-size stone image of Maitreya, said to have been the central image of a geomantic temple dating from the period of the royal dynasty. Formerly, it was flanked by smaller images of the Eight Bodhisattvas, Princess Wengcheng and Minister Gar. In 1265, when Chogyel Phakpa visited Drayab, he identified the main image as Maitreya. Other authorities, such as Karma Chak-me, have stated that a Maitreya temple existed there during the royal dynastic period. At **Kyilechu Nyal**, there is a large stone image of Bhaisajyaguru, the medicine buddha; and at **Langrung-ne Tramo** there is a relief image of Avalokiteshvara, nearby a temple dedicated to the same deity.

Jamdun Bugon Monastery

The Bugon ('son monastery'), properly known as **Jamdun Ganden Shedrub Chokhor**, was founded at Jamdun, near the ancient stone Maitreya image, by Drayab Kyabgon II Ngawang Sonam Lhundrub in 1640. Formerly it housed 1,300 monks and had some 19 branches within the county, including the **Jorkhe Ritro** hermitage, which was once one of the largest nunneries in Tibet, housing 700 nuns at its height. The Bugon was also destroyed twice in the present century by Chao Erh Feng and the Communists. Current rebuilding is under the direction of Drayab Kyabgon IX.

ACCESS Jamdun is reached by jeep from Endun, via **Rangdrub** township. The other outlying townships of the county, such as **Khora**, are accessible on horseback from Endun or Jamdun. **Wakhar** can however be reached by jeep from Endun (27 km). **Khargang** township is reached 14 km from Kyitang, following the Mekong valley downstream.

CHAMDO TO KUNMING
DESCENT OF THE YU-CHU AND
MEKONG GORGES

CONTENTS

T he motor route from Chamdo at the heart of Kham to Kunming in SW China follows the great waterways of E Tibet and the contours of the high ranges dividing them. The initial section runs along the W bank of the Mekong as far as Kyitang and, after crossing the Lana La pass, hugs the Yu-chu through the grasslands as far S as Dzogang. Recrossing the Tsawagang range here via the Dungda La pass, the road then plunges down to cross the Mekong at Drukha Zampa. Reaching the E bank, it abruptly rises through the Markhamgang range and forks, the E branch leading to Batang (on which see below, page 495), and the S branch leading through Markham and Gartok Taking the latter turning, the road eventually rejoins the Mekong at Lagyab Sho above Tasakalho and follows its course downstream as far as Zhokounty (in present day Yunnan). On this section there are spectacular views of the Kawa Karpo glaciers (6,740m). From Zhol, it cuts SE across the watershed to enter the Yangtze river system, fording this mighty river twice: in Gyeltangand Jang Sadam. Finally, the highway leaves the Tibetan area and re-enters the Mekong basin at Dali.

Altogether, the highway traverses two counties which are administered from Chamdo (**Dzogang** and **Markham**), three which are administered from Gyeltang (ie **Jol**, **Gyeltang** and **Balung**), and the **Jang Sadam** (*Ch* Lijiang) region, before heading S to **Dali** and E to **Kunming** City. The overall distance from Chamdo to Kunming is 1,789 km. **Recommended itinerary**: 7.

NB This itinerary can be reversed, and those who have entered Tibet from Kunming have often been impressed by the proximity offered by this approach.

DZOGANG COUNTY

མཛོ་སྒང་

左贡县 Zogang

Population: 32,175   Area: 12,320 sq km

Tsawa Dzogang county comprises the valley of the Salween S of Pasho and those of its tributaries, the Le-chu and the Yu-chu (S of Pomda). At the intersection 13 km S of **Pomda**, take the left (E) road, which continues to run through the Yu-chu valley. Gradually the wide grasslands narrow, and the Yu-chu tapers into a forested gorge. After 29 km, you will pass on the left (E) a turn-off for **Meyul** township.

Temto

The renovated Gelukpa monastery of **Temto** (founded as a branch of Drepung Loseling) is one of the most impressive among the 13 Gelukpa monasteries of

Sketch map: not to scale

DZOGANG & MARKHAM

Yu-chu
To Pasho — Chamdo Airport 25
Pomda 13
Me-yul 22
Temtho 29
Tobang 22 — Sayul 50
Mekong
Wamda 43
To Dzayul — Kyil Lingka 40 — 5,008m / 3,900m — Drukha Zampa
6,090m — To Batang (104 km) 128
Salween
Drakyol 92 — Yu-chu
Gartok 63 — Bumpa
Bum-nye — Pangda 57
Jikdrong 47
4,470m
N — Lagyabsho
Tsakhalo
Salween — To Jol (112 km)
Yangtze
TIB571

this area. Notice the distinctive roadside stupas of the Yu-chu valley, which have a protective wooden pavilion.

At Temto, 22 km S of the Meyul turn-off, there are two branch roads: one to the E leading to **Sayul** (50 km) and **Sanor** on the Mekong, and the other to the SW leading to **Tobang** (22 km).

Wamda

ACCESS The distance from the Pomda intersection to Dzogang is 94 km; and from Chamdo 260 km.

Keeping to the main highway, continue S via Uyak to **Wamda**, the county capital, otherwise known as **Tsawa Dzogang**, which is located on a spur (3,780m) overlooking the Yu-chu, with a backdrop of forest. Timber is plentiful here and this is reflected in the local building construction.

The monastery of **Tsawa Dzogang Sangakling** was founded by Phakpalha of Chamdo, consequent on the conversion of various local Bon monasteries to the Gelukpa tradition.

● **Facilities** Spend the night here at the *Dzogang Guesthouse* (¥15/bed). The exceedingly long main street has a number of small shops and restaurants, government buildings, schools, and the inevitable karaoke bar, Tibetan-owned, and with a surprisingly sophisticated sound system. On the outskirts of town there is a petrol station.

South of Tsawa Dzogang the road branches. Keep to the main road, which leaves the Yu-chu valley to ascend the watershed **Dungda La** pass (5,008m) after 40 km, and enter Markham county.

If instead you continue along the riverside S of Tsawa Dzogang, the Yu-chu gorge deepens and a jeepable dirt road follows the river downstream for 92 km as far as **Drakyol** township, where there is a small Gelukpa monastery. Further S there is no vehicular access as the Yu-chu is abruptly forced to change course by the snow massives of the **Kawa Karpo Range**. The rapid river snakes back upon itself before flowing SW into the

Salween above **Tsawarong** (see above, page 480). Upstream from this confluence are the remote Salween townships of **Kyil Lingka** (Trung Lingka) and **Zha Lingka**, which offer trekking access to Dzayul and to Pasho.

MARKHAM COUNTY

སྨར་ཁམས

芒康县　Markham

Population: 106,706　Area: 12,258 sq km

Markham county is a prosperous and densely populated part of Kham, occupying the high ground (**Markhamgang**) between the Mekong and Yangtze rivers. The farm houses of Markham are for the most part large 3-storey detached buildings of whitewashed adobe and ornate wooden lintels. Trade has been a significant factor in its economy, in that the county straddles the crossroads from Lhasa (via Chamdo), Chengdu (via Batang), and Kunming (via Jol). The capital is located at **Gartok**, 168 km from Tsawa Dzogang, and 104 km from Batang.

Descent from Dungda La pass to the Mekong

Ascending the **Dungda La** pass (5,008m) from Tsawa Dzogang, the highway offers spectacular views of **Mt Dungri Karpo** (6,090m) to the S. A second but lower pass **Joba La** (3,908m) is quickly crossed after **Dempa**, and then the road zigzags down the barren sandstone ravine to **Druka Zampa** bridge, which spans the Mekong. A gradual ascent on the E bank via **Rong-me** township leads across **Lao-shan** pass (4,060m) into the alpine meadows of Markhamgang.

Gartok

The prosperity of the region is instantly apparent. Passing the turn-off for Batang, you soon reach **Gartok**. Its main attraction is the Gelukpa **monastery of Markham**, a beautiful yellow building containing in its inner sanctum a large impressive image of Maitreya, flanked by smaller images of Tsongkhapa and his students. Markham Monastery is affiliated to Drayab, on which see above, page 482.

● **Facilities** Stay at the *Markham Guesthouse*, where the superior rooms are ¥45 (¥15/bed) and inferior dormitory-style beds are ¥8 pp. The town has a number of Sichuan-style restaurants.

The townships of Markham county lying on the Yangtze side of the watershed will be described below (page 486).

Following the highway S from Gartok, along the Drong-chu (Markham Kyilchu) valley, you will pass **Biru** village and 63 km S of Gartok, at **Bum-nye** a turn-off leads E across the river to the farming village of **Pangda**, home of Lhasa's famous merchant Pangdatsang. Motorable country roads link Pangda with **Bumpa** township (57 km) and Jikdrong township (47 km). The **Bum La** pass (4,115m) above Bumpa was held by the Qing emperors as the boundary between independent Tibet and Chinese occupied Tibet from the mid-18th century onwards (although this had little meaning on the ground until the present century).

Staying on the highway, you soon cross **Hung La** pass (4,470m), and the road rejoins the Mekong valley at **Lagyabsho**, some 48 km N of Tasakalho. The descent into Tasakalho is impressive, overlooking the sheer Mekong gorge, and the road tunnels its way through precipitous cliffs.

Tasakalho

Tasakalho (*Ch* Yenching) lies 914m above the Mekong gorge, and the cliffs are so steep that the river cannot be seen from town! Near the riverside are the commercial salt-pans which give Tasakalho its name. The altitude here is relatively low (3,109m), and the climate is warm. Beware of mosquitos in summer. For centuries Tasakalho has been a staging post on the trading route from **Jang** (Lijiang) and **Jol** (Dechen) to Lhasa. In addition to the Tibetan Khampa population, there is a substantial **Jang (Naxi)** community. South of town there is a checkpoint, 12 km below which the road crosses the present day frontier between the TAR and Yunnan province.

● **Facilities** Stay at the *Tasakalho Guesthouse* (¥6/bed). There are small Sichuan and Tibetan-style restaurants in the market, which is well worth a visit.

DECHEN COUNTY

བདེ་ཆེན

德钦县 Deqen

Population: 65,231   Area: 7,164 sq km

Dechen county comprises the Mekong valley S of Tasakalho and the **Kawa Karpo** range (also known as the Minling range; *Ch* Meili) which divides it from the Salween. Its E boundary is formed by the Yangtze. The county capital is located at **Jol**, 112 km S of Tasakalho.

ACCESS The best seasons for driving from Tasakalho to Kunming are spring and autumn. In summer the road surface can be devastated by heavy landslides, necessitating a walk of over 2 days to reach **Jol**. Pack animals can be hired in Tasakalho.

DECHEN AND GYELTANG

Sketch map: not to scale

Hongshan

From Tasakalho, follow the E bank of the Mekong downstream to **Hongshan (Fuchang)** village (40 km), where there is a hospitable roadside inn and the *Markham County Naxi Guesthouse* (beds at ¥2/night). Continue downstream, crossing and recrossing the river, until reaching a point where the road rises high above the river and turns SE for Jol.

Jol

(Dechen; *Ch* Shenping) Pass the night at the county town of **Jol**, located on a steep hillside (3,480m), its slopes and climate strangely reminiscent of Darji-ling.

The main street, leading uphill from the hotel towards the open market has a number of small Sichuan and Yunnan style restaurants. In the wet season, the local economy is centred on mushroom picking, since the **Songrong mushroom** which grows on the river banks and in the forests is exported to Japan, where it is reckoned to have curative effects for the treatment of certain cancers. The monasteries of Jol traditionally belonged to both the Karma Kagyu and the Gelukpa schools. Among them, the most important is **Ganden Dongdrubling**. There are two nature conservation parks: at Kawa Karpo and at Padma.

● **Facilities** The comfortable *Dechen Hotel* has double rooms (¥200) and single rooms (¥80); but the electricity supply is unreliable. The attached bathrooms currently have hot water supplied in thermos bottles. The *Dechen Travel Company*, headed by Mr Tsering Nyima, have an office in the hotel (T 674500).

Mount Padma and Tongtaling Monastery

From Jol, the highway heads SE, crossing the watershed pass between the Mekong and the Yangtze, which offers to the S a spectacular view of the snow peaks of **Mt Padma** (*Ch* Baimang Shan; 4,292m). Descending to the Yangtze basin, via the large Gelukpa monastery of **Tongtaling**, where there are 456 monks, you reach the bustling town of **Baitseilan** (Benzilan). Here, there are plentiful Chinese restaurants.

Above Tongtaling, a **branch road** follows the W bank of the Yangtze upstream to **Derong** county in present day Sichuan (see below, page 499). The **main road** crosses the Yangtze and a SE flowing tributary, at a point made famous by the Long March. From here, it proceeds through Gyeltang county.

MOUNT KAWA KARPO

Across the gorge as you approach Jol, there are truly dramatic views of the **Kawa Karpo** glaciers (6,740m). The astonishing main glacier of Mt Kawa Karpo extends 11,000m almost to the level of the Mekong in the gorge below. From **Melli Dungjang** on the W bank of the river (accessible by ferry), there is a pilgrimage route to the snow range, revered as one of the 25 important meditation sites associated with Padmasambhava in Kham and Amdo. Specifically, this mountain symbolizes the body-aspect of buddha-speech. In the past it has been a stronghold of the Nyingmapa school. Vairocana gave teachings on Dzogchen to his followers at Tsawarong, to the N of the range; and there are branches of **Katok Monastery** in its environs. The most renowned figure in this lineage was Kawakarpowa Namka Gyatso, who, with his teacher Khedrup Yeshe Gyeltsen, expounded the Katok lineage throughout this extreme S region of Kham.

GYELTANG COUNTY

 རྒྱལ་ཐང་

中甸县 Zhongdian

Population: 135,086   *Area:* 11,869 sq km

Gyeltang county is a densely populated area, bounded on the W, S, and E by the bending course of the Yangtze, and comprising the wide fertile plain of the Gyeltang-chu, a major tributary of the Yangtze. Both the county and prefectural capitals are located at **Gyeltangteng**. 184 km SE of Jol, and 193 km NW of Lijiang. Nowadays 40% of the county's population is estimated to be Tibetan.

Gyeltangteng City

The large city of **Gyeltangteng** (*Ch* Zhongdian) lies at the heart of the Gyeltang-chu plain, at an altitude of 3,344m.

Hospital of Tibetan Medicine

The architecture of the city is largely drab and uninspiring Chinese provincial style. Three buildings do however stand out. Among these, the **Hospital of Traditional Tibetan Medicine** located behind the hotel is one of the largest in Tibet. Over 4,800 species of flora, including diverse types of azelia and meconopsis, grow within the prefecture, and many of these have medicinal useage.

The Old Temple

The **Assembly Hall of the 'Old Temple'** is now preserved as a Memorial to the Long March of the Red Army. Tibetan handicrafts are available, particularly the azelia wooden bowls, silver ornaments, and embroidered covers which are made locally.

Gyeltang Sungtseling Monastery

By far the most important site within the valley is **Gyeltang Sungtseling Monastery**, which is the largest Tibetan Buddhist complex in the prefecture, currently housing 600-700 monks. Located some 8 km from the city on an isolated ridge, it has the appearance of a small monastic town. The monastery was originally constructed during the 17th century at the advice of Dalai Lama V, and it traditionally comprised an assembly hall flanked by eight residential colleges (*khangtsang*).

Recently, the **Assembly Hall** and the **Drayab Khangtsang** have been renovated. The former (Dukhang) has an 80-pillared chamber, containing a teaching throne and a series of images depicting Tsongkhapa and his students,

---

NATURE PRESERVES OF GYELTANG COUNTY

Two roads lead from Gyeltangteng. One heads due N to **Wengshui** on the present-day Sichuan border, and thence to **Chaktreng** (see below, page 498), the other is the Kunming highway, which runs SW to **Jang Sadam** (Lijiang). The former is characterized by rich nomadic grasslands of Zhado and Mikzur, and the latter by the spectacular terrain of the Yangtze bend. The landscape of the Yangtze region includes the **Lake Beta Tso** and **Balgo forest nature parks**, and the **Hapa snow range** (5,396m), below which is the renowned '**tiger-leaping gorge**' (*Tib* Takchong Gak). Here the foaming Yangtze rapids cascade 3,250m down a precipitous ravine sloped at an angle of 75-80°. The spectacle is alluring for tourists, but arrange to go with a local guide, since rock slides and sheer cliffs are a hazard for the unprepared traveller. Another attraction is the **Chukar limestone platform** (*Ch* Baishui), where the ridge formation resembles a terraced field or tiers of jade and silver.

Dalai Lama V, and three past lamas of the monastery (one being the late Kangyur Rinpoche). The **upper storey** has a gallery overlooking the main hall, and in its NW corner a protector chapel with a large image of Dharmaraja.

The **Drayab Khangtsang** contains images of Tsongkhapa flanked by his students, and the mundane protector deities Gyel, Se, and Tsen. **Upstairs** is a room where a team of seamstresses are engaged in prepared brocade hangings and ceremonial dance costumes for use at the monastery.

● **Facilities** Accommodation is available at the spacious *Dechen Guesthouse* (¥120/room; ¥60/bed). Cheap restaurants are plentiful on the main street outside the hotel; and here you will also find the government buildings, public security bureau, bookshop and post office.

BALUNG COUNTY

འབའ་ལུང་

维西县 Weixi

Population: 46,974   Area: 1,529 sq km

Balung county occupies the Mekong valley due S of Dechen county. It is a region of great ethnic diversity, the dominant group being the Li (*Ch* Lizu), intermingled with Jang (Naxi), Tibetan, and Han Chinese, amongst others. Terraced farming is the mainstay of the economy here. The county capital is located at **Balung**, known in Naxi language as **Nyinak** and in Chinese as Baohezhen, in the extreme S of the county; and a road connects the capital with Jol, following the E bank of the Mekong. The most important site in Balung is the meditation cave associated with the Chan Buddhist master **Bodhidharma**; as well as the temple of **Shougou** and the ruins of **Gedeng**.

JANG SADAM

འཇང་ས་དམ

(*Chinese name* Lijiang) **Jang Sadam** is the Tibetan name for the narrow peninsula bounded on three sides by the bend of the Yangtze River, to the SE of Gyeltang. The ancient kingdom of Jang Sadam, where the population is predominantly **Naxi** (*Tib* Jang) was for 253 years of its history directly absorbed within the Tibetan Empire from the reign of King Songtsen Gampo onwards, ie from 649 until the disintegration which followed the assassination of Langdarma in 902. Thirteen successive kings of Jang, who ruled from **Bumishi**, were regarded with fraternal respect by the Tibetan monarchs in recognition of their ethnic affinity.

Later, during the Yuan Dynasty (13th century), the capital of Jang was moved

LIJIANG: GATEWAY TO SOUTH-EASTERN TIBET

Travellers arriving in Lijiang from E Tibet are liable to experience culture shock, in that this is the first place on the itinerary completely open to unmonitored individual travel. Package tourists and backpackers come here in great numbers. For travellers intending to visit E Tibet or travel through E Tibet to Lhasa, the advantage of starting here is that it is now possible to fly directly to Lijiang from Hong Kong and principal Chinese cities. **Gyeltang** in SE Kham is therefore only 1 days' drive from Lijiang Airport!

from Bumishi to **Lijiang** by Qubilai Qan; and Tibetan Buddhist influence on the indigenous animism of the Jang people gradually prevailed. The main beneficiaries of this early missionary activity were the Karma Kagyu and the Katokpa branch of the Nyingma school. During the Ming Dynasty, the authority of the successive kings of Jang Sadam was officially recognized; and their influence even spread N into the Dechen area of Kham and Muli. Presently, the majority of **Jang (Naxi)** people reside in the Naxi Autonomous Prefecture of Yunnan county (*Pop* 1,041,676; *Area* 19,594 sq km), which has its capital at Lijiang, but there are also sizeable minority groups as far N as Tasakalho in Markham county of TAR.

Lijiang City

Despite its status as the Naxi capital and the vigorous promotion of the local culture by the Naxi governor of Yunnan, the predominant influence here is clearly Chinese. The exception are the old narrow cobbled streets of the traditional market which are an obvious attraction for visitors.

Bumishi (Baisha) Monastery

Also known as **Liu Lidian Temple** in Chinese ('Coloured Glaze Temple'), the monastery of **Bumishi** stands at the site of the former capital of the Naxi Kingdom on the outskirts of Lijiang. The present building was constructed somewhat later between 1385-1619, in Chinese style. There are three successive halls, the **outermost** containing the temple office and a shop selling Naxi memorabilia. The second and third halls are particularly interesting because they contain original Tibetan-style frescoes. Within the **innermost hall** a central Buddha image has to its rear a series of outstanding murals depicting Avalokiteshvara, Vajrasattva, Karmapa, Vajrasattva (again), and Vajrayogini. To the left near the entrance by contrast there are later Chinese-style paintings.

• **Facilities** There are a number of tourist hotels in Lijiang, the best perhaps being the *Lijiang Binguan* (¥150/room). Restaurants are plentiful, inc some, such as *Mama Fu*, which cater specifically to the western backpacker market.

Lugu Lake

Beautiful **Lugu Lake** straddles the present day frontier between Yunnan and Sichuan provinces. The S shore of the lake lies within **Ninglang** county, in the Yi Autonomous County, and the N shore within the **Muli Tibetan Autonomous County** of Sichuan. The S shore is accessible by road from Lijiang, via **Yongsheng** and **Ninglang** townships. The population here is largely Tibetan, and in the past there were important monasteries constructed near its shores. Most of these were Gelukpa establishments: **Daming Gonpa**, **Shubi Gonpa**, **Ozer Gonpa**, and **Galong Gonpa** (of which only the first two have been renovated), but the Sakya monastery of **Dzembu** was also noteworthy. Ammenities for tourists have been improving in recent years; and local arrangements can be made through the **Lugufu Lake Travel Agency** (head office at Ninglang).

MILI COUNTY

སྨི་ལི

木里 Muli

Population: 112,667   Area: 12,573 sq km

The county of **Mili** lies to the N of Lugu Lake, near the confluence of the Li-chu and the Yalong River. It may be approached from **Ninglang** county in Yunnan via **Lake Lugu**, or by road from **Xichang**, the capital of the Yi Autonomous Prefecture of Liangshan in S Sichuan. To the N of Mili there are three attractive snow peaks, named after the three bodhisattvas, Manjushri, Avalokiteshvara, and Vajrapani; which form a focal point for pilgrimage.

History

Prior to the 16th century the ancient kingdom of Mili was a stronghold of the Karma Kagyu school. The influence of the kings of Jang Sadam who were patrons of the Karma Kagyu, and of Kampo Nenang monastery at Litang (which had been founded by Karmapa I) was instrumental in shaping the early cultural development of Mili.

However, following the expansion of the Gelukpas into Kham during the 15th and 16th centuries, Dalai Lama III Sonam Gyatso oversaw the construction of a large Gelukpa monastery at Litang, and actively encouraged the propagation of his tradition further S in the Li-chu valley. Thus, in 1544, the Gelukpa temple of **Khe'ong Dewachen Sonam Dargyeling** was founded in Mili by Lama Dampa Neten Tsultrim Zangpo. Subsequently, the monastery of **Ganden Shedrub Namgyeling** was founded by Pakti Rabjampa Samten Zangpo in 1596. Through the efforts of their successors and their patrons, including Lama Peljor Gyatso and Khen Rinpoche Lobzang Tutob, the Geluk tradition became the dominant school in the region. In 1640 when Gushi Qan ended the kingdom of Beri, his armies subdued the Kagyu opposition to the Geluk dominance throughout the Litang valley and adjacent areas. Subsequently, Buddhist activity throughout Mili was uniformly sponsored by the Gelukpas of Lhasa and their Qing patrons.

DALI

Those not wishing to fly directly from Lijiang may travel by road to **Dali** and **Kunming**, capital of Yunnan province. **Dali**, 187 km from Lijiang, is situated on the W shore of **Lake Erhai**, at the crossroads leading from Kunming to Tibet (N) and Burma (E). The climate is pleasant (average temperature 15° and average rainfall 1,176 mm).

During the period of the Tang and Song dynasties, Dali was the capital of the **Nan Chao Kingdom**, which came into conflict with the Tibetan Empire of Songtsen Gampo and his successors. The celebrated **Three Pagodas (Sanda)** of Dali date from this era. Later, Dali county fell the authority of neighbouring Jang Sadam. Nowadays, the county (*Pop* 391,765; *Area* 1,062 sq km) is home to more than 20 ethnic minorities, including the Bai, Yi, and Hui.

● **Facilities** Stay at the *Red Camelia Hotel*, the *Erhai Guesthouse*, or the *Dali City Number 2 Hotel* (best rooms ¥160; cheaper rooms ¥78 or 37). The town has western-style restaurants and bars catering to the tourist market.

KUNMING

Kunming City, the capital of Yunnan province lies 412 km E of Dali by rail or road. It is a large modern city with a pleasant climate, varying little from winter to summer. The inner city has a population of 165,562, and an area of 206 sq km; while Outer Kunming has a population of 1,168,320 and an area of

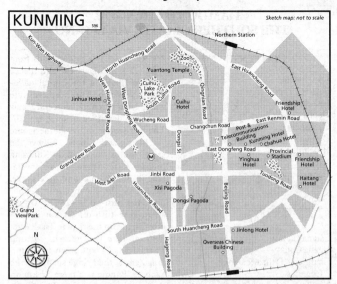

KUNMING 596

Sketch map: not to scale

1,452 sq km. From **Kunming Airport**, domestic flights connect with other major Chinese cities, and international flights depart for Hong Kong, Bangkok, Kuala Lumpur, Singapore, and Rangoon. The railway station has connections to Hanoi.

Local information
● Accommodation

A *Golden Dragon Hotel*, 575 Beijing Rd, T 3133015, F (86-871)-3131082, has 17 storeys, 290 rm, all have attached bath, 3 restaurants (*Lobby Lounge* for snacks, *Yunnan Kitchen Chinese Restaurant* for Chinese, and *Czarina* for international cuisine), room service available, swimming pool, fitness centre, shopping arcade, hairdresser, karaoke, airline offices, and business centre. *King World*, 28 Beijing Rd, T 3138888, F (86-871) 3131910, has 320 rm, attached bathrooms, a revolving rooftop restaurant, Peony Banquet Hall, *Rose Garden Restaurant*, Magnolia function room, business centre and disco-theque. *Kunming Hotel*, W145 Dong Feng Dong Lu, T 3162063, F (86-871) 3138220, has 12 floors, 5 restaurants, bar, shopping arcades, beauty parlour, gym and sauna, mahjong room, travel centre, and business centre; and *Holiday Inn*, 25 Dong Feng East Rd, has 252 rm, 3 restaurants serving Chinese, Japanese, and Western cuisine, lobby lounge, disco/karaoke, swimming pool, sauna and massage centre, health and fitness centre, shopping arcade, and business centre.

B *Green Lake Hotel*, 6 S Cui Hui Rd, T 5158888, F (86-871) 5153286, has 306 rm, attached bathrooms, Chinese restaurant, *Meldevere* coffee shop, *Mezzo Bar*, business centre, and beauty parlour.

● Tourist information
CITS *Yunnan Overseas Travel Corporation*, 154 E Dongfeng Rd, Kunming, T 3188905, F (0086-871) 3132508.

Tourist office *Yunnan Provincial Tourism Bureau*, Huancheng Nanlou St, Kunming, T (0871) 3132895

CHAMDO TO CHENGDU
THE SOUTHERN ROUTE VIA LITANG

There are two motor roads from Chamdo to Dartsedo and thence to Chengdu the capital of Sichuan province. The northern route which leads through Derge and Kandze will be described below, page 507. The first section of the southern route via Batang and Litang follows the same road as the Chamdo-Kunming highway as far as the turn-off for Batang in Markham county (see above, page 486). The distance from Chamdo to the turn-off is 428 km. On reaching the turn-off do not head S into Gartok on the road to Tasakalho. Instead, take the left (E) turning which leads 72 km down to Druparong Zampa, the bridge spanning the Yangtze. Batang is a mere 32 km on the far side of the bridge. The distance from there to Dartsedo (*Ch* Kangding) is 497 km, and from Dartsedo to Chengdu 400 km. All the counties of Kham described in this section are presently administered within the Kandze Autonomous Prefecture of Sichuan province.

Recommended itineraries: 5, 10.

BATANG COUNTY

འབའ་ཐང

巴塘县 Batang

Population: 72,143 *Area: 9,201 sq km*

Batang lies 32 km NE of the confluence of the Batang-chu with the Yangtze. It is an important town, spread out across the fertile and densely populated Batang-chu valley. From the 16th century onwards the Gelukpa tradition established itself in the valley, and two monasteries were constructed, **Batang Chode** (Tsesum Gyashok Kapu Gon) and **Tsesum Serbum Gon**. During the Sino-Tibetan wars of the early 20th century, these were destroyed along with the castles of the Batang chieftains, and gradually repaired over the following decades. One of the Potala Palace's massive applique tangkas was offered to Batang following this reconstruction, and it remains there even now.

The low-lying prosperous Batang valley (2,740m) was one of the few localities in Tibet which had a Chinese settlement prior to the 1950s. There were also American Protestant and French Catholic missions, which focussed largely on medical and educational projects. The work of Shelton at the American mission was particularly respected by the Tibetans.

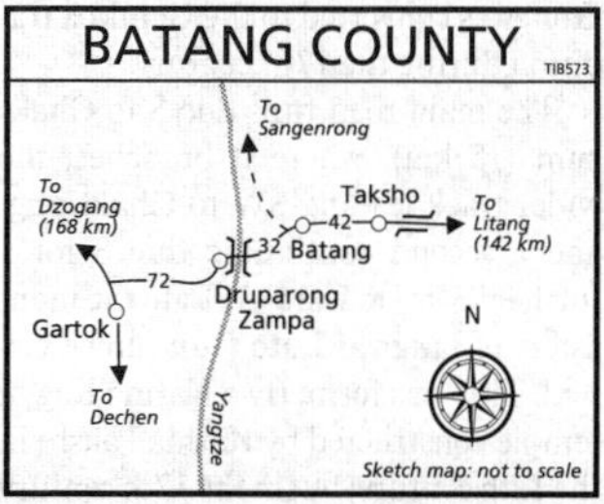
BATANG COUNTY
TIB573
To Sangenrong
To Dzogang (168 km)
Taksho
To Litang (142 km)
42
32 Batang
72
Druparong Zampa
Gartok
N
To Dechen
Yangtze
Sketch map: not to scale

Nowadays, Batang resembles a modern provincial Chinese town, and it has a number of institutions including an important teacher training college. There are also guesthouse and restaurant facilities. Many Bapa (natives of Batang) acquired high bureaucratic positions following the Chinese occupation in consequence of their familiarity with the Chinese language and modern education.

A trail follows the Yangtze upstream from the Batang-chu confluence into the gorge known as **Sangenrong** ('badlands'). Feeder rivers, such as the Karda-chu and the O-chu swell the river's flow on both banks of the inhospitable gorge. The **main highway** runs inland (NE) from Batang, following the Batang-chu upstream as far as **Taksho** (42 km), from where it crosses the watershed between the Batang-chu and Li-chu, and enters the high Litang plain in the headwaters of the Li-chu. 11 km before reaching the town of **Litang**, there is a turn-off on the right, which leads SE to Getse (81 km), where there is an important branch of Katok Monastery. The distance from Batang to Litang is 195 km.

LITANG COUNTY

ལི་ཐང་

理塘县 Litang

Population: 49,126   Area: 14,619 sq km

Litang county occupies the high **Puborgang** range, which forms a watershed between the Yangtze around Batang and the lower Yalong basin (here called Nyachu). The town of **Litang** lies near the source of the Li-chu tributary of the Yalong, and is one of the highest settlements in E Tibet. Guesthouse and restaurant facilities are available. The annual Litang Horse Festival, which begins on 1 Aug, is a great colourful spectacle, attracting visitors from all parts of Kham and even from overseas.

The **Puborgang** area was traditionally a stronghold of the Karma Kagyu and Katokpa branch of the Nyingmapa. In 1165 Karmapa I Dusum Khyenpa founded the monastery of **Kampo Nenang** near Litang, at a site where a large rock reputedly bears the letter KA whenever a new Karmapa appears in the world. He remained there until the age of 74 (ie 1184) and only in his later years did he go on to found the renowned

Karma Gon monastery in Lhato (see above, page 470). Later in the 15th century, Khedrub Yeshe Gyeltsen, a local lama and prolific author, propagated the Katokpa tradition of the Nyingmapa here. Nyingmapas in Litang at the present day maintain strong contacts with the Nyingma monasteries of Nyarong and Sertal.

The Karma Kagyu tradition however was eclipsed in 1580 when Dalai Lama III Sonam Gyatso founded **Litang Chode**, also known as **Ganden Tubchen Chokhorling**. An outstanding image of Jowo Shakyamuni was placed in its Tsuklakhang. Subsequently, in 1640, opposition to the expansion of the Gelukpa order in Litang was suppressed by the Mongol armies of Gushi Qan, and, as an institution, the monastery quickly became the largest in Puborgang, and the dominant influence on local cultural life. In recent years the complex has been renovated under the guidance of Litang Kyabgon Tulku Palden Dorje and Shodruk Tulku. There are two large buildings: the hilltop white **Assembly Hall** (_dukhang_) and the yellow **Tsuklakhang Kungarawa**.

From Litang, the highway leads E to **Nyakchuka** in upper Nyarong (125 km).

South of Litang to Yunnan

Another road leads due S from Litang, following the Li-chu valley downstream through the grasslands to **Gyawa** (30 km). A trail leads SE from here to **Mola** (53 km), where the local monastery, **Wa Gon**, was converted to the Gelukpa tradition during the 17th century.

The main road runs due S to **Chaksum** (15 km), where it branches, the wider track leading SW to **Chaktreng**, and a second continuing due S for a further 73 km to **Lato**. At Lato the monastery of **Jangwar Lato Gon** can be visited. This was formerly a Karma Kagyu temple constructed by Karma Pakshi in the 12th century; but in the 17th century

LITANG COUNTY

TIB573A

Litang — To Nyachuka (125 km)
— 11 —
30
81 Li-chu Gyawa
53 Mola
15
Chaksum
Getse
3
76 Lato
To Sumdo (76 km)
To Mili
Lugu Lake
Ninglang

N

Sketch map: not to scale

it was converted into a Gelukpa monastery by Serkong Onpo. From Lato, a trekking route leads S to **Mili** (see above, page 492).

Taking the **Chaktreng** road from Chaksum, you recross the Yalong-Yangtze watershed, and head SW for 76 km

to **Sumdo** in the upper reaches of the Shuiluo he (a tributary of the Yangtze). Here, the road forks again: the left (E) branch heading downstream into **Dabpa** county (26 km) and the right (SW) heading into the **Chaktreng** valley (67 km).

HORSE FESTIVALS

The horse festival (*ta-gyuk du-chen*) tradition in Central Tibet is said to trace its origins back to King Rabten Kunzang Phak of Gyantse in Western Tibet, who in 1408 organized a religious and secular festival on behalf of his grandfather's memory. It included wrestling, weightlifting, and horse-racing, to which archery on horseback was added in 1447. However, the festival tradition in the Amdo and Kham areas of Eastern Tibet, where horses abound and horse-riding remains a skill acquired at a young tender age, may have had an even longer history. Most festivals, with the exception of Gyantse which coincides with the fourth month of the lunar calendar, are held in the autumn when the grasslands begin to turn yellow and the harvest has been gathered in the villages. Among the sites in Central Tibet, which are renowned for their horse festivals, the Lhasa 4-day event coinciding with the Great Prayer Festival (Monlam Chenmo) is not presently held; but those of Damzhung and Kongpo are still extremely popular. The Damzhung Festival is particularly grand, the 10 km site being covered with the blue appliqued tents of the riders, traders, and locals. The Yak Race is the comic highlight of the event.

In E Tibet, horse festivals nowadays tend to be organized according to the western or modern Chinese calendar. For instance, the well-known Jyekundo Festival begins on 25 July; and the Litang Festival on 1 Aug (National Army Day). In addition to speed-racing, there are other equestrian events, with riders stooping from their galloping steeds to pick up kataks from the ground or twirling Tibetan muskets around their shoulders before shooting at a target on the ground. Tug-of-war and weightlifting add to the spectacle – sometimes with strongarm monks from the local monasteries participating; and there are folk song and dance troupes representing the different regions. A brisk trade is conducted amid the copious drinking of beer, chang, and hard liquor.

DABPA COUNTY

འདབ་པ

稻城县 Daocheng

Population: 26,303   Area: 5,870 sq km

Dabpa county lies on the S bank of the Shuiluo he, a tributary of the Yangtze which rises in Puborgang and flows S to join the Yangtze at the N tip of its bend on the present day Sichuan-Yunnan border. **Dabpa Yangteng Gon** was originally a Kagyu monastery, converted to the Gelukpa school by Lodro Namgyel, a student of Jetsun Jampal Nyingpo in the 17th century. A motorable road continues S from Dabpa, reaching **Dong-nyi** township near the Yunnan border after 104 km, and thence entering Yunnan via Gyeltang county.

CHAKTRENG, DABPA & DERONG COUNTIES

Sketch map: not to scale

CHAKTRENG COUNTY

ཕྱག་ཕྲེང

乡城县 Xiangcheng

Population: 21,112   Area: 4,712 sq km

Chaktreng county, in the middle reaches of the Chaktreng-chu valley, has been a staunchly partisan Gelukpa area since the 17th century when the local Kagyu monastery **Gyazawei Gonpa** was razed to the ground by the Mongol army of Gushi Qan. Pon Khandro, a local chieftain, subsequently constructed the Gelukpa monastery of **Chaktreng Sampeling** on the same site.

The inhabitants of Chaktreng vigorously resisted the Chinese occupation of Chao Erh Feng's army in the Batang area during the early decades of the present century.

Trijang Rinpoche, the late tutor of HH Dalai Lama XIV, was a native of Chaktreng, and many of his most devoted followers hailed from this part of E Tibet and the adjacent areas of Drayab and Gyeltang. The distance from Chaktreng to the Yunnan border is 69 km, and from there it is but a short drive to Gyeltang.

DERONG COUNTY

སྡེ་རོང་

得荣县 Derong

Population: 20,108   Area: 2,244 sq km

Derong county, otherwise known as **Lower Zang (Zang-me)** lies on the banks of the Ding-chu River, S of its confluence with the Mo-chu, and N of its confluence with the Mayi-chu. The distance from Chaktreng to Derong via **Zangang** is 151 km; and, after Derong, the road continues due S, following the W bank of the Ding-chu to its confluence with the Yangtze at **Wakha** on the Yunnan border, near Benzilan.

NYACHUKA COUNTY

ཉག་ཆུ་ཁ

雅江县 Yajiang

Population: 37,703   Area: 6,732 sq km

Taking the main highway E from Litang, after 59 km you will pass through **Nub Golok** township (*Ch* Xi Golok), where a branch of Litang Chode named **Golok Gonsar** was founded in the 17th century by Ripa Sarampa. Then, driving across the Kabzhi La watershed between the Li-chu and Yalong, after 66 km the road descends into **Nyachuka** county. The administrative capital is located at **Pundadrong** in the Yalong valley. There are guesthouse and restaurant facilities; and there are important monasteries such as **Odozangpo Gonpa** of the Sakya school. This is a strategically important intersection where four roads diverge: W to Litang, N to Nyarong and Tawu, S to Bawolung, and E to Minyak and Dartsedo. Among these the N-S roads follow the course of the Yalong River (known here as the Nyak-chu). For a description of the N roads to Tawu (121 km) and Nyarong county (142 km), which

NYACHUKA & GYEZIL

TIB554

Sketch map: not to scale

are important cultural areas for the Nyingmapa and the Bonpo, see below. The S road to **Bawolung** is only motorable in its initial 39 km sector, as far as Lake Malangtso.

Dzongzhab

The E road ascends the **Minyak Rabgang** highlands, which form the watershed between the Yalong and the Gyarong basins. En route you will pass through **Kabzhi Monastery**, which represents the Karma Kagyu tradition. **Dzongzhab** township (*Ch* Xinduqao), 72 km E of Nyachuka, is another important transport station. The valley in which it lies straddles the intersection of four main roads: N to Tawu, Kandze and Derge, S to Gyezil, and E to Dartsedo.

● **Facilities** There are several Sichuan-style restaurants in this bustling market town.

GYEZIL COUNTY

 བརྒྱད་ཞེལ

九龙县 Jiulong

Population: 50,257   Area: 7,478 sq km

Taking the S route from Dzongzhab, you will arrive in **Gyezil** county, traditionally known as **Gyezur**. The road at first follows a feeder river of the Tung-chu (itself a tributary of the Yalong) upstream through S Minyak district. There are fine views of **Mt Minyak Gangkar** (7,556m), the highest snow range in E Tibet; and 6-day treks can be arranged from the Base Camp (5,220m), approached via **Rindrubtang**, 95 km S of Dzongzhab. Important monasteries in the vicinity of Minyak Gangkar include the Gelukpa monastery of **Giwakha Jampaling**, which was founded by Lama Gangringpa, a student of Dalai Lama II; the Karma Kagyu monastery of **Gangkar Gonpa**; and the smaller monasteries of **Nego**, **Tongku** and **Chukmo**, which appear to have been originally of Kagyupa provenance, and later absorbed by the Sakya and Geluk traditions.

South of the Rindrubtang turn-off, the road enters the valley of the Gyezil-chu tributary of the Yalong, and follows it downstream. The administrative capital of Gyezil county is at **Karpo**, 83 km S of Rindrubtang and 176 km S of Dzongzhab. The town is located in the extreme SE of the Tibetan plateau. The population here is predominantly **Yi** rather than Tibetan; and the road itself continues S from Karpo out of Tibetan territory into the **Liangshan** Yi Autonomous Prefecture.

DARDO COUNTY

དར་མདོ

康定县 Kangding

Population: 99,695   Area: 11,125 sq km

Present day **Dardo** county broadly corresponds to the area of the ancient **Chakla Kingdom**, which until the mid-20th century was governed by the Chakla Gyelpo from Dartsedo town. It therefore includes both the Minyak region of the Tibetan plateau and the plunging gorge formed by the Dar-chu and Tse-chu tributaries of the Gyarong. The administrative capital is at **Dartsedo**, 75 km from Dzongzhab (Xinduqiao) and 400 km from Chengdu. **NB** Minyak should not be confused with the medieval kingdom of Minyak (*Ch* Xixia), located in present day Ningxia Province of China, which was founded in 1038 and destroyed by Genghiz Qan in 1227. The survivors of this kingdom are said to have fled into E Tibet, where they intermingled with the local populace in the W of Minyak Rabgang. Some say that the distinctive language of Tawu reflects this intermingling.

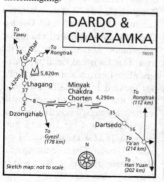

DARDO & CHAKZAMKA

To Tawu
76
Ganthar
72
To Rongtrak
TIB555
4,420m
5,820m
37
Lhagang
8
Minyak Chakdra Chorten
4,290m
To Rongtrak (112 km)
34
Dzongzhab
35
To Gyezil (178 km)
Dartsedo
16
To Ya'an (214 km)
N
To Han Yuan (202 km)

Sketch map: not to scale

North from Dzongzhab

Lhagang

Driving N from the highway intersection 4 km N of **Dzongzhab**, the road passes through **Lhagang** in the Tungchu valley after 37 km.

Lhagang Monastery

At the N end of town surrounded by three hills symbolizing the bodhisattvas Manjushri, Avalokiteshvara, and Vajrapani, is **Lhagang Monastery**, formally known as **Lhagang Gon Tongdrol Samdrubling Chode**. The chapel to the right of the Assembly Hall contains a revered Jowo Shakyamuni image named Semnyi Ngalso (popularly called Lhagang Jowo). According to legend, when Princess Wengcheng travelled to Tibet, she stayed overnight here, and the Jowo Shakyamuni image which she brought as her dowry to Lhasa is said to have spoken out aloud, requesting to be left in that idyllic setting! Subsequently King Songtsen Gampo constructed 108 temples in the direction of China, the last being Lhagang. Later in the 12th century, the original temple was expanded into the form of a monastery by the Kagyupas, and from the 13th century onwards under the influence of Chogyel Phakpa it was gradually absorbed by the Sakyapa school, to which it holds allegiance at the present day.

The renovated **Assembly Hall** in its **lower storey** contains images of the Buddhas of the Three Times, three of the Five Founders of Sakya (Kunga Nyingpo, Sakya Pandita, and Chogyel Phakpa), and a set of the Eight Stupas symbolizing the deeds of the Buddha. In its **upper storey** there are reliquary stupas containing the remains of past teachers associated with the monastery – including Do Khyentse Yeshe Dorje.

The **Jokhang Chapel**, containing the sacred Jowo Semnyi Ngalso image, has an air of great sanctity. Pilgrims from Kham who have seen this image will sometimes say that the blessing resembles that of seeing the Lhasa Jowo image itself! The main image is flanked by others depicting (L): Thousand-armed Avalokiteshvara, Four-armed Avalokiteshvara, and Buddha (twice); and (R): Padmasambhava flanked by Shantaraksita and King Trisong Detsen, Vajrasattva and Tara; and (to the rear): the Sixteen Elders. The ancient murals of this chapel depict the deities of the *four classes of tantra* and the Sukhavati paradise of Amitabha.

Behind the assembly hall compound, which is surrounded by a perimeter wall of prayer wheels, there is a large garden containing 124 stupas of various sizes. One ancient stupa housed here is said to vibrate of its own volition; and there are wonderful views of the snow peak of **Mt Zhara Lhatse** (5,820m) on a clear day to the NE.

Nyingmapa Shedra

On the left side of the road before reaching the monastery, there is a dirt road leading across the fields towards the Nyingmapa Shedra ('college') run by Khenpo Chodrak. Here there are over 100 monks of the Nyingma tradition engaged in the study of classical philosophical texts. There is currently a plan to expand the small temple of the college into a large Lhakhang, which would accommodate an increased number of students. The view from the plain below the college dramatically overlooks the snow range of **Minyak Gangkar** in the distance.

Minyak Pelri Gonpa

A trail NW from the college leads to **Minyak Pelri Gonpa**, a Nyingmapa monastery in a wonderful grassland setting, where the Northern Treasure (*Jangter*) tradition is maintained. For those not wishing to stay in the cramped guesthouse in town, there are wonderful camping grounds to be found beyond the town on the N side.

● **Facilities** The small town has a privately owned guesthouse and a general store.

Mount Zhara Lhatse

Crossing **Drepa La** (4,420m) on an excellent paved road, the sacred snow peak of **Mt Zhara Lhatse** (5,820m) is visible to the NE. This mountain (*Ch* Haitzu Shan) is revered as one of the 25 Padmasambhava sites in E Tibet, specifically representing the body aspect of buddha-mind. According to the ancient pre-Buddhist tradition, the mountain is regarded as an offspring of Nyenchen Tanglha. The beautiful lake **Zhara Yutso** is located on the NE side of the mountain, and around it are many meditation caves associated with Do Khyentse Yeshe Dorje (19th century). On the SW side of the mountain, there are as many as 15 medicinal hot springs. The snow peak remains visible far to the N for those crossing the **Mejesumdo** uplands.

Garthar Chode Monastery

Garthar township (*Ch* Qianning) is located at a road junction, 16 km N of Lhagang, and on the far side of **Drepa La**. There are many government compounds here; some providing guesthouse and dining facilities. Beyond the town the valley widens and the road forks: the left branch heading NW towards **Tawu** (76 km) and the right branch heading in the direction of **Rongtrak** (72 km). Take the latter road and after 9 km you will reach **Garthar Chode Monastery**, located on a hilltop promontory (3,871m) to the N of the road. This renowned Gelukpa monastery, which formerly housed 300 monks, was founded in the 18th century by Dalai Lama VII Kalzang Gyatso, and its construction was sponsored by Emperor Qianlong of the Qing Dynasty. Subsequently, in 1838 Dalai Lama XI was born at Garthar. The road through the **Mejesumdo** uplands to Tawu will be described below, page 550.

Southeast to Dartsedo

Minyak Chakdra Chorten

Heading SE from **Dzongzhab** (Xinduqiao), the highway branches after 8 km, the S dirt track leading to **Gyezil** (see above, page 500) and the E main road leading towards **Dartsedo**. Taking the latter, two minor passes are crossed, and the road enters a wide pasture, flanked by an avenue of planted poplars and willows. The farming villages of **Minyak** have distinctive detached 3-storeyed stone mansions. At **Rilung Drongde** village there is a circular prayer flag formation wound around a central wooden axis, and some fine *mani* stone carvings.

The main landmark in this part of E Minyak however is the enormous white stupa known as **Minyak Chakdra Chorten**, dedicated to the Eight Buddhas of Medicine. The stupa stands beside the highway to the E of the village called Minyak Dem Drongde. The original stupa is attributed to Tangtong Gyelpo; but it has been renovated and reconsecrated several times, by great masters such as the late Panchen Lama X. The adjacent Gelukpa monastery has a small temple depicting images of Shakyamuni and his foremost disciples. From here, it is possible to trek across country towards **Mt Minyak Gangkar** and the various Geluk and Sakya monasteries in its environs.

The highway continues E to cross the **Gye La** pass (4,290m), which the Chinese call Zheduo Shankou. This watershed, which divides the Yalong and the Gyarong basins, is 42 km E of Dzongzhab township and 33 km above Dar-tsedo.

Dartsedo

དར་རྩེ་མདོ

The town of Dartsedo (*Ch* Kangding), altitude 2,590m, lies deep within a gorge at the confluence of the Cheto-chu and Yakra-chu tributaries which form the Dardo River. It was formerly the capital of the **Chakla** Kingdom – one of the five independent kingdoms of Kham, under the hereditary authority of the Chakla Gyelpo. The town prospered as the centre for the tea-trade between Tibet and China. Traders would travel long distances, carrying herbal medicines from the Tibetan plateau to sell in exchange for the tea grown in the Ya'an region, which appealed to the Tibetan palate when blended with salt and butter. The main streets were flanked by large tea warehouses. Nowadays, the profitable tea trade continues, but the town has grown into a large city, containing the Kandze prefectural government as well as the local Dardo county administration. In the past Dartsedo always had the air of a frontier town where Chinese and Tibetans would intermingle. However, the Chinese element of the population has grown considerably in recent years, far outweighing the indigenous element.

Orientation

Descending from the **Gye La** pass, the road plunges into the Dar-chu valley, and on reaching the outskirts of town, passes the entrance to **Lhamotse** and **Dordrak** monasteries on the left. At an important intersection above the town a barrier obstructs the traffic. Continue W of the barrier into the large military compound, located in the NW part of town. Turn S passing through the barrier, and you will enter the city.

Places of interest

The prefectural and county government buildings are located in the uptown area, near **Ngachu Monastery**, as is the *Kangding Hotel*.

Ngachu Monastery (Tenlo Gonsar)

Dartsedo formerly had seven monasteries – three Nyingma, two Sakya and two Geluk. Among these, the largest and best known was the Gelukpa monastery of **Ngachu Gonpa**, founded by Minyakpa Tenpel Nyima in the 17th century as a branch of Drepung Losaling College. The monastery once had over 100 monks. In 1954 the present Dalai Lama stayed there en route to Beijing.

The monastery is located close to the Kangding Hotel and its striking roofs in Sino-Tibetan style are visible from the balconies of that building. The restored **Assembly Hall** contains large images of Jowo Shakyamuni flanked by his foremost students (Shariputra and Maudgalyayana) and of Tsongkhapa flanked by his foremost students (Gyeltsabje and Khedrubje). Other images to the right depict Avalokiteshvara in the form Simhanada and Green Tara. On the sidewalls are images of the protector deities: Dorje Drakden (left) and Shridevi and Dorje Drakden (right). The **Maitreya Hall**, which once housed an enormous 3-storey high image of Maitreya, is yet to be renovated; but a new **Mani Wheel** chapel lies to the left of the courtyard portico. Presently, there are 20 monks here, most of them young novices. Kusho Dardo, the head lama, recently passed away at Nalanda in India.

If you walk down the main street (Shangyang St), you will notice that the **Cheto-chu** River rushes through the middle of the town, hemmed in by steep concrete embankments and small ghats. The sound of its running waters is all-pervasive. Early in the morning the elderly Chinese populace can be seen practising Tai-Chi by the riverside.

Several bridges span the river, linking the government building and open-air market (on the W bank), with the two parallel main streets (on the E bank). The wider of the two main streets (Shangyang St), adjacent to the river, contains shops. The narrower of the two (Sharlam Chen St) has a number of grocery and general stores, some of which sell Tibetan books, artefacts and ready-to-wear clothing. Look out for the Khampa style chubas (for both men and women).

At a large square on the E bank the two roads intersect and the Peoples' Cinema dominates one corner. The corresponding square further downhill on the W bank has government buildings, and below it the Yakra-chu River flows in

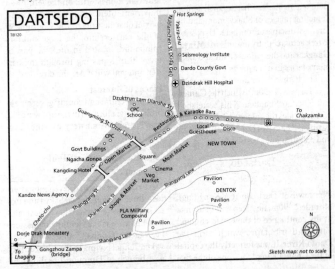

from the N. In this area of town you will find some modern Chinese shops.

Returning to Shangyang St on the E bank, heading downhill after the confluence, you will pass a series of seedy karaoke bars on the left and a series of tea warehouses and go-downs on the right.

There are several schools in town, including the **Tibetan Language University of E Tibet**, which moved here recently from Tawu. Mist permeates the steep walls of the valley, particularly in summertime, and in the winter icy conditions make the main street somewhat slippery.

TIBETAN TEA

Tea has been an indispensable part of the Tibetan diet since the 7th century, and yet it has only recently been grown within the moist low-lying valleys of Dzayul and Pemako in the SW of the country. Instead, the Tibetans have throughout their history relied upon imported tea from China. Following the arrival of the Chinese princesses Wengcheng and Jincheng in imperial Tibet, it was soon realized that the drinking of tea acted as an antedote to the cold and dryness at high altitudes, as well as compensating to some extent for the absence of fruit and vegetables in the Tibetan diet. Nomads and villagers alike drink tea throughout their working day; and, like alcohol in other lands, tea has developed an important social dimension. Whenever Tibetans have guests or visit their relatives or friends, they will offer tea as a courtesy. A cup, once offered, will never be left empty, and will constantly be replenished. If you do not wish to drink it is best to leave the cup full and drain it at the time of departure!

Chinese potentates and emperors, realizing the significance of the tea trade for Tibet, would sometimes exert economic pressures, obliging the Tibetans to trade horses for tea or to pay exorbitant tea taxes to avoid the anguish of a tea embargo! The preferred traditional brand of tea is black, with thick twigs and leaves, which would be imported from Ya'an in Sichuan and other border areas in the form of compressed bricks, packed inside long oblong bamboo cases, and transported by pack animals over immense distances. This tea would be consumed either as a clear black tea (ja-dang) to which a pinch of salt would be added, or as butter tea (so-ja), or more recently, due to Indian influence, as a sweet milk tea (ja ngar-mo). Butter tea is unique to Tibet and particularly well suited to the Tibetan climate. Contrary to the often bandied misconception, most people prefer fresh rather than rancid butter in their tea! The strained black tea is mixed with dri butter and salt in a wooden churn (dong-ma) and then poured into a kettle for heating and serving. Rounds of dri butter are packed and sewn into yak-skin cases (mar-ril) by nomad ladies for the village market and for their own use; and it is important that the supply should never run out! Tea churns made of pine or bamboo consist of an outer cylindrical tube tightly bound with brass hoops at both ends, and an inner wooden piston into which holes are drilled to enable the liquid and air to pass during churning. They come in various sizes: the largest over 1m in height and 30 cm in diameter, and the smaller types 60 cm or 30 cm in height, with proportionate diameters. Butter tea may be consumed from a wooden bowl (which one would normally carry in one's pocket), or mixed with ground roasted barley flour (tsampa) into a dough, which is the staple Tibetan meal.

Nowadays, Chinese jasmin tea is also popular; and drivers will carry a screw-top jar, filled to the brim with this thirst-quenching brew when crossing the dusty roads of the plateau. To be prepared, bring your own screw-top or jam jar!

Excursions

Yakra-chu hot springs Continue out of town from the square on the E bank of the river following the **Yakra-chu** upstream, and you will reach (after 8 km) the Yakra-chu hot springs which have been used as a medicinal spa for centuries. Private bathhouses have been constructed around the sulphurous pools.

Dordrak Gonpa Northeast of town on the **Gye La** road there is an inobtrusive passageway on the right leading to **Dordrak Gonpa**, a branch of the celebrated Dorje Drak monastery of S Tibet. Restoration is on-going; and inside the main temple is a new gilded-copper image of Padmasambhava, flanked by his foremost consorts Mandarava and Yeshe Tsogyel. To the left there are further images of White Tara and Shantaraksita, and to the right King Trisong Detsen and Four-armed Avalokiteshvara. Of the original frescoes, only the magnificent torso of a blue Vajrasattva figure remains; but there are excellent new murals depicting the 25 Disciples of Padmasambhava and the liturgical cycle known as *Lama Sangdu*.

The adjacent **Jokhang** which once housed the canonical texts of the *Kangyur, Tangyur, Nyingma Gyubum* and commentaries, along with the **Gonkhang** and the residence of Gyelse Rinpoche, the head lama, have yet to be restored. Of the original treasures nothing remains. There are presently only 30 monks, in contrast to the 70-100 who once lived here. However a large number of additional monks' quarters have been reconstructed.

In front of Dordrak Gonpa, by the roadside, is the renovated Gelukpa monastery of **Lhamotse**, which contains images of Shakyamuni and Tsongkhapa, each with their foremost students. Originally this monastery was located on the hilltop facing the town, and it has been rebuilt on two subsequent occasions, most recently at its present site.

Local information
● Accommodation
Kangding Hotel, close to Ngachu Monastery, foreign visitors are obliged to stay here. It has comfortable rooms, especially in the new annex to the rear of the main building. There are many guesthouses on the E side of town but these are only for domestic visitors.

● Places to eat
Many Sichuan-style restaurants. The best is situated to the right outside the main entrance of the hotel. Tea houses are on the main street nr the river. Other restaurants can be found on the E bank of the river.

● Banks & money changers
Bank of China is located in the square on the E bank of the river.

● Entertainment
Peoples' Cinema is located on the main square of W bank of river. Karaoke bars can be found on the E bank of the river.

● Hospitals & medical services
There is a hospital located on the square on the E bank of the river.

● Tour companies & travel agents
Kangding Travel Service, T 22928, on main street nr to the river.

● Transport
Road The bus station and petrol station lies at the lower end of town.

CHAKZAMKA COUNTY

ལྕགས་ཟམ་ཁ

泸定县 Luding

Population: 61,563   Area: 1,570 sq km

Below Dartsedo, the paved road follows the Dardo-chu downstream to its confluence with the Gyarong Ngulchu (*Ch* Dadu) in **Chakzamka** county. Here, the road forks, a narrow branch on the left (N) following the rapids upstream to **Rongtrak** in Gyarong (see below, page 507). The main road bears right (S) and shortly thereafter crosses the Gyarong via a new bridge to enter the county capital of **Chakzamka** (*Ch* Luding). This is the last outpost of Tibetan territory (1,100m) on the long highway from Lhasa to Chengdu. The distance from Dartsedo to Chakzamka is 16 km; and from here to Ya'an 214 km.

Chakzam Bridge

The old wooden suspension bridge, which marks the traditional frontier between Tibet and China, has a Chinese style temple on its W bank. Chinese tourists now flock here in great numbers in memory of a heroic episode in the Long March when the Red Army was obliged to take the bridge from the Kuomintang in order to secure its passage NE to Yenan. There is a small museum and S of the bridge a tall but rather nondescript stone column commemorating the martyrs of that occasion. Walk across the bridge, which sways markedly towards the middle, and peer down through the slats of its walkway to observe the torrents of the Gyarong below!

Chakzamka to Chengdu (via Rongtrak, Ya'an, or Hanyuan)

There are three possible routes from Chakzamka to Chengdu, the capital of Sichuan province. The **northern route** follows the W bank of the Gyarong upstream to **Rongtrak** (112 km), where it crosses to the E bank and follows the Tsenlha-chu upstream to the large town of **Tsenlha** (58 km). The watershed pass known as **Balang Shan** (4,237m) is crossed 79 km beyond Tsenlha, and thereafter, the road descends into **Wolong Panda Reserve**. Spend the night here, and drive the following morning to **Chengdu** via **Guan Xian** (156 km).

The **central route**, which is the most direct, crosses **Mt Erhlan Shan** via the 3,000m pass known to Tibetans as

MOUNT EMEI SHAN

An interesting detour to **Emei**, which extends the journey to Chengdu by 1 day, offers you an opportunity to visit the Chinese Buddhist shrines on **Mt Emei Shan** – one of the four sacred Buddhist mountains in China. This peak is dedicated to the bodhisattva Samantabhadra. It has 70 temples and is a veritable treasure-store of medicinal herbs. The peak monastery may be reached on foot or by cable car; and at sunrise the diffracted light sometimes produces the distinctive aura effect known as the "precious light of the Buddha". It is possible to spend several days making a complete pilgrimage circuit of the mountain. The temple of **Wannian Si**, with its life-size image of Samantabhadra riding an elephant, is particularly renowned. Stay at the splendidly tranquil *Hongzhushan Hotel* in Emei. After Emei don't forget to visit the **Temple of the Great Buddha** at **Leshan** – site of the world's largest stone Buddha image (71m). The distance from Han Yuan to Emei is 237 km; and from Emei to Chengdu 296 km.

Khakha Buddha La. Prior to the communist period, the traders, pilgrims and adventurers who walked the tea-trail from Ya'an to Dartsedo via Mt Erhlan Shan were constantly subjected to harassment by brigands. Later, the difficulties faced by the PLA while constructing this road in the 1950s came to inspire a new Chinese proverb comparing any particular hardship to the crossing of Erhlan Shan. From the pass, on a clear day there is a magnificent view of **Mt Minyak Gangkar** (7,556m), the highest mountain in Kham. The distance from Chakzamka to **Ya'an** across the pass is 214 km, and from Ya'an to **Chengdu** 170 km. Recently, this road was closed pending the construction of a new tunnel bore-hole through Mt Erhlan. On its completion, the journey from Chakzamka to Ya'an will be considerably reduced.

The **southern route** from Chakzamka to Ya'an initially follows the Gyarong downstream on its E bank to **Han Yuan** (202 km), before cutting NE to Ya'an (220 km) and on to **Chengdu** (170 km). Both Han Yuan and Ya'an are large uninspiring towns, although the latter is more prosperous, with better accommodation and restaurants. Try the *Ya'an Binguan*, which has attached baths with running hot water!

CHENGDU

Chengdu lies on the Jinjiang (Brocade River), a major tributary of the Minjiang, which flows southwards from Amdo to converge with the Gyarong at Leshan. During the Eastern Han Dynasty, it was formerly known as Jincheng (Brocade Town); and during the Five Dynasties period, it was a capital of China. Later in the 13th century, the Mongol city of Chengdu was visited by Marco Polo. Nothing remains however of the old Tatar city walls and towers, which have been torn down. The narrow streets of the old town rarely preserve their quaint traditional-style wooden houses, but the area of the former imperial palace can be visited.

Chengdu is nowadays the capital of Sichuan Province. As such, it marks the end of the overland road through E Tibet (Kham), but for many it is also the beginning. The routes from **Lhasa to Chamdo** and thence to **Chengdu via Litang or Derge** described in this section of the guide can easily be reversed; and Chengdu has the advantage of being well-connected to the outside world.

As far as E Tibet is concerned, Chengdu is a city of great importance, in that the 19 counties of Kandze Autonomous Prefecture, the 13 counties of Ngawa Autonomous Prefecture; and the Mili Tibetan Autonomous County are all administered from Chengdu. Political and civil offices dealing with the affairs of E Tibet are therefore located here; as are the head offices of cultural organizations such as the Sichuan Nationalities Publishing House and the Sichuan National Minorities Institute.

Places of interest

In the SW is the **Wuhou Temple**, dedicated to Zhu Geliang, who appears as a hero in the Chinese classic novel *Romance of the Three Kingdoms*. The **Wenshu Monastery** on Renmin Bei Rd has a beautiful Buddhist temple; and in the SE, the **Wan Jiang Park** (River View Park) contains three Qing Dynasty buildings and a rare collection of bamboo ('mottled' and 'human face').

In the W of town the **Dufu Caotang** contains the thatched cottage of the Tang Dynasty poet Du Fu (712-770). Du Fu was an empoverished nobleman from Shaoling near Xi'an; but as a poet he is regarded as the archetypal Confucian moralist. His difficult prose style, which focusses on creativity tempered by austere hardships contrasts with the style of his contemporary, Li Po (701-762), a renowned exponent of the Taoist libertine style, emphasizing atmosphere and spontaneity. A Song Dynasty temple complex on the site has a stone image of Du Fu and a museum containing copies of his works and associated paintings.

22 km N of Chengdu is the **Baoguangsi** (Blazing Jewel Temple), which was founded during the Tang Dynasty. The **Lohan Hall** houses 500 arhat images from the Qing period, among the best of traditional Chinese sculpture.

Local information
● Accommodation

A *Chengdu Hotel*, Shudu Dadao Dong Yi Duan, T 4448888, F (86-28) 44416023, 4-star, has 11 storeys, standard room with attached bath at ¥880, 6 restaurants (Chinese, Japanese, Western, Korean BBQ, Beijing Imperial Food and *Cafe de Orchid*), bar, excellent shopping facilities on mezzanine and 9th flr, business centre, travel services, massage and sauna, karaoke and nightclub, swimming pool, billiards, and clinic; **A** *Jinjiang Hotel*, 36 Renmin Nan Rd, T 5582222, F (86-28) 5582348, 4-star (recently refurbished), has 9 storeys, 463 rm (all with attached bath), 7 restaurants (lobby lounge for snacks, ground floor Japanese and Chinese restaurants, 2nd flr group restaurant and 9th flr western and chinese restaurants), room service available, excellent shopping arcade, hairdresser, karaoke, airline offices and business centre; **A** *Minshan Hotel*, 17 Renmin Nan Rd, T 5583333, F (86-28) 5582154, 4-star highrise hotel, standard room with attached bath at ¥800, has lobby snack bar, 2nd flr Cantonese restaurant, among others, with shops, disco, karaoke, sauna and beauty salon.

B *Chengdu Tibet Hotel* (Xizang Fandian), 10 Renmin Bei Rd, T 3333988, F (86-28) 3333526, 3-star, has 359 refurbished rm, Japanese-style 426 rm with attached bath or shower, 8 restaurants and banquet halls (inc *Red Palace Dance-Dinner Restaurant*), lobby bar, business centre, massage and beauty salon, hairdresser, shops and travel services; **B** *Sichuan Hotel*, 31 Zongfu Jie, T 6661115, F (86-28) 66652633, 3-star, has standard rooms with attached bath and good restaurants, centrally located.

C *Jinhe Hotel*, 18 Jinhe Jie, T 6672888, F (86-28) 6662037.

D *Traffic Hotel*, 77 Linjiang Lu, T 5552814, is a backpackers' favourite.

● Airline offices

China South-west Airlines, 15 Renmin Nan Rd (Section Two), T 6665911; **Dragonair**, 65 Renmin Nan Rd (Section Two), T 6679186 x 363.

● Tour companies & travel agents

China International Travel Service, Room 129, *Jinjiang Hotel*, T 5582222, F 6663794; *Golden Bridge Travel Service*, 18 Jinhe St, T 6630370, F (86-28)-6642528; *Guagda Everbright Travel*, *Chengdu Hotel*, Room 115, T 4448888, F (86-28) 44416023.

● Transport

Air There are daily flights from Beijing to Chengdu; and regular departures from Guangzhou, Shanghai, Kunming, Xian, Chongqing, Guilin, Lanzhou, and other major Chinese cities. There are also international connections: thrice weekly from Hong Kong, and once weekly from Bangkok and Singapore, as well as from Kathmandu via Lhasa.

For those wishing to fly directly to Central Tibet, there are daily departures from Chengdu Airport for Lhasa.

CHAMDO TO DERGE
THE CULTURAL HEART OF KHAM

T he northern route from Chamdo to Chengdu via Derge will be described in this and the following sections. The first part of the route follows the highway from Chamdo to Topa and then passes through Jomda county to cross the Yangtze and enter either Derge or Pelyul. From Jomda there is also a side-road leading S into Gonjo county. The distance from Chamdo to Derge is 345 km, and from Topa to Derge, 230 km. Of these four counties, Jomda and Gonjo are currently administered from Chamdo district, within the Tibetan Autonomous Region; while Pelyul and Derge are administered from Dartsedo, within the Kandze Autonomous Prefecture of Sichuan Province.

Recommended itineraries: 5, 8, 10.

JOMDA COUNTY

འཇོ་མདའ

江达县 Jomda

Population: 46,601   *Area:* 13,384 sq km

Jomda county comprises the upper reaches of the Ri-chu around **Chunyido** and of the Ke-chu around **Sibda**, as well as the Do-chu (Tsang-chu valley) and its tributary, the Dzi-chu, which eventually flow into the Yangtze at **Bolo** in Gonjo county. In the extreme NE of the county, **Denkhok Nubma** is more accessible by ferry from Denkhok on the Sichuan side of the border. The county capital is located at **Jomda**, still known locally as Derge Jomda in recognition of the fact that the kingdom of Derge once extended across the W bank of the Yangtze.

ACCESS To reach Jomda from Chamdo, first follow the Derge highway out of town on the E bank of the Dza-chu, and cross the **Tama La** (4,511m) and **Jape La** (4,680m) passes to arrive at **Topa** township in the grasslands of the Drugu-chu valley.

The distance from Chamdo to Topa is 109 km. After Topa the highway crosses **Lazhi La** (4,450m) and enters Jomda county at **Chunyido** township, where there are excellent camping grounds. The distance from Topa to Chunyido is 63 km, and from Lazhi La to Chunyido 40 km.

Dordzang and Dzigar

The main monastery in the Chunyido nomadic area is **Dordzong Gonpa** of the Drukpa Kagyu school. The present incumbent lama resides at Tashijong in India. From Chunyido near the source of the Ri-chu, the highway continues E to **Khargang**, crossing Gele La pass (4,352m) en route and passing through **Tralso**, where there is a small Sakya Monastery. Khargang, on the banks of the Dzi-chu River, is 44 km from Chunyido. A motorable road follows this river upstream for 33 km to **Dzigar**, which is another stronghold of the Drukpa Kagyu school (a branch monastery has been established at Rewalsar in India through the efforts of Lama Wangdor and Dzigar Choktrul).

Trekking

A trekking route crosses Guru La from Dzigar to enter the Ke-chu valley, and head downstream to **Sibda**. Here there are important Kagyu monasteries: **Taklung Gon** and **Cho-ne Gon**. From Sibda, the trekking trail continues following the Ke-chu downstream to **Menda** area, where it merges with the Kyang-chu River of E Zurmang (see above, page 471 and below, page 535).

Jomda town

The highway runs E from Khargang, following the Dzi-chu downstream to the county capital (12 km). **Jomda** is a large town, sprawling along both banks

of the river. The main industries are timber and cement. Passing through town, where there are guesthouse and restaurant facilities, the road descends to **Tangpu** (22 km), where the river converges with the Do-chu.

A motorable side-road runs N from Tangpu to **Terton** township (53 km), where there are a number of important Kagyu monasteries: **Dokhar Gon**, **Gonsar Gon**, and **Kyapje Gon**, among them. It is also possible to trek NE from Terton township to **Denkhok Nubma** on the banks of the Yangtze.

Below Tangpu, the Do-chu is known as the Tsang-chu as far as its confluence with the Yangtze at **Bolo**. The road to Bolo from Tangpu (55 km) passes through **Kutse**, where many of the renowned Derge woodblocks were carved.

Wara Monastery

The highway continues E from Tangpu towards the **Nge La** pass (4,245m). En route you will drive through the beautiful **Wara Gonpa** (3,444m), a significant monastery of the Sakya school, which had its own woodblock edition of the *Kangyur*, prepared during the present century by Jamyang Khyentse Chokyi Lodro. The temple complex at Wara has undergone considerable restoration in recent years. Descending from Nge La pass, the road reaches **Kamtok** on the banks of the Yangtze. The distance from Tangpu to Kamtok is 63 km.

Trekking

Trek upstream through the Yangtze gorge to visit **Onpo-to** township, or cross the Yangtze to enter Derge county at **Kamtok Drukha Zamchen** bridge.

GONJO COUNTY

གོན་འཇོ

贡觉县 Gonjo

Population: 30,428   Area: 4,994 sq km

The county of Gonjo comprises the valleys of the southward-flowing Ri-chu and northward-flowing Mar-chu, which converge above **Akar**, and then flow due E to enter the Yangtze at **Motsa**. It also includes the valley of the Je-chu and adjacent rivers which flow into the Yangtze further SE at **Sangenrong** (the 'badlands'). The county capital is located at **Akar (Gonjo)** on the Mar-chu. The distance from Chunyido to Akar is 82 km.

Akar

At **Tranak**, 3 km E of Chunyido, there is a turn-off on the S side of the road, which runs parallel to the course of the Ri-chu River. Driving along this road, you will cross a 4,064m pass after 5 km, which leads into **Pelha Gon**, and a second pass, **Gyelpo La** (4,472m) after 22 km. Descend into **Kyabal** township (12 km) and **Tsanda**, where a trail follows the Ri-chu upstream to the Nyingmapa monastery of **Nyakla Gonpa**. The motorable track continues downhill from Tsanda to the confluence of the Ri-chu and Mar-chu, and then rises again to reach **Akar**, the county town (40 km from Kyabal), also known nowadays as **Gonjo**.

● **Accommodation** There are spartan guesthouse facilities at Akar.

You can continue driving SE from Akar for 24 km as far as **Lhagyel** in the upper reaches of the Mar-chu, but beyond that point it is necessary to trek SE to reach Lhato township.

Beyond NE Gonjo county, the township of **Bolo** (55 km drive from Tangpu) lies on the W bank of the Yangtze. The township of **Tsepa** is situated on the Tse-chu tributary of the Mar-chu. Further SE, a trail crosses **Pel-yi La** pass (4,642m) to enter the Je-chu valley. Passing through **Jangsum** and **Bumkye** townships, this trail follows the Je-chu downstream to its confluence with the Yangtze in **Sangenrong** ('badlands'), a wild and traditionally lawless part of Kham. The people of Gonjo are regarded as barbarous, headstrong, and somewhat inhospitable, compared to the other inhabitants of Kham.

PELYUL COUNTY

དཔལ་ཡུལ

白玉县 Baiyu

Population: 47,700   Area: 10,646 sq km

At **Kamtok Drukha** two bridges span the swift-flowing waters of the Yangtze. The lower bridge is the original one constructed by the PLA during the occupation of Tibet in 1950. The other is the modern suspension bridge which carries all motor vehicles and pedestrians across the present day border between the Tibetan Autonomous Region and Sichuan. Traditionally, the areas on both banks of the Yangtze belonged to the independent kingdom of **Derge**; and the peoples of Jomda and Pelyul often refer to themselves even now as inhabitants of Derge. Crossing to the E bank of the Yangtze (ie into the Kandze Prefecture of Sichuan Province), there are two motorable roads, one following the river upstream towards Derge (28 km), and the other following the river downstream to Pelyul. Taking the latter road, you will reach **Pelyul** after 87 km.

Pelyul county comprises the lateral valleys of the Horpo-chu and Ngu-chu tributaries of the Yangtze, which between their estuaries demarcate a dramatic section of the awesome gorge, where the river abruptly changes course from SE to SW and again to NW within the distance of 39 km. Two outstanding Nyingmapa monasteries, Katok and Pelyul, are located within the county.

Horpo

ACCESS Driving southwards down the E bank of the Yangtze on a narrow but jeepable road surface, after 32 km you will traverse the estuary of the Mesho-chu. Continue S for a further 10 km to reach the confluence of the Horpo-chu and the Yangtze. **Horpo** township (3,170m) is located a short distance upstream at a point where the Dzin-chu and Horpo-chu streams flow together. The township was formerly one of the 25 districts within the kingdom of Derge, and especially renowned in the past for the high quality of its metalwork.

● **Accommodation** One can stay in the house of the local shopkeeper.

Katok Dorjeden Monastery

ཀཿཐོག་རྡོ་རྗེ་གདན

History

Katok Dorjeden Monastery (4,023m) is located some 853m above Horpo on a hilltop resembling the shape of the Tibetan letter KA, or that of an 'eight-footed lion'. Until 1993 visitors to Katok were obliged to walk 5 hrs or ride on horseback from Horpo. The tranquillity of the remote hilltop monastery was rarely disturbed. Now, following the construction of a jeep

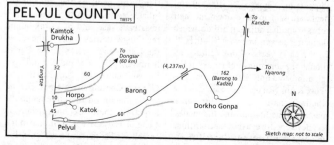

PELYUL COUNTY TIB575

Kamtok Drukha

To Dongsar (60 km)

To Kandze

Yangtze

32   60   (4,237m)   162 (Barong to Kadze)   To Nyarong

10   Horpo   Barong

Katok   60   Dorkho Gonpa

45

Pelyul

N

Sketch map: not to scale

track, the monastery can be reached with ease in 20 mins!

The monastery was founded in 1159 by Katok Dampa Deshek (1122-92). Immediately below the site is a large boulder, in which a local Bonpo divinity is said to have been trapped at the time of the monastery's founding. According to legend, the student and successor of Dampa Deshek called Tsangtonpa helped drag it along to the river bank below the valley where it can still be seen today.

Katok is revered as the main pilgrimage site of buddha-activity in Kham and as the oldest surviving monastery of the Nyingma school, excluding Samye and the temples constructed by the early kings. Dampa Deshek gave teachings continuously to students from all parts of E Tibet and his monastery acquired great prestige both for philosophical studies and meditation practice. It is known to have maintained certain rare lineages of teaching from the 12th century at times when they were lost in central Tibet.

The development of the monastery from its inception was guided by the 13 successors of Katokpa Dampa Deshek, by their students, and the 13 successors of Mokton Jampel Senge. In the 13th century Mani Rinchen of Katok, an associate of the treasure-finder Guru Chowang, is said to have constructed reliquaries for the remains of the first three Katokpa, and then to have flown across to an adjacent hilltop before vanishing into light. During the time of Jampabum, Katokpa III, 100,000 students are said to have flown on their robes to another adjacent hilltop, which thereafter became known as 'Cloth Hill'. In the early years of this century, although the community of monks at Katok numbered only 400, the hermitages above Katok (Ritsip, Bartro and Dechen Choling) continued to produce great masters of meditation, and the monastery developed over a thousand far-flung branches in E Tibet and Central Tibet.

In the 16th century the monastery was expanded by Rigdzin Dudul Dorje, Longsel Nyingpo and Sonam Detsen. Sonam Detsen's successive incarnations, beginning with Drime Zhingkyong Gonpo, maintained the ancient lineage of Katok, and were ably assisted by great scholars of the calibre of Tsewang Norbu (1698-1755) and Gyurme Tsewang Chokdrub (late 18th/early 19th century). More recently, the monastery has been connected with respected figures such as Katok Situ II Chokyi Gyatso (1880-1925) and Khenpo Ngaga (1879-1941), as well as living meditation masters such as Chatrel Senge Dorje.

The site

The track from Horpo to Katok crosses a wooden cantilever bridge over the Dzin-chu and proceeds through lush green countryside, initially on level ground but gradually rising to a steep ascent of 4,023m. On reaching the hilltop, a track to the right leads round the contour of the hill to Katok. On the way it passes a cremation ground, the site from which a former lama, Katok Mani Rinchen, is said to have flown off into space, and the seven damaged stupas which still contain relics of the founders of Katok.

Anyone viewing the majestic setting of Katok's red and white buildings which cover the peaceful mountaintop can appreciate why the concept of 'sacred outlook' or 'pure visionary perception of the landscape' is so significant here. To the right of the hillside are rocks in the shape of Vajrasattva's vase, and of Vajrakila and the Kabgye deities, while to the left of the last of these rocks is the **Bartro** hermitage. Beyond and behind that retreat centre are the **Ritsip** and **Dechen Choling** hermitages. Behind the mountain on the circumambulatory trail, there are impressions in stone of Hayagriva and Simhavaktra, as well as a Padmasambhava footprint.

Two temples have been renovated in recent years, under the auspices of Moktse Tulku, Getse Tulku, and the present Drime Zhingkyong incarnation (who lives in Chengdu). Of these, the large **Assembly Hall (Dukhang)** is for the most part unimpressive, housing new clay images of Padmasambhava and Shakyamuni. However in the course of its reconstruction all the original stones were utilized and thus an original blessing was preserved.

The **Zangdokpelri Temple** is a magnificent and ornate structure overlooking the open courtyard, where religious dances are performed on the 10th day (Tsechu) of the 6th month of the lunar calendar, commemorating the birth of Padmasambhava. Large applique tangkas depicting Katokpa Dampa Deshek and Longsal Nyingpo (founder and restorer of Katok) are erected to the side of the amphitheatre. If you decide to visit Katok at this time, the pageantry and colourful costumes of the dancers and spectators will forever haunt the memory. To visit Katok at other times of the year is to appreciate the tranquillity of this mountaintop bastion of Nyingmapa learning.

A new college (Shedra) is currently under construction on the opposite side of the courtyard from the Zangdokpelri temple. There are over 180 resident monks and 300 affiliated monks, studying philosophical texts of the Nyingma tradition under Khenpo Jamyang, who has authored a *History of Katok Monastery*.

Trekking

Returning to Horpo, you can drive S to Pelyul (45 km), N to Derge (70 km), or else trek through the upper reaches of the Dzin-chu valley to Dzenko and Manigango.

Pelyul

ACCESS Crossing the Horpo-chu near its confluence with the Yangtze, the motor road continues down the E bank as far as **Barna**, where it spans the Ngu-chu tributary, flowing in from the SE. It then follows the latter upstream to **Pelyul** (*Ch* Baiyu), the county capital, 45 km from Horpo.

Pelyul (3,261m) is a large and rapidly expanding town with a considerable Chinese population. Chinese traders and gold-miners fill the streets, alongside somewhat incongruous Khampa inhabitants. Slightly uphill, the **Hospital of Traditional Tibetan Medicine** and its

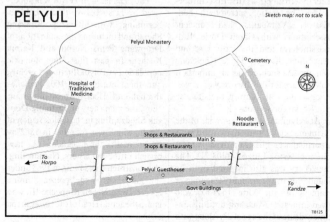

PELYUL — Sketch map: not to scale

Pelyul Monastery

Cemetery

N

Hospital of Traditional Medicine

Noodle Restaurant

Shops & Restaurants

Main St

Shops & Restaurants

To Horpo

Pelyul Guesthouse

Pol

Govt Buildings

To Kandze

TIB125

college are presided over by Dr Phuntsok Rabten, who has struggled heroically to provide a service in great demand by the local Tibetan population.

Dominating the Ngu-chu valley, which is somewhat reminiscent of the Austrian Tyrol, the renovated **Pelyul Monastery** broods over the town on a verdant and picturesque hillside. The former tranquillity of the monastery will be hard to recapture since the sound of music and the radio broadcasts of the town permeate the hillside.

● **Facilities** Stay at the *Pelyul Guesthouse*, on the S bank of the Ngu-chu, which has comfortable rooms, brilliant electrical lighting, a restaurant, and a bath-house with solar heated hot water. The Public Security Bureau is adjacent to the hotel. The main street, on the N bank of the Ngu-chu, has a number of smaller restaurants, serving both Tibetan and Sichuan cuisine; and several shops selling clothing, groceries, electrical goods, and luxury items.

Pelyul Namgyel Jangchubling Monastery

History

The monastery of Namgyel Jangchubling was founded at Pelyul in 1665 by the king of Derge, Lachen Jampa Phuntsok, who appointed Rigdzin Kunzang Sherab (1636-99) as its first throne-holder. The location, sacred to the bodhisattva Vajrapani, had ancient associations with Garab Dorje, Padmasambhava and the latter's second generation disciple, Kyere Chokyong Wangpo. As such, it was an important power place for the discovery of *termas*. Prior to the 17th century, the site also had Kagyu connections.

At Pelyul, the teaching-cycles of the Nyingma school were maintained with a particular emphasis on the *terma*-tradition of Ratna Lingpa (1403-71). The monastery was also inspired from its foundation by the visionary teachings of Namcho Migyur Dorje (1645-67), who lived in nearby **Muksang** until his untimely death at the age of 23. Along with

Katok, it played a major role in the dissemination of the Nyingma Kama (the oral teachings of the Nyingma school), and the xylograph blocks for this collection of oral teachings (20 vols) along with the *Collected Works of Namcho Mingyur Dorje* were prepared and published here under the guidance of the eighth throne-holder, Orgyen Dongak Chokyi Nyima (1854-1906).

The temples of Pelyul were constructed on the slopes below the peak of Dzongnang and the ridge of Dago Osel Lhari. Among them the most important was the **Lhasarkhang** or **Chagrakhang**, constructed by Kunzang Sherab himself and containing a gilded copper image of Shakyamuni in the form of Jowo Yizhin Norbu, as well as frescoes of the Namcho deities. Stupas and reliquary halls housed the remains of past masters including those of Namcho Migyur Dorje. The **Dorsem Lhakhang** with its enormous image of Vajrasattva was constructed by the seventh throne-holder, Gyatrul Pema Dongak Tenzin (1830-91), and the **Terdzokhang** or library by the eighth. The ridge-top temple of **Dago Osel Lhari** contained images, tangkas and frescoes of deities according to the Mahayoga and Anuyoga systems.

The expansion of Pelyul was supervised by 11 successive throne-holders, beginning with Rigdzin Kunzang Sherab and including the emanations of Drupwang Pema Norbu and Karma Kuchen. In past times the monastic population at Pelyul fluctuated greatly, but there were over 100 branches throughout E Tibet, the most important being the monastery of **Tarthang Dongak Shedrupling** in the Golok region of Amdo, which was founded in 1882 by the seventh throne-holder. A new branch of the monastery, **Namdroling**, was constructed in S India in 1963 under the guidance of the present throne holder, Pema Norbu Rinpoche III, who is also the actual Head of the Nyingmapa School.

The site

The monastery (3,261m) is approached from the W end of town via the Hospital of Traditional Tibetan Medicine, and a lane which leads sharply uphill through a timber yard. The reconstruction at Pelyul began in 1981. The new **Assembly Hall** (Dukhang) contains images of Padmasambhava flanked by Shantaraksita and King Trisong Detsen. The skylight murals are exquisitely crafted. In succession (left to right) they depict: (left wall) Karma Chakme, Rongzompa, and Trisong Detsen; (inner wall): Namcho Mingyur Dorje, Longchen Rabjampa, and Rigdzin Kunzang Sherab, and (right wall): Nubchen Sangye Yeshe; Ratnalingpa, and Jamyang Khyentse Wangpo.

150 monks currently live in houses across the hillside, studying under the supervision of Tulku Tubten Pelzang and Chi-me Tulku, who are responsible for the reconstruction pending the exile of Penor Rinpoche in India. Beside the new temple is a chapel containing four large *mani* wheels and a room containing the relics of Namcho Migyur Dorje. Hardly any of the aforementioned xylographs survive, and new blocks are expensive to make.

Higher up on the ridge, the ruined walls of the original massive 2-storey temple are still prominent. Under close inspection, they reveal bullet-holes, as well as Marxist slogans in Chinese from the period of the Cultural Revolution. Above this ruin, on the NW summit is the newly restored hermitage of the late Dzongnang Rinpoche. The meditation retreat centre lies on the upper E side of the ridge.

Pelyul to Kandze road

Following the Ngu-chu valley upstream from Pelyul, the road passes through **Lingtang** and **Barong** (60 km), where forestry is the main industry; and **Zhang Chumdo**, where many small teams of Chinese gold prospectors can be seen spraying the hillside and panning the streams. Crossing the watershed pass (4,237m), the road cuts SE to **Dorkho Gonpa** of the Sakya school (3,612m), before heading NE towards Kandze. On this stretch, there are spectacular upland lakes and variegated grasslands of gentian, meconopsis and edelweiss. A turn-off on the right (E) leads towards Nyarong (see below, page 547). The final watershed pass cuts through the glacial **Kawalungring** range, which divides the Yangtze and Yalong basins. The overall distance from Pelyul to Kandze is 222 km.

DERGE COUNTY

སྡེ་དགེ

德格县 Dege

Population: 91,829   Area: 11,711 sq km

Derge is often regarded as the cultural, if not the geographical, heart of Kham. Traditionally it is the name given to a large independent kingdom, which occupied until recent times present day Jomda, Pelyul, and Sershul counties, in addition to Derge county. The much diminished county of Derge now comprises only the valley of the Zi-chu tributary of the Yangtze, extending from its watershed in the **Tro La** range to its confluence with the Yangtze; and the outlying grasslands of **Yilhun** and **Dzachuka** to the N, and the valley of **Mesho** to the S. The county capital is located at **Derge Gonchen** in the Zi-chu valley – 28 km NE from the Kamtok Drukha Zamchen bridge, 345 km from Chamdo, and 115 km from Pelyul.

Dzongsar

རྫོང་གསར

10 km N of **Horpo** township, and 32 km S of the **Kamtok Drukha** bridge, on the E bank of the Yangtze, the road swerves into a ravine to span the estuary of the **Mesho-chu**. A derelict fortified machine-gun post beside the bridge bears witness to the vigorous resistence maintained by the Khampa Chuzhi Gangdruk organization against the Chinese occupation. Heading inland from the bridge, a new road (constructed in 1992 to facilitate the timber industry) follows the Mesho-chu upstream towards **Dzongsar**, criss-crossing the river and passing through a delightful forest, where bears and wild cats are even now said to roam. Some 60 km along this road, the gorge deepens and you will notice an escarpment with a plunging waterfall to the left. Soon, the valley opens out into cultivated fields, and Dzongsar Monastery appears on the ridge ahead, with the college and village below. The road continues from here on to Mesho.

Dzongsar Tashi Lhatse

This Sakya Monastery was founded in 1253 by Drogon Chogyel Pakpa. During the 19th century, it was renovated and a college (Shedra) was constructed below

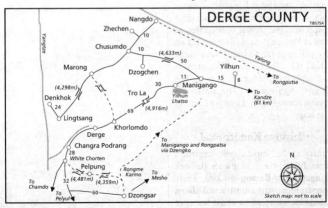

DERGE COUNTY

Sketch map: not to scale

the monastery by the eclectic master Jamyang Khyentse Wangpo (1820-92). He and his incarnation, Dzongsar Khyentse Chokyi Lodro (1896-1959) were among the most prolific teachers and lineage-holders of the combined Sakya, Nyingma, and Kagyu traditions in E Tibet. During the last and the present centuries Dzongsar was one of the most vital and active colleges in the whole of Tibet. The renovated **Assembly Hall** at the monastery is yet to be refurbished. **Upstairs**, the most important chapel contains the reliquaries and images of those two masters, along with an image of Vimalamitra, whose emanations they are said to have been. Rebuilding at Dzongsar is in the capable hands of Dr Lodro Phuntsok who collects many of his medicinal herbs on the grasslands above the monastery.

Pema Shelpuk and Rongme Karmo

4 hrs' trekking above Dzongsar will bring you to the **Pema Shelpuk cave**, associated with Padmasambhava. This power place is one of the 25 important pilgrimage sites in E Tibet, specifically representing the speech aspect of buddha-attributes. Here in the 19th century, the treasure-finder Chogyur Dechen Lingpa (1829-70) discovered an important work entitled *Three Classes of the Great Perfection (Dzogchen Desum)*. Further E from Dzongsar at **Rongme Karmo** 'tiger den', there is another *terma*-site connected with the same master. Here, too, Jamyang Khyentse Wangpo (1820-92) and Jamgon Kongtrul Lodro Thaye (1813-99) redacted a *Means for the Attainment of Dorje Drolo (Drolod Drubthab)* and experienced portentous signs of successful practice, when two huge scorpions appeared in a vision. The scorpion is the hand-emblem of the deity Dorje Drolo. Mipham Rinpoche (1846-1912) also stayed here in retreat for 13 years.

Trekking

From Rongme Karmo there is a trekking route to **Manigango** and **Rongpatsa** via **Dzengko**; and from Pema Shelpuk another trekking route to Pelpung Monastery.

Pelpung Tubden Chokhorling Monastery

From Dzongsar, a 1 day trek leads NW through a pine-clad ravine and across **Ha La pass** (4,359m) to **Pelpung**, located on the knoll of a grassland valley, girded with pine-forest. The grand assembly hall of **Pelpung Tubten Chokhorling Monastery**, which was founded in 1717 by Tai Situ VIII Chokyi Jungne, was the largest Kagyu monastery within the kingdom of Derge, and it rapidly became the most important centre in E Tibet for the study of the Kagyu tradition. Prior to its construction the previous seven incarnations bearing the name Tai Situ lived mostly at **Karma Gon** Monastery in Lhato. The first of these had received the title from the Da Ming emperor in the 15th century. An important woodblock collection for the five anthologies of Jamgon Kongtrul, including the *Store of Precious Treasures (Rinchen Terdzo)* was housed here; but severely damaged in the 1960s. New woodblocks have recently been prepared in Derge to replace the missing volumes.

ACCESS From Pelpung, you can trek back across Ha La to Dzongsar, or alternatively trek W across **Gotse La** pass (4,481m) to **Shigargarba** village and the **White Chorten** which overlooks the confluence of the Pelpung-chu with the Yangtze. Pelpung can also be reached by driving N from Horpo for 54 km, passing the **Kamtok Drukha Zamchen** bridge en route, but staying on the E bank of the Yangtze as far as the **White Chorten**. You would then trek E across Gotse La. The distance from the White Chorten to Derge is 16 km.

SUCCESSIVE INCARNATIONS OF TAI SITU	
Tai Situ I Kyechok Chokyi Gyeltsen	(1377-1488)
Tai Situ II Tashi Namgyel	(1450-1497)
Tai Situ III Tashi Peljor	(1498-1541)
Tai Situ IV Mitruk Chokyi Gocha	(1542-1585)
Tai Situ V Norbu Sampel	(1586-1657)
Tai Situ VI Chokyi Gyeltsen Gelek Pelzangpo	(1658-1682)
Tai Situ VII Mipham Trinle Rabten	(1683-1698)
Tai Situ VIII Chokyi Jungne	(1700-1774)
Tai Situ IX Pema Nyinje Wangpo	(1774-1853)
Tai Situ X Pema Kunzang Chogyel	(1854-1885)
Tai Situ XI Pema Wangchuk Gyelpo	(1886-1852)
Tai Situ XII Pema Dongak Nyinje Wangpo	(b 1954)

Changra Podrang

A short distance N of the White Chorten which marks the beginning of the Pelpung trail, the road passes below the ruins of **Changra Podrang**, the former summer palace of the kings of Derge, where a small temple [Changra Gonpa] has recently been restored. The short drive from here to Derge leaves the Yangtze at its confluence with the Zi-chu, and follows the latter upstream through a prosperous farming belt. The road markers from the Kamtok Drukha Zamchen bridge begin at 980 km and run in descending order, all the way to Chengdu.

Derge

(3,292m) Derge was the largest and most influential of the five kingdoms of Kham. The crafts of Derge, particularly in printing and metal work were renowned throughout Tibet. The independence of the kingdom was firmly maintained until 1865 and sporadically thereafter by its hereditary kings, who have been documented in J Kolmas, *A Genealogy of the Kings of Derge*.

The buildings of Derge are located in a sharp-sided ravine, which abuts the Zi-chu valley. At present, it appears to have lost much of its former grandeur. The best view is to be obtained from the cave of Tangtong Gyelpo, high up on the cliff-face across the Zi-chu. From this vantage point one can clearly discern the ruins of the royal palace and the reconstructed monastery of **Derge Gonchen**. Further downhill in the centre of town is the **Derge Parkhang** and further to the right is the old Tibetan quarter where the houses are clustered around the **Temple of Tangtong Gyelpo**. Below the Parkhang is a large reconstructed stupa – originally founded by Dudul Dorje and later rebuilt by Jamyang Khyentse Wangpo.

The town still has a majority Tibetan population; which is considerably increased in summertime when the **Rain Retreat Festival** attracts visitors from all parts of Kham.

Places of interest

Derge Gonchen Monastery

The ruined monastery was rapidly reconstructed between 1987 and 1988, the internal structures and windows being rebuilt around the shell of the outer walls which largely remained from the past. The **Assembly Hall (Dukhang)** with its high fluted columns is illuminated by windows on the upper level. It leads to a central throne, which is the seat of Sakya Trizin, the head of the Sakyapa school who currently resides at Rajpur in India. Behind the throne is an **inner sanctum** containing enormous clay images of the Buddhas of the Three Times. The antechamber contains on its

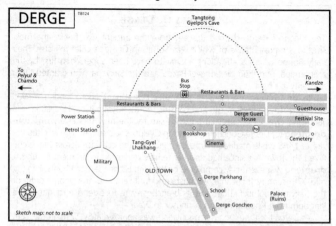

```
DERGE                    TIB124              Tangtong
                                             Gyelpo's Cave

To                                   Bus
Pelyul &                             Stop
Chamdo                                      Restaurants & Bars          To
                                                                       Kandze
                            Restaurants & Bars                      Guesthouse
                                                   Derge Guest
         Power Station                             House           Festival Site
         Petrol Station              Bookshop
                                                            Cemetery
                         Tang-Gyel            Cinema
                         Lhakhang
              Military
                                   OLD TOWN
   N                                    Derge Parkhang
                                                         Palace
                                        School           (Ruins)
Sketch map: not to scale                Derge Gonchen
```

walls a painting of the deer and dharma-wheel motif alongside a list of all those who have made donations towards the rebuilding programme.

Derge Parkhang Printing Press

The celebrated printing press of **Derge Parkhang** is a magnificent 3-storeyed building with original frescoes that were blackened by smoke during the wanton destruction of the 1960s, but recently restored with painstaking care. Beyond the portico, there is an inner courtyard, giving access to the **temple** on the ground level, **the printing works** on the second level, and **the rooftop chapels** on the third level. The temple contains exquisite images of Shakyamuni Buddha, the lineage-holders of the Sakyapa tradition, and its protector deities. **Upstairs**, is the precious collection of xylograph blocks, including the Derge editions of the *Kangyur*, *Tangyur*, *Nyingma Gyudbum* and other works, which are constantly in demand throughout the towns, villages and monasteries of Tibet. The entire printing process can be observed here: from the preparation of the paper and the ink to the carving of the woodblocks and the actual printing and collating of the various texts. The bookshop

(open Mon to Sat) is located in the S wing of the building opposite the Parkhang.

Tangyel Lhakhang

Surrounded by the timber and adobe residential houses of the Tibetan quarter, the **Tangyel Lhakhang** is dedicated to the memory of Tangtong Gyelpo, Tibet's multi-talented bridge-builder, dramatist, engineer and treasure-finder, who consecrated the site of the Gonchen Monastery in 1448. The temple, which was severely damaged during the 1960s, contains a fine characteristic image of this great figure – identified by his reddish brown complexion, white hair and white beard. There is also a large *Mani Wheel* in an adjacent building; and the elderly townspeople devote much time to the circumambulation of the entire complex.

Festivals

Rain Retreat Festival This monastic festival is an occasion for religious dances, depicting the purification of negativity by Shakyamuni over his successive past lives. The performance is held on the open plain by the Zi-chu River, adjacent to the Chinese Martyrs' Cemetery; and colourful tents are pitched on this site for the duration of the festival.

HISTORY OF DERGE

The Kings of Derge claimed descent from the ancient Gar family, the most illustrious representative of which was Songtsen Gampo's chief minister. Their early Bonpo religious affiliations appear to have been superseded first by the Nyingmapa, and then by Chogyel Pakpa and the Sakyapa who granted them authority in Kham.

In the 15th century, the 31st generation descendant, Lodro Tobden, moved his capital to the present site and constructed the royal palace. He also invited Tangtong Gyelpo to select an adjacent site for the new monastery of **Lhun-drupteng** (or Derge Gonchen). Tangtong Gyelpo is said to have consecrated the site in 1448 while meditating in a cave high on the cliff-face across the Zi-chu River. The town has since had another temple dedicated to his memory. **Lhun-drupteng** was eventually completed by the king Lachen Jampa Phuntsok in the mid-17th century. It became the most important centre for the Ngorpa order of the Sakya school in E Tibet and its branches were to extend throughout the kingdom from Khorlomdo and Dzongsar to Wara.

At Derge itself the monastic population was approximately 1700. In the 18th century the king Tenpa Tsering (1678-1738) brought Derge to the height of its power by overpowering the outlying northern districts of **Dzachuka**. Under his auspices, the celebrated printery, **Derge Parkhang**, was established in 1729. Here, the Sakya scholar Zhuchen Tsultrim Rinchen produced his own edition of the *Kangyur* and *Tangyur*, generally regarded as the most accurate in Tibet. However, the collection of xylograph blocks housed at the printery, carved in the style of the **Kutse school**, was also regarded as the most eclectic in Tibet. Works of the Nyingma, Kagyu and Geluk schools were printed alongside those of the Sakyapa. The eclecticism of the kingdom was also reflected in the scope given to non-Sakya traditions, particularly of the Nyingma and Kagyu schools, for their own development.

The kingdom which had survived the campaign of Gushri Qan in the 17th century finally succumbed to Gonpo Namgyel, the chieftain of Nyarong in 1863. However, the latter was defeated by the Tibetan army in 1865 and after an interim period of administration from Lhasa, independence was restored. Later, the armies of Chao Erh Feng occupied the kingdom and it remained in Chinese possession between 1909-1918.

Local information

Below the stupa, the richly decorated Tibetan town gives way to Chinese buildings in drab concrete – the cinema, the shops, the hotel, and government buildings. These lead down to the river front and the main road, flanked on both sides by small restaurants, shops, and bars.

Upper Zi-chu Valley

The highway from Derge to Chengdu (952 km) begins by following the Zi-chu River upstream to its source in the Drida Zelmogang range. This is the name given to the highland region forming a watershed between the upper Yangtze and the upper Yalong. En route it passes through **Khorlomdo**, where there is a small Sakya temple, and the **Kasado** gorge. The ascent to the watershed **Tro La** pass (4,916m), 69 km NE of Derge, is precipitous and switchback, gradually rising above the tree line into a world of jagged snow mountains. There are magnificent views of the Yangtze gorge to the SW. On the far side of Tro La, the landscape is totally different, the enclosed forested valleys giving way to rugged open grassland. The

YANGTZE RIVER

This mighty river (6,300 km) is the longest in Asia and the third longest in the world. There are two main sources: the southern one, known as the Dam-chu (Ulan Muren) rises in the Dangla mountains at 5,486m; and the northern source, known as the Chumar-chu, rises in the Kunluns. These converge above Chumarleb, and flow initially through a spacious lakeland valley. The Yangtze has eight principal tributaries, of which the Yalong, Gyarong, Minjiang, and Jialing all originate on the Tibetan plateau. The upper reaches of the river are inhabited by nomadic peoples, who are largely pastoralists, but also engaged in subsistence farming. South of the Bayankala range, the river forms a narrow gorge, 3-5 km deep in places, and with sheer river-bank peaks as high as 4,900m. Some remote villages are located high up on the river banks. For over 350 km the river flows S through this gorge in close proximity to the Salween and Mekong (which are all within 25-40 km of each other). In winter when the water level is lowest the river is deep blue in colour; but in the rainy season when coffee-coloured alluvium is carried downstream at the rate of 430-500 million tons per annum, its rapid flow increases to more than 2,000 cu m per second.

On reaching the territory of the Jang (Naxi) nationality, at the southernmost outpost of Tibetan culture (now in Yunnan province), the river loops sharply NE to touch the Sichuan border near Mili, and bends back upon itself (SW), before turning E into Dukou. Here, at the confluence of the Yalong, the river widens to 396m and increases to 9m in depth. The other major tributaries – the Gyarong (Dadu) and the Min, which both rise in Amdo, converge together at Leshan in Sichuan province, before emptying into the Yangtze at Yibin.

---

crossroads town of **Manigango** is located in the grassland, 110 km from Derge, and 41 km from Tro La pass.

Yilhun

The grassland region to the NE of Tro La pass is known as **Yilhun**. On the descent, take a turn-off on the right (S) to visit the sacred glacial lake of **Yilhun Lhatso** (*Ch* Xinluhai), situated some 30 km below the pass. This lake is one of the most beautiful in all Tibet – its shores bedecked with carved *mani* stones. The mountains and rocks surrounding the lake are said to assume the divine form of the Cakrasamvara *mandala* to those who have the pure vision to perceive them as such. If you have time, pitch a tent here, and explore the pilgrim's trail along the lake shore.

Manigango

The town of **Manigango**, 11 km below the lake, lies at the junction of three important roads. Derge lies 110 km to

the SW, Jyekundo 429 km to the NW, and Kandze 84 km to the SE. In the meadow above the town there is a branch of Dzogchen Monastery, known as **Yazer Gon**. It was in this locale that Derge Yilhunpa Sonam Namgyel attained the rainbow body accomplishment in 1952. An interesting account of this event is described by Chogyam Trunpa in his autobiography, *Born in Tibet*.

● **Facilities** Stay at either the *Qinghai Guesthouse* or *Sichuan Guesthouse* – the latter has electric blankets on the beds, and an excellent Sichuan-style kitchen beloved by truckers and bus drivers. There are 2 small general stores, selling groceries, liquor, and a few household necessities.

Some 23 km E of Manigango, a motorable road leaves the Kandze highway and the Yi-chu valley, via a side-bridge and heads N to **Yilhun** township. Here, in Aug, there is a small but interesting horse-festival, held on a wide plain below the local monastery and village.

Dzogchen Rudam Orgyen Samten Choling Monastery

ཛོགས་ཆེན་དགོན་པ

ACCESS From Manigango, take the NW route for **Jyekundo**, and cross the Muri La pass (4,633m). After 50 km, you will notice the hamlet of **Dzogchen** coming into view on the left (S) side of the road. Above it you will notice the **Mani Wheel Chapel** of Dzogchen Monastery on a ridge, protruding from a hidden valley to the SW. Leave the highway here and drive across a stream, leading down to the hamlet. The road cuts across a low defile to enter the wonderful valley of **Rudam Kyitram**, where Dzogchen Monastery is located.

History of Dzogchen Monastery

Dzogchen is recognized as the major pilgrimage site of buddha-attributes in E Tibet and as one of the largest monasteries of the Nyingma school in Kham. It lies at an elevation of 4,023m, in the concealed valley of Rudam Kyitram, dominated to the SW by the jagged snow peaks of **Trori Dorje Ziltrom** (5,816m).

The monastery was founded in 1684-85 on the advice of the Dalai Lama V, by the charismatic Dzogchen I Pema Rigdzin (1625-97), and it was subsequently maintained by his students, including Zhechen Rapjam Tenpei Gyeltsen, and by his successive incarnations. Among the latter, Dzogchen II Gyurme Tekchok Tenzin (1699-1758) is known to have inspired the king of Derge to construct the famous **Derge Parkhang**, Dzogchen III Ngedon Tenzin Zangpo (1759-92) built 13 hermitages, colleges and mantra-wheels, Dzogchen IV Migyur Namkei Dorje (b 1793) presided over the monastery when its greatest college was founded, and Dzogchen V Tubten Chokyi Dorje (1872-1935) increased its branches to over 200 throughout Kham, Amdo, and Central Tibet. The mother monastery itself had a population of 1,000 monks. Dzogchen VI Jikdrel Jangchub Dorje (1935-59) died tragically during the resistance to the Chinese occupation of E Tibet, and his reliquary is even now revered in the main temple. Dzogchen Rinpoche VII lives in Karnataka in S India, where he has constructed a branch of the monastery.

At Dzogchen Monastery, two great temples were constructed. The **larger** housed exquisite images of Shakyamuni, Vajradhara and Padmasambhava, alongside the reliquaries of the past emanations of Pema Rigdzin. The **smaller** to the NE contained enormous images of Padmasambhava, Shantaraksita and King Trisong Detsen. In the early 19th century, a college was constructed below the monastery by Gyelse Zhenpen Thaye at a site consecrated by the ancient Nyingma lineage-holder Shrisimha. The college, known thereafter as **Shrisimha**, became renowned for the study of philosophy and Vajrayana until the mid-20th century. It attracted some of the greatest literati of E Tibet, such as Peltrul Rinpoche (1808-87), Mipam Rinpoche (1846-1912) and Khenpo Zhenga (1871-1927), who wrote commentaries on 13 major texts.

Meditation hermitages The monastery was equally renowned for its meditation hermitages and the caves which were inhabited by hermits in the upper reaches of the Rudam Kyitram valley. Important figures such as Dodrub Trinle Ozer (1745-1821), Do Khyentse Yeshe Dorje (b 1800), Peltrul Rinpoche and Mipham Rinpoche passed many years in meditation in this region, the rocks of which are intimately connected with their visionary experiences. It was also here that Peltrul Rinpoche composed his great commentary on the preliminary practices of Buddhist meditation, the *Kunzang Lamei Zhelung* (translated into English under the title "Words of my Perfect Teacher").

The Site

The monastery is located on the N slopes of the Rudam Kyitram valley. The larger of the two temples which formerly housed the relics of past Dzogchen Rinpoches is yet to be restored. The **smaller** one, where the images of Padmasambhava, King Trisong Detsen and Shantaraksita were once enshrined, is undergoing restoration. It has decorative columns at the entrance, protected by silk wrappings, and in its upper storey there is a chapel containing the relics of Dzogchen VI Jikdrel Jangchub Dorje, who was killed in 1959. Religious dancing is still held in the courtyard on the 10th day of the 1st month of the Tibetan calendar.

To the N of these temples is a **Mani Wheel** temple, and to the S are two lower elongated buildings on either side of an open courtyard. Approaching these from the temple, one passes the **Ngakhang** on the left and the **Podrang Khamsum Zilnon** on the right. The latter building, which once housed many chapels, contains in its upper storey the residence of Dzogchen Rinpoche named **Chime Drupei Gatsel**, a library, a printery, and a temporary residence where the present Dzogchen Rinpoche stayed during a recent visit.

Below the monastery and to the right is the **Shrisimha college**, so called because this ancient yogin is said to have appeared in a vision to the college's founder and to have left an impression in a nearby rock. A few buildings within the small campus have been restored by Tulku Kelzang, who has revitalized the college in collaboration with Khenpo Dazer and Khenpo Bentse.

The Cave Hermitages

Heading up the valley from the college towards the cave hermitages and the **Trori** glacier (NW face of Tro La), you first pass, in a clearing, a series of burial stones marking the graves of past monastic preceptors. Above and to the right as you ascend the valley is the ruined hermitage of the monastery where long regulated retreats were once held. Higher up the slope on the same side of the valley are firstly the cave-hermitage of Do Khyentse Yeshe Dorje, known as

the **Tseringma cave** because he is said to have met the deity Tseringma here face to face, and secondly that of Peltrul Rinpoche.

Continuing up the central part of the valley you reach an elevated area where there are well-constructed and active hermitages. On the hillside to the left, high up and across the rushing river is the cave-hermitage known as **Shinje Drupuk** – a former retreat of Dodrub Jigme Trinle Ozer, containing a footprint of Yamantaka which gives the cave its name. Directly opposite the cave site on the right side of the valley is a rock into which the deity Palchen Dupa vanished after appearing in a vision to Dodrub Trinle Ozer. Below this cave is another, approached from the site where Peltrul Rinpoche first taught his celebrated text, *Kunzang Lamei Zhelung*. It contains the meditation-box of Peltrul Rinpoche and naturally produced impressions of Yamantaka which appeared while Dodrub Rinpoche was engaged in practice there. Yet lower down is a **cave of Mipam Rinpoche** containing original but damaged clay relief images of the 25 disciples of Padmasambhava.

From atop these caves one has an excellent view to the N beyond Dzogchen Monastery to the **Kyadrak Senge Dzong** retreat (4,872m) in Dzachuka, the major pilgrimage site representing buddha-body in Kham. There, Padmasambhava himself is reputed to have passed 3 months.

Above the valley in the Rudam Kangtro range are three sacred lakes and on their circuit is a place where Padmasambhava made medicinal myrobalan.

Zhechen Tenyi Dargyeling Monastery

ཞེ་ཆེན་བསྟན་གཉིས་དར་རྒྱས་གླིང་པ

ACCESS Returning to the highway from Dzogchen, drive W for 10 km as far as the transport station at **Chusumdo** (Ch Sansaho). Here, a side-road follows the Nang-chu tributary of the Yalong downstream to its confluence. Some 10 km along this road, you will reach **Zhechen Monastery** on the left (W). This monastery, located in the Nang-chu valley, is situated in a defile between **Bonri** and **Dolmari** hills (3,780m). The site was chosen because on the slopes of Dolmari there were many sacred hermitages and caves associated with Padmasambhava, Yeshe Tsogyel, Vajravarahi, Tangtong Gyelpo and so forth.

History of Zhechen Monastery

The monastery was founded in 1735 by Zhechen Rabjam II, Gyurme Kunzang Namgyel (1710-69). His predecessor, Zhechen Rabjam I Tenpei Gyeltsen (1654-1709), had been a student of Dalai Lama V and Dzogchen Pema Rigdzin. The seat was maintained by his successive emanations, including Zhechen Rabjam III Rigdzin Peljor Gyatso (1771-1809), who constructed the **Pema Choling** hermitage in 1794; and Zhechen Rapjam IV Garwang Chokyi Gyeltsen, as well as by a succession of regents. In the time of the regent Gyeltsab Tendzin Chogyel, 100,000 students gathered from all four Buddhist traditions and also from the Bon to receive his teachings. In more recent years however, the resident population of the mother monastery included about 300 monks. The present Zhechen Rabjam VII, under the guidance of the late HH Dingo Khyentse Rinpoche, constructed a new flourishing branch of the monastery at Boudha in Nepal.

The monastery was known for its fine sculptures, tangkas and murals. Formerly there were two temples with major images of Shakyamuni and Padmasambhava, respectively representing the sutra and mantra traditions. There was also a famous image made of herbs, representing Terdak Lingpa, the founder of Mindroling. Alongside these images were eight reliquaries containing the remains of past Zhechen Rabjam emanations and their regents.

A prestigious college at Zhechen was founded in this century by Gyeltsab III Pema Namgyel (1871-1927), and it rapidly became known in Kham for the excellence of its study programme, largely through the efforts of the late Zhechen Kongtrul (d 1959) and the late Zhechen Rabjam VI (d 1959). Woodblocks were kept for the works of Karma Lingpa and for liturgical texts associated with Mindroling Monastery.

The site

The hill to the right as one approaches from the Chusumdo-Nangdo road, is **Bonri** and the one to the left **Dolmari**. Of the former impressive structures on the slopes of Dolmari, nothing remains. The two original temples are currently undergoing reconstruction. At present there are approximately 200-300 monks affiliated with Zhechen, but few live permanently at the site.

Above the temple is the ruined hermitage, and below and beyond the stream is the **college**, restored through the efforts of the late Lama Gyenpel. The main building of the college contains a shrine with a new Padmasambhava image and a gold-painted footprint of its founder, Zhechen Gyeltsab III.

Sacred caves

Above the monastery on **Dolmari** are many sacred caves and hermitages associated with important historical figures and deities. Among them the following are most notable:

The **Kabgye Drupuk**, where Vajravarahi reputedly appeared in a rock during the meditations of Gyeltsab Gyurme Pema Namgyel. This cave was damaged during the Cultural Revolution, but the earth inside is held by pilgrims to be sacred.

The **Zangdok Pelri Drupuk** of Padmasambhava and Yeshe Tsogyel, where pilgrims go to gather natural medicinal nectar.

The **Khandro Bumgyi Drupuk**, which is adorned with a red and white stupa and a dark blue relief image of Tangtong Gyelpo.

The former **hermitage of Gyeltsab Tenzin Chogyel** and site of the destroyed hermitage of the previous Zhechen Rabjam VI.

The **Osel Drupuk** which has a naturally produced image of the deity Rigdzin Dupa.

Zhechen to Nangdo

10 km N of Zhechen, the Nang-chu flows into the Yalong at **Nangdo**. From here there are trekking routes following the Yalong downstream towards the farming settlements of **Rongpatsa**, and upstream into the sparse grasslands of **Sershul** county. The monasteries of **Drokda Gonpa** and **Samdrub Gonpa** are located downstream around the confluence of the Ding-chu with the Yalong, while **Peni Gonpa** and **Dzechen Gonpa** lie upstream.

Chusumdo to Denkhok

Another motorable trail leads SW from Chusumdo to **Marong**, where Jamgon Kongtrul discovered *termas* in the 19th century. (A trekking route also leads from here across **Le La** pass to **Khorlomdo** near Derge.) The motorable trail then crosses the watershed **Latse Kare La** pass (4,298m) and enters **Lingtsang**, one of the former independent kingdoms of E Tibet, where the Gyelpo (king) claimed descent from Tibet's epic hero Ling Gesar. En route you pass the Nyingmapa monastery of **Dzungo** which spectacularly overlooks the Yangtze from its hilltop pinnacle.

At Lingtsang, there is a large distinctively striped Sakya monastery called **Gotse Gon**. A wide cultivated plain opens out 24 km from Lingtsang, where the road reaches **Denkhok** on the E bank of the Yangtze. Denkhok, the birthplace of the late HH Dingo Khyentse Rinpoche, is nowadays divided into two main sectors – **Denkhok Nubma** lying within the jurisdiction of the Tibetan Autonomous Region on the W bank of the Yangtze, and **Denkhok Sharma** within Sichuan province on the E bank. The Gelukpa monastery of **Chunkor** (a branch of Sershul) is located on the W bank, and the celebrated **Langtang Dolma Lhakhang**, one of Songtsen Gampo's 12 major geomantic temples, is located on the E bank. As its name suggests, it contains an image of Tara (restored).

GRASSLANDS OF DZACHUKA, JYEKUNDO AND NANGCHEN

The upper reaches of the Yalong, Yangtze, and Mekong rivers in the extreme NW of Kham flow through spacious grasslands, largely above the tree line. Here are some of the richest nomadic pastures in Tibet, and a surprisingly large number of monasteries, which minister to the spiritual needs of the nomadic population as well as to the inhabitants of the relatively few agricultural settlements. Driving across the watersheds of these mighty rivers, you will pass through seven counties, one of which (Sershul) is presently administered from Dartsedo (Sichuan), and the remaining six from Jyekundo (Qinghai).

Recommended itinerary: 8.

SERSHUL COUNTY
སེར་ཤུལ

石渠县 Serxu
Population: 68,814   Area: 20,477 sq km

The rich nomadic pastures of **Sershul** extend through the upper reaches of the Yalong as far as the present day Sichuan-Qinghai provincial border. (The actual source of the Yalong lies across the border near **Domda**.) The county capital is located at **Jumang**, now a large sprawling frontier town (generally called Sershul), 139 km from Jyekundo, and 219 km from Manigango. There are 43 monasteries within Sershul county, reflecting all the diverse traditions of Tibetan Buddhism and Bon.

Tsatsha Gon and Junyung

From **Langtang Dolma Lhakhang** at Denkhok in the Yangtze valley, there is an old caravan trail following the Yangtze upstream via the ferry-crossing of **Drenda Druka** to approach Jyekundo from the SE. The main highway however runs NW from **Chusumdo** (*Ch* Sansaho) through the Nang-chu valley, crossing the **Magar Drokra** grassland. After passing the Gelukpa monastery of **Trugu Gonpa** (also pronounced as Jowo) on the left (36 km from Chusumdo), the road leaves the Nang-chu and follows the Tra-chu downstream past the turn-off for **Ralung-kado** village on the right (42 km from Trugu Gonpa), and the important Karma Kagyu monastery of **Tsatsha Gon** after 10 further km.

Here, there is a turn-off on the right, which follows the Tra-chu downstream for 40 km as far as its confluence with the Yalong at **Tung** township. The Nyingmapa monastery of **Tashul** can be visited on this side-road. At Tung township, the Ngoshi-chu tributary also flows into the Yalong from the NW.

Keep to the highway at **Tsatsha Gon**, and the road will continue N to reach the S bank of the Yalong. Following the course of this main waterway upstream, after 38 km (at marker 186), you will arrive at **Rinyur Gonpa** (on the left) and a turn-off (on the right) which leads E to **Arikdza Gonpa** of the Nyingma school.

Further N, the main road passes through **Junyung** township on the left (46 km from Tsatsha Gon). Here there is the Nyingmapa monastery of **Junyung Mehor Sangak Choling** and its retreat hermitage, where the renowned Mipham Rinpoche (1846-1912) studied and practised. At **Junyung**, the Omchung-chu flows into the Yalong from the S via **Bumsar** township, and the Nyingma monastery of **Ponru Gonpa** is located up a lateral valley on the N bank.

The highway continues NW from **Junyung**, following the river bank upstream for a short distance, and then abruptly heads SW following the Omchu tributary upstream to the county capital at **Jumang** (Sershul). If you prefer to continue following the Yalong, a trekking route leads upstream as far as **Gemang**, where there is an important branch of Dzogchen Monastery. Beyond Gemang, the Muge-chu tributary flows in from the NW and you will reach the Gelukpa monastery of **Kabzhi**, where there are 250 monks. From here, you can cross the provincial border to reach the source of the Yalong at **Domda**.

Jumang

Driving S along the main road through the Om-chu valley, 19 km after Junyung, the main road passes the Gelukpa monastery of **Bumnying Gonpa**, where there are 200 monks. The county capital of **Jumang** lies in the same valley, 6 km further S. This is the largest Chinese settlement NW of Kandze, and the nomadic peoples of the grasslands intermingle here with incongruous Chinese immigrants.

● **Facilities** The sprawling main street has a petrol station and bus station at the E end (S side). Across on the N side of the street you will pass in succession: the Cinema, the Book Store, the Post Office, the Public Security Bureau, and a number of general stores and simple Sichuan-style restaurants. At the W end of town, there are 2 hotels, one on either side of the main street. The hotel on the N side also owns the adjacent *Tiemushe Restaurant*.

Sershul Monastery

ACCESS Leaving the capital, the road also leaves the Om-chu valley, and heads NW, passing the small hamlets of Jumang and **Serlha** on the right. From **Deongma** township, 18 km after Jumang, you can see the Nyingma monastery of **Dzakya Gonpa**, in the distance to the NW. Here there are 50 monks.

The great **Sershul Monastery** of the Gelukpas school lies 27 km E of

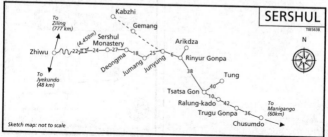

Sketch map: not to scale

Deongma, on the right side of the road. This is currently the largest monastery in Sershul county, with 800 monks, and a grand assembly hall. The rain retreat festival held in Aug is a magnificent spectacle, attracting nomad communities from afar. The hills and plains around the monastery (4,054m) are bare and spacious. Beyond the monastery, the highway heads W for 24 km over a pot-holed and deeply rutted surface to cross the **Ngamba La** pass (4,450m), which divides the Yalong and Yangtze basins, as well as the present day provinces of Sichuan and Qinghai.

JYEKUNDO COUNTY

སྐྱེ་དགུ་མདོ

玉树县 Yushu

Population: 61,976   Area: 13,738 sq km

Jyekundo county is the NW region of Kham, known locally as **Gawa**, which occupies the upper reaches and source feeder rivers of the Yangtze. At the present day the city of Jyekundo is not only the county capital, but also the administrative capital of six counties belonging to the Yushu Tibetan Autonomous Prefecture of Qinghai Province. Here the predominant traditions are those of the Sakyapa and Kagyupa.

Zhiwu

Descending from the **Ngamba La** pass (4,450m) the highway zigzags downhill for 22 km to the township of Zhiwu (*Ch* Xiwu), a low-lying (3,900m) settlement straddling an important crossroads. The township actually falls within Trindu county but is described here for practical reasons. On the descent from the pass there are magnificent views of **Drogon**

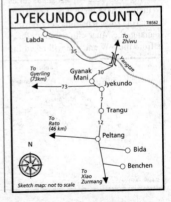

JYEKUNDO COUNTY

Monastery, clinging to the sheer cliff-face above the town, and painted in the distinctive Sakya colours. At the cross-roads, a barrier blocks the road, indicating that you are about to drive from Sichuan into Qinghai. The road to the N (right) leads 777 km to Ziling, and the road to the S (left) leads 48 km to Jyekundo. Southwest of town, is the hilltop monastery of **Nyidzong**, which belongs to the Drigung Kagyu school.

Drogon Monastery

The Sakyapa monastery known as **Drogon Gonpa** originally belonged to the Kadampa tradition, but was converted by Drogon Chogyel Phakpa during the 13th century. From his time until the present, there have been 18 lineage-holders, bearing the title Dro-la or Do-la. The present incumbent is Do-la Jikme Chokyi Nyima, a son of the late HH Dudjom Rinpoche, and father of the present Dudjom Rinpoche. Do-la Jikme was recognized at the age of 7 by the head of the Sakya school; and thereafter educated in Kham. Other teachers associated with Drogon Monastery include Gaden Wangchuk (Ga Tulku) and Ngakpa Ngoten. Currently there are about 70 monks here. The summer festival following the end of the rain retreat is a major event held in the plains below the monastery.

The **main temple** with 38 columns is now being restored. It is planned to install 2-storey images of Shakyamuni, Padmasambhava, and Maitreya in gilded bronze. At present, the smaller **Tsuklakhang** with 16 columns has been undergoing restoration and refurbishment since 1981. The central image, encased in glass, is of the previous Sakya Gongma, and the altar also has colour photographs of the present throne-holders of the Dolma and Phuntsok palaces of Sakya, who respectively reside at Rajpur in India and Seattle in the USA. Alongside these is a photograph of the present Dzongsar Khyentse, a nephew of Do-la Jikme, who now resides in Bhutan and the West. To the left of Sakya Gongma are images of Shakyamuni and the Sixteen Elders, while to the right are an assortment of images, including Tara, Padmasambhava, and Vajrasattva. Below the central image of Sakya Gongma (in the same glass case) are a number of old images including Vajrasattva. Tangkas which decorate the side-walls, including two very old ones depicting Two-armed Mahakala and Vajrabhairava. There are also new images which have been brought from Chamdo, including one of Padmasambhava. On the left is a large Maitreya in a glass case.

Among other restored chapels at Drogon Monastery, visit the **Gonkhang**, containing images of Panjaranatha and the eight classes of spirits (Lhade-gye), the **Mani Wheel Chapel**, and the revered **Vajrayogini Temple**. Below the complex, to the right, is a series of the Eight Stupas symbolizing the major events in the life of the Buddha.

● **Facilities** There are 2 hotels at the N end of town, the *Transport Station Guesthouse* down an alleyway on the right, and a Tibetan family-run hotel called *Mirik Dronkhang* on the left. Stay at the latter! There are a number of small tea-shops and restaurants nr the cross-roads, some serving excellent Muslim tea and lamb dishes.

Yangtze Crossing

Cultivated fields appear around Zhiwu, in contrast to the high grasslands of Dzachuka to the E. The climate is several degrees warmer. The highway to Jyekundo heads S on an excellent paved surface, following the Zhiwuchi-chu downstream to its confluence with the Yangtze after 18 km. En route you will bypass the Kagyupa monasteries of **Bage Gonpa** and **Bambi Gonpa**. Crossing the bridge over the Yangtze at **Druda**, you will notice a trail on the right (W) which follows the course of the Yangtze upstream for 35 km to **Labda** township. En route, you can visit **Tarlam**

Monastery (4,000m), the residence of Pende Rinpoche of the Ngorpa branch of the Kagyu school, who currently resides in France. Other monasteries on that road include Sangda Gonpa and Gara Gonpa.

Gyanak Mani

Continuing on the paved highway, you will reach Jyekundo after 30 km. At the beginning of the descent into Jyekundo valley, the road passes through **Gyanak Mani** – the largest field of *mani* stones in the whole of Tibet. Stop here to circumambulate the field and wander through the lanes between enormous piles of carved stones and prayer flags. Some stones are intricately inscribed with entire sections from the scriptures, and others have bas-relief images of certain meditational deities. The original temple on this site was constructed in the late 13th century by Gyanak Tulku who came here from Chamdo on a return visit from China. The field of stones bears witness to the faith of the Tibetan pilgrims who would travel along the trade routes from Ziling to Lhasa via Jyekundo and make offerings as an expression of their devotion. During the 1960s, many stones were removed for the construction of latrines, but the site has since been reconsecrated, and renovation is supervised by the present incumbent lama, Gyanak Tulku VII.

The **main temple** to the NE of the site contains seven images, viz. (left to right): Doringpa, Shakyamuni, Avalokiteshvara, Padmasambhava, Vajrasattva, Green Tara, and White Tara. There are also stone footprints and handprints of Doringpa. The mani wheel chapel called **Sengzer Dungkhar Chenpo**, reconstructed in 1987, has colour reproductions of the Indian Buddhist masters Vasubandu, Dignaga, Dharmakirtu, Aryadeva, and so forth. The wall on the left has an inscription listing the donors who provided funds for the rebuilding.

Above Gyanak Mani at **Lebkhok** there are rock carvings of Maitreya and rock inscriptions from the royal dynastic period, which have recently been documented.

Jyekundo

Jyekundo (*Ch* Yushu), meaning 'confluence of all attributes or growth', is named after the town's illustrious hilltop monastery, **Jyekundo Dondrubling**. In ancient times, the Bon religion was strong in the region. The earliest Buddhist contact appears to have coincided with the period of King Songtsen Gampo and his Chinese consort Princess Wengcheng, whose child is said to have passed away at nearby **Bida** (see below, page 535). In the 13th century Drogon Chogyel Phakpa consecrated the site for the construction of a Sakya Monastery while en route for Mongolia.

The town of **Jyekundo** (3,700m) quickly sprang up around the monastery as a trading centre, controlling the caravan trails between Ziling and Lhasa; and its traditional summer festival has for centuries attracted crowds of itinerant merchants and pilgrims. Teichman, travelling through Jyekundo in 1919, noticed all sorts of imported goods (tea, textiles, metalware, sugar etc) in the marketplace for sale at cheaper prices than in Dartsedo; and the products of Tibet's nomadic economy: hides, furs, wool, medicines, and so forth attracted the investment of Muslim traders and middlemen. In 1727 the area was nominally brought within the sphere of influence of the Kokonor Muslim territory; but prior to that it had held allegiance to the independent kingdom of Nangchen for centuries. Since 1951 the town has been the capital of Yushu Tibetan Autonomous Prefecture, comprising six counties with a total population of 237,000 and 121 monasteries; and it therefore has a two-tier bureaucracy. The town alone currently has a population of 37,000.

Orientation

Following the Jyeku River upstream from its confluence with the Yangtze, you will soon reach Jyekundo, noticing **Dondrubling Monastery** on the hill to the NE of town. There are two main streets forming a T-junction; and nearby is the confluence of the Jyeku River's two tributaries: the Za-chu which flows from the NW and the Peltang-chu flowing from the SE. West of the T-junction is the Kagyupa **Damko Temple**. The town-residence of Dola Jikme Tulku and the present Dudjom Rinpoche is located down a lane to the SE of town. The road to the S leads out of town in the direction of **Trangu** and **Nangchen**; while the road to the W leads to Lake **Rongpo** and **Drito**.

Jyekundo Dondrubling Monastery

Following the consecration of its site by Drogon Chogyel Phakpa in the 13th century, the monastery was gradually established in two phases: by Dagchen Sherab Gyatso of the Sakya school, and Karmapa VII Chodrak Gyatso of the Kagyu school. The construction was finally completed by Dagchen Palden Chokyong (Ngorpa) of the Ngorpa sub-order of the Sakyapa, to which it now holds allegiance. Until recently there were 16 temples and 1,000 monks. One of these was restored in 1977 and there are currently 140 monks.

The monastery has been visited over its history by illustrious pilgrims, such as the Mongol prince Gaden Qan, and Panchen Lama IX who passed away here in 1937.

The **lower storey** of the temple houses the Delhi edition of the *Kangyur*, a large image of Padmasambhava, and several smaller images including one of Dagchen Palden Chokyong. Murals depict the meditational deities and lineage-holders of the Ngorpa Sakya tradition; and there are tangkas on the side-walls depicting Mahakala and Bhairava. Within its **inner sanctum**, there are images of the Buddhas of the Three Times, the central Shakyamuni being flanked by his foremost students and the Sixteen Elders. **Upstairs** is a small assembly hall, where rain retreat observances are held in summertime. Formerly, the monastery is said to have

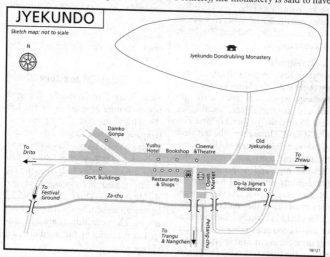

TIB127

held one of the most revered representative objects of buddha-speech in Tibet, the **Chokorma** image, but this no longer survives.

A new protector shrine has recently been renovated to the W of the complex. It is dedicated to Panjaranatha, and has a number of macabre stuffed animals.

Dondrubling Dungkhor

Below, on the approach road to the monastery, there is a Mani Wheel Chapel named **Dondrubling Dungkhor**, which was newly constructed in 1983 by one Tenkyong at the request of Dzongsar Khyentse Rinpoche. The chapel contains images of Avalokiteshvara, Padmasambhava, and White Tara; several tangkas depicting Green Tara, and murals of Vajrasattva, Padmasambhava, Shantaraksita, King Trisong Detsen, and Sachen Kunga Nyingpo. The mantras contained within the wheel include those of the deities Amitayus, Bhaisajyaguru, Vajrapani, Manjushri, Vajrasattva, Padmasambhava, and Sitatapatra; as well as the entire sutra texts of the *Bhadracaryapranidhanaraja* and the *Parinirvanasutra*. Outside the antechamber has paintings of the Four Guardian Kings and the Wheel of Rebirth, as well as a painting of Dondrubling Monastery as it once looked.

Local festivals

South of town in the Peltang-chu valley, there is a wide plain – known as the **Bartang**, which was once used as a military airstrip. Here, starting on each 25 July, the Jyekundo Horse Festival is held. Throughout the last week of July and the 1st week of Aug, colourful applique tents are pitched across the Bartang, and a programme of horse-riding events, and folk dancing attracts people from all corners of the prefecture, and other parts of E Tibet, as far afield as Nakchu. Each year one of the six counties takes it in turn to organize the event, and approximately 60% of the budget (average ¥160,000)

is provided by the prefectural government, the balance being provided by the organizing county. In 1991 all six counties held a joint festival to commemorate the 40th anniversary of the prefecture.

Local information
● Accommodation
The 5-storey *Yushu Hotel* lies to the W of the junction on the N side of the road. Hot showers are sometimes available on each floor of the building.

● Places to eat
There is a restaurant in the hotel; but the best restaurants and shops are outside, clustered around the crossroads and nr the open-air market.

● Entertainment
East, beyond the crossroads are the theatre and city cinema.

● Post & telecommunications
Post Office: the Post Office is located S of the crossroads.

● Shopping
Books can be purchased at a shop immediately to the E of the hotel. South of the crossroads is the open air market. Look out here for nomadic produce: hides, furs, chubas, fresh meat and butter; as well as imported Chinese goods.

● Transport
Road   The bus station is located S of the crossroads.

Trangu Monastery

Some 7 km S of Jyekundo, the road passes **Trangu Monastery** on the left (E). This is the seat of the great contemporary Karma Kagyu scholar and lineage-holder Trangu Rinpoche, who is now based at Rumtek in Sikkim. The renovated **assembly hall** contains exquisite gilded brass images of the Buddhas of the Three Times, flanked by murals depicting the 16 past Karmapas. The outbuildings are still utilized as granaries by the neighbouring village.

Bida Nampar Nangdze Lhakhang

ACCESS At **Peltang**, 19 km S of Jyekundo, the road branches: the left fork leading S towards **Nangchen** (174 km via Kela or 280 km via Zurmang) and the right leading W towards **Dzato** (237 km). If you take the former road, after 1 km a dirt track on the left (E) leads across streams to the **Bida gorge**. Here, surrounded by four sacred peaks, there are rock inscriptions, some revered as naturally produced, which proclaim the site's ancient association with King Songtsen Gampo and Princess Wengcheng. According to legend, the princess lost her baby at this site; and a temple was subsequently commissioned by Lochen Yeshe Yang and erected as a memorial during the reign of King Trisong Detsen. The original images, which depict Vairocana Buddha flanked by the Eight Bodhisattvas, have been 'restored' in recent years. Among them, the central image, which some hold to be natural, is said to contain relics of Kasyapa Buddha and the remains of Princess Wengcheng's deceased child. Most of the rock inscriptions are located immediately behind the temple, and reached via a rear gate. Some have been documented; although there are many unclear expressions. Another set of inscriptions can be seen on a rock to the W of the site. Nowadays, the temple is maintained by the monks of neighbouring Trangu Monastery.

Benchen Monastery

ACCESS Returning to the road from the Bida gorge, turn S and drive past a disused airstrip through a wide plain. A trail then turns off the road to the left (E) to **Benchen Gonpa**, facing into the plain against a backdrop of grassy knolls. This is a monastery of the Karma Kagyu school, the seat of Sangye Nyenpa Rinpoche and Chime Rinpoche. Here the **Assembly Hall** has been restored, and there is a finely crafted row of eight stupas outside, symbolizing the eight major deeds of the Buddha. Within the assembly hall are the reliquaries of previous lamas and the thrones of the present incumbents, both of whom are in exile – in India and England respectively.

NANGCHEN COUNTY
ནང་ཆེན
囊謙县 Nangqen

Population: 67,732   Area: 15,014 sq km

Nangchen was formerly one of the five independent kingdoms of E Tibet. Its territory corresponds to the upper reaches of the five main Mekong feeder rivers: the Ngom-chu, Do-chu, Dza-chu, Tsi-chu and Kyang-chu. As such it includes the region of **Zurmang** in the E and **Nangchen** proper in the W. This area was able to maintain its Kagyupa heritage despite the onslaught of Gushi Qan's armies during the 17th century; and it may in fact have been spared the fate of Litang owing to the nomadic lifestyle of its inhabitants and the inhospitability of the terrain for settlement. Only in a few lower sheltered areas are cultivated fields to be seen; yet the rolling grasslands, dramatic limestone and sandstone cliffs, and pristine nature re-

NANGCHEN & DZATO COUNTIES

TIB562A

Dzato

Rato

172

(4,816m)

35

(5,104m)

Do-chu

Rashi Gonpa

93

(4,267m)

Kharda

(5,000m)

Xiao Zurmang

N

100

61

Sharda

Zurmang Nangyeltse

35

To Riwoche (189km)

Tsi-chu

Zurmang Dutsitil

To Karma Gon

Sketch map: not to scale

serves combine to make Nangchen one of the most interesting and unspoilt parts of Kham. The county capital is located at **Sharda**, 193 km from Jyekundo (via Kela), 160 km from Zurmang Dutsitil, 189 km from Riwoche.

Upper Tsi-chu

To reach Nangchen from Jyekundo by the more direct route, drive W from the **Peltang** intersection for 46 km to **Rato**, crossing the high **Zhung La** watershed pass (4,816m). Then turn S, following the Tsi-chu downstream for 35 km to **Rashi Gonpa**, one of the very few Gelukpa monasteries in Nangchen. Driving SW, cross the Ke La (4,267m) which divides the Tsi-chu from the Dza-chu, to arrive at **Kharda** in the Dza-chu valley, and finally descend to **Sharda**, the county capital, 93 km from Rashi. The river meanders around sandbanks and the tableland mountain known as **Rakjangri** dominates its W bank. This is a natural habitat and breeding ground of the macoques. As you drive into Sharda, the wide and long dusty main street adds to this illusion of the Wild West.

Zurmang Dutsitil Monastery

ཟུར་མང་བདུད་རྩི་མཐིལ

BASICS The village now known as **Xiao Zurmang** lies 120 km S of the Peltang intersection. The road crosses the snow-carpeted Ku La watershed pass which divides the Yangtze and Mekong basins, and a second lesser pass, before descending into the valley of the Kyang-chu, a fast-flowing stream which eventually merges with the Ke-chu at Menda (see above, page 471). A difficult motorable trail follows the river downstream for a further 35 km, on occasions fording it at places where bridges have been damaged by the summer rains. Notice that old carved *mani* stones have been used in places for road construction.

The monastery of **Zurmang Dutsitil** is located on high ground above the road to the right (W). Founded in the 15th century by Trungpa I Kunga Gyeltsen, a close disciple of Trungpa Ma-se of the Karma Kagyu school, the monastery developed into an important meditation and study centre for the nomads and pastoralists of the Nangchen grasslands and surrounding areas. The site was expanded by his successors Trungpa II Kunga Zangpo, Trungpa III Kunga Osel, and Trungpa IV Kunga Namgyel, the last of whom was renowned both for his meditation skills and prolific compositions. In the time of his successor, Trungpa V Tendzin Chogyel, the monastery reached the high point of its development. Exquisite murals depicting the lives of the Buddha were executed in gold line on a red background. After the lifetime of Trungpa VI Lodro Tenpel, in the time of Trungpa VII Jampal Chogyel the site was plundered in 1643 by the Mongol army of Gushi Qan, and the important lamas were briefly incarcerated. Reconstruction of the assembly hall, temples, and the founding of the Zurmang library were undertaken during the late 17th and early 18th century by Trungpa VIII Gyurme Tenpel, who was himself a reputable artist of the **Karma Gadri** school. His successors, Trungpa IX Karma Tenpel and Trungpa X Chokyi Nyima, ensured that the Karma Kagyu tradition was maintained and revitalized in this part of Tibet during a time of increasing strife as Muslim overlords from Kokonor rivalled the Tibetan government and Chinese warlords for control of this important region. Trungpa XI Chokyi Gyatso (1939-87) left Tibet in 1959 and established the **Samye Ling Monastery** in **Scotland**. Later, he founded the worldwide Buddhist organization known as **Dharmadhatu**. The present Trungpa XII is now being educated at **Pelpung** Monastery, near Derge.

Little remains of the grandure of this site, which not so long ago housed 300 monks. The main **assembly hall** is currently undergoing reconstruction. Upstairs are the residential quarters of the Trungpa Tulku and the Chetsang Tulku.

There is an image of Four-armed Mahakala. Above the site is the retreat centre known as **Repuk Dorje Chodzong**; and a ruined fortress.

Below the monastery, the jeepable road continues SW through pine forest for some 30 km, crossing the present day Qinghai-TAR border, to reach **Menda** and the **Lhato** region of Kham.

Zurmang Namgyeltse Monastery

ཟུར་མང་རྣམ་རྒྱལ་རྩེ

The monastery of **Zurmang Namgyeltse** lies 60 km W of Zurmang Dutsitil in the Tsi-chu valley. From Dutsitil, follow the road back upstream in the direction of Xiao Zurmang for 15 km and then turn left (W) after the first pass. The road runs through rich pasturelands where the herds of yak and dri are particularly impressive; and crosses a second pass to enter a narrow gorge. Flowers and medicinal herbs abound in this area. Descending into the Tsi-chu valley, you will pass the Sakyapa monastery of **Dordu Gon**.

ACCESS On reaching the Tsi-chu bridge, leave this trail (which heads downstream on the E bank for **Karma Gon** via Lintrang) and cross the river. The road then forks: upstream (to the right) for **Nangchen** county town (ie Sharda) and downstream to the left for **Da Zurmang** township. The forested Tsi-chu valley is an important nature reserve and you will notice roadside signs prohibiting the killing of animals. Da Zurmang lies only 6 km from the bridge. Here are the grand ruins of the monastery known as Zurmang Namgyeltse.

The original foundation dates from the 15th century when Trungpa Ma-se, a disciple of Karmapa V constructed a 'many-cornered' (*zurmang*) meditation hut here. His disciples gathered in numbers and the local chieftain Adru Shelubum donated his castles (at both Namgyeltse and Dutsitil) to Trungpa Ma-se and his followers. The ruins of the large **assembly hall**, founded by Trungpa V Tendzin Chogyel, convey an impression of the former magnificence of the monastery. It once contained large images of the Buddha of the Three Times and over 40 images of the Karma Kagyu lineage-holders. Three colleges also once existed here: the **Dechen Dratsang** (450 monks) on the higher slopes, the **Lingpa Dratsang** (350 monks) on the lower slopes, and the **Lama Dratsang** (300 monks) adjacent to the assembly hall.

Nowadays there are between 100-200 monks affiliated to Zurmang Namgyeltse, and one temple has been reconstructed. It contains murals depicting Padmasambhava, Simhavaktra, Vajrayogini, Vajravarahi, Cakrasamvara, and various Kagyu lineage-holders including the Zhamarpas. Upstairs a chapel contains newly sculpted clay images of the 16 previous Karmapas.

Zurmang Namgyeltse to Sharda

From Namgyeltse, the distance to Sharda (Nangchen county town) is 100 km. The road crosses the precipitous **Yi gu La pass** (5,000m) – its difficult surface both narrow and gravel-covered. Drive slowly! This is the watershed between the Tsi-chu and Dza-chu rivers, and on the far side, the descent cuts across rolling meadows. Here you rejoin the direct Jyekundo-Nangchen road and enter the wide valley of the Dza-chu, the greatest of the Mekong source rivers. The tableland limestone crags of **Rakjangri** stand out across the sandbanks of the meandering river.

Sharda

Sharda, the county capital of Nangchen, comprises one long and broad main street, where dust and tumbleweed are blown in sporadic gusts. **Tsechu Monastery** of the Karma Kagyu school lies on the outskirts of the town. Formerly this town was the heart of the independent kingdom of Nangchen, to which the 25 clans of the Mekong grasslands held allegiance. The inhabitants of the town are largely engaged in trade, and you may find some interesting Tibetan artefacts here. There are some cultivated barley fields, but agriculture is generally less important to the economy than animal husbandry and lumbering.

● **Facilities** The *Nangchen Guesthouse*, where there are comfortable rooms and friendly maids, is located in a compound on the E side of the main street, nr its middle section, and the Public Security Bureau is on the W side at the extreme S end of the street. Outside the hotel, there are small restaurants, some of them Muslim owned (distinguished by their green banners).

Nangchen to Riwoche

From Nangchen, you can drive S to Riwoche (189 km) when the river levels are low. **NB** This drive is impossible in midsummer during the rainy season. For a description of this route, which crosses the watersheds of the Dza-chu, Do-chu and Ngom-chu, see above, page 535. On the far bank of the Do-chu, above the Nyingma monastery of **Neten Gang**, there are sacred Padmasambhava meditation caves and *terma*-sites in the range known as **Yegyel Namkadzo**. This is the power place representing the attributes-aspect of buddha-speech in E Tibet. Here, in the 19th century Chogyur Dechen Zhikpo Lingpa discovered important *terma*-texts and representative images of Padmasambhava.

DZATO COUNTY

རྫ་སྟོད

杂多县 Zadoi

Population: 37,362   Area: 33,127 sq km

Dzato county is the area around the source of the Dza-chu tributary of the Mekong, far upstream from Nangchen. To reach Dzato, drive W from Peltang in the direction of Nangchen, but do not turn S at the **Rato** turn-off (46 km). Continue due W for a further 172 km, en route crossing the Tsi-chu valley to the N of **Mt Sharpu Karpur** (5,104m), and entering the Dza-chu basin at **Chidza**. This is a sparsely populated nomadic area, and to the W of town, there are trails leading S through the Dangla range, into the Tengchen, Bachen and Sok Dzong counties of the present day Tibetan Autonomous Region (see above).

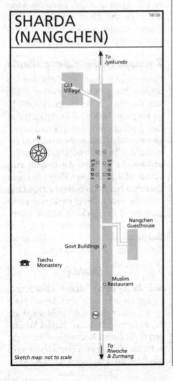

SHARDA (NANGCHEN)   TIB126

To Jyekundo

Old Village

N

Shops

Shops

Nangchen Guesthouse

Govt Buildings

Tsechu Monastery

Muslim Restaurant

Pol

To Riwoche & Zurmang

Sketch map: not to scale

DRITO COUNTY

འབྲི་སྟོད་

治多县 Zhidoi

Population: 89,038   Area: 78,945 sq km

Drito county is the area around the southern source of the Yangtze, the county capital being located at **Gyelje Podrang**, 194 km NW of Jyekundo. To reach Drito, drive W from **Jyekundo** following the Za-chu tributary upstream and passing a grass seed escarpment on the road out of town. On a hill to the N there is a sky burial site.

Ato Monastery

Above **Jalakda**, the road crosses a pass, and descends through an isolated area to **Lake Rongpo** and the township of **Gyelring**, 73 km from Jyekundo. En route, there is also a turn-off on the left, which leads S to the Karma Kagyu monastery of **Ato Gonpa**, the seat of Ato Rinpoche who now resides in England.

Rongpo Nature Reserve

In the vicinity of Lake Rongpo, the **Rongpo Nature Reserve** has the most important breeding site in present day Qinghai province for the Black Necked Crane. There are approximately 69 adult birds and 18 chicks within the reserve, where the marsh is up to 2m deep in places. Other protected species here include the ruddy sheldrake, the bar-head goose, the brown-headed gull, the redshank, and various types of wader and song bird. There is a small barrack-style guesthouse, where the wardens also live. The nests of the Black Necked Crane are protected for several days after hatching by the wardens who camp near the nests to ward off hostile nomad dogs. A guide and photographic permit are available for ¥150 (officially/hour but generally/day!).

Northwest of the marshy lake, there is a *mani* stone wall and **Rongzhi Monastery stands on a hilltop opposite Gyelring** township. A side-road leads N from Gyelring for 45 km towards Hashul and **Bongo Gonpa**.

Gyelje Podrang

Continuing on the main road from **Gyelring**, you will cross a pass and head downstream through the sparsely

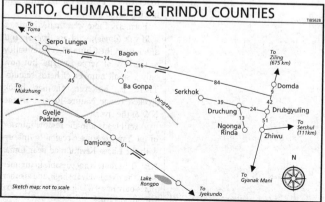

DRITO, CHUMARLEB & TRINDU COUNTIES

TI85628

To Toma

Serpo Lungpa — 16 — 74 — Bagon — 16 —

45

To Mukzhung

Ba Gonpa

Serkhok — 84 —

To Ziling (675 km)

Domda

Gyelje Padrang — 60

Yangtze

Druchung — 39 — 13

9 42

24 — Drubgyuling

Ngonga Rinda

51

Zhiwu

To Sershul (111km)

Damjong — 61

Lake Rongpo

To Jyekundo

To Gyanak Mani

N

Sketch map: not to scale

populated Jong-chu valley, where marmots, hares and pika abound. The Yelung-chu flows in from the SW, and the valley opens out. There are horses in the pastures here and the eroded terrain is evidence of intensive grazing. **Damjong** township is 61 km NW of Gyelring and SE of the Jong-chu valley. **Drito** county town, known as Gyelje Podrang, lies above the confluence of this river and the Nechak-chu, 60 km further NW. It is an unattractive town with a few compounds and a dozen shops. A gravel works depot is located by the riverside.

From Drito, there are routes leading W towards the southern source of the Yangtze in the Dangla range. These eventually link up with the road from Dzato at **Mukzhung** to head S across the range into **Bachen** and **Sok Dzong** counties of the Tibetan Autonomous Region.

A more frequently travelled road follows the Nechak-chu downstream to its confluence with the Yangtze, and the latter upstream to Chumarleb county, 45 km to the NW.

CHUMARLEB COUNTY

ཆུ་དམར་ལེབ

曲麻莱县　Qumarleb

Population: 48,636　Area: 43,123 sq km

The county of **Chumarleb** comprises the area around the northern source of the Yangtze, which flows in a SE course from the Kunlun Mountains. The county capital is located at **Serpo Lungpa**, a new town 45 km from Drito and 270 km from Jyekundo (via Domda).

The hills around Chumarleb have been heavily eroded by the itinerant 70,000 or 80,000 Chinese gold miners who come here during the summer months. The lawlessness of these prospectors is encouraged by the paucity of the police force assigned to monitor them – presently only 40 officers. The town is larger than Drito, and is a centre for the wool and meat trade. Muslim traders come here on trucks to kill sheep; and there are a number of restaurants which have been opened in Chumarleb to serve these butchers and the itinerant mining population.

Formerly there were many herds of wild yak (*drong*), wild ass (*kyang*), and antelope in the Chumarleb River valley to the NW of Serpo Lungpa, but now only a small number of herds remain. There is, however, another Black Necked Crane Nature Reserve to the NW of the river.

A trail leads into the remote interior of the Yangtze source region to link up with the Lhasa-Kermu road near Toma.

NB This route is not passable in summer when the river levels are high, and at other times only in a 4WD jeep with a high-axled support truck.

Chumarleb to Domda

South of the town, there is a good motorable road which runs SE for 199 km to **Domda** (*Ch* Qingshuihe), where it connects with the main Jyekundo-Ziling highway. Head E out of town and turn SE at the road junction. After 16 km (at marker 174) a pass is crossed. To the S, between the road and the Yangtze there are some argali mountain sheep and gazelle. The road now passes through a gorge, where goldminers are encamped near **Bagon** township, 74 km from the pass (around marker 100). A 4 hrs' trek W from Bagon leads to **Ba Gonpa** of the Gelukpa school, where there are 100 monks, and thence to **Gato** near the N bank of the Yangtze.

Staying on the main road, after **Bagon** you climb steeply, crossing a pass after 16 km (marker 84), and then after 20 km, reaching a well-equipped government goldmine. Then, after 12 km (marker 42), the road crosses the south-flowing Gara-chu tributary of the Yangtze, before heading NE up a lateral valley to **Zhakha** township. The final watershed pass crosses the Yangtze-Yalong divide, offering fine views of the rounded peaks of the **Bayankala** range to the N. Thereafter the road descends to the main highway, and **Domda** township (*Ch* Qingshuihe) lies only 9 km to the N, near the northern source of the Yalong River. Gold panning is extensive in this area, where the town has grown up to service the truckers and bus companies which ply the highway from Ziling to Jyekundo. There are several Sichuan and Muslim-style restaurants.

TRINDU COUNTY

ཁྲི་འདུ

称多县 Chindu

Population: 21,917   Area: 9,717 sq km

Trindu county comprises the area around the southern source of the Yalong River. The county capital is located at **Druchung**, 24 km W of the Jyekundo-Ziling highway. To reach Druchung, turn W at the Drigung Kagyu monastery of **Drubgyuling Gonpa**, which adjoins the highway, 51 km N of Zhiwu and 51 km S of Domda.

Drubgyuling Gonpa

སྒྲུབ་བརྒྱུད་གླིང

The **main temple** at Drubgyuling contains many new tangkas flanking a central applique which depicts Drigung Kyopa, with the protector deities below and Vajradhara above. There is a new image of Padmasambhava, as yet unpainted, and many small reliquary stupas. Within the **Gonkhang** there is a larger stupa inset with a photograph of the present Drigung Kyapgon, surrounded by the protector deities of the Drigung Kagyu lineage. There are two other buildings, one of which is the Labrang and the other the residence of Drubgyu Tulku (most senior of the five tulkus of this monastery). Currently there are 200 monks at Drubgyuling.

Druchung town

The town is small, and the community mostly pastoral farmers. Roads lead from here, W to Sekhok (39 km) and SE to Ngonga Rinda (13 km).

TREHOR AND NYARONG
THE YALONG VALLEYS AND GORGES

The middle reaches of the Yalong and the valley of its main tributary, the Zhe-chu, together form the widest cultivated tract of land in Kham, sustaining a large sedentary population, as well as nomadic pastoralists on the high ground. Emerging from the Dzachuka region at Rongpatsa the Yalong flows through this wide valley as far as Kandze where the massive snow range of Kawalungring forces it to change course, cutting S through the Nyarong gorge to converge with the Yangtze at Dukou.

The Zhe-chu and its Nyi-chu tributary both rise in the Dzachuka area to the E of Sershul county, and flow SE in parallel courses to converge at Drango, and then, after meandering through the pleasant Tawu valley, their combined waters flow S to merge with the Yalong above Nyachuka.

Prior to the 17th century, the **Nyarong** valley was a stronghold of the Nyingma and Bon traditions, while the plains to the N were also important for the Sakya and Kagyupa. Further E the peoples of **Tawu**, who speak an extremely idiosyncratic dialect or language, may well be descended from the migrant Minyak (Xixia) population, following the destruction of their kingdom by Genghiz Qan in the 13th century. However, from 1638-41 the Qosot Mongol armies of Gushi Qan forcibly converted many of these Yalong settlements to the Gelukpa tradition, eventually defeating the Bonpo king of Beri in 1641. They then established the five Trehor states: **Beri, Kangsar, Mazur, Trewo**, and **Drango**, which supported a large number of new Gelukpa institutions. Settling there, they intermarried with the local populace, from which time on the local people have been known as the **Trehor Khampa**. Secular arts and crafts also flourished; and the renowned metal work of the region still exhibits many distinctive features – animal motifs and so forth – reminiscent of Scythian or Ordos bronzes.

Nowadays this region includes four counties administered from Dartsedo namely **Kandze** and **Nyarong** in the Yalong valley, and **Drango** and **Tawu** in the Zhe-chu valley.

Recommended itineraries: 5, 8, 10.

KANDZE COUNTY

དཀར་མཛེས

甘孜县 Garze

Population: 48,868 Area: 6,232 sq km

Kandze county extends from the lower Yi-chu valley and **Rongpatsa** township as far as the **Latseka** watershed pass (also known as **Dresel La**) in Trehor. The county capital is located at **Kandze** town, 94 km E of Manigango, and 158 km NW of Tawu.

Yi-chu Valley

Following the Yi-chu downstream from **Manigango**, the highway passes the turn-off for Yilhun township after 15 km and continues along the S bank of the river. Sometimes in the rainy season the river level rises above that of the road! Soon the **Pak-tse Mani Wall** comes into view on the right (S), while, on the distant hilltop across the river, you can see the **Nyaduka Retreat Hermitage**, a branch of Dzogchen Monastery, bedecked in streaming red prayer flags. Thereafter the river cuts NE to join the Yalong, while the road continues due E to Rongpatsa.

KANDZE & NYARONG

TIB563

Manigango — Yilhun — To Dzachuka

15 — 8 — 35 — Rongpatsa

Yangkar — 7 — 6 — 17 — Beri — 13 — Kandze (3,962m)

Dargye Gonpa — 9 — 16 — To Drango (68 km)

To Pelyul (232 km) — 109

Bashok

To Nyachuka

Sketch map: not to scale

N

Yangkar Dorje Phakmo

Some 50 km E of Manigango, the road passes on the left a cave containing an image of the deity Vajravarahi. The pathway leading down to the cave is adorned with prayer flags, but the cave itself lies across a stream and is only accessible in the dry season when the water level is low. This is the most important power place of the Rongpatsa valley.

Rongpatsa

Driving E from Yangkar, the road soon crosses an almost indiscernible pass to enter the wide fertile valley of **Rongpatsa**. Fields of golden barley extend on both sides as far as the distant foothills. To the right (S) you will pass the side-valley leading from **Dzengko** and **Horpo** and the village of **Lakhar**. Just before entering Rongpatsa town (57 km E of Manigango), a turn-off on the left leads towards a ridge overlooking the valley. Here you can visit **Bongen Gonpa**, a finely reconstructed temple in the midst of a flower garden, which is the seat of the late Kalu Rinpoche of the Kagyu and Shangpa Kagyu traditions. The ruins of the original temple still occupy the hillside far to the NE. The present Kalu Rinpoche is currently being educated at Sonada in Darjiling, where his predecessor passed away.

Trekking

Trekking routes follow the Yalong upstream from Rongpatsa in the direction of **Dzachuka**, where there are many monasteries of all the Buddhist traditions and the Bon. The largest Gelukpa Monastery in that vicinity is **Samdrub Gonpa**, a 17th century foundation, which formerly had 700 monks, while the **Lingtsang Katok Gonpa** of the Nyingma school and **Ripu Gonpa** of the Sakya school are also prominant.

Dargye Gonpa

Leaving Rongpatsa, the road passes through **Yartsa** village, where there is a hot spring, and after 6 km runs through a tree-lined avenue to **Dargye Gonpa**. This monastery (3,536m) which represents the Gelukpa school and was founded in 1642, is the oldest of all the 13 so-called Horpa monasteries established by the victorious Mongol forces of Gushi Qan in the 17th century. Its traditional precedence continues, although it is smaller than Kandze Monastery. The most impressive feature of Dargye Gonpa is its enormous assembly hall, approached from named gates in each of the building's four directions. Large teams of volunteer and commissioned craftsmen have been working on the reconstruction of the buildings since 1988; and on its completion, the few surviving images and texts will be transferred there for reconsecration from their present temporary location in smaller rooms to the rear.

Beri

Located 17 km E of Dargye Gonpa on the **Horko plain** (3,536m), **Beri** was the capital of an important Bonpo Kingdom and the cultural centre of this part of Kham until the 17th century. The king of Beri, Donyo Dorje, was defeated by the armies of Gushri Qan between 1639-41, and this event led to the formation of the Trehor states. At Beri, the Bonpo temple was converted into a Gelukpa Monastery, housing 100 monks.

The strategic importance of the town overlooking a narrow part of the Yalong valley, continued to be recognized. In 1918, it was occupied as the front line of defence by the Chinese army, and this subsequently attracted the animosity of the villagers around Dargye Gonpa, who held the Tibetan front line. In 1931 when Beri was assisted in its dispute with Dargye Gonpa by the Chinese governor of Sichuan, the Tibetan forces stationed at Derge came to the assistance of Dargye Gonpa and the attackers were thrust back to Kandze.

Approaching the Beri acropolis from Dargye, the reconstructed buildings of **Beri Gonpa**, where there are more than 200 Gelukpa monks, are visible afar on the N bank of the Yalong. The citadel dominates the road overlooking the river valley from the S bank. Here within a walled town are the ruins of the **Beri Castle** and the renovated **Kablung Monastery**, where there are 50 monks. Kablung, which represents the Nyingma school, is a combined branch of both Katok and Dzogchen, the former tradition being maintained by Norbu Tulku and the latter by Babu Tulku. Extant murals at Kablung depict the *Longchen Nyingtig* tradition. Inland from Beri is the power place of **O Tashi Pema Tsepel** at Lake Tashi Tso, which is frequented by pilgrims at the present day.

Kandze

Kandze (*Ch* Garze), the county capital, is a large provincial town located at 3,581m in the loess hills close to the banks of the Yalong, 13 km E of Beri and 9 km E of the Pelyul turn-off. Two of the five Hor states, Kangsar and Mazur, were formerly located above the gently sloping plain of Kandze; and since the construction of their castles in the 17th century, the town has been the largest and most important in the Trehor region. During the 1909-18 war, the castles were occupied by Chinese garrisons; and today they lie in ruins below **Kandze Monastery**. Apart from this monastery and the historically important **Den Gonpa**, there were several other monasteries of note in the valley. These include Drakar, Nyatso, Khangmar, and Tsitso monasteries of the Gelukpa school; Dontok Monastery of the Sakya school, and Rirak Gonpa of the Kagyu school. Since 1950 the name Kandze has also been given to the Autonomous Prefecture administered from Dartsedo.

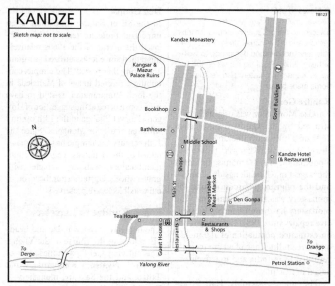

Orientation

At the entrance to town, a bridge spans the Yalong, carrying all traffic across to the N bank. The road then climbs to the N leaving the river, and winds downhill to the crossroads, which marks the town centre. The bus station lies to the right, near the crossroads.

The road to the left from the crossroads leads uphill towards the hilltop **Kandze Monastery**, passing en route a large number of shops, selling traditional Tibetan artefacts and modern Chinese or Indian goods. Further uphill (on the left) there are electrical stores, a photographic studio, a public bathhouse (with hot showers), the post office, and on the right a middle school. At the top of this road, you will pass residential town houses – their horizontal red timbers adorned with flower pots – and climb sharply to the monastery. Alternatively, you can take one of the bridges which span the Kandze-chu to the right of this road. These lead across to a parallel residential street offering good photographic views of the monastery.

Returning downhill to the crossroads, if you go straight ahead, you will pass through the vegetable and meat market. There are some restaurants on this street also, and small shops selling Tibetan artefacts, including old carpets. After the market, a lane to the left leads into the compound of **Den Gonpa**, the oldest temple of Kandze. If you continue along the street from the market you can head out of town right (SE) for Nyarong and Latseka pass, or left along the main paved avenue where the government buildings and the *Kandze Guesthouse* are to be found. The distance from Kandze to Pelyul is 232 km and to Tawu 158 km.

Local information
● Accommodation
The *Kandze Guesthouse* has comfortable rooms in its 2-storey main building, and less comfortable rooms in a rear annex. There is a clean restaurant, where local officials like to hold banquets, and a washroom. There is also accommodation at the bus station.

● Places to eat

Several small restaurants are also to be found adjacent to the bus station, around the intersection, and in the market street. These invariably serve noodles and dumplings, as well as Sichuan dishes. Small tea houses on the road up to Kandze monastery also sell delicious home made bread.

Kandze Gonpa

Kandze Monastery was originally constructed by the Qosot Mongols circa 1642 on a hilltop overlooking their castles of Mazur and Khangsar. It once had a population of 1,500 monks, making it the largest in Kham alongside Chamdo; and the pilgrimage circuit around the monastery was nearly 8 km long. The monastery has been undergoing extensive repairs since 1981. Currently it has an estimated population of 700 monks and three tulkus, one of whom recently returned from India and is actively engaged in teaching.

The main **Assembly Hall** is approached by a long flight of steps. It is a striking building in wood and stone, with a golden roof. Downstairs, the passageways between the red columns lead to the **inner sanctum**, where the images are raised high within glass cabinets. There are three sets of three images, representing the founders of the Kadampa, Gelukpa and Nyingma lineages of Tibetan Buddhism. There are also fine tangkas depicting the meditational deities Guhyasamaja, Cakrasamvara and Yamantaka.

Upstairs are a *Kangyur* library containing old images of Tsongkhapa and Elevenfaced Avalokiteshvara and a **Gonkhang**, entered through a striking black and gold painted doorway, which contains new protector images and a new set of images representing the three aforementioned meditational deities. The **Maitreya Hall** has an enormous central image of Maitreya, flanked by Tsongkhapa, Shakyamuni, Dipamkara and Sitatapatra. On the hillside to the NE of the monastery is a reconstructed white stupa.

Den Gonpa

In the SE of Kandze town there is an important protector temple which survived the events of the 1960s relatively unscathed since it was utilized as a granary during that period. The temple, containing a revered image of Mahakala in the form Panjaranatha, is said to have been constructed at the suggestion of Drogon Chogyel Phakpa in the 13th century while en route for Mongolia. Since the 17th century the temple has been maintained by the Gelukpas. There is a circumambulatory walkway replete with prayer wheels. Upstairs a number of original woodblocks are preserved.

Kandze to Latseka

The highway leaves Kandze and heads SE, rejoining the course of the Yalong. The outlying Gelukpa monasteries of **Drakar**, **Nyatso**, **Khangmar**, and **Tsitso**; and the Sakyapa monastery of **Dontok**, are all to be found in this part of the valley. After 9 km, a side-road leaves the highway on the right, following the river as it changes course to head into **Nyarong**. The highway itself veers steeply to the E, passing through the picturesque farming village of **Puyulung** (*Ch* Lozhling), and you can then see rising on the SE horizon the snow peaks of **Kawalungring** (5,082m), which conceal the entrance to Nyarong. 16 km after the Nyarong turn-off, the road enters a nomadic grassland area and reaches the high Latseka pass (3,962m), which forms a watershed between the Yalong and Zhe-chu rivers.

NYARONG COUNTY

ཉག་རོང

新龙县 Xinlong

Population: 44,000   Area: 9,821 sq km

Nyarong county is the name given to the traditional tribal area of **Upper Nyarong**, in contrast to that of **Lower Nyarong**, which is now under the jurisdiction of **Nyachuka** county. The Yalong River flows through both Upper Nyarong and Lower Nyarong on a southerly course towards its confluence with the Yangtze at **Dukou**. The county capital is located at **Barshok**, 109 km from Kandze.

The isolated Nyarong valley has always been a stronghold of the Nyingmapa school and the pre-Buddhist Bon tradition. During the 19th century, the chieftain of Nyarong, Gonpo Namgyel subdued most of Kham, unifying much of E Tibet under his command during the military campaigns of 1837-63, but he was eventually defeated in 1865 by the Tibetan government and forced to withdraw into the citadels of Nyarong, where he came to an untimely end.

Chakdu Kawalungring

Driving into Nyarong from Kandze, the road follows the E bank of the Yalong downstream through a deep gorge. The most important power-place associated with Padmasambhava in the Nyarong valley is at **Hor Tresho**, also called **Chakdu Kawalungring**, within the Kawalungring range (5,082m). It represents the activity aspect of buddhaspeech; and a nearby monastery is the seat of Chakdu Tulku, now resident in Oregon. At **Da-ge Drongtok Gon**, 46 km from the turn-off, there is an important branch of Katok Monastery.

Barshok

The county capital, **Barshok**, lies 54 km further S, at the heart of Nyarong (*Ch* Xinlong). Here there are guesthouse and restaurant facilities. This was formerly the residence of Nyarong Gonpo Namgyel who unified the upper and lower districts of Nyarong under his command and embarked on a military campaign against the neighbouring independent kingdoms and provinces of Kham. Trehor, Derge, Dzachuka, Lhato, Nangchen, and Jyekundo all succumbed to his forces, as did Batang, Litang, Chaktreng, and Gyeltang in the far S, and Chakla, Trokhyab and Tawu in the E. Only the intervention of the Tibetan government army in 1865 brought an end to this expansion; and Gonpo Namgyel was himself burnt to death when the government forces set fire to his fortress.

Nyarong has produced two outstanding Buddhist masters: the treasurefinder Nyakla Pema Dudul, who lived at **Shunlung** 17 km W of Barshok during the 19th century; and Lerab Lingpa, also known as Terton Sogyel (1856-1926), who hailed from **Karzang Gonpa** and was a close associate of Dalai Lama XIII. The former was one of the few lamas venerated personally by Nyarong Gonpo Namgyel.

Barshok to Nyachuka

From Barshok there is a difficult motorable trail to **Nyachuka**, the capital of lower Nyarong, which straddles the Litang-Dardo highway. The road follows the Yalong downstream SE to its confluence with the Zhe-chu and then due S to Nyachuka. An alternative route from **Tawu to Nyachuka**, following the Zhe-chu (*Ch* Xianshui) downstream, offers easier access to lower Nyarong.

DRANGO COUNTY

 བྲག་འགོ

炉霍县 Luhuo

Population: 37,355   Area: 4,764 sq km

Drango county comprises the valley of the Zhe-chu as far as its confluence with the Nyi-chu tributary, at the county town of the same name. The distance from Kandze to Drango is 93 km, and from Drango to Tawu 72 km.

Joro Lake

On the descent from the watershed **Latseka Pass** (3,962m), also called **Dresel La**, the road passes through sparsely populated nomadic country, dotted with dark yak hair tents. Soon you will reach the ruins of **Joro Gonpa**, a Gelukpa Monastery dating from 1642, where there were once 300 monks. Below the ruins there is a beautiful panorama of an idyllic blue lake, which was once a thriving bird sanctuary. A farming village is located by the lakeside near the road.

Trewo

Below Joro Lake, the road descends for 19 km to **Trewo** (3,612m), where it meets up with the Zhe-chu valley. Trewo, like Khangsar and Mazur at Kandze, was one of the five Trehor kingdoms set up by the Qosot Mongols in this part of Kham. Formerly it had a large citadel with

impressive walls, which was the residence of the chieftain of Hor Trewo. The flat-roofed earthen houses of the Tibetan village are now clustered around the ruins of the castle, and alongside new Chinese compounds with white walls and sloping roofs. Across the river on the N bank of the Zhe-chu is the rebuilt temple of **Dzaleb Gonpa**.

Drango

As the name ('head of the rock') suggests, **Drango** is a strategic location on the mountain slope at the confluence of the Zhe-chu and Nyi-chu rivers. The castle of **Drango Dzong** formerly stood at this vantage point at an elevation of 3,475m. Above it in the 17th century, the Gelukpa monastery of **Drango Gonpa** was constructed. At its high point, this monastery housed 1,000 monks, making it the largest in Kham E of Kandze. In 1863 Drango along with the other Trehor kingdoms and Derge was overwhelmed by the tribal forces of Nyarong Gonpo Namgyel. Then, in 1865 on the defeat of Gonpo Namgyel, the town became a protectorate of Lhasa. Subsequently, the Chinese settlement, **Luho Xian**, was founded in 1894 by Lu Ch'uan-lin who ended the succession of local chieftains.

Orientation Most buildings in Drango are newly constructed, the older town having been devastated by an earthquake in recent decades. Entering the town from the W (49 km from Trewo), the main street runs past a prison and then, on a paved surface, a number of high-rise concrete buildings, including the Bank of China. Reaching the crossroads, which marks the town centre, there are two parallel streets running uphill, both filled with small shops and restaurants. At the upper end of the westernmost of these two streets, turn right and then left to enter the *Drango Guesthouse* compound.

Outside the hotel, turn right and walk along the boulevard running along the

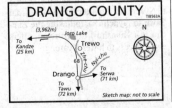

DRANGO COUNTY   TIB563A

To Kandze (25 km)

(3,962m)

Joro Lake

Trewo

N

Zhe-chu

Nyi-chu

68

Drango

To Serwa (71 km)

To Tawu (72 km)

Sketch map: not to scale

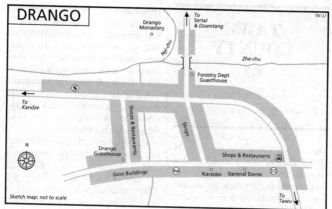

upper end of the two parallel market streets. There are several video parlours, and karaoke bars. Head downhill on this main road, and you will pass the main commercial centre: glass-fronted shops selling textiles, ready-to-wear clothing, shoes etc. The bus station and cinema are located at a roundabout at the bottom of this slope – a barrier on the right pointing the way out of town in the direction of Tawu.

The town evidently has a large Chinese population. Returning uphill to the parallel market streets, turn right and follow the road downhill to the bridge which spans the Zhe-chu River. This is the road leading N to **Serwa** (71 km) and thence to **Sertal** or **Dzamtang** (see below, pages 619 and 621). Before reaching the bridge you will pass a *Forestry Department Guesthouse* on the right. Across the river on the 'head of the rock' promontory, you will notice the rebuilt temples of **Drango Monastery**. There are now three temples which have been renovated, and these are surrounded by smaller residential buildings. Below the promontory the confluence of the Zhe-chu and the Nyi-chu is clearly visible.

● **Accommodation** *Drango Guesthouse*, uphill from town centre, rooms are fine and clean with hot water and showers available on each floor; *Forestry Department Guesthouse*, just before the bridge to Drango Monastery.

● **Places to eat** The guesthouses have a slow service and are more expensive than the roadside Sichuan restaurants and noodle bars.

TAWU COUNTY

ཏ་འུ

道孚县 Daofu

Population: 68,534   Area: 5,099 sq km

The county of **Tawu** comprises the valley of the Zhe-chu (*Ch* Xianshui) below Drango, extending as far S as the river's confluence with the Yalong, and the **Mejesumdo** uplands, which form a watershed between it and the Tung-chu River of Minyak. The county capital is located at **Tawu**, 72 km from Drango and 76 km from Garthar.

The distinctive dialect spoken here may well accord with the legend stating that the displaced inhabitants of Xixia (Minyak) migrated to these parts following their defeat by Genghiz Qan in 1227.

The Tawu valley is one of the most attractive parts of Tibet, the neatly constructed white flat-roofed houses with their horizontal red timbers exuding an air of quiet prosperity. The low altitude of Tawu (3,125m) and the prosperity of the valley have attracted Chinese immigrants since the first Chinese settlement was founded here in 1911 by Chao Erh Feng. Catholic and protestant missions were also based here prior to 1949 with the support of this Chinese community.

Orientation   Entering Tawu from Drango via the **Trongmi** goldfields (72 km), the road crosses to the N bank of the Zhe-chu and passes the *Forestry Department Guesthouse* at the W end of town. Above the main street, on the hillside to the NW you will notice the white gravestones of the Chinese cemetery and the renovated buildings of **Nyitso Gonpa** – a monastery of the Gelukpa school which formerly housed 400 monks.

On both sides of the main street there are small Sichuan-style restaurants. Pass the compound on the right where the Tibetan Language University of E Tibet was based until recently, and on the left a lumber yard. The road forks here; the left branch leading towards the government buildings, the post office, and courts; and the right branch leading to the bus station and the main crossroads at the centre of the town.

Reaching the crossroads, a turning on the left leads uphill to connect with the left branch opposite the law courts. General stores, grocery stores, and vegetable sellers line the main street, near the crossroads. Continue due E from the crossroads to head out of town in the directions of Garthar, SE for Nyachuka and NE for Barkam. A petrol station lies at the extreme E end of town.

● **Facilities** *Tawu Government Guesthouse*, close to the law courts. The rooms are very basic, the toilets outside (as is the norm for transport stations), and the restaurant mediocre. Better to dine outside at the simple street restaurants.

Tawu to Nyachuka, Tu-je Chenpo, and Garthar

Three different roads lead E from Tawu, diverging beyond the petrol station. To the S, a motorable trail follows the Zhe-chu downstream, leaving the Tawu valley at a large white stupa, and heading in the direction of **Drawa** (69 km), where there is a Gelukpa Monastery, and thence to **Nyachuka** (56 km) via the

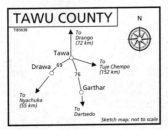

TAWU COUNTY   N

TIBS63B

To Drango (72 km)

Tawa

Drawa   69

To Tuje Chempo (152 km)

76

Garthar

To Nyachuka (55 km)

To Dartsedo

Sketch map: not to scale

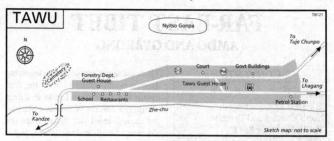

confluence of the Zhe-chu and the Yalong. To the N a trail abruptly crosses the watershed and follows a tributary of the Do-chu River upstream to **Tu-je Chenpo** (*Ch* Qanyiqao) (152 km), from where there are roads E to **Barkham** and W to **Dzamtang** or **Sertal** (see below, pages 621 and 619). Lastly, the main highway runs SE from Tawu, ascending the richly forested watershed region of Mejesumdo, where there are wonderful picnic spots in view of **Mt Zhara Lhatse**. It then crosses the **Nedreheka La** pass (4,115m) to enter the Minyak region of E Tibet at **Garthar**. The distance from Tawu to Dartsedo via Garthar is 240 km.

FAR-EAST TIBET
AMDO AND GYARONG

INTRODUCTION

Far-east Tibet includes **Amdo** or the grassland region around the upper reaches of the Yellow, Min, and Jialing rivers in the NE, and the deep gorges of the **Gyarong** feeder rivers: Ser-chu, Do-chu and Mar-chu further S. Amdo is the region in which the Tibetan population has been most exposed over the centuries to cultural contacts with neighbouring peoples: Tu, Salar, Mongol, Hui, and Chinese; and this intermingling is reflected in the demographic composition of the grasslands. By contrast, the isolated Gyarong valleys remained aloof for centuries from all outside influences and their inhabitants were known for their expressed hostility towards intruders, whether Tibetan, Mongol, Manchu, or Chinese.

There are seven sections in the following description of Far-east Tibet: the first details the route from **Lhasa to Ziling** (Xining) across the W Kokonor plateau; the second, third and fourth trace the old caravan trails and the densely populated valleys to the S, E and N of **Lake Kokonor** and the upper reaches of the Yellow River; the fifth and sixth follow the upper reaches of the Yellow River through **Golok** and the Gyarong feeder rivers through **Sertal** and **Ngawa** as far as **Rongtrak** and **Tsenlha**; and finally, the seventh follows the upper reaches of the Min and Jialing rivers from **Lanzhou to Chengdu** via **Labrang**, **Dzoge**, and **Zungchuka** (*Ch* Songpan).

Presently this entire region of Far-east Tibet comprises 60 counties, of which 37 are within Qinghai province, 8 within Gansu province, and the remainder in Sichuan (13 in the Ngawa Autonomous Prefecture and 2 in the Kandze Autonomous Prefecture).

ACCESS The nearest points of access are the large provincial capital cities: Chengdu, Lanzhou, and Ziling.

Land and life

Geography
The southern border of Amdo is divided from the Salween basin of W Kham by the **Dangla** Mountains, and from the Yangzte and Yalong basins of E Kham by the rolling **Bayankala** Mountains, which form a SE spur of the Kunluns. In the NW, the **Altyn Tagh** range divides the Tsaidam basin of NW Amdo from E Turkestan (*Ch* Xinjiang); and in the NE the **Chokle Namgyel** Mountains (*Ch* Qilian) divide the Kokonor basin of NE Amdo from the Gansu corridor and Mongolia. In the extreme E, the **Min**, **Longmen**, and **Qionglai** mountains

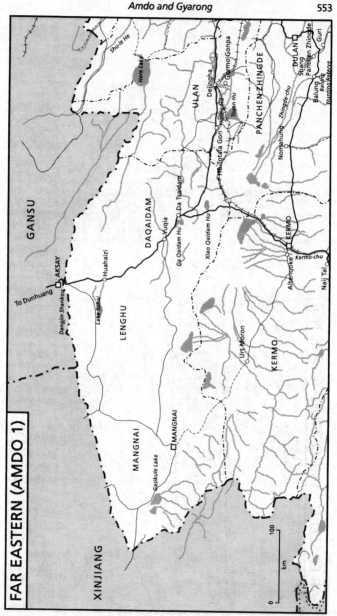

FAR EASTERN (AMDO 1)

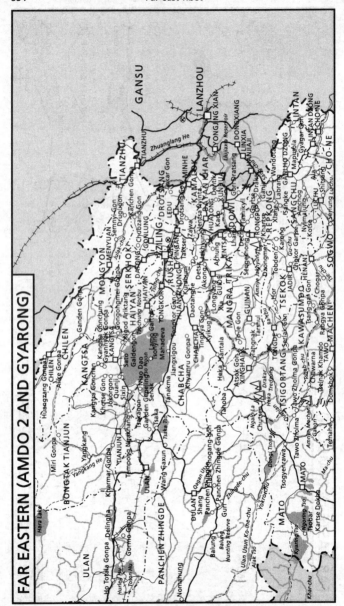

FAR EASTERN (AMDO 2 AND GYARONG)

divide the Amdo grasslands and Gyarong gorges from the Chinese parts of Sichuan and Gansu.

Other ranges internally demarcate the distinct regions of Amdo and Gyarong: the **Kunluns**, which divide the Jangtang Lakes and Yangtze headwaters from the Tsaidam basin; the **Amnye Machen** range which forms the bend of the Yellow River, dividing the nomadic tribes of Golok (S) from those of Banak (N); the **Nyenpo Yurtse** range dividing Golok from Gyarong; and the **Nanshan** range, which divides Kokonor from the Yellow River basin.

The terrain of Far-east Tibet is characterized by its broad valleys, rolling hills and extensive flat tableland. However, there are considerable variations between the deserts of the **Tsaidam** and **Jangtang**, the rich grasslands of **Amdo**, and the forested gorges of **Gyarong**.

In the NW of the region, the intramontane depression of the **Tsaidam** basin is extremely low. The north-westerly parts of the Tsaidam (2,700-3,000m) are characterized by denuded plains of bedrock; while in the lower SE (2,600-2,700m) there are thick Meso-Cenozoic deposits. The terrain therefore varies between gravel, sand and clay deserts, semi-desert tundra, and salt wastelands.

The **Altyn Tagh** Mountains, which divide the NW border of the Tsaidam from the Tarim basin of E Turkestan, extend over 805 km. The western hills are rugged and rocky, above 5,700m with perennial snow peaks and glaciers. In the central part of the range the highest elevation is 4,000m; and in the NE, 5,000m. There are few rivers except in the SW, and the central portion which adjoins the Tsaidam is arid and waterless.

The **Chokle Namgyel** (Qilian) range, dividing the Kokonor basin from the Gobi desert of Mongolia, runs from NW to SE at an average altitude of 5,100m. Many rivers originate from its glaciated peaks, especially the Ruo Shui (known as Etzingol River in Mongolian) which

flows northwards into Mongolia. Around 4,200m there is high altitude pastureland. The area is rich in minerals including iron, chromium, copper, lead, zinc, gold, and coal.

The **Nanshan** range, which divides the Kokonor basin from the Yellow River, has an average altitude of 4,000-5,000m; the higher western peaks being glaciated and exceeding 6,000m. There are a number of tectonic intermontane depressions on both sides of the range, the largest being that of Lake Kokonor to the N. In the lower eastern parts of the range, where the intermontane valleys are more open, humid and warm rains penetrate. Tributaries of the Yellow River rise to the S of the range.

In the S, the **Bayankala** range divides Amdo from Kham. The NW peaks of this range lie S of Kyareng and Ngoreng lakes, at an average altitude of 4,600-5,100m; and they are the source of the Yellow River. The central hills of the range are rounded and rolling. The most renowned peak in the SE is Mt Nyenpo Yurtse (4,947m), the sacred mountain of the Golok, which is surrounded by five lakes.

The **Amnye Machen** range, which forms the bend of the Yellow River, extends from high NW peaks (over 5,100m) to lower SE peaks (4,200m). This range, which is revered as the abode of the protector deity Machen Pomra, has three main snow peaks, all at the NW end. Among these, Mt Dradul Lungshok (6,282m) is the N peak; Mt Amnye Machen is the central peak; and Mt Chenrezik is the S peak. The northern Golok foothills between the Bayankala and Amnyen Machen ranges average 4,200m.

The **Min Shan** range, which demarcates the eastern extremity of the Amdo grasslands, forms the river basins of the Minjiang and Jialing, characterized by strata of red clay, red sandstone and gypsum. This part of the plateau is exposed to higher levels of precipitation, as much as 508 mm.

Flora and fauna

The upper reaches of the Yellow River are predominantly a region of grassy hills and marshlands; but they are not entirely without trees. Small patches of spruce and fir are often found on north-facing slopes, and their presence is important in maintaining the watertables, preventing soil erosion and protecting the local micro-climates. The best quality grassland also contains a wide range of flowers and grasses, but sadly many areas are now becoming overgrazed, and exhibit only a limited diversity of species. Large wild animals have almost disappeared from this region, but smaller mammals such as the pika, mole, vole, rabbit and marmot have proliferated in the absence of predators. Before 1950, this area did support some large herds of yak and sheep, but banditry was rife, and many side-valleys were rarely used for grazing. The modern emphasis on animal husbandry, the new road network and changes in stock management techniques have led to increasingly intensive use of the grasslands and a deterioration in pasture quality.

Many of the marshes have shrunk in size, threatening the habitat of wading-birds, including the well-known Black-necked Crane. In a few places, the thin top-soil has been completely eroded by the action of wind and water, causing some of this rich grassland to turn into semi-desert. Around Lake Kokonor, the plateau vegetation includes tamarisk, haloxylon, feather grass, white willow, craxyweed, astragalus, gentian and allium. Spruce forests are found on the northern slopes of the Nanshan Mountains.

Peoples

The Tibetan population of Amdo comprises the **Drok-ke** speaking nomads of Ranak, Golok, and Ngawa; the **Rong-ke** speaking towns of the Tsong-chu valley, and the **semi Drok-ke** (also called Rongma Drok-ke) speaking settlements of Repkong, Labrang, Luchu and Jo-ne areas. Non-Tibetan languages are also spoken within the Amdo area: particularly among the **Salar** Muslims of Dowi county, the **Tu** of Huzhu and Tianzhou counties, and the **Mongols** of Sogwo county. Further S, in the Gyarong gorges and the lower Min valley, there are Tibeto-Burman populations of the ancient **Qiangic** speaking language group, including those who speak **Tawu-ke** (in Tawu and Rongtrak), **Gyarong-ke** (in Chuchen and Tsenlha), and **Qiang-ke** in Maowen.

YELLOW RIVER

The **Yellow River**, known in Tibetan as **Ma-chu** and in Chinese as **Huang He**, is often regarded (in its lower reaches) as the cradle of Chinese civilization. The world's sixth longest river, it flows 5,464 km (1,167 km in Tibet) from its source in the Bayankala Mountains to its estuary in the E China Sea; and has a drainage area of 745,000 sq km (of which 77,249 km are within Tibet). From its source, the river flows E, traversing **Kyaring** and **Ngoring** Lakes, then turning westwards through the hairpin bend (*khug-pa*), it crosses the **Amnye Machen** range, and flows northwards from **Rabgya**, descending in a series of rapids (fall 2m per km) to **Lanzhou**. From Lanzhou, the river flows E through Ningxia, Mongolia, and the Shanxi, Henan and Shandong provinces of mainland China. The river has an average flow of 1,530 cu m per second, an average annual volume of 48.2 cu km, and an average precipitation of 470 mm (mostly snow-melt in the upper reaches). The Yellow River is the world's muddiest, carrying 1.52 billion tons of silt per year.

The **Qiang** were forced into the mountain fastnesses of the Gyarong and Min valleys by the Qin and Han Emperors following their unification of China in the pre-Christian era. Their **Qiang Long** stone culture is characterized by the construction of large stone watchtowers and sturdy stone dwellings, often containing white quartz rocks which were regarded as sacred artefacts.

The rich pastures of the Amdo grasslands sustain a nomadic population larger than in any other part of Tibet. These nomads, including the **Golok** (S of Amnye Machen) and the **Banak** (N of Amnye Machen) have recently benefitted economically from the reforms in China, but face a long-term threat to their future from environmental deterioration. The education system is basic at best, with Tibetans forced to study Chinese if they wish to advance in their chosen career. There are few employment opportunities in this region, so most children follow their parents and become nomadic pastoralists, while a few, mostly boys, join one of the numerous monasteries that have been rebuilt in the last 10 years. Government funds have been allotted to help rebuild these monasteries, and each site is given a quota of timber and building materials, as well as a construction team, usually composed of Chinese craftsmen. This official help however covers little more than the basic building, and the Tibetans are forced to look to the local communities for the cost of internal and external decoration, and the construction of monastic residences. As a result, most of these monasteries are little more than a concrete shed, only the timber entrance and porch roof supports being made in traditional style. Shrines, statues and murals are generally very poorly executed, although there is now a small body of well-trained artists, centred at the excellent **Schools of Painting in Repkong**. With the exception of the main temples in **Repkong, Labrang** and **Kumbum**, virtually all the original monasteries of Amdo were destroyed in the Maoist era, and the vast bulk of Amdo's artistic heritage has been lost.

History

Tibetan-speaking tribes played an important role in the formation of several Chinese dynasties in the NE; but during the Tang Dynasty, the Tibetan Empire of the **Yarlung kings** consolidated its control over the whole region of Far-east Tibet. Culturally, the peoples of the region have remained within the Tibetan orbit ever since, influenced by both the Bon and the Buddhist traditions. The unifying influence of Tibetan culture withstood the political fragmentation of the region which followed the collapse of the Yarlung Empire in the 9th century; and it was through contact with the Sakyapa and Kagyupa traditions in the grasslands that the Mongol tribes of **Genghiz Qan** and his successors were brought within the fold of Tibetan Buddhism.

For some 500 years (13th-18th century) the Mongol tribes dominated the grasslands, and following the conversion of **Altan Qan** to the Gelukpa school by **Dalai Lama III** in 1580, successive *qans* zealously sought to impose the acceptance of the Gelukpa order upon the diverse cultural traditions of the region. **Gushi Qan** of the Qosot Mongols established his kingdom around Lake Kokonor, and in 1641 aided Dalai Lama V to unify spiritual and temporal power under his authority in Lhasa. His military campaigns directed against the Bonpo and Kagyupa monasteries of Kham in particular were extended into the Gyarong region during the 18th century by **Changkya Qutuktu Rolpei Dorje**, who targetted the Bonpo and Nyingmapa in particular. Despite these efforts, the traditions of the Bonpo, Nyingmapa and Jonangpa remain strong in Gyarong and neighbouring areas at the present day.

Following the pacification of the Mongols by the Manchu emperor **Qianlong** in the 18th century, the political vacuum in the Amdo area was filled by the Muslims, who encroached SW from Ziling towards Jyekundo, dominating the trade routes. From 1727 until the mid-20th century the towns of the grasslands and Tsong-chu valley were controlled by the **Ma** family who looked upon the Kokonor Territory as their own protectorate. Gradually their influence filtered S from Jyekundo into Nangchen, but the nomadic areas of Golok, Sertal, and Gyarong always remained beyond their jurisdiction in the hands of the local Tibetan populace. In 1950, the warlord **Ma Pu-feng** succumbed to the PLA, leaving most of Amdo in the hands of the Communists.

THE WEST KOKONOR PLATEAU

The main highway from Lhasa crosses the border between the Tibetan Autonomous Region and Qinghai at Dang La pass (5,220m), 85 km N of Amdo township; and then runs through the Autonomous Prefecture of West Kokonor to Kermo (*Ch* Golmud) and Ziling. The West Kokonor area, so-called because it lies to the W of Lake Kokonor (*Tib* Tsongon), comprises the sparsely populated and spacious terrain of the Jangtang Lakes and the Tsaidam basin, as well as the source of the Yangtze River. There are eight counties within the prefecture, which is administered from Kermo, 837 km NE of Nakchu and 782 km W of Ziling. The indigenous population of Mongols, Tibetans, and Kazakhs must nowadays contend with widespread Chinese immigration, both official and unofficial. One of the great concerns is the increase in the number of lawless and unaccountable Chinese gold prospectors. **Recommended itinerary: 6.**

SOUTH KERMO COUNTY
ལྡུག་གེར་མོ

南 格 尔 木 Golmud Nan
Population: 49,939   Area: 44,278 sq km

The highway from Lhasa breaches the **Dangla Mountains** at Dang La pass (5,220m), 85 km N of Amdo township, where there is a memorial depicting Chinese soldiers. It then enters the Yangtze basin, following the Bu-chu tributary as far as its confluence with the Kar-chu at **Karchudram Babtsuk** (*Ch* Gaerquyan). En route it passes through Dangla Maktsuk after 19 km, the hot springs of Chutsen, and **Toma** township (*Ch* Wenquan) after 54 further km. From Toma a seasonal side-road leads SW for 88 km to the crystal mines between the glaciers of Mt Janggyen Deuruk Gangri (6,548m) and Mt Kolha Dardong (6,621m) in the Dangla range. Here and around Lake Mirik Gyadram to the SW are the main **southern sources of the Yangtze**: the Kar-chu and the Mar-chu (*Ch* Tuotuohe).

Continuing on the highway from

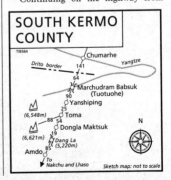

Toma, you will reach **Yanshiping** after 25 km and **Marchudram Babtsuk** (*Ch* Tuotuohe) on the banks of the Mar-chu after 90 km. This last settlement has guesthouse and restaurant facilities; and just to the N of town the road crosses the **first bridge over the Yangtze**.

Northeast of Marchudram Babtsuk, the highway reaches the county border after 64 km; and then traverses the extreme NW of Drito county (see above, page 539) to cross the Chumar River, the **northern source of the Yangtze** which rises in the Kunluns. The main settlement in the Chumar valley is **Chumarhe**, 141 km NE of the border. To the W lie the Jangtang Lakes, and the road in places bypasses small isolated lakes dotted over a fairly barren plain. Occasionally gazelle and kyang (wild ass) can be seen from the road, but wild yak, antelope and argali can only be found in the high plains to the W.

KERMO COUNTY

གེར་མོ་

格尔木市 Golmud

Population: 58,065   *Area:* 51,484 sq km

Kermo county lies between the Kunlun and Tsaidam Pendi ranges. Its rivers which rise on the southern slopes of the Kunluns flow into the salt lakes of the S Tsaidam. The county capital, **Kermo**, is located on the banks of the Kermo-chu at the Qinghai railway terminus. It is an important intersection, in that roads lead N to Gansu and NW to Xinjiang provinces, as well as S to Lhasa and W to Ziling.

Eastern Kunluns

The highway from **Chumarhe** reaches **Budongquan** after 65 km, and, leaving the Yangtze basin, crosses the pass through the Eastern Kunlun Mountains after a further 21 km.

Geography Distinct from the Western Kunluns, which divide the Jangtang Plateau of NW Tibet from the Tarim basin of Central Asia (see above, page 386), the Eastern Kunluns are characterized by their high perennial snow line (5,700-6,000m), low temperatures, aridness,

KERMO COUNTY

TIB564B

To Mangnai (200 km)

Urt Moron

180

Altenquoke

30

To Da Tsaidam (185 km)

Kermo

To Ziling (782 km)

90

Dronglung

68

E Kunluns

21

To Chamarhe (65 km)

Budongquan

N

Sketch map: not to scale

strong winds, intense solar radiation, and brief summers with precipitation under 100mm. The mean July temperature in the higher parts of the range is less than 10°, and the nights can be bitterly cold. The winter is long with severe frosts and strong dust storms (minimum temperature -35°, and wind speed exceeding 20m p/s). The Kunlun landscape largely consists of rock desert and stagnant water pools.

Wildlife is more plentiful here than in the Himalayas and other ranges which have been exploited more on account of their proximity to large centres of population. The ungulates of the Kunluns include the gazelle, wild ass, wild goat, wild yak, blue sheep and argali, while brown bears and wolves are also found in fewer numbers. Waterfowl are frequently seen on the saline lakes around the Kunluns during the migratory season.

Dronglung

From the pass through the E Kunluns, the road descends into the valley known as **Dronglung** ('Wild Yak Valley') to its Tibetan herders (*Mong* Niaj Gol). The Kunlun foothills to the S of this valley still have most of the Jangtang range of mammals in their upper reaches, despite hunting from passing goldminers and occasional professional hunters. Here the temperature range is more extreme: averaging 25-28° in mid-summer, and -9° in mid-winter. After **Naij Tal** township (68 km from the pass), the highway leaves the spectacular plain of the Kunlun snow ranges and, below the Naij Gol River's confluence with the **Kermo-chu**, it descends through a gorge with a hydro-power station to emerge after 90 km at Kermo city on the southern fringe of the Tsaidam desert.

Kermo City

At only 2,800m, **Kermo** (*Ch* Golmud) is a large new town which has developed in recent decades as a centre for potash mining, and (even more recently) oil-re-

fining. Formerly there were barely a dozen houses here! The sprawling concrete buildings and barrack-style compounds abut straight avenues, but there is little of interest in the city itself, its population largely comprising Chinese immigrants. It is however an important transit point for visitors to Lhasa, Ziling or Dunhuang.

Orientation
Approaching the city from the Lhasa road, you will pass a turn-off on the right, which leads to the **railway station** and the **Ziling Bus Station**, and continues E out of town in the direction of Ziling. If you stay on the main road, you will head N onto **Xizang Street**, where the Lhasa Bus Station is located at Zhongshan Park, and thence out of town in the direction of Dunhuang.

A second right-turn leads from Xizang St along **Tsaidam Street**. Take this turn-off and you will soon reach the intersection of **Kunlun Street**. The Bank of China is located on the S side of Tsaidam St after its intersection with Kunlun St. On the E side of Kunlun St itself you will find (in succession) the *Best Cafe*, the *Golmud Hotel*, the *Golmud Hotel Restaurant*, and the open-air market. Continuing E along Tsaidam St you will next arrive at the

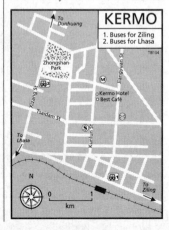

KERMO

1. Buses for Ziling
2. Buses for Lhasa

intersection with **Jiangyuan Street**. The Post Office is located here on the corner.

Local information
● Accommodation
C *Kermo Hotel (Golmud Binguan)*, T 2817, has new rooms (¥40-60/bed) and older rooms (¥16/bed), with erratic hot showers and the *Golmud Hotel Restaurant*.

● Places to eat
Golmud Hotel Restaurant, on Kunlun St, has good and reasonably priced Chinese food. For western food, try the *Best Cafe*, also on Kunlun St (second floor).

● Banks & money changers
Bank of China, Tsaidam St.

● Entertainment
The only forms of entertainment are pool, karaoke, and tourist baiting!

● Hospitals & medical services
Golmud Hospital.

● Shopping
Try the open-air market on Kunlun St and the *Department Store* on Tsaidam St.

● Tour companies & travel agents
CITS, Golmud Branch, based at *Kermo Hotel*, T 2001 ext 254.

● Useful addresses
Police and Public Security: Golmud City Police and Public Security Bureau, Tsaidam St.

● Transport
Road *Tibet Bus Station*, Xizang St, has daily departures for Lhasa. Expect to pay around ¥1,000 inc foreigners' registration fee. The bus station has a foreigners' registration desk. The 1,150 km journey takes between 28 and 35 hrs. **NB** The *Kermo Hotel* is used to foreigners attempting to get to Lhasa and CITS here has had a somewhat chequered history over the years.

Main Bus Station, opp the *Kermo Railway Station*, has daily bus departures for Ziling and Dunhuang (¥40, 13 hrs).

Train There are express and local services to and from Ziling. The former departs *Kermo Railway Station* around 1400, and the latter around 2030. Plans to extend the railway from Kermo to Lhasa have so far floundered on account of the difficulty of laying tracks on a permafrost surface and boring ice tunnels through the Kunluns.

Northern Routes from Kermo

From Kermo, you can drive due E to **Ziling** (782 km), via Dulan; or due N through the Tsaidam Pendi range to **Dunhuang** (524 km) via Lenghu and Aksay. A third and more difficult drive follows the 568 km road to **Mangya** on the Xinjiang border, but parts of this road are seasonal and sealed by the military. Alternatively, take the **train to Ziling**, which runs parallel to the Dunhuang road, before cutting E through Greater Tsaidam, Ulan, and Tianjun counties and skirting the N shore of Lake Kokonor.

MANGNAI DISTRICT

芒崖 Mangnai

Population: 60,665   *Area:* 53,788 sq km

A road runs NW from Kermo via **Altenqoke** and **Urt Moron** (180 km), where there are borax mines. It then continues across the Kermo-Mangnai border, following a seasonal track for some 200 km as it traverses the NW area of the **Tsaidam** desert.

The terrain here is low-lying, arid, waterless, and unpopulated. Sand is blown SW from the Mongolian plateau, and the climate is one of extremes: dry, cold, and windy winters, followed by hot summers. The road surface improves around **Mangnai** (where a side-road from neighbouring Lenghu district connects). The distance from here to the Xinjiang border is 159 km. En route you will pass to the N of Gasikule Lake, where there is a Blacknecked Crane reserve.

Onwards to China From the border, the road crosses the **Altyn Tagh** range to reach **Ruoqiang** in the Qaraqan valley of Xinjiang province, and thence to Korla and **Urumqi**.

GREATER TSAIDAM DISTRICT

大柴旦 Daqaidam

Population: 40,927   *Area:* 36,287 sq km

The main road N from Kermo follows the railway line through the **Tsaidam Pendi** range. En route it crosses a spectacularly long 32 km bridge of salt (*Ch* **Wangzhang** salt-bridge), which is the main scenic attraction of Kermo. The railway then cuts eastwards through S Tsaidam for **Ulan**, while the road head N for the town of **Da Tsaidam** (185 km from Kermo). About 43 km beyond Da Tsaidam, at **Yuqia**, there is a branch road leading W towards **Mangnai** (351 km), while another branch road heads SE from Da Tsaidam to **Delingha** (201 km) and thence to **Ulan** (142 km).

The only fertile tracts are those around the Da Tsaidam and Xiao Tsaidam Lakes; and further E at Hurleg and Toson lakes near **Delingha** railway station. The oil industry has recently become a significant factor for the local economy.

The complexity of the Tsaidam landscape has engendered great variation in climate, soil and vegetation. In general, there is a continental climate, the average precipitation being less than 100 mm (mostly in summer). The NW is particularly arid and waterless. The winters are dry, cold, and windy; while the summers are hot. Strong winds from the Mongolian plateau cover the region with sand. There are, however, some fertile tracts in the piedmont and lakeside areas of this basin; while the SE is a broad saline swamp formed by the rivers draining internally from the Kunluns. Only in the NE, towards the E Nanshan mountains does the climate become milder.

MANGNAI & GREATER TSAIDAM COUNTIES

TIB59B

To Urumqi

Xinjiang Border

N

To Huahaizi (112 km)

159

Mangnai — 351 — Yuqia

43

200   Da Tsaidam   To Delingha (201 km)

Urt Moron   185

210

To Chumarhe (244 km)   Kermo   *Sketch map: not to scale*

LENGHU DISTRICT

冷湖 Lenghu

Population: 21,113   *Area:* 18,720 sq km

PANCHEN ZHINGDE COUNTY

པཎ་ཆེན་ཞིང་སྡེ

都兰县 Dulan

Population: 60,360   *Area:* 53,518 sq km

The **Kermo to Dunhuang** highway enters **Lenghu** district to the N of Da Tsaidam town and Yuqia. It passes through the unpopulated N part of the Tsaidam desert, and after 112 km reaches the township of **Huahaizi**. From here it continues for 55 km to the Qinghai-Gansu provincial border at **Dangjin Shankou** pass, located in a defile between the Altyn Tagh and Chokle Namgyel ranges. The only oasis in these parts is the area close to the shores of **Lake Suhai**. This part of the Tsaidam is largely uninhabited, but there are occasional Kazakh settlements, related to those from neighbouring Aksay in Gansu.

The main highway from Kermo to Ziling runs due E for 782 km. En route, it passes through **Panchen Zhingde (Dulan)** county, which has its capital at Dulan, 354 km from Kermo. The initial stretch of 250 km passes through the barren SE fringe of the Tsaidam. Only occasional desert vegetation on low sand-dunes and stony desert break the horizon as the road runs parallel to the Kunlun. Some 150 km after Kermo, a line of trees to the N marks **Nomahung**, one of the prison farms for which Qinghai is renowned, located nearby a prehistoric archaeological site.

Balung Hunting Ground

Leaving the desert, at Balung hamlet, there is a side-road on the right (S), which leads S into the **Balung Hunting Reserve** of the Kunlun Mountains. Here, over a 66 sq km area, the few remaining large mammals of the Tibetan plateau, including argali, gazelle, white-lipped deer, red deer, corsac foxes, wolves, and marmots, can be shot for hefty fees (ranging from

LENGHU COUNTY

TIB602

To Dunhuang (129 km)

Dangjin Shankou

55

Huahaizi

112

To Mangnai (351 km)

Yugia

43

Da Tsaidam

To Kermo (185 km)

N

Sketch map: not to scale

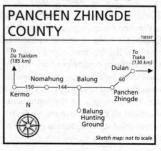

PANCHEN ZHINGDE COUNTY

TIB597

To Da Tsaidam (185 km)

To Tsaka (130 km)

Dulan

Nomahung   Balung   60

150   144   Panchen Zhingde

Kermo

Balung Hunting Ground

N

Sketch map: not to scale

US$10,000 for a white-lipped deer to US$60 for a marmot). Hunting trips are organized from mid-Aug until late-Nov; and from April until late-May. Much better to leave them in peace. Organized hunting of this scale could be halted if ecologically sensitive wildlife tourism could be promoted successfully thoughout the region.

● **Accommodation** is in Mongolian-style yurts and proper kitchen facilities inc refridgeration are available.

Panchen Zhingde Monastery

After Balun, the highway passes through **Shang** (*Ch* Xiang Ride), where there are interesting stone carvings and cliff paintings. A major river cuts through the Kunlun range here, its two sources rising in Alag Lake and Dongi Tsona Lake to the S. This area is said to be the ancestral home of several nomadic Tibetan groups presently living N of Lake Kokonor. These Shang Tibetans were forced northwards en masse into Mongol territory during the 18th century, probably due to pressure from the Goloks. **Panchen Zhingde Monastery**, which was given as a concession to the Dalai Lama, is close to the road. It is run by monks from the Tashilhunpo in Zhigatse, while its patrons are Mongol herdsmen. Further S, at **Guri**, a second hunting park can be visited; and from **Lake Dongi Tsona** there is a route leading to **Tsogyenrawa** on the main Jyekundo-Ziling highway (see below, page 608).

Dulan

The county capital is located 60 km N of Panchen Zhingde, on the banks of the **Qagan Us** River. Situated in the SE corner of the Tsaidam, where irrigated fields and tree plantations have brightened the marshy desert, it is a growing town, inhabited largely by Han Chinese and Hui Muslims. In the hinterland, there are Mongol herdsmen; while Tibetans inhabit the high mountains further S.

ULAN SOK COUNTY

སུན་ལན

乌兰县 Ulan

Population: 74,346   Area: 32,959 sq km

The road and railway links from Da Tsaidam area to Ziling pass through **Ulan Sok Dzong** county. At **Keluke Lake**, between the road and the railway tracks, there are large fish reserves. **Delingha** city, 56 km further E, where the road rejoins the railway track, is a burgeoning Chinese town, while Ulan, the county capital lies 142 km further SE, at the next major intersection of the road and railway tracks.

In this area there are several Mongol settlements which have been hugely expanded by recent Chinese immigration. Further N in Ulan county, the NE Tsaidam desert is largely unpopulated, apart from a few nomadic groups in the upper reaches of the **Yangkang-chu** valley, and to the W of **Hara Lake**.

ACCESS From Ulan to **Tsaka**, on the NE corner of **Tsaka Lake**, the distance is 37 km by road or rail. This road then connects with the main Kermo-Ziling highway and passes into Chabcha county (see below, page 602).

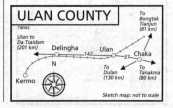

ULAN COUNTY

TIB565

Ulan to Da Tsaidam (201 km)

Delingha —142— Ulan —37— Chaka

To Bongtak Tianjun (81 km)

Kermo

N

To Dulan (130 km)

To Tanakma (80 km)

Sketch map: not to scale

BONGTAK TIANJUN COUNTY

བོད་སྒྲ་ཁེ་ཆེན་རྫོང་

天峻县 Tianjun

Population: 25,258   Area: 22,396 sq km

Tianjun county, which lies to the E of the Tsaidam fringe, comprises the valleys of the NW flowing **Shu-le** River and the SE flowing **Yangkang-chu**. The county capital is located at **Bongtak Tianjun**, on the Ziling-Kermo railway.

ACCESS A road link also connects the town with **Tsaka**, 81 km to the SW, and from Tianjun to **Kangtsa** on the N shore of Lake Kokonor, the distance is 108 km.

A jeepable trail follows the **Yangkang** valley upstream from Bongtak Tianjun, and across the watershed into the **Shu-le** river basin. From here it runs NW, past an area of sulphur mines, and through the **Shu-le Nanshan** branch of the Chokle Namgyel Mountains, into Gansu province.

TSAKA SALT LAKE

From Dulan, a pass leads NE across the attractive Erla hills, to Wang Gaxun and the salt city of **Tsaka** (130 km). Tsaka is encased in salt; vast heaps of it cover the plain, buildings are encrusted, and it is even in the air you breathe. The lake offers spectacular mirages. There is a Mongolian festival here in spring connected to the small monastery in the northern hills. A network of trolley trains carries salt over the lake and a branch line (and road) leads NW to Ulan on the Ziling-Kermo railway. Beyond Tsaka, the highway climbs SE through a semi-desert landscape with spiky tuftgrass, into the grassy pastures of the **Nanshan** (S Kokonor) range. Mongol tents can be seen on this plain and camels are typical. After some 80 km you will reach the Chabcha county border, leaving the W Kokonor region behind.

NORTH KOKONOR AND TSONGKHA

T hise route follows the course of the Qinghai-Gansu railway, and its adjacent valleys. It includes the environs of Lake Kokonor, Tibet's largest lake, and the densely populated Tsong-chu valley, the main artery between the cities of Ziling and Lanzhou, where Tibetan, Mongol, Muslim and Chinese traders have intermingled over the centuries. Also included are the lateral valleys of the Tsong-chu's south-flowing tributaries: Beichuan, Julak-chu, and Zhuang-lang.

A few city-states, ruled by Tibetans, had fleetingly existed in this area from the 4th century onwards, but it was not until the Yarlung Dynasty arose in Central Tibet during the 7th century that Tibetan power was consistently applied throughout the region. During the reign of Relpachen in 823 a peace treaty was signed between Tibet and China, demarcating the border at **Chorten Karpo**, near present day **Yongjing** in Gansu.

The sacred abode of **Dentik** is included among the 25 power places of Amdo and Kham, which were frequented by Padmasambhava and his disciples; and it was here that the refugee monks from Central Tibet fled following the persecution of Buddhism by King Langdarma. Here they transmitted the monastic lineage of Tibetan Buddhism to Lachen Gongpa Rabsel and ensured its continuity through to the present day.

The power vacuum, left in the wake of the Yarlung Empire's disintegration in the 9th century, was subsequently filled by the Tangut Kingdom of **Minyak** (*Ch* Xixia) which emerged towards the end of the 10th century, with its capital in the Ordos desert (modern Ningxia Province). Reaching its zenith in 1038 during the reign of King Si'u Gyelpo, the Tangut Kingdom ruled over Tibetans, Mongols, Turks, Arabs and Chinese. During the last century, Russian explorers discovered relics and books from this little-known civilization, which Genghiz Qan and his armies completely wiped out in 1227. The surviving population are said to have fled to the Tawu and Minyak areas of Kham (on which see above, page 441).

The Mongols ruled the area through a system of princeling chieftains called the **Tu**, who were mostly of Mongol and Arab descent; but who acquired Tibetan Buddhism under the influence of their

LEGENDS OF LAKE KOKONOR

This island has several legendary origins. One, encountered by Abbé Huc, details how the lake was connected to Lhasa by an underground sea, which caused a temple being constructed there to constantly fall down. An old Mongolian shepherd carelessly gave away his secret to a passing lama and the sea flooded out as Kokonor. Another, recounted by Sven Hedin and Dr Rijnhart, recalls a great lama who dug up one white and one black root. He cut the black root, out of which the lake's water fortunately emerged. If he had cut the white root, the lake would have been full of milk and thus unsuitable for use as pastureland! In these legends the island forms the plug which dams the underground sea. In Chinese chronicles over 2,000 years, the island is regarded as the breeding place of the fastest horses on earth; the dragon colts, which were born from mares released on the island. Throughout the centuries important lamas, such as Zhabkar Tsokdruk Rangdrol, have passed periods of time in retreat on Tsonying Mahadeva.

Tibetan subjects. Important lamas of the Karma Kagyu and Sakya schools visited Amdo during this period, and, so, by the time of Tsongkhapa, several large monasteries and many small ones had been established in the Ziling valley and N of the Yellow River. Tsongkhapa himself was taught at the most important of these, **Jakhyung Gonpa**, but it is his birthplace, **Kumbum** in modern Rushar (Huangzhong) county, that later grew into one of the major monasteries of Tibet under both Mongol and Manchu patronage.

Political power remained in the hands of Mongol tribes who became zealous patrons of the Gelukpa school. During the 17th and 18th century, Gushi Qan of the Qosot Mongols and Sonam Rabten of the Dzungars both launched sectarian assaults on Tibet. By the time the Mongol tribes were brought to heel by the Manchus in the mid-18th century, the Kokonor and Tsong-chu areas had fallen under the control of Muslim warlords; and so they remained until the Communist occupation of the present century. It is important to note that despite the variable political climate in Amdo, it was the Tibetan culture which provided a common ground to these disparate populations.

Nowadays, this region comprises 13 counties, of which 12 are in Qinghai and only one in Gansu. The former include all four counties of the Tibetan Autonomous Prefecture of N Kokonor, and all eight counties of Ziling district; while the latter is the remote Tianzhu autonomous county on the Zhuanglang River. **Recommended itineraries**: 6 and 8.

KANGTSA COUNTY
ཁང་ཚ

刚察县　Gangca

Population: 30,975　Area: 9,155 sq km

The county of **Kangtsa** occupies the area around the NW shores of Lake Kokonor and its hinterland. The county capital, Kangtsa, which is part of the North Kokonor Tibetan Autonomous Prefecture, lies 108 km E of Bongtak Tianjun and 110 km NW of Haiyan, on the railway line and northern shore road to Ziling. The most important monastery here is **Kangtsa Gonchen** of the Gelukpa school, located some 25 km NW of the town. Another Gelukpa monastery, **Ganden Gonpa**, is located on the W shore of the lake and may be reached via the railway line to Tainjun, 38 km SW of Kangtsa. Further SE from Kangtsa in the direction of Lake **Tsochung Norbu** (*Ch* Ga hai), there is the Gelukpa monastery of **Ngod Ariktang**, which was built by Rushokpa to fulfil a prophecy made by Dalai Lama III Sonam Gyatso during the 16th century.

Lake Kokonor

The largest lake on the Tibet plateau, known in Mongolian as **Kokonor** and in Tibetan as **Tsongon** (*Ch* Qinghai, *Eng* Blue Lake), gives its name to the present day province of Qinghai. In former times the wide-open shores of this saline lake provided rich pastures for both Tibetan and Mongol nomads. However, the 'vast and magnificent pasturage of Kokonor', where Abbé Huc reported 'vegetation so vigorous that the grass grows up to the stomachs of our camels' and where other visitors of old reported sightings of gazelle and Tibetan wild ass,

has been sadly degraded by intensive grazing and a spread of cultivation near the lake shore. The fields of yellow rape in the summer attract numerous beekeepers from the eastern provinces of China, and groups of hives are scattered all over the plains. At this time, most of the local Tibetans have moved their herds S into the mountains, but a few tents remain near the lake for the whole year. In Aug, a delicious yellow mushroom is sold to passing traffic by Tibetans at the roadside. Fish is also occasionally offered but the official fishing fleet, based at the SE corner of the lake, takes the bulk of the 5,000 ton annual catch of scaleless carp.

Tsonying Mahadeva

There are several small Gelukpa and Nyingma monasteries in the hills around the lake, but the most important religious site is on a small island in the centre, known as **Tsonying Mahadeva**, the 'heart of the lake' (*Ch* Haixin Shan). This temple, inhabited only by a handful of monks, used to be isolated for most of the year, since boats were not permitted on the lake. The monks could therefore only be reached during the 3 month winter period when the lake froze sufficiently deeply for it to be safely crossed.

Nowadays, the island receives regular tourboats from the *Qinghai Lake Guesthouse* and is occasionally visited by fishing vessels. The tour-boat has a capacity of around 60 people and costs

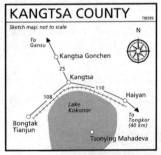

KANGTSA COUNTY　TIB599

Sketch map: not to scale

N

To Gansu

Kangtsa Gonchen

25

Kangtsa

108　　　110　　Haiyan

Lake Kokonor

To Tongkor (40 km)

Bongtak Tianjun

Tsonying Mahadeva

about US$200 to hire for the day, so casual visitors must hope to be able to join a pre-existing tour. Barely an hour is spent on the hill island, but the boat continues to other rocky outcrops where colonies of birds can be found.

● *Qinghai Lake Guesthouse*, with rooms in mock Tibetan-tent style at US$10 a night, is half way along the S shore of the lake at **Jiangxigou** nr Khyamri. Tourists are encouraged to visit the local nomad tents to have some experience of the daily life and the typical nomadic diet of curd, mutton, butter tea, and barley-ale (*chang*). Horse-riding and camel-riding activities are provided, as well as boating and shooting facilities.

Niao Dao

The bird sanctuary, known in Chinese as Niao Dao, is a national reserve located on a peninsula on the W shore of the lake, 53 km by road from the town of **Tanakma** (*Ch* Heimahe). It is also accessible by train from the rail head at **Sixin**. There is a small Nyingma monastery beside *Bird Island Hotel* and the best nesting sites are 16 km further along the peninsula. April, May, June, and early July are the best months for nesting bar-headed geese, gulls, terns and even an occasional black-necked crane, but cormorants are there throughout the summer.

● **Accommodation** At *Bird Island Hotel*.

Tanakma

Tanakma (Heimahe) is a modern roadside town on the SW edge of Kokonor. **Karsho (Garla) Gonpa** of the Gelukpa school, which was founded by Tashi Gyatso, is about 35 km from Tanakma in the direction of the Bird Island Sanctuary. The town itself has two monasteries within reach; the newly-founded Gelukpa Gonpa of **Lamoti**, 2 hrs walk away, and **Gyasho Benkhar (Gyayi) Gonpa**, founded by Jeu Neten Lobzang Nyima in the 16th century, which is several hours walk to the SE.

● **Facilities** Tanakma has several restaurants, small guesthouses and shops.

HAIYAN COUNTY

དཔའ་ཡན

海晏县 Haiyan

Population: 42,582   Area: 4,195 sq km

The county of **Haiyan** occupies the NE shore of Lake Kokonor and in its hinterland there is the source and upper reaches of the Tsong-chu River, which passes through the area traditionally known as Tsongkha via Ziling city to its confluence with the Yellow River near Lanzhou.

The county is nowadays part of the North Kokonor Tibetan Autonomous Prefecture, and its capital is located at **Haiyan town** (Sanjiaocheng), 110 km SE of Kangtsa and 40 km NW of Tongkor (*Ch* Huangyuan). Several years ago, a nuclear research institute located near the lake shore was closed down. Now, as in the past, the **Hudong** pastures by the lake shore provide excellent grazing for nomadic livestock. The main monastery here is **Gonpa Soma** of the Gelukpa school, slightly N of **Bayan** township, in the Tsong-chu valley.

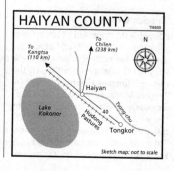

HAIYAN COUNTY

Sketch map: not to scale

TONGKOR COUNTY

སྟོང་སྐོར

湟源县 Huangyuan

Population: 119,572 Area: 1,293 sq km

The county of **Tongkor** is located in the Tsong-chu valley, and now forms part of Ziling district. The county capital, Tongkor, is 40 km equidistant between Haiyan in the NW and Ziling city in the SE.

Tongkor Town

For centuries, this has been an important trading post for the Mongols and Tibetans of Kokonor. Abbé Huc joined a large caravan to Lhasa here in the 1860s, and noted how, even then, the Chinese were 'encroaching on the desert, building houses, and bringing into cultivation portions of the land of grass'. 30 years later, Dr Susie Rijnhart witnessed the second major Muslim rebellion when almost 10,000 Muslims were massacred in the town by a combined force of local Tibetans and the Chinese army sent from Lanzhou.

Here in Tongkor, the rail/road links to the N of Lake Kokonor connect with the main road from the S.

Tongkor Gonpa

Following the main road SW from town, you will pass through several small Chinese farming villages. Then, about 30 km from the town, you will reach the ruins of **Tongkor Gonpa**, founded by Tongkor Yonten Gyatso who was a contemporary of Dalai Lama III Sonam Gyatso. An American visitor, WW Rockhill, noted this monastery as possessing 500 monks at the turn of the century. A few kilometres further on, the tarmac road splits, with the W branch leading over the famous **Nyima Dawa La** ('sun-moon') pass, and the E branch leading to **Trika** county (see below, page 599).

Nyima Dawa La Pass

The **Nyima Dawa La** pass (3,399m), situated 38 km S of Tongkor, was made famous when Princess Wengcheng, en route for Tibet to marry King Songtsen Gampo in the 7th century, looked in a magic mirror with a sun-moon design, which was supposed to show her family home in Changan (modern Xi'an). On seeing only her own reflection, the princess smashed the mirror in despair. The river near the pass, unusually flowing from E to W, is said to be formed from the princess' tears as she continued on her journey to meet Songsten Gampo. Nowadays, two small concrete temples have been constructed on the pass, and the murals are modern, depicting nomad life and the royal couple. On the far side of the pass, the road descends into Chabcha county (see below, page 602).

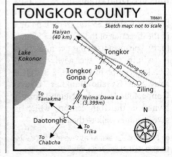

TONGKOR COUNTY

Sketch map: not to scale

ZILING CITY

ཟི་ལིང་

西宁市 Xining Shiqu

Population: 870,201   Area: 430 sq km

Ziling (*Ch* Xining) is the capital of Qinghai province, located at 2,200m on the edge of the Tibetan plateau, in a wide section of the **Tsong-chu** valley, where the **Beichuan** River joins from the NW. The valley floors are well irrigated into a patchwork of fields and trees but the hills nearby are barren, affording only poor grazing. Most heavy industry is located further N in Datong, which also possesses a coal mine, but Ziling itself is largely a residential and market town. The population of Ziling is mostly Muslim, Chinese, Mongol or Tu, and very few Tibetans live in the town itself. It has, however, become an important centre for Tibetan Studies. The Tibetan Nationalities College, the Tsongon Publishing House, and the Gesar Research Institute are in the vanguard of this movement. The average July temperature is 17°.

Ziling has a mean Jan temperature of -7° (min -27), and a mean July temperature of 18° (max 34). The annual precipitation is 366 mm (mostly in summer), and there is little winter precipitation.

ACCESS The distance from Ziling to Tongkor is 40 km, to Repkong 185 km, to Huzhu (Gonlung) 41 km, to Datong (Serkhok) 39 km, and to Lanzhou 280 km.

History

The city developed on the basis of trade between China and Persia, linking with the famous Silk Route to the N. Buddhist pilgrims such as Fa Xian passed this way en route for India, and both the Han and N Wei dynasties sponsored the construction of Chinese-style Buddhist and Daoist temples. Tibetan influence increased following the consolidation of the Yarlung Empire in the 7th century, and later there were influxes of Mongol, Tu, and Muslim groups. Muslim migrants from Central Asia gradually became the dominant sector of the population; and from 1860 onwards, successive uprisings among the Muslims resulted in the destruction of many old settlements in the region. Even Kumbum Monastery itself was badly damaged. The Chinese, calling on their Tu and Tibetan allies, managed to suppress each insurrection with great loss of life, and for decades Muslims were not allowed to reside within the walled city of Ziling. However, by the 1930s, Muslim warlords, in agreement with the Nationalists, once again controlled the entire valley down to the Yellow River.

The Tibetans, to whom the region is known as Tsongkha, largely continued to govern their own affairs, but were forced to allow Muslim trade as far S to Jyekundo. The Mongols were concentrated in outlying parts of Kokonor, Tsaidam and the Kunlun mountains, and were organized into banners or districts, which owed only nominal allegiance to the Ziling *amban* and Muslim government. In recent years there has been an increasing influx of Chinese immigrants from Nanjing in SE China.

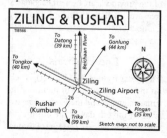

ZILING & RUSHAR

TIB566

To Datong (39 km)   Beichuan River   To Gonlung (44 km)

N

To Tongkor (40 km)   Ziling

Ziling Airport

26   24

Rushar (Kumbum)   To Trika (99 km)   To Pingan (35 km)

Sketch map: not to scale

Orientation

Approaching Ziling city from Tongkor (*Ch* Huangyuan), the road, known as **Qilian Street**, follows the railway and the Tsong-chu River (*Ch* Huangshui) on the N bank and crosses the Beichuan tributary, just upstream from its confluence with the Tsong-chu. **Renmin Park** lies to the S overlooking the confluence. Soon the road passes a turn-off (**Chaoyang Donglu**) which heads N out of town for Datong and the Datong branch railway. The Daoist temple of **Beishan** is located 45 mins walking distance up the mountainside to the N of the road. Continue E along Qilian St, following the N bank of the Tsong-chu, to reach the main **Xining Railway Station**.

Four bridges span the Tsong-chu within the city: the westernmost bridge leads into the W part of town. Here, Xining St, Tongren St, and Huanghe St all run N-S and the lateral roads known as Shengli St, Wusi St, Xiguan St, and Kunlun St bisect them on an E-W axis. **Tongren Street**, in particular, leads S out of town in the direction of Repkong. **Huanghe Street** runs parallel to the W bank of the north-flowing Nanchuan River. **Erlang Park** in the S of the city can be reached via either Tongren St or Huangehe St. The city's best hotel, *Qinghai Hotel*, is located beside the grounds of the park.

Three bridges span the Nanchuan River, leading into the commercial and administrative heart of Ziling. All three of them link up with **Changjiang Street** on the E bank of the Nanchuan, which extends all the way from Qilian St (on the N bank of the Tsong-chu) to the S end of town. The **West Gate Bus Station** (Ximen) is located on this street.

At the city centre is the **Da Xitsa** (Great Cross). The old city which lies to the E of Changjiang St, contains the municipality buildings, the open-air market (one of the most interesting in China), and the **Post Office**. The municipality buildings in particular were constructed on the site of an ancient Buddhist temple attributed to Mar Shakyamuni and his colleagues who maintained the Tibetan monastic tradition here, during the persecution of Buddhism in Central Tibet by Langdarma. The temple, known in Chinese as **Dafusi**, was levelled to make way for the government offices, but one small section was rebuilt in the mid-1980s, and further rebuilding is being carried out at the site. It is only a few hundred metres W of the main Post Office. North from the main Post Office lies the **Public Security Bureau** and at the head of the same road, the *Xining Hotel*.

The **Bank of China** lies further E on Dongguan St in the Muslim quarter. The **Great Mosque**, built originally in the 14th century, is one of the largest in the region; and there are a number of excellent small Muslim restaurants. From here, follow **Jianguo Street** NE to cross the Tsong-chu at the entrance to the main **Xining Railway Station**. The long-distance bus station is located just before the bridge on the right (E) side of the road. The *Yongfu Hotel* is on the opposite side of the road. From the railway station follow Qilian St out of town (N) in the direction of Huzhu county; or follow Bayi St SE in the direction of Lanzhou.

Museums

The *Qinghai Institute for Nationalities* has an interesting exhibition hall; also the *Qinhgai Provincial Museum* houses some of the province's greatest archaeological treasures, including ancient Persian and Chinese artefacts, as well as Buddhist manuscripts.

Local festivals

The *Spring Festival* (*Ch* Caiqing), is held on the 8th day of the 4th month of the lunar calendar; and the *Flower Song* festival on the 6th day of the 6th month. For the 1996 dates of certain traditional

ZILING

Hotels & Restaurants
1. Qinghai Hotel & CAAC
2. Xining Hotel
3. Yongfu Hotel
4. Xining Dasha
5. Peace Restaurant
6. Muslim Restaurant

Buses
B1. Ximen Bus Station
B2. Long Distance Station

Tibetan festivals, see below, **Information for visitors**, page 19.

Local information

● Accommodation

A *Qinghai Hotel (Qinghai Binguan)*, 20 Huanghe Rd, T 6144888, F (86-971)-6144145, is a 3-star hotel with 395 rm, the best in town, with attached bath, USD$40/double room, but remote from city centre in Erlang Park. There is an excellent Chinese restaurant on the second floor, and a lobby bar cum coffee shop. CAAC airline office is located on the first floor; also tour agencies, excellent shopping arcades, business centre, hairdressing and massage service. The karaoke bar and dance hall are located to the rear on the ground floor.

B *Xining Hotel*, T 8245901, is located 5 km W of the railway station. A Russian-style building with double rooms at ¥110. It has attached bathrooms (be careful not to stub your toes on the bathroom door threshold!). The hotel restaurant serves excellent hotpot.

C *Yongfu Hotel*, on Jianguo St nr railway station, has best value. Double rooms at ¥50, with attached bathrooms and good hot water supply, and a coffee shop.

D *Xining Dasha*, on the corner of Jianguo St and Dongguan Dajie, in Muslim quarter, 10 mins walking distance from railway station, has rooms ranging from ¥6 (dorm bed) to ¥57.

● Places to eat

Among the major hotels, the *Qinghai Hotel* is expensive, but offers excellent Chinese cuisine and adequate service. Ziling has many street restaurants of which the cheapest are in the open-air market area nr the **West Gate Bus Station**, and the kebab stalls in the Muslim quarter. For good inexpensive Chinese food, try the *Peace Restaurant*. For excellent Muslim food, try the *Muslim Restaurant*, on the corner of Jianguo St and Dongguan Dajie and for noodle dishes, try the restaurant run by the *Yongfu Hotel*, nr the railway station.

● Airline offices

CAAC, *Qinghai Hotel*, 1st Flr, books flights to Beijing and Xi'an.

● Banks & money changers

Bank of China, Dongguan Dajie. Exchange facilities are also available at the *Qinghai Hotel*, and *Xining Hotel*, while credit card payments are accepted at the *Qinghai Hotel*.

● **Entertainment**

Ziling has the usual turbid nightlife of provincial or frontier towns. The main forms of entertainment are karaoke, disco, and cinema – all located in the downtown area, or in the major hotels. In all, the city has more than 7 theatres and cinemas.

● **Hospitals & medical services**

Peoples' Hospital, Gonghe St.

● **Post & telecommunications**

General Post Office: Bei Dajie. Postal facilities also available in major hotels.

Fax: *Qinghai Hotel Business Centre*, *Xining Hotel Business Centre*.

● **Shopping**

The large open-air market nr the West Gate Bus Station on Changjiang St, has handicraft stalls selling crystal salt carvings and Kunlun jade products, bookshops, traditional medicines, and meat and vegetable markets, as well as textiles of great variety. **NB** Pickpockets are rampant!

For luxury items, inc the hugely popular yak wool sweaters made in the Repkong area, try the shopping arcade in the *Qinghai Hotel*. A visit to the carpet factory is also worthwhile.

Photography: print film and processing are available at photographic shops in town and in the larger hotels.

Stamps: are available at **GPO**, on Dong Dajie; and also at the reception counters or shops in the major hotels.

● **Useful addresses**

Police and Public Security: Foreigners Registration Office, Bei Dajie, N of post office.

● **Tour companies & travel agents**

China International Travel Service: Ziling Branch **(CITS)**, 215 Qiyi Rd, T 8238701 (ext 1307), F (0086) 971-8238721.

● **Tourist offices**

Qinghai Tourist Corporation **(QTC)**, *Qinghai Hotel*, 21 Huanghe Rd, T 6143711, F (0086) 971-8238721.

● **Transport**

Air Ziling is connected to Beijing and Xi'an. The airport lies 24 km E of town on the N bank of the Tsong-chu River.

Road Buses run throughout Qinghai province to and from Kermo (Golmud), Repkong, Lanzhou, Mato, and the Xinjiang border. Long-distance buses leave from the *Main Bus Station* nr the railway station; while local buses leave from the *West Gate (Ximen) Bus Station*. Minibuses and landcoasters can be hired (with driver) from CITS.

Train There are frequent train connections to Lanzhou (4½ hrs); as well as to Beijing, Shanghai, Qingdao, Xi'an, and Kermo (both afternoon express, and morning local services).

RUSHAR COUNTY

ᛞᛁᛦᛠᛞ

湟中县 Huangzhong

Population: 499,504   Area: 2,488 sq km

The county of **Rushar** (*Ch* Huangzhong) lies 26 km SW of Ziling city; only a 40 min bus ride away. The county capital, **Huangzhong**, is a town dominated by Muslim traders, and much of the countryside around consists of Chinese farming villages.

Kumbum Jampaling Monastery

History

At **Rushar Drongdal**, the county boasts the most renowned monastery in Tsongkha, and one of the greatest in all Tibet: that of **Kumbum Jampaling** (*Ch* Taersi), which was founded to commemorate the birthplace of Tsongkhapa in 1560 by Rinchen Tsondru Gyeltsen. The monastery is built around the tree which marks his actual birthplace, where Tsongkhapa's mother, Shingza Acho, had herself built a stupa (*kumbum*) in 1379. Later, in 1583, Dalai Lama III Sonam Gyatso sojourned here, and encouraged Rinchen Tsondru Gyeltsen to build a **Maitreya Temple (Jampa Lhakhang)**, after which the site became known as Kumbum Jampaling. Over subsequent centuries, the monastery developed into a large complex, 41 ha in area.

Kumbum has been sacked and rebuilt several times in its history, particularly during the Muslim rebellion of 1860, when hundreds of monks died protecting the main chapels. It is currently undergoing major restoration work, which is expected to be finished by 1997. Only half of the monks in Kumbum are Tibetan, and most of these come from the Kokonor region or areas to the S of the Yellow River, while Mongol, Tu, and a few Chinese make up the remainder of the monastery's 400 monks. Despite the obvious sanctity and grandure of the complex at Kumbum, the monastery at times has the sad air of a museum, and this is enhanced by the arrival of strident Chinese tourists from Ziling, Lanzhou and other urban areas.

● **Festivals** Festivals and important ceremonies are still held here, notably the *Great Prayer Festival* during the first month of the lunar calendar, the masked dances held in the 4th month, 7th and 9th months; the *Dharmacakra anniversary* (4th day of the 6th month); and the *Anniversary of Tsongkhapa* (25th day of the 12th month).

● **Accommodation** Stay at the *Taer Hotel* (Taersi Binguan), where double rooms are ¥80, and the food is excellent. Muslim street restaurants are also good value.

The site

As one approaches the monastery from town, there are a large number of souvenir stalls selling a range of Tibetan jewellery, both old and new, as well as tangkas and other religious artefacts. By the side of the road you will pass the **Chorten Gobzhi** (1), which is a large stupa with four gates. Then, at the entrance to the monastery are the **Chorten Degye** (2), the eight stupas symbolizing the deeds of the Buddha. The originals were destroyed during the Cultural Revolution, the present set having been reconstructed in the early 1980s. The ticket office and a small guesthouse, known as **Nelenkhang Kakun Gon** (5) are located beside the stupas, and entrance to the following nine main temples and halls is granted for ¥21 (foreigners), and ¥14 (Chinese).

Main temples

The gold-tiled **Tsenkhang Chenmo** (7), constructed in 1692 and rebuilt in 1802, is a protector chapel dedicated to the five aspects of the protector deity Pehar known as Gyelpo Kunga. The **Zhabten**

Lhakhang (9), which was completed in 1717 and consecrated by Dalai Lama VII, contains images of Shakyamuni Buddha with his foremost disciples, along with the Sixteen Elders. The **Jokhang** (17), constructed in 1604, has an exquisite image of Shakyamuni in bodhisattva form, inlaid with pearls and gems, as well as the reliquary of its founder, Ozer Gyatso; and the adjacent **Gonkhang** (29), dated 1594, has images of Tsongkhapa and Yamantaka.

The most sacred temples are those at the heart of the complex: the **Serdong Chenmo** (18) was originally built by Tsongkhapa's mother in 1379 on the spot where a sandalwood tree is said to have sprung from the ground where Tsongkhapa's placenta fell at the time of his birth. The walls are made of aquamarine tiles, and the central gold image of the master, which overlooks the branches of the original tree, is housed in the upper storey below a gilded roof. Adjacent to it is the **Jamkhang** (19), the temple dedicated to Maitreya, containing an image of Maitreya at the age of 12 and the reliquary stupa of Rinchen Tsondru Gyeltsen, which dates from 1583.

The lavish grand assembly hall, **Tsokchen Dukhang** (20), was originally constructed in 1611, but rebuilt in 1776 and again in 1912. The present building has a spacious outer courtyard, and a vast hall with 166 pillars in ornate yellow dragon motifs, and murals depicting the 1,000 buddhas of this age. The volumes of the Tibetan canon are stacked up on the side-walls. The **Jamyang Kunzik Lhakhang** (21) is an elongated building with a Chinese-style roof, dating from 1592. In the centre of its shrine are large images depicting the bodhisattvas, Manjughosa, Avalokiteshvara and peaceful Vajrapani; while to the right are the trio: Simhanada, Sitatapatra and Sarasvati; and to the left, Tsongkhapa flanked by his students and the great scholars of ancient India known as the 'Six Ornaments and Two Supreme Ones'. The protector Dharmaraja stands guard at the side. Lastly, the **Thamche Khyenpei Lhakhang** (22) contains a reliquary stupa of Dalai Lama III (not to be confused with his principal reliquary at Drepung in Lhasa).

The colleges

In addition to those temples there are four colleges: **Champa Dratsang** (3) is for the study of religious dancing. **Menpa Dratsang** (16), the medical college, was built in 1757 and contains images of Tsongkhapa, Bhaisjyaguru, and Shakyamuni, along with a three-dimensional mandala of the Eight Medicine Buddhas. **Gyupa Dratsang** (25), the tantric college, dating from 1649, contains images of Shakyamuni and Maitreya buddhas, the meditational deities Guhyasamaja, Cakrasamvara and Bhairava, and murals depicting the 1,000 buddhas of this age. Finally, **Dukhor Dratsang** (23) for the study of Kalacakra-based astrology and esoteric practices, founded in 1817, contains images of Kalacakra, Shakyamuni, and Avalokiteshvara, as well as some fine old tangkas.

Residential buildings

The building known as **Labrang Tse Tashi Khangsar** (10) is the residence of the presiding abbot of Kumbum; and it was where Dalai Lama V and Panchen Lama VI resided during their historic visits. The original structure dates from 1650 and it was further renovated in 1687.

There are six other residential buildings, each associated with one of the great incarnating lamas of the monastery. The largest is that of the Tulku Akya (**Akya Garwa**; 28), followed by those of Tulku Chesho (**Chesho Garwa**; 24), Tulku Minyak (**Minyak Garwa**; 4), Tulku Patrik (**Patrik Garwa**; 11), Tulku Sertok (**Sertok Garwa**; 13), and the monastic supervisor (**Gonkya Garwa**; 12). Next to the residence of Tulku Akya is the **Dukhor Lolang Kyilkhor** (30), containing a 40 cubit sized three-dimensional mandala of the meditational deity

KUMBUM JAMPALING MONASTERY

N

To Town

Sketch map: not to scale

1. Chorten Gobzhi
2. Chorten Degye
3. Champa Dratsang
4. Minyak Garwa
5. Nelenkhang Kakun Gon (ticket office)
6. Gomangwei Gyencho Zhengsa
7. Tsenkhang Chenmo
8. Dukhor Chorten
9. Zhabten Lhakhang
10. Labrang Tse Tashi Khangsar
11. Patrik Garwa
12. Gonkya Garwa
13. Sertok Garwa
14. Parkhang
15. Chichen (administration)
16. Menpa Dratsang
17. Jokhang
18. Serdong Chenmo
19. Jamkhang
20. Tsokchen Dukhang
21. Jamyang Kunzik Lhakang
22. Thamche Khyenpei Lhakhang
23. Dukhor Dratsang
24. Chesho Garwa
25. Gyupa Dratsang
26. Jetsunpei Gyencho Zhengsa
27. Yarcho Chora
28. Akya Garwa
29. Gonkhang
30. Dukhor Lolang Kyilkhor

TIB102

Kalacakra, which was built in 1987 by Gyabak Lobzang Tenpei Gyeltsen to mark the beginning of the 17th sexagenary year cycle.

Other buildings

Other buildings include the **Parkhang** (14) where woodblock editions of the *Tibetan Canon* and the *Collected Works of Tsongkhapa* are housed; the hillside **Yarcho Chora** (27) or 'summer debating courtyard', the **Dukhor Chorten** (8), the general administrative office known as **Chichen** (15), and two small rooms for moulding tormas and so-called 'butter-sculptures' – the **Gomangwei Gyencho Zhengsa** (6) and the **Jetsunpei Gyencho Zhengsa** (26).

GONLUNG COUNTY

དགོན་ལུང་

Huzhu

互助土族自治县

Population: 356,876   Area: 3,133 sq km

Huzhu county (Gonlung) lies 44 km NE of Ziling in a minor side-valley of the Tsong-chu River. Here the **Tu** peoples, who are of Turkic origin but practitioners of Tibetan Buddhism, are to be found in one of their greatest concentrations. Most of the people wear Chinese clothes, but occasionally Tu women wearing distinctively striped dresses can be seen in the villages.

There are two important monasteries within the county: **Gonlung Jampaling** was founded in 1604 by Gyelse Donyo Chokyi Gyatso. Later, Ngawang Lobzang Chokden, the incarnation of Jamchen Choje Shakya Yeshe (founder of **Sera Monastery** at Lhasa) was invited here by the Manchu emperor, and he constructed a number of temples. His incarnation was Changkya Qutuqtu Rolpei Dorje, the sectarian author and zealot who waged war against the kingdoms of Gyarong (on whom see below, page 630). His incarnation was Tuken Ngawang Chokyi Gyatso, and his the renowned scholar Tuken Qutuqtu Lobzang Chokyi Nyima (b 1737). The latter composed his celebrated philosophical treatise on the schools of Buddhism entitled *Crystal Mirror of Philosophical Systems (Drubta Shelgyi Melong)* at Gonlung in 1801.

Picturesquely situated in a lightly wooded valley, the monastery stretches over the slopes and has seven temples. Its 400 monks are almost entirely of Tu descent, but all speak Amdo Tibetan as well as Chinese. An important ceremony is held here during the prayer festival of the first month of the lunar calendar; while masked dances are held during the 1st, 3rd and 4th months.

The other main Gelukpa monastery of the county is **Chubzang Ganden Migyurling**, which was founded NW of Gonlung, on the plain called Bumlung Tashithang in 1649 by Tolung Chubzang Lalebpa Namgyel Peljor.

● **Festivals** Village folk song fairs are held within the county at **Songshuiwan** and **Weiyuan** in July, and at **Tuguan** in Aug.

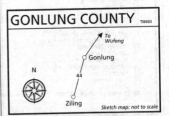

GONLUNG COUNTY TIB603

To Wufeng

Gonlung

44

Ziling

N

Sketch map: not to scale

SERKHOK COUNTY

གསེར་ཁོག

大通县 Datong

Population: 408,602   Area: 2,945 sq km

MONGYON HUI AUTONOMOUS COUNTY

མོང་ཡོན

门源回族自治县 Menyuan

Population: 123,997   Area: 5,497 sq km

Datong is an industrial city 39 km N of Ziling in the valley of the **Beichuan** tributary of the Tsong-chu. The principal monastery here is the **Tsenpo Gon Ganden Damcholing** which was founded in the Serkhok area in 1649 by Tsenpo Dondrub Gyatso, an abbot of Gonlung. Later, it became the seat of the Mindrol Nomenqan incarnations.

The upper reaches of the **Julak-chu** (*Ch* Datong he), which converges with the Tsong-chu at **Minhe**, pass through the area immediately to the S of the Chokle Namgyel range (Qilian). The Gansu corridor and Mongolia lie beyond the range, so this is truly the NE extremity of Amdo. Mongyon county is administered within the N Kokonor Autonomous Prefecture. Its county town is located 74 km N of Datong, and it is largely an area populated by Muslims. There are, however, isolated Gelukpa monasteries, such as **Kanchen Gonpa**, **Semnyi Gon** and **Tetung Drak Gon**, situated on or near the banks of the Julak-chu.

ACCESS Public buses run from Ziling via Datong into the Mongyon area.

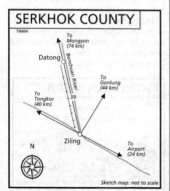

SERKHOK COUNTY

TIB604

To Mongyon (74 km)

Datong

To Gonlung (44 km)

To Tongkor (40 km)

39

Ziling

To Airport (24 km)

N

Sketch map: not to scale

MONGYEN & CHILEN COUNTIES

TIB605

Chilen

Rui Shui

170 Mongyon

Wufeng

74

Datong

Beichuan

Gonlung

To Kamalok

To Haiyan (238 km)

To Ziling

Julak-chu

Tsong-chu

N

Sketch map: not to scale

CHILEN COUNTY
ཆེ་ལེན

祁连县 Qilian

Population: 30,620   Area: 13,575 sq km

TSONGKHA KHAR COUNTY
ཙོང་ཁ་མཁར

平安县 Pingan

Population: 94,527   Area: 671 sq km

Driving NW from Mongyon, the road crosses a watershed between the **Julakchu** tributary of the Tsong-chu and the **Hei** tributary of the Rui Shui. The latter flows NW through the Chokle Namgyel range into Gansu and Inner Mongolia. **Chilen** county lies across the watershed, but deep within the Chokle Namgyel range. It is administered within the N Kokonor Autonomous Prefecture.

ACCESS The distance from Mongyon to the county capital is 170 km, and from Haiyan (Tsolo) 238 km. Buses also run from Ziling to this remote border area.

The Chilen area is sometimes identified with the ancient kingdom of **Bhatahor**, from which the Tibetan imperial armies acquired Shingjachen, a sacred bird-image of the protector deity Pehar, during the 8th century. The Gelukpa temples of **Alike** and **Huangzang** are prominant in this remote outpost.

From Ziling, the Ziling-Lanzhou highway follows the Tsong-chu downstream, parallel to the railway line. En route, it bypasses the new **Ziling Airport**, visible across the river on the N bank, after 24 km; and then, after 35 km it reaches the county capital, **Pingan**. Here, there is a turn-off on the right, which leads S to the Yellow River at Jentsa or Dowi (Xunhua). The small Chinese monastery named **Pei-ma-ssu** ('white horse temple') is situated on **Martsang Drak**, a reddish cliff opposite the town and above a small Tibetan village. Established in the 8th century, one of the legends of this site recounts how a blind foal kicked his mother in anger, and, his sight restored, realized his error, and jumped off the cliff in shame.

NB The birthplace of the present Dalai Lama XIV is located nearby at the village of **Taktser** in an adjacent side-valley. The Dalai Lama's house was reconstructed in 1986, and some of his distant relatives, including the local school teacher, still live in the area. This village is the only destination in the county which requires the foreign traveller to obtain an Alien Travel Permit prior to visiting.

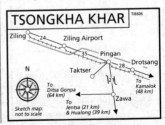

TSONGKHA KHAR TIB606

Ziling —24→ Ziling Airport
—35→ Pingan
Taktser —28→ Drotsang
To Kamalok (48 km)
Zawa
To Ditsa Gonpa (64 km)
To Jentsa (21 km) & Hualong (39 km)
N
Sketch map: not to scale

DROTSANG COUNTY

བྲོ་ཚང་

乐都县 Ledu

Population: 287,008   Area: 2,520 sq km

KAMALOK COUNTY

བ་ཀའ་མ་ལོག

民和县 Minhe

Population: 335,620   Area: 1,681 sq km

Some 28 km downstream from Pingan town, the highway passes through **Drotsang** (Ledu) county. Formerly known as **Neu-be**, this county controls several side valleys of the Tsong-chu River, and one monastery in particular is worthy of a visit. **Drotsang Gonpa** was originally founded in 1387 by the Da Ming emperor as a Karma Kagyu monastery, and was later substantially reconstructed in 1564 by Sherab Chokden (Drepung Samlo Rabjampa) in accordance with a prediction made by Dalai Lama III. It is located 20 km S of Ledu county town, near the large mountain range that separates Ziling district from the Yellow River, on the edge of the agricultural zone. It has a remarkable 360 sq m mural depicting the life of Shakyamuni Buddha.

● **Festival** A festival is held here annually during the 4th month of the lunar calendar.

Kamalok county lies 48 km downstream from Drotsang on the border of present day Qinghai and Gansu provinces. **Minhe**, the new county town, which is situated at the confluence of the Tsong-chu and the Julak-chu tributary (*Ch* Datong he), has a large ferrochrome smelting capacity, and is generally unattractive.

Most of the monasteries in this region are located in the lower **Julak** valley, and although undoubtedly old, they are very small, with only one reconstructed temple and a maximum of 20 monks, many of them of Tu nationality.

At **Liuwan** cemetery, N of Minhe, 1,600 tombs and 30,000 relics have been excavated, including a celebrated clay pot with dancing figurines, which is regarded as a national treasure. This is the largest of many archaeological sites, which have been opened in the Qinghai

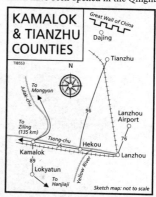

KAMALOK & TIANZHU COUNTIES

TIB553

N

Great Wall of China

Dajing

Tianzhu

To Mongyon

Julak-chu

To Ziling (135 km)

96

Lanzhou Airport

Tsong-chu

Hekou

56

76

Lanzhou

Kamalok

89

Lokyatun

To Hanjiaji

Yellow River

Sketch map: not to scale

DROTSANG COUNTY

TIB607

Sketch map: not to scale

Pingan

28

Drotsang

N

To Kamalok (48 km)

area. A detailed report was published in 1980, including extensive illustrations of the unearthed pottery.

Another road leads SE from Minhe to cross the Yellow River at **Lokyatun** (*Ch* Guanting, 89 km via Gushan and Maying), and then to reach the **Sang-chu** river valley at **Hanjiaji**, SW of Linxia in Gansu province.

TIANZHU AUTONOMOUS COUNTY
བོད་གུༀ

天祝藏族自治县 Tianzhu
Population: 233,896   Area: 6,633 sq km

After Kamalok, the highway crosses the present Qinghai-Gansu border and heads for Lanzhou. At **Hekou** (56 km from Minhe town), it passes the confluence of the Tsong-chu and Yellow rivers, and from there it is but a short drive into the city. From Hekou, there is also a side-road which heads due N, following the **Zhuanglang** tributary upstream to **Tianzhu** (96 km). This autonomous county is the furthest outpost of Tibetan habitation in NE Amdo, and lies not far to the S of Dajing on the **Great Wall of China**. It is also accessible via the Lanzhou-Wuwei railway line, but unlike neighbouring Ziling and Labrang districts it is not yet classed as an open area. Alien travel permit restrictions still apply.

LANZHOU

Like Chengdu, Kunming, and Kathmandu, **Lanzhou** is an important starting point for travellers visiting the Tibetan plateau. It is the hub of the communications network for China's North-western provinces, and most travellers to Amdo in Tibet or the Silk Rd in Xinjiang will pass through here. Two areas of Amdo are currently administered within Gansu province with their centre of government at Lanzhou: the Ganlho Tibetan Autonomous Prefecture (on which see below, page 47) and the Tianzhu Tibetan Autonomous County (on which see above, page 47).

At a low altitude of only 1,600m, Lanzhou is a large elongated industrial town set on the edge of the Tibetan plateau

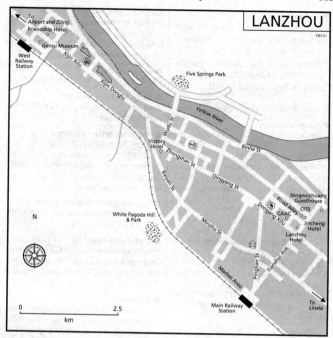

and Ordos desert. Many of the nearby hills are covered in thick deposits of loess, which can be very fertile where irrigated. However, the area around Lanzhou receives little rain, and many parts of Gansu are constantly challenged by desert encroachment.

Orientation

Lanzhou itself sprawls along the S bank of the Yellow River, and grew in importance after the construction of the first bridge in 1385. During the present century, the advent of the railways brought heavy industry to Lanzhou and the urban population rapidly increased. The 500 sq km of the inner city now has a population of 423,875; and its surrounding district (area 1,712 sq km) has a population of 1,450,809. The **airport** is 2 hrs drive (76 km) from the city itself,

up a northern valley, and the journey down to the Yellow River reveals typical small farming of the loess hills.

The **West Railway Station** and the **West Bus Station** (for buses to Labrang) are located at the NW end of town, and nearby are the Gansu Provincial Museum, and the *Friendship Hotel*. The **Main Railway Station** is to the SW of the main shopping area, and connected to it by Pinglian St (where the Post Office is located) and Tianshui Ave. Most hotels are clustered in the area around the Xuguan Traffic Circle on Tianshui Ave, notably the *Lanzhou Fandian*, the *Jingcheng Hotel*, and the *Ningwozhuang Guesthouse*. CITS and CAAC are conveniently here also. Across Central Square on Qingyang St you will find the Bank of China and the Public Security Bureau.

Museums

The *Gansu Provincial Museum*, near *Friendship Hotel*, has an interesting collection of artefacts from the Silk Rd, including neolithic painted pottery. Open 0900 to 1130 and from 1430-1700. Closed on Sun, admission ¥10.

Local information

● **Accommodation**

A *Jincheng Hotel (Jincheng Fandian)*, 363 Tianshui Ave, T 8416638, F (86-931)-8418438 has 136 rm, with attached bath, ¥297/double room, and dorm-style accommodation at ¥24/bed. There are Chinese and Western restaurants, IDD connections, a business centre, currency exchange facilities, ticketing and taxi services, barber and massage parlour, bar, and shopping precinct; **A** *Lanzhou Fandian*, 28 Dongangxilu St, T 8422981, is a 1950s Russian-style building with 80 double rooms at ¥240 (with attached bath) and ¥80 (without attached bath); **A** *Ningwozhuang Park Guesthouse*, Tianshui Ave, T 8426221, ext 444, is a splendid garden hotel, once reserved for party cadres and visiting dignitaries. Double rooms with attached bath over ¥200.

B *Friendship Hotel (Youyi Fandian)*, 14 Xijin St, T 8334711, has 43 double rm at ¥200, and good value dorm-style accommodation at ¥20/bed. The hotel has postal and shopping facilities.

C *Victory Hotel (Shengli Fandian)*, 133 Zhongshan St, T 8421509, has 168 double rm at ¥120, but the dorms (¥12) are usually reserved for Chinese visitors.

● **Places to eat**

Among the major hotels, the *Jincheng* has both Chinese and Western menus, and the *Friendship Hotel* has inexpensive set meals. For local street food, try the restaurants around the Main Railway Station or the lane due E of the Bank of China. Local specialities inc *ruojiabing*, a fiery lamb or pork kebab served in a pitta bread, and *tianpeizi*, a fermented barley dish prepared by Muslims.

● **Airline offices**

CAAC, 46 Dongang Xilu, T 821964, 828174.

● **Banks & money changers**

Bank of China, Pingliang St, T 8485354, has exchange facilities.

● **Post & telecommunications**

General Post Office: Pingliang St, open 0830-1900, and has parcel wrapping service; the Telephone and Telegram Office, on Qingyang St, has IDD facilities. Postal facilities also available in major hotels.

● **Tour companies & travel agents**

Gansu CITS, 361 Tianshui Ave, T 8826181, F 0931-8418556.

● **Useful addresses**

Police and Public Security: Gansu Province Foreigners Registration Office, 38 Qingyang St; Lanzhou City Foreigners Registration Office, 132 Wudu St.

● **Transport**

Air There are daily flights to Beijing (twice), Guangzhou, Shanghai, Xi'an, and Dunhuang. Also less frequent flights to Chengdu, Guilin, Urumqi, Fuzhou, Kunming, and Hong Kong.

Road Buses run from the *West Bus Station* to Linxia, Xiahe, and Ganlho Dzong (Hezuoshen), as well as Wuwei; and from the *East Bus Station* to more remote destinations in Shaanxi and Ningxia provinces. **NB** Foreigners travelling by public bus must pay local travel insurance through the Public Insurance Company of China, 150 Qingyang St, T 8416422 ext 114, or from CITS directly.

Train There are frequent train connections to Kermo via Ziling, and also to Urumqi, Beijing, Chengdu, and Xi'an.

THE YELLOW RIVER BEND:
REPKONG AND SOGWO

There are three routes from Ziling to the Golok region in S Amdo: one via Tsongkha Khar, Bayan Khar or Jentsa, and Repkong; a second via Rushar and Trika; and a third via Chabcha and Mato. The first is described in this section, and the others in the following section.

The ethnic mix to the N and E of **Repkong** is the most complex in Amdo. The Hsuing-nu, distant relatives of the Sodgians, once ruled here, in constant conflict with neighbouring Han China, after which came the Tuyunhun (*Tib* Azha), the Qiang, and then, during the 7th-9th century, the Central Tibetans. The Tangut state to the N and the Mongolian Empire also encompassed this area during the 10th-14th century. There were, additionally, pockets of Hor or Uighur tribes of Turkic origin, who had been dispersed along the oases of the Silk Rd very early, and from the 8th century Arabs and Persians. The Hui Muslims of China, who are mostly of Turkic origin, and the Salar, a distinct tribe exiled from Samarkand, all had a presence. The earlier conquering armies had a tendency to disband at the end of their campaigns, frequently displacing the locals.

After the Ming emperors of China had rescinded the ancient imperial policy of 'using barbarians to rule barbarians', colonial settlements were gradually established in the grasslands, and the agricultural Chinese began to push back the nomadic tribes. Many outlying groups of Amdowa Tibetans became isolated from the rest of the Tibetan population by these large settlements, and at the start of this century in a few regions, Tibetans were becoming a minority. To complicate matters, some Tibetans converted to Islam, often at the point of a sword, and racial intermarriage was commonplace.

The route described in this section comprises six counties, of which three belong to the Tibetan Autonomous Prefecture of S Yellow River (Jentsa, Repkong and Tsekok), two (Bayan Khar and Dowi) are administered directly from Ziling, and one (Sogwo) is a Mongolian Autonomous Prefecture in its own right.

Recommended itineraries: 6, 8, 9, 11.

BAYAN KHAR COUNTY
 བ་ཡན་མཁར

Hualong Hui
Autonomous County

化隆回族自治县

Population: 215,692   Area: 2,732 sq km

From **Pingan** town, a branch road
leads S from the Ziling-Lanzhou highway. Leaving the Tsong-chu valley it
crosses into **Bayan Khar** (Hualong)
county, where virtually half the population is Muslim. Nonetheless, 41,000
Tibetans also live here, the third highest concentration of Tibetans in the
part of Amdo controlled by Qinghai.
Most of Tibetans are in villages far to
the E and W of the county, with the
town itself being predominantly Hui
and Han. The county capital, known as
Hualong, lies 84 km SE of Pingan, on a
south-flowing tributary of the Yellow
River. In the NE of the county, there is
also an important north-flowing tributary of the Tsong-chu.

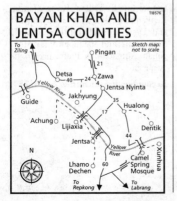

BAYAN KHAR AND JENTSA COUNTIES

TIB576

Sketch map:
not to scale

To Ziling

Pingan
21
Detsa — 40 — 24 Zawa
Jentsa Nyinta
Yellow River
Jakhyung
35
Guide
Hualong
Achung
17
Lijiaxia
44
Jentsa
Dentik
Yellow River
Camel
Lhamo
60
Spring
Dechen
Mosque
Xunhua
N

To Repkong   To Labrang

Jakhyung Shedrubling Monastery

ACCESS The road from Pingan crosses
the watershed, and after passing through
Zawa township (21 km), a rough side-
road heads W to **Xiong Xian** village and
Ditsa Gonpa before linking up with the
Ziling-Trika road (see below, page 599).

The monastery of **Jakhyung Shedrubling** lies to the S of this road on a ridge
overlooking the Yellow River, 24 km beyond Zawa. This is one of the most
historic and renowned Gelukpa monasteries of Amdo, founded in 1349 by Lama
Dondrub Rinchen, the teacher of
Tsongkhapa. The attractive monastery is
situated in a small forest zone, quite
popular with Chinese picnickers from
Ziling at weekends. Small tractors wait
for passengers at the turn-off, and will
charge about ¥8 for the 30 km trip to the
monastery.

Prior to the Gelukpa foundation, an
earlier monastery had been founded on
the same site by Karmapa II, Karmapak-
shi in the 12th century. Later, following
the Gelukpa foundation in 1349, the
monastery was listed, along with Serkhok, Chubzang and Gonlung, as one of
the 'four great monasteries of the N', a
phrase used in Amdo to signify the oldest and most significant Gelukpa institutions of the region. It was here that
Tsongkhapa became ordained as a renunciate, and studied until leaving
Amdo for Lhasa at the age of 16. The
small forest on the eastern slope of the
ridge on which Jakhyung lies is said to
be formed from his hair, and is included
on the 2 hrs circumambulation of the
monastery. There are currently about
500 monks and 10 reconstructed temples. The large assembly hall is brand
new and unimpressive, but the small
temples to the rear have more character.
A green-glazed brick temple houses images of Shakyamuni, Maitreya, and
Tsongkhapa; while another houses a
stupa reliquary (the destroyed original

once held the hair relics of Tsongkhapa), flanked by large images of Jowo Rinpoche, Maitreya and Manjughosa.

From Jakhyung, a 2 hrs walk heads steeply down the barren 'badlands' to the Yellow River.

Detsa Monastery

Ditsa Gompa, some 40 km beyond Jakhyung along the spur road, has a well-respected Gelukpa monastery that was founded in the early 20th century by Sharma Pandita. There are two temples, the larger with a stupa and statue of the founder, along with modern images depicting Jowo Rinpoche, Atisha and Tsongkhapa, and mural panels created by artists from Repkong. The smaller holds a large Avalokiteshvara, a small Manjughosa, and a White Tara. There are currently four lamas and about 300 monks, many of whom come from far afield drawn by the quality of teaching here. Further up-valley en route to **Trika** (*Ch* Guide) is a patch of coniferous forest that must have once covered much of the Lhamori mountain and a small hermitage connected to Kumbum.

Hualong County Town

Returning to the main road from Jakhyung, turn SE and after 4 km there is a major fork at **Jentsa Nyinta** (*Ch* Nangdoi). The SW branch leads directly to the Yellow River at Jentsa where bridges cross to Ljiaxia, Jentsa and the Gu-chu valley; and the SE branch at Dowi (Xunhua) after first passing through Hualong county town. Taking the latter route, you will reach Hualong after 35 km. The town has a large Muslim population, with guesthouses and good noodle restaurants. Bus routes link this town with Ziling, Jentsa, and Rongpo Gyagar.

Dentik

In the NE of Bayan Khar county, on a north-flowing tributary of the Tsongchu, there is the most important pilgrimage site and power place in all of Amdo. **Dentik Sheldrak**, also known as **Dentik Shelgyi Bamgon**, has been revered since the time of Padmasambhava as the foremost power place associated with buddha-mind throughout Kham and Amdo. It was here that Mar Shakyamuni and his colleagues fled from Langdarma's persecution of Buddhism in Lhasa (9th century) in order to conserve the monastic lineage for the sake of posterity.

ACCESS There is a rough road from Hualong that leads E and then S to the village of Korba, 1 hr walking distance from Dentik, but traffic is very infrequent and if you have no transportation, it is much easier to access the site on foot from Dowi (see page 590).

The monastery is spread along the floor of a small side-valley with two simple temples and a number of caves and sacred springs. One of the caves is associated with Lachen Gongpa Rabsel who received the monastic ordination from Mar Sakyamuni and his colleages. Lhalung Pelgyi Dorje, the monk who assassinated Langdarma with an arrow, spent his last years here, although he refused to take part in the ordination of Lachen Gongpa Rabsel because of his crimes. Later, Lu-me and the 10 men of Utsang arrived to receive ordination, and revive monastic Buddhism in Central Tibet.

There are several other monasteries in Far-east Bayan Khar county, including two which represent the Bon tradition, and the **Jampa Bumling** – an extensive Gelukpa establishment, founded by Rinchen Gyatso in the 16th century alongside an earlier Maitreya temple.

Heading S from Hualong county town, the road eventually reaches the N bank of the Yellow River at **Kado Tashi Chodzong** (*Ch* Gando), and crosses over into Dowi county (44 km).

DOWI COUNTY

ཕྱུག

Xunhua Salar
Autonomous County

循化撒拉族自治县

Population: 127,415   Area: 2,132 sq km

The county capital of **Dowi** (Xunhua), traditionally known in Tibetan as Dowi Khar, lies on the S bank of the Yellow River, 44 km SE of Hualong. Since the 14th century the county has been predominantly inhabited by the **Salar**, a very tight-knit band of Central Asian Muslims. A legendary camel carried bags of earth from home, which were matched with earth around a nearby spring, and the tribe's long migration came to an end. The camel appropriately turned to stone!

By the 19th century, the Salar had expanded to include several villages N of the Yellow River, but they were badly defeated by the Chinese armies during the intermittent Muslim wars. The quite large county town is surrounded by fields, both open and enclosed in mud-walled houses, where fruit trees are a speciality.

Despite the Salars' overwhelming dominance in the agriculturally rich valleys, the Tibetans continue to occupy the upper valleys, and several important monasteries can be visited. Above Xunhua town, among the Tibetan farming villages there is a preserved road-side farmhouse, which was the **birthplace of late Panchen Lama X**. It contains a small shrine attended by a caretaker and a courtyard is surrounded by wood-panelled rooms with packed-mud roofs, typical of Amdo hamlets. A footpath leads 1 hr walk over a spur from here to **Bemdo Gonpa**, which was rebuilt quite lavishly in the late 1980s but has not yet regained its religious atmosphere and former importance. Higher up, in the northern mountains, at **Galong**, there are three small Nyingmapa and Gelukpa monasteries.

Routes from Dowi

At the Camel Spring Mosque, 5 km from Xunhua town, three roads split: one road heads N across the Yellow River to Hualong and Ziling, a second cuts SE for Linxia over the mountains, and a third runs SW to Rekpong. To reach **Dentik** on foot (see above, page 589), head E to Dowi and cross the Yellow River by a small bridge. Then, leave the motor road, and take a footpath which heads up a narrow rocky gorge straight ahead, climbing steeply through a series of ridges, 610m above the valley. This trail eventually descends into a narrow side-valley where Dentik is located, 5 hrs walk uphill and 3 hrs walk downhill.

Alternatively, if you take the SE road you will reach **Linxia** after 86 km (via Gangshun Gon, Chorten Rangma, and Hanjiaji). After 8 km due E of Dowi, on a trail which follows the downstream, a side-valley extends SW through a lateral gorge for 12 km, as far as the **Mengda Tianchi Lake**. This lake is revered by Tibetans, who view it as a talismanic power place, and it is now a nature reserve, although its woods are still extensively used by the last Salar village. There is a guesthouse before the lake which hires out horses, for the 4 hrs trail through a craggy mountain gorge to the lakeside.

Lastly, if you take the SW road, you will reach **Baoan** in the upper Gu-chu valley of Repkong, 53 km from Xunhua.

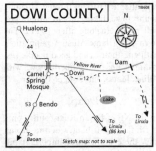

DOWI COUNTY

Sketch map: not to scale

JENTSA COUNTY
གཙན་ཚ

尖扎县 Jainca
Population: 41,528   Area: 1,601 sq km

Jentsa county is located on the S bank of the Yellow River, 17 km SW of the road junction at **Jentsa Nyinta** (see above, page 589). The county town is small and largely Tibetan, but has seen much encroachment from the Hui Muslim traders in recent years. It lies 2 km S of the Yellow River, and NW of **Lhamo Dechen**.

Gur Gonpa of the Gelukpa school (4 km to the W) and **Malho Dorje Drak** of the Nyingma school are both within walking distance of Jentsa town. The latter was where Lhalung Pagyi Dorje remained in retreat during his enforced exile from Central Tibet following his assassination of the apostate king Langdarma during the 9th century.

There are several smaller monasteries of the Gelukpa and Nyingmapa schools in the county, most of them set high up the side-valley between Lijiaxia and Jentsa. Among them, **Gawu Dzongnang**, a Gelukpa institution located a few kilometres S of Lijiaxia, houses a fine set of old tangkas, while three small Gelukpa monasteries: **Gowa**, **Sandrok** and **Ngarong**, with 50-100 monks each, can be accessed on a hill-road, which connects the bridge at Dongma with Jentsa town.

However, the two most significant monasteries within the county are those of Lhamo Dechen and Achung Namdzong.

Lhamo Dechen Monastery

Lhamo Dechen Gonpa, with around 250 monks, is the largest monastery of Jentsa county, located high on a ridge about 25 km SE, E of town. The monastery is sited amidst high altitude Tibetan farming villages with some nearby patches of original forest. It was founded by Lham Shabtrang Karpo, whose most recent incarnation died a few years ago. Although there are five newly constructed main temples and several smaller ones, they are all extremely basic, with the Repkong mural panels as the main point of interest.

Achung Namdzong

The celebrated Nyingma monastery of Achung Namdzong lies within the Nangra curve of the Yellow River, NW of Jentsa town.

ACCESS It can be reached via a rough road that follows the S bank upstream, but the easiest route crosses the Yellow River to reach **Lijiaxia**, a rapidly growing town located beside a new hydro dam. Work on the dam is not yet complete and the Yellow River has been diverted from its bed into a tunnel about 1 km long. About 15 km past the dam, up a side valley to the S, dramatic red mud pinnacles, over 100m high, rise above the valley between the verdant mountains. The road divides here, with the right fork heading into **Jangbula**, a protected forest area, and the left heading up to Achung Namdzong.

Chorten Tang

Overlooking this junction is **Chorten Tang**, the largest nunnery in Central Amdo. Around 200 nuns are based here, but there is only one simple temple, as yet only partially decorated. About 2 km up valley, there is a small Gelukpa temple, named **Tashi Namgyeling**, and, just beside it, the monastery of Achung Namdzong.

Achung

Achung, also known as Dorje Drakra Anchung Namdzong, is one of the 25 important power places of Kham and Amdo, specifically symbolizing the mind aspect of buddha-mind. It was here that the three learned men from Central Tibet, Mar Sakyamuni, Yo Gejung, Tsang Rabsel, stayed when they arrived in Amdo. The main temple was not, however, constructed until 1794. This is the largest Nyingmapa site in Central Amdo, with about 100 monks and a variable number of long-haired mantrins, known as *ngakpa* in Tibetan (pronounced 'ngukwa' or 'hwon' in local Amdo dialect). The mantrins at Achung Namdzong are generally older men who have received some religious instruction in the past, and take a limited number of Vinaya vows in conjunction with their bodhisattva and mantra vows. Most are married farmers or, less frequently, nomads. The 25 branch monasteries of Achung Namdzong are only occasionally attended by the mantrins, although one who lives nearby will act as caretaker and has the keys to the main temple.

Achung Namdzong itself is rare amongst the monasteries of Amdo for the high quality of its construction, particularly the woodwork, which is excellent. **Dolma Lhakang** and **Guru Gonkang** are the two main temples and slightly below them the **Manikhang** has a set of large water-driven prayerwheels. Lama Gurong Tsan, the chief Nyingmapa master of the region, whose 80-year-wold mother also lives here, has overseen the construction, but funds are now short and the temples still require interior decoration.

The spectacular red hill opposite Achung Namdzong, known as **Namdzong Tse**, houses some retreat caves, where traces of original murals can be seen. These are accessible by a steep track on the N side, which should not be attempted during or just after heavy rain.

REPKONG COUNTY
རེབ་གོང་
同仁县 Tongren

Population: 71,842   Area: 3,353 sq km

Central Amdo, the region S of Tsongkha, comprises a large proportion of the Tibetan population of Amdo. Farmers and nomads are spread through the verdant valleys and plains, and there are many monasteries dotted throughout the region. **Repkong** in Central Amdo, just S of the Yellow River, can in many ways be considered the heart of Amdo. Its principal monastery pre-dates Labrang and Kumbum by at least two centuries, and the county itself possesses almost 50 smaller monasteries, mostly of the Gelukpa school.

The main river of Repkong is the Gu-chu, which flows N to converge with

REPKONG COUNTY

the Yellow River near Lhamo Dechen. The '9 side-valleys' that make up the Gu-chu basin vary from rolling grasslands which support nomadic camper groups, through forested gorges, to an agricultural zone near the county town itself. The ethnic mix is also fascinating, for there are four villages inhabited by thoroughly Tibetanized Tu people in the valley while to the E lies Dowi (Xunhua), home of the Muslim Salar and to the N Bayan Khar (Hualong), a Hui autonomous county, and to the S, Sogwo (*Ch* Henan), a Mongol autonomous county.

The capital, **Rongpo Gyakhar**, is both the administrative centre for Repkong County and for the S Yellow River Prefecture. The distance to the capital from Jentsa is 76 km, and from Xunhua 67 km (both via the Bao'an intersection). Another road leads SE via Bao'an for 115 km from the capital to Labrang Monastery.

Gu-chu Caves

The main roads heading S into Repkong from Jentsa and Xunhua meet together at **Bao'an** 16 km N of the county capital. Then, from a cement factory near **Toja**, a road heads E out of the Gu-chu valley. After 7 km it splits, the left fork heading NE to Xunhua (52 km) and the right heading SE to Labrang (100 km). Up a side valley to the S, before reaching this junction, there is a small monastery set on a cliff at the entrance to a vast cave network. The extensive caves (some 20 km from Toja) are said to link up with the cave at Drakar near Labrang in an 8-day underground pothole. There is a natural cave temple dedicated to Cakrasamvara here, and it is one of the 'eight places of spiritual attainment' sited around the Gu-chu valley.

Tashikyil

The road to Labrang climbs for 11 km from the Xunhua turn-off, leaving the Gu-chu valley, and entering a beautiful red sandstone gorge, which is forested in its upper reaches. Eventually it reaches **Zhongpong Chi**, a farming village with two temples, which is the birthplace of Zhabkar Tsokdruk Rangdrol (1781-1851). Above Zhongpong Chi, a 40 min climb reaches **Tashikyil Gonpa**, which is an important hermitage of the Nyingma tradition, maintained by a strong *ngakpa* community. Zhabkar spent many years teaching here, and his stone chairs are still enclosed in ancient groves. There is a small government compound truckstop at Zhongpong Chi, where it may be possible to stay.

Gartse Gonpa

Continuing through the heavily logged gorge from Zhongpong, and crossing a spur, the road then ascends 13 km to the attractive **Gartse Gonpa**. This is revered as one of the eight foremost places of spiritual attainment in Repkong. After Gartse, the road traverses a broad grassy plain beside **Mt Amnye Nyemri**, and then continues across the current provincial frontier (from Qinghai into Gansu) to reach **Ganja**, **Drakar Gonpa** and **Labrang** (see page 637) in Sangchu county. A more indirect trekking route continues across the plain from Gartse to **Dowa** (42 km), and thence to Labrang via Sangke.

Rongpo Gyakhar

After crossing the Yellow River, the road to Repkong enters the Gu-chu valley, and follows the spectacular gorges of that river upstream. After 20 km the valley broadens into the fertile plain, dotted with villages and monasteries, that stretches all the way to **Rongpo Gyakhar**, the county and prefectural capital. According to 1989 statistics, the population of the town is almost 70% Tibetan, but the buildings have a very Chinese appearance. The town has not yet developed as a tourist destination, but this will change next year following the completion of the new high-rise *Huangnan Hotel*, at the top of main street. The open air market, entered by a passageway opposite the old *Huangnan Hotel* is well worth a visit.

Rongpo Gonchen Monastery

Rongpo Gonchen, the principal monastery of Repkong, lies to the S of town. The original buildings were constructed in 1301 by the Sakyapa master Sangda Rinchen, who was an emissary of Drogon Chogyel Phakpa. Later, it was reconstituted as a Gelukpa monastery by Shar Kalden Gyatso during the 16th century. The monastery currently has nine temples and around 400 monks; headed by the important incarnate lamas of Rongpo. The principal tulku, Rongpo Kyabgon VIII, is now a young boy. The previous incumbent passed away in 1978.

There are 35 branch monasteries, most of them in Repkong county, and these are often associated with the other lamas affiliated to the mother monastery: Alak Re Yerchung, Alak Kutso, Alak Rongwo, Alak Tson-de, and so forth. The main N-S road runs between the monastery and a small cliff below which is the old village, complete with Chinese temple and a mosque, on the banks of the Gu-chu.

The site

At its high point, Rongpo Gonchen had four major colleges: a general college known as **Dratsang Tosam Namgyeling**, a tantric college known as **Gyudra Sangchen Chokyi Bangzo**, a Kalacakra college known as **Dudra Sangak Dargyeling**, and a meditation college called **Drubdra Nechok Tashikyil**.

Among the renovated buildings, the **Great Assembly Hall (Tsokchen Du-khang)** is close to the main road, behind a shrine dedicated to the gate-keeper Acala (containing an enormous image of this sword-wielding deity). The main entrance of the monastery is located some distance further S, through a chapel gateway decorated with modern murals. The interior of the Great Assembly Hall is vast and spartan; but its porch contains some interesting murals, which depict the ubiquitous Four Guardian Kings, the dress code for monks, and in addition, the local protector deities of Amdo, known as Amnye Machen and Amnye Shachung. The latter is the name of a sacred snow peak 20 km due E of Repkong.

To the S and slightly uphill from the Great Assembly Hall is the **Khardong Chapel**, containing the reliquary stupa of Rongpo Kyapgon VII. The renovated **Kalacakra College (Du-khor Dratsang)** lies behind it, and contains some beautiful new murals executed by the master artist, Kharsham Gyal, in the Repkong style. There are new images of the kings of Shambhala, yet to be installed, and a few old tangkas, notably a large Tsongkhapa and a depiction of Tsongkhapa flanked by his followers (Je Yabsesum). One of the statues depicts Shar Kalden Gyatso, who established the Gelukpa tradition here in the 16th century.

Far to the right of the Kalacakra College is the **Jampeyang Lhakhang** with its distinctive *gyabib*-style roof. It contains an exquisitely fashioned clay image of Manjughosa, which exhibits all the best hallmarks of Repkong clay sculpture. Above this temple is the **Podrang**, or residence of the present Rongpo Kyapgon VIII, and the restored tantric college or **Gyupa Dratsang**.

Rongpo Gonchen was formerly renowned for its expertise in Tibetan medicine and in painting. Two painting schools known as Sengeshong Yagotsang and Sengeshong Magotsang were established to the N of the monastery and these were given responsibility for the painting and embellishing of different temples and colleges.

SENGESHONG ART SCHOOLS

Slightly N of the town, the two renowned painting schools of Repkong, known as **Sengeshong Yagotsang** and **Sengeshong Magotsang**, are located within their unique idyllic village settings. Almost every house is an artist's studio, and in recent years four artists have become celebrities in their own right: Shawu Tsering of Sengeshong Yagotsang, Gyatso of Sengeshong Magotsang, Kunzang (who resides across the Gu-chu river) and Jigme (now deceased). Their works are on display in the Repkong Art Centre of the Huangnan Tibetan Nationality Autonomous Prefecture in town. More importantly, their work is represented in the stupendous temples of Sengeshong Yagotsang and Magotsang monasteries.

The Repkong school of art, known as Wutun to the Chinese, was established by the 15th century and, by the 18th century, it had spread to cover much of Amdo, as indeed it does today. Almost all of the work executed here over the centuries was lost, unseen by the outside world, during the destruction of Amdo's monasteries in the Cultural Revolution; but due to the dedication of a few elderly masters the tradition is now being carefully handed down to the next generation. The style broadly follows that of Central Tibet, but the infusion of cultures brought by contact with the Mongolians, Tu and neighbouring Chinese makes the work distinct. This is reflected in the ethnic origins of the people of Sengeshong themselves, who are said to have come from Western Tibet and to have intermingled over the centuries with neighbouring communities.

Sengeshong Yagotsang

At **Sengeshong Yagotsang** there is an **Assembly Hall** containing exquisite clay statues, the foremost representing Repkong Kyapgon VII and the founder of Yagotsang. The work is recent, the original having been destroyed by fire in 1946. Alongside the assembly hall is a temple dedicated to the Buddhas of the Three Times, in which the enormous figures of the three buddhas are flanked by the eight standing bodhisattvas. A side chapel dedicated to Tsongkhapa is currently under construction.

Sengeshong Magotsang

At Sengeshong Magotsang, where there are currently 150 monks, the Assembly Hall has original ceiling panels, dating to the 1910s. These survived the ravages of the Cultural revolution because the building was used as a wheat granary during that turbulent period. Alongside it, is a Maitreya temple, containing enormous and outstanding clay images Maitreya, flanked by Manjushri (twice),

Mahakarunika, and Tsongkhapa. The image of Manjushri to the left is upright, as is that of Mahakarunika to the right.

Local information
● **Accommodation**
Foreigners are obliged to stay in the *Huangnan Hotel*, also known as the *Tongren County Guesthouse*, which has a range of rooms from ¥16 upwards, the best with attached baths and running hot water in the evenings. There is a good second floor Chinese restaurant, and a cheaper one on the ground floor (sharing the same kitchen).

● **Places to eat**
As with most Amdo towns, there are mostly Muslim noodle restaurants, and a few more upmarket Chinese ones.

Middle Gu-chu Valley

On the valley floor N of Repkong are the Gelukpa monasteries of **Nyentok** and **Gomar**, both populated with Tu rather than Tibetan monks. Nyentok is small and close to town, while Gomar is 8 km further N and much more impressive. It has newly-built temples, all of a much higher artistic and architectural standard than the normal concrete and brick, and a colourful 7-tiered stupa with temples atop and a good view of the valley.

Upper Gu-chu Valley

The road continues to follow the Gu-chu upstream, into the broad grassy plains of Tobden, Tsekok, and Sogwo. **Jangkya** is the first village, 7 km out of Repkong, and it has a tiny Nyingmapa temple. A few rather tattered original Repkong wall hangings are preserved here, reputedly thanks to them being hidden on Mt Amnye Mori behind the village during the 1960s. The valley to the E contains the affiliated **Jangkya Monastery**, also of the Nyingmapa school, which once housed 125 monks, and a small Gelukpa monastery.

Further S, at **Chukhol Khartse Gonpa**, there are sacred hot springs. **Dardzang** lies higher, above the valley, giving unparalleled views and a tantalizing glimpse of **Mt Amnye Jakhyung**, the prime holy mountain of the region. There are many other significant hills and mountains in the vicinity, and almost every village will have its arrow shrines on a nearby hill, which are attended annually. A few like Amnye Taklung, close to Repkong, are more broadly recognized; and Amnye Shachung is renowned all over Amdo.

Further S, are the traces of the two largest Nyingmapa monasteries in the area: **Repkong Nyingon** of the Mindroling tradition, which had over 1,000 monks; and **Repkong Sibgon** of the *Longchen Nyingtig* tradition, which had over 1,500 monks.

The road continues through partially forested hills past **Dzongmar Monastery** of the Gelukpa school, and then over a pass to **Tobden** (60 km), little more than a restaurant and checkpost on the grasslands. The distance across the watershed from Tobden to Tsekok in the upper Tsechu valley is 38 km.

TSEKOK COUNTY

རྩེ་ཁོག

泽库县 Zekog

Population: 38,675 *Area:* 6,858 sq km

The county of **Tsekok** is a broad grassland which extends hundreds of kilometres through the upper Tsekok valley, N of the sharp bend in the Yellow River. The county town, known as **Jadir**, has an air of the Wild West. Nomads in shaggy sheepskin coats typical of Amdo ride into town on a yak or horse to do the shopping, play pool, and sell a sheep or yakskin. The principal monastery is Sonak Geden Tashi Choling. Also, nearby is a small Gelukpa monastery, named **Tukchen Yonden Dargyeling**, which is affiliated to Rongpo Gonchen. One of its temples is built of stone, all too rare in modern Amdo, and decorated with Repkong-style tangkas which depict Tara, Bhaisajyaguru, Avalokiteshvara, Sitatapatra, Tsongkhapa, and the protectress Shridevi, alongside the standard set of images.

ACCESS The distance from Repkong to Jadir is 98 km, and from Jadir to Sogwo county, 39 km.

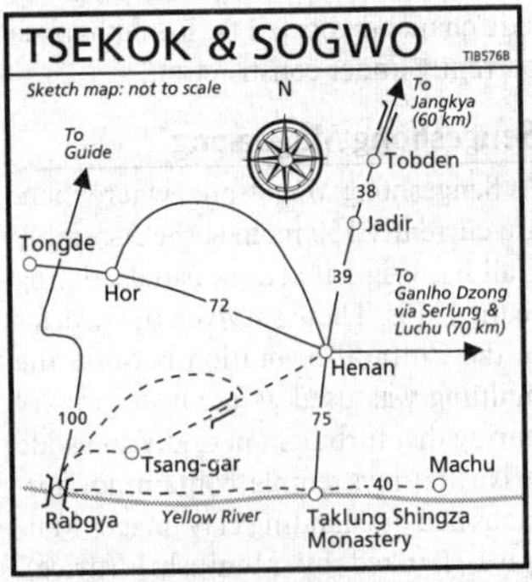
TSEKOK & SOGWO
TIB576B
Sketch map: not to scale
N
To Jangkya (60 km)
To Guide
Tobden
38
Jadir
Tongde
39
Hor
72
To Ganlho Dzong via Serlung & Luchu (70 km)
Henan
100
75
Tsang-gar
Machu
40
Rabgya
Yellow River
Taklung Shingza Monastery

NW of Jadir, there are two rough trails which lead via **Hor** township to **Tongde**, 72 km distant. In this part of the county there are other monasteries of the Gelukpa and Bon tradition. The most significant site in the NW of the county is **Terton Chogar** monastery in Hor township. Here, mantrins and monks of the Nyingma school both attend a 3-storeyed temple and there is the most famous Mani Wall in all of Amdo.

From Tongde, it is possible to drive S through the grasslands into Golok (via Rabgya) or N to Trika and Chabcha.

SOGWO PREFECTURE
སོག་པོ
河南蒙古族自治县 Henan
Population: 20,545   Area: 6,072 sq km

Sogwo prefecture is a region where the dominant population is ethnically Mongol, but so thoroughly integrated with the Amdowa, that only a few distinctive cultural traits remain. The yurt, the round felt tent of the Mongols, is found in abundance here, and slight differences in dress and jewellery can be detected. The best sheepskin coats (*Tib* chuba) are made from the skins of blue sheep, and this region is famous for their production.

Henan

The county capital is located at **Henan** on the lower Tse-chu River, 39 km S of Tsekok. The small monastery of **Laka**, 2 km from that small town, is affiliated to **Tsang-gar Monastery** near Rabgya. It was founded by Laka Tsung, the seventh incarnation of whom is now a boy aged 14.

A difficult trail leads S for 75 km from Henan to **Taklung Shingza Monastery** (*Ch* Xiangza) on the N bank of the Yellow River. This monastery is also known as **Ganden Rabgyuling**. Rough unreliable trails lead upstream to **Rabgya** (and thence to Machen in Golok) and downstream for 40 km through marshland and gorges to **Machu** in present day Gansu province.

Grasslands

ACCESS Public buses also run from Henan, the county capital, to Ganlho Dzong in Gansu, via **Luchu** (70 km).

The grasslands on the road to Luchu are as good as they get in Amdo, but the density of livestock is high and several species of pika (small herbivores) burrow extensively over the terrain. They prefer not to use steeper land, rough shrub or marshlands, so the extension of pastures and drainage of marshes suits them well. As the last remaining mammal predators are eliminated by hunting, they, along with the marmot, have often prospered. Several birds of prey, led by the steppe eagle and the huge lammergeier vulture, as well as songbirds, inhabit the steppe for most of the year nesting in deserted holes and roosting on telephone poles.

The shrub-covered hills between Sogwo and Luchu contain a disputed border, one of many among the present day provincial, prefectural, or county borders throughout the plateau. The monastery of **Serlung** actually marks the end of Mongol territory.

ZILING TO MATO: THE SOUTH KOKONOR REGION AND THE YELLOW RIVER BASIN

The second and third routes from Ziling to the Golok area of S Amdo are described in this section. The second runs from Ziling via Rushar through Trika and Kawasumdo to cross the Yellow River at Rabgya Gonpa. The third runs from Ziling via Tongkor and Nyima Dawa La pass to Daotong and thence via Chabcha to Tsigortang and Mato. This entire area, presently administered within the Tibetan Autonomous Prefecture of S Kokonor, comprises five counties: Trika, Mangra, Kawasumdo, Chabcha and Tsigortang.

Recommended itineraries: 8, 9, 11.

TRIKA COUNTY
ཁྲི་ཀ

貴德縣 Guide

Population: 88,398   Area: 3,408 sq km

Regular buses leave Ziling for **Trika** (*Ch* Guide), taking the Kumbum road for 18 km and then heading S across the **Lhamori** mountains, which comprise three prominent craggy black peaks on the watershed of the Yellow River. Just down from the pass, a rough side-road heads E to Detsa monastery and **Bayan Khar** (see above, page 588), but the main road continues S through a few small Tibetan villages – **Garang**, **Horkya Gon**, and **Akong**, where there was once a Nyingma monastery, and so forth, to the Yellow River. The final stretch is through some very barren rusty brown hills, typical Yellow River scenery.

Guide, 117 km from Ziling, is a fairly large town spread along the S bank of the Yellow River, where it has absorbed sev-

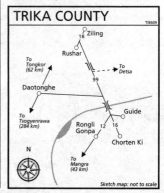

TRIKA COUNTY
TIB609

eral farming villages. Tibetans account for 32% of the population, but only a few live in the town itself, which is predominantly Chinese and Muslim. The houses of this region have very tall outer walls enclosing a courtyard with a few fruit trees or a vegetable plot, and a single-storey house built of mud brick. To the S of town after a thick belt of planted trees is a stony desert stretching towards the distant mountains of **Amnye Jakhyung**.

It is in the upper valleys of this region that most Tibetans can be found, and there are numerous small monasteries, mostly Gelukpa but with some Nyingma and even Bonpo. The most renowned locally is the Gelukpa monastery at **Chorten Ki**, about 16 km S of town, but the easiest to reach is **Renong (Rongzhi Gon)**, 12 km along the main road to the S. There is a hot spring here and it is possible to stay in a guesthouse, at a range of prices, with a piping hot mineral bath in every room. The monastery has little to see apart from a set of Repkong-style tangkas, depicting the preferred deities of the Gelukpa school.

From Trika you can head NW via **Garang** to the **Daotonghe** junction (for Chabcha or N Kokonor). Alternatively, you can continue on the road SW from Trika, to reach Mangra after 55 km.

MANGRA COUNTY

མང་ར

贵南县 Guinan

Population: 56,687   Area: 5,585 sq km

The main road from **Trika** (*Ch* Guide) continues through some fairly barren hills, passing just E of the dam and hydro-electric power plant at **Longyang Xia**, into the county of **Mangra** (55 km). The county town, **Mangra** (known in Chinese as Guinan), is located on the Mangrachu tributary of the Yellow River; and is currently the only district in this prefecture still closed to foreigners.

Mangra is a county of two halves, the northern part being barren, sandy desert, while S of the Mangra-chu, towards the low mountain range that divides it from Kawasumdo, there is some lush grassland.

Mangra town is 36 km off the main road, on a route heading 60 km W to the bridge over the Yellow River at **Atsok Gonpa**. There is another medium-sized Gelukpa monastery, **Lu Gonpa**, in the town.

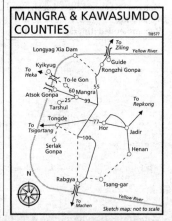

MANGRA & KAWASUMDO COUNTIES

Some 25 km to the SW of town is **Tarshu Gonpa** (also Gelukpa), pleasantly located in the grassy hills, with about 80 monks and an 89-year-old Rinpoche. Further N, **To-le Gonpa** of the Gelukpa school lies on the N bank of the Mangra-chu, much closer to the Yellow River, and there are a couple of small Nyingma temples nearby.

From Mangra the main road leads S into Kawasumdo county (99 km); while branch roads lead W across the Yellow River at Atsok Gonpa into Tsigortang county, and NW crossing the Yellow River at Kyikyug to arrive at Chabcha.

KAWASUMDO COUNTY

གཅ་བ་སུམ་མདོ

同德县 Tongde

Population: 30,063   *Area:* 5,331 sq km

The main road continues S from Mangra, crossing into the Ba-chu valley where a side-road leads to **Tongde** in Kawasumdo county, 99 km from Mangra town. The terrain here is wide open country, populated by many yak herding nomads and the grasslands are dotted with their tents. In summer there are occasional grassland festivals, when scores of tents, including tented monasteries established by monks from nearby monasteries, are pitched together. From Tongde a side-road leads W to cross the Yellow River into Tsigortang County.

The largest monastery, 6 hrs trek over a pass to the SW, is **Serlak Gonpa** of the Gelukpa school, with around 180 monks, headed by Do-me Rinpoche. The small brick and concrete temple of **Gochen Dzong Gon** lies 15 km E of Serlak, visible from the main road across a small river.

Tsang-gar Gonpa

The main road continues S, crossing into the Serchung Nang valley, which flows due S into the Yellow River. Halfway down this valley, up a broad tributary to the E, lies a rough track that leads over a southerly pass to **Tsang-gar Gonpa**, about 20 km from the main road.

Tsang-gar was founded in the early 18th century by a monk from Tashilhunpo known as Tsang Pandita. It now houses over 400 monks and several temples have been constructed, but not yet fully decorated. Some of the monks are 'Sogwo Arig', a Mongolian clan whose main base is in Sogwo (*Ch* 'Henan') county to the E, but who have now fully adopted Tibetan language and culture.

To avoid the steep gorges as the tributaries descend sharply towards the Yellow River, the main road crosses several small ridges before descending to **Rabgya Gonpa**, 371 km from Ziling. There is a small Muslim-run truckstop near the bridge, where it is possible to stay. Although Rabgya is on the N bank of the river, it technically falls within Machen county of Golok, for which reason it is described below, page 606.

CHABCHA COUNTY

ཆབ་ཆ

共和县 Gonghe

Population: 147,188   Area: 16,313 sq km

The third route from Ziling to Golok, follows the highway SW from the city, through **Tongkor** county and **Nyima Dawa La** pass (see above, page 572).

ACCESS Descending from the pass, at **Daotonghe**, 102 km from Ziling, three roads diverge. Head W for **Lake Kokonor** and **Kermo**; or alternatively, head SE for **Trika**. If instead, you continue SW on this road, you will eventually reach **Mato** and **Jyekundo**.

Chabcha

Taking the last of these roads, you will first enter the county of **Chabcha** (*Ch*

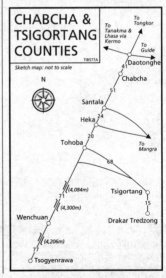

CHABCHA & TSIGORTANG COUNTIES

TIB577A

Sketch map: not to scale

N

To Tanakma & Lhasa via Kermo
To Tongkor
To Guide
Daotonghe
41
Chabcha
51
Santala
Heka 24
20
Tohoba
To Mangra
68
Tsigortang
71 (4,084m)
(4,300m) 15
Wenchuan
Drakar Tredzong
(4,206m)
77
Tsogyenrawa

Gonghe). The county town lies 41 km SW of Daotonghe in the basin between Lake Kokonor and the Yellow River. It is a surprisingly large modern town on the fringe of a semi-desert, and nowadays functions as the administrative capital of the entire S Kokonor prefecture.

One of China's largest dams has created a reservoir here, silting up fast under the heavy sediment load of the river. A small reservoir dam to the W of Chabcha burst in 1993 due to an earthquake, killing over 200 people. Earthquakes are common in this region, and a powerful one also struck in the mid-1980s. There is little of interest in or near town apart from a modern shrine to King Songsten Gampo, which can be seen on the approach to town.

● **Facilities** There are supermarkets, and good guesthouse and restaurant facilities, with one upmarket Sichuan restaurant having pride-of-place.

Atsok Gonpa

At the Santala crossroads, 51 km SW of Chabcha, there is a tiny Nyingma monastery called **Jugho**. From here, and also from Heka, 24 km further on, rough roads head SE to **Atsok Gonpa** beside the banks of the Yellow River, some 2 km S of the road bridge which leads to Mangra (*Ch* Guinan). Atsok Gonpa is an important but small Gelukpa monastery, with an impressively sited set of the eight stupas symbolizing the deeds of Shakyamuni Buddha, and several old tangkas. The monastic community here numbers approximately 70.

Heka

About 4 hrs walk SW of **Heka** is a small Nyingma monastery, but the town itself is just a roadside collection of shops, Muslim restaurants and truckstops, like almost all townships in Amdo. Their attraction lies in the local Tibetans who frequently visit to purchase supplies from the Chinese, Hui and Salar shopkeepers.

The main road continues SW from Heka to **Tohoba** (20 km), and then rises across the **Ngalo La** pass (4,084m), known in Chinese as Waka Sankou. Some 23 km beyond Heka on the main road, there is another turn-off leading SE into Tsigortang county.

TSIGORTANG COUNTY
རྩི་གོར་ཐང་

兴海县 Xinghai

Population: 39,320   Area: 11,621 sq km

The county of **Tsigortang** (*Ch* Xinghai) occupies the NW extremity of the bend of the Yellow River, formed by the Amnye Machen range. The county capital is located at **Xinghai** new town, 68 km SE of **Heka** on a branch road, which leaves the highway at the **Tohoba** bridge. The town is surprisingly attractive, large and situated near the scenic power place of **Drakar Tredzong**. From Xinghai it is also possible to cross the Yellow River at **Tangnak** and head N into Trika or S into Kawasumdo.

Drakar Tredzong

Drakar Tredzong, the celebrated 'white monkey fortress' is classed along with Dentik and Achung Namdzong, as one of the three most important sacred sites in Amdo. A high 5,000m peak with thickly forested slopes and abundant wildlife, it is located only 15 km S of

Tsigortang county town (Xinghai), but transport is irregular. The approach on foot is impressive, and for the last few kilometres the trail joins the pilgrim's route, which is one of the most renowned in Amdo. The air is permeated by aromatic herbs and incense.

There is a large Gelukpa monastery on the S side of the mountain, which was founded in 1923 by Arik Tsang. Currently it has over 300 monks and a hall capable of holding over 1,000. It contains gilded images of Shakyamuni, Padmasambhava, Tsongkhapa, and Arik Tsang; and excellent murals. This is one of the so-called **18 sacred sites of Drakar Tredzong**. Others include a natural image of Tara said to cure infertility (**Dolma Bujin**), the rock impressions of Ling Gesar's horse; a stone image of Avalokiteshvara which is said to have saved the life of an old native inhabitant of Arik; a renowned charnel ground associated with Vajrasana in India; a passageway through which pilgrims squeeze to test their karma in the face of the Lord of Death (**Chogyel Nang**); a hermitage of Yeshe Tsogyel (**Khandro Tsokhang**); a cave where Padmasambhava meditated (**Yamatarkhung**); and the site where he tamed the hostile spirits (**Dresin Tulsa**); a medicinal spring (**menchu**); the summit (**nego**) where there are stone footprints

---

DRAKAR TREDZONG: ABODE OF SOLITUDE

The attractions of **Drakar Tredzong** for the meditator are summarized in the following verse by Zhabkar Tsokdruk Rangdrol:

"Ema! The Trakar Dredzong mountain
Is as beautiful as a heap of precious white crystals.
It is a supreme abode of solitude
Blessed by Padmakara, the Lord of the Victorious Ones.
There are countless miraculously arisen images of deities,
The refuge of all beings, men and gods.
Almost all the practitioners who, after renouncing the world,
Meditated in this place, attained realisation"

M Ricard (transl) *The Life of Shabkar*

of Padmasambhava and many *mani* stones; a natural pillar of crystal in a bottomless cave; the auspicious pass (**Tashi La**) where Tsongkhapa gave wondrous teachings; the place where Tsongkhapa rested; a cave containing a wish-granting 'cow'; the vase and begging bowl of Padmasambhava; and the deep cave (**Dorje Puklam**) at the centre of a natural amphitheatre where Padmasambhava hurled his vajra into the air to create a natural skylight in the cave-roof. These sites can all be visited in the course of a 5-hr pilgrimage.

A number of active retreat hermitages are also found on the mountain, as well as a small camp of Nyingma nuns. Formerly there were also 400 Nyingmapa monks at Drakar Tredzong.

Tohoba to Tsogyenrawa

The main Ziling-Jyekundo road which passes through the far W of Tsigortang county heads SW to **Wenchuan** after crossing the **Ngalo La** pass on Mt Heka and a second pass on Mt Erlan (4,300m). Wenchuan (3,400m) is 71 km from Ngalo La pass.

Wenchuan
The main attraction here is the hot spring, which is yet to be developed.

● **Accommodation** There is a small guesthouse (¥10/bed) amid the usual truckstops and restaurants.

From Wenchuan continue across another pass (4,206m), which leads into the basin of a small lake and over a stony plain to the road junction at **Tsogyenrawa** (*Ch* Huashixia, 77 km). There is a small Nyingma monastery to the SW of Tsogyenrawa, but the main interest is the proximity of Golok. The various routes from here into Amnye Machen, Central Golok, and Mato in Upper Golok are all described in the following section.

GOLOK-SERTAL AND NGAWA: THE AMNYE MACHEN RANGE AND THE GYARONG HEADWATERS

The Bayankala and Amnye Machen ranges of Amdo demarcate the upper reaches of the Yellow River, homeland of the Golok; while the Mardzagang range forms a watershed between the Yellow River and the three main sources of the Gyarong: the Ser-chu, Do-chu, and Mar-chu. This entire region is the domain of independently minded nomadic peoples who have maintained their distinctive cultural traditions for centuries.

Four of the six counties currently included in the Golok Tibetan Autonomous Prefecture of Qinghai occupy the valley of the Yellow River, whereas the other two, Padma and Jigdril along with those of Sertal, Dzamtang, and Ngawa, all lie within the gorges and valleys of the Gyarong source rivers. Nowadays the counties of the Golok Tibetan Autonomous Prefecture are administered from Machen, Sertal from Dartsedo (in the Kandze Tibetan Autonomous Prefecture), and the last two from Barkham, within the Ngawa Tibetan Autonomous Prefecture of Sichuan province. **Recommended itineraries: 9, 11 (also 8).**

MATO COUNTY
ཨ་སྟོད

玛多县 Madoi
Population: 28,492   *Area*: 25,263 sq km

This county, also known as **Machuka**, contains the source of the Yellow River. The county town, **Mato**, lies 331 km NE of Jyekundo and 494 km SW of Ziling. Approaching Mato from Kham (ie from Jyekundo or Sershul via Zhiwu), the road gradually ascends through the rolling swamplands of the upper Yalong to cross the **Bayankala Pass** (5,082m), 61 km beyond **Domda** (*Ch* Qingshuihe). There are fine views of the rolling humps of the Bayankala range to the E of the road; and yellow poppies are commonplace around the pass. After crossing this watershed, a bleak expanse of high altitude lakeland unfolds. The road (currently under repair) descends gradually for 121 km, passing en route a blue stone obelisk (after 29 km) and nomadic camper groups at **Yeniugdo** (51 km), where there is also a small

Nyingma monastery. Foxes are a common sight by the roadside. Soon small lakes appear close to the road on the left and right; and there is a charnel ground marked by prayer-flags. Then, skirting a larger lake on the left, the road enters the valley of the Yellow River. It soon crosses the **first bridge over the Yellow River** and after a further 5 km arrives at Mato town (70 km from Yeniugdo).

Mato Town

Mato is a high altitude town (4,300m), where snow is not uncommon in summertime! Entering the town from the SW, a bypass leads directly ahead, and beyond, to continue in the direction of Ziling. A turn-off on the left leads into the centre of town. Here, on the left side of Main St are the *Mato Military Guesthouse* and the general store; while the post office is on the right. At the head of this road, commanding a T-junction, is the Mato Theatre/ Cinema. Turn left for the *Government Guesthouse* (rooms at ¥25) and Lake Ngoring Tso, and right for the Mato Hospital. Returning to the bypass, the bus station is located on the left towards the Ziling end of the road. The open-air market has an interesting selection of nomadic produce and Golok style clothing. The town itself is small, but its bus station and market are important for the locals.

Ngoring and Kyaring Lakes

Mato county has several marshy plains dotted with tiny lakes and meandering rivers which provide good grasslands for the many nomads around the source of the Yellow River. There are however two particularly large lakes (each 104 sq km in area), known as **Kyaring Tso** and **Ngoring Tso**, through which the Yellow River itself flows. To reach these lakes, take the jeepable road from Mato which follows the Yellow River upstream, for 57 km to Ngoring Tso (the closer of the two lakes). Both lakes provide a rich

MATO COUNTY
TIB553

Lake Ngoring Tso

To Tsogyenrawa (75km)

Yellow River

57

Mato

70

Yeniugdo

51

Obelisk

29

(5,082m)

61

Domda

To Zhiwu & Jyekundo

N

Sketch map: not to scale

fishing ground for Chinese immigrants. Tibetans, even in these remote parts, are reluctant to eat fish.

On a hilltop between the lakes there is a very small reconstructed monastery, said to mark the unknown site of **Gartse Palace**, which, according to old Chinese sources, is where Songsten Gampo met and married Princess Wencheng. The region W of the lakes is in places very marshy and an excellent breeding ground for many of the plateau's bird species, including the rare black-necked crane. It leads over the 'plain of stars' to **Mt Yakra Tatse** (5,442m), near the ham-

let of **Dzomo Manang**, which is just inside Chumarleb county (see above, page 540). This is **Machuka**, the true source of the Yellow River.

Tsogyenrawa

The main highway to Ziling from Mato cuts NE through a fairly flat plain, following a tributary of the Yellow River upstream for 75 km to reach the gorge of **Tsogyenrawa** (*Ch* Huashixia, 4,039m). The town is named after the colourful mountain range below which it lies.

• **Facilities** Here, there is a small town, with

PILGRIMAGE

Throughout the Buddhist world, pilgrimage is an important means of affirming the faith of devotees and above all of accumulating merit (punya) and virtuous actions (kushala), without which progress to enlightenment or buddhahood would not be possible. In Tibet, pilgrimage (ne-khor) has assumed a significant social role, and there is a distinct genre of literature, the pilgrimage guidebook (ne-yig), which describes both the historical background and development of any given site, as well as the manner in which its rocks and contours are to be viewed from the perspective of 'pure vision'. For, the peaks, stones, and rivulets of the most sacred sites are properly viewed as deities or consecrated objects in their own right!

While travelling through remote areas of Tibet, you will occasionally come upon remarkable individuals who are in the course of prostrating hundreds or even thousands of kilometres, all the way from their local villages to Lhasa, the most magnetic of Tibet's pilgrimage places. Often elected by village communities to undertake the pilgrimage, their journey may take several years to complete. Such pilgrims frequently wear leather aprons, knee pads, and hand pads to protect their bodies from exposure to the rough road surfaces, and they may travel in a group, accompanied by an assistant who will arrange food and shelter on their behalf. On reaching the goal of their pilgrimage, the sacred image of Jowo Rinpoche in Lhasa, they will make offerings, and then return home by motor vehicle.

The act of prostration (phyag-tshal) is generally combined with the recitation of the refuge prayer (kyab-dro), through which the Buddhist meditator or practitioner reduces pride, generates humility, and becomes confident in the goals and methods of Buddhism. Outside the Jokhang temple in Lhasa, the flagstones have been worn smooth by centuries of prostrations. Inside, pilgrims will add lumps of butter to the lamps as they proceed from one shrine to the next in a clockwise sequence, occasionally also making monetary offerings, or attaching some metalic or precious object to the wire mesh of a shrine as an act of simple devotion.

This movement of pilgrims around the countryside and its great Buddhist shrines (ne-khor) is nowadays contrasted with the movement of tourists around the very same buildings and locations (ta-khor). If you wish to be taken as a pilgrim rather than a tourist, invariably generating more respect or courtesy, it will be best to assert your status as a 'pilgrim' (ne-khor-wa) rather than a 'tourist' (ta-khor-wa)!

Muslim tea shops, Chinese restaurants, and a simple guesthouse.

Four roads converge at Tsogyenrawa: a side-road leading NW to **Lake Dongi Tsona** and the **Shang** area (on which see above, page 566); another jeep track leading E for 45 km to **Tawo Zholma** village on the Amnye Machen trail; the main highway leading NE to **Ziling** or SW to **Mato**, and a wide gravel road, which leads SE into **Machen** and **Darlag** counties. Tsogyenrawa marks the extremity of the Golok penetration. Further N from here, the nomads belong to the Banak group rather than the Golok.

MACHEN COUNTY

ཨ་ཆེན

玛沁县 Maqen

Population: 37,500   Area: 16,625 sq km

The **Amnye Machen** range, which forms the large bend of the Yellow River, is the ancestral homeland of the **Golok**; and the sacred abode of the protector deity, **Machen Pomra**, revered by Bonpo and Buddhists alike. As recently as 1949 there had been reports suggesting that the highest peak of this isolated range exceeded the height of Mt Everest; and it was only during the 1950s and 1960s that the height was fixed at 6,282m. The county of Machen includes the entire pilgrim's circuit around the range. The county capital is located at **Tawo** (Machen), 209 km from **Tsogyenrawa** (*Ch* Huashixia) and 68 km from **Rabgya Monastery** on the banks of the Yellow River (see below, page 612).

MACHEN COUNTY

TIB574

N

Chabcha

Tohoba — 95

71 — Yellow River

To Lake Dongi Tsona & Pachen Zhingde — Wenchuan

77

Tawo Zholma

45 — Tawo Zholma Monastery

Tsogyenrawa

To Tongde (100km)

(6,282m) — (4,328m) — Rabgya

Mnt Amnye Machen — Chuwarna

Tselnak Khamdo

87 — 116

Yellow River — Domkhok — 68 — Tawo

89 — 33 — 109

Chamalung — (4,670m) — 83

109 — Gabde (Bakchen) — Xia Zangke

53

Dzuktrun — 23 — Darlag (Gyu-me)

Darling Monastery

Sketch map: not to scale

Amnye Machen Circuit

ཨ་སྙེ་རྨ་ཆེན

The traditional starting point for the Bon and Buddhist pilgrims, who all circumambulate the range in a clockwise direction, is the **Chorten Karpo** near **Xueshan** village; although most pilgrims presently set out from **Tawo Zholma** village, 45 km due E of Tsogyenrawa. On the rough road approaching this village, the Amnye Machen range comes into sight in the distance. There are wonderful sunsets to be seen here.

Tawo Zholma (*Ch* Xiao Dawu) is a pastoral commune with only 77 inhabitants, of whom 30 are children attending the local primary school, where there are five teachers. Most of the commune members are of Banak origin, but a transient workforce from Labrang area, and as far away as Shanxi province, contributes to the ethnic mix of the commune. Pack animals for the circuit of the mountain can be arranged in this village. See Dolma Tsering, a native of Dzachuka who has lived here since the late 1950s.

Tawo Zholma Monastery

Fording the **Qushian** River below the village, the trail leads 5 km to **Tawo Zholma Monastery**, a branch of Dodrub Chode of the Nyingma school, which until recently was the seat of the late Thubten Tsering, a charismatic lama descended from Lhalung Peldor, who was also a contemporary of Dodrupchen Rinpoche and a qualified Dzogchen master in his own right. It was he who supervised the temple's reconstruction from 1985 onwards. The local community in the monastery and surrounding village numbers approximately 100. There are a few monks, but the majority of practitioners here are mantrins.

The complex comprises three main buildings, in addition to the lama's residence. Among these, the **main temple** contains excellent new images of Padmasambhava, Shantarakshita and King Trisong Detsen, as well as White Tara, Green Tara, Vairocana, Vajrasattva, Four-armed Avalokiteshvara, Eleven-faced Avalokiteshvara, Machen Pomra, and Tangtong Gyelpo. The vestibule has a large Mani Wheel Chapel in addition to the murals depicting the four guardian kings.

To the left of the temple is a **Reliquary Chapel** containing the consecrated remains of Lama Gyatso (d 1987) and Lama Thubten Tsering. It also has images of Padmasambhava and of the three deities symbolizing longevity: Amitayus, White Tara, and Vijaya. The **Gonkhang**, situated behind the lama's residence, contains a revered central image of Ling Gesar, the hero of Tibetan epic poetry who has many associations with Amnye Machen. Its murals depict (left) Tangtong Gyelpo, and (right) Machen Pomra, complete with retinue. In the **lama's residence** there are images of Padmasambhava, Jigme Lingpa, and Tangtong Gyelpo. Texts are kept here which describe both the Buddhist and Bonpo pilgrimage guides to Amnye Machen.

Approaching the Snow Peaks

The trail climbs steadily from the monastery following the **Niwagu** River upstream. A large *latse* bedecked with mantra-engraved stones and colourful prayer-flags is passed before the low pass of **Drado Wangchuk La**. A trail of steeper gradient then ascends the high **Drakdo Latse Chogon** (4,328m), close to the glaciers. The walk from the monastery to this pass takes 8 hrs. A ridge above the pass leads towards the glaciers and the icy **Tso Karpo** ('white lake'), otherwise known as **Drodu Nyaka** (4,600m). Slightly below the pass, on the S side, there is a field of protuberant glaciers, known as **Rigar Tongka** or **Rigar Tongjung**. This is revered as a sacred site symbolic of the Thousand Buddhas of the present aeon, or of the Sixteen Elders. Golok camper groups are to be found in this vicinity in summertime.

The view of the main peaks of the range is genuinely impressive from this vantage point. The highest of the 14 peaks forming the range is **Dradul Lungshok**, the northernmost peak, which lies close to the trail across the Rigar Tongjung glacier field. The next peak is the dome shaped **Mt Amnye Machen** itself, followed by the pyramid-shaped **Mt Chenrezig**, down the valley, towards Xueshan.

Descending from the pass through the **Zhideka** valley, after 3 hrs, the side-valley of the **Yekhok-chu** joins the circuit from the N. The trail then descends through flower-carpeted grassland to the junction of the **Halong-chu** valley, which leads NW towards the **Amnye Machen Base Camp** (4,600m). Gazelles can frequently be seen in these parts, and there is a sky burial terrace. Deep within the Halong-chu valley near the rocks of **Phawang Serka** and **Phawang Hekar**, there is the **Terdak Phawang Drubzhi**, containing the *termas* of Ling Gesar, the warrior king of Tibetan epic poetry, who is said to have hidden his sword here, pledging 1 day to retrieve it. Even closer to the mountain are the **Ser Tso** ('golden lake') and **Ngon Tso** ('blue lake').

Eastern Part of the Circuit

From the Halong-chu junction to the **Chorten Karpo** at **Chuwarna** (*Ch* Xueshan) village it is an easy 6-hr trek. Here, the **Yonkhok-chu** (*Ch* Qiemuqu) flows from the SW to join the Yekhok-chu, thereby forming the **Tshab-chu** which flows E into the Yellow River. At **Chuwarna** (Xueshan) village there are small shops and a motorable track. Adjacent to the Chorten Karpo is a large wall, known as **Gonying Mani Lhartse**, inscribed with the mantra of the meditational deity Vajrakila. Traditionally, this is the starting point of the circuit for many pilgrims.

Follow the motor road for 4 hrs from Chorten Karpo, passing several nomad houses set among sparse juniper woods in the hills around. At **Tselnak Khamdo**, the road leaves the circuit, and cuts SE for 116 km to **Tawo** (Machen), the capital of the Golok region. Prayer-flags and stone cairns bedeck the trail and the trees along this section of road.

Southern Part of the Circuit

Continuing on to the SW sector of the pilgrims' circuit, the trail passes the entrance to the **Halong Langri-chu** valley, which leads N towards the Base Camp, and then gradually ascends the **Yonkhok-chu** valley, to eventually reach the **Tamchok Gongkha la** pass after some 7 hrs. The broad saddle of the pass stretches for a further 10 km (3 hrs). In summer this area is a carpet of wild flowers set against the imposing snow peaks and many nomads establish camps here. After the saddle one comes to a curious rock formation in the middle of the valley called **Mowatowa**, which houses several meditation caves, including that of the great Nyingmapa meditation master Zhabkar Tsokdruk Rangdrol (1781-1851). The variegated cliffs of **Goku Chenmo** are said to mark the entrance to the 'palace' of the protector **Machen Pomra**.

Some 4 hrs later, the trail reaches the **Dolma Gur-chu** spring, which demarcates the final part of the circuit. Rather than follow the gorge of the Qushian River, the path heads over a spur, where Ling Gesar tied his horse, and then descends back down to **Tawo Zholma Monastery**, about 5 hrs away.

Practicalities

The best months to make this circuit are May/June and Sept/Oct, avoiding the summer rains and the biting cold of winter. A tent and sleeping bag are essential as well as a good supply of food, for apart from being offered tea, tsampa and yoghurt by the occasional nomad, there is no chance of restocking. It is advisable to allow at least a week for the full circuit.

Tawo (Machen) Town

The Golok capital at Tawo is an archetypal image conjured out of the Wild West! Prior to the 1960s when a concerted policy was adopted with a view to settling the nomadic Golok and Banak populations of Amdo, Tawo was but a small hamlet. The prefecture even now has an estimated 88% Tibetan population. Almost half the non-Tibetan population of Golok, ie Han Chinese, Hui and Salar, live here in Tawo, alongside the indigenous Tibetan groups. There are also many itinerant traders and work-unit appointees who come during the seasonal months, for in winter temperatures of -20° are common. Most of the Tibetan nomad families currently have a small disposable income and Tawo, situated on a tributary of the Tshab-chu, is a natural gathering place.

● **Facilities** Stay at the *Machen Hotel*. There are a few Muslim- and Chinese-style restaurants, apart from the hotel restaurant. Take a walk down the main street to inspect the Golok markets, the dusty pool tables, and the Stalinist concrete blocks from which the prefecture is administered.

Roads from Tawo

Various roads diverge at Tawo: W for 122 km to **Chamalung** on the Tsogyenrawa-Darlag road; NW for 118 km to **Chuwarna** (*Ch* Xueshan) on the Amnye Machen pilgrimage circuit; NE for 68 km to **Rabgya Monastery** on the banks of the Yellow River; SW for 83 km to **Gabde**; and SE for 109 km to **Xia Zangke** on the Yellow River.

Rabgya Monastery

Taking the NE road, a southern pass is crossed and this leads into a series of small, lightly-forested gorges to the Yellow River opposite Rabgya. A small enclave on the N bank of the Yellow River belongs to Machen rather than Repkong. It includes the bridge spanning the Yellow River (70

km from Da-re), **Rabgya Monastery**, which is 2 km beyond the bridge and **Mt Khyung-ngon**.

Rabgya Monastery, otherwise known as **Tashi Kundeling**, is an important Gelukpa monastery, founded during the 18th century by a Mongol from Kokonor named Arik Geshe. Even today there are several monks from the Sogwo Mongol prefecture just to the E. The second abbot, Shingza Pandita Lobzang Dargye (1753-1824), is regarded as an incarnation of Tsongkhapa's mother, Shingza Acho, and his subsequent incarnations have presided over the monastery.

The complex has been substantially rebuilt during the last decade, but a few old artworks did survive, including a handful of pillar carpets in the main prayer hall and a set of tangkas. The architecture of the modern temples is functional but unimaginative, except for the artwork which is in the wonderful Repkong style. The broad cliff behind Rabgya is known as **Mt Khyung-ngon** (Blue Garuda) and the walk to the hilltop shrine passes several smaller shrines and caves, giving a good view of the Yellow River.

Temahe

To reach the main Jyekundo-Ziling highway from **Machen**, take the W road out of town and on reaching **Domkhok** (*Ch* Dongqingguo) after 33 km, do not turn NW for Xueshan and Amnye Machen. Instead, turn SW across the **Dramani La** pass (4,760m) for **Temahe** (*Ch* Qamalung), reaching that township after 89 km. There is a small Nyingma monastery here.

Then, head NW over a shallow pass, which can be muddy in summer and snow-bound in winter, to arrive at **Tsogyenrawa** (87 km). This road runs parallel to the southern and western sectors of the Amnye Machen circuit.

GABDE COUNTY
དགའ་བདེ

甘德县 Gade

Population: 22,176   *Area:* 6,554 sq km

Gabde county lies in Central Golok to the S of the Amnye Machen range and within the bend of the Yellow River. It is an important breeding area for the black-necked crane. The county capital is located at **Bakchen** on the Shi-ke-chu, a SE flowing tributary of the Yellow River. Bakchen lies 83 km SW of the prefectural capital Tawo (Machen), and 53 km from Darlag.

ACCESS Gabde can also be approached from Tsogyenrawa on the Jyekundo-Ziling highway. A turn-off at Tsogyenrawa leads SE through **Temahe** (87 km), and **Jang-gegye** (91 km) in the direction of Darlag. Turn NE at Jang-gegye to reach Bakchen after 35 km.

Jonang Gonpa
ཇོ་ནང་དགོན་པ

The largest monastery within the county is the **Jonang Gonpa** situated near Jiangian, in a side-valley SE of Qingzhen on the Machen-Gabde road, about 15 km before the Yellow River. The head lama here is Tashi Gyatso, currently residing in New York.

Shar-o Gonpa

To the SE of Bakchen, accessible only by a little-used side-road, is the small Gelukpa monastery of **Shar-o** (*Ch* Xiagongma), noted for its strict discipline and excellent teachings. The monastery is situated on the ridge N of the Yellow River, at a distance of 46 km down-valley from Gabde.

DARLAG COUNTY
དར་ལག་

达日县 Darlag

Population: 16,184   *Area:* 14,351 sq km

Darlag county straddles the Yellow River due S of the Amnye Machen range in Golok, and extends further S as far as the Mardzagang watersheds, which separate the Yellow River basin from the Ser-chu, Do-chu and Mar-chu tributaries of the Gyarong. The county capital is located at **Gyu-me** on the banks of the Yellow River. The distance from Gyu-me to Gabde is 53 km, to Machen 118 km; to Tsogyenrawa 196 km, to Padma 168 km, and to Jigdril 261 km.

Gyu-me Town

Gyu-me town (3,993m) has two long and wide intersecting streets. Beside the bridge over the Yellow River at Darlag is a small Nyingma monastery, **Wachin Gonpa**, an easy walk from town.

DARLAG & GABDE

TIB572

Sketch map: not to scale

● **Facilities** The *Government Guesthouse* has reasonable rooms (¥30-150), and an excellent restaurant. There are other guesthouses, restaurants and a public cinema lining the two streets.

Darling Monastery

Darling Monastery is situated 15 km W of town in the direction of **Dzuktrun** (*Ch* Jianshe), and a further 7 km along a side-road. For much of the journey the road follows the Yellow River upstream through rich pasture lands. This monastery, which has over 300 monks, is affiliated to Katok in Kham. It has been visited by Moktse Tulku of Katok, who in recent years has been responsible for the reconstruction of the mother monastery (see above, page 515). Within the main temple there are large cast images of Shakyamuni and Padmasambhava, and old tangkas representing the Eight Manifestations of Padmasambhava, as well as the reliquary stupa containing the remains of the previous Lingtrul Rinpoche. The present incumbent, also called Ya Tulku, currently resides in California. In his absence, monastic affairs including reconstruction are in the hands of Tulku Taknyi and Khenpo Peljor.

Above the monastery is a renowned **charnel ground** (*durtro*), to which corpses will be brought for dismemberment and sky burial from all parts of Golok. Here there is a raised platform above the circular dismemberment stones, and on its rear wall there are individually framed paintings of the Hundred Peaceful and Wrathful Deities, who appear to the deceased following death and before rebirth.

Roads from Dzuktrun

Dzuktrun lies 23 km W of Gyu-me, and two roads diverge here: SW to **Sangruma** (50 km) on the Khanglong-chu and SE to **Mopa** (43 km) on the Darlagchu. The Bayankala watersheds are crossed on both these roads: trekking SW to **Arikdza Gonpa** and the Yalong River, or SE to **Ponkor** and the Nyi-chu (50 km).

NB The latter is the main road to Sertal which crosses the Qinghai-Sichuan border, 17 km beyond Ponkor.

South of Darlag

Taking the main road SE from **Gyu-me**, you will pass through **Ozer** (*Ch* Wesai) after 21 km, and **Dernang Gonpa** after a further 39 km. This is an important branch of Katok Monastery, and there are over 200 affiliated monks. Outside the temple by the banks of the Gyu-chu (a tributary of the Yellow River) there is a fine set of stupas symbolizing the deeds of Shakyamuni Buddha.

From Ozer, a trail also follows the Kyilho-chu tributary upstream towards Do Gongma Gon (NE) and Kharsumdo (SE).

At Dernang Gonpa, an incomplete 9-storey tower marks the entrance to the **Padma Bum** region, and a side-trail leads SW, into the upper reaches of the Do-chu valley. Taking the latter, you will reach **Wangchen Drok Gon**, the birthplace of Do Khyentse; and the spectacularly located Nyingmapa monastery of **Tsimda Gonchen**. From here, a hard trek leads to **Dodrub Chode** (*Ch* Zhiqin Temple), on which see below, page 618.

Continuing on the main road from Dernang Gonpa, you will cross into the watershed region (4,465m) between the Gyu-chu and the Mar-chu tributary of the Gyarong. At **Mangdrang**, 46 km further SE, the road bifurcates, leading SE into Padma county and NE into Jigdril county.

JIGDRIL COUNTY
བཅོག་སྐྱིལ

久治县 Jigzhi
Population: 17,962   *Area:* 7,963 sq km

Jigdril county, at the SE extremity of Golok, occupies the watershed between the Yellow River basin and the Nga-chu tributary of the Gyarong. The county capital is located at Drukchen Sumdo, 155 km from Kharsumdo (Mangdrang), and 75 km from Ngawa.

Tarthang Monastery
དར་ཐང་དགོན་པ

From Kharsumdo, where the road branches, take the left fork which heads E over an occasionally snowy pass. In the distance there are views of the Nyenpo Yurtse mountain range. Reaching **Warje** village after 22 km, the road divides again, E for Sogruma and S for Tarthang. Taking the latter, you will enter a side-valley which follows the Mar-chu downstream. After travelling along this rough road for 18 km (sometimes it is impassable in the rainy season), you will arrive at Tarthang Monastery (*Ch* Baiyu), which is the largest in the county.

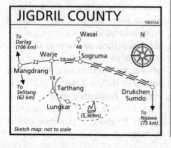

JIGDRIL COUNTY

TIB572A

To Darlag (106 km) ○ — Mangdrang ○ — 22 — Warje — 58 — Sogruma — Wasai ○ 48 N

To Selitang (62 km) — Tarthang ○ — Lungkar ○ — (5,369m) — Drukchen Sumdo — To Ngawa (75 km)

Sketch map: not to scale

History

This monastery, properly known as **Tarthang Dongak Shedrub Dargyeling**, was founded in 1882 by Gyatrul Rinpoche, Pema Dongak Tendzin (1830-91), the seventh throne-holder of the great Nyingmapa monastery of Pelyul in Kham. It quickly became the largest and most influential branch of Pelyul in the entire Golok-Sertal area, with 1,210 monks and 30 incarnate lamas, headed by the Pelyul Choktrul incarnation, who presently resides in Nepal. Among the other important figures connected with this monastery in recent times, special mention should be made of Lama Kunga or Tarthang Tulku, who has established a Nyingma institute and publishing centre (Dharma Publishing) in California. In addition, the charismatic tulku Garwang Nyima is presently responsible for the reconstruction and revitalization of the monastery, which houses over 1,000 monks.

The complex

The **Great Assembly Hall (Tsokchen)** has 140 pillars, and contains large cast images of Jowo Shakyamuni, Padmasambhava, and Amitabha. There are important murals in the Repkong style, the work of the master artist Kalzang, which focus on the meditational deities of the Nyingma lineage.

Alongside the assembly hall, there are two other buildings: the **Serdung Lhakhang**, containing the reliquary stupas of the previous Pelyul Choktrul and of two former monastic preceptors of Tarthang; and the **Teaching Hall (Dukhang)**, with Repkong-style murals which depict the *terma* visions of the Nyingma school, such as the Peaceful and Wrathful Deities according to Karma Lingpa's *Tibetan Book of the Dead*. In front of this complex of buildings there is a **wall of prayer wheels**, over 2 km in length; and beyond that, further down the valley, there is a new

Buddhist Studies College (Shedra), sponsored by Tarthang Tulku in the United States.

After the college and close to the road, there is the magnificent **Zangdok Pelri Lhakhang**. On its **ground floor** there are cast images of the Eight Manifestations of Padmasambhava (made by Chamdo artisans) and clay images of the Twenty-five Disciples of Padmasambhava (made by the Repkong artist Kalzang). The surrounding corridors depict scenes from the *Biography of Padmasambhava* (*Pema Katang*). On the **second floor**, there are images of the Lords of the Three Enlightened Families (ie Manjughosa, Avalokiteshvara, and Vajrapani), along with Tara and Acala. Amitabha is the central image on the **third floor**.

Behind the Zangdok Pelri Lhakhang, there is another temple known as the **Phurba Lhakhang**, dedicated to the meditational deity Vajrakila. Here, the central image depicting Vajrakumara is made of wood and its facial features of clay. To the right of the last two temples and close to the road, there is the residence of Tarthang Tulku (now in the United States) and his sisters.

The township lies beyond the monastery lower down the Mar-chu valley. It contains a small guesthouse run by a Tibetan medical practitioner and his family (¥10/bed).

From Tarthang, it is possible to trek further, following the Mar-chu downstream into Padma county.

Mount Nyenpo Yurtse

From Tarthang Monastery, the trail continues SE to **Lungkar Monastery** of the Gelukpa school, where there are over 200 monks. It then leads to the western edge of **Mt Nyenpo Yurtse** (5,369m), the principal holy mountain of southern Golok, which is revered as the birthplace of the Golok tribes. The 10-15 day pilgrimage circuit is much harder than at Mt Amnye Machen. The snow-capped steep ridges of the mountain are surrounded by marshland and glacial lakes, such as **Tsochen** and **Tsochung** which feed streams flowing N into the Yellow River, or **Tso Nagma** and **Nojin Tso**, which feed streams flowing S into the headwaters of the Gyarong. The **Base Camp** is located at 4,000m. On the S side of the mountain there are three hot springs and a nature reserve for the macaque.

Drukchen Sumdo (Jigdril) Town

After Warje, another steep pass leads to Sogruma (58 km), which has a small **Jonangpa Monastery** (currently under repair) 8 km from the village. A trail leads NW from here to **Wasai** (48 km), but the main road turns SE, crossing five more major passes, which offer increasingly spectacular views of Mt Nyenpo Yurtse's glaciers. After traversing the glacial rivers which flow northwards from this sacred mountain, the road eventually reaches **Drukchen Sumdo**, the county capital of SE Golok.

● **Facilities** The town has a population of only a few thousand, but there are comfortable guesthouse facilities, and a fine Sichuan-style restaurant.

Taklung Gonpa

Located just to the S of Drukchen Sumdo town, and on a side-road, this Nyingma monastery is a branch of Pelyul, under the supervision of Dampuk Rinpoche who has dedicated his recent years to its reconstruction. There is an Assembly Hall, a Zangdok Pelri-style temple; a Potala-style temple, named after the residence of Avalokiteshvara on Mt Potalaka; a protector chapel (Gonkhang), and a large Tara stupa.

The road to Ngawa

A poorly serviced road heads S across the watershed to **Ngawa** (75 km) in the Nga-chu valley, while another with even less traffic heads NE to **Mantang** (43 km) and **Awantsang**, from where it crosses the Yellow River twice en route to Machu in present day Gansu (see below, page 643). Along the Ngawa road, apart from Taklung, there are two other small monasteries: Khangsar (Nyingma) and Ny-inyu (Jonangpa).

PADMA COUNTY
ন্ত্র

班玛县 Baima

Population: 21,777   Area: 6,437 sq km

Padma county, pronounced *Parma*, is one of the most beautiful parts of E Tibet. It lies on the S side of the watershed between the rolling grasslands of the Yellow River basin and the forested gorges of the Gyarong. Specifically it occupies the upper reaches of the Mar-chu and Do-chu rivers. The county capital is located at **Selitang** on the Mar-chu, 168 km SE of Darlag, 217 km SW of Jigdril, and 202 km NW of Ngawa. There are many monasteries in the county, almost all being small Nyingmapa monasteries with between 30 and 150 monks, scattered throughout the valleys.

Selitang

Selitang lies 62 km below **Mangdrang**, in the upper Mar-chu valley. It is a small county town, pleasantly situated amidst coniferous forest, which is being exploited for timber. It also has the air of

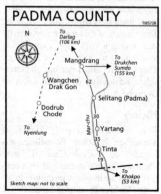

PADMA COUNTY

To Darlag (106 km)

N

Mangdrang

To Drukchen Sumdo (155 km)

Wangchen Drak Gon

62

Selitang (Padma)

Dodrub Chode

30

Yartang

To Nyenlung

35

Tinta

Mar-chu

19

To Khokpo (53 km)

Sketch map: not to scale

a garden town. A branch road leads NE to Tarthang Monastery, following the Mar-chu upstream.

● **Facilities** There is a spartan guesthouse and there are a number of Sichuan-style roadside restaurants.

Further S, the Mar-chu plunges through virgin forest, one of the most spectacular locations in all Tibet. The road runs parallel to the river, passing the villages of **Jangritang**, **Yartang** (30 km), **Bengen**, and **Tinta** (35 km), before crossing the current Qinghai-Sichuan border to enter Ngawa county. Several small Nyingma monasteries are visible, on either side of the road, and even two of the Kagyu school.

The town of Ngawa, 108 km further NE on the Sichuan side of the border, is approached via the Dze-chu tributary which flows into the Mar-chu near **Khokpo**.

Dodrub Chode Monastery

This, the most important monastery in Padma county, may be approached from **Dernang Gonpa** on the road from Darlag to Padma, or from **Padma** itself. Passes lead SW across the watershed into the Do-chu valley. The upper reaches of the Do-chu valley are rich in gold and there is a major mine 8 km S of the village of **Dankar**, where there is an active, newly-constructed Nyingmapa monastery with about 150 monks. The nomads of this region appear wild and unkempt with most men having long hair and heavy silver earrings. There is a trekking route but no motorable road leading down the valley to Dodrub Chode.

History

This monastery, properly known as **Tsangchen Ngodrub Pelbarling**, was founded by Dodrub Chen II Jigme Phuntsok Jungne in the mid-19th century when the monks of its mother monastery, **Yarlung Pemako** in Sertal, fled N to escape the marauding army of Nyarong Gonpo Namgyel (see above, page 448). The tradition maintained here is that of the 18th century treasure-finder Jigme Lingpa, whose *Longchen Nyingtig* cycle is widely practised throughout Tibet. Jigme Lingpa's disciples Dodrubchen I Jigme Trinle Ozer (1745-1821) and Jigme Gyelwei Nyugu returned to their native Kham after receiving the teachings from Jigme Lingpa, and they founded the monasteries of **Dzagya** in Dzachuka and **Drodon Lhundrub** at Sukchen Tago in the Do valley. Dzagya was where the great Paltrul Rinpoche (1808-87) studied under Jigme Gyelwei Nyugu. Dodrubchen then went on to found **Tseringjong Monastery** at Yarlung Pemako (also called **Pemako Tsasum Khandroling** in neighbouring Sertal. It was his successor who moved the monastic community to its present location in Padma county, seeking to avoid the Nyarong incursions, and building anew on the site of an ancient 13th century Sakyapa monastery (once visited by Drogon Chogyel Phakpa).

Subsequently, the new monastery was developed and expanded by Dodrubchen III Tenpei Nyima (1865-1926), the son of the great treasure-finder Dudjom Lingpa (1835-1904). He was a renowned scholar who built the great temples of **Dodrub Chode**, and established a non-sectarian college as well as a meditation hermitage. The woodblocks for his published works were formerly housed here. In all, the monastery had 13 incarnate lamas and 250 monks until the 1950s. The present Dodrubchen Rinpoche IV, Thubten Trinle Pelzangpo (b 1927), resides at the Chorten Monastery in **Gangtok**, Sikkim; and he has also established a Buddhist Temple in Massachusetts.

From Dodrub Chode, a seasonal jeep track heads S to **Nyenlung** into Sertal county, and thence to Sertal itself (65 km from Nyenlung).

SERTAL COUNTY

གསེར་ཐལ

色达县 Sertar

Population: 25,049   Area: 7,454 sq km

Sertal county occupies the valley of the Ser-chu, a major source river of the Gyarong, which drains the grasslands from the NW and, as in neighbouring Dzamtang, its southern portions are densely forested. Since these hills are less steep than the gorges downstream, they have been quite heavily logged, and many convoys of timber trucks can be seen transporting logs to Chengdu. The Pelyul branch of the Nyingmapa school predominates in Sertal county and there are several small monasteries in the villages and on the grasslands further N. The county capital is located at **Gogentang**, within the Kandze prefecture, 126 km SE of the Qinghai-Sichuan border. The distance from Gogentang to Dzamtang is 152 km, to Nyenlung 65 km, and to Drango 149 km.

SERTAL COUNTY

To Dodrub Chode

Ponkor
17   Qinghai-Sichuan border   Nyenlung
53 Nyichu
        Yarlung   65
9   Khenleb   45   19
    Gonpa   Gogentang   27
                Nubzur 13
                Horshe 16
                Sheldrub 10
        N   Yango   To Dzamtang
                Serwa   9
                17   Gyasho
                4,115m
                Nyipa
                        To Likhok and Tsanghu
Sketch map: not to scale
        To Drango
        (54 km from pass)

ACCESS Two motorable roads lead into Sertal county from Golok. The first crosses the Bayankala N of **Ponkor Me-ma** (50 km) on the Nyi-chu, and then, after crossing the Qinghai-Sichuan border, enters the Ser-chu valley above Nyichu township. Below **Nyichu** it follows the Ser-chu downstream to **Gogentang**, the county capital, and thence to **Serwa**, where the Drango road branches off to the S and the Dzamthang/Barkham road to the E.

The second crosses from **Dodrub Chode** into **Nyenlung** township, and thence downstream to Gogentang. Between these two border crossings, equidistant between the Ser-chu and Do-chu valleys is the monastery known as **Dartsang Gonpa**, the seat of Dudjom Lingpa (1835-1904).

Nyichu and Yarlung Pemako

At **Nyichu**, 53 km SE of the border, there are two Nyingma monasteries of note: **Zhichen Kharmar Sang-me Gon** is a branch of Katok, with over 1,000 monks. Beru Rinpoche, the head lama, currently resides in Nepal. He is the father of the present head of the Drukpa Kagyu school. The smaller monastery of **Taklung Gon** is located nearby. About 9 km further SE is the small **Khenleb Gonpa**, a branch of Pelyul, in Khenleb township.

From Khenleb, the road cuts E to **Yarlung**, 45 km distant. Here is the celebrated **Yarlung Pemako Monastery**, founded by Dodrubchen I on his return from Central Tibet. The tradition followed at Yarlung is that of Rigdzin Jigme Lingpa. Nearby, there are smaller branches of Pelyul at **Serto Gonpo Drongrir Nego Gon** and **Ser Shorok Gon**, where there are fewer than 200 and 300 monks respectively.

Gogentang and Ser

Gogentang, the county capital of Sertal, is 19 km E of Yarlung. Here the major landmark is the large white stupa, known as **Gogen Chorten**. A small monastery, named **Ser Gogen Chorten Gon**, lies alongside the stupa.

- **Facilities** The town has the standard up-country guesthouse and restaurant facilities. Buses also run from here to Drango and Barkham.

The neighbouring township of **Ser** has a number of grassland monasteries, which are nearly all branches of Pelyul. Among them the largest are **Raktrom Jampaling**, and **Singsing Dungkar Gon**, which both once had over 1,000 monks. The latter is located not far from the Chorten. Smaller monasteries in this same township include Jekar Luklha Gon in Sholeb (450 monks), Sangsang Dradra Gon (100 monks), Tashul Barmi Gon, Tashul Ogmi Gon, Washul Pon Gonsum, and A'u Sera Gon.

Nyenlung

At Gogentang, a poor road leads N over the grasslands via **Nyenlung** (65 km) to Dodrub Chode in Padma county (see above, page 617), but it receives very little traffic. The monasteries of **Nyenlung Gon** and **Bochung Rusal Me Gon** are located here.

Nubzur and Larung

ACCESS The main road follows the Ser-chu downstream to an important intersection at **Serwa**, above its confluence with the Do-chu. **NB** In the summer months this road can be cut off by the flooding waters of the Ser-chu.

Nubzur (*Ch* Loro) township lies along this road, 27 km SE of Gogentang. Here, the principal monastery is **Ser Nubzur Gon**, which was the original seat of Khenpo Jikpun, also known as Terton Sogyel, the incarnation of Lerab Lingpa. This charismatic lama subsequently founded the monastery of **Larung Gar**, located in a side valley about 15 km S of Gogentang, which has over 2,000 monks and 1,000 nuns. There are no temples as such, since the lama has registered the institution as an educational establishment rather than a monastery. Khenpo Jikpun is well-known for obtaining the 'bird-dogs' of Tibet, a tiny dog which is reputably found in the nest of

cliff-nesting birds, and has the power to detect poison in food! He presented one to the Dalai Lama on a recent visit to India. He has also travelled widely in Europe and North America.

Serwa and Lhartse Sangak Tenpeling

Passing through Horshe township after 13 km, where the monastery of **Horshe Gon** is a branch of Pelyul, the road continues to follow the river downstream via **Sheldrub** (16 km), and **Yango** (10 km), before reaching **Serwa** township (12 km). This important crossroads village has a large guesthouse, small shops, and a restaurant. The monastery of **Serlha Tsechu Jar Gon** is located here.

Taking the E road from Serwa which leads to Dzamtang and Barkham, you will pass through **Gyasho** after 9 km, and **Golatang** after 20 km. Barley is cultivated in these lower reaches of the Ser-chu; and before reaching the wooden barrier which demarcates Kandze and Ngawa prefectures, you will pass by a **Mantra Wheel Chapel (Dungkor)** containing the mantras of Padmasambhava, a white stupa containing an image of Padmasambhava, and 13 km from Serwa, the monastery of **Lhartse Sangak Tenpeling**, which has a high tower replica of **Sekhar Gutok** (see above, page 275), the tower of Milarepa. The tower was rebuilt by the late Panchen Lama X. Above this tower, on the ridge is the Pelyul branch monastery known as **Lhartse Gon**. The road then passes into Dzamtang county.

Likhok and Tsang-chu Valleys

Taking the S road from Serwa, you will reach Drango after 71 km. A stunningly beautiful pass crosses the watershed (4,115m) between the Ser-chu and Nyi-chu rivers after 17 km. The nomads of this area are tough and not particularly hospitable to strangers. Sometimes they will block the road with logs and extract protection money from passing drivers! At **Nyipa**, a branch road on the left leads sharply NE into the **Likhok** and **Tsang-chu** valleys. There are many Nyingmapa monasteries in this area, including **Rahor Gonpa**, in Tsangto township, a branch of Dzogchen which is the seat of Rahor Khenpo Thubten, now resident in Switzerland; and **Khardong Monastery**, the Jangter seat of Lama Chime Rigdzin who also resides in Europe. Other Nyingmapa monasteries in this small area include: Shukgang Gon, Tsangda Gon, Senge Dzong (a branch of Katok in Tsang-me township), Sago Gon, Domang Gon, Dicham Gon, Jangang Gon, and Gochen Gon.

DZAMTANG COUNTY

ཛོམ་ཐང

琅塘县 Zamtang

Population: 34,278   Area: 7,650 sq km

Dzamtang county occupies the valley of the Do-chu, from the grasslands and gorges of its mid-reaches, through its confluence with the Ser-chu, and as far as its confluence with the Mar-chu, at which point it becomes known as the **Gyarong** (*Ch* Dadu) River. It also includes the valley of the north-flowing Dzi-chu, a tributary of the Mar-chu. The county capital is located at **Dzamtang**, 152 km from Sertal, 213 km from Barkham, and 155 km from Drango.

ACCESS Driving into Dzamtang county from Sertal or Drango, via Serwa, a wooden barrier marks the modern border between Kandze and Ngawa prefectures. At the confluence of the Ser-chu and Do-chu rivers, 39 km beyond Serwa, there is a turn-off on the left which follows the Do-chu upstream through a precipitous gorge. In the summer season this road can become impassable due to the damage

DZAMTANG   Sketch map: not to scale

To Dodrub Chode
Yutok
Dzongda
Nada
18
Doto
Do-chu
24
32
28
Dzamtang
N
27
To Gogentang (95 km)
Drukje
Lhartse Sangak Tenpeling (Monastery)
18
To Barkham
Serwa
To-de
Gyasho
Golatang
26
20
9
20
10
Ser-chu
Kandze / Ngawa Prefectural Border
Tsangkhok

TIB560

caused by the swollen river banks. Turn left for Dzamtang or continue due E for Barkham.

Jonangpa Monasteries of the Middle Do-chu Valley

If you head N through the Do-chu gorge, you will pass **Drukje** township after 18 km and reach **Dzamtang**, the county capital, after a further 27 km. There are two main monasteries, both representing the Jonangpa school. Among them, **Dzamtang Chode Gonpa** was founded by Drung Kazhi Rinchenpel, and **Dzamtang Tsangpa Gon**, where there are 1,500 monks, was founded by Ngawang Tendzin Namgyel, whose uncle had been an actual student of Taranatha. Isolated in their remote sanctuaries, the Jonangpas of Dokhok and Markhok successfully survived the persecution and conversion of their mother monastery in Tsang by the Gelukpas during the 17th century.

● **Facilities** There are guesthouse and restaurant facilities.

There are also several small monasteries of the Kagyupa and Nyingmapa schools in the main Do-chu valley.

Yutok

The road bifurcates at Dzamtang, the left branch heading NW to **Doto** (32 km) and **Yutok** (24 km); and the right branch heading NE across the watershed to **Nada** (28 km) and **Dzongda** (18 km) in the Dzi-chu valley. Around Yutok, the Nyingmapa monasteries of **Do Shukchung Gon** and **Do Yutok Gon** each have about 500 monks. A trail leads from Yutok via Shukchung to **Dodrub Chode** (see above, page 618) across the Qinghai border.

Dzi-chu Valley

Driving NE into the Dzi-chu valley, there are minor Nyingma monasteries, such as **Dzika-me Akye Gon**, most of which are branches of Dodrub Chode. The most important sites in this valley, however, are the numerous monasteries of the Jonangpa school, each with around 100 monks, which are affiliated with the two main Jonangpa monasteries at Dzamtang. The land is flatter here, and quite suddenly the forested gorges with their stone and wooded houses blend into the rolling hilly grasslands inhabited only by yak herding nomads.

Lower Do-chu Valley

Heading E from the aforementioned confluence of the Do-chu and Ser-chu rivers (2,896m), the road follows the combined waters of these Gyarong feeder rivers downstream for 122 km as far as their confluence with the Marchu. On this route through the gorges, there are only a very few small roadside settlements. After 26 km, the road passes through **To-de** (2,743m), where a side-road leads SW to **Tsangkhok** (20 km), and after a further 40 km it leaves Dzamtang county for Barkham county.

NGAWA COUNTY

རྔ་བ་

阿坝县 Aba

Population: 39,320   Area: 8,776 sq km

Ngawa county, named after the Nga-chu tributary of the Mar-chu, which flows S from **Mt Nyenpo Yurtse**, is an area where nomadic groups and long-established sedentary communities intermingle. The villages are characterized by large detached adobe farming houses with tapering walls and windows all on one side of the building! Agricultural produce is limited to valley floors and alluvial fans, where fields of barley, rapeseed and beans are planted, but it is animal husbandry and forestry that provide the principal economic outputs. Ngawa has thrived on trade for centuries; and its inhabitants even now frequently undertake business trips to Chengdu and Lhasa. The county capital is located at **Ngawa** (*Ch* Aba); 75 km from Jigdril, 254 km from Barkham, and 157 km from Mewa (*Ch* Hong Yuan).

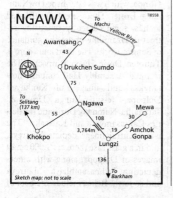

NGAWA

To Machu — Yellow River

Awantsang — 43

Drukchen Sumdo — 75

To Selitang (137 km)

Ngawa — 55

Mewa — 30

Khokpo — 108 — 3,764m — 19 — Amchok Gonpa

Lungzi — 136

To Barkham

Sketch map: not to scale

Upper Ngawa (Ngawa To)

Two roads approach Ngawa from Golok, one following the Mar-chu downstream from Padma, across the Qinghai-Sichuan border, as far as **Khokpo**, where a side-road leaves the Mar-chu and heads NE for 55 km to Ngawa town (total distance 192 km). The other follows the Nga-chu downstream from Jigdril on the SE side of Mt Nyenpo Yurtse, via **Ngato** (total distance 75 km).

The monasteries of Upper Ngawa (Ngato) include **Tsinang Gon** of the Jonang school, and Gelukpa institutions such as **Tsegon Sangchen Tashiling** (founded by Khenchen Ngawang Drakpa), and **Ziwei Ritro Ganden Tashi Choling**. Just before reaching the town, the road leaves a narrow gorge marked by a vast stone cairn in the open hills that lead up towards the sacred Mt Nyenpo Yurtse, just visible in the distance. 15 km NE of town is the famous **Gomang Gonpa**, also known as Gomang Gar Ganden Labsum Zungjuk Dechenling. Most of the Nyingma monasteries of Ngawa are small and located in this northern part of the county.

Middle Ngawa (Ngawa Barma)

The town of **Ngawa** itself (population approximately 15,000) is a typical mix of Chinese compounds, department stores and simple shops, but despite its remote location, it remains an important thriving trading town. In common with most of Amdo, gold is a predominant local product, and large numbers of itinerant Chinese workers visit the area to pan for gold in summer. As in Dzamtang and Sertal, the forested hills on the upper reaches of the Nga-chu tributaries have proved easier to log than the gorges further S, and many hillsides have been stripped bare. There is little evidence of replanting except beside the roads of the valley floor, and the denuded slopes are soon covered with herds of yaks and sheep, making

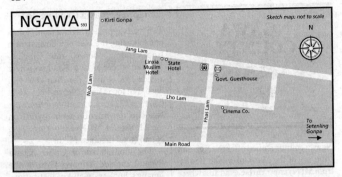

Sketch map: not to scale

N

Kirti Gonpa

Jang Lam

Linxia Muslim Hotel · State Hotel

Nub Lam

Govt. Guesthouse

Lho Lam

Fhas Lam

Cinema Co.

To Setenling Gonpa →

Main Road

regeneration almost impossible. The Public Security Bureau are over-vigilant and may restrict one's movements, even when all travel permits are in order. The town has an interesting leather goods factory and a teacher training college.

● **Facilities** In town there is a large *Government Guesthouse*, and several Sichuan-style restaurants. There is a varied nightlife with lively karaoke bars and discotheques.

Monasteries and temples

Kirti Gonpa

The hills around the town are dotted with more than 30 monasteries of the Nyingma, Sakya, Geluk and Jonang schools of Buddhism, as well as major Bonpo institutions. The largest monastery, Kirti Gonpa, properly known as **Kirti Kalari Gon Tashi Lhundrub**, is located on the western edge of town. It was founded in 1472 by Rongpa Chenakpa, a disciple of Tsongkhapa; and has well over 1,000 monks. The head lama Kirti Tsenzhab Rinpoche currently resides in India. At its entrance is a huge stupa, one of the largest in Amdo, and this is a major destination for pilgrims from all parts of Tibet. The restored murals and images display a high standard of craftsmanship.

Other Gelukpa monasteries near the town include Khashi Ritro Tashi Gepeling, Dongkhu Gon Yulgyel Samtenling, and Namkyak Ritro Namdakling,

the last having been founded by a student of Dalai Lama VII, named Gyakhe Lama.

Narshi Gonpa

The Bonpo monasteries of **Narshi** and **Topgyel** lie just NE of town. Both represent the so-called 'old Bon' tradition, which remains aloof from the 19th century ecumenical movement, according to which great Bonpa masters such as Sharza Tashi Gyeltshen juxtaposed their realizations with those of the various Buddhist traditions. **Narshi Gonpa** is the larger of the two, and its monks are well-versed in dialectics, composition, and the decorative arts.

Setenling Gonpa

The Jonangpa tradition is also represented in the valley itself at **Setenling Gonpa**, which was established by Namnang Dorje. There are 800 affiliated monks, some currently practising retreat in Dzamtang under the guidance of Sangye Dorje. The head lama here is Thubten Dorje Hwon Rinpoche. The restored **Assembly Hall** contains new tangkas and images of Kunkhyen Dolpopa, Jetsun Kunga Drolchok, Taranatha, Namnang Dorje and the deities Cakrasamvara and Kalacakra. The large central image depicts Maitreya, and in a glass case there are 1,000 small images of Dolpopa, along with others depicting Padmasambhava, Maitreya and so forth. Relics include the boot of

Taranatha. There are various collections of texts including the *Kangyur* from Derge and *The Collected Works of Taranatha* (28 vols). Woodblocks for the *Six Yogas of Niguma* are also preserved here.

The **Gonkhang** has a central image of Mahakala in the 'tiger-riding form' Takkiraja; while the meditation hermitage has images of Dolpopa, Taranatha, Namnang Dorje, and the meditational deity Vajrakila. In the **lama's residence**, there is a Jokhang Chapel with fine images, tangkas and books, including one tangka depicting Taranatha surrounded by the so-called *Rinjung Gyatsa* deities.

Lower Ngawa (Nga-me)

The 108 km descent from Ngawa town to **Lungzi** (*Ch* Longriwa) crosses six passes, offering fine views (N) of Mt Nyenpo Yurtse after 20 km, and (S) of the deforested hillsides towards Barkham. Gelukpa monasteries in this area include **Tsakho Gon Ganden Dargyeling**. The highest of the passes on this route (3,764m) is the main watershed dividing the Mar-chu/Nga-chu basin from the Yellow River basin, 56 km S of the town. Crossing this pass, on a hillside just N of the road, is the Gelukpa monastery of **Darchen**, with around 200 monks.

Amchok Gonpa

Further on, about 40 km from the pass, the monastery of **Amchok Gonpa** comes into view in the valley floor far below. At **Lungzi** (*Ch* Longriwa) roads lead S into **Bar-kham** county (136 km) and NE following the Ger-chu tributary of the Yellow River upstream for 49 km to **Mewa** (*Ch* Hongyuan). If you take the latter route, you will reach **Amchok Gonpa** after 19 km. This is a particularly large Gelukpa monastery with two complexes: the Tsenyi Lhakhang for the study of dialectics and the Tenyi Lhakhang for the study of sutra and tantra. Altogether there are over 1,000 monks, under the guidance of Amchok Rinpoche. The present incumbent, Amchok Rinpoche IV, returns regularly from exile.

GYARONG GORGES

S outh of Ngawa, in the precipitous rugged gorges of Trokhyab, the source rivers of the Gyarong converge. This is the beginning of the Gyarong region, which extends through the lower reaches of this river valley as far as Chakzamka, and includes the lateral valleys of the Tsenlha-chu and Somang-chu, as well as the upper reaches of the Trosung-chu.

History

In Gyarong, the indigenous population speak a distinctively archaic Qiangic dialect called **Gyarong-ke**, and they maintained their unique way of life and culture for centuries. Until 1949, the tribes of Gyarong were organized into **eighteen petty kingdoms**. Among them, the **northern group** includes

Trokhyab (Zhousejia), Dzongak (Songang), Barkham, Choktse (Zhoukeji), Somang (Suomo), Zida, Tsakhok (Li dzong/Zagunao), Gyelkha, and Wasi. These are all located around the Dochu/Somang-chu confluence and in the upper Trosung-chu valley.

The **central group** comprises Rabten (Chuchen/Jinchuan), Badi, Pawang (Chuchen), Geshitsa, Rongtrak, and Dardo (Chakla), which are all located in or around the main Gyarong valley; and the **south-eastern group** includes Tsenlha, Dawei, Hva-hva (Hanniu), and Dronba (Muping), which are all located in the Tsenlha valley and the mountains further S.

Traditionally, **Trokyab, Rabden, Tsenlha**, and **Dardo** were the most influential among these 18 kingdoms, which kept the powerful Sino-Manchu armies of Emperor Qianlong at bay for 10 years during the 18th century. Nowadays, both Barkham and Dardo are prefectural capitals, responsible for the administration of those parts of Kham, Amdo and Gyarong presently under the control of Sichuan province. This section, outlining the Gyarong gorge and its adjacent valleys, comprises five present day counties: **Barkham, Chuchen, Rongtrak, Tsenlha**, and **Tashiling**, of which only Rongtrak falls within the Kandze prefecture – the others all being within the Ngawa prefecture. Dardo has already been described (see above, page 501). **Recommended itinerary: 9 (also 5).**

BARKHAM COUNTY

འབར་ཁམས

马尔康县 Markam

Population: 82,075   Area: 7,327 sq km

Barkham county is the northern limit of the Gyarong region and the language here (considered a branch of the archaic Qangic group of Tibeto-Burman) is almost unintelligible to the Amdowa populations further N, and the Khampa peoples to the W. The dress is also distinctive. Most of the women wear multi-coloured embroidered headscarfs and elaborate belts and aprons. Fewer men wear the traditional felt tunic, which is quite distinct from the Tibetan *chuba* or bulky sheepskin coat. The vast majority of men now wear Chinese clothes, and only a small number of traditionalists can be observed in the market. There are almost 40 monasteries in the county, representing the Nyingma, Gelukpa, Sakya, Jonang and Bonpo traditions, several of them in attractive mountain locations.

Ga-ne and Tuje Chenpo Gon

Entering Barkham county from Dzamtang, the road passes first through **Ga-ne** (2,590m), where a bridge spans the river and a side-road leads S to **Tawu** (see above, page 550) in Kham. On the far bank of the Do-chu at Ga-ne, there is a **Mani Wheel Chapel**.

Continuing downstream from Ga-ne for 13 km, the road passes through **Tuje Chenpo** township (*Ch* Guanyinqiao), where another motorable bridge cuts S across the river. Above the town (1½ hrs walking distance), there rises the Nyingmapa monastery of **Tuje Chenpo Gon**, which formerly had over 300 monks, and is revered as one of the major pilgrimage sites in Far-east Tibet. There is a small reconstructed monastery here, with about 70 monks, and although the building itself is unimpressive, the winding path up to it is covered in small shrines where pilgrims leave old bits of clothes, tufts of wool from their sheep and broken jewellery.

The side-road leading southwards from Tuje Chenpo leads to **Akhori Gon** (41 km), a branch of Dzogchen monastery. Across the pass from here (in Rongtrak county), is **Maha Kyilung Gon**, the seat of Zenkar Rinpoche, the incarnation of Do Khyentse Yeshe Dorje. The present incumbent is currently based in England.

BARKHAM
TIB567

To Dzamtang (45 km) — To-de — 26 — 45 — Ga-ne — 13 — Tuje Chenpo — 4 — Trokhyab — 34 — Tsedun Sobdun Gonpa — Mar-chu — Dartsang — Sar Dzong — Dzongkhag — Barkham — To Ngawa (108 km) — To Mewa (49 km) — Lungzi (3,673m) — 15 — 18 — 26 — To Trochu — Lhagyeling — 10 — Chiri — 21 — To Chengdu (328 km)

Do-chu — 20 — Tsangkhok — To Tawu — 41 — Akhori Gon — Tro-ye — Gyarong — 30 — 10 — 15 — 9 — 38 — 17 — Choktse — Somang-chu — Somang — Maha Kyilung Gon — To Chuchen (46 km) — To Tseniha (144 km)

N

Sketch map: not to scale

Trokhyab

Following the main road downstream for 4 km from Tuje Chenpo, you will arrive at **Trokhyab**, once one of the most powerful of the 18 ancient kingdoms of Gyarong, but nowadays having the appearance of a small country village. Some houses have the Tibetan syllable 'Tro' (written *khro*) inscribed on the doors!

Some 34 km further E at **Tro-ye**, the road reaches the confluence of the Do-chu and Mar-chu rivers (2,073m). The gorge here is one of the steepest in Tibet; and a sturdy bridge spans the rapids. Crossing over to the E bank, the main road heads upstream and then E through the valley of the Somang-chu tributary to **Barkham**, the prefectural capital. The distance from the confluence to Barkham is 55 km.

Alternatively, from the confluence at **Tro-ye**, you can take a side-road which leads upstream to **Tsedun Sobdun Gonpa** – the largest Gelukpa monastery in the county, and Khangsar; as well as Jonangpa monasteries such as **Dzago**, **Bala**, and **Tashigang**, all of which are in the Mar-chu valley (and its side-valleys). The Gelukpa monastery of **Datsang**, located above **Sar Dzong** on a west-flowing tributary of the Mar-chu, is also accessible by this route. There are fine views from here of **Mt Shukgopuk** (4,906m) to the SW. Unfortunately, the road does not continue up river to the junction of the Mar-chu and Nga-chu. Visitors and pilgrims to Ngawa are therefore forced to backtrack to Barkham and head for Ngawa via the Somang valley.

Barkham City

ACCESS At **Tro-ye** where the combined waters of the Mar-chu and Do-chu are crossed, the road bifurcates: one trail (S) following the Gyarong downstream into Chuchen county (see below, page 630), and the other (E) following the Somang-chu upstream. The latter passes through several of the ancient Gyarong kingdoms: **Dzonggak** lies 10 km E of the

turn-off, **Barkham** (15 km further E), **Choktse** (9 km further E), and **Somang** (38 km further E). Of these Barkham, which was once one of the smaller of the ancient kingdoms, is now a city replete with high-rise apartment buildings. As the capital of both Barkham county and Ngawa Prefecture, the city is now comparable to Dartsedo in its importance, with a population of approximately 20,000.

The steep-sided valley of the fast-flowing Somang-chu, almost denuded of its original forest, constricts the town into a long thin corridor. Much of the town is composed of administrative buildings and compounds, of uninspired design (large high-rise concrete apartments), but nearby village houses are still constructed in the traditional three storey stone and wood fashion characteristic of most of Gyarong. Alluvial fans on the valley floor and the less steep slopes high above the river provide some rich agricultural land and terraced fields, irrigated by cleverly contoured canals which surround the small hamlets throughout this area.

Places of interest

The small Gelukpa monastery which overlooks the town is little more than a concrete shed, with about 30 attendant monks. **Gyidruk Monastery** of the Nyingma school is located some 3 hrs climb SW of town. It offers spectacular valley views, although the building and its contents are disappointing artistically.

● **Accommodation** The more upmarket *Aba Hotel* (Aba Binguan), with its expensive attached bathrooms, and restaurant/karaoke wing; and the cheaper *Minshan Hotel* (Aba Zhou Minshan Hotel) which has 4-bedded rooms (¥20/bed) and functional hot showers on each floor. There are a number of small guesthouses and street restaurants.

● **Shopping** The town has several industries: handicrafts, Tibetan medicines, matches, and wooden furniture; located alongside the ubiquitous government buildings and shops. Look out for the Minority Handicrafts Shop (Ch

Minzu Yongpin Shangdian) for traditional products, and the Xinhua Bookstore for books on the region. A cinema and sports stadium provide local entertainment.

Upper Somang Valley

From Barkham the road continues to follow the Somang-chu gorge upstream, passing the ancient kingdom of **Choktse** after 9 km. Here there is a turn-off to the S which crosses a pass

and then follows the Tsenlha River (*Ch* Xiaojin) downstream for 144 km to Tsenlha county (see below, page 633).

Continuing E along the Somang-chu, you will pass through the area where, according to one tradition, the great translator Vairocana is said to have meditated and transmitted the Dzogchen teachings during his exile from Central Tibet in the 8th century. Passing **Somang**, another of these ancient king-

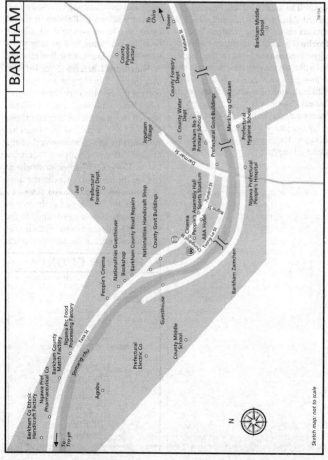

BARKHAM

To Chiro

Tower

County Plywood Factory

Minham St

Barkham Middle School

County Forestry Dept

County Water Dept

Jopatsen Village

Barkham No 1 Primary School

Merkhang Chakzam

Prefectural Govt Buildings

Prefectural Hygiene School

Darmar St

Prefectural Forestry Dept

Jail

Nationalities Guesthouse

People's Cinema

Bookshop

Barkham County Road Repairs

Nationalities Handicraft Shop

County Govt Buildings

Cinema

People's Assembly Hall

Sports Stadium

ABA Hotel

Tundri St

Rigne St

Toogtie St

Ngawa Prefectural People's Hospital

Barkham Zamchen

Guesthouse

County Middle School

Tsoa St

Ngawa County Match Factory

Barkham County Pharmaceutical Co

Ngawa Prc Food Processing Factory

Somang-chu

Agbou

Prefectural Electric Co

Barkham Co Ethnic Handicraft Factory

Ngawa Pref Pharmaceutical Co

To Tro-ye

N

Sketch map: not to scale

doms, after 47 km, you will then after 8 further km reach the major intersection at **Chiro**. The road to the SE leads via Tashiling (Lixian) and Lungu (Wenchuan) to Chengdu (328 km) and the road to the N continues to follow the So-mang-chu upstream to the watershed area.

Taking the latter, you drive through a narrow gorge for 10 km to emerge at **Lhagyeling**. This important Gelukpa monastery once specialized in gold-printed texts, and is one of the oldest in Amdo. The area is densely forested and rugged. After a further 26 km, there is a turn-off on the right (E) which leads to **Trochu** (*Ch* Hei shui) county. Continuing on the main road for a further 18 km, you will cross the watershed between the Gyarong and Yellow river basins (3,673m), and then after 15 km reach **Lungzi** (Longriwa) in the grasslands. From here you can drive NW for 108 km to Ngawa (see above, page 623), or NE through the Ger-chu grasslands to Mewa (Hongyuan).

CHUCHEN COUNTY

ཆུ་ཆེན

金川县 Jinchuan
Population: 85,234   Area: 5,435 sq km

Chuchen county lies deep in the awe-some and unwelcoming Gyarong gorge. Formerly known as **Rabden**, it was at times the most powerful of all the Gyarong kingdoms, and its king was a vigorous proponent of the Bon religion. At **Yungdrung Lhateng**, 15 km S of Rab-den, there was the largest and most im-portant Bonpo Monastery in this part of Tibet. Between 1746-49 and 1771-76 the Sino-Manchu armies of Emperor Qian-long (1736-95) marched into Gyarong, sustained by the messianic zeal of the Mongol lama Changkya Qutuqtu Rolpei Dorje (1717-86) who sought to convert the Bon and other communities of Gyarong to the Gelukpa school by force of arms. The heroic resistance of the Gyarong people owed much to the isolation of the terrain and to their skill at constructing fortified towers – a tra-

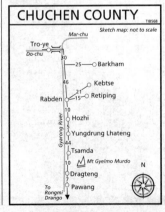

CHUCHEN COUNTY TIB568

Sketch map: not to scale

dition indicative of their Qiang ancestry. The imperial forces were driven back across the **Balang Shan** pass (see below, page 634) in disgrace before eventually returning to destroy the Bonpo monastery with their Portuguese cannons, and achieving a partial conversion to the Gelukpa cause. The present county capital is located at **Chuchen** (*Ch* Jinchuan), formerly Rabden, 46 km S of Tro-ye and 84 km N of Rongtrak.

Rabden Town

The road from the N enters the Gyarong valley at the **Tro-ye** intersection, and heads downstream for 46 km to **Chuchen** (Rabden), passing through **Drukzur** (*Ch* Xiazhai) and **Chingnying**.

• **Accommodation** The small county town has simple guesthouse and Sichuan restaurant facilities. There are also hot springs near the town.

Side-roads lead NE from the town for 21 km to **Rihruntang** (via Kalingka), and for 15 km to **Retiping** (via Wenlin).

Yungdrung Lhateng

Further S, the road passes **Hozhi** after 10 km; and then, after **Dosum**, it reaches the site of the Bon monastery of **Yungdrung Lhateng** (near Kharatang). Following the subjugation of Chuchen and the destruction of this monastery by the forces of Qianlong, a Gelukpa monastery named **Tenpel Gonpa** (*Ch* Guangfasi) was constructed in 1776, and developed with funds directly from from the imperial coffers. Its golden roofs were among the most lavish in Tibet. The wealthy monastery was destroyed during the 1960s and has subsequently been reclaimed by the Bonpos, who have once again resurrected Yundrung Lhateng.

Anying and Tsemda

From here, the road follows the river S. Tall fortified towers are commonplace on both banks of the river, particularly at strategic confluences. Passing through **Anying**, the road reaches the town of **Tsemda** (59 km S of Chuchen), and from here it crosses the modern prefectural boundary to enter Rongtrak county and the Kandze prefecture.

Gyarong Farmhouse

RONGTRAK COUNTY

རོང་བྲག

丹巴县 Danba

Population: 115,719   *Area:* 6,887 sq km

Rongtrak county occupies the Gyarong valley further S from Chuchen. Here the rapids are strong and the sound of rushing waters all-pervasive. The most important pilgrimage centre and power place is **Mt Gyelmo Murdo**, from which the Gyarong region gets its name. Gyarong is a contraction of Gyelmo Tsawarong. This mountain of solid quartz which once reputedly had mantra syllables inscribed in the rock crystal, has sadly been fully exploited for its minerals. The county capital is located at **Rongmi Drango**, 84 km S of Chuchen and 112 km N of Chakzamka.

Dragteng and Pawang

From **Tsemda** in Chuchen county, the road runs due S, passing the sacred **Mt Gyelmo Murdo** on the E bank. Two of the ancient Gyarong kingdoms are passed along this stretch – **Dragteng** after 10 km, and **Pawang** after 7 km. At **Dragteng** there are two major monasteries: the Gelukpa monastery of **Phuntsoling** and a large Bonpo monastery, which was once the principle shrine of the Dragteng kings. Near **Pawang** there is another 18th century Gelukpa monastery and the **Bumzhi Hermitage**, associated with the great translator Vairocana, who is said to have built 100,000 stupas here during the 8th century.

Geshetra

Continuing S from Pawang, after 3 km, a branch road on the NW leads over a high pass to **Geshetra**, another of the ancient Gyarong kingdoms, 44 km distant. In Lower Geshitsa there is the Gelukpa monastery of **Yangra Gon** and the Bon monastery of **Chadolo Gon**. Middle Geshitsa has a large Bonpo monastery named **Taksum Gonpa** (at Cherba township) and a ruined Jangter monastery of the Nyingma school. In Upper Geshitsa there is a Bon monastery name **Halo Gonpa**. Two trails leads from here to **Maha Kyilung Gon**, the seat of Zenkar Rinpoche, incarnation of Do Khyentse Yeshe Dorje (see above, page 627). The first crosses high passes and a hot springs, while the second, the easier route, passes through the Nyingma monastery of **Odu Gonpa**, birthplace of the present Gyatrul Rinpoche.

Rongmi Drango

Some 4 km S of the turn-off from Geshetra, the road reaches the county capital of **Rongmi Drango**, at the confluence of the Gyarong and Tsenlha rivers. Tall 18th century fortifications dominate the landscape of this ancient Gyarong Kingdom. The nearby **Mt Lateng** has three monasteries, situated one above the other on the hillside. The lowest of these is Gelukpa, the second is Nyingma, and the third is **Norbupuk Hermitage**, located at the site of Vairocana's 8th century cave, where a *drubchu* stream attributed to that great master remains ice-cold even in

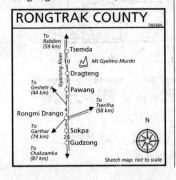

RONGTRAK COUNTY

To Rabden (59 km) — Tsemda

Gyarong River

Mt Gyelmo Murdo

Dragteng

To Geshetra (44 km) — Pawang

To Tsenlha (58 km)

Rongmi Drango

To Garthar (74 km) — Sokpa

Gudzong

To Chakzamka (87 km)

Sketch map: not to scale

summer.

On the W bank of the Gyarong, near Rongmi Drango the main road leads downstream to **Sokpa** (5 km) and **Gudzong** (20 km). Sokpa has a Bonpo monastery named **Taktse Gon**.

ROUTES Four roads diverge at Rongmi Drango (including the road just described from Chuchen). Head downstream (SE) on the W bank of the Gyarong to reach **Chakzamka** (112 km); SW following the Dungku-chu tributary to **Garthar** (74 km); or cross the Gyarong and head NE following the Tsenlha-chu valley to **Tsenlha** (58 km).

Among these, the main road to Chakzamka passes through small villages at km markers 85 and 28. Here there were labour camps during the Cultural Revolution. The low-lying county of Chakzamka (1,829m) has already been described (see above, page 507).

The SW road passes through **Tonggu** township and reaches **Garthar** after 74 km. This was formerly the main motor road to Garthar and Tawu prior to the construction of the **Gya La** route above Dartsedo (see above, page 503).

TSENLHA COUNTY

བཙན་ལྷ

小金县 Xiaojin

Population: 73,891   *Area:* 5,074 sq km

Tsenlha county occupies the valley of the Gyarong river's main tributary, the Tsenlha-chu (*Ch* Xiaojin), which nowadays lies within Ngawa prefecture. The population here is mixed Tibetan and Qiang, and both the Bonpo and Gelukpa traditions have co-existed since the 18th century. The county capital is located at **Drongdal Mezhing**, 58 km NE of Rongtrak, 143 km S of Barkham, and 146 km W of the Wolong Panda Reserve.

Dronang and Tselung

The road from Rongtrak to Tsenlha crosses the Gyarong River above its confluence with the Tsenlha-chu, and follows the latter upstream. At Dronang, 8 km E of Rongmi Drongo, there is **Langchen Gonpa** of the Gelukpa school and a small Jangter monastery of the Nyingma school, as well as a hot spring. Continuing on to **Tselung** (31 km), the road crosses the prefectural border, and after a further 19 km reaches the county capital.

Drongdal Mezhing Town

Drongdal Mezhing (*Ch* Xiaojin) is a picturesque town, located on the steep slopes of the Tsenlha valley, below its confluence with the Bupen-chu. Even the government buildings have assumed the appearance of a pagoda, and the local municipality has taken over the old Catholic Church. Traditionally one of the important kingdoms of Gyarong, Tsenlha entered the mythology of Chinese 20th century history as the place where the participants of the Long

March met up with the Fourth Front Army on 21 June 1935. Some 11 km S of Tsenlha a side-road leads to **Huanniu**, one of the minor kingdoms of ancient Gyarong.

● **Accommodation** Stay at the *Xiaojin Government Zhaodaisuo*, 3 Zhengfu Jie, which has double rooms at ¥6/bed.

Bupen-chu Valley

About 7 km E of town at **Masangtra**, the two tributaries of the Tsenlha-chu converge: the Bupen-chu flowing from the N and the Wangzhing-chu flowing from the E. Taking the former, a road follows the tributary upstream and across the watershed to **Choktsen** (143 km from Tsenlha) and Barkham (see above, page 627). On this road you will pass Bupen (36 km), Chugar (26 km), Tapon (23 km), and **Tsakho Gon**, the seat of Tsongkhapa's great student Tsakho Ngawang Drakpa (15 km). This road appears to get much less traffic than the main Rongtrak route.

Wangzhing-chu Valley

Following the Wangzhing-chu tributary upstream, the road passes through **Wangzhing** township (10 km), Zur (18 km), Dawei (5 km), and Zhilung (23 km). Among these, **Dawei** is one of the

old Gyarong kingdoms. The valleys here are extremely mountainous, with raging rivers flowing through steep-sided gorges. Only a few side-valleys still contain patches of original forest. Many of the villages, often with small Gelukpa or Bonpo temples, are on the flatter slopes, high above the road and are only visible on account of the numerous tall watchtowers found beside nearly every settlement. The village houses of the mixed Tibetan and Qiang population who inhabit this region are characteristically made of stone, their small windows decorated with swastikas.

Balang Shan

From **Dawei**, the road rises gradually over a rough pot-holed surface to cross the high. **Balang Shan** pass (4,487m) after 25 km (marker 203). The pass is often shrouded in mist, obscuring the view of the snow peaks of **Mt Siguniang** (6,250m) to the N, and it is not difficult to visualize the demoralized armies of Qianlong retreating across Balang Shan watershed in disarray.

After crossing the pass, the road enters **Lungu** (Wenchuan) county, and passes through the **Wolong Panda Reserve** (see below, page 656).

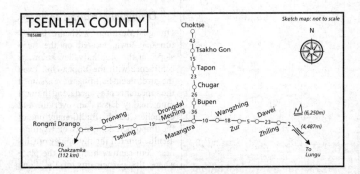

TASHILING COUNTY

བཀྲ་ཤིས་གླིང་

理县 Li Xian

Population: 51,174   Area: 4,569 sq km

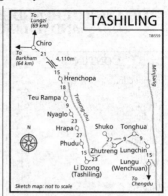

The county of **Tashiling** occupies the valley of the Troksung-chu, a tributary of the Minjiang, which rises S of the **Trakar Shankou** (Partridge Pass) watershed below **Chiro** in Barkham county (see above, page 627). Four of the ancient Gyarong kingdoms are located in this valley. The county capital is located at **Li Dzong**, 186 km SE of Barkham (via Chiro) and 56 km SW of Lungu (Wenchuan).

Trosung-chu Valley

ACCESS From **Chiro**, 64 km E of Barkham, there is an important intersection. Head N for Lhagyeling, Ngawa and the grasslands of Mewa within the Ger-chu valley (a tributary of the Yellow River); or head S across the Gyarong-Minjiang watershed to Chengdu (328 km). The watershed **Trakar Shankou pass** (4,110m) is 21 km from Chiro. Take this latter road, and after crossing the watershed, you will enter the long valley of the Trosung-chu, a major tributary of the Minjiang. Passing **Hrenchopa** (15 km), **Teu Rampa** (18 km), and **Nyaglo** (9 km), where the attractive Nyaglo Lungpa valley extends NE, the road eventually, after a further 23 km, reaches Hrapa, the site of the ancient **Zida** Kingdom of Gyarong.

Li Dzong

Continue on to **Phudu** (27 km) and then climb to Li Dzong, the county capital after 15 km. The village stone houses are typical of the Tibeto-Qiang culture. The main monastery is **Tashiling** of the Gelukpa school. Across the S bank of the Trosung-chu from Li Dzong, there was the ancient Gyarong Kingdom of **Tsakhok** (*Ch* Zagunao).

● **Accommodation** There are simple guesthouse and restaurant facilities.

After Li Dzong, the valley leads NE for 23 km to **Zhutreng** (*Ch* Xuecheng), where the ancient Gyarong kingdoms of **Gyelkha** and **Wasi** were once located. A side-road leads NW for 27 km to Shuko.

Then, after **Tonghua** (9 km), and **Lungchin** (9 km), the road eventually after 15 km reaches the Trosung-chu river's confluence with the Minjiang at **Lungu** or Wenchuan (see below, page 655).

LABRANG TO CHENGDU: THE UPPER MINJIANG AND JIALING VALLEYS

CONTENTS

MAPS

The road from Lanzhou to Chengdu passes through rich grasslands and nature parks interspersed with areas of high Chinese population density. The basins of the Yellow River, the Jialing, and the Minjiang are crossed and recrossed by the network of roads which cover this most E region of Amdo. 14 counties are visited, the first 7 of them currently in the Ganlho Tibetan Autonomous Prefecture of Gansu province, and the others in the Ngawa Tibetan Autonomous Prefecture of Sichuan. **Recommended itineraries: 11 (also 6, 8, 9).**

Bilingsi

The road from Lanzhou to Labrang heads W through **Yongjing** county, where the major attraction is the **Bilingsi Cave** complex. Here there are 183 Buddhist grottoes containing 694 statues and many terracotta sculptures and frescoes. The oldest date from the Western Qin Dynasty, and the greatest period of development occurred during the Tang Dynasty. The largest image is a 27m seated Maitreya.

ACCESS The caves are situated in a 60m high ravine beside the **Liujiaxia** reservoir on the Yellow River, and are accessible by boat. An average 2-way journey from Lanzhou to Bilingsi takes 12 hrs, of which half the time is spent in the boat. Boats depart from the reservoir, 30 mins walk above Yongjing county town. A round-trip will cost around ¥150 for a group of three or four people, but entrance charges to certain groups of caves are extra. It is easy to link up with other Chinese or foreign tour groups at the lake, but the local bus only goes twice a day. Alternatively, stay overnight at *Lidian Hotel* in Yongjing (¥50/double with attached bathroom), or the *Huanghe Hotel* (¥30/room).

Chorten Karpo

South of the Liujiaxia reservoir in Yongjing county, there is the site where **Chorten Karpo** once stood. This structure, constructed in 823, formerly marked the official frontier between Tibet and China, as determined by a peace treaty approved by the Tibetan monarch Relpachen. There is no trace of the stupa today!

Linxia

A newly constructed 1½ km tunnel provides easy access to Linxia county from Lanzhou, avoiding the former route which entailed crossing the reservoir by ferry boat. The direct route from the NE links up with the older road after passing through the fertile loess-covered hills of **Dongxiang** county. The drive is interesting, climbing through high terraces and small villages, each with its distinctive mosque.

Linxia, located in the lower valley of the Sang-chu (*Ch* Daxia), is an extensive county town renowned for its hundreds of mosques and as a trading town throughout the centuries. It is currently accorded priority development as a Special Economic Zone. Brick carving among the Hui community has a long history here, and the houses are well-decorated with flowers. The population pressure is obvious – the markets and bus stations are crowded, and modern construction rampant.

● **Facilities** Stay at the *Linxia Hotel*. Local arrangements can be handled by the *Linxia Travel Company*, T 214496 ext 2888.

Linxia to Dowi

At **Hanjiaji**, 20 km SW of Linxia county town, a side-road heads NW over **Darje La** pass to **Dowi** (Xunhua) county (80 km), and thence to Ziling, while the main road continues up river into the mountains of Central Amdo. Taking the former road, the first stretch is exclusively Muslim, but after the pass there are several small Gelukpa monasteries, including a branch of Rongpo Gonchen (formerly Sakya) which has 50 monks, as well as small Nyingmapa temples. At **Dowi Chorten**, there is a small community of nuns, founded during the 15th century by one Nakjin Rangron. A few hours walk from the top of the pass leads to **Darje Yumtso**, an oracle lake sited at the base of a high mountain. Dowi county which lies on the far side of the pass has already been described (page 590).

SANGCHU COUNTY

བསང་ཆུ་

夏河县 Xiahe

Population: 150,955   *Area:* 8,562 sq km

The county capital of Xiahe is located on the upper reaches of the Sang-chu River, 280 km from Lanzhou. At Km 201 there is a gateway indicating that you are leaving the Muslim area for that of the Tibetans. Then, 6 km further on, a large stupa comes into view, opposite **Sumchu Tampa** monastery. The Tibetan population is now estimated at 45% and there are 35 small monasteries. Dwarfing them all, however, is the monastery of **Labrang Tashikyil**, the largest in Amdo. To reach Labrang, follow the Sang-chu upstream from Linxia city for 71 km to **Wandotang**, the point where the main road leaves the river for **Ganlho Dzong** (**Hezuoshen**) new town. Take the branch road to the W which continues to follow the river upstream all the way to Xiahe (36 km). In this steep gorge, there are a few houses, on either side of **Da-me La** pass (3,698m) and a few small Gelukpa monasteries are interspersed among the hamlets.

SANGCHU COUNTY

Sketch map: not to scale

Xiahe Town

Xiahe (2,920m) sprawls for some 15 km along the banks of the Sang-chu, and is predominantly Hui Muslim at the E end and Tibetan at the W end. In all, the town is well-developed for tourism with several guesthouses, restaurants and souvenir stalls. Once past the monastery, development is restricted, leaving the splendid *Labrang Hotel* attractively isolated in the midst of fields and hamlets. Cycle rickshaws operate along the tarmac road, and the 40 min walk to the hotel passes two nunneries and a Nyingmapa temple on a muddy track.

The winter here is severe, down to -20°, but in the short spring season the hillsides bloom, providing excellent hill walks or horse riding, and summer is very pleasant despite the rain. Autumn is cool and clear, and in this season the dirt roads of Central Amdo are more comfortable to travel along.

Labrang Tashikyil Monastery

History

Labrang Tashikyil (2,820m) is one of six great Gelukpa monasteries in Tibet and, although 90 damaged temples have yet to be restored, it is amongst the handful anywhere in Tibet that survived the Cultural Revolution relatively intact. It was founded in 1709 by Jamyang Zhepa I Ngawang Tsondru (1648-1721), who was revered as an emanation of Tsong-khapa's teacher Umapa Pawo Dorje. Within the Gelukpa hierarchy, the incarnations of Jamyang Zhepa are superceded only by the Dalai Lama and the Panchen Lama. During his studies in Lhasa, where he was a contemporary of Desi Sangye Gyatso, he received his title 'Jamyang Zhepa' (laughing Manjughosa), when a statue of Manjughosa (Jamyang) laughed at his prostrations. Returning to his homeland, he then founded the most powerful monastery in Amdo.

Main buildings

The great temples and colleges of Labrang Tashikyil were constructed by Jamyang Zhepa and his successors. He himself founded the **Dukhang** (3) or assembly hall in 1709, the **Gyupa Dratsang** (9) or tantric college in 1716, the **Tosamling Dratsang** (12) or college of dialectics, and the **Jokhang temple** (1), containing a much revered Jowo Rinpoche image (flanked by 108 others) in 1718.

His successor, Jamyang Zhepa II Konchok Jigme Wangpo (1728-91) founded the **Serkhang Chenmo** (2), also known as Tsegaling, containing an 8-storey high cross-legged image of Maitreya, and in 1763 he founded the **Dukhor Dratsang** (10) for the study of Kalacakra chronology and astrology. Towards the end of his life in 1784 he instituted the medical college, **Menpa Dratsang** (7), which has a fine image of Aksobhya Buddha and is currently the most active of Labrang's colleges.

The tradition was maintained by his successors, Jamyang Zhepa III Kyabchok Jigme Gyatsode (b 1792) and Jam-yang Zhepa IV Kalzang Thupten Wangchuk (b 1855). The latter founded the **Kyedor Dratsang** (11) for the practice of the Hevajra meditational cycle in 1879. It contains images of Hevajra flanked by Guhyasamaja, Kalacakra, Cakrasamvara, and Vajrapani in the form Chakdor Khorchen, as well as Maitreya. The **Gyuto Dratsang** (8) or Upper Tantric College, was built by Jamyang Zhepa V Je Tenpei Gyeltsen Pelzangpo (b 1916), in 1928, as was the **Dolkar Lhakhang** (14) in 1940.

Other temples and buildings

Other important temples at Labrang include **Jamyang Lhakhang** (4), which has a large image of Manjughosa flanked by Maitreya and White Manjushri; the **Dedenling** (5) temple, dedicated to Sukhavati buddhafield and containing an image of Avalokiteshvara in the form Simhanada; **Je Rinpoche Lhakhang** (6), which contains images of

LABRANG TASHIKYIL MONASTERY

TIB610

Ticket office

Main gate

To Labrang Hotel

To Xiahe Town

Kyi-chu River

1. Jokhang
2. Serkhang Chenmo
3. Dukhang
4. Jamyang Lhakhang
5. Dedenling
6. Je Rinpoche Lhakhang
7. Menpa Dratsang
8. Gyuto Dratsang
9. Gyupa Dratsang
10. Dukhor Dratsang
11. Kyedor Dratsang
12. Tosamling Dratsang
13. Gatseling
14. Dolkar Lhakhang
15. Gongtang Chorten
16. printing presses
17. Deyang Podrang
18. School of Buddhist Studies
19. Labrang Museum

Tsongkhapa and Kharsapani; and **Gatseling** (13) containing murals of the three deities of longevity (Amitayus, White Tara and Vijaya) as well as Shakyamuni flanked by the Eight Bodhisattvas, and Tsongkhapa.

There are also two printing presses (16): one for woodblocks and the other for texts printed in movable type. The former contains the *Collected Works of Tsongkhapa* and those of his closest students. The residence of the Jamyang Zhepas called **Deyang Podrang** (17), the **Cham Jangsa** or religious dancing school (18), and the **Labrang Museum and Butter-Sculpture Collections** (19) are also worth a visit. The entire complex can be circumambulated by pilgrims over a 3 km circuit.

Recent renovations at Labrang

At its high-point Labrang Tashikyil Monastery housed 4,000 monks, and when Jamyang Zhepa V passed away in 1947 there were 300 geshes, 3,000 monks and 50-100 incarnate lamas. The present incumbent, Jamyang Zhepa VI, who lives in Lanzhou, presides over a much depleted monastery where there are barely more than 1,000 monks, of whom half are engaged in the study of dialectics and the rest in tantric meditation practice. In April 1985 the **Assembly Hall** (Dukhang) had been destroyed by fire, and the renovated hall (3), which can now be visited, was consecrated only in 1990. It contains a central image of Maitreya, with images of Tsongkhapa, the Eight Bodhisattvas, and Shakyamuni with his two foremost students to the left, and the five stupa reliquaries of the previous Jamyang Zhepa incarnations to the right. The hall itself has 140 pillars and 1,000 small buddha images.

The restored **Gongtang Chorten** (15) is the most recent building within the complex. Funded by a Chinese American devotee and consecrated in 1992 by Gongtang Rinpoche, its **ground floor** contains resplendent images of Sarvavid Vairocana, Manjughosa, Maitreya, and an exquisite reclining white jade Buddha from Burma. There are 21,000 volumes of texts encorporated within the structure. On the **second floor** there is an image of Amitabha, along with the Thousand Buddhas of the Aeon. The gallery offers a wonderful view of the murals downstairs, which depict the diversity of the Buddhist lineages in Tibet. On the **uppermost level** there is an inscription bearing the name of the sponsor.

Admission fees

Guided tours of the monastery (the only means of access) are available at ¥15 pp from the ticket office (closed from noon until 1400), and at ¥5 pp for the Gontang Chorten. The supervisor, Konchok Gyatso, is a close aide of Gontang Rinpoche's. **NB** Internal photography is generally prohibited, except in the museum.

School of Buddhist Studies

Outside the main gate of the monastery, there is an important **School of Buddhist Studies** (Nangten Lobdra), where some of the great contemporary teachers of Labrang, such as Geshe Gendun Gyatso and Geshe Jamyang Gyatso continue to teach.

Festivals at Labrang

The major festivals of the Buddhist calendar are observed at Labrang. During the *Great Prayer Festival*, reminiscent of the identical ceremonies held at Lhasa, on the 13th day of the first lunar month, a large (30 by 20m) applique tangka is displayed on the **Tangka Wall** on the S bank of the Sang-chu River, opposite the monastery. This is followed on the 14th by religious marked dances, on the 15th or full-moon day by *torma* (butter sculpture) offerings, and on the 16th by the procession of a Maitreya image around the monastery.

Sangke Grasslands

The open **Sangke** grasslands, where large horse-racing festivals are held, are located 14 km SW of Labrang. The main festival falls around July and is a highly-organized display of sports in which teams of Tibetans from settlements far and near participate, each with a distinctive hat and coat. A rough road leads over to **Amchog Gonpa** from Sangke's huge open grassy bowl and a large crowd attends, swelled by Chinese and western photographers. White tents mushroom on the hills and a great deal of beer is drunk. The *Labrang Hotel* has a traditional tented camp here on the grasslands, enabling tourists to sample the nomadic life.

Local information
● Accommodation

The most charming *Labrang Hotel* (T 09412-21849) lies at the extreme E end of town (ie 15 km from the extreme W end) beyond the monastery and this is recommended above all others. Formerly the Summer Palace of Jamyang Zhepa, it has been renovated as a Tibetan-style hotel with all modern comforts, set within its own tranquil grounds. There are 106 'luxury' chalets constructed in the style of an ornate Tibetan tented-camp (40 rm at ¥300 pp), and regular double rooms with attached bath (¥700/night). For budget travellers, the *Labrang Monastery Guesthouse* has beds for ¥10/night (no showers).

The Muslim commercial end of town (E) has less appealing hotels: the *Daxia Hotel*, the *Xinhua Hotel*, the *Waterworks Hostel*, and the *Minzu Hotel*. All are inexpensive.

● Shopping

Tibetan carpets may be a good buy here. Some traders and shopkeepers have returned from exile in India over recent years.

● Transport

To reach Xiahe by bus from Lanzhou be prepared for a 7 hr journey, departing at 0730 and stopping over for lunch at Linxia.

Ganja and Drakar Gonpa

ACCESS Buses leave Xiahe every other day for the 115 km (6 hr) journey to **Repkong** although during heavy summer rain the muddy track can become almost impassable. From the eastern edge of town, a road winds over a pass to the **Tsilung** valley, and the hamlet of **Ganja** where (17 km NE) **Drakar Gonpa**, an important Gelukpa monastery and cave-complex, are located. The cave descends along steep muddy tracks through a vast fractured pothole which has legendary underground connections to caves in the Repkong and Sogwo areas (see above, page 587).

Trekking

A long pilgrim's circuit of the mountain passing several lakes starts from the monastery but requires camping equipment for one night at least. There is also a small Bonpo temple on the opposite mountainside.

From Gangja, the road continues across the provincial frontier into Qinghai, and on to **Tashikyil**, **Gartse**, and **Repkong** (see above, page 592).

Labrang to Luchu Valley

There are two routes from Labrang in the Sang-chu (*Ch* Daxia) valley to that of the Lu-chu (*Ch* Tao), which is the principal tributary of the Yellow River in Ganlho prefecture. The first is a rough seasonal road running due S from Labrang to Luchu via **Amchog** (97 km) in the upper reaches of the Lu-chu valley; while the second heads downstream to **Wandotang**, where it rejoins the main road from Lanzhou and Linxia to **Ganlho Dzong** (Hezuoshen, 71 km) and thence to **Lintan** in the mid-reaches of the valley (76 km). The former route which continues S towards Machu county and Dzoge in the Ngawa prefecture will be described first.

Ganlho Dzong

Ganlho Dzong (*Ch* Hezuoshen) is a large city of recent development, 36 km beyond the turn-off for Labrang at Wandotang. Nowadays it functions as the prefectural capital. The local monastery, **Tsogon Geden Choling**, where 200 monks reside, is lost among the largely Chinese and Muslim shops or compounds, but its newly-reconstructed 9-storey tower, still to be decorated, dominates the skyline.

● **Transport** The bus station is an important hub for passengers heading N to Lanzhou, and into the Tibetan areas of Xiahe, Luchu, Lintan, and Dzoge. There is also a private bus station which runs frequent minibuses to Linxia and Labrang.

LUCHU COUNTY

ཀླུ་ཆུ

碌曲县 Luqu

Population: 19,992   Area: 4,253 sq km

The county of **Luchu** occupies the upper reaches of the Lu-chu valley, from **Serlung** near the river's source (on the Qinghai frontier) through to the borders of **Lintan** county in its mid-reaches. The grassland roads leading S from Labrang converge at **Amchog**, 43 km N of Luchu county town. Further S, beyond the Lu-chu valley, there are important roads leading W to Machu, E to Tewo, and S to Dzoge.

Amchog

Amchog (2,835m) can be reached directly from Labrang by driving S through the **Sangke grasslands** (14 km), and then SE for 49 km. Another route leads from Wandotang (at the Labrang turn-off, km marker 223), via **Pongartang** village and across a pass to the prefectural capital of **Ganlho Dzong** (*Ch* Hezuoshen). The distance from the

LUCHU & MACHU COUNTIES

TIB569A

To Sogwo — Amchog
43
Serlung — 45 — Luchu — Shitsang
(4,054m)
To Awentsang — Dzoge Nyima — Taktsang Lhamo
Lake Drangto tso — 19
7 — 8
N — To Denka Gon
To Dzoge

Sketch map: not to scale

turn-off to Ganlho Dzong is 37 km. After Ganlho Dzong, take the SW road, which leads across a 3,048m pass (km marker 271) to Amchog and then links up with the direct road.

At **Amchog**, there is a large village and a Gelukpa monastery named **Amchog Demotang Ganden Chokhorling**, which lies atop a ridge to the W of the motor road.

Luchu Dzong

The pleasant county town of **Luchu** lies 43 km S of the nomadic pastures of Amchog and in the sheltered Lu-chu valley (2,957m). En route you will pass through **Nyimalung** village where there are interesting stone houses and the turn-off for the **Kotse** grassland, before crossing a 3,200m pass. The 106 km drive from Labrang takes approximately 3 hrs.

Formerly Luchu was a stronghold of the Bon tradition, and a major Bonpo monastery survived here until its final conversion by the Gelukpa in 1688, at which time it was renamed **Gegon Ganden Phuntsoling** by Lobzang Dondrub, the lord of neighbouring Cho-ne. Its tranquil setting, 4 km off the road, and mild climate add to its attractions. The population is even now largely Tibetan.

● **Accommodation** The town has simple but clean guesthouse and restaurant facilities.

ROUTES A side-road from Luchu leads upstream from a junction just N of the town for 45 km through a rugged and wide range of hills to **Serlung** on the edge of the Sogwo region. The exact provincial border is marked differently on maps published in Qinghai and Gansu provinces. Yet another side-road heads downstream following the river bank to **Ala** and then via Mapusola to **Lintan** (185 km). The Gelukpa temple of **Shitsang** is located along this road, 13 km down-valley from Luchu.

The main road to the S leaves the valley at Luchu and heads across the watershed (3,414m) between the Lu-chu and Yellow River, eventually

reaching the celebrated monastery of **Taktsang Lhamo** after 98 km. About 10 km out of town on this section of the road there are superb views of the **Ziqing** range to the SW, which hides the Yellow River from view. Three further passes are crossed in close proximity, the highest (4,054m) offering a vista of verdant and cragged terrain as the Ziqing range draws near. Then, at Lake **Drangto Tso**, 79 km S of Luchu (at marker 414), there is a dirt road on the W (right) which leads through the range to Machu on the bank of the Yellow River (see below, page 643).

Taktsang Lhamo Monasteries

About 19 km S of the Machu turn-off (at marker 433), a spectacular mountain view heralds the valley of the **Druk-chu** (*Ch* Bailong), which stretches from the two **Taksang Lhamo** monasteries at its source through **Tewo** and **Drukchu** counties to converge with the Jialing River in **Guangyuan**, Sichuan.

Although **Taktsang Lhamo** (*Ch* Lamosi) officially refers to the cave-shrine beside **Gerda Gonpa**, it is often used to include the neighbouring **Sertang Gonpa**.

The two monasteries, despite their proximity, are nowadays in different provinces, with **Gerda** belonging to Sichuan, while **Sertang** is just inside Gansu. They are both Gelukpa, but Gerda was founded in 1413 as disciples of Tsongkhapa spread throughout Tibet and was for years the most influential monastery in the region. The current Gerda Rinpoche, the 11th, is now in his mid-fifties and lives in India. His residence is being carefully rebuilt and the architecture of the whole monastery is of a higher standard than most new Amdo monasteries.

● **Accommodation** A small trading village, Lhamo, 4 km from the main road, can provide basic food and accommodation and the area has already become a popular stop-over for travellers between Dzoge and Labrang.

MACHU COUNTY

ཨ་ཆུ

玛曲县 Maqu

Population: 36,138   Area: 10,249 sq km

Turning off the main highway at the Lake Drangto Tso intersection, 79 km S of Luchu, a dirt road leads into Machu county. 3 km along this side-road, at Lake Drangto Tso (*Ch* Gahe), there is a small bird sanctuary. Another seasonal road into Machu heads W from Taxtsang Lhamo to reach the banks of the Yellow River.

The capital, **Dzoge Nyima**, is a fairly large town, located on the banks of the Yellow River, and its hinterland contains almost all of the river's first bend as it makes its 'S' curve through Amdo. Much of the terrain is flat, marshy grassland, but a spine of mountains runs down to **Sogtsang** monastery, at the apex of the bend.

There are several Gelukpa monasteries in the county, including **Ngora** to the W of the bridge and **Dzoge Nyima** a short walk from town. The road across the bridge leads to **Awantsang** and Jigdril county in Golok (on which see above, page 606).

LINTANG COUNTY

ལིན་ཐང

临潭县 Lintan

Population: 151,245   Area: 1,399 sq km

The counties of **Lintan** and **Cho-ne** in the mid-reaches of the Lu-chu valley can be reached from Lanzhou (via Kangle) or from Labrang (via Ganlho Dzong). The latter is the more scenic route.

Lintan Dzong

On the way to Lintan, 76 km further SE from Ganlho Dzong, there are a number of small monasteries affiliated to Labrang visible from the road, including **Tashi Gar**. 24 km NE of Lintan Dzong in Gyagartang is the Gelukpa monastery named **Gyagar Gon Shedrub Dargeling**, which was founded by Gyagar Gongma Lobzang Damcho. During the period of the Yarlung Empire, major battles were waged here between the Tibetan and Chinese armies. The county capital, **Lintan Dzong**, is a typically sinicized town with guesthouse and restaurant facilities. Visitors to Lintan generally pass through en route for Cho-ne, 30 km to the SE on the N bank of the Luchu.

LINTAN & CHONE

TIB569B

To Hezuushen (Ganlho Dzong) (76 km)

Lintan
30
Cho-ne
Min Xian

To Shitsang (185 km)

N

Dengka Gon
150
Drukchu

To Wudu

Sketch map: not to scale

CHO-NE COUNTY

ཅོ་ནེ

卓尼县 Jone

Population: 93,168   Area: 4,954 sq km

Cho-ne county on the banks of the Lu-chu is renowned for its ancient monastery. **Cho-ne Gonchen Shedrubling** was originally a Sakyapa monastery, founded by Drogon Chogyel Phakpa and his patron Qubilai Qan in 1295. Subsequently, it was converted to the Gelukpa tradition in 1459 by Choje Rinchen Lhunpo. The colleges at Cho-ne were established in the 18th century by Kunkyen Jigme Wangpo: the school of dialectics (**Tsenyi Dratsang**) in 1714, and the tantric college (**Gyupa Dratsang**) in 1729. The monastery was renowned for its woodblock collection of the *Kangyur* and *Tangyur*, prepared in 1773. Printed copies of this collection are still extant, although the woodblocks have been irreparably damaged. The **town of Cho-ne**, adjacent to the monastery, is fairly large, 374 sq km in area, with a predominantly non-Tibetan population (7,022).

TEWO COUNTY

ཐེ་བོ

迭部县 Tewo

Population: 57,907   Area: 4,927 sq km

As an alternative to going due S through the grasslands to Dzoge, it is possible to detour through the forested counties of **Tewo** and **Drukchu** within the valley of the Druk-chu (*Ch* Bailong), a tributary of the Jialing. To enter the Druk-chu ('white dragon') valley, turn left (E) at the road junction 8 km S of **Taktsang Lhamo monastery** (marker 441). Bee hives are plentiful in this area, and in season you will be able to buy fresh honey at the roadside. This route is the eastern extremity of Amdo and most of the population is highly sinicized. Nonetheless, it is a scenic and historic route, visiting pockets of Amdowa who trace their ancestry back to border armies from the time of the Tibetan kings. The monasteries here are mostly Sakya and Gelukpa.

Following the river's SE course, the road leaves the grasslands and enters forested gorges of Tewo. The county capital is located at **Dengka Gon** within the gorge, 150 km NW of Drukchu. Among other notable sites is the hermitage of **Tratsang Ritro**, which was founded by a lama named Tewo Rabjampa Palden Senge. Another road leads indirectly from Lintan to Tewo, via Jango, Niba and Yiwa.

DRUKCHU COUNTY
འབྲུག་ཆུ

舟曲县 Zhugqu

Population: 146,710   *Area:* 2,972 sq km

Heading SE through the Druk-chu valley, the road leaves Tewo county and enters **Drukchu** county, via Nyiga and Peltsang villages. The county capital, **Drukchu**, is 150 km from Tewo. The terrain ranges from 3,000-4,000m, and a large percentage of the 147,000 local people are even now Tibetans.

Roads From Drukchu, you can continue following the river road downstream to **Wudu** or follow a tributary upstream and across the watershed to Minxian and **Chone** in the Lu-chu valley.

THE FOREST DWELLERS OF DRUKCHU

Formerly this was the wealthiest part of the prefecture because it was an important forest region with a reserve of 156 million cubic metres of wood. The local people had lived by lumbering generation after generation and, at the same time, taken care of the forest which sustained them, so that it never deteriorated and provided a beautiful green environment with scenic waters and roaming pandas. The forest dwellers of Drukchu had a higher living standard than the peasants and nomads. However, great changes have occurred since the establishment of the Bailong Forest Administration Bureau in 1966, and the immigration of 10,000-20,000 lumber workers from Manchuria and Sichuan, plus their families. These alien people have no affinity toward this heavily wooded region. They are active in cutting down trees but have no intention to replant. Consequently, the hills on both sides of the Druk-chu are denuded, and the ecological system endangered. The Tibetan inhabitants are gradually being marginalized and empoverished – all that is left for them is the cultivation of mountain barley. Since the 1950s, the area of forest has shrank by 30% and the reserve of timber has been reduced by 25% due to overcutting. The sand in the river water has increased by 60%, and the water flow volume has reduced by 8%, resulting in increased flooding and drought.

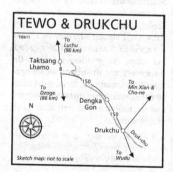

TEWO & DRUKCHU

TIB611

To Luchu (98 km)

Taktsang Lhamo

8

150

To Dzoge (86 km)

N

Dengka Gon

To Min Xian & Cho-ne

150

Druk-chu

Drukchu

To Wudu

Sketch map: not to scale

DZOGE COUNTY

མཛོད་དགེ

若尔盖县 Zoige

Population: 62,877   Area: 11,226 sq km

Crossing the current Gansu-Sichuan provincial border at **Taktsang Lhamo** monastery (see above, page 642), the road follows the Me-chu upstream to Dzoge. This river rises in the Minshan range and flows NW to converge with the Yellow River below Machu. As one crosses the craggy **Amnye Lhago** range (_Ch_ Erlong Shan), which in parts forms this provincial divide, some small remaining clumps of forest are visible on the steeper hills, but the landscape is still primarily grassland. The county capital is located at **Taktsha Gondrong**, in the Me-chu valley. The distance from Taktsang to Dzoge is 78 km via **Zhakdom**.

The terrain around Dzoge consists of high windswept marshland and vast grassland plain (3,292m), with an abundance of medicinal herbs. The horizon is dotted with nomad camps ringed by piles of yak-dung. The topsoil is thin and grazing land is intensively used, which has resulted in severe wind and water erosion in several areas. Everywhere there are molehills and the small holes made by pika, a voracious herbivore, which have added to the deterioration of the range.

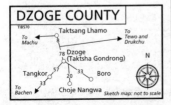

DZOGE COUNTY

TIB570

To Machu ← Taktsang Lhamo → To Tewo and Drukchu

78 Dzoge (Taktsha Gondrong)

Tangkor —57— 20 —33— Boro

To Bachen —33— Choje Nangwa

N

Sketch map: not to scale

Dzoge Town (Taktsha Gondrong)

The land around Dzoge town is classic yak-herding country: shaggy-haired nomads, dressed in little more than filthy sheepskin _chubas_ edged with fur, ride into town to barter skins or shoot pool in the market square, and fights are commonplace. Muslims from Gansu visit regularly to buy wool and carcasses which they transport northwards on ancient Chinese lorries, some of them settling to run the noodle restaurants and tea houses, which are found all over northern Amdo. Most of the Chinese here are administrators or shopkeepers selling a range of cheap nylon and plastic goods, and it is evident that few enjoy their stay. There are local industries based on the traditional nomadic produce: especially milk powder processing and meat canning factories.

Mentsikhang

The town is most famous, however, for its hospital of traditional medicine. This **Mentsikhang** is a teaching hospital with a 4-year study course run by Lopon Tenko, a former pupil of Geshe Lobzang Palden of Labrang who died in 1963 at the age of 88. The medicinal compounding room, the grinding machine, the dispensary, and the library are all open to visitors. On average the hospital treats 80 patients each day, mostly for stomach and liver ailments, as well as arthritis and bronchitis.

● **Facilities** The town has three small guesthouses and simple Sichuan-style restaurants, as well as those owned by the Muslims.

Dzoge Gonsar Gaden Rabgyeling

There are altogether 80 monasteries in Dzoge county, of which only three are Sakya and one Bonpo, the remainder are all Gelukpa. Among them, the best known (but not the largest) is **Dzoge Gonsar Gaden Rabgyeling**, which was consecrated in 1798, the site having been offered by Konchok Rabten, the chieftain of neighbouring Mewa (*Ch* Hongyuan).

Presently there are 100 monks here. The **main temple** has images of Shakyamuni, Tsongkhapa and Maitreya. In the **Gonkhang** there is a Four-armed Mahakala, while the **Mani Wheel Chapel (Dungkhor)** was constructed in 1988. The monastery has an important medical college (**Menpa Dratsang**), under the guidance of Akhu Puntsok. At the entrance to the site there is a large white stupa.

Festivals Small grassland festivals are held in Dzoge county throughout the summer with horse and yak races, weightlifting and traditional dances. The monastery establishes a small tent temple and numerous visitors bring tents in which a great deal

of alcohol is consumed.

Ger-chu Valley

Heading S from Dzoge there are two routes following the tributaries of the Me-chu upstream to **Bozo** (33 km) and **Choje Nangwa** (20 km).

The **main road** however leaves the Me-chu valley, heading SW to **Tangkor** (57 km). Here, it enters the valley of the Ger-chu, a north-flowing tributary of the Yellow River, which merges with the latter at nearby **Sogtsang Gonpa**. This is beehive country and the monastery is visible just to the N of the road. There are also ancient camouflaged village dwellings, their roofs covered in grass and earth for protection. From here to **Mewa** (*Ch* Hongyuan) the distance upstream is only 76 km.

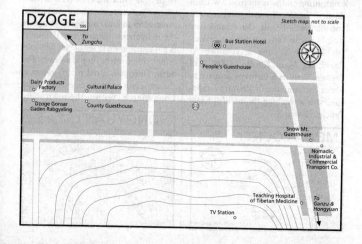

DZOGE

Sketch map: not to scale

To Zungchu

Bus Station Hotel

People's Guesthouse

Dairy Products Factory

Cultural Palace

Dzoge Gonsar Gaden Rabgyeling

County Guesthouse

Snow Mt. Guesthouse

Nomadic, Industrial & Commercial Transport Co.

Teaching Hospital of Tibetan Medicine

To Ganzu & Hongyuan

TV Station

MEWA COUNTY
མེ་བ

红原县 Hongyuan

Population: 24,624   Area: 7,328 sq km

Following the Ger-chu tributary of the Yellow River upstream from **Tongkor**, the road reaches **Bachen** (pronounced Wachen) after 33 km. Here a road branches SE across the watershed between the Yellow River and Minjiang basins to **Zungchu** (*Ch* Songpan), 186 km distant via Mewa and Changla. Some 18 km along this road, you can visit **Mewa Gonpa** of the Nyingma school, the largest monastery in the county, where the *Longchen Nyingtig* and *Choling Tersar* traditions are maintained. The monastery was founded in the 19th century by Do Rinpoche. Presently, there are over 1,300 monks here.

Razhitang Mani Khorlo

Continuing on the main road SW from Bachen, the Ger-chu valley flattens out, and on pools beside the meandering river black-necked cranes can occasionally be seen nesting in summer. At **Razhitang Mani Khorlo**, 2 km S of Bachen, there is a Gelukpa monastery under the guidance of Zhabtra Rinpoche, with a teaching throne of the late Panchen Lama X.

At **Amokok**, 25 km SW of Bachen, a turn-off on the E (marked by stupas and prayer flags to the right of the road) follows the course of the Amo-chu tributary upstream to **Gonlung** and the **Muge** grasslands (25 km).

Gongtang Temple

Back on the main road, the marshy plain around **Mewa town** (*Ch* Hongyuan) supports large numbers of nomads, but the numerous Gelukpa and Nyingmapa monasteries, such as **Regur**, are little more than concrete sheds whose most attractive feature is the decorative field of prayer-flags, sometimes pyramid-shaped, that are found beside them. Approaching the town, just above a little village to the W, is the small temple of **Gongtang**, the summer residence of Gongtang Rinpoche, whose lineage is traced back to Je Gongtangba (1762-1823). Except during his visits, only a handful of monks, of Bonpo and Nyingma traditions as well as Gelukpa, inhabit this site.

Hongyuan

The burgeoning county town of Hongyuan (Km marker 647) is a place where Chinese settlers have established themselves in great numbers, alongside the indigenous nomadic population. It is not uncommon to see horses and yaks tethered in front of shop doorways. The name Hongyuan ('red plain') refers to the associations of the county with the Long March. Within the town there

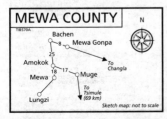

MEWA COUNTY

Bachen
8 — Mewa Gonpa
25
Amokok
18 17 — Muge
Mewa
To Changla
To Tsimule (69 km)
Lungzi

Sketch map: not to scale

HONGYUAN

Sketch map: not to scale

To Youth Palace & Dzoge

Guesthouse

Hongyuan Main St

Pastoral Farm Implement Supply Store

County Guesthouse

Bus Company

is an important *Grasslands Research Institute*.

● **Accommodation** Stay at the *Hongyuan Zhaodaisuo*, which has simple rooms in the main concrete building, alongside an uninspiring restaurant, in an annexe to the rear.

● **Transport** Public transport runs from here to Dzoge, Ngawa, Barkham, and Chengdu from the large bus station.

ROUTES From Mewa, the main road leads SW via **Amchok Gonpa** to **Lungzi** (49 km) where it bifurcates: one branch heading NW to Ngawa and the other due S to Barkham (see above, page 627).

ZUNGCHU COUNTY

ཟུང་ཆུ

松潘县 Songpan

Population: 51,099   Area: 6,517 sq km

Take the side-road at **Bachen** (90 km S of Dzoge and 43 km N of Mewa), and head SE across the watershed between the Yellow River and Minjiang basins. On the first part of the route you will pass through classic Amdo country: low hills, broad grassy valleys and meandering rivers with patches of marsh. Black yak-hair tents, typical of all Tibetan nomads, are abundant here, and the rich grazing land supports vast herds of yak and many sheep and goats. Much of the milk produced in this region is collected in large churns and taken by truck to Mewa, Dzoge, and other centres where it is processed into powdered milk. The remainder is used by the nomads to make butter, cheese and yoghurt, some of which is sold or bartered for tsampa, wheat, tea and salt, the principal constituents of the Tibetan diet.

Serdeutang and Aling

Passing through **Serdeutang**, where there is an attractive Nyingmapa monastery, known locally as Sergyi or Decha, the road then winds its way down from

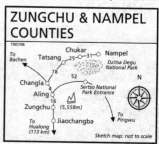

ZUNGCHU & NAMPEL COUNTIES

the grasslands through **Pangzang** village, to enter the forested Minjiang valley. **Aling** on the banks of the Minjiang is an important crossroads town. From here you may follow the Minjiang valley upstream to visit **Nampel** (Nanping) county and the **Jiuzhaigou National Park** (128 km), or S to the county capital of Zungchu (16 km).

Zungchu Town

Zungchu (*Ch* Songpan) has long been an important trading town for Tibetans, Qiang, Chinese and Muslims. Much of the tea trade for E Tibet was centred here, with wool, furs, musk, medicinal herbs and gold also providing important markets. The old city walls, now crumbling and overshadowed by new construction, can still be seen, and the extensive market area still attracts a wide selection of visitors from the hills. The Minjiang River runs through the town, carrying an abundance of logs downstream in defiance of the posters urging conservation and restraint. The population is diverse, but predominantly Muslim, and worshippers can frequently be seen at the **Qingzhen Si Mosque** near the N end of town.

Zungchu is rapidly becoming an important tourist centre for domestic and foreign visitors; and in summer, dozens of minibuses leave daily for the nearby national parks. It is also possible to hire horses and guides for trips into the mountains, lasting up to a week, but be sure you understand the itinerary, what services (eg food and accommodation) are included, and that you see the horses before parting with any money.

• **Facilities** Stay at the *Songpan County Peoples' Government Zhaodaisuo* (Songpan Xian Renmin Zhengfu Zhaodaisuo), which has double rooms with attached bath at ¥18, or ¥10 without; or the *Songzhou Zhaodaisuo*, which has double rooms at ¥16, with communal showers, and running hot water. There are several restaurants in town, mostly serving Muslim and Sichuan cuisine.

Nyenyul Valley

To the W of town, a steep climb and descent leads into the **Nyenyul** valley, where are found several Bonpo temples, including the important **Gyagar Mandi**, which is built on an Indian model, and the Sakya monastery of **Jara**. It is also possible to reach this valley, which has a famous waterfall called **Zhaga Purbu**, and a hot spring, by road from a turn-off a little to the S of Zungchu.

Sertso National Park (*Ch* Huanglong)

Further NE is the **Huanglong National Park** (*Tib* Sertso Rangjung Sungkyong Sakul), a popular destination which can be reached via a pass near the holy Bon mountain called **Mt Shar Dungri** (5,588m), which is the main peak of the Minshan range. A trekking route follows

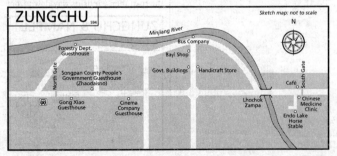

ZUGCHU 594

Sketch map: not to scale

N

Minjiang River

Bus Company

Forestry Dept. Guesthouse

Bayi Shop

North Gate

Songpan County People's Government Guesthouse (Zhaodaisno)

Govt. Buildings

Handicraft Store

South Gate

Café

Gong Xiao Guesthouse

Cinema Company Guesthouse

Lhochok Zampa

Chinese Medicine Clinic

Endo Lake Horse Stable

a tributary of the Minjiang upstream through **Dongna** to **Rongkok**, where you can visit **Rongpa** monastery of the Sakyapa school and **Sebo** monastery of the Gelukpa. En route are the small villages with Bonpo temples, such as **Rinpung** and **Kharchung**.

Alternatively, about 15 km N of Zungchu, a winding road to the E passes over the ridge and descends to the **entrance of the park** on the road to **Pingwu**. It is possible to stay in guesthouses near the park entrance, and walk past the series of small lakes and steep coniferous forests to an impressive alpine meadow, with numerous rhododendron species, at the eastern foot of **Mt Shar Dungri**. The small reconstructed temples here have Tibetan shrines in front, where juniper is burnt, and *lungta* (Tibetan printed prayers) are scattered. Among them the most famous is known in **Sertso Gonpa**. Tibetan and Qiang peoples from various Buddhist traditions gather here during a summer festival, held over a 3-day period from the 15th day of the 6th lunar month.

Several protected species, including the red panda, golden monkey, takin and water deer are supposedly found in the park, but in such small numbers they are unlikely to be seen by the casual visitor. The park, which extends for 9 km, was established as a nature reserve in 1983. It contains a series of variegated lakes suffused with minerals and algae, and (according to one tradition) received its name from the yellowish karst limestone formations which cover the landscape. **Sertso** village at the NE extremity of the park can also be reached by jeep or bus from Aling (52 km) on the Zungchu-Pingwu road.

South from Zungchu

Heading S from Zungchu to Chengdu, the main road follows the Minjiang downstream, passing through **Pata**, **Dongna**, and **Zhenjiangquan**, where there is a side-road leading into the Zhangdu-chu valley, and connecting with the neighbouring Metsa valley in Tro-chu county (see below, page 654).

The main road continues southwards to enter a gorge, and you will pass through **Jiaochangba**, which gives access to the Tungping side-valley. Eventually, you will reach the confluence of the Minjiang and the Tro-chu in Maowen county, 113 km from Zungchu. The county capital of Maowen is located 29 km further S.

NAMPEL COUNTY

ཀྲུན་འཕེལ་

南坪县 Nanping

Population: 62,257   Area: 6,175 sq km

The county of **Nampel** occupies the upper reaches of the Baishui and Fujiang tributaries of the Jialing River. From **Zungchu** head N following the Minjiang upstream via **Aling** to **Changla** (20 km). Instead of turning E here, for the Sertso National Park, continue upstream, to cross the watershed at **Tatsang** (78 km). The county town of Nampel, or Nanping in Chinese, is located 46 km further NE on the Baishui tributary. En route, there is a Bonpo monastery at **Nang-zhi**, and several affiliated nearby temples, notably **Lenri** and **Kyang**, the last having been founded by Kyang Lobzang Gyatso.

Further N, just before reaching the Minjiang watershed, there is the sacred **Mt Jadur** and the large Bonpo monastery of **Gamal Gonchen**, with over 400 monks and a nearby nunnery. Since it is beside the main road to **Dzitsa Degu National Park** (*Ch* Jiuzhaigou), this monastery receives many tour buses, although most visitors stay only a short while. Once over the pass, there are more Bonpo temples, including Lanping and Daju.

Dzitsa Degu National Park (Jiuzhaigou)

ACCESS At **Chukar**, 31 km before Nampel, the road reaches the entrance to the park and a ticket office is located at **Penpo** (Goukou) where the Fujiang river makes a hairpin bend.

Named after its nine largest settlements, this national park is one of the most beautiful areas of the Tibetan plateau. **Dzitsa Degu** is a Y-shaped forested ravine, 30 km long, within the Minshan range. Numerous mineral-tinted pools and lakes, connected by small waterfalls, line the valley bottom, while the forest extends to the snow peaks above. The total area of the park is 720 sq km, and its altitude is in the range 2,000-3,100m. In recent years, the park has been developed as the major tourist destination of northern Sichuan. Entrance to the park costs about US$10, including one night's accommodation, and for longer stays there are several small guesthouses at the junction of the two main valleys, where it is possible to hire horses for journeys in the hills.

Buses run inside the grounds of the park, several times a day from the entrance to the *Nurilang Guesthouse* near **Laga**, passing by the **Shukcho falls**. It takes about 3 hrs to walk this 14 km section. From the guesthouse, which is the focal point for most tourists, there are 2 buses/day running back and forth (SW) to **Ri-tse** (17 km), and on this stretch which is a former panda habitat, you can see the park's largest waterfall. An infrequent bus service also runs from the guesthouse to **Tsoring Lake** (18 km) in the SE. This is the park's largest lake, and on the way there is a stunningly beautiful five-coloured pool. The park is rich is flora including wild roses, clematis, honeysuckle, violet, wild ginger, and above all rhododendron.

● **Accommodation** Stay at the *Nuorilang Guesthouse*, where double rooms with attached bath are at ¥75, and there are three restaurants, or deeper within the park at the *Rhinoceros Lake Lodgings (Xiniu Hai Shishudian)*, the *Ri-tse Guesthouse*, or the Tibetan-run *Minzufeng Hostel*, all of these with minimal facilities but inexpensive. At the entrance to the park there is the *Yangdong Guesthouse*, run by the local Jiuzhaigou Travel Company, and outside the park on the Nampel road there is the plush *Jiuzhaigou Baihe Guesthouse (Baihe Luyou Zhen)*, where rooms with attached bath are at ¥90.

Tangjiahe National Park

Although notionally a panda park, most of the few remaining giant pandas are found further SW at the junction of Pingwu, Nampel, and Qingchuan counties, especially in the **Tangjiahe National Park**. This represents the westernmost penetration of Tibetan influence. But nowadays their tiny Tibetan populations are isolated in the mountain regions, greatly outnumbered by Chinese and Muslim settlements lower down.

● **Transport** From either Pingwu or Nampel, it is possible to reach the main rail-link to Chengdu by local bus.

MAOWEN QIANG AUTONOMOUS COUNTY

 མའོ་ཝུན་

茂汶羌族自治县 Maowen

Population: 102,868   Area: 4,373 sq km

Maowen is the county capital of the Qiang nationality, who are believed to be descendants of the Tibetan tribe that ranged widely across the extreme N and E of the plateau before and during the period of the Tibetan kings. The town is located in the Minjiang valley, 142 km S of Zungchu, and at the confluence of this river with the Tro-chu (*Ch* Heishui). It has an active market, although the *Qiang Handicrafts Shop* on the main street is disappointing.

This is the best place to observe the costumes of the Qiang women, who wear long brightly coloured (often blue) slit dresses, with blue or black trousers underneath, and intricately embroidered collars adorned with heavy amber jewellery. Most wear a black or white turban, or a decorative headscarf.

MAOWEN, TROCHU & LUNGU COUNTIES

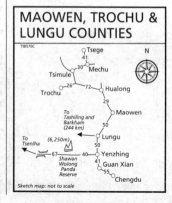

Sketch map: not to scale

The Qiang are renowned for their stone buildings and watchtowers, a culture which they share with the apparently related Qiangic peoples of E Tibet, such as those of Gyarong, and of Tawu and Minyak in Kham. Nowadays they are principally agriculturalists, with wheat and maize as their main crops, although many keep a few domestic animals stabled in large courtyards or the ground floor of their 3-storey stone and timber houses. A large number of these houses have been rebuilt in the last 15 years, and most window and door-frames are painted in bright colours with traditional designs.

Higher up, above the tree-line, on alpine meadows, yak, sheep and goats are pastured by mixed populations of Qiang and Tibetan nomads living in traditional black yak wool tents.

• **Accommodation** Stay at the _Renmin Guesthouse_, at the main crossroads, where double rooms with attached showers are ¥18/night.

TROCHU COUNTY
ཁྲོ་ཆུ

黑水县 Heishui

Population: 49,601   _Area:_ 2,952 sq km

At **Hualong**, 29 km N of Maowen town, where the Tro-chu (_Ch_ Heishui) River flows into the Minjiang, there is a road branching off the Maowen-Zungchu highway, which follows the Tro-chu upstream. To reach **Trochu** county, head W up this side-vallley, passing through Pichi, Serkyu, Gagu, and Shiwar Kazi. The county capital, also known as **Trochu**, is 94 km from the junction at Hualong, on a tributary of the Tro-chu. Many logs are floated downstream, continuing evidence of the massive deforestation which has halved the area's forest cover since 1950.

Muge-chu Valley

Some 26 km before reaching the county capital, the road forks: the W branch leading to the capital and the N branch continuing to climb N through the Tro-chu gorge to **Tsimule**. At Tsimule, two valleys converge: the Muge-chu valley (W) and the Tsagi-chu valley (E). Taking the former, the road (69 km) passes through Chunak, the Bonpo monastery of **Yungdrung Gon**, Muge and Norwa. **Muge Gonpa** in particular is an important Gelukpa institution, and was visited by Mao Tse Tung during the Long March.

Tsagi-chu Valley

The E branch runs N to **Mechu**, where a jeepable loop road heads SE through the Tungping valley to rejoin the Zungchu-Maowen highway at **Jiaochangba** (30 km). Further N of Mechu, the road through the Tsagi-chu valley continues for 41 km, via Natsi and Tsege. These valleys are characterized by small village temples, all recently rebuilt, and mostly of Bonpo origin. There are also a few very small Gelukpa temples, usually attended by a single caretaker or a handful of monks, and which only come to life during village festivals.

LUNGU COUNTY
སྤུང་དག
汶川县 Wenchuan
Population: 87,171   Area: 3,537 sq km

From Maowen the main road to Chengdu continues to follow the steep Minjiang gorge downstream. Although there are patches of forest left on the steeper slopes, most of the mountains were deforested long ago and now exhibit a rich and varied selection of shrubs and wild flowers. The road lies only a few hundred metres above the raging river, and in many places is prone to landslides, particularly in early summer. Precarious bamboo and pulley type suspension bridges span the chasm at intervals, and these are nonchalantly crossed by the locals.

Wenchuan

The county capital, Wenchuan, is located 50 km SW of Maowen at a point where the Troksung-chu flows in from the W. The attractive setting and colourful markets are memorable, but although undeniably a major town, Wenchuan is architecturally uninspiring.

● **Accommodation** Stay at the *Wenchuan County Government Guesthouse*, where there are beds at ¥15.

An important bridge crosses the Minjiang at Wenchuan, and a road leads W to **Tashiling** (Li Xian), **Nyaglo** and **Barkham** (244 km), following the Troksung-chu upstream (see above, page 627). Most villages in this area are situated on flatter ground high above the road, and a few possess the tall stone watchtowers characteristic of the regional Qiang culture.

Wolong Panda Reserve

The road from Wenchuan to Chengdu continues following the course of the Minjiang S for 50 km to **Yenzhing**, where the Pitiao River flows in from the Wolong Panda Reserve.

Wolong lies only 67 km to the E of the **Balang Shan** pass, on the main road from Tsenlha to Chengdu (see above, page 634).

Guan Xian

After Wolong, the road leaves Lungu (Wenchuan) county and in doing so it simultaneously leaves the Tibetan world for that of mainland China. The town of **Guan Xian**, 81 km from Wolong and 55 km NW of Chengdu, has an important irrigation system which has been in use since the Han Dynasty (256 BC). The then governor of Chengdu, Li Bing, con-structed a weir in the Minjiang River at **Dujiangyan** in order to split the river into two channels, diverting much of its flow through the irrigation network of the Chengdu Plain (6,500 sq km). This reduced the annual summer flooding of the valley, and, from that time on, Chengdu became a significant farming region. Models and inscriptions here commemorate Li Bing and his son. The nearby **Two Princes Temple (Erwangsi)** was built in their honour, and there is also a Taoist temple (**Fulongguan**) com-manding the weir. 15 km SE of Guan Xian is the Daoist holy mountain, **Qing-cheng Shan**. The 4 hrs ascent passes several temples and caves which once housed over 500 monks. It is possible to sleep at **Shangqing Gong Temple** and rise early to see dawn at the summit.

THE GIANT PANDAS OF WOLONG

This nature reserve (2,000 sq km) has acquired international renown as the principal breeding ground for the **Giant Panda**, an endangered species whose natural habitat in now confined to a few forested areas of Sichuan, Gansu and Shaanxi provinces. Established in 1983, the **Hetaoping** breeding station within the reserve monitors the greatest concentration of the panda population (overall less than 1,000), but their survival is constantly under threat due to rampant deforestation and the peculiarity of their diet. The arrow bamboo and umbrella bamboo on which they depend have a 50/60 year cycle, at the end of which many pandas die due to starvation.

Apart from the pandas, there are almost 100 species of animals, 230 species of birds, and 4,000 species of plants within the reserve; and the Wolong Museum of Natural History at **Shawan** (Wolong town) is well worth a visit. Here, the Wolong Nature Reserve Administration Office runs a bungalow-style lodge and restaurant. Single rooms with attached baths are ¥30; and doubles without bath ¥15. To reach Shawan from Balang Shan pass, the road follows the **Pitiao** River, a tributary of the Minjiang, downstream for 67 km. From Shawan to the E entrance of the reserve the distance is 40 km, and from there to Chengdu only 136 km. In the NW of the reserve near **Mt Siguniang** (6,250m) there are trekking and camping facilities. The local population is a mix of Tibetan and Qiang.

KATHMANDU VALLEY

CONTENTS

MAPS

INTRODUCTION

The Kathmandu Valley is the cultural and political heart of Nepal. After a long period of isolation throughout the 19th and early 20th centuries (which followed Nepal's unification in the late 17th century), Kathmandu has rapidly become an international centre for tourism. The first surfaced road to reach Kathmandu, that from Raxaul Bazar, was only completed in 1956. Now it also has direct road connections with Uttar Pradesh, Bihar and West Bengal in India, Lhasa in Tibet and Pokhara to its W. Thus, in recent years Kathmandu has become one of the important gateway cities for travel to and from Tibet (along with Chengdu, Lanzhou, Kunming, and Kashgar). Apart from the Kathmandu-Lhasa air route (Tues/Sat), there are two main land routes – via the Arniko Highway (Kathmandu-Dhulikhel-Lamosangu-Barabise-Ta topani-Kodari) and via West Nepal (Kathmandu-Nepalganj- Simikot-Til-Khojarnath). **NB** Each of the three historic towns of the Kathmandu Valley will be described in turn, beginning with Kathmandu, and then continuing with Patan (Lalitpur) and Badgaon (Bhaktapur).

Early history

Kathmandu was founded in 723 AD by the Licchavi king Gunakamadeva at the confluence of the Bagmati and Vishnumati rivers. The hub of the city is the oldest building, the Kasthamandap, which stood at the crossroads of two important trade routes. The name Kathmandu is itself derived from this temple. Later, following Jayasthiti Malla's 14th century unification of the three medieval Newar towns (Kathmandu, Patan and Badgaon or Bhaktapur) which occupy the Valley, Kathmandu became an

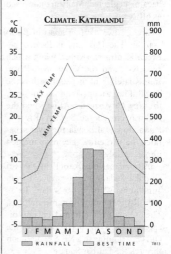

CLIMATE: KATHMANDU

°C / mm — MAX TEMP / MIN TEMP

J F M A M J J A S O N D

RAINFALL / BEST TIME

TIB13

important administrative centre, but the medieval character of the three towns was well preserved. Then, in the late 17th century, consequent on the Gorkha unification of the kingdom of Nepal by King Prithivi Narayan Shah, it naturally became the capital of the newly formed country. This sparked off a long period of expansion.

European influences

In the 19th century the ruling Rana family travelled frequently overseas, as a result of which new European building styles were introduced. The palaces that Jung Bahadur built from 1850 onwards were European in concept and contrasted sharply with the indigenous Newari style. Singha Durbar, a palace with 17 courtyards and over 1,500 rooms, was built within a year (1901). Reputed to have been the largest contemporary building in Asia, it was severely damaged by fire in 1974. Other palaces were built at Patan and Kathmandu but with the eclipse of the Rana family's power in 1951, and the strengthening of the monarchy these became neglected. Many are now used as offices.

There are two distinct areas of Kathmandu. The Old City is located between Kantipath (King's Way), which runs N-S, and the Vishnumati River. Immediately E of the Kantipath is the Tundhikhel, a long parade ground, with the New City beyond. At its S end the highway crosses the Bagmati River to Patan. Today, although the river separates the two cities they have merged imperceptibly.

After the earthquake of 1934, New Rd (Juddha Sadak) was constructed from Tundhikhel W to Durbar Square. Today New Rd is the city's commercial axis. The old trade route from Tibet cuts diagonally across the northern half of the Old City running in a NE-SW direction through the Durbar Square.

KATHMANDU

Pop 727,794; _Area_ 453 sq km; _Alt_ 1,370m.
The description of the Old City of Kathmandu starts at the Kasthamandap, in the SW corner of Durbar Square, and moves NE, broadly following the line of the old Tibet trade road. Some travellers find the increased pollution in the city uncomfortable – some use masks, wear long trousers and avoid sandals.

The figures in brackets refer to the numbers on the map.

Places of interest

Durbar Square and Basantapur Square

This is the spiritual heart of Kathmandu and once the crossroads of important trading routes. The old royal palace was at the centre of the city and surrounded by temples and other important buildings. There are more than 50 monuments in the area; the oldest dates back eight centuries. Many of the old buildings were rebuilt after the 1934 earthquake, not always to the original design. Visit it early in the morning to see men start work and Hindu women arrive at temples to make their offerings of flowers to the gods.

The Durbar Square area in fact comprises three large open areas or squares. In the SW corner is one of Kathmandu's most famous buildings, the **Kasthamandap** (wooden pavillion), which straddles the crossroads of the ancient trade routes, and is one of the grandest temples in Kathmandu. This is the real central point around which the city developed. Widely believed to have been built in 1596 by the king Laksmina Narasimha Malla from the wood of one enormous sal (_shorea robusta_) tree, it is now known to be much earlier, as references to the temple have been found in a manuscript dating from the 12th century. It was originally a resthouse or community centre and so has an open ground floor. Later it was made more ornate and converted into a temple dedicated to Gorakhnath, whose shrine is in the centre of a small enclosure. The Malla kings greatly embellished it. Nowadays, bronze lions guard the entrance, the Hindu epics are portrayed along the cornices of the first floor, and at the four corners there are images of Ganesh. People gather to recite devotional songs although the early morning is the time of greatest activity.

Behind the Kasthamandap on the N side of the square is the **Ashok Vinayaka** (or Maru Ganesh Temple), dedicated to Ganesh (Vinayaka/Ganapati). As the god of good fortune, Ganesh is propitiated by intending travellers at this small but important golden temple, which has a constant stream of worshippers. The gilded roof is a 19th century addition, and the main part of the building is much older.

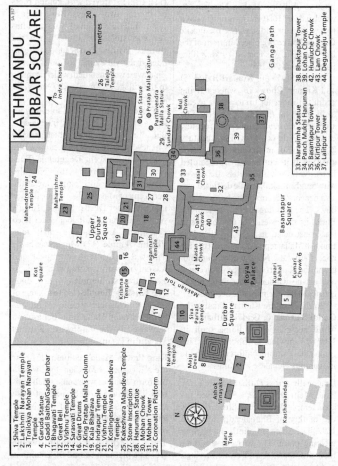

KATHMANDU DURBAR SQUARE

1. Shiva Temple
2. Lakshmi Narayan Temple
3. Trailokya Mohan Narayan Temple
4. Garuda Statue
7. Gaddi Baithal/Gaddi Darbar
8. Bhagavati Temple
12. Great Bell
13. Vishnu Temple
14. Sarasvati Temple
16. Great Drums
17. King Pratap Malla's Column
19. Kala Bhairava
20. Indrapur Temple
21. Vishnu Temple
22. Kotlingeshvara Mahadeva Temple
25. Kakeshvara Mahadeva Temple
27. Stone Inscription
28. Hanuman Statue
30. Mohan Chowk
31. Mohan Tower
32. Coronation Platform

23. Mahavishnu Temple
24. Mahendreshwar Temple
26. Taleju Temple
29. Sundari Chowk

33. Narasimha Statue
34. Panch Mukhi Hanuman
35. Basantapur Tower
36. Kirtipur Tower
37. Lalitpur Tower
38. Bhaktapur Tower
39. Lohan Chowk
42. Hunluche Chowk
43. Lam Chowk
44. Degutaleju Temple

The road to your left as you face the Ashok Vinayaka is Maru Tole which leads to the Vishnumati River and the Svayambhunath temple. The **Shiva Temple** (1) to your right beyond Kasthamandap and Ashok Vinayaka has a nine-step plinth and three roofs. Barbers work on the steps.

Towards Basantapur Square, on your right, is the **Lakshmi Narayan Temple** (2); and to its W side, a small 5-tiered temple dedicated to **Trailokya Mohan Narayan** (3), which is dated 1680, and has a finely carved roof with struts and screens. An exquisite **Garuda Statue** (4), placed in front of the latter temple, was erected by king Bhupalendra Malla in 1689.

To the SE is the **Kumari Bahal** (5) and **Kumari Chowk** (6), where a living goddess resides for up to a dozen years until reaching the age of puberty. The stucco façade has a number of intricately carved windows. This 18th century building and monastic courtyard is guarded at its entrance by two painted lions. Note how the lintels are carved with laughing skulls while deities, doves and peacocks decorate the balcony windows. The building is in the style of the Buddhist monasteries of the valley, and was constructed in 1757 by king Jaya Prakash Malla, reputedly as an act of penance. *Entry Re 1.* **NB** You may not photograph the Kumari who appears on cue at one of the windows. The walls of the courtyard have remarkable decoration.

To the N of the Kumari Bahal is the **Gaddi Baithak**, or **Gaddi Darbar** (7), a white neo-classical building built in 1908 by King Chandra Shumshere. This Rana palace sits uncomfortably with the indigenous Nepalese buildings.

Diagonally across Durbar Square is the large **Maju Deval** (8), a 3-storeyed pagoda temple dedicated to Shiva, built by the mother of Bhupalendra Malla in 1692. The nine-step plinth is a popular meeting place. The eaves of the three roofs are adorned with erotic carvings.

Behind Maju Deval is a small **Narayan Temple** (9) with the **Siva Parvati Temple** (10) to the right. Note the centre window of the upper balcony with its carved and painted deities. The platform of this 18th century temple may have been an older dancing stage.

Makhan Tole

At the SW end of Makhan Tole is the early 18th century **Bhagavati Temple** (11), triple storeyed with golden roofs on the top two storeys. Built by Jaya Jagat Malla, its original Narayana image was stolen in 1766. When the Gorkha Prithivi Narayan Shah conquered the valley in 1767 an image of Bhagavati was installed, which is taken to the village of Nuwakot, 57 km N, for an annual festival.

Proceeding up Makhan Tole, on your left is the **Great Bell** (12), installed by Bahadur Shah in 1797 which is rung whenever offering ceremonies (*puja*) are held at the adjacent **Degutaleju Temple**. The **Great Drums** (16) which also mark worship at this temple, are at the north end of Makhan Tole where it leads into the upper Durbar Square. Twice a year a goat and a buffalo are sacrificed near them. Adjacent is a small stone **Vishnu Temple** (13) which was badly damaged in the 1934 earthquake and was only recently restored with the damaged **Sarasvati Temple** (14) next door. The **Krishna Temple** (15; 1648), one of the few octagonal temples here, was built by Pratap Malla, some believe as a response to the impressive Krishna Mandir in Patan.

King Pratap Malla's column (17) near the NE corner of Makhan Tole, is on a platform it shares with some small temples. The king who built many of these structures, is accompanied by his two wives and sons, and faces his prayer room on the third floor of Degutaleju Temple. The 17th century **Jagannath Temple** (18) on a platform behind the column is the oldest structure in this group and is noted for its erotic carvings at head level. Only the central gate is used.

Behind the column, and forming the S side of the upper square, is **Kala Bhairava** (19), a fearsome image of Shiva the Destroyer, carved out of a single stone. The six-armed, black deity wears a crown and has a garland of skulls. He carries a sword, a severed head, hatchet, shield and a skull (which has become a bowl for devotees' offerings), and he is stamping on a corpse. The image was brought to its present location by Pratap Malla in the second half of the 17th century after being found in a field to the N of the city. A lie told before the image is believed to result in instant death. In the past, those suspected of crimes were brought here and forced to touch the feet of the image, stating their innocence.

The **Indrapur Temple** (20) next to it has a Shiva lingam inside but a Garuda image to the S, suggesting that it may have once been a Vishnu temple. The adjacent **Vishnu Temple** (21) is thought to have existed in Pratap Malla's reign (1641-74).

The **Kotlingeshvara Mahadeva Temple** (22) dedicated to Shiva and with a Nandi bull, differs from the surrounding temples. It is a cube with a bulbous dome in the 16th century Gumbhaj style, similar to early Muslim tombs in India.

The **Mahavishnu Temple** (23) nearby was built by Jaya Jagat Malla in the early 18th century and was also affected by the 1934 earthquake. Another Shiva temple, it has a shikhara (spire) topped by a golden umbrella (a royal insignia).

Upper Durbar Square

Just off the NW corner of Durbar Square is the Kot Square. In 1846 Jung Bahadur Rana, the founder of the Rana Dynasty, murdered all his potential opponents from the local nobility before seizing power. As if commemorating that event, during Durga Puja each year, at this spot, young soldiers attempt to cut off a buffalo head with a single stroke of their kukri. The 16th century **Mahendreshvara Temple** (24) dedicated to Shiva stands just beyond Kot Square and Durbar Square.

The Taleju Temple

To the E of Upper Durbar Square is the **Kakeshvara Mahadeva Temple** (25), dedicated to Shiva, with the magnificent **Taleju Temple** (26) behind, in Trishul Chowk (a courtyard named after Shiva's trident which is stationed at its entrance). Taleju Temple is closed to the public except during the Durga Puja festival, when Hindus may enter. Thus it is open only once a year during the autumn festival of Dasain. The tallest of all the temples on the Hanuman Dhoka site, this Taleju Temple was built in 1564 by King Mahendra Malla and only the royal family and important priests are allowed regular access. Taleju was a patron goddess of the Malla kings who reputedly played cards with the king of Kathmandu, Jayaprakash Malla, within the Hanuman Dhoka complex. The rulers of Bhaktapur and Patan followed suit and established their own Taleju temples alongside their palaces. It has ornately carved beams and brackets and superb window decoration. The extensive use of gilt makes it an even more attractive sight at sunset. It stands 36m high on a 12-stage plinth, soaring above the Hanuman Dhoka complex. 12 miniature temples outside the walls are built on the eighth stage. The temples at the four corners are built in pagoda (mandapa) style.

Hanuman Dhoka Palace

The Royal Palace takes its name from the **Hanuman Statue** (28) at its entrance, which was installed by Pratap Malla in 1672. The monkey god is wrapped in a red cloak, his face smeared

THE 'LIVING GODDESS'

Hindus worship the **Kumari** as the reincarnation of Shiva's consort **Parvati**, Buddhists as **Tara**. The cult was instituted just over 200 years ago by *Jaya Prakash Malla*. All Kumaris are drawn from the Newar Shakya clan of gold and silversmiths and are initiated into the role at the age of 4 or 5. They must meet 32 requirements, including being at least 2 years old, walking, a virgin, in immaculate health, and having an unblemished skin, black or blue eyes, black hair with curls turning to the right, a flawless and robust body, soft and firm hands, eye lashes 'like those of a cow', slender arms, brilliant white teeth and the 'voice of a sparrow'.

Initiation The final examination is a test of nerve. Each suitable candidate is led to the **Taleju temple** at Kalratri in the dead of night and must remain calm and fearless as she walks amidst severed buffalo and goat heads. She confirms her divine right by identifying the clothes of her predecessor from a large assortment of similar articles. The installation ceremony is private. Astrologers then match her horoscope with the king's and she is ensconced in the *bahal*. The royal family consult her before important festive occasions. The bahal is her home until she menstruates or loses her perfection through haemorrhage from a wound or from losing a tooth. To maintain her purity, she is only allowed to leave the *bahal* for religious ceremonies when she is carried through the street in a palanquin or walks on cloth. Her feet must not touch the ground as this would be polluting. Whenever she appears she is dressed in red and has a 'third eye' painted on her forehead. When her reign ends, she leaves the temple with a handsome dowry, is free to marry and live a normal life. Nowadays she is taught to read and write to prepare her for the future.

with red vermilion powder and mustard oil, and has a golden umbrella above. Hanuman, a hero of the Hindu epic *Ramayana*, is worshipped to bring success in war. Nearby, outside the palace wall, is a **Stone Inscription** (27) in 15 languages including French and English, in praise of the goddess Kalika. It was carved on 14 January 1664 during the reign of Pratap Malla, a talented poet and linguist.

The site apparently dates back to the late Licchavi era. Mahendra Malla started the present buildings in the 16th century, and during the 17th century king Pratap Malla added many temples. The S wing was added by Prithivi Narayan Shah in 1771, and the SW wing by King Prithivi Bikram Shah in 1908. Open 1030-1600. Rs 10.

The 'Golden Gate' of the palace is brightly painted in green, blue and gold and it is flanked by two stone lions, one carrying Shiva, the other his consort Parvati. In the niche above the gate is Krishna in his ferocious tantric aspect, flanked by the more gentle, amorous Krishna surrounded by the gopi (cow-girls), and by King Pratap Malla (believed to be an incarnation of Vishnu) and his queen.

In the W wing of Hanuman Dhoka is the **Tribhuvan Museum** dedicated to the king who led a revolt against the Ranas who had built it. The king's bedroom and study have been recreated. See also under **Museums**.

Nasal Chowk

The Golden Gate (Suvarnadvara) leads to Nasal Chowk, the largest of the 10 palace courtyards, where coronations take place. This, along with the **Sundari Chowk** (29), the **Mohan Chowk** (30) and the **Mohan Tower** (31), was originally built by king Pratap Malla in the 17th century. The decorated golden waterspout named Sundhara was built by Pratap Malla, who brought cool clear water from Buddhanilakantha, 9 km N, and bathed, 3.5m below ground level.

The present king Birendra was crowned on the **Coronation Platform** (32) in the centre. Nasal Chowk (meaning Courtyard of the Dancing One) is named after the small figure of Dancing Shiva on the E side of the courtyard. To the left of the entrance is a silver-inlaid stone **Narasimha Statue** (33; 1673), depicting Vishnu in his man-lion incarnation, killing the demon Hiranyakashipu. The open verandah houses the throne and portraits of the Shah kings.

In the NE corner of the complex is the **Panch Mukhi Hanuman** (34), a round 5-storeyed building which only temple priests may enter for worship.

You can climb to the top of the later **Basantapur Tower** (35; 18th century) or Kathmandu Tower, that overlooks the square. It is the 9-storey palace in the SW corner of Nasal Chowk, with beautiful wooden windows and fine carvings on the roof struts. Prithivi Narayan Shah renovated many of the earlier buildings and from 1768 onwards extended the palace to the E. He introduced the fortified tower to Durbar Square, adding the smaller towers which are named after the ancient cities of **Kirtipur** (36) to the NW with its superb copper roof, **Lalitpur** (37) to the SE and **Bhaktapur** (38) to the NE. It once overlooked beautiful gardens with a clear view of the Taleju Temple, all set round the **Lohan Chowk** (39).

The area W of Nasal Chowk was built in the latter half of the 19th century. This includes the **Dahk Chowk** (40), **Masan Chowk** (41), **Hnuluche Chowk** (42) and **Lam Chowk** (43). The **Degutaleju Temple** (44) dedicated to the Mallas' personal goddess was erected by Shiva Singh Malla (r 1578-1620).

Running S from Basantapur Chowk, is Jochen (Freak St) where cheap hotels, restaurants, and hashish shops made it a centre for hippies in the 1960s. The dope peddlars are still active. It is now just a tourist attraction. Thamel and Chetrapati have taken over as the centres for backpackers.

Northeast from Durbar Square

Returning to the NE corner of Durbar Square from Makhan Tole, you can walk to Indra Chowk, Asan Tole and Rani Pokhari Tank. This thoroughfare is the old artery of the city. On your left in the corner of the Square is a Garuda Statue. **Makhan Tole** was the start of the trade route to Tibet and is lined with interesting temples and shops. After the earthquake, New Rd diverted much of its traffic. There are medieval houses with colourful façades, overhanging carved wooden balconies and carved windows. Many of the shops sell tangkas, clothes and paintings.

Indra Chowk, the first crossroads, is at the intersection of Makhan Tole and Shukra Path. The SW corner has a small brass Ganesh shrine. The **Akash Bhairava** Temple to the W has a silver image of the rain god which is displayed outside for a week during Indra Jatra festival. Non-Hindus are not allowed in. The square was a textile market and many shops still specialize in blankets, shawls and cloth. In the NE corner is a **Shiva Temple** as the street runs towards Khel Tole, another market square with Tibetan carpet shops.

Off to the W past a small shrine, smeared with fresh blood, almost halfway between Indra Chowk and Asan is the **Sveta Matsyendranath Temple**, one of the most venerated Buddhist shrines in Kathmandu (equally popular with Hindus). It has a 2-tier bronze roof and two brass lions guard the entrance. The courtyard is filled with small shrines, carved pillars and statues. The image inside the elaborately carved

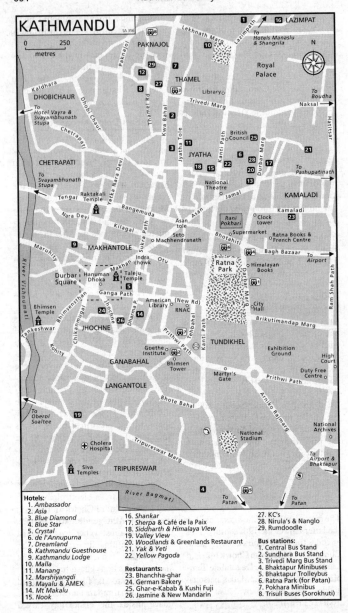

KATHMANDU

SA 356

0   250
metres

PAKNAJOL

Lekhnath Marg

LAZIMPAT

To
Hotels Manaslu
& Shangrila

Royal
Palace

DHOBICHAUR

THAMEL

Thamel Rd

Kwa Bahal

Trivedi Marg

Library

To
Boudha

Naksal

To Hotel Vayra &
Svayambhunath Stupa

Kaldhara

Dhobi Chaur

Chetrapati

Paknajol

Yetka Nara Devi

Jyatha Tole

Kanti Path

British
Council

Durbar Marg

Hattisar

CHETRAPATI

JYATHA

To Pashupatinath

KAMALADI

To
Svayambhunath
Stupa

Tengal

Nara Devi

Raktakali
Temple

Bangemuda

Kilagal

Sukra Path

National
Theatre

Jamal

Asan
tole

Asan

Rani
Pokhari

Clock
tower

Kamaladi

Maruhity

MAKHANTOLE

Seto
Machhendranath

Bhotahiti

Supermarket

Ratna Books &
French Centre

Indra
chowk

Otu

Ratna
Park

Himalayan
Books

Bagh Bazaar

To
Airport

River Vishnumati

Durbar
Square

Hanuman
Dhoka

Taleju
Temple

Ganga Path

Makhan

Dharma P.

American (New Rd)
Library

RNAC

Kanti Path

Durbar Marg

City
Hall

Bhimsen
Temple

Bhimsenthan

Chikanmugal

Jhochne

Prithwi Path

Tehbahal

Brikutimandap Marg

Ram Shah Path

Tankeshwar

Kohity

JHOCHNE

Dharma P.

Goethe
Institute

Bhimsen
Tower

TUNDIKHEL

Exhibition
Ground

High
Court

GANABAHAL

Martyr's
Gate

Prithwi Path

Duty Free
Centre

LANGANTOLE

Bhote Bahal

Arniko Rajmarg

To
Oberoi
Soaltee

Cholera
Hospital

Tripureswar Marg

National
Stadium

National
Archives

To
Airport &
Bhaktapur

Siva
Temples

TRIPURESWAR

To Patan

River Bagmati

To Patan

Hotels:
1. *Ambassador*
2. *Asia*
3. *Blue Diamond*
4. *Blue Star*
5. *Crystal*
6. *de l'Annupurna*
7. *Dreamland*
8. *Kathmandu Guesthouse*
9. *Kathmandu Lodge*
10. *Malla*
11. *Manang*
12. *Marshiyangdi*
13. *Mayalu & AMEX*
14. *Mt Makalu*
15. *Nook*

16. *Shankar*
17. *Sherpa & Café de la Paix*
18. *Siddharth & Himalaya View*
19. *Valley View*
20. *Woodlands & Greenlands Restaurant*
21. *Yak & Yeti*
22. *Yellow Pagoda*

Restaurants:
23. *Bhancha-ghar*
24. *German Bakery*
25. *Ghar-e-Kabab & Kushi Fuji*
26. *Jasmine & New Mandarin*

27. *KC's*
28. *Nirula's & Nanglo*
29. *Rumdoodle*

Bus stations:
1. Central Bus Stand
2. Sundhara Bus Stand
3. Trivedi Marg Bus Stand
4. Bhaktapur Minibuses
5. Bhaktapur Trolleybus
6. Ratna Park (for Patan)
7. Pokhara Minibus
8. Trisuli Buses (Sorokhuti)

shrine is Padmapani Avalokiteshvara in the form of the compassionate and benevolent divinity Matsyendra (*Tib* Phakpa Jamali; see above, page 82). There are 108 paintings of Avalokiteshvara throughout the temple. A colourful procession of the main image around town takes place during the Rath Yatra or chariot festival in Mar/April. The Hindu temple next door on the left is the **Lunchun Lumbun Ajima**, a *shakti* temple with erotic carvings.

Leave Khel Tole and continue walking NE until you reach the next square which is **Asan Tole**. Three temples to Annapurna, Ganesh and Narayan line the square which is regarded as the commercial heart of the Old City with the rice market and bicycle and rickshaw repair shops. You then reach Kantipath and the **Rani Pokhari** tank (1667) built by Pratap Malla's wife in memory of her son. The area is locked except on Diwali, the Festival of Lights (Oct-Nov).

Chetrapati and Thamel

Heading W from Asan Tole, you will reach the crossroads of Bangemudha on Shukra Path. Continue S to return to Indra Chowk or N to reach the tourist heartland of the Old City. If you head N, you will pass on the left a recessed square containing the large **Kathesimbhu Stupa**, and soon reach the **Thahiti Square**, where the traffic moves around yet another stupa. From here, you can turn E along Jatha Rd to Kantipath, passing on the right the entrance to the **Chusya Bahal**. Alternatively, proceeding N from the stupa, you will enter the Thamel area, which is the focal point of the city for tourists. Or, heading W, you will reach the frenetic intersection of Chetrapati where traffic converges from six roads. In **Thamel** there are numerous budget hotels and exotic restaurants featuring sundry cuisines from the four quarters of the earth. The intersection of Thamel Chowk may be reached from

Thahiti Stupa in the S via Kwa Bahal Rd or from Trivedi Marg and the Royal Palace to the E. Two parallel N-S running roads are particularly geared to the tourist industry: Kwa Bahal Rd to the E and Thamel Rd to the W. The former has more shops, selling Nepalese, Tibetan and Bhutanese handicrafts and second-hand trekking equipment, while the latter has many hotels, guesthouses, and restaurants. At the lower end (actually on Chetrapati Rd) is the *Potala Guest House*. The well-known *Kathmandu Guesthouse* lies just NW of the junction of N Thamel Rd, S Thamel Rd, and E Thamel Rd. Heading S or N from this crossroads, you will be mesmerized by the density of the facilities available for the budget tourist – far removed from the ancient culture of the surrounding city. By contrast, at **Bhagavan Bahal** in NE Thamel, there are three active Newar Buddhist shrines which are particularly colourful during Dasain.

If you head W from Thahiti Stupa or from the *Potala Guest House* into **Chetrapati**, there are many more low priced hotels and guesthouses, interspersed with authentic street life. Chetrapati is also interesting as the neighbourhood of brass bandsmen who are in demand during local festivals and Nepalese weddings, especially in Feb. Heading S from the Chetrapati intersection onto Pyaphal Rd, you will eventually reach the Kasthamandap at the SW end of Durbar Square.

Svayambhunath

From Chetrapati or Nardevi you can head W to the banks of the Vishnumati River and to one of the most sacred sites of the Kathmandu Valley on its far bank. The **Svayambhunath Stupa** (*Tib* Phakpa Shangku) is revered as the oldest and one of the two most important sites of Buddhist worship in Kathmandu. It is a major landmark, towering above Padmachala Hill, 175m above the valley and 3 km W of Kathmandu. The

Svayambhunath Stupa, Kathmandu

stupa occupies a site where the Buddha of the previous aeon Vipashyin is said to have thrown a lotus seed into the lake which then filled the valley, causing it to bloom and radiate with a 'self-arising' (*svayambhu*) luminosity, identified with that of the primordial buddha, Vajradhara. The bodhisattva Manjushri is believed to have made this lotus light accessible to worshippers and pilgrims by using his sword to cleave a watercourse for the rivers of the valley, thereby draining the lake. Newar Buddhists hold that the primordial buddha Vajradhara is even now embodied in the timber axis of the stupa.

The earliest historical associations of the site are linked to Vrishadeva, the patriarch of the Licchavi Dynasty, who is said to have built the first shrine, perhaps using a pre-existing projecting stone. Later inscriptions attribute the stupa's construction to his great-grandson King Manadeva I (c 450 AD) and its reconstruction to the Indian master Shantikara, a contemporary of King Amshuvarman. It became a focal point for Indian pilgrims and was frequented by Padmasambhava, Atisha and others. By 1234 it had become an important centre of Buddhist learning, with close ties to Tibet. In 1349 Muslim troops from Bengal ravaged the shrine but it was soon rebuilt with its now familiar tall spire. In 1614 additions and renovations were made by Zhamarpa VI during the reign of Pratap Malla. Access from Kathmandu was improved with the construction of a long stairway and a bridge across the Vishnumati River. Pratap Malla also added two new temple spires and a large vajra placed in front of the stupa. Later repairs were carried out by Katok Tsewang Norbu (1750), Pawo Rinpoche VII (1758), and the Shah kings (1825 and 1983).

The Eastern Stairway The climb up the 400 stone steps is more impressive than the modern road. At the bottom are three painted images symbolizing the Three Precious Jewels of Buddhism, which were erected in 1637 by Pratap Malla and his father. A large footprint in the stone, is said to be either the Buddha's or Manjushri's. At regular intervals are pairs of eagles, lions, horses and peacocks, the vehicles of the peaceful meditational buddhas. **NB** The monkeys can be aggressive: treat with caution.

On entering the compound from the main stairway you see the **Great Vajra** set upon its drum base, symbolizing male skilful means, and the **Bell** alongside, symbolizing female discernment. Around the pedestal are the 12 animals from the Tibetan calendar (hare, dragon, snake, horse, sheep, monkey, bird, dog, pig, mouse, ox, and tiger).

The **stupa** (20m diameter, 10m high) has been a model for subsequent stupas constructed in Nepal. The various tiers of its base and dome respectively symbolize the elements: earth, water, fire, air, and space. Above the dome is the square *harmika*, each side of which has the eyes of the Buddha, gazing compassionately from beneath heavy black eyebrows, fringed by a curtain of blue, green, gold and red material. The 13 steps of the spire surmounting the *harmika* represent the successive bodhisattva and buddha levels, and the crowning canopy represents the goal of buddhahood. On each of the four sides of the stupa, at the cardinal points, there a niche containing a shrine dedicated to one of the meditational buddhas, each with its distinct posture and gesture, deeply recessed and barely visible within a richly decorated gilded copper repoussé. Aksobhya is in the E, Ratnasambhava in the S, Amitabha in the W, and Amoghasiddhi in the N. Vairocana, the deity in the centre, is actually depicted on the E side, along with Aksobhya. The female counterparts of these buddhas are located within the niches of the intermediate directions. The faithful turn the prayer wheels as they walk clockwise round the shrine.

The Vajra at the top of the stairs is flanked by the two white *shikhara* temples, known as Anantapur (SE) and Pratapur (NE), which were built by King Pratap Malla in 1646 to house the protector deities Bhairava and Bhairavi. Circumambulating the stupa clockwise, on the S side, you will pass Newar shrines dedicated to Vasudhara and the nagas (rebuilt in 1983). On the W side, after the rear entrance, there is a museum, a Bhutanese temple of the Drukpa Kagyu school, and Newar temples dedicated to Manjushri and Ajima Hariti. Lastly, on the N side, is a Newar temple dedicated to Cakrasamvara, and a Karma Kagyu temple of the Zhamar school, built in the 1960s by Sabchu Rinpoche. An International Buddhist Library and Pilgrim Guesthouse are located on a side pathway. On a neighbouring hill is another stupa dedicated to Sarasvati, the goddess of discriminative awareness and learning.

GETTING THERE Svayambhu is a comfortable 1 hr walking distance from Durbar Square, along Maru Tole to the river which you cross by a footbridge. There are cremation ghats on the riverbank. The path then leads through a built-up area with a sizeable Tibetan carpet-weaving community, to a meadow. Or take a taxi or rickshaw to the S entrance at the bottom of the hill.

NB If you hire a cycle it is worth paying Rs 1-2 to have it 'minded' by one of the small boys hanging around: this avoids tyres being let down.

New Road, Tripureshwar, and Singha Durbar

The area of S Kathmandu, extending from Jochen (Freak St) towards the Vishnumati and Bagmati rivers is predominantly an untouristed area, where Hindu traditions thrive. There are temples dedicated to Bhimasena, one of the five Pandava brothers whose epic tales are recounted in the *Mahabharata*; the Jaisi Dewal (dedicated to Shiva), and Panchali Bhairava near the ghats of the Bagmati River.

New Road, extending SE from Durbar Square, was constructed in the aftermath of the 1930s earthquake, and is now the city's main commerical thoroughfare. Here, there are supermarkets, textile and clothing stores, jewellers, the **Nepal Bank**, and **Royal Nepal Airlines** on its intersection with Kantipath. If you head N along Kantipath from the intersection you will pass the **Bir Hospital** on the left and **Ratna Park** on the right. If you turn S, you will pass the **GPO**, Bhimsen Tower, Sundhara bathing area, and the **Central Telegraph Office** to the right, with Martyr's Gate and the **National Stadium** on the left. Beyond Martyr's Gate, at the S end of the Ratna Park/Tundikhel parade ground, there is a large military camp, the Singha Durbar Government buildings, the Supreme Court, and the **Archaeology Department** (which must issue certificates before antiques or apparent antiques can be exported).

On the right side of the Bagmati River, lies the **Tripureshvara Temple**. Built in 1818 by Queen Lalitatripurasundari Devi Shah, this is a 3-storey temple in pagoda style, surrounded on four sides by small temples dedicated to Vishnu, Surya, Ganesh and Devi. In the centre of the main temple is a shapeless Shiva lingam without any facial features, which can be circumambulated.

Durbar Marg, Kamaladi, and Bagh Bazaar

Durbar Marg runs parallel to Kantipath, extending from the Royal Palace southwards, as far as the Army Camp at the SE corner of Tundikhel Parade Ground. At its upper end, the road forms a T-junction at the palace gates, with W Trivedi Marg (heading W towards the Immigration Office and Thamel) and E Trivedi Marg (heading towards Nag Pokhari and Boudha). Proceeding southwards on Durbar Marg you will pass the *Yak and Yeti Hotel* on the E and the *Annapurna Hotel* on the right. Jamal Rd cuts SW towards Rani Pokhari tank, while Kamaladi and Bagh Bazaar cut E towards Naksal and Maitidevi districts respectively. In this area there are a number of upmarket hotels and expensive restaurants, including the *Bhancchagar Nepalese Restaurant* on Kamaladi, various airline offices, and travel agencies such as *Adventure Travel*.

Buddhanilakantha

(*Tib* Lu Gang-gyel) Heading NW from the Royal Palace along Lazimpath Rd, you will pass through the diplomatic enclave of Kathmandu. Turn left at the *Hotel Ambassador* to reach the British and Indian Embassies, or right on Lazimpath to reach the US Embassy. Continuing along the latter road, you will eventually reach **Buddhanilkantha**, 9 km N of Kathmandu, which is one of the valley's most photographed sights.

Revered as an emanation of Avalokiteshvara by Newar Buddhists and as Narayana, an incarnation of Vishnu lying on a bed of naga-spirits or snakes by Hindus, this remarkable supine image is the largest stone sculpture of the Kathmandu valley and one of three fashioned by King Vishnugupta in the 7th century. It draws large crowds at **Haribodhini Ekadasi** and **Kartik Purnima**. The 5m monolithic statue is in a small tank at the foot of the Shivapuri Hills and is thought to have come from beyond the valley. In his four hands the deity holds the four attributes: a discus (symbol of the mind), mace (primeval knowledge), conch (the five elements) and lotus seed (universe). Pilgrims descend to the tank by a stone causeway. A priest washes the god's face each morning at around 0900. *Jayasthiti Malla* revived the Vishnu cult at the end of the 14th century pronouncing himself to be an incarnation of Vishnu, a belief held by successive rulers down to the present day. Now, there is a Vishnu shrine in front of each former royal palace in the valley. Since the time of King Pratap Malla (17th century), who dreamt that his successors would die if they were to visit the image, no king of Nepal has ventured into its presence. According to legend, Vishnu sleeps for 4 months of the year and the festival of Budhanilkantha (Nov) celebrates the deity waking from his monsoon slumber.

GETTING THERE Buses run from near the National Theatre to Bansbari. From here it is about an hour's walk. Alternatively, you can walk from Kathmandu or cycle. Further N, the road heads from Buddhanilakantha into the Shivapuri Hills.

Balaju Park

If you head NW from Thamel, passing through Naya Bazaar, you will cross the Vishnumati River and the Ring Rd to reach Balaju. Thus, **Balaju Park** is within walking distance of the city. Alternatively, you can take a taxi, rickshaw or bicycle. The water garden, which is a famous picnic spot, has a series of 22 18th century water spouts carved with crocodile heads and some fish ponds. The modern Olympic size swimming pool is open to the public. By the tank is a typical Nepalese temple flanked by a row of images of Hindu deities including one of the three supine Narayana images attributed to King Vishnugupta (7th century). At 3m in length, it is smaller than the aforementioned Buddhanilakantha image.

Nagarjuna Hill

(*Tib* Langru Lungten) Overlooking Balaju 5 km NW of Kathmandu is **Nagarjuna Hill** (2,188m). It offers a view of the entire valley and a partial vista of the Himalayas, which are somewhat obscured by the Shivapuri range. There is a Buddhist shrine and look-out tower at the summit. The whole hill is covered with thick jungle which is a refuge for deer, pheasant, leopard and wild pigs. Woodcutting is prohibited and penalties strictly enforced. The hill is revered in the Tibetan tradition as the site where the Buddha delivered the *Prophetic Declaration of Goshringa*, although other sources locate this peak in Khotan.

GETTING THERE You can drive to the summit via a dirt road, or go to Balaju (by bicycle or bus from Rani Pokhari) and hike about 1-2 hrs on an easy trail. From Balaju below the hill, a road heads NW towards the Trishuli valley.

Chabahil

If you head E from Naksal area, you will arrive at **Goshala** (where there is a turn-off leading S towards Pashupati and Tribhuvan Airport). Continuing eastwards from this crossroads towards Boudha, you will pass through **Chabahil**, where there is a small but elegant stupa known as **Dhanju Chaitya**, which was originally built by King Dharmadeva. During Licchavi times Chabahil was a village at the crossroads between India and Tibet. Ashoka's daughter Charumati is said to have lived here and with her husband Devapala founded two monasteries. The stupa was rebuilt during the 7th century; and there are even now some old chaityas and statuary at the site, including a 9th century free-standing Bodhisattva.

The Chabahil area is also well known for its **Ganesh Temple**, which is one of the four Ganesh temples protecting the Kathmandu Valley. For the local people, this temple has the reputation of curing sores and pimples. The Ganesh image is reputed to date from the 8th-9th century and once a year is taken around locally in a chariot. The most popular day for devotees is Tues.

Bodhnath Stupa

(*Tib* Chorten Jarung Khashor) About 1 km E of Chabahil, the **Bodhnath Stupa**

(38m high, 100m in circumference) looms above the road, dominating the ancient trade route between Kathmandu and Lhasa. As the largest stupa in Nepal, it is revered by both Tibetan and Newar Buddhists. The former hold it to contain the bone relics of the past Buddha Kashyapa and to have been built by a lowly poultry keeper named Jadzimo with unfledging royal approval. The poultry-keeper's sons are said to have been subsequently reborn as King Trisong Dtesen, Shantaraksita, and Padmasambhava, who together established Buddhism in 8th century Tibet. Newar chronicles, by contrast, hold the stupa to have been constructed by the Licchavi king Manadeva in 500 AD in order to expiate his crime of patricide. The structure was subsequently restored by the Nyingmapa lama Shakya Zangpo in the early 16th century. Later, following the 1852 treaty between Nepal and the Manchus, which ended the Tibeto-Nepalese border wars, the abbotship of Boudha was granted to a Chinese delegate whose descendents, including Chini Lama (*Tib* Gya Lama), continued to hold a privileged position in local affairs.

By its sheer size the Bodhnath Stupa may seem even more impressive than that at Svayambhunath. It too has a hemispherical dome topped by a square *harmika*, above which rise the spire with its 13 steps and the canopy symbolizing the goal of buddhahood. However, it is now almost hidden from distant view by the surrounding buildings, which create an attractive courtyard effect for the stupa itself.

Around the octagonal 3-tiered base of the stupa, there is a brick wall with 147 niches and 108 images of the meditational buddhas, inset behind copper prayer-wheels. Each section of the wall holds four to five such prayer wheels. The main entrance to the stupa is on the S side, and the principal shrine dedicated to the female protectress Ajima/Hariti on the W. Around the stupa there is a pilgrim's circuit, which is densely thronged in the early mornings and evenings by local Tibetan residents and by pilgrims from far-flung parts of the Himalayan region and beyond. Numerous shrines, bookstores, and handicraft shops surround the circuit, the speciality being Newar *cire perdue* silverware. The Tibetan New Year (usually Feb) is celebrated here with special prayers, processions, masked dances and a feast.

In recent years Boudha, once a remote country village, has become a densely populated suburb of Kathmandu. There is a particularly high concentration of Tibetans here, alongside the older Newar and Tamang communities, and this is reflected in the prolific temple-building which the various Tibetan traditions have engaged in since the late 1960s. These shrines and monasteries are too numerous to describe here, but a few of the most important among them, can be mentioned, some with well-structured teaching programmes.

The only temple of importance on the S side of the main road is **Orgyen Dongak Choling**, the seat of the late Dudjom Rinpoche, a charismatic meditation master and scholarly head of the Nyingmapa school, whose mortal remains are interred here in a stupa. Those located to the W of the Stupa include **Jamchen Monastery** (Sakya; under the guidance of Chogyel Trichen), **Sharpa Monastery** and Trulzhik Rinpoche's Monastery (both Nyingma), **Tsechen Shedrubling** (Kagyu), and **Shelkar Chode** (Geluk).

Heading **NW** of the Stupa the following are most important: **Tharlam Monastery** (Sakya), **Karnying Shedrubling** (Karma Kagyu; under the guidance of Chokyi Nyima Rinpoche), **Zhechen Tenyi Dargyeling** (Nyingma; under the guidance of the late Dilgo Khyentse Rinpoche and Zhechen Rabjam Rinpoche), **Nenang Monastery** (Kagyu; under the tradition of Pawo Rinpoche), Bairo Khyentse Rinpoche's monastery

(Kagyu), and **Marpa House** (Kagyu; under the guidance of Khenpo Tsultrim Gyatso).

Close to the Stupa on the **N** side are: **Dabsang Monastery** (Kagyu), **Trangu Tashi** Choling (Kagyu), and **Kyirong Samtenling** (Geluk). To the **E** are: **Tashi Migyur Dorje Gyeltsen Ling** (Sakya, under Tarik Tulku), **Dezhung Monastery** (Sakya), **Leksheling** (Sakya/Kagyu; under Karma Trinle Rinpoche), **Thubten Ngedon Shedrubling** (Kagyu), and **Karma Chokhor Tekchen** Leksheling (Kagyu). Further **N** on or near Mahankal Rd are: **Mahayana Prakash Pelyul Dharmalaya** (Nyingma; under the guidance of Penor Rinpoche). **To Pullahari** (Kagyu; under Jamgon Kongtrul Rinpoche), **International Buddhist Academy** (Sakya; under Khenpo Abe), and the **Drukpa Kagyu Monastery** (under the guidance of Tsoknyi Rinpoche). Mahankal Rd extends **NE** to **Kopan Monastery** (Geluk; under Lama Zopa and Lama Yeshe), and **Ngagi Gonpa** (Kagyu; under Tulku Orgyan). To the extreme **E** of Boudha, on the N side of the main road is **Chubsang Monastery** (Geluk; under Tsibri Chubzang Rinpoche).

GETTING THERE Crowded buses to Boudha leave from Ratna Park and Bagh Bazaar. Better to take a taxi. Alternatively, to walk from Guheshvari Temple at Pashupati head to your left downstream to the bridge, or from Pashupatinath Temple upstream along the W bank. Both paths meet on the N side of the bridge. A footpath leads off to the NE to Boudha, 1.5 km.

Gokarna Park

Less than 3 km NE of Boudha, on the banks of the Bagmati River, is the royal game reserve at **Gokarna**. This has become a favourite picnic spot, offering elephant and horse rides. Overlooking the Bagmati river (and approached from Jorbati via the turn-off to Sundarijal) is the **Gokarneshvara Temple**. Built prior to the 14th century, this temple in

Nepalese pagoda style exhibits some of the finest wood carvings. In Aug-Sept each year thousands of people pay homage here to the memory of their dead fathers. **Jorbati** has become an important base for the Tibetan carpet industry, and **Sundarijal**, 15 km NE, is the most convenient trail-head for the Helambu (*Tib* Yolmo) trek.

Sankhu Vajrayogini

Beyond Gokarna, the main road heads E to Sankhu, the abode of the revered image of the powerful female deity Khadga Vajrayogini. A 2 km ascent on foot leads from the motor terminus to the 3-storeyed temple, in pagoda style, which has an upper roof of gold and lower roof of copper and was renovated in the 17th century. Accommodation is provided for devotees.

Pashupatinath

Some 5 km NE of Kathmandu and near the airport, Nepal's most important Hindu pilgrim site is located on the banks of the Bagmati River, in the dry season no more than a trickle of badly polluted water. Pashupatinath has been designated a world heritage site and as it lies between Kathmandu and the airport, a visit may be combined with a trip to Bodhnath. There is a Tourist Information Unit.

You follow an ancient road which in medieval times linked the royal palace in Durbar Square with the temple complex, crossing the Dhobi Khola by a steel bridge. The road then traverses the Pashupatinath plateau which was the probable site of the Licchavi capital of **Deopatan**. You will pass a large pilgrims' rest-house and a small village before reaching the temple to the right of the road.

Pashupatinath belongs to Shiva, here in his peaceful form as Pashupati, the shepherd or lord of beasts, and to Narayana. Shiva is known by many names, of which Pashupati is one. *Pashu* means "living beings" and *Pati* means "lord". The temple is one of the most important to Hindus in the subcontinent and has been closely associated with orthodox S Indian Shaivism since the visit of Shankacharya. It was reputedly built by a Licchavi king, Supuspadeva, 39 generations before Mandadeva (464-505 AD) but later underwent considerable repair and reconstruction. The main temple was renovated by Queen Gangadevi during the period 1578-1620, turning it into a pagoda of brass and gilt with silver plated gateways. **NB** Non-Hindus are not allowed into this 17th century temple, but you may get a glimpse of the gilt Nandi Bull, Shiva's vehicle, said to be around 300 years old. The black, 4-headed image of Pashupati inside the temple is older, and replaced one destroyed by Muslim invaders in the 14th century.

In the NE of the courtyard is the **Vasuki Temple**, dedicated to the image of the *naga* king Vasuki, whose lower body appears as an intricate tangled body of snakes. Devotees generally circumambulate the Vasuki temple before worshipping Pashupatinath, as Vasuki is considered the main temple's protector. It was constructed by King Pratap Malla during the Malla period.

South of the Pashupatinath courtyard is found the **Kotilingeshvara Temple**, surrounded by many Shiva lingas.

To the left of the temple is a ramp of steps, taken from former Licchavi buildings. This leads to the small hill representing **Mount Kailash**, the mythical centre of the Universe, from which you get a good view of the temple site. There are also good views from the banks of the Bagmati River which is spanned by two bridges.

On the E bank are the Royal Cremation Ghats (steps), especially busy on Sat and at Ekadashi (11th day after full moon), when the river bank resembles Varanasi. South of the ghats is the 6th century **Baccheeshvari Temple** on the W bank. This contains a number of erotic Hindu tantric carvings and it is thought that in the past human sacrifices were made here during the Shivaratri festival. Nearby is a fine but neglected 7th century Buddha statue whilst a little further down the river is the **Rama Temple** where many congregate during the Shivaratri celebration. It contains life-size images of Rama, his consort and three brothers. The upper floor has five dome like structures with gilt finials and commands a very good view of Kathmandu.

On the other bank, to the left is a row of 11 stone chaityas (chapels), each containing a stone lingam and further N, beyond these is the **Hermit's Cave**. Beyond the ghats is the **Gorakhnath Temple**, a tall brick *shikhara* structure with a large brass trident in front, surrounded by lingas. This is one of the oldest temples of Gorakhnath who is considered a guardian deity of the Nath sect. The temple was built by Jayasthiti Malla (1382-95) and contains the footprints of Gorakhnath. A track leads off to the right to the **Vishvarupa Temple** (non-Hindus are not allowed inside). Here is a huge image of Shiva in union with Shakti, almost 6m high.

Just S of Pashupatinath is a cluster of white temples called **Panchadeval** ("five temples"). Built in 1870, the central temple and the four surrounding it all have Shiva lingas as their central shrines. The pilgrim resthouses around the temple are used for homeless old people.

Beyond the Goraknath Temple and down by the Bagmati River on the other side of its meandering loop is the **Guheshvari Temple** (17th century) dedicated to Kali, the goddess of destruction. The arched tubular metal construction covers the main temple. Near the top, four gilded snakes support the roof apex illustrating the *yantra* diagram (geometric triangle). In the centre of the temple is a pool, covered at the base in gold and silver. At the head of the pool is a jar which is worshipped as the goddess Guheshvari and the water from the pool is accepted as her offering. Again, only Hindus are allowed inside to see the gilded shrine room. Thousands of devotees visit Guheshvari daily.

Kirtipur

From Kalimati in the W suburbs of Kathmandu, the main highway to Pokhara and Birganj extends westwards before bifurcating at **Naubase**. Turning SW away from this highway, a side-road leads from Kalimati across the confluence of the Vishnumati and Bagmati rivers to **Tribhuvan University** and the medieval hilltop city of **Kirtipur**. Formerly classed as one of the four cities of the valley, and with a predominantly Newar Buddhist population, Kirtipur suffered in 1767 when its inhabitants vainly attempted to resist the unification of Nepal by Prithivi Narayan Shah. The noses and lips of the city's male inhabitants were brutally severed. Sacred sites at Kirtipur include the **Bagh Bhairava Temple**, where weapons retrieved from that 18th century battle are housed, the **Uma Maheshvara Temple**, and the **Chilandeo Stupa** (attributed to Ashoka).

Chobar Gorge

The striking Chobar gorge is located 6 km SW of Kathmandu. Its origins have been given both Buddhist and Hindu explanations. The former suggests that the bodhisattva Manjushri, wishing to make the sacred lotus flame of Svayambhu accessible to devotees, slashed the valley wall with his flaming sword of discriminative awareness (*prajna*) to drain off the lake that covered the whole area. Chobar Gorge was caused by his powerful blow. Hindus sometimes add that Krishna hurled a thunderbolt at the valley walls. Scientists provide a much more prosaic explanation, but what is certain is that the Kathmandu valley was

drained and now the muddy waters of the Bagmati River flow through it.

Downstream, at the point where the Bagmati emerges from the gorge, is the **Jal Vinayaka Temple** (1602), dedicated to the protector deity Ganesh. A huge rock has a Ganesh carved into it though this is now indistinct and does not resemble the usual image of the elephant-headed deity. A bronze shrew, Ganesh's vehicle in Nepal (as distinct from a rat more common in India), faces the shrine. An earlier Hindu shrine to Shiva and Parvati is believed to be 11th century.

Above the gorge is Chobar village which has a Buddhist temple dedicated to Adinath Lokeshvara (15th century, rebuilt 1642). This triple-roofed temple has numerous vessels for containing water nailed to its walls. The inner sanctum contains an image of **Anandadi Lokeshvara** (replacing the original Phakpa Wati image), and facing the shrine is a stone *shikhara*.

Pharping

(*Tib* Yanglesho) After Chobar, the road climbs to Pikhel and crosses a high ridge. On the way you will pass **Lake Taudaha** – a protected nature park and the only residue of the valley's original lake. Descending from the ridge, you will reach the shaded sacred pools and the Hindu temple dedicated to **Shesh Narayana**, which stands below a steep limestone cliff (18 km from Kathmandu). The cave alongside the temple is revered by Buddhists as the place where Padmasambhava attained his realisation of the Mahamudra teachings. It has an as yet 'unopened' *terma* in its rock walls. Adjacent to the Shesh Narayana Temple, and approached via a flight of steps is the **Buddhist Monastery** under the guidance of Chatrel Rinpoche Sangye Dorje – one of the greatest living masters of the Nyingma school who maintains the Katok and *Longchen Nyingtig* traditions, among others.

The large village of **Pharping** lies a few hundred metres beyond this site, overlooking the Bagmati River. On the ridge above the town, there is an ancient Newar pagoda style temple dedicated to **Phamting Vajrayogini** – one of the four main Vajrayogini shrines of the valley. Higher up the hillside, there is the **Asura Cave**, where Padmasambhava attained realisations by propitiating the meditational deity Vajrakila combined with Yangdak Heruka. There are several Tibetan Buddhist temples and monasteries, which have been constructed on the hillside around and below this cave in recent decades – principally representing the Nyingma and Kagyu traditions. Among them are those under the guidance of Zatrul Rinpoche and Lama Ralo. An exquisite 'self-arising' rock image of Tara, which was not so long ago exposed to the elements has now been encorporated within a large temple complex.

Dakshin Kali

The Hindu temple of Dakshin Kali, 22 km from Kathamndu, is located at the bottom of a steep ravine, 4 km below Pharping. The shrine was built by a Malla king to appease the goddess Kali with a great sacrifice of buffaloes when his country was in the grip of a cholera epidemic 300 years ago. A blood-thirsty slaughter (usually the beheading of chickens) takes place on Tues and Sat mornings in front of the goddess, whose image is on the left of the temple entrance. The path down from the car park crosses a bridge leading to the temple, guarded by lion sculptures, and crowded with worshippers and priests performing rituals.

Museums

National Museum, Chauni, near Svayambhunath Temple. 1030-1630 summer, 1030-1530 winter, Fri till 1430. Closed Tues. Rs 5, Camera Rs 10. Two main buildings in Nepalese style with superb woodcarving. Uniforms, military decorations, leather cannon used in Tibetan war, portraits. The art gallery contains an interesting collection of sculptures dating from 1st century BC including a charming dancing Ganesh, terracottas, paintings and manuscripts. **Natural History Museum**, behind Svayambhunath exhibits flora and fauna of the region. Stuffed animals, large collection of birds and butterflies. Free. Open daily, except Sat and holidays from 1000-1700. **Tribhuvan Museum**, in Hanuman Dhoka Royal Palace. Open daily except Tues and holidays 1000-1700, Rs 10. Photos, portraits, memorabilia of the Late King and country's best collection of coins. Your ticket enables you to climb the Basantapur Tower and look out over the temples of Durbar Square.

Local festivals

The most important of Kathmandu's many festivals are as follows:

Feb: *Basanta Panchami* at Hanuman Dhoka Palace; *Tibetan New Year* at Boudha; *Sivaratri* at Pashupatinath.
Mar-April: *Ghorajatra.*
May: *Buddha Jayanti* at Svayambhunath and Boudha.
June-July: *Tribhuvan Jayanti* at Tripureswar.
Aug: *Gaijatra*; *Pancha Dan* at Svayambhunath.
Sept: *Indrajatra*; *Teej* at Pashupatinath.
Oct: *Bada Dasain*. Government offices remain closed for a week. City is very busy and crowded. Accommodation and transport difficult.
Nov: *Tihar*; *Ekadasi* at Buddhanilakantha and Pashupatinath.
Dec: *Bala Chaturdasi* at Pashupatinath.

Local information

● **Accommodation**
Kathmandu is the only town in Nepal that has a wide range of accommodation. There

is a reservation counter at the airport, for upmarket hotels. Many offer free transfers. In season (Oct-Nov and Feb-Mar) there is heavy demand, so book in advance. Outside the airport you will find touts for the cheaper hotels. Government tax (10-15%). Payment at all except cheapest hotels, with either foreign currency (TCs, cash, credit card) or Rupees with an official exchange receipt (given at any recognized exchange). All **A** category hotels have a/c rooms, restaurants, coffee shop, bar, exchange, travel counter, car hire and most have shops and a swimming pool. Most hotels offer to store baggage for trekkers. **NB** Many visitors to Kathmandu now prefer to stay at hotels in Patan (such as the *Summit Hotel*). For these see the local information for Patan, given below, page 686.

AL *Hotel de l'Annapurna* (Taj Group), Durbar Marg, T 221711, F 225236, 160 rm, best overlooking garden and pool, next to Royal Palace with good Indian restaurant, exclusive shops and cultural centre, extensively remodelled 1993, refurbished rooms rec; **AL** *Soaltee Oberoi*, Tahachal, T 221211, 300 rm, Himalayan Wing – grand, Garden Wing – quieter, 5 km from city centre but free transport to town and airport, Nepal's first casino, mini golf, excellent restaurants and service; **AL** *Yak and Yeti*, Durbar Marg, Lal Durbar, T 413999, F 227781, 255 rm, 15 suites, a recently refurbished Rana palace with some fine woodcarving and excellent restaurants.

A *Dwarika's Kathmandu Village*, Putalisadak, T 412328, 31 rm, traditional Newar carvings and decor, won Heritage Award from Pacific Asia Travel Assoc for cultural sensitivity, 12 rm, no credit cards; **A** *Everest Sheraton*, Baneshwar, T 220567, F 226088, 162 rm, 6 restaurants, Far Pavilions (7th flr) has excellent views and Indian classical music, modern hotel on main road, Nepal's first disco; **A** *Kathmandu*, Maharajgunj, T 410786, F 416574, 120 large rm, Embassy area, modern, clean, friendly, all-Nepalese staff; **A** *Malla*, Lekhnath Marg, W of Royal Palace, T 410966, 75 rm, in traditional style, peaceful garden, cultural shows, *Mountain City* serves good Sichuan dishes; **A** *Shangrila*, Lazimpath, Embassy area, T 412999, F 414184, 50 rm, best face garden, Tibetan style decor, cultural programmes, interesting library, free transport to centre, good restaurants, garden café; **A** *Shankar*, Lazimpat, T 410151, 100 rm, 2 km centre, pleasant 19th century Rana Palace

with large garden, full of character; **A** *Sherpa*, Durbar Marg, T 222585, F 222026, 96 rm, some fine traditional brass and woodwork in modern hotel, roof-top terrace garden, pleasant atmosphere; **A** *Woodlands*, Durbar Marg, T 222683, F 225650, 71 rm, dim and rather decaying interior, overpriced, luxurious lobby but as rooms are dark and drab, not worth the price, restaurant with simple decor but excellent Indian veg, bar, disco.

B *Crystal*, 594 Shukrapath, corner of New Rd, nr Durbar Square, T 223636, 52 rm, all a/c, right by Durbar Square, good views of town from roof terrace and convenient for temple visits, location reflects price, restaurant (Indian, Continental); **B** *Marshyangdi*, Paknajol, Thamel, T 414105, F 410008, 80 rm, modern hotel, popular with groups, well located; **B** *Yellow Pagoda*, Kantipath, T 220392, 51 rm (some refurbished), restaurants, roof garden, central, modern, clean, 1st flr rooms better, food mediocre, overpriced.

C *Ambassador*, Lazimpath, nr Durbar Marg, T 410432, F 413641, 48 rm, good restaurant, bar, exchange, travel, shop, small garden, partly refurbished, rooms do not live up to the impressive entrance lobby; **C** *Durauka's Kathmandu Village Hotel*, T 470770, F 225131, unusual hotel which has beautiful carved wood in rooms (woodworking shop which does restoration on premises), book exchange, no TV and excellent authentic Nepalese cuisine in restaurant (9 courses), necessary to make reservation; **C** *Gautam*, Jyatha, Kantipath, T 215014, good rooms, excellent Kabab Corner, Tandoori dishes rec; **C** *Manang*, Thamel, T 410993, pleasant, friendly hotel which serves good food, freshly prepared and reasonably priced; **C** *Manaslu*, Lazimpat, T 413470, F 228467, down narrow lane nr French Embassy, renovated Rana palace, attractive garden, pleasant, very quiet, excellent service, good restaurant, excellent value; **C** *Tilicho*, Tridevi Marg, Thamel (nr Immigration Office), T 416828/410132, F 227567, roof-top garden and restaurant, deluxe rooms have bath; **C** *Utse*, Jyatha, Thamel, T 226946, F 226945, Tibetan-style hotel which is very pleasant and popular, roof-top garden, small library with newspapers and magazines, helpful staff; **C** *Vajra*, Bijeshwari, T 224719, F 271695, 51 rm, best with bath in new extension, restaurant, roof-top bar, library, river view, distinctive Newari architecture, excellent hotel, built 1980 using traditional designs and materials, surrounded by gardens and trees, centre for cultural programmes, heavily booked, very good value, highly rec.

D *Garuda*, T 416340, restaurant, coffee bar, roof-top terrace, good rooms and view, very clean and friendly, US$20 for room with en-suite bathroom; **D** *Kathmandu Guest House*, nr W end of Tridevi Marg, T 413632, F 417133, 104 rm, some a/c with bath, best in *Maya* apartments upstairs, restaurant, exchange, overseas telephone office, travel, art gallery, reception with TV and English-language, Indian and Nepali newspapers plus a pleasant quiet garden, long established reputation, still popular, in season book more than 1 month in advance, excellent value, old block has 40 rm, some under US$20, eg single room with no facilities, 'Maya' discount card; **D** *Lovers' Nest*, Thamel, T 220541, F 227795, very reasonable and very popular, with roof garden; **D** *Mt Makalu*, 65 Dharmapath, T 214616, 30 rm, breakfast, central, clean, top flr rooms cheaper; **D** *Nook*, Jyatha, T 213627, 24 rm, restaurant, small garden, central but noisy; **D** *Pilgrims Hotel*, Thamel, T 225159, F 229983, clean rooms, very popular with budget travellers; **D** *Potala Tourist Home*, Tridevi Marg, Thamel (nr Immigration Office), T 410303, roof-top garden, free transport to and from airport, set back from street, quiet and friendly; **D** *Snow Lion Guest House*, Chetrapati, T 213922, F 220142, friendly Tibetan hospitality, warm and comfortable; **D** *Tibet Rest House*, Jyatha Tole, Thamel, T 225319, F 226945, is popular with travellers, prices reasonable, friendly Tibetan hospitality; **D** *Tridevi*, T 416742, 30 pleasant rm, clean; **D** *Tushita*, Kantipath, once US embassy, T 216913, rooms with bath, restaurant, art gallery, small garden; **D** *Hotel Harati*, Ikhapokhari, Chetrapati, T 226527, F 223329, 50 rm, some with attached bath, currency exchange facilities, restaurant and coffee bar; **D** *Hotel Ganesh Himal*, Chetrapati, T 223216, F 223315, has rooms with attached bath, friendly service and flexible rates, rec for budget travellers; **D** *Norbulingka Guest House*, Thamel, Gairidhara, T 414799, has 50 rm, some with attached bath, restaurant serving various cuisines, and roof-top beer garden.

Cheaper accommodation There are a lot of inexpensive hotels and guesthouses in Thamel and Chetrapati in the N part of the city, about 15 mins walk from Durbar Square. Along Jochen Rd (Freak St), made popular by 1960s hippies, there are cheap lodges and guesthouses in **E** and **F** categories with fairly basic rooms and few facilities. Rooms nr the top of the building may have views. Heating is non-existent or minimal, so a sleeping bag is necessary in winter. Many have roof-top terraces. There are also good and inexpensive hotels in outlying areas such as Boudha and Chobar.

In Chetrapati and Thamel: E *Earth House Lodge*, T 410500 and **E** *Asia*, Thamel, T 216541 are in Nepalese homes, friendly; **E** *Himalaya Guest House*, Jochen (ask for Himalaya Coffee Bar), friendly, clean, hot showers, rec; **E** *Shakti*, in a garden setting, **E** and **E** *Holy Lodge*, are quiet and pleasant; **E** *Shambala Guest House*, T 212524, some rooms with bath, Tibetan run, roof garden, attractive views; **E** *Hotel My Home*, Thamel, friendly atmosphere, good value, popular with tourists; **E** *Hotel Shree Tibet*, T 419902, F 419361, very clean, reasonably priced, very helpful and friendly; **E** *Kathmandu Lodge*, Pyaphal Tole, off Durbar Square, T 214893, some rooms with bath; **F** *Century Lodge*, T 214341, rooms with bath, good value.

In Durbar Square: E *Kumari Guest House*, basic, hot showers but no safes for luggage, hence insecure, unsatisfactory laundry.

In Bhote Bahal: D *Janak*, large rooms, restaurant; **D** *Sayapatri*, T 223398, breakfast, pleasant garden; **E** *Valley View*, Teku, T 216771, rooms with bath, terrace, clean.

In Boudha: D *Maya Guesthouse*, T 470866, has good, expensive rooms, but wonderful garden and tekking service to Langtang; **D** *Stupa Hotel*, T 470400, is large with a spacious garden; **E** *Snowlion Lodge*, T 4470431, large building with two blocks and restaurant facilities; **E** *Lotus Guesthouse*, clean but simple rooms in excellent location; **E** *Hotel Tashi Delek*, T 471380, and **E** *Bir Restaurant*, T 470790, are located close to the noisy bus stand.

Further away from the centre: rec as a cultural experience, **E** *Catnap*, Chauni, across Vishnumati River, T 272392 and **F** *Peace Lodge* on road to Svayambhunath are fairly quiet.

Youth hostels See under Patan below.

● **Places to eat**

A wide choice of menu at most. Some close at 2200. At top restaurants, a meal for 2 with drinks may cost Rs 1,000. In Thamel and

Chetrapati, a meal may cost Rs 80; a bottle of beer may cost as much; and a Nepalese meal of dhal, bhat, tarkari, around Rs 60 (or more depending on the establishment). **NB** Stomach upsets are common so take extra care.

Highly recommended: *Bhanchhaghar* ('Nepalese Kitchen'), Kamaladi Rd, off Durbar Marg, nr clocktower in a 3-storey Newari house, with bar, T 25172, Res 419323, beautiful, atmospheric surroundings, have your drink seated on cushions upstairs while ordering your meal, not cheap (Rs 600) but excellent authentic Nepali food – an experience; *Nanglo Restaurant and Bar*, on Durbar Marg, offers excellent Nepalese food at reasonable prices, frequented by local business community; *Chimney Restaurant*, Yak & Yeti Hotel, offers excellent but expensive western food as well as Russian dishes; *Naachghar* at the Yak & Yeti serves Nepalese food in a magnificent setting and the *Sunrise*, a café restaurant is more informal but boasts a magnificent view of gardens and a live band in the evenings; *Dairy House*, Thamel, is a simple café offering cheesecake, cheeses, yoghurt, ice cream and butter at reasonable prices; *KC's Consequence*, Balaju (off Ring Rd), T 272274 (closed Sun), for a meal with a difference in rural surroundings, stylish indoors, informal outside and a wide choice, home-grown veg and cuisine influenced by KC's German partner; *Nepalese Kitchen* in Thamel and the Newari *Bhoe Chhen* on Yak and Yeti Rd, offer local dishes, more reasonably priced; *Old Vienna Inn and Gourmet shop* (delicatessen), Thamel, well worth a visit for excellent Viennese food, the Gourmet shop offers an extensive array of European delicacies, inc Bratwurst and Applestrudel; *Restaurant Himalchuli*, Hotel Holiday Inn, Crowne Plaza, has excellent Tibetan momos; and *Tripti*, just off New Rd, serves good economical vegetarian food, delicious taste.

Chinese: *Golden Dragon Restaurant and Bar*, Durbar Marg, Chinese and Thai food, good value; *Golden Gate*, upstairs, opp Indonesian Bank and *Ras Rang*, opp *Ambassador Hotel*; *Nanglo Chinese Restaurant*, Durbar Marg, Chinese with dark decor but good food and prices.

Japanese food rec at: *Fuji*, Royal Palace end of Kantipath, in old Rana, moated bungalow; *Kushi Fuji*, above Tiger Tops office; *Sakura-Ya*, Lazimpat, in beautiful garden, are good but pricey, counter lunches more affordable.

Thai: *Him Thai*, Thamel, and *Ruen Thai*, Durbar Marg, both rec.

Tibetan restaurants, inc: *Lhasa*, where you can sample inexpensive momo and thukpa; *Rum Doodle*, Thamel, T 414336, friendly, hospitable with inexpensive good food and garden; *Utse*, Thamel, is rec (also for Chinese).

Italian restaurants are less expensive, several in Thamel inc: *Al Pollo e Pizzeria Restaurant* and *Mona Lisa*, which has good food and a pleasant atmosphere, tables in garden; and *La Dolce Vita*. *The Pizza Inn*, Thamel (T 222408), has three restaurants on 3 flrs (inc rooftop garden restaurant), which serve Chinese, Italian, Mexican, Nepalese and French cuisine and is highly rec, pleasant atmosphere and friendly service, dishes reasonably priced; *Pizza Maya*, Chetrapati, serves Mexican pasta.

On Durbar Marg: *Café-de-la-Paix* is smart, moderately priced for Nepali and continental dishes; opp is *Nirula's*, fast-food and ice-creams; with the rec *Woodlands*, S Indian restaurant nearby; *Bangalore Coffee House*, for good S Indian food; *Mike's Breakfast*, Seto Durbar, behind *Sherpa Hotel* in Rana cottage for big breakfasts and lunch, highly rec, wonderful garden; *Mike's Cantina*, does Mexican-American food, roof terrace, good views; *Nanglo Pub* has western snacks; *Sunkosi Restaurant*, Naksal (opp *Mike's Breakfast*), very comfortable with very tasty traditional Nepalese and Tibetan food, favoured by locals.

Off Jochen (Freak St): *Himalaya Coffee Bar*, nr Durbar Square, friendly; *Lunchbox*, for good cheap food (poor service); *Narayan's*, Chetrapati, popular moderately priced, Indian restaurant; *Skylab*, behind PO, excellent authentic Nepali dhal bhat, good Chinese, Indian and Continental and small bar, knowledgeable, friendly owner of family business, reasonably priced, rec.

In Thamel: *Boris's*, rec for Russian dishes, popular; *Coppers*, Kaisermahal, has a delicatessen; *Everest Steak House*, for excellent steaks; *KC's* and *Alice's* around the corner is rec for breakfasts, choc cake, western food; bar food at *Spam's Spot* and veg at *Sanghamitra*;

Bakeries: *Krishna Loaf Store*, Kamal Pokhari; *Pumpernickel*, is a popular bakery; *Snowman*, off Jochen Rd, for excellent freshly-baked cake. Other shops rec for cakes, bread and pies are along Maru Tole ('pie alley'). The New Rd *Dairy Shop* sells good cheese.

● **Bars**

Most hotels (*Shankar* and *Yak & Yeti* rec) and restaurants have bars or sell beer (close 2300).

● **Airline offices**

NB You should reconfirm your tickets on arrival in Nepal and about 72 hrs before departure. Flights out of Kathmandu are notoriously overbooked. Check in early. **Royal Nepal Airlines Corp** (RNAC), Kantipath, T 220757, Airport, T 414918; **Indian Airlines**, Durbar Marg, T 411997, at Tribhuvan Airport, T 411933.

On **Kanti Path**: Air India, T 212335; Cathay Pacific, T 226765; TWA, T 214704.

On **Durbar Marg**: Air France, T 223339; Biman, T 222544; British Airways, T 222266; JAL, T 223871; KLM, T 224896; Lufthansa, T 223052; PIA, T 22202; Swissair, T 222452; Thai, T 223565, Airport T 413440.

On **Kamaladi Rd**: Aeroflot, T 212397; and China South-west Airlines, T 419770.

● **Banks & money changers**

Banks: most open 1000-1500 (1430 in winter) Sun-Thur, and up to 1300 Fri. **Citibank**, *Hotel Yak and Yeti*; **NZ Grindlay's Bank**, Kamalpokhari; **Nepal Bank**, New Rd; **Nepal Bank**, Kantipath (open 0900-1300 on Sat, closed Sun and Bank holidays); **Nepal Rashtra Bank**, Baluwater; **Rastriya Baniyya Bank**, Tangal, nr Police HQ; **Standard Chartered Bank**, Durbar Marg. **NB** Carry enough cash outside Kathmandu.

Exchanges: at airport and most hotels will change TCs for guests. **American Express**, Jamal Tol, nr Ratna Park, will make cash advances to card holders, 1000-1300; **Grindlay's** for Visa and Mastercard holders.

Credit Cards: American Express, Jamal, Ratna Park, T 226172 (Sun-Fri 0800-2000, Sat 0930-1700); Visa and MasterCard: *Alpine Travel*, Durbar Marg, T 225020.

● **Culture centres**

Everest Cultural Society, *Annapurna Hotel*, has Nepalese folk dances at 1900 (Rs 250). **New Himalchuli Cultural Group**, *Hotel Shanker*, offers Nepali cultural programme every evening at 1900 (Rs 250). *Hotel Everest*, has a programme of Indian classical music most nights. Regular theatre performances at Kanti Path and Rani Pokhari. Details from Rashtriya Naach Ghar, Kanti Path, nr Rani Pokhari, T 211900, **Royal Nepal Academy**, Kamaldali and the City Hall opp Exhibition Ground. **Arniko Cultural Society** is in Dilli Bazaar and

Chimal Cultural Group in *Manaslu Hotel*. *Hotel Vajra* also organizes regular cultural shows.

Foreign cultural centres & libraries: British Council, Kantipath, 1100-1800 Sun-Fri, closed Sat, English newspapers, reference material plus books on Nepal. **American Library**, New Rd, 1100-1900 Mon-Fri, closed Sat. **Goethe Institute**, nr Bhimsen Tower and GPO, library, film nights (small charge). **CIS Cultural Centre**, Russian Embassy; and French Cultural Centre, Bagh Bazaar.

● **Embassies & consulates**

Australia, Bhatbhateni, T 411578; **Bangladesh**, Naksal, T 414265; **Burma**, Pulchowk, T 521788; **China**, Baluwatar, T 411740; **CIS**, Baluwatar, T 411063; **Denmark**, Meera Home, Kichapokhari, T 215939; **France**, Lazimpat, T 412332; **Germany**, PO Box 226, Gyaneswar, T 412786; **India**, Lainchaur, T 410900; **Italy**, Lalita Niwas Rd, Baluwatar, T 412743; **Japan**, Pani Pokhari, T 414083; **Pakistan**, Pani Pokhari, T 411421; **Sweden**, Meera Home, Kichapokhari, T 215939; **Thailand**, Thapathali, T 213910; **UK**, Lainchaur, T 410583; **USA**, Pani Pokhari, T 411179.

● **Entertainment**

Casinos: *The Soaltee Oberoi*, Rs 100 of free chips within a week of arriving by air (show ticket and passport), gambling with Indian Rupees and US$, blackjack, poker, roulette and pokies (slot machines), open 24 hrs, free transport back to major hotels (2300-0400).

Clubs: Birdwatchers' Club organizes guided tours from *Kathmandu Guest House*, Thamel. There are Bridge and Chess Clubs and branches of Jaycees, Lions and Rotary.

Parks and zoos: *Balaju Water Gardens*, 5 km NW. Also *Ratna Park*, town centre and the quieter *Exhibition Ground*, which occasionally is the venue for fairs.

● **Hospitals & medical services**

Bir Hospital, Kantipath, nr Parade Gr, T 221119; *Kanti Hospital*, Maharajaganj, T 411550; *Teaching Hospital*, Maharajaganj, T 412404; *Himalayan International Clinic*, Iyatha, Thamel, T 25455, F 220143; *Nepal International Clinic*, T 412842.

● **International agencies**

Asian Dev Bank, Babar Mahal; **IMF**, Rastriya Bank; **UN**, Lainchaur; **World Bank**, Kantipath.

● **Libraries**

Indian Cultural Centre and Library, RNAC

Building, Kantipath. *Keshar Library* in a Rana Palace W of New Royal Palace, collected by Samsher Jung Bahadur, a Rana noble and scholar, impressive collection of books and manuscripts on Buddhism, open during office hours, 1000-1600 or 1700, closed Sat. *Tribhuvan University Library*, Kirtipur, open 0900-1800 Sun-Fri, closed Sat.

● **Post & telecommunications**

Stamps at GPO, Sundhara, open Sun-Fri 1000-1700. **NB** Make sure that cards and letters are franked in your presence. Major hotels sell stamps and have post box. American Express, Jamal Tol, Durbar Marg, Kathmandu, has a Poste Restante service for cardholders. GPO Poste Restante not efficient for forwarding mail. Central Telegraph Office, Tripureswar, 200m S of GPO has International Telephone Service Counter open 24 hrs. Phone calls, telex and fax messages may be sent. For International calls T 186, Domestic information T 197 and Domestic trunk calls T 180. It is more convenient to make calls from hotels, or from one of the many business centres which have sprung up throughout the city – even in far-flung suburbs like Boudha, but expect to pay a service charge.

● **Shopping**

Antiques: reliable antiques from *Tibet Ritual Art Gallery* above *Sunkosi Restaurant* and *Potala Gallery*, opp *Yak and Yeti*.

Books: on Trivedi Marg: *Tibet Book Store* (for Buddhism; closed Mon) and *Bookland*, opp Immigration Office; *Kailash*, *Yak & Yeti's* main entrance; *Mandala*, Bidhur, Kantipath; *Himalayan Booksellers*, nr Clock Tower, small but good range; *Everest Books* and *Asia Book House*, off Durbar Marg nr National Theatre in Rani Pokhari; *Ratna Books*, Bagh Bazaar, nr Fr Cultural Centre, wide range, informed, helpful; *Educational Book Shop*, Kantipath, opp New Rd, excellent for educational books; *Pilgrim Book House*, Thamel and elsewhere, a wide selection, but very expensive. Antiquarian bookshop nearby. Thamel has several bookshops which remain open until late, stocking new and second-hand books: *Tantric Book Shop*, 3/394 Thamel, good range; *Global Books*, new and second-hand collection.

Clothing and embroidery: in Thamel and Nepalese caps, between Indra Chowk and Asan Tole.

Handicrafts & textiles: *Tangkas* are available in Thamel, Jochen and Hanuman Dhoka.

Mannie's Art, Sakya Arcade, Durbar Square, rec. Rice paper prints are available in Thamel nr *Kathmandu Guest House*. Good selection in *The Print Shop*, Batik, small oil paintings and greeting cards made of pipal leaf, are popular. Handicrafts and textiles at *Yeshi Phuntsok's* in Thamel. Also from disadvantaged groups: UNCF's Hastakala, opp *Himalaya Hotel*, Women's Skill Development Project, Lazimpat, nr French Embassy and Mahaguthi, Durbar Square.

Jewellery: in Kathmandu ranges in both style and quality. Typically, gem stones and turquoise and coral are used in settings. Several good shops in New Rd, Thamel, especially nr Chetrapati. Visit the Kashmiri Bead Market, crossing of Maru Tole and Indra Chowk, for glittering glass beads.

Khukris: try stalls in Basantapur, nr Hanuman Dhoka.

Maps: see books; a wide selection is available for trekking.

Markets: around Basantapur Square, Indra Chowk and Asan Tole offer good opportunities for browsing for bargains.

Metalwork: Patan is the centre for bronze casting by the cire perdu (lost wax) process. Metal figures of deities, gameboards and pieces for the traditional Nepalese game bagh chal are also available.

Papiermâché masks and puppets: at shops in Kathmandu, Patan, and Bhaktapur. **Thimi** is the manufacturing centre for masks (Ganesh, Bhairava and the Kumari are popular). Some are used in the traditional masked dances in September.

Photography: Kodak and Fuji films are readily available in Kathmandu and processing and printing can now be done with confidence. Send prepaid processing films home.

Stamps & coins: you can pick up stamps and coins in New Rd and Basantapur.

Souvenir shops: in Makhan Tole, between Hanuman Dhoka and Indra Chowk.

Tibetan carpets: Jawalakhel, S of Patan, and Boudha/ Jorbati are the carpetweaving centres in the valley. Most are for wholesale export, but there are also numerous shops. Try Indra Chowk and Durbar Marg.

Terracotta pottery: is particularly good from Bhaktapur and Thimi (on the way) which specialize in little flowerpots often in animal shapes.

● **Sports**

Fishing: Mahseer which can grow up to 40 kg, Asla, a kind of snow trout and other fish in Terai rivers and valley lakes. For permits, apply to National Parks and Wildlife Conservation Department, Babar Mahal. For fishing in Karnali, Babai and Narayani rivers, contact *Tiger Tops* and *West Nepal Adventures*, Durbar Marg, T 222706. Feb-Mar and Oct-Nov are best for fishing. Bring your own tackle.

Golf: two 9-hole golf courses, inc the *Royal Nepal Golf Club*, nr airport. Temporary members welcome.

Jungle safaris: contact *Tiger Tops*, Durbar Marg, T 222706; *Gaida Wildlife Camp*, Durbar Marg, T 215840; *Gokarna Safari Park*, Thapalthali, T 411896; *Elephant Camp*, Durbar Marg, T 213976; *Jungle Safari Camp*, Kantipath.

River rafting: offered on Trisuli, Narayani, Marsyangdi, Set and Sunkoshi. Inflatable rubber rafts for 5 plus guide, for either scenic or 'white water' trips. Trisuli trips (from a few hours to 3 days) are popular as the river runs through forests and villages. The demanding Sunkosi (7-10 days) offers exciting rapids, good birdlife and white beaches for night stops, starting at Dolalghat E of Kathmandu. **NB** Make certain about quality of raft, safety jackets and helmets, arrangements for transportation to and from, and also about camping style and food for longer journeys. Members of Nepal Association of Rafting Agents (NARA) meet all safety and licensing requirements. Report back if not satisfied. Go to a reputable agency and do not risk a cheap offer. Rafting can be combined with trekking or a visit to the Chitwan National Park.

Swimming: National Stadium, Tripureshwar, has a large pool. Open daily except Sun for members and guests. Mon, women only. Large public pool next to Baleju Water Garden, NW Kathmandu. Pools in the *Yak and Yeti* and *Hotel Narayan*, open to non-residents on payment of a fee.

Trekking: excellent opportunities for short or long, easy or difficult. See under **Tour companies & travel agents**.

● **Tour companies & travel agents**

On Durbar Marg: *Adventure Travel*, T 223328; *Himalayan Travels*, T 223803; *Karthak*, T 227233; *Natraj*, Ghantaghar, T 222014; *President*, T 220245, a first class travel service; *Yeti*, T 221234; and *Shambhala Travels and Tours*, T 225166, F 227229 (specialists in Bhutan).

On Ganga Path: *Everest*, T 222217 and Kathmandu, T 212511; *Marco Polo*, Kamalpokhari, T 414192; *Namaste*, Maitighar, Ramshah Path, T 212918; *Nepal Travel Agency*, Ramshah Path, T 412899; *Paramount Nepal Tours*, Lazimpat, PO Box 4749, Kathmandu, T 415078, F 977-1-415078, are very helpful; *Shashi's Holidays*, Ranipokhari, T 216208. Numerous other travel agents on Durbar Marg, Thamel and Kantipath where you might find very competitive rates. Half day tours of city and surroundings and overnight trip to Dhulikhel. Book early during tourist season. **NB** Trekking agents offer inclusive packages for rafting as well as trekking. Notice boards around town publicize courses and cultural events. Trekkers looking for partners use these and the notice board at *Kathmandu Guest House*.

In Patan, see below, page 686.

● **Tourist offices**

Information Centre at New Rd, nr Durbar Square, T 220818, Sun-Thur, 0900-1600 (Fri to 1500). At International Airport, T 410537.

'*Nepal Traveller*', a free magazine, inc practical information and articles of interest. Available from Tripureshwar Marg, 400m from Kantipath roundabout. **Government Department of Tourism**, Tripureshwar (behind stadium), T 211293, 1100-1600 (to 1500 Fri). **Trekking Agents Assoc of Nepal** (TAAN), Gairidhara, T 217804.

● **Useful addresses**

Chamber of Commerce: Nepal Chamber of Commerce, Gangapath.

Fire: T 221177.

Immigration Office (for Visa Renewals and Trekking Permits): Tridevi Marg, nr Thamel, Sun-Thur 1000-1300/1400 and Fri 1000-1200, closed Sat. Be there when the office opens to avoid long queues.

Police: T 216999.

Tourist Police: Basantapur Info Centre, T 220818.

● **Transport**

Local Autorickshaws: metered though fares often negotiable. Fix before starting journey. Extra for night. **Bicycle hire**: Rs 50/day. More expensive mountain bikes from shops around the Thamel, Thahiti Tole and Chetrapati Square areas. Please use lock provided. **Bus**: buses are cheap but very crowded. Buses for Kathmandu Valley leave from Shahid Gate and Ratna Park. **NB** Beware of pickpockets. **Cycle Rickshaw**: rates negotiable, around Rs 3/km. Some may find this uncomfortable. **Motorcycle hire**: Rs 65/hr, Rs 400/day, T 213569. **Taxis**: easily available; metered ones with black registration plates have at long last been installed with efficiently functioning metres. About Rs 80 for a long trip across town but fares double on rainy evenings and at night (T 224374). Out of town/day hire can be expensive, Rs 4,000/day.

Air Royal Nepal Airlines links Kathmandu by flights to Calcutta (Mon, Wed, Sat), Delhi (twice daily), Bombay (Mon, Fri). RNAC also connects Kathmandu with Rangoon, Bangkok, Karachi, Singapore, Shanghai and Osaka. Biman, PIA, Burma, Thai International and China South-west also link Kathmandu with Dhaka, Karachi, Rangoon, Bangkok and Lhasa respectively. RNAC and Lufthanza have flights from London, Paaris and Frankfurt, while Aeroflot link Kathmandu with Moscow. Indian Airlines has an extensive network linking Kathmandu with Delhi and Varanasi daily, Calcutta (Tues, Thur, Fri, Sun) and Patna (Wed, Sat).

RNAC's domestic services (T 223453/226574): Bharatpur (for Chitwan) Mon, Wed, Sat, Sun; Biratnagar (daily except Thur), Lukla (daily) and Pokhara (daily). Also Bhairawa Tues, Thur, Sat, Sun; Jumla, Sat; Tumlingtar Tues, Thur, Sat, Sun. Everest Airways services (T 228392): daily to Bharatpur; Biratnagar and Pokhara and to Jomosom Thur, Fri, Sun; Jumla Fri, Sun; Nepalgunj, Sun. Nepal Airways (T 414488): daily to Lukla, Nepalgunj and Pokhara. RNAC and Everest Air also do 1 hr morning 'Mountain Flights'. **NB** Flights to trekking destinations (Jomosom, Jiri, Manang, Simara) are frequent during the season but the timetable is variable. Kathmandu and Jomosom both have winter weather problems, the former with fog, the latter with wind from the Kali Gandaki gorge. Reservations: RNAC, New Rd, Kathmandu, T 214511. Students (ISI card holders) may get 25% discount. The airport (8 km) bus calls at popular hotels, Durbar Marg, Thamel and Singha Durbar (0800-2200). Sajha Yatayat Tourist bus to New Rd Gate, Rs 25. Taxis available. **Warning** The STOL (Short Take Off and Landing) strip at Lukla for Namche Bazaar and Everest can close due to bad weather. Allow a couple of extra days in case of flight delays.

Train Nearest railhead at Amlekhganj (162 km) in the Terai, is linked with Raxaul Bazaar on the Indian border which is connected with Gorakhpur and Patna.

Points of Entry There are 10 points of entry for foreign tourists: Kakarbhitta with connections from Siliguri and Darjiling into E Nepal; Pashupatinagar from Darjiling into E Nepal, Birganj from Raxaul in Uttar Pradesh for Hetauda and Kathmandu; Sonauli (Belhalia) N of Gorakhpur for Bhairawa and the roads to Pokhara and Kathmandu; Nanpara for Nepalganj and W Nepal; Dhangadhi from Shajahanpur area into Far-west Nepal; Mahendranagar from Pilibith area into Far-west Nepal; Kodari on the Tibetan border providing access from Lhasa via Barabise, and Khojarnath from Purang in Far-west Tibet via Simikot (both with a special permit); and Tribhuvan International Airport.

Road Five main highways converge in the capital: Tribhuvan Raj Path linking Kathmandu with Raxaul at the Indian border (200 km); Arniko Highway linking Kathmandu with Kodari on the Tibetan border (114 km); Prithivi Raj Marg linking Kathmandu and Pokhara (200 km); Mahendra Raj Marg linking the E Terai with the W Terai (1,000 km); and Ring Rd within the Kathmandu valley (32 km). **Bus**: regular bus services from Kathmandu to Pokhara, Sonauli, Birgunj and Kakarbhitta. Most leave from Central Bus Stand (nr City Hall, S of Bagh Bazaar), Sundhara (Bhimsen Tower nr GPO) and Trivedi Marg (E of Kathmandu Guest House). Approximate journey times are in brackets. Some private operators providing Tourist buses include: Memoire, Osho, Student Travel and Swiss. Rs 100 to Pokhara. **Warning** Beware of pickpockets. State buses for Pokhara leave from Sundhara at 0630-0700 and hourly from 0500 from the Central Bus Stand (6-7 hrs). Private buses from Trivedi Marg Rd conditions can be difficult. Bhairawa busses (via Pokhara) leave from Sundhara and Central Bus Stand at 0500 (14 hrs); Kakarbhitta regular busses from Put Sadak at 0430 and 1740 and express busses from Central Bus Stand at 0500 and 1815 (12-14 hrs) (night buses only in winter which can be very cold); Biratnagar busses leave from the Central Bus Stand at 1815 (11 hrs); Birganj busses from Sundhara at 0645 and Central Bus Stand at 0630, 0800, 1900 and 2000 (10 hrs); Trishuli busses from Sorokhuti (Paknajal, Lekhnath Mg) at 0700 and 1200 (5 hrs); Kodari busses from Sundhara at 0600 and Central Bus Stand from 0500 onwards (6 hrs); Gorkha busses from Central Bus Stand at 0815, 1900 (5 hrs); Janakpur busses from Central Bus Stand at 0600 (9-10 hrs); Jiri busses at 0530 (book the day before) 0630, 0800 (10-14 hrs), and Narayanghat busses at 0700 and 1330 (5 hrs).

PATAN

(*Pop* 277,054; *Area* 346 sq km), also known as Lalitpur, is officially the valley's second largest town, although it has now been absorbed into Kathmandu. It has a long history and has long been an important centre of Newar Buddhism. The four earth and brick directional stupas at its four corners are attributed to Emperor Ashoka. Its compact scale and the remarkable vivacity of its Malla temple architecture, give Patan a unique atmosphere.

With a Durbar Square more densely packed with Hindu temples than either Kathmandu or Bhaktapur, and a total of 55 major temples and 136 monasteries, Patan is the artistic and architectural centre of the valley.

Places of interest

Hindu Patan

The palace complex in the centre of the town has changed little in the last century. The main avenue runs from N to S. The **Bhimsena Temple** at the N end has a lion pillar in front of it. Bhimsena in the *Mahabharata* is the exceptionally strong god of traders. The present 3-storeyed marble and gilt-faced building was constructed in 1682 after an earlier one had been destroyed by fire. Next to it is the 2-storey **Vishvanath Temple** (1627) dedicated to Shiva with a *linga* shrine. Two stone elephants guard the entrance and a Nandi bull the rear. The beams and brackets are profusely decorated with erotic carvings.

Set further back from the main thoroughfare, the **Krishna Mandir** (1637) is unlike the Malla temples in using stone in a combination of early Mughal and Nagara architectural styles. Built by the famous Malla king of Patan, Siddhinarasimha Malla, it is one of the best known temples in Nepal, noted for its high quality of stone work. The first three floors have *chattri* pavilions and open colonnaded sides reminiscent of Akbar's Panch Mahal at Fatehpur Sikri. On the second floor is a Shiva *linga*. Capping it is a curvilinear Hindu *shikhara* similar to those in the Kangra Valley of Himachal Pradesh. A golden garuda on a stone pillar faces the temple. Inside are excellent stone bas relief carvings of scenes from the Hindu epics with fine details, the *Mahabharata* stories on the first floor and *Ramayana* on the second. A popular festival is held on Krishnastami in Aug/Sept when a number of devotees gather to pay homage to Krishna.

The **Jagannarayan Temple** (c1565) dedicated to Vishnu, the oldest in the square, comes next. Two stone lions guard the entrance of the 2-storey *shikhara* style temple. The carved roof struts depict Vishnu's incarnations.

The **Yoganarendra Malla Statue** sits

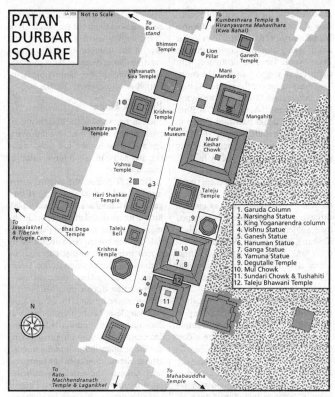

PATAN DURBAR SQUARE

SA 359 Not to Scale

To Bus stand

To Kumbeshvara Temple & Hiranyavarna Mahavihara (Kwa Bahal)

Bhimsen Temple

Lion Pillar

Ganesh Temple

Vishvanath Siva Temple

Mani Mandap

Krishna Temple

1

Jagannarayan Temple

Patan Museum

Mangahiti

Vishnu Temple

Mani Keshar Chowk

2

3

Hari Shankar Temple

Taleju Temple

To Jawalakhel & Tibetan Refugee Camp

9

Bhai Dega Temple

Taleju Bell

10

Krishna Temple

7 8

4

12

5

11

6

N

To Rato Machhendranath Temple & Lagankhel

To Mahabauddha Temple

1. Garuda Column
2. Narsingha Statue
3. King Yoganarendra column
4. Vishnu Statue
5. Ganesh Statue
6. Hanuman Statue
7. Ganga Statue
8. Yamuna Statue
9. Degutalle Temple
10. Mul Chowk
11. Sundari Chowk & Tushahiti
12. Taleju Bhawani Temple

on a pillar facing the palace under a cobra hood, on which sits a bird. A local legend suggests that as long as the bird remains, the king may return to his palace. A window is kept open for his return, and a hookah ready for his use! The 3-storeyed **Hari Shankar Temple** (1705) built by Yoganendra's daughter, has elaborately carved struts and arches. The **Taleju Bell** (1736), cast by Vishnu Malla, hangs between two thick pillars. By ringing the bell, citizens could draw the king's attention to injustices suffered by them. Beside this is the attractive octagonal **Krishna Temple** of Chyasim Deval (1723). In the lower, SW corner stands the Shaivite **Bhai Dega**

Temple, a simple cube topped by an onion dome.

Across the street is the **Royal Palace**. The entrance to its **Sundari Chowk** is guarded by stone statues of Ganesh, Hanuman and Vishnu. The fine 3-storey Palace with carved roof struts has a gilded metal window over the entrance, flanked by carved ivory windows. In the centre is the Tushahiti (tank), a sunken royal bath decorated with fine stone and bronze carvings. There is an incomplete set of Ashta Matrika deities, eight divine mother goddesses who attend Shiva and the god of war, Skanda, the eight Bhairavas and the eight Nagas.

To your left (N) is **Mul Chowk** (1668),

the core of the complex built for Shrinivasa Malla with the small gilded **Vidya Mandir** shrine at the centre. The cloister is a 2-storey building, comprising the Patan Royal Family's residence, with three Taleju temples around the court. Two brass images of the goddess Ganga on a tortoise and Yamuna on the mythical *makara* flank the doorway of the Bhutanese style **Taleju Bhawani** shrine to the S. The **Degutalle Temple** (1640, NE corner) dedicated to the personal deity of the Mallas was destroyed by fire and rebuilt in 1662.

The most northerly and recent courtyard, **Mani Keshar Chowk** (1734) took 60 years to complete, and is entered through a splendid gilded door topped by a golden *torana*. Beyond the Mani Keshar Chowk is the **Mangahiti**, another tank in a lotus pattern with three carved crocodile stone waterspouts, and the **Mani Mandap** (1700) Royal Pavilion adjacent to it.

300m along the road which leads N from Durbar Square, stands the imposing 5-storey **Kumbeshvara Temple** (1392), dedicated to Shiva, the oldest existing temple here. A Shiva *linga* is enshrined in the temple and there are also different forms of Shiva, carved in wood. It is finely proportioned with numerous carvings including figures of Ganesh, Narayana and other deities with small Bhairava and Baglamukhi temples around it. The natural spring which feeds the tank in the courtyard is said to have the glacial Lake Gosainkund as its source. A bath here is considered as holy as the long pilgrimage to that High Himalayan lake. At Janai Purnima in July/Aug, large crowds of pilgrims take a ritual bath and worship a silver and gold *lingam*, placed in the tank. Brahmins and Chettris replace their sacred threads at the festival, amidst frenetic dancing by strikingly dressed *jhankri* (witch doctors).

Agnimath on the outskirts of Patan is worth a visit. It is a very popular place of worship as the sacred fire here has not been allowed to go out for hundreds of years. Only a married priest can take care of the fire. On his death, a new caretaker takes charge of the Agnimath, chosen from the five families of Agnihotras, or caretakers of the fire.

Buddhist Patan

You can visit some of the Buddhist temples and bahals in Patan on a tour starting at Durbar Square and finishing at the zoo and Tibetan refugee camp at Jawalakhel.

Going NW from the Square, a few minutes' walk brings you to the **Hiranyavarna Mahivihara** (Golden Temple), known for its abundant use of gold. The monastery is a triple-roofed pagoda, its gold plating having been dedicated by a rich merchant, and it has a richly embossed silver and gold façade. Decorative lions guard the entrance. Though first documented in 1409, it was renovated by the 11th century King Bhaskaradeva, and presumably was constructed some period before then. Inside, the shrine has a frieze depicting the life of Shakyamuni Buddha where a strong Hindu component of some images indicate the extent of religious cross-fertilization in the valley. There is a rack of prayer wheels and a large suspended bell.

Further N, passing the aforementioned Kumbeshvara Temple, is the **Northern Ashoka Stupa**, the best preserved of the four accredited to the great Mauryan emperor in the 3rd century BC.

To the SE of Durbar Square, and along a SW leading alleyway is the 16th century *shikhara* style **Mahaboudha Temple**, dedicated to the Thousand Buddhas of the Auspicious Aeon. Tightly hemmed in by surrounding buildings the terracotta and tile temple is a little difficult to locate. It is somewhat reminiscent of the great Mahabodhi Temple at Bodhgaya in India. This is a masterpiece of terracotta and each of the 9,000 or so bricks is said to carry an image of the Buddha. In the centre is a gold image of the Buddha. A narrow staircase leads to the upper part. Although it was completely destroyed after the 1934 earthquake, it has been rebuilt exactly like the original. The temple is surrounded by Newar Buddhist craft shops, most of them selling images of Buddhist deities fashioned in the renowned cire perdue ('lost wax') style.

Rato Maysyendranath Temple Heading SW from Durbar Square, you will come to the Rato (Red) Matsyendranath Temple, also known as Bungadya. This is venerated as the abode of the deity Bungamati Avalokiteshvara (also called Karunamaya Avalokiteshvara; *Tib* Bukham Lokeshvara). Legend has it that when Gorakhanath, a disciple of Karunamaya, visited Kathmandu, he was not shown due respect. In his anger he cursed the people and consequently they suffered a long drought. When Karunamaya learned of this, he told Gorakhanath to pardon the people and lift the curse; this was done and rain poured down. In honour of Karunamaya's kindness, the king Narendradeva built this temple. He also instigated the annual chariot festival.

The revered image is worshipped as a god of rain and Hindus also believe that simply seeing the chariot festival of Rato Matsyendranath is enough to attain salvation. The present 3-storeyed temple dates from 1673 and stands in a courtyard filled with sculptures of animals including horses, lions and bulls. Four richly adorned entrances lead into the shrine which houses the large-eyed image, made of clay-covered sandalwood, and decorated with jewellery and garlands. For several weeks from April onwards, the deity is trundled through the streets of Patan in an enormous chariot. This culminates in the Boro Jatra festival when the chariot reaches Jawalakhel.

Heading S from Rato Matsyendranath, you will pass the Patan Hospital and reach the **Southern Ashoka Stupa**, via the district of Lagankhel. At the Patan Industrial Estate in Lagankhel, you can visit an outstanding wood carving factory.

Heading NW from the S side of Durbar Square, you will pass the Patan Hospital and after about 1 km you will reach **Jawalakhel**, where there is a large Tibetan community, and a Tibetan Refugee Camp, now occupied by only the poorest of the exiles. It is possible to visit the camp shop and see Tibetan carpets being weaved, along with blankets, jackets and pullovers; and you can buy them at a competitive price. Closed Sat. Nearby is the Zoo.

The road N from Jawalakhel takes you past the **Western Ashoka Stupa (Pulchowk)** and joins Kopundole Rd, which crosses the Bagmati, a short distance from the centre of Kathmandu.

Sites South of Patan

Some 12 km S of Patan, near Chapagaon is the **Vajravarahi Temple**, sacred to Buddhists as the enlightened consort of the meditational deity Cakrasamvara, and to Hindus as a protector of domestic animals. This temple is set amidst woodlands and attracts innumerable devotees. Outside the temple is an image of a bull.

Buses leave Lagakhel in Patan for Godavari every hour, heading out of town in a SE direction via Dupat district. En route you will pass the **Eastern Ashoka Stupa**, and some of the best forested parts of the valley.

Godavari, 22 km from Kathmandu, is situated below Mt Phulchowki (2,760m), the highest peak on the ridge surrounding the valley. Here the attraction for visitors is the **Royal Botanical Garden** (open daily, 1000-0500; Rs 2). From the base at Godavari it takes 3-4 hrs to hike up the mountain, or 2 hrs scramble on a motorbike, up the rough, winding track to the summit. You can also rent a 4WD vehicle. In a preservation area, **Mt Phulchowki** is a haven for birds and butterflies, with good vegetation and on a clear day, a magnificent panorama of several Himalayan peaks include Ganesh Himal, Langtang, Himalchuli, and Manaslu. The summit has a Buddhist stupa, a Hindu shrine dedicated to the mother goddess Phulchowki Mai, and an army telecommunications tower. If you take a bus to Patan after your hike, it is best to catch the bus before 1700 as services are erratic later.

Museums

National Bronze Museum contains a good collection of ancient statues, paintings and tangkas. Also the **Mani Keshar Chowk Museum** in Durbar Square was restored in 1993 in a project sponsored by the Austrian Government.

Zoos

At Jawalakhel, a small zoo has birds, reptiles and large mammals, including lions, leopards, tigers, elephants and rhinos. Re 0.50. Not recommended as a special trip.

Local festivals

Mar-April: *Ghorajatra*.
April: *Bisket*.
Apr/May: *Rato Matsyendranath*. The month-long festival when the red-faced image of the patron deity of the valley, the God of Rain and Harvest, is taken around the city. His chariot moves by daily stages and may not return for some months. The image is prepared for the event in Pulchowk, when it is washed and repainted awaiting the assembling of the remarkably tall chariot. The procession through the streets is accompanied by musicians and soldiers and the nightly halts are marked by worship and feasting. The arrival in Jawalakhel several weeks later is witnessed by not only the royal family but also by Patan's Kumari, the 'Living Goddess'. Every 12 years, the procession goes to Bungamati,

5 km S of Patan where the image is ensconced in a second home for 6 months. Next in 2003.
July: *Janai Purnima*.
Aug/Sept: *Krishnastami*.

Local information

● **Accommodation**
Hotels in Patan offer an alternative to Kathmandu's pollution, and are becoming increasingly popular.

A *Himalaya*, Sahid Sukra Marg, Pulchowk, 1.5 km SE of Bagmati Bridge, T 523900, 100 rm, modern, tasteful with Himalayan views, free transport to town (10 mins), Japanese owned.

B *Summit*, Kopundole Heights, 2 km SW of Bagmati Bridge, T 521780, F 523737, 64 rm in Garden and Himalaya View wings, 3 km centre, traditional style Newari architecture, good restaurant, pool, beautiful tranquil gardens, mountain and valley views, excellent service, home-grown produce, transport to airport and town centre, experienced trekking organization, English and Dutch management; **B** *Narayani*, at Pulchowk Crossroads, 1 km W of Durbar Square, T 521442, F 521291, 90 rm, restaurant, café, bar, pool, travel, pleasant garden. Facilities of **D** *Oasis*, T 522748, available inc squash and tennis, 22 rm with bath, restaurant, bar, exchange, travel.

Youth hostels **F** *Mahendra Yuvalaya*, Jawalakhel, 15 mins' walk from Patan bus stop, T 521003, rooms and dormitory, quiet.

● **Places to eat**
Summit Hotel Restaurant has excellent Nepalese, Indian, Western and Tibetan cuisine; the *Café de Patan*, SW corner of Durbar Square, is also rec; *The German Bakery*, nr Zoo Roundabout, Jawalakhel, is good for bread, pastries, cakes and cold drinks. Few basic places nr City Gate bus stand.

● **Libraries**
Rastriya Pustakalaya (Nepal National Library), Pulchowk, Patan, books in English, Nepali and Indian languages.

● **Hospitals & medical services**
Patan Hospital, Lagankhel, T 521333.

● **Shopping**
Patan is regarded as the best place for handicrafts in the valley. It has a long metal working tradition and produces fine statues of the Buddha, various bodhisattvas, and Buddhist

tantric deities. Prices for gold plated bronze figurines range from Rs 2,000 to over Rs 10,000. Go to *Gyan Hasta Kala Udhyog*, Mahabauddha Temple, T 525051; or to *Patan Industrial Centre* 1.5 km S of Durbar Square, to see craftsmen at work. The estate also has an excellent wood carving industry. Good variety of metal work and paintings N of Durbar Square. Tibetan crafts in Jawalakhel. South Asian music is available on cassette at the shop adjacent to the Café de Patan. *Arjun* and *Madhu Chandra Art Gallery* are in Durbar Square. In Jawalakhel you will find Tibetan handicrafts, crafts from all over Nepal at *Cheez Beez*, *Mahaguthi* and the *BB Thapa Gallery*. Carpets are good in Mangal Bazaar and you can watch weavers (and buy) in the *Tibetan Refugee Centre*.

● **Transport**

Local Bus: regular bus service from Ratna Park bus stop to Patan Gate from which it is a very short walk to Durbar Square. Fare Rs 2.00. **Taxi**: a taxi will cost around Rs 50 one way. You can also take a **tempo**, **rickshaw**, **cycle** or walk the 5 km.

BHAKTAPUR

(*Pop* 186,385; *Area* 106 sq km), also known as Bhadgaon, is the valley's third major city. Situated about 14 km E of Kathmandu, Bhaktapur developed independently until the Gorkha unification in 1768. After this its growth stopped as Kathmandu became more cosmopolitan and merged with Patan. Consequently it has preserved its medieval character better than Patan and Kathmandu. In the 1970s it benefited from a W German funded restoration project. The town is known for its pottery, weaving and Nepali caps.

On the N bank of the Hanumante River, Bhaktapur was capital of the whole valley from the 14th-16th century and fortified in the 15th century. The original 15th century centre of the city comprised the East Square with its Dattatraya Temple and Pujahari Math, but later Durbar Square became the main focus. The Dattatraya Temple with the Pujahari Math is one of the oldest and most famous temples in Bhaktapur. It is dedicated to both Brahma and Vishnu and noted for its wood carvings, in particular the exquisitely carved peacock window on the eastern wall. In front of the Vishnu Temple is a golden garuda on a stone monolith and the temple is believed to have been built from a single tree.

Bhaktapur is approached from Kathmandu via the Ring Rd which leads through Baneshwar, bypassing Tribhuvan Airport and the walled city of Thimi. Entering Bhaktapur from the W, you pass through a pine grove on a low hill, where two tanks once supplied the population with drinking water. The bus stop is near the walled tank known as **Siddha Pokhari**, considered holy by Hindus and Buddhists. Beyond this the road divides, the left fork running into Durbar Square.

Places of interest

Durbar Square

The 1934 earthquake caused considerable damage to buildings in the square which consequently appears more spacious than its two namesakes in Kathmandu and Patan. It is still an architectural showpiece, exhibiting numerous superb examples of the skills of Nepalese artists and craftsmen over several centuries.

As you enter the outer square from the W end, in front of you is a Shiva/Parvati Temple, while to the right are two smaller temples dedicated respectively to Shiva/Parvati and Shiva. Past the house of a Malla prince on your right are two large stone lions and a small gateway on your left. Two fine stone statues represent the 18-armed Ugrachandi Durga and 12-armed Bhairava. To the left, on the N side of the square, is the ruined palace. Opposite, the minor temples, from right to left, are dedicated to: Rameshvara, Bhadri, Krishna and Shiva.

In the centre of Durbar Square, the most striking feature is a life-size gilded statue of Bhupatindra Malla, seated on a tall stone pillar facing the **Sun Dhoka** (Golden Gate), one of the artistic mas-

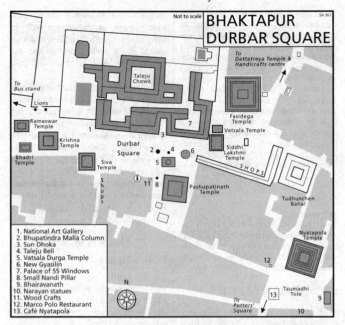

Not to scale

BHAKTAPUR DURBAR SQUARE

SA 361

To Dattatreya Temple &
Handicrafts centre

To
Bus stand

Lions

Rameswar
Temple

Krishna
Temple

Bhadri
Temple

Siva
Temple

Durbar
Square

Taleju
Chowk

Fasidega
Temple

Vatsala Temple

Siddhi
Lakshmi
Temple

SHOPS

Pashupatinath
Temple

Tudhunchen
Bahal

Nyatapola
Temple

Taumadhi
Tole

To
Potters'
Square

N

1. National Art Gallery
2. Bhupatindra Malla Column
3. Sun Dhoka
4. Taleju Bell
5. Vatsala Durga Temple
6. New Gyasilin
7. Palace of 55 Windows
8. Small Nandi Pillar
9. Bhairavanath
10. Narayan statues
11. Wood Crafts
12. Marco Polo Restaurant
13. Café Nyatapola

terpieces of the valley with superb dark
woodcarving set off by the red brick. The
door frame shows many divinities and
mythical creatures. Crowning the gateway are Kali and Garuda, killing ser-
pents. Below Garuda is the 4-headed and
16-armed Taleju Bhavani, the personal
deity of the Malla Dynasty. The gate is
set into glazed brickwork and is similar
to Ghiberti's Florentine masterpiece at
the Baptistry.

The gate leads to the main courtyard of the **Palace of Fifty-five Windows** which was built during the early
15th century but remodelled by Bhupatindra Malla (r 1696-1722) and completed in 1754. The balcony with 55
windows is unique for its marvellous
woodcarving. The small entrance
courtyard leads onto the Mul Chowk
which is guarded and inaccessible.

To the left of the Sun Dhoka, with
another two stone lines in front, is the

National Art Gallery, formerly part of
the palace. Its entrance is flanked by
Hanuman in the tantric form Bhairava
and Vishnu as Narasimha (c1698), and
it has an especially fine collection of
tangkas, palm leaf manuscripts and examples of Bhaktapur's craft heritage.
Strange, colourful Newari animal paintings on the second floor should not be
missed. Open daily 1000-1700 except
Tues and holidays, Rs 5, Camera Rs 10.

The National Wood Carving Museum
in Dattatreya Square is in the restored
Pujari Math which is the museum itself
and has fine examples of arched windows
and roof struts. The woodcarving is the
finest Newari quality and includes the famous Peacock Window. Open daily, except
Tues and holidays, 1030-1600.

**The National Brass and Bronze
Museum** is also in Dattatreya Square
and offers a collection of domestic and
religious metalware. Open daily, except

Tues and holidays, 1000-1700.

Facing the Sun Dhoka, the **Vatsala Durga Temple** temple, intricately carved in the Indian *shikhara* style, was built by Prakash Malla in 1672, Vatsala is another name for Parvati, the consort of Shiva. In front is the large bronze Taleju Bell (Ranjit Malla, 1737) which originally sounded the daily curfew. Popularly known as "The Barking Bell" following a dream visitation the king had, it is rung every morning to mark the worship of Taleju.

Behind this is the 2-storey, 15th century **Yaksheshvara Temple**, also known as the Pashupatinath Temple, noted for the erotic carvings on its roof struts. This is a replica of the famous Pashupatinath Temple near Kathmandu (see above, page 671) and the image in the centre of the temple is identical to that in Pashupatinath. Beside the temple is a tank with a new octagonal 'waiting room' behind, built with German aid (opened 1987), which used materials from the 18th century Gyaslin Mandapa, that had been destroyed in the 1934 earthquake.

Other temples here include the 17th century **Siddhi Lakshmi Temple** with stone attendants lining the steps. To the E of this temple are stone lions and to the N another Vatsala Temple. The temple in the NE corner sits on a six-level platform with an attractive flight of steps flanked by decorative elephants, lions and cows.

Nyatapola Temple, a short walk S of the Square, at the N end of Taumadhi Tole, is Nepal's tallest temple (30m) and one of the only two 5-storey temples in the country built in Nepalese pagoda style. It was founded by King Bhupatindra Malla of Bhaktapur in 1798 and only mildly damaged in the 1934 earthquake. The successive tiled roofs are supported by extravagantly carved and painted beams and struts. Five pairs of stone carved figures line the steps of the five terraces, each thought to be 10 times stronger than the one below. The images of the legendary Bhaktapur wrestlers of enormous strength, Jaya Malla and Phatta Malla, elephants, lions, griffins, Baghini and Singhini, the tiger and lion goddesses are found on the side of the steps. The interior (accessible only to priests) is Sino-Thai in character. It contains the shrine of the Hindu tantric goddess Siddhi Lakshmi who is also carved into the 108 roof struts.

South of the Nyatapola Temple is the **Akasha Bhairava Temple** (17th century) with a dance platform in front and shrines dedicated to Shiva and Narayana behind. A **Jagannath Temple** marks the SW exit from the square to the Potter's Square and Bus Stop. The roof, finials and windows are all made out of gold. On the 13 or 14 April, the image of the Lord Bhairava is taken around the city.

About 3 km to the S from Bhaktapur and overlooking the city is the **Surya Vinayaka Temple**. This is one of the four Ganesh temples of the Kathmandu valley, and it catches the first rays of the rising sun. Tues is a popular day for worshipping Ganesh and this is a popular pilgrimage spot for Hindu devotees.

The **Changu Narayana Temple** is 12 km E of Kathmandu and approximately 5 km N of Bhaktapur, some 125m above the valley floor. The temple sits on the hillock of Dolagiri (1,524m) and dates from the 4th century AD. It can be reached on foot from Bhaktapur, or even from Kathmandu if you are feeling energetic, and may be combined with a visit to the great Stupa of Bodhnath. The walk through cultivated fields of rice up to the low hill is most attractive, especially if you descend at sundown. The old temple destroyed by fire in 1702 was completely rebuilt. Stone elephants guard the entrance to its 2-tiered replacement, dedicated to Narayana or Vishnu. The original structure was possibly the oldest in the valley in the pagoda style. In front is a huge Garuda (c 5th century) with an important Licchavi inscription in Gupta script nearby. There are four pillars capped by a conch and lotus, Vishnu's traditional weapons.

For Bodhnath there is a steep descent to the N to the Manohara River which you cross by a temporary dry season bridge to reach the road. Bodhnath is 6 km to the W. Less than an hour's walk along the ridge to the E brings you to Nagarkot.

Local festivals

April: *Bisket* (Snake slaughter). Special celebrations to commemorate the great battle in the Hindu epic *Mahabharata*. Chariots carrying Bhairava and Bhadrakali are drawn through the narrow streets. A tug-of-war between upper and lower parts of the town decides who will be fortunate for the coming year. A tall wooden pole (sometimes 20m high) is erected near the riverside with cross beams from which two banners, signifying snake demons are hung. On the following day (New Year), it is brought crashing down after another tug-of-war. There is dancing and singing in the street over 4 days.

Local information

● **Places to eat**
Restaurants nr the Dattatreya and Nyatapola Temples and also nr the Bus Stop. There are good views from the balcony of the *Marco Polo* Restaurant nr the Nyatapola Temple. The Bhaktapur speciality is *Jujudhau*, a sweet curd.

● **Cultural centres**
French Cultural Centre, Bagh Bazaar, T 224326, regular French film nights (small charge).

● **Hospitals & medical services**
Hospital at Doodh Pati, T 610676.

● **Shopping**
Particularly good for tangkas, caps, masks and puppets. Puppets made in Bhaktapur often show tribal people with tools of their trade or many-armed deities, clutching little wooden weapons in each hand. *The Handicrafts Centre*, nr Dattatreya Temple. Good tangkas in the Durbar Square and Nepalese caps from shops nr Akasha Bhairavanath Temple. The Potters' Square is worth a visit to see a range lining the square.

Books: *Himalaya Book Store*, Bagh Bazaar, nr Bus Stand.

● **Transport**
Road Bus: minibus from Bagh Bazaar or a trolley from Tripureswar nr the stadium in Kathmandu, gets you to Bhaktapur.

NAGARKOT

Roads lead from the Bhaktapur area NE to Nagarkot and SE to Dhulikhel – both mountain top locations of stunning beuaty. Nagarkot (2,100m), 32 km E of Kathmandu, has the best views of the Himalayas from the Kathmandu Valley – its panorama extending from Annapurna (8,090m) and Macchapuchare (7,059m) in the W, to Everest (8,845m) and Kangchendzonga (8,597m) in the E.

The views can be exceptional at sunrise and sunset. Visibility is good from Oct to Feb but cloud cover can spoil the view at any time, particularly during the monsoon. In April and May it can be quite hazy. The spring flowers and unusual rock formations make short, undemanding treks from Nagarkot particularly attractive. Nagarkot is only a small village with an army camp, a temple and market place and an increasing number of small hotels of varying standards. Local lodges are open all year, with reduced rates off season. Visit recommended as it is particularly relaxing after Kathmandu. Nagarkot is also a popular picnic spot for Nepalis and you may come across groups singing and dancing in traditional Nepali style.

Tours

Tours leaving Kathmandu well before dawn cost around Rs 200. A short 3-day trek is an attractive option. *S Powers*, Yangrima, Kathmandu, F 227628, arranges comfortable trek with sherpas, recommended.

Local information

● **Accommodation**
Many visitors come for an overnight stay. The narrow dirt road off the main road is motorable with difficulty. Most hotels are within a 30 mins walk of the bus stop.

B *Club Himalaya Nagarkot Resort*, above bus stand, has 50 rm, indoor pool, its *Tea House Restaurant* offering full range of meals, book through *Kathmandu Guest House*, T 413632, F 417133.

C *Nagarkot Farmhouse*, conceived and built by an American in conjunction with a Tibetan, is highly rec, 9 rm (best No 9), with bath, good food in Dining Hall which has an open fireplace, small hall for yoga, meditation or small conferences of about 20 people, solar-heated water, 2,000 peach and apple trees have been planted, reasonable rates inc 3 meals/day, reservations: *Hotel Vajra*, T Kathmandu 272719, F 271824, delightful and secluded; **C** *Flora Hill*, T 226893, is modest but relatively comfortable with 13 rm, government run.

D *Taragaon Resort*, road closed by army in 1993, due to reopen; **D** *Nagarkot Cottages* are uphill, simple but clean rooms; **D** *View Point*, T 290870 or Kathmandu 417424, clean if basic rooms with attached bath in cottages up hillside, restaurant, electricity, excellent views from some rooms, now partially blocked by rising *Tushita Hotel View Point* will be adding 2 flrs!, heavily booked in season, offers bus service from Thamel, opp British Council, depart 1330, return 1030 following morning. Also new *Space Holiday Resort* opening shortly.

The rest are basic, **E** and **F** lodges most without electricity. Some on the way up, others nr the Mahakali Temple inc **E** *Galaxy*, 9 rm, with electricity, upstairs rooms are simple but clean with good views; **E** *Bamboo Village* has electricity; **E** *Pheasant Lodge*, above with best rooms in cottages; **F** *Peaceful Cottage* has some clean rooms, very basic, check first, all have restaurants.

● **Places to eat**

The Tea House, in the *Club Himalaya Resort* has an immaculate dining room, and spectacular view on top of hill; *View Point*, with limited menu.

● **Transport**

Road Bus: buses from the main bus stand nr the pond in Bhaktapur leave every few hours (Rs 10, 2-3 hrs with many stops). It takes up to 4 hrs from Kathmandu to the hilltop by bus. **Taxi**: a taxi from Kathmandu (1 hr) cost approximately Rs 500 for the return trip. Taxis are also for hire in Bhaktapur but be prepared to bargain. **Mountain bike**: you can mountain bike up the main road and descend down the track to Sankhu. **Hiking**: the adventurous can hike from Bhaktapur (about 4 hrs). It is also possible to walk back to Bhaktapur (3½ hrs) and Kathmandu (6 hrs). Take plenty of drinking water – it can be hot from Mar onwards.

DHULIKHEL

Located on the Arniko Highway, 34 km E of Kathmandu, this old Newar town, offers panoramic views of 12 peaks over 6,000m in NE Himalaya from Cho Oyu (Jowo Oyuk) in the E to Annapurna in the W. The drive along the highway takes 45 mins, passing Bhaktapur and Banepa, a 14th century capital. The hillside village of Dhulikhel in the Panchkhal valley was known for its fine woodcarving which you can see in the temples and village houses around the square and in the upmarket resorts nearby. The **Bhagavati Temple** is a 30 mins walk. Other trails provide pleasant day hikes: to **Namobuddha**, which is an ancient Buddhist shrine marking the spot where Shakyamuni in a previous life gave his body to a hungry tigress; to **Nagarkot**; or to **Panauti**, an ancient riverside town of temples which is a place of pilgrimage for Hindus.

From Dhulikhel it is possible to continue along the Arniko Highway through Lamosangu, Barabise, and Tatopani to reach the **Tibet border**. Visitors entering Nepal from Tibet on this overland route often prefer to spend their last night in Dhulikhel, rather than Kathmandu, thus avoiding the inevitable culture clash and the pollution of the valley.

KODARI

For information on Kathmandu travel agents who can arrange Tibet visas, see above, page 680. To reach Dram from Kathmandu in 1 day be sure to leave early from Kathmandu. You may have to walk 8 km from the Friendship Bridge at Kodari to reach the Chinese Customs at Dram. Landslides occur frequently in the rainy season both N and S of Kodari.

Local information

● **Accommodation**

A *Himalayan Horizon Resort*, Sun and Snow, T Kathmandu 225092, designed in traditional Newari style with *Terrace Garden Restaurant*, marble-tiled bathrooms with solar heated hot water, restaurant has Newari woodcarvings and serves Moghul as well as unusual Nepali festival food, home-baked bread; **A** *Mountain Resort*, above the village, T Kathmandu 220031, 35 twin-bedded rooms with large windows in thatched cottages, lit by candles and traditional oil lamps, attached bathrooms have running water heated by solar energy, good restaurant and bar in the main house which is built in typical Nepali style, delightful terraced gardens, the *Mountain Resort* has its own fleet of vehicles plus trekking and rafting equipment for excursions.

F *Dhulikhel Lodge* in village, T 61114, basic rooms in converted traditional Newari house with courtyard and restaurant, delicious Nepali dishes, served on low tables in the restaurant or in the garden, photocopies of 1 day trekking route to Namobuddha available from reception.

INFORMATION FOR VISITORS

CONTENTS

Before travelling

Entry requirements

● **Visas**

Visas are required by most nationalities. They are available from Nepalese embassies or consulates, and at the Indian border and Kathmandu airport. The cost of a visa varies according to your country of origin (£20 from UK), and is valid for 30 days. A visa issued on arrival is only valid for 30 days (US$20) but may be extended.

Warning Visa extensions are very time consuming so it is best to get a 30-day visa in advance. From outside your home country it is easiest in Bangkok, Calcutta, Lhasa and New Delhi.

Extensions Beyond 1 month, costs US$2/day. Visas can only be extended further than 3 months through special application. The fourth month is granted at US$3/day. Theoretically only 4 months residence per year is allowed on a tourist visa. It may, however, be possible to return after 1 month stay in India, Thailand or Tibet. Studying, teaching, research (University or Government Institute) may provide grounds for exemption. Kathmandu Immigration Office, Keshar Mahal, Trivedi Marg, Thamel, T 412337. Pokhara Immigration Office is near the lake (extensions up to 6 weeks only). In an emergency local police stations may extend visas or trekking permits for up to 7 days.

Validity A visa is officially only valid for the Kathmandu and Pokhara valleys, and the Royal Chitwan National Park, although in practice this includes all major roads through the country.

Trekking permits NB You must apply for a trekking permit to use trekking routes. This automatically extends your visa. Trekking in two areas require separate permits. Trekking permits cost US$5 per week plus Park entry fee US$13 for Everest and Annapurna. Two photographs are required.

Work permits Work permits are required in Nepal which should normally be obtained before entering the country. Your employer applies for the permit, which can take months. If you arrange to work after arriving in Nepal, you should leave the country while the paperwork is negotiated. It is almost impossible to change a tourist visa into a work permit.

Driving If you are considering driving a car or motorcycle in Nepal you should have an International Drivers Permit.

Student cards An International Student Identity Card (ISIC) can be help to get travel discounts.

Onward travel Visa section of the Chinese Embassy in Kathmandu is open 1000-1200 Mon and Wed. Visas take 4-5 days and cost about US$20; extra US$20 if embassy has to telex Beijing. For special Tibet visa procedures, see above, page 19. Visas for India are required of every nationality, best obtained in your country of origin where possible. Visas for Burma are currently only issued for group tourists, although may be for longer than 7 days. Visas for Thailand are issued without complication, they can be issued at Bangkok Airport for stays of 14 days or less.

● **Vaccinations**

In Kathmandu you can get certain vaccinations free of charge from the *Infectious Diseases Clinic* (T 215550) in Teku or from the *CIWEC Clinic* (T 410983) and *Kalimati Clinic* (T 214743) for a charge.

● **Representation overseas**

Australia, 3rd Level, 377 Sussex St, Sydney, NSW 2000 (T (02) 264 7197); 66 High St, Toowong, Queensland 4006 (T (07) 378 0124); Suite 23, 18-20 Bank Place, Melbourne, Vic 3000 (T (03) 602 1271); 4th Flr, Airways House, 195 Adelaide Tce, Perth, WA 6000 (T (09) 221 1207). *Bangladesh*, Lake Rd, Road No 2, Baridhara Diplomatic Enclave, Dhaka. *Belgium*, M25 Ballegeer, RNCG Office, 20/8 Antwerp. *Burma*, 16 Natmauk Yeiktha (Park Ave), PO Box 84, Rangoon. *Denmark*, 36 Kronprinsessegade, DK 1006, Copenhagen K (T (01) 143175). *France*, 7 Rue de Washington, Paris 75008. *Germany*, Im Hag 15, 5300 Bonn, Bad Godesberg 2 (T 34 3097); Flinschtrasse 63, 6000 Frankfurt am Main (T 06 114 0871); Landsbergerstrasse 191, 8000 Munchen 21 (T 089 570 4406); Handwerkstrasse 5-7, 7000 Stuttgart 80 (T 0711 7864 614 617). *India*, 1 Barakhamba Rd, New Delhi 110001 (T 38 1484); 19 Woodlands, Sterndale Rd, Alipore, Calcutta 700027 (T 45 2024). *Italy*, Piassa Medaglie d'Orro 20, Rome (T 348 176). *Japan*, 16-23 Highashi-Gotanda, 3 chome, Shinagawa-ku, Tokyo 141. *Netherlands*, Prinsengracht 687, Gelderland Bdg, Nl 1017 J V Amsterdam (T 020 25 0388). *Nor-way*, Haakon, VIIs gt-5, 0116 Oslo (T 2 414743). *Pakistan*, 506 84th St, Ataturk Ave, Ramna 6/4, Islamabad 23; Karachi, Memon Cooperative Housing Society, Block 7-8 Modem Club Rd, Karachi 29 (T 201908). *Sri Lanka*, 290 R A de Mel Mawatha, Colombo 7. *Sweden*, Birger Jarlsgatan 64, Karlavagen 97 S-115 22, Stockholm. *Switzerland*, Schanzeigasse 22, CH-8044 Zurich (T 816023). *UK*, 12A Kensington Palace Gardens, London W8 4QU (T 0171 229 6231). *USA*, 1500 Lake Shore Dr, Chicago, IL 60610; Heidelberg College, Tiffin, OH 44883 (T (419) 448 2202); 473 Jackson St, San Francisco, CA 94111 (T (415) 434 1111); 16250 Dallas Parkway, Suite 110, Dallas, Tx 75248 (T (214) 931 1212); 212 15th St NE, Atlanta, GA 30309 (T (404) 892 8152); 2131 Leroy Place NW, Washington, DC 20008 (T (202) 667 4550).

● **Tourist offices**

No official government tourist office overseas, though some tour operators have backing, eg *Promotion Nepal (Europe) Ltd*, 3 Wellington Terrace, Bayswater Rd, London W2 4LW, T 0171 2993528.

● **Specialist tour operators**

UK: *Exodus*, T 0181 675 5550; *Explorasia*, T 0171 6307102; *Himalayan Kingdoms*, T 0117 923 7163; *Promotion Nepal (Europe) Ltd*, T 0171 2293528, Trans Himalaya, T 0181 459 7944.

USA: *Abercrombie & Kent*, T 312 9542944; *Archaeological Tours*, T 212 986 3054; *Distant Horizons*, T 617 2675343; *Mountain Travel*, T 415 5278100; *Tiger Tops International*, T 415 3463402.

Health

See section on health in Introduction, page 39.

Warning When trekking in the monsoon, beware of leeches. They sway on the ground waiting for a passer by and get in boots when you are walking. When they are gorged with blood they drop off. Don't try pulling one off as the head will be left behind and cause infection. Put some salt, or hold a lighted cigarette to it, which will make it quickly fall off. Before starting off in the morning it helps to spray socks and bootlaces with an insect repellent.

● **Health insurance**

Many travel insurances include cover for theft, loss and medical problems. There is a large variety of different insurance covers, so it is recommended that careful consideration is made of all the options. Read the fine print carefully. Many policies exclude dangerous activities which can include trekking.

Money

● Currency
The Nepalese Rupee (Rs) is divided into 100 paisa (p). Major international currencies are readily accepted (many hotels and travel agents ask to be paid in US$). The Indian Rupee is usually accepted at a recognized market rate (NRs 1.6 in 1996). Coins are 5, 10, 25 and 50 paisa and 1 rupee. Notes are 1, 2, 5, 10, 20, 50, 100, 500 and 1,000 Rupees. The last two are often difficult to change outside major towns, so carry smaller notes.

● Cost of living
Cost of living in Nepal is low by western standards. The top of the range hotels and the best restaurants are considerably cheaper than their equivalent in the West.

● Exchange
If travelling or trekking individually you will need cash, as it is impossible to exchange foreign currency or TCs. (Beware of pickpockets at start of trek.) Most TCs are accepted at banks and major hotels.

    NB Only exchange currency at banks and authorized hotels and keep encashment receipts. You need these if you wish to extend your visa and need proof of exchange (US$20 per day). You also require the form if you wish to exchange your rupees to US$ on departure. Only 15% of the total or the last amount exchanged, whichever is greater, will be exchanged. Airport Departure Lounge has a bank.

● Credit cards
Visa, MasterCard and AmEx are widely accepted in main centres, but not outside. In Kathmandu, Visa and MasterCard: *Alpine Travel*, Durbar Marg, T 225020; AmEx: Jamal, Ratna Park, T 226172 (Sun-Thur 0800-2000, Sat 0930-1700).

Getting there

Air
From Europe, North America and Australasia a change of plane and/or airline en route is often necessary. Foreigners must pay for tickets in foreign exchange.

● From Europe
Lufthansa fly Frankfurt to Kathmandu. RNAC fly London, Frankfurt, Dubai, Kathmandu. Aeroflot flights via Moscow.

● From North America
Flights from US E coast usually require transferring in New Delhi to RNAC or Indian Airlines; from W coast in Hong Kong or Singapore. Fares from Canada are similar to USA, westbound from Vancouver or eastbound from Toronto or Montreal. Bangladesh Biman and PIA offer discounted fairs through small agents.

● From Southeast Asia
Thai International and RNAC connect Bangkok with Kathmandu. Direct flights from Singapore (Singapore Airlines) and Hong Kong (also RNAC).

● From India
New Delhi (IA, RNAC, Druk Air) is the main departure point (1 hr). Calcutta (IA, RNAC), Bombay (RNAC) and Varanasi (IA) have direct connections with Kathmandu.

● From other Asian cities
Other departure points for Kathmandu include: Dhaka (Biman, Singapore Airlines), Dubai (RNAC), Karachi (PIA, Lufthansa), Paro (Druk Air), Osaka, Shanghai (both RNAC) and Lhasa (CSWA).

Discounts ISIC card holders under 26 years are eligible for 25% reduction on RNAC on domestic and international flights. Similar discount on certain RNAC and Indian Airlines routes for anyone under 30 years.

Land
There are 21 recognized border crossing points. Eight are normally open, but only three are used by most foreign travellers. **Warning** At Immigration, clerks may demand an unauthorized 'fee' – do not pay unless a receipt is given.

    Both the **Sonauli/Bhairawa** and Raxaul Bazaar/Birganj border posts can be reached from Varanasi and Patna respectively by train or bus. Bus travel is quicker though crowded. In Nepal the government-owned Saja Sewa are a little less crowded than most – good value, 'Tourist Buses' allow seat reservation and have fewer stops. See also Kathmandu section.

From Tibet
The route from Tibet across the Kodari/Khasa border point was opened in 1984 allowing access to Lhasa along the Friendship Highway. However in 1989 this crossing was closed

again to individual travellers due to political troubles in Tibet. In Jun 1991 this road route was reopened to tourists. From the Friendship Bridge on the Nepal side of the border buses run twice a day to Kathmandu and taxis are also available. The road may be blocked by either landslides or snow.

On arrival

● **Airport taxes**
Departure tax for international flights, Rs 700, domestic flights, Rs 30. Please confirm on arrival.

● **Clothing**
The weather ranges from sticky heat in the Terai to freezing in Himalaya. Therefore you should have clothing that will suit your travels. If you intend to trek you should have the correct clothing.

● **Conduct**
When trekking, do not give money, cigarettes, sweets or other items indiscriminately, but do give to pilgrims and holy men who live on alms. Do not swim or bathe nude in rivers or hot springs. Help Nepal retain its beauty and its forests. Burn or bury litter. Do not use firewood or encourage its use. See 'Code of Practice' under Introduction.

Visiting temples or monasteries Some Hindu temples are open to non-Hindus, most are not. Look for signs or ask. Remove shoes and any leather items before entering. Walk on the left of shrines and stupas. Also walk on the left hand side inside monasteries. Buddhist monasteries are open to all. You may even visit the resident lama (priest), offering him a khatak (white ceremonial scarf of silk or cotton – available in Asan, Kathmandu). If you wish to make a contribution, put money in the donation box. It will be used for the upkeep of the temple or monastery.

● **Hours of business**
Bank hours are officially 1000-1500 (1430 in winter) Sun to Thur, and up to 1300 Fri. Kantipath branch of Nepal Bank is open 0900-1300 on Sat, closed Sun. Larger hotels will exchange TCs at bank rates, but usually only for guests. Bank holidays – 8 and 22 Mar, 13 Apr, 8 Nov, 25 and 28 Dec. Government Offices 1000-1700, Sun to Thur. Winter 1000-1600. Fri till 1500. **NB** Sat in Nepal is a rest day and Sun is a full working day for offices and banks. Embassies and international organizations take a 2-day weekend but are open 0900 or 0930 to 1700 or 1730 during the week. Shops are open on Sat and holidays from 1000-1900 or 2000.

● **Official time**
Nepal is 15 mins ahead of Indian Standard Time, and 5 hrs 45 mins ahead of GMT.

● **Photography**
Many Nepalese like being photographed, particularly if you have a Polaroid and can give them a copy. If in any doubt, ask, but you are encouraged not to pay. Most festivals allow photography. Participants sometimes go into a trance and may act unpredictably. It is safest to avoid taking photographs under such circumstances.

● **Shopping and best buys**
Nepal is a shopper's paradise. Remember to bargain except in a 'fixed price' shop. Some do not accept credit cards or TCs. Try to get an idea of the prices being charged for goods before you start bargaining.

Thangkas (paubha in Newari) The professional thangka painters live in Bhaktapur and Boudha.

Rice Paper Prints produced by wooden blocks on locally produced paper of Buddhist and Hindu deities make good gifts. You can buy these (sometimes along with an old block) from Basantapur in Kathmandu or a handicrafts shop.

Tibetan Carpets are handwoven and nowadays use chemical dyes in addition to the traditional vegetable dyes. You will be able to see weavers at work in Bodhnath and Jawalakhel. The traditional designs include dragons, geometric and floral patterns and you can get one small enough to pack easily into a suitcase.

Clothing, both Nepalese and Tibetan, is a popular buy, including Tibet jackets and machine embroidered cloth. Nepalese caps are traditionally made in Bhaktapur.

Tea is grown in E Nepal. Ilam and Mai Valley are recommended brands.

Crafts Other Nepalese crafts include the *khukri*, the traditional Gurkha knife. The genuine ones come with two extra smaller knives for skinning, and the main blade has a notch to stop blood reaching the handle. Woodcarving is centred in Bhaktapur and can be found around Tachupal Tole. The Crafts Centre is in Dattatraya. Tibetan crafts include prayer wheels and other religious items. Check inside the wheel to see if it contains the printed prayer on a roll. Crafts sold around Bodhnath and Svayambhunath are often highly priced. Trinkets and jewellery with turquoise setting are good value while stamps and coins attract collectors. Gold and silver jewellery should only be bought from reputable shops.

Warning The bronze and metal statues, sold as antiques are mostly mass produced and 'aged' which will be obvious from the price. Antiques cannot be taken out of the country, and Nepalese Customs is strict on departure. You need a permit from the Department of Archaeology if you want to take out any article which looks older than 100 years. The office (T 215358) is in the National Archives Bldg, Ram Shah Path. Go between 1000-1300 to pick up the permit by 1700 the same day. The Customs Office, Tripureshwar, T 215525, provides information.

Sending Purchases Home If you cannot carry your goods with you, you can ship them, though it can be risky and expensive. The Foreign Post Office requires inspection by officials before you wrap your purchases for mailing. Reliable packing companies in Kathmandu include Sharma and Sons Packers & Movers (T 411474) and Atlas Packers & Movers (T 221402). DHL international couriers has an office in Durbar Marg.

● **Tipping**
Tipping is becoming more prevalent in Kathmandu. In expensive establishments tip up to 10%, in smaller places the loose change or Rs 10 will be appreciated. **NB** Taxi drivers do not expect a tip.

● **Voltage**
Major towns in Nepal have electricity, 220 volt AC; fluctuations in current are common. A few major hotels have their own generators, as there are frequent power cuts.

● **Weights and measures**
Nepal uses the decimal system, but people often use traditional measures for some purposes, counting in lakhs (100,000) and crores (10 million). For rice, cereals, milk and sugar: 1 mana equals about $\frac{1}{2}$ a litre; 1 paathi equals 3.75 litres, which contains 8 mana; 1 muri equals 20 paathi (75 litres). For vegetables and fruit: 1 pau equals 250g; 1 ser equals 1 kg (4 pau); 1 dharmi equals 3 kg (3 ser). The term mutthara means 'a handful', for vegetables or firewood. For all metals 1 tola equals 11.5g. For precious stones 1 carat equals 0.2g.

Where to stay

Accommodation has been graded from **AL** down to **F**. The price is a guide to what you would pay for the best room (double) remembering that taxes vary and can sometimes add considerably to the basic price. However, hotels in some centres such as Pokhara offer large seasonal discounts. It is always worth asking. Prices in Nepal are almost always now quoted in dollars.

AL: US$110+; **A**: US$70-110; **B**: US$40-70; **C**: US$25-40; **D**: US$15-25; **E**: US$10-15; **F**: below US$10. **NB** In small towns and villages, hot water is provided in buckets. Some places have no electricity.

Food and drink

● **Food**
Real Nepalese food consists of *dhal* (lentils), *bhat* (rice) and *tarkari* (vegetable curry). It can get monotonous. However, Kathmandu has a genuinely cosmopolitan cuisine.

Water buffalo is the usual substitute for beef since cows are sacred and cannot be eaten. You will come across 'buff' curry and even 'buff' burgers or steaks. *Gurr* – made from raw potatoes ground and mixed with spices and then grilled like a large pancake and eaten with cheese. Potatoes are the staple food of the Sherpa although they are a relatively recent introduction. *Momo* or *Kothe* – Tibetan 'dumplings' – steamed or fried meat or vegetables wrapped in dough (like Chinese 'dim sum' or Italian ravioli). *Tsampa* – staple hill country dish of ground grain usually mixed with tea, water or milk. *Tama* – a traditional Nepalese soup made from dried bamboo shoots. *Thukpa* – Tibetan pasta, meat and vegetable soup. *Gundruk* – soup made from dried vegetables.

Other popular local dishes: *Charako sekwa* (grilled chicken) and *charako achar* (marinated, spiced chicken); *golbheda bari* (meatballs); *banel tareko* (fried wild boar).

Desserts: *Dahi* – yoghurt or curd (usually from rich buffalo milk); *Sikarni* (sweet spiced yoghurt); *khuwa* (cheese curd dessert).

● **Drink**
Chiya is local tea prepared with milk and sugar. Coke as well as orange and lemon bottled drinks, are available in the main towns. *Lassi* – a refreshing drink made of curd mixed with water, but make sure the water is safe. The locally produced beer is generally good, espe-

cially refreshing after a day trekking. 'Iceberg' regarded as the best, is the most expensive. 'Leo' and 'Star' beers are good. *Chang* – the home brew made from barley, rye or maize, is the popular alcoholic drink. *Arak* is from potato and *rakshi* from wheat or rice. *Tongba*, made from millet, is the S Tibetan and Sikkimese drink.

Warning See Health section in Introduction for detailed health advice.

● **Eating and drinking customs**
You must not touch somebody else's food. You will notice that the Nepalese, when drinking water from a bottle or tumbler, may pour the liquid into their mouth without their mouth touching the container. In this way they avoid ritual pollution. You should only use your right hand for eating or passing food. The left is considered unclean as it is associated with washing after defecating.

A cup of tea usually starts the morning, followed by a substantial 'brunch' late morning. If you are invited for a meal, socializing takes place before dinner (which may be served late by Western standards), and guests often leave soon after finishing the meal.

The kitchen in a Hindu home is sacred so non-Hindus should ask before entering.

Communications

● **Postal services**
The Central Post Office in Kathmandu has three sections located at the junction of Kanti Path and Kicha-Pokhari Rd. For stamps and Poste Restante go to the GPO, Sundhara, 1000-1700, Sun-Fri. The Poste Restante section is to the left of the main entrance and is efficiently run. You must show your passport for collecting mail. **NB** Ask correspondents to underline your surname or print it in bold block capitals and only your initials. Open Sun-Thur, 1015-1700 (1015-1600, mid-Nov-mid-Feb), 1015-1400 Fri, closed Sat. Hotels will also post, receive and hold mail for guests. The Foreign Post Office, N of GPO, deals only with parcels sent or received from outside Nepal. Open

1000-1700 Sun-Thur, 1000-1200 Fri, closed Sat. Sending a parcel is time consuming so best avoided. They have to be examined and sealed by a Customs Officer.

● **Telephone services**
The Telecommunication Office, Tripureshwar, deals with telephone calls, cables and telex. The international telephone office is open 1000-1700, Sun-Fri. International telephone connections are almost impossible.

Entertainment

● **Newspapers**
Nepal's daily English-language paper *Rising Nepal*, is often difficult to find. The *International Herald Tribune*, *Time*, *Newsweek*, *Statesman*, and *Times of India*, are sold in Kathmandu. *Nepal Traveller*, is a free monthly tourist magazine distributed at many hotels. *Himal Magazine* (six issues annually) is devoted to development and environment issues throughout the Himalaya.

● **Radio**
Radio broadcasts English news at 0800 and 2000.

● **Television**
Nepal TV, morning and evening transmissions only, Star TV.

National holidays

National holidays
Sep/Oct: Dasain.
Oct: Deepavali.
7 Nov: Queen Aishworya's Birthday.
17 Dec: Constitution and King Mahendra Day;
28 Dec: King Birendra's Birthday.
11 Jan: Unity Day (King Prithivi Natham Shah's death anniversary).
9 Feb: Martyrs Day; **18 Feb**: National Democracy Day.
Feb/Mar: Siva Ratri.
Mar: Holi; **8 Mar**: Nepalese Women's Day.
10 Apr: Teachers' Day.

BHUTAN

CONTENTS

OFFICIAL NAME *Druk-Yul*

CAPITAL Thimphu

NATIONAL FLAG Saffron and orange red, divided diagonally, with a white dragon in the centre

OFFICIAL LANGUAGE Dzongkha

MEDIUM OF INSTRUCTION IN SCHOOLS English

BASICS *Population*: 1995, 600,000; Urban 4%; Drukpas 67%; Nepalese origin about 30%. *Population density*: 12.76/sq km. *Birth rate*: 3.9%. *Death rate*: 0.9%. *Life expectancy*: 65%. *Literacy*: 32%, M 54%, F 40%. *GDP*: 500 USD. *Land use*: forested 64.4%, permanent pasture and agriculture 9%, snow/glacier 7.5%, scrub forest 8.1, other 11%. *GNP per capita*: US$700. *Religion*: Buddhist 70%, Hindu 28%, other 2%.

Land and life

Bhutan, dwarfed by its great neighbours India and Tibet, and only one third the size of Nepal, is nonetheless at 47,077 sq km slightly larger than Switzerland. Its official name, Druk-Yul, means 'Land of the Thunder Dragon' (the emblem portrayed on the national flag), and also 'Land of the Drukpa Kagyu school', indicating the tradition of Tibetan Buddhism which has come to dominate Bhutanese religious life since the 17th century. The name Bhutan is probably derived from the Sanskrit *bhotanta*, meaning 'Tibetan frontier'; while the Tibetans often refer to the land as 'Lho-mon', or 'Southern Mon'. A self-imposed isolation and undeveloped infrastructure have ensured that Bhutan remains the most mysterious country in South Asia, notwithstanding recent moves towards modernization. Never colonized, the country is today fully independent and maintains excellent relations with India. Consistently cautious with respect to contact with the outside world,

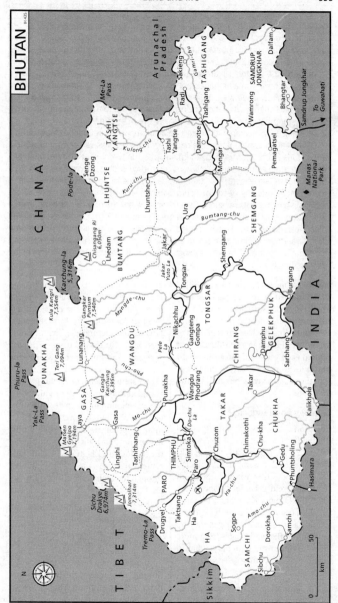

DZONGS

These were originally built as monasteries/fortresses, strategically sited to defend the country from hostile Tibetan armies who sought to reintergrate Bhutan within Tibet. They became centres of religious as well as secular power. Traditionally they have been the centres of artistic and intellectual life and their construction, ornamentation and maintenance have absorbed much of the nation's wealth. The high whitewashed walls are made of earth and stone (mud is trampled into wooden brick moulds, the labour being provided by the community). The wooden windows and balconies (built without nails) are richly ornamented. The interior walls are usually covered with murals depicting episodes in Buddhist legend.

The villagers congregate at the *dzong* for the major festivals and for seasonal agricultural feasts which provide them an opportunity to wear their finest clothes and for merrymaking after the religious ceremony. *Tsechus*, held on the 10th day of the month, are celebrated in different parts of the kingdom, through the year, to commemorate the deeds of Padmasambhava. In the non-religious festivals archery is a highly popular sport. The archers aim at targets at a distance of about 150m and every village has its own range. Religious *Cham* dances can be very colourful and spectacular, performed in special costumes and masks to the accompaniment of drums and cymbals. Mask makers can sometimes be seen at work during festivals. They often enact a ritual purification of negativity and may conclude with the display of a prized *tangka*.

the flow of tourists is tightly controlled by the imposition of high package fees, which provide sufficient foreign exchange to aid development without over-extending the basic ammenities of the country. Less than 4,000 tourists visit Bhutan each year; and the government continues to make great efforts to uphold the country's religious and cultural traditions.

Geology and landscape

Location

Bhutan lies between 89° and 92° E and 27° and 28° N. The Indian states of Sikkim, W Bengal, Assam, and Arunachal Pradesh occupy the entire 605 km length of its W, S, and E borders respectively, while the Dromo, Khangmar, Lhodrak and Tsona counties of Tibet lie to its N, forming a 470 km border. In general, the elevation of the land ranges from more than 7,000m in the N to only 300m in the S.

The Land

In the N, separating the country from Tibet, lies a relatively narrow chain of glacial mountains belonging to the High Himalayan range, with several peaks over 7,000m. From W to E these peaks include: **Jomolhari** (7,313m), the most famous and picturesque; Jichu Drakye (6,974m); Gyelpo Matsen (7,158m); Terigang (7,060m); Jejehangphu Gang (7,158m); Gangphu Gang (7,170m); Dzongaphu Gang (7,060m); and **Gangkar Punsum** (7,540m) which is the highest mountain entirely within the borders of Bhutan. Even higher and more imposing is the massive **Kulha Kangri** (7,554m), slightly to the NE, on the border with Lhodrak. Ancient trade routes traverse these high snow ranges through the high passes: Tremo La, Yak La, Phiru La, Monla Karchung La, and Phode La; while the slightly less daunting passes: Me La, Nyingzang La, and Ngonkha La connect E Bhutan with Tsona and Arunachal. In general, those peaks of the High Himalayan range form a watershed between the N and S flowing tributaries of the Brahmaputra River. All the rivers in Bhutan flow S. Yet among them there are three that originate N of the range in Tibet: the Amo-chu (Torsa), which enters W Bhutan from the Tromo (Chumbi) valley; the Kuru-chu, which enters NE Bhutan from Lhodrak; and the Tawang-chu (Gamri/Drangme), which enters E Bhutan from Tsona. In the far W, the Di-chu (Jaldakha) enters from Sikkim. All other tributaries have their sources within Bhutan. In the extreme NW the alignment of the Tibet-Bhutan border has been repeatedly disputed by China.

The largest part of the country belongs to the middle Himalayan range with altitudes ranging from 1,100 to 4,000m. Here, the Black Mountains form a watershed between W and E Bhutan and are crossed via the **Pele La pass** (3,369m). The rivers of W Bhutan which flow to the W of that pass include the Di-chu (Jaldakha), the Amo (Torsa), the Wang-chu (Raidak) with its Ha (Lhade), Paro, and Thimphu tributaries, and the Puna Tsang-chu (Sankosh). Those flowing E of the pass, which converge to form the Drangme-chu (Manas), include the Tongsar (Tongsa/Mangde) and the Bumtang-chu of Central Bhutan, as well as the Kuru-chu, Kulong-chu, and Tawang-chu (Gamri) of E Bhutan. In the far SE of the country, the Bada-chu and Dhanasiri-chu follow their distinct courses into Assam.

In the more densely populated S border with India, which was established by the British in the 18th and 19th centuries, generally runs along the base of the abruptly rising Himalayan foothills (average altitude 300-1,600m). Here, the aforementioned rivers cut their way through to reach the Brahmaputra River lowlands of W Bengal and Assam, thereby forming the 18 'gates' of the **Duars** (Hindi – gates). All the motor roads from the S pass through the Duars. In the W the boundary with Sikkim was also established by the British and accepted by India; while the boundary to the E currently follows the de-facto Sino-Indian frontier.

The country is divided into 20 administrative districts or 'dzongkhak'; among which Samchi, Chukha, Gelekphuk, and Samdrup Jongkhar border India on the W and S. Those of Ha, Paro, Thimphu, Gasa, Wangdu, Bumtang, Lhuntse, Tashi Yangtse, and Tashigang border Tibet on the N and E. The central districts of Tagkar (Daga), Chirang, Punakha, Tongsar (Tongsa), Shemgang, Pema Gatsel and Mongar lack an external frontier. Motorable roads now link the southern border towns of Phuntsoling, Khalikhola, Gelekphuk (Burgang), and Samdrup Jongkar with the capital and central parts of the country; and there is also a lateral paved road linking the districts of Ha, Paro, Thimphu, Wangdu, Tongsar, Bumtang, Mongar and Tashigang. Apart from the NE roads to Lhuntse and Tashi Yangtse, the N of Bhutan is even now only accessible on ancient trekking and caravan trading routes. In all, the motorable roads cover 2,165 km.

Vegetation

The three vegetation and climatic zones found throughout the Himalayan countries are also apparent in Bhutan. In the S the wet Duars are covered in lush forest with bamboo, fern, hanging plants, and giant orchids amid the banyan, giant sal and teak trees. As you move higher into mountainous terrain, the tropical vegetation gives way to the deciduous and conifer forests of the temperate zone, and there is still a wide range of trees: poplar, ash, aspen, magnolia, oak, and beautiful rhododendron. Above 3,000m bamboo and conifer forests take over, alongside fir, larch, and cypress. At 4,000m birch, pine and rhododendron dominate and then give way to high alpine juniper, edelweiss, blue poppies, gentian, and other medicinal plants. Mosses and lichens can occasionally be found at the highest altitudes in N Bhutan, but it is only in NE Bhutan, bordering on Lhodrak, that the forest penetrates the otherwise bleak N side of the main Himalaya range.

Wildlife

In S Bhutan the forests abound with monkeys, including the rare golden langur, as well as deer, buffalo, wild boar, bears, snakes, leopards, rhino, and even tigers. The mid-mountain belt is home to the red panda, wild boar, Himalayan black bear, pheasant, and hornbill; while remote valleys around Bumtang and Gangteng (Gantey) are the preferred winter destination of the black-necked crane. In N Bhutan, the high alpine valleys are frequented by yaks, tahr, the rare and protected *bharal* blue sheep, the snow leopard, and the takin which live above 4,000m. The **blue sheep** (*Pseudois nayaur*), rare elsewhere in the Himalaya, have thick sheep-like horns but goat-like legs with dark stripes on the flanks. They prefer plateaus for grazing and have a split lip which enables them to pull grass straight out of the ground rather than crop it. Takins (*Budorcas taxicolor*) are larger (over 1m at the shoulders), and short-legged. They have a shaggy dark brown coat with a lighter back; the snout is swollen and their thick horns splay out and then up and back. They live in small herds, often above the tree-line, and in spite of their stocky appearance are remarkably agile on steep slopes. The winter draws them down to bamboo and rhododendron forests, from which they emerge to graze in meadows, morning and evening.

There are also many species of birds and butterflies, fish, such as the celebrated masheer, and various reptiles. Wildlife parks cover much of the border regions. In the extreme N the **Jigme Dorje Wangchuk Sanctuary** occupies 7,813 sq km; and there are at least 11 others covering the mid-mountain belt and the S. Among the latter, the best known is the **Manas Wildlife Sanctuary** (463 sq km), which stretches across the border into Assam, and may be entered from the Indian side (closed at present). In Central Bhutan further wildlife reserves are being established in the Black Mountains and in Ura.

Climate

The monsoon begins in June and lasts until end of Sept when 85% of the annual rainfall is received. The windward south-facing mountain slopes are the wettest areas. The climate within the mountains varies greatly according to sunshine, precipitation and wind conditions, yet it basically resembles the middle European climate.

In the **Duars Plain** and up to 1,500m, the climate is sub-tropical with high humidity and heavy rainfall (2,000-5,000 mm). The climate of the **mid-mountain belt** varies, such that low-lying parts of Punakha, Mongar, Tashigang, and Lhuntse have cool winters and hot summers, whereas the higher valleys of Ha, Paro, Thimphu, Tongsar, and Bumtang, ranging from 3,000-4,500m endure a temperate climate with cold snowy winters and somewhat cooler summers. The rainfall of these mid-mountain valleys averages 1,000 mm-1,500 mm/year; and in the winter snowfall can close many passes. In **N Bhutan**, above 4,500m, an alpine/arctic climate prevails, with most areas permanently covered with snow and ice. Here the winters are severe and the summers generally cool.

The daily air mass exchange between highlands and lowlands often causes stormy winds which frequently prevent rainfall in the middle portions of cross valleys so that between 900 to 1,800m it is quite dry, requiring irrigation for farming, while higher up it is often wet.

Temperature

Across the country, the min temperatures range from -10°C (Paro, Thimphu) to 15°C (Southern Foothills); and the max from 30°C (Southern Foothills) to 35°C (Paro, Thimphu). More specifically, in the mid-mountain belt which is visited by most tour groups, from mid-

Mar to mid-June, the temperature range is 27°C-18°C; in the monsoon season from mid-June to late Sept the range is 24°C-15°C; and in winter from mid-Nov to mid-Mar, the days are dry, averaging 16-18°C, while the nights, early mornings, and evenings are cold. Mountain vistas are best in the Autumn (Oct-mid Nov), and in the Spring.

History

Despite the lack of archaeological research, stone implements found in Bhutan suggest that the mid-mountain belt was inhabited by humans circa 2,000 BC. Bhutan's recorded history dates the establishment of the Buddhist geomantic temples of **Kyerchu** in the W (Paro district) and of **Jampa Lhakhang** in central (Bumtang district) to the reign of the Tibetan king Songtsen Gampo, who unified most of the Tibetan plateau during the 7th century, and constructed such temples in order to stabilize the border regions of his empire (see above). The indigenous inhabitants of Bhutan during that period seem to have been those whose descendents even now occupy much of Central and E Bhutan, the Sharchokpa or 'Easterners', who have affinity with the Monpa of SE Tibet and Arunachal Pradesh. The Tibetan peoples, formerly known in Bhutan as the Ngalong (ie the 'earliest to rise up within the fold of Tibetan Buddhism'), and now known as the Drukpa, appear to have settled there gradually, following the unification of Songtsen Gampo's Empire. During the 8th century, when Buddhism became the established religion of Tibet, Bhutan is believed to have been officially converted to the Tibetan form of Buddhism by the accomplished spiritual master Padmasambhava, at the invitation Sendhaka, the local king of the Bumtang region. Pilgrimage sites associated with Padmasambhava and his followers include **Taktsang** in Paro, **Kurje** in Bumtang, and **Monka Nering Senge Dzong** in Lhuntse.

Following the disintegration of the Tibetan Empire in the 9th century, waves of settlers arrived from Tibet to occupy Bhutan, then known as Lhomon, 'Southern Mon'. Between the 11th and 15th century, the major Tibetan schools of Buddhism, notably the Nyingma, Sakya, Kadam and Kagyu, established monasteries and temples throughout the Bhutanese valleys, as cultural and economic ties with Tibet continued to have paramount importance. Among these, the renowned institutions of the **Nyingma** school included the various branches of the E Tibetan monastery of Katok, such as **Orgyan Tsemo** and **Pang Karpo** in Paro (founded by Katokpa V in the 13th century), as well as **Chidzong** and **Baling** in Shar; the eight monasteries founded by Longchen Rabjampa (14th century) in Central Bhutan, during his sojourn in exile from Tibet; and the sites associated with Guru Chowang (13th century in Lhuntse); Dorjelingpa (14th century in Bumtang, Paro and Shar); the celebrated bridge-building engineer Tangtong Gyelpo (15th century in Paro), and, above all, Pema Lingpa (1450-1521) whose familial and incarnate lineages have continued down to the present day in E Bhutan and the Lhodrak region of S Tibet.

Monasteries of the **Sakya** school were also established in Bhutan at **Lhading**, N of Paro in the 13th century, and by Trinle Rabyang of the Ngor sub-school at **Chizhing** and elsewhere during the 15th century; while the Nenying tradition of the **Kadam** school was strong in W Bhutan during the 15th century.

Among all the diverse traditions of Tibetan Buddhism, the one which exerted the most influence on Bhutanese spiritual and secular life has been the Kagyu school, early branches of which were founded during the 11th-12th century at **Langmoling** in Tang (by Ngok

Choku Dorje), at **Thangkhabe** in Chokhor (by the Karma Kagyu school), and at **Chelkha** in N Paro and **Dongon Dzong** in Thimphu (by Lhanangpa and his followers). In the 14th century, the Barawa sub-school was established at **Drang-gyekha** in Paro by Barawa Gyeltsen Pelzang. Among the many Kagyu sub-schools such as these, dominance in Bhutan was eventually achieved by the **Drukpa** from the 13th century onwards: Lorepa of the Lower Drukpa school founded **Chodrak** in Bumtang, and Chilkarwa of the Upper Drukpa school founded **Chikarkha** in Paro; while various monasteries representative of the powerful Middle Drukpa school were founded throughout W Bhutan by descendents of Drukgom Zhikpo. It was he who succeeded in forging a vital link between W Bhutan and the major Drukpa monastery of **Ralung** in Tibet (see above, page 321). During 15th century, Kunga Peljor of Ralung thrice visited Paro and Bumtang, founding a number of important Drukpa monasteries, including **Do Chorten** in Paro.

Although Bhutan was throughout this period a significant region for Tibetan Buddhist missionary activity, the country clearly lacked political unity – itself perhaps a reflection of the fragile political cohesion of the Sakya, Phakmodru, Ringpung, and Tsangpa dynasties who successively governed Tibet from the 13th-17th century. Then, during the 17th century **Zhabdrung Ngawang Namgyel** (1594-1651), the hierarch of Ralung monastery, which was the principal seat of the Drukpa school in Tibet, founded the Bhutanese unified state. When the Tsangpa ruler of Tibet disputed his incarnate status within the Drukpa school, he fled to the S, to find sanctuary in the ancestral Drukpa domains of W. Bhutan. There, he constructed a series of fortified castles (*dzong*) on the Tibetan model; and successfully repelled five Tibetan and Mongolian attacks between 1616 and 1648. Internally, he defeated a grand coalition of hostile Buddhist schools, known as the 'five groups of lamas', and thus established the whole of W. Bhutan under his rule. Central and E Bhutan were integrated within the new Bhutanese state after his death in 1656.

From 1616 until 1907, Bhutan was governed in accordance with the theocratic system introduced by Zhabdrung Ngawang Namgyel. The spiritual authority of the country was embodied in the person of the **Je Khenpo** ('Chief Monastic Preceptor') and temporal authority in that of the **Desi** ('Regent'), both of whom were subservient to the Zhabdrung and his subsequent incarnations. Three provinces (Dagana, Paro and Tongsar) were created, each under the direct control of a governor (*ponlop*); while the fortified castles which developed as centres of local administration and bastions of Buddhist learning, were governed by the *dzongpon*. This dual system and its legal code based on Buddhist principles endured until 1907 despite the inherent threat of decentralisation frequently posed by powerful provincial governors and local officials during the hiatus following the death of the Zhabdrung and the accession to power of his recognized incarnation. The 18th and 19th century were characterized by internecine disputes instigated by the regents, governors, and dzongpon.

From earliest times until the mid 18th century, the inhabitants of Bhutan had remained firmly within the Tibetan cultural orbit, notwithstanding the aforementioned conflicts. The intractable and virtually impenetrable terrain of S Bhutan ensured that contact with the Indian sub-continent was minimal, with only the Maharaja of neighbouring Cooch Behar having diplomatic relations. This situation rapidly changed with the advent of the British East India Company who, through their quest for trading concessions, forced the Bhutanese to look southwards. Specifically,

Warren Hastings sent a mission into the 'Land of the Thunder Dragon' in the 1770s, headed by George Bogle (who was also ordered to plant potatoes there!). In 1841 the **British** annexed the Duars plain and created the present boundary, agreeing to pay a small annual subsidy as long as the Bhutanese remained peaceful. However, Bhutanese raiders continued to make forays across the border, carrying off Indians as slaves. In 1863, the visit of a British representative who forced his way into Bhutan did not please the Bhutanese, and so he was not treated well. A war followed but the British failed to invade Bhutan. In 1865 the Treaty of Sinchula was ratified, ensuring that the Duars were regained by the British in exchange for monetary compensation to the Bhutanese.

By 1865, the fabric of the dual theocratic system had been worn down in consequence of this period of turmoil, leaving Central and E Bhutan in the power of the provincial governor of Tongsar, Jigme Namgyel. His son, Ugyen Wangchuk, who inherited the governership in 1881, inflicted a severe defeat on the governor of Paro at Thimphu, thereby forging a renewed sense of national unity in 1885. The governor then entered into an increasing co-operation with the British, acting as an intermediary between them and the Tibetans in 1904 at the time of the Younghusband expedition into Tibet. With British support, he was successfully elected as the hereditary monarch of Bhutan in 1907. Secular and religious rule was vested in his family; and the Zhabdrung's theocracy was abruptly and forcefully ended.

In 1910, in return for an increase in its annual subsidy, Bhutan agreed to accept British guidance in its external affairs. Bhutan, however, did not receive help in building roads, expanding communications and developing the economy as did Sikkim which was then a British protectorate. The pace of development was therefore much slower.

Following the death of Ugyen Wangchuk in 1926, his son Jigme Wangchuk became the second king, reigning until his own death in 1952. During this period, western-style schools were established with British aid, and Bhutanese students were encouraged to study in India. Under a 1949 treaty between Bhutan and newly independent India, Bhutan entered a non-binding agreement to 'be guided by the advice' of India in its foreign affairs. It was, however, the third king Jigme Dorje Wangchuk who consciously altered the course of Bhutan's political isolation and began the process of modernisation and economic development in the aftermath of the invasion of Tibet by China in 1959. He initiated a road-building programme, which gradually made the country more accessible to the outside world. Then, in 1971, shortly before his death, he successfully applied for UN membership. The affection with which the third king is regarded in Bhutan is reflected in the grandeur of his impressive **Memorial Chorten**, subsequently erected in Thimphu. The fourth and present king, Jigme Senge Wangchuk, ascended the throne in 1972 at the age of 17. His policy has been to promote socio-economic development, while preserving the Buddhist heritage of Bhutan. Through his efforts, Bhutan has become a member of many international organizations, including the Nonaligned Movement, the South Asian Association for Regional Cooperation, the Asian Development Bank, the Colombo Plan, the World Bank, the International Monetary Fund, and the Universal Postal Union. In addition, Bhutan has full diplomatic relations with India, Pakistan, Bangladesh, Nepal, Maldives, Kuwait, Switzerland, Norway, the European Union, Japan, Sri Lanka, and Thailand.

Prior to the 20th century the inhospitable terrain of S Bhutan remained uninhabited until small numbers of ethnic Nepalis began moving into the foothills. This modest migration continued throughout the first half of the 20th century, as Nepali forest labourers were brought in, later settling as tenant farmers and eventually acquiring Bhutanese nationality in 1958. However, with the recent opening up of the country and the endeavour to develop its infrastructure, large numbers of economic migrants followed in the wake of those early settlers, the majority of them ethnic Nepali. These latecomers were declared illegal immigrants in 1991. The Nepalis are confined to the five southern districts, where they outnumber the indigenous Bhutanese, and are now estimated to comprise 30% of the total national population.

Culture

People and language

There are two main population groups in Bhutan: the Drukpa (approximately 67%) of Tibetan and Monpa origin, and the Lhotsampa (approximately 30%) of Nepalese origin. The remaining 3% of the population comprise indigenous tribal groups, such as the Toktop, Doya, and Lepcha of SW Bhutan, and the Santal who migrated there from N Bihar. Among the two larger groups, the Drukpa include within their numbers the Ngalong of W Bhutan who speak the Tibetan dialect known as Dzongka, now the official language of Bhutan; the 'drokpa' nomads of N Bhutan; the Monpa of Bumtang, Khyeng and Kurto districts whose dialects are related to those of the Monpa of Tawang; and the most populous group, the Sharchokpa of E Bhutan, who speak the proto-Bodic language known as Tsangla. The Nepali speaking Lhotsampa of S Bhutan belong mainly to the high castes and to the Rai, Gurung and Limbu tribes, and because of their different language and religion they have not intermingled with the Drukpa.

Since 1959 immigration from Nepal has been banned and the Govt wishes to avoid a repetition of what happened in Sikkim (where, in 1975 the King was overthrown by the majority Nepali speaking population). The problem of the people of Nepalese origin who left Bhutan since 1991 for refugee camps in SE Nepal is the subject of talks between Nepal and Bhutan.

Bhutan has the lowest population density of any country in South Asia. Most people live along the S border and in the high valleys of the mid-mountain belt, particularly along the E-W trade route that passes through Thimphu and Punakha. In mountain regions the Drukpa are predominant, whilst the S is largely settled by Nepalis.

National language Since the Drukpa share a common heritage of culture, language and religion with Tibet, the written language, here known as 'cho-ke', employs the classical Tibetan script. The colloquial form of Tibetan given national status in Bhutan is, as stated above, known as *Dzongkha*, the dialect of W Bhutan. The teaching of the national language is compulsory at all levels of education, although English is the medium of instruction. Primary education has been encouraged since the 1960s with the opening of state funded schools throughout the country.

Daily life

National dress The people take pride in their clothing which, like the dress worn by the neighbouring Tibetans of Tromo, Khangmar, and Lhodrak, is influenced by the harshness of the Himalayan climate. The men wear a long *kho* or *baku* (robe), hitched up to the knees with a sash, and long boots, while women wear an *onju* or *gyenja* (blouse), a *kira* (ankle-length robe, wrapped around from under the arm, held by silver brooches), a belt, and a *togo* (short jacket). Traditionally, special ceremonial scarves are worn – the king and the

Je Khenpo (Head Monastic Preceptor) wear saffron yellow, the ministers orange, senior officials red and the ordinary subjects white, while the women wear red scarves with woven motifs.

Village houses with mud walls have a lower floor for animals; the upper floor for living is made of wood and bamboo lattices covered with mud plaster. Shuttered windows with a trefoil arch shape are colourfully painted. Roofs are covered with wooden shingles weighted down with stones. In N and Central Bhutan, house walls are made of stone and in the E, bamboo houses are constructed on stilts. Lighting was once provided by oil lamps, but now by kerosene or elecricity.

Religion

Religion plays a crucial role in social affairs. The **Drukpa Kagyu** school of Tibetan Buddhism is the state religion but the **Nyingma** school is also well represented, particularly in central and E districts.

As stated above, there are unique political and military circumstances through which the Drukpa Kagyu, among all the various schools of Tibetan Buddhism, came to dominate the religious life of the country. This school was founded at **Druk** in Tibet by Tsangpa Gya-re Yeshe Dorje (1161-1211), whose foremost students formed its three main branches: the Middle Drukpa school at Ralung, the Upper Drukpa school in W Tibet and Ladakh, and the Lower Drukpa school at Uri and Karpo Cholung. Among these, the Middle Drukpa school first reached Bhutan during the 13th century through the missionary efforts of Drukgom Zhikpo and his descendents, who established strong links between W Bhutan and Ralung. In particular, Kunga Peljor founded a number of Middle Drukpa monasteries in W Bhutan during the 15th century; and it was to these that during the 17th century Zhabdrung Ngawang Namgyel (1594-1651), the hierarch of Ralung monastery, fled to escape the persecution of the King of Tsang, thereby founding the Bhutanese state. In this way, the Drukpa Kagyu school gave its name to the newly emergent state of Bhutan.

There are around 6,000 monks in Bhutan, approximately half being subsidized under the authority of the Je Khenpo (the 'Head Monastic Preceptor') of the Drukpa Kagyu school; and the remainder subsisting on private patronage. Each of the larger dzong houses several hundred monks. By contrast, there are only about 250 nuns. In addition to monastic Buddhism, there are also a number of important reincarnating tulkus who are responsible for maintaining their own distinctive spiritual lineages, whether Bhutanese or Tibetan in origin; and approximately 15,000 respected lay practitioners, known as Ngakpa or Gomchen. Many Nyingma temples are privately owned, and passed on through familial lines of succession from one generation to the next. All those fully engaged in Buddhist practice, whether monastic or not, are highly respected by the people and by the government, for whom they provide spiritual guidance and support through their private meditations, communal prayers, ceremonial rituals, and religious festivals.

The laity, in turn, place great emphasis on the importance of making offerings at their household shrines, performing daily prayers, circumambulating stupas and temples, going on pilgrimage, and sponsoring religious ceremonies. As in other Buddhist countries, there is a universal understanding of the importance of the accumulation of merit for the spiritual well-being and development of each individual in this life and in subsequent lives after death. In S Bhutan, where the dominant population is Nepalese, religious ceremonies correspond to those of contemporary Hindu and Newar society in Nepal.

Religious festivals are important events throughout the Tibetan Buddhist world – commemorating the deeds of the Buddha, or those of the great masters of the past associated with one tradition or another. In Bhutan, in addition to the standard festivals associated with the Buddha's life, the most renowned of these are the Tsechu ('10th day') festivals commemorating the deeds of Padmasambhava, the 8th century master of the Nyingma school who is credited with the introduction of the most profound Buddhist teachings into Tibet and Bhutan. Each 10th day of the lunar calendar is said to commemorate a special event in the life of Padmasambhava; and some of these are dramatized in the context of a religious festival, which may last from 3-5 days (one of which usually but not invariably falls on the 10th day of the lunar month). The regional dzong and remote village communities tend to hold their distinct annual Tsechu festival, providing the local populace with a wonderful occasion to dress up, gather together, and enjoy themselves in a convivial light-hearted atmosphere. It is also an occasion for them to renew their faith and receive blessings by watching the sacred dances, or receiving 'empowerment' from an officiating lama. The dances, each aspect of which has symbolic meaning, are performed by trained monks and laymen wearing ornate costumes, and, in some cases, impressive masks. At Paro, Wangdu, Mongar and Tashigang, among other places, a large painted scroll known as a *Tongdrol* is exhibited for a few hours in the course of the Tsechu festival, enabling the people to throng forward to obtain its blessing on that auspicious day; since such painted scrolls are said to 'confer liberation by their sight alone' (*tongdrol*).

Religious dances (*cham*) may be generally classed according to three distinct themes: morality plays; purificatory rites which exorcise demonic forces; and triumphal celebrations of Buddhism, glorifying the deeds of Padmasambhava, and so forth. Among these, the first type is exemplified by the lewd Dance of the Princes and Princesses (*pho-le mo-le*), in which dancers depict two princes who return from a foreign war to cut off the noses of their adulterous princesses; the Dance of the Stag and Hunting Dogs (*sha-ba sha-khyi*), in which the hermit saint Milarepa saves the life of a hunted stag and converts its pursuing hounds and hunter to Buddhism; and the Dance of the Judgement of the Dead (*raksha marcham*), derived from the *Tibetan Book of the Dead*, in which the executors of the rites of the Lord of Death dramatically pass judgement on two recently deceased individuals, one evil and the other virtuous.

The second type (purificatory dances of exorcism) is exemplified by the famous Black Hat dance (*shanag*) in which dancers wearing large wide-brimmed black hats, high boots, and silk brocade costumes, exorcise demonic forces from the dancing arena, in a parody of the assassination of the apostate 9th century Tibetan king Langdarma; the Dance of the Ging and Tsholing (*ging-dang tsholing*), in which two waves of terrifying deities in the entourage of Padmasambhava successively appear to take possession of the dancing arena; and the dance of the lords of the charnel ground (*durtro dakpo dagmo*), in which the eight great charnel grounds of ancient India are ritually guarded by two skeleton-clad dancers.

The third category is exemplified by the Drum Dance of Damotse Monastery (*damotse ngacham*), in which 12 animal-masked figures in Padmasambhava's entourage enact the victory of Buddhism; the Lute Dance (*dranyen cham*), in which the founding of the Drukpa Kagyu school is celebrated; and the elaborate Dance of Padmasambhava's Eight Manifestations (*gu-ru tsen-gye*). The accompanying orchestra beats out the rhythym of the dance as they play their long horns (*dungchen*), oboes (*gyaling*), drums (*nga*), cymbals (*silnyen/babchal*), shinbone trumpets (*kangling*), conch shells (*dung*), skull-drums (*damaru*), and bells (*drilbu*).

Secular festivals and dances Non-religious festivals include the traditional new year (*losar*) festivals and the recently introduced commemoration days indicative of the modern nation state. The former include the official new year (*gyelpo losar*) held in Feb/Mar, the agricultural new year (*sonam losar*) held in Nov/Dec, and the Nepalese new year in April. The latter include National Day (commemorating the institution of the monarchy on 17 Dec 1907); the King's Birthday (11 Nov), and Coronation Day (2 June). Such secular festivals are occasions for merry-making and archery contests. Secular music and song vary, corresponding to the cultural divide between the Drukpa and Nepalese parts of the country. The instruments, rhythms, ballads, and working songs of the Drukpa reflect the folk and popular culture of Tibet, while those of the Lhotsampa are identical to the music of Nepal.

Crafts

Traditional handicrafts, expensively priced, are made largely for the indigenous market rather than the tourist trade. There is little mechanisation, and no competition to encourage lower pricing. Different parts of the country are renowned for different products: bamboo baskets from Khyeng, brocade from Lhuntse, raw silk from E Bhutan, woodwork from Tashi Yangtse, metalwork from Thimphu, and yak-hair products from the nomadic N. Bhutanese handloom woven fabrics are particularly renowned, each having a distinctive name depending on its unique combination of fibre, colour and pattern. Cotton, wool, silk, yak, and nettle fibres may be used to weave material in striped, banded or checked patterns.

Gold and silver jewellery is made in the Tibetan style, often inset with coral, freshwater pearl, or zi (banded chalcedony/etched agate), and occasionally with turquoise. Wooden drinking bowls, inlaid with silver, and laquered bowls are prized among the woodwork of Tashi Yangtse in E Bhutan. Waterproof bamboo or rattan baskets, including the celebrated round picnic basket, are fashioned in interesting geometric designs in Khyeng; while strong lightweight paper is made from the bark of the Daphne and Edgeworthia shrubs.

Modern Bhutan

Government

The Bhutanese monarchy recognizes the King as both the Chief of State and the Head of Central Government, presiding over a cabinet (*lhengye zhungtsog*) which comprises the Ministers of Home Affairs, Foreign Affairs, Communications, and Social Services, along with representatives or vice-ministers from the Ministries of Finance, Agriculture, Trade & Industry, Tourism, Cultural Affairs, and the Civil Srvice, as well as the Chief of the Royal Bhutan Army and Police. In 1953 King Jigme Dorje Wangchuk (1952-72) inaugurated a National Assembly, the *Tshogdu*, which meets bi-annually at Tashi Chodzong in Thimphu and has some legislative power, in that 100 out of its 150 members are directly elected for a 3-year term by a limited electorate, comprising village elders and heads of households. The remaining members of the National Assembly comprise 10 representing the monastic community and 40 royal appointees. The resolutions passed by the National Assembly are implemented by a nine-member Royal Advisory Council (*lodro'i tsogde*), which the king set up in 1965. There is no written constitution and no independent judiciary, although a high court of six judges was established in 1968 to adjudicate on a modified version of Zhabdrung Ngawang Namgyel's 17th century legal code.

The modern reorganization of Bhutan's system of regional and local government has resulted in a more decentralized multi-tiered administration, at the heart of which is the division of the country into 20 districts (*dzongkhag*). Each district is headed by its own commissioner (*dzongdag*), who is appointed by the king and responsible to the Ministry of Home Affairs. At the regional level, there are four zones (*dzongde*), each comprising four of the aforementioned districts, and presided over by a zonal administrator (*dzongde chichab*); while the districts themselves are subdivided into smaller blocks of hamlets or villages (*gewog*) under the authority of an elected village headman (*gup*). The State Monastic Community, which is represented in the National Assembly and on the Royal Advisory Council, has been subsidized by the government since 1968, and its vast land holdings have been gradually purchased by the government for redistribution among the peasantry. At its head is the Je Khenpo, head of the Drukpa Kagyu school in Bhutan.

After Bhutan joined the UN in 1971, the government sought to exercise an increasing autonomy in its foreign policy, despite the important role which newly independent India had inherited from the British in 1947 as an arbiter of Bhutanese foreign affairs, and the major source of foreign aid. Internally, too, although the present King Jigme Senge Wangchuk continues to wield considerable power, his reign has been marked by a great improvement in the country's infrastructure; in the development of roads, buildings, telecommunications, and an increasing decentralisation of both administrative power and economic decision making. All is now geared towards the development of agriculture, private enterprise and environmental conservation. This does not mean, however, that social services are neglected, and a priority is also given to education and healthcare, which are both free of charge.

Recent developments The early 1990s have been marked by major unrest in the neighbouring Indian state of Assam and other parts of N India. The response of the Bhutanese government was to strengthen its programme of self-reliance and to underline its commitment to maintaining traditional Bhutanese values. The King has toured extensively and renewed support for the wearing of national dress has come from many parts of the country, especially in the S, bordering India. Language posed a particular problem, as English was increasingly becoming the lingua franca of the educated. While promoting the use of Dzongka, the King also took steps to encourage the Hindu population of the S to feel integrated with the Buddhist population, himself taking part in one of the major Hindu festivals.

The Bhutanese have long been wary of the comparatively recent historical trend of Nepali migration, which eventually led to the demise of the monarchy in neighbouring Sikkim, and the incorporation of that country within India. In 1990, a new census declared many people of Nepalese descent to be illegal immigrants. This sparked off anti-government propaganda by dissidents and terrorism, which led many Nepalis to leave the country. By the end of 1992, 70,000 Nepalis had gathered in the refugee camps of E Nepal. Dissidents formed the political organization BNDP. In Sept 1990 violent mass demonstrations were mounted and government offices ransacked in S Bhutan protesting against 'racism', the denial of democratic and human rights, and ethnic cleansing. The King threatened to abdicate but was persuaded to remain by the National Assembly. He then granted amnesty to hundreds of detainees and announced exemption of rural and labour tax in 1992 for all Lhotsampas, encouraging them not to leave the country. Schools, development projects and health services which had been suspended since 1990 because of the unrest, were ordered to reopen in 1993. Bilateral talks are now taking place between the Bhutanese and the Nepalese governments to solve the problem of the people in the camps.

The plea put forward is that without military and economic might, the very survival of the tiny country, the last bastion of Mahayana Buddhism, depends on Bhutan retaining its cultural identity.

Bhutan has played an active part in the SAARC meetings, and has welcomed contacts with the outside world, increasing the tourist quota to 4,000. Satellite dishes are not permitted and there is no national TV but video rental shops flourish and they are uncensored.

Economy

In 1995, the per capita income was estimated at US$500, and the annual growth rate at 5%; although the inflation rate also stood at 11%. As much as 80% of GDP was in the rural sector but this contributed less than 2% of tax revenue. Although these figures tend to place Bhutan among the least developed nations, the country is unlike others within that category, in that there is no famine, little malnutrition, good housing, a favourable ratio of population to cultivated land, with approximately 98% of the land being owned by the peasants who work it. Motorable roads, airline services and modern satellite communication systems now link Bhutan with the outside world, propelling the country rapidly away from its long-sought isolation.

Agriculture

Over 91% of the population depends on agriculture and livestock rearing, which together account for some 50% of GDP,

despite the fact that only 2% of the land is arable. The most important areas of cultivation are in the Duars and the river valleys of Central Bhutan. The main crops are maize (output 40,000 tonnes), and rice (output 43,000 tonnes), cultivated on the valley floors and, wherever possible, on the terraced and irrigated slopes up to 2,400m. Between 2,400m and 2,900m, millet (7,000 tonnes), wheat (5,000 tonnes), buckwheat and barley (4,000 tonnes) are also grown. Hot pepper (output 7,000 tonnes) is the favoured vegetable in kitchen gardens all over the country. Apples (5,000 tonnes) and potatoes (33,000 tonnes) are particularly important cash crops for the mid-mountain belt, while at altitudes between 300m and 1,300m, oranges (62,000 tonnes) and sugarcane (12,000 tonnes) are abundant. Farming is at the subsistence level and in recent years rice has had to be imported. Cattle, pigs, horses, sheep, and goats contribute greatly to the economy; yaks are the main livestock over 3,500m.

The extensive forests, which cover 70% of the land, are scientifically managed, but nonetheless damaged by shifting cultivation in the E and also by ageing and blight. The Bhutanese government is very conservation oriented and is assisted in this task by various international organizations. A small dairy farm was started at Bumtang in Central Bhutan with Swiss help and produces excellent cheese.

The curtailment of trade with Tibet in 1959 encouraged economic dependence on India and smuggling. Even now trade with Tibet is minimal, and restricted to specific trade fairs in Lhodrak and S Tibet, at which Bhutanese delegations are encouraged to participate, and to local cross-border smuggling. In these ways, grain and sugar are carried on yak trains into Tibet and watches, thermos flasks, crockery, and shoes from China are imported. By contrast, trade with India has contributed immensely to Bhutan's economic development, with road building, small cottage industries, fruit processing, and hydro-electric power plant construction expanding rapidly.

Industry and resources

Bhutan has no oil or natural gas. It is mining dolomite (output 50,000 tonnes) and limestone (100,000 tonnes) for export to India, along with gypsum (10,000 tonnes) and slate. It also mines 30,000 tonnes of coal a year. The main industries are timber, which accounts for 15% of GDP, hydro-electricity (output 336,000 kw), cement (output 36 million tonnes) and distillery products (47 million tonnes), but Bhutan is also producing veneer woods and plywood (3 million tonnes), and high density polythene pipe. Its main exports, all to India, are cement, timber, block boards, electricity, cardamom, gypsum, processed food, fruit and alcoholic drinks. The main imports, 60% of which are obtained from India and the remainder through trade with Japan, EU, USA and so forth, are petroleum, fuel, machinery, fabrics, vehicles, and grain.

Development

In 1961, the present king's father initiated a continuing series of 5-year plans, which at the outset focussed on the development of road construction and basic administrative infrastructures. The third and fourth of these plans focused on the economic exploitation of Bhutan's natural resources including forestry, agriculture, mining, and electricity. During the eighties and nineties, these plans have focused on administrative decentralisation, privatisation, health, education, and the strengthening of Bhutan's cultural heritage.

Tourism

This is deliberately kept on a small scale with only 4,000 tourists planned for the year 2000. Although FIT tourism is permitted, this option proves to be extremely expensive, and the majority of visitors are advised to form or join a tour group (which may consist of as few as one or two people only). As late as the early 1960s the only way to Thimphu was either on foot or by pack animal. The building of roads had been forbidden until 1959 and began in 1960 on the issue of a royal decree. By 1964 the first all-weather road had been completed from Paro to the new capital Thimphu; and there are now some 2,165 km of roads (paved and unpaved), linking India with Central Bhutan, and the central valleys with each other.

Since the Tourist Authority of Bhutan requires tourists to pay a fixed daily rate, currently in the region of US$220, which includes accommodation, food, transport, driver and local guide, only affluent tourists from Western countries, virtually all in tour groups, see this marvellous, peaceful country with its charming and friendly people. In general, prices vary according to the season and the group-size, with larger groups being offered greater discounts. Nonetheless, travel in Bhutan still proves to be more expensive than comparable travel in Tibet. Itineraries may be varied to take local festivals into account; but since 1988 most of the important monasteries, temples, and dzong have been denied access to foreign tourists. Permission to visit specific sites may exceptionally be obtained from the Secretary of the Special Commission for Cultural Affairs. Currently only a few sites of historic or cultural importance may be visited, and these are indicated in the course of the regional descriptions which follow.

Since the privatisation of the Bhutan Tourism Corporation Limited (BTCL) in 1992, as many as 28 in-bound tour operators have emerged, competing against each other. Visitors should be aware, however, that BTCL remains one of the few agencies able to handle large groups. Guides are trained by the Tourism Authority of Bhutan, and some have developed a specialized expertise in flora, fauna, Buddhism, and so forth. The continuing construction of tourist hotels suggests that this exclusive destination will continue to open its doors gradually to an increasing number of visitors, and it is rumoured that some of the monasteries open to tourism pre-1988 will once again be made accessible.

Philately

Bhutan joined the Universal Postal Union only in 1969 but since then has made a speciality of exporting stamps, particularly novelty stamps (three-dimensional, circular, on silk and metal) and stamps depicting Buddhist imagery. These are now a significant source of foreign exchange.

REGIONS AND DISTRICTS OF BHUTAN

THIMPHU CITY

ཐིམ་ཕུ

(*Pop* 26,000 approximately; *Alt* 2,350m)
Located 55 km from Paro airport, Thimphu is a relatively new town, having been built by the late King Jigme Dorje Wangchuk to become the new permanent capital from 1955 onwards (the old capital was Punakha). By Bhutanese standards Thimphu is busy and lively, though to an outsider it may appear an uncrowded haven. The population largely comprises civil servants and shopkeepers, although a few families have maintained the traditional agricultural pursuits of the Thimphu valley. The city has seen unprecedented urban development over the recent decades, but the districts of modern Thimphu still bear the names of the important land-owning families of the past: Mutigtang and Kawangjangsa to the W; Chang Zamtog, Samar Szingkha, and Yangchenphu to the S, and Zilungkha, Langjophakha, Hehjong, Belpina, Dechhu, Jongzhina, and Tagbab to the N.

Orientation

The major roads through the city run from S to N. **Dechen lam**, the only main road following the E bank of the Thimphu River, runs from the **Simtokha** intersection S of Thimphu to the **Dechen Choling Palace** complex in the far N of the valley. Bridges link this road with the **Chogyal lam** on the W bank or city side of the river at a southern intersection (known as **Lungten Zampa**) near the Bus Station, and also at a northern intersection near the Tashi Chodzong or Central Government Secretariat.

On the W bank, the principal street is **Nordzin lam**, which is the commercial heart of the city. Nordzin lam is intersected by three roundabouts at its southern, central, and northern points. The southern roundabout (the **Dzogchen lam** intersection) is located near an ornate petrol station, after which the traffic moves through a one-way system, passing grocery stores, the famed *Swiss Bakery*, and the *Taktsang Hotel*. After the second roundabout (the **Chorten lam/Odzin lam** intersection), the traffic moves in both directions. Shops on the left side include handicraft, textile, pharmaceutical and video-rental stores, as well as the *Hotel Norling*, and the Public Library. On the right side, is the Etometho handicraft and tour company, with the Bhutan Tourism Corporation upstairs, a cinema, the polce station, Bank of Bhutan, and State Handicraft Emporium. The final roundabout (at the **Dobum lam/Desi lam** intersection) marks the N end of Nordzin lam, where the Department of Public Works and Housing, and Bhutan Broadcasting Service are located, and from which (along **Drophen lam**) are found the Telecommunication Office, the Satellite Station, the Survey Department, and the Hospital of Traditional Medicine.

There are a number of parallel streets, located between Nordzin lam and Chogyal lam (the river road), among which **Odzin lam** is approachable from the second roundabout. Here are the *Druk Hotel*, the *Jomolhari Hotel*, and the *Druk Sherig Hotel*, as well as some smaller travel agencies, and a religious supply store. On **Gaton lam**, which leads uphill from the N end of Odzin lam to the **Changlingmethang** weekend market and the adjacent riverside sport's field, there are a number of fashionable restaurants. Then, on **Drenton lam**, NE after the second roundabout on Nordzin lam, are the General Post Office and the UN buildings.

All three roads branching westwards from the roundabouts on Nordzin lam lead to the **Memorial Chorten**. Among these, the longest is the residential **Dobum lam**, where one will also find the *Dechen Hotel*, the Ministry of Finance, the Ministry of Trade and Industry, and a swimming pool complex. A southern ring road, called **Gongphel lam**, links the Memorial Chorten with the southern bridge across the Thimphu River, passing through the southern

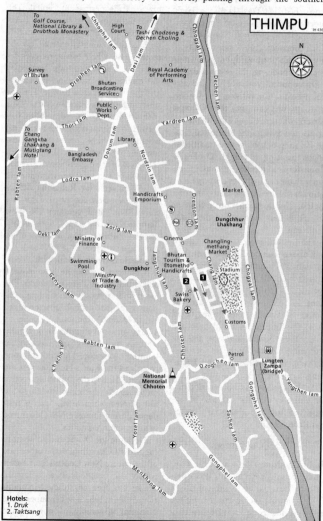

THIMPU

To Golf Course, National Library & Drubthob Monastery

To Tashi Chodzong & Dechen Choling

High Court

Chhophel lam

Desi lam

Chogyal lam

Dechen lam

N

Survey of Bhutan

Bhutan Broadcasting Service

Droshen lam

Royal Academy of Performing Arts

Public Works Dept.

Thori lam

Yardren lam

Dobum lam

Library

To Chang Gangkha Lhakhang & Mutiqtang Hotel

Bangladesh Embassy

Nordzin lam

Rabten lam

Lodra lam

Drenton lam

Market

Deki lam

Zorig lam

Handicrafts Emporium

Ⓢ

Dungchhur Lhakhang

Ministry of Finance

ⓟol

Cinema

Changling-methang Market

Genyen lam

Swimming Pool

Dungkhor

Jangchub lam

Bhutan Tourism & Etometha Handicrafts

Chang lam

Stadium

Chogyal lam

Kharcho lam

Ministry of Trade & Industry

2 **1**

Swiss Bakery

Rabten lam

Chhoten lam

Customs

National Memorial Chhoten

Ozogchen lam

Petrol

Lungten Zampa (bridge)

Yangchen lam

Yoseel lam

Sachey lam

Gongphel lam

Menkhang lam

Gongphel lam

Hotels:
1. *Druk*
2. *Taktsang*

suburbs of Thimphu, known as **Chang Zamtog**. Here are the General Hospital, the Education Department, Save the Children, and the Fire Brigade.

In N Thimphu, the central government buildings of **Tashi Chodzong** are approached, via **Desi lam**, the High Court, and the 9-hole Golf Course (the only one in the country). **Chophel lam**, which demarcates the W side of the Golf course, leads northwards out of town to **Dechen Phodrang**, the original dzong of Thimphu valley (until 1772) and current site of the Central Monastic School. En route, one can visit the **National Library**, where precious Tibetan manuscripts and xylographs are stored, and the Painting School, where traditional tangka painting is taught. **Drubthob Monastery**, a recently reconstructed nunnery, the original 15th century foundation of which is attributed to Tangtong Gyelpo, is located higher up on Ganden lam, on a spur overlooking the Tashi Chodzong.

The western approach roads known as **Ganden lam** and **Thori lam**, run through W Thimphu, where the city's most fashionable residential area, Mutigtang, has undergone great development in recent years. Here are the former *Mutigtang Hotel* (constructed 1974), the Embassy of Bangladesh, the *Kungacholing State Guesthouse*, and the Mutigtang Zoo. Southeast of Mutigthang, is the **Changangkha Lhakhang**, a celebrated 15th century temple of the Drukpa Kagyu school overlooking the entire city, which can also be approached from the Memorial Chorten (via Rabten lam).

Places of interest

Tashi Chodzong, the seat of the Bhutanese central government, was originally constructed on its present site in 1772, following the destruction by fire of the previous complex at Dechen Phodrang. Further restorations were carried out in 1870 and 1897 in the wake of natural disasters; and the present sprawling building with its tiered roof was built between 1962-69 using traditional techniques and modelled on the original after Thimphu had been recognized as the permanent capital. The adobe walls are 2m thick in places. Approached by an avenue of fine rose bushes, the **Dzong** is entered via the eastern gate, where ornate frescoes depict the four guardian kings, flanked by the gatekeepers Acala and Hayagriva, and the yogin Drukpa Kun-le. The distinctive Bhutanese architectural style, with its ornately carved wooden columns and ceilings is seen here at its best advantage. A large central tower, housing temples, separates the southern courtyard of the central administration (flanked by the royal appartments and the **Secretariat for Religious Affairs** from the northern courtyard of the state clergy. The latter contains the **New Temple** (*lhakhang sarpa*), with its impressive Padmasambhava image, originally constructed in 1907, and the **Monastic Assembly Hall**, with its portico depicting elaborate cosmological diagrams and the Wheel of Rebirth. The lower storey of this latter building functions as the summer headquarters of the Central Monk Authority, and it contains a large image of Buddha Shakyamuni; while its upper storey functions as a state tailoring workshop. The gilded throne room and the King's Headquarters are also here. Half of the Dzong is an active monastery to which non-Buddhists are not allowed when monks are in residence during summer. **NB** This is true of all major monasteries.

Opposite the Dzong and adjacent to the SAARC Building on the other side of the river, a **New Central Secretariat** which also functions as a conference centre has been constructed in traditional style in 1993. The **Chamber of the National Assembly**, is now located here.

4 km N of Tashi Chodzong is the **Dechen Choling** royal palace, where the government goldsmiths and silversmiths may be observed at work (**NB** Silversmiths are now also at work in Thimphu itself). En route, it is possible to visit the Forestry Institute at Tagbab. In a meadow further NE of Dechen Choling is the **Pangri Zampa** temple, where Zhabdrung Ngawang Namgyel first lived following his arrival in Bhutan from Tibet in 1616.

In downtown Thimphu, the most significant building of interest is the **Memorial Chorten**, constructed in 1974 by Dung-se Rinpoche Trhinle Norbu, to commemorate the late third king, Jigme Dorje Wangchuk, at the behest of the Royal Grandmother Ashi Phuntsok Chodron. The chorten in its 3-storeys contains enormous three-dimensional mandalas of deities, representing three of the most important 'treasure-cycles' (*terma*) of the Nyingma school of Tibetan Buddhism, namely: the cycle of *Vajrakila: Dagger of Razor-sharp Meteorite* (*Phurpa namchak putri*), which was revealed during the 19th century by Dudjom Lingpa; the cycle of the *Eight Wrathful Meditational Deities: Gathering of the Sugatas* (*Kabgye deshek dupa*), revealed during the 12th century by Nyangrel Nyima Ozer; and the cycle of the *Gathering of the Guru's Intention* (*Lama gongdu*), revealed during the 14th century by Sangye Lingpa.

The 15th century temple known as **Changangkha Lhakhang** in SW Thimphu contains a central image of Avalokiteshvara, and the frescoes at its gate depict Tsangpa Gya-re (1161-1211), the founder of the Drukpa Kagyu school in Tibet.

Local information

● **Accommodation**
In W Thimphu: *Bhutan*, has rooms with terraces, good views; *Zandopelri*, off Thori Lam, Mutigtang, is small and cozy.

In town: *Jomolhari*, T 22747, and *Druk* hotels are conveniently located on Odzin lam, with all modern facilities. The small *Druk Sherig* is the favourite of returning visitors. All have rooms with bath, restaurant, bar, exchange, fax. Other downtown hotels inc the *Taktsang*, *Norling* and *Dechen* on Nordzin lam.

● **Places to eat**
All major hotels offer Indian, Chinese, Continental and a few local dishes inc the fiery *omadasé* (cheese with hot peppers). Non-residents should book in advance at *Zandopelri* and *Druk Sherig*. For *momo*, *chowmien* and *thukpa* the tiny and spartan *Beneez* is excellent. *89* is the favourite of many for its pasta, while the newly opened *Apa* has partries and Chinese dishes as well as a bar and pool tables. For Bhutanese delicacies *Rabten* is the place (on order only). The popular *Swiss Bakery*, a white octagonal cottage off Nordzin lam, nr crossroad, uphill from *Hotel Druk* does Western snacks (closed Thur). *Plum Café* is equally good for snacks as is *Jichudrake Bakery* up the same road for good cakes and bread.

● **Airline offices**
Druk Air, Nordzin lam, in old *Bhutan Hotel*.

● **Banks & money changers**
American Express and Bank of Bhutan, Nordzin lam, 0900-1600. BTCL also changes money.

● **Entertainment**
Thimphu is very quiet by Western standards. Royal Academy of Performing Arts puts on shows.

● **Hospitals & medical services**
General Hospital, T 22496.

● **Post & telecommunications**
Couriers & fax: *DHL*, at *Sonam Peldon Stationery* shop nr Druk Air.
Post Office: Drenton lam, behind bank, 0830-1230, 1330-1630, Sat 0900-1230.

● **Shopping**
Nordzin lam and adjacent streets have rows of neat, traditionally painted shops. Most accept only Bhutanese currency. Usually open 0800-1900, Mon-Sun. Closed on Tues. There is an interesting market at Changlimgethang on Sat and Sun morning.

Books & cards: *Yangchenma Bookshop*, Gaton lam; *Pekhang* and the *Handicrafts Emporium* on Nordzin lam.

Handicrafts: *Handicrafts Emporium*, Nordzin lam, extensive range inc old sculptures, textiles, masks, jewellery and paintings. An excellent handicrafts shop has opened in *Druk Hotel*, American Express accepted. Also, for a wide and great selection of handicrafts and jewellery, do not miss *Druk Trin Cottage Industries* off the main street. *Kelzang Handicrafts and Jewellery*, by Druk Shopping Complex and *Norling Handicrafts*, shop 37, Nordzin lam, are worth a visit. For masks go to *Choeki Handicrafts*.

Maps: newspaper stand nr the cinema hall, which also sells maps of Thimphu and Paro.

Photography: films and processing at *Photofield* and *Sunrise*.

Stamps: for collectors from *Philatelic Bureau*, inside GPO.

Textiles: *Pel Jorkhang*, Crossroads, specializes in local textiles. *Sengay Buddha* and *Dorji Gyeltsen*, shops 33 and 35, Line 2, Nordzin lam, are rec for traditional clothes. Also *Tshering Dolkar* and *Ethometho*, Tourism Bldg by Cinema, for handicrafts and cloth. The latter stocks books, postcards and stamps.

WARNING Do not bargain. Foreigners are not allowed to buy antiques (see Information for visitors below).

● **Sports**
Golf: entrance on Chophel lam, behind Tashi Chodzong. There are also 2 tennis courts, a squash court, and swimming pool.

Health club and hairdresser: *Sakteng Salon* on Gaton lam.

● **Tourist offices**
Tourist Authority of Bhutan (TAB), PO Box 126, T 23251, F 23695.

● **Tour companies & travel agents**
See Information for visitors below.

● **Transport**
Road Most places of interest are now linked by bus. Private vehicle hire with a driver is possible. Paro (59 km, 1½ hrs); Punakha and Wangdu 2 hrs; Phuntsoling, 6 hrs.

WESTERN BHUTAN

Thimphu district

(*Area* 1,620 sq km) This is the district named after the Thimphu River, a tributary of the Wang-chu (Raidak), from which the national capital also gets its name. The district administrative capital (*dzongkhag*) is located in Thimphu city, N of the Changlingmethang market, and beside the river.

Places of interest

North of the city, and across the river from **Dechen Choling** palace complex is the picturesque monastery of **Pangri Zampa**, built in the early 16th century by Ngawang Chogyel, and the original residence of Zhabdrung Ngawang Namgyel in Bhutan. Some 20 km further N, the motor road abruptly ends, close by the monasteries of **Cheri** (dated 1619) and **Tangro** (original construction 13th century, rebuilt 1688). It is from the former that the difficult trekking route to **Lingzhi** in northern Thimphu district begins, crossing the Yele La pass (4,900m) via Shodu and Barshong. Lingzhi, largely a nomadic area, contains the ruins of one of the Zhabdrung's non-monastic fortresses at Yulgyel Dzong, close to the Tibetan frontier.

From Pangri Zampa there is an old trekking route (40 km) which leads into the **Punakha** district to the E. The trek climbs through beautiful rhododendron forests via Kabjisa to Sinchu La pass (3,400m), and thence downhill via Tonshinkha to Sirigang (1,350m), from where there is a motorable road into Punakha.

5 km downstream from Thimphu city, strategically located at the junction of the Paro, Punakha, and Thimphu roads is **Simtoka Dzong** (*srinmo dokha*). Dated 1627, this was the first dzong to be constructed by Zhabdrung Ngawang Namgyel in Bhutan, and since 1961 it has functioned as the national Dzongka

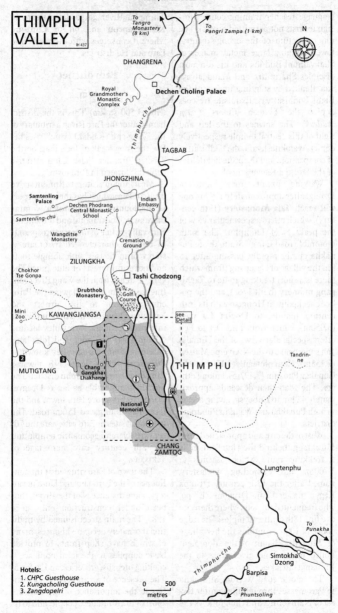

THIMPHU
VALLEY
BH 437

To
Tangro
Monastery
(8 km)

To Pangri Zampa (1 km)

N

DHANGRENA

Royal
Grandmother's
Monastic
Complex

Dechen Choling Palace

TAGBAB

Thimphu-chu

JHONGZHINA

Samtenling
Palace

Dechen Phodrang
Central Monastic
School

Indian
Embassy

Samtenling-chu

Wangditse
Monastery

Cremation
Ground

ZILUNGKHA

Chokhor
Tse Gonpa

Tashi Chodzong

Drubthob
Monastery

Golf
Course

Mini
Zoo

KAWANGJANGSA

see
Detail

THIMPHU

Tandrin-
ne

MUTIGTANG

1

3

Chang
Gangkha
Lhakhang

2

National
Memorial

CHANG
ZAMTOG

Lungtenphu

To Punakha

Simtokha
Dzong

Barpisa

To
Phuntsoling

Thimphu-chu

Hotels:
1. *CHPC Guesthouse*
2. *Kungacholing Guesthouse*
3. *Zangdopelri*

0   500
metres

language teacher training centre (foreign tourists not permitted access). The inner sanctum of the dzong's central tower contains large metal images of Shakyamuni Buddha and his foremost disciples Shariputra and Maudgalyayana, flanked by standing images of the Eight Bodhisattvas. Exquisite frescoes depict the Sixteen Elders (*neten chudruk*). The shrines to the left and right of this central temple respectively depict Avalokiteshvara, the bodhisattva of compassion, and the protector deities of the Drukpa Kagyu school.

Walking uphill from Simtokha Dzong, after approximately 1½ hrs one will reach **Tala Monastery** (19th century), which offers a spectacular view of the peaks N of Thimphu. The main motorable road E from Simtokha to Punakha climbs rapidly, passing after 15 km the village of Oesepang (from which there is a short trekking route to **Tashigang** nunnery (built 1768), and the police checkpoint at **Hongtso** with its 16th century temple, to **Dochu La** pass (3,050m), which from mid-Oct to Feb offers spectacular views of the Himalayan snow peaks to the N: Gyelpo Matsen (7,158m), Kangphugang (7,170m), and Gangkar Punsum (7,497m), among others. The road then descends approximately 42 km to **Lobeysa**, giving access to both Punakha and Wangdu Phodrang districts.

West of the city, and approached from Mutigtang (behind the Hotel), there is a trekking route which ascends to 3,700m. and **Phajoding** monastery, named after the 13th century Drukpa Kagyu master Phajo Drugom Zhikpo, who frequented this site, where there are two fine 18th century temples. The ridge above (4,100m) contains the hermitage of **Thujedra**, haunt of the aforementioned master, and give access to the Jimilangtsho lakes.

The motor road W from Simtokha to Paro passes through the conifer forest of **Namseling**, and then follows the Thimphu River gorge downstream to Khasadrapchu and on to **Chuzom**, where it converges with the roads into Paro and Ha districts.

Paro district

པ་རོ་

(*Area* 1,500 sq km) This is the district named after the Paro River, a tributary of the Wang-chu (Raidak), which rises below the snow-peak of Jomolhari on the Tibetan frontier. The administrative capital is located in Paro town.

Most foreign visitors to Bhutan arrive by air at Paro which has the only airport in the country. Thimphu is a 90 mins drive away. The tranquil and unpolluted Paro valley is one of the most prosperous in Bhutan, characterized by ornate 3-storey farm houses with shingle-roofs and beautiful forests of blue pine. The valley extends from the Wang River confluence at Chuzom, following the Paro-chu upstream to the airport and Rinpung Dzong, from where it divides into two: the main Paro valley leading NW to Drugyel Dzong and Jomolhari base camp, and a side-valley known as **Dopchari**, which leads NE towards Lingzhi in upper Thimphu district. The former is motorable as far as Drugyel Dzong 16 km above Paro town, and the latter has an unpaved 15 km road. The two oldest sites in Paro valley are the 7th century Kyerchu geomantic temple and the 8th century cave hermitage of Taktsang.

The town of Paro situated at the confluence of the Paro-chu and Do-chu valleys, some distance N of the airport, has been under construction only since 1985. The main street is lined by traditional ornately decorated houses, many of which have shop fronts to provide basic supplies to the local populace – cooking utensils, groceries, and so forth. The presence of an archery range testifies to the importance of the national sport of the Bhutanese people; and to its

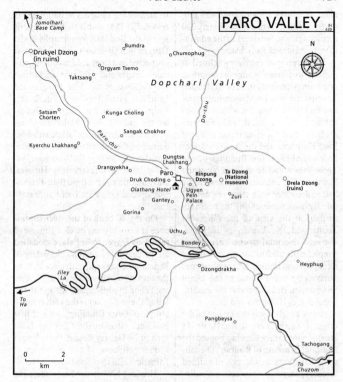

right, there is a lane leading gently up-hill toward the impressive cantilever bridge of Paro Dzong, which is strikingly roofed with shingles.

Places of interest

The vast white **Paro Dzong**, formerly known as Rinpung Dzong, dominates the skyline and life of Paro. The original building on this site had been constructed by a descendent of Phajo Dru-gom Zhikpo, who founded the Drukpa Kagyu school in Bhutan, and it had been the castle of the lords of Humrel until 1645 when it was offered to Zhabdrung Ngawang Namgyel. The following year (1646) the Zhabrung then constructed a more imposing 5-storeyed fortress with

a covered drawbridge on one wall, and, on the other three walls, dungeons, the narrow window slits of which are clearly visible. For 250 years it served as a bastion against invasions from the N. It burnt down in 1905 and all the treasures except the enormous **Tongdrol tangka** (30m x 45m) were destroyed. This tangka depicts Padmasambhava flanked by his two foremost consorts and surrounded by his eight manifestations. On the last day of the Paro Tsechu festival, it is unfurled for a few hours and dances are performed in front of it.

The present dzong was built immediately after the fire and has fine wood-work, large sections of logs slotted into each other, held together without any nails. It houses a state-sponsored monastic community of approximately 200 monks; and also functions as the administrative centre of Paro district.

The interior of the dzong (closed at present to foreign visitors) comprises two main courtyards and a central tower. The first courtyard contains administrative buildings, while the second houses the monastic community and an assembly hall, where the main image is that of Jowo Rinpoche and the frescoes depict Padmasambhava, the Buddhas of the Three Times, and Zhabdrung Ngawang Namgyel. The entrance to this assembly hall is decorated with three cosmological diagrams, representing the world according to the view of the *Kalacakra Tantra*, and the *Treasury of the Abhidharma*. The central tower (*u-tse*) contains temples dedicated to the masters of the Drukpa Kagyu lineage, to the eight stupas symbolizing major events in the life of Shakyamuni Buddha, and to the meditational deities Havagriva and Tara.

Above the dzong is the largest of the original watchtowers (c 1651), or **Ta Dzong**, which since 1968 has housed the **National Museum of Bhutan**. The museum has a varied collection of painted scrolls, applique, postage stamps, sculpture and engraving, silverwork, armour, stuffed animals, and traditional articles in daily use, as well as ancient and modern costumes and jewellery. Outside is a collection of iron chains derived from the eight iron bridges constructed in Bhutan by Tangtong Gyelpo. 0900-1600. Closed Mon. Carry a flashlight (erratic electric supply) and allow 1 hr to see all floors.

The approach road to the National Museum passes in front of **Dungtse Lhakhang**, which lies across the river from Paro town on a geomantic promontory between the Paro and Do rivers. Constructed in 1421 by the celebrated bridge builder Tangtong Gyelpo on the head of a demoness, this temple, like the Memorial Chorten in Thimphu, is located within a stupa. The building was restored in 1841 and is a unique repository of the Buddhist iconography of the Drukpa Kagyu school. The 3 storeys, connected by a steep ladder, contain precious images and paintings, including: the Buddhas of the Five Enlightened Families, as well as Avalokiteshvara, Padmasambhava, and Tangtong Gyelpo on the ground floor, Mahakala along with the hundred peaceful and wrathful deities on the second floor, and meditational deities such as Guhyasamaja, Vajrabhairava, Cakrasamvara, Hevajra, and Kalacakra on the third floor. Permission needed for a visit; flashlight essential.

On the W bank of the river confluence at Paro, you can catch a glimpse of the lovely **Ugyen Pelri Palace** modelled on the heavenly Zangdokpelri palace of Padmasambhava and built circa 1930 by the then district governor of Paro, Tshering Peljor. Slightly upstream and to the left of the main road is the 16th century temple of **Druk Choding**, and S of that building, close to the *Olathang Hotel* turn-off, is **Gantey Resort**, the splendid former residence of the governors of Paro, now also converted into a hotel.

Heading NW up the Paro valley, one reaches the two most sacred sites of this district: **Kyerchu Lhakhang**, and Taktsang hermitage. The former, which is presently closed to foreigners, is located a few kilometres N of Paro town and to the left side of the road amid masses of prayer flags. It is revered as one of the four border-taming geomantic temples (*thadul lhakhang*) built by the Tibetan king **Songtsen Gampo** during the 7th century see above, page 85). Kyerchu is considered to have been constructed specifically on 'the left foot of the supine ogress', who, geomantically speaking, represents the rigours and hostility of the Tibetan landscape, which was to be tamed and civilized by the construction of Buddhist temples at selected power points on its surface.

Paro Taktsang in Bhutan

Later in 13th century, the temple was administered in succession by the Lhapa and the Drukpa Kagyu schools. The gold roof was added in 1830, and in 1839, the site was restored by Sherab Gyeltsen, the 25th Je Khenpo of Bhutan, who commissioned the large central image of Avalokiteshvara. More recently, in 1968, the Queen Mother of Bhutan, had a second temple constructed alongside the original in the same style, but dedicated to the eight meditational deities of the Nyingma school, known as the 'eight transmitted precepts' (*kabgye*). The entire complex of buildings is situated within a decorative courtyard. The ancient temple has outer murals depicting the 12 deeds and past lives of Shaykamuni Buddha, the Sixteen Elders, the protectors Tsheringma and Genyen Dorje Dradul, as well as Padmasambhava, Zhapdrung Ngawang Namgyel, and the aforementioned 25th Je Khenpo. Inside, the images (closed to the public) include a celebrated Jowo image similar to that of the Jokhang in Lhasa, flanked by the eight standing bodhisattvas, as well as numerous images of Avalokiteshvara and his emanation, the Tibetan king Songtsen Gampo.

The **Taktsang hermitage** (Tiger's Lair) is located on the face of a sheer 1,000m cliff above the Paro valley, and to the right side of the road, some 5 km N of Kyerchu. It is an impressive sight but far from inaccessible. During the 8th century, Padmasambhva, the great Buddhist master of Oddiyana, is said to have travelled the length and breadth of the Himalayan regions, from Zahor in the NW through Central Tibet, Nepal, and Bhutan, as far as Kham and Amdo in Eastern Tibet, establishing Buddhism en route. The sacred sites associated with Padmasambhava include some of the most dramatic and remote power places in the region. Taktsang is one of a number of awesome tiger lairs frequented by this master, who, according to legend, is said to have flown there from **Khenpajong** in NE Bhutan on the back of a tigress, in order to subdue negative demons, hostile to Buddhism, through his tiger-riding emanation, known as Dorje Drolod. In 853, one of Padmasambhava's Tibetan students known as Langchen Pelgyi Senge meditated in the main cave at Taktsang, which later came to be known as Taktsang Pelphuk, after hos own name. A recently restored stupa at the entrance to this cave contains his mortal remains. Subsequently many great spiritual masters of Tibet passed periods here in profound meditation – notably 11th and 12th century figures such as Milarepa, Phadampa Sangye, and Machik Labdron, and 14th-15th century figures, such as Tangtong Gyelpo.

On the ascent to Taktsang from the road, you can rest at the *Taktsang Tea House*, which has breathtaking views of the hermitage; it serves refreshments, warm lunches, and sells handicrafts. Although horses can be arranged on request, it is better to walk up as Bhutanese saddles are memorably uncomfortable. The beautiful walk up from the motor road, past the **Satsam Chorten** (10 mins drive from Paro village; 2 hrs from Thimphu) through oaks and pine trees to the *Tea House*, is quite strenuous and usually takes 2 hrs. A further 1 hr walk climbs steeply to a vantage point above Taktsang, from which a flight of cliff-hanging steps leads down towards the cave (3 hrs to reach the highest point).

The entire complex of Taktsang includes 13 holy places, and the earliest buildings (no longer extant) were constructed by Sonam Gyeltsen, a 14th century Nyingmapa lama of Katok monastery in E Tibet. Until the site was offered to Zhapdrung Ngawang Namgyel in 1645, it remained under the authority of Katok, and even in recent centuries its close association with the

latter have been maintained. The present buildings date from 1692, and these have been subsequently restored in 1861-5 and in 1982. There are three temples, the most important of which is the smallest, containing the sacred cave of Padmasambhava. Here a wrathful image of Dorje Drolod riding the tigress guards the approach to the cave, while adjacent murals depict the meditational deity Vajrakila.

Above this shrine is a second temple, containing a 'speaking' image of Padmasambhava, smaller images of the temple's founder Desi IV Tendzin Rabgye (1638-96) and Langchen Pelgyi Senge, and a variety of fine murals, depicting Shakyamuni Buddha, Zhapdrung Ngawang Namgyel, Amitayus, the great religious kings of Tibet, and the three cycles of deities (*Kagong Phursum*) which are also depicted three-dimensionally in the Memorial Chorten of Thimphu (see above, page 722).

The third temple, the largest, has a large image of Padmasambhava and murals depicting him surrounded by his eight manifestations, as well as murals of the *Lama Gongdu* and *Vajrakila* cycles. Smaller shrines above this temple contain further images of Dorje Drolod, Amitayus and Kubera.

The summit of the ridge above Taktsang has three further temple complexes. Among them, **Orgyen Tsemo** with its amazing frescoes of Padmasmbhava and his followers, was a branch of Katok, built in 1408 and restored in 1958. **Ozergang** was constructed in 1646, and **Zangdok Pelri** in 1853. All the sites at Taktsang are visited by pilgrims from Bhutan and the Tibetan Buddhist world, although foreigners are currently only allowed to within 100m of the hermitage complex.

16 km N of Paro, at the end of the motorable road stands the **Drukgyel Dzong** ('fortress of the victorious Drukpas') built to commemorate victory over the Tibetans in 1644, and to protect the

Paro valley from further invasions. The building was ruined by fire in 1951, and in 1985 a shingled roof was added to protect what remains of the building from further ruin. Situated on a hill, it stands against the snow peak of Mt Jomolhari (7,313m), protected by three towers and approached only from one direction, and gives the impression of shutting off the Paro valley. Its position ensured that no one could travel on the Paro-Tibet road without being seen. This has long been the most accessible route from Tibet into Bhutan, leading from Phari in the Tromo region across the Tremo La, and directly to Drugyel Dzong.

In Southern Paro district, a few kilometres above Chuzom, and on the E bank of the Paro River, is **Tachogang Lhakhang** – a celebrated temple constructed by Tangtong Gyelpo circa 1420 to commemorate one of his visionary experiences. The river confluence at **Chuzom**, which marks the southern extremity of Paro district, where the roads from Ha and Thimphu also converge, is indicated by three stupas – respectively in Nepalese, Tibetan, and Bhutanese styles.

Trekking in Northern Paro

1. Drugyel Dzong to upper Thimphu via Mt Jomolhari Base Camp

There is a demanding trek via Jomolhari Base Camp into Northern Thimphu district. It takes around 7 days. Best season: late April, May, Oct. You get excellent views of the mountains and glaciers and pass gorges and waterfalls, cross rivers and see yaks in their pasture and alpine flowers, rhododendrons and orchids according to the season.

From **Drukyel Dzong** in Paro the path rises steadily for some 12 km up to the ruined **Soi Dzong** at the foot of the **Jomolhari** (7,313m), a truly dramatic sight. The base camp at Jomolhari, most sacred of mountains to the Bhutanese, is 3 days trekking from Drugyel Dzong. Then the trail crosses a pass at 4,400m before descending into Thimphu

district to the valley where the hilltop **Lingzhi Dzong** once guarded the frontier with Tibet. From there you have splendid views of the Jichu Drakye (6,974m) and Tseringkhang mountains. The path then continues through yak pastures to the Yele La pass (4,900m) before descending through the spectacular Wang-chu gorge, up to **Dodina** in the upper part of the Thimphu valley.

2. Paro to Ha via the Cheli La

From Paro, most of the early part of this trek is through dense forest. As you reach Cheli La, broad panoramas of the mountains around Jomolhari open out. Above the forest, the trekking is across yak pastures. There are two important passes, the Kale La and Sage La, both important burial areas. Towards the finish, you will descend into deciduous forest and re-enter the Paro Valley. Although comparatively short (under 7 days), the variation in altitude and vegetation plus the rich flora and fauna and stunning views make it an exceptionally good trek in Oct-Nov and April.

3. Paro-Thimphu Trek (Druk Path)

Although most people drive from Paro to Thimphu, you can do a 3-day easy trek along a path, instead of the road, going through a 3,900m pass. It gives the not-so-energetic a wonderful, relaxed insight into Bhutanese life. There are some fine ridge views of the mountains and pleasant stretches through lush forest. In April-May the rhododendrons are in bloom and are a spectacular sight. On the way, there are beautiful lakes and the famous monastery of **Phajoding** (3,058m) with its 18th century temples housing art works and paintings, which can also be visited from Thimphu on a day excursion but involves a 3 hrs climb.

● **Accommodation** *Eye of the Tiger* cottages opp Taktsang monastery are simple but very pleasant; *Gantey Resort*, refurbished and located in an old traditional manor opp the dzong, is charming; *New Druk Hotel*, shaped like a dzong above the airport is very grand;

BTCL *Olathang*, in a beautiful hillside setting overlooking valley, 3 km from the village, pleasant rooms with bath in main building and in 14 cottages spread around the large grounds, restaurant, bar, shop.

● **Shopping** *Chencho Handicrafts*, on the main square, has a very good selection and there is also a small souvenir shop at the airport.

Ha district

(*Area* 2,140 sq km) This is the district named after the Had (or Lhade) River, locally pronounced as 'Ha', which converges with the Paro and Thimphu tributaries of the Wang-chu (Raidak) at Chuzom. The administrative capital is located in **Ha** (2,700m) – the only habitation in the district connected by a motorable road. The population is fairly isolated and, for climatic reasons, engaged for the most part in pastoral farming. According to local legend, the valley was known as Had ('sudden') because two temples, one white and one black, are said to have spontaneously appeared in the valley below Mt Khyungdu (which separates this district from Tibet). Perhaps the most important Buddhist establishment in Ha is the **Gyamdud** monastery, which has had associations with the Barawa and Drukpa Kagyu schools. Formerly, there was an active trade with Tibet through the valley of the Amo-chu (Torsa), which enters W Bhutan from the Dromo (Chumbi) valley and forms the western boundary of Ha district. The village of **Sangbay** is the largest in the Amo valley. A short 7-day trekking route from Paro to SE Ha has already been described (see above).

Samchi district

བསམ་རྩེ

(*Area* 2,140 sq km) This is the westernmost district of Bhutan, which shares its N and W borders with Sikkim, and its S frontier with W Bengal. The administrative capital is located at **Samchi**. The principal river of this district is the Dichu (Jaldakha), which enters from Sikkim and flows into W Bengal. The towns of **Sibsu**, **Chengmari**, and **Samchi** which adjoin the Indian frontier have a large Lhotsampa (ie Nepalese) population, while the more remote village of **Dorokha** in the Amo valley borders on Ha.

Chukha district

ཆུ་ཁ

(*Area* approximately 7,000 sq km) This somewhat sensitive border district provides Bhutan with its main land access to India in the S. The administrative capital was, until the construction of the Chukha hydroelectric plant, located at **Chukha Dzong**, on the Wang-chu (Raidak) River, not far S of Chuzom, where its three main tributaries converge. Following the recent dam construction and the flooding of the Chukha valley, the capital has been moved S to **Phuntsoling**, the largest town, on the Indian border, some 141 km from Chuzom. Located 3-4 hrs by road from Bagdogra Airport in W Bengal, and 4$\frac{1}{2}$ hrs drive from Chuzom, Phuntsoling is a typical frontier town, situated on the left bank of the Amo (Torsa) River, where Bhutanese, Nepalese, Bengali and Indian cultures meet head on. A traditionally painted gateway welcomes visitors to the Bhutanese frontier post. Commercially it is an important town with small-scale industries (dairy, soft drinks, matches). All imported goods to the capital Thimphu transit through Phuntsoling, so each morning trucks (and buses) roar through the streets. The town is not particularly attractive, but has an interesting mix of population and a definite tropical air. There is a newly constructed **Zangdokpelri** temple, modelled on the palace of Padmasambhava, with images of the latter's eight manifestations at ground level, Avalokiteshvara, on the midlevel, and Amitabha on the uppermost level. These three types of images are representative respectively of the three buddha-bodies.

● **Accommodation** Phuntsoling is the usual night halt for travellers entering Bhutan by road from India. Welcomgroup *Druk*, T 2426, and *Namgyel*, PO Box 99, T 2293, are the best hotels with good restaurants. For simple accommodation and good Indian meals *Kunga* opp *Druk* is fine. All are comfortable.

From Phuntsoling, nestling at the foot of the Himalaya, the spectacular 175 km drive to Thimphu and Paro via Chuzom reaches altitudes of 3,000m. Ascending steeply through teak jungle landscape, the first stop is at **Kharbandi Monastery** above the town at 400m, with fine views over the foothills and the Bengal plains. The main temple, constructed in 1967, contains images of Shakyamuni Buddha, Padmasambhava, and Zhabdrung Ngawang Namgyel, as well as paintings depicting the deeds of the Buddha. The complex is encircled by the eight stupas, which symbolize the important events of the Buddha's life. At Kharbandi there is also a police immigration checkpoint, and a technical college.

The road continues to rise through a series of switchback turns, as it leaves the Amo valley behind, and traverses the tropical jungle. At **Gedu** (2,200m) there is a truckers stop and a large plywood factory. Then, entering the misty and humid Wang-chu valley via Taktichu, where leeches abound during the monsoon season, the countryside becomes sparsely populated. A bridge crosses the Wang-chu adjacent to the Chukha hydroelectric plant, after which the road then rises to **Bunakha**, where the Bhutan Tourism Corporation has a small restaurant, and the prosperous farming village of **Chapcha**. At Chapcha La pass (2,900m) the entire Wang-chu gorge is visible, snaking its way southwards to the Bengal plains. On the descent, the road continues to follow the river through a narrow gorge to Chuzom.

Punakha district

(*Area* 6,040 sq km; including Gasa district) The administrative capital is located at Punakha, where the Mo-chu and Pho-chu tributaries of the Puna Tsangchu (Sankosh) converge.

Punakha town is close enough to Thimphu to make a long day-trip feasible. A 2-hr drive on the new road crosses the spectacular **Dochu La pass** (3,050m) with excellent views of the northern peaks early morning from Oct to Mar. The pass is 45 mins' drive from the Simtokha Dzong turn-off to the S of Thimphu. During the ascent, you will pass through the police checkpoint at **Hongtso**, where a large 16th century temple, **Hongtso Lhakhang**, is located, and where the local populace includes many Bhutanese nationals of Tibetan origin. *Dochu La Cafe* at the pass serves refreshments. The long 65 km descent to Lobeysa (1,300m) traverses both temperate and semi-tropical zones, and takes 2½ hrs. The valley here is in a rainshadow area, lower than most midland valleys with a mild climate allowing rice, oranges and a variety of vegetables to be grown. At **Lobeysa**, where the roads to Punakha and Wangdu Phodrang diverge, there is a hilltop **temple associated with Drukpa Kun-le**, the renowned yogin or 'divine madman' of Bhutan, where infertile Bhutanese women will go on pilgrimage. 2 km beyond Lobeysa on the Punakha road is the beautifully located *Zandopelri Hotel* opened in 1994. Punakha town (1,350m) is located some 10 km further N.

The main site at Punakha is the **Dechen Phodrang Dzong**, which stands at the confluence of the Pho-chu (Father) and Mo-chu (Mother) tributaries. Built in 1637, the dzong served as the winter capital of Bhutan for 300 years, despite being damaged by fires in the 17th and 18th century, as well as in 1986, and by floods in 1897 and 1994.

The present king has commissioned extensive restorations. Even now, it functions as the winter headquarters of the Je Khenpo (Head Monastic Preceptor of Bhutan), and, apart fom its courtyard, it is open to foreign visitors only in summer when the monks reside at Thimphu. The original 17th century construction is said to have been predicted by Padmasambhava, who had frequented the site during the 8th century. Within the complex, the first courtyard contains administrative buildings (since the dzong functions as the capital of Punakha district). The second courtyard is occupied mostly by a recently constructed temple, dedicated to the deity Cakrasamvara. A third courtyard contains the large monastic assembly hall, where the main image is of Vajrasattva. The central tower, with its great assembly hall, were chosen as the location for the coronation of Bhutan's first king in 1907. Altogether, there are 21 temples, the most sacred perhaps being the **Machen Lhakhang**, where the body of the Zhabdrung (d 1651) is itself interred. The principal image is a self-originated Avalokiteshvara in the form known as Kharsapani, which the Zhabdrung himself had brought from Ralung, and which the Tibetan armies had unsuccessfully attempted to retrieve in the 17th century. An annual festival is held at Punakha to commemorate these events during the first month of the lunar calendar.

Gasa district

དགར་ས

The northern frontier of Gasa is separated from the Khangmar county of Tibet by the formidable Himalayan snow range, which stretches from Mt Gyelpo Matsen (7,158m) to Mt Zongaphugang (7,060m) and Mt Kulha Kangri (7,554m). Local traders still gain access to Khangmar via the frontier passes of Yak La and Phiru La. Bhutan's highest mountain,

Gangkar Punsum (7,540m) is also located in this district, making the northern reaches attractive to mountaineering expeditions and trekking groups.

Trekking in Gasa district

1. Punakha to Gasa and Laya

The motorable road ceases 30 km N of Punakha Dzong at Tashinthang in the Mo-chu valley, and from that point onwards, the trekking routes to the northern parts of Gasa district begin. It is possible to undertake an 11-day trek to Laya (3,850m), starting and ending in Punakha, with 4 full days in Laya. The first part of this route leads to **Gasa**, a once thriving market, also in the Mo-chu valley, where yak caravans would congregate. Today, with Tibetan trade being severely curtailed, its role has been considerably diminished. There is a dzong at Gasa, now given dzongkhak status, which directly administers the northern settlements of Laya and Lunanang, and a renowned medicinal hotsprings. **Laya** (3,850m), the second highest village in Bhutan, is situated at the foot of Mt Gyelpo Matsen (7,158m), and near the source of the Mo chu. The inhabitants of Laya still worship Bon divinities and guard their villages of painted wooden houses with wood images. Here, yak herders dressed in a very distinctive costume, live and tend their yaks; the women too are more reminiscent of nomadic Tibetan peoples with their long hair and plaited cane pointed hats. You will see herdsmen in blackened yak-hair tents or stone houses, and prayer flags constructed around 'demon-exorcising thread-crosses' made of wood and stone. In the higher reaches there are large flocks of blue sheep, and the takin which is rare elsewhere in the Himalaya. Bears are relatively common, and the guides often make a lot of noise so as not to take them by surprise. Best season: spring and autumn. The monsoon is to be avoided owing to the overwhelming number of leeches between

Punakha and Gasa. The Laya trek can be combined with the Jomolhari trek (see above, page 700), which makes a strenuous 15-day trek crossing several 4,000m passes into Paro.

2. Punakha to Gasa, Laya and Lunanang

One of the most difficult treks of all, this takes 18 days, and is for the very fit, experienced trekker as it crosses five passes over 5,000m. The trail goes first from Punakha to **Laya** (see above) in 4 days. Beyond Laya, there is a demanding 3-day trek, traversing the **Gangla Karchung Pass** (5,100m), which is the first of the three steep passes over 5,000m offering superb views of the E Himalaya. Descending to **Woche** (3,850m) in the beautiful northern region of Lunanang, near the source of the Pho chu, you trek for 2 days through **Thega, Chozo Valley** with its dzong, and to the regional capital **Thanaza** (4,050m). A further 5 days trek to the S crosses Rinchenzo La pass (5,220m) to intersect with the motor road at **Nakarchu Bridge** where you can get transport back to Thimphu or Tongsar. The mountain views, particularly those of Mt Gangkar Punsum (7,239m), are spectacular and you pass lakes, glacial rivers, moraines, beautiful forests with Himalayan birds and flower-filled alpine meadows. Uncertain weather conditions add to the difficulty of this trek. Best season: Aug-Sept. Difficult as it is, some intrepid trekkers prefer to extend the Lunanang trek to over 21 days, by combining it with the Jomolhari trek – altogether 356 km, crossing eight high passes, sometimes known as the 'snowman trek'.

Wangdu district

དབང་འདུས

(*Area* 3,000 sq km) The administrative capital is located at Wangdu Phodrang. The northern extremity of Wangdu district, which borders the Lhodrak county

of Tibet via the Monla Karchung La pass, includes the headwaters of the Mangde chu; but the greater part of the district comprises the mid-reaches of the Puna Tsang-chu (Sankosh) valley, along with those of its Dang-chu and Hang-chu tributaries. In the E of the district the Black Mountains form a watershed between the main rivers of W and E Bhutan.

At Lobeysa to the S of Punakha, there is a southerly turn-off for **Wangdu Phodrang** (9 km distant), which is sometimes referred to as the gateway to Central and E Bhutan. The large dzong, constructed 1638-83, stands impressively on a rocky outcrop, and strategically dominates the main roads which intersect below it: those to Punakha and Thimphu in the N, Chirang in the S, and Tongsar in the E. It is said that the protector deity Mahakala appeared in a vision to Zhabdrung Ngawang Namgyel, exhorting him to build a fortress on a rocky spur where ravens fly off in all four directions. Hence the name Wangdu Phodrang ('palace gathering all within its power'). The dzong, which is only open to foreign visitors during the annual Tsechu ceremony, contains the administrative centre for the whole district, as well as a monastic assembly hall containing large images of the Buddhas of the Three Times. The town at Wangdu is currently under construction. Local handicrafts include bamboo work, as well as stone and slate carving.

● **Accommodation** In town, a small, spartan *Guest House*, with 6 clean rm, some with bath, simple meals, camping on lawn, suitable overnight stop for trekkers. The lovely *Dechen Cottages* in Mendegang, are 15 km before Wangdu, on the Thimphu road.

From the crossroads at the bridge below Wangdu Phodrang, it a 129 km (3½ hrs drive) to Tongsar in Central Bhutan, a 71 km (2½ hrs drive) to Thimphu, or a 4 hrs drive to Chirang in the S. Taking the central road, you drive due E via **Chuzomsa** and **Tikke**, and ascend into the **Black Mountains**. The entire region of the Black Mountains is the preserve of nomadic yak-herders and shepherds; and there is a Yak Dairy Research Station in the isolated valley of **Gogona**.

7 km after the small village of Nobding on the Wangdu-Tongsar raod, there is a turn-off to the right which leads into the glacial **Phobjika valley** (3,000m). This truly spacious valley, unusual in Bhutan but reminiscent of many in Tibet, is the location of the beautiful **Ganteng Gonpa**, the only monastery of the Nyingma school of Tibetan Buddhism on the W side of the Black Mountains. The complex was founded in 1613 by Pema Trhinle, a grandson of the treasure-finder Pema Lingpa, and now has five temples within its central tower. Here the liturgies of Pema Lingpa's tradition are maintained by the monks and by the married Buddhist practitioners, whose families inhabit the large village which surrounds the monastery. The Phobjika valley is also the winter haunt of the amazing black-neck crane, which migrates here from Central Asia and can be seen circling above the fields from Nov-Mar. The higher pastures above the valley are ideal for yaks who subsist on the high-altitude dwarf bamboo which grows in abundance. For those wishing to avoid the motor road, there is an easy 3-4 days trek from Phobjika valley, where you see the beautiful Ganteng monastery, down to **Wangdu Phodrang**, passing through small villages and splendid forests of giant junipers, daphne bushes, rhododendrons and magnolia. The rhododendron season (April) is highly recommended, since you can then see hundreds in bloom.

Returning to the main road, the drive continues eastwards through rhododendron and magnolia forest for 14 km to the watershed at **Pele La** pass (3,300m), which in clear weather offers a splendid view of Jomolhari to the NW. On the far side of the pass, the road descends through the village of Rukubji to the bridge at **Nakarchu**, from where the trekking route to Lunanang can be reached (see above). Beyond Nakarchu, you pass out of Wangdu and into the Tongsar district of Central Bhutan.

The southern road from the bridge at Wangdu follows a newly constructed motor route into Chirang.

Chirang district
རྗི་རང་

(*Area* 800 sq km) The administrative capital of Chirang is located at Damphu. This landlocked district is now linked by a recently constructed motor road which follows the course of the Puna Tsang-chu (Sankosh) with Wangdu Phodrang in the N and Khalikhola on the Indian frontier. Its major villages: **Damphu**, Lamidangra, and Dagapela are in the heart of the orange and cardamom growing part of the country, and the population is predominantly Lhotsampa.

Takar (Daga) district

(*Area* 1,400 sq km) The administrative capital is located at Takar (Daga) on the Takar-chu, a tributary of the Puna Tsang-chu, which rises E of Chuzom. Like Chirang, this district is also known for its orange and cardamom plantations, but the absence of a motorable road has ensured its isolation.

CENTRAL BHUTAN

A trip to Central Bhutan allows you to discover diverse aspects of the country but be prepared for long drives and rustic comfort at the lodges. Allow about 10 days for a worthwhile trip. From June-Sept the roads are sometimes blocked by landslides. The districts comprised within Central Bhutan are those of Tongsar and Bumtang in the N, and those of Gelekphuk and Shemgang in the S.

Tongsar district

ཀྲོང་གསར

(*Area* 1,470 sq km) The administrative capital is located at Tongsar (Tongsa). Bounded on the W by the Black Mountains, which form a watershed between W and E Bhutan, this district corresponds to the valley of the Mangde-chu, an important tributary of the Drangmechu (Manas), rising below Mt Gangkar Punsum.

The central motor road, constructed in 1985, links Wangdu with Tongsar. After the descent from Pele La pass to Nakarchu (see above), you enter into the district of Tongsar, and drive through a narrow gorge to **Chendebji Chorten**. Here, there are two stupas: the older in Nepalese style, which was constructed in 18th century by Lama Shida for geomantic purposes, and the more recent one in Bhutanese style, which dates from 1982. On leaving the gorge, the road then follows the Mangde-chu, and descends dramatically along the edge of a sheer precipice into **Tongsar**, which is visible some 20 km below. At 2,200m, and 130 km E of Wangdu Phodrang, **Tongsar Dzong** is the largest and most impressive dzong in Bhutan, standing on a spur above the deep Mangde gorge and dominated by a two-wing watchtower ('Ta Dzong'), from which all aproaches could be monitored with ease. The original dzong was established by the Zhabdrung in 1647 on the site of a temple founded by his great-grandfather in 1543. Subsequently enlarged in 1652 and 1771, it has also been damaged by an earthquake (1897), and repaired in the present century. This huge, many-levelled fortress has a maze of courtyards and covered passages, and 23 temples, among which those dedicated to Maitreya, Yamantaka, Hevajra, and Kalacakra are most important. A stupa shrine stands on the site where the original 16th century temple once stood; and there is an active printing press, utilising the traditional xylographic method. The monastic community of Tongsar moves in summer to **Kurje Monastery** in Bumtang.

During the 19th century, Tongsar was the seat of the most powerful governor of the country, commading the whole of the central and eastern region. One of these governors (*Tongsar Ponlop*), Ugyen Wangchuck, became the first hereditary King of Bhutan in 1907, for which reason the dzong at Tongsar is revered as the ancestral home of Bhutan's royal family (tourists need a permit to visit).

The new village of Tongsar above the dzong has been under construction since 1982. The shopkeepers of this community, perched on the mountainside, are largely Bhutanese of Tibetan origin.

● **Accommodation** BTCL *Sherubling Lodge*, nr the school, has 6 simple heated rm and 6 cottages with bath, limited catering; *Yangkhyil* in town is simpler but great for excellent meals in its warm kitchen. A new hotel is currently being constructed next to the *Yangkhyil*.

The road from Tongsar to Bumtang extends eastwards for 29 km, as far as **Yutong La** pass (3,400 km), which marks the border between Tongsar and Bumtang districts. En route you will have a stunning view of the Tongsar Dzong before entering the forested approach to the pass.

The southern road from Tongsar follows the Mangde-chu downstream before cutting westwards to Burgang (Gelekphuk) on the Indian frontier, some 237 km distant. For the first 15 km this road runs parallel to the Wangdu road, before turning SE. **Kunga Rabten**, the winter palace of Bhutan's second king lies beside this road, 20 km S of Tongsar. Farming villages are to be seen by the roadside but further S the gorge narrows. The road plunges down to 1,400m, passing through a wild uninhabited region.

Shemgang district

གཞལ་སྒང་

(*Area* 2,540 sq km) The administrative capital is located at Shemgang, some 107 km S of Tongsar on a wind-exposed ridge above the Mangde-chu gorge. The district is characterized by its forested mountain slopes, where the Mangde-chu and Bumtang-chu tributaries of the Drangme-chu (Manas) cut deep gorges, interspersed occasionally with random rice growing areas. Most of Shemgang district may be considered as a botanical paradise, in that it contains carniverous plants, rare species of orchid, and so forth. Descending from 1,900m in the N to 200m in the S, the land is covered by tropical forests, yielding most of Bhutan's bamboo and rattan produce, as well as bananas, mangoes, edible roots, and so forth.

The first temple to be constructed on the site of the recently reconstructed **Shemgang Dzong** dates from a foundation established by the Tibetan lama Drogon Shangkyeme in 1163. The whole of Shemgang and Mongar districts formerly belonged to the ancient region of **Khyeng**, where the inhabitants speak Khyeng-ka, a distinctive dialect of Bumtang-ka. At **Nabji** village near Shemgang an ancient pillar commemorating an 8th century treaty between King Sendhaka and King Nawoche attests to the antiquity of this region. A number of the principalities or enclaves of Khyeng, which are nowadays encorporated within Shemgang district, such as **Buli** and **Nyakhar**, successfully maintained their autonomy until their absorption into the Bhutanese state during the 17th century. These sites, however, are fairly inaccessible in that they are not connected by motorable routes. After passing through Shemgang Dzong, the main road leaves the Mangde-chu valley to enter Gelekphuk district.

Gelekphuk district

དགེ་ལེགས་ཕུག

(*Area* 2,640 sq km) The administrative capital is located at Burgang on the Indian border, 237 km from Tongsar. This district is one of the four which, between them, extend along the entire length of the southern border, and it encorporates within it important border towns, such as **Kalilkhola**, giving road access to Wangdu via the Puna Tsang-chu (Sankosh) valley; **Burgang**, giving road access to Tongsar, and **Sarbhang** (Sapu). The landscape is similar to that of Shemgang district, but the population is largely Lhotsampa.

Bumtang district

བུམ་ཐང་

(*Area* 2,990 sq km) The administrative capital of Bumtang is located at Jakar. Bumtang is the name given to a complex of four sacred valleys which are often regarded as the religious or cultural heart of Bhutan. The district follows the course of the Bumtang-chu, from its sources around Lhedam near the Lhodrak Tibetan border and downstream towards its confluence with the Mangde-chu in Shemgang district. In its mid-reaches there are four rivers which converge to form the 'vase-shaped' bulge of Bumtang, namely: the Chukhar-chu (the main river) which forms the **Chokhor** valley; the Chume-chu which forms the **Chu-me** valley; the Tang-chu forming the **Tang** valley; and the Ura-chu forming the **Ura** valley. All these valleys are wide and gently sloping, offering a sense of spaciousness, almost unequalled elsewhere in the country. Among them, Chokhor and Chu-me are agricultural, while Tang and Ura are largely pastoral valleys. Though accessible by road, most of the interesting temples and beautiful monasteries are only accessible to trekkers. It is also a fantastic area for day-walks. With beautifully painted

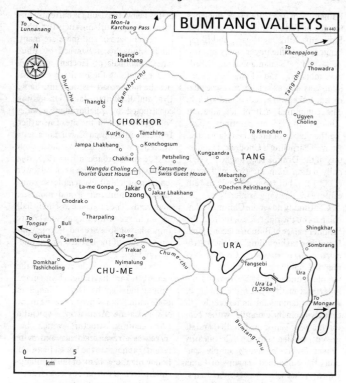

BUMTANG VALLEYS IH 440

To Lunnanang
To Mon-la Karchung Pass
To Khenpajong
Thowadra
N
Ngang Lhakhang
Thangbi
Chamkhar-chu
Dhur-chu
Ugyen Choling
CHOKHOR
Kurje
Tamzhing
Ta Rimochen
Jampa Lhakhang
Konchogsum
Chakhar
Petsheling
Kungzandra
TANG
Wangdu Choling Tourist Guest House
Karsumpey Swiss Guest House
Mebartsho
La-me Gonpa
Jakar Dzong
Jakar Lhakhang
Dechen Pelrithang
Tang-chu
Chodrak
Tharpaling
To Tongsar
Buli
Zug-ne
Chu-me-chu
URA
Shingkhar
Gyetsa
Samtenling
Trakar
Sombrang
Domkhar Tashicholing
Nyimalung
CHU-ME
Tangsebi
Ura
Ura La (3,250m)
To Mongar
Bumtang-chu

0   5
km

wooden house façades, it looks best in the autumn when the buckwheat paints the fields deep orange.

Bumtang is the stronghold of the Nyingmapa school in Bhutan, cheifly on account of the activities of three important Nyingmapa lamas of the 14th and 15th century: Longchen Rabjampa, Dorje Lingpa, and Pema Lingpa – the last of whom was actually born in Bumtang. The construction of the motor road and the implementation of development projects through Swiss and Indian government aid have brought a new prosperity to this once isolated rural area. The following account describes the sights of Bumtang, following the course of the motor road in succession through the valleys of Chu-me, Chokhor, Tang and Ura.

Chu-me Valley

After crossing the Yutong La pass on the drive eastwards from Tongsar (see above), you enter the broad 18 km long Chu-me valley (2,700m) at **Gyetsa**. The land is fertile, yielding crops of wheat, barley, potatoes, and the local staple buckwheat. To the left of the road you will see **Buli Lhakhang**, a shrine established by descendents of Dorje Lingpa in 15th century, and **Samtenling**, one of the monasteries founded by Longchen Rabjampa during his 10 years exile in Bumtang. Higher up the hillside is **Tharpaling**, also founded by Longchen

Rabjampa in 1352. Its lower floor has images of Padmasambhava, Longchen Rabjampa, Trhisong Detsen, and Jikme Lingpa; while the upper storey has images of Samantabhadra, Padmasambhava, and Longchen Rabjampa; as well as splendid frescoes depicting Sukhavati paradise, and so forth. The communal hall of an adjacent school (built 1985) has paintings depicting the lineage of Longchen Rabjampa. Above Tharpaling is **Chodrak**, a monastery of the Drukpa Kagyu school, originally dating from the time of Lorepa (1187-1250) but renovated only in 18th century by Ngawang Trinle.

Continuing down the Chu-me valley, you pass on the right side of the road the summer palace of Bhutan's second king, **Domkhar Tashicholing**, and the hydroelectric power station at **Chorten Nyingpo Lhakhang**, a Drukpa Kagyu temple founded in 1587. Towards the lower end of the valley, the village of **Zug-ne** is famous for its reputedly 7th century geomantic temple (with a central image of Vairocana Buddha) and its woven woollen fabrics. The nearby **Trakar** ('white monkey') temple contains the embalmed remains of Lama Dawa Gyeltsen, the son of Pema Lingpa, whose incarnation lineage has played an important role in the Buddhist tradition of Bumtang and the Lhodrak region of Tibet to the N. At **Nyimalung Monastery** (b 1900) the monastic discipline and liturgies of the Nyingma tradition are particularly renowned. Reaching the lower extremity of Chu-me valley, the road crosses Kiki La pass (2,900m) to enter Chokhor valley.

Chokhor Valley

From Kiki La pass, the entire breadth of Chokhor valley is visible on a clear day. The short 9 km descent brings you to **Jakar Dzong** ('White Bird Fortress'), the administrative capital of the whole Bumtang district, altitude 2,800m. The village of Jakar which occupies the plains below the dzong is currently undergoing rapid urbanisation (by Bhutanese standards), and there are many small shops, mostly owned by Bhutanese nationals of Tibetan origin. A bridge spanning the Bumtang-chu carries the motor road eastward into Tang, Ura, and E Bhutan. Jakar Dzong was constructed by Zhabdrung Ngawang Namgyel in 1646 on the site of an earlier 16th century Drukpa Kagyu monastery. Subsequent rebuilding was undertaken in 1683 and more recently in 1905. It is an elegant building, with a central tower (containing a Maitreya temple) separating the administrative and monastic courtyards. The monastic assembly hall has an image of the meditational deity Vajrakila, while a second temple contains images of the Drukpa Kagyu lineage holders.

On the left side of the road below the dzong is **Jakar Lhakhang**, a Nyingmapa temple founded by Dorje Lingpa in 1445, while 4 km above the dzong to the NW is **La-me Monastery**, a splendid 19th century structure which has served as a royal residence and more recently as home to the Forest Institute. Following the W bank of the Bumtang-chu upstream, you pass by a Swiss dairy farm (where you can buy authentic swiss cheese, honey, and alcoholic fruit drinks), and a mechanical workshop. The **Wangdu Choling Palace** (built 1856) is renowned as the birthplace of the first king's father, and the gardens now contain a splendid tourist guesthouse in traditional design. Upstream from the palace and beyond the archery range is the Bumtang hospital, which was built with Swiss aid in 1988-89, and the **Chakhar** ('iron castle') residence of the 8th century king Sendhaka (see above).

The most ancient of all the temples in Bumtang is probably the 7th century **Jampa Lhakhang**, which like Kyerchu in the Paro valley, was a geomantic temple constructed by the Tibetan king Songtsen Gampo, this time on the 'left

Kuje Temple in Bumtang, Bhutan

knee of the ogress'. It is said that when Padmasambhava taught Buddhism to King Sendhaka during the 8th century, he did so from the temple roof. The original temple contains a large image of Maitreya, flanked by the eight standing bodhisattvas, four on each side. Later 19th century shrines at Jampa Lhakhang include the **Kalacakra Temple**, the **Guru Lhakhang** (with images of Padmasambhava, Avalokiteshvara, and Amitayus), the **Sangye Lhakhang** (with images depicting the Seven Generations of Past Buddhas), and the **Chorten Lhakhang** (dedicated to the relics of a Karma Kagyu lama who passed away in 1940).

North of Jampa Lhakhang is the **Kurje Lhakhang** (named after the site where Padmasambhava is said to have left the imprint of his body in rock). The site has three temples forming a grand complex reminiscent of Samye in Tibet,

and is occupied in summertime by the monks of Tongsar Dzong, who hold their annual Tsechu ceremony here. The oldest temple dating from 1652 contains images (upstairs) of the Buddhas of the Three Times, and (downstairs) the cave containing the body imprint and images depicting the Eight Manifestations of Padmasambhava. An upstairs carving depicts the subjugation of the demon Shelging Karpo by Padmasambhava in the form of a garuda bird, which is said to have occured at this site.

The second temple contains an enomrmous 10m image of Padmasambhava flanked by his eight manifestations, and the third was newly consecrated in 1990. In front of the complex are the **three funeral chortens** of the three past kings of Bhutan.

Thangbi Lhakhang, 1½ hrs walk above Kurje was founded by Zhamar IV of the Karma Kagyu school in 1470. It

Tamzhing Temple in Bumtang, Bhutan

contains images of the Buddhas of the Three Times (downstairs) and of Jowo Rinpoche (upstairs), as well as a large shrine room dedicated to the protector deities.

Following the E bank of the Bumtang-chu upstream from Jakar Dzong, you drive past **Konchoksum Lhakhang**, where there is a celebrated bell with an 8th century inscription, linking it to the royal family of Tibet. The main image is Vairocana Buddha, flanked by Padmasambhava, and Avalokiteshvara, as well as later Nyingmapa masters such as Longchen Rabjampa and Pema Lingpa.

Further N is **Tamzhing Lhakhang**, which was founded in 1501 by Pema Lingpa and maintains the liturgical traditions and spiritual practices of Pema Lingpa at the present day. Long regarded as a branch monastery of **Lhalung**, the residence of the Peling Sungtrul incarnations in Lhodrak, this temple has been revitalized by an influx of Tibetan refugee monks from Lhalung in 1959. It contains (downstairs) images of Padmasambhava and his eight manifestations, and (upstairs) Amitayus. The paintings of Tamzhing are particularly renowned: especially those of the ground floor vestibule, which are among the oldest surviving paintings in Bhutan.

Tang Valley

After crossing the bridge at Jakar, the main road swerves southwards, following the E bank of the Bumtang-chu downstream for 5 km, and then turns NE as far as the sheep-breeding farm of **Dechen Pelrithang**, altitude 2,800m. At this point there is an unpaved turn-off on the left, which leads into the narrow gorge of the Tang valley. The land here is more suited to sheep farming and has been left fairly undeveloped. The most famous site in Tang is **Mebartsho** gorge, where Pema Lingpa is said not only to have discovered *terma* from its depths, but to have done so in public, holding an oil lamp in his hand which remained burning as he emerged from the waters with his treasure! Hence the name of the site Mabartsho ('Blazing Fire Lake'). Pilgrims can still be seen here placing small lighted lamps on the river.

In a recessed cliff, some 1½ hrs walk uphill from Mebartsho, you can visit **Kungzandra Monastery**, founded in

1488 by Pema Lingpa on a site formerly consecrated by Padmasambhava and his student Namkei Nyingpo in person. There are three temples: the **Wangkhang** dedicated to Avalokiteshvara; the **Ozerphuk** dedicated to Pema Lingpa's son Dawa Gyeltsen, who meditated in the grotto here; and the **Khandroma Lhakhang**, containing a gilded copper image of Pema Lingpa.

Driving upstream, you reach the **Rimochen** Temple, founded by Dorje Lingpa and named after the markings left on a large rock by Padmasambhava. The motorable road has its terminus at **Ugyen Choling**, a 19th century palace built on the site of an earlier hermitage, once sanctified by the presence of both Longchen Rabjampa and Dorje Lingpa. A 4 hrs walk upstream from this point brings you to **Thowadra Monastery** (3,400m), occupied since the late 18th century by the followers of Jikme Lingpa and Jikme Kundrol, who maintain the *Longchen Nyingthig* tradition. The site marks the entrance to **Khenpajong**, a hidden land consecrated by Padmasambhava to the E of Lhedam in N Bumtang and in Lhuntse district.

Ura Valley

Ura is the highest of Bumtang's four valleys, and the road climbs from Tang in a series of switchback bends through open countryside. The approach to Ura La pass (3,600m) offers a splendid view of Bhutan's highest peak, Mt Gangkar Punsum. **Ura** village (3,100m) consists of closely built shingled houses, where the community subsists on the basis of pastoral farming and the potato crop. The **Shingkar** monastery, founded by Longchen Rabjampa circa 1350, is 1 hr walking distance form **Sombrang** village.

Trekking in Bumtang district

The four valleys of Bumtang give the visitor an opportunity to explore the remote countryside of Central Bhutan where life has remained virtually unchanged for centuries. You can watch people producing baskets, weaving on traditional looms or making hand-made paper from daphne bark. One easy 5-6 days trek which remains below 3,500m, starts near **Kurje Lhakhang**, and follows the Chamkhar-chu upstream to the old temple of **Ngang Lhakhang**, before crossing a pass into the Tang valley at **Ugyen Choling**. This trek offers sufficient time for the visitor to see the most important sites of the Chokhor valley, which have already been described: Jampa Lhakhang, Kurje Lhakhang, and Tamzhing Lhakhang foremost among them. Note that most of the temples require a permit to be visited. Best season: April-May, late Sept to mid-Nov.

● **Accommodation** The lovely BTCL *Wangdu Choling Lodge*, nr an old 19th century palace is full of charm with its painted bungalows and its large elaborately decorated dining room, heated rooms with attached bath, simple meals (Continental and Bhutanese), handicrafts shop. *Swiss Guest House*, above the Swiss Farm at Karsunphe, recently reconstructed, is simple but has a cosy atmosphere. *Tamzhing Guest-house*, nr Tamzhing monastery, has 8 rm, and a delightfully peaceful atmosphere. **NB** Electricity supply is still erratic in Bumtang.

EAST BHUTAN

The best time for a trip E is April/May and Oct/Nov. The E is wonderful in winter as it is warmer than W Bhutan but there can be snow on the road from Bumtang to Mongar. The region is more densely populated (with the exception of the extreme NE), broadly corresponding to the valleys of the Kuru-chu and Tawang-chu tributaries of the Drangme-chu (Manas).

Mongar district

མོན་འགར

(*Area* 1,830 sq km) The administrative capital of the district is located at Mongar in the valley of the Kuru-chu. In the eastern part of the district, where the people speak Tsangla dialect, the Drangme-chu flows through Damotse (Dametsi). The two rivers converge in the extreme S of the district, where the Khyeng-ka dialect in prevalent.

After leaving Ura valley in Bumtang, the road ascends through conifer forest to the **Tumsing La** pass at 3,800m. From there in 3 hrs you make a dramatic descent to **Namning** (only 700m) and a semi-tropical area; it is a spectacular drive, as the road in places is dug out of the precipitous cliffs. Village houses have roofs made of bamboo matting, and the staple crop is maize. After crossing the Kuru-chu at 650m, the road climbs again for 13 km to reach the town of Mongar (1,700m), 141 km from Ura. On the ascent there is a turn-off on the left for Lhuntse in NE Bhutan.

Mongar (1,600m) is a small, sleepy town built across the open hillside, with a lovely dzong, constructed in 19th century and rebuilt in 1953. As with other dzong, it combines both administrative and monastic functions, housing within it two temples. Prior to its construction, the main dzong of the district was situated to the W of the Kuru-chu river at the low-lying **Shongar Dzong** (now in ruins). The town has a number of shops and an excellent hospital.

● **Accommodation** Mongar has *Shongar Lodge* nr the dzong, this simple BTCL guest house is basic, with electricity and water supply still erratic.

From there you can take a 3-day side trip to **Lhuntse Dzong** (described below), or drive straight to **Tashigang**. The latter road reaches the eastern border of Mongar and Tashigang districts over a 70 km drive. At first it ascends through forested terrain to Kori La pass (2,450m), and therafter descending through **Yadi** village, it cuts a series of switchbacks in the hillside to reach the Tawang-chu (Manas), also known as the Gamri-chu. Following that river upstream, you then

drive into **Damotse Urgyen Choling**, the largest monastery of E Bhutan, which was founded in the late 16th century by a female descendent of Pema Lingpa known as Chodron Zangmo. The monastery has undergone various phases of restoration, and its central tower contains temples dedicated to Padmasambhava and the protector deities of the Everest Range, Tsering Che-nga. At Damotse there are both monastic and mantrin commmunities of Buddhist practitioners.

The southern part of Mongar district, where the Kuru-chu and Drangme-chu rivers have their confluence, is isolated and as yet unconnected by motorable roads. It is a region where the Khyeng-ka dialect predominates.

Lhunste district

(*Area* 2,910 sq km) The administrative capital is at Lhuntse, near the confluence of the Kuru-chu with its Khoma-chu tributary. This densely populated district, formerly called Kurto ('upper Kuru-chu valley') is inhabited by people speaking a dialect of Bumtang-ka. Its mountain villages are known for their fine weaving and the village women spend most of their days at the loom. The steep terrain is really suitable for exploring on foot. The NE of the district is occupied by the sacred hidden land of **Khenpajong**, and the northern border at **Ngortong Zampa** has easy access to the Lhodrak region of Tibet, in that the Kuru-chu which it spans flows directly through that part of southern Tibet into Bhutan. The meagre cross-border traffic is monitored from **Senge Dzong** in the mid-reaches of the Kuru chu. Further NE, Phode La pass (4,965m) separates Bhutan from the **Kharchu** hillside of Lhodrak in Tibet. Significantly, the royal family of Bhutan claims descent from **Dungkar** village in the N of Lhuntse district.

The motor road from the turn-off at Lingmitang below Mongar heads northwards into Lhuntse district, following the forested Kuru-chu gorge upstream, and on to **Lhuntse Dzong**, some 77 km distant. The massive Lhuntse Dzong (altitude 1,700m) was constructed in 1654 on a site of a 16th century temple associated with the descendents of Pema Lingpa. The protector shrine is dedicated to Mahakala, and the main temples to Padmasambhava, Avalokiteshvara, and Aksobhya Buddha. The assembly hall which houses 100 monks contains images of the Buddhas of the Three Times.

Tashigang district

(*Area* 4,260 sq km; including Tashi Yangtse) The administrative capitals of this most densely populated district of Bhutan is located at Tashigang. The valleys which sustain such a large population are those of the Tawang-chu (Manas), also known in Bhutan as the Gamri-chu and the Drangme-chu further downstream, which enters E Bhutan from Tsona county of Tibet. The eastern frontier passes of Nyingzang La and Ngonkha La lead directly to Tawang (disputed territory, now in Arunachal Pradesh), via the Bhutanese settlements of Radi and Sakteng.

From Mongar it is a quick 3 hrs journey to **Tashigang** (altitude 1,150m), the biggest and busiest town in E Bhutan and, after Thimphu, the second largest mountain town of the country. The town looks attractive with its painted houses amid flowering bougainvilleas, its tiny shops, and the 'square' and cafés which hum with activity at the end of the day. Tropical fruits and crops thrive; apple is pressed into juice to produce cider and brandy. The local *endi* silk is spun from silkworms bred on castor oil plants. The impregnable **Tashigang Dzong** which stands on a spur overlooking the Tawang-chu river 400m below, was built

in 1659, and later enlarged and rennovated on two occasions. The temples contained within it include the **Lama Lhakhang** (dedicated to the Eight Vidyadhara masters of Tantric Buddhism in ancient India), the **Guru Lhakhang** (dedicated to Padmasambhava's Eight Manifestations), the **Tsozhing Lhakhang** (dedicated to the Kagyu and Nyingma linages), and the **Gonkhang** (dedicated to the protector Mahakala). With its single courtyard sharing both administrative and monastic functions, this dzong is unique in Bhutan.

● **Accommodation** Tashigang has *Kellling Lodge*. Simple accommodation and meals available at *Ugyen Newly* and social watering hole for expatriate aid workers at the *Punsum*.

The road S from Tashigang to Samdrup Jongkhar district, newly built in 1963-65, covers 180 km in about 6 hrs, following ridges rather than valleys most of the way. En route you pass **Kanglung**, Bhutan's only university campus which was established in 1978; and **Khaling** where there is a school for the blind and a weaving centre. After **Wamrong** and **Trimshing** villages, you pass the **Riserbu** hospital, and the turn-off for Pema Gatsel district before reaching the district frontier at **Deothang** (870m), the last stop before the plains and one-time scene of a British defeat during the Anglo-Bhutanese war of 1865.

Tashi Yangtse district

This newly created district occupies the valley of the Kulong-chu, a major tributary of the Tawang-chu (Manas), which flows through the extreme NE of the country to its confluence at Tashigang. In the extreme NE of the district the Me La pass leads into the Tsona county of Tibet.

From Tashigang, you can take a fascinating day-trip to **Chorten Kora** and **Tashi Yangtse**, driving some 50 km up the Kulong-chu valley. The drive takes about 2 hrs. En route you will pass through **Gom Kora**, a meditation haunt of Padmasambhava, and then enter the Kulong valley at Doksum. The **Tashi Yangtse Dzong** (constructed 1656) is set in the lush gorge of the Kulong-chu at 1,850m. The dzong formerly commanded the trade route between Tashigang and Bumtang via Lhuntse before the advent of the motor road, and it is approached across the river by way of an old drawbridge covered with bamboo mats. Further N the gorge opens out to reveal the huge white stupa of **Chorten Kora**, fashioned in Nepalese style in 1782 to fulfil one of Padmasambhava's prophecies. In Mar, it is the scene of an important religious festival for the inhabitants of E Bhutan.

Pema Gatsel district

དཔལ་དགའ་ཚལ

(*Area* 380 sq km) The administrative capital of this small district is located at Pema Gatsel. Much of the land is occupied by the **Dungsam Wildlife Reserve** (180 sq km), which is named after an ancient kingdom once established in this

region. The northern border of the district is separated from Mongar district by the Drangme-chu (Manas). The main town is approached via a turn-off S of Wamrong on the Tashigang-Samdrup Jongkar road. You will notice that many of the houses in this region are raised on stilts, reminiscent of many parts of Southeast Asia, and roofed with bamboo matting.

Samdrup Jongkhar district

(*Area* 2,340 sq km) The administrative capital is located at Samdrup Jongkhar, 18 km S of Deothang, and 7 hrs drive from Tashigang. With a large Lhotsampa population, **Samdrup Jongkhar** is the tropical gateway to Assam, and has grown into an important market town serving the mountain districts of E Bhutan. Two rivers, which rise further N, flow into Assam through this district: the Bada-chu through the border town of **Bangtar** and the Dhanasiri through the border town of **Daifam**. From Samdrup Jongkhar, one can cross the border and go to Guwahati airport in Assam (special permission needed).

INFORMATION FOR VISITORS

Before travelling

Entry requirements

● Visas

Valid passports and entry visa are essential. There is a fixed government quota on the number of tourists most of which is taken up by tour companies, so virtually the only way to see Bhutan is as a member of a commercially organized tour group. Tour prices, all inclusive, range from US$150-250/day according to the season.

Visas cannot be obtained at Bhutanese embassies. Foreigners can only go through a travel agent abroad or one in Bhutan who will obtain a visa for you and make all your bookings. This can take about 3 weeks (Fax is very reliable within Bhutan). You pay for the visa (US$20, validity 15 days) on arrival in Bhutan. The regulations are simpler for Indian nationals who do not need to go through a travel agent. **NB** Special permission is needed to visit monasteries and dzongs, with the exception of the following: Ta Dzong, Drugyel Dzong and Takstang viewpoint in Paro; Tashi Chodzong, Memorial Chorten, Changlimithang, and Jigmeling temples in Thimphu; Kamji, Chasilakha, and Chime temples in Phuntsoling; Damphu and Lamidara temples in Chirang; Punakha Dzong in Punakha; Wangdu Choling Dzong, Mebartsho gorge, and Ura temple in Bumtang; Mongar Dzong in Mongar; Chorten Kora, Tashi Yangtse Dzong, and Kanglung Zangdokpelri temple in Tashigang; and the Zangdokpelri temple in Samdrup Jongkhar. **Buddhists** may be given special permits to some restricted dzongs and gonpas, permission being granted by the Secretary of the Special Commission for Cultural Affairs.

● Tourist authority

The Tourism Authority of Bhutan (TAB) is the only government body; all other outlets are private travel agents. There is no tourism office abroad. You can write for information to TAB, PO Box 126, Thimphu, T 975 223251, F 223695. Information can also be obtained from Bhutan Embassies/Missions in Dhaka, Kuwait, Delhi, Geneva and New York.

● Embassies abroad

Royal Bhutan Embassy: **India**: Chandra Gupta Marg, Chanakyapuri, T 604076, 609217, F 6876710, New Delhi 11021; 48 Tivoli Court, 1A Ballygunge Circular Rd, Calcutta. **Bangladesh**: 58, Road No 3A, Dhanmondi RA, Dhaka, T 545018. **USA**: 120 E 56th St, New York, NY 10022, T (212) 826 1919, 826 1990, F (212) 826 2998; **Switzerland**:17-19 Chemin Du Champ D'Anier, Ch-12209 Geneva, T (022) 798 7971-73, F (022) 788 2593.

● Tour companies and travel agents

Bhutan: In Thimphu: *Bhutan Himalaya Trekking*, PO Box 236, (code 975) T 223293, F 222897; *BTCL* (Bhutan Tourism Corp Ltd), PO Box 159, T 222647, F 222479; *Chhundu Travels*, PO Box 149, T 222592, F 222645; *Ethometho Tours*, PO Box 360, T 223693, F 222884; *Lhomen Tours and Trekking*, T/F 23243; *Mandala Tours*, PO Box 397, T 223676, F 223675; *Reekor Tours*, PO Box 304, T 222733, F 223541; *Takin Tours*, PO Box 454, T 223129, F 223130; *Yangphel Tours*, PO Box 326, T 223293, F 222897; *YuDruk*, PO Box 140, T 223461, F 222116.

Nepal: *President Travels & Tours*, Durbar Marg, Kathmandu, T (977-1) 226744; *Shambhala Travels and Tours*, Durbar Marg,

Kathmandu, T (977-1)225166, F (977-1) 227229.

India: *Malbros Travels*, 415 Antriksh Bhawan, 22 Kastruba Gandhi Marg, New Delhi, T (91-11) 3722031, F (91-11) 3723292; *Stic Travel Pvt Ltd*, 6 Maker Arcade (GF), Bombay 400005, T (91-22) 2181431; *Stic Travel Pvt Ltd*, 142 Nungambakkam Sigh Raod, Madras 600034, T (91-44) 475332.

Bangladesh: *Vantage Tours & Travels Ltd*, L-270 Office Arcade, *Sonargaon Hotel*, Dhaka, T (880-2) 326920.

Thailand: *Oriole Travel & Tour Co Ltd*, 10/12-13 SS Building, Convent Rd, Bangkok 10500, T (66-2) 235-0411/2, F (66-2) 236-7186.

UK: *Himalayan Kingdoms*, 20 The Mall, Clifton, Bristol, BS8 4DR, T 0117 9237163, F 0117 974 4993, leading specialist in Bhutan treks, including private itineraries for individuals and groups; *Trans Himalaya*, 30 Hanover Rd, London NW10 3DS, T 0181-459-7944, F 0181-459-8017; *Worldwide Safaris*, Chelsea Reach, 2nd Flr, 79-89 Lots Rd, London SW10 0RN, T 0171 3510298; *Karakorum Experience*, 32 Lake Rd, Keswick, Cumbria, CA12 5DQ, T 017687 73966.

USA: *Bhutan Travel*, 120E, 56th St, Suite 1430, New York, NY 10022, T 212 838 6382; *Inner Asia*, 2627 Lombard St, San Francisco, Ca 94123, T 4159220448, F 4153465535; *Mountain Travel*, 6420 Fairmount Ave, El Cerrito, CA 94530, T 415 527 8100.

When to go

Best time for a visit Mar-May and Sept-Nov, either side of the rainy season.

Health

Protection is *recommended* against cholera, typhoid, tetanus, polio, hepatitis, malaria and rabies, and *optional* for meningitis and altitude sickness. Avoid unboiled water and ice-cubes, as well as uncooked vegetables and unpeeled fruit since dysentery is commonplace. At high altitude, drink more liquid to avoid dehydration. See Health in Himalayan Region, Introduction, page 37.

WARNING Thimphu Valley has been experiencing increased incidence of rabies because of the growing number of stray dogs.

Money

● **Currency**
The national currency is the Ngultrum (Nu). 100 Chetrum = 1 Nu. Exchange rate is approximately US$1 = Nu 30. Indian Rupees circulate at par. American Express credit card accepted in a few shops. No other credit card is accepted so far.

● **Exchange**
Bank of Bhutan in Thimphu and Phuntsoling will change TCs and hard currency. The **Bank of Bhutan** has 26 branches across the country. Head Office is at Phuntsoling. Money-changers prefer TCs to currency notes. Carry enough Nu when trekking or touring.

Getting there

Air

The airport is at Paro. **Transport to Thimphu:** 1½ hrs drive by Druk Air coach. Druk Air, the national carrier (2 BAe 146), has connections with Delhi (3 hrs), US$580, via Kathmandu (45 mins) US$330 on Mon and Thur. From Bangkok (4 hrs), US$670, via Calcutta (1½ hrs), US$330 Wed, return Sun, and via Dhaka (1 hr), US$330, Sun, return Wed. **NB** Bad weather can delay flights during monsoons. Dep from Paro 0730; To Paro from Delhi 1125; Kathmandu 1410; Dhaka 1610, Bangkok 1355. **Druk Air** have offices at 48 Tivoli Court, Ballygunge Circular Rd, Calcutta. There are also offices in Delhi, Dhaka, Bangkok and Kathmandu but **note** bookings must be made through your travel agent. Always recheck your flight time. A visa fee of US$20 is payable upon entry at Paro airport; and an airport tax of Nu 300 is payable on departure.

Road

The road from Bagdogra (the nearest Indian airport) enters Bhutan at Phuntsoling, the border town. It is a 3-4 hrs drive from Bagdogra airport which can be reached by plane from Calcutta and Delhi. From Darjiling or Gangtok, it can take 7 hrs to Phuntsoling. It takes about 6 hrs to negotiate the winding 179 km road from Phuntsoling through to Thimphu (or Paro).

Customs

8 mm cameras are allowed. No 16 mm cameras. Permits are needed for video cameras and for filming (for a fee). Contact Tourism Authority of Bhutan (TAB), F 223251. You may not take antiquities, religious artefacts, plants or animal products out of the country – all old items and new tangkas must have a certificate clearing them from the Dept of Antiquities, and all sales receipts should be kept for inspection.

On arrival

● **Clothing**
Cottons and light woollens in summer (June-Sept). Heavy woollens and jackets the rest of the year. Take an umbrella for the monsoons and comfortable shoes. Shorts, revealing clothes or T-shirts are not suitable. For trekking gear, see below, page 745.

● **Hints on social behaviour**
Useful words include – *Kadrinche* (thank you), *Kusuzangpo* (greetings) and *Lasso* (when leavetaking). The interiors of some monasteries were closed because the tourists were disturbing the monks and stealing mementos. When visiting a dzong, **do not** smoke, wear a hat, interrupt prayers or enter the dance area during the *Tsechu* ceremony. Ask before photographing. See also the section on trekking, below, page 695.

● **Official time**
Bhutanese time is 30 mins ahead of Indian National Time or GMT +6 hrs.

● **Photography**
There is some spectacular scenery, but if you go during the wet season make sure to protect film against humidity. Carry plenty of films and batteries. No photography allowed inside temples and dzongs.

● **Safety**
The crime rate in this unspoilt country is very low. However, it is safest to lock precious belongings and money inside a suitcase or a bag before leaving the room.

● **Shopping**
Traditional handicrafts, jewellery, baskets, masks, textiles. Paintings and woodcarving make good buys. See Thimphu Shopping above. Get a receipt and please do not attempt to bargain.

● **Tipping**
Tipping is forbidden by law, but an acknowledgement of good services is always appreciated.

● **Voltage**
220-240 volts, 50 cycles AC. The current is variable and supply sometimes erratic. Flashlights are useful.

● **Weights and measures**
Metric – the same as in India.

Where to stay

Bhutan has only been accepting foreign visitors for the last 15 years and limits the numbers to 3,000-4,000 so there is neither a well developed hotel industry nor category **A-C** hotels. In Phuntsoling, Thimphu and Paro there are some comfortable hotels with Bhutanese decor and modern facilities. BTCL accommodation in Bumtang, Tongsar, Mongar and Tashigang is simpler but has modern plumbing and helpful staff (water and electricity supply can be erratic). Elsewhere Guesthouses are very basic.

Food and drink

● **Food**

Rice is the staple, eaten with spicy and hot vegetables and meat curries; buckwheat pancakes or noodles, and barley or wheat flour are eaten in some high valleys. Hot chillies and melted cheese (*omadasé*) is the national dish. The Tibetan dishes, dumplings (*momo*), and noodle soup (*thukpa*) are great favourites. Pork and beef are the most common meat; chicken is also becoming popular. Yak meat is the favourite but available only in the winter. Delicious fruits are available in season.

● **Drink**

Sweet milk tea, beer and fruit juices are available but no real coffee, only Nescafé. Butter tea is drunk at home for special occasions and local alcoholic drinks (*chang*, *arak* and *tomba*) are brewed or distilled at home. Bottled mineral water can be bought in the towns. Spirits (whisky, gin, fruit brandies and rum) are produced in Bhutan.

Getting around

Road

The road network is not extensive since construction only began in the 1960s. The main lateral road links Thimphu with Tashigang (1965-85); and there are now four main roads linking the mountain areas with the plains: Thimphu-Phuntsoling (1982); Wangdu Phodrang-Khalikhola; Tongsar-Burgang; and Tashigang-Samdrup Jongkhar (1963-65). The principal means of road transport is by public bus. 4WD drive and Japanese cars are available for hire. Cars are always hired with driver.

Trekking

The N and the more remote central and southerly parts of Bhutan are even now only accessible by trekking, which offers not only spectacular scenery but also a chance to see the village people maintaining their ancient skills and crafts. Bhutan is really off-the-beaten-track, has wonderful landscapes, amazing flora and kind, affectionate people who are very proud of their life-style.

Planning a trek

Trekking conditions are very different from Nepal since it is much wetter: the season is much shorter and for some high-altitude treks choosing a period between snow and rain can be difficult. The best months are Mar-April and Oct-Nov. Treks start at 2,400m generally rising to 4,000m quite rapidly. With Bhutan's small, scattered population you might trek for hours, and sometimes days, without seeing a single house, and only passing the odd person with pack animals along the track. The trails are not mapped or well-defined so it is easy to lose one's way; high-altitude rescue is non-existent. It is therefore essential to trek with a reliable local guide.

The fast mountain streams are crossed by ingenious log or liana and split bamboo bridges, while wider rivers may have more substantial wooden ones – often protected by prayer flags. The famous 15th century iron chain bridges were built by Tangtong Gyelpo. The chains were often made in Bhutan (using a small quantity of arsenic to reduce the melting point of iron) and transported great distances. Over 50 bridges were erected across the Himalaya; some had nine lengths of chain suspended to form the frame of a bridge which would then be tied with wire and have matting placed underfoot.

For **accommodation** there are no 'tea houses' or cosy lodges with hot-water to welcome you after a hard day's trek. In the countryside the Bhutanese are fully occupied tending animals and with work in the fields and do not have time, or the need, to take in guests, be they Bhutanese or foreigners – The traces of fire camps in rock shelters provide ample proof of this. Because of the inaccessability of most of the countryside, people are reluctant to sell any food since a shop could be 3 days walk away. In remote areas, barter is a standard mode of exchange; salt or edible oil are more likely to see eggs materialize than a bank-note! It is therefore essential to have tents and provisions.

The economy is not dependent on tourism and so the Bhutanese do not hire themselves as porters; yaks and mules carry all belongings on treks. Since the trekking months coincide with the busy period in the fields, the owners of pack animals have to be contacted well in advance, and be flattered and cajoled before they agree. Moreover, in the course of a single trek, the pack animals will also be changed at the district frontiers.

Trekking in Bhutan is logistically complicated because it is still a wild country. However, tour operators here know the problems well; they will help you with the choice of trek and the season, taking into account your own preferences and physical fitness. Small groups are provided with a guide, helpers, a wonderful cook, tents, mattresses, pack-animals and all the food needed, as there is nothing available on the way; you are advised to bring your own sleeping bags, walking boots and clothing (Gortex recommended), umbrella, flashlight (head-Lamp recommended), medications, sun hat, sun lotion and sun glasses, water flask, and film, batteries etc. In the monsoons some paths can be very muddy and below 2,000m, leeches are problematic.

Ecology and the environment have recently become the main concern of tour operators who do not want trekkers (and local staff) to litter the still pristine countryside. Many treks will take place in the national parks, such as the Jigme Dorje Wangchuk Sanctuary (7,813 sq km) which occupies the entire northern belt of the country. Conservation of flora and fauna is the responsibility of the Royal Society for the Protection of Nature. Please follow the Himalayan Code of Practice, cited above, page 31.

Mountaineering

There are 21 peaks above 7,000m, of which a few are now open to mountaineering groups. Peaks below this elevation can be climbed by trekkers without seeking special permission. For details of climbing fees and orgainisation, refer to BTCL's Bhutan Mountaineering Regulations.

Communications

● **Postal services**

A postal service was introduced in 1962 which covers most of the country. Allow at least 14 days for delivery to Australia and Europe and longer for the Americas. Attractive and highly prized national stamps are sold at the GPO, Thimphu and Philatelic Bureau, Phuntsoling. Courrier services, such as DHL, now operate out of Thimphu.

● **Telephone services**

Most of the country is now internally connected and international phone calls can be made from Paro, Thimphu, Bumtang, Mongar and Tashigang. The connections are excellent and the fax services are also very reliable.

Bhutan international dialling code is 975. Area codes: Thimphu and Paro 2; Tongsar, Bumtang and Gelekphuk 3; Mongar, Tashigang and Samdrup Jongkhar 4.

Entertainment

● **Media**

Kuensel is the only national weekly (English) but international magazines are on sale. BBS is the national radio. BBC and VOA reception is good. Video but no TV.

Holidays and festivals

● **National holidays**

Dates sometimes vary according to the lunar calendar.

1996

19 Feb	Bhutanese New Year
27 April	Death Anniversary of Zhabdrung Ngawang Namgyel
2 May	Birth anniversary of the third King
2 June	Coronation Day
21 July	Death anniversary of the third King
23 Sept	Blessed Rainy Day
21 Oct	Dasain
2 Nov	Descent of Lord Buddha from Tushita
11-13 Nov	Birthday of the present King
16 Dec	Meeting of Nine Evils
17 Dec	National Day

● **Festivals**

Most religious festivals take place in the spring and autumn, see page 000. Check with your travel agent who is sent a list by TAB, well ahead of time. Only authorized festivals are listed.

1996

Punakha: Dromcho 24-28 Feb; Serda 28 Feb
Chorten Kora: 5 Mar; 19 Mar
Gomkora: 27-29 Mar
Paro: Tsechu 30 Mar-3 April
Thimphu: Tsechu 22-24 Sept
Wangdu Phodrang: Tsechu 20-22 Sept
Tongsar: Tsechu 17-20 Dec
Bumtang: Tamzhing Phala Chopa 22-24 Sept; Tangbi Manicham 26-28 Sept; Jampa Lhakhang 26-29 Oct; Kurje Tsechu 26 June
Mongar: Tsechu 17-20 Nov
Tashigang: Tsechu 18-21 Nov
Lhuntse: Tsechu 17-20 Dec
Pema Gatsel: Tsechu 17-20 Nov

GLOSSARY

A

abhidharma A class of Buddhist literature pertaining to phenomenology, psychology, and cosmology

All-surpassing Realisation (*thogal*) A meditative technique within the Esoteric Instructional Class of Atiyoga, the highest teachings of the Nyingma school, through which the buddha-body of form (*rupakaya*) is manifestly realized

amban A Manchu ambassador of the imperial Qing dynasty

Anuttarayogatantra The unsurpassed yogatantras, which focus on important tantric subject matters, such as 'inner radiance' and 'illusory body'

Anuyoga The eighth of the nine vehicles of Buddhism according to the Nyingma school, in which the perfection stage of meditation (*sampannakrama*) is emphasized

apsara Offering goddess, celestial nymph

argali (*Ovis ammon Hodgsoni Blyth*) A type of wild sheep

Arpacana Mantra The mantra of the bodhisattva Manjughosa (*Om Arapacana Dhih*, the recitation of which generates discriminative awareness (*prajna*) and intelligence

Atiyoga The ninth of the nine vehicles of Buddhism according to the Nyingma school, in which the resultant three buddha-bodies (*trikaya*) are effortlessly perfected, and the generation and perfection stages of meditation are both effortlessly present

Avatamsakasutra The title of the longest Mahayana sutra (excluding the Prajnaparamita literature)

B

bahal A Newari temple

bangrim The terraced steps of a stupa, symbolising the bodhisattva and buddha levels

beyul A hidden land conducive to meditation and spiritua life, of which there are several in trhe Hiamlayan region, such as Pemako in SE Tibet, and Khenpajong in NE Bhutan

Bhadracaryapranid-hanaraja The title of an important aspirational prayer which is part of the **Avatamsakasutra**

bharal A species of blue sheep (Tib *nawa*; *Pseudois nayaur* Hodg)

bindu The finial of a stupa, symbolising the buddha-body of actual reality (*dharmakaya*). The term also refers to the generative fluids of human physiology (according to Tibetan medicine and tantra), and to the seminal points of light appearing in the practice of **All-Surpassing Realisation**

bodhicitta (Tib *jangchub sem*) The enlightened mind which altruistically acts in the interest of all beings, combining discriminative awareness with compassion

bodhicitta vow The aspiration to attain full enlightenment or buddhahood for the benefit of all beings

bodhisattva (Tib *Jangchub Sempa*) A spiritual trainee who has generated the altruistic mind of enlightenment (*bodhicitta*) and is on the path to full buddhahood, remaining in the world in order to eliminate the sufferings of others. Ten successive bodhisattva levels (*bhumi*) are recognized

Bodongpa An adherent of the Bodong tradition, stemming from Bodong Chokle Namgyel

body of light The rainbow body of great transformation, in which the impure material body is transformed into one of light, through the practice of the **All-Surpassing Realisation**

Bon An ancient spiritual tradition, predating the advent of Buddhism in Tibet, which is considered by scholars to be of Zoroastrian or Kashmiri Buddhist origin, but which has, over centuries, assimilated many aspects of indigenous Tibetan religion and Buddhism

border-taming temple (Tib *Tadul Lhakhang*) A class of stabilising geomantic temples, reputedly constructed by King Songtsen Gampo in the border regions of Tibet

bumpa The bulbous dome of a stupa

C

calm abiding (Skt *shatipathana*, Tib *zhi-ne*) A state of mind characterized by the stabilisation of atten- tion on an internal object of observation, conjoined with the calming of external distractions to the mind

Caryatantra The name of a class of tantra and the fifth of the nine vehicles according to the Nyingma school. Equal emphasis is placed on internal meditation and external rituals

caterpillar fungus (*Cordiceps sinensis*) A medicinal plant used in the treatment of general debility and kidney disease

cave hermitage (Tib *zimpuk/grubpuk*) A remotely located mountain cave utilized as a hermitage for meditative retreats

chaitya A chapel within a large temple, also used as a synonym for **stupa**

cham Religious dance

chang Barley ale or fortified wine (occasionally made of other grains)

charnel ground A sky burial site, where human corpses are dismembered and compassionately fed to vultures

cho-ke The name given in Bhutan to the classical Tibetan language, which is the medium of Buddhist literature, in contrast to the colloquial Dzongka language/dialect

Chod (*yul*) A meditative rite

('Object of Cutting') in which the egotistical obscurations at the root of all delusions and sufferings are compassionately visualized as a feast-offering on behalf of unfortunate spirits or ghosts, often frequenting **charnel grounds**

chorten See **stupa**

Chosi Nyiden The name given to the combined spiritual and temporal form of government maintained in Tibet from 1641 to 1951, and in Bhutan until 1902

chu river

chuba Tibetan national dress, tied at the waist with a sash. For men it takes the form of a long-sleaved coat, and for women a long dress, with or without sleaves, which may be shaped or shapeless

chulen The practice of subsisting upon nuitritious elixirs and vitamins extracted from herbs and minerals, undertaken for reasons of health or as a spiritual practice

D

dadar An arrow employed in longevty empowerments, marriage and fertility rites, and during harvest festivals

Dasain Principal Hindu festival dedicated to Durga, the consort of Shiva in her wrathful form, slaying the demon Mahisha, which is held in Nepal over a 10-day period in Sept-Oct

de'u Enigmatic riddle of the Bon tradition

debri Mural paintings, frescoes

desi The title of the regents of the Dalai lamas (in Tibet) and

of the Zhabdrungs (in Bhutan), who often wielded considerable political power, particularly during the minority years of the incarnation under their charge

dharma (Tib cho) The theory and practice of the Buddhist doctrine, including its texts and transmissions

discriminative awareness (Skt prajna/Tib sherab) The faculty of intelligence inherent within the minds of all beings, which enables them to examine the characterisrtics of things and events, thus making it possible to make judgements and deliberations

district-controlling temple (Tib Runon Lhakhang) a class of stabilising geomantic temples, reputedly constructed by King Songtsen Gampo in Central Tibet, forming an inner ring around the central Jokhang temple

dogar Tibetan opera

Drepung Zhoton the Yoghurt festival held at Drepung one day prior to the start of the operatic Yoghurt festival of Norbulingka

dri fermale of the yak (Bos grunniens)

Drigungpa An adherent of the Drigung sub-order of the Kagyu school of Tibetan Buddhism

drokpa nomad

drubchu A sacred spring, said to have been brought forth from the ground through the meditative prowess of one of Tibet's great Buddhist masters

drubkhang Meditation hermitage

Drubtab Gyatsa ('Hundred Means for Attainment') A cycle

of short medittative practices contained in the Kangyur, which were translated into Tibetan by Bari Lotsawa

Drukpa Kagyupa An adherent of the Drukpa sub- order of the Kagyu school of Tibetan Buddhism, which predominates in Bhutan

drung story

dukhang The assembly hall of a large monastery, in which the monks affiliated to the various colleges will congregate

Durga puja See **Dasain**

Dzogchen Great Perfection, a synonym for **Atiyoga**

dzong County (administrative unit in Tibet), fortress, castle

dzongkha Colloquial language/dialect of Bhutan

dzongkhak District (administrative unit in Bhutan)

dzongpon District governor (in Bhutan)

E

eight attributes of pure water coolness, sweetness, lightness, softness, clearness, soothing quality, pleasantness and wholesomeness

eight auspicious symbols (Tib tashi tagye) umbrella, fish, conch, eternal knot, vase, wheel, and victory-banner, and flower

eight stupas symbolising the major events of the Buddha's life Eight styles of stupa reliquary, respectively symbolising the Buddha's birth, subjugation of Mara, enlightenment, teaching, descent from Tusita (after teaching his late mother), victory, revelation of miracles, and decease

empowerment (Skt abhiseka/Tib wangkur) A ritual performed by a Buddhist master, which is an essential prerequisite, empowering prospective trainees into the practice of tantra by activating the potential inherent in their mental continuum

emptiness (Skt shunyata/Tib tongpanyi) The absence of inherent existence and self-identity with respect to all phenomena, the ultimate reality underlying all phenomenal appearances

enlightened mind See **bodhicitta**

enlightenment stupa (Tib jangchub chorten) One of the eight types of stupa, this one symbolising the Buddha's enlightenment

eternal knot (Skt srivatsa/Tib palbe'u) One of the **eight auspicious symbols**, and one of the 32 major marks of a buddha's body, some- times rendered in English as 'heart-orb' since it is found at the heart of the Buddha

extensive lineage of conduct The transmission of Mahayana Buddhism which Asanga received in ancient India from Maitreya, and which emphasizes the elaborate conduct and development of the bodhisattva, in contrast to the 'profound lineage of view', which Nagarjuna received from Manjughosa

extraneous emptiness (Tib zhentong) The view that buddha-attributes are extraneously empty of mundane impurities and dualities, but not intrinsically empty in a nihilistic sense

F

Father Class of Unsurpassed Yogatantras One of the three subdivisions of the Unsurpassed Yogatantras (Anuttarayogatantra), according to the later schools of Tibetan Buddhism, exemplified by tantra-texts, such as the *Guhyasamaja* and *Yamari*

four classes of tantra See respectively: **Kriyatantra, Caryatantra, Yogatantra** and **Anuttarayogatantra**

four harmonious brethren (Tib *tunpa punzhi*) An artistic motif symbolising fraternal unity and respect for seniority, in which a partridge, rabbit, monkey, and elephant assist each other to pluck fruits from a tree

G

gakhyil A gemstone emblem comprising two or three segments

Ganden Tripa Title given to the head of the Gelukpa school of Tibetan Buddhism

gandharva (Tib *driza*) Denizens of space or celestian musicians who subsist on odours

garuda A mythological bird normally depicted with an owl-like sharp beak, often holding a snake, and with large powerful wings. In Buddhism, it is the mount of Vajrapani, symbolising the transmutative power which purifies certain malevolent influences and pestilences

Gelukpa An indiguenous school of Tibetan Buddhism, founded in the 14th century by Tsongkhapa, which, from the 17th century onwards, came to dominate the spiritual life of Tibet and Mongolia

generation stage of meditation (Skt *utpattikrama*/Tib *kye-rim*) The creative stage of meditation in which mundane forms, sounds, and thoughts are gradually meditated upon as natural expressions of deities, mantras, and buddha-mind

geshe (Skt *kalyanamitra*) Spiritual benefactor (of the Kadampa tradition), philosophical degree of a scholar-monk, a scholar-monk holding the geshe degree

gesture of calling the earth as a witness to past merits (*bhumisparshamudra*) The hand-gesture of the Buddha utilized during the subjugation of Mara through which he touches the ground, calling the goddess of the earth (Sthavira) to bear witness to his past merits

ghat Steps by the bank of a river, jetty

gomchen Experienced meditator

gongma Chinese emperor

Great Prayer Festival (Tib *Monlam Chenmo*) A festival held in Lhasa during the first month of the lunar calendar, instituted by Tsongkhapa in 1409

Great Seal (Skt *mahamudra*/Tib *chakya chenpo*) The realisation of emptiness as the ultimate nature of reality (according to the sutras), and the supreme accomplishment of buddhahood according to the tantras. The term also refers to the dynamic meditative techniques through which these goals are achieved

Greater Vehicle (Skt *Mahayana*/Tib *Tekpa Chenpo*) The system or vehicle of Buddhism prevailing in Tibet, Mongolia, China, Korea, and Japan, emphasising the attainment of complete liberation of all sentient beings from obscurations and sufferings (rather than the goal of the Lesser Vehicle which is more self-centred and lacks a full understanding of emptiness). The Greater Vehicle includes teachings based on both sutra-texts and tantra-texts

Gu-ge style The artistic style prevalent in Far-west Tibet (Ngari) and adjacent areas of NW India (Ladakh, Spiti), exhibiting Kashmiri influence

gyaphib A Chinese-style pavilion roof

gyelpo losar Official Tibetan New Year, held at the beginning of the first month of the lunar calendar, which normally falls within February or early March

H

harmika The square section of a stupa, above the dome, on which eyes are sometimes depicted

I

incarnation (Tib *yangsi*) The human form taken by an incarnate lama (*tulku*) following his decease in a previous life

Indra Jatra A Hindu festival held in Nepal honour of the god of rain (Aug-Sept)

Industructible Vehicle (Skt *Vajrayana*/Tib *Dorje Tekpa*) The aspect of the **Greater Vehicle** emphasising the fruitional tantra teachings and meditative techniques concerning the unbroken mental continuum from ignorance to enlightenment. It includes the vehicles of **Kriyatantra, Caryatantra, Yogatantra, Anuttarayogatantra, Mahayoga, Anuyoga** and **Atiyoga**

Inner Tantra The three inner classes of tantra. See under **Mahayoga, Anuyoga** and **Atiyoga**

Innermost Spirituality of Vimalamitra (*Bima Nyingthig*) The title of a collection of esoteric instructions belonging to the **man-ngag-de** (esoteric instructional) class of **Atiyoga**, which were introduced to Tibet from India by Vimalamitra during the early 9th century, and later redacted by Longchen Rabjampa in the 14th century

J

Janai Purnima A Hindu festival held at the Kumbeshvara Temple in Patan, Kathmandu, in honour of Mahadeva, when high caste hindus renew their sacred threads

Jatakamala A stylized account of the Buddha's past lives as a bodhisattva, in Sanskrit verse, composed by Ashvaghosa, and translated into Tibetan

Je Khenpo Title of

the chief monastic preceptor of the Drukpa Kagyu school in Bhutan

Jonangpa An adherent of the Jonang school of Tibetan Buddhism

K

kadam (-style) stupa A small rounded stupa, the design of which is said to have been introduced into Tibet by Atisha during the 11th century

Kadampa An adherent of the Kadam school of Tibetan Buddhism, founded by Atisha in the 11th century

Kagyupa An adherent of the Kagyu school of Tibetan Buddhism, founded in Tibet by Marpa during the 11th century

Kalaratri The eighth night of the Hindu festival of **Dasain** (Durga Puja) when animal sacrifices are made in Kathmandu's Taleju Temple

Kangyur An anthology of the translated scriptures of the sutras and tantras, the compilation of which is attributed to Buton Rinchendrub

Karma Gadri A school of art, which evolved in Kham, integrating Tibetan iconography with Chinese landscape themes and perspective

Karma Kagyu A sub-order of the Kagyu school, founded by Karmapa I during the 12th century

kashag The official name of the pre-1959 Tibetan cabinet

khatvanga A hand-emblem, held by Padmasambhava and several wrathful deities, comprising a staff skewered with a stack of three dry skulls and surmounted by an iron trident

kho/baku A woman's dress (in Bhutan)

Khyenri A school of painting associated with the 16th century master Jamyang Khyentse Wangchuk

kira The waistband or cumberband of a Tibetan or Bhutanese **chuba**

Kriyatantra The name of a class of tantra and the fourth of the nine vehicles according to the Nyingma school. Greater emphasis is placed on external rituals than on internal meditation

kumbum A stupa containing many thousands of images, and often multiple chapels, sometimes known as 'Tashi Gomang' stupa

kunzang khorlo (Skt *sarvatobhadra*) A type of geometric poetry in the shape of a wheel, the lines of which read in all directions

kyang The Asiatic wild ass (*Equus hemionus* Pallas)

L

la Mountain pass

la-do A stone assuming the function of a life-supporting talisman (*la-ne*)

la-guk A rite for summoning or drawing in the life-supporting energy or talisman of another

la-shing A tree assuming the function of a life-supporting talisman (*la-ne*)

labrang The residence of an incarnate lama within a monastery

lam road

Lama Chopda A text on the practice of *guruyoga* ('union with the guru'), written by Panchen Lama IV

lama Spiritual mentor (Skt *guru*)

Lamdre A unique collection of meditative practices related to the meditational deity Hevajra, which are pre-eminent in the Sakya school, outlining the entire theory and practice of the **Greater Vehicle**

lamrim (Skt *pathakrama*) The graduated path to enlightenment, and the texts expounding this path

Lato style A localized and less cosmopolitan style of Tibetan panting, associated with sites in the highland region of W Tibet

latse Top of a mountain pass, the cairn of prayer flags adorning a mountain pass

Lesser Vehicle (Skt *Hinayana*/Tib *Tekmen*) The system or vehicle of Buddhism prevalent in Sri Lanka, Thailand and Burma, emphasising the four truths and related teachings through which an individual seeks his own salvation, rather than the elimination of others' sufferings

lhakhang Buddhist temple

lhamo Female deity (Skt *devi*)

life-supporting talisman (Tib *la-ne*) An object imbued with a sympathetic energy force, said to sustain the life of its owner

Ling Gesar The legendary warrior king, who is the hero of Tibetan epic poetry

lingam See **Shiva lingam**

losar Tibetan New Year

lumo Female naga-spirit (Skt *nagini*)

lung-gom A set of meditative practices in which the vital energy (*lung*) of the body, including the respiratory cycle, is controlled and regulated

lungta Tibetan mantras printed on cloth for use as prayer flags, which are activated by the power of the wind, or on paper as an offering to local mountain divinities, in which case they are tossed into the air on a mountain pass

M

Madhyamaka The philosophical system of Mahayana Buddhism based on the Middle Way, which seeks to comprehend, either by means of syllogistic reasoning or by reductio ad absurdum, the emptiness or absence of inherent existence with respect to all phenomena. A distinction is drawn between the ultimate truth, or emptiness, and the relative truth in which all appearances exist conventionally

Mahamudra See **Great Seal**

Mahayoga The name of a class of tantra and the seventh of the nine vehicles according to the Nyingma school, emphasising the generation stage of meditation (*utpattikrama*)

man-ngagde (Skt *upadeshavarga*) The inner- most class of instructions according to **Atiyoga**

mandala (Tib *kyilkhor*) A symbolic two or three dimensional representation of the palace of a given meditational deity, which is of crucial importance during the generation stage of meditation

mani (-stone) wall A wall adorned with stone tablets engraved with the mantras of the deity Avalokiteshvara, embodiment of compassion

Mani Kabum The title of an early Tibetan historical work, said to have been concealed as a terma-text by King Songtsen Gampo in the 7th century, and to have been rediscovered during the 12th century by three distinct treasure-finders (*terton*)

mani prayer-wheel (Tib *dungkhor*) A large prayer wheel containing mantras of the deity Avalokiteshvara, embodiment of compassion

mantra (Tib *ngak*) A means of protecting the mind from mundane influences through the recitation of incantations associated with various meditational deities, thereby transforming mundane speech into buddha-speech. Mantra also occurs as a synonym for tantra

mantra vows The various commitments maintained by those who have been empowered to practice the tantras

mantrin (Tib *ngakpa*) A practitioner of the mantras, who may live as a lay householder rather than a renunciate monk

-me The lower part of a valley

meditational deity (Skt *istadevata*/Tib *yidam*) A peaceful or

wrathful manifestation of buddha-mind, which becomes the object of a meditator's attention, as he or she seeks to cultivate experientially specific buddha-attributes by merging inseperably with that deity

momo A Tibetan dumpling

monk (Skt *bhiksu*/Tib *gelong*) One who maintains the full range of monastic vows as designated in the Vinaya texts

Mother Class of Unsurpassed Yogatantras One of the three subdivisions of the Unsurpassed Yogatantras (Anuttarayogatantra), according to the later schools of Tibetan Buddhism, exemplified by tantra-texts, such as the Cakrasamvara and Hevajra

Mt Potalaka Abode of the deity Avalokiteshvara, said in some sources to be located in S India

mu A 'sky-cord' of light on which the ancient 'immortal' kings of Tibet were said to leave this world at the time of their succession

mumo A female mu spirit, said to cause dropsy

muntsam Meditation retreat in darkness

N

naga A powerful water spirit which may take the form of a serpent or semi-human form similar to a mermaid/man

Nagaraja King of naga spirits

Namchu Wangden A series of vertically stacked letters symbolising elemental power and buddha-attributes

Namgyel Chorten See **Victory Stupa**

nectar (Skt *amrita*/Tib *dutsi*) The ambrosia of the gods which grants immortality, metaphorically identified with the Buddhist teachings

New Translation Schools (Sarmapa) Those maintaining the Buddhsit teachings which were introduced into Tibet from India from the late 10th century onwards, and which are contrasted with th Nyingma school, representing the earlier dissemination of Buddhism. The New Translation Schools include those of the **Kadampa**, **Kagyupa**, **Sakyapa**, **Jonangpa** and **Zhalupa**

ngakpa See **mantrin**

nine (hierarchical) vehicles (Skt *navayana*/Tib *tekpa rimpa gu*) According to the Nyingma school of Tibetan Buddhism, these comprise the three vehicles of pious attendants (*shravaka*), hermit buddhas (*pratyekabuddha*) and bodhisattvas, which are all based on the sutras; as well as the six vehicles of Kriyatantra, Caryatantra, Yogatantra, Mahayoga, Anuyoga, and Atiyoga, which are all based on the tantras. Each of these is entered separately in this glossary

Northern Treasures (Tib *jangter*) The terma tradition derived from Rigdzin Godemchen's 14th century discoveries in the Zangzang area of Northern Tibet

Nyang Chojung Taranatha's history of the Nyang-chu valley

nyenmo A plague-inducing demoness of the soil

Nyingma Gyudbum

The anthology of the Collected Tantras of the Nyingmapa, most of which were translated into Tibetan during 8th-9th centuries and kept unrevised in their original format

Nyingma Kama The anthology of the oral teachings or transmitted precepts of the Nyingma school, accumulated over the centuries, and published most recently by the late Dudjom Rinpoche

Nyingmapa An adherent of the Nyingma school of Tibetan Buddhism, founded in Tibet by Shantaraksita, Padmasambhava, King Trisong Detsen, and Vimalamitra

nyung-ne A purificatory fast (*upavasa*)

O

offering mandala A symbolic representation of the entire universe, which is mentally offered to an object of refuge, such as the Buddha or one's spiritual mentor

onju/gyenja A woman's blouse in Bhutan and Tibet)

Outer Tantra The three outer classes of tantra. See under **Kriyatantra**, **Caryatantra** and **Yogatantra**

P

pagoda A distinctive style of multi-storied tower, temple or stupa

Pala style Bengali style of Buddhist art

pandita Scholar, a Buddhist scholar of ancient India

Parinirvanasutra The sutra expounding the events surrounding the Buddha's decease

Path and Fruit See Lamdre

penma (*Potentilla fructicosa*) A type of

twig used in the constuction of the corbels of certain Tibetan buildings for aesthetic reasons, and to provide a form of ventilation

perfection stage of meditation (Skt *sampannakrama*/Tib *dzog-rim*) The techniques for controlling the movement of vital energy (*vayu*) and bindu within the central channel of the body through which inner radiance (*prabhasvara*) and coemergent pristine cognition (*sahajajnana*) are realized. It is contrasted with the **generation stage of meditation**

Phakmodrupa The dynasty of Tibetan kings who ruled Tibet from Nedong during the 14th-15th centuries

phurba A ritual dagger, which is the hand-emblem of the meditational deity Vajrakila/Vajrakumara, penetrating the obscurations of mundane existence

pilgrim's circuit (Tib *khorlam*) A circumambulatory walkway around a shrine or temple, along which pilgrims will walk in a clockwise direction

place of attainment (Tib *drub-ne*) A sacred power-place where great spiritual masters of the past meditated and attained their realizations

Ponlop The title of a district governor in pre-1902 Bhutan

Prajnaparamita A class of Mahayana literature focussing on the bodhisattva paths which cultivate the 'perfection of discriminative awareness'

prayer flag A flag printed with sacred

mantra syllables and prayers, the power of which is activated by the wind

prayer wheel A large fixed wheel (*dungkhor*) or small hand-held wheel (*tu-je chenpo*), containing sacred mantra-syllables or prayers, the power of which is activated by the spinning motion of the wheel

profound lineage of view The transmission of Mahayana Buddhism which Nagarjuna received in ancient India from Manjughosa, and which emphasizes the profound view of emptiness, in contrast to the 'extensive lineage of conduct', which Asanga received from Maitreya

protecter shrine (*gonkhang*) A temple or chapel dedicated to the class of protector deities (Skt *dharmapala*/Tib *chokyong*)

puja Offering ceremony

Q

qan A Mongol chieftan or king

qutuqtu The Mongol equivalent of **tulku** ('incarnate lama')

R

rainbow body (*ja-lu*) The buddha-body of great transformation, in which the impure material body is transformed into one of light, through the practice of the **All-Surpassing Realisation**

Ranjana (*lantsa*) The medieval Sanskrit script of Newari Buddhism from which the Tibetan capital letter script (*u-chen*) is said to have been derived

Ratnakuta An important section of the Mahayana sutras,

which, along with the prajnaparamita literature, largely represent the second promulgation of the Buddhist teachings

reliquary (*dung-ten*) A stupa containing buddha-relics or the relics/embalmed remains of a great spiritual master

residential college/unit (*khangtsang*) The residential quarters of a large monastic college, often inhabited by monks from one specific region of the country

Ringpungpa The dynasty of Tibetan princes who usurped the power of the Phakmodrupa kings during the late 15th century and ruled much of Tibet from Rinpung in Tsang, until they themselves were usurped by the kings of Tsang, based in Zhigatse

ritual dagger See **phurba**

rongpa villager

runon See **district controlling temple**

S

sacred outlook (*dak-nang*) The pure vision through which all phenomenal appearances, including rocks and topographical features, may assume the forms of deities

Sakyapa An adherent of the Sakya school of Tibetan Buddhism, founded by Gayadhara, Drokmi, and Khon Konchok Gyelpo in the 11th century

sand mandala A two-dimensional representation of the palace of a given meditational deity, made of finely ground coloured powders or sands

sangha The Buddhist monastic community (Tib *gendun*)

self-arising (object/image) (*rang-jung*) A naturally produced object or image, emerging of its own accord from stone, wood, and the like, in which great sanctity is placed

self-arising seed-syllable A (*A rang-jung*) a 'naturally produced' seed-syllable A, indicative of emptiness

self-arising terma stone (*rangjung terdo*) A 'naturally produced' stone, said to have been discovered as **terma**

serdung A reliquary stupa made of gold

Seven Trial Monks The first Tibetan monks ordained in the 8th century by Shantaraksita

sexagenary year cycle (*rab-jung*) The cycle of 60 years on which Tibetan chronology is based (rather than centuries). This system was originally adopted in Tibet from the *Kalacakra Tantra*, and each year of the sixty years was later given a distinctive name combining one of the 12 animals and one of the five elements of the Chinese system

shakti Energy or power inherent in the female consort of the Hindu deity Shiva

Shambhala A mysterious hidden land, often identified with Central Asia, where the *Kalackra Tantra* was disseminated, and from where, it is said, messianic kings will emerge during the next millenium to subdue tyrranical empires on earth

Shangpa Kagyu A branch of the Kagyu school which originated from the

Tibetan yogin Khyungpo Naljor of Shang rather than Marpa

shastra A treatise or commentary elucidating points of scripture or science (Tib *ten-cho*)

shen A type of Bonpo priest

shikhara The curved spire of a Hindu temple

Shiva lingam The Hindu deity Shiva embodied in a phallic emblem

sign of accomplishment A sign or intimation of success in spiritual practice

six-syllable mantra The mantra of the bodhisattva Avalokiteshvara (*Om Mani Padme Hum*), the syllables of which respectively generate com- passion for the sufferings endured by gods, antigods, humans, animals, ghosts, and denizens of the hells

sky-burial site (*dutro*) See **charnel ground**

sok-shing The central pillar of a building or the wooden axis inside an image, which acts as a life-support

sonam losar The agricultural new year, held 1 month prior to the official new year (in Bhutan and parts of Tibet)

stone footprint The imprint of the foot of a great spiritual master of the past, left in stone as a sign of yogic prowess

stupa (Tib *chorten*) The most well-known type of sacred monument in the Buddhist world, symbolising the buddha-body of reality (*dharmakaya*), and holding the relics of the Buddha or some great spiritual master. For illustrations of the eight types of stupa

recognized in the Tibetan world

Sukhavati The buddha-field of Amitabha, the meditational buddha of the west

supine ogress An anthropomorphic description of the dangerous terrain of the Tibetan landscape, which King Songtsen Gampo tamed by constructing a series of geomantic temples

sutra (Tib *do*) The discourses of the Buddha, belonging to either the **Lesser Vehicle** or the **Greater Vehicle**, which were delivered by Shakyamuni Buddha, and which expound the causal path to enlightenment in a didactic manner, in contrast to the tantras

Sutra of the Auspicious Aeon (*Bhadrakalpikasutra*) The title of a sutra enumerating the thousand budhas of this 'auspicious aeon', of whom Shakyamuni was the fourth and Maitreya will be the fifth

swastika (Tib *yungdrung*) A Buddhist symbol of good auspicies, included among the thirty-two excellent major marks of a buddha's body. The inverse swastika is also a Bon symbol

syllable A The seed-syllable inherent in all syllables, which is indicative of **emptiness**

T

tadul See **border taming temple**

talismanic object/place (*la-ne*) See **life-supporting talisman**

tangka Tibetan painted scroll

tangka wall (*goku*) A large wall located

within the grounds of a monastery, on which large applique tangkas are hung during specific festivals

Tangyur An anthology of the translated scriptures of the Indian treatises on Buddhism and classical sciences, the compilation of which is attributed to Buton Rinchendrub

tantra The continuum from ignorance to enlightenment

tantra-text (Tib *gyud*) Canonical texts delivered by the buddhas, which emphasize the resultant approach to buddhahood, in contrast to the causal or didactic approach of the **sutras**

teaching gesture (*dharmacakramudra*) The hand-gesture of the Buddha deity during the teaching of the Buddhist doctrine

terma (Skt *nidhi*) The texts and sacred objects formerly concealed at geomantic power-places on the Tibetan landscape during the 7th-9th centuries, in the manner of a time capsule, which were later revealed in subsequent centuries by the treasure-finders (*terton*) appointed to discover them. Other termas, known as gong-ter, are revealed directly from the nature of buddha-mind

thread-cross (Tib *do*) A wooden framed structure crossed with many layers of coloured threads, used as a device for trapping and exorcising evil forces or demons

three approaches to liberation (Tib *namtar gosum*) As expounded in the

Greater Vehicle, these are: emptiness, aspirationlessness and signlessness

three buddha-bodies (*trikaya*) The buddha-body of actual reality (*dharmakaya*) or emptiness underlying all phenomena; the buddha-body of perfect resource (*sambhogakaya*) whose light-forms appear in meditation to advanced level bodhisattvas; and the buddha-body of emanation (*nirmanakaya*) which manifests materially in the world to guide living beings from suffering

three roots (Skt *trimula*/Tib *tsawa sum*) The spiritual mentor (*lama*) who confers blessing, the meditational deity (*yidam*) who confers spiritual accomplishments, and the dakini (*khandroma*) who embodies enlightened activity

three world systems (*tridhatu*) Those of desire, form and formlessness

three-dimensional palace (*vimana*) The celestial palace of a given meditational deity

thukpa soup, noodle soup

Tishri The title of imperial preceptor to the Mongol Yuan emperors

-to The upper reaches of a valley

togo jacket, shirt

tongdrol Liberation by sight, an object conferring liberation by sight

torana Stucco halo of an image, arched pediment above a gateway

torma (Skt *bali*) Ritual offering-cake

tratsang A college within a large monastery

treasure chest (Tib *terdrom*) Container in which terma are concealed and from which they are subsequently discovered

treasure See **terma**

treasure-finder (Tib *terton*) The prophesied discoverer of a terma-text or terma-object

treasure-site (Tib *terka*) Locations in which terma are concealed and discovered

tsampa The staple Tibetan food consisting of ground and roasted barley flour, which is mixed with tea as a dough

tsatsa Mininiture votive terracotta image, sometimes inserted within a stupa

Tsechu The tenth day of the lunar month, associated with the activities of Padmasambhava, and on which feast-offering ceremonies are held. These may assume the form of grand religious dance performances, for which reason, in Bhutan, the term refers to **cham** festivals

tsewang Longevity empowerment

tshe-chu Water-of-life spring

tsuklakhang large temple (Skt *vihara*)

tulku Incarnate lama, emanation, buddha-body of emanation (*nirmanakaya*)

tummo The name of a yogic practice of the perfection stage of meditation in which an inner heat is generated within the body to burn away all obscurations and generate the coemergence of bliss and emptiness

Tusita A low-level paradise within the world-system of desire (*kamadhatu*) where the future buddha Maitreya is presently said to reside

Twelve Deeds of Shakyamuni The 12 principal sequential acts in the Buddha's life, viz: residence in Tusita paradise, conception, birth, study, marriage, renunciation, asceticism, reaching the point of enlightenment, vanquishing demonic obstacles, perfect enlighten- ment, teaching and final nirvana at the time of death

U

Uchen The Tibetan capital letter script

udumbara lotus A hugh mythical lotus, said to blossom once every 500 years

V

vajra (Tib *dorje*) The indestructible reality of buddhahood, a sceptre-like ritual object symbolizing this indestructible reality, or skillful means

vajra and bell (*vajragantha*) A set of ritual implements, respectively symbolising skilful means and discriminative awareness

Vajra Guru mantra The mantra of Pasmasambhava (*Om Ah Hum Vajra Guru Padma Siddhi Hum*)

vajradhatu (Tib *dorje ying*) The indestructible expanse of reality

Vartula A large script from which the cursive Tibetan U-me script is said to be derived

Victory/Vijaya Stupa (Tib *namgyel chorten*) One of the eight types of stupa, this one symbolising the Buddha's victory over mundane influences

vihara A large Buddhist temple

Vinaya (Tib *dulwa*) The rules of Buddhist monastic discipline, the texts outlining these rules

W

wheel and deer emblem A motif symbolizing the deer park at Rsipatana (Sarnath) where the Buddha gave his first teaching, turning the doctrinal wheel in a deer park

wheel of rebirth (Skt *bhavacakra*/Tib *sidpei khorlo*) A motif depicting the sufferings of the various classes of sentient beings within cyclic existence and the causal processes which give rise to their rebirth

wind-horse See **lungta**

Y

yaksa A type of malevolent mountain spirit

yangdul lhakhang The remote group of 'further taming' geomantic temples, reputedly constructed by King Songtsen Gampo, outside the line of the 'border-taming temples'

yantra Yogic exercises (in Buddhism), a magical geometric diagram (in Hinduism)

Yogatantra The name of a class of tantra and the sixth of the nine vehicles according to the Nyingma school. Greater emphasis is placed on internal meditation than upon external rituals

Yoghurt festival See **Zhoton**

yogin (Tib *neljorpa*) A male practitioner engaged in intensive meditative practices

yogini (Tib *neljorma*) A female practitioner engaged in intensive meditative practices

Z

Zangdok Pelri style A mode of temple construction symbolising the 3-storeyed palace of Padmasambhava

Zhalupa An adherent of the Zhalu tradition, associated with Zhalu Monastery (founded 1040)

Zhidag A type of local divinity

Zhije The meditative technique of 'pacification' introduced to Tibet by Phadampa Sangye

Zhoton The Yoghurt operatic festival, held at Norbulingka in Lhasa in Aug

zi A species of etched agate or banded chalcedony, highly valued in Tibet

Zikpa Ngaden Tsongkhapa's five vsions of diverse aspects of Manjushri

INDEX

MAPS